Klaus Pannen (Ed.)
European Insolvency Regulation

De Gruyter Commentaries
on European Law

De Gruyter Commentaries on European Law

RECHT

De Gruyter Recht · Berlin

European Insolvency Regulation

Edited by

Klaus Pannen

W DE G RECHT

De Gruyter Recht · Berlin

List of Contributors

EIR

Arts 1, 3, 9	Dr. Klaus Pannen
Arts 2, 8, 20, 24 to 26, 39 to 47	Dr. Susanne Riedemann
Arts 5 to 7	Dr. Thomas Ingelmann
Arts 10 to 15	Dr. Reinhard Dammann
Arts 21 to 23	Prof. Dieter Eickmann
Introduction, Arts 4, 16 to 19, 31	Dr. Klaus Pannen/Dr. Susanne Riedemann
Arts 27 to 30, 32 to 38	Dr. Axel Herchen, Judge

German Law

Art 102 Sections 1 to 11 EGInsO	Frank Frind, Judge/Prof. Dieter Eickmann

Country Reports

France	Dr. Reinhard Dammann
Great Britain	Dan Hamilton/Stephen Hair
Hungary	Andrea Csőke/László Csia
Protocols	Stephen Taylor
UNCITRAL	Evan C. Hollander/Richard A. Graham

∞ Printed on acid-free paper which falls within the guidelines of the ANSI to ensure permanence and durability.

ISBN 978-3-89949-207-1

Bibliografische Information der Deutschen Nationalbibliothek

Die Deutsche Nationalbibliothek verzeichnet diese Publikation in der Deutschen Nationalbibliografie; detaillierte bibliografische Daten sind im Internet über http://dnb.d-nb.de abrufbar.

Printed in Germany

Data Conversion: WERKSATZ Schmidt & Schulz, Gräfenhainichen
Printing and Binding: Bercker Graphischer Betrieb GmbH & Co. KG, Kevelaer
Cover Design: deblik, Berlin

Contents – Summary

Annex

Contents

Chapter II. Recognition of Insolvency Proceedings

Foreword

This book is a comprehensive commentary on the EIR in light of recent decisions of the European Court of Justice and decisions of the judicatures of the various Member States of the EU. It contains a commentary on Article 102, Sections 1 to 11 of the German *EGInsO* (The Act Introducing the Insolvency Act), as well as country reports on the international insolvency laws of France, Great Britain, and Hungary. This book also deals with the UNCITRAL Model Law on Cross-Border Insolvency together with detailed references to the international insolvency laws of the U.S.A., and it also includes a discussion of protocols (an example of which is included in the appendix to the country report Great Britain). The appendix to the commentary on Article 3 of the EIR contains an extensive Table of Cases, which sets out over 100 cases from the various Member States, including decisions and literature references.

The contributing authors are all well-respected academics and practitioners in Germany, England, France, Hungary, and the U.S.A. Such diversity ensures that the issues dealt with are being viewed from a variety of angles. Through the cross-border examination of the area by taking into account the decisions of the judicatures of the various Member States, this book attempts to provide a uniform interpretation of the EIR. While thus being tailored to the needs of the European insolvency practitioner, this commentary also serves as a knowledge-base from which further exploration of the material can begin.

May 2007 Dr. Klaus Pannen

List of Abbreviations

AG	Amtsgericht
AHB	Anwaltshandbuch
AJ	Actualité juridique
AktG	Aktiengesetz
ALI	American Law Institute
AnwBl	Anwaltsblatt
Art	Article
AVAG	Anerkennungs- und Vollstreckungsausführungsgesetz
BB	Betriebs-Berater
BGB	Bürgerliches Gesetzbuch
BGBl	Bundesgesetzblatt
BGH	Bundesgerichtshof
BK-InsO/*contributor*	Berliner Kommentar Insolvenzrecht (eds: *Breutigam/Blersch/Goetsch*)
BKR	Bank- und Kapitalmarktrecht
Braun/*contributor* InsO	Insolvenzordnung Kommentar (ed: *Braun*)
Bull civ	Bulletin civil
Bull Joly Sociétés	Bulletin Joly des sociétés
CA	Cour d'appel
Cass ass plén	Cour de cassation assemblée plénière
Cass civ	Chambre civile de la Cour de cassation
Cass com	Chambre commerciale de la Cour de cassation
CCom	Code de commerce
Cf	Confer
CJEL	The Columbia Journal of European Law
COMI	Centre of main interests
DB	Der Betrieb
D-K/D/Ch-*contributor*	*Duursma-Kepplinger/Duursma/Chalupsky* Kommentar zur Europäischen Insolvenzverordnung (2002)
DNotZ	Deutsche Notar-Zeitschrift
DStR	Deutsches Steuerrecht
DZWiR	Deutsche Zeitschrift für Wirtschaftsrecht
ECJ	European Court of Justice
ed	editor
edn	edition
eds	editors
EGBGB	Einführungsgesetz zum Bürgerlichen Gesetzbuch
EGInsO	Einführungsgesetz zur Insolvenzordnung
EIR	EC Regulation on Insolvency Proceedings
ELR	European Law Report
Et seq	And the following
EU	Europäische Union
EuGH	Europäischer Gerichtshof

EuZW	Europäische Zeitschrift für Wirtschaftsrecht
EWCA civ	Court of Appeal Civil Division
EWiR	Entscheidungen zum Wirtschaftsrecht
EWS	Europäisches Wirtschafts- und Steuerrecht
FK-InsO/*contributor*	Frankfurter Kommentar zur Insolvenzordnung (ed: *Wimmer*)
fn	footnote
FS	Festschrift
GBA	Grundbuchamt
GBO	Grundbuchordnung
GbR	Gesellschaft bürgerlichen Rechts
GewArch	Gewerbearchiv: Zeitschrift für Gewerbe- und Wirtschaftsverwaltungsrecht
GKG	Gerichtskostengesetz
GmbH	Gesellschaft mit beschränkter Haftung
GmbHG	Gesetz betreffend die Gesellschaften mit beschränkter Haftung
GmbHR	GmbH-Rundschau
Gottwald/*contributor* InsR-Handb	Insolvenzrechts-Handbuch (ed: *Gottwald*)
GPR	Zeitschrift für Gemeinschaftsprivatrecht
GVG	Gerichtsverfassungsgesetz
GVGA	Geschäftsanweisung für Gerichtsvollzieher
HamburgerKomm-*contributor*	Hamburger Kommentar zum Insolvenzrecht (ed: *A. Schmidt*)
Haß/Huber/Gruber/Heiderhoff-*contributor*	EU-Insolvenzverordnung – Kommentar
Hirte/Bücker-*contributor*	Grenzüberschreitende Gesellschaften (eds: *Hirte/Bücker*)
HK-InsO/*contributor*	Heidelberger Kommentar zur Insolvenzordnung (eds: *Eickmann/Flessner/Irschlinger/ Kirchhof/Kreft/Landfermann/Marotzke/Stephan*)
ICC	International Code Council
InsO	Insolvenzordnung
INSOL	International Federation of Insolvency Professionals International
InsVV	Insolvenzrechtliche Vergütungsverordnung
IntInsR	Internationales Insolvenzrecht
InVo	Insolvenz und Vollstreckung
IPR	Internationales Privatrecht
IPRax	Praxis des Internationalen Privat- und Verfahrensrechts
IPRspr	Die deutsche Rechtsprechung auf dem Gebiet des internationalen Privatrechts
IZVR	Internationales Zivilverfahrensrecht
Jaeger Komm InsO/*contributor*	Jaeger Insolvenzordnung Großkommentar (eds *Henckel/Gerhardt*)
JCl	JurisClasseur
JCl Commercial	JurisClasseur commercial
JCP	JurisClasseur périodique – La semaine juridique
JCP E	JurisClasseur périodique – La semaine juridique, édition entreprise
JDI	Journal du Droit International
JO	Journal officiel
JOR	Jurisprudentie Onderneming & Recht

JZ	Juristenzeitung
KG	Kammergericht / Kommanditgesellschaft
KO	Konkursordnung
Komm	Kommentar
KTS	Zeitschrift für Insolvenzrecht
Kübler/Prütting-*contributor*	Kommentar zur Insolvenzordnung (eds: *Kübler/Prütting*)
LG	Landgericht
Ltd	Private Limited Company
mn	marginal note
MDR	Monatsschrift für Deutsches Recht
Moss/Fletcher/Isaacs-*contributor*	The EC Regulation on Insolvency Proceedings (eds: *Moss/Fletcher/Isaacs*)
MünchKomm BGB/*contributor*	Münchener Kommentar zum Bürgerlichen Gesetzbuch (eds: *Rebmann/Säcker/Rixecker*)
MünchKomm InsO/*contributor*	Münchener Kommentar zur Insolvenzordnung (eds: *Kirchhof/Lwowski/Stürner*)
Musielak ZPO/*contributor*	Kommentar zur Zivilprozessordnung (ed *Musielak*)
NAFTA	North American Free Trade Agreement
NCPC	Nouveau code de procédure civile
Nerlich/Römermann-*contributor* Komm InsO	Insolvenzordnung Kommentar (eds *Nerlich/Römermann*)
NJW	Neue Juristische Wochenschrift
NJW-RR	NJW-Rechtsprechungsreport
No	number
NZG	Neue Zeitschrift für Gesellschaftsrecht
NZI	Neue Zeitschrift für Insolvenzrecht
OGH	Oberster Gerichtshof
OHADA	Organisation pour l'Harmonisation en Afrique du Droit des Affaires
OHG	Offene Handelsgesellschaft
OJ	Official Journal
OLG	Oberlandesgericht
p	page
RabelsZ	Zeitschrift für ausländisches und internationales Privatrecht
RB	Revue Banque
RCDIP	Revue critique de droit international privé
Rev Lamy dr aff	Revue Lamy droit des affaires
Rev proc coll	Revue des procédures collectives
Rev Soc	Revue des sociétés
RIW	Recht der internationalen Wirtschaft
RpflG	Rechtspflegergesetz
RTD com	Revue trimestrielle de droit commercial
Sec	section
StGB	Strafgesetzbuch
TC	Tribunal de commerce
Uhlenbruck Komm InsO/*contributor*	Insolvenzordnung Kommentar (ed: *Uhlenbruck*)

UNCITRAL	United Nations Commission on International Trade Law
vol	volume
vs	versus
wbl	Wirtschaftsrechtliche Blätter
WiRO	Wirtschaft und Recht in Osteuropa
WM	Wertpapiermitteilungen
ZGR	Zeitschrift für Unternehmens- und Gesellschaftsrecht
ZIK	Zeitschrift für Insolvenzrecht und Kreditschutz
ZInsO	Zeitschrift für das gesamte Insolvenzrecht
ZIP	Zeitschrift für Wirtschaftsrecht
ZPO	Zivilprozessordnung
ZustDG	Gemeinschaftsrechtliches Zustellungsdurchführungsgesetz
ZVG	Zwangsversteigerungsgesetz
ZVglRWiss	Zeitschrift für vergleichende Rechtswissenschaft
ZVI	Zeitschrift für Verbraucher- und Privatinsolvenzrecht
ZZP	Zeitschrift für Zivilprozess

Bibliography

Altmeppen Änderungen der Kapitalersatz- und Insolvenzverschleppungshaftung aus „deutsch-europäischer" Sicht, NJW 2005, p 1911; *Altmeppen* Existenzvernichtungshaftung und Scheinauslandsgesellschaften, Crezelius (ed), Festschrift Röhricht (2005) p 3; *Altmeppen* Parteifähigkeit, Sitztheorie und „Centros", DStR 2000, p 1061; *Altmeppen* Schutz vor „europäischen" Kapitalgesellschaften, NJW 2004, p 97; *Altmeppen/Wilhelm* Gegen die Hysterie um die Niederlassungsfreiheit der Scheinauslandsgesellschaften, DB 2004, p 1083; American Law Institute, Principles of Cooperation and Transnational Insolvency Cases Among the Members of the North American Free Trade Agreement (2003), Guidelines Applicable to Court-to-Court Communications in Cross Border Cases (16 May 2000); *Audit* La fin attendue d'une anomalie jurisprudentielle: retour à la lettre de l'article 15 du code civil, Dalloz 2006, p 1846; *Baetge* Zum gewöhnlichen Aufenthalt bei Kindesentführung, IPRax 2001, p 573; *Bähr/Riedemann* Comments on AG Mönchengladbach dated 27/4/2004 – 19 IN 54/04, ZIP 2004, p 1066; *Baird* The Hidden Virtues of Chapter 11: An overview of the Law and Economics of Financially Distressed Firms (March 1997) (Chicago Working Papers in Law and Economics No. 43 (2nd Serie)); *Balz* Das neue Europäische Insolvenzübereinkommen, ZIP 1996, p 948; *Balz* The European Union Convention on Insolvency Proceedings, 70 American Bankruptcy Law Journal (1996), p 485; *Baudenbacher/Buschle* Niederlassungsfreiheit für EWR-Gesellschaften nach Überseering, IPRax 2004, p 26; *Baur/Stürner* Zwangsvollstreckungs-, Konkurs- und Vergleichsrecht; *Baumbach/Hueck* GmbH-Gesetz, Kommentar (18th edn 2006); *Baxter* Eurofood ECJ Decision – Guidelines on COMI, INSOL World – Third Quarter 2006, p 9; *Bayer* Die EuGH-Entscheidung „Inspire Art" und die deutsche GmbH im Wettbewerb der europäischen Rechtsordnungen, BB 2003, p 2357; *Bazinas* EU Regulation on Insolvency Proceedings: A first year and the outlook from Greece, Presented at the International Insolvency Institute 3rd Annual International Insolvency Conference, Fordham University Law School, New York, 9–10 June 2003; *Beck* Verteilungsfragen im Verhältnis zwischen Haupt- und Sekundärverfahren nach der EuInsVO, NZI 2007, p 1; *Beck* Verwertungsfragen im Verhältnis von Haupt- und Sekundärinsolvenzverfahren nach der EuInsVO, NZI 2006, p 609; *Behrens* Das Internationale Gesellschaftsrecht nach dem Überseering-Urteil des EuGH und den Schlussanträgen zu Inspire Art, IPRax 2003, p 193; *Behrens* Gemeinschaftsrechtliche Grenzen der Anwendung inländischen Gesellschaftsrechts auf Auslandsgesellschaften nach Inspire Art, IPRax 2004, p 20; *Behrens* Reaktionen mitgliedstaatlicher Gerichte auf das Centros-Urteil des EuGH, IPRax 2000, p 384; *Berner/Klöhn* Insolvenzantragspflicht, Qualifikation und Niederlassungsfreiheit, ZIP 2007, p 106; *Bernstorff v.* Das Betreiben einer englischen Limited in Deutschland, RIW 2004, p 498; *Beutler/Debus* Comments on Landesgericht Klagenfurt, EWiR Art 3 EuInsVO 3/2005, p 217; *Binge/Thölke* „Everything goes!" – Das deutsche Internationale Gesellschaftsrecht nach „Inspire Art", DNotZ 2004, p 21; *Bismarck von/Schümann-Kleber* Insolvenz eines deutschen Sicherungsgebers – Auswirkungen auf die Verwertung im Ausland belegener Kreditsicherheiten, NZI 2005, p 89; *Bitter* Flurschäden im Gläubigerschutzrecht durch „Centros & Co."?, WM 2004, p 2190; Black's Law Dictionary (7th edn 1999); *Blersch/Goetsch/Haas* Berliner Kommentar zum Insolvenzrecht (April 2006); *Boehmer v.* (Deutsches) Internationales Insolvenzrecht im Umbruch: Grundfragen grenzüberschreitender Insolvenzen, unter Berücksichtigung der UNCITRAL-Modellbestimmungen über grenzüberschreitende Insolvenzverfahren (2006); *Borges* Die Sitztheorie in der Centros-Ära: Vermeintliche Probleme und unvermeidliche Änderungen, RIW 2000, p 167; *Borges* Gläubigerschutz bei ausländischen Gesellschaften mit inländischem Sitz, ZIP 2004, p 733; *Bork* (ed) Handbuch des Insolvenzanfechtungsrechts (2006); *Bork* Die Aufrechnung im internationalen Insolvenzrecht, ZIP 2002, p 690; *Bork* Die Geltendmachung der Existenzvernichtungshaftung in der Insolvenz, KTS 2006, p 39; *Bork* Europarechtswidrige Gesellschafterdarlehen in der Insolvenz, in Schneider (ed), Festschrift Lutter (2000) p 301; *Bormann* Chronik der Rechtsentwicklung: Rumänien, WiRO 2006, p 29; *Böttcher* Gesetz über die Zwangsversteigerung und die Zwangsverwaltung (4th edn 2005); *Braun* Kommentar zur Insolvenzordnung (2004); *Braun/ Heinrich* Finanzdienstleister in der „grenzüberschreitenden" Insolvenz – Lücken im System ? – Ein Beitrag zu der Verordnung (EG) Nr. 1346/2000 des Rates vom 29.5.2000 über Insolvenzverfahren, NZI 2005, p 579; *Brenner* Comments on AG Hamburg dated 14/5/2003 – 67g IN 358/02, EWiR 2003, p 925; *Brenner* Zur Insolvenzfähigkeit ausländischer Gesellschaften mit Inlandssitz, EWiR 2003, p 925; *Breslau/Heron* Interview with the former U.S. President William J. Clinton in The Debriefing: Bill Clinton, Wired Magazine, 8 December 2000, available at: http://www.wired.com/ wired/archive/8.12/clinton.html (citing generally *Robert Wright*, Nonzero: The Logic of Human Destiny (2000)); *Breutigam/Blersch/Goetsch* Berliner Kommentar zum Insolvenzrecht (April 2006); *Buchberger D./Buchberger R.* Das System der „kontrollierten" Universalität des Konkursverfahrens nach der Europäischen Insolvenzverordnung, ZIK 2000, p 149; *Bufford* International Accord, Los Angeles Lawyer, p 33–41 (July–August 2006); *Bufford* International Insolvency Case Venue in The European Union: The Parmalat and Daisytek Controversies, in: The Columbia Journal of European Law Vol. 12 No. 2 2006, p 429; *Bufford/Adler/Brooks/Krieger* International Insolvency (Federal Judicial Center 2001); *Bureau* Comments on Cass com dated 21/3/2006, Bull Joly 2006, p 185; *Bureau* La fin d'un îlot de résistance : Le règlement du Conseil relatif aux procédures d'insolvabilité, RCDIP 2002, p 613; *Burg* Existenzvernichtungshaftung in der Private Limited Company?, GmbHR 2004, p 1379; *Burman* Harmonization of International Bankruptcy Law: a United States Perspective, Fordham L.R, 64, 1996, p 2543; *Carstens* Die internationale Zuständigkeit im europäischen Insolvenzrecht (2005); *Chalupsky* Das europäische Übereinkommen über Insolvenzverfahren, in Baudenbacher (ed), Aktuelle Probleme des Europäischen und Internationalen Wirtschaftsrechts, vol I (1998); *Chaput* Centre des intérêts principaux et catégories juridiques de l'insolvabilité des entreprises (à propos de l'arrêt CJCE du 2 mai 2006), Comments on ECJ dated 2/5/2006, Rev Lamy dr aff Juni 2006, p 26; *Correnti* Einführung in das italienische Insolvenzrecht und seine Reform, ZInsO 2006, p 1020; *Costa* Die Reform des italienischen Insolvenzrechts, ZInsO 2006, p 1071; *Courbe* L'effet international de la faillite: la solution de la Cour de cassation, in Jault-Seseke/Robine (eds) L'effet international de la faillite: une réalité? (2004); *Csia/Martinez Ferber* Comments on Municipality Court Fejer/Székesfehérvár (Hungary) dated 14/6/2004 – 9. Fpk. 01-04-0029116/2, ZInsO 2004, p 861; *Dammann/Podeur* L'affaire Daisytek: l'épilogue. Application par la Cour de cassation du règlement européen relatif aux procédures d'insolvabilité, Banque et droit 2006 n° 109, p 3; *Dammann/Podeur* L'affaire Eurotunnel, première application du règlement CE n° 1346-2000 à la procédure de sauvegarde, Dalloz 2006, p 2329; *Dammann/Podeur* Le mandat ad hoc, une „porte d'entrée" pour l'application aux groupes de sociétés du règlement européen relatif aux procédures d'insolvabilité, Rev Lamy dr aff November 2006, p 104; *Dammann* Comments on CA Versailles dated 15/12/2005, Dalloz 2006, p 379; *Dammann* Comments on ECJ Eurofood, Dalloz 2006, p 1752; *Dammann* Comments on TC Nanterre dated 15/5/2005, Dalloz 2005, p 1787; *Dammann* Conflits de juridictions et Forum shopping, Dalloz 2005, p 1779; *Dammann* Das neue französische Insolvenzrecht RIW 2006, p 16; *Dammann* Das neue französische Insolvenzrecht, ZIP 1996, p 300; *Dammann* L'application du règlement CE n° 1346-2000 après les arrêts *Staubitz-Schreiber* et *Eurofood* de la CJCE, Dalloz 2006, p 1752; *Dammann* L'évolution du droit européen des procédures d'insolvabilité et ses conséquences sur le projet de loi de sauvegarde, Rev Lamy dr aff April 2005, p 18; *Dammann* La future procédure de conciliation, pierre angulaire du projet de loi de sauvegarde des entreprises, Revue Lamy Droit des affaires, Juni 2005, p 5; *Dammann* La loi de sauvegarde des entreprises, Bull Lamy Sociétés Commerciales November 2005, no 184; *Dammann* La mobilité des sociétés et la localisation des actifs, JCP E, March–April 2006; *Dammann* La réforme des sûretés mobilières: une occasion manquée, Dalloz 2006, p 1298; *Dammann* Mobility of companies and localisation of assets, pleading in favor of a dynamic and teleological interpretation of the EC Regulation no 1346/2000 on Insolvency Proceedings, ICC-Conference in Paris on International Insolvency Law, 11 June 2006 (publication in preparation); *Dammann* Vers une interprétation pragmatique du règlement européen des faillites, Banque June 2006; *Dammann/Ollivry* Réflexions sur l'aménagement du principe d'universalité de la faillite, JCP E 2006, p 2628; *Dammann/Podeur* The Eurotunnel case, A success for the Sauvegarde process, Global Turnaround March 2007, p 11; *Dammann/Sénéchal* Procédure secondaire du Règlement (CE) n° 1346/2000: mode d'emploi, Rev Lamy dr aff October 2006; *Dammann/Undritz* Die Reform des französischen Insolvenzrechts im Rechtsvergleich zur InsO, NZI 2005, p 198; *Dassler/Schiffhauer/Gerhardt* Gesetz über die Zwangsversteigerung und die Zwangsverwaltung (1991); *Deipenbrock* Das neue europäische Internationale Insolvenzrecht – von der „quantité négligeable" zu einer „quantité indispensable", EWS 2001, p 113; *Derleder/Knops/Bamberger* Handbuch zum deutschen und europäischen Bankrecht (2004); *Dicey/Morris/Morse* Conflict of Laws: Fourth Cumulative Supplement (1991); *Dierksmeier* Die englische Ltd. in Deutschland – Haftungsrisiko für Berater, BB 2005, p 1516; *Dolinger* The Bustamante Code and the Interamerican Conventions in the Brazilian System of Private International Law, in Kleinheisterkamp/Lorenzo Idiarte (ed) Festschrift für Samtleben – „Avances del Derecho Internacional Privado en América Latina – Liber Americorum Jürgen Samtleben" (eds Kleinheisterkamp/Lorenzo Idiarte) (2002), p 133; *Drobnig* in Kegel/Thieme (eds), Vorschläge und Gutachten zum Entwurf eines EG-Konkursübereinkommens (1988) p 358 et seq; *Drygala* Comments on ECJ dated 30/09/2003 – C-167/01, EWiR 2003, p 1029; *Duursma* Der Anwendungsbereich der Insolvenzverordnung, IPRax 2003, p 505; *Duursma/Duursma-Kepplinger* Gegensteuerungsmaßnahmen bei ungerechtfertigter Inanspruchnahme der internationalen Zuständigkeit gemäß Art 3 Abs 1 EuInsVO, DZWiR 2003, p 447; *Duursma-Kepplinger* Checkliste zur Eröffnung eines Insolvenzverfahrens nach der Europäischen Insolvenzverordnung und zum anwendbaren Recht, NZI 2003, p 87; *Duursma-Kepplinger* Eigentumsvorbehalt und Mobilienleasing in der Insolvenz (2002); *Duursma-Kepplinger* Aktuelle Entwicklungen zur internationalen Zuständigkeit für Hauptinsolvenzverfahren – Erkenntnisse aus Staubitz-Schreiber und Eurofood, ZIP 2007, p 896; *Duursma-Kepplinger/Duursma* Das Schicksal von dinglichen Sicherungsrechten sowie des Eigentumsvorbehalts nach der InsolvenzVO (VO 1346/2000), wbl 2002, p 59; *Duursma-Kepplinger/Duursma* Das Schicksal von dinglichen Sicherungsrechten sowie des Eigentumsvorbehalts nach der Insolvenzverordnung, wbl 2002, p 59; *Duursma-Kepplinger/Duursma/Chalupsky* Europäische Insolvenzverordnung, Kommentar (2002); *Ebenroth* Die Inlandswirkungen der ausländischen lex fori concursus bei Insolvenz einer Gesellschaft, ZZP 101 (1988), p 139 et seq; *Ebke* Das Centros-Urteil des EuGH und seine Relevanz für das deutsche Internationale Gesellschaftsrecht, JZ 1999, p 656; *Ehricke* Das Verhältnis des Hauptinsolvenzverwalters zum Sekundärinsolvenzverwalter bei grenzüberschreitenden Insolvenzen nach der EuInsVO, ZIP 2005, p 1104; *Ehricke* Die neue Europäische Insolvenzverordnung und grenzüberschreitende Konzerninsolvenzen, EWS 2002, p 101; *Ehricke* Die Umsetzung der Finanzsicherheitenrichtlinie (Richtlinie 2002/47/EG) im Rahmen des Diskussionsentwurfs zur Änderung der Insolvenzordnung, ZIP 2003, p 1065 and ZIP 2003, p 1068; *Ehricke* Die Zusammenarbeit der Insolvenzverwalter bei grenzüberschreitenden Insolvenzen nach der EuInsVO, WM 2005, p 397; *Ehricke* Die Zusammenfassung von Insolvenzverfahren mehrerer Unternehmen desselben Konzerns, DZWiR 1999, p 356; *Ehricke* Zum anwendbaren Recht auf ein in einem Clearing-System vereinbartes Glattstellungsverfahren im Fall der Insolvenz ausländischer Clearing-Teilnehmer, WM 2006, p 2109; *Ehricke/Ries* Die neue Europäische Insolvenzverordnung, JuS 2003, p 313; *Eickmann* Zwangsversteigerungs- u. Zwangsverwaltungsrecht, 2nd edn (2004); *Eickmann/Flessner/Irschlinger/Kirchhof/Kreft/Landfermann/Marotzke* Heidelberger Kommentar zur Insolvenzordnung (2006); *Eidenmüller* Beurteilung der Rechtsfähigkeit einer ausländischen Gesellschaft nach dem Recht des Gründungsstaates, JZ 2003, p 526; *Eidenmüller* Der Markt für internationale Konzerninsolvenzen: Zuständigkeitskonflikte unter der EuInsVO, NJW 2004, p 3455; *Eidenmüller* Europäische Verordnung über Insolvenzverfahren und zukünftiges deutsches internationales Insolvenzrecht, IPRax 2001, p 2; *Eidenmüller* Geschäftsleiter- und Gesellschafterhaftung bei europäischen Auslandsgesellschaften mit tatsächlichem Inlandssitz, NJW 2005, p 1618; *Eidenmüller* Mobilität und Restrukturierung von Unternehmen im Binnenmarkt, JZ 2004, p 24; *Eidenmüller* Niederlassungsfreiheit versus Schutz des inländischen Rechtsverkehrs: Konturen des Europäischen Internationalen Gesellschaftsrechts, ZGR 2004, p 159; *Eidenmüller* Unternehmenssanierung zwischen Markt und Gesetz: Mechanismen der Unternehmensreorganisation und Kooperationspflichten im Reorganisationsrecht (1999); *Eidenmüller* Wettbewerb der Gesellschaftsrechte, ZIP 2002, p 2233; *Eidenmüller* Wettbewerb der Insolvenzrechte?, ZGR 2006, p 467; *Emmerich/Sonnenschein* Konzernrecht (6th edn 1997); *Engel* Suggested Clarifications and Reforms for U.S. Chapter 15 and the UNCITRAL Model Law on Cross-Border Insolvency on Which It Is Based: The Pragmatic Cynics' Concerns (prepared for International Insolvency Institute New York Program, 12–13 June 2006), available at: http://www.iiiglobal.org/country/usa/20060620morrison.pdf (last viewed 20 March 2007); *Farley/Leonard/Birch* Cooperation and Coordination in Cross-Border Insolvency Cases (paper delivered on the INSOL conference in May 2006); *Fasquelle* Comments on TC Nanterre dated 19/5/2005, JCP E

2006, p 1412; *Fasquelle* Comments on ECJ dated 2/5/2005 (Eurofood), Bull Joly 2006; *Felsenfeld/Gropper/Beltzer* (eds) A Treatise on the Law of International Insolvency (1999); *Ferid/Sonnenberger* Das französische Zivilrecht (2nd edn 1986); *Fischer* Die Verlegung des Gläubigerschutzes vom Gesellschafts- in das Insolvenzrecht, ZIP 2004, p 1477; *Fleischer* Der Rechtsmissbrauch zwischen Gemeineuropäischem Privatrecht und Gemeinschaftsrecht, JZ 2003, p 865; *Fleischer* Kapitalschutz und Durchgriffshaftung bei Auslandsgesellschaften, in Lutter (ed), Europäische Auslandsgesellschaften in Deutschland (2005) p 49; *Flessner* Das künftige internationale Insolvenzrecht im Verhältnis zum Europäischen Insolvenzübereinkommen. Anwendbares Recht, Reichweite der Anerkennung, Insolvenzplan und Schuldbefreiung, in Stoll (ed), Vorschläge und Gutachten, p 219; *Flessner* Die Unternehmensperspektive im europäischen Insolvenzrecht, in Festschrift für Thomas Raiser zum 70. Geburtstag (2005), p 827; *Flessner* Dingliche Sicherungsrechte nach dem Europäischen Insolvenzübereinkommen, in Basedow/Hopt/Kötz (eds), Festschrift Drobnig (1998) p 277 et seq; *Flessner* in FS Merz (1992), p 93; *Flessner* Internationales Insolvenzrecht in Deutschland nach der Reform, IPRax 1997, p 1; *Fletcher* Insolvency in Private International Law (2005); *Fletcher* The Law of Insolvency (2002); *Florian* Das englische internationale Insolvenzecht (1989); *Forsthoff* EuGH fördert Vielfalt im Gesellschaftsrecht, DB 2002, p 2471; Frankfurter Kommentar zur Insolvenzordnung, edited by Klaus Wimmer (4th edn 2006); *Freitag/Leible* Justizkonflikte im Europäischen Internationalen Insolvenzrecht und (k)ein Ende?, RIW 2006, p 641; *Fritz/Bähr* Die Europäische Verordnung über Insolvenzverfahren – Herausforderung an Gerichte und Insolvenzverwalter, DZWiR 2001, p 221; *Fröhlich/Strasser* Die Limited als Einzelkaufmann mit beschränkter Haftung? Deliktsrechtliche Gegenargumente, ZIP 2006, p 1182; *Galanti* The New EC Law on Bank Crisis, International Insolvency Review 2002, p 49; *Geyrhalter/Gänßler* „Inspire Art" – Briefkastengesellschaften „on the Move", DStR 2003, p 2167; *Geyrhalter/Gänßler* Perspektiven nach „Überseering" – wie geht es weiter?, NZG 2003, p 409; *Giovanoli/Heinrich* (eds) International Bank Insolvencies – A Central Bank Perspective (1999); *Glosband* für Leonard (15. Sep. 2003), Memorandum re Proposed Chapter 15 of the United States Bankruptcy Code, available at http://www.iiiglobal.org/international/cross_border/United_States_Daniel%20Glosband.pdf (last visited April 6, 2007); *Glosband* SPhinX Chapter 15 Opinion Misses the Mark, American Bankruptcy Institute Journal 44 (Dec/Jan 2007), p 44–45, p 84–85; *Goette* Wo steht der BGH nach „Centros" und „Inspire Art"?, DStR 2005, p 197; *Gottwald* FamRZ 2002, p 1423; *Gottwald* Grenzüberschreitende Insolvenzen (1997); *Gottwald* Grenzüberschreitende Insolvenzen (1997); *Gottwald* Insolvenzrechtshandbuch (2006); *Gottwald/Pfaller* Aspekte der Anerkennung ausländischer Insolvenzverfahren im Inland, IPRax 1998, p 170; *Grasmann* Effets nationaux d'une procédure d'exécution collective étrangère (redressement ou liquidation judiciaires, faillite, concordat), RCDIP 1990, p 419; *Grigoleit* Gesellschafterhaftung für interne Einflussnahme im Recht der GmbH (2006); *Gross/Schork* Strafbarkeit des directors einer Private Company Limited by Shares wegen verspäteter Insolvenzantragstellung, NZI 2006, p 10; *Grütters* BB-Forum: Limited auf dem Vormarsch – Serien-Reinfälle nicht ausgeschlossen, BB 2005, p 1523; *Haas* Der Normzweck des Eigenkapitalersatzrechts, NZI 2001, p 1; *Haas* Die Verwertung der im Ausland belegenen Insolvenzmasse im Anwendungsbereich der EuInsVO, in Schilken/Kreft/Wagner/Eckhardt (eds), Festschrift Gerhardt (2004) p 319; *Habersack/Verse* Wrongful Trading – Grundlage einer europäischen Insolvenzverschleppungshaftung, ZHR 168 (2004), p 174; *Haberscheid* Konkursstatut und Wirkungsstatut bei der internationalen und der künftigen innereuropäischen Insolvenzanfechtung, ZZP (114) 2001, p 167; Hamburger Kommentar zum Insolvenzrecht (2006) (ed Schmidt, A.); *Hanisch* Das Recht grenzüberschreitender Insolvenzen – Auswirkungen im Immobiliensektor, ZIP 1992, p 1125; *Hanisch* Stellungnahme zu der Frage, ob und gegebenenfalls in welcher Weise ein in seiner Wirkung territorial beschränktes Sonderinsolvenzverfahren über das Inlandsvermögen eines Schuldners vorzusehen ist, wenn dieser den Mittelpunkt seiner hauptsächlichen im Ausland hat, in Stoll (ed), Vorschläge und Gutachten zur Umsetzung des EU-Übereinkommens über Insolvenzverfahren im deutschen Recht (1997), p 202; *Happ/Holler* „Limited" statt GmbH? – Risiken und Kosten werden gern verschwiegen, DStR 2004, p 730; *Hase v.* Insolvenzantragspflicht für directors einer Limited in Deutschland, BB 2006, p 2141; *Haß/Huber/Gruber/Heiderhoff* EU-Insolvenzverordnung, Kommentar (2005); *Haubold* Europäisches Zivilverfahrensrecht und Ansprüche im Zusammenhang mit Insolvenzverfahren, IPRax 2002, p 157; *Haubold* Mitgliedstaatenbezug, Zuständigkeitserschleichung und Vermögensgerichtsstand im Internationalen Insolvenzrecht, IPRax 2003, p 34; Heidelberger Kommentar zur Insolvenzordnung (4th edn 2006) (eds

Eickmann/Flessner/Irschlinger/Kirchhof/Kreft/Landfermann/Marotzke/Stephan); *Heinz* Englische Limited und Deutsche GmbH – eine vergleichende Darstellung, AnwBl 2004, p 612; *Heiss/Gölz* Zur deutschen Umsetzung der Richtlinie 2001/17/EG des Europäischen Parlaments und des Rates vom 19.3.2001 über die Sanierung und Liquidation von Versicherungsunternehmen, NZI 2006, p 1; *Henry* Comments on Cass com dated 21/3/2006, Dalloz 2006, p 1466; *Henze* Aspekte des Insolvenzrechts an der Schnittstelle zum Gesellschaftsrecht, WM 2006, p 1653; *Herchen* Aktuelle Entwicklungen im Recht der internationalen Zuständigkeit zur Eröffnung von Insolvenzverfahren: Der Mittelpunkt der (hauptsächlichen) Interessen im mittelpunkt der Interessen, ZInsO 2004, p 825; *Herchen* Das Prioritätsprinzip im internationalen Insolvenzrecht, ZIP 2005, p 1401; *Herchen* Das Übereinkommen über Insolvenzverfahren der Mitgliedstaaten der Europäischen Union vom 23.11. 1995 (2000); *Herchen* Die Befugnisse des deutschen Insolvenzverwalters hinsichtlich der „Auslandsmasse" nach In-Kraft-Treten der EG-Insolvenzverordnung (Verordnung des Rates Nr. 1346/2000), ZInsO 2002, p 345; *Herchen* International-Insolvenzrechtliche Kompetenzkonflikte in der Europäischen Gemeinschaft, ZInsO 2004, p 61; *Herchen* Scheinauslandsgesellschaften im Anwendungsbereich der Europäischen Insolvenzverordnung, Comments on High Court of Justice, Chancery Division (Company Court) dated 7/2/2003, ZInsO 2003, p 742; *Herchen* Wer zuerst kommt, mahlt zuerst! – Die Bestellung eines „schwachen" vorläufigen Insolvenzverwalters als Insolvenzverfahrenseröffnung im Sinne der EuInsVO, NZI 2006, p 435; *Herweg/Tschauner* Comments on AG Hamburg dated 1/12/2005 – 67a IN 450/05, EWiR 2006, p 169; *Herweg/Tschauner* Comments on High Court Dublin (Justice Kelly) dated 23/3/2004 – 33/04, EWiR 2004, p 599; *Herweg/Tschauner* Comments on AG Düsseldorf dated 12/3/2004 – 502 IN 126/03, EWiR 2004, p 495; *Hess* Neues deutsches und europäisches Zustellungsrecht NJW 2002, p 2417; *Hess/Laukemann/Seagon* Europäisches Insolvenzrecht nach Eurofood: Methodische Standortsbestimmung und praktische Schlussfolgerungen, IPRax 2007, p 89; *Hinkel* Comments on OLG Frankfurt dated 26/1/2006 – 15 U 200/05 –, ZIP 2006, p 769; *Hinkel/Flitsch* Comments on OLG Frankfurt dated 26/1/2006 – 15 U 200/05 –, EWiR 2006, p 237; *Hintzen* Höhe des Zinsausgleiches nach Einstellung der Zwangsversteigerung, ZInsO 2000, p 205; *Hintzen* Insolvenz und Immobiliarzwangsvollstreckung, Rpfleger 1999, p 256; *Hirsch/Britain* Artfully Inspired – Werden deutsche Gesellschaften englisch?, NZG 2003, p 1100; *Hirte/Bücker* Grenzüberschreitende Gesellschaften – Praxishandbuch für ausländische Gesellschaften mit Sitz im Inland (2nd edn 2006); *Hirte/Mock* Wohin mit der Insolvenzantragspflicht?, ZIP 2005, p 474; *Holzer* Rechte und Pflichten des Geschäftsführers einer nach englischem Recht gegründeten „limited" im Hinblick auf das deutsche Insolvenzverfahren, ZVI 2005, p 457; *Homann* System der Anerkennung eines ausländischen Insolvenzverfahrens, KTS 2000, p 343; *Horn* Deutsches und europäisches Gesellschaftsrecht und die EuGH-Rechtsprechung zur Niederlassungsfreiheit – Inspire Art, NJW 2004, p 893; *Houin* Konkursprobleme des gemeinsamen Marktes, KTS 1961, p 177; *Hub* Die Neuregelung der Anerkennung und Vollstreckung in Zivil- und Handelssachen und das familienrechtliche Anerkennungs- und Vollstreckungsverfahren, NJW 2001, p 3145; *Huber* Der deutsch-englische Justizkonflikt – Kompetenzkonflikte im internationalen Insolvenzrecht, in Lorenz/Trunk/Eidenmüller/Wendehorst/Adolff (eds), Festschrift für Heldrich (2005), p 679; *Huber* Die Europäische Insolvenzverordnung, EuZW 2002, p 490; *Huber* Die Insolvenzantragspflicht der Geschäftsführer von Auslandsgesellschaften, in Lutter (ed), Europäische Auslandsgesellschaften in Deutschland (2005) p 307; *Huber* Gesellschafterdarlehen in der Inlandsinsolvenz von Auslandsgesellschaften, in Lutter (ed), Europäische Auslandsgesellschaften in Deutschland (2005) p 131; *Huber* Internationales Insolvenzrecht in Europa ZZP 114 (2001), p 133; *Huber U.* Inländische Insolvenzverfahren über Auslandsgesellschaften nach der Europäischen Insolvenzverordnung, in Schilken/Kreft/Wagner/Eckhardt (eds), Festschrift Gerhardt (2004) p 397 et seq; INSOL, Transcript of the Open Forum at UNCITRAL – INSOL International Second Multinational Judicial Colloquium (March 1997); International Bar Association, Committee J of the Section on Business Law, "Cross-Border Insolvency Concordat" (adopted by the Council of the Section of Business Law of the International Bar Association on Sept 17, 1995, and by the Council of the International Bar Association on May 31, 1996), available at: http://www.iiiglobal.org/international/projects/concordat.pdf (last viewed April 4, 2007); *Israël* European Cross-Border Insolvency Regulation (2005); *Jacquemont* Comments on Cour de cassation dated 4/9/2003, JDI 2004, p 142; *Jahn* Insolvenzen in Europa (4th edn 2004); *Jahr* Vereinheitlichtes Internationales Konkursrecht in der Europäischen Wirtschaftsgemeinschaft: Der Vorentwurf eines Übereinkommens über den Konkurs, Vergleich und ähnliche Verfahren,

RabelsZ 36 (1972), p 620; *Jault-Seseke* Le sort des salariés, in Jault-Seseke/Robine (eds), L'effet international de la faillite : une réalité ? (2004) p 151; *Jault-Seseke/Robine* Comments on TC Nanterre dated 15/2/2006 (SAS EMTEC), Bull Joly Sociétés 2006, p 575; *Jault-Seseke/Robine* L'interprétation du Règlement n° 1346/2000 relatif aux procédures d'insolvabilité, la fin des incertitudes ?, RCDIP 2006; *Just* Comments on LG Kiel dated 20/04/2005 – 10 S 44/05, ZIP 2006, p 1248; *Kallmeyer* Vor- und Nachteile der englischen Limited im Vergleich zur GmbH oder GmbH & Co. KG, DB 2004, p 636; *Kammel* Die Bestimmung der zuständigen Gerichte bei grenzüberschreitenden Konzerninsolvenzen, NZI 2006, p 334; *Kebekus* Comments on AG Nuremberg dated 1/10/2006, ZIP 2007, p 84; *Kebekus* Hauptinsolvenzverfahren, Sekundärinsolvenzverfahren, Mittelpunkt der hauptsächlichen Interessen/ EMBIC I, EWiR 2004, p 705; *Kegel/Thieme* Vorschläge und Gutachten zum Entwurf eines EG-Konkursübereinkommens (1988); *Keidel/Kuntze/Winkler* Freiwillige Gerichtsbarkeit (2005); *Keller* Die EG-Richtlinie 98/26 vom 19.5.1998 über die Wirksamkeit von Abrechnungen in Zahlungs- sowie Wertpapierliefer- und -abrechnungssystemen und ihre Umsetzung in Deutschland, WM 2000, p 1269; *Keller/Langner* Überblick über EG-Gesetzgebungsvorhaben im Finanzbereich, BRK 2003, p 616; *Kemper* Die Verordnung (EG) Nr. 1346/2000 über Insolvenzverfahren, ZIP 2001, p 1609; *Keppelmüller* An der Schwelle zu einem europäischen Insolvenzrecht?, wbl 1996, p 337; *Keppelmüller* Österreichisches internationales Konkursrecht (1997); *Kessler/Eicke* Die Limited – Fluch oder Segen für die Steuerberatung, DStR 2005, p 2101; *Khairallah* Comments on CA Versailles dated 4/9/2003, RCDIP 2003, p 667; *Khairallah* Comments on Cour de cassation dated 19/11/2002, Dalloz 2003, p 797; *Kieper* Abwicklungssysteme in der Insolvenz – Dargestellt am Beispiel der Eurex Deutschland (2004); *Kindler* „Inspire Art" – Aus Luxemburg nichts Neues zum internationalen Gesellschaftsrecht, NZG 2003, p 1086; *Kindler* Auf dem Weg zur Europäischen Briefkastengesellschaft? – Die „Überseering" – Entscheidung des EuGH und das internationale Privatrecht, NJW 2003, p 1073; *Kindler* Sitzverlegung und internationales Insolvenzrecht, IPRax 2006, p 144; *Klein* Frankreichs Insolvenzrechtsreform setzt auf Vorbeugung, RIW 2006, p 13; *Kleinert/Probst* Endgültiges Aus für Sonderanknüpfungen bei (Schein-) Auslandsgesellschaften – Comments on ECJ dated 30/9/2003 – C-167/01 – Inspire Art, DB 2003, p 2217; *Klöhn* Statische oder formale Lebenssachverhalte als „Interessen" i.S. des Art. 3 I 1 EuInsVO? – Zum Mittelpunkt der hauptsächlichen Interessen einer im Ausland gegründeten Gesellschaft bei Einstellung ihrer werbenden Tätigkeit im Inland, NZI 2006, p 383; *Klöhn* Verlegung des Mittelpunkts der hauptsächlichen Interessen iSd Art 3 Abs 1 S 1 EuInsVO vor Stellung des Insolvenzantrags, KTS 2006, p 259; *Knof* Europäisches Insolvenzrecht und Schuldbefreiungs-Tourismus, ZInsO 2005, p 1017; *Knof* Internationale Zuständigkeit bei Abwicklungstätigkeiten nach Einstellung der werbenden Tätigkeit einer GmbH, Comments on AG Hamburg dated 16/8/2006, NZI 2006, p 653; *Knof Perpetuatio fori* und Attraktivkraft des Erstantrags im Europäischen Insolvenzrecht?, ZInsO 2006, p 754; *Knof/Mock* Comments on ECJ dated 2/5/2006, ZIP 2006, p 911; *Knof/Mock* Zur perpetuatio fori bei Sitzverlegung nach Stellung eines Insolvenzantrags, ZIP 2006, p 189; *Knof/Mock* Zuständigkeit des Insolvenzgerichts auch bei COMI-Verlegung des Schuldners zwischen Antragsstellung und Insolvenzeröffnung („Susanne Staubitz-Schreiber"), Comments on ECJ dated 17/1/2006, ZIP 2006, p 189; *Knöpfel* Gefahren beim Einsatz von Ltd.-Gründungsagenturen: Auftrags- und Beratungsumfang contra Qualifikation?, BB 2006, p 1233; *Kodek* Comments on AG Nuremberg dated 1/10/2006 – 8034 IN 1326/06, EWiR 2007, p 179; *Köke* Die englische Limited in der Insolvenz, ZInsO 2005, p 354; *Kolmann* Kooperationsmodelle im Internationalen Insolvenzrecht – Empfiehlt sich für das deutsche internationale Insolvenzrecht eine Neuorientierung (2001); *Krebber* Europäische Insolvenzverordnung, Drittstaatengesellschaften, Drittstaatensachverhalte under innergemeinschaftliche Konflikte (zur Entscheidung des High Court vom 7.2.2003, In re BRAC Rent-A-Car International Inc.), IPRax 2004, p 540; *Kropholler* Europäisches Zivilprozessrecht, 7th edn (2002); *Kübler* Mittelpunkt der hauptsächlichen Interessen nach Art 3 Abs 1 EuInsVO, in Schilken/Kreft/Wagner/Eckhardt (eds), Festschrift für Gerhardt (2004), p 527; *Kübler/Prütting* Kommentar zur Insolvenzordnung (March 2006); *Kuntz* Die Insolvenz der Limited mit deutschem Verwaltungssitz – EU-Kapitalgesellschaften in Deutschland nach „Inspire Art", NZI 2005, p 424; *Kuntze/Ertl/Hermann/Eickmann* Grundbuchrecht, 5th edn (1999); *Lagarde* Comments on Cour de cassation dated 19/3/1979, RCDIP 1981, p 524; *Lautenbach* Comments on AG Mönchengladbach dated 27/4/2004 – 19 IN 54/04, NZI 2004, p 384; *Legros* Comments on Cass com dated 21/3/2006, JCP E 2006, No 2072; *Lehr* Die neue EU-Verordnung über Insolvenzverfahren und deren Auswirkungen für die Unternehmenspraxis, KTS 2000, p 577; *Leible* Niederlassungsfreiheit und Sitzverlegungsrichtlinie, ZGR 2004, p 531; *Leible/Freitag* Justizkonflikte im Europäischen Internationalen Insolvenzrecht, RIW 2006, p 641; *Leible/Hoffmann* Entscheidungsbesprechung: „Überseering" und das deutsche Gesellschaftskollisionsrecht, ZIP 2003, p 925; *Leible/Hoffmann* Wie inspiriert ist „Inspire Art"?, EuZW 2003, p 677; *Leible/Staudinger* Die europäische Verordnung über Insolvenzverfahren, KTS 2000, p 533; *Leipold* Zum künftigen Weg des deutschen Internationalen Insolvenzrechts (Anwendungsbereich, internationale Zuständigkeit, Anerkennung und Vollstreckung), in Stoll (ed), Vorschläge und Gutachten, p 185; *Leipold* Zuständigkeitslücken im neuen Europäischen Insolvenzrecht, in Lüke/Mikami/Prütting (eds), FS Ishikawa (2001), p 221; *Lemontey* Bericht über das Übereinkommen über den Konkurs, Vergleiche und ähnliche Verfahren, in Kegel/Thieme (eds), Vorschläge und Gutachten zum Entwurf eines EG-Konkursübereinkommen (1988); *Leutner/Langer* Durchgriffshaftung bei Scheinauslandsgesellschaften, ZInsO 2005, p 575; *Lieder* Die Haftung der Geschäftsführer und Gesellschafter von EU-Auslandsgesellschaften mit tatsächlichem Verwaltungssitz in Deutschland, DZWiR 2005, p 399; *Lienhard* Comments on Cass com dated 21/3/2006, Dalloz 2006, AJ p 914; *Lienhard* Comments on CA Versailles dated 15/12/2005, Dalloz 2006, AJ p 142; *Lienhard* Comments on Cour de cassation dated 10/5/2005, Dalloz 2005, p 1414; *Lienhard* Comments on Cour de cassation dated 27/6/2006, Dalloz 2006, AJ p 1816; *Lienhard* Comments on Cour de cassation dated 5/2/2002, Dalloz 2002, AJ p 957; *Lienhard* Comments on TC Nanterre dated 15/12/2006, Dalloz 2006, AJ p 651; *Lienhard* Procédures d'insolvabilité : détermination du centre des intérêts principaux, Comments on TC Nanterre dated 15/2/2006, Dalloz 2006 AJ, p 651; *Lienhard* Procédures d'insolvabilité: déplacement du centre des intérêts principaux du débiteur, Comments on ECJ dated 17/1/2006 Dalloz 2006, AJ p 367; *Liersch* Comments on AG Düsseldorf dated 12/3/2004 – 2004 502 IN 126/03, NZI 2004, p 271; *Liersch* Comments on BGH dated 27/11/2003 – IX ZB 418/02, NZI 2004, p 141; *Liersch* Deutsches internationales Insolvenzrecht, NZI 2003, 302; *Liersch* Nach der Eurofood-Entscheidung des EuGH: Genugtuung, aber auch viel Nachdenklichkeit, NZI 6/2006, V; *Liersch* Sicherungsrechte im Internationalen Insolvenzrecht (2001); *Likillimba* Comments on Cour d'appel de Versailles dated 4/9/2003, JCP E 2003, No 1747; *Linnertz/Scholl* Mehrpersonenlimited oder vorgeschaltete Holding, NZG 2006, p 493; *Loussouarn/Borel/de Vareilles-Sommières* Droit international privé, 8th edn; *Lüer* Einheitliches Insolvenzrecht innerhalb der Europäischen Gemeinschaften – Die Quadratur des Kreises? – Anmerkung zum Entwurf eines Übereinkommens über den Konkurs, Vergleich und ähnliche Verfahren, KTS 1981, p 147; *Lüer* Zur Neuordnung des deutschen Internationalen Insolvenzrechts, in Stoll (ed), Stellungnahmen und Gutachten zur Reform des deutschen Internationalen Insolvenzrechts (1992), p 96; *Lüke* Das europäische internationale Insolvenzrecht, ZZP 111 (1998), p 275; *Lüke* Europäisches Zivilverfahrensrecht – das Problem der Abstimmung zwischen EuInsÜ und EuGVÜ, in Geimer (ed), Festschrift Schütze (1999); *Lurger* Neuere Entwicklungen im österreichischen Handels- und Wirtschaftsrecht, RIW 2005, p 209; *Lutter* (ed) Europäische Auslandsgesellschaften in Deutschland (2005); *Lutter* Überseering und die Folgen, BB 2003, p 7; *Lutter/Hommelhoff* GmbH-Gesetz, Kommentar, 16th edn (2004); *Mankowski* Comments on AG Düsseldorf dated 6/6/2003, EWiR 2003, p 767; *Mankowski* Comments on AG Cologne dated 1/12/2005 – 71 IN 564/05, EWiR 2006, p 109; *Mankowski* Comments on AG Munich dated 4/5/2004 – 1501 IE 1276/04, NZI 2004, p 450; *Mankowski* Comments on CA (Cour d'appel) Versailles dated 4/9/2003 – 05038/03, EWiR 2003, p 1239; *Mankowski* Comments on Court of Appeal (Civil Division) dated 27/7/2005 – [2005] EWCA Civ 974, NZI 2005, p 575; *Mankowski* Comments on High Court of Justice, Chancery Division, Birmingham dated 18.4.2005 – 2375–2382/05, EWiR 2005, p 637; *Mankowski* Comments on High Court of Justice, Chancery Division dated 18/8/2006 – No 5618/06, EWiR 2007, p 177; *Mankowski* Bestimmung des Mittelpunkts der hauptsächlichen Interessen nach Zeitpunkt der Verfahrenseröffnung, Comments on Court of Appeal Civil Division dated 27/7/2005 – [2005] EWCA Civ 974, NZI 2005, p 571; *Mankowski* Die deutsche Ltd.-Zweigniederlassung im Spannungsverhältnis von Gewerbe- und Registerrecht, BB 2006, p 1173; *Mankowski* Entwicklungen im Internationalen Privat- und Insolvenzrecht 2003/2004 (part 1), RIW 2004, p 481; *Mankowski* Entwicklungen im Internationalen Privat- und Prozessrecht (part 2), RIW 2005, p 561; *Mankowski* EuGVÜ-Gerichtsstand für Gesellschafterhaftungsklage des Insolvenzverwalters, NZI 1999, p 56; *Mankowski* Grenzüberschreitender Umzug und das center of main interests im europäischen Internationalen Insolvenzrecht, NZI 2005, p 368; *Mankowski* Klärung von Grundfragen des europäischen Internationalen Insolvenzrechts durch die Eurofood-Entscheidung?, BB 2006, p 1753; *Mankowski* Konkursgründe beim inländischen Partikularkonkurs, ZIP 1995, p 1650; *Mankowski* Comments on AG Cologne dated 1/12/2005, EWiR 2006, p 109; *Mankowski* Mittelpunkt der hauptsächlichen Interessen bei Verlegung des Wohnsitzes nach Antragstellung, Comments on ECJ dated 17/1/2006 – C-1/04 Susanne Staubitz-Schreiber, NZI 2006, p 153; *Mankowski* Zulässigkeit der Verweisung durch deutsches Insolvenzgericht an ausländisches Gericht, Comments on AG Hamburg dated 9/5/2006, NZI 2006, p 486; *Marshall* European Cross Border Insolvency (2005); *Martinez Ferber* European Insolvency Regulation – Substantive Consolidation, the threat of Forum Shopping and a German point of view (2004); *Maul/Schmidt* C. Inspire Art – Quo vadis Sitztheorie?, BB 2003, p 2297; *Mayer* Droit international privé (6th edn 1998); *Meikel* Grundbuchrecht (9th edn 2004); *Meilicke* Der GmbHR-Kommentar, GmbHR 2003, p 1271; *Mélin* Comments on Cour d'appel de Versailles dated 4/9/2003, RJDA 1/04, p 3; *Mélin* Comments on Cour de cassation dated 27/6/2006, JCP E 2006, No 2291; *Mélin* Comments on TC Nanterre dated 19/5/2005, Act proc coll 2005 No 11; *Mélin* La faillite internationale (2004); *Mellert/Verfürth* Wettbewerb der Gesellschaftsformen (2005); *Menjucq* Comments on Cour de cassation dated 14/3/2000, Bull Joly sociétés Juni 2000, p 600; *Menjucq* Comments on Cour de cassation dated 27/6/2006, JCP G 2006 II, No 10147; *Menjucq* Comments on ECJ dated 2/5/2006 (Eurofood), JCP 2006 II, No 10089; *Menjucq* Comments on TC Nanterre dated 15/12/2006, Rev proc coll 2006, p 241; *Menjucq* Comments on TC Nanterre dated 19/5/2005, JCP G II, No 10116; *Menjucq* Aspects de droit international privé relatif aux conflits de compétence et aux conflits de lois, Rev proc coll March 2003, p 49; *Menjucq* Notion autonome du centre des intérêts principaux d'une filiale étrangère d'un groupe, Comments on ECJ dated 2/5/2006, JCP 2006, II, No 10089; *Menjucq* Ouverture, reconnaissance et coordination des procédures d'insolvabilité dans le règlement 1346/2000, Bull Joly Soc 2000, p 1111; *Meyer-Löwy/Plank* Entbehrlichkeit des Sekundärinsolvenzverfahrens bei flexibler Verteilung der Insolvenzmasse im Hauptinsolvenzverfahren, NZI 2006, p 622; *Meyer-Löwy/Poertzgen* Eigenverwaltung (§§ 270 ff InsO) löst Kompetenzkonflikt nach EuInsVO, ZInsO 2004, p 195; *Mittelstädt* Anwendbarkeit der Existenzvernichtungshaftung auf europäische Kapitalgesellschaftern, Bucerius Law Journal 2007, p 7; *Mock* Comments on LG Kiel dated 20/04/2006 – 10 S 44/05, NZI 2006, p 482; *Mock* Safe harbour für Qualifikationsprobleme bei der Insolvenzantragspflicht? NZI 2006, p 24; *Mock/Schildt* Insolvenz ausländischer Kapitalgesellschaften mit Sitz in Deutschland, ZInsO 2003, p 396; *Morscher* Die europäische Insolvenzverordnung (2002); *Mörsdorf-Schulte* Internationaler Gerichtsstand für Insolvenzanfechtungsklagen im Spannungsfeld von EuInsVO, EuGVÜ/VO und autonomem Recht und seine Überprüfbarkeit durch den BGH, IPRax 2004, p 31; *Moss/Fletcher/Isaacs* (eds) The EC Regulation on Insolvency Proceedings, A Commentary and Annotated Guide (2002); *Müller H.-F.* Insolvenz ausländischer Kapitalgesellschaften mit inländischem Verwaltungssitz, NZG 2003, p 414; *Müller K.* Die englische Limited in Deutschland – für welche Unternehmen ist sie tatsächlich geeignet?, BB 2006, p 837; Münchener Kommentar zum Bürgerlichen Gesetzbuch, vol 11 (2006); Münchener Kommentar zur Insolvenzordnung, vol 1 (2001); Münchener Kommentar zur Insolvenzordnung, vol 2 (2003); Münchener Kommentar zur Insolvenzordnung, vol 3 (2003); *Muth* Die Zwangsversteigerung auf Antrag des Insolvenzverwalters, ZIP 1999, p 945; *Nadelmann* Ausländisches Vermögen unter dem Vorentwurf eines Konkursabkommens für die EWG-Staaten, KTS 1971, p 65; *National Bankruptcy Review Commission*, Bankruptcy, the Next Twenty Years, National Bankruptcy Review Commission Final Report (1997) ("NBRC Report"); *Nerlich/Römermann* (eds) Insolvenzordnung (InsO), Kommentar (September 2005); *Niggemann/Blenske* Die Auswirkungen der Verordnung (EG) Nr. 1346/2000 auf den deutsch-französischen Rechtsverkehr, NZI 2003, p 471; *Oberhammer* Europäisches Insolvenzrecht in praxi – „Was bisher geschah", ZInsO 2004, p 761; *Oppermann* Europarecht (1991); *Oppetit* Comments on Cass com dated 11/4/1995, RCDIP 1995, p 742; *Paefgen* Wider die gesellschaftsrechtliche Ausländerphobie, ZIP 2004, p 2253; *Paefgen* Auslandsgesellschaften und Durchsetzung deutscher Schutzinteressen nach „Überseering", DB 2003, p 487; *Pannen* Internationales Insolvenzrecht, in Runkel (ed), Anwaltshandbuch-Insolvenzrecht (2005); *Pannen* Krise und Insolvenz bei Kreditinstituten, Handbuch (2nd edn 2006); *Pannen/Kühnle/Riedemann* Die Stellung des deutschen Insolvenzverwalters in einem Insolvenzverfahren mit europäischem Auslandsbezug, NZI 2003, p 72; *Pannen/Riedemann* Comments on AG Bad Segeberg, dated 24/03/2005 – 17 C 289/04, NZI 2005, p 411; *Pannen/Riedemann* Comments on AG Offenburg dated 2/8/2004 – 2 IN 133/04, EWiR 2005, p 73; *Pannen/Riedemann* Comments on AG

Weilheim i. OB dated 22/6/2005 – IN 260/05, EWiR 2005, p 791; *Pannen/Riedemann* Comments on the opinion of the ECJ Advocate General Francis Geoffrey Jacobs dated 27/9/2005 – C-341/04, EWiR 2005, p 725; *Pannen/Riedemann* Comments on OLG Düsseldorf dated 9/7/2004 – I-3 W 53/04, EWiR 2005, p 177; *Pannen/Riedemann* Checkliste: Die englische „Ltd.“ Mit Verwaltungssitz in Deutschland in der Insolvenz, MDR 2005, p 496; *Pannen/Riedemann* Der Begriff des „centre of main interests“ i.S des Art 3 I 1 EuInsVO im Spiegel aktueller Fälle aus der Rechtsprechung, NZI 2004, p 646; *Pannen/Riedemann* Die deutschen Ausführungsbestimmungen zur EuInsVO – Ein Überblick zu den Regelungen des Art. 102 EGInsO n.F., NZI 2004, p 301; *Pannen/Riedemann/Kühnle* Zur Stellung der Insolvenzgläubiger nach der Europäischen Verordnung über Insolvenzverfahren (EuInsVO), NZI 2002, p 303; *Paulus* „Protokolle“ – ein anderer Zugang zur Abwicklung grenzüberschreitender Insolvenzen, ZIP 1998, p 977; *Paulus* Änderungen des deutschen Insolvenzrechts durch die Europäische Insolvenzverordnung, ZIP 2002, p 729; *Paulus* Grundlagen des neuen Insolvenzrechts – Internationales Insolvenzrecht, DStR 2005, p 334; *Paulus* Anfechtungsklagen in grenzüberschreitenden Insolvenzverfahren, ZInsO 2006, p 295; *Paulus* Comments on AG Munich dated 4/5/2004 – 1501 IE 1276/04, EWiR 2004, p 493; *Paulus* Comments on Landesgericht Leoben dated 31/8/2005 – 17 S 56/05, NZI 2005, p 647; *Paulus* Comments on OLG Vienna dated 09/11/2004 – 28 R 225/04w, NZI 2005, p 62; *Paulus* Banken und Insolvenz – eine internationale Betrachtung, ZBB 2002, p 492; *Paulus* Das inländische Parallelverfahren nach der Europäischen Insolvenzverordnung, EWS 2002, p 497; *Paulus* Der EuGH und das moderne Insolvenzrecht, NZG 2006, p 609; *Paulus* Die europäische Insolvenzverordnung und der deutsche Insolvenzverwalter, NZI 2001, p 505; *Paulus* Europäische Insolvenzverordnung, Kommentar (2006); *Paulus* NZI aktuell 2006, Heft 8, VII; *Paulus* Überlegungen zu einem modernen Konzerninsolvenzrecht, ZIP 2005, p 1948; *Paulus* Zuständigkeitsfragen nach der Europäischen Insolvenzverordnung, ZIP 2003, p 1725; *Pellens/Jödicke/Richard*, Solvenztests als Alternative zur bilanziellen Kapitalerhaltung, DB 2005, p 1393; *Penzlin* Comments on Tribunal de Commerce de Nanterre dated 15/2/2006, EWiR 2006, p 207; *Penzlin/Riedemann* Comments on High Court of Justice Birmingham dated 18/4/2005 – 2375 to 2382/05, NZI 2005, p 469; *Penzlin/Riedemann* Comments on High Court of Justice Birmingham dated 11/05/2005 – 2375 to 2382/05, NZI 2005, p 517; *Penzlin/Riedemann* Klarstellung der Befugnisse englischer Hauptinsolvenzverwalter – MG Rover II, NZI 2005, 515; *Poertzgen/Adam* Die Bestimmung des „centre of main interests“ gem Art 3 Abs 1 EuInsVO, ZInsO 2006, p 505; *Prütting* Aktuelle Entwicklungen des internationalen Insolvenzrechts, ZIP 1996, p 1277; *Radin* Fraudulent Conveyances at Roman Law, 18 Virginia Law Review 109 (1931); *Raimon* Comments on Cour de cassation dated 5/2/2002, JCP E 2003, p 955; *Ramackers* Réflexions critiques sur la Convention européene relative à certains aspects internationaux de la failite, La Semaine Juridique 1993, p 3685; *Reinhart* Sanierungsverfahren im internationalen Insolvenzrecht (1995); *Reisch/Winkler* Die Tücken der Eröffnung eines Parallelverfahrens nach der EuInsVO, ZIK 2004, p 118; *Rémery* Comments on Cass civ dated 19/1/1988, Dalloz 1988, p 565; *Rémery* Comments on Cass civ dated 25/271986, JCP 1987 II, No 20776; *Rémery* Comments on Cour d'appel de Versailles dated 4/9/2003, Rev des sociétés 2003, p 891; *Rémery* Comments on Cour de cassation dated 31/1/1990, Dalloz 1990, p 461; *Rémery* L'application à une filiale du règlement communautaire relatif aux procédures d'insolvabilité, Comments on ECJ dated 2/5/2006, Rev Soc 2006, p 360; *Rémery* Les aspects européens de la déclaration des créances dans une procédure collective ouverte en France, Rev proc coll March 2003, p 66; *Resnick et al* Collier on Bankruptcy (2006); *Riedemann* Auseinanderfallen von Gesellschafts- und Insolvenzstatut. „Inspire Art“ und die Insolvenz über das Vermögen einer englischen „limited“ in Deutschland, GmbHR 2004, p 345; *Riegger* Centros – Überseering – Inspire Art: Folgen für die Praxis, ZGR 2004, p 510; *Ringe* Insolvenzanfechtungsklage im System des europäischen Zivilverfahrensrechts – zugleich Anmerkung zu OLG Frankfurt, Urt. v. 26.1.2006 – 15 U 200/05, ZInsO 2006, p 700; *Ringstmeier/Homann* Masseverbindlichkeiten als Prüfstein des internationalen Insolvenzrechts, NZI 2004, p 354; *Röhricht* Insolvenzrechtliche Aspekte im Gesellschaftsrecht, ZIP 2005, p 505; *Römermann* Die Limited in Deutschland – eine Alternative zur GmbH?, NJW 2006, p 2065; *Römermann/Johnen* Limited vs. GmbH: Einige „Schlachten“ hat die Limited schon gewonnen, den „Krieg“ aber noch nicht, GmbHR 2005, p R305; *Rönnau* Haftung der Direktoren einer in Deutschland ansässigen englischen Private Company Limited by Shares nach deutschem Strafrecht – eine erste Annäherung, ZGR 2005, p 832; *Rosch* Grenzüberschreitende Insolvenzen im Lichte der Verordnung (EG) Nr. 1346/2000, ELR 2000, p 378; *Rossbach* Europäische Insolvenzverwalter in Deutschland (2006); *Roth G* Gläubigerschutz durch Existenzschutz, NZG 2003, p 1081; *Roth G* Qualität und Preis am Markt für Gesellschaftsformen, ZGR 2005, p 348; *Roth W-H* Internationales Gesellschaftsrecht nach Überseering, IPRax 2003, p 117; *Roussel Galle* Comments on Cour de cassation dated 19/11/2002, JDI 2003, p 132; *Roussel Galle* Juris-Classeur Commercial, Procédures Collectives, Redressement et Liquidation judiciaires, Droit communautaire, Fasc 3125; *Runkel* (ed) Anwaltshandbuch – Insolvenzrecht (2005); *Sabel* Hauptsitz als Niederlassung im Sinne der EuInsVO?, NZI 2004, p 126; *Sabel/Schlegel* Comments on High Court of Justice Chancery Division Companies Court (England) dated 7/2/2003 – 0042/2003, EWiR 2003, p 367; *Saenger/Klockenbrink* Anerkennungsfragen im internationalen Insolvenzrecht gelöst? – Zugleich Anmerkung zum Urteil des EuGH v. 2.5.2006 – Rs. C-341/04 (Eurofood/Parmalat), EuZW 2006, p 621; *Saenger/Klockenbrink* Neue Grenzen für ein forum shopping des Insolvenzschuldners? DZWiR 2006, p 183; *Sandrock* Die Schrumpfung der Überlagerungstheorie, ZVglRWiss 102 (2003), p 447; *Sandrock* Sitzrecht contra Savigny?, BB 2004, p 897; *Sandrock* Sitztheorie, Überlagerungstheorie und der EWG-Vertrag – Wasser, Öl und Feuer, RIW 1989, p 505; *Schack* Internationales Zivilverfahrensrecht (2002); *Schall* Englischer Gläubigerschutz bei der Limited in Deutschland, ZIP 2005, p 965; *Schan* Die Entscheidung für Pluralität: kollisionsrecht und Gesellschaftsrecht nach der EuGH-Entscheidung „Inspire-Art", AG 2003, p 661; *Schanze/Jüttner* Anerkennung und Kontrolle ausländischer Gesellschaften – Rechtslage und Perspektiven nach der Überseering-Entscheidung des EuGH, AG 2003, p 30; *Scheel* Konzerninsolvenz – eine vergleichende Darstellung des US-amerikanischen und des deutschen Rechts (1995); *Schelo* Konzerninsolvenz – Alles in einen „Topf"?, NZI Aktuell Heft 12/2005, V; *Schilling* Comments on LG Kiel dated 20/04/2006 – 10 S 44/05, EWiR 2006, p 429; *Schilling* Das englische Insolvenzeröffnungsverfahren im Anwendungsbereich der EuInsVO und im Vergleich mit dem deutschen Insolvenzeröffnungsverfahren, DZWiR 2006, p 143; *Schilling/Schildt* Comments on AG Hamburg dated 14/5/2003 – 67 g IN 358/02, NZI 2003, p 444; *Schilling/Schildt* Insolvenz ausländischer Kapitalgesellschaften mit Sitz in Deutschland, ZInsO 2003, p 396; *Schilling/Schmidt* COMI und vorläufiger Insolvenzverwalter – Problem gelöst?, ZInsO 2006, p 113; *Schilling/Schmidt* Comments on LG Hamburg dated 18/8/2005 – 326 T 34/05, EWiR 2006, p 15; *Schlichte* Existenzvernichtung in der Ltd. & Co. KG, DB 2006, p 2672; *Schlichte* Kapitalerhaltung in der Ltd. & Co. KG, DB 2006, p 1357; *Schlosser* EU-Zivilprozessrecht (2003); *Schmidt H.* Anfechtungsklage des Konkursverwalters und Anwendbarkeit des EuGVÜ, EuZW 1990, 219; *Schmidt* InVO 1999, p 76; *Schmidt J.* Eurofood – Eine Leitentscheidung und ihre Rezeption in Europa und den USA, ZIP 2007, p 405; *Schmidt J.* Insolvenzantragspflicht und Insolvenzverschleppungshaftung bei der „deutschen" Limited – Das LG Kiel auf dem richtigen Weg?, ZInsO 2006, p 737; *Schmidt* Perpetuatio fori im europäischen Insolvenzrecht – Anmerkung zu EuGH, Rs C-1/04, ZInsO 2006, p 88; *Schmidt/Uhlenbruck* (eds) Die GmbH in Krise, Sanierung und Insolvenz, 3th edn (2003); *Schollmeyer* Gegenseitige Verträge im internationalen Insolvenzrecht (1997); *Schön* Die „Existenzvernichtung" der juristischen Person, ZHR 168 (2004), p 268; *Schön* Die Niederlassungsfreiheit von Kapitalgesellschaften im System der Grundfreiheiten, in Schneider (ed), Festschrift Lutter (2000) p 685 et seq; *Schröder/Schneider* Geschäftsführerhaftung bei der Private Limited Company mit Verwaltungssitz in Deutschland, GmbHR 2005, p 1288; *Schulz* (Schein-) Auslandsgesellschaften in Europa – Ein Schein-Problem?, NJW 2003, p 2705; *Schumann* Die englische Limited mit Verwaltungssitz in Deutschland: Kapitalaufbringung, Kapitalerhaltung und Haftung bei Insolvenz, DB 2004, p 743; *Schwerdtfeger/Schilling* Innerstaatlicher Rechtsschutz gegen die Eröffnung eines Hauptinsolvenzverfahrens nach Art 3 Abs 1 EuInsVO in Deutschland, DZWiR 2005, p 370; *Sedláčková/Keller* Tschechien: Insolvenzgesetz – Teil 1: Eröffnungsverfahren, WiRO 2006, p 342; *Smid* Auswirkungen des europäischen internationalen Insolvenzrechts auf die Praxis der deutschen Insolvenzgerichte, InVo 2005, p 437; *Smid* Deutsches und Europäisches internationales Insolvenzrecht, Kommentar (2004); *Smid* EuGH zu »Eurofood«, BGH zur internationalen Zuständigkeit: Neueste Judikatur zur EuInsVO, DZWiR 2006, p 325; *Smid* Europäisches Internationales Insolvenzrecht (2002); *Smid* Internationales Insolvenzrecht im Spiegel ausgewählter Verfahren und Entscheidungen, DZWiR 2006, p 45; *Smid* Judikatur zum internationalen Insolvenzrecht, DZWiR 2004, p 397; *Smid* Vier Entscheidungen englischer und deutscher Gerichte zur europäischen internationalen Zuständigkeit zur Eröffnung von Hauptinsolvenzverfahren, DZWiR 2003, p 397; *Soinne* Droit communautaire des entreprises en difficulté: prospective, Rev proc coll März 2003; *Sonnenberger/Dammann* Französisches Handels- und Wirtschaftrecht (3th edn in preparation); *Spahlinger* Sekundäre Insolvenzverfahren bei grenzüberschreitenden Insolvenzen, Eine vergleichende Untersuchung zum deutschen, US-amerikanischen, schweizerischen und europäischen Recht (1998); *Spindler/Berner* Der Gläubigerschutz im Gesellschaftsrecht nach Inspire Art, RIW 2004, p 7; *Spindler/Berner* Inspire Art – Der europäische Wettbewerb um das Gesellschaftsrecht ist endgültig eröffnet, RIW 2003, p 949; *Staak* Der deutsche Insolvenzverwalter im europäischen Insolvenzrecht – Eine Analyse der EG-Verordnung Nr 1346/2000 des Rates vom 29. Mai 2000 über Insolvenzverfahren unter besonderer Berücksichtigung der Person des deutschen Insolvenzverwalters (2004); *Staudinger* Kommentar zum Bürgerlichen Gesetzbuch mit Einführungsgesetz und Nebengesetzen EGBGB/IPR, Internationales Gesellschaftsrecht (1998); *Steiner/Eickmann* Zwangsversteigerung und Zwangsverwaltung, 9th edn; *Stöber* Zwangsversteigerungsgesetz, 18th edn (2006); *Stoll* (ed) Vorschläge und Gutachten zur Umsetzung des EU-Übereinkommens über Insolvenzverfahren im deutschen Recht (1997); *Stork* Deutsche GmbH vs. englische Ltd. – Wettbewerb der Rechtsordnungen um die beste Gesellschaftsform für den Mittelstand, GewArch 2005, p 265; *Storz* Praxis des Zwangsversteigerungsverfahrens, 10th edn (2007); *Stummel* Konkurs und Integration. Konventionsrechtliche Wege zur Bewältigung grenzüberschreitender Insolvenzverfahren (1991); *Süß* Häufige Probleme mit Zweigniederlassungen englischer Limited Companies, DNotZ 2005, p 180; *Synvet* Comments on Cass civ dated 25/2/1986, RCDIP 1987, p 589; *Taupitz* Das (zukünftige) europäische Internationale Insolvenzrecht – insbesondere aus internationalprivatrechtlicher Sicht, ZZP 111 (1998), p 315; *Teves* Rumänien: Schwerpunkte im Insolvenzgesetz, RIW 2000, p 682; *Thieme* Vermögensgerichtsstände, Inlandsbezug und Partikularkonkurs, Jahresheft der Internationalen Juristenvereinigung Osnabrück (1995/1996), p 44; *Thole* Die internationale Zuständigkeit für insolvenzrechtliche Anfechtungsklagen, ZIP 2006, p 1383; *Thomas/Putzo* Zivilprozessordnung, 27th edn (2005); *Tirado* Die Anwendung der Europäischen Insolvenzverordnung durch die Gerichte der Mitgliedstaaten, GPR 2005, p 39; *Torwegge* UK Company Law Reform Bill – Think Small First!, GmbHR 2006, p 919; *Totty & Moss* Insolvency (1986); *Trunk* Internationales Insolvenzrecht (1998); *Trunk* Regelungsschwerpunkte eines Ausführungsgesetzes zum Europäischen Insolvenzübereinkommen, in Stoll (ed), Vorschläge und Gutachten zur Umsetzung des EU-Übereinkommens über Insolvenzverfahren im deutschen Recht, 1997, p 232; U.N. G.A., 52d Session, Report of the United Nations Commission on International Trade Law on the work of its thirtieth session, (4 July 1997) ("A/52/17"); U.N. G.A., 61st Session, Report of the United Nations Commission on International Trade Law on the work of its thirty-ninth session, (14 July 2006) ("A/61/17"); U.N. G.A., United Nations Commission on International Trade Law, 27th Session, Report of the *Secretariat*, Report on UNCITRAL – INSOL Colloquium on Cross-Border Insolvency (19 May 1994) ("A/CN.9/398"); U.N. G.A., United Nations Commission on International Trade Law, 29th Session, Report of Working Group on Insolvency Law on the work of the eighteenth session (1 December 1995) (A/CN. 9/419); U.N. G.A., United Nations Commission on International Trade Law, 29th Session, Report of Working Group on Insolvency Law on the work of the nineteenth session, (25 April 1996) ("A/CN.9/422"); U.N. G.A., United Nations Commission on International Trade Law, 30th Session, Report of Working Group on Insolvency Law on the work of the twentieth session, (24 October 1996) ("A/CN.9/433"); U.N. G.A., United Nations Commission on International Trade Law, 30th Session, Report of Working Group on Insolvency Law on the work of the twenty-first session (19 February 1997) ("A/CN.9/435"); U.N. G.A., United Nations Commission on International Trade Law, 30th Session, Guide to Enactment of the UNCITRAL Model Law on Cross-Border Insolvency (1997) ("A/CN.9/442"); U.N. G.A., United Nations Commission on International Trade Law, 38th Session, Report of the *Secretariat*, Developments in insolvency law: adoption of the UNCITRAL Model Law on Cross-Border Insolvency, use of cross-border protocols and court-to-court communication guidelines, and case law on interpretation of "centre of main interests" and "establishment" in the European Union (14 April 2005) ("A/CN.9/580"); U.N. G.A., United Nations Commission on International Trade Law, Report of the *Secretariat*, Treatment of Corporate Groups in Insolvency (4 October 2006) ("A/CN.9/WG.V/WP.74/Add.2"); *Uhlenbruck* Insolvenzordnung, Kommentar (2004); *Ulmer* Das Centros-Urteil des EuGH und seine Relevanz für das deutsche Internationale Gesellschaftsrecht, JZ 1999, p 662; *Ulmer* Gläubigerschutz bei Scheinauslandsgesellschaften – Zum Verhältnis zwischen gläubigerschützendem nationalem Gesellschafts-, Delikts-, und Insolvenzrecht und der EG-Niederlassungsfreiheit, NJW 2004, p 1201; *Ulmer* Insolvenzrechtlicher Gläubigerschutz gegenüber Scheinauslandsgesellschaften ohne hinreichende Kapitalausstattung?, KTS 2004, p 291; *Ulmer/Habersack/Winter* Gesetz betreffend die Gesellschaften mit beschränkter Haftung, Kommentar (2005); United Nations Commission on International Trade Law, Legislative Guide on Insolvency Law (Adopted by General Assembly on 2 December 2004); *Urbain-Parléani* La faillite des sociétés, Bref aperçu sur le règlement CE n° 1346-2000 du 29 mai 2000 relatif aux procédures collectives, Rev soc Januar/Februar 2005; *Urban* La protection juridique incertaine des salariés dans une procédure collective transfrontalière JCP 2006 I, p 122; *Vallender* Aufgaben und Befugnisse des deutschen Insolvenzrichters in Verfahren nach der EuInsVO, KTS 2005, p 283; *Vallender* Die Insolvenz von Scheinauslandsgesellschaften, ZGR 2006, p 425; *Vallender* Die Voraussetzungen für die Einleitung eines Sekundärinsolvenzverfahrens nach der EuInsVO, InVo 2005, p 41; *Vallender/Fuchs* Die Antragspflicht organschaftlicher Vertreter einer GmbH vor dem Hintergrund der Europäischen Gerichtsordnung, ZIP 2004, p 829; *Vallender/Heukamp* Die Reform des französischen Unternehmensinsolvenzrechts oder: Rette sich, wer kann! InVo 2006, p 1; *Vallens* Comments on Cour d'appel de Versailles dated 4/9/2003, Dalloz 2003, p 2352; *Vallens* Comments on Cour de cassation dated 27/6/2006, Dalloz 2006, p 2257; *Vallens* Comments on ECJ dated 17/1/2006 (Staubitz-Schreiber), Rev des sociétés 2006, p 346; *Vallens* Comments on ECJ dated 2/5/2006 (Eurofood), JCP E 2006, No 2071; *Vallens* Comments on TC Nanterre dated 15/12/2006, Dalloz 2006, p 793; *Vallens* La maison mère d'un groupe centre des intérêts principaux de ses filiales étrangères, Comments on TC Nanterre dated 15.2.2006, Dalloz 2006, p 793; *Vallens* La mise en œuvre du règlement communautaire sur les procédures d'insolvabilité : questions de procédure, Dalloz 2003, p 1426; *Vallens* Le droit de la faillite en Europe, Les procédures secondaires, Rev proc coll März 2003; *Vallens* Le règlement communautaire sur les procédures d'insolvabilité et les procédures de redressement et de liquidation judiciaire, Rev Lamy dr aff Juli 2002; *Vallens/Dammann* Die Problematik der Behandlung von Konzerninsolvenzen nach der EuInsVO, NZI 2006, p 29; *Van Galen* How to use the European Insolvency Regulation (2005); *Van Galen* The European Insolvency Regulation and Groups of Companies, Arbeitspapier INSOL Europe Annual Congress (Cork, Ireland), 16–18 October 2003; *Vasseur* Comments on Cass com dated 11/4/1995, Dalloz 1995, p 640; *Virgós/Garcimartín* The European Insolvency Regulation: Law and Practice (2004); *Virgós/Schmit* Erläuternder Bericht zu dem EU-Übereinkommen über Insolvenzverfahren, in Stoll (ed), Vorschläge und Gutachten (1997), p 32; *Volders/Rétornaz* Forum shopping et procédures d'insolvabilité, Comments on ECJ dated 17/1/2006 (Staubitz-Schreiber), Rev proc coll 2006, 241; *Wachter* Auswirkung des EuGH-Urteils in Sachen Inspire Art Ltd. auf Beratungspraxis und Gesetzgebung, GmbHR 2004, p 88; *Wachter* Der GmbHR-Kommentar, GmbHR 2006, p 709; *Wachter* Errichtung, Publizität, Haftung und Insolvenz von Zweigniederlassungen ausländischer Kapitalgesellschaften nach „Inspire Art", GmbHR 2003, p 1254; *Wachter* Persönliche Haftung des Gründers einer englischen private limited comapy, BB 2006, p 1463; *Waechter* Der Entwurf des MoMiG und die Auswirkungen auf inländische Zweigniederlassungen von Auslandsgesellschaften, GmbHR 2006, p 793; *Wagner* Insolvenzantragstellung nur im EU-Ausland? Zivil- und strafrechtliche Risiken für den GmbH-Geschäftsführer, ZIP 2006, p 1934; *Walterscheid* Die englische Limited im Insolvenzverfahren, DZWiR 2006, p 95; Webster's Ninth New Collegiate Dictionary (1984); *Wehdeking* Reform des Internationalen Insolvenzrechtes in Deutschland und Österreich, DZWiR 2003, p 133; *Weller* „Inspire Art": Weitgehende Freiheiten beim Einsatz ausländischer Briefkastengesellschaften, DStR 2003, p 1800; *Weller* Das Internationale Gesellschaftsrecht in der neuesten BGH-Rechtsprechung, IPRax 2003, p 324; *Weller* Einschränkung der Gründungstheorie bei missbräuchlicher Auslandsgründung, IPRax 2003, p 520; *Weller* Forum Shopping im Internationalen Insolvenzrecht?, IPRax 2004, p 412; *Weller* Inländische Gläubigerinteressen bei internationalen Konzerninsolvenzen, ZHR 169 (2005), p 570; *Weller* Scheinauslandsgesellschaften nach Centros, Überseering und Inspire Art: Ein neues Anwendungsfeld für die Existenzvernichtungshaftung, IPRax 2003, p 207; *Wenzel* Die Rechtsstellung des Grundpfandrechtsgläubigers im Insolvenzverfahren, NZI 1999, p 102; *Werner* Die Ltd. & Co. KG – eine Alternative zur GmbH & Co. KG?, GmbHR 2005, p 288; *Wessels* International Insolvency Law (2006); *Wessels* Current Topics of International Insolvency Law (2004); *Wessels* Germany and Spain Lead Changes Towards International Insolvency Law in Europe, Paper presented to Insol International Academics meeting on 'Comparative Approaches to Insolvency', Las Vegas, Nevada, USA, 20/21 September 2003 – www.iiiglobal.org; *Wessels* Moving House: Which court can open insolvency proceedings – www.iiiglobal.org; *Wessels* Realisation of the EU Insolvency Regulation in Germany, France and the Netherlands, Paper presented to Insol International Academics meeting on 'Multinational Insolvency Proceedings – Cooperation among Nations', Las Vegas, Nevada, USA, 20/21 September 2003 – www.iiiglobal.org; *Wessels* The European Union Insolvency Regulation: It's first year in Dutch Cases, Third Annual International Insolvency Conference, Fordham University School of Law, New York City June 9–10, 2003, www.iiiglobal.org; *Westbrook* Chapter 15 at Last, 79 American Bankrutpcy Law Journal 713 (2005); *Westbrook* Multinational Enterprises in General Default: Chapter 15, the ALI Principles, and the EU Insolvency Regulation, 76 American Bankrutpcy Law Journal 1 (Winter 2002); *Westermann* Die GmbH in der nationalen und internationalen Konkurrenz der Rechtsformen, GmbHR 2005, p 4; *Westphal* Comments on AG Düsseldorf dated 7/4/2004, EWiR 2004, p 909; *Wiedemann* Reflexionen zur Durchgriffshaftung, ZGR 2003, p 283; *Wienberg/Sommer* Anwendbarkeit von deutschem Eigenkapitalersatzrecht auf EU-Kapitalgesellschaften am Beispiel eines Partikularinsolvenzverfahrens im engeren Sinne nach Art 3 II, IV EuInsVO, NZI 2005, p 353; *Wilhelmi* Das Mindestkapital als Mindestschutz – eine Apologie im Hinblick auf die Diskussion um eine Reform der GmbH angesichts der englischen Limited, GmbHR 2006, p 13; *Willemer* Vis attractiva concursus und die Europäische Insolvenzverordnung (2006); *Wilmowsky v.* KTS 1998, p 343; *Wilmowsky v.* Sicherungsrechte im Europäischen Insolvenzübereinkommen, EWS 1997, p 295; *Wimmer* Anmerkungen zum Vorlage des irischen Supreme Court in Sachen Parmalat, ZInsO 2005, p 119; *Wimmer* Die Besonderheiten von Sekundärinsolvenzverfahren unter besonderer Berücksichtigung des Europäischen Insolvenzübereinkommens, ZIP 1998, p 982; *Wimmer* Die EU-Verordnung zur Regelung grenzüberschreitender Insolvenzverfahren, NJW 2002, p 2427; *Wimmer* Die Richtlinien 2001/17 EG und 2001/14 EG über die Sanierung und Liquidation von Versicherungsunternehmen und Kreditinstituten, ZInsO 2002, p 897; *Wimmer* Die UNCITRAL-Modellbestimmungen über grenzüberschreitende Insolvenzverfahren, ZIP 1997, p 2220; *Wimmer* Die Verordnung (EG) Nr 1346/2000 über Insolvenzverfahren, ZInsO 2001, p 97; *Wimmer* Einpassung der EU-Insolvenzverordnung in das deutsche Recht durch das Gesetz zur Neuregelung des Internationalen Insolvenzrechts, in Gerhardt/Haarmeyer/Kreft (eds), Festschrift Kirchhof (2003) p 521 et seq; *Wimmer* Frankfurter Kommentar zur Insolvenzordnung (2005); *Wittinghofer* Der nationale und internationale Insolvenzverwaltungsvertrag (2004); *Witz/Zierau* Französisches internationales Konkursrecht – Neue Tendenzen und Entwicklungen in der Rechtsprechung der Cour de cassation, RIW 1989, p 929; *Wunderer* Auswirkungen des Europäischen Übereinkommens über Insolvenzverfahren auf Bankgeschäfte, WM 1998, p 793; *Zerres* Deutsche Insolvenzantragspflicht für die englische Limited mit Inlandssitz, DZWiR 2006, p 356; *Ziemons* Freie Bahn für den Umzug von Gesellschaften nach Inspire Art ?!, ZIP 2003, p 1913; *Zimmer* Nach "Inspire Art" – Grenzenlose Gestaltungsfreiheit für Deutsche Unternehmen ?, NJW 2003, p 3585; *Zimmer* Wie es Euch gefällt? Offene Fragen nach dem Überseering-Urteil des EuGH, BB 2003, p 1; *Zöllner* Konkurrenz für inländische Kapitalgesellschaften durch ausländische Rechtsträger, insbesondere durch englische Private Limited Company, GmbHR 2006, p 1.

PART 1

COUNCIL REGULATION (EC) No 1346/2000

of 29 May 2000
on insolvency proceedings

THE COUNCIL OF THE EUROPEAN UNION,

Having regard to the Treaty establishing the European Community, and in particular Articles 61(c) and 67(1) thereof,

Having regard to the initiative of the Federal Republic of Germany and the Republic of Finland,

Having regard to the opinion of the European Parliament[1],

Having regard to the opinion of the Economic and Social Committee[2],

Whereas:

(1) The European Union has set out the aim of establishing an area of freedom, security and justice.

(2) The proper functioning of the internal market requires that crossborder insolvency proceedings should operate efficiently and effectively and this Regulation needs to be adopted in order to achieve this objective which comes within the scope of judicial cooperation in civil matters within the meaning of Article 65 of the Treaty.

(3) The activities of undertakings have more and more cross-border effects and are therefore increasingly being regulated by Community law. While the insolvency of such undertakings also affects the proper functioning of the internal market, there is a need for a Community act requiring coordination of the measures to be taken regarding an insolvent debtor's assets.

(4) It is necessary for the proper functioning of the internal market to avoid incentives for the parties to transfer assets or judicial proceedings from one Member State to another, seeking to obtain a more favourable legal position (forum shopping).

(5) These objectives cannot be achieved to a sufficient degree at national level and action at Community level is therefore justified.

(6) In accordance with the principle of proportionality this Regulation should be confined to provisions governing jurisdiction for opening insolvency proceedings and judgments which are delivered directly on the basis of the insolvency proceedings and are closely connected with such proceedings. In addition, this Regulation should contain provisions regarding the recognition of those judgments and the applicable law which also satisfy that principle.

---

[1] Opinion delivered on 2 March 2000 (not yet published in the Official Journal).

[2] Opinion delivered on 26 January 2000 (not yet published in the Official Journal).

(7) Insolvency proceedings relating to the winding-up of insolvent companies or other legal persons, judicial arrangements, compositions and analogous proceedings are excluded from the scope of the 1968 Brussels Convention on Jurisdiction and the Enforcement of Judgments in Civil and Commercial Matters[3], as amended by the Conventions on Accession to this Convention[4].

(8) In order to achieve the aim of improving the efficiency and effectiveness of insolvency proceedings having cross-border effects, it is necessary, and appropriate, that the provisions on jurisdiction, recognition and applicable law in this area should be contained in a Community law measure which is binding and directly applicable in Member States.

(9) This Regulation should apply to insolvency proceedings, whether the debtor is a natural person or a legal person, a trader or an individual. The insolvency proceedings to which this Regulation applies are listed in the Annexes. Insolvency proceedings concerning insurance undertakings, credit institutions, investment undertakings holding funds or securities for third parties and collective investment undertakings should be excluded from the scope of this Regulation. Such undertakings should not be covered by this Regulation since they are subject to special arrangements and, to some extent, the national supervisory authorities have extremely wide-ranging powers of intervention.

(10) Insolvency proceedings do not necessarily involve the intervention of a judicial authority; the expression 'court' in this Regulation should be given a broad meaning and include a person or body empowered by national law to open insolvency proceedings. In order for this Regulation to apply, proceedings (comprising acts and formalities set down in law) should not only have to comply with the provisions of this Regulation, but they should also be officially recognised and legally effective in the Member State in which the insolvency proceedings are opened and should be collective insolvency proceedings which entail the partial or total divestment of the debtor and the appointment of a liquidator.

(11) This Regulation acknowledges the fact that as a result of widely differing substantive laws it is not practical to introduce insolvency proceedings with universal scope in the entire Community. The application without exception of the law of the State of opening of proceedings would, against this background, frequently lead to difficulties. This applies, for example, to the widely differing laws on security interests to be found in the Community. Furthermore, the preferential rights enjoyed by some creditors in the insolvency proceedings are, in some cases, completely different. This Regulation should take account of this in two different ways. On the one hand, provision should be made for special rules on applicable law in the case of particularly significant rights and legal relationships (e.g. rights in rem and contracts of employment). On the other hand, national proceedings covering only assets situated in the State of opening should also be allowed alongside main insolvency proceedings with universal scope.

(12) This Regulation enables the main insolvency proceedings to be opened in the Member State where the debtor has the centre of his main interests. These proceedings have universal scope and aim at encompassing all the debtor's assets. To protect the diversity of interests, this Regulation permits secondary proceedings to be opened to run

[3] OJ L 299, 31.12.1972, p. 32.

[4] OJ L 204, 2.8.1975, p. 28; OJ L 304, 30.10.1978, p. 1; OJ L 388, 31.12.1982, p. 1; OJ L 285, 3.10.1989, p. 1; OJ C 15, 15.1.1997, p. 1.

in parallel with the main proceedings. Secondary proceedings may be opened in the Member State where the debtor has an establishment. The effects of secondary proceedings are limited to the assets located in that State. Mandatory rules of coordination with the main proceedings satisfy the need for unity in the Community.

(13) The 'centre of main interests' should correspond to the place where the debtor conducts the administration of his interests on a regular basis and is therefore ascertainable by third parties.

(14) This Regulation applies only to proceedings where the centre of the debtor's main interests is located in the Community.

(15) The rules of jurisdiction set out in this Regulation establish only international jurisdiction, that is to say, they designate the Member State the courts of which may open insolvency proceedings. Territorial jurisdiction within that Member State must be established by the national law of the Member State concerned.

(16) The court having jurisdiction to open the main insolvency proceedings should be enabled to order provisional and protective measures from the time of the request to open proceedings. Preservation measures both prior to and after the commencement of the insolvency proceedings are very important to guarantee the effectiveness of the insolvency proceedings. In that connection this Regulation should afford different possibilities. On the one hand, the court competent for the main insolvency proceedings should be able also to order provisional protective measures covering assets situated in the territory of other Member States. On the other hand, a liquidator temporarily appointed prior to the opening of the main insolvency proceedings should be able, in the Member States in which an establishment belonging to the debtor is to be found, to apply for the preservation measures which are possible under the law of those States.

(17) Prior to the opening of the main insolvency proceedings, the right to request the opening of insolvency proceedings in the Member State where the debtor has an establishment should be limited to local creditors and creditors of the local establishment or to cases where main proceedings cannot be opened under the law of the Member State where the debtor has the centre of his main interest. The reason for this restriction is that cases where territorial insolvency proceedings are requested before the main insolvency proceedings are intended to be limited to what is absolutely necessary. If the main insolvency proceedings are opened, the territorial proceedings become secondary.

(18) Following the opening of the main insolvency proceedings, the right to request the opening of insolvency proceedings in a Member State where the debtor has an establishment is not restricted by this Regulation. The liquidator in the main proceedings or any other person empowered under the national law of that Member State may request the opening of secondary insolvency proceedings.

(19) Secondary insolvency proceedings may serve different purposes, besides the protection of local interests. Cases may arise where the estate of the debtor is too complex to administer as a unit or where differences in the legal systems concerned are so great that difficulties may arise from the extension of effects deriving from the law of the State of the opening to the other States where the assets are located. For this reason the liquidator in the main proceedings may request the opening of secondary proceedings when the efficient administration of the estate so requires.

(20) Main insolvency proceedings and secondary proceedings can, however, contribute to the effective realisation of the total assets only if all the concurrent proceedings pending are coordinated. The main condition here is that the various liquidators must cooperate closely, in particular by exchanging a sufficient amount of information. In

order to ensure the dominant role of the main insolvency proceedings, the liquidator in such proceedings should be given several possibilities for intervening in secondary insolvency proceedings which are pending at the same time. For example, he should be able to propose a restructuring plan or composition or apply for realisation of the assets in the secondary insolvency proceedings to be suspended.

(21) Every creditor, who has his habitual residence, domicile or registered office in the Community, should have the right to lodge his claims in each of the insolvency proceedings pending in the Community relating to the debtor's assets. This should also apply to tax authorities and social insurance institutions. However, in order to ensure equal treatment of creditors, the distribution of proceeds must be coordinated. Every creditor should be able to keep what he has received in the course of insolvency proceedings but should be entitled only to participate in the distribution of total assets in other proceedings if creditors with the same standing have obtained the same proportion of their claims.

(22) This Regulation should provide for immediate recognition of judgments concerning the opening, conduct and closure of insolvency proceedings which come within its scope and of judgments handed down in direct connection with such insolvency proceedings. Automatic recognition should therefore mean that the effects attributed to the proceedings by the law of the State in which the proceedings were opened extend to all other Member States. Recognition of judgments delivered by the courts of the Member States should be based on the principle of mutual trust. To that end, grounds for non-recognition should be reduced to the minimum necessary. This is also the basis on which any dispute should be resolved where the courts of two Member States both claim competence to open the main insolvency proceedings. The decision of the first court to open proceedings should be recognized in the other Member States without those Member States having the power to scrutinise the court's decision.

(23) This Regulation should set out, for the matters covered by it, uniform rules on conflict of laws which replace, within their scope of application, national rules of private international law. Unless otherwise stated, the law of the Member State of the opening of the proceedings should be applicable (*lex concursus*). This rule on conflict of laws should be valid both for the main proceedings and for local proceedings; the *lex concursus* determines all the effects of the insolvency proceedings, both procedural and substantive, on the persons and legal relations concerned. It governs all the conditions for the opening, conduct and closure of the insolvency proceedings.

(24) Automatic recognition of insolvency proceedings to which the law of the opening State normally applies may interfere with the rules under which transactions are carried out in other Member States. To protect legitimate expectations and the certainty of transactions in Member States other than that in which proceedings are opened, provisions should be made for a number of exceptions to the general rule.

(25) There is a particular need for a special reference diverging from the law of the opening State in the case of rights in rem, since these are of considerable importance for the granting of credit. The basis, validity and extent of such a right in rem should therefore normally be determined according to the *lex situs* and not be affected by the opening of insolvency proceedings. The proprietor of the right in rem should therefore be able to continue to assert his right to segregation or separate settlement of the collateral security. Where assets are subject to rights in rem under the *lex situs* in one Member State but the main proceedings are being carried out in another Member State, the liquidator in the main proceedings should be able to request the opening of secondary proceedings in the jurisdiction where the rights in rem arise if the debtor has an establish-

ment there. If a secondary proceeding is not opened, the surplus on sale of the asset covered by rights in rem must be paid to the liquidator in the main proceedings.

(26) If a set-off is not permitted under the law of the opening State, a creditor should nevertheless be entitled to the set-off if it is possible under the law applicable to the claim of the insolvent debtor. In this way, set-off will acquire a kind of guarantee function based on legal provisions on which the creditor concerned can rely at the time when the claim arises.

(27) There is also a need for special protection in the case of payment systems and financial markets. This applies for example to the position-closing agreements and netting agreements to be found in such systems as well as to the sale of securities and to the guarantees provided for such transactions as governed in particular by Directive 98/26/EC of the European Parliament and of the Council of 19 May 1998 on settlement finality in payment and securities settlement systems[5]. For such transactions, the only law which is material should thus be that applicable to the system or market concerned. This provision is intended to prevent the possibility of mechanisms for the payment and settlement of transactions provided for in the payment and set-off systems or on the regulated financial markets of the Member States being altered in the case of insolvency of a business partner. Directive 98/26/EC contains special provisions which should take precedence over the general rules in this Regulation.

(28) In order to protect employees and jobs, the effects of insolvency proceedings on the continuation or termination of employment and on the rights and obligations of all parties to such employment must be determined by the law applicable to the agreement in accordance with the general rules on conflict of law. Any other insolvency-law questions, such as whether the employees' claims are protected by preferential rights and what status such preferential rights may have, should be determined by the law of the opening State.

(29) For business considerations, the main content of the decision opening the proceedings should be published in the other Member States at the request of the liquidator. If there is an establishment in the Member State concerned, there may be a requirement that publication is compulsory. In neither case, however, should publication be a prior condition for recognition of the foreign proceedings.

(30) It may be the case that some of the persons concerned are not in fact aware that proceedings have been opened and act in good faith in a way that conflicts with the new situation. In order to protect such persons who make a payment to the debtor because they are unaware that foreign proceedings have been opened when they should in fact have made the payment to the foreign liquidator, it should be provided that such a payment is to have a debt-discharging effect.

(31) This Regulation should include Annexes relating to the organization of insolvency proceedings. As these Annexes relate exclusively to the legislation of Member States, there are specific and substantiated reasons for the Council to reserve the right to amend these Annexes in order to take account of any amendments to the domestic law of the Member States.

(32) The United Kingdom and Ireland, in accordance with Article 3 of the Protocol on the position of the United Kingdom and Ireland annexed to the Treaty on European Union and the Treaty establishing the European Community, have given notice of their wish to take part in the adoption and application of this Regulation.

---

[5] OJ L 166, 11.6.1998, p. 45.

(33) Denmark, in accordance with Articles 1 and 2 of the Protocol on the position of Denmark annexed to the Treaty on European Union and the Treaty establishing the European Community, is not participating in the adoption of this Regulation, and is therefore not bound by it nor subject to its application,

HAS ADOPTED THIS REGULATION:

Introduction

Contents

Index

Bibliography

Balz Das neue Europäische Insolvenzübereinkommen, ZIP 1996, p 948; *Breutigam/Blersch/Goetsch/Haas* Insolvenzrecht, Berliner Kommentar (01/2006); *Burman* Harmonization of International Bankruptcy Law: a United States Perspective, Fordham L.R, 64, 1996, p 2543; *Duursma-Kepplinger/Duursma/Chalupsky* Europäische Insolvenzverordnung, Kommentar (2002); *Dolinger* The Bustamante Code and the Interamerican Conventions in the Brazilian System of Private International Law, in Kleinheisterkamp/Lorenzo Idiarte (eds), „Avances del Derecho Internacional Privado en América Latina – Liber Americorum Jürgen Samtleben" (2002), p 133; *Eidenmüller* Europäische Verordnung über Insolvenzverfahren und zukünftiges deutsches internationales Insolvenzrecht, IPRax 2001, p 2; *Fritz/Bähr* Die Europäische Verordnung über Insolvenzverfahren – Herausforderung an Gerichte und Insolvenzverwalter, DZWiR 2001, p 221; *Gottwald* Grenzüberschreitende Insolvenzen (1997); *Herchen* Das Übereinkommen über Insolvenzverfahren der Mitgliedstaaten der Europäischen Union vom 23.11.1995 (2000); *Houin* Konkursprobleme des gemeinsamen Marktes, KTS 1961, p 177; *Jahr* Vereinheitlichtes Internationales Konkursrecht in der Europäischen Wirtschaftsgemeinschaft: Der Vorentwurf eines Übereinkommens über den Konkurs, Vergleich und ähnliche Verfahren, RabelsZ 36 (1972), p 620; *Kegel/Thieme* (eds) Vorschläge und Gutachten zum Entwurf eines EG-Konkursübereinkommens (1988); *Kübler* Der Mittelpunkt der hauptsächlichen Interessen nach Art 3 Abs 1 EuInsVO, in Schilken et al (eds), Festschrift Gerhardt (2004), p 527;

Leible/Staudinger Die europäische Verordnung über Insolvenzverfahren, KTS 2000, p 533; *Lemontey* Bericht über das Übereinkommen über den Konkurs, Vergleiche und ähnliche Verfahren, in Kegel/Thieme (eds), Vorschläge und Gutachten zum Entwurf eines EG-Konkursübereinkommens (1988); *Liersch* Sicherungsrechte im Internationalen Insolvenzrecht (2001); *Lüer* Einheitliches Insolvenzrecht innerhalb der Europäischen Gemeinschaften – Die Quadratur des Kreises? – Anmerkung zum Entwurf eines Übereinkommens über den Konkurs, Vergleich und ähnliche Verfahren, KTS 1981, p 147; *Nadelmann* Ausländisches Vermögen unter dem Vorentwurf eines Konkursabkommens für die EWG-Staaten, KTS 1971, p 65; *Pannen/Riedemann* Der Begriff des „centre of main interests" iSd Art 3 I 1 EuInsVO im Spiegel aktueller Fälle der Rechtsprechung, NZI 2004, p 646; *Paulus* Europäische Insolvenzverordnung, Kommentar (2006); *Ramackers* Réflexions critiques sur la Convention européenne relative à certains aspects internationaux de la faillite, La Semaine Juridique 1993, p 3685; *Runkel* (ed) Anwaltshandbuch – Insolvenzrecht (2005); *Smid* Europäisches Internationales Insolvenzrecht (2002); *Smid* Deutsches und Europäisches Internationales Insolvenzrecht (2004); *Staak* Der deutsche Insolvenzverwalter im europäischen Insolvenzrecht – Eine Analyse der EG-Verordnung Nr 1346/2000 des Rates vom 29. Mai 2000 über Insolvenzverfahren unter besonderer Berücksichtigung der Person des deutschen Insolvenzverwalters (2004); *Trunk* Internationales Insolvenzrecht (1998); *Vallender* Aufgaben und Befugnisse des deutschen Insolvenzrichters in Verfahren nach der EuInsVO, KTS 2005, p 283; *Virgós/Garcimartín* The European Insolvency Regulation: Law and Practice (2004); *Virgós/Schmit* Erläuternder Bericht, in Stoll (ed), Vorschläge und Gutachten (1997), p 32; *Wessels* Current Topics of International Insolvency Law (2004); *Wessels* International Insolvency Law (2006); *Westbrook* Multinational Enterprises in General Default: Chapter 15, the ALI Principles and the EU Insolvency Regulation, American Bankruptcy Law Journal (Winter 2002); *Wimmer* Die UNCITRAL-Modellbestimmungen über grenzüberschreitende Insolvenzverfahren, ZIP 1997, p 2220; *Wimmer* Die Besonderheiten von Sekundärinsolvenzverfahren unter besonderer Berücksichtigung des Europäischen Insolvenzübereinkommens, ZIP 1998, p 982.

1. Origins of the Regulation

1 In cases of cross-border insolvency in Europe, Council Regulation (EC) No 1346/2000 (the "Regulation" or "the EIR") resolves conflicts among the national law regimes and conflicts of jurisdictions among the courts of the various Member States. It has therefore legitimately been termed a "milestone" along the way to a uniform body of European commercial law.[1] By the time the Regulation came into force on 31 May 2002, this journey had already been a long one.[2]

2 As early as **Art 220 4th dash of the old version of the EEC Treaty**, the Member States undertook, *"as far as is necessary, [to] enter into negotiations with each other with a view to securing for the benefit of their nationals the simplification of formalities governing the reciprocal recognition and enforcement of judgments of courts or tribunals and of arbitration awards."*[3]

3 With the enactment of the Convention on Jurisdiction and the Enforcement of Judgments in Civil and Commercial Matters (**1968 Brussels Convention**) on 27 September 1968[4], the need for a European convention on bankruptcy became critical, because the

[1] *Eidenmüller* IPRax 2001, 2; BK-InsO/*Pannen* Präambel EuInsVO mn 1.

[2] An overview of the legal history of international insolvency law is presented by: *Wimmer* ZIP 1998, 982 et seq; *Leible/Staudinger* KTS 2000, 533, 538; *Staak* Der deutsche Insolvenzverwalter im europäischen Insolvenzrecht, p 5 et seq; and *Trunk* Internationales Insolvenzrecht, p 34 et seq.

[3] Cf *Gottwald* Grenzüberschreitende Insolvenzen, p 14.

[4] On 22 Dec 2000 Council Regulation (EC) No 44/2001 was adopted; it transformed the 1968 Brussels Convention into a European

1968 Brussels Convention expressly excluded bankruptcy, composition and similar proceedings from its scope of application.[5] The original intention had been to regulate bankruptcy law in the 1968 Brussels Convention as well. However, once it became apparent that it would be difficult to reach a consensus in the area of insolvency law, the work on a bankruptcy convention was transferred to a special committee in 1963 in order to avoid undue delays of the work on the 1968 Brussels Convention.[6]

From **1963 to 1980** the preparation of a bankruptcy convention remained in the hands of an autonomous **committee of experts.** Several unpublished drafts were prepared.[7] A **preliminary draft** was published on **16 February 1970**[8] (see mn 5), followed by a **draft version** in **1980**[9] and by a **revised draft version** in **1984.**[10] **4**

The first **published draft** of a bankruptcy convention of **1970** (so-called **preliminary draft**), which included an explanatory report by ***Lemontey***,[11] was premised on a strictly unified and universal proceeding.[12] Independent territorial insolvency proceedings and secondary insolvency proceedings (see Art 3 of the EIR mn 5 on this) were not permitted. However, because of the fundamental disparities between the national insolvency law regimes, numerous exceptions to the principle of universality were provided for.[13] The result of this compromise was a highly complicated regulation of this issue, which has been heavily criticized.[14] **5**

Following the accession of Great Britain, Ireland, and Denmark to the EU, a revised version of the 1970 draft was presented in **1980**[15]; this **draft** adhered to the fundamental principle of a strictly unified and universal proceeding.[16] This draft was also criticized for its complexity and lack of practicability.[17] **In 1984 a revised draft** was presented.[18] **6**

In light of a very modest degree of acceptance by the Member States, the responsible panel of the Council passed a resolution in **March 1986** to stop work on the bankruptcy convention.[19] **7**

In an **informal conference** of the Ministers of Justice of the Community in **San Sebastian** from 25 to 27 May 1989, the decision was made to resume negotiations on the **8**

---

regulation and came into force on 1 March 2001.

[5] D-K/D/Ch-*Duursma* Geschichte mn 9; *Staak* Der deutsche Insolvenzverwalter im europäischen Insolvenzrecht, p 5.

[6] Cf *Paulus* Komm EuInsVO Einl mn 3.

[7] *Staak* Der deutsche Insolvenzverwalter im europäischen Insolvenzrecht, p 6. For a description of the development of the draft versions, see *Houin* KTS 1961, 177 et seq.

[8] Printed in: RabelsZ 36 (1972), 734.

[9] Printed in: ZIP 1980, 582 and ZIP 1980, 811; cf *Lemontey*-Report zum Entwurf eines EG-Konkursübereinkommens, ZIP 1981, 547.

[10] *Staak* Der deutsche Insolvenzverwalter im europäischen Insolvenzrecht, p 6.

[11] Printed in *Kegel/Thieme* Vorschläge und Gutachten (1988), 93 et seq, with the *Lemontey*-Report.

[12] *Paulus* Komm EuInsVO Einl mn 4, *Staak* Der deutsche Insolvenzverwalter im europäischen Insolvenzrecht, p 6 et seq.

[13] *Paulus* Komm EuInsVO Einl mn 4.

[14] *Jahr* RabelsZ 36 (1972), 620 et seq; *Nadelmann* KTS 1971, 65. Critical view: *Paulus* Komm EuInsVO Einl mn 4; D-K/D/Ch-*Duursma* Geschichte mn 9.

[15] Printed in: ZIP 1980, 582 and ZIP 1980, 811; cf *Lemontey*-Report zum Entwurf eines EG-Konkursübereinkommens, ZIP 1981, 547.

[16] *Liersch* Sicherungsrechte im internationalen Insolvenzrecht, p 40; *Paulus* Komm EuInsVO Einl mn 6.

[17] For example *Lüer* KTS 1981, 147, 163. On this see also *Wessels* International Insolvency Law (2006) mn 10435.

[18] The text is printed in: *Kegel/Thieme* Vorschläge und Gutachten (1988), 417 et seq.

[19] *Herchen* Das Übereinkommen über Insolvenzverfahren der Mitgliedstaaten der Europäischen Union vom 23.11.1995, p 21; D-K/D/Ch-*Duursma* Geschichte mn 5.

regulation of cross-border insolvency proceedings. An **ad hoc group "bankruptcy convention"** was created for this purpose and remained active until 1995.[20]

9 The ad hoc group worked on a draft convention on the basis of the former projects. The first preliminary draft was presented in March 1991,[21] and a revised internal draft on 3 April 1992.[22] The basis of the draft was the so-called **Istanbul Convention,**[23] which had been signed by Belgium, Germany, France, Greece, Italy, Luxembourg, Turkey and Cyprus in 1990 (on this, see also mn 15 et seq).[24]

10 Based on the 1992 draft, the **Convention on insolvency proceedings (1995 Insolvency Convention)**[25] was adopted by all of the Member States on 23 November 1995 by the Ministers of Justice of the Member States – with the exception of Ireland, the Netherlands, and Great Britain.[26] The EU Member States were given until 23 May 1996 to sign the 1995 Insolvency Convention. Although Ireland and the Netherlands signed the Convention within the signing period,[27] Great Britain failed to do so by the expiration of the signing period on 23 May 1996. This meant that the enactment of the 1995 Insolvency Convention was thwarted for lack of unanimity (Art 220 EEC Treaty). The reason for Great Britain's refusal to sign was the European import ban on British beef as a protective measure against BSE[28]; unofficial British sources also cited the Gibraltar conflict as a reason.[29] The 1995 Insolvency Convention thus failed.[30]

11 With the coming into force of the **Treaty of Amsterdam** on 1 May 1999, the overall situation in Europe underwent fundamental changes. Since its enactment, the cooperation in civil matters falls within the scope of the Community's jurisdiction. On account of the priority afforded Community law instruments by Art 64 EEC Treaty over (public) international law treaties, the ratification of the 1995 Insolvency Convention was made impossible.[31] The European Parliament therefore requested the Commission to produce a draft regulation or directive on cross-border insolvency proceedings based on the 1995 Insolvency Convention under Art 65 (a) 3rd dash, Art 67 (1) and (2) of the EEC Treaty.[32]

---

20 *Leible/Staudinger* KTS 2000, 533, 535; *Smid* Komm EuInsVO Vor Art 1 EuInsVO mn 1; *Paulus* Komm EuInsVO Einl mn 9; D-K/D/Ch-*Duursma* Geschichte mn 6.

21 Council document 5419/91 DRS 12 (CFC) of 25.3.1991.

22 The text is printed in: ZIP 1992, 1197.

23 The Istanbul Convention was signed on 5 June 1990 in Istanbul but was ratified by Cyprus only. The reciprocal recognition of insolvency proceedings was all that was intended from the outset. On this: *Gottwald* Grenzüberschreitende Insolvenzen, p 15; *Paulus* Komm EuInsVO Einl mn 8; *Staak* Der deutsche Insolvenzverwalter im europäischen Insolvenzrecht, p 10 et seq.

24 *Liersch* Sicherungsrechte im international Insolvenzrecht, p 40.

25 The wording of the European Insolvency Convention is nearly identical to the wording of the Regulation. One can therefore also consult the Explanatory Report to this Convention on Insolvency Proceedings – which was prepared by *Miguel Virgós* and *Etienne Schmit* – for questions regarding the Regulation as well (*Virgós/Schmit* Explanatory Report).

26 The text is printed in: ZIP 1996, 976 and in *Stoll* Vorschläge und Gutachten (1997), p 3 in addition to the Explanatory Report of *Virgós/Schmit*.

27 *Balz* ZIP 1996, 948.

28 *Gottwald* Grenzüberschreitende Insolvenzen, p 15; *Liersch* Sicherungsrechte im internationalen Insolvenzrecht, p 41; *Leible/Staudinger* KTS 2000, 533, 535; *Balz* ZIP 1996, 948; *Fritz/Bähr* DZWiR 2001, 221, 222.

29 *Fritz/Bähr* DZWiR 2001, 221, 222; *Wessels* International Insolvency Law (2006) mn 10437.

30 *Liersch* Sicherungsrechte im internationalen Insolvenzrecht, p 41; *Virgós/Garcimartín* Regulation, p 7; *Kübler* FS Gerhardt (2004), p 527.

31 D-K/D/Ch-*Duursma* Geschichte mn 9.

32 D-K/D/Ch-*Duursma* Geschichte mn 9.

Pursuant to the deliberations of the members of the **ad hoc group "convention on insolvency proceedings"** on 27 January 1999, the majority opted in favour of an EU regulation in close conformity with the 1995 Insolvency Convention. Subsequent to this, Germany and Finland on 27/28 May 1999 made a proposal to the Council for an EU regulation,[33] which was then enacted as Council regulation (EC) No 1346/2000 of 29 May 2000 on insolvency proceedings ("the Regulation" or "the EIR"). The enactment of the Regulation was important for Germany as the German *InsO* (Insolvency Act), which had come into force in 1999, contained no provision for international insolvency proceedings.[34] **12**

On 31 May 2002, the Regulation came into force (Art 47 of the EIR). **13**

2. Parallel Legislation

The Regulation is not the only piece of legislation in the world that was developed to deal with cross-border insolvencies. **14**

Parallel Legislation
- **Istanbul Convention, see mn 15 et seq**
- **UNCITRAL Model Law, see mn 17 et seq**
- **ALI Principles, see mn 22 et seq**
- **Nordic Bankruptcy Convention, see mn 24 et seq**
- **Bustamante Code, see mn 26**
- **Uniform Act of OHADA, see mn 27 et seq**

2.1 Istanbul Convention

Commencing in 1980, the European Council established a committee comprised of governmental specialists and gave it the task of preparing a bankruptcy convention. This led to the signing of the so-called **Istanbul Convention** on 5 June 1990,[35] which dealt with certain international aspects of bankruptcy.[36] However the Istanbul Convention has only been ratified by Cyprus and must therefore be regarded as a failure, Art 34 of it stipulating that it must be ratified by at least three Member States of the European Council.[37] According to Art 44 (1) (k) of the EIR, the Regulation replaces the Istanbul Convention. **15**

The Istanbul Convention had a substantial impact on the further developments of the Regulation. It endorsed, for example, the linking of the main and the optional independent territorial insolvency proceedings.[38] **16**

---

[33] With further references: *Liersch* Sicherungsrechte im internationalen Insolvenzrecht, p 41.

[34] *Smid* Komm EuInsVO Vor Art 1 mn 1.

[35] On this: *Wessels* International Insolvency Law (2006) mn 10436; *Ramackers* La Semaine Juridique 1993, 3685.

[36] European Convention on Certain International Aspects of Bankruptcy, Council of Europe, European Treaty Series – No 136.

[37] D-K/D/Ch-*Duursma* Geschichte mn 9.

[38] *Herchen* Das Übereinkommen über Insolvenzverfahren der Mitgliedstaaten der Europäischen Union vom 23.11.1995, p 22.

2.2 UNCITRAL Model Law

17 The UNCITRAL Model Law[39] was approved by the United Nations General Assembly on proposal by the UNCITRAL Commission on 15 December 1997[40] (detailed discussion on the UNCITRAL Model Law in Part 4). The goals of the Model Law are to:

- recognize foreign insolvency proceedings,
- improve cooperation between the courts, and
- simplify access to the courts by foreign liquidators.[41]

18 Due to the large disparities between the insolvency law regimes throughout the world, a uniform law convention was rejected.[42] The Model Law is a model that may be modified by the respective insolvency law regimes.[43] The enacting states can adapt the provisions of the Model Law to their special needs and legal culture.[44]

19 The Model Law distinguishes between a foreign main proceeding, which is carried out at the centre of the debtor's main interests, and a foreign non-main proceeding, which may be opened wherever the debtor has an establishment.[45]

20 As opposed to the Regulation (Art 16 of the EIR), the Model Law does not provide for the **automatic recognition** of foreign insolvency proceedings.[46] Instead, a **formal recognition procedure** at the request of the foreign liquidator is mandatory (for a detailed discussion on this see Part 4).[47] The court is under an obligation to recognize (the foreign proceedings) if the listed requirements are fulfilled, see Part 4. The court is entitled to refuse recognition if this would infringe public policy.

21 The UNCITRAL Model Law has been adopted in numerous countries using more or less the identical wording, for example in Eritrea, Mexico, Serbia, Montenegro, Japan, South Africa, Romania, Poland, the USA (Chapter 15 US Bankruptcy Code "Ancillary and other Cross-border Cases"), Great Britain, Argentina, and Pakistan.[48]

2.3 ALI Principles

22 In 1994 the North American Free Trade Agreement (**NAFTA**) was entered into between the **USA, Mexico, and Canada.** Pursuant to this, the American Law Institute (ALI) initiated the Transnational Insolvency Project, which led to the publication in 2002 of the "Principles of Cooperation in Transnational Insolvency Cases Among the Members of the North American Free Trade Agreement".[49] The "Guidelines Applicable to Court-to-Court Communications in Cross-Border Cases" are annexed to the "Principles". The

---

[39] Printed in ZIP 1997, 2224 et seq.

[40] *Pannen* in Runkel (ed), AHB-Insolvenzrecht (2005) § 16 mn 58 et seq and 537 et seq; *Wimmer* ZIP 1997, 2220.

[41] *Wimmer* ZIP 1997, 2220, 2220.

[42] *Wimmer* ZIP 1997, 2220, 2221.

[43] *Pannen* in Runkel (ed), AHB-Insolvenzrecht (2005) § 16 mn 58.

[44] D-K/D/Ch-*Duursma* Parallelentwicklungen mn 6.

[45] *Wimmer* ZIP 1997, 2220, 2221.

[46] *Pannen* in Runkel (ed), AHB-Insolvenzrecht (2005) § 16 mn 63, 542.

[47] *Wimmer* ZIP 1997, 2220, 2222.

[48] See UNCITRAL 38th session (Vienna, July 4–15, 2005) Developments in Insolvency Law: adoption of the UNCITRAL Model Law on Cross-Border Insolvency; use of cross-border protocols and *court-to-court* communication guidelines, and case law on interpretation of "centre of main interests" and "establishment" in the European Union (Note by the Secretariat, April 14, 2005 – A/CN.9.580); see on this Part 4 mn 4.

[49] Printed in *Wessels* International Insolvency Law (2006), Appendix VI; see on this *Westbrook* 76 Am Bankr LJ 1. On this: *Burman* Fordham L.R.64 (1996), 2543.

starting point of the "Principles" was the summary and comparison of the insolvency law rules of Mexico, the USA, and Canada.[50]

According to the ALI Principles, there is no **automatic recognition** of insolvency proceedings. Instead, a separate recognition procedure must take place in each of the contracting states.[51] The powers of the liquidator in the other contracting states are defined by the autonomous laws of the respective states. **23**

2.4 Nordic Bankruptcy Convention

The **Nordic Bankruptcy Convention**[52] was entered into on 7 November 1933 between Denmark, Finland, Iceland, Norway, and Sweden. The reason for the convention was the similarity of the legal situations in all of these countries.[53] An insolvency proceeding opened at the debtor's domicile in one of these contracting states is effective in all five contracting states against all of the debtor's assets.[54] Therefore only one insolvency proceeding may be opened. But since the convention only applies in the contracting states, the principle of universality has a limited effect. Although secondary insolvency proceedings may not be opened subsequent to the opening of insolvency proceedings at the domicile of the debtor, any previous proceedings may be continued.[55] The insolvency proceeding and its effects are regulated by the ***lex fori concursus***.[56] The liquidator is granted powers in the other states as well. He may, in particular, request the assistance of the public authorities of the other contracting states.[57] **24**

The Nordic Convention was replaced by the Regulation pursuant to Art 44 (1) (j) of the EIR with respect to Finland and Sweden regarding their relations to each other. **25**

2.5 Bustamante Code

The so-called **Bustamante Code**,[58] the *Código de derecho internacional privado*,[59] was entered into in 1928 by 15 Central and South American countries within the context of the 6th Pan-American Conference.[60] This body of law is premised on the universality of insolvency proceedings.[61] If the debtor has only one domicile, then only one insolvency proceeding can be opened against all of his assets and liabilities in all of the contracting states. If the debtor has several economically independent establishments in various contracting states, then only one request to open a "preventative insolvency proceeding" may be made per member country (Art 415).[62] A parallel insolvency proceeding may be opened if the national courts have international jurisdiction to decide on the claim made by the requesting creditor.[63] **26**

50 *Westbrook* 76 Am Bankr LJ 1.

51 *Westbrook* 76 Am Bankr LJ 1.

52 Printed in *Wessels* International Insolvency Law (2006), Appendix V.

53 *Wessels* International Insolvency Law (2006) mn 10071.

54 *Wessels* International Insolvency Law (2006) mn 10072; *Trunk* Internationales Insolvenzrecht, p 77.

55 *Trunk* Internationales Insolvenzrecht, p 78.

56 *Wessels* International Insolvency Law (2006) mn 10072; *Trunk* Internationales Insolvenzrecht, p 78.

57 *Wessels* International Insolvency Law (2006) mn 10072.

58 On this see also: *Dolinger* FS Samtleben (2002) p 133 et seq.

59 Printed in *Wessels* International Insolvency Law (2006), Appendix IV.

60 *Wessels* International Insolvency Law (2006) mn 10069; *Trunk* International Insolvenzrecht, p 76.

61 *Trunk* Internationales Insolvenzrecht, p 76.

62 *Wessels* International Insolvency Law (2006) mn 10069.

63 *Trunk* Internationales Insolvenzrecht, p 77.

2.6 Uniform Act of OHADA

27 **OHADA** is the French acronym for "*Organisation pour l'Harmonisation en Afrique du Droit des Affaires*", i.e. the Organization for the Harmonisation of Business Law in Africa. It was founded in 1993. Its members are primarily the French-speaking countries of West Africa and the Comoros. To facilitate the harmonization of the laws of the member countries, so-called **Uniform Acts** are being enacted. These can be loosely compared to the EU regulations as they too are directly applicable in the member countries.[64] A common Court of Justice is also intended to ensure uniform interpretation.

28 On 1 January 1999, a **Uniform Act** Organizing Collective Proceedings for Wiping Off Debts came into force, which contains ten provisions in relation to international insolvency proceedings.[65] As opposed to the Regulation, the Uniform Act introduces a **uniform insolvency law regime**, thereby not restricting itself to regulating issues of international procedural law and conflicts of laws. According to Art 247 of the Uniform Act, decisions of a member state that are declared *res judicata* are automatically deemed *res judicata* in all other member states as well. Similar to the Regulation, Art 251 of the **Uniform Act** also allows secondary insolvency proceedings to be opened parallel to main insolvency proceedings. Main insolvency proceedings are opened in the member country in which the debtor has his main establishment (in the case of natural persons) or in which he has his domicile/registered office (in the case of legal entities). A secondary insolvency proceeding may be opened in the other member states. The liquidators are then mutually obliged to provide each other with information (Art 252). The Uniform Act contains provisions similar to the Regulation respecting the right of the creditors to make multiple requests, the equalization of dividends, and the surplus from secondary insolvency proceedings.

29 Although it has adopted nearly all of the fundamental mechanisms of the European Regulation, the OHADA Uniform Act differs significantly from it in that it contains no conflict of laws rules (see Art 4 et seq of the EIR).[66] These are simply not necessary within the scope of applicability of the OHADA because, regardless of which court has jurisdiction in the particular case, the same insolvency law is to be applied.

3. Principles Underlying the Regulation

30 The EIR aims to provide the Europe-wide regulation of:

- jurisdiction,
- applicable laws, and
- recognition.[67]

It is intended to prevent so-called **forum shopping**. It also endeavours to eliminate the incentive for the participants to obtain for themselves, through the application of conflicts of law rules, a more favourable legal position by transferring assets or judicial proceedings from one Member State to another.[68]

---

64 *Wessels* International Insolvency Law (2006) mn 10077.

65 Uniform Act Organizing Collective Proceedings for Wiping Off Debts, printed in *Wessels* International Insolvency Law (2006), Appendix VII.

66 *Wessels* International Insolvency Law (2006) mn 10078.

67 *Paulus* Komm EuInsVO Einl mn 14; BK-InsO/*Pannen* Präambel EuInsVO mn 4.

68 Recital 14 of the EIR.

Principles underlying the Regulation
- **Principle of mutual trust, see mn 31 et seq**
- **Modified universality, see mn 34 et seq**
- **Automatic recognition, see mn 39**
- **Applicability of the *lex fori concursus*, see mn 40**

3.1 Principle of Mutual Trust

The Regulation, both in terms of its conception and in its application, is based on the **principle of mutual trust**, although this is only mentioned as an aside in Recital 22 of the EIR.[69] Neither the automatic recognition nor the principle of priority is conceivable without the principle of mutual trust.[70] **31**

In the opinion of the *OLG* **Vienna** (→ cf Table of Cases Art 3 of the EIR Appendix A mn 13 – High Court of London / Commercial Court of Vienna), because of the **principle of Community-wide trust** in the courts of the Member States ("community trust"), the international jurisdiction of the court opening the proceedings is not to be reviewed.[71] According to the **ECJ** in the **Eurofood/Parmalat** case (→ cf Table of Cases Art 3 of the EIR Appendix A mn 10), this mutual trust is also what makes it possible to create the compulsory system of jurisdiction found in Art 3 of the EIR.[72] **32**

The principle of mutual trust is also a dynamic principle because it must be taken into account when interpreting the Regulation. In the opinion of *Paulus*, this means that the reasons upon which decisions are based must be given in detail and that a certain degree of restraint must be exercised in the unilateral application of national laws.[73] **33**

3.2 Modified Universality

The Regulation is premised on the principle of **"moderate"** or **"modified" universality.**[74] **34**

A fundamental issue in international insolvency law is whether the effects of an insolvency proceeding are to be **universal**, i.e. in all countries where assets of the debtor are situated, or whether territorially restricted insolvency proceedings may be opened in each country.[75] This issue has been discussed in the legal literature under the concepts of **universal vs. territorial** or **unified vs. multiple** insolvency proceedings.[76] Depending on the **35**

---

[69] *Paulus* Komm EuInsVO Einl mn 19; *Smid* Komm EuInsVO Vor Art 1 mn 14.

[70] Similar ECJ C-341/04 dated 2 May 2006, ZInsO 2006, 484, 485 Nr 39 and 42 (→ cf Table of Cases Art 3 Appendix A mn 10); *Wessels* International Insolvency Law (2006) mn 10466.

[71] OLG Vienna dated 9 Nov 2004 – 28 R 225/04w, NZI 2005, 56 with comments by *Paulus* 62 et seq; this decision was affirmed by the OGH in an order dated 17 March 2005 – 8 Ob 135/04t where it was held in particular that the interpretation made by the "Rekursgericht" was not only supported by the wording of art 26 of the EIR but was also in line with Recital 22 of the Regulation, NZI 2005, 465, 466.

[72] ECJ C-341/04 dated 2 May 2006, ZInsO 2006, 484, 485 Nr 40.

[73] *Paulus* Komm EuInsVO Einl mn 20.

[74] BK-InsO/*Pannen* Präambel EuInsVO mn 4; *Smid* Europäisches Internationales Insolvenzrecht, p 5; *Wessels* International Insolvency Law (2006) mn 10456, who also designates it a *"combined model"*.

[75] *Westbrook* 76 Am Bankr LJ 1; *Smid* Komm EuInsVO Vor Art 1 mn 9 and 10.

[76] *Trunk* Internationales Insolvenzrecht, p 11; *Smid* Komm EuInsVO Einl mn 2; *Smid* Europäisches Internationales Insolvenzrecht, p 5.

particular era, the responses to it varied. While legal scholars in the 19th century largely favoured the territoriality of insolvency proceedings,[77] in the 20th century the majority favours universality. In spite of this, most countries adhered for a long time to the principle of territoriality.[78]

36 Although there is now a broad consensus at least in theory that the principle of universality is the better solution in a globalized world, the practical implementation of it seems rather doubtful considering the wide diversity of insolvency law regimes.[79] Instead, a so-called **modified universality** has found favour and is being endorsed by the **UNCITRAL Model Law**, by the **ALI Principles**, and by the **EU Regulation** (see Recital 11 of the EIR).[80] The idea underlying the concept of modified universality is to have one single insolvency proceeding only and to allow other subordinate proceedings in exceptional cases only (see Recital 12 of the EIR as well).

37 Being well aware of the difficulties involved with universally effective insolvency proceedings within the EU, the drafters of the Regulation opted in favour of **modified universality.** The legitimization for this is found in the absence in Europe of a uniform system of secured (property) rights and the widely disparate national law criteria for ascertaining the preferential rights of the various classes of creditors.[81] Although the Regulation essentially endorses the universal effects of the insolvency proceedings, it also allows – in order to take national differences into account – the opening of territorially restricted insolvency proceedings in those Member States in which an establishment of the debtor's is situated (on territorial insolvency proceedings, see Art 3 of the EIR).[82]

38 Universality is thus being restricted ("moderated") in the Regulation by allowing territorial insolvency proceedings. **Territorial insolvency proceedings** are subdivided into **secondary insolvency proceedings** and **independent territorial insolvency proceedings,** on this see Art 3 of the EIR mn 5.

3.3 Automatic Recognition

39 The Regulation's most fundamental characteristic is that a proceeding opened in one Member State will be **automatically recognized** in all other Member States (Art 16 of the EIR).[83] This is a consequence of the principle of universality. Not only the opening judgement must be recognized, but also the decisions to execute and terminate the insolvency proceedings, and insolvency derived proceedings.[84] The only stipulated reason for refusing recognition is the **public policy clause** in Art 26 of the EIR (see the detailed comments on Art 26 of the EIR). The Regulation therefore goes much farther than **Council Regulation (EC) No 44/2001** (Art 32 et seq), which contains a variety of reasons for not recognizing.

3.4 Applicability of the *lex fori concursus*

40 In order to ensure the priority of the main insolvency proceedings, the Regulation provides for the broadest possible applicability of the *lex fori concursus,* i.e. the law of

---

[77] *Westbrook* 76 Am Bankr LJ 1 fn 19.

[78] *Westbrook* 76 Am Bankr LJ 1.

[79] *Pannen* in Runkel (ed), AHB-Insolvenzrecht (2005) § 16 mn 44 (fn 2); *Westbrook* 76 Am Bankr LJ 1.

[80] *Westbrook* 76 Am Bankr LJ 1.

[81] *Virgós/Schmit* Explanatory Report mn 12.

[82] *Pannen* in Runkel (ed), AHB-Insolvenzrecht (2005) § 16 mn 44.

[83] *Pannen* in Runkel (ed), AHB-Insolvenzrecht (2005) § 16 mn 44; *Wessels* International Insolvency Law (2006) mn 10467.

[84] *Wessels* International Insolvency Law (2006) mn 10467.

the Member State in which the proceedings are opened (Art 4 of the EIR).[85] Although it is stipulated that the *lex fori concursus* is to govern, Art 5 to 15 of the EIR provide for numerous exceptions to this (see also sentence 5 of Recital 11 Regulation). These exceptions were introduced to safeguard the trust placed in and the legal certainty of business transactions entered into in Member States other than the one in which the proceedings are opened.[86]

4. Explanatory Report by *Virgós/Schmit*

The Regulation was enacted with 33 **Recitals**. These evince the legislator's intentions and, being the motivating factors behind the legislator,[87] lend support to the interpretation of the Regulation.[88] **41**

The **1995 Draft Convention** was adopted nearly *verbatim* by the Regulation.[89] This is an important point considering that the 1995 Insolvency Convention had been published at that time together with the Explanatory Report by *Virgós* and *Schmit* (so-called **Virgós/Schmit Report**).[90] Judicial opinion and legal academics unanimously hold that this Report is authoritative for the interpretation of the Regulation as well.[91] However the definitions contained in it are not binding.[92] **42**

5. Structure of the Regulation

The Regulation is comprised of 47 articles preceded by 33 **Recitals**. **43**

It is divided into 5 chapters: **44**

- Chapter I: General Provisions
- Chapter II: Recognition of Insolvency Proceedings
- Chapter III: Secondary Insolvency Proceedings
- Chapter IV: Provision of Information for Creditors and Lodgement of Their Claims
- Chapter V: Transitional and Final Provisions

Equally important for the application of the Regulation are the three **Annexes**. These contain respectively a list of insolvency proceedings (Annex A), of winding-up proceedings (Annex B), and of liquidators (Annex C). These lists supplement the legal definitions contained in Art 2 of the EIR and, by dictating which national legal institutions fall within the definitions, they ease the interpretation of these. According to Art 45 of the EIR, the Council, acting by qualified majority on the initiative of one of its members or on a proposal from the Commission, may amend the Annexes. **45**

---

[85] *Pannen* in Runkel (ed), AHB-Insolvenzrecht (2005) § 16 mn 44.

[86] *Virgós/Schmit* Erläuternder Bericht mn 92; *Pannen* in Runkel (ed), AHB-Insolvenzrecht (2005) § 16 mn 44.

[87] *Smid* Komm EuInsVO Vor Art 1 mn 14.

[88] *Vallender* KTS 2005, 283, 288.

[89] *Virgós/Garcimartín* Regulation, p 7.

[90] *Virgós/Schmit* Explanatory Report, in Stoll (ed), Vorschläge und Gutachten zur Umsetzung des EU-Übereinkommens über Insolvenzverfahren im deutschen Recht (1997), 32.

[91] *Smid* Komm EuInsVO Vor Art 1 mn 14; *Virgós/Garcimartín* Regulation, p 7; *Vallender* KTS 2005, 283, 288; BK-InsO/*Pannen* Präambel EuInsVO mn 3 Fn 11; *Pannen/Riedemann* NZI 2004, 646, 651; *Wessels* International Insolvency Law (2006) mn 10439; see for example also: Supreme Court of Ireland to the ECJ dated 27 Jul 2004 – C 341/04, ZInsO 2005, 159, 165 (→ cf Table of Cases Art 3 of the EIR Appendix A mn 10).

[92] *Virgós/Garcimartín* Regulation, p 7.

Chapter I
General Provisions

Article 1
Scope

(1) This Regulation shall apply to collective insolvency proceedings which entail the partial or total divestment of a debtor and the appointment of a liquidator.

(2) This Regulation shall not apply to insolvency proceedings concerning insurance undertakings, credit institutions, investment undertakings which provide services involving the holding of funds or securities for third parties, or to collective investment undertakings.

→ Cf Art 1 UNCITRAL Model Law

Contents

Index

Bibliography

Altmeppen Schutz vor europäischen Kapitalgesellschaften, NJW 2004, p 97; *Altmeppen* Parteifähigkeit, Sitztheorie und „Centros", DStR 2000, p 1061; *Balz* Das neue Europäische Insolvenzübereinkommen, ZIP 1996, p 948; *Baudenbacher/Buschle* Niederlassungsfreiheit für EWR-Gesellschaften nach Überseering, IPRax 2004, p 26; *Bayer* Die EuGH-Entscheidung Inspire Art und die deutsche GmbH im Wettbewerb der europäischen Rechtsordnung, BB 2003, p 2357; *Bazinas* EU Regulation on Insolvency Proceedings: A first year and the outlook from Greece, presented at the International Insolvency Institute 3rd Annual International Insolvency Conference, Fordham University Law School, New York, June 9–10, 2003; *Behrens* Das Internationale Gesellschaftsrecht nach dem Überseering-Urteil des EuGH und den Schlussanträgen zu Inspire Art, IPRax 2003, p 193; *Behrens* Reaktionen mitgliedstaatlicher Gerichte auf das Centros-Urteil des EuGH, IPRax 2000, p 384; *Braun/Heinrich* Finanzdienstleister in der „grenzüberschreitenden" Insolvenz – Lücken im System? – Ein Beitrag zu der Verordnung (EG) Nr. 1346/2000 des Rates vom 29.5.2000 über Insolvenzverfahren, NZI 2005, p 579; *Brenner* Zur Insolvenzfähigkeit ausländischer Gesellschaften mit Inlandssitz, EWiR 2003, p 925; *Breutigam/Blersch/Goetsch/Haas* Berliner Kommentar zum Insolvenzrecht vol I (April 2006) vol III (December 2004); *Carstens* Die internationale Zuständigkeit im europäischen Insolvenzrecht (2005); *Dammann* La future procédure de conciliation, pierre angulaire du projet de loi de sauvegarde des entreprises, Revue Lamy Droit des affaires, Juin 2005, p 5; *Dammann* Das neue französische Insolvenzrecht, ZIP 1996, p 300; *Derleder/Knops/Bamberger* Handbuch zum deutschen und europäischen Bankrecht (2004); *Dicey/Morris/Morse* Conflict of Laws: Fourth Cumulative Supplement (1991); *Duursma-Kepplinger/Duursma/Chalupsky* Europäische Insolvenzverordnung, Kommentar (2002); *Ebke* Das Centros-Urteil des EuGH und seine Relevanz für das deutsche Internationale Gesellschaftsrecht, JZ 1999, p 656; *Eidenmüller* Unternehmenssanierung zwischen Markt und Gesetz: Mechanismen der Unternehmensreorganisation und Kooperationspflichten im Reorganisationsrecht (1999); *Eidenmüller* Europäische Verordnung über Insolvenzverfahren und zukünftiges deutsches Internationales Insolvenzrecht, IPRax 2001, p 2; *Eidenmüller* Beurteilung der Rechtsfähigkeit einer ausländischen Gesellschaft nach dem Recht des Gründungsstaates, JZ 2003, p 526; *Eidenmüller* Mobilität und Restrukturierung von Unternehmen im Binnenmarkt, JZ 2004, p 24; *Flessner* Die Unternehmensperspektive im europäischen Insolvenzrecht, in Damm/Heermann/Veil (eds), Festschrift für Thomas Raiser zum 70. Geburtstag (2005), p 827; *Fletcher* The Law of Insolvency (2002); *Forsthoff* EuGH fördert Vielfalt im Gesellschaftsrecht, DB 2002, p 2471; *Fritz/Bähr* Die Europäische Verordnung über Insolvenzverfahren, DZWiR 2001, p 221; *Galanti* The New EC Law on Bank Crisis, International Insolvency Review 2002, p 49; *van Galen* The European Insolvency Regulation and Groups of Companies, INSOL Europe Annual Congress (Cork, Ireland), October 16–18, 2003; *Giovanoli/Heinrich* (eds) International Bank Insolvencies – A Central Bank Perspective (1999); *Haß/Huber/Gruber/Heiderhoff* EU-Insolvenzverordnung Kommentar (2005); *Heiss/Gölz* Zur deutschen Umsetzung der Richtlinie 2001/17/EG des Europäischen Parlaments und des Rates vom 19.3.2001 über die Sanierung und Liquidation von Versicherungsunternehmen, NZI 2006, p 1; *Herchen* Scheinauslandsgesellschaften im Anwendungsbereich der Europäischen Insolvenzverordnung, Comments on High Court of Justice, Chancery Division (Company Court) dated 7.2.2003, ZInsO 2003, p 742; *Hirsch/Britain* Artfully Inspired – Werden deutsche Gesellschaften englisch?, NZG 2003, p 1100; *Huber* Internationales Insolvenzrecht in Europa, ZZP 114 (2001), p 133; *Huber* Die Europäische Insolvenzverordnung, EuZW 2002, p 490; *Keller/Langner* Überblick über EG-Gesetzgebungsvorhaben im Finanzbereich, BKR 2003, p 616; *Kemper* Die Verordnung (EG) 1346/2000 über Insolvenzverfahren, ZIP 2001, p 1609; *Kleinert/Probst* Endgültiges Aus für Sonderanknüpfungen bei (Schein-) Auslandsgesellschaften, DB 2003, p 2217; *Knof/Mock* Zur perpetuatio fori bei Sitzverlegung nach Stellung eines Insolvenzantrags, ZIP 2006, p 189; *Krebber* Europäische Insolvenzverordnung, Drittstaatengesellschaften, Drittstaatensachverhalte und innergemeinschaftliche Konflikte (zur Entscheidung des High Court vom 7.2.2003, In re BRAC Rent-A-Car International Inc.), IPRax 2004, p 540; *Leible/Hoffmann* Wie inspiriert ist Inspire Art?, EuZW 2003, p 677; *Leible/Hoffmann* Entscheidungsbesprechung: „Überseering" und das deutsche Gesellschaftskollisionsrecht, ZIP 2003, p 925; *Leible/Staudinger* Die europäische Verordnung über Insolvenzverfahren, KTS 2000, p 533; *Liersch* Deutsches Internationales Insolvenzrecht, NZI 2003, p 302; *Lurger* Neuere Entwicklungen im österreichischen Handels- und Wirtschaftsrecht, RIW 2005, p 209; *Lutter* Überseering und die Folgen, BB 2003, p 7; *Mankowski* Entwicklungen im Internationalen Privat- und Prozessrecht (Teil 2), RIW 2005, p 561; *Mankowski* Entscheidungsbesprechung: Grenzüberschreitender Umzug und das center of main interests im europäischen Internationalen Insolvenzrecht, NZI 2005, p 368; *Marshall* European Cross Border Insolvency (2004); *Mock/Schildt* Insolvenz ausländischer Kapitalgesellschaften mit Sitz in Deutschland, ZInsO 2003, p 396; *Moss/Fletcher/Isaacs* (eds) The EC Regulation on Insolvency Proceedings, A Commentary and Annotated Guide (2002); *Pannen* Internationales Insolvenzrecht, in Runkel (ed), Anwaltshandbuch-Insolvenzrecht (2005); *Pannen* Krise und Insolvenz bei Kreditinstituten, Handbuch, 2nd edn (2006); *Pannen/Riedemann* Der Begriff des „centre of main interests" i.S des Art 3 I 1 EuInsVO im Spiegel aktueller Fälle aus der Rechtsprechung, NZI 2004, p 646; *Paulus* Die europäische Insolvenzverordnung und der deutsche Insolvenzverwalter, NZI 2001, p 505; *Paulus* Europäische Insolvenzverordnung, Kommentar (2006); *Riedemann* Entscheidungsbesprechung: Das Auseinanderfallen von Gesellschafts- und Insolvenzstatut, GmbHR 2004, p 345; *Roth* Internationales Gesellschaftsrecht nach Überseering, IPRax 2003, p 117; *Sabel/Schlegel* Zum Anwendungsbereich der EGV 1346/2000, EWiR 2003, p 367; *Schanze/Jüttner* Anerkennung und Kontrolle ausländischer Gesellschaften – Rechtslage und Perspektiven nach der Überseering-Entscheidung des EuGH, AG 2003, p 30; *Schmidt* Perpetuatio fori im europäischen Insolvenzrecht – Anmerkung zu EuGH, Rs C-1/04, ZInsO 2006, p 88; *Schulz* (Schein-) Auslandsgesellschaften in Europa – Ein Schein-Problem?, NJW 2003, p 2705; *Smid* Deutsches und Europäisches Internationales Insolvenzrecht (2004); *Smid* Vier Entscheidungen englischer und deutscher Gerichte zur europäischen internationalen Zuständigkeit zur Eröffnung von Hauptinsolvenzverfahren, DZWiR 2003, p 397; *Spindler/Berner* Inspire Art – Der europäische Wettbewerb um das Gesellschaftsrecht ist endgültig eröffnet, RIW 2003, p 949; *Spindler/Berner* Der Gläubigerschutz im Gesellschaftsrecht nach Inspire Art, RIW 2004, p 7; *Staak* Der deutsche Insolvenzverwalter im europäischen Insolvenzrecht (2004); *Tirado* Die Anwendung der Europäischen Insolvenzverordnung durch die Gerichte der Mitgliedstaaten, GPR 2005, p 39; *Ulmer* Das Centros-Urteil des EuGH und seine Relevanz für das deutsche Internationale Gesellschaftsrecht; JZ 1999, p 662; *Virgós/Garcimartín* The European Insolvency Regulation: Law and Practice (2004); *Virgós/Schmit* Erläuternder Bericht zu dem EU-Übereinkommen über Insolvenzverfahren, in Stoll (ed), Vorschläge und Gutachten (1997) p 32; *Weller* Scheinauslandsgesellschaften nach Centros, Überseering, Inspire Art: Ein neues Anwendungsfeld für die Existenzvernichtungshaftung, IPRax 2003, p 207; *Weller* Das Internationale Gesellschaftsrecht in der neuesten BGH-Rechtsprechung, IPRax 2003, p 324; *Weller* Einschränkung der Gründungstheorie bei missbräuchlicher Auslandsgründung, IPRax 2003, p 520; *Wehdeking* Reform des Internationalen Insolvenzrechts in Deutschland und Österreich, DZWiR 2003, p 133; *Wessels* Current Topics of International Insolvency Law (2004), *Wessels* The European Union Insolvency Regulation: Its first year in Dutch Cases, Third Annual International Insolvency Conference, Fordham University School of Law, New York City June 9–10, 2003, www.iiiglobal.org; *Wessels* Current Topics of International Insolvency Law (2004); *Wessels* Realisation of the EU Insolvency Regulation in Germany, France and the Netherlands, Paper presented to Insol International Academics meeting on 'Multinational Insolvency Proceedings – Cooperation among Nations', Las Vegas, Nevada, USA, 20–21 September 2003 – www.iiiglobal.org; *Wessels* Germany and Spain lead changes towards International Insolvency Law in Europe, Paper presented to Insol International Academics meeting on 'Comparative Approaches to Insolvency', Las Vegas, Nevada, USA, 20–21 September 2003 – www.iiiglobal. org; *Wessels* Moving House: Which court can open insolvency proceedings – www.iiiglobal.org; *Wimmer* Die Richtlinien 2001/17 EG und 2001/24 EG über die Sanierung und Liquidation von Versicherungsunternehmen und Kreditinstituten, ZInsO 2002, p 897; *Wimmer* Die UNCITRAL-Modellbestimmungen über grenzüberschreitende Insolvenzverfahren, ZIP 1997, p 2220; *Ziemons* Freie Bahn für den Umzug der Gesellschaften nach Inspire Art ?!, ZIP 2003, p 1913; *Zimmer* Wie es Euch gefällt? Offene Fragen nach dem Überseering-Urteil des EuGH, BB 2003, p 1; *Zimmer* Nach „Inspire Art" – Grenzenlose Gestaltungsfreiheit für Deutsche Unternehmen?, NJW 2003, p 3585.

I. Introduction

1 A distinction must be drawn between the Regulation's **scope of application** in terms of **subject matter** (see mn 6 et seq), **persons/entities** (see mn 93 et seq), **territory** (see mn 112 et seq), and **time** (see mn 104 et seq).

2 Art 1 (1) of the EIR – in interaction with Annexes A and B[1] – is a provision regarding **subject matter.**[2] It covers all **collective insolvency proceedings** that require an insolvency on the part of the debtor and that entail the partial or total divestment of a debtor and

[1] Modified *inter alia* by Council Regulation (EC) No. 603/2005 of April 12, 2005, Official Journal of the European Union, L 100/1 (for an overview of the changes hitherto see Art 45 of the EIR mn 6 et seq).

[2] *Bazinas* EU Regulation on Insolvency Pro-

the appointment of a liquidator.[3] Because collective insolvency proceedings must be involved, it does not cover proceedings to satisfy one (or several) individual debtor(s).[4] **Compulsory execution measures** are governed within Europe by the provisions of Council Regulation (EC) No 44/2001.[5]

The **territorial scope of application** (see mn 112 et seq) is not expressly regulated. Undisputed is that the Regulation applies throughout the EU with the exception of Denmark.[6] It does not, however, apply to **purely domestic matters of a Member State.** What is essential is a foreign element. But whether a so-called **"qualified" foreign connection** is required, or whether a **"simple" foreign connection** will suffice (mn 118 et seq), is unsettled. **3**

The scope of application in terms of **time** follows from Art 43 and Art 47 of the EIR. The Regulation governs insolvency proceedings opened after 31 May 2002 (see Art 43 of the EIR mn 3 et seq and Art 47 of the EIR mn 1 et seq). In the new Member States that joined the European Union through the enlargement process, the Regulation is law whose application is immediate and mandatory.[7] **4**

The **areas exempted from the scope of the Regulation's application** are set out in Art 1 (2) of the EIR.[8] According to Art 1 (2) of the EIR, the Regulation does not apply to insolvency proceedings concerning insurance undertakings, credit institutions, investment undertakings which provide services involving the holding of funds or securities for third parties, or to collective investment undertakings (see mn 23 for definitions).[9] Significant to the aforementioned exemptions are Directive 2001/24/EC of 4 April 2001 on the reorganisation and winding-up of credit institutions (OJ L 125 p 15)[10] and Directive 2001/17/EC of 19 March 2001 on the reorganisation and winding-up of insurance undertakings (OJ L 110 p 28).[11] **5**

---

ceedings: A first year and the outlook from Greece, p 8; *Huber* EuZW 2002, 490, 491.

3 See *Pannen* in Runkel (ed), AHB-Insolvenzrecht (2005) § 16 mn 29; *Smid* Komm EuInsVO Art 1 mn 1.

4 *Paulus* Komm EuInsVO Art 1 mn 8.

5 Council Regulation (EC) No 44/2001 of 22 December 2000 on jurisdiction and the recognition and enforcement of judgments in civil and commercial matters (OJ L 12, 16 Jan 2001, p 1).

6 *Pannen* in Runkel (ed), AHB-Insolvenzrecht (2005) § 16 mn 25; on this, see also: OLG Frankfurt dated 24 Jan 2005 – 20 W 527/04, ZInsO 2005, 715; *Tirado* GPR 2005, 39, 39.

7 Art 1 (2) of the Accession Treaty, OJ L 236 of 23.9.2003, p 17, 22, in connection with art 2 of these Acts, OJ L 236 of 23 Sep 2003, p 33/ Act concerning the conditions of accession of the Czech Republic, the Republic of Estonia, the Republic of Cyprus, the Republic of Latvia, the Republic of Lithuania, the Republic of Hungary, the Republic of Malta, the Republic of Poland, the Republic of Slovenia and the Slovak Republic and the adjustments to the Treaties on which the European Union is founded, OJ of 23 Sep 2003; Protocol concerning the conditions and arrangements for admission of the Republic of Bulgaria and Romania to the European Union, OJ of 21 Jun 2005 L 157/29; *Paulus* Komm EuIns-VO Einl mn 14.

8 *Pannen* in Runkel (ed) AHB-Insolvenzrecht (2005) § 16 mn 40; *Pannen* Krise und Insolvenz bei Kreditinstituten (2006), p 212.

9 On this, see also: *Wessels* Germany and Spain changes towards International Insolvency Law in Europe, p 1; *Braun/Heinrich* NZI 2005, 578, 579.

10 In depth: *Pannen* Krise und Insolvenz bei Kreditinstituten 2006, p 211. This contains, *inter alia*, a synopsis on implementing the Directive in Germany (p 239 et seq); also: *Wessels* Current Topics of International Insolvency Law, p 259 et seq; in depth on this: *Giovanoli/Heinrich* International Bank Insolvencies – A Central Bank Perspective, p 321 et seq.

11 On this *Heiss/Gölz* NZI 2006, 1; FK-InsO/*Wimmer* Anhang 1 mn 222 et seq and mn 233 et seq, *Wimmer* ZInsO 2002, 897; and BK-InsO/*Pannen* Art 1 EuInsVO mn 18 et seq.

II. Scope of Application – Subject Matter

1. Article 1 (1) of the EIR

6 The Regulation applies to **collective insolvency proceedings** that require an insolvency on the part of the debtor and that entail the partial or total divestment of a debtor and the appointment of a liquidator (Art 1 (1) of the EIR). The full scope of the Regulation's application (in terms of subject matter) can only be attained, however, if Art 1 is read in conjunction with Art 2 (a) (b) and (c) of the EIR (together with Annexes A, B, and C).[12]

7 Because insolvency proceedings vary quite considerably in the Member States, a **wide definition** of insolvency proceedings was chosen.[13] The definition is purely descriptive.[14] The underlying objectives of the proceedings are not even hinted at. While in Germany the satisfaction of the creditors plays the leading role (Sec 1 *InsO*), the primary importance of the proceedings in France and Spain is the reorganization of the business enterprise and the salvaging of jobs.[15]

8 Terms such as:

- **"collective insolvency proceedings"**[16] (i.e. the affected creditors may pursue the satisfaction of their claims through insolvency proceedings only);[17]
- **"insolvency"**[18] (this is defined pursuant to the laws of the state in which the proceedings are opened[19]); or
- **"divestment"** (this means that the debtor's power to administer and dispose of his assets passes to another person);[20] or
- **"liquidator"** (effectively excludes from the definition of Art 1 of the EIR all proceedings intended by operation of law to collectively settle all of the debtor's debts without the assistance or the control of a neutral third party)[21]

are subject to interpretation. In order to facilitate the application of the Regulation, the insolvency and winding-up proceedings referred to in Art 2 (a) sentence 2 and in Art 2 (c) of the EIR are listed **exhaustively**[22] in Annexes A and B.[23] Art 2 (b) of the EIR de-

---

12 Moss/Fletcher/Isaacs-*Fletcher*, Regulation, mn 3.02.

13 D-K/D/Ch-*Duursma-Kepplinger* Art 1 mn 11.

14 *Paulus* Komm EuInsVO Art 1 mn 2.

15 *Paulus* Komm EuInsVO Art 1 mn 2; see also the company-oriented perspective pursued in France and other countries in *Flessner* FS Raiser 2005, pp 827, 829 et seq.

16 *Moss/Smith* in Moss/Fletcher/Isaacs, Regulation, mn 8.04 infer from the term "collective" that the Regulation is not applicable to proceedings aimed to benefit to one single creditor; concurring: *Virgós/Garcimartín* Regulation, p 18.

17 *Virgós/Schmit* Explanatory Report mn 49; Moss/Fletcher/Isaacs-*Moss/Smith*, Regulation, mn 8.04.

18 This term, which the Regulation does not define more precisely, is to be so construed that the proceedings must ensue from a financial crisis on the part of the debtor (national laws must therefore be consulted for a more precise definition of this), and they may not be based on any other grounds. It therefore follows that the Regulation will not apply, for example, in English law where a winding-up is ordered in the interests of the public, or if such proceedings are based on any other facts that "do not constitute insolvency", Moss/Fletcher/Isaacs-*Moss/Smith*, Regulation, mn 8.04.

19 *Virgós/Schmit* Explanatory Report mn 49; Moss/Fletcher/Isaacs-*Moss/Smith*, Regulation, mn 8.04; *Staak* Der deutsche Insolvenzverwalter im europäischen Insolvenzrecht, p 19; *Virgós/Garcimartín* Regulation, p 28.

20 *Virgós/Schmit* Explanatory Report mn 49.

21 *Paulus* Komm EuInsVO Art 1 mn 11.

22 *Wessels* The Regulation, It's first year in Dutch Cases, p 3; Moss/Fletcher/Isaacs-*Fletcher*, Regulation, mn 3.02.

23 This method of listing all pertinent proceedings by name in the list is based on the meth-

fines "liquidator" for the purposes of the Regulation as any person or body whose function is to administer or liquidate assets of which the debtor has been divested, or to supervise the administration of his affairs. These persons or bodies are listed in Annex C of the EIR, see also Art 2 of the EIR mn 5.

Because the lists contained in these annexes are exhaustive, the definition of insolvency proceedings contained in Art 1 (1) of the EIR is not necessary for determining the scope of the Regulation's applicability in terms of subject matter. The definition is to be understood in such a way that it is directed at the Member States, prescribing to them which proceedings may be included in Annexes A and B of the EIR.[24] The annexes to the Regulation may be amended through the simplified procedure laid down in Art 45 of the EIR.[25] They may be amended or augmented by a resolution with a qualified majority, see on this Art 45 of the EIR mn 2 et seq.[26] **9**

The **country recognizing the proceedings does not review** whether a particular foreign insolvency proceeding listed in Annex A or B complies with the definition in Art 1 (1) of the EIR; this is an unsettled point.[27] Conferring on the other Member States such a right to review would run contrary to legal certainty. **10**

However, the definition may become significant if a Member State has included proceedings in the annexes that can be resorted to both in the case of an insolvency as well as for matters unrelated to an insolvency; an example of this is the compulsory winding-up proceeding pursuant to English and Irish law.[28] Only proceedings based on the insolvency of the debtor should fall within the scope of the Regulation's applicability.[29] In such cases, the laws of the Member State must require that the reasons for opening proceedings be stated in the decision to open proceedings (in the form of a kind of "labelling" in the opening decision).[30] On this, see the UK case ***Re Marann Brooks CSV Ltd***[31] (mn 18). **11**

Proceedings that are not expressly listed in the annexes are not subject to the Regulation even if they meet the criteria of Art 1 (1) of the EIR.[32] **12**

a) Examples of types of proceedings (not) subject to the Regulation

(1) Examples of proceedings not subject to the Regulation

The English **administrative receivership** proceeding[33] is not listed in the annexes even though it certainly would comply with the definition in Art 1 (1) of the EIR.[34] The legal **13**

---

odology of the Istanbul Convention, Moss/Fletcher/Isaacs-*Fletcher*, Regulation, mn 3.06.

24 *Virgós/Schmit* Explanatory Report mn 48; Moss/Fletcher/Isaacs-*Fletcher*, Regulation, mn 3.02; MünchKomm InsO/*Reinhart* Art 1 EuInsVO mn 2.

25 Cf *Bazinas* EIR and the outlook from Greece, p 8 (mn 20); *Pannen* in Runkel (ed), AHB-Insolvenzrecht (2005) § 16 mn 32.

26 *Pannen* in Runkel (ed), AHB-Insolvenzrecht (2005) § 16 mn 32.

27 D-K/D/Ch-*Duursma-Kepplinger* Art 1 mn 16; *Pannen* in Runkel (ed), AHB-Insolvenzrecht (2005) § 16 mn 32; *Kemper* ZIP 2001, 1609, 1611; FK-InsO/*Wimmer* Anhang 1 mn 71; *Eidenmüller* IPRax 2001, 2, 4; **contra:** *Bazinas* EIR and the outlook from Greece, p 8 (mn 20).

28 *Virgós/Schmit* Explanatory Report mn 49; MünchKomm InsO/*Reinhart* Art 1 EuInsVO mn 2; *Paulus* Komm EuInsVO Art. 1 mn 7.

29 *Virgós/Schmit* Explanatory Report mn 49; MünchKomm InsO/*Reinhart* Art 1 EuInsVO mn 2.

30 D-K/D/Ch-*Duursma-Kepplinger* Art 1 mn 23.

31 (2003) B.C.C. 239, Chancery Division, December 4, 2004; on this, see also *Marshall* European Cross Border Insolvency, No. 2.002.

32 Moss/Fletcher/Isaacs-*Fletcher*, Regulation, mn 3.02.

33 Moss/Fletcher/Isaacs-*Fletcher*, Regulation, mn 3.03; MünchKomm InsO/*Reinhart* Art 1 EuInsVO mn 2.

34 MünchKomm InsO/*Reinhart* Art 1 EuInsVO mn 2.

literature explains the failure to classify it as an "insolvency proceeding" by the fact that the "receiver's" main concern is the safeguarding of the interests of the creditors of the floating charge, and therefore no collective insolvency proceedings are taking place.[35]

14 This exclusion should be kept in mind particularly by English advisors in the case of a cross-border insolvency: It may be advisable to request an "administration" (which is governed by the Regulation) rather than an "administrative receivership" (which does not fall within the scope of the Regulation).[36]

15 Also outside the scope of the Regulation are, for example, the French ***"règlement amiable"***,[37] which are pure pre-insolvency composition proceedings, and the Austrian pre-bankruptcy proceedings known as **company reorganization proceedings pursuant to the Austrian *URG*.**[38]

(2) Reorganization proceedings motivated by politico-industrial reasons and the German debtor in possession proceeding

16 The Regulation also governs proceedings whose purpose is the reorganization of the debtor enterprise. Particularly the French and Italian reorganization proceedings, which are motivated by politico-industrial reasons, have been included in Annex A (***redressement judiciaire*** and the ***amministrazione straordinaria***).[39]

17 According to the wording of Art 1 (1) of the EIR, the Regulation only governs proceedings that entail the appointment of a liquidator. However, the German debtor in possession proceedings, the so-called ***Eigenverwaltung*** pursuant to Sec 270 et seq *InsO*, also fall within the scope of the Regulation's application.[40] This follows from Art 2 (b) of the EIR. According to this section, "liquidator" also includes persons who merely supervise the business activities of the debtor, for example the German *Sachwalter* (custodian) in debtor in possession proceedings (see on this Art 2 of the EIR mn 8).[41]

b) Cases involving Article 1 (1) of the EIR

(1) Re Marann Brooks CSV Ltd

18 The English case ***Re Marann Brooks CSV Ltd***[42] deals with the concept of insolvency proceedings as understood by Art 1 (1) of the EIR. The court came to the conclusion that the Regulation does not apply to a request "to wind up a company in the public interest under s. 124 A of the Insolvency Act 1986". In Nos 25 and 32 of the judgement, Justice Patten holds:

---

[35] *Fritz/Bähr* DZWiR 2001, 221, 223; furthermore, the court in most cases does not participate in the receivership process, Moss/Fletcher/Isaacs-*Fletcher*, Regulation, mn 3.03.

[36] See also Moss/Fletcher/Isaacs-*Fletcher*, Regulation, mn 3.03.

[37] On this, see *Dammann* ZIP 1996, 300, 301; *Staak* Der deutsche Insolvenzverwalter im europäischen Insolvenzrecht, p 19; *Virgós/Garcimartín* Regulation, p 18.

[38] D-K/D/Ch-*Duursma-Kepplinger* Vorbemerkung zur EuInsVO mn 28.

[39] MünchKomm InsO/*Reinhart* Art 1 EuInsVO mn 3.

[40] MünchKomm InsO/*Reinhart* Art 1 EuInsVO mn 4; **contra:** D-K/D/Ch-*Duursma-Kepplinger* Art 1 mn 29.

[41] MünchKomm InsO/*Reinhart* Art 1 EuInsVO mn 4; *Paulus* Komm EuInsVO Art 1 mn 11.

[42] (2003) B.C.C. 239, Chancery Division, December 4, 2004; on this, see also *Marshall* European Cross Border Insolvency, No. 2.002.

"25. If one took the list in Annex A in isolation from the other provisions of the Regulation, the reference to winding-up by or subject to the supervision of the court, would, on the face of it, include petitions brought under Section 124 (A). ... It is clear, however, as I have already indicated, that the purpose and basis of a winding-up petition brought under Section 124 (A) is to curtail the operation of the company on public interest grounds. It is not a condition precedent to the exercise of that jurisdiction that the company should itself be insolvent, and in many cases the companies wound up on these grounds will be solvent ... **19**

32. ... Although Annex A, as I have indicated, refers to winding-up by the court in general terms, without specific reference to insolvency, the provisions of the articles themselves do refer to insolvency proceedings and, more to the point, the definition of insolvency proceedings in Article 1 is to insolvency proceedings entailing the partial or total divestment of a debtor. It seems to me, therefore, that, construing Annex A by reference to the terms of the articles themselves, it is confined to insolvency proceedings, i.e. winding-up proceedings, brought on grounds of insolvency and not on public interest grounds." **20**

(2) Re Rechtbank Almelo

In the judgement ***Rechtbank Almelo*** (decision of the Netherlands),[43] the debtor made a request for *Schuldsanering*, i.e. debt restructuring. The request was denied because the debtor was indebted (stemming from a criminal sentence) to a German creditor. It was argued that the Regulation did not apply to the *Schuldsanering* proceedings and therefore the Dutch proceedings would only relate to Dutch debts. The court referred, however, to Annex A of the EIR according to which *"De schuldsaneringsregeling natuurlijke personen"* fall within the scope of applicability of the Regulation. **21**

2. Article 1 (2) of the EIR, Exemptions

a) General

According to Art 1 (2) of the EIR, the Regulation does **not** apply to insolvency proceedings concerning insurance undertakings, credit institutions, investment undertakings which provide services involving the holding of funds or securities for third parties, or to collective investment undertakings.[44] **22**

As to which debtor enterprises are exempt from the scope of the Regulation's application is to be determined by the EU directives relevant to them:[45] **23**

- The definition of **credit institutions** is found in Art 1 No 1 of Directive 2000/12/EC of 20 March 2000[46] relating to the taking up and pursuit of the business of credit institutions.[47] According to this, a credit institution is "any undertaking whose activity is to receive deposits or other refundable funds and to grant loans for its own account".[48]

---

43 A description is also found in *Marshall* European Cross Border Insolvency, No 2.005; see also *Mankowski* RIW 2005, 561, 577.

44 Cf *Wessels* Germany and Spain lead changes towards International Insolvency Law in Europe, p 1; *Virgós/Garcimartín* Regulation, p 18.

45 On this, see also *Braun/Heinrich* NZI 2005, 578, 581.

46 OJ L 126, 26.5.2000, p 1.

47 *Virgós/Garcimartín* Regulation, p 27.

48 Moss/Fletcher/Isaacs-*Moss/Smith*, Regulation, mn 8.09.

- The definition of **insurance undertakings** stems from the amended directives on the carrying out of the business of direct insurance, one excluding and one including life insurance.[49]
- The definition of **investment firms** stems from Art 4 (1) No 1 of Directive 2004/39/EC of 21 April 2004 on markets in financial instruments.[50] These include "any legal person[51] whose regular occupation or business is the provision of one or more investment services to third parties and/or the performance of one or more investment activities on a professional basis."
- **Undertakings for collective investments in transferable securities** is defined in the Directive on the coordination of laws, regulations and administrative powers relating to these institutions.[52] According to Art 1 (2) of Council Directive 85/611/EEC of 20 December 1985, these are undertakings whose sole object is the collective investment in transferable securities of capital raised from the public and which operate on the principle of risk-spreading and the units of which are, at the request of holders, repurchased or redeemed, directly or indirectly, out of those undertakings' assets, provided that they are not excluded pursuant to Art 2 of Council Directive 85/611/EEC from the application of the directive.[53] Such undertakings for collective investment may be constituted under the law of contract (as common funds managed by management companies), or trust law (as unit trusts), or under statute (as investment companies), Art 1 (3) of Council Directive 85/611/EEC.[54]

b) Directives on banking and insurance crises

24 Directive 2001/24/EC of 4 April 2001 on the reorganization and winding-up of credit institutions (OJ L 125 p 15) and Directive 2001/17/EC of 19 March 2001 on the reorganization and winding-up of insurance undertakings (OJ L 110 p 28) – hereinafter referred to as the Directives – are important to those areas exempted from the Regulation via Art 1 (2) of the EIR.[55] They apply to credit institutions and insurance undertakings. In the case of undertakings for collective investment and investment undertakings, the "general provisions" of international insolvency law apply.[56] In Germany, Secs 335 et seq *Ins*O apply in this connection.[57]

25 Unlike the Regulation, the Directives are based on strictly unified and universally effective proceedings. There is no place whatsoever for secondary insolvency proceedings.[58]

---

[49] Directive 73/239/EEC of 24 Jul 1973 as amended by Directive 95/26/EC for direct insurances other than life insurance, and the first Directive 79/267/EEC of 5 Mar 1979 as amended by Directive 95/26/EC for life insurance.

[50] OJ L 145, 30.4.2004, p 1.

[51] Certain restrictions apply to natural persons, see *Braun/Heinrich* NZI 2005, 578, 581.

[52] Directive 85/611/EEC of 20 Dec 1985 as amended by Directive 95/26/EC.

[53] This concerns, for example, closed-end funds.

[54] On this see *Braun/Heinrich* NZI 2005, 578, 582.

[55] On this *Heiss/Gölz* NZI 2006, 1; FK-InsO/*Wimmer* Anhang 1 mn 222 et seq and mn 233 et seq, *Wimmer* ZInsO 2002, 897 and BK-InsO/*Pannen* Art 1 EuInsVO mn 18 et seq; *Liersch* NZI 2003, 302 et seq, *Wessels* Current Topics of International Insolvency Law, p 259 et seq.

[56] *Braun/Heinrich* NZI 2005, 578, 582.

[57] *Braun/Heinrich* NZI 2005, 578, 582.

[58] *Virgós/Garcimartín* Regulation, p 18.

(1) Directive 2001/24/EC of 4 April 2001 on the reorganization and winding-up of credit institutions (OJ L 125 p 15)

(a) General

Directive 2001/24/EC (hereinafter referred to as the **Banking Crisis Directive**, see Annex 3) is one of the action plans for financial markets that was ratified at the EU summit in Lisbon;[59] underlying its enactment is the extensive harmonization of banking law that has taken place through the banking law coordination directives (Council Directive 77/780/EEC of 12 December 1997, OJ L 322 p 30, Council Directive 89/646/ EEC of 15 December 1989, OJ L 386 p 1) and through Directive 2000/12/EC relating to the taking up and pursuit of the business of credit institutions. A credit institution and its branch offices are a unit that must also be subject to a uniform supervision. For this reason, reorganization and winding-up proceedings must be dealt with in a uniform manner. **26**

Although there is a good degree of conformity between the provisions of the Regulation and the Banking Crisis Directive, there are also significant **differences:** **27**

- Where the Banking Crisis Directive applies, **secondary insolvency proceedings are not permitted.**[60]
- Furthermore, European bank insolvency proceedings link international jurisdiction to the **home Member State** and not to the "centre of main interests" as does the Regulation in Art 3 with its wide scope for interpretation.[61]

Secondary insolvency proceedings in relation to the assets of a branch office of a credit institution in another Member State will not be permitted.[62] During the deliberations on the Banking Crisis Directive, controversial debates took place on whether secondary insolvency proceedings should be permitted.[63] Germany in particular was opposed to strictly unified proceedings from the outset.[64] **28**

The European legislators decided against permitting secondary insolvency proceedings. In their opinion, a credit institution and its branch offices form a unit that must be **29**

---

59 In the action plan implementing the framework for financial markets of 11 May 1999 (Communication from the Commission of 11 May 1999, printed in ZBB 1999, 254), various political goals and special measures for improving the single market for financial services providers were proposed for implementation by 2004. The action plan contains a list of priorities and a time schedule for legislative and other measures. On this, see: *Keller/Langner* BKR 2003, 616 et seq.

60 See *Wimmer* ZInsO 2002, 897 et seq; *Braun/Heinrich* NZI 2005, 578, 580; *Pannen* Krise und Insolvenz bei Kreditinstituten (2006), 215; also the synopsis by *Wessels* Current Topics of International Insolvency Law, p 279. However, in the case of non-EU bank insolvencies, secondary insolvency proceedings are permissible from the perspective of German law. This follows from an inversion of the conclusion found in Sec 46e (2) KWG.

61 *Pannen* Krise und Insolvenz bei Kreditinstituten (2006), 213 et seq.

62 This was justified by the fact that the earlier law, which allowed secondary insolvency proceedings, led to disparate reorganization measures and to prejudicial results for some creditors; on this: *Hirte/Heinrich* in Derleder/Knops/Bamberger p 60 mn 52.

63 Cf *Galanti* International Insolvency Review 2002, 49, 51; *Wessels* Current Topics of International Insolvency Law (2004), 277.

64 On this: *Wimmer* ZInsO 2002, 897, 901 et seq; *Wimmer* FK-InsO Anhang 1, mn 227. It was argued that, although the area of bank supervision law has been harmonized to a large degree in respect of credit institutions, this is only a small part of the entire area of law important to creditors of credit institutions.

subject to uniform supervision (Recital 3 of the Banking Crisis Directive).[65] They further argued that this principle of "unity" should not be waived if reorganization measures are to be resorted to or winding-up proceedings opened.[66]

30 The reorganization or winding-up measures of the responsible authorities in the home Member State should be recognized in the other Member States without the need for any further formalities. The law of the home Member State applies both to reorganization measures and to winding-up proceedings. In Art 9 of the Directive, the principle of the unity and universality of the proceedings is expressly proclaimed. Only the public authorities of the home Member State are authorized to decide on the opening of winding-up proceedings in respect of a credit institution including its branch offices in other Member States.

31 As opposed to a regulation that is automatically in force in other Member States,[67] the Banking Crisis Directive must be **implemented** into the national laws of the individual Member States.[68] The European provisions were transformed into national law in Germany with the "Law to amend international insolvency law" of 14 March 2003[69] in Sec 335 et seq *InsO*,[70] and with the "Law to implement provisions on supervising the reorganization and winding-up of insurance undertakings and credit institutions" of 10 December 2003.[71]

32 Therefore, from the perspective of German law in the case of international bank insolvencies:

- both autonomous German international insolvency law (Sec 335 et seq *InsO*)
- and the relevant provisions of the German *Kreditwesengesetz* (*KWG* – Banking Act) apply.[72]

For questions of interpretation, the Banking Crisis Directive is to be consulted as a supplementary source. The Regulation and German provisions implementing it in Art 102 *EGInsO* (amended version) do not apply.[73]

(b) Implementation in the individual Member States

33 Directive 2001/24/EC on the reorganization and winding-up of credit institutions (Banking Crisis Directive) was implemented in the EU Member States as follows.

(The following information shows the status as of 1 Februar 2007):

(i) Austria

34 Bundesgesetz, mit dem die Konkursordnung, die Ausgleichsordnung, das Insolvenzrechtseinführungsgesetz, das Bankwesengesetz und das Versicherungsaufsichtsgesetz

---

[65] On this, see also: *Wessels* Current Topics of International Insolvency Law, 270.

[66] Recital 4 of the Banking Crisis Directive.

[67] Cf art 249 (2) EEC Treaty.

[68] *Wessels* Current Topics on International Insolvency Law, p 259. Pursuant to art 34 (1) of the Banking Crisis Directive, the Directive had to be implemented by 5 May 2004. See mn 33 et seq as to the status of implementation in the Member States.

[69] BGBl I 2003 p 345.

[70] Explanatory Statement on the Governmental Draft, BT-Drucks. 15/16, p 14.

[71] BGBl I 2003 p 2478.

[72] BK-InsO/*Pannen* Vorbem zu §§ 335 et seq mn 5.

[73] For the German provisions implementing the Regulation, see *Pannen/Riedemann* NZI 2004, 301 et seq.

geändert werden (Bundesgesetz über das Internationale Insolvenzrecht – IIRG) (BGBl. für die Republik Österreich Teil I Nr. 36 vom 13/06/2003, p. 189).[74]

(ii) Belgium

Loi du 6 décembre 2004 modifiant notamment, en matière de procédures d'insolvabilité, la loi du 22 mars 1993 relative au statut et au contrôle des établissements de crédit et la loi du 9 juillet 1975 relative au contrôle des entreprises d'assurances (p 85856). **35**

Loi du 19 novembre 2004 modifiant la loi du 22 mars 1993 relative au statut et au contrôle des établissements de crédit, la loi du 9 juillet 1975 relative au contrôle des entreprises d'assurances, la loi du 2 août 2002 relative à la surveillance du secteur financier et aux services financiers et la loi du 28 avril 1999 visant à transposer la Directive 98/26/CE du 19 mai 1998 concernant le caractère définitif du règlement dans les systèmes de paiement et de règlement des opérations sur titres (p 85854).

(iii) Bulgaria

The Directive 2001/24/EC has been implemented into Bulgarian law in a new act on credit institutions (in force since the accession treaties of the Bulgarian Republic to the European Union; printed in Official journal No 105 of 22.12.2006). **36**

(iv) Cyprus

The Banking (Amendment) Law (Ap. 2) of 2004 [Ο περί Τραπεζικών Εργασιών (Τροποποιητικός) (Αρ. 2) Νόμος του 2004]. **37**

(v) Czech Republic

Zákon ze dne 19. srpna 2005 o doplňkovém dozoru nad bankami, spořitelními a úvěrními družstvy, institucemi elektronických peněz, pjišťovnami a obchodníky s cennými papíry ve finančních konglomerátech a o změně některých dalších zákonů (zákon o finančních konglomeraátech). **38**

(vi) Denmark

Bekendgorelse om lovvalg mv. ved penge- og realkreditinstitutters samt udstedere af elektroniske penges betalingsstandsning, tvangsakkord, tvangsoplosning eller konkurs. **39**

(vii) Estonia

Krediidiasutuste seaduse ja äriseadustiku muutmise seadus – 1/01/2005. **40**

Krediidiasutuste seadus – 1/05/2005.

(viii) Finland

Laki säästöpankkilain muuttamisesta – 19/05/2004 = Lag om ändring av sparbankslagen – 19/05/2004. **41**

Laki luottolaitostoiminnasta annetun lain 12 §:n muuttamisesta – 19/05/2004 = Lag om ändring av 12 § kreditinstitutslagen – 19/05/2004.

---

[74] On this see also: *Lurger* RIW 2005, 209, 212;
Wehdeking DZWiR 2003, 133, 139 et seq.

Laki liikepankeista ja muista osakeyhtiömuotoisista luottolaitoksista annetun lain muuttmisesta of 19/05/2004 = Lag om ändring av lagen om affärsbanker och andra kreditinstitut I aktiebolagsform – 31/05/2004.

Laki osuuspankeista ja muista osuuskuntamuotoisista luottolaitoksista annetun lain muuttamisesta – 19/05/2004 = Lag om ändring av lagen om andelsbanker och andra kreditinstitut i andelslagsform – 19/05/2004.

Laki ulkomaisen luotto- ja rahoituslaitoksen toiminnasta Suomessa annetun lain muuttamisesta – 19/05/2004 = Lag om ändring av lagen om utländska kreditinstituts och finansiella institutes – 19/05/2004.

Laki talletuspankin toiminnan väliaikaisesta keskeyttämisestä annetun lain muuttamisesta – 19/05/2004 = Lag om ändring av lagen om temporärt avbrytande av en depositionsbanks verksamhet – 19/05/2005.

(ix) **France**

42 Ordonnance, 2004-1127, du 21 octobre 2004, portant transposition de la directive 2001/24/CE du Parlement européen et du Conseil du 4 avril 2001 concernant l'assainissement et la liquidation des établissements de crédit.

Décret en Conseil d'Etat 2005-468 du 12 mai 2005 pris pour l'application des articles L 613-31-1 à L 613-31-10 du code monétaire et financier et relatif à l'assainissement et à la liquidation des établissements de crédit communautaires.

(x) **Germany**

43 Gesetz zur Neuregelung des Internationalen Insolvenzrechts vom 14. März 2003 (BGBl. I S 345).

Gesetz zur Umsetzung aufsichtrechtlicher Bestimmungen zur Sanierung und Liquidation von Versicherungsunternehmen und Kreditinstituten vom 16. Dezember 2003 (BGBl. I S 2478).

(xi) **Greece**

44 Εξυγίανση και εκκαθάριση των πιστωτικών ιδρυμάτων και άλλες διατάξεις (νόμος υπ' αριθ. 3458) (*Reorganisation and winding-up of credit institutions and other provisions (law Nr. 3458)*).

(xii) **Hungary**

45 Évi CXX. törvény a tőkepiacról – 18/12/2001.

Évi CXXIV. törvény a Pénzügyi Szervezetek Állami Felügyeletér´´ ol** – 21/12/1999.

Évi CXLV. törvény a cégnyilvántartásról, a cégnyilvánosságról és a bírósági cégeljárásról – 09/12/1997.

Évi CXXXII. törvény a külföldi székhelyű vállalkozások magyarországi fióktelepeiről és kereskedelmi képviseleteiről – 10/12/1997.

Évi XIII. törvényerejű rendelet a nemzetközi magánjogról – 31/05/1979.

Évi IV. törvény a Magyar Köztársaság Polgári Törvénykönyvéről – 11/08/1959.

Évi XLIX. törvény a csődeljárásról, a felszámolási eljárásról és a végelszámolásról – 22/10/1991.

Évi CXII. törvény a hitelintézetekről és pénzügyi vállakozásokról – 12/12/1996.

Évi XXXIX. törvény a hitelintézetekrõl és a pénzügyi vállalkozásokról szóló.

Évi CXII. törvény módosításáról – 17/06/2003.

(xiii) **Ireland**

European Communities (Reorganisation and Winding-up of Credit Institutions) Regulations 2004 of 04/05/2004. **46**

(xiv) **Italy**

Decreto Legislativo 9 luglio 2004 – Attuazione della direttiva 2001/24/CE in materia di risanamento e liquidazione degli enti creditizi. **47**

(xv) **Latvia**

Grozījumi Kredītiestāžu likumā, Publicēts: Latvijas Vēstnesis 92 10.06.2005. **48**

Grozījums Kredītiestāžu likumā, Publicēts: Vēstnesis 90 04.06.2004.

Grozījumi Kredītiestāžu likumā, Publicēts: Vēstnesis 180 12.11.2004.

Kredītiestāžu likums, Publicēts: Vēstnesis 163 24.10.1995.

(xvi) **Lithuania**

Lietuvos Respublikos akcinių bendrovių įstatymo pakeitimo įstatymas Nr. IX-1889 – 11/12/2203. **49**

Lietuvos Respublikos civilinio kodekso pavirtinimo, įsigaliojimo ir įgyvendinimo įstatymas Nr. VIII-1864 – 18/07/2000.

Lietuvos Respublikos Lietuvos banko įstatymo 8, 11, 42, 43, 45, 46 ir 47 straipsnių pakeitimo įstatymas Nr. IX-2069 – 23/03/2004.

Lietuvos Respublikos bankų įstatymas Nr. IX-2085 – 30/03/2004.

Lietuvos Respublikos Įmonių bankroto įstatymas Nr. IX-216 – 5/07/2003.

Lietuvos Respublikos įmonių bankroto įstatymo 10 ir 14 straipsnių pakeitimo ir 32 straipsnio papildymo įstatymas Nr. IX-1600 – 5/06/2003.

Įmonių bankroto įstatymo 1 straipsnių pakeitimo įstatymas Nr. IX-1711 – 04/07/2003.

Įmonių bankroto įstatymo 4, 10 ir 18 straipsnių pakeitimo įstatymas Nr. IX-1463 – 03/04/2003.

Įmonių bankroto įstatymo 10, 11, 13, 19, 23, 27, 32 straipsnių pakeitimo ir papildymo įstatymas Nr. IX-1332 – 28/01/2003.

Įmonių bankroto įstatymo 11 ir 22 straipsnių papildymo įstatymas Nr. IX-1272 – 10/12/2002.

Įmonių bankroto įstatymo 2, 6, 7, 8, 9, 10, 11, 12, 15, 26, 29, 32, 35, 37 straipsnių pakeitimo ir papildymo bei įstatymo ketvirtuoju (1) skirsniu ir 13(1) straipsnių įstatymas Nr. IX-1200 – 19/11/2002.

Įmonių bankroto įstatymo 11 ir 31 straipsnių pakeitimo įstatymas Nr. IX-665 – 17/12/2001.

(xvii) **Luxemburg**

50 Loi du 19 mars 2004 portant transposition dans la loi modifiée du 5 avril 1993 relative au secteur financier de la directive 2001/24/CE du Parlement européen et du Conseil du 4 avril 2001 concernant l'assainissement et la liquidation des établissements de crédit (Mémorial A no. 45 du 29/03/2004 p. 708).

(xviii) **Malta**

51 Regolamenti ta' l-2004 dwar Istituzzjonijiet ta' Kreditu (Riorganizzazzjoni u Stralç) (*Credit Institutions (Reorganisation and Winding-up) Regulations*).

(xix) **The Netherlands**

52 Wet van 7/4/2005 tot wijziging van het Wet toezicht kredietwezen 1992 en van de Faillissementswet in verband met de uitvoering van richtlijn nr 2001/24/EG van het EP en de Raad van de EU van 4/4/2001 betreffende de sanering en de liquidatie van kredietinstellingen (PbEG L 125).

Besluit van 27/4/2005, houdende vaststelling van het tijdstip van inwerkingtreding van de Wet van 7/4/2005 tot wijziging van het Wet toezicht kredietwezen 1992 en van de Faillissementswet in verband met de uitvoering van richtlijn nr 2001/24/EG van het EP en de Raad van de EU van 4/4/2001 betreffende de sanering en de liquidatie van kredietinstellingen (PbEG L 125).

(xx) **Poland**

53 Ustawa z 21 sierpnia 1997 Prawo o publicznym obrocie papierami wartościowymi – 21/08/1997.

Ustawa z 29 sierpnia 1997 Prawo bankowe – 29/08/1997.

Ustawa z 28 lutego 2003 Prawo upadłościowe i naprawcze – 28/02/2003.

(xxi) **Portugal**

54 Decreto-Lei n° 199/2006 de 25 de Outubro – Regula a liquidação de instituições de crédito e sociedades financeiras com sede em Portugal e suas sucursais criadas noutro Estado membro, transpondo para a ordem jurídica interna a Directiva n° 2001/24/CE, do Parlamento Europeu e do Conselho, de 4 de Abril, relativa ao saneamento e à liquidação das instituições de crédito.

(xxii) **Romania**

55 No information available.

(xxiii) **Slovakia**

56 Zákon č. 603/2003 Z. z., ktorým sa mení a dopĺňa zákon č. 483/2001 Z. z. o bankách a o zmene a doplnení niektorých zákonov v znení neskorších predpisov – 03/12/2003.

Zákon Národnej rady Slovenskej republiky č. 566/1992 Zb. o Národnej banke Slovenska – 18/11/1992.

Zákon č. 149/2001 Z. z., ktorým sa mení a dopĺňa zákon Národnej rady Slovenskej republiky č. 566/1992 Zb. o Národnej banke Slovenska v znení neskorších predpisov a ktorým sa mení a dopĺňa zákon č. 21/1992 Zb. o bankách v znení neskorších predpisov – 06/04/2001.

Zákon č. 483/2001 Z. z. o bankách a o zmene a doplnení niektorých zákonov – 05/10/2001.

Zákon č. 7/2005 Z. z. o konkurze a reštrukturalizácii a o zmene a doplnení niektorých zákonov – 09/12/2004.

(xxiii) Slovenia

Zakon o spremembah in dopolnitvah zakona o prisilni poravnavi, stečaju in ikvidaciji – 12/06/1997. **57**

Zakon o spremembah in dopolnitvah zakona o prisilni poravnavi, stečaju in likvidaciji – 23/06/1999.

Zakon o delovnih razmerjih – 24/04/2002.

Zakon o mednarodnem zasebnem pravu in postopku (ZMZPP) – 30/06/1999.

Stvarnopravni zakonik – 27/09/2002.

Zakon o bančništvu – uradno prečiščeno besedilo – 17/06/2004.

Zakon o finančnih zavarovanjih – 22/04/2004.

Zakon o spremembah in dopolnitvah zakona o bančništvu – 08/04/2004.

Zakon o prisilni poravnavi, stečaju in likvidaciji – 07/12/1993.

Zakon o gospodarskih družbah – 27/05/1993.

Zakon o bančništvu – 19/01/1999.

(xxv) Spain

Ley 6/2005, de 22 de abril, sobre saneamiento y liquidación de las entidades de crédito (Official Spanish Gazette (BOE) 23-04-2005). **58**

(xvi) Sweden

Lag (2005 : 1047) om internationella förhållande rörande försäkringsföretags och kreditinstituts insolvens. **59**

(xxvii) United Kingdom

The Credit Institutions (Reorganisation and Winding-up) Regulations 2004 of 01/04/2004. **60**

(2) Directive 2001/17/EC of 19 March 2001 on the reorganization and winding-up of insurance undertakings (OJ L 110 p 28)

(a) General

Directive 2001/17/EC of 19 March 2001 on the reorganization and winding-up of insurance undertakings (**Insurance Crisis Directive**, see Annex 4)[75] adheres to – as does the Banking Crisis Directive, see mn 26 above – the **principle of unified and universal** proceedings. The goal is an EU-wide automatic recognition of reorganization and winding-up proceedings of insurance undertakings. Only the responsible authorities of the **61**

[75] In detail: *Wessels* Current Topics of International Insolvency Law, p 293 et seq.

home Member State are authorized to open winding-up proceedings.[76] Secondary insolvency proceedings at the location of the branch office are not permitted.[77]

62 Reorganization and winding-up measures are governed by the law of the home Member State of the insurance undertaking concerned, Art 4 (2) and Art 9 of the Insurance Crisis Directive.[78] However, the Insurance Crisis Directive deviates from the **home State principle** in Arts 19 to 26 thereof. These exceptions are equivalent to those found in Arts 5 to 15 of the EIR.[79]

63 The European provisions were transformed into national law in **Germany** with the "Law to amend international insolvency law" of 14 March 2003[80] in Sec 335 et seq *InsO*, and with the "Law to implement provisions on supervising the reorganization and winding-up of insurance undertakings and credit institutions"[81] of 10 December 2003.[82]

(b) Implementation in the individual Member States

(i) Austria

64 1. Bundesgesetz, mit dem die Konkursordnung, die Ausgleichsordnung, das Insolvenzrechtseinführungsgesetz, das Bankwesengesetz und das Versicherungsaufsichtsgesetz geändert werden (Bundesgesetz über das Internationale Insolvenzrecht – IIRG) BGBl. für die Republik Österreich Teil I n° 36 vom 13/06/2003 p 189.

(ii) Belgium

65 1. Loi du 19 novembre 2004 modifiant la loi du 22 mars 1993 relative au statut et au contrôle des établissements de crédit, la loi du 9 juillet 1975 relative au contrôle des entreprises d'assurances, la loi du 2 août 2002 relative à la surveillance du secteur financier et aux services financiers et la loi du 28 avril 1999 visant à transposer la Directive 98/26/CE du 19 mai 1998 concernant le caractère définitif du règlement dans les systèmes de paiement et de règlement des opérations sur titres.

2. Wet van 6 december 2004 tot wijziging, wat insolventieprocedures betreft, van inzonderheid de wet van 22 maart 1993 op het statuut van en het toezicht op de kredietinstellingen en de wet van 9 juli 1975 betreffende de controle der verzekeringsondernemingen.

(iii) Bulgaria

66 1. Insurance Code 23.12.2005 in force as of 01.01.2006, amended; Commerce Act (18.06.1991), Law on the Financial Supervision Commission (28.01.2003), Code on International Private Law (17.05.2005), Ordinance No 21 on the Own Funds and Solvency Margin of Insurers and Health Insurance Companies (16.3.2005). (Code on International Private Law: the decisive provisions are Art 56 and Art 58; Commerce act: the decisive provisions are Art 12, Art 267, Art 268, Art 269, Art 614, Art 620, Art 635, Art 645, Art 646–649, Art 658, Art 637–639, Art 685–695, Art 720–722, Art 723,

---

[76] *Wessels* Current Topics of International Insolvency Law, p 299.

[77] *Virgós/Garcimartín* Regulation, p 18; *Wessels* Current Topics of International Insolvency Law, p 298.

[78] *Heiss/Gölz* NZI 2006, 1, 2.

[79] *Heiss/Gölz* NZI 2006, 1, 2.

[80] BGBl I 2003 p 345.

[81] BGBl I 2003 p 2478.

[82] For the implementation in Germany, see *Heiss/Gölz* NZI 2006, 1; for the implementation in the Netherlands, see *Wessels* Current Topics of International Insolvency Law, p 301 et seq.

Art 724–726, Art 732, Art 744; Law on the Financial Supervision Commission: the decisive provisions are Art 16 and Art 24–25).

(iv) **Cyprus**

1. Ο περί της Ασκήσεως Ασφαλιστικών Εργασιών και 'Αλλων Συναφών Θεμάτων (Τροποποιητικός) (Αρ.3) Νόμος του 2004. **67**

(v) **Czech Republic**

1. Zákon č. 363/1999 Sb., o pojišťovnictví a o změně některých souvisejících zákonů (zákon o pojišťovnictví). **68**

2. Zákon, kterým se mění zákon č. 363/1999 Sb., o pojišťovnictví a o změně některých souvisejících zákonů (zákon o pojišťovnictví), ve znění pozdějších předpisů, a některé další zákony.

3. Concordance table 32001L0017_041215.

4. Zákon o konkursu a vyrovnání.

5. Zákon č. 97/1963 Sb., o mezinárodním právu soukromém a procesním.

6. Zákon č. 377/2005 Sb., o doplňkovém dozoru nad bankami, spořitelními a úvěrními družstvy, institucemi elektronických peněz, pojišťovnami a obchodníky s cennými papíry ve finančních konglomerátech a o změně některých dalších zákonů (zákon o finančních konglomerátech).

(vi) **Denmark**

1. Concordance table. **69**

2. Lov om finansiel virksomhed. ref: Lov n° 453 af 10/06/2003 p 2822.

3. Bekendtgorelse om registrering af aktiver i forsikringsselskaber m. v. ref: BEK n° 562 af 19/06/2003 (SG(2003)A/06211 du 09/07/2003).

(vii) **Estonia**

1. Kindlustustegevuse seadus. **70**

2. Kindlustustegevuse seadus 1.

(viii) **Finland**

1. Lag om ändring av lagen om arbetspensionsförsäkringsbolag. **71**

2. Laki vakuutusyhdistyslain muuttamisesta.

3. Lag om ändring av lagen om försäkringsföreningar.

4. Laki vakuutusyhtiölain muuttamisesta.

5. Lag om ändring av lagen om försäkringsbolag.

6. Laki ulkomaisista vakuutusyhtiöistä annetun lain muuttamisesta.

7. Lag om ändring av lagen om utländska försäkringsbolag.

8. Laki työeläkevakuutusyhtiöistä annetun lain muuttamisesta.

9. – Concordance table.

(ix) France

72 1. Ordonnance n° 504 du 7/6/2004 portant transposition de la directive 2001/17/CE concernant l'assainissement et la liquidation des entreprises d'assurances.

2. Décret n° 2005-8 du 5 janvier 2005 portant transposition de la directive 2001/17/CE du Parlement européen et du Conseil concernant l'assainissement et la liquidation des entreprises d'assurance et modifiant le code des assurances, le code de la mutualité et le code de la sécurité sociale (partie réglementaire).

(x) Germany

73 1. Gesetz zur Umsetzung aufsichtrechtlicher Bestimmungen zur Sanierung und Liquidation von Versicherungsunternehmen und Kreditinstituten. BGBl Teil I n° 59 vom 16/12/2003 S. 2478.

(xi) Greece

74 Presidential Decree 332/2003 "Compliance with the provisions of Directive 2001/17/EC on the reorganisation and winding-up of insurance undertakings" of 5/12/2003.

(xii) Hungary

75 1. 2003. évi LX. törvény a biztosítókról és a biztosítási tevékenységrõl.

2. A Kormány 235/2003. (XII. 17.) Korm. rendelete a biztosítók éves beszámoló készítési és könyvvezetési kötelezettségének sajátosságairól szóló 192/2000. (XI. 24.) Korm. rendelet módosításáról.

3. A Kormány 192/2000. (XI. 24.) Korm. rendelete a biztosítók éves beszámoló készítési és könyvvezetési kötelezettségének sajátosságairól.

4. 1991. évi XLIX. törvény a csődeljárásról, a felszámolási eljárásról és a végelszámolásról.

(xiii) Ireland

76 European Communities (Reorganisation and Winding-up of Insurance Undertakings) Regulations 2003. Publication reference in the Official Journal: Statutory Instrument No. 168 of 2003.

(xiv) Italy

77 1. Decreto legislativo 9 aprile 2003 n. 93 – Attuazione della direttiva 2001/17/CEE in materia di risanamento e liquidazione delle imprese di assicurazione GURI – Serie generale n° 98 del 29/04/2003.

(xv) Latvia

78 1. Apdrošināšanas sabiedrību un to uzraudzības likums.

2. Grozījumi Apdrošināšanas sabiedrību un to uzraudzības likumā.

3. Grozījumi Apdrošināšanas sabiedrību un to uzraudzības likumā.

(xvi) Lithuania

79 1. Draudimo priežiūros komisijos nutarimas Nr. N-20 „Dėl draudimo įmonių turto, dengiančio draudimo techninius atidėjinius, sąrašo tvarkymo taisyklių patvirtinimo".

2. Draudimo įstatymas Nr. IX-1737.

3. Lietuvos Respublikos Įmonių bankroto įstatymas Nr. IX-216.

4. LIETUVOS RESPUBLIKOSDARBO KODEKSO PATVIRTINIMO, ĮSIGALIOJIMO IR ĮGYVENDINIMOĮSTATYMAS IX-926.

5. Lietuvos Respublikos civilinio kodekso patvirtinimo, įsigaliojimo ir įgyvendinimo įstatymas Nr. VIII-1864.

(xvii) **Luxemburg**

Loi du 11 mars 2004 relative à l'assainissement et la liquidation des entreprises d'as- **80**
surances et modifiant la loi modifiée du 6 décembre 1991 sur le secteur des assurances.

(xviii) **Malta**

1. Chapter 403 Insurance Business Act.

2. Insurance Business Act (CAP. 403) Insurance Business (Reorganisation and Wind- **81**
ing-Up of Insurance Undertakings) Regulations, 2004.

3. Special Funds (Regulation) Act.

(xix) **The Netherlands**

1. – Besluit van 10/3/2004, houdende vaststelling van het tijstip van inwerkingtreding **82**
van de wet van 21/2/2004 tot wijziging van de Wet toezicht verzekeringsbedrijf 1993 en van de Faillissementswet in verband met de uitvoering van richtlinijn n° 2001/17/EG betreffendede sanering en de liquidetie van verzekeringsondernemingen (PbEG L 110). ref: Staatsblad n° 101 van 18/3/2004.

2. Wet van 21/2/2004, houdende wijziging van de Wet toezicht verzekeringsbedrijf 1993 en van de Faillissementswet in verband met de uitvoering van richtlinijn n° 2001/17/EG betreffendede sanering en de liquidetie van verzekeringsondernemingen (PbEG L 110). ref: Staatsblad n° 86 van 9/3/2004.

(xx) **Poland**

1. Ustawa z 22 maja 2003 o nadzorze ubezpieczeniowym i emerytalnym oraz Rzeczni- **83**
ku Ubezpieczonych.

2. Ustawa z 22 maja 2003 o działalności ubezpieczeniowej.

3. Ustawa z 22 stycznia 1999 o ochronie informacji niejawnych.

4. Ustawa z 28 lutego 2003 Prawo upadłościowe i naprawcze.

(xxi) **Portugal**

1. Decreto-Lei n° 90/2003, de 30 de Abril Diario da Republica I Serie A n° 100 de **84**
30/04/2003 p 2768.

2. Decreto-Lei n° 267/2003, de 27 de Outubro 2003 Diário da republica I Serie A n° 249 de 27/10/2003 p 7136 (SG(2003)A/11393 du 21/11/2003).

(xxii) **Romania**

Law no. 503 of 17th November 2004 regarding the financial recovery and winding-up **85**
of insurance undertakings (Published in The Official Journal of Romania, Part no. 1193/14 December 2004) and Law No 32/2000 on Insurance Undertakings and Insurance Supervision (Published in the Official Journal no 148/10 April 2000) as amended.

(xxiii) Slovakia

86 1. Zákon č. 95/2002 Z. z. o poisťovníctve a o zmene a doplnení niektorých zákonov.

2. Zákon č. 96/2002 Z. z. o dohľade nad finančným trhom a o zmene a doplnení niektorých zákonov.

3. Zákon č. 430/2003 Z. z., ktorým sa mení a dopĺňa zákon č. 381/2001 Z. z. o povinnom zmluvnom poistení zodpovednosti za škodu spôsobenú prevádzkou motorového vozidla a o zmene a doplnení niektorých zákonov v znení neskorších predpisov a o zmene a doplnení niektorých zákonov.

4. Zákon č. 186/2004 Z. z., ktorým sa mení a dopĺňa zákon č. 95/2002 Z. z. o poisťovníctve a o zmene a doplnení niektorých zákonov v znení zákona č. 430/2003 Z. z. a o zmene a doplnení niektorých ďalších zákonov.

5. Zákon č. 645/2004 Z. z., ktorým sa mení a dopĺňa zákon č. 95/2002 Z. z. o poisťovníctve a o zmene a doplnení niektorých zákonov v znení neskorších predpisov a ktorým sa dopĺňa zákon č. 381/2001 Z. z. o povinnom zmluvnom poistení zodpovednosti za škodu spôsobenú prevádzkou motorového vozidla a o zmene a doplnení niektorých zákonov v znení neskorvších predpisov.

6. Zákon č. 7/2005 Z. z. o konkurze a reštrukturalizácii a o zmene a doplnení niektorých zákonov.

(xxiv) Slovenia

87 1. Zakon o gospodarskih družbah.

2. Zakon o zavarovalništvu.

3. Zakon o prisilni poravnavi, stečaju in likvidaciji.

4. Zakon o spremembah in dopolnitvah zakona o prisilni poravnavi, stečaju in likvidaciji.

5. Zakon o spremembah in dopolnitvah zakona o prisilni poravnavi, stečaju in likvidaciji.

6. Zakon o delovnih razmerjih.

7. Zakon o spremembah in dopolnitvah zakona o obveznih zavarovanjih v prometu

8. Stvarnopravni zakonik.

9. Pomorski zakonik – uradno prečiščeno besedilo.

10. Zakon o spremembah in dopolnitvah zakona o zavarovalništvu.

11. Concordance table.

(xxv) Spain

88 Ley 34 de 4/11/2003, de modificación y adaptación a la normativa comunitaria de la legislación de seguros privados. BOE n° 265 de 05/11/2003 p 39190.

(xxvi) Sweden

89 Lag (2005:1047) om internationella förhållande rörande försäkringsföretags och kreditinstituts insolvens.

(xxvii) United Kingdom

1. Insurers (Reorganisation and Winding-Up) Ordinance 2004. **90**

2. The Insurers (Reorganisation and Winding-Up) Regulations 2003 SI n° 1102 of 14/04/2003.

3. SI 2005 n° 1998 Insurers (Reorganisation and Winding-Up) (Lloyd's) Regulations 2005.

c) Case involving the exemption in Article 1 (2) of the EIR

In the English case ***Dobb White & Co.***,[83] the **exemption in Art 1 (2) of the EIR** was a **91**
decisive factor.

The Financial Services Authority (FSA) petitioned for winding-up proceedings against **92**
an accounting firm operating in the form of a partnership and requested insolvency proceedings against the partners. It was contended, *inter alia*, in the petitions that the partnership was linked to an unauthorized collective investment program. The FSA maintained that the requests did not fall within the exemption set out in Art 1 (2) of the EIR, i.e. respecting "collective investment undertakings". The court referred to No 60 of the Virgós/Schmit Report and held that the exemption "collective investment undertakings" was restricted to undertakings that were authorized and as such fall within the definition set out in the amended version of Council Directive 85/611/EEC of 20 December 1985 on the coordination of laws, regulations and administrative provisions relating to undertakings for collective investment. According to the court, an unauthorized undertaking of this kind would not fall within the exemption and the Regulation therefore applied to insolvency requests.

III. Scope of Application – Persons/Entities

1. Concept of Debtor

The **term debtor** is not defined in the Regulation. As to who a debtor is within the **93**
meaning of Art 1 (1) of the EIR is determined by the national law of the country in which the proceedings are opened.[84] On this point, see the general discussion on insolvency capacity in the individual Member States in Art 3 of the EIR mn 14.

The Regulation governs all insolvency proceedings regardless of whether the debtor is **94**
a **natural person, a legal entity, a state-owned enterprise, a businessperson** (*Kaufmann*) **or a private individual.**[85]

By contrast, many European insolvency regimes distinguish between the bankruptcy **95**
of a businessperson and that of a non-business person, see on this the Overview of Insolvency Capacity in Art 3 of the EIR mn 14.[86] Furthermore, even if a Member State only allows for the bankruptcy of businesspersons, that Member State is still obliged to recog-

[83] UK High Court of 2 Dec 2003 (unreported), comments on the case by *Gabriel Moss* QC (Deputy High Court Judge) at http://www.iiiglobal.org; a discussion is also found in *Marshall* European Cross Border Insolvency, No 2.009.

[84] *Virgós/Garcimartín* Regulation, p 26.

[85] Recital 9 of the Regulation; *Virgós/Garcimartín* Regulation, p 26.

[86] For example in Greece, Luxembourg, and Italy only businessmen have insolvency capacity.

nize insolvency proceedings of another Member State involving a non-businessperson (cf Art 16 of the EIR mn 37 et seq). France, for example, must recognize German insolvency proceedings against a consumer even though insolvency proceedings in France may only be opened against a private person if that person is a businessperson.[87]

96 The ECJ decision ("Inspire Art"[88]) must be taken into account in this context. As a result of this decision, foreign companies (for example an English limited liability company in Germany) will be regarded by the courts as having insolvency capacity.[89]

2. Pseudo Foreign Corporations

97 A **pseudo foreign corporation** is understood as a company that, apart from its legal form and its incorporation, has no connection to the foreign country in which it was established.[90]

98 The Regulation applies to pseudo foreign corporations;[91] such matters are definitely not of a purely **"domestic nature"** (see mn 117). There is a foreign connection because of the disparity between the company's legal and actual corporate domicile. The actual relocation of the company in the sense of the entirety of its assets cannot be treated differently than the relocation of a part of the assets.[92]

99 In the **"Inspire Art"** decision,[93] the ECJ decided for the third time in five years – after the **"Centros"**[94] and the **"Überseering"** decisions[95] – in favour of a company's freedom of establishment. Any corporate enterprise incorporated in a Member State may, based on its freedom of establishment – Arts 43, 46, 48 EEC Treaty, move its corporate domicile and its activities to any other Member State. The relocation of the corporate domicile to another Member State is still allowed even if the capitalization requirements[96] imposed by the latter country are more cumbersome than those of the country of incorporation.[97] EU-foreign companies with limited liability must be tolerated in every other

87 *Paulus* Komm EuInsVO Einl mn 37.

88 ECJ of 30 Sep 2003, C-167/01, ZIP 2003, 1885.

89 E.g. AG Duisburg NZI 2003, 658, 659; dissenting opinion: AG Hamburg ZIP 2003, 1008 according to which a limited liability company, although having insolvency capacity, should not have this as a "pseudo foreign company"; critical of this: *Brenner* EWiR 2003, 925 on Art 3 of the EIR = NJW 2003, 2835.

90 *Weller* IPRax 2003, 207.

91 Cf *Herchen* ZInsO 2003, 742 et seq.

92 *Herchen* ZInsO 2003, 742, 744.

93 ECJ of 30 Sep 2003 C – 167/01, ZIP 2003, 1885. On this, e.g.: *Altmeppen* NJW 2004, 97; *Kleinert/Probst* DB 2003, 2217; *Ziemons* ZIP 2003, 1913; *Bayer* BB 2003, 2357; *Zimmer* NJW 2003, 3585; *Leible/Hoffmann* EuZW 2003, 677; *Spindler/Berner* RIW 2003, 949; *Spindler/Berner* RIW 2004, 7; cf also art 4 of the EIR mn 19 with further references.

94 ECJ of 9 Mar 1999 C-212/97, NJW 1999, 2027 = RIW 1999, 447. On this: *Altmeppen* DStR 2000, 1061; *Behrens* IPRax 2000, 384; *Ebke* JZ 1999, 656; *Ulmer* JZ 1999, 662; cf also Art 4 of the EIR mn 20 with further references.

95 ECJ of 5 Nov 2002 C-208/00, NJW 2002, 3614 = IPRax 2003, 65. On this: *Roth* IPRax 2003, 117; *Weller* IPRax 2003, 207; *Weller* IPRax 2003, 324; *Forsthoff* DB 2002, 2471; *Behrens* IPRax 2003, 193; *Eidenmüller* JZ 2003, 526; *Leible/Hoffmann* ZIP 2003, 925; *Baudenbacher/Buschle* IPRax 2004, 26; *Zimmer* BB 2003, 1; cf also Art 4 of the EIR mn 20 with further references.

96 Great Britain, Ireland, and France have either no or only nominal requirements respecting the minimum capitalization of companies with limited liability. Spain demands EUR 3,006, Portugal EUR 5,000 minimum capital. Other examples in *Altmeppen* NJW 2004, 97 fn 2.

97 Which means an open season on "societas shopping"; see also: *Bayer* BB 2003, 2357; *Eidenmüller* JZ 2004, 24; *Leible/Hoffmann* EuZW 2003, 677, 682; *Spindler/Berner* RIW 2003, 949; *Ziemons* ZIP 2003, 1913, 1920.

Member State even if the reason for the incorporation in the foreign country was, from the outset, to elude the stricter incorporation laws of the country where residence is being taken up.[98] Since the "Inspire Art" decision, the **law of the state of incorporation** governs basically all company law issues.[99] For details on this, see Art 4 of the EIR mn 19 et seq.

Thus, for example, pseudo foreign corporations in Germany – which is currently experiencing a downright "boom" on English limited liability companies – have insolvency capacity.[100] According to Art 4 (2) (a) of the EIR, the insolvency capacity of the debtor is ascertained according to the *lex fori concursus*, therefore pursuant to German law in this case. Secs 11 and 12 of the German *InsO* determine which persons and which assets have insolvency capacity. **100**

The foreign corporate enterprise is not included here. The view held in the interim by the 2nd Division for Civil Matters of the German Federal Supreme Court (*BGH*)[101] – which holds that a private limited company that moves its head office to Germany will be recognized in Germany as a "*GbR*" (civil law partnership) or, if a commercial activity is being conducted, as an "*oHG*" (general partnership) – cannot be adhered to in the face of the unequivocal decisions of the ECJ[102] since the *BGH*'s view is based on the corporate domicile theory. However, since the ECJ decisions "Überseering" and "Inspire Art", company law issues are being determined pursuant to the law of the place of incorporation (above). **101**

Insolvency capacity is basically put on the same footing as legal capacity.[103] Since the "Inspire Art" decision, the private limited company with its head office in Germany has, as a foreign legal entity, legal capacity and therefore also **insolvency capacity** in Germany.[104] **102**

In the case of pseudo foreign corporations, there is a disparity between the law governing the insolvency and that governing the company (see Art 4 of the EIR mn 15 et seq as well).[105] According to private international law, the law governing the company is that of the country in which the company was established, thus English law in the case of a limited liability company incorporated in England. According to Art 4 (1) of the EIR, however, German law as the *lex fori concursus* is the law governing the insolvency provided that there is German international jurisdiction pursuant to Art 3 of the EIR and German insolvency proceedings are pending. **103**

---

98 Inspire Art, mn 137, cf moreover: Inspire Art, mn 95 et seq ECJ of 30 Sep 2003 C-167/01.

99 *Spindler/Berne* RIW 2003, 949, 951; *Bayer* BB 2003, 2357, 2363; *Baudenbacher/Buschle* IPRax 2004, 26, 27.

100 E.g. also AG Duisburg of 14 Oct 2003 – 63 IN 48/30, NZI 2003, 658, 659. BGH of 14 Mar 2005, ZIP 2005, 805; cf Table of Cases Art 3 of the EIR Appendix B No 34.

101 BGHZ 151, 204 = NJW 2002, 3529 = NZG 2002, 1009. See on this: *Kindler* IPRax 2003, 41.

102 *Leible/Hoffmann* EuZW 2003, 677, 681; *Hirsch/Britain* NZG 2003, 1100, 1101; *Spindler/Berner* RIW 2003, 949, 950; *Weller* IPRax 2003, 520, 522; *Mock/Schildt* ZInsO 2003, 396, 399. **Contra:** AG Hamburg of 14 May 2003, IPRax 2003, 534, 535 (use of the modified corporate domicile theory).

103 BK-InsO/Goetsch § 11 mn 2.

104 *Hirsch/Britain* NZG 2003, 1100, 1101; *Lutter* BB 2003, 7, 9; *Schanze/Jüttner* AG 2003, 30, 32; *Schulz* NJW 2003, 2705; *Weller* IPRax 2003, 520, 522. Also LG Hannover of 2 Jul 2003 – 20 T 39/03, NZI 2003, 608.

105 *Riedemann* GmbHR 2004, 345, 346.

IV. Scope of Application – Time Element

1. General

104 The Regulation came into force on **31 May 2002**. All of its parts are binding, and it is directly applicable, Art 47 of the EIR.

105 The Regulation is applicable to all insolvency proceedings opened after 31 May 2002 in the Member States with the exception of Denmark, Art 43 sentence 1 of the EIR (see on this Art 43 of the EIR mn 3).[106] Determinative is the time at which the opening becomes effective through an act of the sovereign state, Art 2 (f) of the EIR.[107]

106 The bilateral conventions between Member States have automatically lost their validity, Art 44 of the EIR.

107 According to Art 43 sentence 2 of the EIR, legal acts carried out by the debtor prior to the coming into force of the Regulation continue to be governed by the law applicable to them.[108] Which legal acts are affected and at which time they were carried out are determined by the *lex fori concursus*,[109] see Art 43 of the EIR mn 11 et seq as well.

2. Order of the LG Wuppertal of 14 August 2002, ECJ Decision Susanne Staubitz-Schreiber

108 Problematical in this context is the order of the *LG* (Regional Court) of Wuppertal, Germany of 14 August 2002,[110] which by way of an order of reference from the German *BGH* of 27 November 2003[111] was also dealt with by the ECJ[112], see case Susanne Staubitz-Schreiber in Art 3 of the EIR mn 73 (cf Table of Cases Art 3 of the EIR Appendix A mn 17). On 6 December 2001, the debtor made a request to the insolvency court with international and territorial jurisdiction to open insolvency proceedings over her assets; the request was denied pursuant to Sec 26 *InsO* on 10 April 2002 for insufficiency of assets. The special appeal (*sofortige Beschwerde*) filed by the debtor was dismissed by an order of the *LG* on 14 August 2002. The court held that there was no longer German international jurisdiction because the debtor had moved her habitual residence on 1 April 2002 to Spain. According to the court, her centre of main interests (COMI) as understood by Art 3 (1) of the EIR was now located there. Those provisions of German national law contrary to this (Sec 4 *InsO* in conjunction with Sec 261 (3) No 2 *ZPO*), which hold that the jurisdiction of the court will not be affected by a subsequent cessation of the circumstances that gave rise to such jurisdiction, have, in the opinion of the court, been superseded as of 31 May 2002. The court found no transitional provision in the Regulation for "old cases" (Art 43 of the EIR seems not to have been considered by the *LG*). The decisive point in time, according to the court, for determining international jurisdiction was not the time at which the request was made but rather the point in time at which the decision on the special appeal was rendered on 14 August 2002. For a detailed discussion on this, see Art 3 of the EIR mn 15 and Art 43 of the EIR mn 15.

---

[106] *Virgós/Garcimartín* Regulation, p 30.

[107] *Pannen* in Runkel (ed), AHB-Insolvenzrecht (2005) § 16 mn 19.

[108] *Virgós/Garcimartín* Regulation, p 31.

[109] *Virgós/Schmit* Explanatory Report mn 306.

[110] LG Wuppertal ZInsO 2002, 1099; on this, see *Carstens* Die internationale Zuständigkeit im europäischen Insolvenzrecht, p 36 et seq.

[111] BGH ZIP 2004, 94.

[112] The proceedings there were conducted under the file no. C-1/04 (Staubitz-Schreiber), OJ 2004 C 71/13 p 10.

Legal precedent and literature in Germany takes the stance that the only point in time for determining jurisdiction is the time at which the request is made,[113] whereas the courts and legal writers in England and the Netherlands hold as decisive the time at which the decision opening proceedings is made unless the relocation of the domicile evidently constitutes an abuse of the law.[114] By order dated 27 November 2003, the *BGH* referred the question to the ECJ.[115] The strongest argument put forth by the *BGH* for maintaining the jurisdiction of the court at which the request is made was the objective set out in Recital 4 of the EIR, namely the prevention of forum shopping. But on the other hand, according to the *BGH*, the fact that the debtor would no longer be permanently present in the earlier location, and having brought his remaining assets to the new location, could make the insolvency proceedings more cumbersome. **109**

The ECJ rendered its decision on the reference order on 16 January 2006[116], see case Susanne Staubitz-Schreiber (→ cf Table of Cases Art 3 of the EIR Appendix A mn 17). Concurring with the closing submissions of the Advocate General *Colomer*,[117] the ECJ held in favour of the **continued validity** of the originally-established jurisdiction. The court's main argument was that a change of jurisdiction would contradict the objectives of the Regulation, particularly the prevention of forum shopping.[118] According to the ECJ, the debtor, by moving the centre of his main interests to another Member State in the time between the filing of the request to open proceedings and the issuing of the decision to open proceedings, would otherwise be free to choose the legal venue and the applicable law (Recital 25 of the Regulation). The court also found that, by adhering to the originally-established jurisdiction of the court first seized of the matter, a higher degree of legal certainty would be afforded to the creditors whose assessment of the risks associated with an insolvency of the debtor was done so in relation to the location where the debtor had his centre of main interests at the time of entering into legal relationships with him (Recital 27 of the Regulation). **110**

Although a relocation of the COMI prior to the making of a request is generally acceptable, a relocation will be disregarded if it amounts to a mere sham, i.e. if it is an arbitrary act made only a few weeks or months prior to the making of an insolvency request instead of one being done for sound business reasons.[119] For a detailed discussion on this, see Art 3 of the EIR mn 69 et seq as well. **111**

---

[113] AG Celle NZI 2005, 410; LG Hamburg NZI 2005, 645; *Mankowski* NZI 2005, 368; *Mankowski* NZI 2005, 575, 576, cf Table of Cases Art 3 of the EIR Appendix B No 73 and Appendix A mn 1.

[114] Cf for Great Britain: Geveran Trading Co Ltd. v. Skjevesland [2003], BPIR 73 (Registrar Jacques) und [2003], BCC 391 (High Court), Shierson v Vlieland-Boddy [2005], EWCA Civ 974 = NZI 2005, 571. The Netherlands: Gerechtshof Amsterdam dated 17 Jun 2003, JOR 2003/186; Hooge Rad dated 9 Jan 2004, Zaaknr. R03/091HR, available at www.rechtspraak.nl.; *Dicey/Morris/Morse* Conflict of Laws, Fourth Cumulative Supplement (1991) mn 31-090; *Fletcher* Law of Insolvency, p 839; Moss/Fletcher/Isaacs-*Moss/Smith,* Regulation, mn 8.44; *Wessels* Moving House: Which court can open insolvency proceedings, p 4 et seq.

[115] BGH ZIP 2004, 94 et seq = NZI 2004, 139 with an explanatory note by *Liersch*.

[116] ECJ of 17 Jan 2006, Susanne Staubitz-Schreiber, C-1/04, ZIP 2006, 188 et seq; with an explanatory note by *Knof/Mock* ZIP 2006, 189 et seq; *Schmidt* ZInsO 2006, 88 et seq.

[117] ECJ opinion, ZInsO 2005, 1099 et seq = NZI 2005, 544 et seq.

[118] ECJ of 17 Jan 2006, Susanne Staubitz-Schreiber, C-1/04, ZIP 2006, 188 et seq; with an explanatory note by *Knof/Mock* ZIP 2006, 189 et seq; *Schmidt* ZInsO 2006, 88 et seq.

[119] High Court of Justice Leeds ("Ci4net") ZIP 2004, 1769; and *Wessels*, Current Topics of International Insolvency Law, 170; Haß/

V. Scope of Application – Territorial

1. Introduction

112 The Regulation itself does not expressly regulate the territorial scope of its application.[120] This can be inferred, however, from the recitals in conjunction with the regulatory mechanisms of some of its individual provisions.[121] The Regulation only regulates the intra-Community effects of insolvency proceedings.[122] It only applies if the debtor's "centre of main interests" is located within the Community.[123]

113 The Regulation applies to all Member States of the EU (with the exception of Denmark, Recital 33 of the EIR). Art 44 of the EIR consequently lists all conventions, treaties, and contracts that have been partially repealed and replaced by the Regulation.[124] There are special arrangements with Denmark, Ireland, and the United Kingdom (see Art 69 EEC Treaty). Ireland and the United Kingdom take part in the adoption of the Regulation, Denmark does not (Recitals 32 and 33 of the EIR). Denmark will most likely enter into a bilateral treaty with the EU on the basis of the Regulation; on the still existing Nordic Bankruptcy Convention, see Introduction mn 24.

114 A case decided by the *OLG* (**Higher Regional Court**) **Frankfurt/Main**[125] is interesting in this context. According to this decision, the Regulation is not relevant in relation to Denmark. A decision of the Danish bankruptcy court cannot therefore be declared enforceable by the presiding judge of a civil chamber pursuant to Art 25 of the EIR, Art 31 et seq of the 1968 Brussels Convention, Sec 1 (1a) and Sec 11 et seq of the German Act on the Recognition and Enforcement of Foreign Judgments (*AVAG*). Instead, an action must be brought before a trial court to obtain a judicially enforceable instrument (authorizing execution).[126]

115 The Regulation does not apply to **purely domestic matters** or to the insolvency of a debtor whose centre of interests is located in a **non-EU country**.

116 Disputed is whether the Regulation applies when the only foreign connection is to a non-EU country, there being no other connection to an EU country (so-called "simple" foreign connection, see mn 120 et seq).[127]

2. Purely Domestic Matters

117 The Regulation only applies to cases involving cross-border insolvencies.[128] It does not apply to those involving **domestic matters** only.[129]

Huber/Gruber/Heiderhoff-*Haß/Herweg* Art 3 EuInsVO mn 17 with further references.

120 *Herchen* ZInsO 2005, 742, 743; MünchKomm InsO/*Reinhart* Art 1 EuInsVO mn 1.

121 MünchKomm InsO/*Reinhart* Art 1 EuInsVO mn 1.

122 *Virgós/Schmit* Explanatory Report mn 11.

123 *Virgós/Schmit* Explanatory Report mn 11.

124 *Paulus* Komm EuInsVO Einl mn 33.

125 OLG Frankfurt/Main of 24 Jan 2005 – 20 W 527/04, ZInsO 2005, 715.

126 In this regard, German autonomous international insolvency law applies, thus sec 353 (1) InsO which refers to secs 722 and 723 *ZPO*. Outside the scope of application of the Regulation, an insolvency-law judgement can only be enforced in Germany if a German court has issued a so-called *Vollstreckungsurteil*, i.e. an enforcement judgement authorizing execution of a foreign judgement.

127 So High Court of Justice (London) ZIP 2003, 813 ("BRAC-Budget"); *Herchen* ZInsO 2003, 742 et seq; **contra** *Balz* ZIP 1996, 948; *Eidenmüller* IPRax 2001, 2, 5; *Pannen/Riedemann* NZI 2004, 646, 651: a "qualified foreign connection" is necessary).

128 *Carstens* Die internationale Zuständigkeit im internationalen Insolvenzrecht, p 28.

129 See also Recitals 2 and 3 of the Regulation; *Huber* ZZP 114 (2001), 133, 136.

3. Foreign Connection Requirement

The Regulation only applies to cases involving cross-border insolvencies.[130] The problem, however, is defining what a cross-border connection is. **118**

A cross-border connection definitely exists if the debtor has assets in a foreign country, or if there are foreign creditors. The Regulation even applies to pseudo foreign corporations (see mn 97 et seq). **119**

Disputed is whether the Regulation will apply when the only foreign connection is to a non-EU country, there being no other connection to a Member State (so-called "simple" foreign connection).[131] It would be correct to insist on there being a "qualified" foreign connection:[132] **120**

For reasons of legal certainty, however, it would be advisable to refrain from broadening the scope of applicability of the Regulation to non-Member States, as was done in the "BRAC Rent-A-Car" case, although this may make economic sense in some instances. The Regulation makes no provision whatsoever for international insolvency law issues arising between EU Member States and non-EU countries.[133] This is solely a matter for the international insolvency law regimes of the respective Member States.[134] **121**

4. Re BRAC Rent-A-Car

In the English decision **BRAC Rent-A-Car,**[135] a large, US-registered company was placed under "administration order" in England, see case BRAC Rent-A-Car (→ cf Table of Cases Art 3 of the EIR Appendix A mn 3). The debtor company was a member of a corporate group whose individual companies were involved in reorganization proceedings under Chapter 11 of the US Bankruptcy Code. The Chancery Division of the High Court of Justice assumed[136] that such proceedings did not afford the debtor any protection, at least not in England and Wales pursuant to English precedent, from enforcement measures (meaning that the "automatic stay" of Chapter 11 proceedings could not apply) and assumed international jurisdiction to open main insolvency proceedings. The court did not consider the issue of whether secondary insolvency proceedings (aimed at winding-up the company) within the meaning of Art 3 (2) and Art 27 of the EIR should be opened parallel to the Chapter 11 proceedings. **122**

Although the USA does not belong to the EU, and is therefore outside the scope of the Regulation's application, the court assumed that the COMI as understood by the Regulation was in England, justifying this on the following grounds: **123**

"The company[137] *is incorporated in Delaware, and has its registered address in the United States. However, that is not an address from which it trades, and it has never trad-* **124**

---

130 *Huber* ZZP 114 (2001), 133, 136.

131 So High Court of Justice (London) ZIP 2003, 813 ("BRAC-Budget"); *Herchen* ZInsO 2003, 742 et seq; **contra** *Balz* ZIP 1996, 948; *Eidenmüller* IPRax 2001, 2, 5; *Pannen/ Riedemann* NZI 2004, 646, 651: a "qualified foreign connection" is necessary.

132 *Pannen/Riedemann* NZI 2004, 646, 651.

133 *Balz* ZIP 1996, 948; *Eidenmüller* IPRax 2001, 2, 5; also: *Leible/Staudinger* KTS 2000, 533, 538. Undecided in: D-K/D-Ch-*Duursma-Kepplinger* Art 1 mn 52.

134 In Germany, secs 335 et seq InsO apply in this regard.

135 Also called BRAC. High Court of Justice Chancery Division Court (England; The Honourable Mr. Justice Lloyd), of 7 Feb 2003 – 0042/2003; ZIP 2003, 813 with an explanatory note by *Sabel/Schlegel* EWiR 2003, 367.

136 On account of the decision Banque Indosuez v Ferromet, (1993) BCLC 112.

137 Author's note: this means BRAC Rent-A-Car International Inc.

ed in US. Its operations are conducted almost entirely in the UK. ... It trades from an address in Hemel Hempstead, in England. ... It has no employees in the US, and all its employees work in England, with contracts of employment governed by English law, apart from a small number in branch office in Switzerland. Its trading activities are carried out by way of contracts with subsidiaries and franchisees. All of these are governed by English law ..."[138]

125 One of the liquidators appointed to the proceedings emphasized **the advantages** of this approach in the following statements:

126 *"Braci should be a template for consensual cross-border restructurings. It establishes what can be achieved with the European Regulation. The only alternative for Budget Rentacar was Provisional Liquidation in the UK, which would have made a sale of the business virtually impossible."*[139]

127 With this decision, the English court brought about the automatic stay without infringing precedent on its own English jurisdiction.[140] If this decision is followed, main insolvency proceedings as understood by the Regulation can be opened in all EU-Member States against each and every non-EU pseudo foreign corporation whose de facto head office is located in the European Union.

5. Non-EU Matters

128 Furthermore, the Regulation only applies to insolvency proceedings involving cross-border matters **within the EU with the exception of Denmark**. According to Recital 14 of the EIR, the centre of the debtor's main interests must be located in the Community.

129 If such centre of interests is located in a **non-EU country**, the Regulation does not apply.[141] If the debtor operates an establishment outside the EU, but his centre of interests is located within a Member State, the Regulation remains applicable for the purposes of opening main insolvency proceedings.[142]

130 The territorial aspect of the scope of the Regulation's application played a role especially in the decision in the BRAC Rent-A-Car case, see above mn 122 et seq.

131 The international insolvency law regimes of each Member State must find their own way of dealing with international insolvency-law issues concerning non-EU countries. The options include adopting the **UNCITRAL Model Law**[143] (see the comments on this in Part 4) as a supplementary source, entering into bi- and multilateral conventions, or by treating non-EU States the same as the Member States. The last option would mean aligning the respective international insolvency laws with the Regulation.

---

[138] High Court of Justice Chancery Division Companies Court (England; The Honourable Mr. Justice Lloyd) of 7 Feb 2003 – 0042/2003, ZIP 2003, 813 f.

[139] Cited according to: *Willcock* INSOL World – Third Quartal 2003, 8, 9.

[140] *Smid* DZWIR 2003, 397, 403.

[141] *Leible/Staudinger* KTS 2000, 533, 538; *Huber* ZZP 114 (2001), 133, 137.

[142] *Leible/Staudinger* KTS 2000, 533, 538.

[143] About the UNCITRAL-Model Law cf *Wimmer* ZIP 1997, 2220.

VI. Insolvencies of Corporate Groups

Although the insolvency of corporate groups is extremely relevant to cross-border insolvencies,[144] it is not expressly dealt with in the Regulation.[145] It particularly does not deal with the fact that, in the case of cross-border corporate groups, the COMI of the subsidiaries is located at the head office (corporate domicile) of the group's parent company.[146] On this see Art 3 of the EIR mn 46 et seq. **132**

Considering that **corporate-group insolvencies** are the very epitome of cross-border insolvencies, the problem of establishing international jurisdiction for the opening of main insolvency proceedings within the meaning of Art 3 of the EIR has become extremely pressing especially in these cases (on this issue, see Art 3 of the EIR mn 47). **133**

The issue of who may be a debtor must be answered by the national insolvency laws. It is therefore quite conceivable that national laws would allow insolvency proceedings to be opened against the assets of a corporate group.[147] For the opening or joining together of insolvency proceedings against a main debtor or a joint and several debtor that is a corporate (legal) entity of a consolidated group, the general rule applies: for every affected debtor with its own legal personality jurisdiction must be determined in accordance with the Regulation. **134**

Article 2
Definitions

For the purposes of this Regulation:

(a) "insolvency proceedings" shall mean the collective proceedings referred to in Article 1(1). These proceedings are listed in Annex A;

(b) "liquidator" shall mean any person or body whose function is to administer or liquidate assets of which the debtor has been divested or to supervise the administration of his affairs. Those persons and bodies are listed in Annex C;

(c) "winding-up proceedings" shall mean insolvency proceedings within the meaning of point (a) involving realising the assets of the debtor, including where the proceedings have been closed by a composition or other measure terminating the insolvency, or closed by reason of the insufficiency of the assets. Those proceedings are listed in Annex B;

(d) "court" shall mean the judicial body or any other competent body of a Member State empowered to open insolvency proceedings or to take decisions in the course of such proceedings;

---

[144] *Paulus* NZI 2001, 505, 508 regards this as a „veritable sin of omission". On this see also *Ehricke* EWS 2002, 101 et seq, and *van Galen*, The European Insolvency Regulation and Groups of Companies, Work paper INSOL Europe Annual Congress (Cork, Ireland), October 16–18, 2003; *Willcock* INSOL World – Second Quarter 2004, 6 et seq.

[145] *Virgós/Garcimartín* Regulation, p 27; *Virgós/Schmit* Explanatory Report mn 76.

[146] *Ehricke* EWS 2002, 101, 103.

[147] The above-cited wording in the Explanatory Report must be so understood that cross-border insolvency issues are only governed by the Regulation insofar as they concern the same debtor as defined by the national insolvency law. *Eidenmüller* IPRax 2001, 2, 4.

(e) "judgment" in relation to the opening of insolvency proceedings or the appointment of a liquidator shall include the decision of any court empowered to open such proceedings or to appoint a liquidator;

(f) "the time of the opening of proceedings" shall mean the time at which the judgment opening proceedings becomes effective, whether it is a final judgment or not;

(g) "the Member State in which assets are situated" shall mean, in the case of:

- **tangible property, the Member State within the territory of which the property is situated,**
- **property and rights ownership of or entitlement to which must be entered in a public register, the Member State under the authority of which the register is kept,**
- **claims, the Member State within the territory of which the third party required to meet them has the centre of his main interests, as determined in Article 3(1);**

(h) "establishment" shall mean any place of operations where the debtor carries out a non-transitory economic activity with human means and goods.

→ Cf Art 2 UNCITRAL Model Law

Contents

Index

Bibliography

Carstens Die internationale Zuständigkeit im europäischen Insolvenzrecht (2005); *Dammann* L'application du règlement CE n° 1346-2000 après les arrêts Staubitz-Schreiber et Eurofood de la CJCE, Dalloz 2006, p 1752; *Dammann/Podeur* L'affaire Daisytek: l'épilogue. Application par la Cour de cassation du règlement européen relatif aux procédures d'insolvabilité, Banque & Droit N° 109 September–October 2006, p 3; *Duursma-Kepplinger/Duursma/Chalupsky* Europäische Insolvenzverordnung, Kommentar (2002); *Ehricke* Die neue Europäische Insolvenzverordnung und grenzüberschreitende Konzerninsolvenzen, EWS 2002, p 101; *Eidenmüller* Europäische Verordnung über Insolvenzverfahren und zukünftiges deutsches internationales Insolvenzrecht, IPRax 2001, p 2; *Gottwald* Grenzüberschreitende Insolvenzen (1997); *Haß/Huber/Gruber/Heiderhoff* Kommentar zur Verordnung (EG) Nr. 1346/2000 über Insolvenzverfahren (EuInsVO) (2005); *Herchen* Das Prioritätsprinzip im internationalen Insolvenzrecht, ZIP 2005, p 1401; *Huber* Internationales Insolvenzrecht in Europa, ZZP 114 (2001), p 133; *Kebekus* Comments on Amtsgericht Nürnberg dated 1.10.2006, ZIP 2007, p 84; *Kübler* Mittelpunkt der hauptsächlichen Interessen nach Art 3 Abs 1 EuInsVO, in Schilken/Kreft/Wagner/Eckhardt (eds), Festschrift Gerhardt (2004), p 527 et seq; *Laukemann* Rechtshängigkeit im europäischen Insolvenzrecht, RIW 2005, p 104; *Lüke* Das europäische internationale Insolvenzrecht, ZZP 111 (1998), p 275; *Mankowski* Klärung von Grundfragen des europäischen Internationalen Insolvenzrechts durch die Eurofood-Entscheidung?, BB 2006, p 1753; *Moss/Fletcher/Isaacs* (eds) The EC Regulation on Insolvency Proceedings (2002); Münchener Kommentar zur Insolvenzordnung, vol 3 (2003); *Pannen/Riedemann* Comments on Opinion of Advocate General Francis Geoffrey Jacobs dated 27.9.2005 – C-341/04, EWiR 2005, p 725; *Paulus* Europäische Insolvenzverordnung, Kommentar (2006); *Paulus* Die Europäische Insolvenzverordnung und der deutsche Insolvenzverwalter, NZI 2001, p 505; *Poertzgen/Adam* Die Bestimmung des "centre of main interests" gem. Art. 3 Abs. 1 EuInsVO, ZInsO 2006, p 505; *Runkel* (ed) Anwaltshandbuch – Insolvenzrecht (2005); *Sabel* Hauptsitz als Niederlassung im Sinne der EuInsVO?, NZI 2004, p 126; *Smid* Europäisches Internationales Insolvenzrecht (2002); *Smid* Deutsches und Europäisches Internationales Insolvenzrecht, Kommentar (2004); *Vallender* Aufgaben und Befugnisse des deutschen Insolvenzrichters in Verfahren nach der EuInsVO, KTS 2005, p 283; *Virgós/Garcimartín* The European Insolvency Regulation: Law and Practice (2004); *Virgós/Schmit* Explanatory Report, in Stoll (ed), Vorschläge und Gutachten (1997), p 32; *Wessels* International Insolvency Law (2006).

1. Overview

1 Art 2 of the EIR is a so-called **definition norm** containing the **statutory definitions** of key terms used throughout the Regulation. The intention is to ensure the most uniform interpretation possible of these terms in all of the various countries.[1] The interpretation of these terms is a matter for the **ECJ**.[2]

2. Art 2 (a) of the EIR – "insolvency proceedings"

2 "**Insolvency proceedings**" are defined in Art 2 (a) of the EIR as proceedings:

- that fulfil the conditions of Art 1 (1) of the EIR and
- that are listed in Annex A of the EIR, which forms an integral part of the Regulation.

3 Only those proceedings listed in Annex A of the EIR benefit from the **automatic recognition** provided for in Art 16 of the EIR.[3] The Regulation does not apply to proceedings that, although they fulfil the requirements of Art 1 of the EIR, are not listed in Annex A of the EIR.[4] This "**closed-list system**"[5] provides legal certainty as it enables the parties applying it to ascertain exactly which proceedings fall within the scope of the Regulation's application.

4 According to Art 45 of the EIR, the Council, acting by qualified majority on the initiative of one of its members or on a proposal from the Commission, may amend the Annexes. This has already been done on several occasions since the Regulation has come into force. For example, the French *procédure de sauvegarde* pursuant to Art L 620-1 to L 620-2 *Code de commerce* was added to Annex A of the EIR. What is not considered an insolvency proceeding within the meaning of Art 2 (a) of the EIR is, however, the composition proceeding under French law, although it plays an important role in practical terms and can be opened instead of reorganization proceedings.[6] (On the amendments to the Regulation, see the discussion of Art 45 of the EIR mn 6 et seq).

3. Art 2 (b) of the EIR – "liquidator"

5 The term "**liquidator**" is to be understood in a broad sense.[7] Pursuant to Art 2 (b) of the EIR, a "**liquidator**" is any person or body whose function is to administer the assets of which the debtor has been divested, or to supervise the administration of his affairs.

These persons or bodies are listed in Annex C of the EIR, which can also be amended pursuant to Art 45 in the same manner as Annex A of the EIR.[8]

---

[1] Cf *Paulus* Komm EuInsVO Art 2 mn 1; *Smid* Komm EuInsVO Art 2 mn 1.

[2] *Smid* Komm EuInsVO Art 2 mn 1.

[3] *Virgós/Schmit* Explanatory Report mn 61; *Virgós/Garcimartín* Regulation, p 29; *Eidenmüller* IPRax 2001, 2, 4; *Wessels* International Insolvency Law (2006) mn 10518.

[4] Moss/Fletcher/Isaacs-*Fletcher*, Regulation, mn 3.03; *Wessels* International Insolvency Law (2006) mn 10518.

[5] *Virgós/Garcimartín* Regulation, p 30.

[6] *Dammann* Dalloz 2006, 1752, 1759.

[7] *Virgós/Schmit* Explanatory Report mn 63; *Wessels* International Insolvency Law (2006) mn 10519.

[8] *Wessels* International Insolvency Law (2006) mn 10519.

6 The appointing of a liquidator is mandatory since Art 2 (a) and Art 1 (1) of the EIR stipulate that insolvency proceedings must be collective proceedings that demand the full or partial divestment of the debtor.[9]

7 Should the **court** itself take over the administration of the debtor's assets, then it too may be regarded as a **liquidator** within the meaning of Art 2 (b) of the EIR provided that the court is listed in Annex C as a possible liquidator.[10] This is not the case in Germany or France. By contrast, the *Konkursgericht* (bankruptcy court) in Austria is included in the list of "liquidators" pursuant to Art 2 (b) in conjunction with Annex C of the EIR.

8 In Germany, the debtor could theoretically also be classified as a liquidator in the **debtor in possession** *(Eigenverwalter)* constellation pursuant to Sec 270 et seq *Ins*O.[11] This follows from the fact that the debtor in this situation is entitled to administer and dispose of the insolvency estate under the supervision of a *Sachwalter* (Sec 270 (1) sentence 1 *Ins*O). However, because Annex C of the EIR only includes the ***Sachwalter***[12] (the custodian pursuant to the *Ins*O) in the debtor in possession situation, the debtor cannot be regarded as a liquidator.

9 The definition of liquidator in Art 2 (b) of the EIR poses difficulties in the case of the English **administration proceedings**. The question is whether the **directors** of the company, who function as administrators, may be regarded as liquidators. Although the administrator is explicitly listed in Annex C of the EIR, some argue that such an administrator must, in addition, also comply with the elements of Art 2 (b) of the EIR.[13] If all of the persons or bodies listed in Annex C of the EIR were automatically considered liquidators, then the statutory definition in Art 2 (a) of the EIR would be rendered superfluous. The drafters of the Regulation could have been content with the Annexes. Instead, the fact that they included the definitions in Art 2 (a), (b), and (c) of the EIR indicates that the elements of these provisions must be complied with in every concrete case. The same holds true for all of the Annexes; on this, see Art 1 of the EIR mn 18 et seq (in the **Marann Brooks CSV Ltd** case).

4. Art 2 (c) of the EIR – "winding-up proceedings"

10 According to Art 2 (c) of the EIR, **"winding-up proceedings"** are collective insolvency proceedings within the meaning of Art 2 (a) of the EIR that involve the realization of the debtor's assets even if the proceedings have been closed by a **composition** or other measure terminating the insolvency, or closed because of insufficiency of assets. The proceedings relevant here are listed in Annex B of the EIR. This provision defines the type of proceedings permissible as secondary insolvency proceedings pursuant to Art 3 (2) and Art 27 of the EIR[14] since secondary insolvency proceedings may only take the form of winding-up proceedings.

11 During the course of deliberations on the **1995 Draft convention on insolvency proceedings,**[15] many of the Member States wished to restrict the scope of the convention to

[9] *Virgós/Schmit* Explanatory Report mn 63; D-K/D/Ch-*Duursma-Kepplinger* Art 2 mn 4.

[10] *Smid* Komm EuInsVO Art 2 mn 5; *Virgós/Schmit* Explanatory Report mn 63; D-K/D/Ch-*Duursma-Kepplinger* Art 2 mn 6; *Wessels* International Insolvency Law (2006) mn 10519.

[11] *Paulus* Komm EuInsVO Art 2 mn 7.

[12] On this, see also: AG Cologne of 23 Jan 2004, ZIP 2004, 471, 472 (→ cf Table of Cases Art 3 of the EIR Appendix A mn 2).

[13] *Paulus* Komm EuInsVO Art 2 mn 8.

[14] *Virgós/Schmit* Explanatory Report mn 64.

[15] For the history of the Regulation, see the Introduction at mn 1 et seq.

winding-up proceedings.[16] By way of compromise, it was finally agreed that main insolvency proceedings could also be geared to the reorganization of the debtor but that secondary insolvency proceedings could not; these must result in a winding-up.[17] The reason for this is that secondary insolvency proceedings geared to the reorganization of the debtor could pose problems of compatibility and coordination with the main insolvency proceedings.[18]

12 This restriction does not apply, however, to **independent territorial insolvency proceedings** per Art 3 (4) of the EIR; these may also be opened as reorganization proceedings. If main insolvency proceedings are opened subsequent to these proceedings, the liquidator of the main insolvency proceedings can request that the earlier proceedings be converted to winding-up proceedings if it can be demonstrated that the conversion is in the interests of the creditors of the main insolvency proceedings.[19]

13 The fact that secondary insolvency proceedings must be winding-up proceedings creates no difficulties in Member States that have separate forms of proceedings, such as France or Italy. For Germany, the proceedings listed in Annex B of the EIR are the *Konkursverfahren,* the *Gesamtvollstreckungsverfahren,* and the *Insolvenzverfahren.* An *Insolvenzverfahren* (insolvency proceeding) pursuant to the German *InsO* may be a winding-up or a reorganization proceeding. In contrast to other legal systems, German insolvency law (as is the case in Spanish law: *concurso* in Annex A and B of the EIR) does not distinguish from the outset between winding-up and reorganization proceedings.

14 The Explanatory Report states that the fact that a winding-up proceeding can be closed on the basis of an agreement with the creditors, or through another measure that terminates the debtor's insolvency, does not affect its character as a proceeding if the primary purpose of the proceeding is the winding-up (realization) of the debtor's assets.[20] The controversy is whether an **insolvency plan proceeding** under German law should be regarded as a winding-up proceeding within the meaning of the Regulation.[21]

- One view suggests that the concept of insolvency proceedings should be teleologically limited to exclude cases with insolvency plans geared toward reorganization of the debtor enterprise, since such insolvency plans are obviously not winding-up proceedings.[22]
- The contrary, and more convincing, approach is one that views Sec 217 et seq *InsO* as also being applicable within the context of secondary insolvency proceedings.[23] This is justifiable on the basis that the actual outcome of a proceeding is irrelevant to the decision as to whether it is a winding-up proceeding.[24] Furthermore, Annex B of the EIR refers indiscriminately to the German *Insolvenzverfahren* (which would also include an insolvency plan proceeding).

15 The fact that secondary insolvency proceedings must be winding-up proceedings does not prevent the ordering of **debtor in possession** proceedings[25] (see the *AG* Cologne decision "Automold").

[16] *Virgós/Schmit* Explanatory Report mn 51.
[17] *Virgós/Schmit* Explanatory Report mn 51.
[18] *Virgós/Schmit* Explanatory Report mn 51.
[19] *Pannen* in Runkel (ed), AHB-Insolvenzrecht (2005) § 16 mn 306, 607.
[20] *Virgós/Schmit* Explanatory Report mn 64.
[21] On this, cf e.g.: *Smid* Komm EuInsVO Art 2 mn 11; *Paulus* Komm EuInsVO Art 2 mn 11; *Kübler* FS Gerhardt (2004), p 527, 536 et seq.
[22] *Smid* Komm EuInsVO Art 2 mn 11.
[23] *Paulus* Komm EuInsVO Art 2 mn 1; *Paulus* NZI 2001, 505, 514; *Kübler* FS Gerhardt (2004) p 527, 536 et seq.
[24] *Paulus* Komm EuInsVO Art 2 mn 11.
[25] Cf *Kübler* FS Gerhardt (2004) p 527, 538; *Sabel* NZI 2004, 126 et seq.

Example

(AG Cologne "Automold" → cf Table of Cases Art 3 of the EIR Appendix A mn 2)

Upon request by the German managing director and the English liquidator in the main proceedings, the *AG* Cologne opened secondary insolvency proceedings on 23 January 2004. The court also issued – upon application – a debtor in possession order and, absent a contrary provision in German law, awarded the powers of administration and disposal to the English liquidators. The *AG* Cologne held that the debtor in possession constellation leads, via a coordinated handling of the insolvency, to higher proceeds from the liquidation; the court also argued that the English liquidators were already familiar with the matter.

References: AG Cologne, order dated 23 January 2004 – 71 IN 1/04 ZIP 2004, 471 = NZI 2004, 151 = ZInsO 2004, 216 = DZWiR 2004, 434.

In secondary insolvency proceedings, a **reorganization by way of a transfer (asset deal)** can also take place instead of a direct winding-up or an insolvency plan.[26] Although there is normally an "interim phase" where the business continues operating, the legal entity will ultimately be wound up since, pursuant to the **asset deal,** its assets are being transferred. **16**

5. Art 2 (d) of the EIR – "court"

The Regulation does not provide for any kind of uniform competence in terms of judicial functions in insolvency matters.[27] The term **"court"** is defined in Art 2 (d) of the EIR as any judicial body or any other competent body of a Member State that is empowered to open insolvency proceedings or to take decisions in the course of such proceedings. In compliance with Recital 10 of the EIR, the term "court" must be given a broad meaning.[28] It is not restricted to the public courts or institutions whose functions are equivalent to a court or a public authority, as was required in the earlier drafts of the 1995 Draft convention on insolvency proceedings.[29] **17**

"In the course of the proceedings" means a court that has a direct influence on the insolvency proceedings concerned.[30] A court dealing with civil law matters that, for example, interrupts a civil proceeding pursuant to Sec 240 of the German *ZPO* is not a "court" within the meaning of Art 2 (d) of the EIR even though the decision it makes is made "in the course of the proceedings".[31] **18**

The fact that the definition of "court" in Art 2 (d) of the EIR is not restricted to state institutions has particularly astounding repercussions in English law. A "meeting of creditors" in conjunction with a "voluntary agreement" made pursuant to the Insolvency Act 1986 is understood in English legal writings as a court if it is authorized to petition **19**

[26] *Kübler* FS Gerhardt (2004) p 527, 540.

[27] This follows from the principle of proportionality that must be adhered to with respect to encroachments on the national insolvency laws of Member States, see *Smid* Europäisches Internationales Insolvenzrecht, p 58.

[28] *Virgós/Schmit* Explanatory Report mn 66, *Wessels* International Insolvency Law (2006) mn 10521.

[29] *Virgós/Schmit* Explanatory Report mn 66.

[30] *Paulus* Komm EuInsVO Art 2 mn 12.

[31] *Paulus* Komm EuInsVO Art 2 mn 12.

for the winding-up of the company.[32] Since the enactment of the insolvency law reform on 15 September 2003, the directors of a company are also authorized to open administration proceedings without the participation of a court. This constitutes a so-called **"out of court appointment"**. The managing director can therefore qualify as a "court" within the meaning of Art 2 (d) of the EIR.[33]

6. Art 2 (e) of the EIR – "judgment"

20 A "**judgement**" in relation to the opening of insolvency proceedings or the appointment of a liquidator includes the decision of any court empowered to open such proceedings or to appoint a liquidator. As with the term "court", this term is to be given a broad meaning.[34]

21 The English version of the Regulation differs in this definition from the other versions: "Judgement [...] shall include the decision of any court". This could be construed to mean that other bodies or persons, as per the definition in Art 2 (d) of the EIR, would be in a position to open insolvency proceedings or to appoint a liquidator[35] (see mn 17 above).

22 In the **ECJ** decision **Eurofood/Parmalat** (→ cf Table of Cases Art 3 of the EIR Appendix A mn 10), the appointing of a **provisional liquidator**[36] was also regarded as an **opening of proceedings** within the meaning of Art 16 of the EIR.[37] The appointment would then prevent the opening of (other) main insolvency proceedings.[38]

23 The concept of **opening insolvency proceedings** contemplated by Art 16 of the EIR is to be understood to include not only those opening judgements defined formally as such by the law of the Member State applicable to the court issuing the judgement, but it also includes a judgement that is made in response to a request stemming from the debtor's insolvency to open one of the proceedings set out in Annex A of the EIR if such judgement leads to the divestment of the debtor and if, pursuant to it, one of the liquidators named in Annex C of the EIR is appointed.[39] According to Art 2 (e) of the EIR, a judge-

[32] Moss/Fletcher/Isaacs-*Moss/Smith*, Regulation, mn 8.19; *Smid* Komm EuInsVO Art 2 mn 12.

[33] *Paulus* Komm EuInsVO Art 2 mn 13; *Wessels* International Insolvency Law (2006) mn 10521. For an example of an out-of-court appointment, see the case Hans Brochier Holdings Ltd (→ cf Table of Cases Art 3 of the EIR Appendix B No 97, 98, 100 and 101), on this *Kebekus* note on AG Nürnberg of 1 Oct 2006, ZIP 2007, 84.

[34] *Virgós/Schmit* Explanatory Report mn 67; D-K/D/Ch-*Duursma-Kepplinger* Art 2 mn 12; *Wessels* International Insolvency Law (2006) mn 10522.

[35] Moss/Fletcher/Isaacs-*Moss/Smith*, Regulation, mn 8.20.

[36] It is irrelevant whether a "strong" or "weak" liquidator is appointed as long as this is provided for in law, as is the case in German law (secs 21, 22 InsO). All that is important is whether a decision has been made to appoint a liquidator.

[37] ECJ of 2 May 2006 – C-341/04 (Eurofood IFSC Ltd.), NZI 2006, 360 et seq (→ cf Table of Cases Art 3 of the EIR Appendix A mn 10 – Eurofood/Parmalat); also Advocate General *Jacobs* in his opinion ZIP 2005, 1641; *Laukemann* RIW 2005, 104, 112.

[38] With the same result: High Court Dublin "Eurofood/Parmalat II" ZIP 2004, 1223, 1224; ECJ, C-341/04 (→ cf Table of Cases Art 3 of the EIR Appendix A mn 10); moreover Municipality Court of Prague "Aircraft" ZIP 2005, 1431 (→ cf Table of Cases Art 3 of the EIR Appendix A mn 1); *Pannen/Riedemann* EWiR 2005, 725, 726.

[39] ECJ C-341/04 of 2 May 2006, ZInsO 2006, 484 (→ cf Table of Cases Art 3 of the EIR Appendix A mn 10 – Eurofood/Parmalat);

ment also includes the appointment of a liquidator, whereby Art (2) (b) in conjunction with Annex C of the EIR also mentions the German ***vorläufigen Insolvenzverwalter*** (temporary administrator); on this see also Art 3 of the EIR mn 9 or Art 16 of the EIR mn 32 et seq.

7. Art 2 (f) of the EIR – "the time of the opening of proceedings"

Art 2 (f) of the EIR regulates the ascertainment of the "**time of the opening of proceedings**". This plays a decisive role in the application of many of the provisions of the Regulation. Since the ECJ's decision in Eurofood/Parmalat,[40] the **ordering of a temporary administrator** can also be regarded as the **opening of proceedings**, see mn 22. **24**

The time of the opening of proceedings is the point in time at which the **decision to open** (or the ordering of a temporary administrator) becomes **effective** pursuant to the law of the opening Member State, regardless of whether the decision is final or not. According to the wording of Art 2 (f) of the EIR, it is therefore irrelevant whether or not the opening decision is final or *res judicata*.[41] A decision that is not *res judicata* will thus suffice even if it is effective in the opening State only.[42] The issue of the effectiveness of the decision is a matter for the *lex fori concursus*.[43] **25**

The **determination of the time of the opening of proceedings** is relevant *inter alia* for the following articles of the Regulation: **26**

- **Art 3 (3) of the EIR:** once main insolvency proceedings have been opened, secondary insolvency proceedings only may be opened.
- **Art 5 of the EIR:** third party rights *in rem* are not affected by the opening of the proceedings if they are situated in another Member State at the time of the opening of the proceedings.
- **Art 7 of the EIR:** the opening of the proceedings does not affect the rights of a conditional seller if the property is situated in another Member State at the time of the opening of the proceedings.
- **Art 16 of the EIR:** as soon as a main insolvency proceeding has effectively been opened, its recognition is mandatory in all other Member States.
- **Art 18 (2) sentence 1 of the EIR:** the liquidator in secondary insolvency proceedings may in any other Member State claim that moveable property has been removed after the opening of the insolvency proceedings from the territory of the State of the opening of proceedings to the territory of that other Member State.
- **Art 20 of the EIR:** a duty to return pursuant to Art 20 (1) of the EIR only exists if the creditor's claim has been satisfied after the opening of proceedings.

It is difficult to define the time at which some forms of proceedings are opened, for example the "creditor's voluntary winding-up" pursuant to English law.[44] The question **27**

Poertzgen/Adam ZInsO 2006, 505, 508; on this, see also: *Mankowski* in BB 2006, 1753 et seq, who draws special attention to the consequences of dogmatically treating the provisional opening of insolvency proceedings as equivalent to the final opening of such.

[40] ECJ of 2 May 2006 – C-341/04 (Eurofood IFSC Ltd.), NZI 2006, 360 et seq (→ cf Table of Cases Art 3 of the EIR Appendix A mn 10 – Eurofood/Parmalat).

[41] *Smid* Komm EuInsVO Art 2 mn 16.

[42] *Paulus* Komm EuInsVO Art 2 mn 15.

[43] *Paulus* Komm EuInsVO Art 2 mn 15.

[44] *Virgós/Schmit* Explanatory Report mn 68.

is whether the normal criterion should be applied in such a case, or whether the approval of the proceedings and the appointment of the liquidator is decisive.[45] According to the Explanatory Report, the time of the approval by the court is only relevant to the exercising of the powers of the liquidator in the territory of another Member State. For all other matters, the normal definition applies.[46]

28 Problematic for determining the time of the opening of proceedings are the so-called **relation back principles**, which exist in English, Irish, Welsh, and Czech law (on this see Art 3 of the EIR mn 89).[47] The opening of insolvency proceedings in such constellations is retroactive to the point in time at which the request was made.[48] However, the ECJ's decision in Eurofood/Parmalat (→ cf Table of Cases Art 3 of the EIR Appendix A mn 10) is to be so understood that **retroactive fictions of national law** are to be **disregarded**; for a detailed discussion on this see Art 3 of the EIR mn 89 et seq.[49]

8. Art 2 (g) of the EIR – "the Member State in which assets are situated"

29 Art 2 (g) of the EIR concerns the location of assets. The location of an asset is decisive for the application of various provisions of the Regulation:[50]

- **Art 5 of the EIR:** third party rights *in rem* that are situated in another Member State at the time of the opening of the proceedings are not affected by the opening of the proceedings.
- **Art 7 of the EIR:** the opening of the proceedings does not affect the rights of a conditional seller if the property is situated in another Member State at the time of the opening of the proceedings.
- **Article 17 (2) sentence 2 of the EIR:** any restriction of the creditors' rights only has an effect on those assets situated within the territory of another Member State in respect of those creditors who have given their consent.
- **Article 18 (1) sentence 2 of the EIR:** the liquidator in the main insolvency proceedings is entitled to remove assets belonging to the insolvency estate from the territory of the Member State in which they are situated.
- **Art 20 (1) of the EIR:** the duty to return only exists if the satisfaction has been obtained from property in the insolvency estate in another Member State.

30 For the application of these provisions, the definitions in Art 2 (g) of the EIR provide a certain degree of assistance.[51] They also ensure that the localization of assets takes place in a consistent manner in all Member States. Without the definitions, the provisions of the autonomous Member States would apply. The Regulation is content, however, with adopting the established rules of international private law of the Member States.[52]

---

45 *Virgós/Schmit* Explanatory Report mn 68.
46 *Virgós/Schmit* Explanatory Report mn 68.
47 Haß/Huber/Gruber/Heiderhoff-*Huber* Art 2 EuInsVO mn 3.
48 E.g. High Court Dublin "Eurofood/Parmalat" ZIP 2004, 1223; Municipality Court of Prague of 26 Apr 2005, ZIP 2005, 1431, cf Table of Cases Art 3 of the EIR Appendix A mn 1, on this *Herchen* ZIP 2005, 1401.
49 *Mankowski* BB 2006, 1753, 1757.
50 *Virgós/Schmit* Explanatory Report mn 69.
51 *Virgós/Schmit* Explanatory Report mn 69.
52 *Virgós/Schmit* Explanatory Report mn 69.

8.1 Tangible property

In the case of "**tangible property**", the first dash of Art 2 (g) of the EIR presumes that such property is located in the Member State in which it is actually situated.[53] Such a localization should give rise to relatively few problems in practical terms.[54] **31**

What the Regulation does not do, however, is to define "**tangible property**" or specify the law pursuant to which it could be ascertained. The assumption simply cannot be made that all property that does not fall within Art 2 (g) second or third dash of the EIR (on this see mn 35 et seq and 39 et seq) is to be regarded as tangible property. **32**

In practice, every Member State will have to rely on its own property laws. This naturally gives rise to a danger that an asset will be classified in various ways, which renders the application of the aforementioned provisions more difficult. **33**

From the German perspective, tangible property is that which is defined by **Sec 90** ***BGB***.[55] This includes **securities** provided that they are not found in collective safekeeping (because then, pursuant to Art 9 of Directive 2002/47/EC on financial collateral arrangements, that law will govern in which the "relevant account" is being maintained).[56] Notwithstanding Sec 90a *BGB*, **animals** are also deemed as property (objects).[57] **34**

8.2 Property or rights whose ownership / entitlement must be entered in a public register

Property or rights whose ownership or entitlement must be entered in a **public register** are deemed to be situated in the country authorized to keep the register. **35**

Examples of this include registers for ships and aircraft, and registers for intangible assets such as patents and securities.[58] Also included are legal rights ensuing from compulsory executions (Secs 828 et seq, 857 of the German *ZPO*.) **36**

Decisive for locating such property or rights is not the **State in which the register is actually situated** but the State under whose **supervision** the register is being kept.[59] Such a disparity exists, for example, in the case of a register of a consulate or an international centralized register.[60] **37**

A "**public register**" within the meaning of Art 2 (g) of the EIR does not necessarily have to be kept by a public authority. It must be accessible to the public and the registration in it must have an effect on third parties.[61] **38**

8.3 Claims

Claims are presumed to be situated in that State in whose territory the party with the performance obligation (and not the insolvency debtor) has his centre of main interests as per Art 3 (1) of the EIR.[62] **39**

The term **claim** is not to be understood as the entire (contractual) obligation or the indebtedness arising from it, but simply the debt claim against the third party debtor.[63] **40**

---

[53] *Virgós/Schmit* Explanatory Report mn 69.

[54] D-K/D/Ch-*Duursma-Kepplinger* Art 2 mn 16.

[55] *Paulus* Komm EuInsVO Art 2 mn 18.

[56] *Paulus* Komm EuInsVO Art 2 mn 18.

[57] *Paulus* Komm EuInsVO Art 2 mn 18.

[58] *Virgós/Schmit* Explanatory Report mn 69.

[59] *Virgós/Schmit* Explanatory Report mn 69; D-K/D/Ch-*Duursma-Kepplinger* Art 2 mn 16.

[60] *Virgós/Schmit* Explanatory Report mn 69.

[61] *Virgós/Schmit* Explanatory Report mn 69.

[62] *Virgós/Schmit* Explanatory Report mn 69.

[63] D-K/D/Ch-*Duursma-Kepplinger* Art 2 mn 16; *Smid* Komm EuInsVO Art 2 mn 20.

For the localization of claims and the ascertainment of the COMI, reference can therefore be made to the submissions on Art 3 of the EIR. If the COMI of the third party debtor is located outside the scope of the Regulation's application (e.g. in Switzerland), then the Regulation does not apply; instead, the autonomous international insolvency law is to apply.[64]

41 The definition in Art 2 (g) of the EIR does not distinguish between certificated and uncertificated debt claims: claim entitlements arising from bearer securities, bills of exchange, and other negotiable instruments are included, but interests in corporate entities are not.[65]

8.4 Diverse Assets

42 Art 2 (g) of the EIR says nothing about those assets that are not mentioned in it. Copyrights or more general kinds of intangible property, for example, cannot be classified in one of the three categories[66] unless they are registered in a public register (then Art 2 (g) 2nd dash of the EIR applies).

43 One possible solution would be to deem the *situs* of strictly personal (nontransferable) rights as being there where the legal holder is located, and the *situs* of other rights as being there where the legal object in which the right exists is located.[67]

44 Certain kinds of property, for instance **software** or **legal interests and membership rights**, will still be difficult to localize:

- If the software is not stored on a data carrier, then the location of the computer will have to be determinative.[68]
- In the case of legal interests and membership rights, it can be assumed that these are situated at the COMI of the company regardless of whether they are evidenced in a document or not.[69]

9. Art 2 (h) of the EIR – "establishment"

9.1 General

45 The term **"establishment"** is defined in Art 2 (h) of the EIR. This term is central to the application of the entire Regulation since, pursuant to Art 3 (2) of the EIR, the opening of territorial insolvency proceedings is conditioned on the existence of an establishment.[70]

46 The definition of establishment was the subject of intensive **controversial** debate from the very beginning.[71] Central to the debate was whether secondary insolvency proceedings could be opened based solely on the existence of assets, or whether the debtor should have to have an establishment.[72] The broad definition adopted by Art 2 (h) of the

---

64 *Paulus* Komm EuInsVO Art 2 mn 23.

65 Haß/Huber/Gruber/Heiderhoff-*Huber* Art 2 EuInsVO mn 6; MünchKomm InsO/*Reinhart* Art 2 EuInsVO mn 4.

66 *Paulus* Komm EuInsVO Art 2 mn 25.

67 *Paulus* Komm EuInsVO Art 2 mn 25.

68 *Paulus* Komm EuInsVO Art 2 mn 26.

69 *Paulus* Komm EuInsVO Art 2 mn 26; contra MünchKomm InsO/*Reinhart* Art 2 EuInsVO mn 4: situation at the domicile of the company.

70 D-K/D/Ch-*Duursma-Kepplinger* Art 2 mn 21; *Smid* Komm EuInsVO Art 2 mn 21; Münch Komm InsO/*Reinhart* Art 2 EuInsVO mn 5; Moss/Fletcher/Isaacs-*Moss/Smith*, Regulation, mn 8.25.

71 *Virgós/Schmit* Explanatory Report mn 70.

72 *Virgós/Schmit* Explanatory Report mn 70; cf also *Ehricke* EWS 2002, 101, 104; *Huber* ZZP 114 (2001), 133, 142; *Lüke* ZZP 111 (1998), 275, 299.

EIR is therefore a compromise: the mere existence of assets (e.g. a **bank account**[73]) does not constitute an establishment, which means that territorial proceedings cannot be opened.[74] In other words, there is no jurisdiction for the assets on their own.[75] As a result of this compromise, the term establishment was given an even broader definition than it had been in the 1968 Brussels Convention for example.[76]

The term "establishment" as per Art 2 (h) of the EIR must be **distinguished** from that **47**
used in Art 5 (5) of the **1968 Brussels Convention** (respectively **Council Regulation** (EC) **No 44/2001**). In the deliberations on the 1995 Draft convention on insolvency proceedings, the adoption of the concept of establishment as used in the 1968 Brussels Convention and as construed by the ECJ was explicitly rejected, there being a fear of an excessively restrictive interpretation of the concept of establishment.[77] The result of this would have been that territorial proceedings could only seldom be opened.[78] The ECJ interpreted the term "establishment" in Art 5 (5) of the 1968 Brussels Convention as being the centre of business activities that clearly operates on a permanent basis as a branch establishment of a parent company, that has a management body, and that is legally equipped (authorized) to transact with third parties in such a way that these parties, although they know that a legal relationship is likely being established with the parent company in a foreign country, do not have to turn to the parent company but are entitled to conclude transactions at this centre of business activities, this being the parent company's branch establishment.[79] A subsidiary was also regarded as an establishment (within the meaning of the 1968 Brussels Convention) of its parent company. The ECJ (in the **SAR Schotte/ Parfums Rothschild** case) regarded a subsidiary company as an establishment within the meaning of Art 5 (5) of the 1968 Brussels Convention.[80] The concept of establishment as understood by Art 5 (5) of the 1968 Brussels Convention would collide with the general jurisdiction provisions in Art 3 of the EIR, which considers each company an independent legal entity.[81] The ECJ ruling in SAR Schotte/Parfums Rothschild cannot be used for interpreting the term establishment within the scope of application of the Regulation.[82]

The concept of establishment in the Regulation is completely independent of that **48**
found in Art 5 (5) of the 1968 Brussels Convention and of the definitions found in various national laws. Hence it must be interpreted **independent from national laws.**[83]

Underlying the definition of establishment in Art 2 (h) of the EIR is the idea that the **49**
same insolvency laws that apply to national market participants should also apply to foreign business participants who operate a national establishment since both are operating on the same market.[84] For assessing their risks, it is therefore irrelevant for potential creditors whether an establishment is dependent on a national or on a foreign enterprise.[85]

---

[73] *Pannen* in Runkel (ed), AHB-Insolvenzrecht (2005) § 16 mn 114.

[74] *Virgós/Schmit* Explanatory Report mn 70.

[75] D-K/D/Ch-*Duursma-Kepplinger* Art 2 mn 22.

[76] *Virgós/Schmit* Explanatory Report mn 70; *Carstens* Die internationale Zuständigkeit im europäischen Insolvenzrecht, p 73; *Lüke* ZZP 111 (1998), 275, 299.

[77] *Virgós/Schmit* Explanatory Report mn 70; D-K/D/Ch-*Duursma-Kepplinger* Art 2 mn 23.

[78] *Virgós/Schmit* Explanatory Report mn 70.

[79] ECJ of 22 Jan 1978 – 33/78 (*Somafer/Saarferngas*) RIW 1979, 56.

[80] ECJ of 9 Dec 1987 – 218/86 (*Schotte/Parfums Rothschild*).

[81] Moss/Fletcher/Isaacs-*Moss/Smith*, Regulation, mn 8.31.

[82] *Ehricke* EWS 2002, 101, 106.

[83] *Carstens* Die internationale Zuständigkeit im europäischen Insolvenzrecht, p 73; *Ehricke* EWS 2002, 101, 104; *Smid* Komm EuInsVO Art 2 mn 21.

[84] *Virgós/Schmit* Explanatory Report mn 71.

[85] *Virgós/Schmit* Explanatory Report mn 70.

9.2 Elements of the Provision

50 **An establishment is a**

- **place of operations where the debtor carries out an economic activity**
- **that is non-transitory**
- **with human means and goods.**

9.2.1 Place of operations

51 The **place of operations** denotes a place at which **economic activities** are being carried out on the open market. The Regulation thus distinguishes this from the mere existence of assets, which was not politically enforceable as a connecting factor for the opening of territorial proceedings (see mn 46 above).[86] The mere existence of assets (e.g. **bank account** or **securities**) does not suffice for a finding of an establishment.[87]

52 The activities may be of a

- commercial,
- industrial,
- self-employed, or
- non-commercial nature.[88]

The activity need not be geared to **profit making.**[89]

53 A **large construction site** (if the project management utilizes machines and employs persons on a permanent basis and a certain degree of organization can be determined),[90] **doctors' medical practices, law firms,** and **warehouses** for example can be classified as establishments.[91]

54 The fact that a debtor stores goods in the warehouse of a third party will not suffice.[92]

9.2.2 Non-transitory nature

55 The economic activity of the debtor must not be of mere transitory nature. A certain degree of **permanence** is therefore required.[93] The legislators did not stipulate a minimum time period.[94] It depends on the circumstances in the individual case. Decisive is whether the place of operations, in terms of the legal relations involved, is not of a mere transitory nature; the personal intentions of the debtor are not determinative.[95]

---

86 *Carstens* Die internationale Zuständigkeit im europäischen Insolvenzrecht, p 74.

87 *Carstens* Die internationale Zuständigkeit im europäischen Insolvenzrecht, p 76.

88 *Carstens* Die internationale Zuständigkeit im europäischen Insolvenzrecht, p 74; *Virgós/Schmit* Explanatory Report mn 71; *Smid* Komm EuInsVO Art 2 mn 22.

89 *Lüke* ZZP 111 (1998), 275, 299.

90 *Carstens* Die internationale Zuständigkeit im europäischen Insolvenzrecht, p 77.

91 *Smid* Komm EuInsVO Art 2 mn 22; Moss/Fletcher/Isaacs-*Moss/Smith*, Regulation, mn 8.27; *Paulus* Komm EuInsVO Art 2 mn 36.

92 Moss/Fletcher/Isaacs-*Moss/Smith*, Regulation, mn 8.27.

93 *Carstens* Die internationale Zuständigkeit im europäischen Insolvenzrecht, p 74.

94 *Virgós/Schmit* Explanatory Report mn 71.

95 *Carstens* Die internationale Zuständigkeit im europäischen Insolvenzrecht, p 75.

9.2.3 Utilization of human means and goods

The requirement that human means and goods must be utilized means, in effect, that a minimum amount of organization must be present. [96] Both human means and goods must be utilized, i.e. the requirements are **cumulative.**[97] **56**

Sole distributors, commercial agents, or commercial brokers are not establishments within the meaning of Art 2 (h) of the EIR since they generally act independent of the debtor.[98] **57**

The German word *"Personal"* (staff/employees) means that persons must be engaged for whom the debtor is responsible, either as an employer or as a principal.[99] **58**

Example of the requirement of utilizing human means **59**

It does not suffice for a finding of an establishment that the owner of a summer residence keeps a current (drawing) bank account in the same Member State (which could be considered an economic activity). What is missing in this situation is a personal, active activity, and therefore the existence of an establishment must be rejected.[100] This is different, however, if a caretaker or a gardener were being engaged.[101]

Other examples:

- In the **Werlin** case (→ cf Table of Cases Art 3 of the EIR Appendix B No 8), the *situs* of an establishment of a company registered in England was considered to be in Belgium. The court held that the economic activities carried out by the company in Belgium were sufficient to affirm the existence of an establishment.
- In the **Pittagold case** (→ cf Table of Cases Art 3 of the EIR Appendix B No 11), business activities also carried out in Belgium by a company registered in England were deemed sufficient for the finding of an establishment.
- In the **Conception Enterprises Ltd.** case (→ cf Table of Cases Art 3 of the EIR Appendix B No 16), the court had to decide whether to open proceedings in respect of a debtor resident in Great Britain and registered in Dover/Kent; the debtor had an establishment in Belgium. The Belgian court opened a territorially restricted proceeding. The court relied on the fact that an establishment had been opened and registered in Belgium, and that this establishment also had a representative in Belgium. The Belgian court nevertheless admitted that the Belgian branch establishment was nothing more than a **"mailbox"**.
- In the case **Procureur des Konings v BVHE** (→ cf Table of Cases Art 3 of the EIR Appendix B No 17), business activities carried out in Belgium by the Belgian subsidiary of a Dutch parent company were deemed sufficient for the finding of an establish-

---

96 *Virgós/Schmit* Explanatory Report mn 71; *Smid* Komm EuInsVO Art 2 mn 22.

97 *Paulus* Komm EuInsVO Art 2 mn 29; *Carstens* Die internationale Zuständigkeit im europäischen Insolvenzrecht, p 75.

98 Münch Komm InsO/*Reinhart* Art 2 EuInsVO mn 5; *Pannen* in Runkel (ed), AHB-Insolvenzrecht (2005) § 16 mn 114.

99 Moss/Fletcher/Isaacs-*Moss/Smith*, Regulation, mn 8.29.

100 Moss/Fletcher/Isaacs-*Moss/Smith*, Regulation, mn 8.31.

101 *Carstens* Die internationale Zuständigkeit im europäischen Insolvenzrecht, p 77.

ment even though the COMI of the subsidiary was in the Netherlands and main insolvency proceedings had not been opened there.

- In the **Crisscoss Telecommunications** case (→ cf Table of Cases Art 3 of the EIR Appendix A mn 6), the Italian court held that the head office in Italy of Crisscross Telecommunications Italy S.r.l. was not an establishment within the meaning of Art 2 (h) of the EIR. The court held that this characteristic could not be attributed to a head office that was merely registered at the registered office of the statutory auditors, who themselves first became aware of their actual legal incapacity with the opening of the insolvency proceedings.
- In the **Hans Brochier Holdings Ltd** case (→ cf Table of Cases Art 3 of the EIR Appendix B No 101), the English court refused to find in favour of an establishment of the debtor in England. This was a "mailbox company" that operated in Germany although its registered office was in England.
- In the **BenQ Mobile Holding B.V.** case (→ cf Table of Cases Art 3 of the EIR Appendix B No 102), the court concluded that the debtor maintained an establishment in Germany, giving the following reasons for this:
  - The debtor was carrying on economic activities that were not merely transitory.
  - Business decisions of the debtor were being prepared and implemented from Munich.
  - A certain degree of permanence was intended for the economic activity.
  - The economic activity was directed to the outside world and ascertainable by third parties.
  - The economic activity was effected using human means and goods.

  The court also held that the definition of establishment in Art 2 (h) of the EIR contained no indication that the utilization of human means is restricted to one's own employees nor that it may not be performed by other persons, for example on an order/commission basis or on the basis of business management contracts.

9.3 Insolvencies of Corporate Groups / Subsidiaries

60 A **subsidiary** cannot be classified as an establishment of its parent company within the meaning of Art 2 (h) of the EIR.[102]

61 Were the debtor's subsidiary regarded as its establishment, then secondary insolvency proceedings could be opened in the State concerned. The advantage here would be a coordination between the main and secondary insolvency proceedings, particularly via the **cooperation and communication duties** pursuant to Art 31 of the EIR.[103]

62 The wording of Art 2 (h) of the EIR does not *a priori* preclude the conclusion that a subsidiary can be an establishment if the requirements of Art 2 (h) have been fulfilled. This is because no inference can be drawn directly from the definition that an establishment cannot be an independent legal subject.

63 However, the consequences of classifying a subsidiary as an establishment are far more extensive than the benefits brought about by a better coordination of the insolvency proceedings. Such a classification would result, namely, in the consolidation of the

---

[102] *Ehricke* EWS 2002, 101, 104; *Vallender* KTS 2005, 283, 303; *Gottwald* Grenzüberschreitende Insolvenzen, p 21 et seq; *Smid* Komm EuInsVO Art 2 mn 23; *Pannen* in Runkel (ed), AHB-Insolvenzrecht (2005) § 16 mn 114.

[103] *Ehricke* EWS 2002, 101, 104.

various insolvency estates. According to the systematic of the Regulation, the main and secondary insolvency proceedings actually involve one debtor only even though – for practical reasons – the insolvency estates are administered separately for the duration of the secondary insolvency proceedings. This is clearly illustrated by Art 35 of the EIR, which provides that any assets remaining in the secondary insolvency proceedings must be transferred to the liquidator in the main insolvency proceedings. The same holds true for the equalization of dividends contemplated by Art 20 (2) of the EIR, which is illustrative of the unified nature of the insolvency estates.

A consolidation of the insolvency estates of various separate legal subjects would also be contrary to the systematic underlying the Regulation. According to the ECJ in the **Eurofood/Parmalat** case, it follows from the Regulation's system of determining jurisdiction that independent judicial competence exists for every debtor that is an independent entity.[104] The COMI must therefore be ascertained independently for each legal subject or company in a corporate group.[105] **64**

- In the **Telia v Hillcourt** case (→ cf Table of Cases Art 3 of the EIR Appendix B No 7), the court refused to qualify the English subsidiary of a Swedish parent company as an establishment of the parent company, the reason being that each company in the group must be treated as a separate legal entity. There was therefore no "establishment" in England.

The implementation of a corporate insolvency by classifying one subsidiary as an establishment would also contradict the intentions of the drafters of the Regulation, which was to consciously refrain from regulating the issue of insolvencies of corporate groups.[106] This intention is clearly demonstrated by the fact that the Member States expressly rejected the concept of establishment found in Art 5 (5) of the 1968 Brussels Convention – which allows a subsidiary to be classified as an establishment – and replaced this with a new, independent concept. **65**

For these reasons, a subsidiary cannot constitute an establishment. Prevailing academic opinion also holds that independent companies cannot be classified as establishments within the meaning of Art 2 (h) of the EIR.[107] This also applies to subsidiaries that are fully controlled by their parent company.[108] Such control does nothing to change the submissions made above. **66**

The interests held by a parent company in its subsidiary are, however, to be allocated to the main insolvency proceedings.[109] But since they only represent a part of the assets, secondary insolvency proceedings cannot be opened in relation to these. **67**

Secondary insolvency proceedings may, however, be opened in certain situations in respect of a subsidiary. If the COMI of a subsidiary is held to be situated at the register- **68**

---

[104] ECJ of 2 May 2006 – C-341/04 (Eurofood IFSC Ltd), NZI 2006, 360 et seq Nr 30. (→ cf Table of Cases Art 3 of the EIR Appendix A mn 10 – Eurofood/Parmalat).

[105] *Virgós/Schmit* Explanatory Report mn 76; *Smid* Komm EuInsVO Art 2 mn 23.

[106] *Virgós/Schmit* Explanatory Report mn 76; *Carstens* Die internationale Zuständigkeit im internationalen Insolvenzrecht, p 78; *Pannen* in Runkel (ed), AHB-Insolvenzrecht (2005) § 16 mn 114 fn 13.

[107] D-K/D/Ch-*Duursma-Kepplinger* Art 2 mn 29; *Gottwald* Grenzüberschreitende Insolvenzen, p 21 et seq; *Huber* ZZP 114 (2001), 133, 142; *Pannen* in Runkel (ed), AHB-Insolvenzrecht (2005) § 16 mn 114; *Vallender* KTS 2005, 283, 303. **Contra** *Paulus* NZI 2001, 505, 509; *Paulus* Komm EuInsVO Art 2 mn 34.

[108] D-K/D/Ch-*Duursma-Kepplinger* Art 2 mn 29.

[109] D-K/D/Ch-*Duursma-Kepplinger* Art 27 mn 27.

ed office of its parent company in another Member State (e.g. **ISA/Daisytek**, → cf Table of Cases Art 3 of the EIR Appendix A mn 15) and **MG Rover** (→ cf Table of Cases Art 3 of the EIR Appendix A mn 16), then secondary insolvency proceedings may be opened against the assets of the subsidiary at its place of operations provided that the definition of establishment has been complied with.[110] This provides better protection for any existing local creditors as local laws would then govern the distribution of the insolvency estate.[111]

69 According to the *AG* **Cologne** (**"Automold"**, → cf Table of Cases Art 3 of the EIR Appendix A mn 2),[112] the **head office**, in particular, can also be classified as an **establishment.**[113]

Article 3
International jurisdiction

(1) The courts of the Member State within the territory of which the centre of a debtor's main interests is situated shall have jurisdiction to open insolvency proceedings. In the case of a company or legal person, the place of the registered office shall be presumed to be the centre of its main interests in the absence of proof to the contrary.

(2) Where the centre of a debtor's main interests is situated within the territory of a Member State, the courts of another Member State shall have jurisdiction to open insolvency proceedings against that debtor only if he possesses an establishment within the territory of that other Member State. The effects of those proceedings shall be restricted to the assets of the debtor situated in the territory of the latter Member State.

(3) Where insolvency proceedings have been opened under paragraph 1, any proceedings opened subsequently under paragraph 2 shall be secondary proceedings. These latter proceedings must be winding-up proceedings.

(4) Territorial insolvency proceedings referred to in paragraph 2 may be opened prior to the opening of main insolvency proceedings in accordance with paragraph 1 only:

a) where insolvency proceedings under paragraph 1 cannot be opened because of the conditions laid down by the law of the Member State within the territory of which the centre of the debtor's main interests is situated; or

b) where the opening of territorial insolvency proceedings is requested by a creditor who has his domicile, habitual residence or registered office in the Member State within the territory of which the establishment is situated, or whose claim arises from the operation of that establishment.

---

110 So *Paulus* Komm EuInsVO Art 2 mn 36; *Dammann* Dalloz 2006, 1752, 1757; *Dammann/Podeur* Banque & Droit 2006 (109), 3, 4.

111 *Dammann* Dalloz 2006, 1752, 1757; *Dammann/Podeur* Banque & Droit 2006 (109), 3, 4.

112 AG Cologne dated 23 Jan 2004 – 71 IN 1/04, NZI 2004, 151.

113 On this, see also: *Vallender* KTS 2005, 283, 303; *Sabel* NZI 2004, 126 et seq.

Contents

Index

Bibliography

Baetge Zum gewöhnlichen Aufenthalt bei Kindesentführung, IPRax 2001, p 573; *Bähr/Riedemann* Comments on AG Mönchengladbach of 27.4.2004 – 19 IN 54/04, ZIP 2004, p 1066; *Balz* Das neue Europäische Insolvenzübereinkommen, ZIP 1996, p 948; *Baxter* Eurofood ECJ Decision – Guidelines on COMI, INSOL World – Third Quarter 2006, p 9; *Breutigam/Blersch/Goetsch/Haas* Insolvenzrecht, Berliner Kommentar (01/2006); *Borges* Gläubigerschutz bei ausländischen Gesellschaften mit inländischem Sitz, ZIP 2004, p 733; *Bork* Handbuch des Insolvenzanfechtungsrechts (2006); *Bormann* Chronik der Rechtsentwicklung: Rumänien, WiRO 2006, p 29; *Brenner* Comments on AG Hamburg of 14.5.2003 – 67g IN 358/02, EWiR 2003, p 925; *Bufford* International Insolvency Case Venue in The European Union: The Parmalat and Daisytek Controversies, The Columbia Journal of European Law Vol. 12 No. 2 2006, p 429; *Carstens* Die Internationale Zuständigkeit im europäischen Insolvenzrecht (2005); *Correnti* Einführung in das italienische Insolvenzrecht und seine Reform, ZInsO 2006, p 1020; *Costa* Die Reform des italienischen Insolvenzrechts, ZInsO 2006, p 1071; *Csia/Martinez Ferber* Comments on Municipality Court Fejer/ Székesfehérvár (Hungary) of 14.6.2004 – 9. Fpk. 01-04-0029116/2, ZInsO 2004, p 861; *Dammann* Vers une interprétation pragmatique du règlement européen des faillites, Revue banque Juin 2006 N° 681 p 47; *Dammann* L'application du règlement CE n° 1346-2000 après les arrêts Staubitz-Schreiber et Eurofood de la CJCE, Dalloz 2006, p 1752; *Dammann/Podeur* L'affaire Daisytek: l'épilogue. Application par la Cour de cassation du règlement européen relatif aux procédures d'insolvabilité, Banque & Droit N° 109 September–October 2006, p 3; *Dammann* L'affaire *Eurotunnel*, première application du règlement CE n° 1346-2000 à la procédure de sauvegarde, Dalloz 2006, p 2329; *Dicey/Morris/Morse* Conflict of Laws: Fourth Cumulative Supplement (1991); *Duursma/ Duursma-Kepplinger* Gegensteuerungsmaßnahmen bei ungerechtfertigter Inanspruchnahme der internationalen Zuständigkeit gemäß Art 3 Abs 1 EuInsVO, DZWiR 2003, p 447; *Duursma/Duursma-Kepplinger* Der Anwendungsbereich der Insolvenzverordnung, IPRax 2003, p 505; *Duursma-Kepplinger/Duursma/Chalupsky* Europäische Insolvenzverordnung, Kommentar (2002); *Duursma-Kepplinger* Aktuelle Entwicklungen zur internationalen Zuständigkeit für Hauptinsolvenzverfahren – Erkenntnisse aus Staubitz-Schreiber und Eurofood, ZIP 2007, p 896; *Ehricke* Die neue Europäische Insolvenzverordnung und grenzüberschreitende Konzerninsolvenzen, EWS 2002, p 101; *Ehricke/ Ries* Die neue Europäische Insolvenzverordnung, JuS 2003, p 313; *Eidenmüller* Europäische Verordnung über Insolvenzverfahren und zukünftiges deutsches internationales Insolvenzrecht, IPRax 2001, p 2; *Eidenmüller* Der Markt für internationale Konzerninsolvenzen: Zuständigkeitskonflikte unter der EuInsVO, NJW 2004, p 3455; *Emmerich/Sonnenschein* Konzernrecht, 6th edn (1997); *Haß/Huber/Gruber/Heiderhoff* EU-Insolvenzverordnung, Kommentar (2005); *Fletcher* Law of Insolvency (2002); *Fletcher* Insolvency in Private International Law (2005); *Gottwald* Grenzüberschreitende Insolvenzen (1997); *Gottwald* Insolvenzrechts-Handbuch (2003); Hamburger Kommentar zum Insolvenzrecht (2006) (ed *Schmidt, A.*); *Hanisch* Stellungnahme zur Frage, ob und gegebenenfalls in welcher Weise ein in seiner Wirkung territorial beschränktes Sonderinsolvenzverfahren über das Inlandsvermögen eines Schuldners vorzusehen ist, wenn dieser den Mittelpunkt seiner hauptsächlichen Interessen im Ausland hat, in Stoll (ed), Vorschläge und Gutachten (1997), p 202; *Haubold* Europäisches Zivilverfahrensrecht und Ansprüche im Zusammenhang mit Insolvenzverfahren, IPRax 2002, p 157; *Haubold* Mitgliedstaatenbezug, Zuständigkeitserschleichung und Vermögensgerichtsstand im Internationalen Insolvenzrecht, IPRax 2003, p 34; Heidelberger Kommentar zur Insolvenzordnung, 4th edn (2006) (eds *Eickmann/Flessner/Irschlinger/Kirchhof/Kreft/Landfermann/Marotzke/Stephan*); *Herchen* Scheinauslandsgesellschaften im Anwendungsbereich der Europäischen Insolvenzverordnung, ZInsO 2003, p 742; *Herchen* International-Insolvenzrechtliche Kompetenzkonflikte in der Europäischen Gemeinschaft, ZInsO 2004, p 61; *Herchen* Aktuelle Entwicklungen im Recht der internationalen Zuständigkeit zur Eröffnung von Insolvenzverfahren: Der Mittelpunkt der (hauptsächlichen) Interessen im Mittelpunkt der Interessen, ZInsO 2004, p 825; *Herchen* Das Prioritätsprinzip im internationalen Insolvenzrecht, ZIP 2005, p 1401; *Herchen* Wer zuerst kommt, mahlt zuerst!, NZI 2006, p 435; *Herweg/Tschauner* Comments on AG Düsseldorf of 12.3.2004 – 502 IN 126/03, EWiR 2004, p 495; *Herweg/Tschauner* Comments on High Court Dublin (Justice Kelly) of 23.3.2004 – 33/04, EWiR 2004, p 599; *Herweg/Tschauner* Comments on AG Hamburg of 1.12.2005 – 67a IN 450/05, EWiR 2006, p 169; *Hess/Laukemann/Seagon* Europäisches Insolvenzrecht nach Eurofood: Methodische Standortsbestimmung und praktische Schlussfolgerungen, IPRax 2007, p 89; *Hinkel* Comments on OLG Frankfurt of 26.1.2006 – 15 U 200/05 –, ZIP 2006, p 769; *Hinkel/Flitsch* Comments on OLG Frankfurt of 26.1.2006 – 15 U 200/05 –, EWiR 2006, p 237; *Hirte/Bücker* Grenzüberschreitende Gesellschaften – Praxishandbuch für ausländische Gesellschaften mit Sitz im Inland, 2nd edn (2006); *Huber* Internationales Insolvenzrecht in Europa, ZZP 114 (2001), p 133; *Huber* Die Europäische Insolvenzverordnung, EuZW 2002, p 490; *Huber* Der deutsch-englische Justizkonflikt – Kompetenzkonflikte im internationalen Insolvenzrecht, in Lorenz/Trunk/Eidenmüller/Wendehorst/Adolff (eds), Festschrift für Heldrich (2005), p 679; *Israël* European Cross-Border Insolvency Regulation (2005); *Jahn* Insolvenzen in Europa, 4th edn (2004); *Kammel* Die Bestimmung der zuständigen Gerichte bei grenzüberschreitenden Konzerninsolvenzen, NZI 2006, p 334; *Kindler* Sitzverlegung und internationales Insolvenzrecht, IPRax 2006, p 144; *Klöhn* Statische oder formale Lebenssachverhalte als "Interessen" iS des Art 3 I 1 EuInsVO? – Zum Mittelpunkt der hauptsächlichen Interessen einer im Ausland gegründeten Gesellschaft bei Einstellung ihrer werbenden Tätigkeit im Inland, NZI 2006, p 383; *Klöhn* Verlegung des Mittelpunkts der hauptsächlichen Interessen iSd Art 3 Abs 1 S 1 EuInsVO vor Stellung des Insolvenzantrags, KTS 2006, p 259; *Knof* Europäisches Insolvenzrecht und Schuldbefreiungs-Tourismus, ZInsO 2005, p 1017; *Knof/Mock* Comments on ECJ dated 17.1.2006 – C-1/04, ZIP 2006, p 189; Kodek Comments on AG Nürnberg dated 1.10.2006 – 8034 IN 1326/06, EWiR 2007, p 179; *Krebber* Europäische Insolvenzverordnung, Drittstaatengesellschaften, Drittstaatensachverhalte und innergemeinschaftliche Konflikte, IPRax 2004, p 540; *Kropholler* Europäisches Zivilprozessrecht: Kommentar zu EuGVÜ und Lugano-Übereinkommen, 6th edn (1998); *Kübler* Mittelpunkt der hauptsächlichen Interessen nach Art 3 Abs 1 EuInsVO, in Schilken/Kreft/Wagner/Eckhardt (ed) Festschrift Gerhardt (2004), p 527; *Kübler/Prütting* Kommentar zur Insolvenzordnung (March 2006); *Laukemann* Rechtshängigkeit im europäischen Insolvenzrecht, RIW 2005, p 104; *Lautenbach* Comments on AG Mönchengladbach dated 27.4.2004 – 19 IN 54/04, NZI 2004, p 384; *Leible/Staudinger* Die europäische Verordnung über Insolvenzverfahren, KTS 2000, p 533; *Leipold* Zuständigkeitslücken im neuen Insolvenzrecht, in Lüke/Mikami/Prütting (eds) Festschrift Ishikawa (2001), p 221; *Liersch* Comments on BGH dated 27.11.2003 – IX ZB 418/02, NZI 2004, p 141; *Liersch* Comments on AG Düsseldorf dated 12.3.2004 – 2004 502 IN 126/03, NZI 2004, p 271; *Liersch* Nach der Eurofood-Entscheidung des EuGH: Genugtuung, aber auch viel Nachdenklichkeit, NZI 6/2006, p V; *Lüke* Europäisches Zivilverfahrensrecht – das Problem der Abstimmung zwischen EuInsÜ und EuGVÜ, in Geimer (ed) Festschrift Schütze (1999); *Mankowski* EuGVÜ-Gerichtsstand für Gesellschafterhaftungsklage des Insolvenzverwalters, NZI 1999, p 56; *Mankowski* Comments on AG Düsseldorf dated 6.6.2003, EWiR 2003, p 767; *Mankowski* Comments on CA (Cour d'appel) Versailles dated 4.9.2003 – 05038/03, EWiR 2003, p 1239; *Mankowski* Comments on AG München dated 4.5.2004 – 1501 IE 1276/04, NZI 2004, p 450; *Mankowski* Grenzüberschreitender Umzug und das center of main interests im europäischen Internationalen Insolvenzrecht, NZI 2005, p 368; *Mankowski* Entwicklung im Internationalen Privat- und Prozessrecht 2004/2005 (Teil 2), RIW 2005, p 561; *Mankowski* Comments on High Court of Justice, Chancery Division, Birmingham dated 18.4.2005 – 2375-2382/05, EWiR 2005, p 637; *Mankowski* Comments on Court of Appeal (Civil Division), dated 27.7.2005 – [2005] EWCA Civ 974, NZI 2005, p 575; *Mankowski* Comments on AG Cologne dated 1.12.2005 – 71 IN 564/05, EWiR 2006, p 109; *Mankowski* Klärung von Grundfragen des europäischen Internationalen Insolvenzrechts durch die Eurofood – Entscheidung?, BB 2006, p 1753; *Marshall* European Cross Border Insolvency (May 2007); *Martinez Ferber* European Insolvency Regulation – Substantive Consolidation, The Threat of Forum Shopping and a German Point of View (2004); *Meyer-Löwy/Poertzgen* Eigenverwaltung (§§ 270 ff InsO) löst Kompetenzkonflikt nach EuInsVO, ZInsO 2004, p 195; *Meyer-Löwy/Plank* Entbehrlichkeit des Sekundärinsolvenzverfahrens bei flexibler Verteilung der Insolvenzmasse im Hauptinsolvenzverfahren, NZI 2006, p 622; *Mörsdorf-Schulte* Internationaler Gerichtsstand für Insolvenzanfechtungsklagen im Spannungsfeld von EuInsVO, EuGVÜ/VO und autonomem Recht und seine Überprüfbarkeit durch den BGH, IPRax 2004, p 31; *Morscher* Die europäische Insolvenzverordnung (2002); *Moss/Fletcher/Isaacs* (eds) The EC Regulation on Insolvency Proceedings (2002); Münchener Kommentar zum Bürgerlichen Gesetzbuch, vol 11 (2006); Münchener Kommentar zur Insolvenzordnung, vol 1 (2001); Münchener Kommentar zur Insolvenzordnung, vol 3 (2003); *Oberhammer* Europäisches Insolvenzrecht in praxi – "Was bisher geschah", ZInsO 2004, p 761; *Pannen* Krise und Insolvenz bei Kreditinstituten, 2nd edn (2006); *Pannen/Riedemann* Die deutschen Ausführungsbestimmungen zur EuInsVO – Ein Überblick zu den Regelungen des Art 102 EGInsO nF, NZI 2004, p 301; *Pannen/Riedemann* Der Begriff des "centre of main interests" iSd Art 3 I 1 EuInsVO im Spiegel aktueller Fälle der Rechtsprechung, NZI 2004, p 646; *Pannen/Riedemann* Comments on AG Offenburg dated 2.8.2004 – 2 IN 133/04, EWiR 2005, p 73; *Pannen/Riedemann* Comments on the Opinion of Advocate General Francis Geoffrey Jacobs dated 27.9.2005 – C-341/04, EWiR 2005, p 725; *Pannen/Riedemann* Comments on AG Weilheim i. OB dated 22.6.2005 – IN 260/05, EWiR 2005, p 791; *Pannen/Riedemann/Kühnle* Zur Stellung der Insolvenzgläubiger nach der Europäischen Verordnung über Insolvenzverfahren (EuInsVO), NZI 2002, p 303; *Paulus* "Protokolle" – ein anderer Zugang zur Abwicklung grenzüberschreitender Insolvenzen, ZIP 1998, p 977; *Paulus* Die Europäische Insolvenzverordnung und der deutsche Insolvenzverwalter, NZI 2001, p 505; *Paulus* Zuständigkeitsfragen nach der Europäischen Insolvenzverordnung, ZIP 2003, p 1725; *Paulus* Comments on AG Munich dated 4.5.2004 – 1501 IE 1276/04, EWiR 2004, p 493; *Paulus* Europäische Insolvenzverordnung, Kommentar (2006); *Paulus* Überlegungen zu einem modernen Konzerninsolvenzrecht, ZIP 2005, p 1948; *Paulus* Comments on Landesgericht Leoben of 31.8.2005 – 17 S 56/05, NZI 2005, p 647; *Paulus* Anfechtungsklagen in grenzüberschreitenden Insolvenzverfahren, ZInsO 2006, p 295; *Paulus* NZI aktuell 2006, Heft 8, VII; *Paulus* Der EuGH und das moderne Insolvenzrecht, NZG 2006, p 609; *Pellens/Jödicke/Richard* Solvenztests als Alternative zur bilanziellen Kapitalerhaltung, DB 2005, p 1393; *Penzlin* Comments on Tribunal de Commerce de Nanterre of 15.2.2006, EWiR 2006, p 207; *Penzlin/Riedemann* Comments on High Court of Justice Birmingham of 18.4.2005 – 2375 to 2382/05, NZI 2005, p 469; *Poertzgen/Adam* Die Bestimmung des "centre of main interests" gem Art 3 Abs 1 EuInsVO, ZInsO 2006, p 505; *Riedemann* Auseinanderfallen von Gesellschafts- und Insolvenzstatut. "Inspire Art" und die Insolvenz über das Vermögen einer englischen "limited" in Deutschland, GmbHR 2004, p 345; *Ringe* Insolvenzanfechtungsklage im System des europäischen Zivilverfahrensrechts – zugleich Anmerkung zu OLG Frankfurt, Urt v 26.1.2006 – 15 U 200/05, ZInsO 2006, p 700; *Runkel* (ed), Anwaltshandbuch – Insolvenzrecht (2005); *Sabel* Hauptsitz als Niederlassung im Sinne der EuInsVO?, NZI 2004, p 126; *Sabel/Schlegel* Comments on High Court of Justice Chancery Division Companies Court (England) of 7.2.2003 – 0042/2003, EWiR 2003, p 367; *Saenger/Klockenbrink* Anerkennungsfragen im internationalen Insolvenzrecht gelöst? – Zugleich Anmerkung zum Urteil des EuGH v 2.5.2006 – Rs C-341/04 (Eurofood/Parmalat), EuZW 2006, p 621; *Saenger/Klockenbrink* Neue Grenzen für ein forum shopping des Insolvenzschuldners? DZWiR 2006, p 183; *Schelo* Konzerninsolvenz – Alles in einen „Topf"?, NZI Aktuell Heft 12/2005, p V; *Schilling* Das englische Insolvenzeröffnungsverfahren im Anwendungsbereich der EuInsVO und im Vergleich mit dem deutschen Insolvenzeröffnungsverfahren, DZWiR 2006, p 143; *Schilling/Schmidt* COMI und vorläufiger Insolvenzverwalter – Problem gelöst?, ZInsO 2006, p 113; *Schilling/Schmidt* Kurzkommentar zu LG Hamburg, Beschl v 18.8.2005 – 326 T 34/05, EWiR 2006, p 15; *Schmidt, H.* Anfechtungsklage des Konkursverwalters und Anwendbarkeit des EuGVÜ, EuZW 1990, p 219; *Schmidt, J.* Perpetuatio fori im europäischen internationalen Insolvenzrecht, ZInsO 2006, p 88; *Schmidt J.* Eurofood – Eine Leitentscheidung und ihre Rezeption in Europa und den USA, ZIP 2007, p 405; *Schwerdtfeger/Schilling* Innerstaatlicher Rechtsschutz gegen die Eröffnung eines Hauptinsolvenzverfahrens nach Art 3 Abs 1 EuInsVO in Deutschland, DZWiR 2005, p 370; *Sedláčková/Keller* Tschechien: Insolvenzgesetz – Teil 1: Eröffnungsverfahren, WiRO 2006, p 342; *Smid* Deutsches und Europäisches internationales Insolvenzrecht, Kommentar (2004); *Smid* Judikatur zum internationalen Insolvenzrecht, DZWiR 2004, p 397; *Smid* Internationales Insolvenzrecht im Spiegel ausgewählter Verfahren und Entscheidungen, DZWiR 2006, p 45; *Smid* EuGH zu »Eurofood«, BGH zur internationalen Zuständigkeit: Neueste Judikatur zur EuInsVO, DZWiR 2006, p 325; *Stoll* (ed) Vorschläge und Gutachten zur Umsetzung des EU-Übereinkommens über Insolvenzverfahren im deutschen Recht (1997); *Taupitz* Das (zukünftige) europäische Internationale Insolvenzrecht – insbesondere aus internationalprivatrechtlicher Sicht, ZZP 111 (1998), p 315; *Teves* Rumänien: Schwerpunkte im Insolvenzgesetz, RIW 2000, p 682; *Thole* Die internationale Zuständigkeit für insolvenzrechtliche Anfechtungsklagen, ZIP 2006, p 1383; *Tirado* Die Anwendung der Europäischen Insolvenzverordnung durch die Gerichte der Mitgliedstaaten, GPR 2005, p 39; *Uhlenbruck* Insolvenzordnung, Kommentar (2004); *Vallender* Aufgaben und Befugnisse des deutschen Insolvenzrichters in Verfahren nach der EuInsVO, KTS 2005, p 283; *Vallender* Die Insolvenz von Scheinauslandsgesellschaften, ZGR 2006, p 425; *Vallender* Die Voraussetzungen für die Einleitung eines Sekundärinsolvenzverfahrens nach der EuInsVO, InVO 2005, p 41; *Vallender/Fuchs* Die Antragspflicht organschaftlicher Vertreter einer GmbH vor dem Hintergrund der Europäischen Gerichtsordnung, ZIP 2004, p 829; *Vallens/Dammann* Die Problematik der Behandlung von Konzerninsolvenzen nach der EuInsVO, NZI 2006, p 29; *Virgós/Garcimartín* The European Insolvency Regulation: Law and Practice (2004); *Virgós/Schmit* Erläuternder Bericht zu dem EU-Übereinkommen über Insolvenzverfahren, in Stoll (ed), Vorschläge und Gutachten (1997), p 32; *Weller* Forum Shopping im Internationalen Insolvenzrecht?, IPRax 2004, p 412; *Weller* Inländische Gläubigerinteressen bei internationalen Konzerninsolvenzen, ZHR 169 (2005), p 570; *Wessels* International Insolvency Law (2006); *Wessels* Current Topics of International Insolvency Law (2004); *Wessels* Moving House: Which court can open insolvency proceedings – www.iiiglobal.org; *Willemer* Vis attractiva concursus und die Europäische Insolvenzverordnung (2006); *Wimmer* Anmerkung zum Vorlagebeschluss des irischen Supreme Court in Sachen Parmalat, ZInsO 2005, p 119; *Wittinghofer* Der nationale und internationale Insolvenzverwaltungsvertrag (2004).

1. Overview

1 Art 3 of the EIR regulates **international jurisdiction** for cross-border insolvencies within Europe[1] with the exception of Denmark[2] (→ on the territorial scope of application, see also **OLG Frankfurt**, Table of Cases Art 3 of the EIR Appendix B No 65).

It specifies which Member State has international jurisdiction to open insolvency proceedings, whereas **local jurisdiction** is determined pursuant to national law.[3] (See mn 14 for an overview of local jurisdiction in the various Member States.) Art 3 of the EIR establishes an automatic **decision-making power** and not a mere **power to recognize,** i.e. no special recognition or publication of the decision has to be made in the other Member States.[4] An insolvency proceeding opened by a court that has jurisdiction pursuant to Art 3 of the EIR must be recognized along with all of its effects in all of the other Member States, → e.g. cf Table of Cases Art 3 of the EIR Appendix B No 10 – BABCOCK. If a court of a Member State assumes international jurisdiction pursuant to Art 3 (1) of the EIR, then no verification of such jurisdiction by a court of another Member State is made (see Art 16 of the EIR mn 15).[5]

2 The determination of international jurisdiction simultaneously determines the applicable law (***lex fori concursus*** = the law of the country in which the insolvency proceedings are being opened[6]), which governs both the procedural and the substantive law effects of the proceedings (see Arts 4, 28 of the EIR). Exemptions from the applicability of the *lex fori concursus* are delineated in Arts 5 to 15 of the EIR, which provides that the particular national laws are applicable in these specific instances.

3 Art 3 (1) of the EIR distinguishes between jurisdiction to open **universal proceedings** (**main insolvency proceedings**, sub 1) and **territorial proceedings** (subs 2–4) with cross-border effects (see Illus 1, mn 4). While universal insolvency proceedings cover the entire assets of the debtor **worldwide**[7], only those assets situated in the country in which the proceedings are opened are caught by territorial proceedings.[8]

4 In addition to regulating international jurisdiction, Art 3 of the EIR also regulates the **relationship** between **main and territorial insolvency proceedings** and the requirements pursuant to which they may be opened, on this see mn 116 et seq.

---

[1] The Regulation does not apply to insolvency proceedings relating to the assets of insurance undertakings, credit institutions and investment undertakings, see Art 1 (2) of the EIR, Recital 9 of the EIR. A detailed discussion of this is found in Art 1 of the EIR mn 22.

[2] For the special position of Denmark, see *Israël* European Cross-Border Insolvency Regulation (2005) p 253.

[3] *Huber* EuZW 2002, 490, 492; *Pannen* in Runkel (ed), AHB-Insolvenzrecht (2005) § 16 mn 76.

[4] *Balz* ZIP 1996, 948, 951; Moss/Fletcher/Isaacs-*Moss/Bayfield*, Regulation, mn 5.28; *Virgós/Garcimartín* Regulation, p 188; *Israël* European Cross-Border Insolvency Regulation (2005) 263 et seq; *Pannen* in Runkel (ed), AHB-Insolvenzrecht (2005) § 16 mn 70; *Smid* Komm EuInsVO Art 3 mn 3.

[5] *Pannen* in Runkel (ed), AHB-Insolvenzrecht (2005) § 16 mn 94. A lack of jurisdiction may only be claimed using the remedies available in the country in which the proceedings were opened; in detail on this, see: *Duursma/Duursma-Kepplinger* DZWiR 2003, 447, 450; *Virgós/Garcimartín* Regulation, p 186; ECJ C-341/04 (Eurofood/Parmalat), judgement dated 2 May 2006, ZInsO 2006, 484 (→ see Table of Cases Art 3 of the EIR Appendix A mn 10).

[6] *Pannen* in Runkel (ed), AHB-Insolvenzrecht (2005) § 16 mn 66.

[7] Not only Europe-wide. E.g. also concurring: *Virgós/Garcimartín* Regulation, p 54. The Regulation can only ensure universality within the EU (with the exception of Denmark); outside the EU, the respective national laws govern.

[8] *Pannen* in Runkel (ed), AHB-Insolvenzrecht (2005) § 16 mn 66.

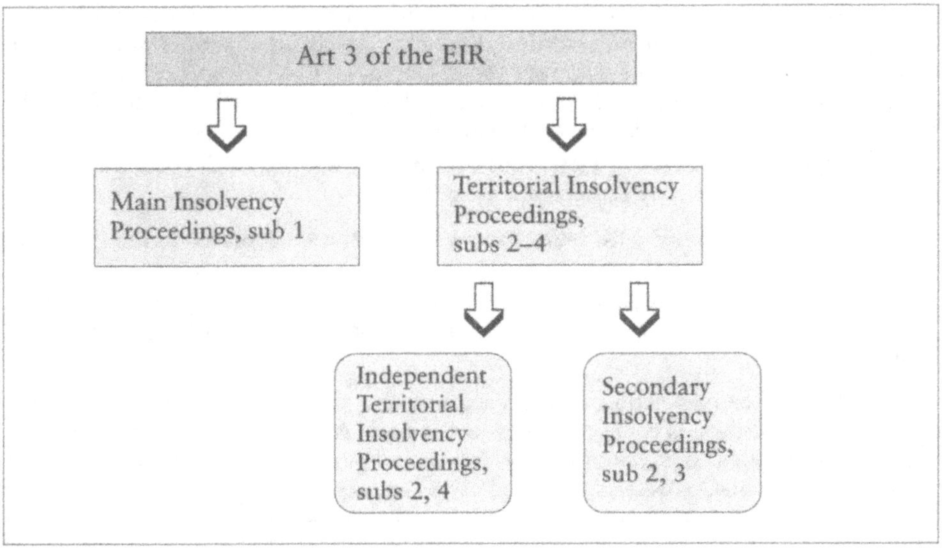

Illus 1 Structure of Art 3 of the EIR

Pursuant to Art 3 (2) of the EIR, **territorial insolvency proceedings** are subdivided into secondary (territorial) insolvency proceedings (sub 3) and isolated independent territorial insolvency proceedings (sub 4). The key distinction between them is that secondary (territorial) insolvency proceedings (hereinafter: **secondary insolvency proceedings**) may only be opened parallel to main insolvency proceedings, whereas isolated independent territorial insolvency proceedings (hereinafter: **independent territorial insolvency proceedings**) may also be opened independent of main insolvency proceedings under certain conditions, on this mn 131. **5**

Independent territorial insolvency proceedings are insolvency proceedings opened prior to main insolvency proceedings in a country in which an establishment is located (Art 3 (4) of the EIR), → cf Table of Cases Art 3 of the EIR Appendix B No 8 – **Werlin Corporation Ltd.** **6**

Secondary insolvency proceedings are insolvency proceedings carried out in the place where the debtor has an establishment and are only opened after main insolvency proceedings have been opened (Art 3 (3) of the EIR).[9] The connecting factor vital to allowing independent territorial or secondary insolvency proceedings is the existence of an **establishment,** see on this mn 119 et seq.

2. Main Insolvency Proceedings

The court of the Member State in which the debtor has his **"centre of main interests"** (**COMI**) has international jurisdiction to open main insolvency proceedings (detailed discussion on this at mn 15 et seq). Only **one** main insolvency proceeding may be opened. The Regulation does not allow for the opening of two main insolvency proceedings[10] **7**

---

[9] BK-InsO/*Pannen* Art 3 EuInsVO mn 16.

[10] Moss/Fletcher/Isaacs-*Moss/Smith*, Regulation, mn 8.33; *Israël* European Cross-Border Insolvency Regulation (2005) 263 et seq;

(see ***ISA/Daisytek***,[11] → a detailed discussion is found in the Table of Cases Art 3 of the EIR Appendix A mn 15). If more than one country claims international jurisdiction to open main insolvency proceedings, then those proceedings validly opened first must be recognized as the main insolvency proceedings (**principle of priority**),[12] Recital 22 of the EIR.[13] On the principle of priority, see also mn 88.

8 In **Germany**, the connecting factors for determining international and local jurisdiction to open main insolvency proceedings are different:

- According to Art 3 of the EIR, **international jurisdiction** is connected to the "centre of main *interests*",
- whereas **local jurisdiction** pursuant to Sec 3 (1) sentence 2 of the German *InsO* (Insolvency Act) is connected to the "centre of the debtor's independent, economic *activities*".

Should a lack of jurisdiction arise on account of a discrepancy between the factors upon which jurisdiction is connected, then in Germany **Art 102 Sec 1 *EGInsO***[14] applies, which holds that local jurisdiction is to be determined pursuant to the criteria of Art 3 of the EIR. Sec 3 (1) *InsO* is being superseded in this respect.[15]

Example

(From the *AG* Hamburg, → cf Table of Cases Art 3 of the EIR Appendix B No 83)

In the case of an English limited liability company operating exclusively in Germany, the German insolvency courts retain international jurisdiction for the opening of main insolvency proceedings within the meaning of Art 3 (1) sentence 1 of the EIR even if the economic activities completely ceased prior to the insolvency request due to the fact that the debtor's "interests", as understood by Art 3 of the EIR, virtually "continue in effect". If the debtor no longer carries on any activities within the meaning of Sec 3 (1) sentence 2 *InsO* in Germany, which means there would be no national jurisdiction, then pursuant to Art 102 (2) *EGInsO* that court in whose district (*Bezirk*) the debtor has the centre of his main interests has exclusive local jurisdiction for the insolvency proceedings.

Herchen ZInsO 2004, 61, 62; *Smid* Komm EuInsVO Art 3 mn 7; *Wessels* International Insolvency Law (2006) mn 10548.

[11] High Court of Leeds ZIP 2003, 1362, also NZI 2004, 219 = ZIP 2004, 963 – "ISA I"; AG Düsseldorf ZIP 2003, 1363; NZI 2004, 269 = ZIP 2004, 623; ZIP 2004, 866 – "ISA II"; on the French "ISA-decision" cf Cour d'Appel Versailles, ZIP 2004, 377; on the "ISA-case" , cf e.g. *Herchen* ZInsO 2004, 61; *Paulus* ZIP 2003, 1725; *Paulus* EWiR 2003, 709; *Mankowski* EWiR 2003, 767; *Mankowski* EWiR 2003, 1239; *Smid* DZWiR 2003, 397; *Pannen/Riedemann* NZI 2004, 301 et seq; *Bufford* Columbia Journal of European Law (CJEL) Vol 12, No 2 2006, 429, 453. → cf also Table of Cases Art 3 of the EIR mn 15.

[12] *Huber* ZZP 114 (2001), 133, 144.

[13] *Eidenmüller* IPRax 2001, 2, 7; *Herchen* ZInsO 2004, 61, 64; *Leible/Staudinger* KTS 2000, 533, 545; BK-InsO/*Pannen* Art 3 EuInsVO mn 13; *Pannen/Riedemann* NZI 2004, 301, 302.

[14] On this, see *Pannen/Riedemann*, NZI 2004, 301 et seq.

[15] BK-InsO/*Pannen* Art 3 EuInsVO mn 1a; *Pannen/Riedemann* NZI 2004, 301, 302.

2.1 Concept of Debtor

The phrase **"centre of main interests"** describes the place where the debtor customarily – which is therefore ascertainable to third parties – pursues the administration of his interests. The word **"interests"** comprises not only commercial or professional activities. Even persons in their private capacities fall within the scope of Art 3 of the EIR.[16] The Regulation therefore applies to both **natural persons** and to **legal entities** regardless of whether these are business persons or persons in their private capacities.[17] **9**

The Regulation does not apply to insolvency proceedings regarding the assets of **insurance undertakings, credit institutions, and investment undertakings** (see Art 1 (2) of the EIR, on this Art 1 of the EIR mn 22).[18] **10**

Whether or not the debtor has **capacity for insolvency proceedings** is determined in each case pursuant to the *lex fori concursus* (Art 4 (a) of the EIR) of the Member State in which the proceedings are being opened or in which an opening is being sought. Where for example the laws applicable pursuant to Arts 3 and 4 of the EIR of a Member State stipulate that for the opening of insolvency proceedings the person must be a businessperson (*Kaufmann*),[19] then, even if the Regulation governs, insolvency proceedings cannot be opened in that Member State against the assets of a non-businessperson. **11**

Insolvency capacity is therefore determined in accordance with the national law applicable pursuant to the international jurisdiction. The debtor's **establishment**[20] is not afforded its own legal personality; it only serves as a connecting factor for the admissibility of territorial insolvency proceedings. **12**

Insolvency capacity is defined differently in the various Member States (on this see the overview below at mn 14). The application of the private international law rule for main and territorial proceedings (Art 28 of the EIR) can lead to a situation where a debtor has insolvency capacity pursuant to the law of the country in which the main insolvency proceedings are opened but not pursuant to the law of the country in which his establishment, as per Art 2 (h) of the EIR, is located, and the other way around. This conflict becomes particularly relevant in connection with the opening of **independent territorial insolvency proceedings**, on this mn 128. Art 3 (4) (a) of the EIR prescribes that independent territorial insolvency proceedings may only be opened if main insolvency proceedings cannot be opened "because of the conditions laid down by the law of the Member State within the territory of which the centre of the debtor's main interests is situated." This would be the case where main insolvency proceedings cannot be opened in the country where the debtor has his **COMI** (on this mn 15 et seq) because he lacks insolvency capacity. This Member State would have to recognize the insolvency proceedings opened against a debtor who, according to their own law, does not have insolvency capacity (Art 16 (1) subs 2 of the EIR).[21] **13**

---

16 *Virgós/Schmit* Explanatory Report mn 32, 75.

17 See on this Recital 9 of the EIR.

18 Cf on this *Pannen* Krise und Insolvenz bei Kreditinstituten, 217.

19 As is the case e.g. in France, Art L 620-2 (1) Code de commerce: see *Jahn* Insolvenzen in Europa, p 107; the provisions of other Member States are set out in detail in the overview at mn 14.

20 For detailed discussion on the concept, see Art 2 (h) of the EIR.

21 *Pannen/Riedemann/Kühnle* NZI 2002, 303.

Example:

- **Unlike Germany, only businesspersons in Belgium have insolvency capacity (see mn 14). But should a non-businessperson with an establishment in Belgium have his COMI in Germany, then main insolvency proceedings opened in Germany must nevertheless be recognized in Belgium.**
- **Small entrepreneurs in Italy have no insolvency capacity. Small entrepreneurs are those whose investments in the operation as a whole do not exceed € 300,000, or whose gross annual revenues – on the average of the last three years or since the commencement of the business activities – do not exceed a total of € 200,000 (Art 1 *Legge fallimentare*). Should an Italian small entrepreneur with an establishment in Germany become insolvent, then main insolvency proceedings may not be opened in Italy. However, independent territorial insolvency proceedings in respect of the assets of the establishment may be opened in Germany pursuant to Art 3 (4) (a) of the EIR.**

2.2 Overview of Jurisdiction and Insolvency Capacity Within the Scope of Application of the EIR

14

Member State	Local Jurisdiction	Insolvency Capacity
Austria	In the case of bankruptcy and composition proceedings, the issue of jurisdiction is governed by Sec 63 et seq, Sec 182 of the *Konkursordnung* (*"KO" RGBl 1914/337* as amended in *BGBl I 2002/75*), and Sec 76 of the *Ausgleichsordnung* (*"AO" RGBl 1914/337* as amended in *BGBl I 2002/75*). According to Sec 63 (1) *KO*, the court of first instance (insolvency court/regional court) in whose district (*Sprengel*) the insolvent debtor operates his business enterprise, or where his habitual residence is located if he has no such operation, has jurisdiction for the bankruptcy proceedings. If the debtor is not operating a business enterprise, then the bankruptcy court is that district court with local jurisdiction at the time at which the request is made. (Debt settlement proceedings) (Sec 182 1st half sentence *KO*).	In addition to legal entities, commercial/business enterprises, and estates of deceased persons, natural persons also have insolvency capacity. (Secs 67, 181 et seq *Konkursordnung* (*"KO" RGBl 1914/337* as amended by *BGBl I 2002/75*). Bankruptcy proceedings in respect of natural persons who do not operate a business enterprise are termed debt settlement proceedings (Secs 25, 181 et seq *KO*). *(http://ec.europa.eu/civiljustice/bankruptcy/bankruptcy_aus_de.htm; MünchKomm/InsO/Augustin Art 102 EGInsO Anhang II Österreich mn 1)*

Member State	Local Jurisdiction	Insolvency Capacity
	The debtor is entitled to request from the court with jurisdiction to open bankruptcy proceedings (settlement court) that settlement proceedings should be opened instead of bankruptcy proceedings (Sec 1 *AO*). *(MünchKomm/InsO/Augustin Art 102 EGInsO Anhang II Österreich mn 4; http://www.ris.bka.gv.at/bundesrecht/; http://ec.europa.eu/civiljustice/bankruptcy/bankruptcy_aus_de.htm; Jahn/Sahm-Helfrich Insolvenzen in Europa p 360 et seq)*	
Belgium	The commercial court of the place in which the debtor has his domicile or registered office (corporate domicile) on the day on which proceedings are instituted has jurisdiction to open the proceedings. *(MünchKomm/InsO/Verdonck Art 102 EGInsO Anhang II Belgien mn 7)* Information is available from the commercial court in the location of the registered office as to whether bankruptcy proceedings have been opened against a business enterprise. *(Jahn/Sahm-Arts Insolvenzen in Europa p 16)*	Debt composition and bankruptcy proceedings are only available to businesspersons. The proceedings may be opened against the assets of a businessperson who has ceased making payments and who is no longer creditworthy (Art 1 of the Belgian Commercial Code – *Wetboek van Koophandel/Code de Commerce* – defines who/what is a businessperson in relation to both legal entities and natural persons). *(MünchKomm/InsO/Verdonck Art 102 EGInsO Anhang II Belgien mn 1–3)*
Bulgaria	No information.	No information.

Member State	Local Jurisdiction	Insolvency Capacity
Cyprus	No information.	Bankruptcy proceedings may be instituted against the assets of natural persons – including the partners of general commercial partnerships and limited commercial partnerships – who commit acts constituting grounds for insolvency, such as the failure to pay debts, or who declare to the court that debts cannot be paid, or who themselves make a request for bankruptcy proceedings. *(http://ec.europa.eu/youreurope/nav/de/business/life-events/insolvency-bankruptcy/cy/index_de.html)*
Czech Republic	The jurisdiction of the insolvency court in terms of subject matter and locality is determined by the provisions of the Civil Proceedings Code (Secs 9 (3) (f), Secs 84–89 CPC); generally the county court where the debtor's domicile is located has jurisdiction. *(Sedláckková/Keller WiRO 2006, p 342)*	All natural persons and legal entities whose general jurisdiction is located within the Czech Republic have bankruptcy capacity. *(Jahn/Sahm-Payne Insolvenzen in Europa p 511)* The inability to pay debts or overindebtedness on the part of the debtor constitute financial deterioration and are thereby grounds for bankruptcy; overindebtedness, however, only applies to legal entities and natural persons that are businesspersons. *(Jahn/Sahm-Payne Insolvenzen in Europa p 511; Sedláckková/Keller WiRO 2006, p 342, 344)* According to Sec 6 of the Insolvency Act, public-law legal entities (primarily the Czech state), decentralized public corporations, public universities, etc. have no bankruptcy capacity.

Member State	Local Jurisdiction	Insolvency Capacity
		(Sec 6 of Act No 182/2006 Sb, that came into force on 1 July 2007; in detail on this see Sedláčková/Keller WiRO 2006, p 342 et seq)
Estonia	The regional courts have jurisdiction for these matters pursuant to Sec 4 (1) of the Estonian Insolvency Act. According to Sec 4 (2) of the Estonian Insolvency Act, the insolvency court in whose district the debtor's general jurisdiction is located has local jurisdiction. *(Insolvency Act of 22 January 2003 – RT I 2003, 17, 95 – in force since 1 January 2004, as amended on 15 Jun 2005, which came into force on 1 Jan 2006 – RT I 2005, 39, 308)*	When the claim is over a certain amount, both legal entities and natural persons have insolvency capacity. *(Jahn/Sahm-Bergmann/Vallikivi Insolvenzen in Europa p 111)*
Finland	Upon request by the debtor, the district courts in Finland, as courts of first instance, review whether the requirements have been met for executing reorganization proceedings in the case of business enterprises, or those required for composition proceedings in the case of persons in their private capacities. *(MünchKomm/InsO/Sedig/Sundström Art 102 EGInsO Anhang II Finnland mn 5)* In the case of bankruptcy proceedings, the district court in the place where the business enterprise has its actual head office, or the district court in the place of residence in the case of persons in their private capacities, has jurisdiction.	Finnish insolvency law applies to both business enterprises and persons in their private capacities. *(Jahn/Sahm-Virri Insolvenzen in Europa p 121 et seq; MünchKomm/InsO/Sedig/Sundström Art 102 EGInsO Anhang II Finnland mn 1)*

Member State	Local Jurisdiction	Insolvency Capacity
	(MünchKomm/InsO/Sedig/ Sundström Art 102 EGInsO Anhang II Finnland mn 7)	
France	In the case of commercial/business enterprises and the professional classes, the commercial courts have jurisdiction. Since there is no commercial court in some French departments, the *Tribunal de Grande Instance* has jurisdiction there. *(http://ec.europa.eu/civiljustice/ bankruptcy/bankruptcy_fra_de. htm; MünchKomm/InsO/ Augustin Art 102 EGInsO Anhang II Frankreich mn 1–4)* *Code de commerce* *Art L 621-2 (1)*: The commercial court has jurisdiction if the debtor is a businessperson or if he is registered in the list of professionals. The *Tribunal de Grande Instance* has jurisdiction in the other Cases. *Décret n° 2005-1677 of 28 December 2005* Art 1: Unless something to the contrary is provided for in Art 343, the court with local jurisdiction for the proceedings regulated in the fourth book of the Commercial Code is that court in whose district the debtor, a legal entity, has its registered office; or in whose district the debtor, a natural person, has registered the address of his business enterprise or business activities. In the absence of a domicile in France, then that court has jurisdiction in whose district the debtor's centre of main interests in France is located.	Insolvency law only applies to traders, persons registered in the craftsmen's register, farmers, other persons carrying on an independent professional activity, including an independent professional person with a statutory or regulated status or whose designation is protected, as well as private-law entities *(Art L 620-2 of the French Commercial Code).* *(http://ec.europa.eu/civiljustice/ bankruptcy/bankruptcy_fra_de. htm; MünchKomm/InsO/Augustin Art 102 EGInsO Anhang II Frankreich mn 1–4)*; For natural persons who are not businesspersons, the French consumer protection code provides for proceedings before the commission for overindebtedness (Art L 331-1 – L. 333-8 *Code de la Consommation*) *(Jahn/Sahm-Weber Insolvenzen in Europa p 190 et seq; http://ec.europa.eu/civiljustice/ bankruptcy/bankruptcy_fra_de. htm)*

Member State	Local Jurisdiction	Insolvency Capacity
	Natural persons who are manifestly unable in good faith to discharge their entire private debts may seek assistance from the commission for overindebtedness provided for in each department. *(MünchKomm/InsO/Augustin Art 102 EGInsO Anhang II Frankreich mn 1–4; Jahn/Sahm-Weber Insolvenzen in Europa p 191)*	
Germany	The insolvency court in the district (*Bezirk*) where the debtor's general jurisdiction is located has local jurisdiction (Sec 3 (1) sentence 1 *InsO*). If the centre of the debtor's independent, economic activities is located in another place, then the insolvency court in whose district this place is located has exclusive jurisdiction (Sec 3 (1) sentence 2 *InsO*). If more than one court has jurisdiction, then the court at which the opening was first requested has jurisdiction (Sec 3 (2) *InsO*)	According to Sec 11 *InsO*, natural persons as well as legal entities have insolvency capacity. An association without legal capacity will be treated in this regard the same as a legal entity (sub 1). Insolvency proceedings may also be instituted against the assets of a company without legal personality, against a deceased's estate, and against the common property of a jointly administered marital community of property (sub 2, Nos 1 and 2). Insolvency proceedings may also be opened against the assets of legal entities and companies without legal personality after they have been dissolved provided that the distribution of the assets has not yet been completed (sub 3). Public law entities, however, have no insolvency capacity (Sec 12 *InsO*).
Greece	Upon the request of a creditor or a debtor, or by the court on its own motion, the opening of bankruptcy proceedings is effected through a judgement of the regional court in whose district the businessperson's domicile is located.	Bankruptcy proceedings may only be instituted in the case of businesspersons (Art 525 Sec 1 of the Greek Commercial Code).

Member State	Local Jurisdiction	Insolvency Capacity
	(MünchKomm/InsO/Zerey Art 102 EGInsO Anhang II Griechenland mn 2)	
Hungary	In the case of composition and bankruptcy proceedings, the local jurisdiction of the court is determined by the registered office/domicile of the debtor; in the case of winding-up proceedings, however, the commercial court at which the company to be wound up is registered always has jurisdiction. *(MünchKomm InsO/Pesser-Müller Art 102 EGInsO Anhang II Ungarn mn 5)*	Those organisations (with or without legal personality) that are listed in the law have insolvency capacity pursuant to Hungarian insolvency law. This includes all of the various corporate forms, even one-person companies, but it does not include natural persons. *(MünchKomm InsO/Pesser-Müller Art 102 EGInsO Anhang II Ungarn mn 6)*
Ireland	A request to open insolvency proceedings must be made to the High Court of Dublin. *(Jahn/Sahm-Grehan Insolvenzen in Europa p 223)*	According to Irish law, sole proprietors, natural persons, and companies have insolvency capacity. In the case of natural persons, proceedings are governed by the Bankruptcy Act of 1988 and the Bankruptcy Rules that came into force on 24 April 1998; in the case of companies, by the insolvency provisions in the Companies Act (1963–2001). *(MünchKomm/InsO/Grehan Art 102 EGInsO Anhang II Irland mn 1; Jahn/Sahm-Grehan Insolvenzen in Europa p 223; http://ec.europa.eu/civiljustice/bankruptcy/bankruptcy_ire_de.htm)*
Italy	For the opening of bankruptcy proceedings, the regional court has jurisidiction in whose district the entrepreneur's head office is located.	Only entrepreneurs who are involved in trading activities have bankruptcy capacity; excepted from this are public-law corporations, small entrepreneurs, large enterprises in crisis.

Member State	Local Jurisdiction	Insolvency Capacity
	(Jahn/Sahm-Moser Insolvenzen in Europa p 240; Correnti ZInsO 2006, 1020, 1023)	*(MünchKomm/InsO/Schaub/ Jakobs Art 102 EGInsO Anhang II Italien mn 4–5; Jahn/Sahm-Moser Insolvenzen in Europa p 235)* Small entrepreneurs ("*piccoli imprenditori*") are those whose investments in the operation as a whole do not exceed € 300,000, and/or whose gross annual revenues – calculated on the average of the last three years or since the commencement of the business activities – do not exceed a total of € 200,000 (Art 1 *LF* = *Legge fallimentare*). *(Costa ZInsO 2006, 1071, 1077; Correnti ZInsO 2006, 1020, 1022)* In addition, clubs/societies and endowments that carry out trading activities and cartels with external activities have insolvency capacity. *(MünchKomm/InsO/Schaub/ Jakobs Art 102 EGInsO Anhang II Italien mn 8)*
Latvia	No information.	Insolvency law in Latvia only applies to companies. *(Jahn/Sahm-Sabitov/Grunte Insolvenzen in Europa p 274)*
Lithuania	The request to open bankruptcy proceedings is made to the county court that has jurisdiction in the place of the debtor company's registered office/principle place of business. *(Jahn/Sahm-Karvele Insolvenzen in Europa p 286)*	Bankruptcy proceedings in Lithuania are only applicable to business enterprises. *(Jahn/Sahm-Karvele Insolvenzen in Europa p 286)*

Member State	Local Jurisdiction	Insolvency Capacity
Luxembourg	The district court (*"tribunal d'arrondissement"*), which deals with commercial law matters (commercial court), has local jurisdiction. In the case of businesspersons and legal entities, the request must be made at the commercial court of the judicial district in which the business person's head office is located or in which the business enterprise has its registered office/principal place of business. *(http://ec.europa.eu/civiljustice/bankruptcy/bankruptcy_lux_de.htm)*	There are five different types of insolvency proceedings in Luxembourg. Three of these concern businesspersons only (natural persons and legal entities); one proceeding is only available to natural persons who are not businesspersons. *(http://ec.europa.eu/civiljustice/bankruptcy/bankruptcy_lux_de.htm)*
Malta	The Civil Court, First Hall, i.e. the first chamber of the upper civil court of first instance, has jurisdiction in respect of commercial traders (Sec 478 of Chapter 13 of the Laws of Malta). Natural persons or their creditors may also institute proceedings at the First Hall of the Civil Court. *(http://ec.europa.eu/civiljustice/bankruptcy/bankruptcy_mlt_de.htm)*	Natural persons, legal entities, and partnerships all have insolvency capacity. The insolvency of natural persons and partnerships is regulated in the Commercial Code (Sec 477 et seq of Chapter 13 of the Laws of Malta). Chapter 386 of Title II, Part V of the Companies Act governs the insolvencies of corporate enterprises. *(http://ec.europa.eu/civiljustice/bankruptcy/bankruptcy_mlt_de.htm)*
The Netherlands	The insolvency court is the "*rechtbank*" (official name: *arrondissementsrechtbank* = district court) of the district in which the natural person's domicile is located or in which the company's registered office is located (Art 2 *Faillissementswet*).	According to the Dutch bankruptcy regulation (*Wet op het Fallissement en de Surséance van Betaling – Faillissementswet, "Fw"*), persons in their private capacities, legal entities, and business enterprises that do not operate as a legal entity, for example the sole proprietorship, have insolvency capacity.

Member State	**Local Jurisdiction**	**Insolvency Capacity**
	(Mincke Einführung in das niederländische Recht, JuS – Schriftenreihe (2002), mn 398; http://ec.europa.eu/civiljustice/bankruptcy/bankruptcy_net_de.htm)	*(http://ec.europa.eu/civiljustice/bankruptcy/bankruptcy_net_de.htm;* *Jahn/Sahm-Hagedorn/Rhein Insolvenzen in Europa p 307)* The bankruptcy regulation envisions three different types of judicial insolvency proceedings: bankruptcy (Art 6 *Fw*), debt composition (Art 214 *Fw*), and debt reorganization (Art 284 *Fw*). *(http://ec.europa.eu/civiljustice/bankruptcy/bankruptcy_net_de.htm)*
Poland	The bankruptcy petition is to be made to the *Rayongericht* – insolvency and reorganization department – where the insolvent debtor's registered office/principal place of business is located (jurisdiction over subject matter is regulated in Art 18 of the Polish Insolvency Regulation). *(Jahn/Sahm-Siekierzyński/Reith Insolvenzen in Europa p 405)* According to Art 19 of the Polish Insolvency Regulation, the insolvency court in whose district the debtor's main business operations are located has exclusive local jurisdiction. If the debtor has several business operations that are located in the districts of various courts and it is not possible to designate one of these as the main business operation, then all courts have local jurisdiction. In such a case, it is at the requesting party's discretion where the matter is to be decided.	Only economic/business entities have bankruptcy capacity. This means private-law business entities and incorporated companies only. Hence public-law corporations and certain state-owned utilities and service enterprises named in the Bankruptcy Regulation do not have bankruptcy capacity. Natural persons also have no bankruptcy capacity unless they carry out an activity for which a trade registration is required. *(Jahn/Sahm-Siekierzyński/Reith Insolvenzen in Europa p 389 and 402)* A request to open bankruptcy proceedings can nevertheless be made against a natural person if this person has ceased exercising his economic activities and one year has not yet lapsed since the day on which the registration of the business enterprise was cancelled in the regional court register or in any other register. *(Jahn/Sahm-Siekierzyński/Reith Insolvenzen in Europa p 403)*

Member State	Local Jurisdiction	Insolvency Capacity
Portugal	The court at the place of the main branch establishment or at the registered office of the business enterprise has jurisdiction for issuing orders based on a request for reorganization measures and for opening bankruptcy proceedings. *(Jahn/Sahm-Ennes Insolvenzen in Europa p 416)*	The Portuguese Insolvency Act of 23 April 1993 (*No. 132/93, Código dos Processos Especiais de Recuperação da Empresea e da Falência*) regulates the reorganization and the bankruptcy of business enterprises. *(Jahn/Sahm-Ennes Insolvenzen in Europa p 415; http://ec.europa.eu/civiljustice/bankruptcy/bankruptcy_por_en.htm#1)*
Romania	The insolvency court as understood by the Romanian Insolvency Act is the court of justice, whereby the Romanian law governing the jurisdiction and organization of courts subdivides the courts into three levels (local/magistrate courts, county courts, and appellate courts). Exclusive local jurisdiction in Romania is based on the domicile of the debtor (Art 6 of the Insolvency Act). *(Teves RIW 2000, 681, 682)*	The scope of application of the Romanian Insolvency Act of 29 June 1995 (Official Journal of Romania No. 130/29 June 1995) was augmented by the new Romanian Insolvency Act No 85/2006. It now covers, in addition to businesspersons, all private-law legal entities that carry on economic activities regardless of whether they do so as natural persons or commercial enterprises. *(Bormann WiRO 2006, 29)* No provision is made for consumer insolvency proceedings. *(Bormann WiRO 2006, 221)*
Slovakia	No information.	According to the law on bankruptcy and composition proceedings of the Slovak Republic, a debtor may be either a legal entity or a natural person (entrepreneurs and non-entrepreneurs). *(Jahn/Sahm-Poláková/Čarnogurský Insolvenzen in Europa p 475)*
Slovenia	No information.	No information.

Member State	Local Jurisdiction	Insolvency Capacity
Spain	The commercial court of the judicial district in which the debtor's principal interests are centred has jurisdiction. In the case of legal entities, this is presumed to be where their registered office/principal place of business is located. A relocation of this registered office/ principal place of business in the last 6 months is invalid. *(Insolvency regulation 1346/00; Jahn/Sahm-Helfrich Insolvenzen in Europa p 505)*	A debtor may be a natural person or a legal entity as long as such person or entity is afforded its own legal personality. Bankruptcy proceedings may not be opened against agencies or departments of the public administration authorities. *(Konkursgesetz Nr. 22/2003 vom 09.07.2003; MünchKomm InsO/ Volz/Oliver Art 102 EGInsO Anhang II Spanien mn 1–6; http://ec.europa.eu/civiljustice/ bankruptcy/bankruptcy_spa_de. htm)*
Sweden	The local/magistrates court in whose judicial district the debtor has his domicile has jurisdiction. *(MünchKomm/InsO/Csatho Art 102 EGInsO Anhang II Schweden mn 6)*	Proceedings in Sweden are in the form of bankruptcy proceedings and are applicable to both natural persons and legal entities. The law dealing with the discharging of residual debts contemplates such proceedings in the case of natural persons. In the case of business enterprises, company reconstruction proceedings may be sought pursuant to the law on this. *(MünchKomm/InsO/Csatho Art 102 EGInsO Anhang II Schweden mn 2–5; Jahn/Sahm/ Herrmann Insolvenzen in Europa p 429 et seq)*
United Kingdom		
England & Wales	For debt claims above a certain amount, the Chancery Division of the High Court of Justice of England and Wales (highest civil court of first instance) has jurisdiction to open insolvency proceedings. Otherwise the County Court has jurisdiction for insolvency matters.	Consumer insolvency ("bankruptcy") proceedings can be opened in respect of natural persons. *(MünchKomm InsO/Pesser-Müller Art 102 EGInsO Anhang II England und Wales mn 1, 39 et seq;*

Member State	Local Jurisdiction	Insolvency Capacity
	(Insolvency Act 1986 Chapter VI No 117; http://ec.europa.eu/civiljustice/bankruptcy/bankruptcy_eng_de.htm)	*http://ec.europa.eu/civiljustice/bankruptcy/bankruptcy_eng_de.htm)* Businesspersons have insolvency capacity in accordance with the so-called Insolvency Act 1986, Secs 122, 123, and 84. *(MünchKomm InsO/Pesser-Müller Art 102 EGInsO Anhang II England und Wales mn 1, 4 et seq; http://ec.europa.eu/civiljustice/bankruptcy/bankruptcy_eng_de.htm)*
Scotland	No information.	The English Insolvency Act 1986 applies generally in Scotland. In the case of consumer insolvencies (*sequestration*), the Bankruptcy (Scotland) Act 1985 (as amended) also applies, particularly Sec 7. *(MünchKomm InsO /Pesser-Müller Art 102 EGInsO Anhang II England und Wales mn 2; http://ec.europa.eu/civiljustice/bankruptcy/bankruptcy_sco_de.htm)* Consumers and entrepreneurs have insolvency capacity. *(http://ec.europa.eu/civiljustice/bankruptcy/bankruptcy_sco_de.htm)*
Northern Ireland	No information.	Both natural persons and legal entities have insolvency capacity. *(http://ec.europa.eu/civiljustice/bankruptcy/bankruptcy_nir_de.htm#1.)*

Member State	Local Jurisdiction	Insolvency Capacity
Gibraltar	The general rule applies: legal actions against natural persons must be lodged at the court in whose jurisdiction the natural person's domicile is located. In the case of legal entities, the court's jurisdiction is determined by the *situs* of the registered office/principal place of business. *(http://ec.europa.eu/civiljustice/jurisdiction_courts/jurisdiction_courts_gib_de.htm#B.)*	The law in Gibraltar contemplates insolvency proceedings for both consumers and business enterprises; hence insolvency proceedings can be opened in respect of the assets of both natural persons and legal entities. *(http://ec.europa.eu/civiljustice/bankruptcy/bankruptcy_gib_de.htm)*

2.3 Centre of Main Interests = COMI

2.3.1 Concept

The connecting factor for assuming international jurisdiction to open insolvency proceedings is the **centre of main interests** (**COMI**).[22] This concept is not legally defined in the Regulation. **15**

The drafters of the EIR presumed that the debtor can only have **one centre** (which can already be inferred from the use of the term "main" in the wording of Art 3 of the EIR). For this reason, it is only possible to have one main insolvency proceeding pursuant to which the debtor's entire national and foreign assets are liquidated[23] (→ cf Table of Cases Art 3 of the EIR Appendix A mn 15, **ISA/Daisytek**). Parallel to **main insolvency proceedings, territorial proceedings** within the meaning of Art 3 (2)–(4) of the EIR may be conducted in the place where the debtor has an establishment (**secondary and independent territorial insolvency proceedings**, on this see mn 116 et seq). **16**

Various criteria are used to determine the **centre of main interests** (**COMI**) (detailed discussion on this in mn 34 et seq). This concept, which is decisive for determining international jurisdiction in the case of European insolvencies, is the subject of controversial discussion. Considerations such as **"forum shopping"** in the case of insolvencies of corporate groups, the governing **principle of priority**, and the "race to open first" associated with it are also important aspects of this controversy.[24] **17**

---

[22] The phrase originates from the European Convention on Certain International Aspects of Bankruptcy signed in Istanbul on 5 June 1990; on this, see: *Balz* ZIP 1996, 948, 949. The phrase "centre of main interests" is also in the UNCITRAL Model Law.

[23] BK-InsO/*Pannen* Art 3 EuInsVO mn 3; D-K/D/Ch-*Duursma-Kepplinger* Art 3 mn 6; *Paulus* Komm EuInsVO Art 3 mn 2; *Wessels* Current Topics of International Insolvency Law, 161; *Virgós/Schmit* Explanatory Report mn 73; *Virgós/Garcimartín* Regulation, p 37; ECJ "Susanne Staubitz-Schreiber" ZIP 2006, 188 (→ cf Table of Cases Art 3 of the EIR Appendix A mn 17); with annotation by *Knof/Mock* ZIP 2006, 189; HK-InsO/*Stephan* Art 3 EuInsVO mn 2.

[24] E.g. *Kübler* FS Gerhardt, p 527 et seq; *Weller* IPRax 2004, 412 et seq; *Pannen/Riedemann* explanatory note on AG Offenburg

18 According to **Recital 13 of the EIR**, the **COMI** is the "place where the debtor conducts the administration of his interests on a regular basis and is therefore ascertainable by third parties."[25] The Explanatory Report on the EU Draft Convention on Insolvency Proceedings (from 1995)[26] also utilizes this – objective – criteria to determine the centre of main interests.[27] The reason for adopting this objective perspective is that, because insolvency is a real risk, creditors must be able to assess this risk in conjunction with objective criteria ascertainable to them. According to this view, the insolvency proceedings must therefore be conducted at a place known and ascertainable to potential creditors of the debtor.

With respect to these individual criteria:

- for consumers, see mn 19 et seq below;
- for persons engaged in business activities, see mn 27 et seq;
- for companies, see mn 30 et seq;
- for corporate groups, see mn 46 et seq.

2.3.2 Ascertaining the *situs* of the COMI

2.3.2.1 Consumers

19 In the case of **consumers**, assuming they have insolvency capacity pursuant to the *lex fori concursus* (see the Overview at mn 14), the connecting factor for international jurisdiction to open main insolvency proceedings is also the "centre of main interests" (COMI). However it is uncertain just where this centre of interests is, in the case of **persons who are not carrying out business activities.**

> **→ On this, see the Table of Cases Art 3 of the EIR Appendix B,**
> - **No 2 (Court of Assen, *Schuldsaneringsregeling*),**
> - **No 3 (High Court of Justice, Chancery Division, Geveran Trading Co Ltd v Skjevsland),**
> - **No 5 (*LG* Wuppertal),**
> - **No 6 (Swedish Court of Appeal, Brynervall v Johannson),**
> - **No 26 (Court of Appeal, Amsterdam, M. van Dulvenbode v W. J. M. van Andelte & J. J. van der Veen),**
> - **No 27 (Swedish Court of Appeal, Vikingson).**

20 In some cases it is linked to the **domicile**[28] (→ ***AG*** **Celle**, Table of cases Art 3 of the EIR Appendix B No 73; ***LG*** **Wuppertal**, cf Table of Cases Art 3 of the EIR Appendix B

dated 2 Aug 2004 – 2 IN 133/04 (→ cf Table of Cases Art 3 of the EIR Appendix A mn 14 – HUKLA), EWiR 2005, 73.

[25] *Klöhn* KTS 2006, 259, 277; *Pannen* in Runkel (ed), AHB-Insolvenzrecht (2005) § 16 mn 92; *Smid* Komm EuInsVO Art 3 mn 9.

[26] Explanatory Report by *Virgós/Schmit*.

[27] *Virgós/Schmit* Explanatory Report mn 75; *Smid* Komm EuInsVO Art 3 mn 9.

[28] See AG Celle, ZInsO 2005, 895 = NZI 2005, 410 (→ cf Table of Cases Art 3 of the EIR Appendix B No 73); LG Wuppertal, ZInsO 2002, 1099 (→ cf Table of Cases Art 3 of the EIR Appendix B No 5); Moss/Fletcher/Isaacs-*Moss/Smith*, Regulation, mn 8.41; *Balz* ZIP 1996, 948, 949; *Wimmer* ZInsO 2001, 97, 99; *Smid* Komm EuInsVO Art 3 mn 15; → cf also Table of Cases Art 3 of the EIR Appendix B No 26, Court of Appeal Amsterdam of 17 Jun 2003: The Court of Appeal in Amsterdam had to decide a case in which a Dutch debtor had manifestly given

No 5), and in others it is linked to the **place of habitual residence**[29] (→ see **Court of Assen**, judgement of 5 June 2002, Table of Cases Art 3 of the EIR Appendix B No 2). Neither the wording of Art 3 (1) of the EIR nor Recital 13 allows an inference to be made either in favour of the domicile or the habitual residence.[30]

The Explanatory Report to the Draft Convention on Insolvency Proceedings (the so-called Virgós/Schmit Report) also fails to clarify this issue as it refers to the **"habitual domicile"**.[31]

In some respects this wording combines both approaches ("habitual" and "domicile"), thus providing no solution.[32]

21 If the connection was being made to the **domicile**, then this would accord with **German law** (Sec 3 *InsO* in conjunction with Sec 13 *ZPO*).[33] However, the factors used to evaluate this on the various national levels are not the same for an assessment on the European level based on Art 3 of the EIR. Determining the domicile causes difficulty as the exact meaning of the term varies from one Member State to another.[34] For this very reason, it would seem incorrect to use this concept at the European level.[35] The term "domicile" also has a comparatively formalized meaning, whereas the concept of a "COMI" in the Regulation contains a certain degree of flexibility.

22 Consistency with private international law is also a reason to refrain from using the domicile as a decisive criteria; many of the provisions in the Rome Convention 1980,[36] for example, turn on the habitual residence of the person concerned.[37] In addition, throughout Council Regulation (EC) No 1347/2000,[38] the legislator linked decision-making powers to the habitual residence of the applicant and/or of the opposing party, Art 2 (1) (a) Council Regulation (EC) No 1347/2000. In both international private law

---

up her occupation and moved to Longueville, France one year before the insolvency request. The court in the Netherlands held that the move to another country on its own does not necessarily mean that the debtor's COMI was no longer in the Netherlands.

29 Also *Carstens* Die internationale Zuständigkeit im europäischen Insolvenzrecht (2005) 59; *Mankowski* NZI 2005, 368, 369 et seq; *Wessels* Current Topics of International Insolvency Law, 164; *Taupitz* ZZP 111 (1998) 315, 326 et seq; *Leible/Staudinger* KTS 2000, 533, 543; *Huber* ZZP 114 (2001) 133, 140; *Paulus* NZI 2001, 505, 509; D-K/D/Ch-*Duursma-Kepplinger* Art 3 mn 20–22; HamburgerKomm-*Undritz* Art 3 mn 8; *Paulus* Komm EuInsVO Art 3 mn 24.

30 *Carstens* Die internationale Zuständigkeit im europäischen Insolvenzrecht (2005) 57.

31 *Virgós/Schmit* Explanatory Report mn 75; *Israël* European Cross-Border Insolvency Regulation (2005) 258.

32 Also *Knof* ZInsO 2005, 1017, 1018; *Wessels* Current Topics of International Insolvency Law, 163.

33 On this, see MünchKomm InsO/*Ganter* § 3 mn 17.

34 The German InsO makes a connection to the domicile (permanent residence) (Sec 3 InsO in conjunction with Sec 13 ZPO), whereas Austrian insolvency law, for example, makes a connection to habitual residence (Sec 63 of the Austrian KO); see *Knof* ZInsO 2005, 1017, 1022; AG Celle, ZInsO 2005, 895 = NZI 2005, 410 (→ Table of Cases Art 3 of the EIR Appendix B No 73). On this issue, also see: *Carstens* Die internationale Zuständigkeit im europäischen Insolvenzrecht (2005) 55.

35 AG Celle, ZInsO 2005, 895 = NZI 2005, 410 (→ Table of Cases Art 3 of the EIR Appendix B No 73).

36 Convention on the law applicable to contractual obligations signed on 19 June 1980 in Rome, also known as the Rome Convention 1980.

37 *Leible/Staudinger* KTS 2000, 543.

38 Council Regulation (EC) No 1347/2000 of 29 May 2000 on jurisdiction and the recognition and enforcement of judgments in matrimonial matters, OJ L 160 p 19.

and international civil procedural law, the criteria "habitual residence" has, in the interim, strongly superseded the criteria "domicile" as a connecting factor.[39]

23 A **systematic interpretation** of Art 3 (1) of the EIR also speaks in favour of locating the COMI in the case of consumers at the **place of their habitual residence.** An approach similar to the one applied to companies and legal entities is being used: the actual administrative head office is decisive for ascertaining where the COMI is (see mn 41 et seq).[40]

24 A **teleological interpretation** also confirms this. The purpose of using the COMI as a connecting factor for determining international jurisdiction is to choose a place that is easily and clearly ascertainable.[41] Although it is possible to have many domiciles, more than one "habitual residence" is hardly conceivable.[42] Judges and creditors are also spared the problem of having to deal with the various national definitions of domicile.[43]

25 The centre of interests in the case of natural persons who are not carrying on business activities is therefore generally the **place of the habitual residence.**[44] It also represents the centre of the debtor's life and activities.[45]

26 According to the rules of private international law, **two conditions** must be fulfilled to establish a **habitual residence:**

- The residency must be on a **permanent** basis, i.e. it must have already existed for a longer period of time or is, under the given circumstances, to continue on for a longer period of time. In any other case, the necessary social integration in the respective surroundings cannot be presumed.[46] A duration of 6 months is generally deemed necessary.[47] A shorter period may also suffice provided that it was intended to be permanent from the outset.[48]
- Secondly, the **centre of the person's existence**, i.e. the focus of his/her life, must be in the respective country.

2.3.2.2 Natural persons involved in business activities

27 In the case of **natural persons involved in business activities** (→ see Table of Cases Art 3 of the EIR Appendix B No 39, highest court of the Netherlands – **Fortis v Vennick;** Table of Cases Art 3 of the EIR Appendix A mn 17 – **Susanne Staubitz-Schreiber**), the issue is whether the centre of main interests is simultaneously the habitual residence. The term "interests" has a wide meaning encompassing not only commercial, trading, or occupational activities but **also general economic activities.**[49]

---

[39] *Carstens* Die internationale Zuständigkeit im europäischen Insolvenzrecht (2005) 57.

[40] *Carstens* Die internationale Zuständigkeit im europäischen Insolvenzrecht (2005) 58.

[41] *Carstens* Die internationale Zuständigkeit im europäischen Insolvenzrecht (2005) 59.

[42] *Carstens* Die internationale Zuständigkeit im europäischen Insolvenzrecht (2005) 59.

[43] *Carstens* Die internationale Zuständigkeit im europäischen Insolvenzrecht (2005) 59.

[44] Also HamburgerKomm-*Undritz* Art 3 mn 8; *Virgós/Schmit* Explanatory Report mn 75; AG Celle ZInsO 2005, 895 = NZI 2005, 410 (→ cf Table of Cases Art 3 of the EIR Appendix B No 73); *Wessels* Current Topics of International Insolvency Law, 162 et seq; contra MünchKomm InsO/*Reinhart* Art 3 of the EIR mn 2 with further references.

[45] *Israël* European Cross-Border Insolvency Regulation (2005) 257 et seq; *Mankowski* NZI 2005, 368, 369 et seq; *Virgós/Garcimartín* Regulation, p 43.

[46] OLG Rostock IPRax 2001, 588, 589.

[47] BGH NJW 1981, 520; OLG Hamm NJW 1974, 1053; *Baetge* IPRax 2001, 573, 574.

[48] See BGH NJW 1981, 520.

[49] MünchKomm InsO/*Reinhart* Art 3 EuInsVO mn 2; Moss/Fletcher/Isaacs-*Moss/Smith*, Regulation, mn 8.40.

28 In the case of persons carrying on occupational activites, then the place where such activities are carried out is the overriding factor. It is therefore generally not necessary to resort to the domicile or the place of the habitual residence.[50] In the case of **businesspersons, sole proprietors,** and **freelancers,** the **place of the business establishment,** the **law firm,** or the **occupational activities**[51] is therefore decisive.[52] This applies even more so in the case of persons involved in commercial activities as it is often these very occupational activities that are the reason for the insolvency.[53] For reasons of practicality, it is **irrelevant** in the individual case whether the debt obligations stem predominantly from the occupational or the private sphere.[54]

29 If a sole proprietor has **more than one establishment**, the location of the **main establishment** is decisive.[55] This is because the centre of the economic activities, as opposed to one single establishment per Art 2 (h) of the EIR, can only be the main establishment. This is supported by the fact that, when viewed objectively, the main establishment is the place where the entrepreneur of a sole proprietorship makes fundamental decisions.

2.3.2.3 Companies

30 For **companies** and **legal entities**, there is a **rebuttable presumption** that the place of the registered office is the centre of main interests (Art 3 (1) sentence 2 of the EIR). This wording is intended to avoid the difficulties that have arisen in conjunction with Art 53 of the 1968 Brussels Convention[56] pertaining to the ascertainment of domicile.[57]

31 In the case of companies and legal entities whose registered office **coincides** with the place where the operative business is being conducted, the ascertainment of the centre of main interests poses no problems since insolvency proceedings are to be opened for all legal subjects there where the centre of their main interests are located.[58] The legal presumption only becomes relevant if there is a discrepancy between the registered office and the centre of interests; on ascertaining the COMI in general see mn 19 et seq, and for corporate group insolvencies see mn 46 et seq.

---

[50] Moss/Fletcher/Isaacs-*Moss/Smith,* Regulation, mn 8.41; D-K/D/Ch-*Duursma-Kepplinger* Art 3 mn 19.

[51] In Fortis v Vennink (→ cf Table of Cases Art 3 of the EIR Appendix B No 39), the Court of Appeal in Amsterdam held in conformity with Art 3 (1) of the EIR that the debtor's COMI was in the Netherlands based on the fact that he, amongst other things, executed bank transactions there. The court took notice of the debtor's argument that he resided in Belgium but nevertheless held that Art 3 (1) of the EIR does not prescribe that the place where a natural person is resident automatically constitutes his/her COMI.

[52] Moss/Fletcher/Isaacs-*Moss/Smith,* Regulation, mn 8.41; *Carstens* Die internationale Zuständigkeit im europäischen Insolvenzrecht (2005) 52 et seq; *Pannen* in Runkel (ed), AHB-Insolvenzrecht (2005) § 16 mn 90; *Paulus* Komm EuInsVO Art 3 mn 25; *Smid* Komm EuInsVO Art 3 mn 15.

[53] *Huber* ZZP 114 (2001) 133, 140.

[54] Also *Paulus* Komm EuInsVO Art 3 mn 25.

[55] *Mankowski* NZI 2005, 368, 370; *Wessels* Current Topics of International Insolvency Law, 164.

[56] As of 1 March 2002, the 1968 Brussels Convention has been replaced by Council Regulation (EC) No 44/2001.

[57] MünchKomm InsO/*Reinhart* Art 3 EuInsVO mn 2; *Kropholler* EuGVÜ Art 53 mn 2; *Herchen* ZInsO 2004, 825, 828.

[58] *Virgós/Schmit* Explanatory Report mn 74.

2.3.2.4 Court's obligation to review on its own motion

32 The issue here is how to construe the relationship between sentences 1 and 2 of Art 3 (1) of the EIR.[59] One possible construction is to give sentence 1 priority, the court then always being obliged to ascertain the centre of main interests. Another way would be to give sentence 2 priority, i.e. make a presumption in favour of the registered office until it is rebutted by one of the parties (**true legal presumption**).

33 The **prevailing view** holds that because the state alone is entitled – and thus obligated – to institute proceedings *ex officio*, the legal presumption does not function to relieve the court of its duty to ascertain the centre of main interests on its own motion.[60] The problem is, however, that if the court is always obliged make such an ascertainment, then the legal presumption, which is actually meant to provide guidance,[61] is robbed of all practical meaning.[62] Therefore **some scholars** suggest that the court may refrain from making a review where there is no indication whatsoever for a discrepancy between the registered office and the COMI.[63] But this view is also not convincing because there is no reason for making an exception to the above-referred to "*ex officio* principal". Sentence 2 therefore only applies **if the COMI cannot be ascertained pursuant to a review made by the court on its own motion;** in other words, where the court, based on its own review, is uncertain and therefore must resort to the presumption.[64]

2.3.2.5 Criteria for ascertaining the COMI

34 The phrase "centre of main interests" (COMI) as understood by Art 3 (1) sentence 1 of the EIR, which is decisive for establishing international jurisdiction to open main insolvency proceedings, is **subject to various interpretations.**[65]

2.3.2.5.1 Head-office functions / mind of management / place of strategic controlling decisions

35 In deciding which aspects are decisive for ascertaining the COMI, the "head-office functions" are sometimes relied on, at other times the "mind of management" is referred

---

[59] MünchKomm BGB/*Kindler* IntInsR mn 146; *Wessels* Current Topics of International Insolvency Law, 171. → see on this AG Cologne, Table of Cases Art 3 of the EIR Appendix B No 86.

[60] *Gottwald* Grenzüberschreitende Insolvenzen (1997) 20; *Huber* ZZP 114 (2001) 133, 141; *Vallender/Fuchs* ZIP 2004, 829, 831; HK-InsO/*Stephan* Art 3 EuInsVO mn 6; *Herchen* ZInsO 2004, 825, 826; *Borges* ZIP 2004, 733, 737; *Smid* Komm EuInsVO Art 3 mn 13.

[61] Also *Carstens* Die internationale Zuständigkeit im europäischen Insolvenzrecht (2005) 63 et seq.

[62] AG Munich "Hettlage" NZG 2004, 782 = NZI 2004, 450 (→ cf Table of Cases Art 3 of the EIR Appendix A mn 12), with explanatory note by *Mankowski* NZI 2004, 450, 451.

[63] Held by D-K/D/Ch-*Duursma-Kepplinger* Art 3 mn 25, fn 60 in whose opinion the narrowing of the duty to review does not relate generally to the issue of international jurisdiction but is limited exclusively to the issue of domicile, and therefore all other requirements for jurisdiction must still be ascertained on the court's own motion; *Vallender/Fuchs* ZIP 2004, 829, 831.

[64] Cf in particular *Gottwald* Grenzüberschreitende Insolvenzen (1997) 20; *Virgós/Garcimartín* Regulation, p 44; Moss/Fletcher/Isaacs-*Fletcher*, Regulation, mn 3.12; *Huber* ZZP 114 (2001) 133, 141. Contra: *Carstens* Die internationale Zuständigkeit im europäischen Insolvenzrecht (2005) 66.

[65] *Pannen/Riedemann* NZI 2004, 646.

to.[66] These approaches regard internal corporate factors as being decisive, especially the place where strategic decisions are being made.

36

→ See the Table of Cases Art 3 of the EIR

- **Appendix A mn 2: Automold**
- **Appendix A mn 3: BRAC-Rent-A-Car**
- **Appendix A mn 4: Ci4net.com Inc**
- **Appendix A mn 5: Collins & Aikmann**
- **Appendix A mn 6: Crisscross Telecommunications Group**
- **Appendix A mn 7: EMBIC**
- **Appendix A mn 8: EMTEC**
- **Appendix A mn 9: Enron Directo SA**
- **Appendix A mn 10: Eurofood /Parmalat**
- **Appendix A mn 11: Eurotunnel**
- **Appendix A mn 12: Hettlage**
- **Appendix A mn 14: Hukla**
- **Appendix A mn 15: ISA/Daisytek**
- **Appendix A mn 16: MG Rover**
- **Appendix A mn 19: Zenith**
- **Appendix B No 14: Norse Ferries and Cenargo Navigation Ltd**
- **Appendix B No 29: Cirio Del Monte**
- **Appendix B No 53: Parmalat Ungarn**
- **Appendix B No 59: AIM Underwriting Agencies Ltd**
- **Appendix B No 67: Re Parkside Flexibles SA**
- **Appendix B No 76: AvCraft International Ltd**
- **Appendix B No 77: Sendo Ltd**

Particularly – but not only – English courts in the past leaned towards a **broad** interpretation of the concept of the COMI, which allows international jurisdiction to be easily assumed especially in the case of corporate group insolvencies.[67] Although this approach was originally found in English judgements only,[68] it is increasingly finding 37

[66] AG Weilheim "AvCraft International Ltd" ZIP 2005, 1611 (→ cf Table of Cases Art 3 of the EIR Appendix B No 76); with annotation by *Pannen/Riedemann* EWiR 2005, 791 et seq, who moreover enhance the relevancy of objective criteria; also High Court of Justice Leeds "ISA I" ZIP 2003, 1362 (→ cf Table of Cases Art 3 of the EIR Appendix A mn 15); and ZIP 2004, 963; also High Court of Justice Birmingham "Rover" ZIP 2005, 1610 et seq (→ cf Table of Cases Art 3 of the EIR Appendix A mn 16), with rejecting annotation: *Penzlin/ Riedemann* NZI 2005, 469 et seq; Tribunale di Parma "Eurofood/Parmalat I" ZIP 2004, 1220 (→ cf Table of Cases Art 3 of the EIR Appendix A mn 10); AG Munich "Hettlage" NZG 2004, 782 = NZI 2004, 450 1611 (→ cf Table of Cases Art 3 of the EIR Appendix A mn 12).

[67] On this see e.g. *Sabel* NZI 2004, 126 et seq; *Vallender* reported in *Rein* NZI 2004, 310 and *Mankowski* EWiR 2003, 1239 et seq who speaks of "insolvency tourism", "insolvency imperialism", and even an "aggressive self-serving interpretation". See also *Herchen* ZInsO 2004, 825, 826.

[68] E.g. High Court of Justice Birmingham "Rover" ZIP 2005, 1610 et seq; High Court of Justice Leeds "ISA I" ZIP 2003, 1362

more followers on the continent.[69] According to this approach, the place where **strategic controlling decisions**[70] are made is decisive, i.e. the place at which the head-office functions[71] are exercised or where the **mind of management**[72] is located. But such an approach not only facilitates **forum shopping,** it also makes it much easier to contemplate doing it before the insolvency proceedings have even been instituted, especially in the case of **insolvencies of corporate groups**; on corporate group insolvencies, see mn 46 et seq.[73]

38 **Example:**

Using this approach, insolvency proceedings in respect of a German GmbH (limited liability company) may, for example, be conducted in England pursuant to English insolvency law (the *lex fori concursus* as per Art 4 of the EIR would be English law[74]) although the debtor has neither assets, creditors, employees, nor economic activities with outward effects there.[75]

39 The **following criteria** have been developed primarily for ascertaining the *situs* of the **mind of management:**[76]

- The place where the debtor makes fundamental **administrative decisions.** This is to be understood as the place where the debtor customarily, and thus ascertainable to outside third parties, carries out the administration of his interests.[77] According to this

(→ cf Table of Cases Art 3 of the EIR Appendix A mn 15).

69 AG Munich "Hettlage" IPRax 2004, 433 (→ cf Table of Cases Art 3 of the EIR Appendix A mn 12); AG Offenburg NZI 2004, 673 (→ cf Table of Cases Art 3 of the EIR Appendix A mn 14 – HUKLA), on this *Pannen/Riedemann* EWiR 2005, 73 et seq; AG Siegen "Zenith" NZI 2004, 673, 674 (→ cf Table of Cases Art 3 of the EIR Appendix A mn 19); Tribunale di Parma "Eurofood/Parmalat I" ZIP 2004, 1220 (→ cf Table of Cases Art 3 of the EIR Appendix A mn 10); Municipality Court Fejér/Székesfehérvár "Parmalat Hungary/Slovakia" ZInsO 2004, 861 (→ cf Table of Cases Art 3 of the EIR Appendix B No 53); Tribunal de Commerce de Nanterre "EMTEC" (→ cf Table of Cases Art 3 of the EIR Appendix A mn 8) with explanatory note by *Penzlin* EWiR 2006, 207; on this see also www.globalturnaround.com. France Survey: French U-Turn on the European Regulation, May 2006.

70 Cf the opinion of *Stephen Taylor*, reproduced in *Leithaus* NZI 2004, 194, 195.

71 Moss/Fletcher/Isaacs-*Moss/Smith*, Regulation, mn 8.39.

72 *Stephen Taylor*, reproduced in *Leithaus* NZI 2004, 194, 195.

73 *Braun* NZI 2004, V, VI; *Vallender* cited in *Rein* NZI 2004, 310; see on this also *Oberhammer* ZInsO 2004, 761, 767 et seq.

74 But for all company-law related issues, German law – as the law pursuant to private international law that governs the company – applies (since the "Inspire Art" decision of the ECJ of 30 Sept 2003 – C 167/01, the law of the forum where the company was incorporated and not the place of its domicile applies); in the case of a disparity between the law pursuant to private international law that governs the company and that which governs the insolvency, see *Riedemann* GmbHR 2004, 345 et seq.

75 *Sabel* NZI 2004, 126, 127. In the German Automold case (→ cf Table of Cases Art 3 of the EIR Appendix A mn 2), an order of the AG Cologne dated 23 Jan 2004 – 71 IN/04 (ZIP 2004, 471), the creditors' meeting of the English main insolvency proceedings was even carried out in Germany.

76 See *Martinez Ferber* European Insolvency Regulation (2004) 22 et seq; for a detailed listing of the criteria for the "MG Rover" case (→ Table of Cases Art 3 of the EIR Appendix A mn 16) see *Penzlin/Riedemann* NZI 2005, 469, 470.

77 See on this: High Court of Justice Birmingham "Rover" ZIP 2005, 1610 (→ cf Table of Cases Art 3 of the EIR Appendix A mn 16); Case Enron Directo Sociedad Limitada (→ cf Table of Cases Art 3 of the EIR Appendix A mn 9) and the case Crisscross Telecommunications (unreported) (→ cf Table of Cases

view, the place where the insolvency debtor makes **strategic controlling decisions**, or the place where the **accounting** takes place, are decisive.[78]

- In the **Crisscross Telecommunications Group**[79] case (→ cf Table of Cases Art 3 of the EIR Appendix A mn 6), the *situs* of the centre of main interests for all eight group companies from various EU-Member States and Switzerland was found to be in England based on the finding that **"headquarter activities"** had taken place in London and that the vast majority of transactions had been carried out through **bank accounts** kept in England.
- In the **Norse Ferries and Cenargo Navigation Ltd** case (→ cf Table of Cases Art 3 of the EIR Appendix B No 14), the fact that **management board meetings** took place in England played an important role.
- The Italian court in the **Cirio del Monte** case (→ cf Table of Cases Art 3 of the EIR Appendix B No 29) held that the COMI of a Dutch company was in Italy based on the fact that the debtor was being **controlled** by an Italian parent company.
- In the **Enron Directo SA** case (→ cf Table of Cases Art 3 of the EIR Appendix A mn 9), the *situs* of the COMI was held to be in England because, *inter alia*, the "headquarter functions" were carried out in London. **Fundamental strategic decisions** and **relevant personnel decisions** were being made there. In addition, **payments** were being made through the Citibank Madrid (a dependent establishment of the Citibank International plc London).[80]
- In **ISA/Daisytek** (→ cf Table of Cases Art 3 of the EIR Appendix A mn 15), the *situs* of the COMI of a German company was held to be in England[81] because **financial, contractual, guarantee, and supply activities/duties** were in fact being made and controlled by the **international management body in England**. For expenditures in excess of € 5,000, for example, **consent had to be obtained**. In addition, the **bank accounts** of the German company were kept with German branch establishments of an English bank.[82]
- In the **Hettlage** order (→ cf Table of Cases Art 3 of the EIR Appendix A mn 12), the COMI of an Austrian debtor was held to be in Germany because the court found that that was the **place where the administration of the economic interests** was located. The court held that, from an economic point of view, the economic activities of the debtor were carried out in Germany. Both the responsible management body and head of sales, which managed the operative business, was located in Germany.
- Decisive for the ascertainment of the COMI in the **AIM Underwriting Agencies** case (→ cf Table of Cases Art 3 of the EIR Appendix B No 59) was the finding by the

---

Art 3 of the EIR Appendix A mn 6); *Smid* DZWiR 2004, 397, 400; *Fritz/Bähr* DZWiR 2001, 221, 224.

[78] Cf Enron Directo Sociedad Limitada (→ cf Table of Cases Art 3 of the EIR Appendix A mn 9); and the decision in re Crisscross Telecommunications (unreported) (→ cf Table of Cases Art 3 of the EIR Appendix A mn 6), moreover *Kübler* FS Gerhardt (2004) p 527, 541, with annotation on the Hettlage-decision of the AG Munich ZIP 2004, 962; on this, see also: *Tirado* GPR 2005, 39, 46.

[79] The London High Court, Chancery Division, dated 20 May 2003, unreported. Cf on this also *van Galen*, The European Insolvency Regulation and Groups of Companies, paper INSOL Europe Annual Congress (Cork, Ireland), October 16–18, 2003; *Pannen/Riedemann* NZI 2004, 646, 648.

[80] Cf *Pannen/Riedemann* NZI 2004, 646, 648.

[81] Cf judgement on the administration order dated 16 May 2003 – No. 861 – 876/03, printed in ZIP 2004, 963 et seq. On this see also *Pannen/Riedemann* NZI 2004, 646, 648.

[82] Cf *Pannen/Riedemann* NZI 2004, 646, 648.

court that the English managing director executed the business of the debtor (an Irish "Ltd.") from London and that he would have been the only person authorized to **sign** on behalf of the company.

- The presumption in Art 3 (1) sentence 2 of the EIR was deemed rebutted in the **HUKLA** case (→ cf Table of Cases Art 3 of the EIR Appendix A mn 14) because the court found that both the **organisation** and **sales activities** were being managed from Germany and that the business records were also found there.[83]
- In **MG Rover** (→ cf Table of Cases Art 3 of the EIR Appendix A mn 16),[84] the COMI of the National Sales Companies ("NSC") was held to be in England because, *inter alia*, **fundamental decisions** for the NSC were being made **in England** by the **management** of other companies in the group.[85]

• Place of **financing** and **financial planning**, and **supervision of the debtor;**[86]

- In **MG Rover** (→ cf Table of Cases Art 3 of the EIR Appendix A mn 16)[87], the COMI of the National Sales Companies was also held to be in England because, in the court's opinion, the **budgeting**, the **financial control**, and the **financing** of the NSC was being carried out from England.[88]
- In the **EMTEC** case (→ cf Table of Cases Art 3 of the EIR Appendix A mn 8), the COMI was held to be in France because, *inter alia*, the financial management was situated there.

• Place where **marketing decisions** are made and where the **corporate identity** is created;[89]

- In **MG Rover** (→ cf Table of Cases Art 3 of the EIR Appendix A mn 16),[90] another reason why the court found that the COMI of the National Sales Companies was in England was because the NSC had not presented an autonomous image to the outside world nor did they have an independent status. The **advertising brochures**, for example, were designed and produced in England. The **website** was operated in England, and other **marketing decisions** were also made from England.[91]

---

83 On this *Pannen/Riedemann* EWiR 2005, 73.

84 On this in detail *Penzlin/Riedemann* NZI 2005, 469 et seq.

85 High Court of Justice Birmingham dated 18 Apr 2005, NZI 2005, 467 et seq (→ cf Table of Cases Art 3 of the EIR Appendix A mn 16), at point 11 "... *I have not the slightest doubt that all effective management decisions, other than those which can be described as routinely operative, are taken at Longbridge or by personnel appointed by and supervised from Longbridge ...*".

86 Cf on this High Court of Justice Birmingham "Rover" ZIP 2005, 1610 = NZI 2005, 467 et seq (→ cf Table of Cases Art 3 of the EIR Appendix A mn 16); Cour d'appel de Versailles dated 4 Sep 2003, ISA Daisytek SAS – 05038/03 – with explanatory note by *Mankowski* EWiR 2003, 1239 (→ cf Table of Cases Art 3 of the EIR Appendix A mn 15).

87 On this in detail *Penzlin/Riedemann* NZI 2005, 469 et seq.

88 High Court of Justice Birmingham dated 18 Apr 2005, NZI 2005, 467 et seq (→ cf Table of Cases Art 3 of the EIR Appendix A mn 16), mn 12.

89 See High Court of Justice Leeds "ISA-Daisytek" ZIP 2004, 963, 965, point 13 of the detailed English original version (→ cf Table of Cases Art 3 of the EIR Appendix A, mn 15); High Court of Justice Birmingham "Rover" ZIP 2005, 1610, 1611; *Mankowski* EWiR 2005, 637, 638; *Mankowski* speaks of a "uniform group image under one single name", see *Mankowski* BB 2006, 1753, 1755.

90 On this in details *Penzlin/Riedemann* NZI 2005, 469 et seq.

91 High Court of Justice Birmingham dated 18 Apr 2005, NZI 2005, 467 et seq (→ cf Table of Cases Art 3 of the EIR Appendix A mn 16), mn 13.

- The **advertising** in the **Hettlage** case (→ cf Table of Cases Art 3 of the EIR Appendix A mn 12) was also designed by the responsible departments of the parent company.

• Primary place of **financial independence**, especially in the case of main suppliers and main creditors;[92]

- In the **MG Rover** case (→ cf Table of Cases Art 3 of the EIR Appendix A mn 16),[93] the National Sales Companies primarily sold products of the English group's head company and were integrated in the Rover affiliation. The group's head company was the **main supplier** and the **main creditor** of NSC.[94]

• **International group structure** and the **network of the business enterprise**[95] (for international insolvencies of corporate groups, see mn 46 et seq and the **ECJ decision Eurofood/Parmalat** in which this criteria was rejected as a connecting factor for ascertaining the *situs* of the COMI at → Table of Cases Art 3 of the EIR Appendix A mn 10).

- In the **EMTEC** case (→ cf Table of Cases Art 3 of the EIR Appendix A mn 8), the court held that the debtor's COMI was in France although the registered office of the holding company was in the Netherlands. This was based on the **controlling position** that the affiliated companies, EMTEC International and EMTEC France, exercised over the debtor. The court held that this could be deduced from the **group's structure.** The debtor, so the court, was being controlled by EMTEC International, EMTEC France, and their subsidiaries to a considerable degree. In the court's opinion, these companies were, *inter alia*, responsible for managing finances, supplying goods, corporate policy, and for the supply agreements of the debtor company.
- In the **MG Rover** decision (→ cf Table of Cases Art 3 of the EIR Appendix A mn 16)[96], Judge Norris refers to the international structure of the group as an argument in favour of locating the COMI in the United Kingdom.[97]
- In the **Parmalat** insolvency proceedings (→ cf Table of Cases Art 3 of the EIR Appendix A mn 10), the COMI was held to be with the Italian parent company in Italy because the activities of the subsidiary were being carried out exclusively in the interests of the parent company, the Italian parent company had full control, and because the directives in conjunction with all fundamental decisions stemmed from Italy.

• Place where **fundamental contracts** of the debtor are being negotiated and concluded;[98]

---

[92] On this see the case High Court of Justice Birmingham "Rover" ZIP 2005, 1610, 1611; Cour d'appel de Versailles dated 4 Sep 2003, ISA Daisytek SAS – 05038/03 – with explanatory note by *Mankowski* EWiR 2003, 1239 (→ cf Table of Cases Art 3 of the EIR Appendix A mn 15).

[93] On this in detail *Penzlin/Riedemann* NZI 2005, 469 et seq.

[94] High Court of Justice Birmingham dated 18 Apr 2005, NZI 2005, 467 et seq (→ cf Table of Cases Art 3 of the EIR Appendix A mn 16), mn 14.

[95] Cf High Court of Justice Birmingham "Rover" – dated 18 Apr 2005, 2375 – 2382/05 – reported by *Dammann* NZI 2005, 467 = reported by *Mankowski* ZIP 2005, 1610, 1611; *Mankowski* EWiR 2005, 637 (→ cf Table of Cases Art 3 of the EIR Appendix A mn 16).

[96] On this in detail *Penzlin/Riedemann* NZI 2005, 469 et seq.

[97] High Court of Justice Birmingham dated 18 Apr 2005, NZI 2005, 467 et seq (→ cf Table of Cases Art 3 of the EIR Appendix A mn 16), mn 16.

[98] Cour d'appel de Versailles dated 4 Sep 2003, ISA Daisytek SAS – 05038/03 – with explanatory note by *Mankowski* EWiR 2003, 1239 (→ cf Table of Cases Art 3 of the EIR Appendix A mn 15).

- In the **AvCraft Internation Ltd** case (→ cf Table of Cases Art 3 of the EIR Appendix B No 76), the presumption in Art 3 (1) sentence 2 of the EIR was rebutted since all administrative transactions such as the **maintenance of legal relationships** to third parties, **purchasing**, and personnel and accounting were being carried on from an outside location.
- A relevant criterion for ascertaining the COMI in the **Crisscross Telecommunications Group** case (→ cf Table of Cases Art 3 of the EIR Appendix A mn 6) was the fact that most customers had entered into **contracts, which were subject to English law**, with English companies.[99]
- In **BRAC Rent-A-Car** (→ cf Table of Cases Art 3 of the EIR Appendix A mn 3), the *situs* of the COMI was justified based on the fact that, *inter alia*, the fundamental contracts were subject to English law:

  "The company[100] *is incorporated in Delaware, and has its registered address in the United States. However, that is not an address from which it trades, and it has never traded in US. Its operations are conducted almost entirely in the UK. ... It trades from an address in Hemel Hempstead, in England. ... It has no employees in the US, and all its employees work in England, with contracts of employment governed by English law, apart from a small number in branch office in Switzerland. Its trading activities are carried out by way of contracts with subsidiaries and franchisees. All of these are governed by English law..."*[101]

• The place where **management employees** of the debtor live and carry out their day to day business.[102]

- In the **MG Rover** case (→ cf Table of Cases Art 3 of the EIR Appendix A mn 16),[103] the COMI of the National Sales Companies ("NSC") was held to be in the United Kingdom because, *inter alia*, **British citizens** were active in the respective management organs of all NSC, and in five of these they formed a majority.[104]
- In the **Sendo Ltd** decision (→ cf Table of Cases Art 3 of the EIR Appendix B No 77), the COMI was presumed to be in Great Britain (*inter alia*) because the managing directors **lived** there.
- In the **Eurotunnel** insolvency proceedings (→ cf Table of Cases Art 3 of the EIR Appendix A mn 11), one of the reasons why the COMI was presumed to be in France was because the strategic and operative management of the various group companies was being discharged in Paris by a common body made up of **French citizens**.

2.3.2.5.2 Conciliatory approach

40 A **conciliatory approach** is one which is based on **internal circumstances** and asks whether the conclusion it reaches is confirmed by the **external circumstances**.[105] If it is

---

[99] *Pannen/Riedemann* NZI 2004, 646, 648.

[100] Meaning BRAC Rent-A-Car Internaional Inc.

[101] High Court of Justice Chancery Division Companies Court (England; The Honourable Mr. Justice Lloyd), dated 7 Feb 2003 – 0042/2003, ZIP 2003, 813 et seq.

[102] *Martinez Ferber* European Insolvency Regulation (2004) p 23; *Penzlin* EWiR 2006, 207.

[103] On this in details *Penzlin/Riedemann* NZI 2005, 469 et seq.

[104] High Court of Justice Birmingham dated 18 Apr 2005, NZI 2005, 467 et seq (→ cf Table of Cases Art 3 of the EIR Appendix A mn 16), mn 11.

[105] MünchKomm BGB/*Kindler* IntInsR mn 144.

not, then the legal presumption in Art 3 (1) sentence 2 of the EIR should apply, which therefore means that the registered office is determinative.[106] The followers of this approach also find support for it by the fact that the registered office is discernible to every creditor. According to them, this approach would also accord with Recital 13 of the EIR since only it enables the creditors to calculate the legal risks in the event of an insolvency. The place where a company customarily carries out the administration of its interests – which therefore makes it ascertainable for third parties – determines, according to this approach, where its actual centre of its interests is located.

2.3.2.5.3 Objective criteria, business activity theory, ECJ in the Eurofood/Parmalat case

Another approach is based on **purely objective criteria** from a creditor's point of view **(business activity theory)**.[107] This approach is affirmed by the ECJ in the **Eurofood/Parmalat** judgement of 2 May 2006 – C-341/04 (→ cf Table of Cases Art 3 of the EIR Appendix A mn 10 – Eurofood/Parmalat) in the case of international jurisdiction in relation to a company in a corporate group;[108] on this, see mn 46 et seq. **The ECJ**[109] **clearly rejects the mind of management / head-office functions approach.** **41**

The centre of main interests pursuant to the **business activity theory** is the **place of the business activities**, on this see mn 49 below.[110] According to this theory, the Regulation is based on the assumption that, from the creditor's point of view, the place where business activities are being carried out is ascertainable as the centre of every company's interests.[111] Such an objective standard is very much in line with the aims of the Regulation.[112] **42**

Principally decisive for ascertaining the COMI are such objective criteria as **customer relations, a company's objects, employment of persons, bookkeeping, and bank accounts.**[113] According to this approach, international jurisdiction must be found at a place known to the creditors, this enabling them to estimate legal and eco- **43**

---

[106] *Virgós/Garcimartín* Regulation, p 44; MünchKomm BGB/*Kindler* IntInsR mn 144.

[107] *Israël* European Cross-Border Insolvency Regulation (2005) 258; *Bähr/Riedemann* ZIP 2004, 1065; *Pannen/Riedemann* NZI 2004, 646, 651; *Pannen/Riedemann* note on AG Offenburg, order of 2 Aug 2004 – 2 IN 133/04, EWiR 2005, 73; *Vallender* KTS 2005, 283, 292. This interpretation is affirmed by the ECJ in the Eurofood judgement of 2 May 2006 – C-341/04 (→ cf Table of Cases Art 3 of the EIR Appendix A mn 10 – Eurofood/Parmalat) in the case of international jurisdiction in relation to a company of a corporate group; on this, see mn 55.

[108] Cf *Mankowski* BB 2006, 1753, 1754.

[109] ECJ C-341/04 dated 2 May 2006, ZInsO 2006, 484. Cf on this critical: *Paulus* NZG 2006, 609, 612; approving: *Mankowski* BB 2006, 1753 et seq.

[110] So AG Mönchengladbach "EMBIC I" ZIP 2004, 1064 (→ cf Table of Cases Art 3 of the EIR Appendix A mn 7); with explanatory note by *Bähr/Riedemann* ZIP 2004, 1066, 1067; *Mankowski* EWiR 2005, 637, 638; *Weller* IPRax 2004, 412, 415 et seq cf also Hans Brochier Holdings Ltd (→ cf Table of Cases Art 3 of the EIR Appendix B No 97).

[111] Cf Recital 13 of the EIR; *Virgós/Schmit* Explanatory Report mn 76; Moss/Fletcher/Isaacs-*Fletcher*, Regulation, mn 3.10; *Smid* DZWiR 2006, 45, 46. Also High Court of Justice Chancery Division in Re Parkside Flexibles SA (→ Table of Cases Art 3 of the EIR Appendix B mn 67).

[112] *Bähr/Riedemann* ZIP 2004, 1066, 1067.

[113] *Marshall* European Cross Border Insolvency (2005) mn 1.006; Moss/Fletcher/Isaacs-*Moss/Smith*, Regulation, mn 8.39; *Bähr/Riedemann* ZIP 2004, 1066, 1067.

nomic risks.[114] The **place where the debtor's assets are mainly situated** may also be decisive.[115]

The moving of the administrative head office by **merely moving the business records** to another place does not amount to a relocation of the centre of the debtor's main interests pursuant to Art 3 (1) of the EIR (→ cf Table of Cases Art 3 of the EIR Appendix B No 89 – ***LG* Leipzig**).

Example:

In the AvCraft International Ltd case[116] (→ cf Table of Cases Art 3 of the EIR Appendix B No 76), the *AG* Weilheim lists the points that it considers decisive for a finding of German international jurisdiction. Objective criteria seem to be decisive. Tangible property and where it is situated (in this case the decision of the *AG* Weilheim turns on the *situs* of the production facilities) is one of the things to be taken into account in arriving at the ascertainment. The employment of salaried employees is an act that is also ascertainable for third parties. Decisive is the place at which the "day to day business" is being conducted, or the place where the "economic activities" of the debtor are taking place (affirmed by the *AG* Weilheim based on the criteria: purchasing and operative business).

44 In the Eurofood/Parmalat judgement of 2 May 2006 – C 341/04 (→ cf Table of Cases Art 3 of the EIR Appendix A mn 10), the **ECJ** did not set out **any criteria for ascertaining the COMI**, so that a number of references to the ECJ can be reckoned with.[117]

45 The **business activity theory** is preferable since only by relying on objective circumstances can the creditors be afforded the best possible protection.[118] A test using an objective third party ensures not only legal certainty, but it also makes the ascertainment of jurisdiction transparent and predictable for all outsiders. This is particularly relevant in light of the fact that, according to Art 4 of the EIR, jurisdiction also determines which law is applicable (*lex fori concursus*).

---

[114] *Virgós/Schmit* Explanatory Report mn 75; *Wessels* Current Topics of International Insolvency Law, 165; MünchKomm BGB/*Kindler* IntInsR mn 152; Moss/Fletcher/Isaacs-*Fletcher*, Regulation, mn 3.12; *Pannen/Riedemann* NZI 2004, 646, 656; *Marshall* European Cross Border Insolvency (2005) mn 1.006.

[115] An initiative pertaining to the Regulation that was submitted to the Council by the Federal Republic of Germany and the Republic of Finland on 26 May 1999 proposed this criterion for the wording of Recital 13 as an additional 3rd sentence; this is discussed in OJ C 221/8. This proposal was not, however, taken into account by the Council in the implementation of the Regulation; for more details on this, see: *Kübler* FS Gerhardt (2004) p 527, p 552 et seq; going further: *Poertzgen/Adam* ZInsO 2006, 505, 507; *Martinez Ferber* European Insolvency Regulation (2004) p 22.

[116] ZIP 2005, 1611; on this *Pannen/Riedemann* EWiR 2005, 791.

[117] *Mankowski* BB 2006, 1753, 1754.

[118] MünchKomm BGB/*Kindler* IntInsR mn 144; Moss/Fletcher/Isaacs-*Moss/Smith*, Regulation, mn 8.38; HamburgerKomm-*Undritz* Art 3 mn 34; BK-InsO/*Pannen* Art 3 EuInsVO mn 6a; *Pannen/Riedemann* EWiR 2005, 791; *Virgós/Schmit* Explanatory Report mn 75; Haß/Huber/Gruber/Heiderhoff-*Haß/Huber* Art 3 EuInsVO mn 15; confirmed by Eurofood, ECJ C-341/04, dated 2 May 2006, ZInsO 2006, 484 (→ cf Table of Cases Art 3 of the EIR Appendix A mn 10).

2.3.2.6 Insolvency of corporate groups

→ See the Table of Cases Art 3 of the EIR 46

- Appendix A mn 2: **Automold**
- Appendix A mn 3: **BRAC-Rent-A-Car**
- Appendix A mn 4: **Ci4net.com Inc**
- Appendix A mn 5: **Collins & Aikmann**
- Appendix A mn 6: **Crisscross Telecommunications Group**
- Appendix A mn 7: **EMBIC**
- Appendix A mn 8: **EMTEC**
- Appendix A mn 9: **Enron Directo SA**
- Appendix A mn 10: **Eurofood /Parmalat**
- Appendix A mn 11: **Eurotunnel**
- Appendix A mn 12: **Hettlage**
- Appendix A mn 14: **HUKLA**
- Appendix A mn 15: **ISA/Daisytek**
- Appendix A mn 16: **MG Rover**
- Appendix A mn 19: **Zenith**
- Appendix B No 14: **Norse Ferries and Cenargo Navigation Ltd**
- Appendix B No 29: **Cirio Del Monte**
- Appendix B No 53: **Parmalat Ungarn**
- Appendix B No 59: **AIM Underwriting Agencies Ltd**
- Appendix B No 67: **Re Parkside Flexibles SA**
- Appendix B No 76: **AvCraft International Ltd**
- Appendix B No 77: **Sendo Ltd**

The Regulation does **not specifically provide for** Cases involving **corporate consolidations** (in the form of parent companies and subsidiaries).[119] This is surprising considering that insolvencies of corporate groups are the very epitome[120] of cross-border insolvency proceedings.[121] The Regulation only regulates insolvency proceedings opened against an individual legal subject that involves legal issues in another Member State.[122] It in no way allows an inference to be drawn that the COMI of the subsidiaries of cross-border groups of companies is located at the registered office of the group's parent company.[123] The European legislators made the assumption based on the vast differences in the substantive laws of the Member States that a universal insolvency law regime would not be possible.[124] For this reason, whenever the Regulation applies, jurisdiction pur-

[119] *Virgós/Schmit* Explanatory Report mn 76; *Virgós/Garcimartín* Regulation, p 46; Moss/Fletcher/Isaacs-*Moss/Smith*, Regulation, mn 8.56; D-K/D/Ch-*Duursma-Kepplinger* Art 1 mn 48; *Bähr/Riedemann* ZIP 2004, 1066, 1067.

[120] *Mankowski* NZI 2004, 450, 452.

[121] Also BK-InsO/*Pannen* Art 3 EuInsVO mn 12; *Pannen/Riedemann* NZI 2004, 646, 647.

[122] Moss/Fletcher/Isaacs-*Fletcher*, Regulation, mn 3.15; D-K/D/Ch-*Duursma-Kepplinger* Art 1 mn 48.

[123] *Ehricke* EWS 2002, 101, 103.

[124] See Recital 11 of the EIR; Haß/Huber/Gruber/Heiderhoff-*Haß/Herweg* Art 3 EuInsVO

suant to Art 3 of the EIR must be determined separately **for each individual company in the corporate group.**[125] A unified **"group jurisdiction"** can therefore only be found if the centre of main interests (COMI) for all of the companies of the group can be localized at one single place, i.e. at the place where the group's management is located.[126] The existence of such a jurisdiction would make sense considering that the insolvency of one company in a group often has a domino effect, triggering the insolvency of all other units, or vital units, of the group; one group jurisdiction would also make the reorganization of the group as a whole considerably easier.[127]

47 The insolvency of groups such as **ISA/Daisytek,**[128] **Collins & Aikman,**[129] **Eurofood/Parmalat,**[130] **Hettlage,**[131] **Zenith,**[132] and **MG Rover**[133] have raised the highly disputed issue of how to ascertain the centre of main interests in the case of group insolvencies, especially that of foreign subsidiaries. Since most international groups are so-called **qual-**

mn 55; *Moss/Smith* in Moss/Fletcher/Isaacs-*Moss/Smith,* Regulation, mn 8.58 hold that a future revision of the Regulation should deal with this.

125 *Virgós/Schmit* Explanatory Report mn 76; *Mankowski* BB 2006, 1753, 1754; ECJ "Eurofood/Parmalat" ZInsO 2006, 484, 486 (→ cf Table of Cases Art 3 of the EIR Appendix A mn 10); *Duursma-Kepplinger/Duursma* IPRax 2003, 505, 510; *Eidenmüller* NJW 2004, 3455; *Oberhammer* ZInsO 2004, 761, 767; *Paulus* ZIP 2005, 1948; *Schilling/Schmidt* ZInsO 2006, 113, 115 et seq.

126 Haß/Huber/Gruber/Heiderhoff-*Haß/Herweg* Art 3 EuInsVO mn 56; *Wessels* Current Topics of International Insolvency Law, 165.

127 *Schelo* NZI Aktuell Heft 12/2005, V; *Virgós/Garcimartín* Regulation, p 61.

128 "ISA I" – High Court of Justice Leeds dated 16 May 2003 – 861-876/03 ZIP 2003, 1362; "ISA II" – AG Düsseldorf dated 6 Jun 2003 – 502 IN 126/03 ZIP 2003, 1363; AG Düsseldorf dated 12 Mar 2004 502 IN 126/03 ZIP 2004, 623; "ISA III" – Cour d'appel Versailles dated 4 Sep 2003 – 05038/03, ZIP 2004, 377 (→ cf Table of Cases Art 3 of the EIR Appendix A mn 15).

129 "Collins & Aikman I" – High Court of Justice London dated 15 Jul 2005 – 4697–4712/05 and 4717–4725/05, *Marshall* European Cross Border Insolvency, No 2.035/4; critical on this *Paulus* NZI 2005, 647; "Collins & Aikman II" – AG Cologne dated 10 Aug 2005 – 71 IN 416/05 ZIP 2005, 1566 = NZI 2005, 564 = NZG 2005, 858 = EuZW 2005, 704 = DZWiR 2006, 218; on this *Schilling/ Schmidt* DZWiR 2006, 219;"Collins & Aikman III" – High Court of Justice London dated 9 Jun 2006 – 4697, 4698, 4700, 4705, 4711, 4717–4719, 4721, 4722 of 2005, ZIP 2006, 2093; cf *Meyer-Löwy/Plank* NZI 2006, 622; (→ cf Table of Cases Art 3 of the EIR Appendix A mn 5).

130 "Eurofood/Parmalat I" – Tribunale di Parma dated 19 Feb 2004 – 53/04 ZIP 2004, 1220; Tribunale di Parma dated 15 Jun 2004 – 93/04 ZIP 2004, 2295; "Eurofood/Parmalat II" – High Court Dublin dated 23 Mar 2004 – 33/04 ZIP 2004, 1223; "Eurofood/Parmalat III" – Supreme Court of Ireland dated 27 Jul 2004 – 147/04 NZI 2004, 505; ECJ Advocate General *Jacobs* opinion dated 27 Sep 2005 – "Eurofood/ Parmalat IV" ZIP 2005, 1878; ECJ dated 2 May 2006 – C-341/04 ZInsO 2006, 484 = IPRax 2007, 120 (→ cf Table of Cases Art 3 of the EIR Appendix A mn 10).

131 "Hettlage I" – AG Munich dated 4 May 2004 – 1501 IE 1276/04 ZInsO 2004, 691; "Hettlage II" – Landesgericht Innsbruck dated 11 May 2004 – 9 S 15/04, ZIP 2004, 1721 (→ cf Table of Cases Art 3 of the EIR Appendix A mn 12).

132 AG Siegen dated 1 Jul 2004 – 25 IN 154/04 NZI 2004, 673; Landesgericht Klagenfurt dated 2 Jul 2004 – 41 S 75/04h NZI 2004, 677 (→ cf Table of Cases Art 3 of the EIR Appendix A mn 19).

133 "MG Rover I" – High Court of Justice Birmingham dated 18 Apr 2005 – 2375–2382/05 ZIP 2005, 1610; "MG Rover II" – High Court of Justice Birmingham dated 11 May 2005 NZI 2005, 515; High Court of Justice Birmingham dated 30 Mar 2006 – 2377/2006 NZI 2006, 416 (→ cf Table of Cases Art 3 of the EIR Appendix A mn 16).

ified de facto groups, meaning that the individual companies are completely controlled by the parent company through either a sole or controlling interest in the subsidiary company, the strategic decision-making powers of the individual group companies are vested in the group's parent company, while its actual (de facto) activities are being executed at the registered office of the group company. This disparity raises the question as to which country has international jurisdiction for the insolvency proceedings involving the assets of the subsidiary companies.

The issue becomes particularly pertinent in light of the **principle of priority** (on this, see mn 88 and the ECJ in the Eurofood/Parmalat case (→ cf Table of Cases Art 3 of the EIR Appendix A mn 10) according to which jurisdiction, once having been assumed for main insolvency proceedings in respect of a legal entity, must be recognized in every other Member State.[134] A review may only be made for reasons of **public policy** (Art 26 of the EIR), but this will rarely be relevant to a mistaken assumption of jurisdiction.[135] A violation of public policy can only be found if the decision rendered in another Member State violates a fundamental legal principle and therefore conflicts in an unacceptable manner with the laws of the enforcing country.[136] In terms of insolvency law, this means that the recognition of insolvency proceedings may be denied if, for example, the decision to open proceedings was rendered in obvious **violation of the concerned person's fundamental right to be heard by the court.**[137] **48**

Example:

***OLG/OGH* Vienna (→ cf Table of Cases Art 3 of the EIR Appendix A mn 13)**

On 27 March 2003, the High Court of Justice in London opened bankruptcy proceedings in respect of the assets of the debtor with a short reference to Art 3 (1) of the EIR. Having no knowledge of these proceedings, an Austrian bank, which had been

---

134 Haß/Huber/Gruber/Heiderhoff-*Haß/Herweg* Art 3 EuInsVO mn 59; *Israël* European Cross-Border Insolvency Regulation (2005) p 264; a decision of the Municipality Court of Prague is important in this connection; the court held that, pursuant to Czech law, the appointment of a temporary administrator constitutes an effective opening for an assertion of priority (Municipality Court of Prague, "Aircraft" ZIP 2005, 1431 → cf Table of Cases Art 3 of the EIR Appendix A, mn 1; see also *Herchen* ZIP 2005, 1401; *Smid* DZWiR 2006, 45, 57; *Smid* Komm EuInsVO Art 3 mn 19.

135 *Knof/Mock* ZIP 2006, 189, 190; Austrian OGH NZI 2005, 465 (→ cf Table of Cases Art 3 of the EIR Appendix A mn 10); *Herchen* ZIP 2005, 1401, 1404; *Wessels* Current Topics of International Insolvency Law, 27; Moss/ Fletcher/Isaacs-*Moss/Smith*, Regulation, mn 8.206; *Smid* DZWiR 2006, 45, 47; *Smid* DZWiR 2006, 325, 326; contra in extreme cases: *Morscher* Die europäische Insolvenzverordnung p 21; see on this *Carstens* Die internationale Zuständigkeit im europäischen Insolvenzrecht (2005) 93 et seq.

136 ECJ "Krombach/Bamberski" NJW 2000, 1853, 1854; *Virgós/Schmit* Explanatory Report mn 206; cf also *Kammel* NZI 2006, 334, 338.

137 ECJ C-341/04, judgement of 2 May 2006, ZInsO 2006, 484 (→ cf Table of Cases Art 3 of the EIR Appendix A, mn 10). However in its decision of 27 Jun 2006, the Cour de cassation was of the opinion that the failure to hear the personnel representative prior to the opening of reorganization proceedings (which pursuant to art L 621-1 Code de commerce leads to the annulment of the opening order) is not a manifest violation of a person involved in such proceedings' fundamental right to be heard; on this, see *Dammann/Podeur* Banque & Droit 2006 (109), 6, who are of the opinion that the provisions of art L 621-1 Code de commerce do not fall within the fundamental principles set out in art 26 of the EIR.

trying for a considerable time to collect on debts owed by the debtor, filed a bankruptcy petition at the *Handelsgericht* in Vienna on 26 November 2003. By order dated 28 January 2004, the *Handelsgericht* opened bankruptcy proceedings against the assets of the debtor.

By order dated 9 November 2004, the *OLG* in Vienna recognized the bankruptcy proceedings in England as main insolvency proceedings within the meaning of Art 3 (1) of the EIR. The court saw no violation of public policy as per Art 26 of the EIR since, in the court's opinion, such a violation would demand a serious disregard of fundamental Community law. An infringement of the jurisdiction provisions of the Regulation would, in itself, certainly not amount to a violation of public policy. The court also held that the (absence of) reasons of the High Court of Justice also did not qualify as a violation of public policy since no fundamental principles of fair procedure had been breached by them.

49 There are basically **three approaches to ascertaining the COMI in the case of group companies.** The **Supreme Court of Ireland**[138] requested a clarification of this central issue from the **ECJ** in the form of a preliminary ruling. The ECJ[139] rendered its decision on this on 2 May 2006 (→ cf Table of Cases Art 3 of the EIR Appendix A mn 10 – **Eurofood/Parmalat**), the court thereby endorsing the **business activity theory** (see mn 41 and 44).

The three approaches are to be distinquished as follows:

50 According to the **first approach**, the interests of the group as a whole are to be given priority over the interests of the creditors of the subsidiary companies. Pursuant to this approach (see also mn 53 below), decisive for ascertaining the COMI is the place where the so-called **head-office functions**[140] – business, sales, and personnel management – are being discharged, i.e. the place where strategic decisions, and thus the control over the subsidiaries, are being made.[141] In centrally controlled affiliations of companies, this so-called **mind of management** is generally found at the **headquarters** of the group, which is generally the registered office of the parent company.[142] This results in effect in a unified

[138] Supreme Court of Ireland "Eurofood/Parmalat III" ZIP 2004, 1969 (→ cf Table of Cases Art 3 of the EIR Appendix A mn 10).

[139] ECJ C-341/04 dated 2 May 2006, ZInsO 2006, 484 (→ cf Table of Cases Art 3 of the EIR Appendix A mn 10).

[140] AG Munich "Hettlage" IPRax 2004, 433 (→ cf Table of Cases Art 3 of the EIR Appendix A mn 12) approving: *Paulus* EWiR 2004, 493; AG Offenburg NZI 2004, 673 (→ cf Table of Cases Art 3 of the EIR Appendix A mn 14 – HUKLA); AG Siegen NZI 2004, 673, 674 (→ cf Table of Cases Art 3 of the EIR Appendix A mn 19 – Zenith); High Court of Justice Birmingham "Rover" ZIP 2005, 1610 et seq (→ cf Table of Cases Art 3 of the EIR Appendix A mn 16); *Fletcher* Insolvency in Private International Law (2005) mn 7.70, 7.77; *Paulus* ZIP 2003, 1725, 1727; also for the Tribunale di Parma "Eurofood/Parmalat I" (→ cf Table of Cases Art 3 of the EIR Appendix A mn 10), the High Court of Justice Leeds "ISA I" (→ cf Table of Cases Art 3 of the EIR Appendix A mn 15) and the Municipality Court Fejér/Székesfehérvár "Parmalat Hungary/Slovakia" (→ cf Table of Cases Art 3 of the EIR Appendix B No 53) was the mind of management decisive; Tribunal de Commerce de Nanterre "EMTEC" (→ cf Table of Cases Art 3 of the EIR Appendix A mn 8), with explanatory note by *Penzlin* EWiR 2006, 207.

[141] *Penzlin/Riedemann* NZI 2005, 469, 470; *Weller* ZHR 169 (2005), 570, 579; *Wessels* Current Topics of International Insolvency Law, 182.

[142] AG Offenburg NZI 2004, 673 (→ cf Table of Cases Art 3 of the EIR Appendix A mn 14); on this *Pannen/Riedemann* EWiR

group jurisdiction at the centre of interests of the parent company.[143] Often, however, this place is not readily ascertainable to creditors, but is rather a matter of internal organizational structures.

The **business-activity-theory** localizes the centre of main interests at the **place of the economic (business) activities.**[144] According to this theory, the Regulation is based on the assumption that, from the creditors' point of view, the place where business activities are being carried out is ascertainable as the centre of every company's interests.[145] It further contends that international jurisdiction must be at the place known to the creditors, thus enabling them to estimate the legal and economic risks.[146] A unified international jurisdiction at the registered office of the group's parent company will, according to this theory, only be found in exceptional Cases if the controlling position of the group's parent company is outwardly ascertainable to the creditors.[147] **51**

For **ascertaining the COMI of a corporate group**, the **conciliatory approach** concerns itself with the **organization** of the group.[148] If the group presents itself as a functional unit (**centralized group**[149]) whose decisions are directed and controlled by the parent company, then it would appear correct to place the COMI at the place of the parent company. But if it is a heterogeneous (**decentralized**) **group**, then the presumption in sentence 2 of Art 3 of the EIR should be applied, i.e. the COMI of the subsidiary company should be located at the registered office of such subsidiary.[150] Such a differentiation could also find support in the fact that in the case of centralized groups with their uniform **corporate identity**, the way the individual group companies present themselves to the outside world (logo and design) is also uniform, and it is thus objectively ascertainable to the creditors where the COMI of the group is located. This would then allow ample opportunity for making an individual assessment of the potential risks. **52**

In order to comment on the various advocated theories, the following **three basic points** should be kept in mind. Each of them throws a different light on the particular theory. **53**

- Firstly, a centralized winding-up of a corporate group not only makes economic sense, but, because it increases the insolvency estate that is liable for satisfying claims, it may

2005, 73; *Oberhammer* ZInsO 2004, 761, 767.

[143] An exception to the above principle was made in the BRAC Rent-A-Car case where the COMI was presumed at the registered office of the subsidiary, High Court of Justice "Re BRAC Rent-A-Car" ZIP 2003, 813 = [2003] EWHC (Ch) 128 = 2 All E.R. 201 (→ cf Table of Cases Art 3 of the EIR Appendix A mn 3); with explanatory note by *Sabel/Schlegel* EWiR 2003, 367; *Pannen/Riedemann* NZI 2004, 646, 649.

[144] So AG Mönchengladbach "EMBIC I" ZIP 2004, 1064 (→ cf Table of Cases Art 3 of the EIR Appendix A mn 7); with explanatory note by *Bähr/Riedemann* ZIP 2004, 1066, 1067; *Mankowski* EWiR 2005, 637, 638; *Pannen/Riedemann* NZI 2004, 646, 651; *Pannen/Riedemann* Comments on AG Offenburg, dated 2 Aug 2004 – 2 IN 133/04, EWiR 2005, 73; *Weller* IPRax 2004, 412, 415 et seq.

[145] Cf Recital 13 of the EIR *Virgós/Schmit* Explanatory Report mn 76; Moss/Fletcher/Isaacs-*Fletcher*, Regulation, mn 3.10; *Smid* DZWiR 2006, 45, 46.

[146] *Virgós/Schmit* Explanatory Report mn 75; *Wessels* Current Topics of International Insolvency Law, 165; MünchKomm BGB/*Kindler* IntInsR mn 152; Moss/Fletcher/Isaacs-*Fletcher*, Regulation, mn 3.12; *Pannen/Riedemann* NZI 2004, 646, 651.

[147] *Herchen* ZInsO 2004, 825, 826; *Virgós/Garcimartín* Regulation, p 47; *Lautenbach* NZI 2004, 384, 386.

[148] *Paulus* Komm EuInsVO Art 3 mn 30–42.

[149] On the structuring of corporate groups, see *Emmerich/Sonnenschein* Konzernrecht § 4 I.

[150] *Paulus* ZIP 2005, 1948, 1952.

also be extremely advantageous to the creditors in some Cases.[151] A splitting up of the economic unity into the individual group companies for procedural law reasons would put at risk that additional value that the group – as a unified whole – is attributed with.[152] Another reason for supporting a centralized winding-up is the fact that groups, for strategical reasons, commonly shift profits and losses amongst the group companies, and they do so without the creditors being able to know about it or prevent it in any way.[153] In the event of an insolvency, the assets that should be there to satisfy the creditors' claims are often no longer in existence at the particular group company.

- Secondly, the creditor's assessment of the risk must be taken into account. Special, objective criteria should be used to ascertain the COMI since this is the only way to ensure that the creditors are able to assess their risk when they enter into business relations with a company.[154]
- The third thing to bear in mind is that the drafters of the Regulation consciously refrained from establishing a group jurisdiction in the case of insolvencies of corporate groups, but rather favoured a separate ascertainment of jurisdiction for each company for insolvency law purposes as well.[155] Recital 13 of the EIR makes it clear that any group-internal matters that are not ascertainable by third parties are irrelevant for the determination of the centre of main interests.

In light of these, the "mind of management" approach must be discarded.[156] For one thing it would create a group jurisdiction for the purposes of insolvency proceedings. Secondly, a connecting factor would be presumed that is not readily ascertainable for the creditors, which would run contrary to the recitals of the Regulation. The **trust created – *ex ante* the establishing of the business relationship** – in the insolvency law regime applicable at the actual place of the economic activities would be frustrated were an exception to be made in the case of centrally organized corporate groups.[157] There is also the possibility that main insolvency proceedings would be conducted at a place where neither employees, assets, nor creditors of the subsidiary exist.[158]

The conciliatory approach (see mn 52) is also not convincing considering the **minimal protection to creditors** that it offers. It is generally the small creditors and the employees who do not profit from a group jurisdiction, and it is especially these who warrant protection. And it is this specific group of creditors that is not in a position to look for contractual partners or to sustainably enforce their rights in another Member State. The

151 *Vallens/Dammann* NZI 2006, 29, 30; HamburgerKomm-*Undritz* Art 3 mn 14; *Eidenmüller* NJW 2004, 3455, 3456.

152 *Virgós/Garcimartín* Regulation, p 46; *Paulus* ZIP 2005, 1948, 1953; *Paulus* NZI aktuell 2006, Heft 8, VII.

153 *Pellens/Jödicke/Richard* DB 2005, 1393, 1394; *Paulus* ZIP 2005, 1948, 1953.

154 *Virgós/Schmit* Explanatory Report mn 75; Virgós/*Garcimartín* Regulation, p 46; *Weller* IPRax 2004, 412, 416.

155 Cf *Virgós/Schmit* Explanatory Report mn 76; also *Gottwald* Grenzüberschreitende Insolvenzen (1997) 21 et seq; *Eidenmüller* IPRax 2001, 2, 4; Moss/Fletcher/Isaacs-*Moss/Smith*, Regulation, mn 8.56; *Herchen* ZInsO 2004, 825, 827; *Weller* IPRax 2004, 412, 415.

156 Dissenting opinion in *Paulus* ZIP 2005, 1948, 1952: it is appropriate to deem the centre of main interests at the place of the parent company in Cases where the group operates as a single functional unit; see also *Eidenmüller* NJW 2004, 3455, 3458 et seq who prefers to find this at the administrative head office of the company.

157 *Virgós/Garcimartín* Regulation, p 46 et seq; *Weller* ZHR 169 (2005) 570, 582; *Kübler* FS Gerhardt (2004) p 527, 551.

158 Cf *Weller* ZHR 169 (2005), 570, 579; *Bähr/Riedemann* ZIP 2004, 1066; *Wimmer* ZInsO 2005, 119, 122.

necessity of this was also acknowledged in the **MG Rover**[159] case (→ cf Table of Cases Art 3 of the EIR Appendix A mn 16). The group consisted of an English parent company that had eight wholly-owned subsidiaries in other Member States. The English court decided on the basis of the "mind of management" approach that the COMI of the parent and all of the subsidiaries was located in England and opened one main insolvency proceeding for all of the companies there. Following the opening of the proceedings, the High Court of Justice issued another order.[160] It was stipulated as part of the powers of the English liquidator that employee claims were to be satisfied in the order of priority to which they were entitled pursuant to the national laws. It was not the protection of the creditors that the court had in mind, but rather the prevention of secondary insolvency proceedings, which, in the opinion of the court, would have led to a shattering of the group.[161] This case clearly illustrates that the protection of the creditors plays a subordinate role in the case of a group jurisidiction; although it may, admittedly, lead to a higher dividend in some Cases, it generally only benefits the secured creditors.

As a result, the only really convincing approach for the localisation of the COMI is the one based on the **economic business activity** of the individual group companies.[162] Only this approach affords small creditors and especially employees – who operate under the assumption that national insolvency law governs their contractual partners – the necessary protection from the consequences of an insolvency. Only the safeguarding of this assumption assures a maximum of creditor protection. But if, on the other hand, it is ascertainable to outside parties that the economic activities are being managed by the parent company, then the COMI of the group company can also be found at the registered office of the parent company. The result of such international, corporate-group insolvency law is that a liquidator is forced to apply various national, complex company laws at the same time. This presupposes the existence of "transnational corporate-group liquidators"[163] who are willing and able to take on such a case. **54**

The **ECJ**[164] came, in effect, to the same conclusion (→ cf Table of Cases Art 3 of the EIR Appendix A mn 10 – **Eurofood/Parmalat**).[165] According to this, the presumption found in Art 3 (1) sentence 2 of the EIR, i.e. that the centre of main interests is in the Member State in which the registered office is situated, can only be rebutted if there are **objective elements ascertainable by third parties** that prove that the actual location is not that of the registered office.[166] This should apply especially in Cases where the company is not involved in any activities at its registered office (**mailbox/sham companies**). To rebut the presumption, it is not enough – and here the judgement effectively holds against the "mind of management" approach – that the economic decisions of the subsidiaries can be controlled by the parent company.[167] What is meant by "third parties" in the decision are, in keeping with *Virgós/Schmit*, primarily the (potential) creditors.[168] **55**

---

[159] High Court of Justice Birmingham "MG Rover" NZI 2005, 467; with explanatory note by *Penzlin/Riedemann* NZI 2005, 469.

[160] High Court of Justice Birmingham "MG Rover II" NZI 2005, 515.

[161] HamburgerKomm-*Undritz* Art 3 mn 30; *Virgós/Garcimartín* Regulation, p 46.

[162] AG Mönchengladbach "EMBIC I" ZIP 2004, 1064 (→ cf Table of Cases Art 3 of the EIR Appendix A mn 7); *Bähr/Riedemann* ZIP 2004, 1066, 1067; *Mankowski* EWiR 2005, 637, 638; *Weller* IPRax 2004, 412, 415 et seq; also Recital 13 of the EIR; *Virgós/Schmit* Explanatory Report mn 76; *Kübler* FS Gerhardt (2004) p 527, 555.

[163] *Oberhammer* ZInsO 2004, 761, 770.

[164] ECJ C-341/04 dated 2 May 2006, ZInsO 2006, 484. Cf on this critical *Paulus* NZG 2006, 609, 612.

[165] Cf also *Kammel* NZI 2006, 334, 338.

[166] *Kammel* NZI 2006, 334, 336.

[167] *Kammel* NZI 2006, 334, 336.

[168] *Virgós/Schmit* Explanatory Report, mn 75; concurring: His Honour Judge Howarth in

56 The ECJ[169] in the **Parmalat/Eurofood** decision of 2 May 2006 also held (→ cf Table of Cases Art 3 of the EIR Appendix A mn 10) that proceedings once opened must be recognized in all other Member States without any verification of this. This raises the question of how the directions of the ECJ can be enforced if a court does not comply with them, i.e. if a court holds pursuant to the "mind of management" approach that the COMI is at the place of strategic decision making. The ECJ replied to this in the judgement that, in such a situation, it would be open to the Member States to construe such a proceeding that was opened too quickly as a violation of public policy (Art 26 of the EIR), and therefore they would not have to recognize it. The "public policy objection" must, however, be based on a manifest infringement of a fundamental legal rule or of a right considered fundamental.[170]

57 Another reason to contain the spreading of the "mind of management" approach is to **prevent forum shopping,** thus curtailing[171] the propagation of **"insolvency tourism and insolvency imperialism"**.[172] "Forum shopping" refers to consciously "searching" for the insolvency law regime most advantageous for the company. And a less than optimal coordination of the legal regimes makes it even easier for courts to declare the COMI at a place that the debtors wants.[173] There is a particularly high danger of this in relation to corporate group insolvencies as there are a number of group companies each of which would be eligible as the group domicile. One very good reason to curtail this is that it would otherwise force creditors to assess the risks in conjunction with their undertaking on the basis of a hypothetical insolvency law regime, thereby exposing them to an excessive amount of potential manipulation.[174] In summary, a unified group jurisdiction would encourage forum shopping and would significantly emaciate the effectiveness of the Regulation.[175]

2.3.3 Situations involving non-European companies

58 **→ See the Table of Cases Art 3 of the EIR**

- **Appendix A mn 3 BRAC Rent-A-Car**
- **Appendix A mn 4 Ci4net.com Inc**

59 In **BRAC Rent-A-Car** (→ cf Table of Cases Art 3 of the EIR Appendix A mn 3), the High Court of Justice had to deal with the question of whether the Regulation also

Skjevesland v Geveran Trading Company Ltd. [2002] EWHC 2898 (Ch) – quoted in BeckRS 2005, 09991 (→ cf Table of Cases Art 3 of the EIR Appendix B No 3); in the "Eurofood/Parmalat" case (→ cf Table of Cases Art 3 of the EIR Appendix A mn 10), the High Court of Ireland held that which the third parties (creditors) actually ascertained as determinative, whereas the Tribunale di Parma focussed on what the third parties should have ascertained; see *Marshall* European Cross Border Insolvency (2005) mn 2.038, 2.068 et seq; *Saenger/Klockenbrink* EuZW 2006, 363, 364; *Pannen/Riedemann* NZI 2004, 646, 651.

[169] ECJ C-341/04 dated 2 May 2006, ZInsO 2006, 485 = IPRax 2007, 120 (→ cf Table of Cases Art 3 of the EIR Appendix A mn 10 – Eurofood/Parmalat); comments on this *inter alia* by *Baxter* INSOL WORLD III 2006, 9 et seq.

[170] *Kammel* NZI 2006, 334, 338.

[171] Recital 4 of the EIR.

[172] *Mankowski* EWiR 2003, 1239.

[173] *Weller* IPRax 2004, 412, 413; Hamburger-Komm-*Undritz* Art 3 mn 103; *Wessels* Current Topics of International Insolvency Law, 238; *Virgós/Garcimartín* Regulation, p 46; *Kübler* FS Gerhardt (2004) p 527, 554.

[174] *Kindler* IPRax 2006, 114, 115.

[175] *Virgós/Garcimartín* Regulation, p 47.

applied **in relation to non-EU countries.** The BRAC Rent-A-Car International Inc.[176] was one of the largest globally operating car rental firms, which was founded in the US state of Delaware and had its registered office there. Chapter 11 proceedings had already been opened in the USA against the company and against other companies of the group. The company had no employees in the USA. Most of the employees were found in England. The business activities were also carried out in England. The company requested the opening of insolvency proceedings pursuant to which (main) insolvency proceedings were opened in the USA.

By order dated 14 January 2003, the High Court of Justice issued an "administration order" with which main insolvency proceedings were opened parallel to the US insolvency proceedings. This would appear to be the first time that a court held the Regulation applicable to a non-EU country.[177] The court found that because the business operations were executed exclusively in England, the presumption in Art 3 (1) sentence 2 of the EIR had been rebutted. If this decision is followed, main insolvency proceedings as per the Regulation could be opened in each EU Member State against every **non-EU pseudo foreign corporation** whose actual administrative head office is located in the European Union.[178] **60**

The decision **Ci4net.com Inc** (→ cf Table of Cases Art 3 of the EIR Appendix A mn 4) follows in the footsteps of this judgement. The debtor was a company founded and registered in the USA and operated in the Internet sector. The business activities, which had ceased long before the request was made, were ultimately obviously carried out primarily in England. By order dated 20 May 2004, the High Court of Justice in Leeds nevertheless opened main insolvency proceedings in England. It affirmed its international jurisdiction, concurring with both the grounds for and the result of the decision of the High Court of Justice in London. **61**

Decisive is whether the **cross-border element of the Regulation** commands a foreign connection to another EU Member State (so-called **qualified foreign connection**[179]) or merely a connection to any foreign country (**simple foreign connection**[180]), on this see Art 1 of the EIR mn 118 et seq as well. The issue becomes vital in Cases such as BRAC Rent-A-Car (→ cf Table of Cases Art 3 of the EIR Appendix A mn 3) that involve the cross-border insolvency of a non-European company. **62**

---

[176] High Court of Justice Chancery Division Companies Court dated 7 Feb 2003 – 42/03 "Re BRAC Rent-A-Car" ZIP 2003, 813 = [2003] EWHC (Ch) 128 = [2003] 2 All E.R. 201 (→ cf Table of Cases Art 3 of the EIR Appendix A mn 3); on this also *Pannen/Riedemann* NZI 2004, 646, 649.

[177] Following in the footsteps of this judgement is the High Court of Justice Leeds in the matter "Ci4net" ZIP 2004, 1769 (→ cf Table of Cases Art 3 of the EIR Appendix A mn 4), commented on by *Westpfahl/Wilkens* EWiR 2004, 848. The debtor in this case, although founded and registered in the USA, operated mainly in England. The High Court of Justice justified the international jurisdiction of the English courts on the grounds that the presumption in Art 3 (1) sentence 2 of the EIR had been rebutted; approving: *Herchen* ZInsO 2004, 830; *Krebber* IPRax 2004, 540; critical: *Westpfahl/Wilkens* EWiR 2004, 848, 849; dissenting opinion: *Smid* DZWiR 2003, 302.

[178] *Pannen/Riedemann* NZI 2004, 646, 649.

[179] *Balz* ZIP 1996, 948, 949; *Ehricke/Ries* JuS 2003, 313; D-K/D/Ch-*Duursma-Kepplinger* Art 1 mn 3; *Smid* Komm EuInsVO Art 3 mn 6a.

[180] *Huber* ZZP 114 (2001), 136, 138 et seq; *Krebber* IPRax 2004, 540 et seq; *Hauboldt* IPRax 2003, 34; Haß/Huber/Gruber/Heiderhoff-*Huber* Art 1 EuInsVO mn 19 et seq.

63 **In some Cases**, the existence of a **"simple" foreign connection** is found to be sufficient.[181] These Cases justify this on the provisions of Art 3 (1) of the EIR, which for the opening of insolvency proceedings prescribes nothing more than the existence of the centre of main interests in a Member State. It is then argued that this also warrants the equal treatment of Cases involving European and non-European factual situations.[182]

64 To be kept in mind is that the Regulation itself does **not regulate** international insolvency law issues arising between EU Member States and non-EU countries. Because some of the provisions of the Regulation stipulate that in certain situations the laws of other Member States (Arts 5, 7–11, 13, 15 of the EIR) are to apply, it could logically be inferred that the existence of a cross-border, inner-Community element is imperative.[183] But from the same wording chosen by the legislators, the inference could also be made that these provisions do not apply when a connection to a non-European country (simple foreign connection) exists. Therefore an adequate answer to this question cannot be derived from the **underlying logic of the Regulation.**

65 Invoking the provisions of Art 3 (1) of the EIR is questionable considering that Art 3 merely regulates jurisdiction, which says nothing about the application of the Regulation in any particular case.

66 Furthermore, the kind of **practical considerations** raised in the BRAC Rent-A-Car decision cannot, at least on their own, answer the question on the scope of the Regulation's territorial applicability.

67 Support for the necessity of a **qualified foreign connection,** i.e. that there must be a relationship to an EU Member State, could be found in Art 65 of the EEC Treaty. This provision clothes the Community with competence only to the extent necessary for a **proper functioning of the single European market.** Some conclude that this provision operates to divest the Community legislator of any legislative competence regarding matters that have a simple foreign connection only.[184]

68 **Reasons of legal certainty** also speak against broadening the scope of applicability of the Regulation to non-Member States,[185] as was done in the BRAC Rent-A-Car case (→ cf Table of Cases Art 3 of the EIR Appendix A mn 3) even though it may make economic sense in some instances, on this see Art 1 of the EIR mn 121 above.

2.3.4 Relocation of domicile / shifting the COMI

69 **Relocating the domicile** or **shifting the COMI** of the debtor's raises the issue of whether the court at which the request to open proceedings was made retains jurisdiction, or whether a change of jurisdiction takes place. The points in time that may be determinative for a change of jurisdiction are:

- **the coming into existence of the debt,**
- **the lodging of the insolvency request, or**
- **the opening of the insolvency proceedings.**

---

[181] In the decision High Court of Justice "Re BRAC Rent-A-Car" ZIP 2003, 813 = [2003] EWHC (Ch) 128 = 2 All E.R. 201 (→ cf Table of Cases Art 3 of the EIR Appendix A mn 3); *Herchen* ZInsO 2003, 742, 746; *Herchen* ZInsO 2004, 825, 830.

[182] So in particular in the decision High Court of Justice "Re BRAC Rent-A-Car" ZIP 2003, 813 = [2003] EWHC (Ch) 128 = 2 All E.R. 201 (→ cf Table of Cases Art 3 of the EIR Appendix A mn 3).

[183] *Huber* ZZP 114 (2001) 133, 138 et seq relies on this argument.

[184] Also *Duursma-Kepplinger/Duursma* IPRax 2003, 505, 506; and *Mock/Schildt* in Hirte/Bücker Grenzüberschreitende Gesellschaften § 17 mn 10 et seq.

[185] *Pannen/Riedemann* NZI 2004, 646, 651.

The **time at which the debt came into existence** cannot serve as a connecting factor since instead of upholding one of the fundamental goals of the Regulation, namely the prevention of jurisdictional conflicts, it would increase the chances of it.[186] **70**

→ See the Table of Cases Art 3 of the EIR

- **Appendix A mn 17: Susanne Staubitz-Schreiber**
- **Appendix B No 5: *LG* Wuppertal**
- **Appendix B No 26: M. van Dulvenbode v W. J. M. van Andelte & J. J. van der Veen**
- **Appendix B No 64: Shierson v Vlieland-Boddy**
- **Appendix B No 73: AG Celle**

2.3.4.1 Outline of the problem

Until the ECJ **decision "Susanne Staubitz-Schreiber"** (→ cf Table of Cases Art 3 of the EIR Appendix A mn 17), the treatment of a **relocation of the domicile after the opening of the proceedings** was much in dispute. **71**

- **Legal precedent and literature in Germany** hold that the **time of the lodging of the request** is solely decisive for establishing jurisdiction,[187]
- whereas the **courts and legal scholars in England and the Netherlands** consider the **time of the opening decision** as decisive, unless the relocation of the domicile evidently constitutes an abuse of the law.[188]

By order dated 27 November 2003, the ***BGH*** referred the question to the ECJ.[189] The strongest argument put forth by the *BGH* for retaining the jurisdiction of the court at which the request is made was the objective set out in Recital 4 of the EIR, namely the prevention of **forum shopping.** The court also conceded, however, that the fact that the debtor would no longer be permanently present in the earlier location, and since he would have brought his remaining assets to the new location, could make the insolvency proceedings more cumbersome. **72**

---

186 AG Celle – individuals – ZInsO 2005, 895 = NZI 2005, 410 (→ cf Table of Cases Art 3 of the EIR Appendix B No 73); also High Court of Justice Chancery Division dated 26 Nov 2004 (→ cf Table of Cases Art 3 of the EIR Appendix B No 65, Shierson v Vlieland-Boddy); *Knof* ZInsO 2005, 1017, 1023; *Mankowski* NZI 2005, 368, 369.

187 AG Celle, ZInsO 2005, 895 = NZI 2005, 410 (→ cf Table of Cases Art 3 of the EIR Appendix B mn 73); LG Hamburg – individuals – NZI 2005, 645; *Mankowski* NZI 2005, 368; *Mankowski* NZI 2005, 575, 576.

188 For Great Britain: Geveran Trading Co Ltd. v. Skjevesland [2003] BPIR 73 (Registrar Jacques) and [2003] BCC 391 (High Court) (→ cf Table of Cases Art 3 of the EIR Appendix B No 3), Shierson v Vlieland-Boddy [2005], EWCA Civ 974 = NZI 2005, 571 (→ cf Table of Cases Art 3 of the EIR Appendix B No 64: In this case the court held that the time of the opening of the main proceedings was decisive for ascertaining the COMI.) Netherlands: Gerechtshof Amsterdam dated 17 Jun 2003, JOR 2003/186 (→ cf Table of Cases Art 3 of the EIR Appendix B No 26); Hooge Rad 9 Jan 2004, Zaaknr. R03/091HR, available at: www.rechtspraak. nl.; *Dicey/Morris/Morse* Conflict of Laws, Fourth Cumulative Supplement (1991) mn 31-090; *Fletcher* Law of Insolvency p 839; Moss/Fletcher/Isaacs-*Moss/Smith,* Regulation, mn 8.44; *Wessels* Moving House: Which Court Can Open Insolvency Proceedings, p 4 et seq.

189 BGH, ZIP 2004, 94 et seq = NZI 2004, 139 with explanatory note by *Liersch*. (→ cf Table of Cases Art 3 of the EIR Appendix A mn 17).

2.3.4.2 ECJ decision "Susanne Staubitz-Schreiber"

73 On 17 January 2006, the ECJ rendered its preliminary ruling (detailed discussion on this in Table of Cases Art 3 of the EIR Appendix A mn 17).[190] Concurring with the opinion of the Advocate General *Colomer*,[191] the ECJ held in favour of retaining the originally-established jurisdiction – so-called ***perpetuatio fori***. The court's main argument was that a change of jurisdiction would contradict the aims of the Regulation, particularly the prevention of forum shopping.[192] According to the ECJ, the debtor – by moving the centre of his main interests to another Member State in the time between the lodging of the request to open proceedings and the issuing of the opening decision – would otherwise be free to choose the legal venue and the applicable law.[193] The court also found that an adherence to the originally-established jurisdiction of the court first seized of the matter would afford a higher degree of legal certainty to the creditors whose assessment of the risks associated with an insolvency of the debtor was done so in relation to the location where the debtor had his centre of main interests at the time of entering into legal relationships with him.[194]

2.3.4.3 Legal conclusions

74 Although a relocation of the COMI prior to the making of a request is **generally acceptable**, such a relocation will be **disregarded** if it constitutes a **mere sham**, i.e. if it is an arbitrary act done only a few weeks or months prior to the making of an insolvency request instead of being done for sound business reasons.[195]

75 Because the court originally seized of the matter retains jurisdiction for deciding on the opening of proceedings in a case where the centre of main interests is relocated to another Member State after the lodging of the request but before the opening of the insolvency proceedings, it does not automatically follow that this **court also has jurisdiction over the insolvency requests that are lodged after the debtor relocated.** Separate

[190] ECJ "Susanne Staubitz-Schreiber" ZIP 2006, 188 et seq; with explanatory note by *Knof/Mock* ZIP 2006, 189; *Schmidt* ZInsO 2006, 88; *Kindler* IPRax 2006, 114 et seq; *Dammann* Dalloz 2006, 1752, 1758; *Duursma-Kepplinger* ZIP 2007, 896 et seq.

[191] ECJ, opinion of the Advocate General ZIP 2005, 1641 = ZInsO 2005, 1099 et seq = NZI 2005, 544.

[192] ECJ "Susanne Staubitz-Schreiber" ZIP 2006, 188 (→ cf Table of Cases Art 3 of the EIR Appendix A mn 17); comments by: *Knof/Mock* ZIP 2006, 189 et seq; *Schmidt* ZInsO 2006, 88; *Kindler* IPRax 2006, 114 et seq; *Vogl* EWiR 2006, 161; *Saenger/Klockenbrink* DZWiR 2006, 183, 184; also: *Laukemann* who finds that the action is pending in an insolvency proceeding as soon as the request has been made, *Laukemann* RIW 2005, 104, 110.

[193] ECJ dated 17 Jan 2006, point 25, printed in ZIP 2006, 188, 188 (→ cf Table of Cases Art 3 of the EIR Appendix A mn 17).

[194] ECJ dated 17 Jan 2006, point 27, printed in ZIP 2006, 188, 189 (→ cf Table of Cases Art 3 of the EIR Appendix A mn 17).

[195] High Court of Justice in Leeds "Ci4net" ZIP 2004, 1769 (→ cf Table of Cases Art 3 of the EIR Appendix A mn 4); *Wessels* Current Topics of International Insolvency Law, 170; Haß/Huber/Gruber/Heiderhoff-*Haß/Herweg* Art 3 EuInsVO mn 17 with further reasons. French and Italian law expressly regulate the ostensible relocation of domicile. Pursuant to Art 1 (2) of Décret no 2005-1677 of 28 Dec 2005, the court in the district in which the domicile was originally located retains sole jurisdiction in the case of a relocation of the domicile of a legal entity in the six months prior to the invocation of the court. According to Art 9 of the Legge fallimentare, a relocation of domicile made up to one year prior to the lodging of the insolvency request is disregarded for the purposes of determining jurisdiction.

opening proceedings are instituted for each insolvency request made. Only once the proceedings are opened will all of the requests be bundled into one single proceeding.

It would also seem appropriate to apply the jurisdiction rule in Art 3 (1) of the EIR to insolvency requests made after the insolvent debtor has moved away. This would curtail forum shopping by ensuring that the debtor was not given the opportunity, through the lodging of an insolvency request (for example by satisfying all of the claims), to freely select the laws of a Member State most advantageous for him. **76**

Accordingly, the **court originally seized of the matter retains jurisdiction, even after the first request has been discharged, for insolvency requests that have been lodged (but not yet discharged) in the interim.**[196] This approach does justice to the intentions of the drafters of the Regulation, this being the improvement of the efficiency and the effectiveness of cross-border insolvency proceedings.[197] **77**

2.3.5 The admissibility of an "international referral"

→ See Table of Cases Art 3 of the EIR Appendix B No 94: *AG Hamburg*

The Regulation is as silent on the issue of **negated jurisdiction**, i.e. where both courts refuse to assume international jurisdiction, as it is in the case where both courts claim international jurisdiction. Although Recital 6 of the EIR speaks of "provisions governing jurisdiction", no provision is made for the reversed situation of a lack of jurisdiction. Therefore the question is how to deal with the case where the court invoked declines jurisdiction. Unclear is whether an "international referral" is possible. **78**

The Regulation does not oppose the making of such an **"international referral"** (→ cf Table of Cases Art 3 of the EIR Appendix B No 93, ***AG Hamburg***). Recital 3 of the EIR speaks of a "coordination of the measures to be taken regarding an insolvent debtor's assets".[198] A "coordination" would include a transferring of a proceeding to the competent court as soon as it becomes known that jurisdiction has been declined. This also follows from Recital 8 of the EIR. This prescribes a bundeling of the laws and the effects of the proceedings for the sake of an efficient execution of insolvency proceedings. Recital 22 of the EIR also lends support in its emphasis of the mutual trust that should exist between the courts of the Member States. In adherence to this principle, it must be possible to rely on the integrity of an insolvency court invoked pursuant to the Regulation not to arbitrarily assume or decline its jurisdiction but to deal with a referral with the care it is due, and that the court receiving the referral will continue to further these proceedings.[199] If there are factors indicating that another insolvency court has European jurisdiction, then the court being invoked must investigate this. Support for this interpretation is also found in Germany in Art 102 Sec 2 *EGInsO*.[200] **79**

The necessity of an **"international referral"** can also be seen – at least from the German perspective – from the fact that, should there be a referral or retraction of the **80**

---

196 Cf also BGH dated 2 Mar 2006 ZIP 2006, 767, 768 et seq = ZInsO 2006, 431, 433; on this *Smid* DZWiR 2006, 325, 328.

197 Cf on this BGH dated 2 Mar 2006 ZIP 2006, 767, 768 = ZInsO 2006, 431, 433.

198 AG Hamburg dated 9 May 2006, NZI 486, 487 (→ cf Table of Cases Art 3 of the EIR Appendix B No 93).

199 AG Hamburg dated 9 May 2006, NZI 486, 487 (→ cf Table of Cases Art 3 of the EIR Appendix B No 93).

200 AG Hamburg dated 9 May 2006, NZI 486, 486 (→ cf Table of Cases Art 3 of the EIR Appendix B No 93).

request, a managing director could otherwise not be able to fulfill his obligation to request insolvency proceedings pursuant to Sec 64 *GmbHG* (German Limited Liability Companies Act).[201] The duty to request, as understood by German company law, should also be considered as having been satisfied for the purposes of the Regulation even when the request is lodged at a – possibly foreign – insolvency court that lacks jurisdiction.[202]

81 Nevertheless, pursuant to Recital 15 of the EIR in conjunction with Art 4 of the EIR, the referral has **no binding effect** on the court receiving it.[203]

2.3.6 Ceasing business operations

82 **→ See the Table of Cases Art 3 of the EIR**

- **Appendix B No 83: *AG Hamburg***

83 The ascertainment of the centre of interests becomes problematic if the debtor has **ceased business operations** at the time of making the insolvency request. **Determinative here is whether there is still a centre of interests at the time when the economic activities cease, or whether the presumption in Art 3 (1) sentence 2 of the EIR is revived**, and therefore a presumption in favour of the registered office of the company is to be made.

84 The point in time for ascertaining the centre of interests is the **moment at which the request to open insolvency proceedings** is lodged.[204] If business operations have ceased, then the centre of main interests established prior to the cessation remains in effect.[205] Where Sec 3 of the German *InsO* applies, then the registered office is decisive if the debtor has already ceased business operations and the company has been completely dissolved.[206] But if the company is still being wound up, general opinion holds that this is still an "activity" within the meaning of Sec 3 (2) *InsO*, and the place where this is taking place is thus decisive.[207] However, the standards developed for national law are only applicable to issues of international jurisdiction to a limited degree.[208] The phrase **"centre of main interests"** as used in the Regulation is therefore an autonomous, uniform concept of Community law whose meaning is independent of national laws.[209] The

201 AG Hamburg dated 9 May 2006 NZI 486, 487 (→ cf Table of Cases Art 3 of the EIR Appendix B No 93); dissenting opinion *Mankowski* NZI 2006, 488: the managing director should only be liable if he intentionally made the request to the wrong court in order to slow down the processing of his request. But a mere wrong assessment of the situs of the COMI does not amount to an infringement of the duty to make the request.

202 AG Hamburg dated 9 May 2006, NZI 486, 487 (→ cf Table of Cases Art 3 of the EIR Appendix B No 93).

203 AG Hamburg dated 9 May 2006, NZI 486, 487 (→ cf Table of Cases Art 3 of the EIR Appendix B No 93).

204 Cf the opinion of the Advocate General *Colomer* ZIP 2005, 1641, 1645; AG Celle – Individual – ZInsO 2005, 895 = NZI 2005, 410 (→ cf Table of Cases Art 3 of the EIR Appendix B No 73); *Herchen* ZInsO 2004, 825, 829 et seq; *Liersch* NZI 2004, 141, 142.

205 AG Hamburg – Ltd in Germany – ZIP 2005, 2275 et seq; approving *Klöhn* NZI 2006, 383 et seq; with the same result, without explicitly dealing with the problem – AG Hamburg – Ltd in Germany – NZI 2003, 442, 443; contra *Brenner* EWiR 2003, 925 et seq.

206 BayObLG NZI 1999, 457; Uhlenbruck-*Uhlenbruck* InsO § 3 mn 3.

207 OLG Braunschweig ZIP 2000, 1118; MünchKomm InsO/*Ganter* § 3 mn 8.

208 So also AG Hamburg dated 1 Dec 2005 ZIP 2005, 2275 et seq = ZInsO 2005, 1282 et seq = NZG 2006, 439 et seq; see on this the commentar on Art 102 EGInsO sec 1 mn 2.

209 *Virgós/Garcimartín* Regulation, p 37; Also ECJ Eurofood / Parmalat, C-341/04, ZInsO

concept of **"activities"** pursuant to national law can also **not** be equated to the **"interests"** in conjunction with cross-border insolvencies Cases. Recital 13 of the EIR alone demonstrates that the European legislators wished to take a creditor-based perspective, and that the Regulation aims at creating legal certainty through the predictability of international jurisdiction and the governing law.[210] Therefore the necessity of being able to ascertain the centre of main interests for third parties is being expressly referred to; only a definition of "interests" that also – and perhaps only – includes static or formal matters of daily life, such as the existence of debts or the situs of objects, will do justice to the aims of the Regulation.[211] The same must also hold true in order to prevent forum shopping.[212]

Example from the *AG Hamburg*, Table of Cases Art 3 of the EIR Appendix B No 83 **85**

In the case of an English limited liability company operating exclusively in Germany, the German insolvency courts retain international jurisdiction for the opening of main insolvency proceedings within the meaning of Art 3 (1) sentence 1 of the EIR even if the economic/business activities have completely ceased prior to the insolvency request.

2.4 Conflicts of Jurisdiction

The Regulation contains no provision for solving **conflicts of jurisdictions.** Conflicts **86** are to be resolved in keeping with Recital 22 of the EIR – as well as Council Regulation (EC) No 44/2001 – according to the **principle of priority** (see mn 88).[213]

According to this, if a court has assumed international jurisdiction for opening main **87** insolvency proceedings, then another court can only assume jurisdiction for secondary insolvency proceedings pursuant to Art 3 (2) of the EIR. The other courts of the Member State are prohibited from reviewing the factual grounds for the assumption of jurisdiction of the court concerned. This also complies with the aims of the regulation, to create efficiency and legal certainty with respect to the ascertainment of international jurisdiction and to avoid lengthy disputes over the jurisdiction issue. The only time that an

2006, 484, point 31 (→ cf Table of Cases Art 3 of the EIR Appendix A mn 10).

210 Moss/Fletcher/Isaacs-*Fletcher* Regulation mn 3.10; *Pannen/Riedemann* NZI 2004, 646, 656.

211 AG Hamburg – Ltd in Germany – ZInsO 2005, 1282, 1283 = NZG 2006, 439, 440 = ZIP 2005, 2275, 2276 (→ cf Table of Cases Art 3 of the EIR Appendix B No 83); comments: *Herweg/Tschauner* EWiR 2006, 169 et seq; *Klöhn* agrees with the result reached on the facts by the AG Hamburg, but he points out that in this case, the main reason for the decision was the fact that none of the interests involved were supporting England as a venue for the insolvency proceedings, KTS 2006, 259, 280, 288; *Klöhn* NZI 2006, 368.

212 Recital 4 of the EIR.

213 The issue of the principle of priority within the scope of application of the Regulation was also referred by the Supreme Court of Ireland in Eurofood/Parmalat NZI 2005, 505, 510 to the ECJ for a decision. The core issue is whether the court still has jurisdiction pursuant to Art 3 of the EIR (in conjunction with Art 16 of the EIR if the company neither has its registered office nor administers its main interests in the opening country; see ECJ C-341/04, judgement of 2 May 2006, ZInsO 2006, 485 et seq (→ cf Table of Cases Art 3 of the EIR Appendix A mn 10); *Wessels* Current Topics of International Insolvency Law, 176 et seq; *Virgós/Garcimartín* Regulation, p 51.

assumption of jurisdiction would appear to warrant review is when there is a fear that public policy has been breached, particularly an infringement of the right to be heard[214] or the right to obtain a fair trial.[215]

2.4.1 The validity of the principle of priority

88 The **principle of priority** has been applied by courts in numerous decisions. Insolvency proceedings opened later in time were stayed on account of the previously opened main insolvency proceedings, or the opening of another main insolvency proceeding was denied.[216]

→ For examples of the principle of priority, see also Table of Cases Art 3 of the EIR:

- **Appendix A mn 1, Aircraft**
- **Appendix A mn 2, Automold**
- **Appendix A mn 5, Collins & Aikman**
- **Appendix A mn 7, EMBIC**

---

[214] Such an infringement is to be affirmed especially when one of the company's organs involved in the proceeding is not heard, as was decided by the High Court Dublin in "Eurofood/Parmalat II" ZIP 2004, 1223, 1227 (→ cf Table of Cases Art 3 of the EIR Appendix A mn 10); on this: *Herweg/Tschauner* EWiR 2004, 599 et seq; AG Düsseldorf "ISA" ZIP 2004, 623, 624 et seq (→ cf Table of Cases Art 3 of the EIR Appendix A mn 15); comments: *Herweg/Tschauner* EWiR 2004, 495 et seq; *Liersch* NZI 2004, 271, 272; also: *Herchen* ZInsO 2004, 61, 64 et seq; *Weller* IPRax 2004, 412, 416 et seq; *Israël* European Cross Border Insolvency Regulation (2005) 261. However in its decision of 27 Jun 2006, the Cour de cassation holds that the failure to hear a workers' representative prior to the opening of reorganization proceedings (which pursuant to Art L 621-1 Code de commerce would lead to the nullity of the opening order) does not infringe persons affected by such proceedings' fundamental right to be heard; on this, see: *Dammann/Podeur* Banque & Droit 2006 (109), 6.

[215] A breach of the right to a fair trial may be found if documents relevant for determining international jurisdiction are withheld from individual parties to the proceedings, and through this abuse of the law their decision is being affected. The Supreme Court of Ireland in "Eurofood/Parmalat III" NZI 2004, 505, 510 had referred this issue to the ECJ for a decision, which was affirmed by the ECJ in "Eurofood", judgement of 2 May 2006, ZInsO 2006, 485 (→ cf Table of Cases Art 3 of the EIR Appendix A mn 10).

[216] The AG Cologne in "Automold" ZIP 2004, 471 (→ cf Table of Cases Art 3 of the EIR Appendix A mn 2) recognized the opening of main insolvency proceedings by an English court and opened secondary insolvency proceedings in Germany; on this, see also: *Sabel* NZI 2004, 126, 128; *Meyer-Löwy/Poertzgen* ZInsO 2004, 195. The Cour d'appel de Versailles had set aside the previously opened main insolvency proceedings of the Tribunal de commerce de Pontoise (Cour d'appel de Versailles "ISA III" ZIP 2004, 377, confirmed by the Cour de cassation, 27 Jun 2006 03-19863 (→ cf Table of Cases Art 3 of the EIR Appendix A mn 15), on this *Dammann/Podeur* Banque & Droit 2006 (109), 3; critical: *Mankowski* EWiR 2003, 1239 et seq. The AG Düsseldorf (→ cf Table of Cases Art 3 of the EIR Appendix A mn 15) also stayed opened main insolvency proceedings (AG Düsseldorf "ISA" (→ cf Table of Cases Art 3 of the EIR Appendix A mn 15), with comments by *Mankowski* EWiR 2003, 767) after finding out about the previously opened main insolvency proceedings (printed in ZIP 2004, 623, approving: *Herweg/Tschauner* EWiR 2004, 495 et seq). → cf Table of Cases Art 3 of the EIR Appendix B No 4, SARL Bati-France.

- **Appendix A mn 10, Eurofood / Parmalat**
- **Appendix A mn 15, ISA / Daisytek**
- **Appendix B No 4, SARL Bati-France**

2.4.2 The applicability of the "relation back principle"

An interesting issue is the **effectiveness** of the so-called **"relation back principles"** developed in English, Irish, and Welsch law.[217] According to the "relation back principle", the opening of insolvency proceedings is effective retroactive to the point in time at which the request was made. The appointment of an "administrator" arguably also takes effect retroactive to the time of the lodging of the request. Despite the validity of the principle of priority, the High Court of Dublin[218] (→ cf Table of Cases Art 3 of the EIR Appendix A mn 10, **Eurofood/Parmalat**) and the Municipality Court of Prague (→ Table of Cases Art 3 of the EIR Appendix A mn 1, **Aircraft**) nevertheless assumed jurisdiction in Cases where, although they had not opened proceedings first, the insolvency request at issue in each case had been lodged before the request was made to the court that opened proceedings first. In reference order issued by the Supreme Court of Ireland,[219] the court affirms the effectiveness of the "relation back principle" stating in support of it that the drafters of the Regulation were aware of this principle and their failure to regulate this illustrates their acceptance of it.[220] The ECJ's decision, however, in the Eurofood/Parmalat case (→ Table of Cases Art 3 of the EIR Appendix A mn 10) is to be so understood that **retroactive fictions of national law** are to be disregarded.[221] **89**

The court found that the application of such national rules would mean that a national court, contrary to the principle of priority and despite the existence of earlier opened main insolvency proceedings, could decide that it had international jurisdiction; in other words, the ascertainment of international jurisdiction would be at the discretion of the national courts. In addition, main insolvency proceedings that had been opened earlier would be robbed of any effect. Adherence to such retroactively effective legal fictions of national law would also lead to uncertainty of the law, which is clearly not what the drafters of the Regulation desired. The court argued that the mere lodging of a request to open insolvency proceedings in a Member State that endorses the "relation back principles" would operate to block the courts of the other Member States, although a summary review had not yet been made by a state authority to assess their own jurisdiction and although it would not yet be clear if the requirements to open proceedings in that Member State have been satisfied.[222] For the sake of a predictable and efficient determination of international jurisdiction, the "relation back principle" should be disregarded.[223] **90**

---

[217] Term taken from Sec 220[2] Companies Act 1963.

[218] High Court Dublin "Eurofood/Parmalat" ZIP 2004, 1223 (→ cf Table of Cases Art 3 of the EIR Appendix A mn 10); with explanatory note by *Herweg/Tschauner* EWiR 2004, 599.

[219] Supreme Court of Ireland "Eurofood/Parmalat III" NZI 2004, 505, 510 (→ cf Table of Cases Art 3 of the EIR Appendix A mn 10).

[220] Cf the Request of the High Court of Dublin for a preliminary ruling by the ECJ "Eurofood/Parmalat II" ZIP 2004, 1223, 1224 (→ cf Table of Cases Art 3 of the EIR Appendix A mn 10).

[221] *Mankowski* BB 2006, 1753, 1757.

[222] Cf *Eidenmüller* NJW 2004, 3455, 3457; *Schilling/Schmidt* ZInsO 2006, 113, 115.

[223] Also *Mankowki* BB 2006, 1753, 1757.

2.4.3 The concept of opening insolvency proceedings – temporary administrator

91 By application of and adherence to the **principle of priority**, jurisdiction to open main insolvency proceedings must, in compliance with Art 16 of the EIR, be recognized in the other Member States. In the **Eurofood/Parmalat** decision (→ cf Table of Cases Art 3 of the EIR Appendix A mn 10), the ECJ dealt with the issue of whether the requesting of the appointment of a **"provisional liquidator"** could be considered as an **opening of proceedings** within the meaning of Art 16 of the EIR.[224] The appointment of a **provisional liquidator**[225] is also a decision ("judgement") that must, in compliance with Art 16 (2) of the EIR, be recognized in all other Member States, which then serves to block the opening of (any further) main insolvency proceedings.[226] The concept of opening insolvency proceedings contemplated by Art 16 of the EIR is to be understood to include not only those opening judgements defined formally as such by the law of the Member State applicable to the court issuing the judgement, but also a judgement that is made in response to a request stemming from the debtor's insolvency to open one of the proceedings set out in Annex A of the EIR if such judgement leads to the divestment of the debtor and if, pursuant to it, one of the liquidators named in Annex C of the EIR is appointed.[227] According to Art 2 (e) of the EIR, the term "judgement" also includes the appointment of a liquidator, and Art 2 (b) in conjunction with Annex C of the EIR also names the **German *"vorläufigen Insolvenzverwalter"*** (temporary administrator). This construction also seems correct for the sake of preventing forum shopping and for avoiding the appointment of a multiplicity of temporary administrators, which would in turn lead to conflicts of jurisdictions (for a detailed discussion on this, see Art 16 of the EIR mn 32 et seq).

Deeming the appointment of a temporary administrator as the opening of insolvency proceedings within the meaning of Art 16 of the EIR is most welcoming from a German point of view. Such an interpretation is also to be seen in light of the principle of priority and the race to open first which goes along with it in the case of international group insolvencies. While in Germany the opening proceedings often take many weeks (one important reason being to take advantage of the period during which compensation of lost wages due to insolvency is granted), insolvency proceedings are opened in other Member State directly after the request is made. The ability to "block" the COMI

224 ECJ dated 2 May 2006 – C-341/04 (Eurofood IFSC Ltd), NZI 2006, 360 et seq (→ cf Table of Cases Art 3 of the EIR Appendix A mn 10 – Eurofood/Parmalat); also Advocate General *Jacobs* in his opinion ZIP 2005, 1641; *Laukemann* RIW 2005, 104, 112.

225 It is immaterial whether a "strong" or "only" a weak administrator is appointed as long as this is provided for by law, as is the case in German law (secs 21, 22 InsO). All that counts is that there has been a decision to appoint the liquidator.

226 With the same result High Court Dublin "Eurofood/Parmalat II" ZIP 2004, 1223, 1224; ECJ, C-341/04 (→ cf Table of Cases Art 3 of the EIR Appendix A mn 10); and Municipality Court of Prague "Aircraft" ZIP 2005, 1431 (→ cf Table of Cases Art 3 of the EIR Appendix A mn 1); *Eidenmüller* NJW 2004, 3455, 3457 fn 32; *Pannen/Riedemann* EWiR 2005, 725, 726; *Schilling/Schmidt* ZInsO 2006, 113, 114; *Wessels* Current Topics of International Insolvency Law, 176, 234; *Schilling* DZWiR 2006, 143, 147; *Israel* European Cross-Border Insolvency Regulation (2005) 260 et seq.

227 ECJ C-341/04, judgement of 2 May 2006, ZInsO 2006, 484 (→ cf Table of Cases Art 3 of the EIR Appendix A mn 10 – Eurofood/Parmalat); *Poertzgen/Adam* ZInsO 2006, 505, 508; on this, see also: *Mankowski* in BB 2006, 1753 et seq who draws special attention to the consequences of dogmatically treating the provisional opening of insolvency proceedings as equivalent to the final opening of such.

through the ordering of a temporary administrator would, from a German point of view, put a considerable damper on the much discussed race to open first.[228]

The divestment required by the ECJ must – in the interests of legal certainty and in light of efficient and effective cross-border insolvency proceedings envisioned by the drafters of the Regulation[229] – be so understood that the appointing of a German **weak administrator** will satisfy this as well;[230] (see on this Art 16 of the EIR mn 36). The German temporary administrator is named in Annex C of the EIR. Annex C has a constitutive effect, i.e. it establishes rights. No further distinctions are made to the terms listed in it.[231] There is therefore no need to distinguish between the various strengths of the temporary administrator in Germany.[232] **92**

Unclear, however, is how the **problems consequential** to this will be dealt with by the ECJ in light of the Eurofood/Parmalat decision (→ cf Table of Cases Art 3 of the EIR Appendix A mn 10). For one thing, the temporary administrator, in all its various forms, must be subsumed under both substantive requirements of the ECJ.[233] Secondly, an answer must be found to the question of whether the "provisional" opening of main insolvency proceedings is to be understood as an "opening" for the purposes of Arts 4, 5, 6, 7, 14, 20, 21, 22, 24, 27, 40 of the EIR, which would mean that they would have to be applied.[234] Another example of a problem in this connection is the way to deal with secondary insolvency proceedings that were opened after the appointment of a temporary administrator of main proceedings when the opening of such main insolvency proceedings is ultimately denied.[235] How this will be dealt with will depend in particular on whether or not the denial of the (provisional) main insolvency proceedings simultaneously nullifies the **reason for opening insolvency proceedings**[236] pursuant to Art 27 of the EIR.[237] **93**

Also to be kept in mind is that the **temporary administrator** up to now has not yet been recognized as being entitled pursuant to Art 29 (a) of the EIR to request the opening of secondary insolvency proceedings.[238] It remains open whether this should take place through a reversal of the existing rule, or whether a distinction is to be made between the various sets of facts and rules.[239] In addition, the risk of a dispute between the temporary administrators would be even higher if the provisional opening was not recognized as such.[240] **94**

In the interests of a uniform interpretation of a European law, Art 102 Sec 3 *EGInsO* should now be so understood that a temporary administrator is also entitled to appeal if a German court, despite the earlier appointment of a (foreign) temporary administrator, **95**

---

228 *Pannen/Riedemann* EWiR 2005, 725, 726.

229 Recital 2 of the EIR.

230 Also *Herchen* in NZI 2006, 435, 437; *Knof/Mock* ZIP 2006, 911, 912; *Mankowski* BB 2006, 1753, 1758; contra *Smid* DZWiR 2006, 325, 327; *Paulus* NZG 2006, 609, 613.

231 *Mankowski* BB 2006, 1753, 1758.

232 *Mankowski* BB 2006, 1753, 1758.

233 Cf *Knof/Mock* ZIP 2006, 911, 912; *Mankowski* BB 2006, 1753, 1757.

234 On this also *Liersch* NZI 6/2006, V, VI; *Mankowski* BB 2006, 1753, 1758.

235 *Mankowski* BB 2006, 1753, 1757 et seq; cf *Liersch* NZI 6/2006, V, VI.

236 For a detailed discussion of the reason for opening insolvency proceedings, see Art 27 mn 30 et seq.

237 On this issue, see also *Mankowski* BB 2006, 1753, 1757 et seq who opts for retaining the reason for opening insolvency proceedings.

238 So explicitly *Virgós/Schmit* Explanatory Report, mn 226, 262; *Leible/Staudinger* KTS 2000, 533, 570; *Vallender* InVO 2005, 41, 42, 45.

239 Also *Mankowski* BB 2006, 1753, 1757.

240 *Schilling/Schmidt* EWiR 2006, 15, 16; *Mankowski* BB 2006, 1753, 1758.

wants to open main insolvency proceedings since not only the opening of main insolvency proceedings constitutes a judgement within the meaning of Art 16 (1) of the EIR, but the appointment of a temporary administrator satisfies this as well.[241]

2.5 International Jurisdiction for Insolvency-related Proceedings

96 **→ On the international jurisdiction for insolvency-related proceedings, see for example the Table of Cases Art 3 of the EIR Appendix B No 86, *OLG Frankfurt***

On the face of its wording, the rule on international jurisdiction found in Art 3 of the EIR only concerns the opening of insolvency proceedings. This does not deal with the issue of international jurisdiction for actions brought by the liquidator or by individual creditors of the insolvency proceedings.[242] These include in particular actions of the liquidator to **avoid** (set aside) a legal transaction of the debtor's, a debtor's action for **separate satisfaction or preferential treatment** (*Aussonderung* or *Absonderung*), for a **declaratory judgement** on a claim's inclusion in the schedule of creditors' claims, and for **liability claims** against the liquidator or against the management or the managing director. The question from both the liquidator's and the creditors' point of view is which place is decisive for establishing the international jurisdiction for such actions.

97 Both Art 3 and Art 25 (1) subpara 2 of the EIR are silent on the international jurisdiction for judgements directly ensuing from the insolvency proceedings. Art 25 (1) subpara 2 of the EIR merely provides for a simplified recognition of such judgements; it provides no solution, however, on the issue of which principles are to be applied to ascertain international jurisdiction. This **regulatory gap** therefore needs to be filled.

98 Three **solutions** are conceivable:

- the application of national provisions on jurisdiction, see mn 99 et seq
- the application of Council Regulation (EC) No 44/2001, see mn 101 et seq, or
- an analogous application of Art 3 of the EIR, see mn 110 et seq.

2.5.1 National provisions on jurisdiction

99 Up to now, the **national provisions on jurisdiction** have been invoked for determining international jurisdiction.[243] This has been justified with the argument that the regulatory scope of the Regulation only extends to areas actually regulated by it. And since it is silent on the issue of jurisdiction for insolvency-related proceedings, then it is argued that national law must apply.

100 Speaking against this, however, is the danger of conflicts of jurisdictions caused by each Member State regulating international jurisdiction pursuant to its own autonomous laws. And the principle of priority can only apply if the criterium for jurisdiction is identical for each Member State. It is also argued that resorting to national jurisdictions

---

[241] Also *Mankowski* BB 2006, 1753, 1758; *Knof/Mock* ZIP 2006, 911, 912.

[242] *Smid* Komm EuInsVO Art 3 mn 4; D-K/D/Ch-*Duursma-Kepplinger* Art 25 mn 22: *Adolphsen* in Bork, Handbuch des Insolvenzanfechtungsrechts p 657.

[243] BGH ZIP 1990, 246, 246 et seq; on this *Balz* EWiR 1990, 257; explanatory note by *H. Schmidt* EuZW 1990, 219; BGH ZIP 2003, 1419, 1420; OLG Hamm EuZW 1993, 519; OLG Zweibrücken EuZW 1993, 165; see also *Adolphsen* in Bork, Handbuch des Insolvenzanfechtungsrechts p 658 et seq.

would be contrary to the intentions of the drafters of the Regulation,[244] this being a seamless, unified regulation of international jurisdiction, which already follows from Recital 6 of the EIR.[245] Also speaking against an application of national laws is that it would enable the Member States to enact extensive national laws on jurisdiction for insolvency-related proceedings (a so-called ***vis attractiva concursus***), which could make it nearly impossible to standardize direct jurisdiction rules in Europe.[246] From an unintentional regulatory gap in the Regulation, a national mandate to form a *vis attractiva concursus* cannot be inferred.[247]

2.5.2 Application of Council Regulation (EC) No 44/2001

The provisions of Council Regulation (EC) No 44/2001 are sometimes invoked for **101** determing jurisdiction for insolvency-related proceedings (→ cf Table of Cases Art 3 of the EIR Appendix B No 86, *OLG* **Frankfurt**).[248]

Because insolvency proceedings are a special part of civil law and because the Regula- **102** tion wishes to specifically regulate the international jurisdiction of the courts in this area, a graduated relationship exists between the regulations: Council Regulation (EC) No 44/2001 regulates civil and commercial disputes in general, and the EIR, as the *lex specialis*, governs the special area of insolvency law (→ cf Table of Cases Art 3 of the EIR Appendix B No 86, *OLG* **Frankfurt**).[249] Although the wording of Art 1 (2) (b) of Council Regulation (EC) No 44/2001 excludes bankruptcy, composition proceedings and similar proceedings from the scope of its applicability, it does not do so for insolvency-related proceedings for which it would logically be applicable.

Two different approaches are possible for applying Council Regulation (EC) No 44/ **103** 2001:

- **One approach**[250] separates the jurisdiction regime from the enforcement regime. With respect to jurisdiction in the case of insolvency-related proceedings only, the **jurisdiction rules** of Council Regulation (EC) No 44/2001 are invoked supplementarily. Because of the low recognition hurdle contained in the EIR, this leads to a privileged position for insolvency-related decisions.[251]
- **Another approach**[252] would apply Council Regulation (EC) No 44/2001 entirely. The issue here, however, is the meaning which should then be attributed to Art 25 (1) subpara 2 of the EIR. An exclusive application of Council Regulation (EC) No 44/2001 could only be justified by the fact that there is a gap in respect of the relevant jurisdiction issue, and a strived-for synchronization between the jurisdiction of a court closely involved with the matter and the recognition.

---

244 Cf also Haß/Huber/Gruber/Heiderhoff-*Haß/Herweg* Art 3 EuInsVO mn 20; *Adolphsen* in Bork, Handbuch des Insolvenzanfechtungsrechts p 661.

245 *Adolphsen* in Bork, Handbuch des Insolvenzanfechtungsrechts p 661; Haß/Huber/Gruber/Heiderhoff-*Gruber* Art 3 EuInsVO mn 22.

246 D-K/D/Ch-*Duursma-Kepplinger* Art 25 mn 26; *Adolphsen* in: Bork, Handbuch des Insolvenzanfechtungsrechts p 662.

247 *Adolphsen* in Bork, Handbuch des Insolvenzanfechtungsrechts p 662; contra *Mörsdorf-Schulte* IPRax 2004, 31, 36.

248 Also *Thole* ZIP 2006, 1383 et seq.

249 OLG Frankfurt/M, judgement of 26 Jan 2006 – not yet res judicata, an appeal against the decision is pending at the BGH (IX ZR 39/06) – ZIP 2006, 769, 771.

250 See in *Thole* ZIP 2006, 1383, 1384.

251 See in *Thole* ZIP 2006, 1383, 1384.

252 MünchKomm-*Reinhart* InsO Art 25 EuInsVO mn 7; *Leipold* FS Ishikawa (2001) p 221, 231; see also in *Thole* ZIP 2006, 1383, 1384.

104 A recent decision of the *OLG* Frankfurt (→ cf Table of Cases Art 3 of the EIR Appendix B No 86, ***OLG* Frankfurt**)[253] applied Council Regulation (EC) No 44/2001 as a whole. It restricted the exemption of bankruptcy in Art 1 (2) (b) of Council Regulation (EC) No 44/2001 to the collective insolvency proceedings in an attempt to do justice to the unification of jurisdiction provisions that Council Regulation (EC) No 44/2001 strives for. The court held that the Regulation made no provision for international jurisdiction for avoidance actions (*Insolvenzanfechtungsklage*). It also argued that an analogy to Art 3 of the EIR could not be made absent an unintentional regulatory gap. The court argued further that Recital 6 of the EIR was to be construed solely in conjunction with recognition and enforcement and, like Art 25 (1) subpara 2 of the EIR, little could be inferred from it about international jurisdiction. However, according to the *OLG* Frankfurt, Art 25 of the EIR still remains applicable to recognition and enforcement.[254]

105 The argumentation of the *OLG* Frankfurt is not convincing. In its 1979 decision in *Gourdain vs Nadler*,[255] the ECJ interpreted Art 1 (2) (b) of the 1968 Brussels Convention (now Council Regulation (EC) No 44/2001) to the effect that judgements associated with insolvency proceedings are excluded from the scope of applicability of the Convention if they stem directly from these proceedings and remain well within the ambit of bankruptcy or composition proceedings. This clearly includes insolvency-related proceedings as understood by Art 25 of the EIR. Therefore Council Regulation (EC) No 44/2001 cannot be invoked for the international jurisdiction of insolvency-related proceedings.[256]

106 Applying the jurisdiction provisions of Council Regulation (EC) No 44/2001 would also lead to serious problems in practice. For most insolvency-related proceedings (e.g. avoidance actions), Art 2 of Council Regulation (EC) No 44/2001 would have to be applied, meaning that the court of the defendant would have jurisdiction. Because Art 4 (2) sentence 2 (m) of the EIR prescribes the application of the *lex fori concursus* with respect to creditors' avoidance proceedings, the court seized of the matter would therefore not be able to apply its own law.

107 Another problem is when the local law of the party opposing the avoidance, as the *lex causae*, applies instead of the *lex fori concursus*; in such a case, the court could refuse to make any review of the foreign avoidance right based on the argument that the legal transaction in issue is neither avoidable nor open to attack in any way pursuant to its own law.[257]

---

[253] OLG Frankfurt/M, judgement of 26 Jan 2006 – not yet res judicata, an appeal against the decision is pending at the BGH (IX ZR 39/06) – ZIP 2006, 769 = ZInsO 2006, 715 = NZI 2006, 648; on this: *Hinkel/Flitsch* EWiR 2006, 237; *Smid* DZWiR 2006, 325; *Ringe* ZInsO 2006, 700; *Thole* ZIP 2006, 1383, 1385 et seq.

[254] OLG Frankfurt/M, judgement of 26 Jan 2006 – not yet res judicata, an appeal against the decision is pending at the BGH (IX ZR 39/06) – ZIP 2006, 769, 769; *Thole* ZIP 2006, 1383, 1386.

[255] Judgement of the ECJ "Gourdain ./. Nadler" EC reports 1979, 733 = RiW 1979, 273, 274 et seq; different: OLG Frankfurt/M, judgement of 26 Jan 2006 – not yet res judicata, an appeal against the decision is pending at the German BGH (IX ZR 39/06) – ZIP 2006, 769 = ZInsO 2006, 715 = NZI 2006, 648; on this: *Hinkel/Flitsch* EWiR 2006, 237; *Smid* DZWiR 2006, 325; *Ringe* ZInsO 2006, 700; *Thole* ZIP 2006, 1383, 1385 et seq.

[256] D-K/D/Ch-*Duursma-Kepplinger* Art 25 mn 35; *Smid* Komm EuInsVO Art 25 mn 10; Haß/Huber/Gruber/Heiderhoff-*Gruber* Art 25 EuInsVO mn 25 und 26; *Adolphsen* in Bork, Handbuch des Insolvenzanfechtungsrechts p 661.

[257] *Adolphsen* in Bork, Handbuch des Insolvenzanfechtungsrechts p 665.

Having one court competent for the insolvency proceedings and a different one for the insolvency-related proceedings would also considerably increase the liquidator's workload.[258] **108**

For these reasons, **the application of Council Regulation** (EC) No **44/2001** should be rejected. **109**

2.5.3 Analogous application of Art 3 of the EIR

In order to avoid **conflicts of jurisdictions** and to counter contradictory assessments, it would seem appropriate to determine **international jurisdiction for insolvency-related proceedings** analogous to that of the **opening of the proceedings.**[259] Because jurisdiction for insolvency-related proceedings is not provided for, the Regulation contains a regulatory gap. That such a gap was not intentional is evidenced by the fact that in Recital 6 of the EIR, the drafters provided that the Regulation also regulated the jurisdiction issue for these very kinds of judgements. The fact that Art 18 (2) sentence 2 of the EIR stipulates the powers of the liquidator of a territorial insolvency proceeding with respect to avoidance actions does nothing to detract from this. The inversion of this – namely that for actions other than the territorial insolvency proceedings jurisdiction is determined not in accordance with the Regulation but rather by Council Regulation (EC) No 44/2001 – holds no weight. Although it is evident that the drafters were generally aware of the problem of insolvency-related proceedings,[260] it cannot be surmised – especially in light of Recital 6 of the EIR – that they did not want to extend the rule on international jurisdiction to insolvency-related proceedings as well. **110**

The scope of application of Art 3 of the EIR therefore extends to the determination of international jurisdiction for the opening of the proceedings as well as (in analogous application) to the determination of jurisdiction for insolvency-related proceedings, a so-called ***vis attractive concursus*** **of European law.**[261] In addition, a presumption in favour of such a **bundling or concentration of jurisdiction** is not contrary to the intentions of the drafters. Recital 6 of the EIR explicitly states that the provisions of the Regulation are also to govern judgements made directly on the basis of the insolvency proceedings. The underlying logic applied by the drafters also speaks in favour of an application of the Regulation: only an analogous application of Art 3 of the EIR accords with the provisions of Art 25 subpara 2 of the EIR, which directly prescribes that the recognition and enforcement of these very proceedings is to be alleviated.[262] **111**

Notable is, however, that the broad interpretation of the *vis attractiva concursus* contemplated in the draft versions of the Convention on Insolvency Proceedings was not adopted in the Regulation. But this does not prevent the recognition of insolvency-related proceedings altogether as justice may still be done to the expressed intentions of the **112**

---

[258] *Adolphsen* in Bork, Handbuch des Insolvenzanfechtungsrechts p 664.

[259] Also *Paulus* Komm EuInsVO Art 25 mn 21; *Carstens* Die internationale Zuständigkeit im europäischen Insolvenzrecht p 110.

[260] Cf OLG Frankfurt ZIP 2006, 769, 771, with explanatory note by *Ringe* ZInsO 2006, 700 et seq; and *Thole* ZIP 2006, 1383 et seq; *Smid* DZWiR 2006, 325, 328.

[261] Cf Haß/Huber/Gruber/Heiderhoff-*Haß/Herweg* Art 3 EuInsVO mn 23; Kübler/Prütting-*Kemper* EuInsVO Art 3 mn 11; *Paulus* ZInsO 2006, 295, 298; *Paulus* Komm EuInsVO Art 25 mn 21; *Carstens* Die internationale Zuständigkeit im europäischen Insolvenzrecht p 110; *Hinkel/Flitsch* EWiR 2006, 237 et seq; contra OLG Frankfurt ZIP 2006, 769, 771.

[262] Also *Leipold* FS Ishikawa (2001), p 221, 234; *Willemer* Vis attractiva concursus und die Europäische Insolvenzverordnung (2006) p 91; *Adolphsen* in Bork, Handbuch des Insolvenzanfechtungsrechts p 662.

legislator by a **restrictive application of the *vis attractiva concursus*.** This then raises the question **of which proceedings are to be considered insolvency-related proceedings, thus falling within the scope of application of Art 3 of the EIR.**

113 A circumscription of these proceedings is also important considering the fact that judgements rendered pursuant to the Regulation are **more easily recognized and enforced** (Art 25 subpara 2 of the EIR) than those rendered pursuant to Council Regulation (EC) No 44/2001. Furthermore, jurisdiction pursuant to Art 3 of the EIR is **exclusive** as opposed to that of Art 2 of Council Regulation (EC) No 44/2001, which is also a sound reason for an exact delimitation.

114 The insolvency-related proceedings pursuant to the Regulation must be limited to such proceedings that are mandatorily dependent on already-opened insolvency proceedings and that adhere to the aims of insolvency proceedings, i.e. a uniform satisfaction of the creditors (principle of *par conditio creditorum*). Only in such Cases does it appear not only appropriate but, in light of the aforementioned restriction to certain defined insolvency-related proceedings and in the interests of the parties to the proceedings, also necessary to subject these proceedings to the exclusive jurisdiction of the Regulation. Such proceedings include **suits brought by the liquidator based on avoidance actions**[263] since these directly foster the equal treatment of creditors and the satisfaction of the claims pursuant to the insolvency proceedings. Actions brought by the creditors aimed at having a **claim allocated to the schedule of creditors' claims** and those **ensuing from entitlements to separate satisfaction or preferential treatment** (*Aussonderung* and *Absonderung*) also constitute insolvency-related actions as their objects are solely of an insolvency law nature. **Actions involving the liquidator's liability** for damages are also related to the insolvency proceedings as the direct and only reason for such actions is the implementation of the insolvency proceedings. On the other hand, actions arising from **managing directors' liability, in particular the liability for delayed filing for insolvency, and from equity-replacing shareholder contributions**, or from **shareholders' liability**, especially the piercing of corporate veil because of an intervention threatening the existence of the subsidiary, are governed solely by Council Regulation (EC) No 44/2001.[264]

115 The legal consequences of assuming international jurisdiction for insolvency-related proceedings in accordance to Art 3 of the EIR (analogous) is that the courts of the country that opened proceedings also have **international jurisdiction** for decisions derived directly from the insolvency proceedings. **Jurisdiction, in terms of the subject matter, territory, and function,** follows the law of the country in which the proceedings are opened (*lex fori concursus*).

[263] D-K/D/Ch-*Duursma-Kepplinger* Art 25 mn 54; *Haubold* IPRax 2002, 157, 163; also *Paulus* NZI 2001, 505, 512; Kübler/Prütting-*Kemper* EuInsVO Art 3 mn 10; *Carstens* Die internationale Zuständigkeit im europäischen Insolvenzrecht p 110.

[264] Cf OLG Jena NZI 1999, 81; OLG Koblenz NZI 2002, 56; *Mankowski* NZI 1999, 56 et seq; and D-K/D/Ch-*Duursma-Kepplinger* Art 25 mn 54; for the *wrongful trading* claims and the *action en comblement du passif* cf ECJ "(Gourdain ./. Nadler)" EC reports 1979, 733 = RiW 1979, 273, 274 et seq.

3. The Opening of Territorial Insolvency Proceedings (Art 3 (2)–(4) of the EIR)

3.1 General

→ **For examples of territorial insolvency proceedings, see also Table of Cases Art 3 of the EIR:** 116

- **Table of Cases Art 3 of the EIR Appendix A mn 2: Automold**
- **Table of Cases Art 3 of the EIR Appendix A mn 5: Collins & Aikman**
- **Table of Cases Art 3 of the EIR Appendix A mn 15: ISA / Daisytek**
- **Table of Cases Art 3 of the EIR Appendix B No 4: SARL Bati-France**
- **Table of Cases Art 3 of the EIR Appendix B No 8: Werlin Corporation Ltd**
- **Table of Cases Art 3 of the EIR Appendix B No 17: Procureur des Konings v BVHE**
- **Table of Cases Art 3 of the EIR Appendix B No 58: Zenith**

Art 3 (2) of the EIR regulates the international jurisdiction for opening **territorial insolvency proceedings**, see mn 4 et seq. Since main insolvency proceedings may only be opened in a Member State in whose territory the debtor's centre of main interests is located, the courts of the other Member States are not authorized to open main insolvency proceedings. They may, however, open territorial insolvency proceedings (Art 3 (2) of the EIR). 117

The subject matter of such territorial insolvency proceedings is restricted to assets located in this Member State.[265] All of the assets of the debtor in the country of the establishment (subs 2 sentence 2) are included in the proceedings. The proceedings – as with main insolvency proceedings – are governed by the law of the country in which the proceedings are opened. Although the universal effects of main insolvency proceedings opened after the opening of territorial proceedings are restricted by the territorial proceedings, the territorial proceedings still serve to supplement and foster the main insolvency proceedings.[266] 118

Only those Member States in whose sovereign territory the debtor has an **establishment** are authorized to open territorial proceedings.[267] The concept of "establishment" is defined in Art 2 (h) of the EIR. This is defined as "any place of operations where the debtor carries out a non-transitory economic activity with human means and goods."[268] The concept of establishment is loosely defined in the Regulation.[269] Required, however, is the carrying out of economic activities on the market, a minimum of organisation, and a certain degree of permanence. In the **Werlin Corporation Ltd** case (→ cf Table of Cases Art 3 of the EIR Appendix B No 8) for example, on the request of a Belgian creditor, territorial insolvency proceedings (independent territorial insolvency proceedings pursuant to the Regulation) were opened in England for the reasons set out in Art 3 (4) (b) of the 119

---

265 See *Virgós/Garcimartín* Regulation, p 162 et seq; *Wessels* Current Topics of International Insolvency Law, 140; Moss/Fletcher/Isaacs-*Moss/Smith*, Regulation, mn 8.60.

266 Cf HK-InsO/*Stephan* Art 3 EuInsVO mn 14; *Virgós/Garcimartín* Regulation, p 156.

267 Moss/Fletcher/Isaacs-*Moss/Smith*, Regulation, mn 8.59.

268 Cf on the concept of establishment: *Hanisch* Stellungnahme, 202, 207 et seq; Moss/Fletcher/Isaacs-*Moss/Smith*, Regulation, Art 3 mn 8.61 et seq.

269 Cf *Smid* Komm EuInsVO Art 2 mn 21, Art 3 mn 30.

EIR in respect of a company registered in England. The court held that the economic activities carried out by the company in Belgium were sufficient to affirm the existence of an establishment. On this, see also → Table of Cases Art 3 of the EIR Appendix B No 17, **Procureur des Konings v BVHE.**

120 What is not sufficient is the mere existence of assets in a country.[270] Hence, debtors' assets that are located in a country where the debtor has no establishment cannot be made the subject matter of territorial proceedings. These assets will rather be included in the main insolvency proceedings if such have been opened.[271] For a detailed discussion on the concept of "establishment", see Art 2 of the EIR mn 45 et seq.

121 The question arises as to whether legally **independent, foreign subsidiaries** of the debtor constitute "establishments" within the meaning of Arts 2 (h) and 3 (2) of the EIR. This is decisive for deciding whether territorial proceedings can be opened in the particular state in respect of the assets of the subsidiaries. **Prevailing opinion** holds that independent subsidiary companies **are not establishments of the parent company.**[272] This appears correct in light of the fact that, pursuant to Art 32 of the EIR, the creditor is entitled to assert his claims both in territorial and in main insolvency proceedings. If they were considered establishments, the creditors of the subsidiary would have an additional defendant at their disposal (i.e. the parent company) who was not the debtor. Art 32 of the EIR imperatively presupposes that a subsidiary company is not deemed an establishment of the debtor's. A subsidiary will still not be considered an establishment even if it is 100 % controlled by the main debtor.[273] The inclusion of subsidiaries in the concept of an establishment would also run contrary to the legislator's intention, i.e. to consciously refrain from creating a unified jurisdiction for corporate groups. But a subsidiary will be considered an establishment within the meaning of Arts 2 (h) and 3 (2) of the EIR if, against its own (autonomous) assets in the country of the parent company, insolvency proceedings are opened on account of the courts there having determined that the centre of main interests of the subsidiary is at the registered office of the parent.[274] In this case, a conflict with Art 32 of the EIR is not to be expected.

122 Another question is whether it is possible after the opening of main insolvency proceedings to still set up an establishment in another Member State through some kind of

[270] *Virgós/Schmit* Explanatory Report mn 80; *Marshall* European Cross Border Insolvency (2005) mn 1.008; *Israel* European Cross-Border Insolvency Regulation (2005) 291; *Smid* Komm EuInsVO Art 2 mn 21.

[271] *Virgós/Schmit* Explanatory Report mn 81.

[272] *Virgós/Garcimartín* Regulation p 48; *Smid* Komm EuInsVO Art 2 mn 23; D-K/D/Ch-*Duursma-Kepplinger* Art 2 mn 29.

[273] Cf *Gottwald* Grenzüberschreitende Insolvenzen (1997) 21 et seq; D-K/D/Ch-*Duursma-Kepplinger* Art 27 mn 25 und 26.

[274] See the decision of the AG Cologne "Automold" ZIP 2004, 471 (→ cf Table of Cases Art 3 of the EIR Appendix A mn 2) in which the court deemed the administrative head office and the main place of activities of a (independently operating) subsidiary, against whose assets main insolvency proceedings had been opened in England, as an establishment within the meaning of Art 2 (h) of the EIR, and opened secondary insolvency proceedings pursuant to which a "debtor in possession" (*Eigenverwaltung*) order was made and transferred the power to administer and dispose of the subsidiary's assets to the liquidator in the main proceedings. The possibility of opening secondary insolvency proceedings at the registered office of an independent subsidiary was also allowed for by the Austrian LG Innsbruck in "Hettlage" ZIP 2004, 1721 (→ cf Table of Cases Art 3 of the EIR Appendix A mn 12); *Eidenmüller* NJW 2004, 3455, 3458; *Huber* FS Heldrich (2005) p 679, 691; on this, see also: Haß/Huber/Gruber/Heiderhoff-*Haß/Herweg* Art 3 EuInsVO mn 43; *Marshall* European Cross Border Insolvency (2005) mn 2.052.

corresponding activity.[275] But since this would probably be done primarily for the purposes of forum shopping, it should not be allowed.

There are **two types of territorial insolvency proceedings**: The first are **secondary insolvency proceedings** pursuant to Art 3 (3) of the EIR, and the second are independent **territorial insolvency proceedings** pursuant to Art 3 (4) of the EIR, which are independent of the main insolvency proceedings (see mn 128 et seq). Secondary insolvency proceedings presuppose that main insolvency proceedings have been opened in respect of the debtor's assets. In the absence of this, independent territorial insolvency proceedings may be opened but only under the additional conditions set out in Art 3 (4) (a) and (b) of the EIR. **123**

3.2 Secondary Insolvency Proceedings

Art 3 (3) of the EIR stipulates that once main insolvency proceedings have been opened, only **secondary insolvency proceedings** may be opened. In the case of secondary insolvency proceedings, the grounds for the insolvency need not be demonstrated nor proven as long as main insolvency proceedings have been opened[276] (on the problems arising from deeming the temporary administration as the opening of insolvency proceedings, see mn 91 et seq above). The effects of these proceedings are restricted to the assets situated in the respective Member State (Art 3 (2) sentence 2 of the EIR). This provision reflects the general principle underlying the Regulation, namely that the interests of the domestic creditors are to be protected particularly through the law applicable to the insolvency proceedings. The opening of secondary insolvency proceedings can also be used as a defense against encroachments of foreign (corporate) group proceedings.[277] Such a move may also be justified if the debtor's assets are so interlocked that a unified liquidation appears too difficult.[278] **124**

Secondary insolvency proceedings must be in the form of **winding-up proceedings** (Art 3 (3) sentence 2 of the EIR).[279] As set out in Art 2 (c) of the EIR, this is to be understood as an insolvency proceeding that results in the "realising" of the debtor's assets. The proceedings may be closed via **composition proceedings, an insolvency plan**, or through any other measure terminating the insolvency proceedings, such as a stay of proceedings due to insufficiency of assets. Annex B of the EIR contains an exhaustive list of winding-up proceedings. The *Insolvenzverfahren* under German law is listed there. This means that, for example, German **"debtor in possession"** (*Eigenverwaltung*) proceedings can be ordered in conjunction with secondary insolvency proceedings. **125**

Example **126**

→ See Table of Cases Art 3 of the EIR Appendix A mn 2: Automold

Upon request by the German managing director and the English liquidator, the *AG* Cologne opened secondary insolvency proceedings on 23 January 2004. The court

275 *Marshall* European Cross Border Insolvency (2005) mn 1.008.

276 *Balz* ZIP 1996, 948 (953).

277 Cf *Oberhammer* ZInsO 2004, 761, 770.

278 See Haß/Huber/Gruber/Heiderhoff-*Haß/Herweg* Art 3 EuInsVO mn 45; it also makes sense if there are a large number of creditors, see *Virgós/Garcimartín* Regulation, p 156.

279 *Penzlin* holds that, in light of Art 34 (1) of the EIR, a reorganization is also possible in addition to a winding-up as long as an understanding has been reached with the liquidator in the main proceedings; already in: *Penzlin* EWiR 2006, 207, 208; *Penzlin/Riedemann* NZI 2005, 517, 518.

also issued – upon application – a "debtor in possession" order and, in the absence of contrary a provision in German law, awarded the powers of administration and disposal to the English liquidators. The *AG* Cologne held that the "debtor in possession" constellation leads, via a coordinated handling of the insolvency, to higher proceeds from the liquidation; the court also argued that the English liquidators were already familiar with the matter.

127 Pursuant to Art 33 of the EIR, the liquidator in the main proceedings can cause a **stay** of the secondary insolvency proceedings; he must, however, take all measures necessary to safeguard the interests of the creditors of the secondary insolvency proceedings (see discussions on Art 33 of the EIR). But the court of the secondary insolvency proceedings is not afforded the same rights as those of the liquidator in the main proceedings, the purpose of the stay being the safeguarding of the outcome of the main insolvency proceedings.[280]

3.3 Characteristic Features of Independent Territorial Insolvency Proceedings (Art 3 (4) of the EIR)

128 **→ For examples of independent territorial insolvency proceedings, see also:**

- **Table of Cases Art 3 of the EIR Appendix B No 8: Werlin Corporation Ltd**
- **Table of Cases Art 3 of the EIR Appendix B No 17: Procureur des Konings v BVHE**

129 What distinguishes **independent territorial insolvency proceedings** from secondary insolvency proceedings is that the courts may, under certain conditions, order the opening of such proceedings even though main insolvency proceedings have not yet been opened. This may be because main insolvency proceedings simply do not exist, or because the main proceedings have not been recognized for the reasons set out in Art 26 of the EIR.[281]

130 In order to uphold the principle of universality of the main insolvency proceedings, independent territorial insolvency proceedings may only be opened under the aforementioned conditions. The Regulation itself does not regulate the implementation of the proceedings; this is a matter for the laws of the respective Member States.

131 Art 3 (4) (a) and (b) of the EIR regulates **two types of Cases for independent insolvency proceedings:**

- Subsection (a) adresses those Cases where the opening of main insolvency proceedings is not possible because of the conditions laid down by the laws of the individual Member States. A common case of this is when the applicable law provides that the debtor must be a businessperson (*Kaufmann*), and the debtor does not fulfill this requirement. Main insolvency proceedings can therefore not be opened due to the lack of insolvency capacity on the part of the debtor, see the example above at mn 13.

---

280 Landesgericht Leoben NZI 2005, 646 (→ cf Table of Cases Art 3 of the EIR Appendix A mn 5 – Collins & Aikman), with explanatory note by *Paulus* NZI 2005, 647; see also *Smid* DZWiR 2006, 325, 329.

281 Cf also *Paulus* Komm EuInsVO Art 3 mn 56.

- Subsection (b) is conditioned on either the creditor or the claim having a connection to the establishment situated in the particular Member State (→ cf Table of Cases Art 3 of the EIR Appendix B No 8 – **Werlin Corporation Ltd**).

Such is the case if the creditor has his domicile, habitual residence, or registered office in the concerned Member State, or if he has a claim arising from the operation of that establishment and such claim must be satisfied in the country of the establishment. The question as to when this is the case can be assessed, because of the identical wording, using the principles developed in connection with Art 5 No 3 of the 1968 Brussels Convention.[282] Precedent holds that a claim is based on an obligation arising from the operation of an establishment if it concerns **contractual or extra-contractual rights and obligations in relation to the actual managing of the establishment** itself.[283] Certain is, however, that the place of performance of the obligation cannot be the decisive factor since the place of performance – pursuant to Council Regulation (EC) No 44/2001 as well – only affords the creditor a supplementary legal venue, the creditor still being able to seek legal redress from the courts having jurisdiction in the forum of the establishment. Also, in light of the fact that Art 3 of the EIR is especially aimed at safeguarding the interests of national creditors, and must therefore uphold the trust they placed in the originally established jurisdiction, all that is relevant is whether the claim arises from the operation of the establishment; the place where the obligation was performed is immaterial.

The conflict of laws rule in Art 4 of the EIR applies to independent territorial insol- **132**
vency proceedings as well, so that the determination of whether there is a reason for opening insolvency proceedings must be made pursuant to the ***lex fori*** governing the independent territorial insolvency proceedings.[284]

Just how the **reason for insolvency** is to be ascertained poses problems (concerning **133**
the procedural costs, cf Art 27 of the EIR mn 16).

- Where the **inability to pay debts** is used as a reason to open proceedings, there is a debate as to whether this should be assessed **in relation to the establishment alone**, or whether it should be assessed **on a worldwide basis**.[285] In support of a worldwide assessment is the fact that the establishment is not afforded its own legal personality and that it is always possible for the main establishment to transfer funds to the branch establishment.[286] If this was adhered to, the creditor who requested the opening of independent territorial insolvency proceedings would have to prove that the debtor – on a worldwide basis – is unable to fulfill its debt obligations.[287] A creditor would hardly be in a position to provide such proof in the case of a globally operating enterprise, or it would necessitate extensive investigations.[288] In a case involving similar facts, the German ***BGH*** held that only the payment abilities of the German establishment, the main establishment, and at most the establishments in other European countries needed to be taken into account for the assessment.[289] For pragmatic rea-

282 MünchKomm InsO/*Reinhart* Art 3 EuInsVO mn 10.

283 *Kropholler* EuGVÜ Art 5 mn 91; and ECJ "Somafer/Saar-Ferngas" EC reports 1978, 2183 = RiW 1979, 273.

284 Moss/Fletcher/Isaacs-*Moss/Smith*, Regulation, mn 8.60.

285 BK-InsO/*Pannen* Art 3 EuInsVO mn 32 et seq.

286 *Wimmer* ZIP 1998, 982, 986.

287 *Wimmer* ZIP 1998, 982, 986; BK-InsO/*Pannen* Art 3 EuInsVO mn 33.

288 *Wimmer* ZIP 1998, 982, 986.

289 BGH ZIP 1991, 1014, 1015.

sons, the **inability to pay debts** for the purposes of establishing a reason to open insolvency proceedings should thus be assessed **in relation to the establishment.**[290]

- By contrast, **overindebtedness** must be assessed in relation to the legal entity behind the establishment. This is because only the legal entity behind the establishment can ever be overindebted.[291] Overindebtedness, as a reason to open insolvency proceedings, can therefore only be ascertained on the basis of worldwide assets and liabilities.[292]

134 There is no requirement that the proceedings must take the form of winding-up proceedings. If main insolvency proceedings are opened after the opening of independent territorial insolvency proceedings, then the provisions applying to secondary insolvency proceedings in Arts 31 to 35 of the EIR apply to the extent possible considering the progress of the proceedings. If the isolated independent territorial insolvency proceedings are not winding-up proceedings, then the liquidator in the main insolvency proceedings is entitled to request a conversion into winding-up proceedings if it is in the interests of the creditors (see discussions on this in Art 37 of the EIR).

3.4 Liquidators' Duty to Cooperate and Communicate

135 If both main and secondary insolvency proceedings have been opened, then in the interests of a best-possible liquidation of the debtor's assets, it is necessary that the liquidators cooperate and communicate with each other (see Art 31 Regulation).[293] It is particularly important that the liquidators of the main insolvency proceedings be able to influence the independent territorial insolvency proceedings in order to ensure the predominant position of the main proceedings.[294] But an insolvency court is not empowered to order the conclusion of a cooperation agreement.[295]

136 Because the Regulation opted against a group jurisdiction in the case of corporate groups, it is extremely important that the liquidators in these constellations cooperate with each other. For a detailed discussion on this, see Art 31 of the EIR.

137 One proposed solution takes the form of private law agreements between the liquidators and the insolvency courts, so-called **protocols.**[296] This kind of agreement was developed in Anglo-American law, and is commonly used there in cross-border insolvency Cases.[297] For a detailed discussion on this, see Part 3, 4).

---

[290] *Wimmer* ZIP 1998, 982, 987; cf also MünchKomm InsO/*Reinhart* Art 3 EuInsVO mn 11; *Virgós/Garcimartín* Regulation, p 156; BK-InsO/*Pannen* Art 3 EuInsVO mn 33.

[291] *Wimmer* ZIP 1998, 982, 986.

[292] *Wimmer* ZIP 1998, 982, 987; BK-InsO/*Pannen* Art 3 EuInsVO mn 37.

[293] The Regulation provides in Art 31 a duty to cooperate and to communicate information between the main and territorial insolvency proceedings, Moss/Fletcher/Isaacs-*Moss/Smith*, Regulation, mn 8.56; *Pannen* in Runkel (ed), AHB-Insolvenzrecht (2005) § 16 mn 237 et seq.

[294] Cf on this in details the comments on Art 31 EuInsVO.

[295] Landesgericht Leoben NZI 2005, 646 (→ cf Table of Cases Art 3 of the EIR Appendix A mn 5 – Collins & Aikman).

[296] For a detailed discussion on "protocols", see Haß/Huber/Gruber/Heiderhoff-*Haß/Herweg* Art 3 EuInsVO mn 65-70; also on this topic: *Wittinghofer* Der nationale und internationale Insolvenzverwaltungsvertrag (2004).

[297] *Paulus* ZIP 1998, 977, 979–982.

Appendix A to Art 3 of the EIR

Table of Cases
Landmark Judgements in Long Version

Contents

1

Aircraft	
Preliminary comments/ company	The debtor is a natural person with a participating interest in several companies whose registered offices are primarily in Hamburg. One of these is an interest in the Aircraft KG whose assets include two airplanes. The debtor administers his interests and real property from Hamburg, where he spends two thirds of the year. In the other third, he resides in the Czech Republic.
Proceedings	On 11 February 2005, one of the creditors requested insolvency proceedings at the Municipality Court of Prague. On 2 March 2005, the debtor himself requested insolvency proceedings at the *Amtsgericht* Hamburg. Pursuant thereto, the *AG* Hamburg ordered an expert report. By order dated 08 March 2005, the Municipality Court of Prague appointed a temporary administrator. The *Amtsgericht* Hamburg then opened main insolvency proceedings on 16 March 2005. An appeal of an insolvency creditor against the opening of the main proceedings was dismissed by the *Landgericht* on 18 August 2005 on the grounds that it was inadmissible, there being no right of appeal pursuant to Sec 32 *InsO* and Art 102 § 3 *EGInsO*. The court also held that the appeal lacked merit as the principle of priority only applies once the proceedings have been opened. → *References: AG Hamburg dated 16 Mar 2005, unreported; on this Herchen ZIP 2005, 1401, 1405 et seq; LG Hamburg dated 18 Aug 2005 – 326 T 34/05 ZIP 2005, 1697 = ZInsO 2005, 1052 = NZI 2005, 645, on this Schilling/Schmidt EWiR 2006, 15.* On 26 April 2005, the Prague Municipality Court also opened main insolvency proceedings in respect of the debtor's assets. Relying on the legal fiction of retroactive effect in Sec 82 (1) of

(Aircraft cont.)	
	the Czech Code of Civil Procedure, the court held that the making of the request, i.e. on 11 February 2005, amounted to the opening insolvency proceedings as per Art 16 of the EIR. The proceedings opened by the *Amtsgericht* Hamburg could therefore, so the court, only constitute secondary insolvency proceedings. → *References: Municipality Court Prague dated 26 Apr 2005 – 78 K 6/05-127 ZIP 2005, 1431; on this Herchen ZIP 2005, 1401.*

2

Automold	
Preliminary comments/ company	The Automold GmbH is a supplier of synthetic automobile parts. One hundred percent of its equity interests are held by an English limited liability company. Production was carried out by 103 employees exclusively in Germany. All personnel and financial decisions are being made by the management of the English company.
Proceedings	On 19 December 2003, the High Court of Justice in Birmingham opened main insolvency proceedings against the assets of the German company. The court was of the opinion that the centre of main interests was situated in England. → *References: High Court of Justice in Birmingham dated 19 Dec 2003, unreported.* Upon request by the German managing director and the English liquidator, the *AG* Cologne opened secondary insolvency proceedings on 23 January 2004. The court also issued – upon application – a "debtor in possession" order and, absent a provision to the contrary in German law, awarded the powers of administration and disposal to the English liquidators. The *AG* Cologne held that the "debtor in possession" constellation leads, via a coordinated handling of the insolvency, to higher proceeds from the liquidation; the court also argued that the English liquidators were already familiar with the matter. → *References: AG Cologne dated 23 Jan 2004 – 71 IN 1/04 ZIP 2004, 471 = NZI 2004, 151 = ZInsO 2004, 216 = DZWiR 2004, 434 = EWiR 2004, 601 with explanatory note by Blenske p 601; on this see also Meyer-Löwy/Poertzgen ZInsO 2004, 195; Smid DZWiR 2004, 397, 406; Sabel NZI 2004, 126.*

3

BRAC Rent-A-Car	
Preliminary comments/ company	In BRAC Rent-A-Car, the High Court of Justice had to deal with the question of whether the EIR also applied in relation to non-EU countries, or whether the foreign connection has to lie within the Community. The BRAC Rent-A-Car International Inc. was one of the largest globally operating car rental firms, incorporated and with its registered office in the US state of Delaware. The company had no employees in the USA; the majority of these were situated in England. The economic activities were therefore carried out from England.
Proceedings	Chapter 11 proceedings had already been opened in the USA against the company and against other companies of the group. The company itself requested the opening of insolvency proceedings in England. By order dated 14 January 2003, the High Court of Justice in London issued an "administration order" with which main insolvency proceedings were opened parallel to the US insolvency proceedings. The High Court assumed that the Chapter 11 reorganisation proceedings did not afford the debtor any protection against enforcement measures, at least not in England and Wales pursuant to English precedent. This appears to be the first time that a court held the Regulation applicable to a non-EU country. The court found that, because the business operations were executed exclusively in England, the presumption in Art 3 (1) sentence 2 of the EIR had been rebutted and the centre of main interests was thereby situated in England. The court held that in order to establish international jurisdiction pursuant to the Regulation, all that was required was a relevant connection in terms of international insolvency law to a non-EU country, e.g. assets or an establishment in the USA, and that a qualified foreign connection was not required. → *References:* *"BRAC Rent-A-Car" – High Court of Justice Chancery Division Companies Court dated 7 Feb 2003 – 42/03 ZIP 2003, 813 = [2003] EWHC (Ch) 128 = [2003] 2 All E.R. 201; with explanatory note by Herchen ZInsO 2003, 742; Herchen ZInsO 2004, 825, 830; Smid DZWiR 2003, 397; on this see also Sabel/Schlegel EWiR 2003, 367; Pannen/ Riedemann NZI 2004, 646; Krebber IPRax 2004, 540.*

4

Ci4net.com Inc	
Preliminary comments/ company	The debtor was a company founded and registered in the USA and operating in the Internet sector. The business activities, which had ceased long before the request was made, were ultimately obviously carried out primarily in England.
Proceedings	A creditor of the company had lodged an insolvency request in England. The sole managing director of the debtor had contested

(Ci4net.com Inc cont.)	
	the international jurisdiction of the English courts, arguing that the centre of main interests was not located in England but rather in the USA and Spain because of his change of location. By order dated 20 May 2004, the High Court of Justice in Leeds nevertheless opened main insolvency proceedings against the assets of the debtor in England. It affirmed its international jurisdiction, concurring with both the grounds and the result of the decision of the High Court of Justice in London, thereby following the precedent set in the BRAC Rent-A-Car case (see mn 3). The court held that the presumption in Art 3 (1) sentence 2 of the EIR, which presumes that the centre of main interests is at the location of the registered office, is just one of many factors to be taken into consideration in ascertaining this centre. The court did not offer any detailed reason for finding that the presumption had been rebutted. → *References: High Court of Justice Leeds Chancery Division Companies Court dated 20 May 2004 – 556 and 557/2004 ZIP 2004, 1769, on this Westpfahl/Wilkens EWiR 2004, 847; Klöhn KTS 2006, 259.*

5

Collins & Aikman	
Preliminary comments/ company	The Collins & Aikman Cooperation Group operates as a supplier of interior fixtures in the automotive sector. The company's head office is in the USA, it operates throughout the world in 17 countries, and employs approx. 23,000 persons. The European group of companies operates in ten different countries. Around 4,000 employees are employed at 24 locations here.
Proceedings	Chapter 11 proceedings pursuant to the US Bankruptcy Code were opened in respect of the US corporate group. On 15 July 2005, the High Court of Justice in London opened main insolvency proceedings ("administration") in respect of all of the European companies in the group. With its decision, the court affirmed a group jurisdiction. → *References: "Collins & Aikman I" – High Court of Justice London dated 15 Jul 2005 – 4697-4712/05 and 4717-4725/05, Marshall European Cross Border Insolvency, No. 2.105; critical Paulus NZI 2005, 647.* On 18 July 2005, the management of one of the group companies that was registered in the German *Handelsregister* of the *AG* Cologne requested the opening of insolvency proceedings from the court. The management thereby wished to comply with its duty to request insolvency proceedings pursuant to Sec 64 (1) of the German *GmbHG*. The intention was not to request the opening of secondary insolvency proceedings. The *AG* Cologne

(Collins & Aikman cont.)

denied a need to grant protection of a legal right and dismissed the request as inadmissible. The court held that by lodging the request in England, the management body had already fulfilled its duty pursuant to the *GmbHG*, and there was no need to make a further request.

→ *References:* *"Collins & Aikman II" – AG Cologne dated 10 Aug 2005 – 71 IN 416/05 ZIP 2005, 1566 = NZI 2005, 564 = NZG 2005, 858 = EuZW 2005, 704 = DZWiR 2006, 218; on this Schilling/Schmidt DZWiR 2006, 219.*

In conjunction with one of the Austrian companies in the group, the English liquidators invoked Art 33 of the EIR and requested the staying of the secondary insolvency proceedings altogether. Pleading in the alternative, the liquidation of the entire assets were to be stayed and the liquidator in the secondary insolvency proceedings was to be put under an obligation to conclude a co-operation agreement with the liquidator. The *Landesgericht* Leoben denied all of the requests on 31 August 2005.

→ *References:* *Landesgericht Leoben dated 31 Aug 2005 – 17 S 56/05 ZInsO 2005, 1176; critical on this Sommer ZInsO 2005, 1137 and Paulus NZI 2005, 646, 647.*

To prevent the fragmentation of the insolvency estate, oral agreements were entered into with a number of creditors and creditors' committees in the other Member States, agreeing to refrain from opening secondary insolvency proceedings in order to attain the best possible results. The liquidators in the main proceedings were of the opinion that the opening of such proceedings and the engaging of local liquidators necessitated by this would hinder their goals and would thwart the success of their plans to – on a group-wide basis – negotiate with the companies, to transact sales, and to finance the administration. Included in these agreements was an undertaking that if secondary insolvency proceedings were not requested, efforts would be made – at the respective forums – to obtain or to take into account as far as possible the better position that the creditors probably would be entitled to pursuant to their own national laws. With only a few minor exceptions, the creditors did not make use of secondary insolvency proceedings or any other unity-disrupting measures but rather supported the strategy proposed by the liquidators in the main insolvency proceedings. The High Court of Justice sanctioned the methods of the liquidators through a so-called "approved judgement" of 9 June 2006.

→ *References:* *"Collins & Aikman III" – High Court of Justice London dated 9 Jun 2006 – 4697, 4698, 4700, 4705, 4711, 4717–4719, 4721, 4722 in 2005, ZIP 2006, 2093; on this Mankowski EWiR 2006, 623; Meyer-Löwy/Plank NZI 2006, 622.*

6

Crisscross Telecommunications Group	
Preliminary comments/ company	The Crisscross Telecommunications Group was a Europe-wide operating corporate group of eight companies in the telecommunications sector.
Proceedings	By order dated 20 May 2005, the High Court of Justice in London opened main insolvency proceedings in England. For all eight group companies from various Member States and Switzerland, the court ascertained the centre of main interests in England where only one subsidiary, which was not the parent company, was registered. The court justified the *situs* of the centre of main interests in England by the fact that the management, administrative, and accounting functions had been carried out in London. The other main reason the court gave for this finding was that the majority of transactions were being made via bank accounts held in England, and that most of the customers had entered into contracts governed by English law with one of the English companies. Similar to the "Enron Directo SA" decision, the carrying out of "headquarter" activities was enough in the court's opinion to rebut the presumption in Art 3 (1) of the EIR (see Art 3 of the EIR mn 35 et seq). → *References: High Court of Justice London dated 20 May 2003, unreported. Description of the case by Martinez Ferber European Insolvency Regulation, p 40; on this, see also van Galen The European Insolvency Regulation and Groups of Companies, INSOL Europe Annual Congress Paper, 2003, p 3; see also Pannen/Riedemann* NZI 2004, 646.

7

EMBIC	
Preliminary comments/ company	The EMBIC Garantie Versicherungs-Vertrieb GmbH sold insurance policies for used motor vehicles in Germany. Employees, personnel accounting, business bank accounts, and customer relations were all managed in Germany. One hundred percent of the business interests were held by English Warrenty Holdings International Limited. Approval for payments over 750 British pounds had to be obtained from the English company. The English company itself is now insolvent.
Proceedings	The management of EMBIC lodged an insolvency request in England on 8 April 2004. The debtor was supposed to be heard on 28 April 2004. On 14 April 2004, a request to open secondary insolvency proceedings in the "debtor in possession" (*Eigenverwaltung*) constellation was lodged in Germany at the *Amtsgericht* Mönchengladbach. The *Amtsgericht* was also petitioned to await the

(EMBIC cont.)	
	decision of the English court in case the court would wish to deny the request to open secondary insolvency proceedings because of the absence of main proceedings. The *AG* Mönchengladbach, however, interpreted the request to open secondary insolvency proceedings as a request to open main proceedings based on the fact that the English court had not yet opened main proceedings. In the opinion of the court, the decisive place for ascertaining the centre of main interests is the place where the company conducts its economic activities. The court held that it was not ascertainable to third parties that strategic business decisions were being made in England. Taken as a whole, the fact that the employees, personnel accounting, business bank accounts, and existing customer relations were all in Germany justified, in the opinion of the court, a finding of the centre of main interests for EMBIC in Germany. → *References: "EMBIC I" – AG Mönchengladbach dated 27 Apr 2004 – 19 IN 54/04 ZIP 2004, 1064 with explanatory note by Bähr/Riedemann, p 1066; NZI 2004, 383 with explanatory note by Lautenbach, p 384 et seq; NZG 2004, 1016; DZWiR 2004, 437; on this Kebekus EWiR 2004, 705.*

8

EMTEC	
Preliminary comments/ company	The holding company of the EMTEC Group is a Dutch company that does not carry out any operations and does not employ any persons. It is the sole shareholder of the central French companies EMTEC International, EMTEC France, and MPOTEC GmbH ("debtor"). In conjunction with the purchase of the French group by a French investor, the Dutch holding company was interposed for legal reasons related to tax and trademark issues. The EMTEC Group markets (data) storage media of various kinds in France and the rest of Europe and is the owner of the trademark.
Proceedings	The *Tribunal de Commerce* in Nanterre initially opened insolvency proceedings against EMTEC International and EMTEC France. On 31 January 2006, the management of the debtor together with seven other European subsidiaries of EMTEC France lodged an insolvency request in Nanterre. In all cases, the *Tribunal de Commerce de Nanterre* opened reorganization proceedings ("*redressement judiciaire*") as main insolvency proceedings pursuant Art 3 (1) sentence 1 of the EIR. Even though the registered office of the holding company was in the Netherlands, the court held that the COMI was in France. This was based on the controlling function that the affiliated companies, EMTEC International and EMTEC France, exercised over the debtor. The

(EMTEC cont.)	
	court held that this could be deduced from the group's structure. The debtor, in the court's opinion, was being controlled by EMTEC International, EMTEC France, and their subsidiaries to a considerable degree. The court found that the companies were, *inter alia*, responsible for managing finances, supplying goods, corporate policy, and for the supply agreements of the debtor company. The *Tribunal de Commerce* held that the supervision of all main insolvency proceedings, and thus the centralization of these, by one single court simplifies the group-wide reorganization via the creation of one universal reorganization plan. The court's arguments also took the creditors' interests into account. They found that, from the point of view of the employees, corporate decision-making was being made from France. The court held that it was forseeable, at least for the main creditors, that the COMI was located at the corporate domicile of the subsidiary companies in France. The court expressly relies on the ECJ decision in Staubitz-Schreiber and on the opinion made by the Advocate General in Eurofood/Parmalat (see this case). → *References: Tribunal de Commerce de Nanterre dated 15 Feb 2006 – PCL 2006J00174, Marshall European Cross Border Insolvency, No. 2.058; on this Penzlin EWiR 2006, 207.*

9

Enron Directo SA	
Preliminary comments/ company	The Enron Directo Sociedad Limitada belonged to the Enron Group, which operates in the energy and raw material sector on a worldwide scale. The administration of the European companies was conducted centrally by an English company. The registered office, assets, customer pool, and employees of Enron Directo SA were all situated in Spain.
Proceedings	Chapter 11 proceedings were opened in the USA in respect of the assets of the group's holding company. On 4 June 2002, the High Court of Justice in London opened main proceedings in respect of the assets of Enron Directo. The High Court was of the opinion that the centre of main interests of Enron Directo was located in England. The court held that the presumption of Art 3 (1) sentence 2 of the EIR had been rebutted by the fact that the essential functions of the enterprise, such as management, personnel decisions, and accounting, were being managed from London.

(Enron Directo SA cont.)	
	→ <u>*References:*</u> *High Court of Justice London dated 4 Jun 2002, unreported; in Internet the "skeleton argument" is available under "www.iiiglobal.org/country/european_union/ Enron_Directo_Skel.pdf"; Martinez Ferber European Insolvency Regulation, p 41; on this see also Pannen/Riedemann NZI 2004, 648.*

10

Eurofood/Parmalat	
Preliminary comments/ company	The Parmalat S.p.A. is a large Italian grocery group operating internationally. In 1997, the group founded the subsidiary Eurofood IFSC Limited (hereinafter "Eurofood"). It is a financing company for the capital market with its registered office in Dublin, Ireland. Eurofood has neither employees nor business premises. The registered office was a law firm in Dublin.
Proceedings	On 23 December 2003, the so-called *"lex parmalat"* was enacted in Italy. According to this, a company can apply to the Italian Industry Minister for an extraordinary administration order, a so-called *"amministrazione straordinaria"*. The court then simply sanctions the ministerial decision. In the time following this, main insolvency proceedings were opened under Art 3 (1) of the EIR in respect of numerous European subsidiaries. On 24 December 2003, *"amministrazione straordinaria"* proceedings pursuant to the *"lex parmalat"* were allowed in respect of the assets of Eurofood IFSC Ltd. A special commissioner was also appointed at the same time. On 27 January 2004, a temporary administrator ("provisional liquidator") with far reaching powers of disposal was appointed for Eurofood in Ireland without the court having dealt with Art 3 (1) of the EIR. By appeal dated 30 January 2004, the special commissioner in Italy objected to this decision. At the same time, the *Tribunale di Parma* on 19 February 2004 sanctioned the Industry Minister's decision on extradordinary administration, which had been made pursuant to a request of the commissioner's, thus opening main insolvency proceedings against Eurofood in Italy. The Italian court was of the opinion that the presumption in Art 3 (1) sentence 2 of the EIR had been rebutted since the actual management of the enterprise in Parma had been ascertainable to third parties particularly through the payment guarantee of Parmalat S.p.A. → <u>*References:*</u> *"Eurofood / Parmalat I" – Tribunale di Parma dated 19 Feb 2004 – 53/04 ZIP 2004, 1220 with explanatory note by Riera/Wagner EWiR 2004, 597.*

(Eurofood/Parmalat cont.)	
	The *Tribunale di Parma* also opened main insolvency proceedings against the assets of the German Parmalat GmbH. The court held that the presumption in Art 3 (1) sentence 2 of the EIR had also been rebutted here by such things as the German subisidiary being bound by directives, the structuring of the shareholders' rights in the articles of association, and the negotiations of the creditors with the Italian group's parent company. → *References: Tribunale di Parma dated 15 Jun 2004 – 93/04 ZIP 2004, 2295 with explanatory note by Bauer/Schlegel EWiR 2004, 1181.* On 23 March 2004, the High Court of Dublin in the Eurofood case decided that the appointment of the "provisional liquidator" on 27 January 2004 already amounted to the opening of main insolvency proceedings. The court based this on the retroactive effect of the insolvency request pursuant to Irish law. They found that the presumption in Art 3 of the EIR had not been rebutted because in the telephone conferences with investors, the Italian directors had only been linked into the telephone connection from Italy. The court did not consider the point emphasized by the *Tribunale di Parma*, i.e. that the payment guarantee of the Parmalat S.p.A. was ascertainable to third parties. → *References: "Eurofood/Parmalat II" – High Court Dublin, dated 23 Mar 2004 – 33/04 ZIP 2004, 1223 with explanatory note by Herweg/Tschauner EWiR 2004, 599; critical Kübler FS Gerhardt, p 527, 546 et seq.* After the Italian special commissioner had appealed against the decision of the High Court Dublin, the Supreme Court of Ireland referred several questions arising from its judgement of 27 July 2004 concerning the interpretation of Art 3 (1) of the EIR in the case of corporate group insolvencies to the ECJ for a preliminary ruling pursuant to Arts 68 and 234 EEC Treaty. → *References: "Eurofood / Parmalat III" – Supreme Court of Ireland dated 27 Jul 2004 – 147/04 NZI 2004, 505; ZIP 2004, 1969; DZWiR 2005, 60 with explanatory note by Smid DZWiR 2005, 64; on this see also Herweg/Tauschner EWiR 2004, 973; Wimmer ZInsO 2005, 119.* On 2 May 2006, the ECJ passed judgement on the conflicts of jurisdictions between the courts of the various EU Member States in relation to the insolvency of the Parmalat Group. The court adhered for the most part to the opinion of the Advocate General *Jacobs*. → *References: ECJ, opinion of the Advocate General dated 27 Sep 2005 – "Eurofood / Parmalat IV" ZIP 2005, 1878, on this Pannen/Riedemann EWiR 2005, 725.*

(Eurofood/Parmalat cont.)	
	With this decision, the ECJ held against the creation, in the case of group insolvencies, of jurisdiction for the group at the registered office of the parent company, emphasizing that the Regulation does not contemplate a group COMI. According to the court, the presumption in Art 3 (1) sentence 2 of the EIR can only be rebutted if there are objective elements ascertainable by third parties that demonstrate that the COMI is not at the registered office of the company. For the ECJ, the fact that substantial management decisions are being made for a national subsidiary by a parent company that is domiciled in a different Member State (in the sense of a negative demarcation) would not be an objective sign ascertainable to third parties particularly if the subsidiary was conducting business activities in that particular (inland) country. The court found that a rebuttal would only be plausible if the subsidiary carried out no activities whatsoever at its registered office. According to the ECJ, the presumption in Art 3 (1) sentence 2 of the EIR has the same effect as a legal norm. The court held that the COMI in the Eurofood IFSC Ltd. case was located in Ireland and not in Italy. → *References: "Eurofood / Parmalat" – ECJ dated 2 May 2006 – C-341/04 ZInsO 2006, 484 = ZIP 2006, 907 = NZI 2006, 360 = DZWiR 2006, 329 = NZG 2006, 633 = BB 2006, 1762 = EuZW 2006, 337= IPRax 2007, 120; Poertzgen/Adam ZInsO 2006, 505 et seq; Mankowski BB 2006, 1753; Kammel NZI 2006, 334; Herchen NZI 2006, 435; Smid DZWiR 2006, 325; Knof/Mock ZIP 2006, 911; Freitag/Leible RIW 2006, 641; Baxter INSOL III 2006, 9 et seq; Dammann/Podeur Banque et droit N° 109, 3 et seq; Dammann Dalloz 2006, 1752; Schmidt J. ZIP 2007, 405; Hess/Laukemann/Seagon IPRax 2007, 89; Dammann/Podeur Global Turnaround March 2007, 11.*

Eurotunnel		11
Preliminary comments/ company	The Eurotunnel PLC is a holding company under English law with its registered office in England. Together with the Eurotunnel SA (company under French law), it is one of the holding companies of the Eurotunnel Group. The group also has other subsidiaries in Spain, Germany, Belgium, and in the Netherlands.	
Proceedings	Because of financial difficulties, representatives of seventeen companies of the Eurotunnel Group from various Member States (including Eurotunnel PLC) requested on 11 July 2006 the opening of special protective proceedings (*"procédure de sauvegarde"* – special insolvency proceedings where the inability to pay debts or over-indebtedness are not required) from the *Tribunal de commerce*	

(Eurotunnel cont.)	
	in Paris.The French *Tribunal* assumed international jurisdiction pursuant to Art 3 of the EIR for the seventeen companies and opened the protective proceedings. Taking into account the submissions made by the ECJ in the Eurofood case, the concept of the COMI has, in the opinion of the *Tribunal de commerce*, a special meaning and must be uniformly interpreted independent of national laws and according to objective factors ascertainable to third parties that prove that, in reality, the situation does not accord with the one that is supposed to be reflected by the registered office. The court found that several concurring elements ascertainable to third parties proved that the COMI of the various companies of the Eurotunnel Group was in France. The following are some of the aspects that were taken into account in coming to this decision: – The strategic and operative management of the various group companies was discharged by a joint council in Paris comprised of French citizens. – The managing of finances and the accounting also took place in France. – The majority of the activities, employees, and assets were located in France. – The negotiations on debt restructuring took place in Paris. → *References: Tribunal de commerce Paris dated 2 Aug 2006 – 2006047554, Dalloz 2006, 2329 "Eurotunnel", with explanatory note by Dammann/Podeur.*

12

Hettlage	
Preliminary comments/ company	The Austrian debtor operates in the textile industry and runs thirteen sale outlets in Austria. It is a subsidiary of the German Hettlage KG a.A. The management of the business, sales, and purchasing was the responsibility of the German parent company, as was accounting and controlling, organisation, computer technology, personnel, and other services.
Proceedings	On 4 May 2004, the *Amtsgericht* Munich opened main insolvency proceedings against the Austrian subsidiary. The court held that the centre of main interests was in Germany as essential services were being rendered by the German parent company, and Germany was the place where the economic interests were being administered. Relying on the judgement of the High Court of Leeds dated 16 May 2003 ("ISA I"), the court held that the presumption in Art 3 (1) sentence 2 of the EIR had been rebutted.

(Hettlage cont.)	
	→ <u>References:</u> *"Hettlage I" – AG Munich dated 4 May 2004 – 1501 IE 1276/04 ZInsO 2004, 691 = ZIP 2004, 962; on this Mankowski NZI 2004, 450; Paulus EWiR 2004, 493; Weller IPRax 2004, 412.* Upon request by the German liquidator in the main insolvency proceedings, the *Landesgericht* of Innsbruck, Austria opened secondary insolvency proceedings on 11 May 2004. → <u>References:</u> *"Hettlage II" – Landesgericht Innsbruck dated 11 May 2004 – 9 S 15/04, ZIP 2004, 1721; KTS 2005, 223; on this Bähr/Riedemann EWiR 2004, 1085.*

13

High Court of London/Commercial Court Vienna	
Preliminary comments/ company	The debtor is a natural person who works in England. He was also the managing director of a *GmbH* registered in Vienna.
Proceedings	On 27 March 2003, the High Court of Justice in London opened bankruptcy proceedings in respect of the assets of the debtor with a short reference to Art 3 (1) of the EIR. Being unaware of these proceedings, an Austrian bank that had been trying for a considerable time to collect on debts owed by the debtor filed a bankruptcy petition at the Commercial Court in Vienna on 26 November 2003. By order dated 28 January 2004, the Commercial Court opened bankruptcy proceedings against the assets of the debtor. Although the Austrian liquidator became aware of the English bankruptcy proceedings after the Austrian proceedings had been opened, he continued on with his activities. In the course of the continued bankruptcy proceedings, he requested the release of a claim of the debtor's against a bank in Prague. Both the Czech bank and the English liquidator appealed against the release of the claim. By order dated 9 November 2004, the *OLG* in Vienna recognized the bankruptcy proceedings in England as main insolvency proceedings pursuant to Art 3 (1) of the EIR. The court saw no violation of public policy as per Art 26 of the EIR since, in the court's opinion, such a violation would demand a serious disregard of fundamental Community laws. An infringement of the jurisdiction provisions of the Regulation would, in itself, certainly not amount to a violation of public policy. The court also held that the (absence of) reasons of the High Court of Justice also did not qualify as a violation of public policy since no fundamental principles of fair procedure had been breached by them. The

(High Court of London/Commercial Court Vienna cont.)	
	OLG Vienna therefore decided that the Commercial Court of Vienna could either set aside the proceedings in Austria based on the insufficiency of the national assets to cover the costs of the proceedings, or could restrict the effects of the proceedings *ex post facto* to Austria. → *References: OLG Vienna dated 9 Nov 2004 – 28 R 225/04w NZI 2005, 56 with explanatory note by Paulus p 62 et seq.* The highest Austrian Court, the *OGH*, affirmed the decision of the *OLG* Vienna by order dated 17 March 2005. → *References: OGH dated 17 Mar 2005 – 8 Ob 135/04t NZI 2005, 465.*

14

HUKLA	
Preliminary comments/ company	The debtor is the HUKLA-Werke GmbH Wien. It operates as a sales company in Austria in the mattress and upholstered furniture sector. Business and sales management was under the responsibility of the German parent company, the HUKLA-Werke GmbH. The business records and the accounting books of the Austrian subsidiary were also kept in Germany.
Proceedings	On 2 August 2004, the *AG* Offenburg opened main insolvency proceedings in Germany against the Austrian subsidiary. The presumption in Art 3 (1) sentence 2 of the EIR was deemed by the court as having been rebutted because both the organisation and sales activities were being managed from Germany, and the business records were also situated there. The centre of administrative and economic activities was therefore located in Germany. → *References: AG Offenburg dated 2 Aug 2004 – 2 IN 133/04 NZI 2004, 673; on this Pannen/Riedemann EWiR 2005, 73.*

15

ISA/Daisytek	
Preliminary comments/ company	The Daisytek Group is a commercial group operating in the computer sector, more specifically computer parts/accessories, on a worldwide basis.
Proceedings	On 7 May 2003, Chapter 11 proceedings were opened in the USA in respect of the assets of the group's parent company. According to the management's plan, the winding-up of the European subsidiaries was to be made entirely pursuant to

(ISA/Daisytek cont.)	
	English law. To this end, the group's management lodged insolvency requests in England in respect of the assets of both the English intermediate holding company and the subsidiaries operating in Germany and in France. Thereupon, the High Court of Justice in Leeds opened main insolvency proceedings on 16 May 2003 against the assets of the English, the German, and the French companies. → *References: "ISA I" – High Court of Justice Leeds dated 16 May 2003 – 861 bis 876/03 ZIP 2003, 1362; Judgement on the administration order in ZIP 2004, 963 = NZI 2004, 219. On this Paulus EWiR 2003, 709; Smid DZWIR 2003, 397; Herchen ZInsO 2004, 61.* The German management also requested the opening of insolvency proceedings in Germany. The *AG* Düsseldorf assumed jurisdiction and on 19 May 2003, unaware that English proceedings had been opened, appointed a temporary administrator. Once they became aware of this, the court issued a so-called "clarification order" *(Klarstellungsbeschluss)* on 6 June 2003 in which it set out that the failure to hear the German managing director constituted a breach of Art 26 of the EIR, and thereupon opened a second main proceeding on 10 July 2003. → *References: "ISA II" – AG Düsseldorf dated 6 Jun 2003 – 502 IN 126/03 ZIP 2003, 1363; DZWiR 2003, 437; on this Mankowski EWiR 2003, 767 and 2003, 1239; Herchen ZInsO 2004, 61; Smid DZWiR 2003, 397.* However, because participation rights had been granted by the High Court, the *AG* Düsseldorf was forced to recognize the English main insolvency proceedings and did so by order dated 12 March 2004. By order dated 7 April 2004, the German main proceedings were stayed pursuant to Art 102 § 4 (1) sentence 1 *EGInsO*, and secondary insolvency proceedings were opened as per the request. → *References: AG Düsseldorf dated 12 Mar 2004 502 IN 126/03 ZIP 2004, 623 with explanatory note by Herweg/Tauschner EWiR 2004, 495; Weller IPRax 2004, 412. AG Düsseldorf dated 7 Apr 2004 – 502 IN 124/03 ZIP 2004, 866 with explanatory note by Westpfahl/Wilkens EWiR 2004, 909.* According to the *OLG* Düsseldorf, the German secondary insolvency proceedings do not conflict with the order of enforcement of the English opening decision (administration order). → *References: OLG Düsseldorf dated 9 Jul 2004 – I-3 W 53/04 ZInsO 2004, 867; ZIP 2004, 1514; DZWiR 2004, 428; NZI 2004, 628; on this Pannen/Riedemann EWiR 2005, 177.*

(ISA/Daisytek cont.)	
	On 26 May 2003, the *Tribunal de commerce* Pontoise opened main insolvency proceedings parallel to this. These proceedings were set aside by the *Cour d'appel* Versailles on 4 September 2003 pursuant to an appeal of the English liquidators, and the court then recognized the English main proceedings in compliance with Art 16 of the EIR. This decision was conclusively affirmed by the *Cour de cassation* on 27 June 2006 citing the exact wording of the Eurofood decision. → *References:* *"ISA III" – Cour d'appel Versailles dated 4 Sep 2003 – 05038/03, ZIP 2004, 377; on this Mankowski EWiR 2003, 1239 sowie ZInsO 2004, 825, 829; Sabel NZI 2004, 126, 127. Cour de cassation dated 27 Jun 2006, 03-19863, available at www.legifrance.gouv.fr; see also Dammann/Podeur, Banque & Droit 2006 (109), 3 et seq.*

16

MG Rover	
Preliminary comments/ company	The MG Rover Group Limited is a corporate group in the automotive sector with its registered office in Longbridge, England. The subsidiary, MG Rover Group Overseas Holding Limited, is one of the English companies of the English group. This English intermediate holding company holds a one hundred percent interest in eight sales companies in the EU. These are situated in Germany, France, the Netherlands, the Benelux countries, Spain, Italy, Portugal and Ireland.
Proceedings	On 8 April 2005, the High Court of Justice in Birmingham opened "administration" proceedings against the assets of the group parent company, the Rover Group. The High Court also opened main insolvency proceedings ("administration orders") in England on 18 April 2005 against the eight foreign subsidiaries. The court justified this on the basis of the management and finance structure of the company and as being in the interests of the creditors. The court argued that since the "head office functions" of the company were located in England, the High Court would have jurisdiction. They also held that a liquidation within the framework of a single "administration" would bring better results; the consequences of not doing this would most likely be the shattering of the other EU associations. → *References:* *"MG Rover I" – High Court of Justice Birmingham dated 18 Apr 2005 – 2375 bis 2382/05 ZIP 2005, 1610; EWiR 2005, 637; NZI 2005, 467 with explanatory note by Penzlin/Riedemann p 469 et seq; on this also Mankowski, EWiR 2005, 63; Dammann RB 2006 No 681, 47 et seq.*

(MG Rover cont.)	
	By order dated 11 May 2005, the High Court of Justice elucidated the rights and obligations of the English liquidators in the main insolvency proceedings. The court deemed this necessary in light of the large number of foreign parties to the proceedings. It issued a so-called "supplemental order" for each of the eight sales companies. These "supplemental orders" set out the goals of the English insolvency proceedings, the effects of a moratorium, and the general powers of the liquidator in the main insolvency proceedings pursuant to the Insolvency Act 1986. The court also affirmed that the claims of the employees of the eight associated companies could be satisfied in the order of priority that they would have had pursuant to the national insolvency law applicable to opened secondary insolvency proceedings. By putting the creditors of the EU associates in a better position, the idea was to eliminate any incentive to open secondary insolvency proceedings in the respective Member State. The court hereby wished to prevent the uncoordinated destruction of the MG Rover Group and to ensure a proper and coordinated winding-up aimed at maximizing the proceeds from the various liquidations. → References: *"MG Rover II" – High Court of Justice Birmingham dated 11 May 2005, NZI 2005, 515 with explanatory note by Penzlin/Riedemann p 517 et seq.* Secondary proceedings were nevertheless requested and, in the interim, have been opened in Germany and in the Netherlands. On 30 March 2006, the High Court in Birmingham in the Rover case approved the making of special payments in order to prevent the opening of secondary insolvency proceedings. The court argued that the making of special payments to individual creditors was permissible pursuant to Sec 65 (3) of the Insolvency Act 1968 if, taking in account all of the circumstances in the individual case, the opening of secondary insolvency proceedings that is planned by one of these creditors would prove detrimental. → References: *High Court of Justice Birmingham dated 30 Mar 2006 – 2377/2006 NZI 2006, 416 with explanatory note by Mankowski p 418 et seq.*

17

Susanne Staubitz-Schreiber	
Preliminary comments/ company	The debtor lived in Germany and traded as a sole proprietor in telecommunication equipment and parts.
Proceedings	On 6 December 2001, the debtor requested the opening of insolvency proceedings at the court with international and local jurisdiction in respect of her assets. The request was dismissed on 10 April 2002 pursuant to Sec 26 *InsO* for insufficiency of assets. → References: *AG Wuppertal dated 10 Apr 2002 – 145 IN 489/01.* The special appeal (subject to a time limit) lodged by the debtor against the decision of the *Amtsgericht* Wuppertal was dismissed by the *Landgericht* Wuppertal on 14 August 2002, the court arguing that by moving her domicile and the place of her economic activities to Spain on 1 April 2002 German international jurisdiction no longer existed; the COMI as understood by Art 3 (1) of the EIR was now located in Spain. → References: *LG Wuppertal dated 14 Aug 2002 – 6 T 495/02 ZInsO 2002, 1099; on this Carstens Die internationale Zuständigkeit im europäischen Insolvenzrecht (2005), p 36 et seq.* By way of a reference from the German *BGH* of 27 November 2003, the order of the *Landgericht* Wuppertal was also dealt with by the ECJ. The order raised the issue whether there is a change of international jurisdiction to open insolvency proceedings pursuant to Art 3 of the EIR when the debtor in the time period between the lodging of the request and the making of the decision to open insolvency proceedings moves the centre of his main interests to another Member State. → References: *BGH 9. Zivilsenat, reference for of preliminary ruling by the ECJ dated 27 Nov 2003 – IX ZB 418/02, 229 NZI 2004, 139 with explanatory note by Liersch p 141 et seq; ZIP 2004, 94 = ZInsO 2004, 34 = ZVI 2003, 655 = DZWiR 2004, 416 = NJW-RR 2004, 848; on this Weller IPRax 2004, 412; Mankowski EWiR 2004, 229.* The judgement of the ECJ of 17 January 2006 – "Susanne Staubitz-Schreiber" – is the ECJ's first decision ever made on the EIR. The court holds in this judgement that, for the ascertainment of the centre of main interests within the meaning of Art 3 (1) of the EIR, only those circumstances at the time at which the request is made are decisive, and any subsequent relocation of the centre to another Member State does not bring about a change of jurisdiction. Concurring with the opinion of the Advocate General, the ECJ held in favour of the continued validity of the originally-established jurisdiction. The court's main argument was that a

(Susanne Staubitz-Schreiber cont.)	
	change of jurisdiction would contradict the objectives of the Regulation, particularly the prevention of forum shopping. The court also found that, by adhering to the originally-established jurisdiction of the court first seized of the matter, a higher degree of legal certainty would be afforded to the creditors whose assessment of the risks associated with a potential insolvency of the debtor was done in relation to the location where the debtor had his centre of main interests at the time of entering into legal relationships with him (Recital 27 of the EIR). They also held that such an approach also promotes the goal of improving the efficiency and effectiveness of cross-border proceedings (Recitals 2 and 8 of the EIR). The creditors would otherwise be at the mercy of the debtor's whims, always having to challenge him wherever he chose to settle down, either for long or for short, which would most likely lead to a protraction of the proceedings. → *References: "Susanne Staubitz-Schreiber" – ECJ dated 17 Jan 2006 – C-1/04, ABl EU 2006 C 60, p 3; ZIP 2006, 188 with explanatory note by Knof/Mock p 189 et seq; ZInsO 2006, 86 with explanatory note by Schmidt p 88 et seq; IPRax 2006, 149 = ZVI 2006, 108 = NZI 2006, 153 = DZWiR 2006, 196; on this Kindler IPRax 2006, 114; Penzlin EWiR 2006, 207; Mankowski NZI 2006, 154; Vogl EWiR 2006, 141; Dammann Dalloz 2006 1752 et seq; ECJ (Advocate General Colomer) opinion 6.9.2005 ZInsO 2005, 1099 = NZI 2005, 544 = ZVI 2005, 476.* Based on the decision rendered by the ECJ, the *BGH* passed judgement in the Staubitz-Schreiber case on 9 February 2006. The headnote reads: The court of a Member State in which the request to open insolvency proceedings is made retains jurisdiction for the decision to open insolvency proceedings when the debtor moves its centre of main interests to another Member State after the time of making the request but before the opening of the proceedings. → *References: BGH 9. Zivilsenat dated 9 Feb 2006 – IX ZB 418/02 ZIP 2006, 529; DZWiR 2006, 211; NZI 2006, 297; ZInsO 2006, 321.*

18

Vierländer Bau Union Ltd	
Preliminary comments/ company	The debtor was founded in July 1999 in England in the form of an English limited liability company and operated exclusively in Germany as a manufacturer of so-called double bottoms/floors. The incorporation was carried out by an English agency.

(Vierländer Bau Union Ltd cont.)	
Proceedings	After the discontinuation of the business operations of the Vierländer Bau Union Limited, a German social security authority lodged an insolvency request. By order dated 14 May 2003, the *AG* Hamburg declared its international jurisdiction based on Art 3 (1) of the EIR. The court rested its jurisdiction on the fact that both the business and the administrative activities of the debtor took place exclusively in Germany. The centre of its main interests was thus in Germany. The court found that the purported registered office of the debtor in England was obviously nothing more than a "mailbox". The request was then denied based on the insufficiency of the assets to cover the costs of the proceedings. → *References: AG Hamburg dated 14 May 2003 – 67g IN 358/02 ZIP 2003, 1008 = IPRax 2003, 534 = BB 2003, 1457 = NZG 2003, 732 = NJW 2003, 2835 = NZI 2003, 442 with explanatory note by Mock/Schildt NZI 2003, 444; critical Brenner EWiR 2003, 925.*

19

Zenith	
Preliminary comments/ company	The debtor is the Austrian Zenith-Maschinenfabrik Austria GmbH. It is a subsidiary of the German Zenith-Maschinenfabrik GmbH.
Proceedings	On 7 June 2004, an insolvency request was lodged against the assets of the German parent company. The *AG* Siegen opened main insolvency proceedings against the assets of the Austrian company on 1 July 2004. The court assumed jurisdiction pursuant to Art 3 (1) of the EIR. The court held that the centre of main interests of the subsidiary was located in Germany since the business transactions were conducted solely by the parent company and its managing directors. They also found that there was no own management in Austria, and that the debtor's production was destined almost exclusively for the German parent company. → *References: AG Siegen dated 1 Jul 2004 – 25 IN 154/04 NZI 2004, 673 = NZG 2005, 92, EWiR 2005, 175 with explanatory note by Mankowski p 175 et seq; KTS 2005, 219 with explanatory note by Strasser p 219 et seq.* Secondary insolvency proceedings were opened in Austria on 2 July 2004 by the *Landesgericht* in Klagenfurt. → *References: Landesgericht Klagenfurt dated 2 Jul 2004 – 41 S 75/04h NZI 2004, 677; EWiR 2005, 217 with explanatory note by Beutler p 217 et seq.*

Appendix B to Art 3 of the EIR

Table of Cases (short version) – Listed According to Date

No	Date	Court/ Country/ Name/ Reference(s)	Headnote/Guiding sentence/ Summary
1	04.06.2002	High Court of Justice London *United Kingdom* **Enron** "www.iiiglobal.org/country/european_union/Enron_Directo_Skel.pdf"; *Martinez Ferber* European Insolvency Regulation, p 41; on this NZI 2004, 648.	See Appendix A – Table of Cases – Long version mn 9.
2	05.06.2002	Court of Assen The *Netherlands* **Schuldsaneringsregeling** Schuldsanering 2002/6, No 164.	On 30 May 2002, the debtor requested consumer debt-remission proceedings (*schuldsaneringsregeling*). The Court of Assen decided that the COMI was located in the Netherlands. The court acknowledged that the requesting party was officially registered in Hungary and spent a large part of the year in various hotels there, hence outside of the Netherlands. At this point in time, however, Hungary was not yet a Member State of the EU. In its decision, the court also took into account the fact that the debtor spent the remainder of his time in the Netherlands where he – shortly before the hearing – had been treated in a hospital, and that he lived with his wife in their common house in the Netherlands.

No	Date	Court/ Country/ Name/ Reference(s)	Headnote/Guiding sentence/ Summary
3	15.07.2002 11.11.2002	High Court of Justice Chancery Division *United Kingdom* **Geveran Trading Co Ltd v Skjevsland** [2003] B.C.C. 209, 391; *Marshall* European Cross Border Insolvency, No 2.068.	The decision of the English High Court involved a debtor who was a Norwegian citizen. He had been living for 3 years in England prior to lodging the insolvency request; he also resided in Spain and in Switzerland. The court held that the COMI was neither in Spain nor in Switzerland. The English court therefore did not apply the Regulation but rather a provision of English law on national jurisdiction (Sec 265 Insolvency Act 1986). Because the debtor's last domicile was in England, the English court assumed jurisdiction.
4	16.07.2002	Charleroi Commercial Court *Belgium* **SARL Bati-France** R.D.C 2004/8, 811; *Marshall* European Cross Border Insolvency, No 2.120.	The company registered in France conducted its business in Belgium. Reorganization proceedings were opened against the company in France in April 2001; these were followed by winding-up proceedings in March 2002. Although the Regulation had not yet come into force, both types of proceedings were listed in Annex A of the EIR. In June 2002, the Belgian court appointed a temporary administrator in respect of the assets of SARL Bati-France, who instigated the opening of insolvency proceedings in Belgium. Despite the submissions of the temporary administrator that the COMI of the Belgium and not in France, the Belgian court refused to open main insolvency

No	Date	Court/ Country/ Name/ Reference(s)	Headnote/Guiding sentence/ Summary
			proceedings. The court argued that after main insolvency proceedings had been opened in another Member State only secondary proceedings could be requested. In addition, because the French proceedings were opened prior to the coming into force of the EIR, the Belgian court was forced, through an interpretation of Art 43 of the EIR, to determine the extent to which the EIR was to apply.
5	14.08.2002	*LG* Wuppertal *Germany* **Germany/Spain** ZInsO 2002, 1099; IPRspr 2002, No 231, 589.	1. If the debtor moves his domicile to Spain after having lodged the insolvency request in Germany, then the German court does not have jurisdiction for the opening of the insolvency proceedings; the Spanish court that is competent at the place of the debtor's domicile has jurisdiction. 2. Because the Regulation is directly applicable and because of the general superiority of Community law over national law, the Regulation has priority over any contradictory provisions of national law. This means that the provisions of Secs 2 and 3 of the German *InsO* dealing with the jurisdiction of the insolvency courts do not apply sofar they are incompatible with the Regulation, which came into force on 31 May 2002.

No	Date	Court/ Country/ Name/ Reference(s)	Headnote/Guiding sentence/ Summary
6	02.10.2002	Swedish Court of Appeal *Sweden* **Brynervall v Johannson** unreported; (Ö 8546-02); but see *Marshall* European Cross Border Insolvency, No 2.064.	The case involves a request to open insolvency proceedings against the assets of a private person in Sweden. The request to open was rejected by the Swedish Court because, in the court's opinion, the debtor did not have enough assets in Sweden for a finding that his COMI or an establishment was located there.
7	16.10.2002	High Court of Justice Chancery Division London *United Kingdom* **Telia v Hillcourt** [2003] B.C.C. 856 Ch D; *Marshall* European Cross Border Insolvency, No 2.076.	In Telia vs Hillcourt, the English High Court dealt with the meaning of the concept of "establishment" as understood by the Regulation. The court refused to recognize the establishment of a subsidiary in England as also being an establishment of the Swedish parent company, which itself had no "establishment" in England.
8	25.11.2002	Brussels Commercial Court *Belgium* **Werlin Corporation Ltd.** unreported; *Marshall* European Cross Border Insolvency, No 2.088.	In the Werlin case, on the request of a Belgian creditor, territorial proceedings (independent territorial insolvency proceedings as per the Regulation) were opened against a company registered in England under the conditions of Art 3 (4) (b) of the EIR. The court held that the economic activities carried out by the company in Belgium were sufficient to affirm the existence of an establishment. The court emphasized that independent territorial insolvency proceedings were to be restricted to the assets in Belgium.

No	Date	Court/ Country/ Name/ Reference(s)	Headnote/Guiding sentence/ Summary
9	04.12.2002	High Court of Justice Chancery Division *United Kingdom* **Marann Brooks CSV** [2003] B.C.C. 239; *Marshall* European Cross Border Insolvency, No 2.005.	It was decided in the Marann Brooks case that the opening of insolvency proceedings for the common good did not fall within the scope of the Regulations's application because such a proceeding was not a collective insolvency proceeding. The intention of the drafters of the Regulation was to regulate cross-border insolvencies. It was not intended to apply to requests whose main concern was not the insolvency of the debtor but rather the safeguarding of the common good. The court relied primarily on the recitals of the Regulation.
10	10.12.2002	AG Duisburg *Germany* **BABCOCK** NZI 2003, 160; NJW-RR 2003, 556; ZInsO 2003, 476; DZWiR 2003, 435; DZWiR 2003, 397; on this ZInsO 2004, 825.	1. The opening of insolvency proceedings by a German court comprises, pursuant to German law, the entire domestic and foreign assets of the debtor unless, as an exception, independent territorial insolvency proceedings restricted to domestic assets are being conducted. 2. The foreign effect of the opening of main insolvency proceedings must be recognized in compliance with the Regulation (Arts 16, 17 of the EIR) in all other EU Member States without the need of any further formality. Thus all of the debtor's assets in the European Union are subject to the insolvency seizure/attachment of assets pursuant to German law. The prohibition of regular (individual) execution measures against the insolvency estate (Sec 89 *InsO*) also applies directly.

No	Date	Court/ Country/ Name/ Reference(s)	Headnote/Guiding sentence/ Summary
			3. Assets that have passed to the debtor via a merger will also be included in the insolvency estate even if – judging by outward appearances – they are still being allocated to the assets of the extinguished, transferring legal entity based on the fact that they are, for example, still being used by the previous company or because registrations in public registers have not been corrected.
11	12.12.2002	Brussels Commercial Court *Belgium* **Pittagold Ltd** unreported; *Marshall* European Cross Border Insolvency, No 2.086.	Commercial Court of Brussels: Pursuant to a request of a Belgian social security authority, independent territorial insolvency proceedings were opened pursuant to Art 3 (4) (b) of the EIR against the assets of a company registered in England. The business activities carried out in Belgium by the company registered in England were considered sufficient for a finding of an establishment. The court also affirmed that the proceedings were restricted to the assets situated in Belgium.
12	2003	Athens Multi-Member Court of First Instance *Greece* Decision No 693/2003 DEE 1/2004; *Marshall* European Cross Border Insolvency, No 2.077.	A company registered in Germany entered into a contract with a Greek utilities enterprise obligating itself to perform certain services. The German company maintained an office in Greece for the on-site management of the project. In order to execute the project, the German company entered into delegation (to another posting) contracts with a Greek private person and his

No	Date	Court/ Country/ Name/ Reference(s)	Headnote/Guiding sentence/ Summary
			successor company. When the German company failed to pay the agreed salaries, it was declared insolvent by a German court and a liquidator was appointed to deal provisionally with the main insolvency proceedings. The successor company requested the opening of secondary insolvency proceedings in Greece, one of the goals being to obtain an injunction to prevent the temporary administrator from removing the assets situated in Greece to Germany. The German company petitioned for a referral to the ECJ for a decision on whether the office in Greece constituted an establishment within the meaning of the Regulation. The Greek court considered the application admissible but dismissed it in all other respects since, in the court's opinion, the meaning of "establishment" can clearly be deduced from Art 2 (h) of the EIR.
13	07.02.2003	High Court of Justice Chancery Division *United Kingdom* **BRAC Rent-A-Car** ZIP 2003, 813; EWiR 2003, 367; [2003] 2 All E.R. 201; *Marshall* European Cross Border Insolvency, No 2.011; on this EWiR 2003, 367; NZI 2004, 649; DZWiR 2003, 397; IPRax 2004, 540.	See Appendix A – Table of Cases – Long version mn 3.

No	Date	Court/ Country/ Name/ Reference(s)	Headnote/Guiding sentence/ Summary
14	20.02.2003	High Court of Justice Chancery Division *United Kingdom* **Norse Ferries and Cenargo Navigation Ltd** unreported; *Marshall* European Cross Border Insolvency, No 2.035.	The companies in this case were business enterprises registered both on the Isle of Man and in Hong Kong. The company on the Isle of Man operated ferries, which serviced a route through the Irish Sea. The company in Hong Kong was a pure property-holding company that owned two ferries that were not, however, operated by them. Because the COMI was found to be in England, the High Court placed the companies under administration. In its decision, the court took into consideration the fact that the management board meetings were held in England. With respect to the pure property-holding company, the court held that what is decisive is not the place where the most important assets are located but rather the place of administrative activities.
15	20.02.2003	Commercial Court of Tongeren *Belgium* **Computer Trade International SPRL (Rechtsbank van Koophandel Tongeren)** unreported; *Marshall* European Cross Border Insolvency, No 2.100.	The Belgian court in Tongeren had to decide in a case in which main insolvency proceedings had already been opened in another Member State, namely Luxembourg, the debtor's registered office being located there. But the court held that the COMI was located in Belgium. Disregarding the decision of the court in Luxembourg, the Belgian court opened another main insolvency proceeding in Belgium.

No	Date	Court/ Country/ Name/ Reference(s)	Headnote/Guiding sentence/ Summary
16	18.03.2003	Belgian Court *Belgium* **Conception Enterprises Ltd.** unreported; *Marshall* European Cross Border Insolvency, No 2.090.	The court had to decide whether to open proceedings in respect of a debtor resident in Great Britain and registered in Dover/Kent; the debtor had an establishment in Belgium. The Belgian court opened a territorially restricted proceeding (secondary insolvency proceedings). The court relied on the fact that an establishment had been opened and registered in Belgium and that this establishment also had a representative in Belgium. The Belgian court nevertheless had to admit that the Belgian branch establishment was nothing more than a "mail-box".
17	31.03.2003	Commercial Court of Tongeren *Belgium* **Procureur des Konings v BVHE** A.R. A/03/1126; *Marshall* European Cross Border Insolvency, No 2.089.	The debtor is a subsidiary with a registered office in Belgium and belongs to a company registered in the Netherlands. The Belgian tax authorities requested the opening of insolvency proceedings against the subsidiary in Belgium. Although the COMI of the subsidiary was obviously in the Netherlands, main insolvency proceedings were not opened there. The Belgian court deemed the business activities of the subsidiary in Belgium as sufficient for the finding of an establishment within the meaning of Art 3 (4) (b) of the EIR. Based on the finding that the requesting creditor was domiciled in Belgium and that the claim being

No	Date	Court/ Country/ Name/ Reference(s)	Headnote/Guiding sentence/ Summary
			asserted was for unpaid value added tax, the commercial court opened independent territorial insolvency proceedings pursuant to Art 3 (4) (b) of the EIR before main insolvency proceedings had been opened in the Netherlands.
18	08.04.2003	Court of Appeal of The Hague *Netherlands* **Interexx Enterprises** unreported; *Marshall* European Cross Border Insolvency, No 2.026.	In the Interexx Enterprises case, the Court of Appeal of The Hague had to decide whether the COMI was located in the Netherlands or in England. While the Interexx Enterprises Ltd claimed that their statutory domicile was in Cardiff, England, one of the creditors insisted on opening the insolvency proceedings under Dutch law. The court of first instance in Rotterdam opened the proceedings; the court of appeal dealt with the request of Interexx to set aside the judgement. After reviewing the facts, the court of appeal came to the conclusion that the Companies House in Cardiff served as a central registry for companies with limited liability and therefore could not function as the debtor's COMI. The debtor (as of 3 July 2001 or 7 March 2001) had ceased business activities and the order to do this had come from the managing director of Interexx from the Netherlands. The managing director was fully authorized to do this and lived in the Netherlands. Based on these facts, the court decid-

No	Date	Court/ Country/ Name/ Reference(s)	Headnote/Guiding sentence/ Summary
			ed to refuse Interexx's request and to find that the COMI was also located in the Netherlands.
19	14.05.2003	*AG* Hamburg *Germany* **Vierländer Bau Union** ZIP 2003, 1008; BB 2003, 1457; NZG 2003, 732; NJW 2003, 2835; IPRax 2003, 534, 520; EWiR 2003, 925; NZI 2003, 444.	See Appendix A – Table of Cases – Long version mn 18.
20	16.05.2003	High Court of Justice Leeds *United Kingdom* **ISA-Daisytek I** ZIP 2003, 1362; 2004, 963; NZI 2004, 219, 648; NZG 2004, 340; [2003] B.C.C. 562; on this EWiR 2003, 709; DZWIR 2003, 397; ZInsO 2004, 61.	See Appendix A – Table of Cases – Long version mn 15.
21	19.05.2003	*AG* Düsseldorf *Germany* **ISA/Daisytek II-Provisional Liquidator**	See Appendix A – Table of Cases – Long version mn 15.

No	Date	Court/ Country/ Name/ Reference(s)	Headnote/Guiding sentence/ Summary
22	20.05.2003	High Court of Justice London *United Kingdom* **Crisscross Telecommunications** unreported; *Marshall* European Cross Border Insolvency, No 2.037; But on this NZI 2004, 648.	See Appendix A – Table of Cases – Long version mn 6.
23	27.05.2003	German *BGH* *Germany* **Private Person as debtor** ZIP 2003, 1419; ZInsO 2003, 707; IPRax 2004, 59, 31; BB 2003, 1810; DZWIR 2003, 469; KTS 2003, 629; WM 2003, 1542; NZI 2003, 545.	1. Even after the coming into force of the civil procedures reform of 27 July 2001 (*BGBl* I 1887), an appeal (on questions of law only) can still be based on the court of first instance having incorrectly denied its international jurisdiction (following a judgement of the *BGH* of 28 November 2002 – III *ZR* 102/2, ZIP 2003, 685, 686 et seq). 2. Sec 19a of the German *ZPO* establishes neither local nor German international jurisdiction over legal suits of the liquidator at the seat of the insolvency court.
24	30.05.2003	Court of Appeal of Sweden *Sweden* **Radaflex OY** *Marshall* European Cross Border Insolvency, No 2.027; (Ö 4105-03).	The debtor is a company registered in Finland with a branch establishment in Sweden. The debtor company lodged an insolvency request against itself at a Swedish court. It alleged that no business activities, no assets and also no debts existed in Finland. However, the com-

No	Date	Court/ Country/ Name/ Reference(s)	Headnote/Guiding sentence/ Summary
			pany in Sweden still owed outstanding wages to former employees in addition to other debts. The court denied the request claiming that it did not have jurisdiction based on the fact that the registered office was located in Finland. The Court of Appeal of Svea set aside the decision of the first instance court and referred the debtor to the original court that had opened the main insolvency proceedings.
25	06.06.2003	AG Düsseldorf *Germany* **ISA/Daisytek II** ZIP 2003, 1363; DZWiR 2003, 437; On this: EWiR 2003, 767 and 1239; DZWIR 2003, 397; ZInsO 2004, 61.	See Appendix A – Table of Cases – Long version mn 15.
26	17.06.2003	Court of Appeal of Amsterdam *Netherlands* **Netherlands/France** **(M. van Dulvenbode v W. J. M. van Andelte & J. J. van der Veen)** JOR 2003/186.	The Court of Appeal in Amsterdam had to decide a case in which a Dutch debtor had manifestly given up her occupation and moved to Longueville, France one year before the insolvency request. The court in the Netherlands held that the move alone to another country does not necessarily mean that the debtor's COMI was no longer in the Netherlands.

No	Date	Court/ Country/ Name/ Reference(s)	Headnote/Guiding sentence/ Summary
27	17.06.2003	Court of Appeal of Sweden *Sweden* **Sweden/Denmark/UK (Vikingson)** *Marshall* European Cross Border Insolvency, No 2.066; (Ö 817-03).	A creditor requested from a Swedish court the opening of insolvency proceedings against the assets of an individual person. The debtor alleged that the centre of his main interests was located in London and that he had no establishment in Sweden. The creditor insisted that the COMI was located in Sweden. The Court of Appeal of Svea took into account the fact that the debtor had cancelled his registration at the Swedish residents' registration office, and then alleged that he first moved to Denmark and to England. The court found, however, that the address in England was nothing more than a postal address. Furthermore, the wife was still living with the three common children in the house in Sweden in which the debtor had formerly lived. The house belonged to a company that, as found by the court, was attributable to the debtor's assets. The court of appeal thus held that the COMI was located in Sweden.
28	10.07.2003	AG Düsseldorf *Germany* **ISA-Daisytek-Opening of the 2nd Main insolvency proceedings**	See Appendix A – Table of Cases – Long version mn 15.

No	Date	Court/ Country/ Name/ Reference(s)	Headnote/Guiding sentence/ Summary
29	13.08.2003	Court of Rome *Italy* **Ciro Del Monte** unreported; *Marshall* European Cross Border Insolvency, No 2.039.	A company with its registered office in the Netherlands was controlled by the Italian parent company, which later became insolvent. The court in Rome placed the entire company in Italy under "extraordinary administration" as the COMI pursuant to Art 3 of the EIR was held to be located there. In order to include the company registered in the Netherlands in the "extraordinary administration" of the Italian group, this company was also declared insolvent (reason for insolvency: inability to pay debts). The Italian court interpreted the COMI in light of general principals of Italian law as well, specifically Art 9 of the *Legge fallimentare* 1942 (insolvency act). Relying on this provision, the court focussed not on the individual activities of the company but rather on the uniform conduct of a corporate group that has a parent company that exercises management control of the group. The requirement in the EIR, i.e. the *situs* of the COMI must be ascertained separately for each entity, was not complied with by the court.
30	04.09.2003	Cour d'Appel de Versailles *France* **ISA-Daisytek**	See Appendix A – Table of Cases – Long version mn 15.

No	Date	Court/ Country/ Name/ Reference(s)	Headnote/Guiding sentence/ Summary
		ZIP 2004, 377; [2004] I.L.Pr. 6; on this EWiR 2003, 1239; NZI 2004, 126, 127; ZInsO 2004, 826, 127.	
31	12.09.2003	AG Duisburg *Germany* **English Private Limited Company** NZI 2003, 610.	1. A foreign corporation that establishes a legally independent branch establishment in Germany is required by law to have this establishment registered in that German commercial registry with local jurisdiction (Secs 13d to 13g *HGB*). The same holds true especially if the establishment is the de facto main establishment. 2. Such a branch establishment is also being represented at the insolvency court by the so-called "permanent representative" contemplated by Sec 13e II 4 No 3 *HGB*. 3. If the German branch establishment has not been registered, then that person who, at the time of applying to register the establishment as a trade *(gewerberechtliche Anmeldung)*, depicts himself vis-à-vis the public-administration authorities as the person with unrestricted powers of representation, then he will also be treated as such by the insolvency court until the contrary is proven.

No	Date	Court/ Country/ Name/ Reference(s)	Headnote/Guiding sentence/ Summary
32	18.09.2003	German BGH *Germany* **Private person as debtor** ZIP 2003, 2123; ZInsO 2003, 1043; ZVI 2003, 666; NZI 2004, 21; EWiR 2004, 293; NJW-RR 2004, 134.	The debtor's duty to provide information and to cooperate pursuant to Sec 97 *InsO* also includes the granting of a so-called "foreign power of attorney" if there are indications that the debtor has assets in a foreign country and the powers of the liquidator are not being automatically recognized there.
33	02.10.2003	Belgian Court *Belgium* **Electra Airlines Compagnie** unreported; *Marshall* European Cross Border Insolvency, No 2.041.	The Belgian court had to make a decision regarding the debtor, ELECTRA Airlines Compagnie, which had its registered office in Greece and a business branch with a registered office in Brussels, Belgium. Despite the fact that the debtor had only one registered business office in Belgium, the court assumed jurisdiction and opened main insolvency proceedings in Belgium.
34	14.10.2003	*AG* Duisburg *Germany* **Private Limited Company** NZI 2003, 658; IPrax 2005, 151; IPRspr 2003, No 220, 717; GmbHR 2004, 121; on this IPRax 2005, 134.	1. The recognition of the legal capacity and the legal form of companies established in another EU Member State, which is derived from the right of establishment that exists within the European Union, applies not only to the creation of such companies but also to their dissolution, winding-up, and the legal termination of them. 2. If a company has been extinguished pursuant to the

No	Date	Court/ Country/ Name/ Reference(s)	Headnote/Guiding sentence/ Summary
			law of the country of incorporation that is relevant to it, then such status is legally binding everywhere within the European Union. 3. According to English law, a company that has been deleted from the company register by the registrar because the business activities have ceased is deemed dissolved once the deletion has been publicly announced. The effect of the dissolution is that the company ceases to exist in legal terms. According to German law, the company no longer has insolvency capacity as a legal entity.
35	23.10.2003	*LG* Düsseldorf *Germany* **ISA-Daisytek**	See Appendix A – Table of Cases – Long version mn 15.
36	27.11.2003	German *BGH* *Germany* **Staubitz-Schreiber-request for preliminary rulings** NZI 2004, 139; ZIP 2004, 94; ZInsO 2004, 34; ZVI 2003, 655; DZWiR 2004, 416; NJW-RR 2004, 848; BB 2004, 127; on this IPRax 2004, 412; EWiR 2004, 229.	See Appendix A – Table of Cases – Long version mn 17.

No	Date	Court/ Country/ Name/ Reference(s)	Headnote/Guiding sentence/ Summary
37	08.12.2003	Brussels Commercial Court *Belgium* **Eurogyp** *Marshall* European Cross Border Insolvency, No 2.040.	The court in Brussels dealt with a case in which the debtor enterprise, SPRL EUROGYP, had its registered office in Brussels and moved this afterwards to Paris. Since then, the company could not be located. However, the debtor continued to make turnover-tax returns and retained its turnover-tax identification number. The court had reason to believe that the relocating of the registered office had never really been a relocation of the COMI; its doing so had rather been a sham. Since the COMI continued to be in Brussels, the court assumed jurisdiction for the opening of main insolvency proceedings in Belgium.
38	19.12.2003	High Court of Justice Birmingham *United Kingdom* **Automold** unreported	See Appendix A – Table of Cases – Long version mn 2.
39	09.01.2004	Highest Court of the Netherlands *Netherlands* **Fortis v Vennink** AN 7896 Zaaknr R03/091 HR; *Marshall* European Cross Border Insolvency, No 2.063.	The highest court of the Netherlands had to decide in a case in which the Fortis Bank in March 2003 lodged a request at the court in Alkmaar to open main insolvency proceedings against the assets of its debtor who resided in Deurle, Belgium. The debtor had resided earlier in the Netherlands and carried

No	Date	Court/ Country/ Name/ Reference(s)	Headnote/Guiding sentence/ Summary
			out his trading interests there. The court allowed the bank's request; the debtor appealed the decision. On 7 August 2003, the Court of Appeal of Amsterdam criticized the international jurisdiction on its own motion and decided, in accordance with Art 3 (1) of the EIR, that the debtor's COMI was in the Netherlands, one reason being that he carried out his banking transactions there. The court took notice of the debtor's argument that he resided in Belgium but nevertheless held that Art 3 (1) of the EIR does not prescribe that the place where a natural person is resident automatically constitutes his COMI; Art 3 of the EIR contains no presumption with respect to natural persons.
40	23.01.2004	*AG* Cologne *Germany* **Automold** DZWiR 2004, 434; ZInsO 2004, 216; NZI 2004, 151; ZIP 2004, 471; EWiR 2004, 601; NJW-RR 2004, 1055; on this DZWiR 2004, 397, 406; ZInsO 2004, 195; NZI 2004, 126.	See Appendix A – Table of Cases – Long version mn 2.
41	27.01.2004	High Court *Ireland*	See Appendix A – Table of Cases – Long version mn 10.

No	Date	Court/ Country/ Name/ Reference(s)	Headnote/Guiding sentence/ Summary
		Eurofood/Parmalat – Provisional Liquidator [2004] B.C.C. 383; *Marshall* European Cross Border Insolvency, No 2.020, Appendix 2 No 2.136 et seq.	
42	19.02.2004	Tribunal di Parma *Italy* **Eurofood/Parmalat I – Opening of the Main insolvency proceeding** ZIP 2004, 1220; [2004] I.L.PR. 14; on this EWiR 2004, 597.	See Appendix A – Table of Cases – Long version mn 10.
43	12.03.2004	*AG* Düsseldorf *Germany* **ISA-Daisytek – Recognition of the english Main insolvency proceeding** ZIP 2004, 623; on this EWiR 2004, 495; IPRax 2004, 412.	See Appendix A – Table of Cases – Long version mn 15.
44	18.03.2004	Tribunal di Milano *Italy* **Crisscross Telecommunications** unreported;	The *Tribunal di Milano* had to decide on the opening of secondary insolvency proceedings against the assets of the Crisscross Telecommunications Italy S.r.l., which was being managed from its registered office in Milan and which was subject to the main insolvency proceedings opened

No	Date	Court/ Country/ Name/ Reference(s)	Headnote/Guiding sentence/ Summary
		Marshall European Cross Border Insolvency, No 2.037.	in England against the company (see Apendix A, Criss-cross Telecommunications mn 6). The court came to the conclusion that the company's head office in Milan was not an establishment within the meaning of Art 2 (h) of the EIR; the court held that this characteristic could not be attributed to a head office that was merely registered at the registered office of the statutory auditors, and who themselves had first been made aware of their actual legal incapacity with the opening of the insolvency proceedings.
45	19.03.2004	Supreme Court *Netherlands* **Rechtbank Almelo (Hoge Raad)** R 03/096 HR; *Marshall* European Cross Border Insolvency, No 2.003; also see on this *Mankowski* RiW 2005, 561, 577.	In the Rechtbank Almelo case, the debtor made a request for "debt restructuring" (*Schuldsanering* / discharge of residual debt). The request was denied because the debtor was indebted to a German creditor and this debt stemmed from a criminal sentence. This constitutes grounds for denying the *Schuldsanering* under Dutch law. The debtor argued that the *Schuldsanering* proceedings did not fall within the scope of application of the Regulation and therefore the Dutch proceedings would only relate to Dutch debts. The court held, however, that the "*De schuldsanerings-regeling natuurlijke personen*" was contained in Annex A of the EIR and is thus governed by it.

No	Date	Court/ Country/ Name/ Reference(s)	Headnote/Guiding sentence/ Summary
46	23.03.2004	High Court Dublin *Ireland* **Eurofood/Parmalat II** ZIP 2004, 1223; [2004] B.C.C. 383; *Marshall* European Cross Border Insolvency, No 2.020, Appendix 2 No 2.136 et seq; on this EWiR 2004, 599.	See Appendix A – Table of Cases – Long version mn 10.
47	07.04.2004	*AG* Düsseldorf *Germany* **ISA/Daisytek** **Dismissal of the German main insolvency proceeding and opening of a secondary insolvency proceeding** ZIP 2004, 866; on this EWiR 2004, 909.	See Appendix A – Table of Cases – Long version mn 15.
48	27.04.2004	*AG* Mönchengladbach *Germany* **EMBIC I** ZIP 2004, 1064; NZI 2004, 383; DZWIR 2004, 437; NZG 2004, 1016; on this ZIP 2004, 1066; NZI 2004, 384; EWiR 2004, 705.	See Appendix A – Table of Cases – Long version mn 7.

No	Date	Court/ Country/ Name/ Reference(s)	Headnote/Guiding sentence/ Summary
49	04.05.2004	*AG* Munich *Germany* **Hettlage I** ZIP 2004, 962; ZInsO 2004, 691; on this ZIP 2004, 1066; IPRax 2004, 412, 433.	See Appendix A – Table of Cases – Long version mn 12.
50	11.05.2004	*LG* Innsbruck *Austria* **Hettlage II** ZIP 2004, 1721; KTS 2005, 223; on this EWiR 2004, 1085.	See Appendix A – Table of Cases – Long version mn 12.
51	20.05.2004	High Court of Justice Leeds *United Kingdom* **Ci4NET.com** ZIP 2004, 1769; on this EWiR 2004, 847; KTS 2006, 259.	See Appendix A – Table of Cases – Long version mn 4.
52	24.05.2004 16.06.2004 24.06.2004	Rechtbank Hertogenbosch *Netherlands* **Transbus International Ltd** JOR 2004, 212; JOR 2004, 213; JOR 2004, 214;	Transbus International Ltd – an English company under administration in England since March 2004 – had *inter alia* an establishment in the Netherlands. This Dutch establishment operated under the company names "Dennis Spezialist Vehicles" and "Dennis Benelux" from business loca-

No	Date	Court/ Country/ Name/ Reference(s)	Headnote/Guiding sentence/ Summary
		Marshall European Cross Border Insolvency, No 2.082.	tions in Nuenen. The establishment was declared insolvent on 24 May 2004; secondary insolvency proceedings were opened against its assets by the court in Hertogenbosch pursuant to Art 3 (2) in conjunction with Art 27 of the EIR. After two of the English liquidators were appointed from the same chartered accountants' firm, it was decided that the liquidator of the Dutch establishment should also be appointed from this firm.
53	14.06.2004	Municipality Court of Fejer *Hungary* **Parmalat** unreported;	The centre of main interests of a debtor company incorporated in Slovakia is located in Hungary if the most important business decisions are being made in Hungary, the company's finances are being managed from Hungary, and this was ascertainable for third parties
54	15.06.2004	Tribunale Civile Parma *Italy* **Eurofood / Parmalat** ZIP 2004, 2295; on this EWiR 2004, 1181.	See Appendix A – Table of Cases – Long version mn 10.
55	16.06.2004	Rechtbank Hertogenbosch *Netherlands* **Transbus International Ltd**	See Appendix B No 52.

No	Date	Court/ Country/ Name/ Reference(s)	Headnote/Guiding sentence/ Summary
		JOR 2004, 212; JOR 2004, 213; JOR 2004, 214; *Marshall* European Cross Border Insolvency, No 2.082.	
56	24.06.2004	Rechtbank Hertogenbosch *Netherlands* **Transbus International Ltd** JOR 2004, 212; JOR 2004, 213; JOR 2004, 214; *Marshall* European Cross Border Insolvency, No 2.082.	See Appendix B No 52.
57	01.07.2004	*AG* Siegen *Germany* **Zenith AG** NZI 2004, 673; NZG 2005, 92; KTS 2005, 219; EWiR 2005, 175; on this KTS 2005, 219; EWiR 2005, 175.	See Appendix A – Table of Cases – Long version mn 19.
58	02.07.2004	*Landesgericht* Klagenfurt *Austria* **Zenith** NZI 2004, 677; EWiR 2005, 217; on this EWiR 2005, 217.	The opening of main insolvency proceedings in an EU Member State (here: Germany) does not impede the opening of secondary insolvency proceedings in the Member State in which the company has its registered office (here: Austria).

No	Date	Court/ Country/ Name/ Reference(s)	Headnote/Guiding sentence/ Summary
59	02.07.2004	High Court of Justice Chancery Division *United Kingdom* **AIM Underwriting Agencies Ltd** [2005] I.L.Ps 22; *Marshall* European Cross Border Insolvency, No 2.047.	The Irish public limited company, Aim Underwriting Agencies (Ireland) Ltd, was a wholly owned subsidiary of an English company and was founded to execute the business of the parent company as an insurance broker primarily in South Africa, the Far East, and in India. The COMI for the English limited company was held to be in England. Decisive for the court was that the English managing director had controlled the business of the subsidiary from London, and that he was the only person who would have been authorized to sign on behalf of the company. The court relied in part on the criteria set out in the BRAC case (see Appendix A, BRAC Rent-A-Car, mn 3), weight being given *inter alia* to the fact that the only creditor was the parent company and they were obviously aware of the actual circumstances; thus there were no other creditors warranting protection.
60	09.07.2004	*OLG* Düsseldorf *Germany* **ISA/Daisytek** Effects of the opening of secondary insolvency proceedings.	See Appendix A – Table of Cases – Long version mn 15.

No	Date	Court/ Country/ Name/ Reference(s)	Headnote/Guiding sentence/ Summary
		DZWiR 2004, 428; ZIP 2004, 1514; ZInsO 2004, 867; NZI 2004, 628; on this EWiR 2005, 177.	
61	27.07.2004	Supreme Court of Ireland (Dublin) *Ireland* **Eurofood/Parmalat III** NZI 2004, 505; ZIP 2004, 1969; DZWiR 2005, 60; on this EWiR 2004, 973; DZWiR 2005, 64; ZInsO 2005, 119.	See Appendix A – Table of Cases – Long version mn 10.
62	02.08.2004	*AG* Offenburg *Germany* **HUKLA AG** NZI 2004, 673; on this EWiR 2005, 73.	See Appendix A – Table of Cases – Long version mn 14.
63	09.11.2004	*OLG* Vienna *Austria* **High Court London/ Commercial Court Vienna** NZI 2005, 56; on this NZI 2005, 62.	See Appendix A – Table of Cases – Long version mn 13.

No	Date	Court/ Country/ Name/ Reference(s)	Headnote/Guiding sentence/ Summary
64	26.11.2004 27.07.2005	High Court of Justice Chancery Division *United Kingdom* **Shierson v Vlieland-Boddy (Vlieland-Boddy I)** [2004] All E.R.(D) 420 (Nov); *Marshall* European Cross Border Insolvency, No 2.019. Court of Appeal (Civil Division) *United Kingdom* **Shierson v Vlieland-Boddy (Vlieland-Boddy II)** [2005] All E.R.(D) 391 (Jul); *Marshall* European Cross Border Insolvency, No 2.073.	The focus in Shierson v Vlieland-Boddy was on the issue of the *situs* of the COMI of a natural person. The court in this case deemed the time of the opening of the main proceedings as decisive for the ascertainment of the COMI. The reference date for this was the date of the hearing on the insolvency request and not the date on which the request was lodged or the date on which the obligations arose. With respect to the ascertainment of the COMI, the High Court did not rely on the impression received by third parties, holding that the Regulation did not prohibit a change of the COMI and that creditors were always exposed to the risk of such a change. Creditors could therefore not be given any assurance that a specific insolvency law regime applied unless the COMI had not been changed. Hence, the court must ascertain the COMI on the basis of the facts obtained in each case at the given time.
65	24.01.2005	*OLG* Frankfurt *Germany* **Scope of application of the EIR** ZInsO 2005, 715; DZWiR 2006, 50.	The Regulation is not relevant in relation to Denmark. A decision of the Danish bankruptcy court can therefore not be declared enforceable by the presiding judge of a civil chamber pursuant to Art 25 of the EIR, Art 31 et seq of the 1968 Brussels Convention, Sec 1 (1) (a) and Sec 11 et seq of the German

No	Date	Court/ Country/ Name/ Reference(s)	Headnote/Guiding sentence/ Summary
			AVAG. Instead, an action must be brough before a trial court to obtain a judgement for enforcement (authorizing execution of the foreign judgement).
66	03.02.2005	Swedish Court of Appeal *Sweden* **Kosingen Ltd** *Marshall* European Cross Border Insolvency, No 2.028 (Ö 21-05).	Kosingen Ltd is a company with its registered office in England and a postal address in Spain. Public authorities lodged a request to the regional court for a declaration that Kosingen Ltd was insolvent. The public authority claimed that Kosingen Ltd held a participating interest in a Swedish company and exercised this in the form of a limited partnership (Top Emblem KB). Kosingen Ltd made no appearance at the hearing, and the regional court assumed jurisdiction and allowed the request.
67	09.02.2005	High Court of Justice Chancery Division *United Kingdom* **Re Parkside Flexibles SA** unreported; *Marshall* European Cross Border Insolvency, No 2.050.	In the Parkside case, the High Court issued an insolvency order against a company's subsidiary that was registered in Poland; the English parent company had already been placed under insolvency administration in England. Despite the fact that the registered office of the establishment was in Poland and that, based on the facts at hand, the presumption in Art 3 (1) sentence 2 of the EIR could not clearly be rebutted, the court came to the conclusion that the COMI was located in England. Decisive

No	Date	Court/ Country/ Name/ Reference(s)	Headnote/Guiding sentence/ Summary
			for this decision was the impression that had been conveyed to outside third parties – especially third party creditors – regarding the COMI of the company.
68	23.02.2005	*OGH* Vienna *Austria* **Austrian procedural law** ZfRV 2005, 117.	1. According to Sec 4 (1) of the *IPRG* (Federal Act on Private International Law), the foreign law applicable must be ascertained by the court on its own motion; to this end, the court may – again on its own motion – also make use of the procedural inquiry measures listed in the act, including the cooperation of the parties, as admissible aids. The measure to be taken depends on the circumstances in the individual case. The court is not obliged to take any particular inquiry measure. It is at the court's discretion just how it procures the requisite knowledge of the foreign law. All of the information procured, including the aid proffered by the parties, may be reviewed by the party applying it at their full discretion. 2. The inability to ascertain the foreign law constitutes a special kind of procedural defect to be construed as an error of law and thus giving rise to grounds for appeal and leading to the setting aside of the judgement at first instance. Because the foreign law is not construed as a fact, the resubmission of sources of knowledge in the appeal pleadings is not prohibited.

No	Date	Court/ Country/ Name/ Reference(s)	Headnote/Guiding sentence/ Summary
			3. If one of the parties to the proceedings submits legal documents to clarify any issues fundamental to the decision, then this party cannot consider himself aggrieved if the court's decision rests on these submissions. This still applies even if, in the appeal submissions made by this party, the correctness of the relevant submissions was not doubted.
69	25.02.2005	*AG* Saarbrücken *Germany* **Limits of the court's investigation in respect of English limited liability companies** ZInsO 2005, 727; ZIP 2005, 2027; on this EWiR 2005, 701.	1. An English limited liability company has insolvency capacity in Germany. 2. If an English limited liability company was incorporated for abusive purposes, this can be raised by the liquidator in opened proceedings and may, in the given case, lead to the nonrecognition of the limitation of liability and, in certain circumstances, to the imposition of personal liability on the subscribing shareholders. Such substantive-law discretionary powers are not conferred on the insolvency court.
70	08.03.2005	High Court *Ireland* **Cedarlease Ltd** [2005] IEHC 67; *Marshall* European Cross Border Insolvency, No 2.118.	In the case of Cedarlease Ltd, a company registered in Ireland and operating in the automobile sector, the High Court of Ireland had to decide on the insolvency request made in England by a higher official of the English tax office. The tax office was claiming outstanding value-added tax liabilities, including penalties for late reporting and interest, in the

No	Date	Court/ Country/ Name/ Reference(s)	Headnote/Guiding sentence/ Summary
			amount of £ 911,167.65. In its decision, the court observed the long-standing legal custom which prohibits the conducting of legal procedures for enforcing, either directly or indirectly, tax revenues of a foreign country. The High Court nevertheless decided that the EIR conferred such jurisdiction on the court. It deemed such legal custom as inapplicable to the extent to which it conflicted with the Regulation. Although the Regulation does not expressly grant the creditor from another Member State the right to initiate main insolvency proceedings, any view to the contrary would thwart the goals of the EIR. The court therefore opened the proceedings requested by the English tax office.
71	17.03.2005	*OGH* Vienna *Austria* **High Court London/ Commercial Court of Vienna** NZI 2005, 465.	See Appendix A – Table of Cases – Long version mn 13.
72	18.04.2005	High Court of Justice Birmingham *United Kingdom* **MG Rover I** NZI 2005, 467; EWiR 2005, 637; ZIP 2005, 1610; on this NZI 2005, 469.	See Appendix A – Table of Cases – Long version mn 16.

No	Date	Court/ Country/ Name/ Reference(s)	Headnote/Guiding sentence/ Summary
73	18.04.2005	*AG* Celle *Germany* EuZW 2005, 415; NZI 2005, 410; ZInsO 2005, 895; on this ZInsO 2005, 1017.	1. For ascertaining the centre of the debtor's main interests pursuant to Art 3 (1) of the EIR, the time of the making of the request and not the time at which the debtor's obligation arose is decisive. Whether the time of the opening of the insolvency proceedings is decisive in certain circumstances need not be answered here. 2. With respect to natural persons, the centre of their main interests within the meaning of Art 3 of the EIR is generally their domicile. 3. Should the debtor move his domicile to another Member State shortly before the making of the request, then the current domicile will generally be decisive.
74	26.04.2005	Municipality Court Prague *Czechia* **Aircraft** ZIP 2005, 1431; DStZ 2005, 687; on this ZIP 2005, 1401.	See Appendix A – Table of Cases – Long version mn 1.
75	11.05.2005	High Court of Justice Chancery Division, Birmingham *United Kingdom* **MG Rover II** NZI 2005, 515; on this NZI 2005, 517.	See Appendix A – Table of Cases – Long version mn 16.

No	Date	Court/ Country/ Name/ Reference(s)	Headnote/Guiding sentence/ Summary
76	22.06.2005	*AG* Weilheim *Germany* **AvCraft International Ltd** ZIP 2005, 1611; EWiR 2005, 791; on this EWiR 2005, 791.	The presumption found in Art 3 (1) sentence 2 of the EIR, pursuant to which the centre of the debtor's main interests are presumed to be the place of its registered office, is rebutted if all administrative transaction, such as the maintenance of legal relationships to third parties, purchasing, and personnel and accounting, are being carried on from an outside location. The *AG* Weilheim lists the factors it considers decisive for a finding in favour of German international jurisdiction. Perfectly in line with Recital 13 of the EIR, these appear to be objective criteria. Tangible property and where it its situated (the decision of the *AG* Weilheim turns on the *situs* of the production facilities) is one of the things to be taken into account in arriving at the ascertainment. The employment of salaried employees is an act that is also ascertainable for third parties. Decisive is the place from which the "day to day business" is being conducted, or the place where the "economic activities" of the debtor are taking place (affirmed by the *AG* Weilheim with the criteria: purchasing and operative business). On the other hand, the place where the accounting is being carried out or the place of strategic decision-making, criteria also referred to by the *AG* Weilheim to

No	Date	Court/ Country/ Name/ Reference(s)	Headnote/Guiding sentence/ Summary
			ascertain the COMI, are more conclusive to the "mind of management" – or "head office functions" theories.
77	29.06.2005	High Court of Justice Chancery Division *United Kingdom* **Sendo Limited** *Marshall* European Cross Border Insolvency, No 2.053.	Sendo Limited was the sole independent manufacturer of telephone earpieces for mobile telephones in Great Britain. The main company was registered in the Cayman Islands in the commercial register, but the COMI was assumed to be located in England. The company heads therefore requested an administration order from the English High Court. The company had numerous establishments in other states. For the purposes of winding up the operations, a serie of secondary insolvency proceedings were requested by the liquidators. The COMI was deemed to be located in Great Britain since the managing directors lived there, the employees were there, and the operative business was carried out there.
78	15.07.2005	High Court of Justice Chancery Division *United Kingdom* **Collins & Aikman I** NZI 2005, 647.	See Appendix A – Table of Cases – Long version mn 5.

No	Date	Court/ Country/ Name/ Reference(s)	Headnote/Guiding sentence/ Summary
79	27.07.2005	Court of Appeal (Civil Division) *United Kingdom* **Shierson v Vlieland-Boddy (Vlieland-Boddy II)** [2005] All E.R. (D) 391 (Jul). *Marshall* European Cross Border Insolvency, No 2.073.	See Appendix B No 64.
80	10.08.2005	*AG* Cologne *Germany* **Collins & Aikman II** ZIP 2005, 1566; NZI 2005, 564; NZG 2005, 858; EuZW 2005, 704; DZWiR 2006, 218; on this DZWiR 2006, 219.	See Appendix A – Table of Cases – Long version mn 5.
81	18.08.2005	*LG* Hamburg *Germany* **Aircraft** NZI 2005, 645; DZWiR 2006, 47; ZIP 2005, 1697; ZIP 2005, 1401.	See Appendix A – Table of Cases – Long version mn 1.
82	31.08.2005	*LG* Leoben *Austria* **Collins & Aikman** ZInsO 2005, 1176; ZInsO 2005, 1137; NZI 2005, 646.	See Appendix A – Table of Cases – Long version mn 5.

No	Date	Court/ Country/ Name/ Reference(s)	Headnote/Guiding sentence/ Summary
83	01.12.2005	*AG* Hamburg *Germany* **English Limited** ZIP 2005, 2275; ZInsO 2005, 1282; NZI 2006, 120; NZG 2006, 439; EWiR 2006, 169; on this NZI 2006, 383.	In the case of an English limited liability company operating exclusively in Germany, the German insolvency courts retain international jurisdiction for the opening of main insolvency proceedings within the meaning of Art 3 (1) sentence 1 of the EIR even if the economic activities have completely ceased prior to the insolvency request.
84	01.12.2005	*AG* Cologne *Germany* **Establishment of an EU foreign company** ZIP 2006, 628; NZI 2006, 57; EWiR 2006, 109; EuZW 2006, 63; on this EWiR 2006, 109.	1. The opening of secondary insolvency proceedings against the assets of the branch establishment of a foreign company from an EU Member State presupposes that main insolvency proceedings have been opened in another Member State against the assets of the company. Without this, the insolvency court is not in a position to review the requirements for allowing secondary insolvency proceedings. 2. Although the insolvency court is obliged, on its own motion, to review both its international and its national jurisdiction, the court's duty pursuant to Sec *5 InsO* to make such an official review is not yet imposed on it in conjunction with the admission proceedings in which the insolvency court is first confronted with the issue of its own jurisdiction. The same applies in the case of an insolvency request in respect of the assets of a foreign company.

No	Date	Court/ Country/ Name/ Reference(s)	Headnote/Guiding sentence/ Summary
85	17.01.2006	*ECJ* *European Union* **Susanne Staubitz-Schreiber** ZIP 2006, 188; ZInsO 2006, 86; IPRax 2006, 149; ZVI 2006, 108; NZI 2006, 153; DZWiR 2006, 196; on this ZIP 2006, 189; ZInsO 2006, 88; EWiR 2006, 207.	See Appendix A – Table of Cases – Long version mn 17.
86	26.01.2006	*OLG* Frankfurt *Germany* **International jurisdiction for avoidance actions brought by the liquidator** ZIP 2006, 769; ZInsO 2006, 715; NZI 2006, 648; on this EWiR 2006, 237; DZWiR 2006, 325; ZInsO 2006, 700; ZIP 2006, 1383.	1. The Regulation makes no provision for international jurisdiction in respect of avoidance actions brought by the liquidator. 2. In the absence of an unintentional regulatory gap, the determination of international jurisdiction for those insolvency-related proceedings (avoidance actions) cannot be made on the basis of an analogy with Art 3 (1) of the EIR.
87	09.02.2006	BGH 9. Zivilsenat *Germany* **Susanne Staubitz-Schreiber** ZIP 2006, 529; DZWiR 2006, 211; NZI 2006, 297; ZInsO 2006, 321.	See Appendix A – Table of Cases – Long version mn 17.

No	Date	Court/ Country/ Name/ Reference(s)	Headnote/Guiding sentence/ Summary
88	15.02.2006	Tribunal de Commerce de Nanterre *France* EMTEC *Marshall* European Cross Border Insolvency, No 2.058; on this EWiR 2006, 207.	See Appendix A – Table of Cases – Long version mn 8.
89	27.02.2006	*LG* Leipzig *Germany* **Moving the administrative head office/forum shopping** ZInsO 2006, 378.	1. The moving of the administrative head office by moving the business records only to another place will not constitute a relocation of the centre of the debtor's main interests pursuant to Art 3 (1) of the EIR. 2. International jurisdiction as between Germany and France is determined pursuant to Art 3 of the EIR. The courts of the Member State within the territory of which the centre of a debtor's main interests is situated have jurisdiction to open insolvency proceedings.
90	02.03.2006	German *BGH* *Germany* **Change of an architect's domicile subsequent to the first insolvency request**	The court of a Member State in whose territory the debtor has his centre of main interests at the time of lodging the request to open insolvency proceedings retains jurisdiction for other opening requests made to it after the debtor has

No	Date	Court/ Country/ Name/ Reference(s)	Headnote/Guiding sentence/ Summary
		ZIP 2006, 767; ZInsO 2006, 431; DZWiR 2006, 254; NZI 2006, 364; EuZW 2006, 382; BB 2006, 963.	moved the centre of his main interests to another Member State but before the first request has been conclusively (*res judicata*) adjudicated.
91	29.3.2006	Tribunal de grande instance (TGI) Lure *France* **Energotech** unreported; Summary and short annotation in Dalloz 2006, 1043; *Marshall* European Cross Border Insolvency, No 2.059.	The COMI is located at the debtor's actual center of business management. The main factors used to determine its location include: – The meeting place of the management board; – The law governing the most important contracts; – The location of the business contacts of the customers; – The place where business policies are decided; – The existence of a preliminary authorisation of the parent company to conclude financial agreements; – The location of the creditor bank; – The location of centralised management of purchase and personnel policy, of bookkeeping and computer systems operations. In this case the COMI of the Polish subsidiary Energotech was located in France at the main office of the parent company.

No	Date	Court/ Country/ Name/ Reference(s)	Headnote/Guiding sentence/ Summary
92	30.03.2006	High Court of Justice Birmingham *United Kingdom* **MG Rover** NZI 2006, 416.	See Appendix A – Table of Cases – Long version mn 16.
93	02.05.2006	ECJ *European Union* **Eurofood/Parmalat** ZInsO 2006, 484; ZInsO 2006, 907; NZI 2006, 360; DZWiR 2006, 329; NZG 2006, 633; BB 2006, 1762; EuZW 2006, 337; on this ZInsO 2006, 505; BB 2006, 1753; NZI 2006, 334; NZI 2006, 435; DZWiR 2006, 325; ZIP 2006, 911.	See Appendix A – Table of Cases – Long version mn 16.
94	09.05.2006	*AG* Hamburg *Germany* **Permissability of a referral by a German court to a foreign court** NZI 2006, 486; ZInsO 2006, 559; EWiR 2006, 433; ZIP 2006, 1105; on this EWiR 2006, 433.	1. If a winding-up is primarily carried out by a liquidator residing in a foreign country, without there being any indications of surreptitiously obtained jurisdiction, and if the debtor has no inland assets worthy of mention, then the insolvency court at the location of the liquidator has jurisdiction for insolvency proceedings involving the debtor. 2. An "international referral" is possible within the scope of application of the Regulation.

No	Date	Court/ Country/ Name/ Reference(s)	Headnote/Guiding sentence/ Summary
95	09.06.2006	High Court of Justice London *United Kingdom* **Collins & Aikman III**	See Appendix A – Table of Cases – Long version mn 5.
96	2.08.2006	Tribunal de commerce Paris *France* **Eurotunnel** *Dalloz 2006, 2329.*	See Appendix A – Table of Cases – Long version mn 11.
97	15.08.2006	*AG* Nürnberg *Germany* **Hans Brochier Holdings Ltd** ZIP 2007, 81.	The opening of English main insolvency proceedings in respect of the assets of the Hans Brochier Holdings Ltd, which operated nearly exclusively in Germany, infringes public policy in Germany and is therefore not to be recognized, based on the findings that: – the court had not made an independent review of its jurisdiction, but it rather based its decision to open insolvency proceedings solely on the unsubstantiated allegations of the requesting party, – the decision rested on representations made by the requesting party that were contradictory to the facts, – the decision was unfounded, – the liquidator was not impartial since he had been appointed pursuant to an application of the managing director of the insolvency debtor and was being advised by the long-standing legal advisors of the insolvency debtor.

No	Date	Court/ Country/ Name/ Reference(s)	Headnote/Guiding sentence/ Summary
98	15.8.2006	High Court of Justice London *United Kingdom* **Hans Brochier Holdings Ltd** NZI 2007, 187; EWiR 2007, 177.	The COMI of Hans Brochier Holdings Ltd is and has at all material times been in Germany. The appointment of the English liquidator was therefore invalid for the purposes of Art 3 (1) of the EIR and did not give rise to main proceedings in England and Wales.
99	16.08.2006	*AG* Hamburg *Germany* **International jurisdiction in the case of winding-up activities after the economic activities of a GmbH have ceased** NZI 2006, 652; ZInsO 2006, 1006; ZIP 2006, 1642.	1. The territorial applicability of the Regulation commands that the insolvency case have a cross-border element. The existence of a creditor with a habitual residence, domicile, or registered office in another Member State suffices for this. 2. Winding-up activities carried out in another Member State after the cessation of the economic activities at the location of the registered office will, at best, give rise to a change of international jurisdiction only if the winding-up activities are objectively ascertainable for third parties. This generally entails the termination of pending transactions and the taking up of new transactions where required by these, and the administration and preservation of the debtor's assets or comparable matters that are situated in, or have been brought into, another Member State.
100	01.10.2006	*AG* Nürnberg *Germany* **Hans Brochier Holdings Ltd**	The statutory presumption in Art 3 (1) sentence 1 of the EIR – which holds that the centre of main interests in the case of cross-border insolvency

No	Date	Court/ Country/ Name/ Reference(s)	Headnote/Guiding sentence/ Summary
		ZIP 2007, 83; EWiR 2007, 179.	proceedings is at the location of the debtor's registered office – is deemed as rebutted if all business decisions are been made at an establishment in another Member State, if nearly all of the employees work in this Member State, and if the operative business is being managed from there.
101	08.12.2006	High Court of Justice London *United Kingdom* **Hans Brochier Holdings Ltd** NZI 2007, 187.	The appointment of the secondary proceeding's liquidator for Hans Brochier Holdings Ltd was void *ab initio* and invalid on the basis that the Company does not have and did not have any establishment in England or Wales within the meaning of Art 2 (2) (h) of the EIR.
102	5.2.2007	*AG* Munich *Germany* **BenQ Mobile Holding BV** ZIP 2007, 495.	The AG Munich has international jurisdiction under Art 3 (2) and (3) of the EIR, because the debtor had an establishment in Germany. This is the result of following considerations: – the debtor had a non-transitory economic activity in Germany; – the business decisions were made and implemented in Munich; – the economic activity was on a continuing basis; – the economic activity was exerciced externally and ascertainable by third parties; – the economic activity was carried-out using human resources and goods. The definition of establishment in Art (2) (h) of the EIR does

No	Date	Court/ Country/ Name/ Reference(s)	Headnote/Guiding sentence/ Summary
			not point out that the use of human resources only corresponds to the debtor's own employees as opposed to other persons, such as those working on the basis of an agency or a commission contract.

Article 4
Law applicable

1. Save as otherwise provided in this Regulation, the law applicable to insolvency proceedings and their effects shall be that of the Member State within the territory of which such proceedings are opened, hereafter referred to as the "State of the opening of proceedings".

2. The law of the State of the opening of proceedings shall determine the conditions for the opening of those proceedings, their conduct and their closure. It shall determine in particular:
(a) against which debtors insolvency proceedings may be brought on account of their capacity;
(b) the assets which form part of the estate and the treatment of assets acquired by or devolving on the debtor after the opening of the insolvency proceedings;
(c) the respective powers of the debtor and the liquidator;
(d) the conditions under which set-offs may be invoked;
(e) the effects of insolvency proceedings on current contracts to which the debtor is party;
(f) the effects of the insolvency proceedings on proceedings brought by individual creditors, with the exception of lawsuits pending;
(g) the claims which are to be lodged against the debtor's estate and the treatment of claims arising after the opening of insolvency proceedings;
(h) the rules governing the lodging, verification and admission of claims;
(i) the rules governing the distribution of proceeds from the realisation of assets, the ranking of claims and the rights of creditors who have obtained partial satisfaction after the opening of insolvency proceedings by virtue of a right in rem or through a set-off;
(j) the conditions for and the effects of closure of insolvency proceedings, in particular by composition;
(k) creditors' rights after the closure of insolvency proceedings;
(l) who is to bear the costs and expenses incurred in the insolvency proceedings;
(m) the rules relating to the voidness, voidability or unenforceability of legal acts detrimental to all the creditors.

Contents

Index

Bibliography

Altmeppen Schutz vor „europäischen" Kapitalgesellschaften, NJW 2004, p 97; *Altmeppen* Änderungen der Kapitalersatz- und Insolvenzverschleppungshaftung aus „deutsch-europäischer" Sicht, NJW 2005, p 1911; *Altmeppen* Existenzvernichtungshaftung und Scheinauslandsgesellschaften, in Crezelius (ed), Festschrift Röhricht (2005) p 3; *Altmeppen/Wilhelm* Gegen die Hysterie um die Niederlassungsfreiheit der Scheinauslandsgesellschaften, DB 2004, p 1083; *Balz* Die neue Europäische Insolvenzverordnung, ZIP 1996, p 948; *Baumbach/Hueck* GmbH-Gesetz, Kommentar, 18th edn (2006); *Bayer* Die EuGH-Entscheidung „Inspire Art" und die deutsche GmbH im Wettbewerb der europäischen Rechtsordnungen, BB 2003, p 2357; *Behrens* Das Internationale Gesellschaftsrecht nach dem Überseering-Urteil des EuGH und den Schlussanträgen zu Inspire Art, IPRax 2003, p 193; *Behrens* Gemeinschaftsrechtliche Grenzen der Anwendung inländischen Gesellschaftsrechts auf Auslandsgesellschaften nach Inspire Art, IPRax 2004, p 20; *Berner/Klöhn* Insolvenzantragspflicht, Qualifikation und Niederlassungsfreiheit, ZIP 2007, p 106; *Binge/Thölke* „Everything goes!" – Das deutsche Internationale Gesellschaftsrecht nach „Inspire Art", DNotZ 2004, p 21; *Bitter* Flurschäden im Gläubigerschutzrecht durch „Centros & Co."?, WM 2004, p 2190; *Borges* Die Sitztheorie in der Centros-Ära: Vermeintliche Probleme und unvermeidliche Änderungen, RIW 2000, p 167; *Borges* Gläubigerschutz bei ausländischen Gesellschaften mit inländischem Sitz, ZIP 2004, p 733; *Bork* Europarechtswidrige Gesellschafterdarlehen in der Insolvenz, in Schneider (ed), Festschrift Lutter (2000) p 301; *Bork* Die Geltendmachung der Existenzvernichtungshaftung in der Insolvenz, KTS 2006, p 39; *Bork* Die Aufrechnung im internationalen Insolvenzrecht, ZIP 2002, p 690; *Breutigam/Blersch/Goetsch/Haas* Insolvenzrecht, Berliner Kommentar (01/2006); *Burg* Existenzvernichtungshaftung in der Private Limited Company?, GmbHR 2004, p 1379; *Chalupsky* Das europäische Übereinkommen über Insolvenzverfahren, in Baudenbacher (ed), Aktuelle Probleme des Europäischen und Internationalen Wirtschaftsrechts, vol I (1998); *Dierksmeier* Die englische Ltd. in Deutschland – Haftungsrisiko für Berater, BB 2005, p 1516; *Drygala* Comments on ECJ of 30.09.2003 – C-167/01, EWiR 2003, p 1029; *Duursma-Kepplinger/Duursma/Chalupsky* Europäische Insolvenzverordnung, Kommentar (2002); *Ehricke/Ries* Die neue Europäische Insolvenzverordnung, JuS 2003, p 313; *Eidenmüller* Europäische Verordnung über Insolvenzverfahren und zukünftiges deutsches internationales Insolvenzrecht, IPRax 2001, p 2; *Eidenmüller* Wettbewerb der Gesellschaftsrechte, ZIP 2002, p 2233; *Eidenmüller* Mobilität und Restrukturierung von Unternehmen im Binnenmarkt, JZ 2004, p 24; *Eidenmüller* Niederlassungsfreiheit versus Schutz des inländischen Rechtsverkehrs: Konturen des Europäischen Internationalen Gesellschaftsrechts, ZGR 2004, p 159; *Eidenmüller* Geschäftsleiter- und Gesellschafterhaftung bei europäischen Auslandsgesellschaften mit tatsächlichem Inlandssitz, NJW 2005, p 1618; *Eidenmüller* Wettbewerb der Insolvenzrechte?, ZGR 2006, p 467; *Fischer* Die Verlegung des Gläubigerschutzes vom Gesellschafts- in das Insolvenzrecht, ZIP 2004, p 1477; *Fleischer* Kapitalschutz und Durchgriffshaftung bei Auslandsgesellschaften, in Lutter (ed), Europäische Auslandsgesellschaften in Deutschland (2005), p 49; *Fleischer* Der Rechtsmissbrauch zwischen Gemeineuropäischem Privatrecht und Gemeinschaftsrecht, JZ 2003, p 865; *Fletcher* Insolvency in Private International Law (2005); *Forsthoff* EuGH fördert Vielfalt im Gesellschaftsrecht, DB 2002, p 2471; *Fritz/Bähr* Die Europäische Verordnung über Insolvenzverfahren – Herausforderung an Gerichte und Insolvenzverwalter, DZWiR 2001, p 221; *Fröhlich/Strasser* Die Limited als Einzelkaufmann mit beschränkter Haftung? Deliktsrechtliche Gegenargumente, ZIP 2006, p 1182; *Geyrhalter/Gänßler* Perspektiven nach „Überseering" – wie geht es weiter?, NZG 2003, p 409; *Geyrhalter/Gänßler* „Inspire Art" – Briefkastengesellschaften „on the Move", DStR 2003, p 2167; *Goette* Wo steht der BGH nach „Centros" und „Inspire Art"?, DStR 2005, p 197; *Gottwald* Insolvenzrechtshandbuch, 3rd edn (2006); *Gottwald* Grenzüberschreitende Insolvenzen (1997); *Gottwald/Pfaller* Aspekte der Anerkennung ausländischer Insolvenzverfahren im Inland, IPRax 1998, p 170; *Grigoleit* Gesellschafterhaftung für interne Einflussnahme im Recht der GmbH, (2006); *Gross/Schork* Strafbarkeit des directors einer Private Company Limited by Shares wegen verspäteter Insolvenzantragstellung, NZI 2006, p 10; *Grütters* BB-Forum: Limited auf dem Vormarsch – Serien-Reinfälle nicht ausgeschlossen, BB 2005, p 1523; *Haas* Der Normzweck des Eigenkapitalersatzrechts, NZI 2001, p 1; *Haas* Die Verwertung der im Ausland belegenen Insolvenzmasse im Anwendungsbereich der EuInsVO, in Schilken et al (ed), Festschrift Gerhardt (2004), p 319 et seq; *Habersack/Verse* Wrongful Trading – Grundlage einer europäischen Insolvenzverschleppungshaftung, ZHR 168 (2004), p 174; *Haberscheid* Konkursstatut und Wirkungsstatut bei der internationalen und der künftigen innereuropäischen Insolvenzanfechtung, ZZP (114) 2001, p 167; *Happ/Holler* „Limited" statt GmbH? – Risiken und Kosten werden gern verschwiegen, DStR 2004, p 730; *Haß/Huber/Gruber/Heiderhoff* EU-Insolvenzverordnung (2005); Heidelberger Kommentar zur Insolvenzordnung, 4th edn (2006); *Heinz* Englische Limited und Deutsche GmbH – eine vergleichende Darstellung, AnwBl 2004, p 612; *Henze* Aspekte des Insolvenzrechts an der Schnittstelle zum Gesellschaftsrecht, WM 2006, p 1653; *Hirte/Bücker* Grenzüberschreitende Gesellschaften, 2nd edn (2006); *Hirte/Mock* Wohin mit der Insolvenzantragspflicht?, ZIP 2005, p 474; *Holzer* Rechte und Pflichten des Geschäftsführers einer nach englischem Recht gegründeten „limited" im Hinblick auf das deutsche Insolvenzverfahren, ZVI 2005, p 457; *Horn* Deutsches und europäisches Gesellschaftsrecht und die EuGH-Rechtsprechung zur Niederlassungsfreiheit – Inspire Art, NJW 2004, p 893; *Huber* Internationales Insolvenzrecht in Europa, ZZP (114) 2001, p 133; *Huber* Die europäische Insolvenzverordnung, EuZW 2002, p 490; *Huber* Gesellschafterdarlehen in der Inlandsinsolvenz von Auslandsgesellschaften, in Lutter (ed), Europäische Auslandsgesellschaften in Deutschland (2005), p 131; *Huber* Die Insolvenzantragspflicht der Geschäftsführer von Auslandsgesellschaften, in Lutter (ed), Europäische Auslandsgesellschaften in Deutschland (2005), p 307; *Israël* European Cross-Border Insolvency Regulation (2005); *Just* Comments on LG Kiel dated 20.04.2005 – 10 S 44/05, ZIP 2006, p 1248; *Kallmeyer* Vor- und Nachteile der englischen Limited im Vergleich zur GmbH oder GmbH & Co. KG, DB 2004, p 636; *Kemper* Die Verordnung (EG) Nr. 1346/2000 über Insolvenzverfahren, ZIP 2001, p 1609; *Keppelmüller* Österreichisches Internationales Konkursrecht (1997); *Kessler/Eicke* Die Limited – Fluch oder Segen für die Steuerberatung, DStR 2005, p 2101; *Kindler* „Inspire Art" – Aus Luxemburg nicht Neues zum internationalen Gesellschaftsrecht, NZG 2003, p 1086; *Kindler* Auf dem Weg zur Europäischen Briefkastengesellschaft? – Die „Überseering"-Entscheidung des EuGH und das internationale Privatrecht, NJW 2003, p 1073; *Kleinert* Endgültiges Aus für Sonderanknüpfungen bei (Schein-) Auslandsgesellschaften, DB 2003, p 2217; *Kleinert/Probst* Endgültiges Aus für Sonderanknüpfungen bei (Schein-) Auslandsgesellschaften – Anmerkung zu dem EuGH-Urteil vom 30.9.2003 – Rs. C-167/01 – Inspire Art, DB 2003, p 2217; *Knöpfel* Gefahren beim Einsatz von Ltd.-Gründungsagenturen: Auftrags- und Beratungsumfang contra Qualifikation?; BB 2006, p 1233; *Köke* Die englische Limited in der Insolvenz, ZInsO 2005, p 354; *Kuntz* Die Insolvenz der Limited mit deutschem Verwaltungssitz – EU-Kapitalgesellschaften in Deutschland nach „Inspire Art", NZI 2005, p 424; *Lehr* Die neue EU-

Verordnung über Insolvenzverfahren und deren Auswirkungen für die Unternehmenspraxis, KTS 2000, p 577; *Leible* Niederlassungsfreiheit und Sitzverlegungsrichtlinie, ZGR 2004, p 531; *Leible/Hoffmann* Wie inspiriert ist „Inspire Art"?, EuZW 2003, p 677; *Leible/Staudinger* Die europäische Verordnung über Insolvenzverfahren, KTS 2000, p 533; *Leutner/Langer* Durchgriffshaftung bei Scheinauslandsgesellschaften, ZInsO 2005, p 575; *Lieder* Die Haftung der Geschäftsführer und Gesellschafter von EU-Auslandsgesellschaften mit tatsächlichem Verwaltungssitz in Deutschland, DZWiR 2005, p 399; *Linnertz/Scholl* Mehrpersonenlimited oder vorgeschaltete Holding, NZG 2006, p 493; *Lutter* (ed) Europäische Auslandsgesellschaften in Deutschland (2005); *Lutter/Hommelhoff* GmbH-Gesetz, Kommentar (16th edn 2004); *Mankowski* Entwicklungen im Internationalen Privat- und Insolvenzrecht 2003/2004 (Teil 1), RIW 2004, p 481; *Mankowski* Die deutsche Ltd.-Zweigniederlassung im Spannungsverhältnis von Gewerbe- und Registerrecht, BB 2006, p 1173; *Maul/C Schmidt* Inspire Art – Quo vadis Sitztheorie?, BB 2003, p 2297; *Meilicke* Der GmbHR-Kommentar, GmbHR 2003, p 1271; *Mellert/Verfürth* Wettbewerb der Gesellschaftsformen (2005); *Mittelstädt* Anwendbarkeit der Existenzvernichtungshaftung auf europäische Kapitalgesellschaften, Bucerius Law Journal 2007, p 7; *Mock* Comments on LG Kiel dated 20.04.2006 – 10 p 44/05, NZI 2006, p 482; *Mock/Schildt* Insolvenz ausländischer Kapitalgesellschaften mit Sitz in Deutschland, ZInsO 2003, p 396; *Mock/Schildt* Comments on AG Hamburg, dated 14.5.2003 – 67g IN 358/02, NZI 2003, p 444; *Moss/Fletcher/Isaacs* (eds) The EC Regulation on Insolvency Proceedings (2002); *H-F Müller* Insolvenz ausländischer Kapitalgesellschaften mit inländischem Verwaltungssitz, NZG 2003, p 414; *K Müller* Die englische Limited in Deutschland – für welche Unternehmen ist sie tatsächlich geeignet?, BB 2006, p 837; Münchener Kommentar zum Bürgerlichen Gesetzbuch, vol 11 (2006); Münchener Kommentar zur Insolvenzordnung, vol 1 (2001); Münchener Kommentar zur Insolvenzordnung, vol 3 (2003); *Oppermann* Europarecht (1991); *Paefgen* Auslandsgesellschaften und Durchsetzung deutscher Schutzinteressen nach „Überseering", DB 2003, p 487; *Paefgen* Wider die gesellschaftsrechtliche Ausländerphobie, ZIP 2004, p 2253; *Pannen/Riedemann* Checkliste: Die englische „Ltd." Mit Verwaltungssitz in Deutschland in der Insolvenz, MDR 2005, p 496; *Pannen/Riedemann* Comments on AG Bad Segeberg dated 24.03.2005 – 17 C 289/04, NZI 2005, p 411; *Paulus* Europäische Insolvenzverordnung, Kommentar (2006); *Penzlin/Riedemann* Comments on High Court of Justice Birmingham dated 11.5.2005 – 2375 to 2382/05, NZI 2005, p 517; *Riedemann* Das Auseinanderfallen von Gesellschafts- und Insolvenzstatut, GmbHR 2004, p 345; *Riegger* Centros – Überseering – Inspire Art: Folgen für die Praxis, ZGR 2004, p 510; *Röhricht* Insolvenzrechtliche Aspekte im Gesellschaftsrecht, ZIP 2005, p 505; *Römermann* Die Limited in Deutschland – eine Alternative zur GmbH?, NJW 2006, p 2065; *Römermann/Johnen* Limited vs. GmbH: Einige „Schlachten" hat die Limited schon gewonnen, den „Krieg" aber noch nicht, GmbHR 2005, p R305; *Rönnau* Haftung der Direktoren einer in Deutschland ansässigen englischen Private Company Limited by Shares nach deutschem Strafrecht – eine erste Annäherung, ZGR 2005, p 832; *G Roth* Gläubigerschutz durch Existenzschutz, NZG 2003, p 1081; *G Roth* Qualität und Preis am Markt für Gesellschaftsformen, ZGR 2005, p 348; *W-H* Roth Internationales Gesellschaftsrecht nach Überseering, IPRax 2003, p 117; *Runkel* (ed) Anwaltshandbuch – Insolvenzrecht (2005); *Sandrock* Sitztheorie, Überlagerungstheorie und der EWG-Vertrag – Wasser, Öl und Feuer, RIW 1989, p 505; *Sandrock* Die Schrumpfung der Überlagerungstheorie, ZVglRWiss 102 (2003), p 447; *Sandrock* Sitzrecht contra Savigny?, BB 2004, p 897; *Schall* Englischer Gläubigerschutz bei der Limited in Deutschland, ZIP 2005, p 965; *Schanze/Jüttner* Anerkennung und Kontrolle ausländischer Gesellschaften – Rechtslage und Perspektiven nach der Überseering-Entscheidung des EuGH, AG 2003, p 30; *Schanze/Jüttner* Die Entscheidung für Pluralität: Kollisionsrecht und Gesellschaftsrecht nach der EuGH-Entscheidung „Inspire-Art", AG 2003, p 661; *Schilling* Comments on LG Kiel dated 20.04.2006 – 10 S 44/05, EWiR 2006, p 429; *Schlichte* Kapitalerhaltung in der Ltd. & Co. KG, DB 2006, p 1357; *Schlichte* Existenzvernichtung in der Ltd. & Co. KG, DB 2006, p 2672; *Schmidt/Uhlenbruck* (eds) Die GmbH in Krise, Sanierung und Insolvenz (3th edn 2003); *J Schmidt* Insolvenzantragspflicht und Insolvenzverschleppungshaftung bei der „deutschen" Limited – Das LG Kiel auf dem richtigen Weg?, ZInsO 2006, p 737; *Schön* Die „Existenzvernichtung" der juristischen Person, ZHR 168 (2004), p 268; *Schön* Die Niederlassungsfreiheit von Kapitalgesellschaften im System der Grundfreiheiten, in Schneider (ed), Festschrift Lutter (2000), p 685 et seq; *Schröder/Schneider* Geschäftsführerhaftung bei der Private Limited Company mit Verwaltungssitz in Deutschland, GmbHR 2005, p 1288; *Schulz* (Schein-) Auslandsgesellschaften in Europa – Ein Schein-Problem, NJW 2003, p 2705; *Schumann* Die englische

Limited mit Verwaltungssitz in Deutschland: Kapitalaufbringung, Kapitalerhaltung und Haftung bei Insolvenz, DB 2004, p 743; *Smid* Deutsches und Europäisches Internationales Insolvenzrecht, Kommentar (2004); *Spindler/Berner* Inspire Art – Der europäische Wettbewerb um das Gesellschaftsrecht ist endgültig eröffnet, RIW 2003, p 949; *Spindler/Berner* Der Gläubigerschutz im Gesellschaftsrecht noch Inspire Art, RIW 2004, p 7; *Staudinger* Kommentar zum Bürgerlichen Gesetzbuch mit Einführungsgesetz und Nebengesetzen EGBGB/IPR, Internationales Gesellschaftsrecht (1998); *Stoll* (ed) Vorschläge und Gutachten zur Umsetzung des EU-Übereinkommens über Insolvenzverfahren im deutschen Recht (1997); *Stork* Deutsche GmbH vs. englische Ltd. – Wettbewerb der Rechtsordnungen um die beste Gesellschaftsform für den Mittelstand, GewArch 2005, p 265; *Süß* Häufige Probleme mit Zweigniederlassungen englischer Limited Companies, DNotZ 2005, p 180; *Taupitz* Das (zukünftige) europäische Internationale Insolvenzrecht – insbesondere aus international-privatrechtlicher Sicht, ZZP (111) 1998, p 315; *Torwegge* UK Company Law Reform Bill – Think Small First!, GmbHR 2006, p 919; *Ulmer* Gläubigerschutz bei Scheinauslandsgesellschaften – Zum Verhältnis zwischen gläubigerschützendem nationalem Gesellschafts-, Delikts-, und Insolvenzrecht und der EG-Niederlassungsfreiheit, NJW 2004, p 1201; *Ulmer* Insolvenzrechtlicher Gläubigerschutz gegenüber Scheinauslandsgesellschaften ohne hinreichende Kapitalausstattung?, KTS 2004, p 291; *Ulmer/Habersack/Winter* Gesetz betreffend die Gesellschaften mit beschränkter Haftung, Kommentar (2005); *Vallender* Die Insolvenz von Scheinauslandsgesellschaften, ZGR 2006, p 425; *Vallender* Aufgaben und Befugnisse des deutschen Insolvenzrichters in Verfahren nach der EuInsVO, KTS 2005, p 283; *Vallender/Fuchs* Die Antragspflicht organschaftlicher Vertreter einer GmbH vor dem Hintergrund der Europäischen Insolvenzverordnung, ZIP 2004, p 829; *Virgós/Garcimartín* The European Insolvency Regulation: Law and Practice (2004); *Virgós/Schmit* Erläuternder Bericht zu dem EU-Übereinkommen über Insolvenzverfahren, in Stoll (ed), Vorschläge und Gutachten (1997), p 32; *von Bernstorff* Das Betreiben einer englischen Limited in Deutschland, RIW 2004, p 498; *von Hase* Insolvenzantragspflicht für directors einer Limited in Deutschland, BB 2006, p 2141; *Wachter* Errichtung, Publizität, Haftung und Insolvenz von Zweigniederlassungen ausländischer Kapitalgesellschaften nach „Inspire Art", GmbHR 2003, p 1254; *Wachter* Auswirkung des EuGH-Urteils in Sachen Inspire Art auf Beratungspraxis und Gesetzgebung, GmbHR 2004, p 88; *Wachter* Der GmbHR-Kommentar, GmbHR 2006, p 709; *Wachter* Persönliche Haftung des Gründers einer englischen private limited company, BB 2006, p 1463; *Walterscheid* Die englische Limited im Insolvenzverfahren, DZWiR 2006, p 95; *Weller* Scheinauslandsgesellschaften nach Centros, Überseering und Inspire Art: Ein neues Anwendungsfeld für die Existenzvernichtungshaftung, IPRax 2003, p 207; *Weller* „Inspire Art": Weitgehende Freiheiten beim Einsatz ausländischer Briefkastengesellschaften, DStR 2003, p 1800; *Weller* Einschränkung der Gründungstheorie bei missbräuchlicher Auslandsgründung?, IPRax 2003, p 520; *Wessels* Current Topics of International Insolvency Law (2004); *Werner* Die Ltd. & Co. KG – eine Alternative zur GmbH & Co. KG?, GmbHR 2005, p 288; *Westermann* Die GmbH in der nationalen und internationalen Konkurrenz der Rechtsformen, GmbHR 2005, p 4; *Wiedemann* Reflexionen zur Durchgriffshaftung, ZGR 2003, p 283; *Wienberg/Sommer* Anwendbarkeit von deutschem Eigenkapitalersatzrecht auf EU-Kapitalgesellschaften am Beispiel eines Partikularinsolvenzverfahrens im engeren Sinne nach Art 3 II, IV EuInsVO, NZI 2005, p 353; *Wilhelmi* Das Mindestkapital als Mindestschutz – ein Apologie im Hinblick auf die Diskussion um eine Reform der GmbH angesichts der englischen Limited, GmbHR 2006, p 13; *Wimmer* Die Verordnung (EG) Nr. 1346/2000 über Insolvenzverfahren, ZInsO 2001, p 97; *Zerres* Deutsche Insolvenzantragspflicht für die englische Limited mit Inlandssitz, DZWiR 2006, p 356; *Ziemons* Freie Bahn für den Umzug von Gesellschaften nach Inspire Art?!, ZIP 2003, p 1913; *Zimmer* Nach „Inspire Art": Grenzenlose Gestaltungsfreiheit für deutsche Unternehmen, NJW 2003, p 3585; *Zöllner* Konkurrenz für inländische Kapitalgesellschaften durch ausländische Rechtsträger, insbesondere durch englische Private Limited Company, GmbHR 2006, p 1.

I. Introduction

1 Art 4 of the EIR regulates the **law applicable** to the insolvency proceedings and its effects. As the "basic conflict of laws rule"[1] of the Regulation, it therefore determines the **law that governs the insolvency.**

2 According to Art 4 of the EIR, the law of the State in which the proceedings are opened (***lex fori concursus***) is applicable to the insolvency proceeding and its effects.[2]

The *lex fori concursus* regulates:
- **the proceedings to open the proceedings,**
- **the opening,**
- **the conduct and the closing of the proceedings, and**
- **the entire effects ensuing from the insolvency proceedings.**[3]

3 The *lex fori concursus* applies unless the Regulation stipulates something to the contrary (see the **exceptions** in Arts 5 to 15 of the EIR, on this mn 35).

4 For **main insolvency proceedings**, the law of the State in which the main proceedings were opened applies. For **territorial insolvency proceedings** (both secondary insolvency proceedings and independent territorial insolvency proceedings), the law of the Member State in which the territorial insolvency proceedings were opened applies (see also mn 7).[4] That the particular *lex fori concursus* applies to territorial insolvency proceedings as well follows *inter alia* from the inclusion of Art 4 in Chapter I "General Provisions" of the Regulation.[5]

5 Art 4 of the EIR constitutes a **referral to certain substantive law provisions**[6] and not to the foreign law in its entirety; this arises from the wording of Art 4 (1) of the EIR, which invokes the insolvency laws of the Member States and does not refer to a conflict of laws rule. Therefore any form of *renvoi* – either back to the law of the forum or forward to another foreign law – provided for by the provisions of private international law of the Member States is not permitted.[7]

---

[1] D-K/D/Ch-*Duursma-Kepplinger* Art 4 mn 5, 7; *Smid* Komm EuInsVO Art 4 mn 1; *Paulus* Komm EuInsVO Art 4 mn 1; *Virgós/Schmit* Explanatory report mn 90; *Huber* ZZP (114) 2001, 133, 151; MünchKomm InsO/*Reinhart* Art 4 EuInsVO mn 1; *Wessels* Current Topics of International Insolvency Law, 134; Gottwald/*Gottwald* InsR-Handb (2006), § 129, mn 52 speaks of a basic rule ("*Grundregel*").

[2] *Wimmer* ZInsO 2001, 97, 100; *Lehr* KTS 2000, 577, 579; HK-InsO/*Stephan* Art 4 EuInsVO mn 1; *Huber* ZZP (114) 2001, 133, 151; *Kemper* ZIP 2001, 1609, 1615; *Vallender* KTS 2005, 283, 290.

[3] *Vallender* KTS 2005, 283, 290; *Wessels* Current Topics of International Insolvency Law, 134; MünchKomm InsO/*Reinhart* Art 4 EuInsVO mn 1.

[4] That the *lex fori concursus* applies to independent territorial insolvency proceedings is not specifically provided for but follows from Recital 23 of the EIR; also: MünchKomm InsO/*Reinhart* Art 4 EuInsVO mn 1, Art 28 EuInsVO mn 2; *Wessels* Current Topics of International Insolvency Law, 29; MünchKomm BGB/*Kindler* IntInsR mn 200; Haß/Huber/Gruber/Heiderhoff-*Haß/Huber* Art 4 mn 2, 5; *Smid* Komm EuInsVO Art 4 mn 1.

[5] MünchKomm BGB/*Kindler* IntInsR mn 200.

[6] *Virgós/Schmit* Explanatory report mn 87; *Paulus* Komm EuInsVO Art 4 mn 1; *Smid* Komm EuInsVO Art 4 mn 1; *Leible/Staudinger* KTS 2000, 533, 549; D-K/D/Ch-*Duursma-Kepplinger* Art 4 mn 2; MünchKomm InsO/*Reinhart* Art 4 EuInsVO mn 1; MünchKomm BGB/*Kindler* IntInsR mn 19.

[7] *Virgós/Schmit* Explanatory report mn 87; *Leible/Staudinger* KTS 2000, 533, 549; D-K/D/Ch-*Duursma-Kepplinger* Art 4 mn 2; MünchKomm BGB/*Kindler* IntInsR mn 199.

By stipulating that the law that governs the insolvency also governs its effects, assurance is being made that – via Arts 16 and 17 of the EIR – such effects automatically extend to all of the other Member States. A different rule applies if independent territorial insolvency proceedings (Art 3 (4) of the EIR) have previously been opened in another Member State, or if secondary insolvency proceedings (Art 3 (2) and (3), Art 17 (2), Art 27, Art 28 of the EIR) are opened after the main insolvency proceedings have been opened. In such a case, the law of the State in which the **territorial insolvency proceedings** are opened governs (so-called *lex fori concursus particularis* or the *lex fori concursus secundarii*).[8] The consequence of this is a disparity between the *lex fori concursus* of the main and the territorial insolvency proceedings. 6

II. Scope of Application

1. Main and Territorial Insolvency Proceedings

The general principle, i.e. that the *lex fori concursus* governs, applies both to the main insolvency proceedings as well as to the territorial insolvency proceedings.[9] Art 28 of the EIR thus confirms that the law governing the secondary insolvency proceedings is that of the Member State in whose territory the secondary insolvency proceedings have been opened.[10] The inference can be drawn from both the intentions of the drafters of the Regulation and the logic underlying it – namely that territorial insolvency proceedings are only to be treated differently with respect to the conditions under which they may be opened – that the principle of the *lex fori concursus* also applies to independent territorial insolvency proceedings; already discussed at mn 4 above.[11] 7

Since the respective *lex fori concursus* governs both the main and the territorial insolvency proceedings, a disparity arises between the law applicable to the secondary and that applicable to the main insolvency proceedings; see mn 15 et seq. This constitutes a break in the uniformity of the various proceedings. In order to provide the creditors with the most comprehensive protection possible and to ensure the smoothest possible processing of the parallel proceedings, the liquidators of the individual proceedings are obliged to communicate and cooperate with each other (cf Art 31 of the EIR and the detailed discussions on it).[12] 8

2. Scope of Application in Terms of Subject Matter

a) Procedural and substantive law effects

The law governing the insolvency regulates the **effects** of the insolvency proceedings both in terms of their **procedural-law** and **substantive-law** aspects.[13] This allows for the circumvention of the difficult problem of having to differentiate between the procedural and substantive-law effects of the insolvency proceedings, and therefore creates legal cer- 9

---

[8] D-K/D/Ch-*Duursma-Kepplinger* Art 4 mn 10.

[9] *Virgós/Schmit* Explanatory report mn 23, 3; D-K/D/Ch-*Duursma-Kepplinger* Art 4 mn 1; *Leible/Staudinger* KTS 2000, 533, 549; *Fritz/Bähr* DZWiR 2001, 221, 226; MünchKomm InsO/*Reinhart* Art 4 EuInsVO mn 1.

[10] *Virgós/Schmit* Explanatory report mn 98; D-K/D/Ch-*Duursma-Kepplinger* Art 4 mn 4; *Chalupsky* in Baudenbacher, p 346.

[11] Cf arts 3 (3) and (4) of the EIR, and Recital 23 of the EIR.

[12] Also Haß/Huber/Gruber/Heiderhoff-*Haß/Huber* Art 4 EuInsVO mn 6.

[13] D-K/D/Ch-*Duursma-Kepplinger* Art 4 mn 9.

tainty in this respect.[14] The reference to all of the effects of the insolvency proceedings guarantees the strived-for harmonization of decisions.[15]

b) Restriction to insolvency-law related matters (classification problem)

aa) Scope of the governing insolvency law

10 The scope of application of Art 4 of the EIR extends, as per its wording, to "insolvency proceedings and their effects". As welcoming as this provision is, it is still difficult in some cases to decide exactly what the *lex fori concursus* encompasses.[16]

11 For deciding what falls within insolvency law, the decisive factor is not whether the provision is contained in insolvency legislation.[17] In which piece of legislation for example provisions dealing with the liability of the company's executive officers or the preparation of a social plan are found is not determinative.[18] The restriction of the *lex fori concursus* to the various pieces of insolvency legislation would be tantamount to an invitation to the Member States to shift to these insolvency acts those regulations advantageous to them for the purpose of realizing their own individual conceptions of insolvency law.[19]

12 According to Art 4 (2) sentence 1 of the EIR, the *lex fori concursus* governs the conditions for opening the proceedings, as well as their conduct and their closure. The **catalogue of examples** set out in subpara 2 serves as an **interpretative guide.**[20] For those matters not listed in the example catalogue, the central **issue** is one of **classification,** namely which matters fall within the ambit of insolvency law and its effects, and are thus governed by the *lex fori concursus*, and which do not.[21]

13 What is decisive is whether a set of facts is to be considered an **insolvency-law matter** within the meaning of the Regulation; or whether such set of facts, although associated with the cross-border insolvency, do not constitute any special effects of the insolvency proceedings and are not closely connected to its organization.[22] The latter are not subject to the *lex fori concursus* but are rather determined pursuant to the classification rule that would normally be invoked outside the insolvency. For determining what falls within insolvency law, a Regulation-autonomous interpretation must be made.[23] It must be asked for each individual set of facts or for each law whether it is a **specific insolvency law matter** (and therefore caught by the *lex fori concursus*), or whether it concerns another area of law that only takes on insolvency-law relevance because of the debtor's insolvency (and therefore the conflict of laws rules of the particular Member State apply).[24]

14 Although the aims of the Regulation – namely uniformity, the harmonization of decisions, and the equal treatment of creditors throughout the Community – would appear to demand a wide interpretation of the concept of "insolvency law and its effects",[25] a

---

[14] D-K/D/Ch-*Duursma-Kepplinger* Art 4 mn 9.
[15] *Leible/Staudinger* KTS 2000, 533, 550; D-K/D/Ch-*Duursma-Kepplinger* Art 4 mn 1.
[16] Haß/Huber/Gruber/Heiderhoff-*Haß/Huber* Art 4 EuInsVO mn 10; D-K/D/Ch-*Duursma-Kepplinger* Art 4 mn 6; *Paulus* Komm EuInsVO Art 4 mn 2.
[17] BK-InsO/*Pannen* Art 4 EuInsVO mn 5; *Paulus* Komm EuInsVO Art 4 mn 2; *Riedemann* GmbHR 2004, 345, 349.
[18] BK-InsO/*Pannen* Art 4 EuInsVO mn 5; *Paulus* Komm EuInsVO Art 4 mn 2; *Riedemann* GmbHR 2004, 345, 349.
[19] Also *Paulus* Komm EuInsVO Art 4 mn 2.
[20] *Virgós/Schmit* Explanatory report mn 91.
[21] *Paulus* Komm EuInsVO Art 4 mn 2; *Leible/Staudinger* KTS 2000, 533, 549.
[22] D-K/D/Ch-*Duursma-Kepplinger* Art 4 mn 6.
[23] *Mankowski* RIW 2004, 481, 486; *Paulus* Komm EuInsVO Art 4 mn 4.
[24] *Paulus* Komm EuInsVO Art 4 mn 4.
[25] D-K/D/Ch-*Duursma-Kepplinger* Art 4 mn 7;

restrictive approach should be taken in deciding what matters fall within insolvency law. This ensures the most comprehensive safeguarding of the interests of the parties to the proceedings, especially the creditors, who have relied on the applicability of a certain specific body of law. Certain matters may therefore only be classified as **insolvency law matters** within the meaning of Art 4 of the EIR if they demonstrate a **particularly close connection to the insolvency proceedings.**[26] Such a connection should be found particularly if:

- the legal norm itself is meant to fulfil an insolvency-political goal, as for example the principle of *par condition creditorum*,[27] or
- the legal norm is required to enable the insolvency proceedings to fulfil their purpose.[28]

A useful – although not always reliable – guideline for classifying legal norms as insolvency laws are the constructions and examples listed in Art 4 (2) of the EIR, which provide at least a framework for what can be understood as insolvency-law matters.[29] When making the classification, the following questions should always be asked:

- is a de facto insolvency a required element of the norm, or
- does the norm itself serve a direct insolvency-political goal?[30]

Only if one of these is affirmed it is to be classified as insolvency law and therefore as a part of the *lex fori concursus*.

bb) Demarcation between the law governing the company and the insolvency

The classification of a set of facts as an insolvency law matter is particularly difficult in the case of insolvencies of pseudo foreign corporations; detailed discussion on this at mn 72 et seq.[31] Pseudo foreign corporations are understood as companies incorporated under the laws of a Member State but which have no other connection to this (incorpo- **15**

Haß/Huber/Gruber/Heiderhoff-*Haß/Huber* Art 4 EuInsVO mn 11.

[26] See also Haß/Huber/Gruber/Heiderhoff-*Haß/Huber* Art 4 EuInsVO mn 11.

[27] See also *Virgós/Garcimartín* Regulation, p 72.

[28] D-K/D/Ch-*Duursma-Kepplinger* Art 4 mn 7; examples of this are such norms pursuant to which the debtor is divested of his powers of administration and disposal once proceedings are opened; in Germany Sec 80 *InsO*.

[29] Cf *Paulus* Komm EuInsVO Art 4 mn 6.

[30] Haß/Huber/Gruber/Heiderhoff-*Haß/Huber* Art 4 EuInsVO mn 11; *Virgós/Schmit* Explanatory report mn 90; D-K/D/Ch-*Duursma-Kepplinger* Art 4 mn 7; *Haas* NZI 2001, 1, 10.

[31] In Germany, this issue is principally discussed in connexion with the English Limited, see on this for example: *Römermann/Johnen* GmbHR 2005, R305; *Grütters* BB 2005, 1523; *Gross/Schork* NZI 2006, 10; *Rönnau* ZGR 2005, 832; *Wachter* GmbHR 2006, 709; *Süß* DNotZ 2005, 180; *Linnertz/Scholl* NZG 2006; 493; *Knöfel* BB 2006, 1233; *Mankowski* BB 2006, 1173; *Pannen/Riedemann* MDR 2005, 496; *Riedemann* GmbHR 2004, 345; *Zerres* DZWiR 2006, 356; *Altmeppen/Wilhelm* DB 2004, 1083; *Borges* ZIP 2004, 733; *Burg* GmbHR 2004, 1379; *Schumann* DB 2004, 743; *Schall* ZIP 2005, 965; *Paefgen* DB 2003, 487; *Wachter* GmbHR 2003, 1254; *Wachter* GmbHR 2004, 88; *Dierksmeier* BB 2005, 1516; *Fröhlich/Strasser* ZIP 2006 1182; *Geyrhalter/Gänßler* DStR 2003, 2167; *Heinz* AnwBl 2004, 612; *von Hase* BB 2006, 2141; *Kallmeyer* DB 2004, 636; *Köke* ZInsO 2005, 354; *Kuntz* NZI 2005, 424; *Lieder* DZWiR 2005, 399; *K Müller* BB 2006, 837; *Römermann* NJW 2006, 2065; *Riegger* ZGR 2004, 510; *Schlichte* DB 2006, 1357; *Stork* GewArch 2005, 265; *Wienberg/ Sommer* NZI 2005, 353; *Walterscheid* DZWiR 2006, 95; *Wachter* BB 2006, 1463; *Werner* GmbHR 2005, 288 (Ltd & Co KG); *Zöllner* GmbHR 2006, 1; *von Bernstorff* RIW 2004, 498.

rating) State because all of their business activities are carried out in a different Member State. In the case of an insolvency of a pseudo foreign corporation, a disparity can arise between the law governing the company and that governing the insolvency;[32] on pseudo foreign corporations in Germany, see the detailed discussion at mn 72.

Pseudo foreign corporations

Disparity between the law governing the company and that governing the insolvency

- **Law governing the company:** according to the "incorporation theory" (on this see mn 19 et seq), the company law of the State in which the company was incorporated applies.
- **Law governing the insolvency:** as *lex fori concursus*, the law of the Member State in which the proceedings were opened applies.

16 The problem that arises here is the categorization of certain legal provisions as company or insolvency law; such provisions concern creditor protection under company law and are always of prime importance in insolvency proceedings. Examples of such norms are those that impose liability on the managing directors or the shareholders and that link (as an element of the norm) the latter's misconduct to the crisis being experienced by the company;[33] in-depth discussion on this at mn 81 et seq.

17 The **liability of the managing director** is an insolvency law matter since it is precisely the manager's conduct in the company's crisis that is being punished, although it is questionable whether this demonstrates the required "particularly close connection" to insolvency law. The reimbursement of payments made on shareholders' loans, if such a legal construction is contemplated at all in the respective national law regimes,[34] or the imposition of personal liability (through a piercing of the corporate veil) on the shareholders also pose problems of classification. Such a classification must take into account the basic freedoms envisioned by the EEC Treaty and the more recent decisions of the ECJ on the company's right of establishment (Art 43, 48 EEC Treaty). The classification of such provisions is of utmost importance because, should they not be classified as insolvency law, they could only be applied if the opening of the insolvency proceedings takes place in the Member State from which such provisions originate (*lex fori concursus*).[35] The classification must be made in each individual case and is dependent on which types of companies in which Member State insolvency proceedings are being opened; detailed discussion on classification with an overview of opinions at mn 72 to 102.

If a norm is classified as insolvency law, then its application follows from Art 4 of the
18 EIR. But if it is classified as company law, then the law of the forum of the incorporation applies. If the norm is classified as general substantive law, then the general conflict of laws rule applies; detailed discussion on this at mn 74.

[32] *Virgós/Garcimartín* Regulation, p 81; *Riedemann* GmbHR 2004, 345 et seq.

[33] In Germany sec 64 (1) and (2) GmbHG; in England: sec 213, 214 IA 1986; in France: "*action en comblement du passif*" pursuant to art L 624-3 Code de Commerce.

[34] In Germany sec 32a and 32b GmbHG.

[35] See also on this Haß/Huber/Gruber/Heiderhoff-*Haß/Huber* Art 4 EuInsVO mn 12 et seq.

aaa) Development of the ECJ decisions on the right of establishment; corporate domicile theory, incorporation theory

19 Since the "Inspire Art" judgement of the ECJ,[36] the so-called **incorporation theory** applies.[37] Pursuant to the incorporation theory, the law of the forum in which the company was incorporated governs all company-law related issues.[38] Therefore, in the event of a (national) insolvency in a Member State concerning the assets of a foreign corporation, a disparity arises between the law governing the company (foreign law as the law of the incorporation) and the law governing the insolvency; for a detailed discussion on pseudo foreign corporations in Germany, see mn 72 to 102.

20 Prior to the ECJ decisions in the Centros,[39] Überseering,[40] and the Inspire Art[41] cases, the so-called **corporate domicile theory**[42] had been favoured particularly on the European continent.

21 According to the **corporate domicile theory**, a company with a domestic administrative head office only has legal capacity if it was incorporated pursuant to national law.[43] The registered office has only evidentiary significance here. The corporate domicile theory presupposes that every company has a main administrative head office in a certain State. Should there be more than one of these, the main one must be ascertained. The ascertainment of this main administrative head office is the central problem of the corporate domicile theory.[44] According to the **incorporation theory**, the legal form of the company is recognized through the eyes of the laws of the forum in which the company was incorporated, whereby the registered office is determinative.[45] In contrast to the incorporation theory, which allows a relocation of the administrative head office to another Member State, the corporate domicile theory dictates that a company forfeits its legal capacity when it relocates its administrative head office to a foreign country. Likewise, a foreign company that relocates to a Member State would be deprived of its legal capacity.[46]

22 The ability to shield national company laws through the corporate domicile theory was brought to an end by the three leading decisions **Centros**, **Überseering**, and **Inspire Art**, all judgements of the ECJ[47] dealing with a company's right of establishment.[48]

---

[36] ECJ dated 30 Sep 2003 – C – 167/01, ZIP 2003, 1885. On this see for instance: *Altmeppen* NJW 2004, 97; *Kleinert/Probst* DB 2003, 2217; *Ziemons* ZIP 2003, 1913; *Bayer* BB 2003, 2357; *Zimmer* NJW 2003, 2385.

[37] *Spindler/Berner* RIW 2003, 949, 951.

[38] *Spindler/Berner* RIW 2003, 949, 951; *Bayer* BB 2003, 2357, 2363.

[39] ECJ dated 9 Mar 1999 – C-212/97, NJW 1999, 2027.

[40] ECJ dated 5 Nov 2002 – C-208/00, NJW 2002, 3614 = IPRax 2003, 65.

[41] ECJ dated 30 Sep 2003 – C-167/01, ZIP 2003, 1885.

[42] Cf *Mellert/Verfürth* Wettbewerb der Gesellschaftsformen (2005), p 30; on the corporate domicile theory see also *Staudinger/Großfeld* IntGesR (1998) mn 25, 72; MünchKomm BGB/*Kindler* IntGesR mn 401 with further references.

[43] *Schön* FS Lutter (2000) p 685, 686; *Borges* RIW 2000, 167; 170; Hirte/Bücker-*Hirte* § 1 mn 2.

[44] *Borges* RIW 2000, 167, 170.

[45] *Sandrock* RIW 1989, 505, 512.

[46] Hirte/Bücker-*Hirte* § 1 mn 2 with further references.

[47] ECJ "Inspire Art" NJW 2003, 3331 = EuZW 2003, 687, cf Art 4 of the EIR fn 36; ECJ "Überseering" NJW 2002, 3614 = EuZW 2002, 754, cf Art 4 of the EIR fn 36; ECJ "Centros" NJW 1999, 2027 = EuZW 1999, 216, cf Art 4 of the EIR fn 36.

[48] *Fleischer* in Lutter (ed), Europäische Auslandsgesellschaften in Deutschland (2005), 49, 94 et seq; *Behrens* IPRax 2003, 193, 195; *Sandrock* BB 2004, 897, 901.

- **In the Centros judgement,**[49] **the ECJ dealt with cases of relocation and the cross-border relocation of the registered office to another Member State. The court ruled that it was not a wrongful exploitation of the right of establishment if for the incorporation of a company, a company law regime was chosen that afforded the incorporating party the greatest degree of freedom and if a branch establishment was then opened in a Member State other than the one in which it was incorporated. The court held that a refusal to register the company constitutes an infringement of the right of establishment guaranteed in Arts 43 and 48 of the EEC Treaty.**
- In the **Überseering** case,[50] a German court had deprived a Dutch company of its legal capacity and its capacity to sue and be sued because it relocated its **main administration** to Germany. The ECJ also considered this an infringement of Art 43 and 48 of the EEC Treaty and held that each and every European company is entitled to exercise its right of establishment, and the exercising of this right may not be hindered by depriving it of its legal capacity and its capacity to sue and be sued. Not only the setting up of branch establishments was held to be protected by the right of establishment, but the State to which the company is relocating must also recognize the company in the form it is in pursuant to the law of the forum of its incorporation.
- The judgement in the **Inspire Art** case[51] dealt with the situation in which a foreign company in the Netherlands, although not being denied recognition in general, was being required to affix a special supplement to its name pursuant to Dutch law and to fulfil minimum capital requirements pursuant to the applicable national laws. The failure to fulfil these requirements would have resulted in personal liability being imposed on the managers. The ECJ also regarded this as an infringement of the right of establishment. The court held that neither the imposition of personal liability nor the fulfilment of minimum capital requirements was permissible. The ECJ has hereby vehemently restricted the ability of the Member States to enforce national, protectionary interests on foreign companies.

23 The result of these decisions of the ECJ is that the corporate domicile theory, which had originally been favoured in many EU countries, is no longer applicable. A company with a foreign legal form must be recognized as having legal capacity in all other Member States.

24 The recognition of the legal capacity and the legal form of companies established in another EU Member State, which is derived from the right of establishment that exists within the European Union, applies not only to the **creation** of such companies but also to their **dissolution, winding-up,** and the **legal termination** of them. If a company has been extinguished pursuant to the laws of the country of incorporation relevant to it, then such status is legally binding everywhere within the European Union. Where a company was **dissolved** *ex officio* pursuant to the laws of the forum of its incorporation, its

---

[49] ECJ dated 9 Mar 1999 – C-212/97 "Centros" NJW 1999, 2027 = EuZW 1999, 216; *Borges* RIW 2000, 167; *Mellert/Verfürth* Wettbewerb der Gesellschaftsformen (2005), p 42 with more references.

[50] ECJ dated 5 Nov 2002 – C-208/00 "Überseering" NJW 2002, 3614 = EuZW 2002, 754; *Mellert/Verfürth* Wettbewerb der Gesellschaftsformen (2005), p 47 with more references; *Schanze/Jüttner* AG 2003, 30.

[51] ECJ dated 30 Sep 2003 – C-167/01 "Inspire Art" NJW 2003, 3331 = EuZW 2003, 687; *Mellert/Verfürth* Wettbewerb der Gesellschaftsformen (2005), p 52 with further references; *Schanze/Jüttner* AG 2003, 661; *Maul/C Schmidt* BB 2003, 2297.

insolvency capacity and legal capacity were denied by the *AG* Duisburg in an order dated 14 October 2003[52] (→ cf Table of Cases Art 3 of the EIR Appendix B No 34).

Example:

In Great Britain, a company that has been deleted from the company register by the Registrar of Companies, either because the business activities have ceased or for failure to submit the annual returns, is deemed dissolved once the deletion has been publicly announced.[53] The effect of the dissolution is that the company ceases to exist in legal terms. According to German law, the company has no longer insolvency capacity as a legal entity.[54] **25**

bbb) Compatibility of applying company laws with the right of establishment pursuant to Articles 43 and 48 of the EEC Treaty

As the ECJ has not yet conclusively ruled on the classification of those legal provisions that impose liability, the specific liability elements of such provisions must be reviewed based on a Regulation-autonomous interpretation as to whether they have a particular insolvency-law character, which would result in the application of Art 4 of the EIR.[55] It is therefore possible that similar elements of a certain kind of liability will be assessed differently in the various Member States. **26**

Each element (of the liability) must be interpreted in isolation and categorized as insolvency, or company law, and, if necessary, it must be tested against the right of establishment; for detailed discussion of the German perspective, see mn 72 et seq. **27**

If one wishes to examine the liability elements found in company law to determine their compatibility with European law, then the **scope of the protection** offered by the right of establishment under European law must first be ascertained.[56] Only outside the scope of this protection can national law still apply autonomously pursuant to the corporate domicile theory.[57] Some are of the opinion that the scope of the right of establishment only extends to the fundamental aspects of the company, hence only to its incorporation, organization, and dissolution in terms of company law.[58] The issue of the equal treatment of corporations would then have nothing to do with the right of establishment.[59] This approach should be rejected. According to the wording of the Überseering decision, a company incorporated under foreign law is to be recognized in full as **28**

---

[52] AG Duisburg dated 14 Oct 2003 NZI 2003, 658; (→ cf Table of Cases Art 3 of the EIR Appendix B No 34.

[53] *Happ/Holler* DStR 2004, 730, 736.

[54] AG Duisburg NZI 2003, 658; (→ cf Table of Cases Art 3 of the EIR Appendix B No 34; LG Duisburg ZIP 2007, 926.

[55] In Gourdain v Nadler, the ECJ classified the French imposition of personal liability occasioned by a piercing of the corporate veil, *action en comblement de passif social,* as insolvency law, see ECJ EC reports 1979, 733, 743 et seq ("... its legal justification is found solely in bankruptcy law within the meaning of the convention."); the proceeding was, however, an isolated decision and was based on the autonomous interpretation of the terminology of the 1968 Brussels Convention. No inferences can be drawn from this as to the classification of German provisions. Also: *Ulmer* NJW 2004, 1201, 1207 fn 61; contra: *Zimmer* NJW 2003, 3585, 3590.

[56] *Fleischer* in Lutter (ed), Europäische Auslandsgesellschaften in Deutschland (2005), 49, 95 et seq.

[57] *Fleischer* in Lutter (ed), Europäische Auslandsgesellschaften in Deutschland (2005), 49, 95.

[58] *Altmeppen* NJW 2004, 97, 99; *Altmeppen/Wilhelm* DB 2004, 1083, 1086; *Altmeppen* NJW 2005, 1911, 1913; *Altmeppen* FS Röhricht (2005) p 3, 15 et seq.

[59] *Altmeppen* NJW 2004, 97, 100.

such.[60] The ECJ is even clearer in the Inspire Art decision in which it rules that "minimum capital (both at the time of incorporation and during the company's existence) and the liability of the managing directors" constitute a restriction of the right of establishment guaranteed by Arts 43 and 48 of the EEC Treaty.[61] That body of private international European company law created through the decisions of the ECJ applies therefore not only to the incorporation of the company but also to the entire body of law governing the company.[62]

29 Because the decisions of the ECJ on the right of establishment apply to the entire body of law governing the company, some legal writers argue that the liability provisions of (national) company law would be being "strangled by the right of establishment".[63] The attempt is being made to evade this by deliberately narrowing the law governing the company by transferring creditor protection provisions to tort, or insolvency law (for a detailed discussion on foreign companies in Germany, see mn 72 et seq).[64] This overlooks, however, that the protection afforded by the right of establishment is not norm-related but rather to the effects ensuing from such norm.[65] The question must therefore be asked – independent of which area of the law the norm is classified as – whether insolvency is one of the required elements of the norm, or whether the norm itself serves a direct insolvency-political purpose.[66]

30 If one concludes that a norm does trigger the protection afforded by Arts 43 and 48 of the EEC Treaty, then the first question to be asked is whether an application of the norm is nevertheless **justified**. The ECJ allows a justification in two possible ways:

- First, the application of national creditor-protection law is possible in cases of abuse of the law and fraud/deceit.[67] But such an abuse of law is not found simply because a citizen of a Member State chooses a company law regime that affords him the largest possible degree of freedom but who then sets up a branch establishment in a different Member State.[68] The right to do this is the very manifestation of the right of establishment guaranteed by Arts 43 and 48 of the EEC Treaty. In the result, a justification based on an abuse of the law has a very narrow scope of application.[69] Furthermore, the Member States are disposed of a wide variety of measures to combat fraudulent conduct should it be proven in a given case.[70]

---

[60] ECJ "Überseering" NJW 2002, 3614 mn 80; see also Art 4 of the EIR fn 40.

[61] ECJ "Inspire Art" NJW 2003, 3331 mn 104; see also Art 4 of the EIR fn 36.

[62] *Ulmer* NJW 2004, 1201, 1209; *Fleischer* in Lutter (ed), Europäische Auslandsgesellschaften in Deutschland (2005), 49, 96; *Riegger* ZGR 2004, 510, 524; *Leible* ZGR 2004, 531, 534.

[63] *Fleischer* in Lutter (ed), Europäische Auslandsgesellschaften in Deutschland (2005), 49, 97.

[64] *Paefgen* ZIP 2004, 2253, 2255; *Ulmer* NJW 2004, 1201, 1205; *Schanze/Jüttner* AG 2003, 661, 670.

[65] *Spindler/Berner* RIW 2004, 7, 9; *Fleischer* in Lutter (ed), Europäische Auslandsgesellschaften in Deutschland (2005), 49, 98.

[66] Haß/Huber/Gruber/Heiderhoff-*Haß/Huber* Art 4 EuInsVO mn 11; *Virgós/Schmit* Explanatory report mn 90; D-K/D/Ch-*Duursma-Kepplinger* Art 4 mn 7; *Haas* NZI 2001, 1, 10.

[67] "[...] the national courts are entitled in cases of abuse of the law or fraudulent conduct on the part of the concerned parties, which is ascertained on the basis of objective criteria, to refuse to invoke the relevant Community law [...]"; see ECJ dated 9 Mar 1999 C-212/97 "Centros" NJW 1999, 2027 mn 25; on this, see also: *Fleischer* JZ 2003, 865.

[68] ECJ "Centros" NJW 1999, 2027 mn 27; see also Art 4 of the EIR fn 39.

[69] *Ulmer* NJW 2004, 1201, 1203; *Fleischer* in Lutter (ed), Europäische Auslandsgesellschaften in Deutschland (2005), 49, 101.

[70] ECJ "Centros" NJW 1999, 2027 mn 39; on the theoretical basis, see *Fleischer* JZ 2003, 865, 870; Hirte/Bücker-*Forsthoff* § 2 mn 46–52.

- Secondly, there may be cases in which an application of national law is justified. But being an encroachment on the right of establishment, such an application must be reviewed using the so-called **Gebhard Formula** (four requirements: 1. encroachment in a non-discriminatory manner, 2. justification for mandatory reasons of public interest, 3. appropriateness, and 4. necessity).[71] The protection of creditors is recognized by the ECJ as being a "mandatory reason of public interest".[72] What causes the most problems here is the requirement of necessity.[73] The choice of what, in the opinion of the ECJ, would be the mildest means of providing such protection is the relevant matter here. In the Inspire Art case, the court had to deal with the issue of creditor protection manifested in the form of minimum capital requirements. The court held that the enforcement of such requirements was inconsistent with, and hence an encroachment on, the right of establishment.[74] The ECJ was of the opinion that an **information model** publicizing the company was the mildest means of providing the creditors with protection.[75]

Some legal writers advocate the view that company law is applicable via a special connecting factor.[76] The basic idea is that the law of the forum of incorporation applies in general, but that national company-law provisions could be applied if the application of foreign company law would lead to unacceptable gaps in liability in comparison to the national provisions on creditor protection.[77] This view is being criticized as not complying with the requirements of legal certainty and the binding nature of laws.[78] This especially holds true if the foreign law affords protection to creditors in a manner different to that of national law.[79] Special connecting factors are, therefore, not permissible or only to a **very limited** extent. **31**

Another manifestation of the right of establishment is found in European law itself. This is found primarily in the impact of the directives through which the European Council pursuant to Art 44 (1) of the EEC Treaty is to design the right of establishment.[80] Pursuant to Art 44 (2) (g) of the EEC Treaty, the protection of creditors is also **32**

---

71 ECJ dated 30 Nov 1995 – C-55/94 "Gebhard" NJW 1996, 579; ECJ "Centros" NJW 1999, 2027 mn 34; ECJ "Inspire Art" NJW 2003, 3331 mn 133; see also *Leible/Hoffmann* EuZW 2003, 677, 682; for a detailed description of the justification, cf Hirte/Bücker-*Forsthoff* § 2 mn 53–84.

72 ECJ "Inspire Art" NJW 2003, 3331 mn 135, cf Art 4 of the EIR fn 36; ECJ "Überseering" NJW 2002, 3614 mn 92, cf Art 4 of the EIR fn 40; ECJ "Centros" NJW 1999, 2027 mn 35, cf Art 4 of the EIR fn 39.

73 In-depth on this *Fleischer* in Lutter (ed), Europäische Auslandsgesellschaften in Deutschland (2005), 49, 103.

74 ECJ "Inspire Art" NJW 2003, 3331 mn 141, see also Art 4 of the EIR fn 36.

75 ECJ dated 30 Sep 2003 – C-167/01 "Inspire Art" NJW 2003, 3331 mn 135 with reference to ECJ "Centros" dated 9 Mar 1999 – C-212/97 NJW 1999, 2027 mn 36.

76 *Altmeppen* NJW 2004, 97, 102; *Altmeppen* NJW 2005, 1911, 1913; *Altmeppen/Wilhelm* DB 2004 1083, 1088 et seq; *Forsthoff* DB 2002, 2471, 2477; *Eidenmüller* ZIP 2002, 2233, 2242; *Eidenmüller* JZ 2004, 24, 28; *Sandrock* ZVglRWiss 102 (2003), 447, 458.

77 *Schulz* NJW 2003, 2705, 2707; *Eidenmüller* JZ 2004, 24, 28; *Behrens* IPRax 2004, 20, 25; *Bayer* BB 2003, 2357, 2364; *Riegger* ZGR 2004 510, 524; *Sandrock* ZVglRWiss 102 (2003), 447, 473.

78 *Kleinert* DB 2003, 2217, 2218; *Wachter* GmbHR 2003, 1254; *Paefgen* ZIP 2004, 2253, 2258; *Horn* NJW 2004, 893, 894; also *Ebert/Levedag* GmbHR 2003, 1337; *Geyrhalter/Gänßler* DStR 2003, 2167, 2171; *Kleinert/Probst* DB 2003, 2217, 2218; *Borges* ZIP 2004, 733, 743.

79 *Sandrock* BB 2004, 897, 898; *Schulz* NJW 2003, 2705, 2707.

80 For an in-depth discussion on this, see: *Schön* ZHR 168 (2004), 268, 293–296 who describes this way as the "self-healing powers of European Community law"; critical: *Fleischer* in Lutter (ed), Europäische Auslandsgesellschaften in Deutschland (2005), 49, 109 et seq.

supposed to be one of the aims of this provision. But whether it really is possible to build "a grand construction of Community-wide creditor protection out of fragments and legal splinters of policy guidelines" [81] is very doubtful and should be rejected for reasons of practicality. The last way that European law influences the right of establishment is through Council Regulation (EC) No 1346/2000 itself, which therefore clarifies the fundamental question as to what is to be understood by insolvency law pursuant to Art 4 of the EIR. This must be reviewed in the individual case in accordance with the principles set out above (see mn 15 et seq above).

ccc) The most important types of European companies with limited liability and the elements of the liability associated with them

33 Considering that a disparity may arise between the law governing the company and governing the insolvency, the most important forms of European companies are being outlined briefly below.

34 The information for the following overview was taken *inter alia* from: *Mellert/Verfürth* Wettbewerb der Gesellschaftsformen, Chapter 2 (2005); *Hirte/Bücker* Grenzüberschreitende Gesellschaften, Sec 4–Sec 10 (2006).

Company Form	Incorporation	Liability for Acts of Executive Officers	Shareholder's Liability
		Germany	
GmbH (Gesellschaft mit beschränkter Haftung)	• Articles of association signed and recorded by a notary • Registration in the commercial register • Minimum share capital € 25.000 • Duration: approx. 2 to 6 weeks • Costs: approx. € 300	Managing Directors • Breaching the duty of care of a prudent and conscientious manager (Sec 43 (2) GmbHG) • Delayed filing for insolvency (Sec 64 GmbHG)	Basically limited liability Exceptions: • Piercing the corporate veil (abuse of the law, commingling of private and company assets) • Subsistence-destroying acts • Equity-replacing shareholder loans
AG (Aktiengesellschaft)	• Articles of association signed and recorded by a notary	Management Board • Breaching the duty of care of a prudent and con-	Basically limited liability Exceptions:

[81] *Fleischer* in Lutter (ed), Europäische Auslandsgesellschaften in Deutschland (2005), 49, 109.

	• Registration in the commercial register • Minimum share capital € 50.000 • Duration: approx. 2 to 6 weeks • Costs: approx. € 500	scientious manager (Sec 93 (2) AktG) • Delayed filing for insolvency (Sec 92 AktG) Supervisory Board • For breaches of duties of care, the same provisions apply as for the management board (Secs 116, 93 AktG)	• Piercing the corporate veil (abuse of the law, commingling of private and company assets) • Subsistence-destroying acts • Equity-replacing shareholder loans

Company Form	**Incorporation**	**Liability for Acts of Executive Officers**	**Shareholder's Liability**
		Great Britain	
Ltd. (Private Company Limited by Shares)	• Memorandum and articles of association • Written form without notarized recording • Registration in the commercial register • No minimum share capital • Duration: approx. 8 days • Costs: approx. € 30	Directors • Liability for breaching certain duties owed to the company • Liability for *ultra vires* acts • Liability for fraudulent or wrongful trading • Liability for tortious acts and unlawful dividend distributions Secretary • Liability for breaches of obligations	Basically limited liability (Salomon doctrine) Exceptions: • Piercing the corporate veil • Shadow directors
PLC (Public Company Limited by Shares)	• Memorandum and articles of association	Directors • Liability for breaching certain	Basically limited liability (Salomon doctrine)

	• Written form without notarized recording • Minimum of 2 incorporators • Registration in the commercial register • Minimum share capital: approx. € 75.000 • Duration: approx. 2 weeks • Costs: approx. € 75	duties owed to the company • Liability for *ultra vires* acts • Liability for fraudulent or wrongful trading • Liability for tortious acts and unlawful dividend distributions Secretary • Liability for breaches of obligations	Exceptions: • Piercing the corporate veil • Shadow directors

Company Form	Incorporation	Liability for Acts of Executive Officers	Shareholder's Liability
		France	
SARL (Société à responsabilité limitée)	• Company charter (in written form signed by hand) • Registration in the commercial register • No minimum share capital • Duration: approx. 2 weeks • Costs: approx. € 210	Management • Liability for infringements of statutory provisions and the company's charter • Liability for incorrect management • Liability for disregarding the company's interests • Liability for irretrievable debts caused by management error that	Basically limited liability Exceptions: • If a shareholder acts as a managing director and in breach of duty (*gérance de fait*, Art L 652-1) • Based on façade company (*fictivité*) or commingling of private and company assets (*confusion de patrimoines*, Art L 621-2)

		leads to insolvency (*action en comblement du passif*; Art L 651-2 Code de commerce)	
SA (Société anonyme)	• Company charter (in written form signed by hand) • Minimum of 7 incorporators • Registration in the commercial register • Minimum share capital: For a public SA: € 225.000 For a normal SA: € 37.000 • Duration: approx. 2 weeks • Costs: approx. € 290	Management Board and Administrative Board • Liability for infringements of statutory provisions and the company's charter • Liability for incorrect management • Liability for disregarding the company's interests • Liability for irretrievable debts caused bymanagement error that leads to insolvency (*action en comblement du passif*; Art L 651-2) Supervisory Board • Liability for own breaches of duties	Basically limited liability Exceptions: • If a shareholder acts as a managing director and in breach of duty (*gérance de fait*, Art L 652-1) • Based on façade company (*fictivité*) or commingling of private and company assets (*confusion de patrimoines*, Art L 621-2)
SAS (Société par actions simplifiée)	• Company charter (in written form signed by hand) • Registration in the commercial register • Minimum share capital € 37.000	Depends on the structure of the SAS (whether an administrative board exists or not) – see the information on the SARL or the SA	Basically limited liability Exceptions: • If a shareholder acts as a managing director and in breach of duty (*gérance de fait*, Art L 652-1)

	• Duration: approx. 2 weeks • Costs: approx. € 290		• Based on façade company (*fictivité*) or commingling of private and company assets (*confusion de patrimoines*, Art L 621-2)

Company Form	Incorporation	Liability for Acts of Executive Officers	Shareholder's Liability
		The Netherlands	
BV (Besloten vennootschap met beperkte aansprakelijkheid)	• Draft of the company charter: Issuance of a clearance certificate from the Ministry of Justice • Notarized act of incorporation • Registration in the commercial register • Minimum share capital: € 18.000 • Duration: approx. 2 to 10 weeks • Costs: approx. € 1.000 to 1.550	Management and Supervisory Board • Liability for improper fulfilment of obligations • Tort liability on the part of the managing directors for tortious acts • In the event of insolvency, liability may be imposed on the managing director for company's inability to pay its debts if the managing director has seriously breached his duties in the three years prior to the opening of insolvency and there is some probability that this caused the insolvency • Liability for delayed filing for insolvency	Basically limited liability Exceptions: • Those persons who acted on behalf of the company prior to registration are liable to third parties for damages if the company is not able to fulfil these obligations and such persons knew this or should have known it • Liability for prohibited profit distributions

		• Liability for misrepresentation of the company's situation in the annual financial statements	
NV (Naamloze vennootschap)	• Draft of the company charter: Issuance of a clearance certificate from the Ministry of Justice • Notarized act of incorporation • Registration in the commercial register • Minimum share capital: € 40.000 • Duration: approx. 2 to 10 weeks • Costs: approx. € 1.000 to 1.550	Management and Supervisory Board • Liability for improper fulfilment of obligations • Tort liability on the part of the managing directors for tortious acts • In the event of insolvency, liability may be imposed on the managing director for company's inability to pay its debts if the managing director has seriously breached his duties in the three years prior to the opening of insolvency and there is some this probability that caused the insolvency • Liability for delayed filing for insolvency • Liability for misrepresentation of the company's situation in the annual financial statements	Basically limited liability Exceptions: • Those persons who acted on behalf of the company prior to registration are liable to third parties for damages if the company is not able to fulfil these obligations and such persons knew this or should have known it • Liability for prohibited profit distributions

Company Form	Incorporation	Liability for Acts of Executive Officers	Shareholder's Liability
Luxembourg			
S.à.r.l. (société à responsabilité limitée)	• Company charter recorded by a notary • Minimum registered capital: approx. € 12.400 • Duration: approx. 4 weeks • Costs: € 400 plus fiscal charges of 0.5 % of the share capital	Managing Directors • Liability for breach of company law or the company's charter • Extending the insolvency to the managing directors if the company was used as a shield • Liability for irretrievable debts caused by management errors that leads to insolvency (*action en comblement du passif*)	Basically limited liability Exceptions: • Piercing the corporate veil in respect of shareholders who have acted like an administrator and in breach of duty (*administrateur de fait*)
S.A. (société anonyme)	• Incorporation by notarized recording • Minimum registered capital: approx. € 30.986.69 • Deposit of the company charter in the commercial registry • Costs: minimum € 1.509,87 (depends on amount of paid-in capital)	Administrative Board • Liability for breach of company law or the company's charter • Extending the insolvency to the managing directors if the company was used as a shield • Liability for irretrievable debts caused by management errors that lead to insolvency (*action en comblement du passif*)	Basically limited liability Exceptions: • Piercing the corporate veil in respect of shareholders who have acted like an administrator and in breach of duty (*administrateur de fait*)

Company Form	Incorporation	Liability for Acts of Executive Officers	Shareholder's Liability
		Spain	
S.R.L. (Sociedad de responsabilidad limitada)	• Notarized recording of company charter • Registration in the commercial register • Minimum share capital: € 3.005,06 • Duration: several days • Costs depend on the amount of the share capital	Administrator • Liability for at least negligent breaches of the duty of care • Liability for violations of law or the company's charter • Liability for reducing share capital below the statutory minimum	Basically limited liability
S.A. (Sociedad anónima)	• Notarized recording of company charter • Registration in the commercial register • Minimum share capital: € 60.101,21 • Costs depend on the amount of the share capital	Administrator • Liability for each act of negligence in fulfilling statutory obligations and those found in the company's charter	Basically limited liability

Company Form	Incorporation	Liability for Acts of Executive Officers	Shareholder's Liability
European Company Forms			
SE (European Public Limited Company)	• Formation via a merger or by converting an existing public limited company into an SE; forming a holding SE or a subsidiary SE • Minimum share capital: € 120.000	• Liability for the acts of executive officers for breaches of duty is determined for both dual-tiered and single-tiered SEs by the law of the Member State of registration	Basically limited liability

c) **Restrictions to the law governing the insolvency (Arts 5 to 15 of the EIR)**

35 The law that governs the insolvency pursuant to Art 4 of the EIR applies only to the extent not otherwise determined by the Regulation. Arts 5 to 15 of the EIR contain **restrictions** that, although they concern the effects of the insolvency proceedings, are treated in a special way due to their proximity to specific areas of substantive law, and because the application of foreign law to these matters would result in serious complications and to impracticable results.[82] In derogation from Art 4 of the EIR, specific areas of national law continue to apply in the cases set out in Arts 5 to 15 of the EIR.

III. The Catalogue of Examples in Art 4 (2) of the EIR

36 Art 4 (2) of the EIR contains **examples of the rule**. It is a non-exhaustive list of matters to which the law of the State in which the proceedings are opened (*lex fori concursus*) applies.[83] The *lex fori concursus* regulates the conditions under which insolvency proceedings may be opened, their conduct, and their closure.

37 Falling within the conditions for **opening insolvency proceedings** are such things as:

- the reasons for opening,
- entitlement to make the request,
- insolvency capacity,
- the required number of creditors, or
- the minimum debt amount.[84]

---

[82] See *Virgós/Schmit* Explanatory Report, mn 92; on the particular relevance for banks of the protection of rights *in rem* from the dangers of the debtor's insolvency and from encroachments by third parties that is anchored in art 5 of the EIR, see Moss/Fletcher/Isaacs-*Fletcher*, Regulation, 35 et seq; also: *Virgós/Schmit* Explanatory Report, mn 97.

[83] *Lehr* KTS 2000, 579.

[84] *Paulus* Komm EuInsVO Art 4 mn 9.

The **selection** and the **appointment** of the liquidator of the main and secondary insolvency proceedings are determined pursuant to the law of the opening State.[85]

The question is whether not only the **right to request** but also the **duty to request** (e.g. Sec 64 of the *GmbHG*) also falls within scope of application of Art 4 of the EIR; on this, see mn 81 et seq. **38**

The **conducting** and the **closure of the insolvency proceedings** also encompasses: **39**

- the social compensation plan proceedings,
- the conducting of the creditors' meetings, or
- the implementation of the debt adjustment plan.[86]

1. Insolvency Capacity (Art 4 (2) sentence 2 (a) of the EIR)

Insolvency capacity must be ascertained pursuant to the law of the opening State. Thus the *lex fori concursus* applies.[87] The issue of insolvency capacity may be regulated differently in the individual Member States. In some Member States, for example, insolvency proceedings may not be opened against public law corporations, and in other States insolvency proceedings may not be opened against natural persons who are not businesspersons,[88] → see the Overview of Insolvency Capacity, Art 3 of the EIR, mn 14. **40**

Therefore – assuming there is international jurisdiction pursuant to Art 3 of the EIR – insolvency proceedings may be opened in a Member State against the assets of a debtor who lacks insolvency capacity in another Member State.[89] The other Member States must recognize the foreign insolvency proceedings.[90] If main insolvency proceedings at the place where the COMI (see Art 3 of the EIR, mn 15 et seq) is located cannot be opened because the debtor lacks insolvency capacity, then independent territorial insolvency proceedings may, as an exception, be opened in another Member State (Art 3 (4) of the EIR).[91] This is conditioned on the debtor having an "establishment" (see Art 2 of the EIR, mn 45 et seq) (Art 3 (2) sentence 1 of the EIR) in this State and on the debtor having insolvency capacity according to the insolvency law of the State in which the independent territorial insolvency proceedings are opened. **41**

Insolvency capacity is determined in Germany pursuant to Sec 11 et seq *InsO* (an Overview of Insolvency Capacity in the various Member States is listed in Art 3 of the EIR mn 14). Since the Inspire Art decision of the ECJ (see above at mn 22), **English limited liability companies** also have insolvency capacity in Germany.[92] **42**

---

85 *Vallender* KTS 2005, 283, 310.

86 *Paulus* Komm EuInsVO Art 4 mn 13.

87 Gottwald/*Gottwald* InsR-Handb (2006), § 130 mn 21.

88 This is the case in France, Greece, Italy, Luxembourg, Portugal, and Spain. Pursuant to art 2083 *Codice Civile,* insolvency proceedings may not be opened in Italy against the assets of a small businessperson (*piccolo imprenditori*) (see Art 3 of the EIR mn 14).

89 *Paulus* Komm EuInsVO Art 4 mn 4; Gottwald/*Gottwald* InsR-Handb (2006), § 130 mn 21.

90 Cf Art 16 (1) of the EIR.

91 *Virgós/Schmit* Explanatory report mn 91 in connexion with mn 85 und 148.

92 See for instance AG Saarbrücken dated 25 Feb 2005, ZInsO 2005, 727 (→ cf Table of Cases Art 3 of the EIR Appendix B No 69); AG Hamburg dated 14 May 2003, ZIP 2003, 1008 = IPRax 2003, 534 = BB 2003, 1457 = NZG 2003, 732 = NJW 2003, 2835 = NZI 2003, 442 with explanatory note by *Mock/Schildt* NZI 2003, 444 (→ cf Table of Cases Art 3 of the EIR Appendix A mn 18).

2. Assets Eligible For Inclusion in the Insolvency Estate (Art 4 (2) sentence 2 (b) of the EIR)

43 According to Art 4 (2) sentence 2 (b) of the EIR, the *lex fori concursus* also determines which assets belong to the insolvency estate.[93]

44 **In dispute**[94] is whether the *lex fori concursus* also determines whether **assets** that are **exempt from execution pursuant to the law of their *situs*** are to be included in the insolvency estate. Some[95] argue that the *lex situs* should override. This approach is not commendable, however, because the drafters of the Regulation expressly included all exceptions to an application of it in Arts 5 to 15 of the EIR.[96] The result of this is that property may be included in the insolvency estate that is actually exempt from execution pursuant to the respective national laws (e.g. in Germany pursuant to Sec 811 *ZPO*, Sec 36 *InsO*).[97] Thus the principle of universality overrides, in this respect, the protection from execution afforded the debtor by national law. The issue of the **non/executionability** of certain assets is determined according to the *lex fori concursus*.[98]

45 The applicable *lex fori concursus* determines whether after the opening of the insolvency proceedings acquired objects (**new acquisitions**) are to be included in the insolvency estate, although the special connecting factors found in Arts 5 and 7 of the EIR could apply.[99] In German law, new acquisitions are included in the insolvency estate. In the case of main insolvency proceedings in Germany, property that was acquired in another Member State could thus be included in the insolvency estate.[100]

46 It must be kept in mind that when both main and secondary insolvency proceedings have been opened, a different decision may be reached in each proceeding on which assets of the same debtor belong to the insolvency estate. This is because a different *lex fori concursus* governs each proceeding.[101] For this reason, Art 12 of the EIR contains a uniform rule in the case of **community patents and trade marks** that such property can never be included in the estate of the secondary insolvency proceedings but must always be allocated to the estate of the main proceedings.

3. Powers of the Debtor and the Liquidator (Art 4 (2) sentence 2 (c) of the EIR)

47 According to Art 4 (2) sentence 2 (c) of the EIR, the powers – and the duties – of the **liquidator** –[102] are determined pursuant to the *lex fori concursus*.

48 Art 18 (3) of the EIR also stipulates that the liquidator must comply with the **law of the Member State** within the territory of which he intends to take action, in particular with regard to procedures for the realisation of assets. Where a temporary administrator has been appointed, Art 38 of the EIR also provides that this person, in order to ensure the preservation of the debtor's assets, is empowered to request any measures to secure

---

[93] Whether assets form part of the insolvency estate is determined in Germany by whether – pursuant to sec 36 InsO in conjunction with sec 811, 850 et seq ZPO – they can be liquidated in regular (individual) execution proceedings.

[94] On this *Paulus* Komm EuInsVO Art 4 mn 19; MünchKomm BGB/*Kindler* IntInsR mn 216.

[95] *Haas* FS Gerhardt (2004) p 319, 323 et seq infers from Art 18 (3) of the EIR that the *lex rei sitae* is decisive.

[96] MünchKomm BGB/*Kindler* IntInsR mn 216.

[97] *Gottwald/Pfaller* IPRax 1998, 174; *Paulus* Komm EuInsVO Art 4 mn 19.

[98] *Paulus* Komm EuInsVO Art 4 mn 19.

[99] MünchKomm BGB/*Kindler* IntInsR mn 217.

[100] *Paulus* Komm EuInsVO Art 4 mn 18.

[101] *Gottwald/Pfaller* IPRax 1998, 174; MünchKomm BGB/*Kindler* IntInsR mn 216.

[102] *Paulus* Komm EuInsVO Art 4 mn 21.

and preserve any of the debtor's assets situated in another Member State provided for under the law of that State.

The validity of legal acts made by the **debtor** and his general powers in the insolvency proceedings are governed by the *lex fori concursus*. Acts carried out by the debtor after the opening of the proceedings are generally invalid pursuant to the laws of most legal systems. Art 14 of the EIR protects the rights of third-party purchasers in the acquisition of immovable property and certain legal transactions whose registration is mandatory. For the protection of the purchaser in such cases, the *lex fori concursus* is superseded by the law of the State in which the immovable asset is situated (*lex rei sitae*) or the State under whose authority the register is kept. **49**

4. Set-off (Art 4 (2) sentence 2 (d) of the EIR)

Art 4 (2) sentence 2 (d) of the EIR provides that the conditions under which **set-offs** are valid are determined by the *lex fori concursus*. **50**

In dispute is whether this also means the **substantive law conditions** for a set-off or only the **procedural admissibility** of the set-off in the insolvency proceedings. Some argue that the wording of the provision "conditions under which set-offs may be invoked" does not allow the inference that only procedural admissibility is meant here.[103] In their opinion, it is clear that the Regulation did not wish to differentiate between substantive and procedural law. Accordingly, both the conditions for and the effects of a set-off would be subject to the law of the State in which the proceedings were opened. Others are of the opinion that the provision only deals with the procedural admissibility in the insolvency proceedings, and the substantive-law effects are to be assessed pursuant to general conflicts of laws rules.[104] They argue that based on the wording of the provision – which provides in Art 4 (1) of the EIR that the *lex fori concursus* applies to the insolvency proceedings and [their] effects and then sets this out in concrete terms in subpara 2 where it states that the law of the opening State determines the conditions for the opening of those proceedings, their conduct and their closure and, in particular, the conditions under which a set-off may be invoked – Art 4 (2) sentence 2 (d) of the EIR must be interpreted restrictively to mean the effects of the opening of the insolvency proceedings only and thus the restriction in terms of its procedural admissibility in the insolvency proceedings.[105] This can also be supported by a systematic argument: Art 6 of the EIR restricts the scope of applicability of the law governing the insolvency. If a set-off is not permitted by the law of a particular Member State, then the law that applies to the principal claim pursuant to general conflict of laws rules (Art 32 (1) No 4 *EGBGB*, Art 10 (1) (d) of the Rome Convention 1980) has priority over the law governing the insolvency. The Regulation must therefore be presuming that the creation of the (civil law) right of set-off was already established pursuant to the law governing the principal claim.[106] Furthermore, it would not seem appropriate to grant the creditor a right of set-off via **51**

[103] So in particular *Gottwald* Grenzüberschreitende Insolvenzen (1997), 36; *Leible/Staudinger* KTS 2000, 533, 555; *Taupitz* ZZP (11) 1998, 315, 343 et seq; *Eidenmüller* IPRax 2001, 2, 6; D-K/D/Ch-*Duursma-Kepplinger* Art 4 mn 16; *Huber* EuZW 2002, 490, 493 et seq; *Huber* ZZP 114 (2001) 133, 161.

[104] So *Bork* ZIP 2002, 690, 692 et seq; *Ehricke/Ries* JuS 2003, 313, 316; MünchKomm InsO/*Reinhart* Art 4 EuInsVO mn 6; Haß/Huber/Gruber/Heiderhoff-*Haß/Herweg* Art 4 EuInsVO mn 32.

[105] Also *Bork* ZIP 2002, 690, 692; *Ehricke/Ries* JuS 2003, 313, 316.

[106] On this, see also *Bork* ZIP 2002, 690, 692.

the *lex fori concursus* that he would not have been entitled to pursuant to general conflict of laws rules. This would create an unjustifiable privilege on the part of the creditor.

52 Both in terms of its wording and the logic underlying the Regulation, Art 4 (2) sentence 2 (d) of the EIR only applies to the **procedural-law insolvency effects** of a set-off, whereas the **substantive-law conditions** for a set-off are determined, on the other hand, in accordance with general conflict of laws rules.

53 Art 6 (2) of the EIR makes it clear that, in spite of a permissible set off, an act detrimental to the creditors can be avoided. Art 6 (2) of the EIR therefore expressly refers to Art 4 (2) sentence (m) of the EIR.

5. Effects of the Insolvency Proceedings on Current Contracts (Art 4 (2) sentence 2 (e) of the EIR)

54 Art 4 (2) sentence 2 (e) of the EIR determines the fate of current contracts, i.e. that they are subject to the *lex fori concursus* and not the *lex contractus* with its own respective insolvency law rules.[107] This includes in particular the rights of the liquidator and the contractual partners of the debtor to prematurely terminate the contractual relationship.[108]

55 Arts 7 (1), 8, and 10 of the EIR contain **exceptions** to the applicability of the *lex fori concursus* for contracts in which a **reservation of title** has been agreed (Art 7 (1) of the EIR), in contracts for **immoveable property** (Art 8 of the EIR), and for **contracts of employment** (Art 10 of the EIR). The use of the word "solely" makes clear that only national contract law applies in each case, including national insolvency laws.[109] The purpose of this provision is to avoid conflicts between the laws of the opening State and the provisions of the *lex contractus*, thereby safeguarding the interests of the creditors.[110] The need to ensure reliance on national laws also applies with respect to relationships with non-EU countries, only in this case the particular (private international) conflict of laws rules of the country in which the contract was entered into are to be invoked.[111]

6. Effects of the Opening of Insolvency Proceedings on Proceedings Brought by Individual Creditors (Art 4 (2) sentence 2 (f) of the EIR)

56 The law governing the insolvency determines how the opening of insolvency proceedings affects procedures brought by individual creditors (Art 4 (2) sentence 2 (f) of the EIR). Excepted from this are pending lawsuits. Art 15 of the EIR provides that the effects of insolvency proceedings on such pending lawsuits is governed solely by the law of the State in whose courts the lawsuit is pending (*lex fori processus*).[112] The generic nature of the term used in the German version – *Rechtsverfolgungsmaßnahme* – must be interpreted broadly and includes provisional remedies in particular.[113]

---

[107] On this, see also *Virgós/Garcimartín* Regulation, p 122.

[108] Gottwald/*Gottwald* InsR-Handb (2006), § 131 mn 43; D-K/D/Ch-*Duursma-Kepplinger* Art 4 mn 18.

[109] *Virgós/Garcimartín* Regulation, p 123.

[110] *Virgós/Garcimartín* Regulation, p 124.

[111] *Fletcher* Insolvency in Private International Law (2005), p 277; *Virgós/Garcimartín* Regulation, p 124.

[112] MünchKomm InsO/*Reinhart* Art 4 EuInsVO mn 4.

[113] D-K/D/Ch-*Duursma-Kepplinger* Art 4 mn 19.

7. Insolvency Claims and Insolvency-Estate Liabilities (Art 4 (2) sentence 2 (g) of the EIR)

According to Art 4 (2) sentence 2 (g) of the EIR, the *lex fori concursus* governs which claims are to be lodged against the debtor's estate and how claims arising after the opening of the insolvency proceedings are to be treated. For the creditors, the latter determines what effect the opening of insolvency proceedings has on the value of a particular claim.[114] **57**

The *lex fori concursus* also regulates the treatment of **post-adjudication claims against the insolvency estate.** **58**

8. Lodging, Verification and Admission of Claims (Art 4 (2) sentence 2 (h) of the EIR)

The *lex fori concursus* applies in general to the **lodging, verification**, and **admission** of claims against the insolvency estate (Art 4 (2) sentence 2 (h) of the EIR). Arts 32 and 39 to 42 of the EIR contain uniform, substantive-law conditions for the exercising of creditors' rights and for the lodging of claims (see the various discussions on these). But whether there is a claim at all against the insolvency estate is determined, on the other hand, according to the law applicable pursuant to general conflict of laws rules (*lex causae*).[115] **59**

9. Distribution of Proceeds, Ranking of Claims (Art 4 (2) sentence 2 (i) of the EIR)

The law of the State in which proceedings are opened determines both the distribution of proceeds and the ranking of the creditors' claims amongst each other (Art 4 (2) sentence 2 (i) of the EIR).[116] The substantive-law legitimization for a particular ranking is determined, in turn, in accordance with the law that applies pursuant to general conflicts of law rules. **60**

If both secondary and main insolvency proceedings have been opened, an identical claim may be ranked differently pursuant to the laws governing the different proceedings.[117] This conflict can only be resolved through an intense and well-coordinated communication and cooperation between the liquidators of the various proceedings, as it is contemplated by Art 31 of the EIR; see also Art 31 of the EIR mn 6 et seq. **61**

A disparity between the law governing the secondary and the main insolvency proceedings may be an incentive to the employees to request the opening of secondary insolvency proceedings. Such secondary insolvency proceedings would provide a framework for dealing with employee claims since such claims could then be dealt with pursuant to the law of the Member State in which these proceedings were opened (Art 28 of the EIR).[118] This often puts the employees in a better position. **62**

---

114 Cf Moss/Fletcher/Isaacs-*Toube/Segal/Marshall*, Regulation, mn 6.24.

115 *Israël* European Cross-Border Insolvency Regulation (2005) 275.

116 Cf *Israël* European Cross-Border Insolvency Regulation (2005) 276; Moss/Fletcher/Isaacs-*Toube/Segal/Marshall*, Regulation, mn 6.26.

117 Cf *Virgós/Garcimartín* Regulation, p 80.

118 This was discussed by Judge *Norris* in the MG Rover decision of the High Court of Justice in Birmingham in an order dated 11 May 2005 – 2375 to 2382/05, NZI 2205, 515 et seq (with comments by *Penzlin/Riedemann*). → see Table of Cases Art 3 of the EIR Appendix A mn 16.

10. Closing the Insolvency Proceedings (Art 4 (2) sentence 2 (j) of the EIR)

63 Supplementary to subs 1, Art 4 (2) sentence 2 (j) of the EIR stipulates that the closing of proceedings, for example through a discharge of residual debt or an insolvency plan,[119] is also governed by the *lex fori concursus*.[120]

64 With respect to the territorial effects of a discharge of residual debt, Art 17 (2) sentence 2 of the EIR restricts in effect the applicability of the law governing the insolvency.

11. Creditors' Rights After Closure of Insolvency Proceedings (Art 4 (2) sentence 2 (k) of the EIR)

65 According to Art 4 (2) sentence 2 (k) of the EIR, the rights of the creditors after the closure of the proceedings is governed by the *lex fori concursus*. This primarily concerns the issue of a **discharge of residual debt** in favour of the debtor after the closure of the proceedings.[121]

12. Costs of the Insolvency Proceedings (Art 4 (2) sentence 2 (l) of the EIR)

66 According to Art 4 (2) sentence 2 (l) of the EIR, the law of the State in which proceedings are opened determines which party is to bear the **costs and the expenses of the insolvency proceedings.**

67 Discrepancies could arise here depending on whether the law of the State in which main proceedings were opened or that in which the territorial insolvency proceedings were opened is decisive. Restrictions could also arise from Art 5 of the EIR. Should the law of the opening State demand procedural costs for secured creditors that exceed the costs demanded by the State in which the secured property is situated, then the higher costs could not be demanded as this would constitute an encroachment on the intrinsic value of the security.[122]

13. Legal Acts Detrimental to the Creditors (Art 4 (2) sentence 2 (m) of the EIR)

68 According to Art 4 (2) sentence 2 (m) of the EIR, the *lex fori concursus* determines which legal acts that are detrimental to the creditors are void, voidable, or unenforceable. This concerns both the requirements for establishing voidness or for voidability, and the effects of such.[123]

69 The scope of Art 4 (2) sentence 2 (m) of the EIR is restricted by Art 13, which provides that the *lex fori concursus* does not apply if the person who benefits from the act detrimental to the creditors can prove that the act itself is subject to the law of a Member State other than that of the State of the opening of proceedings and that this law does not allow any means whatsoever of challenging that act.[124] The use of the phrase

---

[119] *Paulus* Komm EuInsVO Art 4 mn 33.

[120] The concept of "closure of insolvency proceedings" is therefore to be understood in a broad sense; all measures ending the proceedings that are contemplated by the law must be considered, see also *Virgós/Garcimartín* Regulation, p 83 et seq.

[121] D-K/D/Ch-*Duursma-Kepplinger* Art 4 mn 26; *Virgós/Schmit* Explanatory report mn 91; *Paulus* Komm EuInsVO Art 4 mn 34.

[122] On this cf MünchKomm InsO/*Reinhart* Art 4 EuInsVO mn 15; Haß/Huber/Gruber/Heiderhoff-*Haß/Huber* Art 4 EuInsVO mn 45.

[123] D-K/D/Ch-*Duursma-Kepplinger* Art 4 mn 28.

[124] But this does not result in a change of governing law. Art 13 of the EIR (law governing the effects = *lex causae*) simply serves to set aside the application of the *lex fori concursus* in the given case; on this, see the Expla-

"does not allow any means" makes it clear that it is not enough that the legal act simply be inviolable pursuant to the avoidance provisions of the *lex causae*, but such things as a lack of intention and immorality must also not be present.[125] The benefiting party should be able to rely on the fact that a legal act, which is valid and indefeasible pursuant to the law normally applicable, will not be interfered with through the provisions of a foreign *lex fori concursus*. What is involved here is a defence that must be raised by the benefiting party (party disputing the avoidance). This party also has the burden of submitting and proving all of the facts and circumstances.[126]

After insolvency proceedings have been opened, the creditor's reliance on the validity of his legal transactions pursuant to the *lex causae* does not warrant protection. Consequently, Art 13 of the EIR does not apply to dispositions that have taken place after the opening of the proceedings.[127] **70**

If both main and territorial insolvency proceedings are being conducted at the same time, the ascertainment of the applicable law must be based on whether the insolvency estate of the main or that of the territorial insolvency proceedings is being diminished through the act detrimental to the creditors.[128] **71**

IV. Classification of the Legal Elements of Liability in the Case of Pseudo Foreign Corporations using the German *GmbHG* as an Example / Law Governing the Company vs the Law Governing the Insolvency

The insolvency of a foreign company in Germany raises the question of whether German creditor protection law should apply to the foreign company operating in Germany.[129] Whether German creditor protection law will apply depends on the particular conflict of laws rule. And which conflict of laws rule applies depends on how the applicable legal norm is being classified, i.e. as **insolvency law, substantive law**, or **company law**;[130] see mn 15 et seq above. **72**

By a classification as **insolvency law**, the relevant conflict of laws rule is Art 4 of the EIR with its reference to the *lex fori concursus*. **73**

By a classification as substantive law (e.g. tort law), the general conflict of laws rule found in Art 40 *EGBGB* applies in Germany, which results in the application of national law. **74**

Only if the legal norm is classified as **company law** must such a norm be tested against the ECJ decisions dealing with the right of establishment, and an application of **75**

natory Report, mn 136; *Huber* ZZP 114 (2001) 165; also: Moss/Fletcher/Isaacs-*Fletcher*, Regulation, mn 4.08. The latter consider it possible to take the law governing the claim into consideration in the *lex fori concursus*; see Moss/Fletcher/Isaacs-*Fletcher*, Regulation, mn 4.09.

125 *Virgós/Schmit* Explanatory report mn 137; *Habscheid* ZZP (114) 2001, 167, 176.

126 *Virgós/Schmit* Explanatory report mn 136; *Leible/Staudinger* KTS 2000, 533, 556; Gottwald/*Gottwald* InsR-Handb (2006), § 131 mn 76.

127 *Virgós/Schmit* Explanatory report mn 138.

128 *Virgós/Schmit* Explanatory report mn 91; on this, see also D-K/D/Ch-*Duursma-Kepplinger* Art 4 mn 28.

129 On the criminal liability of the executive officers of a pseudo foreign corporation for delayed filing for insolvency using the English limited liability company in Germany as an example, see *Gross/Schork* NZI 2006, 10; *Rönnau* ZGR 2005, 832.

130 According to *Kindler*, a legal norm can be classified in several different ways and can then be applied within the framework of "multiple connecting factors", see *Kindler* NZG 2003, 1086, 1090.

such a norm to European foreign companies can only be made if this is justified in light of the right of establishment.

76 The issue of how to classify some of the various legal elements constituting liability is the subject of heated dispute, and a final decision on it has not yet been reached by the highest court. The problem is being discussed in Germany primarily in connection with the English Private Company Limited by Shares.[131]

77 The following table illustrates the various opinions currently being propounded in German legal literature; a detailed discussion on this is found at mn 78 to 102.

	Company Law	**Insolvency Law**	**Tort Law**
Provision of Capital	Not applicable: ECJ "Inspire Art" NJW 2003, 3331 mn 104, 141.		
Preservation of Capital	Not applicable: *Mellert/Verfürth* Wettbewerb der Gesellschaftsformen (2005), 248; *Paefgen* DB 2003, 487, 490; *Ulmer* NJW 2004, 1201, 1208; *Schumann* DB 2004, 743, 744 et seq; *Bayer* BB 2003, 2357, 2364; *Röhricht* ZIP 2005, 505, 511; *Wachter* GmbHR 2004, 88, 91; Eidenmüller ZGR 2004, 159, 181; *Fischer* ZIP 2004, 1477, 1479; *Geyrhalter/Gänßler* DStR 2003, 2167, 2170; *Holzer* ZVI 2005, 457, 468; *Kindler* NJW 2003, 1073, 1079; *Lieder* DZWiR 2005, 399, 407; *Meilicke* GmbHR 2003, 1271, 1272; *Paefgen* ZIP 2004, 2253, 2259; *Westermann* GmbHR 2005, 4, 15;		

[131] On the discussion concerning the Limited in Germany, see: *Pannen/Riedemann* MDR 2005, 496; *Riedemann* GmbHR 2004, 345; *Zerres* DZWiR 2006, 356; *Altmeppen/Wilhelm* DB 2004, 1083; *Borges* ZIP 2004, 733; *Burg* GmbHR 2004, 1379; *Schumann* DB 2004, 743; *Schall* ZIP 2005, 965; *Paefgen* DB 2003, 487; *Wachter* GmbHR 2003, 1254; *Wachter* GmbHR 2004, 88; *Dierksmeier* BB 2005, 1516; *Fröhlich/Strasser* ZIP 2006 1182; *Geyrhalter/Gänßler* DStR 2003, 2167; *Heinz* AnwBl 2004, 612; *von Hase* BB 2006, 2141; *Kallmeyer* DB 2004, 636; *Köke* ZInsO 2005, 354; *Kuntz* NZI 2005, 424; *Lieder* DZWiR 2005, 399; *K Müller* BB 2006, 837; *Römermann* NJW 2006, 2065; *Riegger* ZGR 2004, 510; *Schlichte* DB 2006, 1357; *Stork* GewArch 2005, 265; *Wienberg/Sommer* NZI 2005, 353; *Walterscheid* DZWiR 2006, 95; *Wachter* BB 2006, 1463; *Werner* GmbHR 2005, 288 (Ltd & Co KG); *Zöllner* GmbHR 2006, 1; *von Bernstorff* RIW 2004, 498.

	Company Law	**Insolvency Law**	**Tort Law**
	Applicable: *Bitter* WM 2004, 2190, 2194 et seq; *Altmeppen/Wilhelm* DB 2004, 1083, 1088 et seq; *Altmeppen* NJW 2004, 97, 102 who want to apply the capital preservation rules as a form of a special connecting factor.		
Right to Request Opening of Proceedings		*Pannen/Riedemann* MDR 2005, 496, 498; *Riedemann* GmbHR 2004, 345, 348; *Mock/Schildt* ZInsO 2003, 396, 399; *H.-F. Müller* NZG 2003, 414, 416; *Holzer* ZVI 2005, 457, 463; *G Roth* NZG 2003, 1081, 1085; Hirte/Bücker-*Mock/Schildt* § 17 mn 64.	
Duty to Request Opening of Proceedings	*Vallender/Fuchs* ZIP 2004, 829, 830; *Ulmer* NJW 2004, 1201, 1207; *Ulmer* KTS 2004, 291, 301; *Schumann* DB 2004, 743, 746; *Mock/Schildt* ZInsO 2003, 396, 399; *Fischer* ZIP 2004, 1477, 1481; *Geyrhalter/Gänßler* DStR 2003, 2167, 2171; *Hirte/Mock* ZIP 2005, 474, 475; *von Hase* BB 2006, 2141, 2147; *K Müller* BB 2006, 837, 839; *Paefgen* ZIP 2004, 2253, 2260; *J Schmidt* ZInsO 2006, 737, 740; *Berner/Klön* ZIP 2007, 106, 111; Hirte/Bücker-*Mock/Schildt* § 17 mn 79.	*Pannen* in Runkel (ed), AHB-Insolvenzrecht (2005) s 16 mn 146; *Pannen/Riedemann* MDR 2005, 496, 498; *same* NZI 2005, 413, 414; *Riedemann* GmbHR 2004, 345, 348; *Zerres* DZWiR 2006, 356, 360; *Borges* ZIP 2004, 733, 739; *Zimmer* NJW 2003, 3585, 3589; *H-F Müller* NZG 2003, 414, 416; *Weller* IPRax 2003, 520, 522; *Eidenmüller* NJW 2005, 1618; 1620; *Röhricht* ZIP 2005, 505, 508; *Wachter* GmbHR 2003, 1254, 1257; *Holzer* ZVI 2005, 457, 464; *Kuntz* NZI 2005, 424, 427; *Vallender* ZGR 2006, 425, 455; *Walterscheid* DZWiR 2006; 95, 98; *Wachter* BB 2006, 1463, 1464 et seq; *G Roth* NZG 2003, 1081, 1085; *Schilling* EWiR 2006, 429; *Leutner/Langer* ZInsO 2005, 575, 577; *Paulus* Komm EuInsVO Art 4 mn 10; *K Schmidt* in Schmidt/Uhlenbruck (ed), Die GmbH in Krise, Sanierung und Insolvenz (2003), 889.	

	Company Law	**Insolvency Law**	**Tort Law**
Delayed Filing for Insolvency	*Ulmer* NJW 2004, 1201, 1207; *Ulmer* KTS 2004, 291, 301; *Schumann* DB 2004, 743, 746; *Mock/Schildt* ZInsO 2003, 396, 400; *Spindler/Berner* RIW 2004, 7, 12; *Schall* ZIP 2005, 965, 974 et seq; *Bitter* WM 2004, 2190, 2199; *von Hase* BB 2006, 2141, 2146; *Kuntz* NZI 2005, 424, 428; *K Müller* BB 2006, 837, 839; *Paefgen* ZIP 2004, 2253, 2260; *J Schmidt* ZInsO 2006, 737, 740; *Mock* NZI 2006, 484, 485; *Berner/Klöhn* ZIP 2007, 106, 114; Hirte/Bücker-*Mock/Schildt* § 17 mn 84 et seq; **Applicable as a special connecting factor:** *Altmeppen/Wilhelm* DB 2004, 1083, 1088; *Altmeppen* NJW 2004, 97, 100 et seq.	*Wilhelmi* GmbHR 2006, 13, 17; *Zerres* DZWiR 2006, 356, 360; *H-F Müller* NZG 2003, 414, 417; *Eidenmüller* NJW 2005, 1618; 1621; *Röhricht* ZIP 2005, 505, 508; *Wachter* GmbHR 2003, 1254, 1257; *Habersack/Verse* ZHR 168 (2004), 174, 207; *Weller* DStR 2003, 1800, 1804; *Goette* DStR 2005, 197, 200; *Holzer* ZVI 2005, 457, 467; *Lieder* DZWiR 2005, 399, 405; *Vallender* ZGR 2006, 425, 455 *Walterscheid* DZWiR 2006, 95, 98; *Wachter* BB 2006, 1463, 1465; *G Roth* NZG 2003, 1081, 1085; *Schilling* EWiR 2006, 429; *Leutner/Langer* ZInsO 2005, 575, 577; MünchKomm BGB/*Kindler* IntGesR mn 646.	*Pannen/Riedemann* MDR 2005, 496, 498; *Pannen/Riedemann* NZI 2005, 413, 414; *Riedemann* GmbHR 2004, 345, 348; *Zimmer* NJW 2003, 3585, 3590; *Schanze/Jüttner* AG 2003, 661, 670; *Bayer* BB 2003, 2357, 2365; *Zöllner* GmbHR 2006, 1, 7.
Payment Prohibition	Hirte/Bücker-*Mock/Schildt* § 17 mn 89.	*Röhricht* ZIP 2005, 505, 510; *Goette* DStR 2005, 197, 200; *Lieder* DZWiR 2005, 399, 406; *Vallender* ZGR 2006, 425, 455 et seq; *Leutner/Langer* ZInsO 2005, 575, 577; *Paulus* Komm EuInsVO Art 4 mn 10; MünchKomm BGB/*Kindler* IntGesR mn 625.	
Capital Substitution Law (overall)	**Not applicable:** Haß/Huber/Gruber/Heiderhoff-*Haß/Huber* Art 4 mn 15; *Mellert/Verfürth* Wettbewerb der Gesellschaftsformen (2005), p 248; Hirte/Bücker-*Mock/Schildt* s 17 mn 115; *Wachter* GmbHR 2004, 88, 92; *Geyrhalter/Gänßler* NZG 2003, 409, 411 et seq; *Heinz* AnwBl 2004, 612, 617; *Holzer* ZVI 2005, 457, 468; *Kallmeyer* DB 2004, 636, 639; *Köke* ZInsO 2005, 354, 356; *Paefgen* ZIP 2004, 2253, 2261; *Kessler/Eicke* DStR 2005, 2101, 2106.		

	Company Law	Insolvency Law	Tort Law
Judge-Made Rules	**Not applicable:** *Pannen/Riedemann* MDR 2005, 496, 498; *Paefgen* DB 2003, 487, 490; *Ulmer* NJW 2004, 1201, 1207; *Ulmer* KTS 2004, 291, 299; *Schumann* DB 2004, 743, 748; *Borges* ZIP 2004, 733, 743; *Zimmer* NJW 2003, 3585, 3589; *Schall* ZIP 2005, 965, 975; *Röhricht* ZIP 2005, 505, 512; *Fischer* ZIP 2004, 1477, 1480; *Geyrhalter/Gänßler* NZG 2003, 409, 411 et seq; *Lieder* DZWiR 2005, 399, 407; *Meilicke* GmbHR 2003, 1271, 1272; *Westermann* GmbHR 2005, 4, 15; *Zöllner* GmbHR 2006, 1, 6; Hirte/Bücker-*Mock/Schildt* § 17 mn 115; Hirte/Bücker-*Forsthoff/Schulz* s 16 mn 41. **Applicable:** *Forsthoff* DB 2002, 2471, 2477; *W-H Roth* IPRax 2003, 117, 125; *Altmeppen* NJW 2004, 97, 103; *Altmeppen/Wilhelm* DB 2004, 1083, 1088 who want to apply legal precedent in the form of a special connecting factor; concurring: *Eidenmüller* ZIP 2002, 2233, 2242; *Eidenmüller* ZGR 2004, 159, 181 who wants to apply the provisions also in the form of a special connecting factor if in the individual case the law of the incoporating forum has no compatible provision.		

	Company Law	Insolvency Law	Tort Law
Amended Statutory Rules	**Company-law preliminary question:** *Riedemann* GmbHR 2004, 345, 348; *H-F Müller* NZG 2003, 414, 417; *K Müller* BB 2006, 837, 838; *Meilicke* GmbHR 2003, 1271, 1272; Hirte/Bücker-*Mock/Schildt* § 17 mn 115; formerly also concurring: *Pannen/Riedemann* MDR 2005, 496, 498.	*Ulmer* KTS 2004, 291, 299; *Röhricht* ZIP 2005, 505, 512 et seq; *Fischer* ZIP 2004, 1477, 1480; *Lieder* DZWiR 2005, 399, 407; *Wienberg/Sommer* NZI 2005, 353, 356; *Walterscheid* DZWiR 2006; 95, 98; *Zöllner* GmbHR 2006, 1, 6; v Gerkan/Hommelhoff-*Haas* Handbuch des Kapitalersatzrechts (2002), mn 15.18; MünchKomm BGB/*Kindler* IntGesR mn 708 et seq.	
Subsistence-Destroying Acts	**Classification as company law:** *Altmeppen* FS Röhricht (2005) p 3, 19; *Burg* GmbHR 2004, 1379, 1380; *Ulmer* NJW 2004, 1201, 1207; *Ulmer:* KTS 2004, 291, 304; *Schumann* DB 2004, 743, 748; *Spindler/Berner* RIW 2004, 7, 11; *Schall* ZIP 2005, 965, 975; *Eidenmüller* NJW 2005, 1618; 1620; *Bitter* WM 2004, 2190, 2197; *Goette* DStR 2005, 197, 200; *Köke* ZInsO 2005, 354, 356; *Kindler* NJW 2003, 1073, 1079; *Kuntz* NZI 2005, 424, 432; *K Müller* BB 2006, 837, 839; *Paefgen* ZIP 2004, 2253, 2260; *Westermann* GmbHR 2005, 4, 15; *Walterscheid* DZWiR 2006; 95, 99; *Zöllner* GmbHR 2006, 1, 8; *Bayer* BB 2003, 2357, 2364 et seq; *Eidenmüller* ZIP 2002, 2233, 2242; *Schulz* NJW 2003, 2705, 2707; *Leutner/Langer* ZInsO 2005, 575, 576; *Schön* ZHR (168) 2004, 268, 290 et seq; **Applicable:** Justified: *Binge/Thölke* DNotZ 2004, 21, 26; *Drygala* EWiR 2003, 1029, 1030; *Bitter* WM 2004, 2190, 2197 et seq; *Leutner/Langer* ZInsO 2005, 575, 576.	*Wilhelmi* GmbHR 2006, 13, 17; *Röhricht* ZIP 2005, 505, 514 et seq; *Weller* IPRax 2003, 207, 210; *Wachter* GmbHR 2003, 1254, 1257; *Lieder* DZWiR 2005, 399, 406; *G Roth* NZG 2003, 1081, 1085; *Horn* NJW 2004, 893, 899; *Fleischer* in Lutter (ed), Europäische Auslandsgesellschaften in Deutschland (2005), 49, 128; *Zimmer* NJW 2003, 3585, 3589 ("also").	*Zimmer* NJW 2003, 3585, 3588; *Schanze/Jüttner* AG 2003, 661, 670; *Dierksmeier* BB 2005, 1516, 1520; *Bayer* BB 2003, 2357, 2365.

	Company Law	Insolvency Law	Tort Law
	Special connecting factor: *Altmeppen/Wilhelm* DB 2004, 1083, 1088; *Altmeppen* NJW 2004, 97, 101; *Borges* ZIP 2004, 733, 741; *Fischer* ZIP 2004, 1477, 1481; *Eidenmüller* ZIP 2002, 2233, 2242; *Horn* NJW 2004, 893, 899; *Kindler* NZG 2003, 1086, 1090; MünchKomm BGB/*Kindler* IntGesR mn 617 (multiple connecting factors); *Schulz* NJW 2003, 2705, 2707; Public policy: *Paefgen* DB 2003, 487, 491; *Paefgen* ZIP 2004, 2253, 2262; *Schulz* NJW 2003, 2705, 2707.		
Other Piercing of the Corporate Veil	*Paefgen* DB 2003, 487, 490; *Weller* IPRax 2003, 520, 523; *Ulmer* KTS 2004, 291, 304; *Bitter* WM 2004, 2190, 2196; *Geyrhalter/Gänßler* NZG 2003, 409, 411; *Horn* NJW 2004, 893, 899; *Borges* ZIP 2004, 733, 743; *Leutner/Langer* ZInsO 2005, 575, 576; *Fleischer* in Lutter (ed), Europäische Auslandsgesellschaften in Deutschland (2005), 49, 121, 123; Hirte/Bücker-*Forsthoff/Schulz* s 16 mn 82, 84; MünchKomm BGB/*Kindler* IntGesR mn 614 et seq.		*Zimmer* NJW 2003, 3585, 3588 et seq.

1. Provision and Preservation of Capital

Since the Inspire Art decision (at mn 22 above), the **provision of capital,** and particularly the current minimal capital requirements of € 25,000 (Sec 5 (1) *GmbHG*), are – as company law provisions – not applicable to foreign companies operating in Germany; only the law of the forum of incorporation applies to this aspect of the company.[132] The entire incorporation process and the legal capacity of the company is governed solely by the law of the place of incorporation. **78**

[132] ECJ "Inspire Art" NJW 2003, 3331 mn 104, 141, see also Art 4 of the EIR fn 36.

79 The **preservation of capital** is also allocated to the law of the forum that governs the company,[133] and therefore German company law provisions on this are not applicable to pseudo foreign corporations operating in Germany.[134] Being a matter closely intertwined with the sensitive areas of the financial system and liability aspect of the company, which has a major impact on incorporation and therefore on the exercising of the right of establishment, the preservation of capital falls within the protection afforded by the right of establishment.[135] There is also no need for a justification vis-à-vis the right of establishment since the law of the forum governing the incorporation contains its own rules restricting the distribution of funds.

2. Right to File for Insolvency

80 The **right to request** the opening of insolvency proceedings is regulated in German law in Sec 15 *InsO*. It stipulates that both creditors and debtors are entitled to make the request. This right to request is a provision falling within insolvency law. It is applicable in conjunction with Art 4 of the EIR.[136]

3. Duty to File for Insolvency and Liability for Delayed Filing for Insolvency

81 **In dispute** is the classification of the managing director of a German GmbH's **duty to request the opening of proceedings** pursuant to Sec 64 (1) *GmbHG* and the **liability for delayed filing for insolvency** associated with it pursuant to Sec 823 (2) *BGB* in conjunction with Sec 64 (1) *GmbHG*, and the payment prohibition pursuant to Sec 64 (2) *GmbHG*.

a) Duty to request the opening of insolvency proceedings

82 The managing director of a German GmbH is under a duty to request the opening of insolvency proceedings once the company becomes insolvent (Sec 64 *GmbHG* in conjunction with Secs 17, 19 *InsO*). Pursuant to Sec 64 (1) *GmbHG*, the request must be made no later than 3 weeks subsequent to the occurrence of the reason for opening insolvency proceedings. The issue of whether the duty to request is to be classified as insolvency law arises primarily because of its placement in the act governing the GmbH rather than in the act governing insolvency.

---

[133] BGHZ 148, 167, 168.

[134] *Mellert/Verfürth* Wettbewerb der Gesellschaftsformen (2005), p 248; Hirte/Bücker-*Forsthoff/Schulz* § 16 mn 37 et seq; *Paefgen* DB 2003, 487, 490; *Ulmer* NJW 2004, 1201, 1208; *Schumann* DB 2004, 743, 744 et seq; *Bayer* BB 2003, 2357, 2364; *Röhricht* ZIP 2005, 505, 511; *Wachter* GmbHR 2004, 88, 91; *Eidenmüller* ZGR 2004, 159, 181; *Fischer* ZIP 2004, 1477, 1479; *Geyrhalter/Gänßler* DStR 2003, 2167, 2170; *Holzer* ZVI 2005, 457, 468; *Kindler* NJW 2003, 1073, 1079; *Lieder* DZWiR 2005, 399, 407; *Meilicke* GmbHR 2003, 1271, 1272; *Paefgen* ZIP 2004, 2253, 2259; *Westermann* GmbHR 2005, 4, 15; contra: *Bitter* WM 2004, 2190, 2194 et seq; *Altmeppen/Wilhelm* DB 2004, 1083, 1088 et seq; *Altmeppen* NJW 2004, 97, 102 who wants to apply the capital preservation rules via a special connecting factor. On capital preservation in the case of a Ltd. & Co. KG, see: *Schlichte* DB 2006, 1357, 1360.

[135] *Fleischer* in Lutter (ed), Europäische Auslandsgesellschaften in Deutschland (2005), 131, 117.

[136] *Pannen/Riedemann* MDR 2005, 496, 498; *Riedemann* GmbHR 2004, 345, 348; *Mock/Schildt* ZInsO 2003, 396, 399; *H-F Müller* NZG 2003, 414, 416; *Holzer* ZVI 2005, 457, 463; *G Roth* NZG 2003, 1081, 1085; Hirte/Bücker-*Mock/Schildt* § 17 mn 64.

Some are of the opinion that the duty to request the opening of insolvency proceedings should be categorized under **company law.**[137] This view fails to appreciate, however, that it is not the place where a rule is found that is decisive but rather its substantive content. The close link between the right to make the request and the duty to make it, and thus its classification as an **executive officer's duty under insolvency law,** clearly supports a classification as insolvency law.[138] This is especially true considering that the requirements for opening insolvency proceedings are closely connected to the aims envisioned by the provisions of the various individual *lex fori concursus*, and a review of such requirements in relation to the right of establishment would be a direct encroachment on the guaranteed freedom afforded to the various Member States to design their national insolvency laws as they see fit.[139] **83**

b) Liability for delayed filing for insolvency

What continues to be heavily disputed is the **liability** arising from a breach of the duty to make a timely request to open insolvency proceedings. The managing director who fails to comply with this duty is personally liable for damages pursuant to Sec 823 (2) *BGB* in conjunction with Sec 64 (1) *GmbHG*. This liability is closely linked with the duty to request the opening of insolvency proceedings. **84**

Because the duty to make the request is found in a separate company law act, some legal writers are of the opinion that the liability for delayed filing for insolvency should be classified as **company law.**[140] This argument is not convincing: the "random" regulation of the duty to request in a separate act cannot on its own justify a classification **85**

[137] *Vallender/Fuchs* ZIP 2004, 829, 830; *Ulmer* NJW 2004, 1201, 1207; *Ulmer* KTS 2004, 291, 301; *Schumann* DB 2004, 743, 746; *Mock/Schildt* ZInsO 2003, 396, 399; *Fischer* ZIP 2004, 1477, 1481; *Geyrhalter/Gänßler* DStR 2003, 2167, 2171; *Hirte/Mock* ZIP 2005, 474, 475; *von Hase* BB 2006, 2141, 2147; *K Müller* BB 2006, 837, 839; *Paefgen* ZIP 2004, 2253, 2260; *J Schmidt* ZInsO 2006, 737, 740; *Berner/Klöhn* ZIP 2007, 106, 111; Hirte/Bücker-*Mock/Schildt* § 17 mn 79; with a reference to: *Huber* in Lutter (ed) Europäische Auslandsgesellschaften in Deutschland (2005) 307, 307 et seq, 320 et seq. *Zöllner* GmbHR 2006, 1, 7 declares the duty to request the opening of insolvency proceedings as applicable via a special connecting factor.

[138] *Pannen* in Runkel (ed), AHB-Insolvenzrecht (2005) § 16 mn 146; *Pannen/Riedemann* MDR 2005, 496, 498; *Pannen/Riedemann* NZI 2005, 413, 414; *Riedemann* GmbHR 2004, 345, 348; *Zerres* DZWiR 2006, 356, 360; *Borges* ZIP 2004, 733, 739; *Zimmer* NJW 2003, 3585, 3589; *H-F Müller* NZG 2003, 414, 416; *Weller* IPRax 2003, 520, 522; *Eidenmüller* NJW 2005, 1618, 1620; *Röhricht* ZIP 2005, 505, 508; *Wachter* GmbHR 2003, 1254, 1257; *Holzer* ZVI 2005, 457, 464; *Kuntz* NZI 2005, 424, 427; *Vallender* ZGR 2006, 425, 455; *Walterscheid* DZWiR 2006; 95, 98; *Wachter* BB 2006, 1463, 1464 et seq; *G Roth* NZG 2003, 1081, 1085; *Schilling* EWiR 2006, 429; *Leutner/Langer* ZInsO 2005, 575, 577; *Paulus* Komm EuInsVO Art 4 mn 10; *K Schmidt* in Schmidt/Uhlenbruck (ed), Die GmbH in Krise, Sanierung und Insolvenz (2003), 889.

[139] *Paulus* Komm EuInsVO Art 4 mn 11.

[140] *Ulmer* NJW 2004, 1201, 1207; *Ulmer* KTS 2004, 291, 301; *Schumann* DB 2004, 743, 746; *Mock/Schildt* ZInsO 2003, 396, 400; *Spindler/Berner* RIW, 7, 12; *Schall* ZIP 2005, 965, 974 et seq; *Bitter* WM 2004, 2190, 2199; *von Hase* BB 2006, 2141, 2146; *Kuntz* NZI 2005, 424, 428; *K Müller* BB 2006, 837, 839; *Paefgen* ZIP 2004, 2253, 2260; *J Schmidt* ZInsO 2006, 737, 740; *Mock* NZI 2006, 484, 485; *Berner/Klöhn* ZIP 2007, 106, 114; Hirte/Bücker-*Mock/ Schildt* § 17 mn 84 et seq; applicable as special connecting factor *Altmeppen/Wilhelm* DB 2004, 1083, 1088; *Altmeppen* NJW 2004, 97, 100 et seq.

under company law. What is decisive is whether such a norm regulates a problem that is specific to insolvency law.[141] A decision along these lines was reached, however, by the *AG* Bad Segeberg in Germany.[142] According to the court, the liability for delayed filing for insolvency pursuant to German law was not applicable. The court held that liability could only be imposed pursuant to the provisions of the law governing the incorporation of the company. The judgement was not upheld, however, on appeal.[143]

86 Coming closer to the point, but equally unconvincing, is the classification of the liability for delayed filing for insolvency as **insolvency law**. Some support this with a reference to the insolvency-law duty to make the request.[144] It is argued that the core of the reproach giving rise to the liability for damages lies in the breach of the insolvency law norm found in Sec 64 (1) *GmbHG*. But to conclude that the liability for delayed filing for insolvency should be classified under insolvency law merely because the duty to request the insolvency is also classified under insolvency law, and thus arrive at a uniform classification,[145] seems somewhat superficial.

87 More convincing is to classify the liability for delayed filing for insolvency as **tort law** since the underlying norm, Sec 823 (2) *BGB*, is regulated in the part of the *BGB* dealing with tort law.[146] Sec 64 (1) *GmbHG* would then be construed as a protectionary insolvency law within the meaning of Sec 823 (2) *BGB*.[147] The protection that the liability serves is regulated via tort law, which is being applied via Art 40 of the German *EGBGB*.

88 In a decision dated 20 April 2006, the ***LG* Kiel**[148] dealt with the issue of imposing liability for delayed filing for insolvency on pseudo foreign corporations in Germany. The court first concluded that the duty to request was to be classified as insolvency law. They reasoned that Sec 64 (1) GmbHG serves the protection of creditors by preserving the insolvency estate (that is liable for satisfying claims) and by keeping insolvent companies out of the stream of commerce. And although the court did not deal directly with the issue of whether the liability for delayed filing for insolvency should be classified specifically as insolvency law or as tort law, it affirmed that it does apply but left it open whether the application takes place via Art 4 of the EIR or via Art 40 *EGBGB*.[149]

---

[141] *Pannen/Riedemann* MDR 2005, 496, 498; BK-InsO/*Pannen* Art 4 EuInsVO mn 5.

[142] AG Bad Segeberg dated 24 Mar 2005 NZI 2005, 411, with explanatory note by *Pannen/Riedemann*.

[143] LG Kiel dated 20 Apr 2006 ZIP 2006, 1248, with explanatory note by *Just*.

[144] *Wilhelmi* GmbHR 2006, 13, 17; *Zerres* DZWiR 2006, 356, 360; *H-F Müller* NZG 2003, 414, 417; *Eidenmüller* NJW 2005, 1618, 1621; *Röhricht* ZIP 2005, 505, 508; *Wachter* GmbHR 2003, 1254, 1257; *Habersack/Verse* ZHR 168 (2004), 174, 207; *Weller* DStR 2003, 1800, 1804; *Goette* DStR 2005, 197, 200; *Holzer* ZVI 2005, 457, 467; *Lieder* DZWiR 2005, 399, 405; *Vallender* ZGR 2006, 425, 455; *Walterscheid* DZWiR 2006, 95, 98; *Wachter* BB 2006, 1463, 1465; *G Roth* NZG 2003, 1081, 1085; *Schilling* EWiR 2006, 429; *Leutner/Langer* ZInsO 2005, 575, 577; MünchKomm BGB/*Kindler* IntGesR mn 646; MünchKomm BGB/*Kindler* IntInsR mn 209.

[145] *Zerres* DZWiR 2006, 356, 360.

[146] *Pannen/Riedemann* MDR 2005, 496, 498; *Pannen/Riedemann* NZI 2005, 413, 414; *Riedemann* GmbHR 2004, 345, 348; *Zimmer* NJW 2003, 3585, 3590; *Schanze/Jüttner* AG 2003, 661, 670; *Bayer* BB 2003, 2357, 2365; *Zöllner* GmbHR 2006, 1, 7.

[147] Since BGH NJW 1959, 623; *Lutter/Kleindiek* in Lutter/Hommelhoff (eds), GmbHG, § 64 mn 41; *Roth/Altmeppen* GmbHG, § 64 mn 61 with further references.

[148] LG Kiel dated 20 Apr 2006 ZIP 2006, 1248, with explanatory note by *Just*.

[149] Some authors, however, read the court's reasons as a classification of the liability for delayed filing for insolvency as insolvency law, see: *Just* ZIP 2006, 1251, 1252; *Mock* NZI 2006, 484, 485; *Schilling* EWiR 2006, 429.

c) **Payment prohibition**

The **classification** of the **payment prohibition** once insolvency has been ascertained pursuant to Sec 64 (2) *GmbHG* is in dispute. Because the insolvency of the company is a prerequisite to Sec 64 (2) *GmbHG*, the majority is – convincingly – of the opinion that the payment prohibition is to be classified as insolvency law whose application takes place via Art 4 of the EIR.[150] Although some prefer to justify this on the basis of a special connecting factor, the result is still an application.[151] A special connecting factor should be rejected in any case for the reasons stated above (mn 31), but especially because it is just not necessary since Art 4 of the EIR, as a conflict of laws rule, serves the very purpose. **89**

4. **Equity Substitution Law**

Equity substitution law[152] is regulated twice in German law. Once in the so-called "judge-made rules", which were influenced by the capital preservation provisions analogous to Secs 30 and 31 of the *GmbHG*, and secondly through an express regulation of it in the so-called "amended statutory rules" (Sec 32a, 32b *GmbHG* and Sec 172a *HGB*, etc.). These are flanked by the provisions of the German Insolvency Act (Sec 39 (1) No 5, Sec 135 *InsO*). The basic concept behind the equity substitution doctrine is that shareholders are to be held responsible for the consequences of financing decisions. Should the company experience a "crisis", the shareholder must decide whether to wind up the company in a proper manner or to supply it with equity.[153] If he decides to secure the company's existence by granting it a loan or by executing some other economically comparable transaction, then he must accept the consequences that such a loan will be subordinated in the event of insolvency. The shareholder must also reimburse the company in full (Sec 135 *InsO*) for any loans paid back to him in the year prior to the filing of the request, and up to the amount in which they were paid out of the preserved share capital (Sec 31 (1) *GmbHG* by way of analogy) for those paid back to him in the last 10 years (Sec 31 (5) *GmbHG*).[154] **90**

In order to determine whether the **equity substitution law** can be applied, the first question that must be asked is whether there must be **uniform** compliance with the **two areas of the law**, or whether the two areas can be complied with **separately**. **91**

- If the **uniform approach** is taken, then – because of the origins in the provisions dealing with capital preservation – there can be no application to pseudo foreign corporations.[155]

---

150 *Röhricht* ZIP 2005, 505, 510; *Goette* DStR 2005, 197, 200; *Lieder* DZWiR 2005, 399, 406; *Vallender* ZGR 2006, 425, 455 et seq; *Leutner/Langer* ZInsO 2005, 575, 577; *Paulus* Komm EuInsVO Art 4 mn 10; MünchKomm BGB/*Kindler* IntGesR mn 625; contra: Hirte/Bücker-*Mock/Schildt* § 17 mn 89.

151 See *Zöllner* GmbHR 2006, 1, 7, who, with a reference to *Huber* in Lutter (ed), Europäische Auslandsgesellschaften in Deutschland (2005) 307, 342, wants to justify an application through a special connecting factor.

152 Fundamental on this: BGHZ 31, 258; *Lutter/Hommelhoff* GmbHG, § 32a/b; *Hueck/Fastrich* in Baumbach/Hueck, GmbHG, § 32a with further references.

153 HamburgerKomm-*J-S Schröder* § 135 mn 4 with further references.

154 The claim for repayment of payments made on loans that contravene European law is also determined pursuant to the general rules, see: *Bork* FS Lutter (2000) p 301.

155 Against an application in the case of a uniform approach because of an infringement of the right of establishment are: Haß/Huber/Gruber/Heiderhoff-*Haß/Huber* Art 4 EuInsVO mn 15; *Mellert/Verfürth* Wettbewerb der Gesellschaftsformen (2005), p 248; Hirte/Bücker-*Mock/Schildt* s 17

• The only convincing approach is a **diversified approach** since the legal effects of the amended statutory rules (subordinations, avoidance) are matters of insolvency law; whereas the judge-made rules, on account of the analogy to the non-applicable capital preservation rules, reclassify shareholder loans as equity.[156]

92 With the diversified approach, the majority is of the opinion that the **judge-made rules**, on account of the aforementioned doubts as to the compatibility of the capital preservation rules with the right of establishment, **do not apply.**[157] What **do apply**, however, are the **amended statutory rules** whose legitimization is fundamentally based on insolvency-law arguments.[158] This results in an application of these rules via the referral to the *lex fori concursus* in Art 4 of the EIR. Support for this is particularly found in the direct references in Art 4 (2) sentence 2 (g), (i), and (m) of the EIR to the legal effects of the amended statutory rules:

(1) by determining which claims are to be lodged in the insolvency proceedings;

(2) by determining the ranking of these;

(3) by determining which legal acts are voidable.

93 Despite the consensus on the classification as insolvency law, there is still strong opinion in the legal literature against the application of the amended statutory rules. The argument is that the categorization of loans as substituted equity constitutes a **preliminary question** of company law, and that the amended statutory rules would only apply if

---

mn 115; *Wachter* GmbHR 2004, 88, 92; *Geyrhalter/Gänßler* NZG 2003, 409, 411 et seq; *Heinz* AnwBl 2004, 612, 617; *Holzer* ZVI 2005, 457, 468; *Kallmeyer* DB 2004, 636, 639; *Köke* ZInsO 2005, 354, 356; *Paefgen* ZIP 2004, 2253, 2261; *Kessler/Eicke* DStR 2005, 2101, 2106.

[156] Basic on this *Huber* in Lutter (ed), Europäische Auslandsgesellschaften in Deutschland (2005), 131, 141; also *Fischer* ZIP 2004, 1911, 1912; *Haas* NZI 2001, 1, 10; Gottwald/*Huber* InsR-Handb (2006) § 50 mn 5; *K Schmidt* ZHR 168 (2004), 493, 497; *Ulmer* NJW 2004, 1201, 1207; *Ulmer* KTS 2004, 291, 298 et seq; *Walterscheid* DZWiR 2006, 95; *Wienberg/Sommer* NZI 2005, 353; *Zimmer* NJW 2003, 3585, 3589; *Zöllner* GmbHR 2006, 1, 5.

[157] *Pannen/Riedemann* MDR 2005, 496, 498; *Paefgen* DB 2003, 487, 490; *Ulmer* NJW 2004, 1201, 1207; *Ulmer* KTS 2004, 291, 299; *Schumann* DB 2004, 743, 748; *Borges* ZIP 2004, 733, 743; *Zimmer* NJW 2003, 3585, 3589; *Schall* ZIP 2005, 965, 975; *Röhricht* ZIP 2005, 505, 512; *Fischer* ZIP 2004, 1477, 1480; *Geyrhalter/Gänßler* NZG 2003, 409, 411 et seq; *Lieder* DZWiR 2005, 399, 407; *Meilicke* GmbHR 2003, 1271, 1272; *Westermann* GmbHR 2005, 4, 15; *Zöllner* GmbHR 2006, 1, 6; Hirte/Bücker-*Mock/Schildt* s 17 mn 115; Hirte/Bücker-*Forsthoff/Schulz* s 16 mn 41; contra: *Forsthoff* DB 2002, 2471, 2477; *W-H Roth* IPRax 2003, 117, 125; *Altmeppen* NJW 2004, 97, 103; *Altmeppen/Wilhelm* DB 2004, 1083, 1088 who wish to apply the judge-made rules in the form of a special connecting factor; concurring: *Eidenmüller* ZIP 2002, 2233, 2242; *Eidenmüller* ZGR 2004, 159, 181 who wishes to apply the provisions also in the form of a special connecting factor if in the individual case the law of the forum of the incorporation has no compatible provision.

[158] *Pannen/Riedemann* MDR 2005, 496, 498; *Riedemann* GmbHR 2004, 345, 348; *Ulmer* NJW 2004, 1201, 1207; *H-F Müller* NZG 2003, 414, 417; *Ulmer* KTS 2004, 291, 299; *Röhricht* ZIP 2005, 505, 512; *Fischer* ZIP 2004, 1477, 1480; *Lieder* DZWiR 2005, 399, 407; *K Müller* BB 2006, 837, 838; *Meilicke* GmbHR 2003, 1271, 1272; *Wienberg/Sommer* NZI 2005, 353, 356; *Walterscheid* DZWiR 2006, 95, 98; *Zöllner* GmbHR 2006, 1, 6; Hirte/Bücker-*Forsthoff/Schulz* § 16 mn 60; v Gerkan/Hommelhoff-*Haas* Handbuch des Kapitalersatzrechts (2002), mn 15.18; MünchKomm BGB/*Kindler* IntGesR mn 708 et seq.

the law governing the incorporation of the company also contained rules comparable to German equity substitution law.[159] This approach is unconvincing for two reasons:[160]

- Firstly, an equity-replacing loan involves a set of facts that must be interpreted. A loan generally "replaces" equity if the company is in a "crisis"[161] and the shareholders cover the capital requirements of the company by way of a loan.[162] For such a finding, there is certainly no need to resort to company law. Even the referral, which existed in Sec 32a of the *KO*, is no longer to be found in the *InsO*. Thus all of the factual requirements are regulated in Sec 39 (1) No 5 and Sec 135 *InsO*, and there is no need to clarify any preliminary (factual) question pursuant to the law of the forum of incorporation.
- Secondly, no objections to an application of the amended statutory rules to foreign companies are to be found from the point of view of European law either. The national insolvency law that is to be applied via Art 4 of the EIR is perfectly consistent with the system of guaranteed freedoms.[163] There is no apparent reason why the right of establishment should be violated through a "surprising"[164] avoidance provision.

The amended statutory rules, as insolvency law provisions, are therefore applicable to foreign companies.[165]

The application of national avoidance provisions nevertheless remain subject to the **94**
proviso in Art 13 of the EIR. According to Art 13 of the EIR, the avoidance laws of the *lex fori concursus*, and thus Sec 135 *InsO* as well, are not applicable if:

(1) the avoidable act is subject to the law of a Member State other than that of the State of the opening of proceedings, and
(2) in the State of such act, there is no means of challenging it.

Art 13 of the EIR constitutes a defence that only needs to be observed if the party **95**
disputing the avoidance raises it in the proceedings.[166] If it is raised, Sec 135 *InsO* will not apply if the loan contract is subject to foreign law. Whether an individual (choice of law) agreement in the contract will suffice, or whether the general rules of Arts 27 and 28 *EGBGB* must apply, is **disputed**. An agreement between the parties is being allowed in

---

159 *H-F Müller* NZG 2003, 414, 417; *K Müller* BB 2006, 837, 838; *Meilicke* GmbHR 2003, 1271, 1272; Hirte/Bücker-*Mock/Schildt* § 17 mn 115; formerly also concurring: *Pannen/Riedemann* MDR 2005, 496, 498; *Riedemann* GmbHR 2004, 345, 348.

160 The following is in agreement with the convincing argumentation of *Huber* in Lutter (ed), Europäische Auslandsgesellschaften in Deutschland (2005), p 131, 171–181.

161 On the concept of "crisis": *Lutter/Hommelhoff* GmbHG, § 32a/b mn 18 et seq; *Hueck/Fastrich* in Baumbach/Hueck, GmbHG, § 32a mn 48.

162 *Huber* in Lutter (ed), Europäische Auslandsgesellschaften in Deutschland (2005), 131, 176 et seq.

163 In detail on this problem: Hirte/Bücker-*Mock/Schildt* § 16 mn 48–54; *Huber* in Lutter (ed), Europäische Auslandsgesellschaften in Deutschland (2005), 131, 186–188.

164 *Müller* NZG 2003, 414, 417.

165 Already: *Ulmer* KTS 2004, 291, 299; *Röhricht* ZIP 2005, 505, 512 et seq; *Fischer* ZIP 2004, 1477, 1480; *Lieder* DZWiR 2005, 399, 407; *Wienberg/Sommer* NZI 2005, 353, 356; *Walterscheid* DZWiR 2006, 95, 98; *Zöllner* GmbHR 2006, 1, 6; v Gerkan/Hommelhoff-*Haas* Handbuch des Kapitalersatzrechts (2002), mn 15.18.
On the application of the amended statutory rules for the Ltd. & Co KG cf *Schlichte* DB 2006, 1357, 1361 et seq.

166 *Paulus* Komm EuInsVO Art 13 mn 4; *Smid* Komm EuInsVO Art 13 mn 7; D-K/D/Ch-*Duursma-Kepplinger* Art 13 mn 14; Haß/Huber/Gruber/Heiderhoff-*Haß/Herweg* Art 13 EuInsVO mn 10.

some instances.[167] The more convincing approach, however, would be not to allow this considering that the very intent and purpose of the Regulation is to prevent the choosing of which law applies. Therefore which law is to govern the loan contract must be ascertained. But if the law governing the individual contract is silent on the repayment of payments made on shareholder loans, then there are strong arguments in favour of not permitting an avoidance in such a case. On the issue of subordination in the insolvency proceedings, however, Art 13 of the EIR has no impact.

96 On 23 May 2007, the German Government presented a draft bill to modernize GmbH law and to combat abusive practices (***MoMiG***).[168] This draft bill is intended to abolish the judge-made rules through a supplement to Sec 30 (1) *GmbHG*. The amended statutory rules are to be incorporated in the German *InsO* independent of the legal form of the company. The consequences of the amendment, and in part the reason for it, is to make **the entire body of "new" equity substitution law applicable** to pseudo foreign corporations.[169]

5. Piercing the Corporate Veil

97 Also in dispute is the imposition of personal liability when there is a **piercing of the corporate veil.** A distinction is being drawn here between the imposition of liability for subsistence-destroying acts, which were developed by the German *BGH* (Federal Supreme Court), and the imposition of general personal liability in cases where the corporate veil is being pierced.

a) Subsistence-destroying acts

98 Liability for **subsistence-destroying acts**, which was developed by the *BGH*,[170] concerns a claim that can be asserted by the creditors of the company against the controlling shareholders. This applies subsidiarily if the capital preservation rules of Sec 30 et seq *GmbHG* cannot be invoked.[171] What is required is an act that harms the company's substance in a manner that endangers its existence.[172] Although every deviation from the company's objects prejudices the company's interests, and hence harms the company's substance, a subsistence-destroying act will only be found in the special case where the company's ability to pay its debts is being impaired.[173]

99 In order to answer the question as to the classification in conjunction with Art 4 of the EIR, the doctrinal basis of the liability must first be clarified.[174] The liability is predominantly considered a direct liability (towards the creditors) which is arrived at through a teleological (utilitarian) interpretation of the general rule of limited liability, or it is considered an unconscionable injury pursuant to Sec 826 *BGB*. Those who see the

---

[167] *Paulus* Komm EuInsVO Art 13 mn 6.

[168] For the following discussions and for an overview and review of the reporter's draft, see: *Scholz/Schmidt*, GmbHG (2006), §§ 32a, 32b mn 238–258 with further reasons.

[169] Reasons of the reporter's Draft, p 36, 83.

[170] For the basic principles of the liability for subsistence-destroying acts, see BGH "Bremer Vulkan" BGHZ 149, 10, 16; BGH "KBV" BGHZ 151, 181, 186. For an in-depth discussion of the liability for subsistence-destroying acts, see with further reasons: *Lutter/Hommelhoff* GmbHG, § 13 mn 17 et seq; *Hueck/Fastrich* in Baumbach/Hueck, GmbHG, s 13 mn 15 et seq; *Bork* KTS 2006, 39 et seq.

[171] BGH ZIP 2005, 117.

[172] BGH "Bremer Vulkan" BGHZ 149, 10, 16; BGH "KBV" BGHZ 151, 181, 186.

[173] *Grigoleit* Gesellschafterhaftung, p 285.

[174] On the existing opinions, cf *Bork* KTS 2006, 39 et seq.

doctrinal basis in Sec 826 *BGB* impose liability under tort law via Sec 40 *EGBGB*.[175] What speaks against this, however, is the fact that the liability is being imposed for a breach of the so-called "functional principle" of corporations, which allows the sanction of the piercing of the corporate veil to be categorized specifically as company law.[176] By contrast, the teleological interpretation of the basic rule of limited liability leads to a piercing of the corporate veil and hence the imposition of general personal liability pursuant to Sec 128 *HGB*. The result is a classification of the liability for subsistence-destroying acts as company law.[177] Also supporting such a classification as company law is the fact that it was developed to compensate for withdrawals of assets the indemnification of which is not possible via the capital preservation provisions, and thus to supplement the capital protection system. The *BGH*[178] has also now concurred in the teleological interpretation of Sec 13 (2) *GmbHG*. The view taken by the *BGH* is convincing because the "separation principle", which dictates that the company is a separate legal subject from its shareholders, is only intended to protect the shareholders of a GmbH from personal liability to the extent to which they do not "abuse" this legal form. If they do this, then they expose themselves to the general rules.

The majority is of the opinion that liability for subsistence-destroying acts is applicable to pseudo foreign corporations. Some favour a **classification as insolvency law.**[179] A weighty argument in support of this is its functional similarity with the avoidance provisions found in insolvency law.[180] This is unconvincing, however, since the liability for subsistence-destroying acts focuses directly on the breach of specific company-law duties and there is no mandatory requirement that it has to cause the insolvency.[181] Therefore the majority are of the opinion that it is to be classified as company law. Some justify this using the so-called "Gebhard Formula",[182] others via a special connecting factor,[183] **100**

---

175 Cf *Zimmer* NJW 2003, 3585, 3588; *Schanze/Jüttner* AG 2003, 661, 670; *Dierksmeier* BB 2005, 1516, 1520; *Bayer* BB 2003, 2357, 2365.

176 *Altmeppen* NJW 2004, 97, 101.

177 *Altmeppen* FS Röhricht (2005) p 3, 19; *Burg* GmbHR 2004, 1379, 1380; *Ulmer* NJW 2004, 1201, 1207; *Ulmer* KTS 2004, 291, 304; *Schumann* DB 2004, 743, 748; *Spindler/Berner* RIW 2004, 7, 11; *Schall* ZIP 2005, 965, 975; *Eidenmüller* NJW 2005, 1618, 1620; *Bitter* WM 2004, 2190, 2197; *Goette* DStR 2005, 197, 200; *Köke* ZInsO 2005, 354, 356; *Kindler* NJW 2003, 1073, 1079; *Kuntz* NZI 2005, 424, 432; *K Müller* BB 2006, 837, 839; *Paefgen* ZIP 2004, 2253, 2260; *Westermann* GmbHR 2005, 4, 15; *Walterscheid* DZWiR 2006, 95, 99; *Zöllner* GmbHR 2006, 1, 8; *Bayer* BB 2003, 2357, 2364 et seq; *Eidenmüller* ZIP 2002, 2233, 2242; *Schulz* NJW 2003, 2705, 2707; *Leutner/Langer* ZInsO 2005, 575, 576; *Schön* ZHR (168) 2004, 268, 290 et seq; *Fleischer* in Lutter (ed) Europäische Auslandsgesellschaften in Deutschland (2005) 49, 128 et seq.

178 BGHZ 151, 181, 187.

179 *Wilhelmi* GmbHR 2006, 13, 17; *Röhricht* ZIP 2005, 505, 514 et seq; *Weller* IPRax 2003, 207, 210; *Wachter* GmbHR 2003, 1254, 1257; *Lieder* DZWiR 2005, 399, 406; *G Roth* NZG 2003, 1081, 1085; *Horn* NJW 2004, 893, 899; *Fleischer* in Lutter (ed) Europäische Auslandsgesellschaften in Deutschland (2005) 49, 128; *Zimmer* NJW 2003, 3585, 3589 also approves a classification as insolvency law.

180 So *Weller* IPRax 2003, 207, 210; *Röhricht* ZIP 2005, 505, 514.

181 *Wiedemann* ZGR 2003, 283, 293; *Mittelstädt* Bucerius Law Journal 2007, 7, 9.

182 *Binge/Thölke* DNotZ 2004, 21, 26; *Drygala* EWiR 2003, 1029, 1030; *Bitter* WM 2004, 2190, 2197 et seq; *Leutner/Langer* ZInsO 2005, 575, 576.

183 *Altmeppen/Wilhelm* DB 2004, 1083, 1088; *Altmeppen* NJW 2004, 97, 101; *Borges* ZIP 2004, 733, 741; *Fischer* ZIP 2004, 1477, 1481; *Eidenmüller* ZIP 2002, 2233, 2242; *Horn* NJW 2004, 893, 899; MünchKomm BGB/*Kindler* IntGesR mn 617; *Kindler* NZG 2003, 1086, 1090 (multiple point of contact "*Mehrfachanknüpfung*"); *Schulz* NJW 2003, 2705, 2707.

and some on the basis of the public policy proviso[184] found in Art 6 *EGBGB*. Only a small minority would like to reject an application based on an infringement of the right of establishment.[185] A classification as company law is already convincing on account of the dogmatic anchoring of the liability for subsistence-destroying acts in the general requirements for piercing the corporate veil, with the consequences ensuing from Sec 128 *HGB*. For a justification vis-à-vis the right of establishment, an examination must be made to determine whether the liability serves the same function for the foreign companies. This – as a teleological interpretation of the „separation principle" – is not specific to German law; all that is required is a limitation of liability.

101 Because of the specific creditor-protection aspect of the liability for subsistence-destroying acts, the majority of arguments support a justification and thus an application to pseudo foreign corporations, especially if the foreign law provides no adequate protection.[186]

b) General piercing of the corporate veil

102 As with the liability for subsistence-destroying acts, the **general piercing of the corporate veil** (and the ensuing imposition of personal liability) also involves cases of teleologically interpreting Sec 13 (2) *GmbHG*, which results in an allocation of these matters to the law governing the company.[187] A classification as tortious liability,[188] which is favoured by some, is not convincing as the cases falling with it relate directly to problems specific to the limitation of liability in relation to limited liability companies. These cases deal with liability for actual undercapitalization[189] and liability for the commingling of private and company assets (*Vermögensvermischung*) or for concealing the separation of the company from its shareholders (*Sphärenvermischung*).[190] In the result, an argument in favour of an application to pseudo foreign corporations is unconvincing because, by ignoring the limitation of liability in those specific cases of a general piercing of the corporate veil, an encroachment is being made on the privilege afforded by the limitation of the liability. The constraining of such privilege must, as with the recognition of incorporation procedures, remain a matter of company law and therefore be subject to the law of the forum that governs the incorporation. As opposed to the liability for subsistence-destroying acts, the issues of sufficient capitalization and the scope of the "separation principle" are liability-law connecting factors that are closely linked to the financial system of the company. It is therefore highly unlikely that this would not be regarded as an encroachment on the right of establishment; a justification is highly improbable.

---

[184] *Paefgen* DB 2003, 487, 491; *Paefgen* ZIP 2004, 2253, 2262; *Schulz* NJW 2003, 2705, 2707; *Mittelstädt* Bucerius Law Journal 2007, 7, 11.

[185] *Schlichte* DB 2005, 2672, 2675.

[186] Also *Fleischer* in Lutter (ed), Europäische Auslandsgesellschaften in Deutschland (2005) 49, 126 et seq.

[187] *Paefgen* DB 2003, 487, 490; *Weller* IPRax 2003, 520, 523; *Ulmer* KTS 2004, 291, 304; *Bitter* WM 2004, 2190, 2196; *Geyrhalter/Gänßler* NZG 2003, 409, 411; *Horn* NJW 2004, 893, 899; *Borges* ZIP 2004, 733, 743; *Leutner/Langer* ZInsO 2005, 575, 576; *Fleischer* in Lutter (ed), Europäische Auslandsgesellschaften in Deutschland (2005), 49, 121, 123; Hirte/Bücker-*Forsthoff/Schulz* § 16 mn 82, 84; MünchKomm BGB/*Kindler* IntGesR mn 614 et seq.

[188] *Zimmer* NJW 2003, 3585, 3588 et seq.

[189] Cf *Lutter/Hommelhoff* GmbHG, § 13 mn 7 with further references; *Hueck/Fastrich* in Baumbach/Hueck, GmbHG, § 13 mn 16; *Roth/Altmeppen* GmbHG, § 13 mn 116 et seq.

[190] Cf *Lutter/Hommelhoff* GmbHG, § 13 mn 13 with further references; *Hueck/Fastrich* in Baumbach/Hueck, GmbHG, § 13 mn 14; *Roth/Altmeppen*, GmbHG, § 13 mn 112 et seq.

Article 5
Third parties' rights in rem

1. The opening of insolvency proceedings shall not affect the rights in rem of creditors or third parties in respect of tangible or intangible, moveable or immoveable assets – both specific assets and collections of indefinite assets as a whole which change from time to time – belonging to the debtor which are situated within the territory of another Member State at the time of the opening of proceedings.

2. The rights referred to in paragraph 1 shall in particular mean:

(a) the right to dispose of assets or have them disposed of and to obtain satisfaction from the proceeds of or income from those assets, in particular by virtue of a lien or a mortgage;

(b) the exclusive right to have a claim met, in particular a right guaranteed by a lien in respect of the claim or by assignment of the claim by way of a guarantee;

(c) the right to demand the assets from, and/or to require restitution by, anyone having possession or use of them contrary to the wishes of the party so entitled;

(d) a right in rem to the beneficial use of assets.

3. The right, recorded in a public register and enforceable against third parties, under which a right in rem within the meaning of paragraph 1 may be obtained, shall be considered a right in rem.

4. Paragraph 1 shall not preclude actions for voidness, voidability or unenforceability as referred to in Article 4(2)(m).

Contents

Index

Bibliography

Balz Das neue Europäische Insolvenzübereinkommen, ZIP 1996, p 948; *D. Buchberger/R. Buchberger* Das System der „kontrollierten" Universalität des Konkursverfahrens nach der Europäischen Insolvenzverordnung, ZIK 2000, p 149; *Drobnig* in Kegel/Thieme (eds), Vorschläge und Gutachten zum Entwurf eines EG-Konkursübereinkommens (1988), p 358 et seq; *Duursma-Kepplinger* Eigentumsvorbehalt und Mobilienleasing in der Insolvenz (2002); *Duursma-Kepplinger/Duursma* Das Schicksal von dinglichen Sicherungsrechten sowie des Eigentumsvorbehalts nach der InsolvenzVO (VO 1346/2000), wbl 2002, p 59; *Duursma-Kepplinger/Duursma/Chalupsky* Europäische Insolvenzverordnung, Kommentar (2002); *Ebenroth* Die Inlandswirkungen der ausländischen lex fori concursus bei Insolvenz einer Gesellschaft, ZZP 101 (1988), p 139 et seq; *Eidenmüller* Europäische Verordnung über Insolvenzverfahren und zukünftiges deutsches internationales Insolvenzrecht, IPRax 2001, p 2; *Flessner* Dingliche Sicherungsrechte nach dem Europäischen Insolvenzübereinkommen, in Basedow/Hopt/Kötz (eds), Festschrift Drobnig (1998), p 277 et seq; *Flessner* Internationales Insolvenzrecht in Deutschland nach der Reform, IPRax 1997, p 1; *Flessner* Das künftige internationale Insolvenzrecht im Verhältnis zum Europäischen Insolvenzübereinkommen. Anwendbares Recht, Reichweite der Anerkennung, Insolvenzplan und Schuldbefreiung, in Stoll (ed), Vorschläge und Gutachten, p 219; *Fritz/Bähr* Die Europäische Verordnung über Insolvenzverfahren, DZWiR 2001, p 221; *Gottwald* Grenzüberschreitende Insolvenzen (1997); *Haas* Die Verwertung der im Ausland belegenen Insolvenzmasse im Anwendungsbereich der EuInsVO, in Schilken/Kreft/Wagner/Eckhardt (eds), Festschrift Gerhardt (2004), p 319; *Herchen* Das Übereinkommen über Insolvenzverfahren der Mitgliedstaaten der EU vom 23.11.1995 (2000); *Huber* Internationales Insolvenzrecht in Europa, ZZP 114 (2001), p 133; *Kemper* Die Verordnung (EG) Nr. 1346/2000 über Insolvenzverfahren, ZIP 2001, p 1609; *Keppelmüller* An der Schwelle zu einem europäischen Insolvenzrecht? wbl 1996, p 337; *Keppelmüller* Österreichisches internationales Konkursrecht (1997); *Kolmann* Kooperationsmodelle im internationalen Insolvenzrecht (2001); *Kübler/Prütting* Kommentar zur Insolvenzordnung (March 2006); *Lehr* Die neue EU-Verordnung über Insolvenzverfahren und deren Auswirkungen für die Unternehmenspraxis, KTS 2000, p 577; *Leible/Staudinger* Die europäische Verordnung über Insolvenzverfahren, KTS 2000, p 533; *Liersch* Sicherungsrechte im Internationalen Insolvenzrecht (2001); Münchener Kommentar zur Insolvenzordnung, vol 1 (2001); *Nerlich/Römermann* (eds) Insolvenzordnung (InsO), Kommentar (May 2003); *Paulus* Die europäische Insolvenzverordnung und der deutsche Insolvenzverwalter, NZI 2001, p 505; *Prütting* Aktuelle Entwicklungen des internationalen Insolvenzrechts, ZIP 1996, p 1277; *Schack* Internationales Zivilverfahrensrecht (2002); *Stummel* Konkurs und Integration. Konventionsrechtliche Wege zur Bewältigung grenzüberschreitender Insolvenzverfahren (1991); *Taupitz* Das (zukünftige) europäische Internationale Insolvenzrecht – insbesondere aus internationalprivatrechtlicher Sicht, ZZP 111 (1998) p 315; *Uhlenbruck* Insolvenzordnung, Kommentar (2004); *Virgós/Schmit* Erläuternder Bericht zu dem EU-Übereinkommen über Insolvenzverfahren, in Stoll (ed), Vorschläge und Gutachten (1997) p 32; *Virgós/Garcimartín* The European Insolvency Regulation: Law and Practice (2004); *Von Wilmowsky* Sicherungsrechte im Europäischen Insolvenzübereinkommen, EWS 1997, p 295; *Wimmer* Die EU-Verordnung zur Regelung grenzüberschreitender Insolvenzverfahren, NJW 2002, p 2427; *Wimmer* Die Richtlinien 2001/17 EG und 2001/14 EG über die Sanierung und Liquidation von Versicherungsunternehmen und Kreditinstituten, ZInsO 2002, p 897; *Wunderer* Auswirkungen des Europäischen Übereinkommens über Insolvenzverfahren auf Bankgeschäfte, WM 1998, p 793.

1. Introduction

1.1 General

1 The primary purpose of rights *in rem* is to provide the secured creditor – in the event of a financial crisis on the part of their debtors – with a secured right in real or personal property, thus affording him preferential satisfaction out of the assets of the insolvent debtor.[1] From such a secured creditor's point of view, the legal validity of the secured right is of crucial importance in the event of insolvency.[2] Secured rights therefore

[1] Cf MünchKomm BGB/*Kindler* IntInsR mn 253.

[2] *Virgós/Schmit* Explanatory report mn 24; *Wimmer* NJW 2002, 2427, 2429; *v. Wilmowsky* EWS 1997, 295 et seq; *Taupitz* ZZP 111 (1998) 315, 329 et seq; *Lehr* KTS 2000,

generally aim at minimizing the risk of deficiencies in the case of an insolvency, although secured rights in conjunction with loans may be dealt with in different ways by the various Member States.[3] And in no way is this incompatible with the debtor's interests. The debtor knows, at the time of obtaining the loan, that he can only obtain the loan by providing the security stipulated in the loan agreement, and he agrees to providing such security by signing the agreement. To deny the entire legal validity of such security in the face of the debtor's financial crisis would be tantamount to exonerating the debtor from his contractual obligations without there having been any discrimination whatsoever of the creditors.

International insolvency law must, however, take into account that creditors with secured rights in real or personal property ("secured creditors") are treated differently in the various Member States, and that by recognizing such secured rights, the principle of equal treatment of creditors cannot be upheld. The reason for creating secured rights, i.e. to minimize the risk of deficiencies in the case of insolvency, exists regardless of where insolvency proceedings are opened. The question as to whether the security granted to a creditor in a State outside the one in which insolvency proceedings are opened was done so effectively, or whether it is enforceable, must be answered in isolation from this. It is true that, because the law of the place where the security is located (*lex rei sitae*) governs, it is more difficult for the liquidator acting in another legal system to know and to ascertain which law governs the security. But the situation for the secured creditors would be worse – and it would also run contrary to their need for legal certainty – because it would either be impossible or extremely difficult for them to predict the law that would apply in the event of the debtor's insolvency.[4] **2**

International insolvency law must therefore find a way to balance the opposing interests between the need for certainty on the one hand and the optimizing of the insolvency estate on the other hand. It must regulate whether and, if applicable, how restrictions imposed by the foreign insolvency law affect secured rights situated in a national territory.[5] The comments made by *Duursma-Kepplinger*[6] – that a well-functioning credit system without adequate protection of the security attached to such credit is inconceivable – is heading in the right direction: **3**

The answer to the question – protection of certainty or optimizing the insolvency estate? – decides in essence on a company's creditworthiness, and therefore often on its ability to survive, at least in the case of a company with a weak equity base. **4**

1.2 Current Opinions and Justifying the Privilege

Within the framework of universal insolvency proceedings, contrary positions are being taken in response to the tension that exists between protecting legal certainty on the one hand and optimizing the insolvency estate on the other hand in association with secured rights *in rem*:[7] **5**

577, 579; MünchKomm BGB/*Kindler* IntInsR mn 253.

[3] D-K/D/Ch-*Duursma-Kepplinger* Art 5 mn 1; see also *Virgós/Schmit* Explanatory report mn 97; *Drobnig* in Kegel/Thieme (eds), Vorschläge und Gutachten, 358 et seq; *v. Wilmowsky* EWS 1997, 295; *Taupitz* ZZP 111 (1998) 330.

[4] Regarding this problem see *Huber* ZZP 114 (2001), 133, 153; *Haas* FS Gerhardt (2004) p 319, 328.

[5] *Wimmer* NJW 2002, 2427, 2429.

[6] D-K/D/Ch-*Duursma-Kepplinger* Art 5 mn 2.

[7] See for instance *Kuhn/Uhlenbruck* Art 237, 238 mn 76, 92.

- The first position adheres rigorously – even with respect to secured rights *in rem* situated outside of the opening State – to the concept of universality, and therefore to the application of the *lex fori concursus generalis*, which means that both the property law as well as the insolvency law of the State in which the insolvency proceedings have been opened applies.[8] Accordingly, the legal validity of the secured rights *in rem* is assessed pursuant to the *lex fori concursus*.
- According to the other position, secured rights situated in a State outside of the State in which insolvency proceedings are opened are always subject to the law that governs such secured right.[9] Therefore the question as to whether the secured right was validly created or whether it is effective, and the effects that an insolvency has on this right, are always determined pursuant to the laws of the place where they are situated (*lex rei sitae*) regardless of where the insolvency proceedings have been opened.[10]

6 Pursuant to Art 5 (1) of the EIR, the opening of insolvency proceedings does not affect the rights *in rem* of creditors or third parties in respect of tangible or intangible, moveable or immoveable assets belonging to the debtor that are situated within the territory of another Member State at the time of the opening of proceedings. Art 5 (1) of the EIR thus protects creditors who have secured their rights pursuant to the law, i.e. the *lex rei sitae*, of a Member State other than the opening State.[11] Art 5 of the EIR is therefore an exception to the rule found in Art 4 (1) of the EIR, i.e. that the *lex fori concursus* applies.[12]

7 The aim of Art 5 of the EIR is to safeguard commercial transactions in the State in which assets are situated and to assure legal certainty with respect to the rights that exist in such assets.[13]

8 The legal literature in some instances assumes that the substantive law governing the secured property is to be invoked for deciding whether the secured right has been validly created.[14] Others hold the view that the conflict of laws rules of the opening State apply,[15] because the issue here is the inviolability of the foreign secured rights in the opening State.[16] This is founded on the argument that Art 5 (1) of the EIR only excludes the applicability of the opening State's special insolvency-specific conflict of laws rules and not its conflict of laws rules in general. The general conflict of laws rules of the

---

[8] See for instance *Kuhn/Uhlenbruck* Art 237, 238 mn 76, 92.

[9] *Ebenroth* ZZP 101 (1988), 139 et seq.

[10] *v. Wilmowsky* EWS 1997, 296 et seq.

[11] This also corresponds to the provisions of German private international law; art 43 (1) of the Introductory Act to the German Civil Code (*EGBGB*) provides that rights to property are governed by the law of the state within whose territory the property is situated (*lex rei sitae*). *Lehr* KTS 2000, 577, 579.

[12] *Smid* Komm EuInsVO Art 5 mn 1; Moss/Fletcher/Isaacs-*Moss/Smith*, Regulation, mn 8.83.

[13] *Virgós/Schmit* Explanatory report mn 97.

[14] *Wimmer* NJW 2002, 2427, 2429; *Wimmer* ZInsO 2002, 897, 903.

[15] *Liersch* Sicherungsrechte im Internationalen Insolvenzrecht (2001), 45, assumes that the private international law of the state of *situs* is authoritative and refers, *inter alia*, to *Taupitz* ZZP 111 (1998) 315, 334 et seq, who, however, clearly assumes that the private international law of the Member State of the opening of proceedings applies; see also *Wunderer* WM 1998, 793, 198; *Liersch* and *Wunderer* are obviously the only authors who assume that the private international law of the state of *situs* is authoritative, but ultimately also arrive at the *lex rei sitae*.

[16] *Leible/Staudinger* KTS 2000, 533, 551; *Eidenmüller* IPRax 2001, 2, 6, mn 29; *Herchen* 35; D-K/D/Ch-*Duursma-Kepplinger* Art 5 mn 44.

opening State often, however, refer to the *lex rei sitae*,[17] which has been recognized by all EU Member States.[18]

The one point that is certainly undisputed is that, through Art 5 of the EIR, rights *in rem* are not affected by the opening of insolvency proceedings. This raises the issue as to whether only the property law of the forum that governs the security applies,[19] or the property law of the forum that governs the security together with this forum's insolvency law.[20] **9**

Prevailing opinion holds that the wording "shall not affect" is to be so understood that secured rights *in rem* are completely inviolable by the foreign insolvency proceeding.[21] **10**

This may not be the best conclusion since secured rights *in rem* may, in some circumstances, be afforded wider protection than they would if insolvency proceedings were opened in the State in which the property is situated.[22] **11**

Art 5 (1) of the EIR is therefore considered by some academics as a conflict of laws rule that refers to the law of the place where the property is situated. And because this in turn refers to the *lex rei sitae*,[23] the assessment in terms of insolvency law should be made pursuant to its insolvency law.[24] **12**

The prevailing opinion counters this line of reasoning by pointing out that the EIR consciously opted for another solution. In the deliberations on the insolvency convention, the idea of subjecting rights *in rem* to an insolvency-law review pursuant to the *lex rei sitae* was rejected.[25] It was also pointed out that secondary insolvency proceedings **13**

---

[17] *Taupitz* ZZP 111 (1998) 315, 335; *Huber* ZZP 114 (2001) 133, 154; see also the Reasons of Governmental Draft concerning a Statute for a Revision of the International Insolvency Law BT-Drs. 15/16 p 12.

[18] Recital 8 of the EU Directive on the Provision of Financial Security.

[19] *Von Wilmowsky* EWS (1997) 295 et seq; *Taupitz* ZZP 111 (1998) 334; *Leible/Staudinger* KTS 2000, 551; *Herchen* 55, 76 et seq; *Kolmann* Kooperationsmodelle (2001) 302 et seq, particularly 308; *Huber* ZZP 114 (2001) 154; *Duursma-Kepplinger/Duursma* wbl 2002, 63 et seq; *Duursma-Kepplinger* Eigentumsvorbehalt und Mobilienleasing 211 et seq.

[20] See *Flessner* in Stoll (ed), Vorschläge und Gutachten, 222; *Flessner* IPRax 1997, 7; *Flessner* FS Drobnig, 281 et seq; *D. Buchberger/R.Buchberger* ZIK 2000, 187; *Fritz/Bähr* DZWiR 2001, 228; see also the opinion of *Gottwald* Grenzüberschreitende Insolvenzen (1997) 31 et seq (under the heading "Insolvenzkollisionsrecht") and *Keppelmüller* wbl 1996, 341, particularly mn 43; *Keppelmüller* Internationales Konkursrecht (1997) 182 et seq according to which art 5 (1) of the EIR itself contains an implied reference to the *lex rei sitae*; regarding the draft of 1980 and 1984, see also *Stummel* Konkurs und Integration (1991) 115.

[21] *Balz* ZIP 1996, 950; *Wunderer* WM 1998, 798; *Leible/Staudinger* KTS 2000, 550; *Taupitz* ZZP 1998, 325, 335; *Paulus* NZI 2001, 505, 513; Kübler/Prütting-*Kemper* InsO Art 102 EGInsO mn 142; *Kemper* ZIP 2001, 1609, 1615 et seq; Nerlich/Römermann-*Mincke* InsO Art 102 EGInsO mn 188; MünchKomm InsO/*Reinhart* Art 5 EuInsVO mn 1; MünchKomm BGB/*Kindler* IntInsR mn 268.

[22] *Drobnig* in Stoll (ed), Stellungnahmen und Gutachten zur Reform des deutschen Internationalen Insolvenzrechts, 1992, 179 et seq; *Leible/Staudinger* KTS 2000, 533, 552; critical: MünchKomm InsO/*Reinhart* Art 5 EuInsVO mn 2; *Virgós/Schmit* Explanatory report mn 97.

[23] Recital 8 of the EU Directive on the Provision of Financial Security.

[24] *Keppelmüller* Internationales Konkursrecht (1997), 182; *D. Buchberger/R. Buchberger* ZIK 2000, 187 who obviously mean a reference to the foreign law in its entirety (including its conflict of laws rules); *Flessner* FS Drobnig, 283 et seq; *Fritz/Bähr* DZWiR 2001, 227; contra: *Haas* FS Gerhardt (2004), 319, 328.

[25] *Kolmann* Kooperationsmodelle (2001) 308; *Wimmer* NJW 2002, 2427, 2430 fn 55; *Virgós/Schmit* Explanatory report mn 97.

could always be requested as long as the debtor had an establishment in the other State. According to this view, Art 5 of the EIR is to be viewed as a substantive law rule that exempts certain rights *in rem* from the scope of applicability of the *lex fori concursus*.[26] *Reinhart*[27] correctly points out that creditors entitled to secured rights *in rem* in business interests/shares of a subsidiary located in a foreign country, i.e. a subsidiary that is not an establishment of the debtor, can still enforce those secured rights even if they would be subject to insolvency-law restrictions in the State in which such secured rights were created. An objective reason for favouring the security provided on credit by foreign debtors over that provided by their domestic counterparts is not apparent.

14 The stance often taken in response to this argumentation is that the secured right itself is unaffected by the foreign insolvency proceedings; only the property in which the secured right exists is affected by the insolvency proceedings.[28] The secured property becomes part of the insolvency estate because of the principle of universality.[29] From a purely practical point of view, however, it would be problematic to include encumbered property in the foreign insolvency proceedings if there is no restricting of the rights *in rem* in such property when these rights have not been redeemed at the expense of the foreign insolvency estate.[30]

15 And when secured rights have not been redeemed, the question arises as to who has the right to liquidate (dispose of) the property.[31]

16 **Position taken:** Prevailing opinion correctly holds that Art 5 of the EIR is a substantive-law norm[32] and not a conflict of laws rule because it is not a provision that specifies which law applies to third party *in rem* rights but merely precludes the applicability of the *lex fori concursus*.

1.3 Right to Liquidate

17 According to Art 5 (1) of the EIR, secured rights in another Member State are unaffected by the opening of insolvency proceedings. But this does not automatically mean that the property concerned is exempt from liquidation in every case. The liquidation should simply not – because of the issue of inviolability – be made in conjunction with the main insolvency proceedings. If secondary insolvency proceedings are opened in the Member State of the secured property, the liquidator in these proceedings is authorized to liquidate if this is provided for in the *lex fori concursus secundarii*. Recital 25 advises the liquidator in the main insolvency proceedings to request the opening of secondary proceedings in the State where the property is situated. Any surplus from the secondary insolvency proceedings must, upon the closing of these proceedings, be transferred to the liquidator in the main insolvency proceedings (Art 35 of the EIR).

18 If secondary insolvency proceedings cannot be opened due to a lack of an establishment within the meaning of Art 2 (h) of the EIR, the creditor must liquidate the secured property himself if he is authorized to do so by local law.[33] The surplus must be trans-

[26] *Paulus* Komm EuInsVO Art 5 mn 1.

[27] MünchKomm InsO/*Reinhart* Art 5 EuInsVO mn 2.

[28] *Taupitz* ZZP 111 (1998) 315, 339; MünchKomm BGB/*Kindler* IntInsR mn 268.

[29] *Leible/Staudinger* KTS 2000, 533, 553; *Liersch* 46, *Herchen* 68; *Paulus* NZI 2001, 505, 513; *Schack* Internationales Zivilverfahrensrecht (2002) mn 1097.

[30] See proposal of D-K/D/Ch-*Duursma-Kepplinger* Art 5 mn 43; see also MünchKomm InsO/*Reinhart* Art 5 EuInsVO mn 3.

[31] *Paulus* Komm EuInsVO Art 5 mn 19 and 22.

[32] Also: MünchKomm BGB/*Kindler* IntInsR mn 274; *Paulus* Komm EuInsVO Art 5 mn 1; Haß/Huber/Gruber/Heiderhoff-*Huber* Art 5 EuInsVO mn1; *Smid* Komm EuInsVO Art 5 mn 15.

[33] *Paulus* Komm EuInsVO Art 5 mn 24.

ferred to the liquidator in the main insolvency proceedings. If he is not authorized to liquidate and if there are no secondary insolvency proceedings, the liquidator in the main insolvency proceedings has the right to liquidate (based on Art 4 of the EIR).[34]

2. Connecting Factors in Art 5 EIR (Summary)

Any proceeds from a liquidation that are not needed to satisfy the secured claims always belong to the insolvency estate of the main proceedings.[35] **19**

The creditor's or third party's right *in rem* is, pursuant to Art 5 of the EIR, not affected by the opening of insolvency proceedings under the following conditions: **20**

2.1 Opening of Insolvency Proceedings in an EU Member State

Insolvency proceedings must have been opened in a Member State of the EU against the assets of a debtor. According to the decision of the ECJ in Eurofood/Parmalat, the appointing of a temporary administrator already constitutes the opening of proceedings within the meaning of the EIR.[36] **21**

2.2 Existence of Right *in rem* Prior to Opening of Proceedings

Art 5 of the EIR only protects those rights *in rem* that existed prior to the opening of the insolvency proceedings. For rights created after the opening of proceedings, Art 4 of the EIR applies.[37] The same holds true for rights created by the liquidator.[38] Pursuant to Art 2 (f) of the EIR, the time of the opening proceedings is the time at which the judgement opening proceedings becomes effective, whether such judgement is final or not (on this, see Art 2 of the EIR mn 24 et seq). The time of creation of the right *in rem* is ascertained in accordance with the law – as determined by the conflict of laws rules of the State in which the court is located – that governs at the place of the secured property, usually the *lex rei sitae*.[39] **22**

2.3 Encumbered Property Situated in the EU But Outside the State of the Proceedings

Art 5 of the EIR only protects rights *in rem* in property if the encumbered property is situated in the EU but outside of the EU Member State in which proceedings were opened. Whether the property is situated in another Member State is a matter to be determined at the time of the opening of proceedings.[40] The legal definition of "the Member State in which assets are situated" is found in Art 2 (g) of the EIR (on this, see Art 2 of the EIR mn 29 et seq). According to this provision: **23**

- tangible property is found in the Member State within the territory of which the property is situated;

---

[34] Similar argumentation *Paulus* Komm EuIns-VO Art 5 mn 25.

[35] With same result: *Paulus* Komm EuInsVO Art 5 mn 24.

[36] Cf ECJ dated 2 May 2006 – C-341/04 (Eurofood IFSC Ltd), NZI 2006, 360 et seq (→ cf Table of Cases Art 3 of the EIR Appendix A mn 10); in-depth on the conditions, Art 3 of the EIR mn 91 et seq.

[37] D-K/D/Ch-*Duursma-Kepplinger* Art 5 mn 6; *Virgós/Schmit* Explanatory report mn 96.

[38] D-K/D/Ch-*Duursma-Kepplinger* Art 5 mn 7.

[39] MünchKomm BGB/*Kindler* IntInsR mn 260 and 262.

[40] MünchKomm BGB/*Kindler* IntInsR mn 263.

- property and rights ownership of or entitlement to which must be entered in a public register are found in the Member State under the authority of which the register is kept;
- claims are found in the Member State within the territory of which the third party required to meet them has the centre of his main interests, as determined in Article 3 (1) of the EIR.

24 If the encumbered property is situated outside the EU, Art 5 of the EIR does not apply.[41] This does not hold true only when the property has been brought into the EU by the time the insolvency proceedings are opened.[42]

25 The *situs* of the encumbered property must not be chosen with the intention to deceive.[43] Should an intent to deceive be found, then Art 4 of the EIR applies.[44]

2.4 The Limits of Art 5 EIR

26 Art 5 (4) of the EIR makes it clear[45] that the creditor's secured rights *in rem* do not enjoy unlimited protection. Via Art 4 (2) sentence 2 (m) of the EIR, an "appropriate abuse-control"[46] takes place – pursuant to the law that, according to the State in which the main proceedings are opened, governs the insolvency – in respect of assertions of voidness, unenforceability, and voidability in terms of insolvency law.

27 The creditor may, however, rely on Art 13 of the EIR with the result that, should the requirements of this provision be fulfilled, an avoidance action will fail.[47]

28 Art 5 (1) of the EIR only protects rights *in rem* from the effects caused by the opening of insolvency proceedings but not from the effects of judicial orders (reducing secured claims or secured rights) or insolvency plans[48] made during the proceedings. Logically, the secured creditor should redeem his secured rights (or have them redeemed) before the court has a chance to make such an order that could lower the value of his security.

3. Rights *in rem*

29 While Art 5 (1) of the EIR outlines the things and the rights in which rights *in rem* may exist, Art 5 (2) of the EIR sets out examples of rights *in rem*, as illustrated by the wording "in particular"[49], without this constituting a legal definition. Art 5 of the EIR does not, therefore, contain a definition of "rights *in rem*" as this would have been too risky: legal constellations not considered rights *in rem* pursuant to the law of the State in which the property is situated would be regarded as such and rights *in rem* that did not meet these requirements would not.[50] The result is that every property right capable of constituting a right *in rem* is included.[51] Whether an agreement creates a right *in rem*

---

[41] *Virgós/Schmit* Explanatory report mn 94; *Paulus* Komm EuInsVO Art 5 mn 4; *Smid* Komm EuInsVO Art 5 mn 2; MünchKomm BGB/*Kindler* IntInsR mn 264.

[42] *Paulus* Komm EuInsVO Art 5 mn 3, 10.

[43] *Virgós/Schmit* Explanatory report mn 105; MünchKomm BGB/*Kindler* IntInsR mn 265. MünchKomm InsO/*Reinhart* Art 5 EuInsVO mn 28.

[44] MünchKomm InsO/*Reinhart* Art 5 EuInsVO mn 28.

[45] *Paulus* Komm EuInsVO Art 5 mn 28; MünchKomm InsO/*Reinhart* Art 5 EuInsVO mn 7.

[46] *Herchen* 166.

[47] See MüKo-Reinhart Art 5 EuInsVO mn 7.

[48] *Herchen* 94 et seq.

[49] MünchKomm BGB/*Kindler* IntInsR mn 255.

[50] *Virgós/Schmit* Explanatory report mn 100; Moss/Fletcher/Isaacs-*Moss/Smith*, Regulation, mn 8.88.

[51] *Paulus* Komm EuInsVO Art 5 mn 6.

within the meaning of Art 5 (1) of the EIR is a matter to be decided by the national law that governs pursuant to the conflict of laws rules commonly applicable to rights *in rem* prior to the opening of insolvency proceedings, which is the *lex rei sitae* in most cases.[52] One exception to this is found in Art 5 (3) of the EIR: a right recorded in a public register and enforceable against third parties under which a right *in rem* within the meaning of Art 5 of the EIR may be obtained is – immediately and irrespective of national law – considered a right *in rem*.[53]

Pursuant to the Explanatory Report, a right *in rem* is characterized by the following:[54] **30**

a) It is directly and immediately linked to the thing that is the object (purpose) of the **31** right *in rem* and that serves the satisfaction of the underlying claim regardless of whose property the concerned thing belongs to and regardless of the relationship that exists between the legal holder and another person.

b) The absolute nature of the right conferred on the party entitled to it means that he **32** can bring an action based on this right against anyone who disregards or prejudices it without his consent (a common example of such a right is the action to recover possession of an object), that the right *in rem* remains in existence even when the thing itself is sold to a third party (it is enforceable *erga omnes* subject to the special protection afforded to the buyer in good faith), and that it continues to exist even when individual legal actions are brought by third parties and in the case of collective insolvency proceedings (through the right to preferential treatment (*Absonderung*) or the individual satisfaction in conjunction with such proceedings).

The right *in rem* must be directly and immediately linked to the thing/right regardless **33** of who the thing/right belongs to, and it must be absolute and enforceable against everyone.[55] Because they are exceptions to Art 4 of the EIR, rights *in rem* must be construed narrowly.[56]

To make sure that floating charges were covered by Art 5 of the EIR, Ireland and **34** Great Britain insisted on the clarification found in Art 5 (1) of the EIR according to which rights *in rem* may exist not only in specific assets, but also in collections of indefinite assets as a whole which change from time to time.[57]

Article 6
Set-off

1. The opening of insolvency proceedings shall not affect the right of creditors to demand the set-off of their claims against the claims of the debtor, where such a set-off is permitted by the law applicable to the insolvent debtor's claim.

2. Paragraph 1 shall not preclude actions for voidness, voidability or unenforceability as referred to in Article 4(2)(m).

---

[52] MünchKomm InsO/*Reinhart* Art 5 EuInsVO mn 5; *Virgós/Schmit* Explanatory report mn 100; *Haas* FS Gerhardt (2004), 319, 331.

[53] *Virgós/Schmit* Explanatory report mn 101.

[54] *Virgós/Schmit* Explanatory report mn 103.

[55] MünchKomm InsO/*Reinhart* Art 5 EuInsVO mn 6.

[56] MünchKomm BGB/*Kindler* IntInsR mn 255.

[57] *Virgós/Schmit* Explanatory report mn 104; MünchKomm InsO/*Reinhart* Art 5 EuInsVO mn 6; MünchKomm BGB/*Kindler* IntInsR mn 259; *Smid* Komm EuInsVO Art 5 mn 15; Moss/Fletcher/Isaacs-*Moss/Smith*, Regulations, mn 8.89.

Contents

Index

Bibliography

Balz Das neue Europäische Insolvenzübereinkommen, ZIP 1996, p 948; *Bork* Die Aufrechnung im internationalen Insolvenzverfahrensrecht, ZIP 2002, p 690; *Duursma-Kepplinger/Duursma/Chalupsky* Europäische Insolvenzverordnung, Kommentar (2002); *Ehricke/Ries* Die neue Europäische Insolvenzverordnung, JuS 2003, p 313; *Eidenmüller* Europäische Verordnung über Insolvenzverfahren und zukünftiges deutsches internationales Insolvenzrecht, IPRax 2001, p 2; *Florian* Das englische internationale Insolvenzecht (1989); *Gottwald* Grenzüberschreitende Insolvenzen (1997); *Fritz/Bähr* Die Europäische Verordnung über Insolvenzverfahren – Herausforderung an Gerichte und Insolvenzverwalter, DZWiR 2001, p 221; *Haß/Huber/Gruber/Heiderhoff* EU-Insolvenzverordnung, Kommentar (2005); *Huber* Internationales Insolvenzrecht in Europa, ZZP 114 (2001), p 133; *Kemper* Die Verordnung (EG) Nr. 1346/2000 über Insolvenzverfahren, ZIP 2001, p 1609; *Kolmann* Kooperationsmodelle im internationalen Insolvenzrecht (2001); *Leible/Staudinger* Die europäische Verordnung über Insolvenzverfahren, KTS 2000, p 533; Münchener Kommentar zur Insolvenzordnung, vol 1 (2001); *Paulus* Banken und Insolvenz – eine internationale Betrachtung, ZBB 2002, p 492; *Paulus* Europäische Insolvenzverordnung, Kommentar (2006); *Schack* Internationales Zivilverfahrensrecht (2002); *Smid* Deutsches und Europäisches Internationales Insolvenzrecht, Kommentar (2004); *Taupitz* Das (zukünftige) europäische Internationale Insolvenzrecht – insbesondere aus internationalprivatrechtlicher Sicht, ZZP 111 (1998), p 315; *Virgós/Schmit* Erläuternder Bericht zu dem EU-Übereinkommen über Insolvenzverfahren, in Stoll (ed), Vorschläge und Gutachten (1997), p 32; *Von Wilmowsky* KTS 1998, p 343; *Wunderer* Auswirkungen des Europäischen Übereinkommens über Insolvenzverfahren auf Bankgeschäfte, WM 1998, p 793.

1. Overview

1 Art 6 of the EIR regulates a set-off similar to the way Art 5 of the EIR regulates rights *in rem* and Art 7 of the EIR the reservation of title.[1] Set-off is the subject matter of two different provisions in the EIR.

- The first one, Art 4 (2) of the EIR, provides that the conditions for determining the validity of a set-off are found in the law that governs the insolvency (Art 4 (2) sentence 2 (d) of the EIR[2]).

---

[1] Cf *Virgós/Schmit* Explanatory report mn 107.

[2] Cf the comments at Art 4 of the EIR mn 50 et seq.

- The second one, Art 6 of the EIR, contains a special rule that applies when the set-off situation is established prior to the opening of insolvency proceedings. According to Art 6 (1) of the EIR, a creditor's right to set off his claim against a claim of the debtor is not affected by the opening of insolvency proceedings if the set-off is permitted by the law that governs the insolvent debtor's claim. One of the goals of Art 6 of the EIR is to uphold the securing-like nature of a set-off.[3] Should the set-off fail pursuant to the law governing the insolvency proceedings, Art 6 of the EIR allows the invoking of the law applicable to the principal claim (*Hauptforderung*) together with its insolvency law.

By way of explanation, the European definition of "principal claim" and "counterclaim" does not coincide with the terminology customarily used in German-speaking legal circles. The debtor's claim against which the set-off is being made (passive claim) is termed the *"Gegenforderung"* (counterclaim), while the *"Hauptforderung"* (principal claim) describes the claim of the creditor who is seeking a set-off (active claim).[4]

2. Art 6 of the EIR as an Exception to Art 4 (2) of the EIR

2.1 Dogmatic Classification

Because Art 4 (2) sentence 2 (d) of the EIR contains the simple wording "the conditions under which set-offs may be invoked", the majority of legal writers[5] construe this to mean that both the substantive validity of a set-off as well as its effectiveness (enforceability) in the event of insolvency proceedings is governed by the *lex fori concursus* of the opening State. A differentiation – such as that found in German law – is also not to be found in every legal system.[6] And alone the wording of Art (4) sentence 2 (d) of the EIR does not allow any clear conclusion to be drawn. This approach would also mean a change in the governing law when insolvency proceedings are opened: when the debtor is solvent, the set-off is governed solely by the law applicable to the principal claim, and in the event of an insolvency by the civil law (in respect of permissibility in terms of insolvency law) of the opening State.[7] **2**

The opposing view holds that the wording of Art 4 (2) sentence 2 (d) of the EIR must be understood as distinguishing between the substantive-law validity of a set-off and its effectiveness (enforceability) in insolvency proceedings.[8] According to this view, despite an extensive allocation of the *lex fori concursus*, not all of the conditions for a set-off are to be assessed pursuant to the law governing the insolvency. Similar to German international insolvency law,[9] a distinction must also be made – where the EIR applies – be-

---

[3] See on this Recital 26 of the EIR, in which this "guarantee function" is mentioned.

[4] *Smid* Komm EuInsVO Art 6 mn 2; D-K/D/Ch-*Duursma-Kepplinger* Art 6 mn 1.

[5] Prevailing opinion: see *Gottwald* Grenzüberschreitende Insolvenzen (1997) 36; *Huber* ZZP 114 (2001), 133, 161; *Leible/Staudinger* KTS 2000, 533, 555; *Taupitz* ZZP 111 (1998), 315, 343.

[6] *Florian* Das englische internationale Insolvenzrecht (1998), 87 who comments that, although no differentiation is made in England in the case of avoidance actions, a distinction is being drawn between a set-off in bankruptcy proceedings and a set-off during normal legal proceedings.

[7] *Bork* ZIP 2002, 690, 692.

[8] *Von Wilmowski* KTS 1998, 343, 357 et seq; *Herchen* Das Übereinkommen über Insolvenzverfahren (2000), 134 et seq; *Kolmann* Kooperationsmodelle (2001), 310 et seq.

[9] Which has developed a "combined solution" pursuant to which "whether" a set-off is permitted is determined by the law governing the insolvency proceedings, and the "how", i.e. the actual requirements for it, is determined pursuant to the contract law governing the principal claim against which a set-off is

tween the right of set-off pursuant to substantive law and the permissibility of the set-off in an insolvency proceeding, the rule in Art 4 (2) sentence 2 (d) of the EIR referring to the latter.

3 Even if a uniform application of the *lex fori concursus* appears to make the conducting of the proceedings easier and appears to do more justice to the equal treatment of creditors, Art 4 (2) sentence 2 (d) of the EIR must not be construed in isolation but must be read together with Art 4 (1) of the EIR.

4 According to Art 4 (1) of the EIR, the law of the State of the opening of proceedings applies to "insolvency proceedings and their effects". This general rule of Art 4 (1) of the EIR is particularized in subsection 2 sentence 2 (d) thereof. According to the latter, the law of the State of the opening of proceedings governs the opening,[10] the conduct, and the closing of insolvency proceedings, and "in particular the conditions under which set-offs may be invoked". In this context, Art 4 (2) sentence 2 (d) of the EIR must be so understood that only the **effects of the insolvency proceedings** are to be governed by the *lex fori concursus.*[11] The civil-law validity is not governed by the *lex fori concursus.* It only determines whether a set-off is permissible in the insolvency proceedings.[12]

5 According to Art 6 of the EIR, a set-off is still permitted even after insolvency proceedings have been opened if the law governing the principal claim (*Hauptforderung*) continues to permit a set-off. This makes sense if the EIR presumes that the creation under civil law of the right of set-off is being assessed pursuant to the law governing the principal claim. And this is exactly what is intended here, namely the reliance on the applicability of this law. Also speaking in favour of a differentiation is the absence of an apparent reason as to why the European legislators would have wanted to cause a change of the governing law when insolvency proceedings are opened. The harmonization of international insolvency law does not compel the application of the civil law of the *lex fori concursus.*[13]

6 Therefore, Art 4 of the EIR only regulates the hurdles that must be overcome to permit a set-off in the insolvency proceedings, but it does not regulate the civil-law requirements for validly establishing the set-off. The civil-law requirements for validly establishing a set-off are thus a matter for the law governing the principal claim. The hurdles that must be overcome in order to permit a set-off in the insolvency proceedings is a matter for the *lex fori concursus.*

2.2 Connection to a Member State and to a non-EU country

7 Although Art 4 (2) sentence 2(d) of the EIR stipulates that the law of the opening State determines the permissibility – for the purposes of the insolvency proceedings – of the set-off, Art 6 of the EIR sets up a special rule. Art 6 of the EIR states that a set-off

being made. On this BGHZ 38, 256; BGHZ 95 256, 273; *v Wilmowsky* KTS 1998, 343, 344 et seq. The phrase "combined solution" is found in D-K/D/Ch-*Duursma-Kepplinger* Art 6 fn 5.

10 According to the decision of the ECJ in Eurofood/Parmalat, a proceeding in already opened within the meaning of the EIR when a temporary administrator has been appointed. See ECJ dated 2 May 2006 – C-341/04 (Eurofood IFSC Ltd), NZI 2006, 360 et seq (→ cf Table of Cases Art 3 of the EIR Appendix A mn 10).

11 *Bork* ZIP 2002, 690, 692; *Ehricke/Ries* JuS 2003, 313, 316; MünchKomm InsO/*Reinhart* Art 4 EuInsVO mn 6; Haß/Huber/Gruber/Heiderhoff-*Haß/Herweg* Art 4 EuInsVO mn 32.

12 See also *von Wilmowsky* KTS 1998, 343, 360.

13 On the whole issue see *Bork* ZIP 2002, 690, 692 et seq; *Kolmann* Kooperationsmodelle (2001), 214 et seq; contra: *Huber* ZZP 114 (2001), 133, 161 referring to *Gottwald* Grenzüberschreitende Insolvenzen 36 and *Taupitz* ZZP 111 (1998) 315, 343.

will also be permitted if this is permitted by the law governing the insolvent debtor's claim.[14] Art 6 of the EIR regulates not only the substantive-law hurdles for permitting a set-off.[15] It also guarantees the reliance that the creditor placed in the applicability of the law pursuant to which the claim was created and in the ability to enforce the set-off also provided for by this law.[16] But the special rule found in Art 6 of the EIR only applies if the *lex fori concursus* does not permit the set-off and the insolvent debtor's claim is governed by the law of the Member State.[17] In the result, the law that is more set-off "friendly" will always prevail.[18] The application of this set-off "friendlier" law presupposes, however, that it is the law of a State that falls within the scope of the EIR's application. If the set-off "friendlier" law is not the law of a State that falls within the scope of the EIR's application, the issue of whether a set-off is permitted is governed exclusively by the rules of private international law of the State in which the insolvency proceedings have been opened.[19]

3. Decisive Point in Time

The requirement remains, however, that the mutual claims must have been created prior to the opening[20] of the insolvency proceedings.[21] Although this is being criticized[22] for violating the principle of equal satisfaction of creditors, it is a desirable solution from the point of view of safeguarding commercial transactions. The ascertainment of the time of creation is, on the other hand, a matter for the law governing the contractual claim. **8**

Should the set-off situation arise after the opening of proceedings, then Art 4 (2) sentence 2(d) of the EIR applies exclusively, i.e. the law of the State of the proceedings.[23] In the case of cross-border insolvencies, the substantive validity is therefore not determined pursuant to the law governing the set-off but rather by the law governing the insolvency proceedings (Art 4 (2) sentence 2 (d) of the EIR), unless of course it involves a right of set-off already in existence prior to the opening of proceedings.

The requirements for enforcing a set-off must be proven by the debtors of the insolvent debtor.[24]

---

[14] As to the terms "principal claim" and "counterclaim" see *von Wilmowsky* KTS 1998, 343 fn 2.

[15] *Leible/Staudinger* KTS 2000, 533, 555 et seq; *von Wilmowsky* KTS 1998, 343, 360 et seq; *Bork* ZIP 2002, 690, 694.

[16] MünchKomm InsO/*Reinhart* Art 6 EuInsVO mn 1; *Paulus* Komm EuInsVO Art 6 mn 1.

[17] *Schack* mn 1099; *Huber* ZZP 114 (2001) 133, 161; *Taupitz* ZZP 111 (1998) 315, 343.

[18] *Schack* mn 1099, *Huber* ZZP 114 (2001), 133; *Bork* ZIP 2002, 690, 694; *von Wilmowsky* KTS 1998, 343, 361; D-K/D/Ch-*Duursma-Kepplinger* Art 6 mn 13.

[19] *Bork* ZIP 2002, 690, 695; *Virgós/Schmit* Explanatory report mn 93; D-K/D/Ch-*Duursma-Kepplinger* Art 6 mn 3 MünchKomm InsO/*Reinhart* Art 6 EuInsVO mn 2: it can also be the law of a non-EU State (disputable); *Paulus* ZBB 2002, 492, 496: for a German creditor, this provision is interesting if the main insolvency proceedings are opened in another Member State, whose law forbids set-off. In this case, a German creditor can make use of sec 94 et seq InsO, if German law applies to the claim.

[20] In-depth on opening of insolvency proceedings, see Art 2 of the EIR mn 24 et seq. Cf ECJ dated 2 May 2006 – C-341/04 (Eurofood IFSC Ltd), NZI 2006, 360 et seq (→ cf Table of Cases Art 3 of the EIR Appendix A mn 10).

[21] *Virgós/Schmit* Explanatory report mn 110; *Leible/Staudinger* KTS 2000, 533, 555; *Huber* ZZP 114 (2001) 133, 161; MünchKomm InsO/*Reinhart* Art 6 EuInsVO mn 3; *Fritz/Bähr* DZWiR 2001, 1609, 1617.

[22] *Kemper* ZIP 2001, 1609, 1617.

[23] *Virgós/Schmit* Explanatory report mn 110; MünchKomm InsO/*Reinhart* Art 6 EuInsVO mn 3.

[24] *Paulus* Komm EuInsVO Art 6 mn 5.

4. Agreed Set-Off

9 A contractually agreed set-off must be based on an agreement that complies with the law applicable to it pursuant to the 1980 Rome Convention.[25] Commensurate with the legal concept underlying Art 5 of the EIR, the set-off agreement is governed by the law of the State that applies to this agreement provided that the claims to be set-off were created prior to the opening of insolvency proceedings.[26]

5. Connecting Factors in Art 6 of the EIR (Summary)

5.1 Application of the Set-Off "Friendlier" Law

10 The general rule is that the set-off is subject to the law that governs the insolvency proceedings (Art 4 (2) sentence 2 (d) of the EIR[27]). If a set-off is not possible pursuant to this rule, Art 6 of the EIR – as an exception to this rule – stipulates that the set-off is not affected by the opening of insolvency proceedings if such set-off is permitted by the law applicable to the principal claim (law governing the set-off). Therefore, if the set-off is not permitted pursuant to the law governing the insolvency proceedings, then the law governing the set-off no longer plays a role. But if the set-off is permitted by the law governing the insolvency proceedings, then a right of set-off pursuant to the law governing the set-off remains intact. The condition is, however, that the claim already existed at the time of the opening of insolvency proceedings (detailed discussion above at mn 1 et seq).

5.2 Limits to Art 6 (2) of the EIR

11 An attempt is being made here to protect the creditors by subjecting the issues of voidness, voidability, or unenforceability – in conjunction with a set-off as well – to the law of the State of the opening of proceedings (Art 6 (2) in conjunction with Art 4 (2) sentence 2 (m) of the EIR). Accordingly, the provisions dealing with avoidance in set-off situations that have been brought about in a disloyal manner or subsequent to the insolvency, or those dealing with a prohibition of set-off, remain in force in such cases.[28] What is unclear is whether a mere invocation of Art 4 (2) sentence 2 (m) of the EIR operates to exclude the application of Art 13 of the EIR, the "cumulation principle"[29] in the law of rescission. But since Art 13 EIR explicitly refers to Art 4 (2) sentence 2 (m) of the EIR, its wording alone speaks in favour of applying it whenever Art 4 (2) sentence 2 (m) of the EIR applies. Therefore both provisions should be applied whenever the issue involves creditors' avoidance actions (*Insolvenzanfechtung*) or other similar actions.[30] Art 6 (2) of the EIR also wishes to provide protection via the provisions dealing with creditors' avoidance actions (*Insolvenzanfechtung*). The EIR has, however, with respect to the issue of creditors' avoidance actions, clearly opted for the "cumulation principle". And in the absence of an explicit exhortation from the legislator, there is no apparent reason why this principle should not apply in this situation.

---

[25] *Virgós/Schmit* Explanatory report mn 110.

[26] *Virgós/Schmit* Explanatory report mn 110.

[27] See the comments at Art 4 of the EIR mn 50 et seq.

[28] *Balz* ZIP 1996, 948, 950; MünchKomm InsO/*Reinhart* Art 6 EuInsVO mn 4.

[29] See the comment on this at Art 13 of the EIR mn 3. See also *Smid* Komm EuInsVO Art 13 mn 6 with further references.

[30] Also held, without discussion, by *Wunderer* WM 1998, 793, 797.

Article 7
Reservation of title

1. The opening of insolvency proceedings against the purchaser of an asset shall not affect the seller's rights based on a reservation of title where at the time of the opening of proceedings the asset is situated within the territory of a Member State other than the State of opening of proceedings.

2. The opening of insolvency proceedings against the seller of an asset, after delivery of the asset, shall not constitute grounds for rescinding or terminating the sale and shall not prevent the purchaser from acquiring title where at the time of the opening of proceedings the asset sold is situated within the territory of a Member State other than the State of the opening of proceedings.

3. Paragraphs 1 and 2 shall not preclude actions for voidness, voidability or unenforceability as referred to in Article 4(2)(m).

Contents

Index

Bibliography

Duursma-Kepplinger/Duursma/Chalupsky Europäische Insolvenzverordnung, Kommentar (2002); *Eidenmüller* Europäische Verordnung über Insolvenzverfahren und zukünftiges deutsches internationales Insolvenzrecht, IPRax 2001, p 2; *Huber* Internationales Insolvenzrecht in Europa, ZZP 114 (2001), p 133; Münchener Kommentar zur Insolvenzordnung, vol 1 (2001); *Paulus* Europäische Insolvenzverordnung, Kommentar (2006); *Taupitz* Das (zukünftige) europäische Internationale Insolvenzrecht – insbesondere aus internationalprivatrechtlicher Sicht, ZZP 111 (1998), p 315; *Virgós/Schmit* Erläuternder Bericht zu dem EU-Übereinkommen über Insolvenzverfahren, in Stoll (ed), Vorschläge und Gutachten (1997), p 32.

1. Introduction

With respect to a reservation of title, Art 7 of the EIR represents an **exception to the principle that the *lex fori concursus* applies** (Art 4 of the EIR); Art 7 (1) of the EIR deals with the insolvency of the **conditional purchaser**, Art 7 (2) of the EIR with the insolvency of the **conditional seller**. 1

2 Art 7 of the EIR presupposes – as does Art 5 of the EIR in the case of rights *in rem* – that the reservation of title has been validly established prior to the opening of insolvency proceedings and that the property subject to the reservation of title ("secured property") is situated in a Member State other than the one in which insolvency proceedings have been opened. Art 7 (2) of the EIR also demands that the secured property has already been delivered.

3 **Conclusion:** A reservation of title validly created in a Member State is always immune from an insolvency and must be observed by the liquidator in the other Member State in which insolvency proceedings have been opened. The intention is to protect the legal position acquired by the particular non-debtor prior to the opening of proceedings. This serves to protect the trust placed in, and the legal certainty of the laws of, a Member State other than the State of the opening of proceedings, and the interests of commercial transactions (object of the rule).[1]

2. Reservation of Title

4 Art 7 of the EIR does not provide a definition of reservation of title. Whether a reservation of title exists is a matter to be decided by the law of the place where the property is situated (*lex rei sitae*).[2] But whether this reservation of title has been effectively agreed is determined by the law of the State where the property was situated at the time the right was acquired.

Prevailing opinion holds that Art 7 of the EIR does not apply to extended forms of reservations of title (renewed, enlarged reservation of title). Being secured rights *in rem*, these extended forms are governed by Art 5 of the EIR.[3]

3. *Situs* of the Property

5 The secured property must be situated in a Member State other than the one in which insolvency proceedings have been opened.[4]

If the purchased or sold property finds its way to another Member State after the opening of proceedings, then Art 4 of the EIR applies without restriction.[5] If the property is situated in a non-EU country, the legal situation is governed by the autonomous international insolvency law of the opening State.[6]

4. Insolvency of the Conditional Purchaser

6 In the event of insolvency on the part of the conditional purchaser, the rights of the seller are, pursuant to Art 7 (1) of the EIR, exempted from the insolvency effects of the

1 *Virgós/Schmit* Explanatory report mn 112; *Paulus* Komm EuInsVO Art 7 mn 1.

2 D-K/D/Ch-*Duursma-Kepplinger* Art 7 mn 5; MünchKomm InsO/*Reinhart* Art 7 EuInsVO mn 1; *Taupitz* ZZP (1998) 342; *Eidenmüller* IPRax 2001, 6; *Huber* ZZP 114 (2001), 154, 159.

3 *Paulus* Komm EuInsVO Art 7 mn 3; D-K/D/Ch-*Duursma-Kepplinger* Art 7 mn 32 et seq.

4 *Virgós/Schmit* Explanatory report mn 112; *Paulus* Komm EuInsVO Art 7 mn 4.

5 *Virgós/Schmit* Explanatory report mn 112; *Paulus* Komm EuInsVO Art 7 mn 4.

6 *Paulus* Komm EuInsVO Art 7 mn 4.

lex fori concursus, i.e. the rights of the seller ensuing from the reservation of title are unaffected.[7] The rights of the conditional purchaser are determined – providing that all other requirements have been met – pursuant to the *lex rei sitae*. This rule will likely prove to be of little relevance since the purchaser generally has the secured property in his possession, which means that the secured property is not situated in a Member State other than the opening State.[8]

5. Insolvency of the Conditional Seller

Prevailing opinion[9] holds that Art 7 (2) of the EIR is a substantive-law rule that applies when insolvency proceedings are opened against the assets of a conditional seller provided that the property has been delivered prior to the opening: in such a case, the EIR stipulates that the opening of insolvency proceedings may not effect a rescission or a termination of the sale contract nor stand in the way of the purchaser's acquisition of ownership.[10] If the property is situated in a Member State other than the opening State, Art 7 (2) of the EIR prevents the legal consequences set out there even if such consequences would have occurred pursuant to either the *lex rei sitae* or the law of the place where proceedings were opened.[11] **7**

The property concerned must also have been delivered in a Member State and not in a non-EU country.[12]

6. Art 7 (3) of the EIR

Art 7 (3) of the EIR is comparable to Art 5 (4) of the EIR. Therefore the submissions made on this can be referred to accordingly.[13] **8**

Article 8
Contracts relating to immoveable property

The effects of insolvency proceedings on a contract conferring the right to acquire or make use of immoveable property shall be governed solely by the law of the Member State within the territory of which the immoveable property is situated.

---

[7] *Virgós/Schmit* Explanatory report mn 113; MünchKomm InsO/*Reinhart* Art 7 EuInsVO mn 1.

[8] MünchKomm InsO/*Reinhart* Art 7 EuInsVO mn 1.

[9] *Virgós/Schmit* Explanatory report mn 112; MüKo MünchKomm InsO/*Reinhart* Art 7 EuInsVO mn 2; D-K/D/Ch-*Duursma-Kepplinger* Art 7 mn 22; critical: *Paulus* Komm EuInsVO Art 7 mn 11, in both cases with further references.

[10] *Virgós/Schmit* Explanatory report mn 114; MünchKomm InsO/*Reinhart* Art 7 EuInsVO mn 7; D-K/D/Ch-*Duursma-Kepplinger* Art 7 mn 23.

[11] MünchKomm InsO/*Reinhart* Art 7 EuInsVO mn 7; D-K/D/Ch-*Duursma-Kepplinger* Art 7 mn 23.

[12] *Paulus* Komm EuInsVO Art 7 mn 9.

[13] Also *Virgós/Schmit* Explanatory report mn 112, 115; see comments at Art 5 of the EIR mn 26.

Contents

Index

Bibliography

Balz Das neue Europäische Insolvenzübereinkommen, ZIP 1996, p 948; *Bismarck von/Schümann-Kleber* Insolvenz eines deutschen Sicherungsgebers – Auswirkungen auf die Verwertung im Ausland belegener Kreditsicherheiten, NZI 2005, p 89; *Blersch/Goetsch/Haas* Berliner Kommentar zum Insolvenzrecht (April 2006); *Braun* Kommentar zur Insolvenzordnung (2004); *Chalupsky* Das europäische Übereinkommen über Insolvenzverfahren, in Baudenbacher (ed), Aktuelle Probleme des Europäischen und Internationalen Wirtschaftsrechts, vol 1 (1998); *Duursma-Kepplinger/Duursma/Chalupsky* Europäische Insolvenzverordnung, Kommentar (2002); *Ehricke/Ries* Die neue Europäische Insolvenzverordnung, JuS 2003, p 313; *Eickmann/Flessner/Irschlinger/Kirchhof/Kreft/Landfermann/Marotzke* (eds) Heidelberger Kommentar zur Insolvenzordnung (2006); *Fletcher* Insolvency in Private International Law (2005); Frankfurter Kommentar zum Insolvenzrecht (2005); *Fritz/Bähr* Die Europäische Verordnung über Insolvenzverfahren – Herausforderung an Gerichte und Insolvenzverwalter, DZWiR 2001, p 221; *Gottwald* Grenzüberschreitende Insolvenzen (1997); *Gottwald* Insolvenzrechtshandbuch (2006); Hamburger Kommentar zum Insolvenzrecht (2006); *Haß/Huber/Gruber/Heiderhoff* EU-Insolvenzverordnung, Kommentar (2005); *Hanisch* Das Recht grenzüberschreitender Insolvenzen – Auswirkungen im Immobiliensektor, ZIP 1992, p 1125; *Huber* Internationales Insolvenzrecht in Europa, ZZP 114 (2001) p 133; *Kemper* Die Verordnung (EG) Nr. 1346/2000 über Insolvenzverfahren, ZIP 2001, p 1609; *Kolmann* Kooperationsmodelle im internationalen Insolvenzrecht (2001); *Kübler/Prütting* Kommentar zur Insolvenzordnung, vol 3 (March 2006); *Leible/Staudinger* Die europäische Verordnung über Insolvenzverfahren, KTS 2000, p 533; *Liersch* Deutsches Internationales Insolvenzrecht, NZI 2003, p 302; *Morscher* Die europäische Insolvenzverordnung (2002); *Moss/Fletcher/Isaacs* (eds) The EC Regulation on Insolvency Proceedings (2002); Münchener Kommentar zum BGB (2006); Münchener Kommentar zur Insolvenzordnung vol 3 (2003); *Paulus* Europäische Insolvenzverordnung, Kommentar (2006); *Runkel* (ed) Anwaltshandbuch – Insolvenzrecht (2005); *Smid* Deutsches und Europäisches internationales Insolvenzrecht, Kommentar (2004); *Stoll* (ed) Vorschläge und Gutachten zur Umsetzung des EU-Übereinkommens über Insolvenzverfahren im deutschen Recht (1997); *Taupitz* Das (zukünftige) europäische Internationale Insolvenzrecht – insbesondere aus internationalprivatrechtlicher Sicht, ZZP 111 (1998), p 315; *Virgós/Garcimartín* The European Insolvency Regulation: Law and Practice (2004); *Virgós/Schmit* Erläuternder Bericht zu dem EU-Übereinkommen über Insolvenzverfahren, in Stoll (ed), Vorschläge und Gutachten (1997), p 32; *Wessels* Current Topics of International Insolvency Law (2004).

1. Overview

Art 8 of the EIR creates an exception in the case of **immoveable property** to the applicability of the ***lex fori concursus*** (= the law governing the insolvency, see Art 4 of the EIR mn 10 et seq) within the scope of the Regulation's application: pursuant to Art 8 of the EIR, the effects of insolvency proceedings on agreements for immoveable property are not subject to the ***lex fori concursus*** but to the ***lex rei sitae***.[1] For certain types of contracts (for contract types, see mn 7 et seq), the provisions of Art 8 of the EIR serve the **safeguarding** of interests at the **place where real property is located.**[2] **1**

Art 4 of the EIR basically provides that the law of the State in which proceedings are opened (*lex fori concursus*) governs these insolvency proceedings. The *lex fori concursus* determines, in particular, the impact of the insolvency proceedings on the debtor's current contracts (Art 4 (2) sentence 2 (e) of the EIR – see mn 54 et seq). Art 8 of the EIR constitutes an **exception** to Art 4 of the EIR and suspends in respect of immoveable property the law of the Member State in which the proceedings were opened. According to Art 8 of the EIR, the **law of the State in which the property is situated**, i.e. the ***lex rei sitae***, applies.[3] **2**

Example

In the event of a foreign insolvency involving real property situated in Germany, German law applies with regard to the effects of the insolvency proceedings on the German contract for acquisition or use (i.e. Sec 103 et seq *Ins*O).[4]

The liquidator is given the task of deciding – pursuant to the insolvency law of the Member State whose law governs – whether contracts are to be fulfilled or terminated. **3**

Art 8 of the EIR applies irrespective of whether insolvency proceedings are pending against the assets of the **debtor** or the **creditor** to the contract.[5] Equally irrelevant for an application of Art 8 of the EIR is whether the debtor is the owner, seller, landlord, or lessor of the property.[6] **4**

The exception to Art 4 of the EIR that is contained in Art 8 of the EIR is to be construed **narrowly**.[7] The exception **only concerns** the effects that insolvency proceedings have on **certain contracts**. It does **not** concern other aspects of validity of the law governing the insolvency pursuant to Art 4 of the EIR. Art 8 of the EIR has **no impact** for example on: **5**

---

[1] BK/*Pannen* Art 8 EuInsVO mn 2; *Virgós/Garcimartín* Regulation, p 124; *Wessels* Current Topics of International Insolvency Law (2004), p 14.

[2] *Virgós/Schmit* Explanatory report mn 118; *Paulus* Komm EuInsVO Art 8 mn 1; D-K/D/Ch-*Duursma-Kepplinger* Art 8 mn 8; Haß/Huber/Gruber/Heiderhoff-*Huber* Art 8 EuInsVO mn 2; MünchKomm InsO/*Reinhart* Art 8 EuInsVO mn 1; Kübler/Prütting-*Kemper* EuInsVO Art 8 mn 1; *Smid* Komm EuInsVO Art 8 mn 1; HamburgerKomm-*Undritz* Art 8 mn 1; BK-InsO/*Pannen* Art 8 EuInsVO mn 1; *Huber* ZZP 114 (2001) p 133, 163; *Ehricke/Ries* JuS 2003, 313, 317; Moss/Fletcher/Isaacs-*Moss/Smith*, Regulation, mn 8.109.

[3] Also *Paulus* Komm EuInsVO Art 8 mn 1; Haß/Huber/Gruber/Heiderhoff-*Huber* Art 8 EuInsVO mn 1; *Smid* Komm EuInsVO Art 8 mn 1; MünchKomm InsO/*Reinhart* Art 8 EuInsVO mn 1; HamburgerKomm-*Undritz* Art 8 mn 1; HK-InsO/*Stephan* Art 8 EuInsVO mn 1; *Virgós/Garcimartín* Regulation, p 124.

[4] BK-InsO/*Pannen* Art 8 EuInsVO mn 5.

[5] Kübler/Prütting-*Kemper* EuInsVO Art 8 mn 3.

[6] *Smid* Komm EuInsVO Art 8 mn 3.

[7] *Virgós/Garcimartín* Regulation, p 123.

- the ranking of claims pursuant to Art 4 (2) sentence 2 (i) of the EIR,[8]
- the issue of whether legal actions are void, voidable, or unenforceable pursuant to Art 4 (2) sentence 2 (m) of the EIR,[9]
- the creditors' rights after the closure of the insolvency proceedings.[10]

In relation to such matters, the ***lex fori concursus*** also applies to real property.[11]

2. Contractual Forms

6 Art 8 of the EIR applies to contracts that confer the right to acquire or use immoveable property (see mn 16 et seq). Art 8 of the EIR is conditioned on the contracts already being in existence at the time at which the insolvency proceedings are opened[12] (see mn 12 et seq).

2.1 Types of Contracts

7 Art 8 of the EIR applies to all contracts that confer the right to acquire or use immoveable property and to all other contracts aimed to procure such a right.[13] Contracts for **acquisition** are those whose intention is to alter the scope of powers in terms of property law, for example **sale or gratuitous/donation contracts.**[14]

8 The contractual **use** of immoveable property is, for the purposes of the Regulation, effected via **renting, leasing,**[15] a **usufructuary lease, or a hereditary tenancy.**[16] The term "use" in Art 8 of the EIR is broader than that used in Sec 100 *BGB*.[17]

---

8 *Virgós/Garcimartín* Regulation, p 123.

9 *Virgós/Garcimartín* Regulation, p 123.

10 *Virgós/Garcimartín* Regulation, p 123.

11 *Virgós/Garcimartín* Regulation, p 123.

12 *Smid* Komm EuInsVO Art 8 mn 2.

13 *Paulus* Komm EuInsVO Art 8 mn 3.

14 *Virgós/Schmit* Explanatory report mn 119; *Paulus* Komm EuInsVO Art 8 mn 3; D-K/D/Ch-*Duursma-Kepplinger* Art 8 mn 1; Haß/Huber/Gruber/Heiderhoff-*Huber* Art 8 EuInsVO mn 4; HK-InsO/*Stephan* Art 8 EuInsVO mn 2; BK-InsO/*Pannen* Art 8 EuInsVO mn 3; HamburgerKomm-*Undritz* Art 8 mn 2; *Balz* ZIP 1996, 948, 950; *Taupitz* ZZP 111 (1998) p 315, 345; *Leible/Staudinger*, KTS 2000, p 533, 557 Fn 180; *Kemper* ZIP 2001, 1609, 1616; *Huber* ZZP 111 (2001), p 133, 163; *Fritz/Bähr* DZWiR 2001, 221, 228; *Morscher* Die europäische Insolvenzverordnung p 40; *Kolmann* Kooperationsmodelle im internationalen Insolvenzrecht p 319; *Chalupsky* in Baudenbacher p 356; Moss/Fletcher/Isaacs-*Moss/Smith*, Regulation, mn 8.110.

15 *Virgós/Schmit* Explanatory report mn 119; D-K/D/Ch-*Duursma-Kepplinger* Art 8 mn 1; FK-InsO/*Wimmer* Anhang I nach § 358 mn 43; *Smid* Komm EuInsVO Art 8 mn 8; HamburgerKomm-*Undritz* Art 8 mn 2; MünchKomm InsO/*Reinhart* Art 8 EuInsVO mn 1; Kübler/Prütting-*Kemper* EuInsVO Art 8 mn 4; BK-InsO/*Pannen* Art 8 EuInsVO mn 3; *Huber* ZZP 114 (2001) p 133, 163; *Balz* ZIP 1996, 948, 950; *Gottwald* Grenzüberschreitende Insolvenzen p 37 (on Art 8 of the 1995 Insolvency Convention); Haß/Huber/Gruber/Heiderhoff-*Huber* Art 8 EuInsVO mn 4; Gottwald/*Gottwald* InsR-Handb § 131 mn 48; Moss/Fletcher/Isaacs-*Moss/Smith*, Regulation, mn 8.109; *Morscher* Die europäische Insolvenzverordnung p 40.

16 *Paulus* Komm EuInsVO Art 8 mn 3; FK-InsO/*Wimmer* Anhang I nach § 358 mn 43; *Smid* Komm EuInsVO Art 8 mn 7; Haß/Huber/Gruber/Heiderhoff-*Huber* Art 8 EuInsVO mn 4; MünchKomm InsO/*Reinhart* Art 8 EuInsVO mn 1; HamburgerKomm-*Undritz* Art 8 mn 2; Kübler/Prütting-*Kemper* EuInsVO Art 8 mn 4; *Gottwald* Grenzüberschreitende Insolvenzen p 37 (on Art 8 of the 1995 Insolvency Convention); *Balz* ZIP 1996, 948, 950.

17 MünchKomm BGB/*Kindler* IntInsR mn 316.

This applies not only to **synallagmatic contracts.** Art 8 of the EIR even applies to incomplete bilateral or unilateral contracts.[18] In the case of **mixed-type contracts,** i.e. contracts that link the acquisition or use of real property to another undertaking, such as the erection of a building, an examination must be made to determine whether that part of the contract protected by Art 8 of the EIR can be separated out. If a separation is possible, the different parts will be subject to different laws. If separation is not possible, then the *lex fori concursus* must be applied.[19] **9**

Art 8 of the EIR applies not only to contracts falling within the law of obligations, but it also covers **contracts under property law,** such as legal dispositions (*Verfügungen*) under German law.[20] The norm encompasses all property-law dispositions, the property-law notification system, and other registers.[21] The acquisition of real property from an insolvency debtor who has been divested of his powers of disposition is protected by the law of the State in which the property is situated (Art 14 of the EIR); under German law, Secs 892 et seq and 878 *BGB* apply.[22] **Priority notices** (e.g. in a land register) are also dealt with pursuant to the *lex rei sitae.* The protection afforded by the doctrine of good faith only ends once the notification of pending insolvency proceedings has been entered (in a public register) pursuant to Art 22 of the EIR and – in Germany – Sec 346 *InsO*.[23] **10**

Art 8 of the EIR **does not apply**, however, to contracts that grant a **secured right** to immoveable property.[24] The same holds true for **assignments for security purposes** of claims to rental payments as these are not geared to the acquisition or use of the immoveable property.[25] **11**

2.2 Time Factor

Art 8 of the EIR only applies to contracts that were already entered into, and thus legally existent, **on the date on which the** insolvency proceedings **were opened.**[26] Although the provision's wording is silent on the time factor, the foregoing can be inferred from the objectives of the norm.[27] Such an inference is also in line with the logic under- **12**

---

[18] D-K/D/Ch-*Duursma-Kepplinger* Art 8 mn 1, 5; Haß/Huber/Gruber/Heiderhoff-*Huber* Art 8 EuInsVO mn 4; HK-InsO/*Stephan* Art 8 EuInsVO mn 2; Kübler/Prütting-*Kemper* EuInsVO Art 8 mn 4.

[19] *Paulus* Komm EuInsVO Art 8 mn 3.

[20] D-K/D/Ch-*Duursma-Kepplinger* Art 8 mn 12 et seq; Gottwald/*Gottwald* InsR-Handb § 131 mn 46; *Smid* Komm EuInsVO Art 8 mn 5; Kübler/Prütting-*Kemper* EuIns-VO Art 102 mn 147; *Hanisch* ZIP 1992, 1125, 1130; *Kemper* ZIP 2001, 1609, 1616; contra: Braun/*Liersch* InsO § 336 InsO 12 and *Morscher* Die europäische Insolvenzverordnung p 40, with further references.

[21] D-K/D/Ch-*Duursma-Kepplinger* Art 8 mn 12 et seq; Gottwald/*Gottwald* InsR-Handb § 131 mn 46; *Smid* Komm EuInsVO Art 8 mn 5.

[22] Gottwald/*Gottwald* InsR-Handb § 131 mn 46; Kübler/Prütting-*Kemper* EuInsVO Art 102 mn 147; *Hanisch* ZIP 1992, 1125, 1130.

[23] Gottwald/*Gottwald* InsR-Handb § 131 mn 46; *Kemper* ZIP 2001, 1609, 1616.

[24] *Paulus* Komm EuInsVO Art 8 mn 4; *v Bismarck/Schümann-Kleber* NZI 2005, 89, 92; MünchKomm InsO/*Reinhart* Art 8 EuInsVO mn 2; HamburgerKomm-*Undritz* Art 8 mn 3.

[25] *Paulus* Komm EuInsVO Art 8 mn 4; Münch-Komm InsO/*Reinhart* Art 8 EuInsVO mn 2; *von Bismarck/Schümann-Kleber* NZI 2005, 89, 92.

[26] *Virgós/Schmit* Explanatory report mn 116 and 118; Haß/Huber/Gruber/Heiderhoff-*Huber* Art 8 EuInsVO mn 5; D-K/D/Ch-*Duursma-Kepplinger* Art 8 mn 3; Kübler/Prütting-*Kemper* EuInsVO Art 8 mn 5; *Smid* Komm EuInsVO Art 8 mn 2; HK-InsO/*Stephan* Art 8 EuInsVO mn 3.

[27] *Virgós/Schmit* Explanatory report mn 116 und 118; HK-InsO/*Stephan* Art 8 EuInsVO mn 3; D-K/D/Ch-*Duursma-Kepplinger* Art 8 mn 3.

lying the Regulation. Art 4 (2) sentence 2 (e) of the EIR, as a norm of general application, subjects the effects of the insolvency proceedings on current contracts to the insolvency law of the State in which proceedings were opened. Since Art 8 of the EIR is a special connecting factor to this norm, then only those contracts that exist on the date on which proceedings were opened are included.[28]

13 For contracts that the liquidator enters into during the insolvency proceedings, Art 8 of the EIR does not apply.[29]

14 The application of Art 8 of the EIR is conditioned firstly upon the **opening** of insolvency proceedings as per Art 3 in conjunction with Art 2 (a) of the EIR. In this connection, the recent ECJ decision in **Eurofood/Parmalat** must be taken into account (cf Table of Cases Art 3 of the EIR Appendix A mn 10).

15 In this decision, the ECJ ruled that the date on which a request is filed to appoint a **provisional liquidator** can be regarded as the **opening of proceedings** within the meaning of Art 16 of the EIR.[30] The concept of opening insolvency proceedings contemplated by Art 16 of the EIR is to be understood to include not only those opening judgements defined formally as such by the law of the Member State applicable to the court issuing the judgement, but also a judgement that is made in response to a request stemming from the debtor's insolvency to open one of the proceedings set out in Annex A of the EIR if such judgement leads to the divestment of the debtor and if, pursuant to it, one of the liquidators named in Annex C of the EIR is appointed.[31] As a result, the ordering of the temporary administration can also be regarded as the date of the "opening of proceedings" within the meaning of the Regulation. The same applies within the scope of application of Art 8 of the EIR.

3. Immoveable Property

16 The contract for the acquisition or use must relate to **immoveable property**. This property must be situated in a Member State other than the opening State.[32]

17 As to what exactly is meant by "immoveable property" is **in dispute**.

- One **approach** prefers an **autonomous interpretation**. According to this approach, the State in which the property is situated should not be permitted to define "immoveable property". The concept must be defined **autonomously** and **uniformly for all Member States**. This should be based on an **"observance of average European concepts"** or on a synopsis.[33] It is argued that the fact that the legal concept of immoveable property

[28] Haß/Huber/Gruber/Heiderhoff-*Huber* Art 8 EuInsVO mn 5; *Smid* Komm EuInsVO Art 8 mn 2.

[29] D-K/D/Ch-*Duursma-Kepplinger* Art 8 mn 3; Haß/Huber/Gruber/Heiderhoff-*Huber* Art 8 EuInsVO mn 5; *Liersch* NZI 2003, 302, 304 (concerning sec 336 InsO).

[30] ECJ dated 2 May 2006 – C-341/04 (Eurofood IFSC Ltd.), NZI 2006, 360 et seq → cf Table of Cases Art 3 of the EIR Appendix A mn 10 – Eurofood/Parmalat).

[31] ECJ C-341/04, judgement of 2 May 2006, ZInsO 2006, 484 → cf Table of Cases Art 3 of the EIR Appendix A, mn 10 – Eurofood/Parmalat); on this, see also: *Mankowski* BB 2006, 1753 et seq who draws special attention to the consequences of dogmatically treating the provisional opening of insolvency proceedings as equivalent to the final opening of such.

[32] Haß/Huber/Gruber/Heiderhoff-*Huber* Art 8 EuInsVO mn 6.

[33] Haß/Huber/Gruber/Heiderhoff-*Huber* Art 8 EuInsVO mn 3; D-K/D/Ch-*Duursma-Kepplinger* Art 8 mn 4; *Smid* Komm EuInsVO Art 8 mn 4; HK-InsO/*Stephan*

varies from Member State to Member State is a point in favour of the creation of a **uniform definition** of immoveable property. While one Member State has a broad definition of it, another Member State construes "immoveable property" more narrowly. Such divergent laws could therefore lead to a highly inconsistent application of the Regulation.

According to this approach, the term "immoveable property" refers primarily to **real property/real estate**. The categorization of business enterprises, ships, and aircraft (see mn 18 below) poses a problem for the advocators of this view, who would not classify ships and aircraft as immoveable property anyway (argumentation based on Art 11 of the EIR).[34]

- The **other approach**, which is **preferable**, advocates an application of the **law of the State in which the property is situated.**[35] What constitutes "immoveable property" is defined by the **laws of the Member State** in which the property is **situated.** In support of such an approach is the legal certainty afforded by an application via the existing legal regimes of the Member States. The autonomous interpretation, on the other hand, gives rise to the problem of who is supposed to provide the "uniform definition" of immoveable property for all of the Member States, and who should review this and how should it be reviewed. As the term is not defined in the Regulation itself, and is therefore not mandatory written law in all of the Member States, the enforcement of a uniform definition could prove to be highly difficult and problematic. Furthermore, it may be possible that immoveable property would be dealt with differently before and after insolvency proceedings have been opened in one and the same Member State. In the final analysis, it is better to define immoveable property pursuant to the **law of the State in which it is situated.** This upholds the purpose of Art 8 of the EIR, namely to subject contracts for the use of acquisition of immoveable property to the law of the State in which such property is situated. Only for immoveable property defined as such and situated in a Member State does this Member State have laws. And such laws are exactly what Art 8 of the EIR is invoking. A definition of this concept for the entire EU that is broader than the definition contained in the laws of Member State could lead to conflicts. For the "excess portion", the Member State would have no applicable law.

The immoveable property must be **real property**. This can be inferred from Arts 11 **18**
and 14 of the EIR, which clearly distinguishes this from ships and aircraft.[36]

The debtor need not be the **owner** of the immoveable property in order for it to be **19**
included in the insolvency estate;[37] the provision applies equally for insolvencies of the seller or the purchaser, and for insolvencies of lessors and lessees.[38] The debtor may also be a landlord or a lessor.[39]

Art 8 EuInsVO mn 4; Gottwald/*Gottwald* InsR-Handb § 131 mn 45; MünchKomm BGB/*Kindler* IntInsR mn 315.

[34] Cf also MünchKomm BGB/*Kindler* IntInsR mn 315.

[35] *Paulus* Komm EuInsVO Art 8 mn 5.

[36] *Paulus* Komm EuInsVO Art 8 mn 6; Braun/*Liersch* InsO § 336 InsO 15; Haß/Huber/Gruber/Heiderhoff-*Huber* Art 8 EuInsVO mn 3.

[37] D-K/D/Ch-*Duursma-Kepplinger* Art 8 mn 2; HK-InsO/*Stephan* Art 8 EuInsVO mn 2; Haß/Huber/Gruber/Heiderhoff-*Huber* Art 8 EuInsVO mn 4; *Smid* Komm EuInsVO Art 8 mn 3.

[38] D-K/D/Ch-*Duursma-Kepplinger* Art 8 mn 2; *Smid* Komm EuInsVO Art 8 mn 3.

[39] *Smid* Komm EuInsVO Art 8 mn 3.

4. Legal Consequences

20 The applicable law is the **law** of the territory in which the immoveable property is **situated.** The "legal consequence" therefore contemplated by the norm is the application of the ***lex rei sitae***, which means that the law of the State in which the property is situated governs. The basic rule pursuant to Art 4 (2) sentence 2 (e) of the EIR is that *lex fori concursus*, the law of the State in which the proceedings were opened, applies to the debtor's current contracts. Art 8 of the EIR is therefore an **exception to this rule.**[40]

21 The referral to the ***lex rei sitae*** means the invoking of the national insolvency laws of the respective State in which the property is situated and the treatment of unfulfilled contracts pursuant to it, which in German law is Sec 103 et seq *InsO.*[41]

22 The reason for invoking the *lex rei sitae* lies in the particularly close connection that exists between legal rights in real property and the legal regime in which the property is situated.[42] The transparency afforded by the application of national law, in particular for rental contracts or (usufructuary) leases, is one good reason to apply the *lex rei sitae*; otherwise it would not be possible to provide tenants, in particular, with protection from the impact of foreign insolvency proceedings.[43]

23 The various procedures in conjunction with the **different types of proceedings** (e.g. winding-up, restructuring, consumer proceedings) that are found within the legal regime of the Member State in which the property is situated must be complied with.[44]

24 The application of Art 8 of the EIR does not necessarily have to put the creditor in a better position than he would be in pursuant to the *lex fori concursus*; the law of the State in which the property is situated may even contain **stricter provisions.** As opposed to Art 11 of the EIR, the effects ensuing from the *lex fori concursus* do not constitute an upper limit for the effects ensuing from the laws of the place where the property is situated.[45]

5. Avoidance Actions

25 Contrary to Arts 5 and Art 7 of the EIR, Art 8 of the EIR **does not expressly** state that contracts for immoveable property are voidable pursuant to Art 13 of the EIR. But even without being expressly mentioned, such contracts are **voidable.**[46]

---

[40] *Virgós/Schmit* Explanatory report mn 118; D-K/D/Ch-*Duursma-Kepplinger* Art 8 mn 7, 8; FK-InsO/*Wimmer* Anhang I nach § 358 mn 43; Haß/Huber/Gruber/Heiderhoff-*Huber* Art 8 EuInsVO mn 7; HK-InsO/*Stephan* Art 8 EuInsVO mn 5; BK-InsO/*Pannen* Art 8 EuInsVO mn 2; Kübler/Prütting-*Kemper* EuInsVO Art 8 mn 6; Gottwald/*Gottwald* InsR-Handb § 131 mn 45; *Pannen* in Runkel (ed), AHB-Insolvenzrecht (2005) § 16 mn 313 (on sec 336 InsO); Moss/Fletcher/Isaacs-*Moss/Smith*, Regulation, mn 8.109; *Morscher* Die europäische Insolvenzverordnung p 40.

[41] *Paulus* Komm EuInsVO Art 8 mn 7; Braun/*Liersch* InsO § 336 InsO 12.

[42] FK-InsO/*Wimmer* Anhang I nach § 358 mn 44; HK-InsO/*Stephan* Art 8 EuInsVO mn 2.

[43] FK-InsO/*Wimmer* Anhang I nach § 358 mn 43; HK-InsO/*Stephan* Art 8 EuInsVO mn 1; BK-InsO/*Pannen* Art 8 EuInsVO mn 1.

[44] *Paulus* Komm EuInsVO Art 8 mn 9.

[45] D-K/D/Ch-*Duursma-Kepplinger* Art 8 mn 8; HK-InsO/*Stephan* Art 8 EuInsVO mn 5.

[46] *Smid* Komm EuInsVO Art 8 mn 3; *Paulus* Komm EuInsVO Art 8 mn 10; Haß/Huber/Gruber/Heiderhoff-*Huber* Art 8 EuInsVO mn 7.

What is disputed, however, is **which legal regime** is to determine the voidability. **26**

- **Some** argue that the **law of the State in which the property is situated** governs the avoidance.[47]
- The **preferred view** is that the avoidance is governed by the **law of the opening State** and **not** by the ***lex rei sitae***.[48] The logic underlying Art 4 (2) of the EIR can be drawn on to support the latter view. Avoidance actions brought by creditors of the insolvency are special, separate matters that are not subject to the exception found in Art 8 of the EIR.[49] Art 4 (2) sentence 2 (m) of the EIR is the *lex specialis* to Art 8 of the EIR.[50] Art 8 of the EIR merely supersedes Art 4 (2) sentence 2 (e) of the EIR.[51] The avoidance is thus determined in accordance with Art 4 (2) sentence 2 (m) of the EIR.[52] Art 13 of the EIR also speaks in favour of an application of the *lex fori concursus*. This provision stipulates when Art 4 (2) sentence 2 (m) of the EIR does not apply. The matter dealt with in Art 8 of the EIR is not listed here, which supports the argument that Art 4 (2) sentence 2 (m) of the EIR applies.

Article 9
Payment systems and financial markets

1. Without prejudice to Article 5, the effects of insolvency proceedings on the rights and obligations of the parties to a payment or settlement system or to a financial market shall be governed solely by the law of the Member State applicable to that system or market.

2. Paragraph 1 shall not preclude any action for voidness, voidability or unenforceability which may be taken to set aside payments or transactions under the law applicable to the relevant payment system or financial market.

Contents

[47] *Paulus* Komm EuInsVO Art 8 mn 10.

[48] MünchKomm BGB/*Kindler* IntInsR mn 322; *Smid* Komm EuInsVO Art 8 mn 9; D-K/D/Ch-*Duursma-Kepplinger* Art 8 mn 10; Haß/Huber/Gruber/Heiderhoff-*Huber* Art 8 EuInsVO mn 7.

[49] *Smid* Komm EuInsVO Art 8 mn 9; D-K/D/Ch-*Duursma-Kepplinger* Art 8 mn 10; Haß/Huber/Gruber/Heiderhoff-*Huber* Art 8 EuInsVO mn 7.

[50] MünchKomm BGB/*Kindler* IntInsR mn 322.

[51] MünchKomm BGB/*Kindler* IntInsR mn 322.

[52] Haß/Huber/Gruber/Heiderhoff-*Huber* Art 8 EuInsVO mn 7; D-K/D/Ch-*Duursma-Kepplinger* Art 8 mn 8.

Index

Bibliography

Balz Das neue Europäische Insolvenzübereinkommen, ZIP 1996, p 948; *Breutigam/Blersch/Goetsch* Berliner Kommentar zum Insolvenzrecht (April 2006); *Bork* Die Aufrechnung im internationalen Insolvenzverfahrensrecht, ZIP 2002, p 690; *Braun* Kommentar zur Insolvenzordnung (2004); *Chalupsky* Das europäische Übereinkommen über Insolvenzverfahren, in Baudenbacher (ed), Aktuelle Probleme des Europäischen und Internationalen Wirtschaftsrechts, vol 1 (1998); *Duursma-Kepplinger/Duursma/Chalupsky* Europäische Insolvenzverordnung, Kommentar (2002); *Ehricke* Zum anwendbaren Recht auf ein in einem Clearing-System vereinbartes Glattstellungsverfahren im Fall der Insolvenz ausländischer Clearing-Teilnehmer, WM 2006, p 2109; *Ehricke/Ries* Die neue Europäische Insolvenzverordnung, JuS 2003, p 313; Heidelberger Kommentar zur Insolvenzordnung, 4th edn (2006) (eds *Eickmann/Flessner/Irschlinger/Kirchhof/Kreft/Landfermann/Marotzke*); Frankfurter Kommentar zum Insolvenzrecht (2005); *Gottwald* Grenzüberschreitende Insolvenzen (1997); *Gottwald* Insolvenzrechtshandbuch (2006); Hamburger Kommentar zum Insolvenzrecht (2006) (ed *Schmidt, A.*); *Haß/Huber/Gruber/Heiderhoff* EU-Insolvenzverordnung, Kommentar (2005); *Huber* Internationales Insolvenzrecht in Europa, ZZP 114 (2001) p 133; *Keller* Die EG-Richtlinie 98/26 vom 19.5.1998 über die Wirksamkeit von Abrechnungen in Zahlungs- sowie Wertpapierliefer- und -abrechnungssystemen und ihre Umsetzung in Deutschland, WM 2000, p 1269; *Kemper* Die Verordnung (EG) Nr. 1346/2000 über Insolvenzverfahren, ZIP 2001, p 1609; *Kieper* Abwicklungssysteme in der Insolvenz – Dargestellt am Beispiel der Eurex Deutschland (2004); *Kübler/Prütting* Kommentar zur Insolvenzordnung, vol 3 (March 2006); *Leible/Staudinger* Die europäische Verordnung über Insolvenzverfahren, KTS 2000, p 533; *Morscher* Die europäische Insolvenzverordnung (2002); *Moss/Fletcher/Isaacs* (eds) The EC Regulation on Insolvency Proceedings (2002); Münchener Kommentar zur Insolvenzordnung, vol 3 (2003); *Niggemann/Blenske* Die Auswirkungen der Verordnung (EG) Nr. 1346/2000 auf den deutsch-französischen Rechtsverkehr, NZI 2003, p 471; *Pannen* Krise und Insolvenz bei Kreditinstituten (2006); *Paulus* Europäische Insolvenzverordnung, Kommentar (2006); *Paulus* Grundlagen des neuen Insolvenzrechts – Internationales Insolvenzrecht, DStR 2005, p 334; *Runkel* (ed) Anwaltshandbuch – Insolvenzrecht (2005); *Smid* Deutsches und Europäisches Internationales Insolvenzrecht (2004); *Stoll* (ed) Vorschläge und Gutachten zur Umsetzung des EU-Übereinkommens über Insolvenzverfahren im deutschen Recht (1997); *Virgós/Garcimartín* The European Insolvency Regulation: Law and Practice (2004); *Virgós/Schmit* Erläuternder Bericht zu dem EU-Übereinkommen über Insolvenzverfahren, in Stoll (ed), Vorschläge und Gutachten (1997), p 32; *Wessels* International Insolvency Law (2006); *Wimmer* Die EU-Verordnung zur Regelung grenzüberschreitender Insolvenzverfahren, NJW 2002, p 2427; *Wimmer* Die Verordnung (EG) Nr. 1346/2000 über Insolvenzverfahren, ZInsO 2001, p 97.

1. Overview

1 According to Recital 27 of the EIR, payment systems and financial markets are areas requiring special protection. Art 9 of the EIR contains a **special connecting factor**[1] for parties to:

- a **payment system**, or
- a **settlement system**, or
- a **financial market.**

2 Therefore the *lex fori concursus* does not apply to these matters, but rather the law that governs the system or market.[2] The special conflict of laws rule contained in Art 9 of the EIR involves cases in which the – deemed relevant – reference point of the system or market is in a Member State other than the State in which proceedings were opened.[3] The operators of such systems are being dealt with as if the insolvency proceedings had been opened in the Member State where the market is located.[4]

3 The objective of the provision is to avoid the problems that would arise from a conflict between the two legal systems (*lex fori concursus* / law of the system or the financial market) and to ensure legal certainty in commercial transactions.[5] The mobility and reliability of the systems, as well as the trust placed in the mechanisms associated with these, are being protected by subjecting the effects of the insolvency proceedings exclusively to the law that applies to the payment/processing system and to the financial market.[6] By applying the law that governs the system or market, the risk remains transparent and calculable.[7] Art 9 of the EIR prevents any negative consequences or restrictions on payment systems and financial markets that could possibly arise or be imposed by a foreign legal regime[8]; a frictionless functioning of the system or the market is thus being guaranteed.[9]

---

1 This special connecting factor can be compared with the conflicts of laws rule contained in sec 340 InsO in German law; see *Pannen* Krise und Insolvenz bei Kreditinstituten p 230; *Ehricke* WM 2006, 2109, 2113.

2 HK-InsO/*Stephan* Art 9 EuInsVO mn 1; *Smid* Komm EuInsVO Art 9 mn 2; MünchKomm InsO/*Reinhart* Art 9 EuInsVO mn 1; Haß/Huber/Gruber/Heiderhoff-*Huber* Art 9 EuIns-VO mn 1; D-K/D/Ch-*Duursma* Art 9 mn 1; *Gottwald* Grenzüberschreitende Insolvenzen p 37 (on Art 9 of the 1995 Insolvency Convention); Gottwald-*Gottwald* Insolvenzrechtshandbuch (2006) § 131 mn 62; *Bork* ZIP 2002, 690, 692; *Huber* ZZP 114 (2001), p 133, 163; *Niggemann/Blenske* NZI 2003, 471, 476; *Paulus* DStR 2005, 334, 337; *Paulus* Komm EuInsVO Art 9 mn 4; *Wessels* International Insolvency Law (2006) mn 10690; *Kieper* Abwicklungssysteme in der Insolvenz, p 180.

3 *Huber* ZZP 114 (2001), p 133, 138 et seq.

4 Haß/Huber/Gruber/Heiderhoff-*Huber* Art 9 EuInsVO mn 1; *Balz* ZIP 1996, 948, 951.

5 *Virgós/Schmit* Explanatory report mn 121.

6 *Virgós/Schmit* Explanatory report mn 120; HK-InsO/*Stephan* Art 9 EuInsVO mn 1; *Smid* Komm EuInsVO Art 9 mn 1; *Paulus* Komm EuInsVO Art 9 mn 1; MünchKomm InsO/*Reinhart* Art 9 EuInsVO mn 1; Haß/Huber/Gruber/Heiderhoff-*Huber* Art 9 EuInsVO mn 1; Kübler/Prütting-*Kemper* EuInsVO Art 9 mn 1; D-K/D/Ch-*Duursma* Art 9 mn 1, 7; *Huber* ZZP 114 (2001), 133, 164; *Kieper* Abwicklungssysteme in der Insolvenz, p 180.

7 Haß/Huber/Gruber/Heiderhoff-*Huber* Art 9 EuInsVO mn 1; D-K/D/Ch-*Duursma* Art 9 mn 6; *Wimmer* ZInsO 2001, 97, 101.

8 BK-InsO/*Pannen* Art 9 EuInsVO mn 1.

9 *Virgós/Schmit* Explanatory report mn 120; FK-InsO/*Wimmer* Anhang I nach § 358 mn 45; HK-InsO/*Stephan* Art 9 EuInsVO mn 2; Haß/Huber/Gruber/Heiderhoff-*Huber* Art 9 EuInsVO mn 1.

4 In addition to the conflict of laws rule contained in Art 9 (1) of the EIR[10], Art 9 (2) broadens the special connecting factor even further:[11]

With respect to the

- voidness,
- voidability, or
- the unenforceability on account of a detriment to the creditors,

the **law governing the contract** also applies instead of the *lex fori concursus.*[12] The relationships within a system or a market should be subject to a uniform body of law.[13]

5 Art 9 of the EIR applies to both **main** and **territorial insolvency proceedings** (Art 3 (1) or (2)–(4) of the EIR).[14] For main insolvency proceedings within the meaning of Art 3 (1) of the EIR, Art 9 of the EIR applies since such proceedings cover the entire domestic and foreign assets of the debtor. In the case of territorial proceedings pursuant to Art 3 (2) to (4) of the EIR, the payment system or the financial market must exist in the Member State in which the territorial proceedings are opened as such proceedings only cover those assets situated in the State in which these proceedings are opened.[15]

6 The significance of Art 9 of the EIR is somewhat diminished, however, by Art 1 (2) of the EIR, which provides that the Regulation does not apply to **credit institutions** and **investment undertakings,** these being typical parties to financial and settlement systems; see Art 1 of the EIR mn 22 et seq.[16]

2. Relationship to Directive 98/26/EC (Finality Directive)

7 Art 9 of the EIR must be considered[17] in conjunction with **Directive 98/26/EC** on settlement finality in payment and securities settlement systems ("Finality Directive").[18] According to Recital 27 of the EIR, the provisions of the Finality Directive have precedence over the provisions of the Regulation.[19]

8 The Finality Directive serves to protect and harmonize financial systems and markets.[20]

---

[10] HK-InsO/*Stephan* Art 9 EuInsVO mn 1; Kübler/Prütting-*Kemper* EuInsVO Art 9 mn 1; D-K/D/Ch-*Duursma* Art 9 mn 1; *Smid* Komm EuInsVO Art 9 mn 1.

[11] *Kieper* Abwicklungssysteme in der Insolvenz, p 180.

[12] HK-InsO/*Stephan* Art 9 EuInsVO mn 1; *Gottwald* Grenzüberschreitende Insolvenzen p 37 (on Art 9 of the 1995 Insolvency Convention).

[13] *Gottwald* Grenzüberschreitende Insolvenzen p 37 (on Art 9 of the 1995 Insolvency Convention).

[14] D-K/D/Ch-*Duursma* Art 9 mn 9; Kübler/Prütting-*Kemper* EuInsVO Art 9 mn 4; *Kieper* Abwicklungssysteme in der Insolvenz, p 179.

[15] Kübler/Prütting-*Kemper* EuInsVO Art 9 mn 4.

[16] D-K/D/Ch-*Duursma* Art 9 mn 2; Braun/*Liersch* InsO § 340 mn 7; *Kieper* Abwicklungssysteme in der Insolvenz, p 178.

[17] Directive 98/26/EC of the European Parliament and of the Council of 19 May 1998 on settlement finality in payment and securities settlement systems, OJ L 166 of 11 June, 1998 pp 0045–0050.

[18] *Virgós/Garcimartín* Regulation, p 127; Haß/Huber/Gruber/Heiderhoff-*Huber* Art 9 EuInsVO mn 2; HamburgerKomm-*Undritz* Art 9 mn 3.

[19] *Paulus* Komm EuInsVO Art 9 mn 1; Haß/Huber/Gruber/Heiderhoff-*Huber* Art 9 EuInsVO mn 2; HK-InsO/*Stephan* Art 9 EuInsVO mn 3; *Virgós/Garcimartín* Regulation, p 127; *Leible/Staudinger* KTS 2000, 533, 560.

[20] HK-InsO/*Stephan* Art 9 EuInsVO mn 3; D-K/D/Ch-*Duursma* Art 9 mn 1; *Pannen* in Runkel (ed), AHB-Insolvenzrecht (2005) § 16 mn 301.

It governs both national and cross-border payment systems.[21] Art 9 of the EIR, on the other hand, is restricted to cross-border payment/settlement systems and financial markets. But because it also covers financial markets, which the Finality Directive does not, it actually has a broader scope of application than the Finality Directive.[22] **9**

Directive 98/26/EC and the Regulation therefore supplement each other to provide comprehensive protection for payment/settlement systems and financial markets in the event of insolvency of one of their participants. However, where the regulatory content of the two laws is identical, the Finality Directive is only to be consulted for purposes of interpreting Art 9 of the EIR.[23] **10**

According to Art 10 of Directive 98/26/EC, this directive only applies to systems that are depicted as such by the Member States and systems that the Commission has been notified of. Art 9 of the EIR contains no such restriction.[24] Art 9 of the EIR therefore applies to **inter company netting agreements,**[25] **forward transactions using clearing systems,** or **commodity futures exchanges** as well.[26] Through Art 9 of the EIR, a special provision has also been created vis-à-vis Art 6 of the EIR.[27] **11**

Sec 340 (3) *InsO* is the **German provision implementing** the **Finality Directive,** which had previously been implemented[28] in **Art 102 Sec 4 of the *EGInsO* (old version)** through the *Gesetz zur Änderung insolvenzrechtlicher und kreditwesenrechtlicher Vorschriften* of December 8, 1999.[29] According to Sec 340 (2) of the *InsO*, the effects of insolvency proceedings on the rights and obligations of participants in a payment or securities delivery and settlement system (see Sec 1 (16) *KWG*) is governed by the law of the State that applies to this system. With respect to the legal effects of insolvency proceedings against a foreign institution that takes part in a national (German) system, national (German) law will apply. In this respect, German law supersedes the foreign *lex fori concursus.*[30] **12**

3. Art 9 (1) of the EIR

According to Art 9 (1) of the EIR, the effects of insolvency proceedings on the rights and obligations of parties to a **payment or settlement system** (see mn 14 et seq) or to a **financial market** (see mn 18 et seq) are governed solely by the law applicable to that system or market. **13**

---

[21] See Recital 6 of Directive 98/26/EC.

[22] Kübler/Prütting-*Kemper* EuInsVO Art 9 mn 3.

[23] Kübler/Prütting-*Kemper* EuInsVO Art 9 mn 3.

[24] Haß/Huber/Gruber/Heiderhoff-*Huber* Art 9 EuInsVO mn 4; MünchKomm InsO/*Reinhart* Art 9 EuInsVO mn 2; *Paulus* Komm EuIns-VO Art 9 mn 2; *Niggemann/Blenske* NZI 2003, 471, 477.

[25] For example in the Babcock case → cf Table of Cases Art 3 of the EIR Appendix B No 10.

[26] *Paulus* Komm EuInsVO Art 9 mn 2.

[27] *Niggemann/Blenske* NZI 2003, 471, 477.

[28] See the reasons for the governmental draft bill, BT-Drucks 15/16, p 20.

[29] BGBl I p 2384.

[30] *Keller* WM 2000, 1269, 1280. The Regulation also applies in reverse cases where German institutions participate in foreign systems. Furthermore, sec 340 (3) InsO also applies to activities within the meaning of sec 46a KWG or to comparable activities pursuant to foreign law.

3.1 Payment and Settlement Systems

14 The definition of "**payment and settlement system**" is not found in Art 9 of the EIR nor in any other provision of it.[31] Thus Directive 98/26/EC can be resorted to.[32] Art 2 (a) of this directive contains a definition of the term "**system**".[33] Summarized, a "system" within the meaning of Directive 98/26/EC is a formal agreement between at least three participants on common rules and standardized arrangements for the execution of payment or transfer orders between the participants, such agreement being governed by the laws of a Member State (where at least one of the participants has its head office) chosen by the participants.[34]

15 "**Payment systems**" refers to agreements on the settlement of payment processes between financial services institutions.[35] These include such things as technical and formal issues of transfer, conditions, and costs of order execution; system operating times and processing periods.[36]

16 The concept of "payment and settlement systems" includes such things as **liquidation contracts** and **netting agreements**[37] and, assuming that the security is located in this Member State, the alienation of securities as well (Recital 27 of the EIR).[38]

---

31 HK-InsO/*Stephan* Art 9 EuInsVO mn 4; Kübler/Prütting-*Kemper* EuInsVO Art 9 mn 5; MünchKomm InsO/*Reinhart* Art 9 EuInsVO mn 2; Haß/Huber/Gruber/Heiderhoff-*Huber* Art 9 EuInsVO mn 2.

32 *Smid* Komm EuInsVO Art 9 mn 4; Kübler/Prütting-*Kemper* EuInsVO Art 9 mn 5; HK-InsO/*Stephan* Art 9 EuInsVO mn 4; D-K/D/Ch-*Duursma* Art 9 mn 1; Haß/Huber/Gruber/Heiderhoff-*Huber* Art 9 EuInsVO mn 2; MünchKomm InsO/*Reinhart* Art 9 EuInsVO mn 2; Moss/Fletcher/Isaacs-*Moss/Smith*, Regulation, mn 8.113; *Virgós/Garcimartín* Regulation, p 128.

33 According to art 2 (a) of Directive 98/26/EC, the word "**system**" means "a formal agreement
– between three or more participants, without counting a possible settlement agent, a possible central counterparty, a possible clearing house or a possible indirect participant, with common rules and standardised arrangements for the execution of transfer orders between the participants,
– governed by the law of a Member State chosen by the participants; the participants may, however, only choose the law of a Member State in which at least one of them has its head office, and
– designated, without prejudice to other more stringent conditions of general application laid down by national law, as a system and notified to the Commission by the Member State whose law is applicable, after that Member State is satisfied as to the adequacy of the rules of the system.
Subject to the conditions in the first subparagraph, a Member State may designate as a system such a formal arrangement whose business consists of the execution of transfer orders as defined in the second indent of (i) and which to a limited extent executes orders relating to other financial instruments, when that Member State considers that such a designation is warranted on grounds of systemic risk.
A Member State may also on a case-by-case basis designate as a system such a formal arrangement between two participants, without counting a possible settlement agent, a possible central counterparty, a possible clearing house or a possible indirect participant, when that Member State considers that such designation is warranted on grounds of systemic risk."
According to art 2 (2) (e) of Directive 98/26/EC, "**clearing house**" means an "entity responsible for the calculation of the net positions of institutions, a possible central counterparty (art 2 (c) of Directive 98/26/EC) and/or a possible settlement agent (art 2 (d)) of Directive 98/26/EC)."

34 Kübler/Prütting-*Kemper* EuInsVO Art 9 mn 5; HK-InsO/*Stephan* Art 9 EuInsVO mn 4; D-K/D/Ch-*Duursma* Art 9 mn 3; Haß/Huber/Gruber/Heiderhoff-*Huber* Art 9 EuInsVO mn 2.

35 D-K/D/Ch-*Duursma* Art 9 mn 4; *Smid* Komm EuInsVO Art 9 mn 5; Haß/Huber/Gruber/Heiderhoff-*Huber* Art 9 EuInsVO mn 2.

36 D-K/D/Ch-*Duursma* Art 9 mn 4.

Securities settlement systems are involved with the transfer and delivery of concrete securities portfolios.[39] The entities operating the securities settlement systems are, for example, **DBC**[40] in Germany, the **Österreichische Kontrollbank** in Austria, **Sicovam** in France, and the two **International Central Securities Depositaries (ICSDs)**,[41] **Euroclear** in Belgium and **CEDEL**[42] in Luxembourg.[43] **17**

3.2 Financial Market

As with "payment and settlement systems", the Regulation contains no legal definition of **"financial market"**.[44] **18**

According to the *Virgós/Schmit* Report (see Introduction at mn 42), a **financial market** is to be understood as a market of a Member State in which financial instruments, other financial assets, or commodities forwards and options are being traded; which functions regularly; whose operating and accessing conditions are defined in a set of regulations; and which is subject to the laws, including any relevant supervision by the responsible authorities, of this Member State.[45] This definition is similar to the definition of **"regulated market"**[46] in the Council Directive on investment services in the securities field (93/22/EEC)[47].[48] **19**

---

[37] According to art 2 (k) of Directive 98/26/EC, netting is "the conversion into one net claim or one net obligation of claims and obligations resulting from transfer orders which a participant or participants either issue to, or receive from, one or more participants with the result that only a net claim may be demanded or a net obligation be owed."

[38] *Virgós/Schmit* Explanatory report mn 120; see also FK-InsO/*Wimmer* Anhang I nach § 358 mn 45; BK-InsO/*Pannen* Art 9 EuInsVO mn 3; HK-InsO/*Stephan* Art 9 EuInsVO mn 2, 4; Haß/Huber/Gruber/Heiderhoff-*Huber* Art 9 EuInsVO mn 1; D-K/D/Ch-*Duursma* Art 9 mn 1; *Smid* Komm EuInsVO Art 9 mn 3; *Wessels* International Insolvency Law (2006) mn 10690; *Morscher* Die europäische Insolvenzverordnung p 40.

[39] *Smid* Komm EuInsVO Art 9 mn 6; Haß/Huber/Gruber/Heiderhoff-*Huber* Art 9 EuInsVO mn 2; D-K/D/Ch-*Duursma* Art 9 mn 5.

[40] Deutsche Börse Clearing AG.

[41] International Central Securities Depositories.

[42] Centrale de Livraison de Valeurs.

[43] D-K/D/Ch-*Duursma* Art 9 mn 5.

[44] MünchKomm InsO/*Reinhart* Art 9 EuInsVO mn 2; HK-InsO/*Stephan* Art 9 EuInsVO mn 5; Moss/Fletcher/Isaacs-*Moss/Smith*, Regulation, mn 8.113.

[45] *Virgós/Schmit* Explanatory report mn 120; see also Kübler/Prütting-*Kemper* EuInsVO Art 9 mn 6; BK-InsO/*Pannen* Art 9 EuInsVO mn 2; Haß/Huber/Gruber/Heiderhoff-*Huber* Art 9 EuInsVO mn 3; *Wessels* International Insolvency Law (2006) mn 10691; *Pannen* in Runkel (ed), AHB-Insolvenzrecht (2005) § 16 mn 300.

[46] Within the meaning of art 1 no 13 of Directive 93/22/EEC, the term "regulated market" means a market for the instruments listed in Section B of the Annex which:
– appears on the list provided for in article 16 drawn up by the Member State which is the home Member State as defined in article 1 (6) (c);
– functions regularly,
– is characterized by the fact that regulations issued or approved by the competent authorities define the conditions for the operation of the market, the conditions for access to the market and, where Directive 79/279/EEC is applicable, to the conditions governing admission to listing imposed in that Directive and, where that Directive is not applicable, the conditions that must be satisfied by a financial instrument before it can be effectively dealt in on the market,
– requires compliance with all the reporting and transparency requirements laid down pursuant to articles 20 and 21."

[47] Council Directive 93/22/EEC of 10 May 1993 on investment services in the securities field, OJ L 141 p 27.

[48] Kübler/Prütting-*Kemper* EuInsVO Art 9 mn 6; HK-InsO/*Stephan* Art 9 EuInsVO mn 5; *Pannen* Krise und Insolvenz bei Kreditinstituten p 231.

20 It seems sensible to interpret "financial market" as a generic term encompassing other financial market systems that are exposed to a similar risk in the event of insolvency.[49]

3.3 Parties

21 Parties to a payment and settlement system and to a financial market within the meaning of Art 9 of the EIR include all participants in these systems/markets.[50] This means banks in particular.[51]

3.4 Opening Insolvency Proceedings

22 Art 9 (1) of the EIR only applies if insolvency proceedings exist.[52] The consequences of Art 9 of the EIR only begin to operate against payment and settlement systems or financial markets once insolvency proceedings have been opened (for the definition of "opening insolvency proceedings", see Art 2 of the EIR mn 24 et seq[53]). The system or the market must thus have been agreed to before the insolvency proceedings have been opened.[54]

4. Legal Consequences

23 Art 9 (1) of the EIR provides that the effects of the insolvency proceedings are subject to the laws of the Member State that governs the system or the market in issue. This rule is subject only to the exception regarding rights *in rem;* see mn 30.

4.1 Validity of the "*lex rei sitae*"

24 The rights and obligations of the parties to a payment system or a financial market are to be governed solely – as is the case prior to the opening of insolvency proceedings – by the law of the State in which the respective system or market is located.[55] Because of this special connecting factor, the *lex fori concursus* does not apply; instead, the law chosen per contract to govern that system or market, i.e. the *lex rei sitae*, applies.[56]

---

[49] MünchKomm InsO/*Reinhart* Art 9 EuInsVO mn 3.

[50] Kübler/Prütting-*Kemper* EuInsVO Art 9 mn 6; HK-InsO/*Stephan* Art 9 EuInsVO mn 2; *Morscher* Die europäische Insolvenzverordnung p 40.

[51] *Wessels* International Insolvency Law (2006) mn 10691; D-K/D/Ch-*Duursma* Art 9 mn 4.

[52] HK-InsO/*Stephan* Art 9 EuInsVO mn 7; Kübler/Prütting-*Kemper* EuInsVO Art 9 mn 7.

[53] It is also possible that "preliminary insolvency proceedings" may be deemed "opened insolvency proceedings" within the meaning of the Regulation.

[54] *Virgós/Schmit* Explanatory report mn 120; HK-InsO/*Stephan* Art 9 EuInsVO mn 7; *Wessels* International Insolvency Law (2006) mn 10690.

[55] *Smid* Komm EuInsVO Art 9 mn 2; *Paulus* Komm EuInsVO Art 9 mn 4; HK-InsO/*Stephan* Art 9 EuInsVO mn 1; *Paulus* DStR 2005, 334, 337; *Wimmer* NJW 2002, 2427, 2429; *Pannen* in Runkel (ed), AHB-Insolverzrecht (2005) § 16 mn 299; *Wessels* International Insolvency Law (2006) mn 10690; *Morscher* Die europäische Insolvenzverordnung p 40; *Virgós/Garcimartín* Regulation, p 126.

[56] HK-InsO/*Stephan* Art 9 EuInsVO mn 1; *Smid* Komm EuInsVO Art 9 mn 2; *Niggemann/Blenske* NZI 2003, 471, 476; *Gottwald* Grenzüberschreitende Insolvenzen p 37 (on Art 9 of the 1995 Insolvency Convention).

The goal here is to ensure that relationships in these systems are subject to a uniform legal regime.[57] Both the operators and the participants in these systems and markets should be able to rely on the application of an insolvency law regime whose rules they are familiar with from the outset;[58] the security and mobility of the systems and markets is thus being guaranteed.[59] This also strengthens the system's autonomy. Art 9 of the EIR builds on the Finality Directive (see above mn 7 et seq), which provides that the same law that governs the participants also governs the system (Art 8 of Directive 98/26/EC).[60] **25**

For the entire legal relationship, the law of the Member State in which the system was agreed or where the market exists[61] applies exclusively, including this State's insolvency laws.[62] This avoids any disruptive conflicting laws, especially in relation to netting, closing out in the event of default, and the treatment of mutual agreements.[63] **26**

The particular *lex rei sitae* that governs the system or the market is subject to the **parties' free disposition** (here the freedom to choose applicable law). This is restricted, however, to the law of a Member State in which at least one of the participants has its head office.[64] Generally the law of the place in which the technical clearing house is located is agreed.[65] The special connecting factor contemplated by Art 9 of the EIR only applies if the law of a Member State of one of the participants or of the system/financial market has been agreed on. Otherwise the special connecting factor does not operate and the connection to *lex fori concursus* remains.[66] Such a constraint corresponds to the material harmonization contained in Art 3 (1) of the Finality Directive for the treatment of these systems in the event of insolvency.[67] **27**

If the law of a State is agreed in which none of the participants has its head office, then, via general conflict of laws rules, the law of the State to which the contract is most closely connected applies subsidiarily (in Germany Art 28 *EGBGB* applies). This is generally the law applicable in the place of the registered office of the operator of the system.[68] **28**

A derogation from the general applicability of the *lex fori concursus* does not affect the issue of the **ranking of the claim**. Art 4 (2) sentence 2 (i) of the EIR must be observed in this regard.[69] **29**

---

[57] FK-InsO/*Wimmer* Anhang I nach § 358 mn 45; *Gottwald* Grenzüberschreitende Insolvenzen p 37 (on Art 9 of the 1995 Insolvency Convention).

[58] HK-InsO/*Stephan* Art 9 EuInsVO mn 2; FK-InsO/*Wimmer* Anhang I nach § 358 mn 45; D-K/D/Ch-*Duursma* Art 9 mn 7; *Huber* ZZP 114 (2001), p 133, 164; *Wimmer* ZInsO 2001, 97, 101; *Ehricke* 2006, 2109, 2113; *Wimmer* NJW 2002, 2427, 2429.

[59] *Virgós/Schmit* Explanatory report mn 120; HamburgerKomm-*Undritz* Art 9 mn 1; Gottwald-*Gottwald* Insolvenzrechtshandbuch (2006) § 131 mn 62; *Kemper* ZIP 2001, 1609, 1617.

[60] *Niggemann/Blenske* NZI 2003, 471, 476, in particular concerning Art 8, 7 und 9 of the Directive 98/26/EC.

[61] MünchKomm InsO/*Reinhart* Art 9 EuInsVO mn 4; Kübler/Prütting-*Kemper* EuInsVO Art 9 mn 8; BK-InsO/*Pannen* Art 9 EuInsVO mn 3; *Wessels* International Insolvency Law (2006) mn 10691; Moss/Fletcher/Isaacs-*Moss/Smith*, Regulation, mn 8.112.

[62] Kübler/Prütting-*Kemper* EuInsVO Art 9 mn 8; D-K/D/Ch-*Duursma* Art 9 mn 7; Balz ZIP 1996, 948, 950; *Wessels* International Insolvency Law (2006) mn 10691.

[63] *Kieper* Abwicklungssysteme in der Insolvenz, p 180.

[64] HK-InsO/*Stephan* Art 9 EuInsVO mn 6; D-K/D/Ch-*Duursma* Art 9 mn 8; *Ehricke* WM 2006, 2109, 2113.

[65] D-K/D/Ch-*Duursma* Art 9 mn 8.

[66] D-K/D/Ch-*Duursma* Art 9 mn 6; MünchKomm InsO/*Reinhart* Art 9 EuInsVO mn 4.

[67] MünchKomm InsO/*Reinhart* Art 9 EuInsVO mn 4.

[68] *Ehricke* WM 2006, 2109, 2113.

[69] *Paulus* DStR 2005, 334, 337.

4.2 Exception: Rights *in rem*

30 The invocation of Art 5 of the EIR is intended to make it clear that rights *in rem* of any kind in the debtor's assets to which creditors or third parties are entitled are always afforded the same protection within the scope of the Regulation's application. As with all other areas where the Regulation applies, rights *in rem* – in instances where Art 9 of the EIR applies – are not affected by the law that governs the payment system or the financial market.[70] Rights *in rem* that were established pursuant to a system within the meaning of Art 9 (1) of the EIR and that were situated in a Member State other than the opening State at the time when insolvency proceedings were opened are not affected by the opening of proceedings.[71] Instead, such rights are governed by the law of the State in which they are situated.[72]

31 The law of the place where such right is situated will apply regardless of who the creditor is, or which institution it is, in whose favour the security was provided.[73] Because rights *in rem* affect third parties, a uniform treatment of them ensures certainty of commercial transactions.[74]

32 In particular, a collateral (*in rem*) security held by a third party in a securities portfolio is not affected by the opening of insolvency proceedings against the holder of the securities or the participants in the securities settlement systems.[75]

33 Rights *in rem* can only be exposed to the effects of an insolvency if the insolvency is being conducted within the framework of secondary insolvency proceedings pursuant to Art 3 (2) and (3) of the EIR in the State where such rights are situated. This presupposes that the conditions for opening such proceedings have been met and the laws of this State allow the inclusion of rights *in rem* in the insolvency proceedings.[76]

5. Effects of Art 9 (2) of the EIR

34 Within the scope of the Regulation's application, the voidness, voidability, or unenforceability of the debtor's acts are usually governed by the *lex fori concursus*, as set out in Art 5 (4), Art 6 (2), and Art 7 (3) of the EIR. Art 9 (2), however, states that the *lex rei sitae* applies to the effects of such acts of an insolvent participant.[77] According to Art 9 (2) of the EIR, the adjudication of detrimental acts is governed solely by the law of the

[70] *Virgós/Schmit* Explanatory report mn 124; BK-InsO/*Pannen* Art 9 mn 4; MünchKomm InsO/*Reinhart* Art 9 EuInsVO mn 5; Haß/Huber/Gruber/Heiderhoff-*Huber* Art 9 EuInsVO mn 5; HK-InsO/*Stephan* Art 9 EuInsVO mn 8; D-K/D/Ch-*Duursma* Art 9 mn 9; *Huber* ZZP 114 (2001), p 133, 164; *Balz* ZIP 1996, 948, 951; *Kemper* ZIP 2001, 1609, 1617; *Chalupsky* in Baudenbacher p 357.

[71] HK-InsO/*Stephan* Art 9 EuInsVO mn 8; Kübler/Prütting-*Kemper* EuInsVO Art 9 mn 9; *Niggemann/Blenske* NZI 2003, 471, 476.

[72] Kübler/Prütting-*Kemper* EuInsVO Art 9 mn 9.

[73] *Virgós/Schmit* Explanatory report mn 124.

[74] *Virgós/Schmit* Explanatory report mn 124.

[75] *Smid* Komm EuInsVO Art 9 mn 7.

[76] Kübler/Prütting-*Kemper* EuInsVO Art 9 mn 9.

[77] HK-InsO/*Stephan* Art 9 EuInsVO mn 9; MünchKomm InsO/*Reinhart* Art 9 EuInsVO mn 6; Kübler/Prütting-*Kemper* EuInsVO Art 9 mn 10; Haß/Huber/Gruber/Heiderhoff-*Huber* Art 9 EuInsVO mn 6; *Balz* ZIP 1996, 948, 951; *Wessels* International Insolvency Law (2006) mn 10693.

State in which the payment system or the financial market exists or is being operated;[78] therefore either the law agreed per contract applies or the *lex rei sitae* applies.[79]

This special regulation constitutes a derogation from the general systematic of the Regulation.[80] On account of Art 9 (2) of the EIR, Art 4 (2) sentence 2 (m) and Art 13 of the EIR are made inoperable.[81] **35**

The idea behind being able to declare payments or transactions that are executed pursuant to such a system or market – which could possibly harm the creditors as a whole – as void, voidable, or unenforceable is to provide certainty with respect to commercial transactions.[82] The security of the systems encompassed by Art 9 of the EIR therefore has priority even over the protection from detrimental acts against the creditors as a whole.[83] **36**

Article 10
Contracts of employment

The effects of insolvency proceedings on employment contracts and relationships shall be governed solely by the law of the Member State applicable to the contract of employment.

Contents

Index

[78] BK-InsO/*Pannen* Art 9 EuInsVO mn 5; Haß/Huber/Gruber/Heiderhoff-*Huber* Art 9 EuInsVO mn 6; D-K/D/Ch-*Duursma* Art 9 mn 11; *Morscher* Die europäische Insolvenzverordnung p 41.

[79] HK-InsO/*Stephan* Art 9 EuInsVO mn 9.

[80] Haß/Huber/Gruber/Heiderhoff-*Huber* Art 9 EuInsVO mn 6.

[81] BK-InsO/*Pannen* Art 9 EuInsVO mn 5; Haß/Huber/Gruber/Heiderhoff-*Huber* Art 9 EuInsVO mn 6; D-K/D/Ch-*Duursma* Art 9 mn 12, 13; *Kemper* ZIP 2001, 1609, 1617; *Chalupsky* in Baudenbacher p 362.

[82] *Virgós/Schmit* Explanatory report mn 122; D-K/D/Ch-*Duursma* Art 9 mn 10.

[83] Kübler/Prütting-*Kemper* EuInsVO Art 9 mn 10.

Bibliography

Chaput Centre des intérêts principaux et catégories juridiques de l'insolvabilité des entreprises (à propos de l'arrêt CJCE du 2 mai 2006), Comments on ECJ 2.5.2006, Rev Lamy dr aff Juni 2006, p 26; *Dammann* L'application du règlement CE n° 1346-2000 après les arrêts *Staubitz-Schreiber* et *Eurofood* de la CJCE, Dalloz 2006, p 1752; *Duursma-Kepplinger/Duursma/Chalupsky* Europäische Insolvenzverordnung, Kommentar (2002); *Haß/Huber/Gruber/Heiderhoff* EU-Insolvenzverordnung, Kommentar (2005); *Jault-Seseke* Le sort des salariés, in Jault-Seseke/Robine (eds), L'effet international de la faillite: une réalité ? (2004), p 151; *Jault-Seseke/Robine* Comments on TC Nanterre 15.2.2006 (SAS EMTEC), Bull Joly Sociétés 2006, p 575; *Kübler/Prütting* Kommentar zur Insolvenzordnung (March 2006); *Lienhard* Procédures d'insolvabilité : détermination du centre des intérêts principaux, Comments on TC Nanterre 15.2.2006, Dalloz 2006, AJ p 651; *Menjucq* Notion autonome du centre des intérêts principaux d'une filiale étrangère d'un groupe, Comments on ECJ 2.5.2006, JCP 2006, II, No 10089; *Moss/Fletcher/Isaacs* (eds) The EC Regulation on Insolvency Proceedings, A Commentary and Annotated Guide (2002); Münchener Kommentar zum Bürgerlichen Gesetzbuch, vol 4 and 11 (2006); Münchener Kommentar zur Insolvenzordnung, vol 3 (2003); *Nerlich/Römermann* (eds) Insolvenzordnung (InsO), Kommentar (May 2003); *Niggemann/Blenske* Die Auswirkungen der Verordnung (EG) Nr. 1346/2000 auf den deutsch-französischen Rechtsverkehr NZI 2003, p 471; *Paulus* Europäische Insolvenzverordnung, Kommentar (2006); *Rémery* L'application à une filiale du règlement communautaire relatif aux procédures d'insolvabilité, Comments on ECJ 2.5.2006, Rev Soc 2006, p 360; *Roussel Galle* Juris-Classeur Commercial, Procédures Collectives, Redressement et Liquidation judiciaires, Droit communautaire, Fasc 3125; *Sonnenberger/Dammann* Französisches Handels- und Wirtschaftsrecht (3rd edn in preparation); *Uhlenbruck* Insolvenzordnung, Kommentar (2004); *Urban* La protection juridique incertaine des salariés dans une procédure collective transfrontalière JCP 2006 I, No 122; *Vallens* La maison mère d'un groupe centre des intérêts principaux de ses filiales étrangères, Comments on TC Nanterre dated 15.2.2006, Dalloz 2006, p 793; *Virgós/Schmit* Erläuternder Bericht zu dem EU-Übereinkommen über Insolvenzverfahren, in Stoll (ed), Vorschläge und Gutachten (1997), p 32; *Volders/Rétornaz* Forum shopping et procédures d'insolvabilité, Comments on ECJ 17.1.2006 (Staubitz-Schreiber), Rev proc coll 2006, p 241.

1. The Issue

1 The status of **employees** in insolvency proceedings is the subject of special legislative protection, which varies greatly in some instances from one Member State to the other. The key issues here include the ranking of the employees, special laws protecting against (unlawful) dismissals, guarantee institutions, and the fate of **employment contracts** in conjunction with an asset deal (reorganisation per transfer of assets) or with a sale of parts of a company. French law, for instance, protects **employees** through a so-called *superprivilège*, whereas German law in the *InsO* regards wage claims as unsecured claims against the insolvency estate. Inconsistencies could arise in the case of **insolvencies of corporate groups** where, for example, a court orders a reorganisation per transfer of assets in respect of a foreign company pursuant to which only some of the employees are to be taken over. Conflicts can also arise between special insolvency law provisions and general **employment law** provisions. Finally, the so-called ***lois de police*** contain numerous substantive law provisions whose socio-political goal is the protection of **employees.** The restricting of the scope of application of the *lex fori concursus* by Art 10 of the EIR must be considered in light of the foregoing.

2. Objects of the Rule

Art 10 of the EIR is regarded as a **special conflict of laws rule.** The law that is to govern the **employment contract** and the employment relationship is determined pursuant to the private international law of the State in which insolvency proceedings are opened. This is found in Recital 28 of the EIR.[1] Therefore, and most importantly, Art 6 of the Rome Convention of June 19, 1980, which applies in all Member States, is applicable. Although the parties are entitled to a certain extent to agree on which law is to govern the **employment contract**, certain compulsory protection provisions of the State in which the work is performed, such as **dismissal protection provisions**, cannot be contracted away, and will therefore apply via the referral contained in Art 10 of the EIR.[2] If no law has been chosen, then the law of the State in which the **employee** habitually performs his work applies. **2**

Art 10 of the EIR constitutes a **protectionary norm** in terms of private international law. The employee and the employment relationship are being protected from the effects of an insolvency proceeding conducted pursuant to a foreign legal regime. The rule can also be applied in the case of employee insolvencies, although this will likely have little significance in practical terms.[3] **3**

3. Scope of Application

Art 10 of the EIR applies in the case of **main insolvency proceedings** pursuant to Art 3 (1) of the EIR, thereby restricting the universal character of the proceedings in respect of employment relationships that are subject to the law of another Member State. An application of this **protectionary norm** is also conceivable in conjunction with **secondary or independent territorial insolvency proceedings** if the **employment contract** is governed by the laws of another Member State.[4] **4**

4. Conditions for Protection

4.1 Employment Contract and Employment Relationship

These terms are to be construed autonomously.[5] Hence the *lex fori concursus* is not to be consulted on this. *Kindler* speaks of an "observance of average European concepts".[6] The decisive factor should be whether an **authority to issue directives** can be demonstrated. In conformity with the ECJ's decision on Art 39 of the EEC Treaty, economic and personal dependence on the **employer** are also factors to be taken into account.[7] *Paulus* holds that collective agreements are also encompassed in this concept.[8] **5**

---

1 Cf MünchKomm BGB/*Kindler* IntInsR mn 335; D-K/D/Ch-*Duursma-Kepplinger* Art 10 mn 1.

2 On this problem: D-K/D/Ch-*Duursma-Kepplinger* Art 10 mn 7 et seq. Another argument in favour of this interpretation is provided by art 7 of the Rome Convention.

3 Cf *Paulus* Komm EuInsVO Art 10 mn 2; Kübler/Prütting-*Kemper* EuInsVO Art 10 mn 2.

4 Cf Kübler/Prütting-*Kemper* EuInsVO Art 10 mn 2.

5 Cf D-K/D/Ch-*Duursma-Kepplinger* Art 10 mn 5.

6 MünchKomm BGB/*Kindler* IntInsR mn 337, also D-K/D/Ch-*Duursma-Kepplinger* Art 10 mn 5.

7 Proofs of this: D-K/D/Ch-*Duursma-Kepplinger* Art 10 mn 6.

8 *Paulus* Komm EuInsVO Art 10 mn 3.

4.2 Date of Concluding Employment Contract

6 Prevailing opinion holds that Art 10 of the EIR should only apply to **employment contracts** that have already been concluded prior to the **opening of insolvency proceedings**. Although Art 10 of the EIR contains no such requirement, this can be inferred – so say the advocates of this approach – from the logic underlying the provision. They reason that an insolvency proceeding can only produce effects if it has been opened and if the contract of employment already exists at the **time of such opening**.[9] The point in time at which the contract is concluded is determined by the *lex contractus*.[10] The broad interpretation afforded the concept of "insolvency proceedings" by the ECJ in the Eurofood decision of 2 May 2006 should be given special attention in this regard.[11] But whether the **time of the opening of the proceedings** is to be determined pursuant to the *lex fori concursus* was left open by the ECJ.[12]

7 Such an approach is, however, disputable. If an **employment contract** only becomes effective a short time after **proceedings are opened**, for example through the occurrence of a condition precedent, the **employee** would be deprived of the protection afforded (via conflicts of laws rules) by Art 10 of the EIR. It is also not really clear why an **employee** who is hired after proceedings have been opened, for instance in conjunction with a debtor in possession constellation, should not be given the protection envisioned by Art 10 of the EIR should the law governing his **employment contract** differ from that of the *lex fori concursus*.

4.3 Effects of Insolvency Proceedings on the Employment Relationship

8 Art 10 of the EIR provides what effects the insolvency has on employment law issues: the *lex contractus* governs the continuation of the employment relationship, the **dismissal conditions and required notice periods**, and the legal effects of the dismissal. Because substantive insolvency laws often provide for a simplified form of dismissal, Art 10 of the EIR is meant to protect the **employee** from such. The liquidator must comply with the relevant **dismissal conditions** under the employment and insolvency laws of the legal regime concerned, including its procedural rules. This includes such things as the creation of a social plan and fulfilling obligations to advise **employees** and their representatives. Failure to comply with these requirements can lead to the annulment of dismissals and to claims for damages. The liquidator under French law may also be held liable under criminal law (so-called *délit d'entrave*). Art 10 of the EIR also applies in the case of modifications to, or transfers of, operating facilities within the framework of reorganization proceedings.[13]

9 Other insolvency law issues, such as whether the **employees'** claims are afforded preferential rights and which priority such a preferential right should be given, are deter-

---

[9] Cf the argumentation of Kübler/Prütting-*Kemper* EuInsVO Art 10 mn 4; see also D-K/D/Ch-*Duursma-Kepplinger* Art 10 mn 3; Haß/Huber/Gruber/Heiderhoff-*Huber* Art 10 EuInsVO mn 3.

[10] Cf MünchKomm BGB/*Kindler* IntInsR 339.

[11] ECJ C-341/04 of 2 May 2006. For discussions in German literature, see Table of Cases Art 3 of the EIR Appendix A mn 10 above. Discussions in French literature: Dalloz 2006 Jur p 1752 with comments by *Dammann*; Rev Soc 2006, 360 with comments by *Rémery*; JCP 2006, II, 10089 with comments by *Menjucq*. JCP E 2006 no 2071 with comments by *Vallens*; Rev Lamy dr aff Juni 2006, 26 with comments by *Chaput*.

[12] As per the Opinion of the Advocate General *Francis Geoffrey Jacobs* on 27 Sept 2005 C-341/04, ZIP 2005, 1878, no 89 et seq.

[13] Cf MünchKomm BGB/*Kindler* IntInsR mn 340.

mined by the law of the State in which proceedings were opened.[14] In addition to the ranking of claims, the *lex fori concursus* also determines the lodging, verification, and admission of **wage claims**. The *lex fori concursus* determines whether **wage claims** are ordinary (non-preferred) claims against the insolvency estate or preferred claims against the insolvency estate. In dispute is whether the exemption from execution of a part of **wage claims** is governed by the *lex contractus* or the *lex fori concursus.*[15]

The claim to payment of compensation for lost wages due to insolvency must be reviewed irrespective of Art 10 of the EIR. The Regulation does not deal with this issue at all.[16] Council Directive 80/987/EEC of 20 October 1980 applies here, as amended by Directive 2002/74/CE of 23 September 2002. According to Art 8 of this directive, the guarantee institution of the State in which the **employee** habitually works is responsible.[17] The guarantee institutions legally represent the **employees** and are therefore obliged to lodge the employees' claims within the requisite period. The ranking of such claims is then determined pursuant to Art 4 of the EIR.[18] Not covered by Art 10 of the EIR are issues arising from the area of "works/industrial constitution law" (generally employees participation rights etc.) and those concerning retirement pensions.[19] **10**

5. Legal Consequences

The referral in Art 10 of the EIR relates to the Member State's **employment-contract laws** and to such State's employment-related insolvency laws that are applicable to the **employment contract.**[20] This law supersedes the *lex fori concursus*. This follows from the use of the word "exclusively."[21] There is thus no cumulative effect even if the dismissal protection provisions of the *lex fori concursus* applicable to the **employee** go further than those contained in the employment and insolvency laws of the *lex contractus*. **11**

Should the conflicts of laws rules of the opening State contain a referral to the laws of a non-EU country, then the issue becomes whether Art 10 of the EIR applies. Academic opinion is divided on this issue. Some are of the opinion that Art 4 of the EIR would then apply.[22] *Reinhart* distinguishes between whether the habitual workplace is in a non-EU country or not.[23] *Kindler* is of the – correct – opinion that in the event of a referral to a non-EU country, the autonomous insolvency conflicts of laws rules are always applicable.[24] This can be inferred from the Regulation's territorial scope of application.[25] **12**

---

[14] See Recital 28 of the EIR.

[15] *Virgós/Schmit* Explanatory report mn 128 opt for the first option; *Paulus* Komm EuInsVO Art 10 mn 9 opts for the second solution.

[16] Cf D-K/D/Ch-*Duursma-Kepplinger* Art 10 mn 14.

[17] See JCl Commercial, Procédures Collectives, Redressement et Liquidation judiciaire, Droit communautaire, Fasc 3125 (*Roussel Galle*) no 98; MünchKomm BGB/*Kindler* IntInsR mn 341.

[18] Cf *Jault-Seseke* Dalloz 2004, 151, 160.

[19] Cf *Uhlenbruck* Komm InsO Art 10 EuInsVO mn 2.

[20] See D-K/D/Ch-*Duursma-Kepplinger* Art 10 mn 10; *Virgós/Schmit* Explanatory report mn 125; *Niggemann/Blenske* NZI 2003, 477; Nerlich/Römermann-*Mincke* Komm InsO Art 10 EuInsVO mn 3.

[21] Cf D-K/D/Ch-*Duursma-Kepplinger* Art 10 mn 10.

[22] Cf for instance *Moss/Fletcher/Isaacs-Fletcher*, Regulation, mn 4.33.

[23] MünchKomm InsO/*Reinhart* Art 10 EuInsVO mn 2.

[24] Cf *Paulus* Komm EuInsVO Art 10 mn 4; MünchKomm BGB/*Kindler* IntInsR mn 345.

[25] D-K/D/Ch-*Duursma-Kepplinger* Art 10 mn 12.

6. Practical Solutions

13 In practice, the following problems may arise.[26] If **main insolvency proceedings** are opened in a State with very liberal insolvency-related **dismissal laws**, such as England, coordination difficulties could arise in the case of **employees** working in another State in which insolvency-related dismissals are subjected to strict conditions. This is the case in France for instance.[27] During the so-called observation phase, dismissals may only be made on extraordinary grounds, and they must also be applied for at court. For non-compliance with this procedure, criminal sanctions may be imposed.[28] The only remedy in such a case is to open **secondary insolvency proceedings.** This course was taken in the *Sendo* case.

14 Problems may also arise in the case of **insolvencies of corporate groups.** In judgements passed down on 15 February 2006, the Commercial Court in Nanterre opened separate insolvency proceedings in respect of eight foreign companies of the French EMTEC group.[29] In separate orders dated 3 May 2006, the court ordered the sale of the respective companies as part of an asset deal. Under French insolvency law, the potential purchaser commits himself in his offer to take over a certain number of **employees,** although differentiations according to categories can be made. All **employees** not taken over are dismissed by the liquidator at the expense of the insolvency estate. Such a bankruptcy-law provision constitutes an exception to the protective provisions of employment law, whereby all **employees** must automatically be taken over in the event of company takeovers.[30] In the individual orders of 3 May 2006, which are to be recognised without formalities in other Member States as per Art 25 of the EIR, the dismissals of the **employees** that were not taken over were in fact approved, but the execution of such dismissals had to be carried out by the liquidator pursuant to the law governing the employment contract as is required by Art 10 of the EIR. Caution should therefore be exercised here to ensure that the timing of the acquisition of the company does not collide with provisions of employment law. This employment law problem can be solved by opening **secondary insolvency proceedings.** This of course complicates the sale of those assets subject to the *lex fori concursus* of the **secondary insolvency proceedings.**

---

[26] For the problem in German-Dutch legal relations, see for example: Moss/Fletcher/Isaacs-*Moss/Smith*, Regulation, mn 8.116.

[27] On this problem, see also: *Urban* JCP 2006 I 122 and *Jault-Seseke*, Dalloz 2004, 151.

[28] Overview of French insolvency law: *Sonnenberger/Dammann*, Französisches Handels- und Wirtschaftrecht (3rd edn in preparation) no VIII 36 et seq.

[29] Cf Dalloz 2006 AJ p 651 comments *Lienhard*; Dalloz 2006, 793 comments *Vallens*; Rev proc coll 2006, 241 Anm *Volders/Rétornaz*; Bull Joly Sociétés 2006, 575 § 122 comments *Jault-Seseke/Robine*.

[30] See art L 122-12 Code du travail. On this idiosyncracy of French insolvency law: *Sonnenberger/Dammann* Französisches Handels- und Wirtschaftrecht (3rd edn in preparation) no VIII 51 et seq. This is one of the main advantages of acquiring the company as part of a *plan de cession* as, in contrast to German law, dismissed employees cannot sue at the employment court to be subsequently taken over by the acquirer. An exception is made in the case of dismissals that the court does not include at all in the *plan de cession.* On German law, see: sec 613 (a) BGB and MünchKomm BGB/*Müller-Glöge* sec 613a BGB mn 1 et seq.

Article 11
Effects on rights subject to registration

The effects of insolvency proceedings on the rights of the debtor in immoveable property, a ship or an aircraft subject to registration in a public register shall be determined by the law of the Member State under the authority of which the register is kept.

Contents

Index

Bibliography

Duursma-Kepplinger/Duursma/Chalupsky Europäische Insolvenzverordnung, Kommentar (2002); *Haß/Huber/Gruber/Heiderhoff* EU-Insolvenzordnung, Kommentar (2005); *Kübler/Prütting* Kommentar zur Insolvenzordnung (March 2006); Münchener Kommentar zum Bürgerlichen Gesetzbuch, vol 11 (2006); Münchener Kommentar zur Insolvenzordnung, vol 3 (2003); *Nerlich/Römermann* (eds) Insolvenzordnung (InsO), Kommentar (May 2003); *Paulus* Europäische Insolvenzverordnung, Kommentar (2006); *Roussel Galle* Juris-Classeur Commercial, Procédures Collectives, Redressement et Liquidation judiciaire, Droit communautaire, Fasc 3125; *Virgós/Schmit* Erläuternder Bericht zu dem EU-Übereinkommen über Insolvenzverfahren, in Stoll (ed), Vorschläge und Gutachten (1997), p 32.

1. Issue and Demarcation

The EIR represents a compromise between the **principle of universality** and the **principle of territoriality**. It is a theme that runs throughout the entire Regulation. Art 11 of the EIR deals with the problem of **rights** that are **subject to registration** pursuant to the *lex fori concursus* in a register of another Member State that has no comparable institution. The problem here stems from the divergent structures and concepts of registrable property rights that are found in the various Member States. The *lex fori concursus* may contain **rights subject to registration** (privileges, preferential rights, rights of retention, etc.) that are completely unknown to the other Member States. **1**

Art 11 of the EIR effectively concerns the scope of the universal effects of the *lex fori concursus* of the main insolvency proceedings with regard to the registration of rights to **immoveable property** (real estate), **ships**, or **aircraft** in a **public register**. It primarily concerns the problem of adaptations of laws; indirectly it concerns the recognition and validity of **rights subject to registration** through the *lex libri*. **2**

3 Art 11 of the EIR does not concern the protection of third parties or creditors who have had their rights registered in such a **register.** It is therefore not related to Art 5 of the EIR, which protects **third party rights *in rem*** that are situated in a Member State other than the opening State. Such is the case, for example, when these rights are registered in a public register being kept by this other Member State; Art 2 (g) of the EIR.

2. Objects of the Rule

4 Because of the wide variety of registration requirements and types of property law regimes in the individual Member States, Art 11 of the EIR attempts to restrict certain insolvency law effects that are inconsistent with foreign registration requirements. It is therefore a **conflict of laws rule.**[1] The idea is to prevent the making of **unknown types of registrations.**[2] This is intended to ensure reliance on the content and the legal effects of **public registers.** It also fosters legal certainty in general and provides protection to business transactions. Although this may complicate the processing of the insolvency in some cases, and may even restrict the **liquidator's powers of disposal** with respect to **real estate, ships,** and **aircraft** under insolvency law, it simply has to be accepted.

3. Conditions for Protection

5 **Public register.** "Public register" is defined in Art 2 (g) of the EIR. It is not restricted to registers that are kept by public authorities or by courts. It suffices if such registers are accessible to the public, and if the registrations have an impact on the rights of third parties.[3]

6 **Effects of insolvency proceedings on the rights of the debtor.** The scope of application of the **conflict of laws rule** should not be limited to whether or not the right is capable of registration. *Kindler* is correct in his assumption that the substantive-law effects also fall within the ambit of Art 11 of the EIR.[4]

4. Scope of the Provision

7 The scope of Art 11 of the EIR in relation to Art 4 of the EIR is the subject of dispute. Art 11 of the EIR provides that the right of the Member State in which the register is kept applies. What is missing, however, is the word "exclusively", as in Art 10 of the EIR. The wording itself does not indicate whether the ***lex libri*** supersedes or replaces the *lex concursus.*

8 Some legal academics hold that this is an editorial oversight.[5] Accordingly, the law of the State in which the register is kept should apply exclusively.[6]

9 The opposing view, which is preferable, advocates a cumulative application of the law governing the insolvency and that governing the register (prevailing opinion).[7] Art 4

[1] Kübler/Prütting-*Kemper* EuInsVO Art 11 mn 1.
[2] See D-K/D/Ch-*Duursma-Kepplinger* Art 11 mn 5.
[3] See D-K/D/Ch-*Duursma-Kepplinger* Art 11 mn 1.
[4] MünchKomm BGB/*Kindler* IntInsR mn 353.
[5] MünchKomm InsO/*Reinhart* Art 11 EuInsVO mn 1.
[6] Also Kübler/Prütting-*Kemper* EuInsVO Art 11 mn 9.
[7] Cf D-K/D/Ch-*Duursma-Kepplinger* Art 11

of the EIR applies in general. The law of the register-keeping State has a corrective influence on the admissibility of certain registrations required under insolvency law that are incompatible with the ***lex libri***. Art 11 of the EIR thereby creates an "upper limit".[8] This means that all insolvency-related registrations required by the foreign main proceedings that contravene the laws of the registry-keeping State cannot be effected.

In absence of an exact counterpart to a registration in the ***lex libri***, the registrar is **10**
obliged to make an adjustment to approximate – through the registration – the ***lex fori concursus*** as closely as possible.[9] If the effects of an insolvency-law registration go beyond those of a comparable registration of the ***lex libri***, then the insolvency-law registration cannot be made. Art 11 of the EIR thus functions as an upper limit.

Article 12
Community patents and trade marks

For the purposes of this Regulation, a Community patent, a Community trade mark or any other similar right established by Community law may be included only in the proceedings referred to in Article 3(1).

Contents

Index

Bibliography

Duursma-Kepplinger/Duursma/Chalupsky Europäische Insolvenzverordnung, Kommentar (2002); Münchener Kommentar zum Bürgerlichen Gesetzbuch, vol 11 (2006); Münchener Kommentar zur Insolvenzordnung, vol 3 (2003); *Paulus* Europäische Insolvenzverordnung Kommentar (2006).

mn 1; Nerlich/Römermann-*Mincke* Komm InsO Art 11 EuInsVO mn 3; *Paulus* Komm EuInsVO Art 11 mn 6; Münch Komm/*Kindler* IntInsR mn 354; *Virgós/Schmit* Explanatory Report mn 129; JCl Commercial, Procédures Collectives, Redressement et Liquidation judiciaire, Droit communautaire, Fasc 3125 (*Roussel Galle*) No 103.

[8] A fitting expression coined by D-K/D/Ch-*Duursma-Kepplinger* Art 11 mn 7, which Haß/Huber/Gruber/Heiderhoff-*Huber* Art 11 EuInsVO mn 4, have taken over.

[9] See Münch Komm BGB/*Kindler* IntInsR mn 355.

1. Issue

1 Art 2 (g) of the EIR contains provisions dealing with the **localization of assets.** These rules are important since the opening of secondary insolvency proceedings causes a splitting of the debtor's assets into separate insolvency estates. This departure from the **principle of universality** aims to protect local interests, especially those of employees and national creditors.

2 However some Europe-wide recognised **intangible rights**, such as **Community patents** and trade marks and other industrial property rights, would be difficult to split up amongst the various insolvency estates involved in an international insolvency. The solution to this problem is found in Art 12 of the EIR.

2. Objects of the Rule

3 Through Art 12 of the EIR, all Europe-wide recognized industrial **proprietary rights** are included exclusively in the main insolvency proceedings. Seen this way, Art 12 of the EIR, in contrast to Art 2 (g) of the EIR, provides that such protected (industrial) property rights cannot – for insolvency law purposes – be allocated to the insolvency estate of the secondary insolvency proceedings. Art 12 of the EIR is therefore not a conflict of laws rule.[1]

3. Conditions

4 Included are **Community patents**[2], **Community trade marks**[3], and any other similar right established by Community law. Hence, **Community designs**[4] and the **protection of plant varieties** are included as well.[5]

4. Legal Consequences

5 The aforementioned **intangible property rights** are to be included exclusively in main insolvency proceedings pursuant to Art 3 (1) of the EIR. They are therefore excluded from the assets of the secondary or independent territorial insolvency proceedings, and thus cannot be liquidated in conjunction with these proceedings.

6 *Paulus* holds that this provision, as an exception to Art 5 of the EIR, should be widened to cover the **secured rights** in such Community rights.[6]

---

[1] Cf MünchKomm BGB/*Kindler* IntInsR mn 356; MünchKomm InsO/*Reinhart* Art 10 EuInsVO mn 1.

[2] *Kindler* suggests including all patents that are issued by the European Patents Office for the whole of the European Community, MünchKomm BGB/*Kindler* IntInsR mn 357. A proposal for a directive is currently being discussed.

[3] See Council Regulation (EC) No 40/94 on the Community trade mark that came into force on 15 March 1994. Details in D-K/D/Ch-*Duursma-Kepplinger* Art 12 mn 5.

[4] See Council Regulation (EC) No 6/2002 on Community designs that came into effect on 6 Mar 2002. Details in D-K/D/Ch-*Duursma-Kepplinger* Art 12 mn 9.

[5] For details, see: MünchKomm BGB/*Kindler* IntInsR mn 357 et seq.

[6] See *Paulus* Komm EuInsVO Art 12 mn 4.

Article 13
Detrimental acts

Article 4(2)(m) shall not apply where the person who benefited from an act detrimental to all the creditors provides proof that:
- **the said act is subject to the law of a Member State other than that of the State of the opening of proceedings, and**
- **that law does not allow any means of challenging that act in the relevant case.**

Contents

Index

Bibliography

Dammann Das neue französische Insolvenzrecht RIW 2006, p 16; *Duursma-Kepplinger/Duursma/Chalupsky* Europäische Insolvenzverordnung, Kommentar (2002); *Haß/Huber/Gruber/Heiderhoff* EU-Insolvenzverordnung, Kommentar (2005); *Kübler/Prütting* Kommentar zur Insolvenzordnung (March 2006); Münchener Kommentar zum Bürgerlichen Gesetzbuch, vol 11 (2006); Münchener Kommentar zur Insolvenzordnung, vol 3 (2003); *Nerlich/Römermann* (eds) Insolvenzordnung (InsO), Kommentar (May 2003); *Paulus* Europäische Insolvenzverordnung, Kommentar (2006); *Roussel Galle* Juris-Classeur Commercial, Procédures Collectives, Redressement et Liquidation judiciaire, Droit communautaire, Fasc 3125; *Sonnenberger/Dammann* Französisches Handels- und Wirtschaftrecht (3rd edn in preparation).

1. Issue

Similar to the ***actio pauliana*** known to Roman law, nearly every European insolvency law regime allows the liquidator to have certain legal acts – that are executed in a specified period before proceedings are opened and that are detrimental to all the creditors – **1** avoided, annulled, or declared unenforceable. This includes such things as gratuitous dispositions, contracts that are clearly overly advantageous to the creditors, the satisfaction of claims that are not due or the satisfaction of claims that are due using uncommon means of payment, or the granting of **mortgages** and **liens** to secure existing claims. The conditions, time periods, and legal consequences of such **avoidance** or **annulment actions** vary, however, considerably from one Member State to the other (in German law see Sec 129 et seq *InsO,* in French law Art L 632-1 et seq *Code de commerce*[1]). And although each Member State has developed its own system to protect the creditors as a whole from detrimental legal acts, there is also the idea that trust must be placed in the validity of legal acts subject to the laws of another Member State.

2 A disparity between the **law governing the insolvency** and the ***lex causae* of the legal act** gives rise to the necessity of finding the best way to resolve the tension between the interests of the parties benefiting from such acts that are not challengeable pursuant to the *lex causae,* and the protection of the creditors as a whole who are able to challenge these legal acts under the *lex fori concursus.* A number of solutions are conceivable. An exclusive application of the *lex fori concursus* or the *lex causae* would lead to unfair results. An unrestricted accumulation of both legal regimes would lead to the application of the body of law most prejudicial to an avoidance, which would be (excessively) adverse to the principle of equitable satisfaction of all insolvency creditors.

2. Objects of the Rule

3 Art 13 of the EIR successfully combines an application of both the *lex fori concursus* and the *lex causae* to balance out the various interests.[2] The right of avoidance, and all aspects of it, is governed exclusively by the *lex fori concursus* (Art 4 (2) sentence 2 (m) of the EIR). However, the party benefiting from the legal act in question is granted the right to raise a defence if he can prove that the **detrimental act** cannot be challenged in any way by the ***lex causae*** governing such act. What is involved here is a two-tiered connection system – a connection to the *lex fori concursus* linked to a corrective through the *lex causae.* The *lex causae* therefore serves a blocking function only,[3] which in effect prevents the unrestricted cumulative applicability of both legal regimes.

3. Scope of Application

3.1 Reference to Member States

4 The first dash in Art 13 of the EIR provides that "the said act is subject to the law of a Member State other than that of the State of the opening of proceedings". Should the law of a non-EU country apply to the legal transaction in issue, Art 13 of the EIR does not apply. In this case, the **avoidance** is governed exclusively by the law that governs the insolvency pursuant to the laws of the opening State.

1 On the nullity of legal acts during the *période suspecte*, see: *Dammann* RIW 2006, 16; and *Sonnenberger/Dammann* Französisches Handels- und Wirtschaftsrecht (3rd edn in preparation) no VIII 16 et seq.

2 Critical: MünchKomm InsO/*Reinhart* Art 13 EuInsVO mn 1. Also critical: Nerlich/Römermann-*Mincke* Komm InsO Art 13 EuInsVO mn 4; Haß/Huber/Gruber/Heiderhoff-*Gruber* Art 13 EuInsVO mn 2.

3 Cf MünchKomm BGB/*Kindler* IntInsR mn 366 et seq; D-K/D/Ch-*Duursma-Kepplinger* Art 13 mn 1 et seq.

5 The law applicable to the detrimental act is determined pursuant to the general **conflict of laws rules** of the State in which insolvency proceedings are opened. Through a choice of law clause, it is therefore always open to the parties to agree on an applicable *lex causae* that is prejudicial to avoidances. *Duursma-Kepplinger* sees a possible manipulation of the *lex causae* here; she suggests that such an abusive choice of law through the *lex fori concursus* should not be allowed.[4] But whether this type of forum shopping really constitutes abuse is somewhat doubtful.[5] Unequivocal proof that such a choice of law is an abuse of the law would have to be rendered by the liquidator, which would prove in most cases to be a very difficult task.

3.2 Application in Main and Territorial Insolvency Proceedings

6 Art 13 of the EIR applies to both **main** and **secondary/independent territorial insolvency proceedings** since the *lex causae* may differ from the *lex concursus particularis* as well as from the *lex concursus secondarii*.[6] The liquidator of the secondary or independent territorial insolvency proceedings must prove that the legal act in question has diminished the separate insolvency estate of the secondary or independent territorial insolvency proceedings. The liquidator of the secondary proceedings is also entitled to assert an **avoidance action** in another Member State pursuant to Art 18 (2) of the EIR, always provided that the separate insolvency estate he administers has been harmed.[7] Art 13 of the EIR will not, however, be applicable in **secondary** or **independent territorial insolvency proceedings** if the **avoidance** is made in relation to property situated outside the territory of the opening State.[8]

3.3 Avoidance Actions Distinguished From Other Types of Annulment Proceedings

7 Art 13 refers to Art 4 (2) sentence 2 (m) of the EIR, which describes classic insolvency-law **avoidance actions**.[9] The decisive factor is the detriment to all creditors. The norm provides that **voidness**, **voidability**, and **unenforceability** are the legal consequences of such acts. This could give rise to problems of distinguishment. Some legal systems automatically **void** any **secured rights** that have been granted within a specific period prior to the opening of insolvency proceedings. Whether such legal provisions are avoidance actions within the meaning of Art 4 (2) sentence 2 (m) of the EIR is debatable.[10] If they are not, then Art 13 of the EIR will not apply. A similar problem arises for instance with the dogmatic classification of Art L 650 C. *com.* with regard to the **creditor's liability for the negligent granting of loans.**[11] This claim forms part of the debtor's assets, is sued upon by the liquidator, and leads to the **avoidance** of the guarantees that were granted. Although the action serves the protection of the creditors as a whole, it is not a classic **avoidance action** within the meaning of Art 4 (2) sentence 2 (m) of the EIR. Art 13 of the EIR can therefore not be applied.

---

4 D-K/D/Ch-*Duursma-Kepplinger* Art 13 mn 16.

5 Concurring: *Paulus* Komm EuInsVO Art 10 mn 6.

6 D-K/D/Ch-*Duursma-Kepplinger* Art 13 mn 4.

7 Cf MünchKomm BGB/*Kindler* IntInsR mn 371 et seq; Haß/Huber/Gruber/Heiderhoff-*Gruber* Art 13 EuInsVO mn 15.

8 Cf Kübler/Prütting-*Kemper* EuInsVO Art 13 mn. 3.

9 *Paulus* interprets the scope of application much wider. He speaks of an insolvency-law repayment/recovery claim. Classification is a matter for the *lex fori concursus*. *Paulus* Komm EuInsVO Art 13 mn 2.

10 On the various opinions, see: D-K/D/Ch-*Duursma-Kepplinger* Art 13 mn 21.

11 More on this: *Dammann* RIW 2006, 16, 17 et seq; and *Sonnenberger/Dammann* Französisches Handels- und Wirtschaftrecht (3rd edn in preparation) no VIII 18 et seq.

4. Conditions for Protection

4.1 An Act Detrimental to All Creditors

8 Art 13 presupposes the existence of a **detrimental legal act** within the meaning of Art 4 (2) sentence 2 (m) of the EIR that is void, voidable or unenforceable. It concerns an **avoidance** or **annulment action,** which is generally asserted by the liquidator or other responsible bodies.

4.2 Date of the Action in Question

9 It must be assumed from the logic underlying the **avoidance** or **annulment action** that only such legal acts are involved that were executed prior to the opening of the insolvency proceedings. The very purpose of Art 13 of the EIR is to protect, in some circumstances, the trust placed by the party disputing the avoidance in the continued existence of these legal acts.[12]

4.3 Unchallengeability of the Legal Act

10 Two phrases must be examined more closely in this connection: "does not allow any means" and "in the relevant case".

11 The phrase "does not allow any means" should be construed broadly. The party disputing the avoidance must first prove that an insolvency-law **avoidance** or **annulment action** is bound to fail under the *lex causae*. He must also prove that there is no reason to avoid such action based on an infringement of other general substantive laws of this legal system. Examples of such general substantive law include the general ***actio pauliana***[13] under civil law, the creditor's avoidance of certain debtor transactions, an avoidance based on a lack of intent, unconscionability, and mistake. However, statutory limitations of actions play no role here (prevailing opinion).[14]

12 The phrase "in the relevant case" allows the assumption that the review *in concreto* must be made by taking into account all of the concrete accompanying circumstances.[15]

5. Legal Consequences

13 Art 13 of the EIR entails a defence that must be raised by the party disputing the avoidance. *Duursma-Kepplinger* accurately refers to it as a kind of "veto".[16] It therefore does not have to be examined by the court on its own motion.[17] The party disputing the avoidance bears the burden of submitting and proving all of the facts, even if the applicable law contains a burden of proof rule to the contrary.[18]

---

[12] Cf MünchKomm BGB/*Kindler* IntInsR mn 374.

[13] Affirmed by French legal scholars; see JCl Commercial, Procédures Collectives, Redressement et Liquidation judiciaire, Droit communautaire, Fasc 3125 (*Roussel Galle*) no 105.

[14] Cf MünchKomm BGB/*Kindler* IntInsR mn 377. Kübler/Prütting-*Kemper* EuInsVO Art 13 mn 7. Contra: Haß/Huber/Gruber/Heiderhoff-*Gruber* Art 13 EuInsVO mn 6.

[15] Cf D-K/D/Ch-*Duursma-Kepplinger* Art 13 mn 21; MünchKomm BGB/*Kindler* IntInsR mn 378.

[16] D-K/D/Ch-*Duursma-Kepplinger* Art 13 mn 15.

[17] Cf Haß/Huber/Gruber/Heiderhoff-*Gruber* Art 13 EuInsVO mn 10.

[18] *Paulus* Komm EuInsVO Art 13 mn 4.

If the defence is successful, then, pursuant to Art 13 of the EIR, Art 4 (2) sentence 2 (m) of the EIR does not apply. The *lex fori concursus* is thus replaced by the *lex causae*. And the legal act in question continues to exist (blocking function of the *lex causae*). **14**

6. International Jurisdiction for Avoidance Actions

15 The Regulation does not regulate the international jurisdiction for **avoidance actions.** Art 25 of the EIR merely provides that judgements derived directly from the insolvency proceedings and closely linked to them are recognized in other Member States without any additional formalities. These include **avoidance actions.** But this does not automatically determine jurisdiction.

16 Although some advocate an application of Council Regulation (EC) No 44/2001,[19] the prevailing view favours – via a reference to Recital 6 of the EIR – an application of Art 3 (1) of the EIR.[20] *Kindler* advocates an analogous application of this provision.[21] This view should be endorsed. It makes no real sense, in the case of **avoidance actions** that are closely linked with the insolvency proceedings, to provide for a jurisdiction different than that determined for the opening of the insolvency proceedings. Art 3 (2) of the EIR applies analogously in the case of **avoidance actions** pursuant to secondary insolvency proceedings.

7. Practical Solutions

17 Before the main liquidator requests the opening of **secondary insolvency proceedings** (Art 29 of the EIR), the effects of this on any **avoidance actions** should be reviewed. The following should be kept in mind here: the **avoidance action** always relates to the diminishment of the particular insolvency estate. Therefore the splitting of the debtor's assets amongst two separate insolvency estates can have negative repercussions. And the law governing the avoidance also changes (*lex concursus secundarii*). This can prove either advantageous or disadvantageous. One need only be reminded of time limits and satisfying the requirements of the claim, to name a few. The liquidator in the main insolvency proceedings is deprived of his ability to act because the action can only be asserted by the liquidator of the secondary insolvency proceedings. Repayment/recovery claims ensuing from a **voidance** of certain legal acts fall within the separate assets of the secondary insolvency proceedings. And even though a global lodging of all of the claims of the **main insolvency proceedings** allows the liquidator in the main insolvency proceedings to protect the rights of the creditors of the **main insolvency proceedings,** the ranking of such claims in the secondary insolvency proceedings is governed by the *lex fori concursus secundarii.* There is a thus a real danger of distortions in favour of the creditors of the **main insolvency proceedings.**

18 Another practical point should be kept in mind. In Arts 5 and 7, the Regulation grants **creditors with secured rights** and **sellers with reserved titles** a particularly strong position when the property in issue is located in another Member State at the time of the

---

[19] MünchKomm InsO/*Reinhart* Art 13 EuInsVO mn 4.

[20] Cf Haß/Huber/Gruber/Heiderhoff-*Gruber* Art 13 EuInsVO mn 22.

[21] Cf MünchKomm BGB/*Kindler* IntInsR mn 385.

opening of proceedings. Such property is not affected by the opening of the proceedings. Art 6 of the EIR contains another special provision in the case of **set-offs**. There is, however, one important exception: **avoidance actions** pursuant to Art 4 (2) sentence 2 (m) of the EIR are possible in all three cases. Hence Art 13 of the EIR is also applicable in all of these cases.

Article 14
Protection of third-party purchasers

Where, by an act concluded after the opening of insolvency proceedings, the debtor disposes, for consideration, of

- **an immoveable asset, or**
- **a ship or an aircraft subject to registration in a public register, or**
- **securities whose existence presupposes registration in a register laid down by law,**

the validity of that act shall be governed by the law of the State within the territory of which the immoveable asset is situated or under the authority of which the register is kept.

Contents

Index

Bibliography

Chaput Centre des intérêts principaux et catégories juridiques de l'insolvabilité des entreprises (à propos de l'arrêt CJCE du 2 mai 2006), Comments on ECJ dated 2.5.2006, Rev Lamy dr aff Juni 2006, p 26; *Dammann* L'application du règlement CE n° 1346-2000 après les arrêts *Staubitz-Schreiber* et *Eurofood* de la CJCE, Dalloz 2006, p 1752; *Dammann* La réforme des sûretés mobilières: une occasion manquée, Dalloz 2006, p 1298; *Duursma-Kepplinger/Duursma/Chalupsky* Europäische Insolvenzverordnung, Kommentar (2002); *Ferid/Sonnenberger* Das französische Zivilrecht, 2nd edn (1986); *Haß/Huber/Gruber/Heiderhoff* EU-Insolvenzverordnung, Kommentar (2005); *Kübler/Prütting* Kommentar zur Insolvenzordnung (March 2006); *Menjucq* Notion autonome du centre des intérêts principaux d'une filiale étrangère d'un groupe, Comments on ECJ dated 2.5.2006, JCP 2006, II, No 10089; Münchener Kommentar zum Bürgerlichen Gesetzbuch, vol 11 (2006); Münchener Kommentar zur Insolvenzordnung, vol 3 (2003); *Nerlich/Römermann* (eds) Insolvenzordnung (InsO), Kommentar (May 2003); *Paulus* Europäische Insolvenzverordnung, Kommentar (2006); *Rémery* L'application à une filiale du règlement communautaire relatif aux procédures d'insolvabilité, Comments on ECJ dated 2.5.2006, Rev Soc 2006, p 360; *Roussel Galle* Juris-Classeur

Commercial, Procédures Collectives, Redressement et Liquidation judiciaire, Droit communautaire, Fasc 3125; *Sonnenberger/Dammann* Französisches Handels- und Wirtschaftrecht (3rd edn in preparation); *Vallens* La maison mère d'un groupe centre des intérêts principaux de ses filiales étrangères, explanatory comments on TC Nanterre dated 15.2.2006, Dalloz 2006, p 793.

1. Issue

Practice has shown that the notification of the decisions opening main insolvency proceedings is sometimes carried out with a considerable time delay in other Member States. Because the opening of proceedings generally leads to the partial or full divestment of the debtor or to restrictions of his rights of disposition, the problem arises in the case of international insolvencies of how to protect *bona fide* third parties who, being unaware that insolvency proceedings have been opened, acquire property for valuable consideration that is situated in another Member State. It also gives rise to the question of whether the *bona fide* acquisition by the third party is governed by the law applicable to the insolvency, or whether a connecting factor under property law to the *lex rei sitae* or to the *lex libri* is more fitting.[1] **1**

2. Objects of the Rule

Art 14 of the EIR regulates such matters but only with respect to the **acquisition for valuable consideration of ships or aircraft** that are subject to registration in a public register, and with respect to **securities** whose existence presupposes registration in a register laid down by law. Art 14 of the EIR is thus a provision for the protection of the *bona fide* third party purchaser who has relied on the completeness of the entries in the register in question. **2**

However, Art 14 of the EIR goes beyond protecting the reliance on such register entries. It also protects the *bona fide* acquisition of **immoveable assets** even if such rights do not have to be registered in a registry. This presupposes, however, that a *bona fide* acquisition of unregistered real property is permissible pursuant to the *lex rei sitae*.[2] The practical relevance of this provision can be seen in French law for example, pursuant to which title to real property, in contrast to German law, is acquired automatically with the conclusion of the purchase transaction (principle of consensus).[3] **3**

3. Scope of Application

Art 14 of the EIR only applies if the State of the *situs* or the State where the register is kept is a Member State.[4] **4**

---

[1] On this, see the references in: D-K/D/Ch-*Duursma-Kepplinger* Art 14 mn 2.

[2] Cf MünchKomm BGB/*Kindler* IntInsR mn 386; D-K/D/Ch-*Duursma-Kepplinger* Art 14 mn 3.

[3] Generally on this: *Ferid/Sonnenberger* Das französische Zivilrecht, 2nd ed (1986), mn 2 G 201 et seq.

[4] Cf MünchKomm BGB/*Kindler* IntInsR mn 401; Haß/Huber/Gruber/Heiderhoff/Heiderhoff-*Gruber* Art 14 EuInsVO mn 13.

4. Conditions for Protection

5 In order for Art 14 of the EIR to apply, the debtor must have – pursuant to the *lex rei sitae* or the *lex libri* and for the benefit of a third party and after the opening of insolvency proceedings – **validly disposed** of immoveable property, a ship or an aircraft subject to registration in a public register, or securities whose existence presupposes registration in a register laid down by law. As a conflict of laws rule, Art 14 of the EIR determines the law according to which the validity of the legal act is to be judged.

6 A **legal act** not only comprises the transfer of ownership but also the granting of rights *in rem* within the meaning of Art 5 of the Regulation.[5] This includes such things as land charges (*Grundschuld*) and mortgages (on land).[6]

7 It must also be a legal act in exchange for **consideration**. Prevailing opinion holds that Art 14 of the EIR also applies to mixed dispositions, i.e. dispositions that are partly gratuitous and partly for valuable consideration.[7] The same should also apply in the case of a sale below value.[8] By contrast, gratuitous disposals are governed by the *lex fori concursus*. These are void, voidable, or unenforceable if they are detrimental to all creditors, Art 4 (2) of the Regulation. *Bona fide* third parties can in certain circumstances raise the defence found in Art 13 of the Regulation. The classification of the consideration is made pursuant to the law governing the main insolvency proceedings.[9]

8 Art 14 of the EIR only relates to legal acts that were made **after insolvency proceedings were opened.** The broad interpretation of the concept of "insolvency proceedings" by the ECJ in the Eurofood decision of 2 May 2006 should be taken into account in this regard.[10] But whether the **time of the opening of the proceedings** is to be determined pursuant to the *lex fori concursus* was left open by the ECJ.[11]

9 **Disposable objects** within the meaning of the second dash of Art 14 of the EIR are **ships** and **aircraft** subject to registration in a public register. Dash three relates to **securities** whose existence presupposes registration in a register laid down by law. This includes such things as – since 1983 in France – de-materialized shares and other securities.[12] Finally, Art 14 of the EIR applies to **immoveable property** whether it is registered in a register or not. Consequently, disposals of moveable property other than the

---

[5] Cf MünchKomm InsO/*Reinhart* Art 14 EuInsVO mn 2.

[6] Cf Haß/Huber/Gruber/Heiderhoff-*Gruber* Art 14 EuInsVO mn 7.

[7] Cf MünchKomm BGB/*Kindler* IntInsR mn 390; D-K/D/Ch-*Duursma-Kepplinger* Art 14 mn 8 f.

[8] By contrast, *Paulus* Komm EuInsVO Art 14 mn 5 considers this questionable.

[9] Cf D-K/D/Ch-*Duursma-Kepplinger* Art 14 mn 8.

[10] ECJ C-341/04 of 2 May 2006. For discussions from German legal literature, see Table of Cases Art 3 of the EIR Appendix A mn 10 above. Discussions from French legal literature: Dalloz 2006, Jur p 1752 *Dammann*; Rev Soc 2006 p 360 with comments by *Rémery*; JCP 2006, II, no 10089 with comments by *Menjucq*. JCP E 2006, no 2071 with comments by *Vallens*; Rev Lamy dr aff June 2006, p 26 with comments by *Chaput*.

[11] As per the Opinion of the Advocate General *Francis Geoffrey Jacobs* on 27 Sept 2005 C-341/04, ZIP 2005, 1878, no 89 et seq.

[12] See JCl Commercial, Procédures Collectives, Redressement et Liquidation judiciaire, Droit communautaire, Fasc. 3125 (*Roussel Galle*) no 98; Circulaire No 2006-19 of the French Justice Minister dated 15 Dec 2006, Bulletin officiel du Ministère de la Justice dated 28 Feb 2007 Art 3.2.2.2 last dash. On laws relating to negotiable instruments and other securities under French law in general, see: *Ferid/Sonnenberger* Das französische Zivilrecht, 2nd ed 1986, mn 2 M 401 et seq and *Sonnenberger/Dammann* Französisches Handels- und Wirtschaftrecht (3rd edn in preparation) no III.

property set out in the second and third dashes of Art 14 of the EIR are governed by the *lex fori concursus* (Art 4 in some circumstances in conjunction with Art 13 of the EIR).

The assets must form part of the **insolvency estate.** Whether such is the case is determined pursuant to the *lex fori concursus.*[13] An example from French insolvency law illustrates the restriction of the scope of application of Art 14 of the EIR. According to French doctrine, property that is delivered subject to a reservation of title is not included in the insolvency estate. The same applies in the case of liens on fungible goods within the meaning of Art 2341 CC.[14] **10**

5. Legal Consequences

Art 14 of the EIR is a conflict of laws rule that refers to the substantive insolvency laws of the State in which the register is kept or the immoveable property is situated (referral to specific substantive law provisions), and thus supersedes the *lex fori concursus.* The *bona fide* purchaser is being dealt with as if domestic insolvency proceedings had been opened.[15] What is being protected is the good faith placed in a register in cases where there has been a failure to register the notification of the opening of proceedings in that register of the other Member State. Not to be forgotten is that the insolvency law provisions of the State in which the register is kept or the immoveable asset is situated may in fact be less favourable to the *bona fide* third party than would the *lex fori concursus* of the main insolvency proceedings.[16] **11**

6. Practical Consequences

In view of the protection afforded by Art 14 of the Regulation, it is in the best interests of the liquidator in the main insolvency proceedings to register the opened insolvency proceedings in the corresponding register of the affected Member State as quickly as possible. **12**

Finally, just how important Art 14 of the EIR will be in practical terms depends on whether the applicable insolvency law of the affected Member State contemplates the protection of *bona fide* third-party purchasers at all. If there is a referral to French insolvency law for example, Art 14 of the EIR would probably play a very minor role. French law does not provide any special protection to third parties for dispositions concluded by the debtor without the permission of the judge of the insolvency proceedings after such proceedings have been opened.[17] **13**

---

[13] Cf Haß/Huber/Gruber/Heiderhoff-*Gruber* Art 14 EuInsVO mn 11.

[14] In the version of the *ordonnance* of 23 Mar 2006, on this, see *Dammann* Dalloz 2006, 1298, 1299 no 7.

[15] See MünchKomm BGB/*Kindler* IntInsR mn 395 et seq; D-K/D/Ch-*Duursma-Kepplinger* Art 14 mn 15; dissenting opinion: Haß/Huber/Gruber/Heiderhoff-*Gruber* Art 14 EuInsVO mn 15 who favours the inclusion of all provisions based on good faith.

[16] Cf MünchKomm BGB/*Kindler* IntInsR mn 396; D-K/D/Ch-*Duursma-Kepplinger* Art 14 mn 17; Haß/Huber/Gruber/Heiderhoff-*Gruber* Art 14 EuInsVO mn 18.

[17] In French law, see Art L 622-7 Code de commerce, which, as part of the *procédure de sauvegarde* and the *procédure de redressement judiciaire,* voids all disposals outside of the normal course of business that are made without the permission of the insolvency judge. Commencing with the opening of *liquidation judiciaire*, the debtor is repre-

Article 15
Effects of insolvency proceedings on lawsuits pending

The effects of insolvency proceedings on a lawsuit pending concerning an asset or a right of which the debtor has been divested shall be governed solely by the law of the Member State in which that lawsuit is pending.

Contents

Index

Bibliography

Chaput Centre des intérêts principaux et catégories juridiques de l'insolvabilité des entreprises (à propos de l'arrêt CJCE du 2 mai 2006), Comments on ECJ dated 2.5.2006, Rev Lamy dr aff Juni 2006, p 26; *Dammann* L'application du règlement CE n° 1346-2000 après les arrêts *Staubitz-Schreiber* et *Eurofood* de la CJCE, Dalloz 2006, p 1752; *Duursma-Kepplinger/Duursma/Chalupsky* Europäische Insolvenzverordnung, Kommentar (2002); *Haß/Huber/Gruber/Heiderhoff* EU-Insolvenzverordnung Kommentar (2005); *Kübler/Prütting* Kommentar zur Insolvenzordnung (March 2006); *Menjucq* Notion autonome du centre des intérêts principaux d'une filiale étrangère d'un groupe, Comments on ECJ dated 2.5.2006, JCP 2006, II, No 10089; *Moss/Fletcher/Isaacs* (eds) The EC Regulation on Insolvency Proceedings, A Commentary and Annotated Guide (2002); Münchener Kommentar zum Bürgerlichen Gesetzbuch, vol 11 (2006); *Nerlich/Römermann* (eds) Insolvenzordnung (InsO), Kommentar (May 2003); *Paulus* Europäische Insolvenzverordnung Kommentar (2006); *Rémery* L'application à une filiale du règlement communautaire relatif aux procédures d'insolvabilité, Comments on ECJ dated 2.5.2006, Rev Soc 2006, p 360; *Vallens* La maison mère d'un groupe centre des intérêts principaux de ses filiales étrangères, Comments TC Nanterre dated 15.2.2006, Dalloz 2006, p 793; *Virgós/Schmit* Erläuternder Bericht zu dem EU-Übereinkommen über Insolvenzverfahren, in Stoll (ed), Vorschläge und Gutachten (1997), p 32.

sented by the *liquidateur* and can no longer make any dispositions that affect creditors. Prevailing opinion holds that such disposals are *inopposable*, see Cour de cassation of 26 Apr 2000, Revue de jurisprudence de droit des affaires (RJDA) 7–8/00 no 783. For German law, see: Kübler/Prütting-*Kemper* EuInsVO Art 14 mn 6; Nerlich/Römermann-*Mincke* Art 14 EuInsVO mn 2.

1. Issue

It is often the case in international insolvencies that at the time at which the main proceedings are opened, other **procedures** have already been **brought by individual creditors** against the debtor in another Member State, or a lawsuit concerning an asset or a right which the debtor has been divested of is already pending. **1**

The problem here is how to coordinate these proceedings with the insolvency proceeding with its claim to universality. **2**

2. Objects of the Rule

The *lex fori concursus* determines how the opening of insolvency proceedings affects **procedures brought by individual creditors;** Art 4 (2) sentence 2 (f) of the EIR. Expressly excluded from this, however, are the **effects on pending lawsuits** regulated in Art 15 of the EIR.[1] **3**

Art 15 of the EIR is a **special conflict of laws rule** that refers to the law of the Member Sate in which the lawsuit is pending, the so-called ***lex fori processus.*** What is being protected here is the need for **legal clarity and legal certainty** in relation to procedural law.[2] How the opening of insolvency proceedings affects the fate of national proceedings is therefore governed exclusively by the *lex fori processus.* The individual substantive-law possibilities within this body of law may vary considerably. These primarily concern a possible suspension of the proceedings[3] and the jurisdiction of the court. Art 15 of the EIR in effect allows the trial court to continue to apply the law of its own forum.[4] **4**

3. Scope of Application

Art 15 of the EIR applies in the event that **main insolvency proceedings** are opened. It may also be applicable to **secondary or independent territorial insolvency proceedings** that have been opened in another Member State. Proceedings pending in a Member State may affect assets in the insolvency estate of the secondary or independent territorial insolvency proceedings.[5] On the other hand, Art 15 of the EIR will not apply to secondary or independent territorial insolvency proceedings if the lawsuit is pending in the territory of another Member State.[6] **5**

The effects of individual execution measures concerning assets that are included in the debtor's insolvency estate are governed by *lex fori concursus*; Art 4 (2) sentence 2 (f) of the EIR. Art 15 of the EIR is thus an exception to the rule. Its scope of application is restricted to **other pending lawsuits concerning an asset or a right of which the debtor has been divested.** **6**

---

1 *Virgós/Schmit* Explanatory report mn 142; D-K/D/Ch-*Duursma-Kepplinger* Art 15 mn 1.

2 See MünchKomm BGB/*Kindler* IntInsR mn 402.

3 See Moss/Fletcher/Isaacs-Moss/Smith, Regulation, mn 8.130.

4 Kübler/Prütting-*Kemper* Art 15 EuInsVO mn 1.

5 Cf Nerlich/Römermann-*Mincke* Komm InsO Art 15 EuInsVO mn 1; MünchKomm BGB-*Kindler* IntInsR mn 411; Haß/Huber/Gruber/Heiderhoff-*Gruber* Art 15 EuInsVO mn 4.

6 Cf Kübler/Prütting-*Kemper* Art 15 EuInsVO mn 2.

4. Requirements

7 The question as to **which assets form part of the insolvency estate is governed** by the *lex fori concursus*, Art 4 (2) sentence 2 (b) of the EIR. *Kindler* and *Duursma-Kepplinger* accurately refer to this as a kind of "pre-selection".[7] All legal procedures concerning the issue of the inclusion of the asset itself in the insolvency estate are subject to Art 15 of the EIR.[8] This generally involves actions for separation of third-party property from the insolvent's estate *(Aussonderung)* and actions claiming preferential satisfaction *(Absonderung)*.[9] Any suspension of the proceedings is therefore governed by the *lex fori processus*. These various connecting factors to the *lex fori concursus* or to the *lex fori processus* are not without their problems. Where an asset or a right is not included in the insolvency estate at all, Art 15 of the EIR will not apply. The proceedings in which this is ascertained, however, are governed by the *lex fori processus*. If the proceedings concern rights *in rem* within the meaning of Arts 5 or 7 of the EIR, *Paulus* prefers the exclusive application of the *lex fori processus*.[10] Although this may at first glance appear correct, what may actually be involved is an **asset-related lawsuit** as the granting of secured rights is challengeable pursuant to Art 4 (2) sentence 2 (m) of the EIR.

8 The term "**lawsuit**" must be construed autonomously without reference to a national legal system.[11] It encompasses both "active" proceedings in which the debtor is the claimant, as well as "passive" proceedings in which the debtor is the defendant.[12] It includes declaratory actions and provisional remedies, but does not include proceedings for non-contentious matters,[13] arbitration proceedings, or enforcement measures that pursuant to Art 4 (2) sentence 2 (f) of the EIR are governed by the *lex fori concursus*.[14]

9 The term "**pending**" is to be interpreted autonomously, independent of how it is understood by the laws of the individual Member States.[15] It suffices if the claimant has done everything required to institute proceedings, having at least filed the statement of claim at the court.[16] The courts should arguably be able to take into account the definition of "pending" in Art 30 of Council Regulation (EC) No 44/2001.[17]

10 The lawsuit must already be pending **when insolvency proceedings are opened.** Whether the time at which proceedings are opened is a matter to be determined by the *lex fori concursus* was left open by the ECJ in the Eurofood decision of 2 May 2006.[18]

---

[7] Cf MünchKomm BGB/*Kindler* IntInsR mn 409; D-K/D/Ch-*Duursma-Kepplinger* Art 15 mn 11.

[8] Cf D-K/D/Ch-*Duursma-Kepplinger* Art 15 mn 10; MünchKomm BGB/*Kindler* IntInsR mn 410.

[9] Cf Haß/Huber/Gruber/Heiderhoff-*Gruber* Art 15 EuInsVO mn 3.

[10] *Paulus* Komm EuInsVO Art 15 mn 4.

[11] Prevailing opinion, see: MünchKomm BGB/*Kindler* IntInsR mn 404; D-K/D/Ch-*Duursma-Kepplinger* Art 15 mn 25; Haß/Huber/Gruber/Heiderhoff-*Gruber* Art 15 EuInsVO mn 5; *Paulus*, on the other hand, in Komm EuInsVO Art 15 mn 3 seems to want to invoke the *lex fori processus*.

[12] Cf D-K/D/Ch-*Duursma-Kepplinger* Art 15 mn 20.

[13] MünchKomm BGB/*Kindler* IntInsR mn 406.

[14] Cf D-K/D/Ch-*Duursma-Kepplinger* Art 15 mn 27.

[15] Prevailing opinion, cf Kübler/Prütting-*Kemper* EuInsVO Art 15 mn 4; Haß/Huber/Gruber/Heiderhoff-*Gruber* Art 15 EuInsVO mn 7.

[16] Cf D-K/D/Ch-*Duursma-Kepplinger* Art 15 mn 15 et seq.

[17] See Kübler/Prütting-*Kemper* EuInsVO Art 15 mn 4; *Paulus* Komm EuInsVO Art 15 mn 5; Haß/Huber/Gruber/Heiderhoff-*Gruber* Art 15 EuInsVO mn 7. In the Eurofood judgement of 2 May 2006 (ECJ C-341/04 NZI 2006, 360), the ECJ relied on the judicial decisions on Council Regulation (EC) No 44/2001 in order to define "public policy" in art 26 of the EIR more precisely.

[18] ECJ 2 May 2006, ZInsO 2006, 360. As per the Opinion of the Advocate General

5. Legal Consequences

Art 15 of the EIR is a **special conflict of laws rule.** The *lex fori processus* determines the law applicable to the pending lawsuit. It concerns a **referral to specific substantive law provisions.**[19] The relevant provisions may be found in procedural law as well as in insolvency law.[20] **11**

The *lex fori processus* governs, in particular, all procedural-law matters in conjunction with the **opening of an insolvency proceeding,** such as whether the proceedings are to be continued or suspended, and at which point in time and by whom the proceedings are to be resumed. A cumulative application of the *lex fori concursus* and the *lex fori processus* is not possible. **12**

6. Practical Solutions

The application of Art 15 of the EIR can lead to practical problems where the respective law regime contemplates different types of insolvency proceedings. A winding-up of the debtor, which leads to a full divestment, cannot be compared to reorganisation proceedings pursuant to which the debtor-in-possession continues to operate his business under the supervision of the liquidator or the court. It therefore makes sense to take these differences into account and, as far as is possible, to "adapt" the *lex fori processus* to the *lex fori concursus* to ensure that the legal effects do not run contrary to the objects of the main insolvency proceedings.[21] **13**

Francis Geoffrey Jacobs on 27 Sep 2005, C-341/04, ZIP 2005, 1878, no 89 et seq. For discussions from German legal literature on the Eurofood decision, cf Table of Cases Art 3 of the EIR Appendix A mn 10 above. Discussions from French legal literature: Dalloz 2006 Jur p 1752 *Dammann*; Rev Soc 2006 p 360 with comments by *Rémery*; JCP 2006, II, no 10089 with comments by *Menjucq*; JCP E 2006, no 2071 with comments by *Vallens*; Rev Lamy dr aff June 2006, p 26 with comments by *Chaput*.

19 Prevailing opinion, cf MünchKomm BGB/*Kindler* IntInsR mn 414 et seq; D-K/D/Ch-*Duursma-Kepplinger* Art 15 mn 6; Haß/Huber/Gruber/Heiderhoff-*Gruber* Art 15 EuInsVO mn 10.

20 Cf Kübler/Prütting-*Kemper* EuInsVO Art 15 mn 5.

21 D-K/D/Ch-*Duursma-Kepplinger* Art 15 mn 20 et seq.

Chapter II

Recognition of Insolvency Proceedings

Article 16
Principle

1. Any judgment opening insolvency proceedings handed down by a court of a Member State which has jurisdiction pursuant to Article 3 shall be recognised in all the other Member States from the time that it becomes effective in the State of the opening of proceedings.

This rule shall also apply where, on account of his capacity, insolvency proceedings cannot be brought against the debtor in other Member States.

2. Recognition of the proceedings referred to in Article 3(1) shall not preclude the opening of the proceedings referred to in Article 3(2) by a court in another Member State. The latter proceedings shall be secondary insolvency proceedings within the meaning of Chapter III.

→ Cf Art 15 et seq UNCITRAL Model Law

Contents

Index

Bibliography

Balz Das neue Europäische Insolvenzübereinkommen, ZIP 1996, p 948; Beck Verwertungsfragen im Verhältnis von Haupt- und Sekundärinsolvenzverfahren nach der EuInsVO, NZI 2006, p 609; *Carstens* Die internationale Zuständigkeit im europäischen Insolvenzrecht (2005); *Dammann/Podeur* L'affaire Daisytek : l'épilogue. Application par la Cour de cassation du règlement européen relatif aux procédures d'insolvabilité, Banque & droit N° 109 September–October 2006, p 3; *Deipenbrock* Das neue europäische Internationale Insolvenzrecht – von der „quantité négligeable" zu einer „quantité indispensable", EWS 2001, p 113; *Duursma-Kepplinger/Duursma/Chalupsky* Europäische Insolvenzverordnung, Kommentar, (2002); *Duursma-Kepplinger/Duursma* Das Schicksal von dinglichen Sicherungsrechten sowie des Eigentumsvorbehalts nach der Insolvenzordnung, wbl 2002, p 59; *Ehricke/Ries* Die neue Europäische Insolvenzverordnung, JuS 2003, p 313; *Eidenmüller* Der Markt für internationale Konzerninsolvenzen: Zuständigkeitskonflikte unter der EuInsVO, NJW 2004, p 3455; *Freitag/Leible* Justizkonflikte im Europäischen Internationalen Insolvenzrecht und (k)ein Ende?, RIW 2006, p 641; *Fritz/Bähr* Die Europäische Verordnung über Insolvenzverfahren – Herausforderung an Gerichte und Insolvenzverwalter, DZWiR 2001, p 221; *Gottwald* Insolvenzrechts-Handbuch (2006); *Gottwald* Grenzüberschreitende Insolvenzen (1997); *Haß/Huber/Gruber/Heiderhoff* EU-Insolvenzverordnung, Kommentar (2005); Heidelberger Kommentar zur Insolvenzordnung (2006) (eds *Eickmann, Flessner, et al*); *Herchen* Aktuelle Entwicklungen im Recht der internationalen Zuständigkeit zur Eröffnung von Insolvenzverfahren: Der Mittelpunkt der (hauptsächlichen) Interessen im Mittelpunkt der Interessen, ZInsO 2004, p 825; *Herchen* Das Prioritätsprinzip im internationalen Insolvenzrecht, ZIP 2005, p 1401; *Herchen* Wer zuerst kommt, mahlt zuerst! – Die Bestellung eines „schwachen" vorläufigen Insolvenzverwalters als Insolvenzverfahrenseröffnung im Sinne der EuInsVO, NZI 2006, p 435; *Huber* Internationales Insolvenzrecht in Europa, ZZP 114 (2001) p 133; *Huber* Die Europäische Insolvenzverordnung, EuZW 2002, p 490; *Huber* Der deutsch-englische Justizkonflikt – Kompetenzkonflikte im Internationalen Insolvenzrecht, in Lorenz (ed), Festschrift für Heldrich (2005) p 695; *Israel* European Cross-Border Insolvency Regulation (2005); *Jahn* Insolvenzen in Europa (2004); *Kemper* Die Verordnung (EG) Nr. 1346/2000 über Insolvenzverfahren, ZIP 2001, p 1609; *Keppelmüller* An der Schwelle zu einem europäischen Insolvenzrecht?, wbl 1996, p 337; *Laukemann* Rechtshängigkeit im europäischen Insolvenzrecht, RIW 2005, p 104; *Leible/Freitag* Justizkonflikte im Europäischen Internationalen Insolvenzrecht, RIW 2006, p 641; *Leible/Staudinger* Die europäische Verordnung über Insolvenzverfahren, KTS 2000, p 533; *Leipold* Zum künftigen Weg des deutschen Internationalen Insolvenzrechts (Anwendungsbereich, internationale Zuständigkeit, Anerkennung und Vollstreckung), in Stoll (ed), Vorschläge und Gutachten, p 185; *Lüke* Das europäische internationale Insolvenzrecht, ZZP 111 (1998) p 275; *Mankowski* Klärung von Grundfragen des europäischen Internationalen Insolvenzrechts durch die Eurofood-Entscheidung?, BB 2006, p 1753; *Morscher* Die europäische Insolvenzverordnung (EuInsVO) (2002); *Moss/Fletcher/Isaacs* (eds) The EC Regulation on Insolvency Proceedings (2002); Münchener Kommentar zum Bürgerlichen Gesetzbuch, vol 11 (2006); *Pannen/Riedemann* Comments on the Opinion of the Advocate General Francis Geoffrey Jacobs dated 27.9.2005 – C-341/04, EWiR 2005, p 725; *Pannen/Riedemann* Die deutschen Ausführungsbestimmungen zur EuInsVO – Ein Überblick zu den Regelungen des Art. 102 EGInsO nF, NZI 2004, p 301; *Pannen/Riedemann/Kühnle* Zur Stellung der Insolvenzgläubiger nach der Europäischen Verordnung über Insolvenzverfahren (EuInsVO), NZI 2002, p 303; *Paulus* Europäische Insolvenzverordnung, Kommentar (2006); *Paulus* Der EuGH und das moderne Insolvenzrecht, NZG 2006, p 609; *Paulus* Zuständigkeitsfragen nach der Europäischen Insolvenzverordnung, ZIP 2003, p 1725; *Paulus* Comments on OLG Vienna dated 9.11.2004, NZI 2005, p 62; *Poertzgen/Adam* Die Bestimmung des „centre of main interests" gem Art 3 Abs 1 EuInsVO, ZInsO 2006, p 505; *Rossbach* Europäische Insolvenzverwalter in Deutschland (2006); *Runkel* (ed) Anwaltshandbuch – Insolvenzrecht (2005); *Sabel* Hauptsitz als Niederlassung im Sinne der EuInsVO?, NZI 2004, p 126; *Schilling* Das englische Insolvenzeröffnungsverfahren im Anwendungsbereich der EuInsVO und im Vergleich mit dem deutschen Insolvenzeröffnungsverfahren, DZWiR 2006, p 143; *Schilling/Schmidt* COMI und vorläufiger Insolvenzverwalter – Problem gelöst?, ZInsO 2006, p 113; *Schmidt* Eurofood – Eine Leitentscheidung und ihre Rezeption in Europa und den USA, ZIP 2007, p 405; *Schwerdtfeger/Schilling* Innerstaatlicher Rechtsschutz gegen die Eröffnung eines Hauptinsolvenzverfahrens nach Art 3 Abs 1 EuInsVO in Deutschland, DZWiR 2005, p 370; *Smid* Deutsches und Europäisches Internationales Insolvenzrecht, Kommentar (2004); *Smid* Vier Entscheidungen englischer und deutscher Gerichte zur europäischen internationalen Zuständigkeit, DZWIR 2003, p 397; *Smid* EuGH zu »Eurofood«, BGH zur internationalen Zuständigkeit: Neueste Judikatur zur EuInsVO, DZWiR 2006, p 325; *Stoll* (ed) Vorschläge und Gutachten zur Umsetzung des EU-Übereinkommens über Insolvenzverfahren im deutschen Recht (1997); *Tirado* Die Anwendung der Europäischen Insolvenzverordnung durch die Gerichte der Mitgliedstaaten, GPR 2005, p 39; *Vallender* Die Voraussetzungen für die Einleitung eines Sekundärinsolvenzverfahrens nach der EuInsVO, InVo 2005, p 41; *Vallender* Aufgaben und Befugnisse des deutschen Insolvenzrichters in Verfahren nach der EuInsVO, KTS 2005, p 283; *Van Galen* How to Use the European Insolvency Regulation (2005); *Virgós/Schmit* Erläuternder Bericht zu dem EU-Übereinkommen über Insolvenzverfahren, in Stoll (ed), Vorschläge und Gutachten, p 32; *Virgós/Garcimartín* The European Insolvency Regulation: Law and Practice (2004); *Weller* Forum Shopping im Internationalen Insolvenzrecht?, IPRax 2004, p 412; *Wessels* International Insolvency Law (2006); *Wessels* Current Topics of International Insolvency Law (2004); *Wimmer* Frankfurter Kommentar (2005); *Wimmer* Einpassung der EU-Insolvenzverordnung in das deutsche Recht durch das Gesetz zur Neuregelung des Internationalen Insolvenzrechts, in Gerhardt/Haarmeyer/Kreft (eds), Festschrift Kirchhof (2003) p 521 et seq.

1. Introduction

1 Art 16 et seq of the EIR regulate the transborder recognition of insolvency proceedings. These provisions are understood as a "basic principle" of the EIR, being the very heart of it in terms of procedural law matters.[1]

2 Art 16 of the EIR primarily prescribes (as do Art 17 and Art 25 of the EIR) the **recognition** and **extension** of the effects throughout Europe of the main insolvency proceedings,[2] which adhere to the so-called **principle of universality**.[3] An insolvency

[1] *Morscher* EuInsVO p 22; *Kemper* ZIP 2001, 1609, 1613; *Leible/Staudinger* KTS 2000, 533, 560; also Moss/Fletcher/Isaacs-*Moss/Smith*, Regulation, mn 8.132; *Smid* Komm EuInsVO Art 16 mn 1.

[2] The concept of universality depicts the total seizure of the debtor's insolvency assets from which the idea of one single (unified) bankruptcy, in procedural law terms, arises; it is also in line with Recital 12 of the EIR; for an in-depth discussion on this, see: *Smid* Komm EuInsVO Einleitung 1, 2 mn 2 with further substantiation; *Wessels* International Insolvency Law (2006) mn 10464.

[3] The effects of the main insolvency proceedings are universal. On this, see Art 3 EuInsVO mn 7 et seq They are intended to encompass the debtor's entire assets – worldwide (and not just Europe-wide) – and all of the creditors, see *Virgós/Schmit* Explanatory Report mn 73; *Virgós/Garcimartín* Regulation, p 54. The EIR can, however, only guarantee the universal effect of the proceedings within the EU (with the exception of Denmark); the respective national laws apply outside the EU.

proceeding opened pursuant to Art 3 (1) of the EIR must therefore be recognized throughout the EU (with the exception of Denmark[4]) without the need for any further formalities (see Art 17 (1) of the EIR).[5] With the coming into force of the EIR on 31 May 2002 (Art 47 of the EIR), a preliminary **exequatur procedure**[6] is no longer necessary, at least not amongst the Member States of the EU.[7] But since the EIR does not adhere strictly to the principle of universality, it is also possible to open territorially-restricted secondary insolvency proceedings parallel to the main insolvency proceedings; see Art 3 of the EIR mn 3.[8]

To be subsumed within the broad definition of **insolvency proceedings,**[9] as understood in Art 16 of the EIR, are the **main insolvency proceedings** and all **territorial insolvency proceedings**, which also must be automatically recognized without any further formalities.[10] **3**

The EIR also prescribes the mandatory recognition of the **judgements** of a court, whose decision to open insolvency proceedings is recognized in accordance with Art 16 of the EIR, that concern the **course and closure** of insolvency proceedings; the same applies to a **composition** approved by such a court (Art 25 (1) subpara 1 of the EIR). Art 25 (1) subpara 1 sentence 2 of the EIR provides that the **enforcement** of these judgements is to be executed in accordance with Arts 31 to 51 (with the exception of Art 34 (2)) of the **Brussels Convention on Jurisdiction and the Enforcement of Judgements in Civil and Commercial Matters.** Commencing with the enactment of **Council Regulation (EC) No 44/2001**[11] of 22 December 2000, the subject matter of these provisions is now regulated in Arts 38 to 52 of Council Regulation (EC) No 44/2001; for an in-depth discussion on this, see Art 25 of the EIR mn 37. **4**

Furthermore, judgements **deriving directly** from the insolvency proceedings and those **closely linked** to it (Art 25 (1) subpara 2 of the EIR) also **must be recognized** even if they **5**

---

4 On the position of Denmark, see Recital 33 of the EIR; Moss/Fletcher/Isaacs-*Moss/Bayfield*, Regulation, mn 5.26; *Israel* European Cross-Border Insolvency Regulation (2005) 253 et seq; *Carstens* Die internationale Zuständigkeit im internationalen Insolvenzrecht (2005) 26 et seq; An identical treaty is still supposed to be entered into with Denmark, *Gottwald* InsR-Handb (2006) § 129 mn 3; also in-depth: FK-InsO/*Wimmer* Anhang I nach § 358 mn 2; *Paulus* Komm EuInsVO Einl mn 13.

5 Siehe auch *Virgós/Schmit* Explanatory report mn 143; *Virgós/Garcimartín* Regulation, p 186; Moss/Fletcher/Isaacs-*Moss/Bogden*, Regulation, mn 8.140; *Smid* Komm EuInsVO Art 16 mn 1; *Wessels* International Insolvency Law (2006) mn 10733.

6 An exequatur procedure is a proceeding to execute foreign judicial enforceable instruments in a national territory (exequatur); prior to the coming into force of the EIR, it was necessary in France for example to obtain an order of enforcement via the exequatur procedure to be able to enforce the effects of foreign insolvency proceedings.

7 *Paulus* EuInsVO Art 16 mn 2; D-K/D/Ch-*Duursma-Kepplinger/Chalupsky* Art 16 mn 2; Haß/Huber/Gruber/Heiderhoff-*Gruber* Art 16 EuInsVO mn 3; *Herchen* ZIP 2005, 1401, 1402; *Pannen/Riedemann/Kühnle* NZI 2002, 303; FK-InsO/*Wimmer* Anhang I nach § 358 mn 32; on this, see also *Dammann/Podeur* Banque & droit no 109 2006, 3, 5.

8 On this, see also *Leible/Staudinger* KTS 2000, 533, 543; *Deipenbrock* EWS 2001, 113, 117.

9 Art 1 (1) of the EIR defines collective proceedings as falling within the concept of insolvency proceedings; see Art 1 of the EIR mn 6 et seq.

10 *Virgós/Schmit* Explanatory report mn 143, 144; *Paulus* EuInsVO Art 16 mn 1.

11 Council Regulation (EC) No 44/2001 of 22 Dec 2000 on jurisdiction and the recognition and enforcement of judgments in civil and commercial matters came into force on 1 Mar 2002 in all Member States of the European Union with the exception of Denmark (art 76 of said Regulation).

have been rendered by another court; the same applies to **preservation measures taken after the request to open insolvency proceedings** (Art 25 (1) subpara 3 of the EIR).

6 Not to be overlooked in this regard is that Art 1 (1) No 2 of the 1968 Brussels Convention excludes bankruptcy, composition proceedings, and similar proceedings from the scope of application of the 1968 Brussels Convention. Consequently, legal actions that are based directly on insolvency law and that are closely linked to the insolvency proceedings do not fall within the scope of application of the 1968 Brussels Convention (according to Art 68 of Council Regulation (EC) No 44/2001, any references to the 1968 Brussels Convention are deemed as references to the new Council Regulation (EC) No 44/2001). The exclusion from application contained in Art 1 (1) No 2 of the 1968 Brussels Convention is now found in Art 1 (1) (b) of Council Regulation (EC) No 44/2001. Art 25 (1) subpara 3 of the EIR provides that judgements relating to preservation measures that are taken by a court with Art 3 of the EIR jurisdiction after the request to open insolvency proceedings must also be recognized. The recognition and enforcing of judgements not named in Art 25 (1) of the EIR are, pursuant to Art 25 (2) of the EIR, governed by the 1968 Brussels Convention (now Council Regulation (EC) No 44/2001) within the scope of its applicability. The reason for this provision was to make sure that there were no regulatory gaps in the transition from the 1968 Brussels Convention (now Council Regulation (EC) No 44/2001) to the EIR.[12]

7 Whereas Art 25 of the EIR regulates the recognition of an array of insolvency-related judgements, **Art 16 of the EIR** is solely concerned with the **recognition** of the **opening of proceedings**, i.e. the effects ensuing from the order to open insolvency proceedings. Through the recognition of such a proceeding, the legal effects conferred on such a proceeding by the laws of the State in which they are opened are extended to all other Member States (**extension of effects**).[13]

8 According to Art 4 (1) of the EIR, the **insolvency law of the Member State in which the proceedings are opened** governs the proceedings and its effects, provided that nothing to the contrary is found in the EIR (so-called *lex fori concursus*).[14] The *lex fori concursus* (see Art 4 of the EIR mn 56) governs all the procedural and substantive law effects that the insolvency proceedings have on the persons and legal relationships affected by them; all of the requirements for opening, conducting, and closing insolvency proceedings are also determined in compliance with it.[15]

2. Recognition of the Foreign Insolvency Proceeding in a Member State

9 As already implied by its heading, Art 16 of the EIR establishes the **principle of automatic recognition,** i.e. the automatic recognition by all other Member States of insolvency proceedings opened by a court with international jurisdiction per Art 3 of the EIR or by any other competent body of a Member State (Art 2 (d) of the EIR).[16] The decision of the court must be recognized as soon as it becomes **effective** in the opening State.

---

[12] *Virgós/Schmit* Explanatory report mn 197; in detail on this *Fritz/Bähr* DZWIR 2001, 221, 225.

[13] Cf Recital 22 of the EIR.

[14] *Van Galen* How to use the European Insolvency Regulation (2005) mn 3.1; cf in detail Art 4 of the EIR mn 6 et seq.

[15] Recital 23 of the EIR.

[16] *Gottwald* Grenzüberschreitende Insolvenzen (1997) 16; *Pannen* in Runkel (ed), AHB-Insolvenzrecht (2005), § 16 mn 70; HK-InsO/*Stephan* Art 16 EuInsVO mn 1.

2.1 Proceedings That Must Be Recognized Pursuant to Art 1 of the EIR

The recognition provisions of the EIR only apply to insolvency proceedings falling within its scope of application. The foreign proceeding wishing to be recognized must therefore be an insolvency proceeding within the meaning of Art 1 of the EIR, which means a proceeding listed in Annex A or Annex B of the EIR (Art 2 (a) and (c) of the EIR). Art 2 (a) defines insolvency proceedings as the **collective insolvency proceedings** referred to in Art 1 of the EIR; these presuppose the insolvency of the debtor and entail the partial or total divestment of a debtor and the appointment of a liquidator. The proceedings not listed in the Annexes do **not** profit from the recognition provisions of the EIR and do not stand in the way of the recognition of one of the proceedings listed in the Annexes, even if they were opened at an earlier point in time.[17] **10**

2.2 Effective Opening Judgement

In order to recognize an insolvency proceeding against the assets of a debtor, the judgement opening such proceedings must be **effective** pursuant to the *lex fori concursus* of the State in which the proceedings are opened. The judgement need not be ***res judicata*** either **formally** or in a **substantive-law** sense.[18] "Preliminary" judgements are already considered effective, i.e. judgements that can be appealed against in the ordinary courts;[19] more important for the determination of **effectiveness** is whether the decision **produces effects** in the State in which the proceedings are opened.[20] "Effects" are those that ensue directly from the opening judgement.[21] **11**

In **German law**, the issuing of the opening order pursuant to Secs 27, 5 (2) sentence 1 *InsO*, or the point in time of the debtor's divestment and deprival of rights of disposition, would constitute an effective opening; on this point see also the **Eurofood/Parmalat** decision of the ECJ according to which the ordering of a provisional administration can also constitute insolvency proceedings within the meaning of the EIR (→ cf Table of Cases Art 3 of the EIR Appendix A mn 10). **12**

Because the recognition occurs by operation of law, the effects of the insolvency proceedings are "activated" in all other Member States **simultaneous** to the effective opening of insolvency proceedings in the opening State.[22] **13**

The **publication** of the opening judgement, i.e. the **public notification** and **registration in a public register** provided for in Arts 21 and 22 of the EIR, is for the sake of publicity only and is not a requirement for recognition within the meaning of Art 16 of the EIR.[23] **14**

---

17 *Virgós/Schmit* Explanatory report mn 145; HK-InsO/*Stephan* Art 16 EuInsVO mn 3.

18 MünchKomm BGB/*Kindler* IntInsR mn 423; *Smid* Komm EuInsVO Art 16 mn 4; *Leible/Staudinger* KTS 2000, 533, 560; *Huber* ZZP 114 (2001) 133, 145; *Huber* EuZW 2002, 490, 494.

19 *Smid* Komm EuInsVO Art 16 mn 8.

20 *Virgós/Schmit* Explanatory report mn 147; *Kemper* ZIP 2001, 1609, 1613 et seq; *Fritz/Bähr* DZWiR 2001, 221, 225.

21 MünchKomm BGB/*Kindler* IntInsR mn 423.

22 *Virgós/Schmit* Explanatory report mn 68, 143; *Virgós/Garcimartín* Regulation, p 193; *Smid* Komm EuInsVO Art 16 mn 9; Moss/Fletcher/Isaacs-*Moss/Smith*, Regulation, mn 8.132; *Wessels* Current Topics of International Insolvency Law, 136.

23 *Virgós/Schmit* Explanatory report mn 29; Moss/Fletcher/Isaacs-*Moss/Smith*, Regulation, mn 8.133; D-K/D/Ch-*Duursma-Kepplinger/Chalupsky* Art 16 mn 16; *Wessels* Current Topics of International Insolvency Law, 136.

2.3 Court Having Jurisdiction

15 The opening of insolvency proceedings by a **court with jurisdiction** pursuant to Art 3 of the EIR must, according to Art 16 of the EIR, be **automatically** recognized in all other Member States. The term "**court**" must be understood here in a **functional** sense,[24] and according to Art 2 (d) of the EIR, it includes any judicial body or any other competent body of a Member State that is empowered to open insolvency proceedings or to take decisions in the course of such proceedings. The formulation "court [...] which has jurisdiction" is somewhat misleading as it is sometimes being erroneously understood as conferring **jurisdiction on the second State to review jurisdiction.**[25] The requirements for the jurisdiction of the opening court **may not be reviewed** in the recognizing State,[26] although such a subsequent review is not expressly prohibited by the EIR. Some argue that **allowing the second State to review** would help prevent the "race" to obtain the first opening judgement, and the overhasty and often unnecessary insolvency requests (motivated by forum shopping) associated with this.[27] Such a **subsequent review** is, however, **precluded** based on the fact that it encroaches on the principle of **Community trust.**[28] This is also in line with Recital 22 of the EIR (which expressly emphasizes the mutual trust in the insolvency laws of the respective Member States).[29] The basis of the principle of mutual trust is that a court of a Member State has to review its own jurisdiction pursuant to Art 3 (1) of the EIR when a request is made to it to open main insolvency proceedings, i.e. it must review whether the debtor's **COMI** is in this Member State.[30] Allowing the other Member States to **make a second review** would run contrary to the intentions of the drafters of the EIR, this being the creation of **legal certainty** through the **principle of priority,**[31] a concept that can already be gleaned from the history of the EIR. Even if the principle of priority was not expressly stipulated in the EIR,[32] Art 16 (1) sub-

---

[24] *Smid* Komm EuInsVO Art 16 mn 5; *Huber* ZZP 114 (2001), 133, 145; *Huber* EuZW 2002, 490, 494.

[25] See *Smid* DZWiR 2003, 397, 401; *Mankowski* RIW 2004, 587, 597 et seq.

[26] *Huber* ZZP 114 (2001), 133, 146; *Smid* Komm EuInsVO Art 16 mn 5; BK-InsO/*Pannen* Art 16 EuInsVO mn 3; MünchKomm BGB/*Kindler* IntInsR mn 424.

[27] See *Smid* DZWiR 2003, 397, 401; *Mankowski* RIW 2004, 587, 597 et seq.

[28] ECJ dated 2 May 2006 "Parmalat/Eurofood" – C-341/04 (→ cf Table of Cases Art 3 of the EIR Appendix A mn 10); *Virgós/Schmit* Explanatory report mn 79 Nr 1 b), 147, 79; MünchKomm BGB/*Kindler* IntInsR mn 424; *Pannen* in Runkel (ed), AHB-Insolvenzrecht (2005), § 16 mn 73; D-K/D/Ch-*Duursma-Kepplinger/Chalupsky* Art 16 mn 14; *Virgós/ Garcimartín* Regulation, p 186, 211; *Tirado* GPR 2005, 39, 40; *Wessels* Current Topics of International Insolvency Law, 27; *Wessels* Insolvency Law mn 10467.

[29] The safeguarding of Community trust is legally anchored in German law in art 102 sec 2 EGInsO. This provision enables a foreign insolvency court to comprehend why a German insolvency court assumed jurisdiction pursuant to art 3 of the EIR: Art 102 sec 2 EGInsO prescribes that the opening order must include a short description of the factual basis of, and the legal considerations for, taking jurisdiction; on this: *Pannen/Riedemann* NZI 2004, 301, 302 et seq.

[30] ECJ dated 2 May 2006 "Parmalat/Eurofood" – C-341/04 – ZInsO 2006, 484, 487 (→ cf Table of Cases Art 3 of the EIR Appendix A mn 10); *Virgós/Schmit* Explanatory report mn 79 Nr 1 a); *Wimmer* FS Kirchhof (2003) p 521, 525.

[31] *Virgós/Schmit* Explanatory report mn 202; ECJ ZInsO 2006, 484, 487; *Herchen* ZIP 2005, 1401 et seq; *Ehricke/Ries* JuS 2003, 313, 314; *Huber* FS Heldrich (2004) p 679, 681 et seq.

[32] But e.g. in art 27 of the Council Regulation (EC) No 44/2001 of 22 December 2000 on jurisdiction and the recognition and enforcement of judgments in civil and commercial matters or art 11 of the Council Regulation (EC) No 1347/2000 of 29 May 2000 on jurisdiction and the recognition and enforce-

para 1 of the EIR operates to provide just such a rule in favour of the first-rendered opening judgement: this provision commands that every judgement to open main insolvency proceedings made by a court of a Member State with jurisdiction to do this must be recognized the moment that such judgement becomes effective in the State in which it was rendered. This is bolstered by Art 3 (3) of the EIR, which provides that any proceeding opened **after** the main insolvency proceedings can only be a secondary insolvency proceeding and not a main proceeding.[33] The same conclusion can be drawn from Art 16 (2) of the EIR, which states that the recognition of foreign main insolvency proceedings does not impede the opening of another territorial insolvency proceeding. It can be deduced from this that the opening of another main insolvency proceeding is not permitted.[34] The **ECJ**[35] finds support for this view in the wording of Art 26 of the EIR as well. According to Art 26 of the EIR, a refusal to recognize a foreign judgement is only permitted if such judgement infringes the **public policy** of the recognizing State (see Art 26 of the EIR mn 1 et seq). Reversing this, the conclusion can be drawn that in all other cases a proceeding must still be recognized even if the national court considers the foreign judgement incorrect in terms of its subject matter. This is in opposition to a view favoured by some legal writers,[36] whose argument turns on the wording of Art 16 of the EIR, "a court [...] which has *jurisdiction* pursuant to Article 3". The **valid existence** of jurisdiction is therefore **not a prerequisite to recognition**; it suffices if the opening court considered itself competent on account of Art 3 of the EIR.[37] Hence, the wording of Art 16 (1) sentence 1 of the EIR – "a court [...] which has jurisdiction pursuant to Article 3" – must be subjected to a **teleological (utilitarian) interpretation.**[38]

But should a party hold that the COMI of the debtor is situated in a Member **16**
State other than one in which the main insolvency proceedings were opened, then the jurisdiction assumed by the opening court can be challenged using the **legal remedies available** under the national laws of this Member State.[39] A debtor in Germany would have a right of appeal pursuant to Sec 34 (2) *InsO*.

A successful appeal that causes the judgement to subsequently **forfeit its effectiveness** **17**
leads to the *ex post facto* cancellation of the reason for recognition, which in turn results in a cancellation of the automatic recognition.[40]

Insolvency proceedings inconsistent with the principle of priority are to be discontinu- **18**
ed in Germany pursuant to Art 102 Sec 4 (1) *EGInsO*.[41] A detailed discussion of Art 102 Sec (4) *EGInsO* is found at mn 1.

---

ment of judgments in matrimonial matters and in matters of parental responsibility for children of both spouses.

33 Also *Freitag/Leible* RIW 2006, 641, 644.

34 *Huber* ZZP 114 (2001), 133, 145.

35 ECJ dated 2 May 2006 "Parmalat/Eurofood" – C-341/04 – ZInsO 2006, 484, 488; (→ cf Table of Cases Art 3 of the EIR Appendix A mn 10).

36 See *Mankowski* EWiR 2003, 767, 768; *Mankowski* RIW 2004, 587, 597 et seq; *Smid* DZWiR 2003, 397, 401.

37 *Virgós/Schmit* Explanatory report mn 202; *Lüke* ZZP 111 (1998) 275, 286 et seq; *Vallender* KTS 2005, 283, 301.

38 MünchKomm BGB/*Kindler* IntInsR mn 424.

39 ECJ dated 2 May 2006 "Parmalat/Eurofood" – C-341/04 (→ cf Table of Cases Art 3 of the EIR Appendix A mn 10); *Virgós/Schmit* Explanatory report mn 202; *Schwerdtfeger/Schilling* DZWIR 2005, 230; LG Hamburg NZI 2005, 645; FK-InsO/*Wimmer* Anhang I nach § 358 mn 29; *Sabel* NZI 2004, 126, 127.

40 Cf *Virgós/Schmit* Explanatory report mn 147, note "as long as"; HK-InsO/*Stephan* Art 16 EuInsVO mn 6.

41 *Pannen/Riedemann* NZI 2004, 301, 303.

2.4 Main Insolvency Proceedings at the Centre of Main Interests

19 The duty to recognize insolvency proceedings that is imposed by Art 16 of the EIR extends to proceedings opened in a Member State and those based on the jurisdiction provisions of Art 3 of the EIR. The duty to recognize therefore relates to both **main insolvency proceedings** as well as to **independent territorial insolvency proceedings and secondary insolvency proceedings.**

20 In order for a proceeding to be recognized as a **main insolvency proceeding,** it is **not** necessary that the opening order **expressly state** that the proceedings opened are main insolvency proceedings.[42] The judgement opening main insolvency proceedings therefore does not need to be formally described as such. The only way a foreign judgement will **not** be regarded as a judgement opening main insolvency proceedings is if the opening order contains concrete, manifest grounds indicating that the order – as an exception – concerns a national independent territorial insolvency proceeding only.[43]

21 If the opening court is unaware of the transborder dimensions of the case, perhaps because it assumes that the debtor only has assets within the State and no other foreign connection is evident, the opening of such a proceeding is to be regarded as the opening of main insolvency proceedings.[44]

2.5 Territorial Insolvency Proceedings, Art 16 (2) of the EIR

22 Art 16 (2) of the EIR repeats and supplements the rule already contained in Art 3 (2) of the EIR, pursuant to which parallel proceedings are permitted. According to Art 3 (2) sentence 1 of the EIR, the courts of a Member State other than the one in which the debtor's centre of main interests is situated only have international jurisdiction to open insolvency proceedings if the debtor has an **establishment**[45] within the territory of this Member State. A (secondary) proceeding opened pursuant to this provision may, in all cases, only be a territorially restricted proceeding whose effects are limited to the State in which it is opened (Art 3 (2) sentence 2 of the EIR); see Art 3 of the EIR mn 116 et seq.

23 In the case of territorial insolvency proceedings per Art 3 (2) and (3) of the EIR, the provisions of the EIR, especially the provisions of Chapter III of it, govern not only the opening of them but also the course of such proceedings. Furthermore, the opening of secondary insolvency proceedings in effect restricts the universal scope of the main insolvency proceedings, the assets situated in the State of the territorial insolvency proceedings no longer being comprised within the main proceedings.[46] The scope of the universal effect of the divestment in conjunction with the main insolvency proceedings (Art 17 (1) of the EIR) is being **restricted** by the effects of the secondary insolvency proceedings to a degree relative to the insolvency assets belonging to such secondary proceedings.[47] The liquidator appointed to the main insolvency proceedings is being deprived of his powers of disposition in relation to the assets situated within the territory of the Member State of the secondary insolvency proceedings and for the duration of

[42] *Herchen* ZInsO 2004, 825; cf on German law AG Duisburg dated 10 Dec 2002, "BABCOCK" ZInsO 2003, 476 (→ cf Table of Cases Art 3 of the EIR Appendix B Nr 10).

[43] Also *Paulus* ZIP 2003, 1725, 1727; following him: AG Cologne dated 23 Jan 2004, "Automold" NZI 2004, 151, 152 (→ cf Table of Cases Art 3 of the EIR Appendix A mn 2).

[44] Also *Herchen* ZInsO 2004, 825; Haß/Huber/Gruber/Heiderhoff-*Gruber* Art 16 EuInsVO mn 16.

[45] Cf for the concept of establishment Art 2 of the EIR mn 45 et seq

[46] *Wessels* Current Topics of International Insolvency Law, 137.

[47] *Beck* NZI 2006, 609, 610; D-K/D/Ch-*Duursma-Kepplinger/Chalupsky* Art 16 mn 31.

such proceedings.[48] Apart from a refusal to recognize based on Art 26 of the EIR (public order proviso), these parallel proceedings may not be challenged either and therefore must be recognized pursuant to Art 16 of the EIR without any further formalities.

2.6 Public Policy

In observation of the **public order proviso** found in Art 26 of the EIR, another Member State within the scope of application of the EIR may only refuse to recognize a proceeding if such recognition would be manifestly contrary to that State's public policy, in particular its fundamental principles or the constitutional rights and liberties of the individual.[49] A finding of such an infringement can lead to a blocking of the effects of the insolvency proceeding.[50] An infringement of public policy will only be found, however, in **a very narrow set of circumstances.**[51] The infringement must be so obvious that an informed user would automatically draw this conclusion.[52] There is a wide consensus that an erroneous assumption of international jurisdiction does not constitute an infringement of public policy.[53] **24**

The court that is reviewing its own jurisdiction to open proceedings pursuant to Art 3 (1) of the EIR must do so in observation of the **principle of Community trust** and **basic procedural guarantees**, particularly the right to a fair trial.[54] As a by-product of Art 6 of the CPHRFF, the right to a fair trial is a fundamental human procedural right and thereby forms a part of each State's public order regardless of such State's national constitutional laws.[55] An infringement of the public order can be found in a breach of the right to be heard, this being an integral part of all Member States' common fundamental procedural principles.[56] An erroneous assumption of a court's own jurisdiction to open proceedings does not, however, constitute a breach of the right to a fair trial because, although it probably makes it more difficult for the parties to access a court, it does not completely prevent them from asserting their rights.[57] **25**

It would also be unacceptable to refuse recognition of one of the reorganization proceedings listed in Annex A of the EIR based on the argument that the creditors are thereby being put in a worse position than they would be in in the case of a winding-up.[58] **26**

For a detailed discussion of the public order issue, see the comments on Art 26 of the EIR. **27**

---

[48] *Virgós/Schmit* Explanatory report mn 156.

[49] See art 26 EuInsVO. OLG Düsseldorf dated 9 Jul 2004 "ISA/Daisytek" (→ cf Table of Cases Art 3 of the EIR Appendix A mn 15).

[50] *Virgós/Schmit* Explanatory report mn 209.

[51] FK-InsO/*Wimmer* Anhang I nach § 358 mn 34 and 82; *Kemper* ZIP 2001, 1609, 1614.

[52] *Kemper* ZIP 2001, 1609, 1614; FK-InsO/*Wimmer* Anhang I nach § 358 mn 82.

[53] D-K/D/Ch-*Duursma-Kepplinger/Chalupsky* Art 16 mn 15; *Eidenmüller* NJW 2004, 3455, 3457; *Huber* ZZP 114 (2001) 133, 146; Moss/Fletcher/Isaacs-*Moss/Smith*, Regulation, mn 8.205; *Sabel* NZI 2004, 126, 127; *Leible/Staudinger* KTS 2000, 533, 568.

[54] ECJ dated 2 May 2006 "Parmalat/Eurofood" – C-341/04 (→ cf Table of Cases Art 3 of the EIR Appendix A mn 10); *Herchen* ZIP 2005, 1401, 1404.

[55] So already ECJ dated 28 Mar 2000 – C 7/98 ("Dieter Krombach/André Bamberski"), EC reports 2000, I-1935, TZ 37 et seq; *Heß* IPRax 2001, 301, 303; *Leipold* in Stoll (ed), Vorschläge und Gutachten (1997), p 185, 193.

[56] Art 6, 25 Convention for the Protection of Human Rights and Fundamental Freedoms; on this *Paulus* ZIP 2003, 1725, 1729; *Weller* IPRax 2004, 412, 417; *Poertzgen/Adam* ZInsO 2006, 505, 509; ECJ dated 2 May 2006 "Parmalat/Eurofood" – C-341/04 (→ cf Table of Cases Art 3 of the EIR Appendix A mn 10).

[57] OLG Vienna "High Court London/Handelsgericht Wien" NZI 2005, 56, 59; with annotation by *Paulus* (→ cf Table of Cases Art 3 of the EIR Appendix A mn 13).

[58] *Balz* ZIP 1996, 948, 953; *Huber* ZZP 114 (2001) 133, 146.

3. Decisive Point in Time for Recognition

28 Because the principle of priority applies in conjunction with the EIR,[59] the ascertainment of the time of the opening of the main insolvency proceedings as understood by Art 3 (1) of the EIR plays an extremely vital role. Although Recital 22, Art 2 (f), Art 3 (1) sentence 1, and Art 16 (1) of the EIR all turn explicitly on the time of the **opening of proceedings**, the concept of **"opening of insolvency proceedings"** is not defined more precisely; see Art 2 of the EIR mn 24 et seq.

29 The confusion surrounding this concept is augmented by the fact that national perceptions of when an insolvency proceeding is deemed opened vary from one Member State to the other. While the point in time at which the judgement is rendered is decisive in German law, Sec 220 (2) of the Irish Companies Act 1963 provides that the court order ordering the opening of the proceedings is retroactive to the time of the making of the insolvency request, the so-called **"relation back principle"** (detailed discussion in Art 3 of the EIR at mn 89 et seq). However, the ECJ's decision in the **Eurofood/Parmalat** case (→ cf Table of Cases Art 3 of the EIR Appendix A mn 10) is to be so understood that **retroactive fictions of national law** are to be disregarded.[60]

30 In the **Eurofood/Parmalat** decision (→ cf Table of Cases Art 3 of the EIR Appendix A mn 10), the ECJ dealt with the issue of whether the appointment of a **provisional liquidator** made at the time of the request to open proceedings can be considered as an **opening of proceedings** within the meaning of Art 16 of the EIR.[61]

31 The ECJ stressed that the concept of "judgement opening insolvency proceedings" found in Art 16 (1) of the EIR must be autonomously construed independent of national laws and concluded that the appointment of a "provisional liquidator"[62] constitutes a judgement pursuant to Art 16 (1) of the EIR; it therefore must be recognized in all Member States and prevents the opening of a (further) main insolvency proceeding.[63]

3.1 Provisional Liquidator

32 According to Art 2 (e) of the EIR, a judgement also includes the appointment of a liquidator, whereby Art (2) (b) in conjunction with Annex C of the EIR also lists the German ***"vorläufigen Insolvenzverwalter"*** (provisional liquidator). This construction also seems correct for the sake of preventing forum shopping and for avoiding the appointment of a multiplicity of provisional liquidators, which would in turn lead to

---

[59] ECJ C-341/04, dated 2 May 2006 "Eurofood/Parmalat" ZInsO 2006, 484, 487 (→ cf Table of Cases Art 3 of the EIR Appendix A mn 10); on the principle of priority see in detail Art 3 of the EIR mn 88 et seq.

[60] *Mankowski* BB 2006, 1753, 1757.

[61] ECJ dated 2 May 2006 – C-341/04 (Eurofood IFSC Ltd), NZI 2006, 360 et seq (→ cf Table of Cases Art 3 of the EIR Appendix A mn 10 – Eurofood/Parmalat); see also the Opinion of Advocate General *Jacobs* ZIP 2005, 1641; *Laukemann* RIW 2005, 104, 112; *Laukemann* RIW 2005, 104, 112.

[62] It is irrelevant whether a strong or weak liquidator is appointed as long as this is provided for in law, as is the case in German law (secs 21, 22 InsO). All that is important is whether a decision has been made to appoint a liquidator.

[63] With same result: High Court Dublin "Eurofood/Parmalat II" ZIP 2004, 1223, 1224 (→ cf Table of Cases Art 3 of the EIR Appendix A mn 10); ECJ C-341/04; and Municipality Court Prague "Aircraft" ZIP 2005, 1431 (→ cf Table of Cases Art 3 of the EIR Appendix A mn 1); *Eidenmüller* NJW 2004, 3455, 3457 Fn 32; *Pannen/Riedemann* EWiR 2005, 725, 726; *Schilling/Schmidt* ZInsO 2006, 113, 114; *Wessels* Current Topics of International Insolvency Law, 176, 234; *Schilling* DZWiR 2006, 143, 147; *Israel* European Cross-Border Insolvency Regulation (2005) 260 et seq; *Poertzgen/Adam* ZInsO 2006, 505, 508.

conflicts of jurisdictions. A decisive factor for the ECJ here was that the recognition must "be made as soon as possible in the course of the proceedings" in order to prevent competing assumptions of jurisdiction by the courts of the various Member States.[64] This does justice to the intentions of the drafters of the EIR, namely the efficient and effective operation of cross-border insolvency proceedings.[65] Deeming the **appointment of a provisional liquidator** as the **opening of insolvency proceedings** within the meaning of Art 16 of the EIR is most welcoming from a German point of view. While in Germany the opening proceedings often take many weeks (one important reason being to take advantage of the period for compensation of lost wages due to insolvency), insolvency proceedings are opened in other Member States directly after the request is made. The ability to "block" the COMI through the ordering of a provisional liquidator would, from a German point of view, put a considerable damper on the much discussed race to open first.[66]

The concern expressed by some with respect to the rather low level of review associated **33**
with the appointment of a provisional administration[67] can be assuaged by recalling that the court that appointed the provisional liquidator still has to review whether the requirements for opening main insolvency proceedings do indeed exist. If the provisional administration was not considered an opening of proceedings, a decision made by a court to assume jurisdiction via the appointment of a provisional liquidator could be undermined by a premature opening of main insolvency proceedings in another Member State, which would only serve to fuel the race between creditors and debtors to find the insolvency forum best suited to their interests. The appointment of a provisional liquidator[68] pursuant to Secs 21 and 22 of the German *Ins*O therefore constitutes a decision to open proceedings within the meaning of Art 16 (1) of the EIR, which must be recognized by all courts/bodies of the other Member States and which prevents them from opening main insolvency proceedings.[69] Even though the submissions made by the ECJ concerning the position of the provisional liquidator are indeed welcoming, since it provides Germany with a competitive edge, it remains to be seen whether the race to be the first to open proceedings will not simply be transformed into a race to be the first to appoint a provisional liquidator.

3.2 Divestment of the Debtor

A decision that must be recognized within the meaning of Art 16 of the EIR pre- **34**
supposes not only the appointment of a liquidator but the **divestment** of the debtor as well.[70]

---

[64] ECJ C-341/04, dated 2 May 2006, ZInsO 2006, 485 et seq (→ cf Table of Cases Art 3 of the EIR Appendix A mn 10).

[65] Recital 2 of the EIR.

[66] *Pannen/Riedemann* EWiR 2005, 725, 726.

[67] *Smid* Komm EuInsVO Art 38 mn 3; the same writer is also sceptical about whether, in the case of a German provisional liquidator, there can be a total divestment of the debtor at all, in: DZWiR 2006, 325, 326.

[68] It is irrelevant whether a strong or weak liquidator is appointed as long as this is provided for in law, as is the case in German law (secs 21, 22 InsO). All that is important is whether a decision has been made to appoint a liquidator particularly since no distinction between these is being made in Annex C of the EIR.

[69] Already *Pannen/Riedemann* EWiR 2004, 725, 726; *Schilling/Schmidt* ZInsO 2006, 113.

[70] ECJ C-341/04 dated 2 May 2006, ZInsO 2006, 485 et seq (→ cf Table of Cases Art 3 of the EIR Appendix A mn 10).

35 In the **Eurofood/Parmalat** decision, the ECJ[71] assumes that the appointment of the Irish "provisional liquidator" satisfies the requisite total divestment of the debtor.[72] Whether the appointment of a **German provisional liquidator** in and of itself results in such a divestment is the subject of debate. But in order to resolve this, the meaning of "divestment" must first be ascertained. The drafters of the EIR included this factual element in Art 1 (1) of the EIR as a component of the definition of "insolvency proceedings": such proceedings entail the partial or total divestment of the debtor. This means that the debtor's powers of administration and disposal in respect of his assets are vested in total or in part in another person, the liquidator, or are restricted through the interference of the liquidator and the supervision of the debtor's legal acts.[73]

36 These requirements are already satisfied by the **"weak"** German provisional liquidator pursuant to Sec 21 (2) No 2 2nd alternative *InsO*, whose consent must be obtained in order to lend validity to the debtor's dispositions.[74] Although the powers of administration and disposal remain with the debtor when a "weak" provisional liquidator has been appointed, he is still a liquidator for the purposes of Art 2 (b) of the EIR. A contrary view[75] holds that the German weak provisional liquidator does not satisfy the requisite divestment of the debtor. An in-depth discussion of this issue is found in Art 3 of the EIR at mn 91 et seq.

4. Lack of Debtor's Insolvency Capacity in Another Member State (Art 16 (1) subpara 2 of the EIR)

37 It can be implied from Art 16 (1) subpara 2 of the EIR that the **insolvency capacity** of the debtor is a matter for the respective *lex fori concursus*, i.e. its concrete determination is left to the laws of the particular Member State and must therefore be recognized by the other Member States (see the description of insolvency capacity in the various Member States in Art 3 of the EIR at mn 14). The provision reiterates and supplements what is already found in Art 4 (2) sentence 2 (a) of the EIR. The insolvency proceedings must be recognized in the other Member States even if the opened proceedings would not be permitted in the recognizing State due to a lack of insolvency capacity (Art 16 (1) subpara 2 of the EIR). This is the case for example when the national law stipulates that the debtor must be a businessperson (merchant) in order to have insolvency capacity.[76]

38 If the debtor fails to satisfy the requirements for establishing **insolvency capacity** pursuant to the law of the Member State with jurisdiction pursuant to Art 3 (1) of the EIR, then main insolvency proceedings cannot be opened there. It is possible in such a case to open **independent territorial insolvency proceedings**; Art 3 (2) of the EIR, Art 4

[71] ECJ C-341/04 dated 2 May 2006, ZInsO 2006, 485 et seq (→ cf Table of Cases Art 3 of the EIR Appendix A mn 10).

[72] The task of the English provisional liquidator is to preserve the debtor's assets in the time between the request to open insolvency proceedings and the opening order; more details on this: *Rossbach* Europäische Insolvenzverwalter in Deutschland, p 98 with further substantiation.

[73] *Virgós/Schmit* Explanatory report mn 49 c).

[74] See also *Herchen* NZI 2006, 435, 437.

[75] *Smid* DZWiR 2006, 325, 326.

[76] In the case of merchant bankruptcies in France, non-businesspersons have no insolvency capacity, Jahn/Sahm-*Weber*, Insolvenzen in Europa, 166; natural persons in Hungary also lack insolvency capacity even if they are active as entrepreneurs, Jahn/Sahm-*Nagy/Müller/Hegybányai*, Insolvenzen in Europa, 536 with further examples; *Virgós/Schmit* Explanatory Report mn 143; Moss/Fletcher/Isaacs-*Moss/Smith*, Regulation, mn 8.134.

of the EIR (see the discussions on Art 3 of the EIR at mn 128 et seq). The effects of such independent territorial insolvency proceedings are restricted to the State in which they are opened; they do not extend to the sovereign territories of other States. They only relate to assets situated in this State.

5. Legal Consequences of Recognition

The existence of an effective judgement of a court of a Member State with jurisdiction pursuant to Art 3 of the EIR causes the **automatic recognition** of the opened insolvency proceedings. This judgement is afforded the same legal status – *res judicata* – in the recognizing Member State that it has in the State in which it was rendered. This automatic effect means that there is no need in the entire territory of the European Union for:[77] 39

- a separate recognition procedure or
- a recognition decision.[78]

As a result of the universal scope of the effects (seizure/attachment of the assets) of the main insolvency proceedings, the pursuing of **individual legal actions** (by individual creditors) is thwarted not only in the State in which the main proceedings were opened but in every other Member State as well. The extensive **powers of the liquidators** to perform administrative acts and liquidation transactions in the other Member States is also a product of this so-called **extended model (of the applicable *lex fori concursus*)** (Art 18 (1) in conjunction with Art 4 (2) sentence 2 (c) of the EIR).[79] 40

6. Recognition and Execution of Other Judgements

All judgements that concern the course and the closure of insolvency proceedings must be recognized without any further formalitites in the other Member States (Art 25 (1) of the EIR). See the in-depth discussions on Art 25 of the EIR. 41

7. Insolvency-related Proceedings

What must be recognized by Art 16 is the opening judgement of a court with jurisdiction pursuant to Art 3 of the EIR, since the provision of international jurisdiction in Art 3 of the EIR, according to its wording, only concerns the opening of an insolvency proceeding. **Insolvency-related proceedings** are not listed in the Annexes to the EIR. Art 25 (1) subpara 2 of the EIR provides for a simplified recognition of judgements derived directly from the insolvency proceedings. As to whether all or only certain kinds of insolvency-related proceedings are subsumed within the meaning of "judgements" in Art 25 (1) of the EIR is the subject matter of debate. For an in-depth discussion of the issue of international jurisdiction in relation to insolvency-related proceedings, see Art 3 of the EIR mn 96 et seq; on the question of their recognition, see Art 25 of the EIR mn 14 et seq. 42

---

[77] With the exception of Denmark since the EIR does not apply to this Member State, see Recital 33 of the EIR.

[78] See MünchKomm BGB/*Kindler* IntInsR mn 434.

[79] So qualified in *Virgós/Schmit* Explanatory report mn 153; D-K/D-Ch-*Duursma-Kepplinger/Chalupsky* Art 16 mn 34. See also on this Art 17 of the EIR mn 6 et seq.

Article 17
Effects of recognition

1. The judgment opening the proceedings referred to in Article 3(1) shall, with no further formalities, produce the same effects in any other Member State as under this law of the State of the opening of proceedings, unless this Regulation provides otherwise and as long as no proceedings referred to in Article 3(2) are opened in that other Member State.

2. The effects of the proceedings referred to in Article 3(2) may not be challenged in other Member States. Any restriction of the creditors' rights, in particular a stay or discharge, shall produce effects vis-à-vis assets situated within the territory of another Member State only in the case of those creditors who have given their consent.

→ Cf Art 15 et seq UNCITRAL Model Law

Contents

Index

Bibliography

Balz Das neue Europäische Insolvenzübereinkommen, ZIP 1996, p 948; *Duursma-Kepplinger* Checkliste zur Eröffnung eines Insolvenzverfahrens nach der Europäischen Insolvenzverordnung und zum anwendbaren Recht, NZI 2003, p 87; *Duursma-Kepplinger/Duursma* Das Schicksal von dinglichen Sicherungsrechten sowie des Eigentumsvorbehalts nach der Insolvenzordnung, wbl 2002, p 59; *Duursma-Kepplinger/Duursma/Chalupsky* Europäische Insolvenzverordnung, Kommentar, (2002); *Ehricke* Das Verhältnis des Hauptinsolvenzverwalters zum Sekundärinsolvenzverwalter bei grenzüberschreitenden Insolvenzen nach der EuInsVO, ZIP 2005, p 1104; *Eidenmüller* Europäische Verordnung über Insolvenzverfahren und zukünftiges deutsches internationales Insolvenzrecht, IPRax 2001, p 2; *Fritz/Bähr* Die Europäische Verordnung über Insolvenzverfahren – Herausforderungen an Gerichte und Insolvenzverwalter, DZWiR 2001, p 221; *Gottwald* Insolvenzrechts-Handbuch (2006); *Gottwald* Grenzüberschreitende Insolvenzen (1997); *Haß/Huber/Gruber/Heiderhoff* EU-Insolvenzverordnung, Kommentar (2005); Heidelberger Kommentar zur Insolvenzordnung (2006) (eds *Eickmann/Flessner/Irschlinger/Kirchhof/Kreft/Landfermann/Marotzke/Stephan*); *Homann* System der Anerkennung eines ausländischen Insolvenzverfahrens, KTS 2000, p 343; *Huber* Internationales Insolvenzrecht in Europa, ZZP 114 (2001), p 133; *Israël* European Cross-Border Insolvency Regulation (2005); *Kemper* Die Verordnung (EG) Nr. 1346/2000 über Insolvenzverfahren, ZIP 2001, p 1609; *Keppelmüller* An der Schwelle zu einem europäischen Insolvenzrecht?, wbl 1996, p 337; *Leible/Staudinger* Die europäische Verordnung über Insolvenzverfahren, KTS 2000, p 533; *Lüke* Das europäische internationale Insolvenzrecht, ZZP 111 (1998), p 275; *Moss/Fletcher/Isaacs* (eds) The EC Regulation on Insolvency Proceedings (2002); Münchener Kommentar zur Insolvenzordnung, vol 3 (2003); *Pannen/Riedemann* Comments on OLG Düsseldorf dated 9.7.2004 – I-3 W 53/04, EWiR 2005, p 177; *Pannen/Kühnle/Riedemann* Die Stellung des deutschen Insolvenzverwalters in einem Insolvenzverfahren mit europäischem Auslandsbezug, NZI 2003, p 72; *Paulus* Europäische Insolvenzverordnung, Kommentar (2006); *Ringstmeier/Homann* Masseverbindlichkeiten als Prüfstein des internationalen Insolvenzrechts, NZI 2004, p 354; *Smid* Deutsches und Europäisches Internationales Insolvenzrecht, Kommentar (2004); *Stoll* (ed) Vorschläge und Gutachten zur Umsetzung des EU-Übereinkommens über Insolvenzverfahren im deutschen Recht (1997); *Taupitz* Das (zukünftige) europäische Internationale Insolvenzrecht – insbesondere aus international-privatrechtlicher Sicht, ZZP 111 (1998), p 315; *Virgós/Garcimartín* The European Insolvency Regulation: Law and Practice (2004); *Virgós/Schmit* Erläuternder Bericht zu dem EU-Übereinkommen über Insolvenzverfahren, in Stoll (ed), Vorschläge und Gutachten (1997), p 32; *Wessels* International Insolvency Law (2006); *Wimmer* Die Verordnung (EG) Nr 1346/2000 über Insolvenzverfahren, ZInsO 2001, p 97.

1. Overview

Art 17 of the EIR regulates the **extension of the effects** of a judgement opening insolvency proceedings that is rendered pursuant to the EIR. A distinction is being made in Art 17 of the EIR between the extension of the effects of: **1**

- **main insolvency proceedings** (Art 17 (1) of the EIR) and
- **territorial insolvency proceedings** (Art 17 (2) of the EIR).[1]

By distinguishing between the effects of the main and territorial insolvency proceedings, Art 17 of the EIR embodies the principle of **modified universality** that is endorsed by the EIR.[2] **2**

2. Effects of Opened Main Insolvency Proceedings (Art 17 (1) of the EIR)

The effects of main insolvency proceedings opened pursuant to Art 3 (1) of the EIR are **universal**, encompassing within the insolvency proceedings the debtor's entire assets and all of his creditors.[3] This ensures a unified administration and liquidation of the debtor's assets pursuant to the laws of the State in which the proceedings are opened (*lex fori concursus*).[4] The **principle of automatic recognition**[5] leads to the extension of **3**

[1] *Virgós/Schmit* Explanatory report mn 150; *Smid* Komm EuInsVO Art 17 mn 1; *Paulus* Komm EuInsVO Art 17 mn 1; *Virgós/Garcimartín* Regulation, p 190 et seq; *Wessels* International Insolvency Law (2006) mn 10746; *Eidenmüller* IPRax 2001, 2, 7; *Huber* ZZP 114 (2001), 133, 147.

[2] *Smid* Komm EuInsVO Art 17 mn 1; *Homann* KTS 2000, 343, 369 speaks here of a "controlled universality"; for a discussion on modified universality, see Introduction mn 34 et seq.

[3] *Virgós/Schmit* Explanatory report mn 151; *Virgós/Garcimartín* Regulation, p 191; *Duursma-Kepplinger/Duursma* wbl 2002, 59, 60; *Huber* ZZP 114 (2001), 133, 147; *Keppelmüller* wbl 1996, 337, 342.

[4] D-K/D/Ch-*Duursma-Kepplinger/Chalupsky* Art 17 mn 2.

[5] Haß/Huber/Gruber/Heiderhoff-*Haß/Gruber* Art 17 EuInsVO mn 1.

the effects of the insolvency proceedings to all other Member States.[6] The scope of the effects ensues directly from the opening judgement.[7] The insolvency laws of the opening State – the *lex fori concursus* – are in effect being exported.[8]

2.1 Principle of Automatic Recognition

4 The recognition of an opening judgement made pursuant to Art 3 (1) of the EIR produces its effects according to Art 17 (1) of the EIR without the need for any "further formalities".[9] This means a recognition of the insolvency proceedings *ipso jure* on account of the EIR without the need to initiate a separate, preliminary **exequatur procedure.**[10] The **effectiveness** of the opening judgement is all that matters here and not whether it is formally *res judicata.*[11]

5 When a court or a public authority is confronted with the recognition of an insolvency proceeding that has been opened in another Member State, the only matters open for review by it are whether the opening order was made within the scope of the EIR's applicability and whether there is a reason to refuse recognition pursuant to Art 26 of the EIR.[12] What is not open to review, however, is whether the court that assumed jurisdiction pursuant to Art 3 of the EIR was justified in doing so.[13]

2.2 Extension of the Effects

6 According to Art 17 of the EIR, the judgement produces the same effects in the recognising State that it does in the opening State.[14] It is **not equivalent** to a national proceeding but is rather a complete **extension** of the effects of the judgement to the entire territory of the EU ("**theory of extension of effects**"[15] or the "**extension theory**"[16]).[17]

---

[6] *Paulus* Komm EuInsVO Art 17 mn 1; *Virgós/Schmit* Explanatory report mn 151; *Fritz/Bähr* DZWIR 2001, 221, 225.

[7] *Virgós/Garcimartín* Regulation, p 191; in Germany, these are mainly the divesting of the debtor of his assets, the appointment of the liquidator, and prohibiting the pursuance of individual legal remedies, on this, see: *Kemper* ZIP 2001, 1609, 1614.

[8] *Paulus* Komm EuInsVO Art 17 mn 1.

[9] *Virgós/Schmit* Explanatory report mn 143, 152; Moss/Fletcher/Isaacs-*Moss/Bayfield*, Regulation, mn 5.32; Gottwald/*Gottwald* InsR-Handb (2006) § 129 mn 32; *Huber* ZZP 114 (2001), 133, 146 et seq; *Fritz/Bähr* DZWiR 2001, 221, 225; *Kemper* ZIP 2001, 1609, 1614; *Ringstmeier/Homann* NZI 2004, 354, 355.

[10] *Virgós/Schmit* Explanatory report mn 152; *Wessels* International Insolvency Law (2006) mn 10733; MünchKomm InsO/*Reinhart* Art 17 EuInsVO mn 1; Haß/Huber/Gruber/Heiderhoff-*Haß/Gruber* Art 17 EuInsVO mn 1; *Paulus* Komm EuInsVO Art 17 mn 2; *Gottwald* Grenzüberschreitende Insolvenzen (1997) 25; *Balz* ZIP 1996, 948, 951; *Leible/Staudinger* KTS 2000, 533, 561; *Lüke* ZZP 111 (1998), 275, 285.

[11] *Balz* ZIP 1996, 948, 951; *Fritz/Bähr* DZWIR 2001, 221, 225.

[12] *Virgós/Schmit* Explanatory report mn 152; *Smid* Komm EuInsVO Art 17 mn 4; Haß/Huber/Gruber/Heiderhoff-*Haß/Gruber* Art 17 EuInsVO mn 1; D-K/D/Ch-*Duursma-Kepplinger/Chalupsky* Art 17 mn 5.

[13] D-K/D/Ch-*Duursma-Kepplinger/Chalupsky* Art 17 mn 5; *Lüke* ZZP 111 (1998), 275, 287. The assumed jurisdiction can only be reviewed through the allowed legal remedies, cf *Lüke* ZZP 111 (1998), 275, 286.

[14] *Virgós/Garcimartín* Regulation, p 191; MünchKomm InsO/*Reinhart* Art 17 EuIns-VO mn 1; Haß/Huber/Gruber/Heiderhoff-*Haß/Gruber* Art 17 EuInsVO mn 2.

[15] *Gottwald* Grenzüberschreitende Insolvenzen (1997) 25; Haß/Huber/Gruber/Heiderhoff-*Haß/Gruber* Art 17 EuInsVO mn 2; *Paulus* Komm EuInsVO Art 17 mn 2; *Balz* ZIP 1996, 948, 951; *Huber* ZZP 114 (2001), 133, 147.

[16] *Virgós/Schmit* Explanatory report mn 153; *Fritz/Bähr* DZWIR 2001, 221, 225 ("Aus-

Included in these effects of the opening order, is the seizure of the debtor's assets, pursuant to the specific provisions of the governing insolvency law.[18]

The **substantive** and **procedural law effects** of the insolvency proceedings are therefore determined in accordance with the law of the State in which the proceedings are opened.[19] Which law that is, is determined, in turn, pursuant to the conflict of laws rule found in Art 4 et seq of the EIR.[20] The (foreign) *lex fori concursus* will apply even if the divestment (of the debtor) contemplated by the governing law is more onerous than that provided for under national insolvency law.[21] **7**

The **principle of automatic recognition** in conjunction with the **extension of the effects of the insolvency proceedings** forms the basis of the universality of the main insolvency proceedings.[22] The moment it is rendered, the opening judgement is effective – to the extent provided for by the provisions of the *lex fori concursus* – in all Member States. This particularly includes the seizure/attachment of the debtor's assets, the appointment of a liquidator, the prohibition on pursuing individual legal remedies,[23] and the creditor's obligation to return assets[24] acquired after the opening of the proceedings.[25] **8**

2.3 Restriction of the Effects Through Territorial Insolvency Proceedings

In the second half-sentence of Art 17 (1) of the EIR, the universality of main insolvency proceedings is being restricted – in addition to other restrictions contemplated by the EIR ("unless this Regulation provides otherwise") – through the opening of territorial insolvency proceedings (in this case, secondary insolvency proceedings[26]).[27] The effects of such proceedings could be described as being "superimposed" on those of the main insolvency proceedings.[28] The special connecting factors found in Art 5 et seq of the EIR, and the special rules pursuant to Art 18 (1) sentence 2 and (3) of the EIR, all fall within this proviso.[29] **9**

---

dehnungsmodell" "extension model"); *Virgós/Garcimartín* Regulation, p 191 ("*extension model*"); also *Wessels* International Insolvency Law (2006) mn 10747.

17 *Virgós/Schmit* Explanatory report mn 153; *Smid* Komm EuInsVO Art 17 mn 5; *Wimmer* ZInsO 2001, 97, 99.

18 MünchKomm InsO/*Reinhart* Art 17 EuInsVO mn 1.

19 *Virgós/Schmit* Explanatory report mn 90, 153; D-K/D/Ch- *Duursma-Kepplinger/Chalupsky* Art 17 mn 7; *Smid* Komm EuIns-VO Art 17 mn 6.

20 Haß/Huber/Gruber/Heiderhoff-*Haß/Gruber* Art 17 EuInsVO mn 3; MünchKomm InsO/*Reinhart* Art 17 EuInsVO mn 1.

21 Haß/Huber/Gruber/Heiderhoff-*Haß/Gruber* Art 17 EuInsVO mn 2.

22 *Virgós/Schmit* Explanatory report mn 154; D-K/D/Ch-*Duursma-Kepplinger/Chalupsky* Art 17 mn 8.

23 *Smid* Komm EuInsVO Art 17 mn 10.

24 *Duursma-Kepplinger/Duursma* wbl 2002, 59, 61.

25 *Virgós/Schmit* Explanatory report mn 154; D-K/D/Ch-*Duursma-Kepplinger/Chalupsky* Art 17 mn 8.

26 For a discussion on the terms territorial- and secondary insolvency proceedings, see Art 3 of the EIR mn 4 and 5.

27 Haß/Huber/Gruber/Heiderhoff-*Haß/Gruber* Art 17 EuInsVO mn 4; *Smid* Komm EuInsVO Art 17 mn 8; MünchKomm InsO/*Reinhart* Art 17 EuInsVO mn 2; *Wessels* International Insolvency Law (2006) mn 10748; *Israel* European Cross-Border Insolvency Regulation (2005) 264; *Virgós/Garcimartín* Regulation, p 193; *Huber* ZZP 114 (2001), 133, 147; *Kemper* ZIP 2001, 1609, 1614; *Keppelmüller* wbl 1996, 337, 344; *Leible/Staudinger* KTS 2000, 533, 562; *Pannen/Kühnle/Riedemann* NZI 2003, 72, 73.

28 *Israel* European Cross-Border Insolvency Regulation (2005) 264; *Balz* ZIP 1996, 948, 952.

29 *Huber* ZZP 114 (2001), 133, 147 et seq.

10 The superimposition on the effects of the main insolvency proceedings caused by the aforementioned special connecting factors or through the opening of secondary insolvency proceedings does not, however, operate to deprive the main insolvency proceedings altogether of their effects in the recognizing State (in which secondary insolvency proceedings have been opened). The reference in the second half-sentence of Art 17 (1) of the EIR must therefore be construed **narrowly.**[30] It is for example conceivable that the liquidator in the main insolvency proceedings – in connection with an asset that belongs to the insolvency estate of the main proceedings – also participates in the territorial proceedings. Art 35 of the EIR (pursuant to which a surplus in the territorial proceedings is transferred to the insolvency estate of the main proceedings) implies for instance that the powers of the liquidator in the main insolvency proceedings must also be recognized in the State of the territorial proceedings.[31]

11 In cases where the **territorial proceedings come to an end,**[32] the effects of the **divestment pursuant to the main insolvency proceedings** are automatically extended anew to the debtor's entire assets – including those that were part of the (former) secondary insolvency proceedings.[33] Independent of the effects that secondary insolvency proceedings have, an order opening foreign main insolvency proceedings is still enforceable even if the secondary insolvency proceedings is still pending. This is justified by the fact that, firstly, it is not included in Art 26 of the EIR as a reason to refuse recognition and, secondly, because it seems legitimate in the interests of full creditor protection.[34]

3. Effects of Opened Territorial Insolvency Proceedings (Art 17 (2) of the EIR)

12 Art 17 (2) of the EIR regulates the effects of opened territorial insolvency proceedings. Territorial insolvency proceedings (independent territorial and secondary insolvency proceedings, see Art 3 of the EIR mn 4 and 5) suspend the universal effects of the main insolvency proceedings.[35]

3.1 Territorial Restriction of the Divestment (of the Debtor)

13 Opened **territorial insolvency proceedings** are **automatically recognized** in the other Member States. Art 17 (2) sentence 1 of the EIR provides that the effects of the territorial proceedings may not be challenged (**"principle of Community trust"**[36]).[37] This means,

[30] MünchKomm InsO/*Reinhart* Art 17 EuInsVO mn 2.

[31] Haß/Huber/Gruber/Heiderhoff-*Haß/Gruber* Art 17 EuInsVO mn 5; MünchKomm InsO/*Reinhart* Art 17 EuInsVO mn 2.

[32] Ended, that is, without the insolvency estate having been liquidated, the proceeds distributed, nor any surplus in the secondary insolvency proceedings having been transferred to the liquidator in the main proceedings.

[33] OLG Düsseldorf ZIP 2004, 1514, 1515; Haß/Huber/Gruber/Heiderhoff-*Haß/Gruber* Art 17 EuInsVO mn 6; *Smid* Komm EuInsVO Art 17 mn 11.

[34] OLG Düsseldorf ZIP 2004, 1514, 1515; Haß/Huber/Gruber/Heiderhoff-*Haß/Gruber* Art 17 EuInsVO mn 6.

[35] *Smid* Komm EuInsVO Art 17 mn 12.

[36] D-K/D/Ch-Duursma-Kepplinger/Chalupsky Art 17 mn 15; *Duursma-Kepplinger* NZI 2003, 87, 88.

[37] MünchKomm InsO/*Reinhart* Art 17 EuInsVO mn 3; D-K/D/Ch-*Duursma-Kepplinger/Chalupsky* Art 17 mn 15; Haß/Huber/Gruber/Heiderhoff-*Haß/Gruber* Art 17 EuInsVO mn 8; *Virgós/Schmit* Explanatory report mn 156; *Virgós/Garcimartín* Regulation, p 193 et seq; Moss/Fletcher/Isaacs-*Moss/Smith*, Regulation, mn 8.150; *Balz* ZIP 1996, 948, 951; *Fritz/Bähr* DZWIR 2001, 221, 230; *Kemper* ZIP 2001, 1609, 1614; *Leible/Staudinger* KTS 2000, 533, 562; *Pannen/Kühnle/Riedemann* NZI 2003, 72, 76.

on the one hand, that a creditor may not be denied participation in territorial insolvency proceedings,[38] and, on other hand, that any benefits such creditor has obtained through the participation in these proceedings may no longer be retracted.[39]

The divestment of the debtor that is triggered by the opening of territorial proceedings only affects the debtor's assets "situated" inland (opening State).[40] The same holds true for all property situated inland at the time of the opening of the proceedings even if such property is removed to a foreign country without the liquidator's consent after such opening, which means that the return of such property can be demanded.[41] The place in which property is situated is ascertained pursuant to Art 2 (g) of the EIR ("the Member State in which assets are situated", see discussions on Art 2 of the EIR mn 29 et seq).[42] Assets situated in a foreign country at the time of the opening of the territorial proceedings are not affected by the opening of such proceedings.[43] **14**

In addition, the opened territorial proceedings operate, through the local divestment, to restrict the universal effects of the main insolvency proceedings.[44] The assets situated in the State of the territorial proceedings are not affected by the effects of the attachment/seizure of the main insolvency proceedings.[45] One could also describe this as a kind of "**territorial priority**".[46] Constraints are being placed on such priority, however, by the provisions of Art 35 of the EIR, which provides that any surplus in the territorial proceedings belongs to the insolvency estate of the main proceedings and must be returned to the liquidator of the main insolvency proceedings.[47] **15**

If territorial insolvency proceedings are opened in addition to main insolvency proceedings, the first sentence of Art 17 (2) of the EIR provides that the effects of the main insolvency proceedings are suspended for the duration of the territorial insolvency proceedings.[48] The decision to open main insolvency proceedings can, however, still be declared enforceable during the period of the secondary insolvency proceedings.[49] **16**

A problem arising from this concerns the question of the legal remedies available to the liquidator in the secondary insolvency proceedings if the liquidator in the main insolvency proceedings makes an unlawful use of the enforcement order of the main **17**

---

[38] According to arts 32 and 39 of the EIR, the creditors may lodge all of their claims in territorial insolvency proceedings.

[39] Haß/Huber/Gruber/Heiderhoff-*Haß/Gruber* Art 17 EuInsVO mn 8; MünchKomm InsO/*Reinhart* Art 17 EuInsVO mn 3; the liquidator is not entitled to demand that a creditor return that which has been obtained pursuant to the territorial proceedings, see OLG Cologne ZIP 1989, 321.

[40] D-K/D/Ch-*Duursma-Kepplinger/Chalupsky* Art 17 mn 15; *Virgós/Schmit* Explanatory report mn 156; *Huber* ZZP 114 (2001), 133, 148.

[41] *Virgós/Schmit* Explanatory report mn 156; *Leible/Staudinger* KTS 2000, 533, 562 et seq; on this, see also *Balz* ZIP 1996, 948, 951.

[42] Haß/Huber/Gruber/Heiderhoff-*Haß/Gruber* Art 17 EuInsVO mn 7; D-K/D/Ch- *Duursma-Kepplinger/Chalupsky* Art 17 mn 15.

[43] *Leible/Staudinger* KTS 2000, 533, 563.

[44] *Virgós/Schmit* Explanatory report mn 156; *Smid* Komm EuInsVO Art 17 mn 12.

[45] D-K/D/Ch-*Duursma-Kepplinger/Chalupsky* Art 17 mn 16; *Paulus* Komm EuInsVO Art 17 mn 4.

[46] *Smid* Komm EuInsVO Art 17 mn 12.

[47] D-K/D/Ch-*Duursma-Kepplinger/Chalupsky* Art 17 mn 16; Haß/Huber/Gruber/Heiderhoff-*Haß/Gruber* Art 17 EuInsVO mn 9; Huber ZZP 114 (2001), 133, 148; *Smid* Komm EuInsVO Art 17 mn 12; *Virgós/Schmit* Explanatory report mn 156.

[48] *Pannen/Riedemann* EWiR 2005, 177, 178; *Virgós/Schmit* Explanatory report mn 163 ("the direct powers [...] no longer apply").

[49] Held by the OLG Düsseldorf in an order dated 9 July 2004, NZI 2004, 628, 629; on this: *Pannen/Riedemann* EWiR 2005, 177 et seq; on the rights of the liquidator in the main insolvency proceedings, see also: *Ehricke* ZIP 2005, 1104, 1106 et seq; dissenting opinion: *Paulus* Komm EuInsVO Art 17 mn 5.

proceedings.[50] As to which legal remedies are permissible is a matter for the national law of the State in which the secondary insolvency proceedings were opened (*lex fori concursus secundarii*).

3.2 Idiosyncrasies of Stays (of Payment) or Discharges (of Residual Debt)

18 Art 17 (2) sentence 2 of the EIR regulates the situation where the *lex fori concursus secundarii* grants the debtor a stay (of payment) or a discharge (of residual debt). In order to safeguard the interests of the creditors, the effects of such measures are not unrestrictedly extended to the other Member States but are restricted primarily to the in inland[51] situated assets.[52] An extension of the effects of a stay or a discharge of residual debt to assets situated in a foreign country is only possible when this is consented to by the **individual** creditors.[53]

19 Although on the one hand the creditors are entitled to satisfy their claims out of the debtor's assets that are situated in another Member State,[54] they are not prevented on the other hand from waiving their rights completely by granting their consent to a stay or a discharge of residual debt.[55] But it is only when all of the creditors consent to the discharge of residual debt or to a stay of payment will this have universal effect and therefore apply outside of the territory of the territorial insolvency proceedings.[56] A **majority decision** will not suffice.[57] **Silence** cannot not be deemed as consent.[58]

20 The "stay or discharge" set out in Art 17 (2) sentence 2 of the EIR are examples of restrictions of the creditors' rights. Other restrictions are conceivable and are also governed by this provision.[59] Other restrictions that have been suggested here are agreements to an **insolvency plan**, or a **composition.**[60]

---

[50] For the German perspective on this problem, see, *Pannen/Riedemann* EWiR 2005, 177, 178 who suggest the *Vollstreckungsabwehrklage* (action objecting to the judgement claim) pursuant to Sec 767 ZPO, or the so-called *Vollstreckungserinnerung* (complaint against an enforcement measure) pursuant to Sec 148 (2) sentence 2 InsO, 89 (3) InsO, 766 ZPO as permissible legal remedies.

[51] = the State in which the secondary insolvency proceedings are opened.

[52] Haß/Huber/Gruber/Heiderhoff-*Haß/Gruber* Art 17 EuInsVO mn 10; *Smid* Komm EuIns-VO Art 17 mn 14; Moss/Fletcher/Isaacs-*Moss/Smith*, Regulation, mn 8.151; *Huber* ZZP 114 (2001), 133, 148; *Leible/Staudinger* KTS 2000, 533, 563; *Taupitz* ZZP 111 (1998), 315, 347.

[53] D-K/D/Ch-*Duursma-Kepplinger/Chalupsky* Art 17 mn 17; *Eidenmüller* IPRax 2001, 2, 9; Haß/Huber/Gruber/Heiderhoff-*Haß/Gruber* Art 17 EuInsVO mn 10; *Paulus* Komm EuInsVO Art 17 mn 8; *Taupitz* ZZP 111 (1998), 315, 347 et seq; *Virgós/Garcimartín* Regulation, p 194; *Virgós/Schmit* Explanatory report mn 157; *Wimmer* ZInsO 2001, 96, 99.

[54] D-K/D/Ch-*Duursma-Kepplinger/Chalupsky* Art 17 mn 18; *Paulus* Komm EuInsVO Art 17 mn 8; *Virgós/Schmit* Explanatory report mn 157; D-K/D/Ch-*Duursma-Kepplinger/Chalupsky* Art 17 mn 18.

[55] *Virgós/Schmit* Explanatory report mn 157.

[56] D-K/D/Ch-*Duursma-Kepplinger/Chalupsky* Art 17 mn 18; Haß/Huber/Gruber/Heiderhoff-*Haß/Gruber* Art 17 EuInsVO mn 10; *Paulus* Komm EuInsVO Art 17 mn 8.

[57] D-K/D/Ch-*Duursma-Kepplinger/Chalupsky* Art 17 mn 18; Haß/Huber/Gruber/Heiderhoff-*Haß/Gruber* Art 17 EuInsVO mn 10; *Huber* ZZP (114) 2001, 133, 149; *Virgós/Garcimartín* Regulation, p 194; *Virgós/Schmit* Explanatory report mn 157; *Smid* Komm EuInsVO Art 17 mn 12.

[58] Haß/Huber/Gruber/Heiderhoff-*Haß/Gruber* Art 17 EuInsVO mn 10.

[59] *Paulus* Komm EuInsVO Art 17 mn 8.

[60] *Balz* ZIP 1996, 948, 951; on this and in particular on the insolvency plan, see also *Eidenmüller* IPRax 2001, 2, 13.

The provisions of Art 17 (2) sentence 2 of the EIR must be read in conjunction with **Article 34 (2) of the EIR** since the latter also deals with **stays** and **discharges.**[61] There are, however, differences between Art 34 and Art 17 of the EIR.[62] In contrast to Art 34 (2) of the EIR, Art 17 (2) sentence 2 of the EIR does not limit itself to secondary insolvency proceedings but applies to independent territorial insolvency proceedings as well;[63] Art 17 (2) sentence 2 of the EIR therefore only applies if main insolvency proceedings have been opened.[64] Furthermore, Art 17 (2) sentence 2 of the EIR speaks of assets that are "situated" in another Member State, whereas Article 34 (2) of the EIR refers to the debtor's assets "not covered by those [secondary insolvency] proceedings".[65] **21**

Article 18
Powers of the liquidator

1. The liquidator appointed by a court which has jurisdiction pursuant to Article 3(1) may exercise all the powers conferred on him by the law of the State of the opening of proceedings in another Member State, as long as no other insolvency proceedings have been opened there nor any preservation measure to the contrary has been taken there further to a request for the opening of insolvency proceedings in that State. He may in particular remove the debtor's assets from the territory of the Member State in which they are situated, subject to Articles 5 and 7.

2. The liquidator appointed by a court which has jurisdiction pursuant to Article 3 (2) may in any other Member State claim through the courts or out of court that moveable property was removed from the territory of the State of the opening of proceedings to the territory of that other Member State after the opening of the insolvency proceedings. He may also bring any action to set aside which is in the interests of the creditors.

3. In exercising his powers, the liquidator shall comply with the law of the Member State within the territory of which he intends to take action, in particular with regard to procedures for the realisation of assets. Those powers may not include coercive measures or the right to rule on legal proceedings or disputes.

→ On Art 18 (1) of the EIR cf Art 5 UNCITRAL Model Law

Contents

[61] *Virgós/Schmit* Explanatory report mn 157; *Paulus* Komm EuInsVO Art 17 mn 7; on this, see also Moss/Fletcher/Isaacs-*Moss/Smith*, Regulation, mn 8.153.

[62] D-K/D/Ch-*Duursma-Kepplinger/Chalupsky* Art 17 mn 18; dissenting opinion: MünchKomm InsO/*Reinhart* Art 17 EuInsVO mn 4 who speaks of a "repetition" but arrives in effect at the same conclusion.

[63] MünchKomm InsO/*Reinhart* Art 17 EuInsVO mn 4.

[64] Haß/Huber/Gruber/Heiderhoff-*Haß/Gruber* Art 17 EuInsVO mn 11; MünchKomm InsO/*Reinhart* Art 17 EuInsVO mn 3.

[65] On this see *Eidenmüller* IPRax 2001, 2, 9.

Index

Bibliography

Balz Das neue Europäische Insolvenzübereinkommen, ZIP 1996, p 948; *Breutigam/Blersch/Goetsch* Berliner Kommentar zum Insolvenzrecht (April 2006); *Duursma-Kepplinger/Duursma/Chalupsky* Europäische Insolvenzverordnung, Kommentar (2002); *Ehricke/Ries* Die neue Europäische Insolvenzverordnung, JuS 2003, p 313; Frankfurter Kommentar zum Insolvenzrecht (2005); *Fritz/Bähr* Die Europäische Verordnung über Insolvenzverfahren – Herausforderung an Gerichte und Insolvenzverwalter, DZWiR 2001, p 221; *Gottwald* Grenzüberschreitende Insolvenzen (1997); *Gottwald* Insolvenzrechtshandbuch (2006); *Haas* Die Verwertung der im Ausland belegenen Insolvenzmasse im Anwendungsbereich der EuInsVO, in Schilken/Kreft/Wagner/Eckardt (eds), Feschrift Gerhardt (2004) p 319; Hamburger Kommentar zum Insolvenzrecht (2006) (ed *Schmidt, A.*); Heidelberger Kommentar zur Insolvenzordnung, 4th edn (2006) (eds *Eickmann/Flessner/Irschlinger/Kirchhof/Kreft/Landfermann/Marotzke/Stephan*); *Herchen* Das Übereinkommen über Insolvenzverfahren der Mitgliedstaaten der Europäischen Union vom 23.11.1995 (2000); *Huber* Internationales Insolvenzrecht in Europa, ZZP 114 (2001) p 133; *Kemper* Die Verordnung (EG) Nr. 1346/2000 über Insolvenzverfahren, ZIP 2001, p 1609; *Kübler/Prütting* Kommentar zur Insolvenzordnung, vol 3 (2006); *Lehr* Die neue EU-Verordnung über Insolvenzverfahren und deren Auswirkungen für die Unternehmenspraxis, KTS 2000, p 577; *Leible/Staudinger* Die europäische Verordnung über Insolvenzverfahren, KTS 2000, p 533; *Lüke* Das europäische internationale Insolvenzrecht, ZZP 111 (1998), p 275; *Moss/Fletcher/Isaacs* (eds) The EC Regulation on Insolvency Proceedings (2002); Münchener Kommentar zum Bürgerlichen Gesetzbuch, vol 11 (2006); Münchener Kommentar zur Insolvenzordnung, vol 3 (2003); *Nerlich/Römermann* Kommentar zur Insolvenzordnung (April 2006); *Pannen/Kühnle/Riedemann* Die Stellung des deutschen Insolvenzverwalters in einem Insolvenzverfahren mit europäischem Auslandsbezug NZI 2003, p 72; *Paulus* Die europäische Insolvenzverordnung und der deutsche Insolvenzverwalter, NZI 2001, p 505; *Paulus* Europäische Insolvenzverordnung, Kommentar (2006); *Penzlin/Riedemann* Klarstellung der Befugnisse englischer Hauptinsolvenzverwalter – MG Rover II, Anmerkung, NZI 2005, p 515; *Runkel* (ed) Anwaltshandbuch – Insolvenzrecht (2005); *Smid* Deutsches und Europäisches Internationales Insolvenzrecht (2004); *Staak* Der deutsche Insolvenzverwalter im europäischen Insolvenzrecht (2004); *Stoll* (ed) Vorschläge und Gutachten zur Umsetzung des EU-Übereinkommens über Insolvenzverfahren im deutschen Recht (1997); *Taupitz* Das (zukünftige) europäische Internationale Insolvenzrecht – insbesondere aus internationalprivatrechtlicher Sicht, ZZP 111 (1998), p 315; Uhlenbruck Insolvenzordnung, Kommentar (2003); *Virgós/Garcimartín* The European Insolvency Regulation: Law and Practice (2004); *Virgós/Schmit* Erläuternder Bericht zu dem EU-Übereinkommen über Insolvenzverfahren, in Stoll (ed), Vorschläge und Gutachten, p 32 (1997); *Wessels* International Insolvency Law (2006); *Wimmer* Die Verordnung (EG) Nr. 1346/2000 über Insolvenzverfahren, ZInsO 2001, p 97.

1. Overview

Art 18 of the EIR concerns the **recognition of the appointment of a liquidator** and of his **powers in the other Member States.**[1] The EIR provides for a system of **automatic recognition**[2] in all EU Member States of insolvency proceedings opened in one of these States.[3] The same automatic recognition applies to the appointment of the liquidator and to the exercising of his powers. The recognition of an insolvency proceeding opened in another Member State triggers the recognition of the appointment of the liquidator and the recognition of his powers in all other Member States.[4] There is no need for an **exequatur procedure**[5] or for a **public notification** pursuant to Art 21 of the EIR.[6] **1**

Art 18 of the EIR does not contain an exhaustive list of all of the powers conferred on the liquidator by the EIR;[7] it merely sets out general rules clarifying the actions that the liquidator may take in the *other* Member States.[8] **2**

[1] With exception of Denmark, cf Art 1 of the EIR mn 113.

[2] For a detailed discussion on the recognition of insolvency proceedings, see the discussions on Art 16 of the EIR mn 9 et seq, on the main insolvency proceedings mn 19 et seq, on territorial insolvency proceedings mn 22 et seq.

[3] *Virgós/Schmit* Explanatory report mn 160; D-K/D/Ch-*Duursma-Kepplinger/Chalupsky* Art 18 mn 6; HamburgerKomm-*Undritz* Art 18 mn 1; *Huber* ZZP 114 (2001), 133, 149.

[4] *Virgós/Schmit* Explanatory report mn 160; FK-InsO/*Wimmer* Anhang I nach § 358 mn 35; D-K/D/Ch-*Duursma-Kepplinger/Chalupsky* Art 18 mn 3.

[5] An "exequatur" or an exequatur procedure is governed in the given case by Council Regulation (EC) No 44/2001 (in arts 38–52).

[6] *Virgós/Schmit* Explanatory report mn 160; FK-InsO/*Wimmer* Anhang I nach § 358 mn 35; D-K/D/Ch-*Duursma-Kepplinger/Chalupsky* Art 18 mn 6.

[7] The powers of the liquidator in the MG Rover case were ordered by the High Court of Justice in Birmingham in so-called "supplemental orders" (independent orders listing the range of powers of the liquidator in the main proceedings pursuant to the Insolvency Act 1986). See the comments on this esp by *Penzlin/Riedemann* NZI 2005, 515, 517; on the MG Rover case → cf Table of Cases Art 3 of the EIR Appendix A mn 16.

[8] D-K/D/Ch-*Duursma-Kepplinger/Chalupsky* Art 18 mn 1.

3 Art 18 of the EIR distinguishes between the **liquidators in the main insolvency proceedings**[9] and those in **territorial insolvency proceedings**[10].[11]

4 The **object** of the provision is to enforce the law that governs the insolvency.[12] The recognition of the liquidator's powers in all of the other Member States is indispensable for this. Art 18 of the EIR therefore makes complete the automatic recognition of the foreign insolvency proceedings within the scope of the EIR's applicability.[13]

5 **Art 18 (1) of the EIR** regulates the powers of the liquidator in the main insolvency proceedings. **Art 18 (2) of the EIR** regulates the powers of the liquidator in secondary and in independent territorial insolvency proceedings.[14] Both of these are **specific provisions of substantive law.**[15]

6 The liquidator in the main insolvency proceedings is entitled in the territory of another Member State to exercise all of the powers conferred on him by the **law of the opening of proceedings.**[16] The liquidator's **powers**, i.e. the **kinds** and the **scope** of them, are always governed by the *lex fori concursus*; hence the **duties** imposed on the liquidator are also determined by this law[17] (Art 18 (1) of the EIR). The liquidator in the territorial proceedings is empowered to **claim through the courts or out of court** property that has been **removed** to another Member State; he is also entitled, in the interests of the creditors, to bring avoidance actions (Art 18 (2) of the EIR).

7 **Art 18 (3) sentence 1 of the EIR** imposes a statutory duty on the liquidator to comply with the laws of the Member State in whose territory he intends to take action. This applies especially to the **procedures for realizing** assets of the insolvency estate. The liquidator is explicitly prohibited from using coercive measures in this territory or from ruling (conclusively) on legal proceedings or disputes (Art 18 (3) sentence 2 of the EIR). Art 18 (3) of the EIR is a **conflict of laws rule.**[18]

8 In order for the liquidator to take action in another Member State, he may have to give **proof**[19] of his appointment in the manner contemplated by **Art 19 of the EIR.**[20]

---

[9] Art 18 (1) and (3) of the EIR.

[10] Art 18 (2) and (3) of the EIR.

[11] *Virgós/Garcimartín* Regulation, p 195. For the definition of main insolvency proceedings, see the discussions on Art 3 of the EIR mn 7 et seq, for secondary insolvency proceedings see Art 3 of the EIR mn 124 et seq, and for independent territorial insolvency proceedings see Art 3 of the EIR mn 128 et seq.

[12] MünchKomm BGB/*Kindler* IntInsR mn 458.

[13] MünchKomm BGB/*Kindler* IntInsR mn 458; *Smid* Komm EuInsVO Art 18 mn 1.

[14] D-K/D/Ch-*Duursma-Kepplinger/Chalupsky* Art 18 mn 2; MünchKomm BGB/*Kindler* IntInsR mn 459.

[15] MünchKomm BGB/*Kindler* IntInsR mn 460, 470; Uhlenbruck Komm InsO/*Lüer* Art 18 EuInsVO mn 1; *Smid* Komm EuInsVO Art 18 mn 1.

[16] *Virgós/Schmit* Explanatory report mn 159; Kübler/Prütting-*Kemper* EuInsVO Art 18 mn 4; *Wimmer* ZInsO 2001, 97, 99.

[17] *Virgós/Schmit* Explanatory report mn 159.

[18] MünchKomm BGB/*Kindler* IntInsR mn 474; D-K/D/Ch-*Duursma-Kepplinger/Chalupsky* Art 18 mn 2.

[19] On the proof of the liquidator's appointment, see the discussions on Art 19 of the EIR mn 4 et seq.

[20] D-K/D/Ch-*Duursma-Kepplinger/Chalupsky* Art 18 mn 6; *Paulus* Komm EuInsVO Art 18 mn 1; *Balz* ZIP 1996, 948, 952; *Kemper* ZIP 2001, 1609, 1615; *Leible/Staudinger* KTS 2000, 533, 561; Gottwald/*Gottwald* InsR-Handb (2006) § 132 mn 57.

2. The Concept of Liquidator in Art 18 of the EIR

9 The term "**liquidator**" as understood in Art 18 of the EIR must be construed broadly. The **definition** in **Art 2 of the EIR** is to be enlisted for this.[21] According to Art 2 (b) of the EIR, a "liquidator" is any person or body whose function is to administer or liquidate assets of which the debtor has been divested, or to supervise the administration of his affairs. The persons or bodies referred to here are listed in Annex C to the EIR.[22]

10 In the United Kingdom for instance, the term "liquidator" in Annex C of the EIR includes the:

- Liquidator,
- Supervisor of a voluntary arrangement,
- Administrator,
- Official receiver,
- Trustee,
- Provisional liquidator,[23]
- Judicial factor.

3. Territory of Another Member State Within the Meaning of Art 18 of the EIR

11 Art 18 of the EIR concerns the **actions of a liquidator** of opened insolvency proceedings that are taken **in the territory of *another* Member State.** "Another" Member State means one of the States of the European Union that falls within the scope of application[24] of the EIR other than the one in which insolvency proceedings that the acting liquidator has been appointed to are opened.

4. Main Insolvency Proceedings – Art 18 (1) of the EIR

12 Art 18 (1) of the EIR regulates the powers of the liquidator in main insolvency proceedings when he intends to take action in a Member State other than the one of the opening of proceedings.

4.1 Opening of Main Insolvency Proceedings

13 In order for Art 18 (1) of the EIR to apply, main insolvency proceedings[25] must have been **opened.** The court with jurisdiction for this is determined pursuant to Art 3 (1) of the EIR. According to the ECJ (**Eurofood/Parmalat**), the **opening of proceedings** within the meaning of the EIR presupposes the divestment of the debtor (of his assets) and the

---

[21] *Virgós/Schmit* Explanatory report mn 158; *Smid* Komm EuInsVO Art 18 mn 3; D-K/D/Ch-*Duursma-Kepplinger/Chalupsky* Art 18 mn 3.

[22] On the concept of "liquidator", see the in-depth discussions on Art 2 of the EIR mn 5 et seq.

[23] Kübler/Prütting-*Kemper* EuInsVO Art 18 mn 2 holds that the German "*vorläufige Insolvenzverwalter*" (provisional liquidator) does not fall within the scope of application of Art 18 of the EIR.

[24] Pursuant to Recital 33 of the EIR, Denmark did not participate in the adoption of the EIR. The EIR therefore does not apply to Denmark. On this, see Art 1 of the EIR mn 113.

[25] On the concept of "main insolvency proceedings", see the discussions on Art 3 of the EIR mn 7 et seq.

appointment of one of the liquidators listed in Annex C of the EIR.[26] Such a divestment means that the debtor is divested of his powers to administer his assets.[27]

14 Pursuant to Arts 16 and 17 of the EIR, an automatic (mandatory) recognition of the main insolvency proceedings takes place in all other Member States.[28] According to Art 16 (1) subpara 2 of the EIR, main insolvency proceedings, including the powers conferred on the liquidator of these proceedings by the law governing the insolvency, must even be recognized in a Member State where the debtor would lack insolvency capacity according to the laws of such State[29] (→ see the Overview of Insolvency Capacity within the scope of application of the EIR in Art 3 of the EIR mn 14).

4.2 Scope of the Powers of the Liquidator in the Main Insolvency Proceedings

15 Pursuant to the 1st half-sentence of Art 18 (1) sentence 1 of the EIR, the **powers of the liquidator in the main insolvency proceedings** are governed by the law of the State of the opening of proceedings (see mn 16 et seq). Art 18 (1) sentence 2 of the EIR also grants the liquidator in the main proceedings special powers of intervention. However these powers of the liquidator are subject to the restrictions found

- in the 2nd half-sentence of Art 18 (1) sentence 1 of the EIR (see mn 24 et seq), and
- in Art 18 (3) of the EIR (on this, see mn 43 et seq).

4.2.1 Principle

16 Within the confines provided by the EIR, the liquidator in the main insolvency proceedings is entitled to exercise his powers not only in the State in which the proceedings are opened but in all other Member States – with the exception of Denmark[30] – as well.[31] This follows from the principle of automatic recognition of the insolvency proceedings.[32] The recognition of main insolvency proceedings opened in a Member State triggers the automatic recognition of the appointment and of the powers of the liquidator in those proceedings.[33]

17 The liquidator in the main insolvency proceedings must adhere to the **law of the State of the opening of proceedings** (1st half-sentence of Art 18 (1) sentence 1 of the EIR) – the so-called ***lex fori concursus generalis***. Because this follows already from the general conflict of laws rule found in Art 4 (1) of the EIR,[34] Art 18 of the EIR has a mere clari-

---

[26] Cf ECJ, dated 2 May 2006 – C-341/04 (Eurofood IFSC Ltd.), NZI 2006, 360 et seq → cf Table of Cases Art 3 of the EIR Appendix A mn 10.

[27] ECJ, dated 2 May 2006 – C-341/04 (Eurofood IFSC Ltd.), NZI 2006, 360 et seq → cf Table of Cases Art 3 EuInsVO Appendix A mn 10).

[28] On the automatic recognition of main insolvency proceedings, see the in-depth discussions on Art 16 of the EIR mn 1 et seq.

[29] D-K/D/Ch-*Duursma-Kepplinger/Chalupsky* Art 18 mn 9.

[30] Pursuant to Recital 33 of the EIR, Denmark did not participate in the adoption of the EIR. The EIR therefore does not apply to Denmark.

[31] *Virgós/Schmit* Explanatory report mn 161; D-K/D/Ch-*Duursma-Kepplinger/Chalupsky* Art 18 mn 7; *Virgós/Garcimartín* Regulation, p 195; *Pannen* in Runkel (ed), AHB-Insolvenzrecht (2005) § 16 mn 265.

[32] *Virgós/Schmit* Explanatory report mn 160; FK-InsO/*Wimmer* Anhang I nach § 358 mn 35; D-K/D/Ch-*Duursma-Kepplinger/Chalupsky* Art 18 mn 3.

[33] *Virgós/Schmit* Explanatory report mn 160; FK-InsO/*Wimmer* Anhang I nach § 358 mn 35; D-K/D/Ch-*Duursma-Kepplinger/Chalupsky* Art 18 mn 3; *Smid* Komm EuInsVO Art 18 mn 4.

[34] D-K/D/Ch-*Duursma-Kepplinger/Chalupsky* Art 18 mn 5; MünchKomm BGB/*Kindler* IntInsR mn 460, 464; MünchKomm InsO/

fying function with respect to the powers of the liquidator. This is because Art 4 (2) sentence 2 (c) of the EIR already confers such legal powers.[35] The liquidator in the main insolvency proceedings is entitled in the territory of *another* Member State to exercise all of the **powers** conferred on him by the *lex fori concursus generalis*.[36] Not only the rights but also the **duties** of the liquidator are determined by the *lex fori concursus generalis*.[37]

The liquidator in the main insolvency proceedings may take all measures necessary for: **18**

- inspecting,
- taking inventory,
- preserving, and
- taking possession

of assets situated in another Member State[38] (the *lex fori concursus generalis* determining the extent of the powers and the manner of their exercise).[39]

4.2.2 Special interventionary powers

The extension of the effects of the (debtor's) divestment associated with the main insolvency proceedings to all other Member States imposes an immediate obligation on the liquidator in the main proceedings to physically record/itemize, preserve, and liquidate the entire insolvency estate.[40] **19**

In this context, Art 18 (1) sentence 2 of the EIR allows the liquidator to **remove assets** from the territory of the Member State in which they are situated.[41] This right to remove is a clarification only and was made to eliminate any doubts on this issue, and hence has a mere declaratory effect.[42] It follows already from Arts 3 (1), 4, 16, and 17 of the EIR.[43] Because of their universal validity, the main insolvency proceedings encompass the entirety of the debtor's assets regardless of which State they are situated in.[44] **20**

If an insolvency asset is situated outside the territory of the State of the proceedings, the liquidator is empowered pursuant to Art 18 (1) sentence 2 of the EIR to remove this asset **21**

Reinhart Art 18 EuInsVO mn 1; *Smid* Komm EuInsVO Art 18 mn 2; Kübler/Prütting-*Kemper* EuInsVO Art 18 mn 5; BK-InsO/*Pannen* Art 18 mn 1; *Ehricke/Ries* JuS 2003, 313, 318; *Gottwald* Grenzüberschreitende Insolvenzen p 26 (on Art 18 of the 1995 Convention on Insolvency Proceedings); *Virgós/Garcimartín* Regulation, p 196; Gottwald/*Gottwald* InsR-Handb (2006) § 132 mn 56; *Staak* Der deutsche Insolvenzverwalter im europäischen Insolvenzrecht, p 141.

35 FK-InsO/*Wimmer* Anhang I nach § 358 mn 35; MünchKomm InsO/*Reinhart* Art 18 EuInsVO mn 1; *Paulus* Komm EuInsVO Art 18 mn 3.

36 *Virgós/Schmit* Explanatory report mn 159.

37 *Virgós/Schmit* Explanatory report mn 159; MünchKomm BGB/*Kindler* IntInsR mn 464; Kübler/Prütting-*Kemper* EuInsVO Art 18 mn 5; Moss/Fletcher/Isaacs-*Moss/Bayfield*, Regulation, mn 5.50; *Taupitz* ZZP 111 (1998), 315, 339.

38 FK-InsO/*Wimmer* Anhang I nach § 358 mn 35; Kübler/Prütting-*Kemper* EuInsVO Art 18 mn 5.

39 *Virgós/Schmit* Explanatory report mn 159; FK-InsO/*Wimmer* Anhang I nach § 358 mn 35.

40 HamburgerKomm-*Undritz* Art 18 mn 3.

41 But only to the extent permitted by the *lex fori concursus*. Sec 148 InsO applies in Germany for example. See *Paulus* Komm EuInsVO Art 18 mn 4.

42 *Virgós/Schmit* Explanatory report mn 161; D-K/D/Ch-*Duursma-Kepplinger/Chalupsky* Art 18 mn 9; *Balz* ZIP 1996, 948, 951; *Leible/Staudinger* KTS 2000, 533, 562; *Pannen* in Runkel (ed), AHB-Insolvenzrecht (2005) § 16 mn 70.

43 D-K/D/Ch-*Duursma-Kepplinger/Chalupsky* Art 18 mn 9.

44 *Taupitz* ZZP 111 (1998), 315, 339.

from the State in which it is situated and bring it into the territory of the State of the proceedings.[45] This takes place, however, **subject to the provisions of Arts 5 and 7 of the EIR.**[46] Rights *in rem* belonging to creditors or third parties, or a reservation of title validly established before the opening of insolvency proceedings, in/to property that is situated in the territory of a Member State other than the State of the opening of proceedings at the time of the opening of such, are not affected by the proceedings.[47] But it is only the right *in rem* itself or the reservation of title that is excluded from the effects of the insolvency proceedings,[48] and not the property itself to which the right *in rem* or the reservation of title is attached. However, the **protection of the right *in rem* or the reservation of title** may in some cases be **extended** to the property itself. This will always be the case if the removal, destruction, or liquidation of the property concerned would frustrate, or at least interfere with, the rights *in rem* (e.g. registrable usufructuary rights[49]).[50]

22 If it is possible, however, to safeguard the right *in rem* in full independence of the property concerned, then Art 5 of the EIR does not prevent the liquidator of the main proceedings from removing the property.[51] If required by the right *in rem* in question, the removal of this property to another State can be made to depend on the consent of the holder of the right *in rem*.[52]

23 Although the creditors could prevent the liquidator in the main proceedings from removing this property by requesting the opening of secondary insolvency proceedings that cover such property, this could only be done if the conditions of Art 3 (2) and (3) of the EIR are being satisfied.[53]

4.2.3 Constraints pursuant to the 2nd half-sentence of Art 18 (1) sentence 1 of the EIR

24 In addition to the barrier represented by Arts 5 and 7 of the EIR (above at mn 21), the powers of the liquidator in the main insolvency proceedings are subject to two further constraints found in the 2nd half-sentence of Art 18 (1) sentence 1 of the EIR:[54]

---

[45] MünchKomm BGB/*Kindler* IntInsR mn 462; *Paulus* NZI 2001, 505, 513.

[46] See on this the commentaries on arts 5 and 7 of the EIR.

[47] *Virgós/Schmit* Explanatory report mn 161; D-K/D/Ch-*Duursma-Kepplinger/Chalupsky* Art 18 mn 10; MünchKomm BGB/*Kindler* IntInsR mn 466; Kübler/Prütting-*Kemper* EuInsVO Art 18 mn 7; HamburgerKomm-*Undritz* Art 18 mn 3; Moss/Fletcher/Isaacs-*Moss/Smith*, Regulation, mn 8.157; *Staak* Der deutsche Insolvenzverwalter im europäischen Insolvenzrecht, p 142.

[48] The liquidator is entitled in Germany for example to demand the costs of determining the legal status of the property and of the rights in such property *(Feststellungskosten)* or the costs of realizing the property *(Verwertungskosten)* pursuant to sec 171 InsO.

[49] I.e. rights to which the undisturbed use of the encumbered property itself is indispensable for the creditors or third parties. In such a case, the liquidator is obliged to refrain from any disturbance whatsoever, and a removal of such property to another State is prohibited per art 5 of the EIR. MünchKomm BGB/*Kindler* IntInsR mn 466; D-K/D/Ch-*Duursma-Kepplinger/Chalupsky* Art 18 mn 10.

[50] D-K/D/Ch-*Duursma-Kepplinger/Chalupsky* Art 18 mn 10; Kübler/Prütting-*Kemper* EuInsVO Art 18 mn 7; MünchKomm BGB/*Kindler* IntInsR mn 466; *Smid* Komm EuInsVO Art 18 mn 6; *Taupitz* ZZP 111 (1998), 315, 339.

[51] D-K/D/Ch-*Duursma-Kepplinger/Chalupsky* Art 18 mn 10.

[52] *Virgós/Schmit* Explanatory report mn 161; MünchKomm BGB/*Kindler* IntInsR mn 466; D-K/D/Ch-*Duursma-Kepplinger/Chalupsky* Art 18 mn 10.

[53] *Virgós/Schmit* Explanatory report mn 161.

[54] Also *Virgós/Schmit* Explanatory report mn 162; MünchKomm BGB/*Kindler* IntInsR mn 461.

- First, the powers of the liquidator in the main proceedings are being restricted by the **commencement of a secondary insolvency proceeding** (see mn 25 et seq).
- Second, **provisional preservation measures** taken prior to the opening of secondary insolvency proceedings could also restrict the powers of the foreign liquidator (see mn 31 et seq).[55]

4.2.3.1 Secondary insolvency proceedings

According to Art 18 (1) sentence 1 of the EIR, the liquidator may exercise the powers conferred on him in all Member States as long as **secondary insolvency proceedings** as understood by Art 3 (2) of the EIR have not been opened there.[56] **25**

As soon as secondary insolvency proceedings are opened, the liquidator in the main insolvency proceedings no longer has any direct powers in respect of the assets that are situated within the territory of the State of the secondary insolvency proceedings. Henceforth, the powers conferred on the **liquidator of the secondary proceedings** by the *lex fori concursus secundarii* are **exclusively** applicable to such assets.[57] In the Member State in which the secondary insolvency proceedings are opened, the effects of the main insolvency proceedings are **suspended *ex nunc***.[58] **26**

This does not mean that the liquidator in the main proceedings is robbed entirely of his ability to influence the debtor's assets situated in the other Member State. It only means that this influence must be exercised within the constraints placed on this liquidator by the EIR for the purposes of coordinating the second and main insolvency proceedings. Arts 31 to 37 of the EIR afford the liquidator in the main insolvency proceedings **indirect ways of intervening**;[59] see the discussions on these articles. **27**

Within the territory of the secondary insolvency proceedings, the powers of the liquidator of the main proceedings are being superseded by those of the liquidator of the secondary proceedings in the same way that the effects of the main insolvency proceedings are being superseded by those of the secondary insolvency proceedings.[60] The EIR adheres here to the principle of **modified universality**;[61] the **principle of universality** generally enjoys priority over the **principle of territoriality**.[62] That is why the liquidator in the main proceedings has a dominating position vis-à-vis the liquidator of the secondary proceedings.[63] The liquidator of the main insolvency proceedings has considerable ways of intervening available to him, especially those facilitating the collaboration between the main and secondary insolvency proceedings.[64] **28**

---

55 FK-InsO/*Wimmer* Anhang I nach § 358 mn 35; MünchKomm BGB/*Kindler* IntInsR mn 461; D-K/D/Ch-*Duursma-Kepplinger/Chalupsky* Art 18 mn 11.

56 *Virgós/Schmit* Explanatory report mn 163; *Smid* Komm EuInsVO Art 18 mn 7.

57 *Virgós/Schmit* Explanatory report mn 163; MünchKomm InsO/*Reinhart* Art 18 EuInsVO mn 1; D-K/D/Ch-*Duursma-Kepplinger/Chalupsky* Art 18 mn 12.

58 D-K/D/Ch-*Duursma-Kepplinger/Chalupsky* Art 18 mn 12.

59 *Virgós/Schmit* Explanatory report mn 163; D-K/D/Ch-*Duursma-Kepplinger/Chalupsky* Art 18 mn 12; *Staak* Der deutsche Insolvenzverwalter im europäischen Insolvenzrecht, p 142.

60 *Virgós/Schmit* Explanatory report mn 163; MünchKomm BGB/*Kindler* IntInsR mn 467; *Taupitz* ZZP 111 (1998), 315, 339.

61 On the concept of modified universality, see the discussions on Art 3 of the EIR mn 34.

62 On these principles, see the Introduction at mn 30 et seq as well.

63 MünchKomm BGB/*Kindler* IntInsR mn 467; *Lehr* KTS 2000, 577, 583.

64 Nerlich/Römermann-*Mincke* InsO Art 18 EuInsVO mn 8; MünchKomm BGB/*Kindler* IntInsR mn 467; *Lüke* ZZP 111 (1998), 275,

29 The liquidator in the main proceedings has the following powers:

- the independent **right of request** (Art 29 (a) of the EIR) see mn 30;
- the **duty to cooperate and communicate** (Art 31 of the EIR);
- the **right to propose** the liquidation or use of the assets of the secondary insolvency proceedings (Art 31 (3) of the EIR);
- the **right to lodge claims** in all proceedings (Art 32 (3) of the EIR);
- the **right to request the stay of the liquidation process** (Art 33 of the EIR); and
- the **right to propose** the **closing of the proceedings** (Art 34 (1) of the EIR).

If there is a **surplus** in the secondary insolvency proceedings, the liquidator in the secondary insolvency proceedings must surrender this to the liquidator in the main proceedings (Art 35 of the EIR). The liquidator in the main proceedings is also entitled to request the conversion of independent territorial insolvency proceedings into secondary insolvency proceedings (Art 37 of the EIR). Art 38 of the EIR empowers the liquidator in the main insolvency proceedings to request preservation measures.[65]

30 It is open to the liquidator in the main insolvency proceedings to request the opening of secondary insolvency proceedings (Art 29 (a) of the EIR).[66] Although by opening secondary insolvency proceedings the liquidator in the main proceedings forfeits the rights conferred on him by the *lex fori concursus generalis* to take action in the concerned Member State,[67] the opening of secondary insolvency proceedings can, according to the Virgós/Schmit Report, be an "auxiliary proceeding" facilitating a more efficient administration of the assets of the insolvency estate. This may be necessary:

- if the debtor's assets are too complex to allow an administration of them as one unit, or
- if the legal regimes concerned are so vastly different that the extension of the *lex fori concursus* to the other States in which the assets are situated would lead to difficulties.[68]

4.2.3.2 Provisional preservation measures

31 According to Art 18 (1) sentence 1 of the EIR, the **rights of the liquidator in the main proceedings** are also being **restricted** in cases where preservation measures resorted to in conjunction with the opening of the secondary insolvency proceedings run contrary to his powers.

32 The preservation measures contemplated by Art 18 (1) sentence 1 (at the end) of the EIR, which are contrary to the exercise of the powers of the liquidator in the main proceedings, concern **provisional measures** taken before the opening of the secondary insolvency proceedings.[69] The purpose of this provision is the interim preservation of the

303; *Pannen* in Runkel (ed), AHB-Insolvenzrecht (2005) § 16 mn 237 et seq.

[65] D-K/D/Ch-*Duursma-Kepplinger/Chalupsky* Art 18 mn 13; MünchKomm BGB/*Kindler* IntInsR mn 467; *Lüke* ZZP 111 (1998), 275, 303 et seq.

[66] *Virgós/Schmit* Explanatory report mn 163; *Fritz/Bähr* DZWIR 2001, 221, 234.

[67] The Automold case (→ cf Table of Cases Art 3 of the EIR Appendix A mn 2) must be referred to here; in this case, the liquidator in the main insolvency proceedings in England – via the debtor in possession constellation in respect of the debtor's assets in Germany – acquired considerable powers to intervene in these secondary proceedings as well. This operated to unite the various powers. But consequently, in the State of the secondary insolvency proceedings, the *lex fori concursus secundarii* governed.

[68] *Virgós/Schmit* Explanatory report mn 33.

[69] *Virgós/Schmit* Explanatory report mn 163; D-K/D/Ch-*Duursma-Kepplinger/Chalupsky* Art 18 mn 14; *Smid* Komm EuInsVO Art 18 mn 8; MünchKomm BGB/*Kindler* IntInsR mn 468.

insolvency estate in view of the imminent opening of secondary insolvency proceedings.[70] In the absence of such protection, the liquidator in the main insolvency proceedings, in cases of forthcoming but not yet opened secondary insolvency proceedings, could try to attach the assets situated in this State. To prevent the shrinking of the insolvency estate of the secondary proceedings even before its opening, the powers of the liquidator in the main proceedings are being restricted through such provisional preservation measures.[71]

5. Territorial insolvency proceedings – Art 18 (2) of the EIR

Art 18 (2) of the EIR concerns the powers of the liquidator in territorial insolvency proceedings that are opened by a court with jurisdiction pursuant to **Art 3 (2) of the EIR.**[72] **33**

As with Art 18 (1) of the EIR, Art 18 (2) of the EIR is also a **specific provision of substantive law.**[73] **34**

5.1 Opening of Territorial Insolvency Proceedings

Art 18 (2) of the EIR applies to territorial insolvency proceedings opened pursuant to Art 3 (2) of the EIR. Falling within such proceedings are **secondary insolvency proceedings**[74] within the meaning of Art 3 (2) and (3) of the EIR and **independent territorial insolvency proceedings**[75] within the meaning of Art 3 (2) and (4) of the EIR. **35**

These territorial proceedings are **automatically recognized** pursuant to Arts 16 and 17 of the EIR in all other Member States.[76] **36**

5.2 Scope of the Powers

The appointment and the powers of the liquidator in the territorial proceedings are **automatically recognized** in the other Member States. The scope of the powers of the liquidator in the territorial proceedings are, however, considerably more narrow than those of the liquidator in the main proceedings. The **extent** of the powers of administration and disposal of the liquidator of the territorial proceedings are directly proportionate to the proceedings on which they are based. These powers are therefore territorially restricted.[77] The kind and the scope of the powers of: **37**

- the secondary insolvency proceedings are always determined pursuant to the *lex fori concursus secundarii.*
- the independent territorial insolvency proceedings are determined pursuant to the *lex fori concursus particularis* (Art 28 of the EIR).[78]

---

[70] D-K/D/Ch-Duursma-Kepplinger/Chalupsky Art 18 mn 14.

[71] MünchKomm BGB/*Kindler* IntInsR mn 468; D-K/D/Ch-*Duursma-Kepplinger/Chalupsky* Art 18 mn 14.

[72] In conjunction with subpara 3 in the case of secondary insolvency proceedings, or in conjunction with subpara 4 in the case of independent territorial insolvency proceedings.

[73] MünchKomm BGB/*Kindler* IntInsR mn 470.

[74] On the concept of secondary insolvency proceedings, see the discussions on Art 3 of the EIR mn 124 et seq.

[75] On the concept of independent territorial insolvency proceedings, see the discussions on Art 3 of the EIR mn 128 et seq.

[76] On the automatic recognition of territorial proceedings, see the in-depth discussions in Art 16 of the EIR mn 3.

[77] *Virgós/Schmit* Explanatory report mn 165; D-K/D/Ch-*Duursma-Kepplinger/Chalupsky* Art 18 mn 24; *Herchen* Das Übereinkommen über Insolvenzverfahren der Mitgliedstaaten der Europäischen Union vom 23.11.1995, p 188.

[78] D-K/D/Ch-*Duursma-Kepplinger/Chalupsky* Art 18 mn 24.

38 Art 18 (2) sentence 1 of the EIR is triggered as soon as property belonging to these territorial proceedings is removed to another Member State after the proceedings have been opened.[79] The **object** of Art 18 (2) sentence 1 of the EIR is therefore to reclaim assets belonging to the insolvency estate of the territorial proceedings when, after proceedings have been opened, these have been removed or with the intent to deceive the creditors of these proceedings from the State of such proceedings.[80] The **reclaiming measures** taken by the liquidator in the territorial proceedings to reclaim property situated in a foreign country that would, under normal circumstances, be included in the territorial proceedings are – subject to Art 13 of the EIR – governed by the *lex fori concursus secundarii* or *particularis* (Art 28 and Art 4 (2) sentence 2 (m) of the EIR).[81]

39 According to Art 18 (2) sentence 1 of the EIR, the liquidator in territorial proceedings can claim in every other Member State that **moveable property**[82] was removed from the territory of the State of the opening of proceedings to the territory of that other Member State after the opening of the insolvency proceedings. The liquidator is entitled to **assert** such claim **in or out of court.**[83] An **assertion in court** means that the action must be brought in the State in which the property is situated (avoidance actions are separately regulated in Art 18 (2) sentence 2 of the EIR); the concept of an **out of court assertion** must be construed broadly in order to afford the liquidator of the territorial proceedings the latitude required for reclaiming the property.[84]

40 Art 18 (2) sentence 2 of the EIR also confers on the liquidator in the territorial proceedings the right to assert an **avoidance action** in the interests of the creditors. Voidability is determined pursuant to the *lex fori concursus* (Art 4 (2) sentence 2 (m) and Art 13 of the EIR). Art 18 (2) sentence 2 of the EIR concerns **moveable property** only. The property must, absent the avoidable act, have been situated at the time of the opening of the territorial proceedings within the territory of such proceedings.[85]

41 Art 18 (2) sentence 1 and sentence 2 of the EIR are **exceptions** to the principle that prohibits the liquidators of territorial proceedings from taking action in another Member State.[86]

42 Whether the liquidator in territorial proceedings is afforded **additional powers** besides the two provisions in Art 18 (2) of the EIR is debatable. One view holds that Art 18 (2) of the EIR contains examples only, it thus being conceivable that the liquidator in the territorial proceedings could be afforded additional powers.[87] But because Art 18 (2) of the EIR is an exception, a broadening of the scope of the liquidator's powers should be rejected.[88]

---

[79] *Virgós/Schmit* Explanatory report mn 165.

[80] *Virgós/Schmit* Explanatory report mn 224; D-K/D/Ch-*Duursma-Kepplinger/Chalupsky* Art 18 mn 25 et seq; MünchKomm BGB/*Kindler* IntInsR mn 470; *Fritz/Bähr* DZWIR 2001, 221, 234.

[81] D-K/D/Ch-*Duursma-Kepplinger/Chalupsky* Art 18 mn 26.

[82] Only this property is covered by art 18 (2) sentence 1 of the EIR.

[83] FK-InsO/*Wimmer* Anhang I nach § 358 mn 35; D-K/D/Ch-*Duursma-Kepplinger/Chalupsky* Art 18 mn 25; HamburgerKomm-*Undritz* Art 18 mn 6; *Huber* ZZP 114 (2001) p 133, 148.

[84] Kübler/Prütting-*Kemper* EuInsVO Art 18 mn 16. It includes in any case mediation and arbitration proceedings.

[85] Kübler/Prütting-*Kemper* EuInsVO Art 18 mn 17.

[86] *Virgós/Schmit* Explanatory report mn 165; MünchKomm BGB/*Kindler* IntInsR mn 471; D-K/D/Ch-*Duursma-Kepplinger/Chalupsky* Art 18 mn 24.

[87] MünchKomm InsO/*Reinhart* Art 18 EuInsVO mn 3.

[88] MünchKomm BGB/*Kindler* IntInsR mn 472.

6. Procedures for Realizing Assets – Art 18 (3) of the EIR

Art 18 (3) of the EIR applies to **main** and to **territorial insolvency proceedings.**[89] **43**

According to Art 18 (3) sentence 1 of the EIR, in exercising his powers, the liquidator **44** must comply with the law of the Member State within the territory of which he intends to take action, in particular with regard to procedures for the realization of assets. He must refrain from using **coercive measures** and from ruling on **legal procedures or disputes** (Art 18 (3) sentence 2 of the EIR).

Unlike Art 18 (1) and (2) of the EIR, Art 18 (3) of the EIR is a **conflict of laws rule.** **45** Art 18 (3) of the EIR operates to restrict Art 4 (2) sentence 2 (c) of the EIR.[90]

6.1 Law of the State in Which the Property is Situated

In the exercising of his powers outside the opening State, in particular with regard to **46** procedures for the realization of assets, the liquidator (despite the general applicability of the *lex fori concursus*) must comply with the law of the Member State concerned (*lex rei sitae*).[91] According to Art 18 (3) sentence 1 of the EIR, regarding procedures for the realization of an asset of the insolvency estate, he must comply with the law of the Member State within the territory of which he intends to take action.[92]

In addition to the *lex fori concursus*, the liquidator must therefore also comply with **47** the insolvency-specific laws of the *lex rei sitae*.

- The first step involves a review pursuant to the *lex fori concursus* of which powers the liquidator has and how these may be exercised.
- The second step involves adapting the realization procedure to the laws of the place where the property is situated.[93]

According to the 2nd half-sentence of Art 18 (3) sentence 1 of the EIR, "**whether**" the property is to be realized is governed by the *lex fori concursus*. The law governing the opening of the proceedings determines the extent of the liquidator's powers and the kinds of measures for exercising it. By contrast, "**how**" such powers/measures are to be implemented is governed by the *lex rei sitae*.[94] The procedures for realizing assets are also governed by the *lex rei sitae*.[95]

---

[89] D-K/D/Ch-*Duursma-Kepplinger/Chalupsky* Art 18 mn 27, 30; MünchKomm BGB/*Kindler* IntInsR mn 463, 473 sowie 474; *Paulus* Komm EuInsVO Art 18 mn 18.

[90] MünchKomm BGB/*Kindler* IntInsR mn 474; HamburgerKomm-*Undritz* Art 18 mn 7.

[91] This is also in line with the principle of comity found in public international law, see *Paulus* Komm EuInsVO Art 18 mn 19.

[92] *Virgós/Schmit* Explanatory report mn 164; MünchKomm BGB/*Kindler* IntInsR mn 474; FK-InsO/*Wimmer* Anhang I nach § 358 mn 35; D-K/D/Ch-*Duursma-Kepplinger/Chalupsky* Art 18 mn 19, 29; *Smid* Komm EuInsVO Art 18 mn 10; HamburgerKomm-*Undritz* Art 18 mn 7; MünchKomm InsO/*Reinhart* Art 18 EuInsVO mn 4; *Virgós/Garcimartín* Regulation, p 198; *Wimmer* ZInsO 2001, 97, 99; *Gottwald* Grenzüberschreitende Insolvenzen p 26 (on art 18 of the 1995 Draft Convention on Insolvency Proceedings); *Staak* Der deutsche Insolvenzverwalter im europäischen Insolvenzrecht, p 143.

[93] Kübler/Prütting-*Kemper* EuInsVO Art 18 mn 9; HamburgerKomm-*Undritz* Art 18 mn 9.

[94] MünchKomm BGB/*Kindler* IntInsR mn 469; Nerlich/Römermann-*Mincke* InsO Art 18 EuInsVO mn 6.

[95] *Virgós/Schmit* Explanatory report mn 164; HamburgerKomm-*Undritz* Art 18 mn 9; Kübler/Prütting-*Kemper* EuInsVO Art 18 mn 8; *Leible/Staudinger* KTS 2000, 533, 562.

48 In **each case**, the liquidator must first review how the realization is to be carried out pursuant to the law of the opening State. The realization procedures pursuant to this law include such issues of whether the property should be liquidated by way of a private sale or through a public sale/auction.[96] If the *lex fori concursus* prescribes a court-ordered sale/auction, then the details of such sale/auction procedure are determined by the *lex rei sitae*; if a private sale is prescribed, then the procedure of such sale transaction is determined as well by the *lex rei sitae*.[97] Should the *lex fori concursus* permit a private sale but the *lex rei sitae* only allows a sale by court-ordered auction, then pursuant to Art 18 (3) of the EIR the realization can only be made by way of a court-ordered auction.[98] It may be necessary in some cases to make an adaptation pursuant to private international law; this means a selection of the realization procedure of the *lex rei sitae* that most closely resembles that of the *lex fori concursus*.[99] The liquidator must also comply with the **public-law provisions** of the *lex rei sitae* that deal with specific realization measures.

49 The issue of the **(non-)executionability** of certain assets is determined in accordance with the *lex fori concursus*;[100] however, this is in dispute. Also see the in-depth discussion in Art 4 of the EIR mn 44.

50 The liquidator is entitled to **remove** the **debtor's assets** to another Member State; see Art 18 (1) sentence 2 of the EIR. This power may only be exercised, however, in compliance with the provisions dealing with the free movement of goods in Art 23 et seq EEC Treaty. An object that is a historical or cultural treasure of a Member State may, for example, be protected by an import/export ban pursuant to Art 30 EEC Treaty. In such a situation, the liquidator is unable to exercise his general powers to remove such property to another Member State.[101]

6.2 No Coercive Measures and Rulings on Legal Proceedings or Disputes

51 According to Art 18 (3) sentence 2 of the EIR, the liquidator may not use coercive measures in the exercising of his powers outside of the opening State.[102] The general principle applies which **prohibits coercive measures in the territory of another Member State.** Art 18 (3) of the EIR therefore expressly prohibits the liquidator from directly using any coercive measures. Any kind of force or coercive measure whatsoever is prohibited.[103] The liquidator must make use of the **legal remedies** available in the other Member State.[104] If the assets are not being surrendered voluntarily, or where the liqui-

---

[96] *Virgós/Schmit* Explanatory report mn 164; MünchKomm BGB/*Kindler* IntInsR mn 469; Nerlich/Römermann-*Mincke* InsO Art 18 EuInsVO mn 6; D-K/D/Ch-*Duursma-Kepplinger/Chalupsky* Art 18 mn 19; *Wimmer* ZInsO 2001, 97, 99.

[97] Kübler/Prütting-*Kemper* EuInsVO Art 18 mn 9; *Virgós/Schmit* Explanatory report mn 164; FK-InsO/*Wimmer* Anhang I nach § 358 mn 35; *Leible/Staudinger* KTS 2000, 533, 562.

[98] *Paulus* Komm EuInsVO Art 18 mn 20; *Haas* FS Gerhardt, 319, 338.

[99] *Balz* ZIP 10996, 948, 952; Kübler/Prütting-*Kemper* EuInsVO Art 18 mn 9.

[100] *Paulus* Komm EuInsVO Art 4 mn 19.

[101] *Virgós/Schmit* Explanatory report mn 164; D-K/D/Ch-*Duursma-Kepplinger/Chalupsky* Art 18 mn 21; HamburgerKomm-*Undritz* Art 18 mn 8.

[102] *Pannen/Kühnle/Riedemann* NZI 2003, 72, 74; *Wessels* International Insolvency Law, mn 10759; Moss/Fletcher/Isaacs-*Moss/Smith*, Regulation, mn 8.165.

[103] *Virgós/Schmit* Explanatory report mn 164; D-K/D/Ch-*Duursma-Kepplinger/Chalupsky* Art 18 mn 17; *Smid* Komm EuInsVO Art 18 mn 9; *Gottwald* Grenzüberschreitende Insolvenzen p 25 (on Art 18 of the 1995 Draft Convention on Insolvency Proceedings); *Wimmer* ZInsO 2001, 97, 100; Gottwald/*Gottwald* InsR-Handb (2006) § 132 mn 59; *Staak* Der deutsche Insolvenzverwalter im europäischen Insolvenzrecht, p 144.

[104] MünchKomm BGB/*Kindler* IntInsR mn 469; D-K/D/Ch-*Duursma-Kepplinger/Chalupsky*

dator must otherwise intervene in the interests of third-party rights, then he must invoke the **courts or public authorities** of the State in which the property is situated so that they can take the necessary enforcement measures.[105] The (mandatory) recognition of the insolvency proceedings and of the appointment of the liquidator places the foreign public authorities under an obligation to carry out such coercive measures.[106] Should the liquidator wish to avoid resorting to the legal remedies of the foreign State, it may be possible to cooperate with the debtor, for example by obtaining a power of attorney or authorization from the debtor to collect the property situated in the foreign country.[107]

If the foreign opening order issued pursuant to the *lex fori concursus* functions in Germany as a **judicially enforceable instrument** (*Vollstreckungstitel*) against the debtor in respect of his assets in the insolvency estate, then the enforcement of the foreign opening order can be executed in Germany in accordance with Art 102 Sec (8) *EGInsO* by a simplified exequatur procedure pursuant to Council Regulation (EC) No 44/2001[108].[109] **52**

Art 18 (3) sentence 2 of the EIR also prohibits the liquidator from ruling on **legal proceedings or disputes.** **53**

Art 18 (3) of the EIR does not affect the fact that **assets** situated in a foreign country can **belong to the insolvency estate.**[110] **54**

7. Objections to the Foreign Liquidator's Actions

The EIR makes no provision for "**objections**" or "**appeals**" against the exercise of the powers of the (foreign) liquidator. The Virgós/Schmit Report suggests that the general provisions therefore apply to this matter.[111] The bodies of the State in which the powers are to be exercised must decide whether the exercising of the power concerned infringes national public policy.[112] A distinction must also be made as to whether: **55**

- the appeal is directed against the subject matter of the power or
- against the manner of its exercise.

If the "objection" is directed at the **subject matter of the power being exercised,** i.e. an objection that the measure planned by the liquidator is not justified, then the **courts of the State of the opening of the proceedings** have jurisdiction.[113] But if it is an appeal against the manner of exercising such measure, then the courts or the bodies of the State in which the liquidator has taken action have jurisdiction.[114] **56**

Art 18 mn 18; *Virgós/Schmit* Explanatory report mn 164; *Pannen/Kühnle/Riedemann* NZI 2003, 72, 74; *Paulus* Komm EuInsVO Art 4 mn 21.

105 *Virgós/Schmit* Explanatory report mn 164; MünchKomm BGB/*Kindler* IntInsR mn 469; FK-InsO/*Wimmer* Anhang I nach § 358 mn 35.

106 MünchKomm BGB/*Kindler* IntInsR mn 469; Nerlich/Römermann-*Mincke* InsO Art 18 EuInsVO mn 5; *Pannen/Kühnle/Riedemann* NZI 2003, 72, 74.

107 *Pannen/Kühnle/Riedemann* NZI 2003, 72, 74.

108 Council Regulation (EC) No 44/2001 of 22 December 2000 on jurisdiction and the recognition and enforcement of judgments in civil and commercial matters.

109 FK-InsO/*Wimmer* Anhang I nach § 358 mn 35.

110 *Virgós/Schmit* Explanatory report mn 164; MünchKomm BGB/*Kindler* IntInsR mn 476.

111 *Virgós/Schmit* Explanatory report mn 166; D-K/D/Ch-*Duursma-Kepplinger/Chalupsky* Art 18 mn 31.

112 *Paulus* Komm EuInsVO Art 18 mn 22.

113 *Virgós/Schmit* Explanatory report mn 166, *Paulus* Komm EuInsVO Art 18 mn 22.

114 *Paulus* Komm EuInsVO Art 18 mn 23.

8. Appendix – Overview of Liquidators' Powers – Powers and Duties of the Liquidator in the Main, Secondary, and Independent Territorial Insolvency Proceedings Pursuant to the EIR

57 The following table compares the powers and duties of the liquidator in main, secondary, and independent territorial insolvency proceedings pursuant to the provisions of the EIR. The powers and duties set out here are not exhaustive.

Proceeding / Rule	Main Insolvency Proceedings	Secondary Insolvency Proceedings	Independent Territorial Insolvency Proceedings
Art 4 (1) and (2) of the EIR	*lex fori concursus generalis* → **General regulating of the powers and duties of the liquidator**	*lex fori concursus secundarii* → **General regulating of the powers and duties of the liquidator**	*lex fori concursus particularis* → **General regulating of the powers and duties of the liquidator**
Art 18 (1) sentence 1, 1st 1/2 sentence of the EIR	Applicability of the *lex fori concursus generalis* in the territory of another Member State → **Clarification of the powers, see mn 17**	–	–
Art 18 (1) sentence 1, 2nd 1/2 sentence, 1st alternativ of the EIR	Opening of secondary insolvency proceedings → **Restriction of the powers of the liquidator in the main proceedings, see mn 25 et seq**	–	–

Proceeding / Rule	Main Insolvency Proceedings	Secondary Insolvency Proceedings	Independent Territorial Insolvency Proceedings
Art 18 (1) sentence 1, 2nd 1/2 sentence, 2nd alternative of the EIR	Preservation measures to the contrary **→ Restriction of the powers of the liquidator in the main proceedings,** see mn 31	–	–
Art 18 (2) sentence 1 of the EIR	–	Claiming the removal of insolvency assets **→ Power of the liquidator in the secondary proceedings,** see mn 38	Claiming the removal of insolvency assets **→ Power of the liquidator in the independent territorial proceedings,** see mn 39
Art 18 (2) sentence 2 of the EIR	–	Asserting avoidance actions **→ Power of the liquidator in the secondary proceedings,** see mn 40	Asserting avoidance actions **→ Power of the liquidator in the independent territorial proceedings,** see mn 40
Art 18 (3) of the EIR	Restriction of the *lex fori concursus generalis* esp in relation to realization, coercive measures, and legal proceedings **→ Restriction of the powers of the liquidator in the main proceedings,** see mn 44	Restriction of the *lex fori concursus secundarii* esp in relation to realization, coercive measures, and legal proceedings **→ Restriction of the powers of the liquidator in the secondary proceedings,** see mn 44	Restriction of the *lex fori concursus particularis* esp in relation to realization, coercive measures, and legal proceedings **→ Restriction of the powers of the liquidator in the independent territorial proceedings,** see mn 44

Proceeding / Rule	Main Insolvency Proceedings	Secondary Insolvency Proceedings	Independent Territorial Insolvency Proceedings
Art 20 (1) of the EIR	Claim to return of that obtained after opening of proceedings → **Right of recovery,** see Art 20 of the EIR mn 5 et seq	–	–
Art 21 (1) of the EIR	Public notification of the opened proceedings → **Right of request of the liquidator in the main proceedings,** see Art 21 of the EIR mn 2	Public notification of the opened proceedings → **Right of request of the liquidator in the secondary proceedings,** see Art 21 of the EIR mn 2	Public notification of the opened proceedings → **Right of request of the liquidator in the independent territorial proceedings,** see Art 21 of the EIR mn 2
Art 21 (2) of the EIR	Public notification of the opened proceedings → **Duty of the liquidator in the main proceedings**	Public notification of the opened proceedings → **Duty of the liquidator in the secondary proceedings**	Public notification of the opened proceedings → **Duty of the liquidator in the independent territorial proceedings**
Art 22 (1) of the EIR	Registration of the opened proceedings in a public register → **Right of request of the liquidator in the main proceedings**	–	–
Art 22 (2) of the EIR	Registration of the opened proceedings in a public register → **Duty of the liquidator in the main proceedings**	–	–

Proceeding / Rule	**Main Insolvency Proceedings**	**Secondary Insolvency Proceedings**	**Independent Territorial Insolvency Proceedings**
Art 29 (a) of the EIR	Right to request the opening of secondary insolvency proceedings **→ Right of request of the liquidator in the main proceedings**	–	–
Art 31 (1) of the EIR	Communicating with the liquidator(s) in the secondary proceedings **→ Duty of the liquidator in the main proceedings,** see Art 31 of the EIR mn 6 et seq	Communicating with the liquidator in the main proceedings **→ Duty of the liquidator in the secondary proceedings,** see Art 31 of the EIR mn 6 et seq	–
Art 31 (2) of the EIR	Cooperating with the liquidator(s) in the secondary proceedings **→ Duty of the liquidator in the main proceedings,** see Art 31 of the EIR mn 32 et seq	Cooperating with the liquidator in the main proceedings **→ Duty of the liquidator in the secondary proceedings,** see Art 31 of the EIR mn 32 et seq	–
Art 31 (3) of the EIR	Proposals on liquidating the assets of the various secondary insolvency proceedings **→ Power of the liquidator in the main proceedings,** see Art 31 of the EIR mn 40	Giving liquidator in the main proceedings opportunity to make liquidation proposals **→ Duty of the liquidator in the secondary proceedings,** see Art 31 of the EIR mn 41	–

Proceeding / Rule	Main Insolvency Proceedings	Secondary Insolvency Proceedings	Independent Territorial Insolvency Proceedings
Art 32 (2) of the EIR	Reciprocal lodging of claims **→ Power/duty of the liquidator in the main proceedings**	Reciprocal lodging of claims **→ Power/duty of the liquidator in the secondary proceedings**	–
Art 32 (3) of the EIR	Liquidator's participation in proceedings on the same basis as a creditor **→ Power of the liquidator in the main proceedings**	Liquidator's participation in proceedings on the same basis as a creditor **→ Power of the liquidator in the secondary proceedings**	–
Art 33 (1) of the EIR	Stay of liquidation of the assets of the secondary insolvency proceedings **→ Right of request of the liquidator in the main proceedings**	–	–
Art 33 (2) 1st dash of the EIR	Termination of stay of liquidation **→ Right of request of the liquidator in the main proceedings**	–	–
Art 33 (2) 2nd dash of the EIR	–	Termination of stay of liquidation **→ Right of request of the liquidator in the secondary proceedings**	–

Proceeding / Rule	**Main Insolvency Proceedings**	**Secondary Insolvency Proceedings**	**Independent Territorial Insolvency Proceedings**
Art 34 (1) subpara 1 of the EIR	Proposal to close secondary proceedings via measures other than liquidation **→ Right of request of the liquidator in the main proceedings**	–	–
Art 34 (1) subpara 2 of the EIR	Consent to proposal to close secondary proceedings via measures other than liquidation **→ Power of the liquidator in the main proceedings**	–	–
Art 34 (3) of the EIR	Proposal or consent to close secondary proceedings via measures other than liquidation during the stay of liquidation **→ Power of the liquidator in the main proceedings**	–	–
Art 35 of the EIR	Claim to surplus of assets in the secondary insolvency proceedings **→ Right of the liquidator in the main proceedings**	Transfer of a surplus of assets **→ Duty of the liquidator in the secondary proceedings**	–

Proceeding / Rule	**Main Insolvency Proceedings**	**Secondary Insolvency Proceedings**	**Independent Territorial Insolvency Proceedings**
Art 37 of the EIR	Converting a reorganization proceeding into a winding-up proceeding **→ Right of request of the liquidator in the main proceedings**	–	–
Art 38 of the EIR	Requesting provisional preservation measures **→ Right of request of the temporary administrator in the main proceedings**	–	–
Art 40 (1) of the EIR	Informing the creditors **→ Duty of the liquidator in the main proceedings,** see Art 40 of the EIR mn 1	Informing the creditors **→ Duty of the liquidator in the secondary proceedings,** see Art 40 of the EIR mn 1	Informing the creditors **→ Duty of the liquidator in the independent territorial proceedings,** see Art 40 of the EIR mn 1

Article 19
Proof of the liquidator's appointment

The liquidator's appointment shall be evidenced by a certified copy of the original decision appointing him or by any other certificate issued by the court which has jurisdiction.

A translation into the official language or one of the official languages of the Member State within the territory of which he intends to act may be required. No legalisation or other similar formality shall be required.

Contents

Index

Bibliography

Duursma-Kepplinger/Duursma/Chalupsky Europäische Insolvenzverordnung, Kommentar (2002); Frankfurter Kommentar zum Insolvenzrecht (2005) *Haß/Huber/Gruber/Heiderhoff* EU-Insolvenzverordnung, Kommentar (2005); *Kübler/Prütting* Kommentar zur Insolvenzordnung (March 2006); *Moss/Fletcher/Isaacs* (eds) The EC Regulation on Insolvency Proceedings (2002); Münchener Kommentar zum Bürgerlichen Gesetzbuch, vol 11 (2006); *Nerlich/Römermann* (eds) Insolvenzordnung (InsO), Kommentar (March 2003); *Penzlin/Riedemann* Klarstellung der Befugnisse englischer Hauptinsolvenzverwalter – MG Rover II, NZI 2005, p 515; *Paulus* Europäische Insolvenzverordnung, Kommentar (2006); *Smid* Deutsches und Europäisches internationales Insolvenzrecht, Kommentar (2004); *Virgós/Garcimartín* The European Insolvency Regulation: Law and Practice (2004); *Virgós/Schmit* Erläuternder Bericht zu dem EU-Übereinkommen über Insolvenzverfahren, in Stoll (ed), Vorschläge und Gutachten (1997), p 32; *Wessels* International Insolvency Law (2006).

1. Overview

According to the **principle of universality,** the opening of main insolvency proceedings is effective throughout the entire European Union. No further formalities are needed. Such proceedings are recognized automatically (see Art 16 of the EIR mn 9 et seq). This enables the liquidator to take action in all Member States and to exercise the powers conferred on him by the *lex fori concursus* (Art 18 of the EIR). In practice, however, the liquidator must provide proof in the other Member States of his appointment in order to manifest such powers.[1] Art 19 of the EIR provides a simplified and inexpensive mechanism for the liquidator to prove his appointment.[2] **1**

Art 19 of the EIR primarily concerns the **liquidator in the main insolvency proceedings** who is acting within the ambit of the main insolvency proceedings on an international basis. Art 19 of the EIR also applies to **liquidators in secondary insolvency proceedings** who are making use of the transborder powers afforded to them by Art 18 (2) of the EIR (return of insolvency assets that were removed to another Member State).[3] **2**

Art 19 of the EIR is equally **applicable** to the German ***vorläufiger Verwalter*** (provisional liquidator) listed in Annex C of the EIR.[4] **3**

---

1 *Virgós/Garcimartín* Regulation, p 200.

2 MünchKomm BGB/*Kindler* IntInsR mn 477; Moss/Fletcher/Isaacs-*Moss/Smith*, Regulation, mn 8.170.

3 D-K/D/Ch-*Duursma-Kepplinger/Chalupsky* Art 19 mn 1; *Smid* Komm EuInsVO Art 19 mn 2; Kübler/Prütting-*Kemper* EuInsVO Art 19 mn 1; Haß/Huber/Gruber/Heiderhoff-*Gruber* Art 19 EuInsVO mn 1; MünchKomm BGB/*Kindler* IntInsR mn 480.

4 *Paulus* Komm EuInsVO Art 19 mn 2.

2. Proof of Liquidator's Appointment

4 According to Art 19 (1) of the EIR, the liquidator's appointment is to be evidenced by a **certified copy** of the decision appointing him or by any **other certificate issued by the court which has jurisdiction.** Examples of such proof in German law, for instance, would be a copy of the order ordering the opening of insolvency proceedings pursuant to Sec 27 (2) *InsO*, or a so-called *Bestellungsurkunde* (certificate of appointment) pursuant to Sec 56 (2) sentence 1 *InsO*).[5]

5 Art 19 (1) of the EIR contains a rule similar to Art 2 of the Istanbul Convention of 1990,[6] which, unlike the Draft Community convention of 1982, considers it unnecessary to insist on a standardized form of attestation of the liquidator's appointment.[7] This is being criticized by some legal writers.[8]

6 A public notification of the opening judgement is not required to prove the liquidator's appointment;[9] this notification pursuant to Art 21 of the EIR is merely an optional right of request afforded to the liquidator. According to Art 19 (2) sentence 2 of the EIR, a **legalisation** or other **similar formality** is also not required. The **apostille** provided for in the 1961 Hague Convention Abolishing the Requirements of Legalisation For Foreign Public documents is, for example, not required.[10] The same holds true for the legalisation of foreign public documents provided in Sec 13 of the German *Konsulargesetz* and the judicial review of the authenticity of foreign public documents in compliance with Sec 438 of the German *ZPO*.[11]

7 The **costs** of the certification are considered costs of the insolvency estate.[12]

3. Translation

8 According to Art 19 (2) sentence 1 of the EIR, a **translation** into the official language or one of the official languages of the Member State within the territory of which the liquidator intends to act may be required. This translation must satisfy the requirements of this State applying to the translation of official documents.[13]

9 The question is whether this translation must be certified considering that Art 19 (2) of the EIR does not require this.[14] Provided that a parallel may be drawn at all to Art 48 (2) of the 1968 Brussels Convention (now Art 55 (2) of Council Regulation (EC) No 44/2001), the Explanatory Report holds that the translation would have to be certified by a person authorized to do so in a Member State (State of the opening of proceedings or the Member State in which the liquidator intends to exercise his powers).[15]

[5] MünchKomm BGB/*Kindler* IntInsR mn 482.

[6] *Smid* Komm EuInsVO Art 19 mn 5.

[7] *Virgós/Schmit* Explanatory report mn 167.

[8] So Nerlich/Römermann-*Mincke* Komm InsO Art 19 EuInsVO mn 1.

[9] D-K/D/Ch-Duursma-Kepplinger/Chalupsky Art 19 mn 2.

[10] *Virgós/Schmit* Explanatory report mn 169; D-K/D/Ch-*Duursma-Kepplinger/Chalupsky* Art 19 mn 5; *Wessels* International Insolvency Law (2006) mn 10766.

[11] MünchKomm BGB/*Kindler* IntInsR mn 486; FK-InsO/*Wimmer* Art 102 EGInsO Anhang I mn 83.

[12] MünchKomm BGB/*Kindler* IntInsR mn 483; *Virgós/Garcimartín* Regulation, p 200; D-K/D/Ch-*Duursma-Kepplinger/Chalupsky* Art 19 mn 4.

[13] *Virgós/Schmit* Explanatory report mn 169; *Virgós/Garcimartín* Regulation, p 200; *Wessels* International Insolvency Law (2006) mn 10766.

[14] Nerlich/Römermann-*Mincke* Komm InsO Art 19 EuInsVO mn 3.

[15] *Virgós/Schmit* Explanatory report mn 169; auch: D-K/D/Ch-*Duursma-Kepplinger/Chalupsky* Art 19 mn 6; Nerlich/Römermann-*Mincke* Komm InsO Art 19 EuInsVO

The **costs of the translation** and the **costs of certifying the translation** are considered costs of the insolvency estate.[16] **10**

4. Proof of the Scope of the Liquidator's Powers

The EIR is silent on the manner in which the liquidator is to prove the scope of his powers.[17] A liquidator asserting the powers conferred on him by the *lex fori concursus* in another Member State should be able to prove such powers in cases where they are being doubted or where an objection to these powers is being made.[18] A certificate issued by the court that appointed the liquidator that lists the powers to which he is entitled may suffice here.[19] The actual need for such a certificate is being doubted – albeit unjustifiably – by some legal writers;[20] an elucidation of the liquidator's powers having proven efficient enough in practice. **11**

On 11 May 2005, the High Court of Justice in Birmingham in the MG Rover case thus issued the so-called "supplemental orders" (→ cf Table of Cases Art 3 of the EIR Appendix A mn 16)[21] in order to elucidate the powers conferred on the English "joint administrator" pursuant to English law, after this court had opened main insolvency proceedings against eight companies of the MG Rover Group.[22] This elucidation was requested by the English liquidators for practical reasons; it enabled them to evidence their legal position and the powers conferred on them more easily towards the foreign participants in the proceedings, who were often unfamiliar with the idiosyncrasies of English "administration proceedings".[23] **12**

Although the liquidators in the main proceedings had only requested a supplementation of the opening order, the High Court considered it expedient, in European insolvency proceedings involving a multitude of foreign participants, to expressly set out in "supplemental orders" the powers of the liquidators in the main proceedings.[24] These "supplemental orders" describe the goals of the English insolvency proceedings, the effects of a moratorium, and the general powers of the liquidator in the main insolvency proceedings pursuant to the Insolvency Act 1986. This is necessary considering that the concise wording of the English law – "the affairs, business and property of the Company be managed by the administrators" – is very much in need of interpretation.[25] **13**

The question is whether proof of the scope of the liquidator's powers must always be made in such "supplemental orders". In light of the universal effects of the main insolvency proceedings, an **informal** (non-standardized) declaration by the court of the opening of proceedings would seem to suffice.[26] **14**

---

mn 4; MünchKomm BGB/*Kindler* IntInsR mn 485.

16 MünchKomm BGB/*Kindler* IntInsR mn 483; Nerlich/Römermann-*Mincke* Komm InsO Art 19 EuInsVO mn 5; D-K/D/Ch-*Duursma-Kepplinger/Chalupsky* Art 19 mn 4.

17 *Virgós/Schmit* Explanatory report mn 170; *Virgós/Garcimartín* Regulation, p 200.

18 *Virgós/Schmit* Explanatory report mn 170.

19 *Virgós/Schmit* Explanatory report mn 170; *Virgós/Garcimartín* Regulation, p 200.

20 Moss/Fletcher/Isaacs-*Moss/Smith*, Regulation, mn 8.170.

21 High Court of Justice Birmingham dated 11 May 2005 – 2375 to 2382/05, NZI 2005, 515 with explanatory note by *Penzlin/Riedemann.*

22 High Court of Justice Birmingham 8.4.2005, NZI 2005, 467 with explanatory note by *Penzlin/Riedemann.*

23 *Penzlin/Riedemann* NZI 2005, 515, 518.

24 *Penzlin/Riedemann* NZI 2005, 515, 518.

25 *Penzlin/Riedemann* NZI 2005, 515, 518.

26 Nerlich/Römermann-*Mincke* Komm InsO Art 19 EuInsVO mn 6; MünchKomm BGB/*Kindler* IntInsR mn 488.

Article 20
Return and imputation

1. A creditor who, after the opening of the proceedings referred to in Article 3(1) obtains by any means, in particular through enforcement, total or partial satisfaction of his claim on the assets belonging to the debtor situated within the territory of another Member State, shall return what he has obtained to the liquidator, subject to Articles 5 and 7.

2. In order to ensure equal treatment of creditors a creditor who has, in the course of insolvency proceedings, obtained a dividend on his claim shall share in distributions made in other proceedings only where creditors of the same ranking or category have, in those other proceedings, obtained an equivalent dividend.

Contents

Index

Bibliography

Balz Das neue Europäische Insolvenzübereinkommen, ZIP 1996, p 948; *Beck* Verteilungsfragen im Verhältnis zwischen Haupt- und Sekundärverfahren nach der EuInsVO, NZI 2007, p 1; *Duursma-Kepplinger/Duursma/Chalupsky* Europäische Insolvenzverordnung, Kommentar (2002); Frankfurter Kommentar zum Insolvenzrecht (2005); *Huber* Die Europäische Insolvenzverordnung, EuZW 2002, p 490; *Kolmann* Kooperationsmodelle im internationalen Insolvenzrecht (2001); *Leible/Staudinger* Die europäische Verordnung über Insolvenzverfahren, KTS 2000, p 533; *Lüer* Zur Neuordnung des deutschen Internationalen Insolvenzrechts, in Stoll (ed), Stellungnahmen und Gutachten zur Reform des deutschen Internationalen Insolvenzrechts (1992), p 96; *Lüke* Das europäische internationale Insolvenzrecht, ZZP 111 (1998), p 275; *Mankowski* Klärung von Grundfragen des europäischen Internationalen Insolvenzrechts durch die Eurofood-Entscheidung?, BB 2006, p 1753; *Meyer-Löwy/Plank* Entbehrlichkeit des Sekundärinsolvenzverfahrens bei flexibler Verteilung der Insolvenzmasse im Hauptinsolvenzverfahren?, NZI 2006, p 622; *Moss/Fletcher/Isaacs* (eds) The EC Regulation on Insolvency Proceedings (2002); Münchener Kommentar zur Insolvenzordnung, vol 3 (2003); *Pannen/Riedemann/Kühnle* Zur Stellung der Insolvenzgläubiger nach der Europäischen Verordnung über Insolvenzverfahren (EuInsVO), NZI 2002, p 303; *Paulus* Änderungen des deutschen Insolvenzrechts durch die Europäische Insolvenzverordnung, ZIP 2002, p 729; *Paulus* Europäische Insolvenzverordnung, Kommentar (2006); *Smid* Europäisches Internationales Insolvenzrecht (2002); *Smid* Deutsches und Europäisches Internationales Insolvenzrecht (2004); *Virgós/Schmit* Erläuternder Bericht zu dem EU-Übereinkommen über Insolvenzverfahren, in Stoll (ed), Vorschläge und Gutachten, p 32 (1997); *Virgós/Garcimartín* The European Insolvency Regulation: Law and Practice (2004); *Wessels* Current Topics of International Insolvency Law (2004); *Wessels* International Insolvency Law (2006).

1. Overview

The EIR endeavours to provide the highest degree of **uniformity and equality** with respect to the **satisfaction of all creditors.**[1] According to Recital 21 of the EIR, the distribution of the proceeds must be coordinated in order to ensure an equal treatment of the creditors. Art 20 of the EIR, in combination with Arts 32, 35, and 39 of the EIR, guarantees this **equal treatment of creditors** (*par conditio creditorum*)[2], and together with Art 35 of the EIR, which provides for the transfer of a surplus in the secondary insolvency proceedings to the liquidator in the main proceedings, it is in this aspect the most important provision of the EIR. The object of Art 20 of the EIR is to guarantee a unified system of collective distribution.[3] **1**

Even though the **main insolvency proceeding** is effective in all Member States, a creditor could, for example, take advantage of the time gap, which inevitably occurs between the opening of the proceedings in one Member State and its effects in another Member State, to initiate individual execution measures.[4] Because of this, Art 20 of the EIR imposes a duty on the creditor to return the satisfaction obtained on any insolvency assets situated in another Member State after the opening of the insolvency proceedings (on the concept of "opening" of insolvency proceedings, see Art 2 of the EIR mn 24). **2**

The **right** to make **multiple lodgements** of claims, which every creditor is entitled to pursuant to Art 32 (1) of the EIR, presupposes a built-in corrective mechanism to prevent the multiple satisfaction of such claims. This is accomplished through the system of equalization of dividends found in Art 20 (2) of the EIR.[5] **3**

Art 20 of the EIR corresponds more or less to the equalization rule developed in the decisions of the German *BGH* in cases of cross-border insolvency proceedings.[6] **4**

---

1 *Leible/Staudinger* KTS 2000, 533, 563.

2 *Wessels* Current Topics of International Insolvency Law, p 139.

3 *Virgós/Garcimartín* Regulation, p 248.

4 MünchKomm InsO/*Reinhart* Art 20 EuInsVO mn 1.

5 *Paulus* Komm EuInsVO Art 20 mn 2.

6 *Balz* ZIP 1996, 948, 952 with reference to BGHZ 88, 147 = ZIP 1983, 961; BGHZ 95, 256 (270) = NJW 1985, 2897. Sec 237 KO allowed, in foreign bankruptcy proceedings with universal effects, individual execution measures only in respect of judicially enforceable instruments in existence prior to the opening of proceedings. The InsO contains nothing comparable to sec 237 KO. Hence, individual execution measures are now completely precluded. On this, see also: *Leible/Staudinger* KTS 2000, 533, 563 and *Paulus* ZIP 2002, 729, 733.

2. Claim for Return Pursuant to Art 20 (1) of the EIR

5 Because the assets of the debtor in the European Community constitute one unified insolvency estate, the main insolvency proceedings with their **universal effects** operate to encompass all of the debtor's assets regardless of where they are situated.[7] After the **opening** of insolvency proceedings (on the question of when proceedings are **opened** within the meaning of the EIR, see Art 2 of the EIR mn 24) creditors are prohibited from totally or partially satisfying their claims through voluntary payments by the debtor or through individual execution measures, as such satisfaction would violate the principle of collective satisfaction of all creditors.[8] Should this nevertheless happen, Art 20 (1) of the EIR imposes an **obligation on such creditors to return** to the liquidator that which has been "obtained"; the sole exception to this are proceeds obtained through the liquidation of the rights referred to in Arts 5 and 7 of the EIR.[9]

2.1 Requirements

6 The **requirements of the claim for return** are set out in the wording of Art 20 (1) of the EIR: a (total or partial) **satisfaction** must have taken place after the **opening** of the insolvency proceedings from an **asset** of the debtor that is situated in **another Member State.**

7 Whether the requirements of Art 20 (1) of the EIR have been met is determined primarily by the *lex fori concursus* within the meaning of Art 4 of the EIR.[10] The issues involved here are mainly the determination of who the creditors are, and whether the asset is one to be included in the insolvency estate (see mn 8).

2.1.1 Satisfaction on an asset of the insolvency estate

8 Which **assets belong to the insolvency estate** is, pursuant to Art 4 (2) sentence 2 (b) of the EIR, a matter for *lex fori concursus.*

9 The **types and manner** of satisfaction are irrelevant.[11] The example mentioned in the provision – enforcement – is intended to make clear that even a legally obtained satisfaction will have no priority over the *par conditio creditorum.*[12] The satisfaction may have been effected via an enforcement measure or through a voluntary payment by the debtor. Art 20 (1) of the EIR applies even where proportional satisfaction has been obtained pursuant to **independent territorial insolvency proceedings.**[13] But where satisfaction has been obtained pursuant to **secondary insolvency proceedings,** Art 20 of the EIR **does not apply;** this is expressly provided for in Art 20 (2) of the EIR.[14]

---

[7] FK-InsO/*Wimmer* Art 102 EGInsO mn 102; *Wessels* International Insolvency Law (2006) mn 10769.

[8] *Virgós/Schmit* Explanatory report mn 172; *Leible/Staudinger* KTS 2000, 533, 563; *Wessels* International Insolvency Law (2006) mn 10769.

[9] *Pannen/Riedemann/Kühnle* NZI 2002, 303, 306; *Wessels* International Insolvency Law (2006) mn 10768.

[10] *Paulus* Komm EuInsVO Art 20 mn 4.

[11] *Paulus* Komm EuInsVO Art 20 mn 6.

[12] *Paulus* Komm EuInsVO Art 20 mn 6.

[13] *Paulus* Komm EuInsVO Art 20 mn 6.

[14] Moss/Fletcher/Isaacs-*Moss/Smith*, Regulation, mn 8.175.

2.1.2 In another Member State

Art 20 (1) of the EIR only applies if the State of the opening of proceedings and the State of the *situs* of the property are not the same. The determination of the *situs* of the property is made in accordance with Art 2 (g) of the EIR. **10**

If the State of the opening of proceedings and the State in which the property is situated are the same, any obligation to return will be governed by the applicable *lex fori concursus*.[15] **11**

Art 20 (1) of the EIR does not apply to situations in which property of the insolvency estate is situated in a **non-EU country**. This is inferable not only from the wording "within [the territory] of another Member State", but also from the basic non-applicability of the EIR in non-EU countries (on this, see Art 3 of the EIR mn 58 et seq).[16] In such a case, the autonomous law of the particular State together with its private international law rules are applicable.[17] **12**

2.1.3 After the opening of insolvency proceedings

Art 20 (1) of the EIR only applies if insolvency proceedings have already been **opened**. These insolvency proceedings must be **main insolvency proceedings** within the meaning of Art 3 (1) of the EIR. Only these proceedings operate to prohibit individual execution measures throughout the Community.[18] Any compulsory execution measures or payments by the debtor that were made **shortly before the opening of proceedings** may only be challenged via an avoidance action; Art 4 (2) sentence 2 (m) of the EIR provides that the *lex fori concursus* governs creditors' avoidance actions.[19] **13**

The determination of the **point in time at which proceedings are opened** is extremely vital to the application of Art 20 (1) of the EIR (on this, see Art 3 of the EIR mn 24 and Art 16 of the EIR mn 28 et seq). According to the decisions of the ECJ, an opening of proceedings within the meaning of Art 16 of the EIR presupposes the divestment of the debtor and the appointment of one of the liquidators listed in Annex C of the EIR.[20] Such a divestment means that the debtor is divested of his powers to administer his assets.[21] Thus, the appointment of a provisional liquidator can be sufficient. **14**

The application of Art 20 (1) of the EIR is made difficult by the so-called "relation back principle",[22] or retroactive legal fiction, found in English, Welsh, and Irish law. In the **Eurofood/Parmalat** decision of the ECJ (→ cf Table of Cases Art 3 of the EIR Appendix A mn 10), although the court did not expressly address this issue,[23] the **15**

---

[15] *Smid* Komm EuInsVO Art 20 mn 4; *Paulus* Komm EuInsVO Art 20 mn 7; *Wessels* International Insolvency Law (2006) mn 10770.

[16] *Smid* Komm EuInsVO Art 20 mn 5; D-K/D/Ch-*Duursma-Kepplinger/Chalupsky* Art 20 mn 16.

[17] D-K/D/Ch-*Duursma-Kepplinger/Chalupsky* Art 20 mn 16.

[18] D-K/D/Ch-*Duursma-Kepplinger/Chalupsky* Art 20 mn 11.

[19] D-K/D/Ch-*Duursma-Kepplinger/Chalupsky* Art 20 mn 13.

[20] Cf ECJ dated 2 May 2005 – C-341/04 (Eurofood IFSC Ltd.), NZI 2006, 360 et seq → cf Table of Cases Art 3 of the EIR Appendix A mn 10).

[21] ECJ dated 2 May 2005 – C-341/04 (Eurofood IFSC Ltd.), NZI 2006, 360 et seq → cf Table of Cases Art 3 of the EIR Appendix A mn 10).

[22] Concept found in sec 220 [2] Companies Act 1963. According to the relation back principle, the opening of insolvency proceedings are effective retroactive to the point in time at which the request was made. On this, see Art 3 of the EIR mn 89 et seq.

[23] ECJ dated 2 May 2005 – C-341/04 (Eurofood IFSC Ltd.), NZI 2006, 360 et seq → cf Table of Cases Art 3 of the EIR Appendix A mn 10).

decision must be so understood to mean that **retroactive fictions of national law** are to be disregarded.[24]

16 Art 20 (1) of the EIR does not only command a determination of the **point in time at which the proceedings are opened.** The **point in time of the satisfaction** must also be determined. Decisive here is the time of fulfilment of the claim, which is ascertained pursuant to the law governing the claim, regardless of whether the satisfaction was obtained pursuant to a compulsory execution measure or via a voluntary payment of the debtor.[25]

2.2 Subject Matter of the Claim for Return

17 **What the claim for return actually entails** is not defined more precisely in Art 20 (1) of the EIR. It merely states that **what has been obtained** must be returned to the liquidator.

18 Prevailing opinion holds that **"liquidator"** in this provision is to be understood as the **liquidator in the main insolvency proceedings.**[26] The claim for return follows from the universality of the main insolvency proceedings, such proceedings encompassing all of the debtor's assets.[27] Also speaking in favour of a return to the liquidator in the main insolvency proceedings is the fact that secondary insolvency proceedings have probably not yet been opened in the Member State in which the property of the insolvency estate is situated. Another approach would be that the creditor returns that which has been obtained to the liquidator under whose jurisdiction the property at issue falls.[28] If secondary insolvency proceedings have been opened, then the Member State in which the claim for return is situated should then be applicable (third dash of Art 2 (g) of the EIR).[29] If the claim for return is situated in the State of the secondary insolvency proceedings, then the claim for return should – by way of subrogation – become vested in the liquidator in the secondary insolvency proceedings.[30]

19 The **party opposing** a claim for return is the creditor who obtained the benefit.[31]

20 The claim for return provided for in Art 20 (1) of the EIR is independent of national law. Because Art 20 (1) of the EIR is a standardized provision of Community-law, it is irrelevant to an application of it whether the law of the Member State in question contains a comparable claim or whether such law structures the claim differently. Art 20 (1) of the EIR is neither a conflict of laws rule nor is it a provision of international procedural law.[32] The claim for return in Art 20 (1) of the EIR rather forms the **basis of a claim *sui generis* in Community law** aimed at preventing an inequitable treatment of creditors.[33] There is therefore no need to invoke national laws dealing with claims for return, which would be hard to do anyway since most national insolvency laws lack such a claim. It would also be difficult to construct such a right from general principles of unjust enrichment.[34]

---

[24] *Mankowski* BB 2006, 1753, 1757.

[25] MünchKomm InsO/*Reinhart* Art 20 EuIns-VO mn 3.

[26] D-K/D/Ch-*Duursma-Kepplinger/Chalupsky* Art 20 mn 18; *Smid* Komm EuInsVO Art 20 mn 9; *Kolmann* Kooperationsmodelle im internationalen Insolvenzrecht (2001), 315.

[27] *Smid* Komm EuInsVO Art 20 mn 11.

[28] MünchKomm InsO/*Reinhart* Art 20 EuInsVO mn 2.

[29] MünchKomm InsO/*Reinhart* Art 20 EuInsVO mn 2.

[30] MünchKomm InsO/*Reinhart* Art 20 EuIns-VO mn 2.

[31] *Smid* Komm EuInsVO Art 20 mn 10.

[32] MünchKomm InsO/*Reinhart* Art 20 EuInsVO mn 1.

[33] *Smid* Komm EuInsVO Art 20 mn 11; D-K/D/Ch-*Duursma-Kepplinger/Chalupsky* Art 20 mn 20.

[34] MünchKomm InsO/*Reinhart* Art 20 EuInsVO mn 1.

21 The claim for return refers first and foremost to the property obtained directly from the insolvency estate.[35] But if such property has already been liquidated, and therefore can no longer be returned, the claim for return then encompasses the **proceeds** of such liquidation.[36] The EIR is silent however on the details of the claim for return, thus leaving a number of issues unresolved. The most problematic cases are those in which the creditor obtained either less or more money than the liquidator would have obtained pursuant to the insolvency proceedings.[37] Does the creditor then have to return the **substitute value** of the asset or the **money obtained** for it? Art 20 (1) of the EIR must be interpreted on its own in this regard. It is irrelevant here whether the national law in question confers special rights on the liquidator in this constellation, because the claim for return constitutes the basis of a claim pursuant to Community law. The wording of Art 20 (1) of the EIR – "shall return what he has obtained to the liquidator" – illustrates that the debtor, if that which has been obtained no longer exists, is under an obligation to return its equivalent.[38] It does not appear to impose any liability for damages over and above this.[39] This means that a creditor who obtains a lesser amount for the property of the insolvency estate is not liable for the **difference** between the amount obtained and the normal price. But if he obtains a better price, then the insolvency estate would benefit from the excess amount. According to *Paulus*, the further obligations of the debtor are determined in accordance with the **principles of unjust enrichment** (in Germany in Secs 818 and 819 *BGB*).[40]

22 Also debatable is whether the creditor must compensate for **usage** or reimburse **interest**. This is to be presumed considering the immediate connection that such things have to the particular asset.[41] A clarification of this issue or the development of judicial guidelines by the ECJ remains to be seen.[42]

Equally unresolved is the question of whether the creditor is entitled to deduct the costs incurred for obtaining the satisfaction.[43] If the creditor has transacted in good faith, i.e. he had no knowledge of the opening of the proceedings, he is entitled to deduct the **costs**, but he will not be able to do so if he resumed the individual execution measures despite his being informed of the opening of the proceedings.[44]

2.3 Exceptions

23 Art 5 of the EIR (third parties' rights in rem) and Art 7 of the EIR (reservation of title) are exceptions to Art 20 (1) of the EIR. A creditor who enforces his right to separate his property out of the insolvency estate *(Aussonderungsrecht)*, or whose claim is satis-

---

[35] *Smid* Komm EuInsVO Art 20 mn 13; D-K/D/Ch-*Duursma-Kepplinger/Chalupsky* Art 20 mn 24.

[36] *Virgós/Schmit* Explanatory report mn 172; *Pannen/Riedemann/Kühnle* NZI 2002, 303, 306; D-K/D/Ch-*Duursma-Kepplinger/Chalupsky* Art 20 mn 24; *Smid* Komm EuInsVO Art 20 mn 13; *Wessels* International Insolvency Law (2006) mn 10771.

[37] D-K/D/Ch-*Duursma-Kepplinger/Chalupsky* Art 20 mn 24.

[38] *Wessels* International Insolvency Law (2006) mn 10771.

[39] D-K/D/Ch-*Duursma-Kepplinger/Chalupsky* Art 20 mn 24.

[40] *Paulus* Komm EuInsVO Art 20 mn 9 (who justifies this on the basis of wanting to close this "inviting gap"); dissenting opinion: MünchKomm InsO/*Reinhart* Art 20 EuIns-VO mn 4.

[41] See also D-K/D/Ch-*Duursma-Kepplinger/Chalupsky* Art 20 mn 24.

[42] Cf MünchKomm InsO/*Reinhart* Art 20 EuInsVO mn 4.

[43] *Virgós/Garcimartín* Regulation, p 244.

[44] *Virgós/Garcimartín* Regulation, p 244.

fied by the liquidation of property in which he has a secured right *in rem*, does not unjustly enrich himself at the expense of the insolvency estate.[45]

24 A party entitled to a right of separation (*Aussonderungsrecht*) or to preferential treatment (*Absonderungsrecht*) must only return the portion in excess of the claim.[46]

3. Equalization of Dividends Pursuant to Art 20 (2) of the EIR

3.1 General

25 The EIR expressly allows the opening of parallel insolvency proceedings (Art 3 of the EIR). On account of the different distribution procedures, **separate distributions** are made to the creditors of the secondary and those of the main insolvency proceedings.[47] A creditor who obtains satisfaction from an insolvency proceeding opened in another Member State is not acting unlawfully, he is simply enforcing the rights afforded to him by Art 32 (1) of the EIR to make multiple lodgements of claims.[48] This creditor is entitled to retain that which he obtained pursuant to the distribution made in the first proceeding.[49] But in order to ensure the equal treatment of all creditors in the European Union, a creditor who has obtained such payment may only participate in other distributions once the claims of the creditors of the same ranking have obtained satisfaction to an equal degree.[50] The object of Art 20 (2) of the EIR is found directly in its wording – "In order to ensure equal treatment of creditors ...".

26 The equalization of dividends commands a thorough knowledge of the claims that have been lodged in the other proceedings, and the dividends already attained.[51] But how this is to take place is not defined in the EIR. The general duty to cooperate and communicate found in Art 31 of the EIR will certainly be applicable here.[52] According to Art 31 (1) sentence 2 of the EIR, the liquidators are under a **duty to communicate** to each other any information that may be relevant to the other proceedings. Knowledge of dividends already obtained undoubtedly constitutes such information.[53]

27 The mechanism envisioned by Art 20 (2) of the EIR corresponds to the so-called "**hotchpot rule**" found in common law.[54]

28 Debatable is whether **dividends obtained in non-EU countries** must also be taken into account in the equalization of dividends. Some argue that the wording of Art 20 (2) of the EIR does not differentiate between dividends obtained within Member States and those obtained in non-EU Member States.[55] Art 20 (2) of the EIR does speak, however, of "insolvency proceedings" whose statutory definition is found in Art 2 (a) of the EIR with its reference to Art 1 (1) of the EIR and Annex A of the EIR. Since Annex A of the EIR only contains insolvency proceedings of the Member States, dividends obtained from non-EU countries could only be taken into account pursuant to **autonomous inter-**

---

45 *Virgós/Schmit* Explanatory report mn 173.
46 *Leible/Staudinger* KTS 2000, 533, 563; *Huber* EuZW 2002, 490, 496; *Pannen/Riedemann/Kühnle* NZI 2002, 303, 306.
47 *Beck* NZI 2007, 1, 6.
48 *Virgós/Schmit* Explanatory report mn 174.
49 *Virgós/Schmit* Explanatory report mn 174; Recital 21 of the EIR.
50 *Virgós/Schmit* Explanatory report mn 174; *Virgós/Garcimartín* Regulation, p 248.
51 *Beck* NZI 2007, 1, 6.
52 *Beck* NZI 2007, 1, 6 and 7.
53 *Beck* NZI 2007, 1, 6.
54 Moss/Fletcher/Isaacs-*Moss/Smith*, Regulation, mn 8.177, with a reference to *Cleaver vs. Delta American Re* [2001] 2 AC 328, PC; *Wessels* International Insolvency Law (2006) mn 10774.
55 MünchKomm InsO/*Reinhart* Art 20 EuInsVO mn 6.

national insolvency law.[56] This leads, however, to a disparate treatment of dividends allocated pursuant to insolvency proceedings in Member States and than those pursuant to insolvency proceedings in non-EU countries. Creditors who have obtained a dividend in a non-EU country may be put in a better position than the other creditors, which violates the **principle of equal treatment of creditors.**[57] In order to prevent this, it is preferable to extend the application of Art 20 (2) of the EIR to insolvency proceedings conducted in non-EU countries as well.[58] An equalization of the dividends obtained in a non-EU country could certainly be provided for through the respective *lex fori concursus*.

3.2 Basic Equalization Rules

The calculation procedure follows the four following rules:[59] **29**

- No creditor may obtain more than 100 % of his claim.
- The original amount of the claim (100 % of its original value) must always be asserted and not the residual amount of it (amounts obtained in other proceedings are not being deducted), otherwise the equal treatment of creditors participating in several proceedings would not be guaranteed.[60]

  Example: Creditor X obtains in Member State Y 5 % of 100 % of his claim. If he can obtain a dividend of 8% in Member State Z, the remaining 3 % (8 %–5 %) is deducted from 100 % and not from 95 % (100 %–5 %). Otherwise, creditor X would obtain a total of 7.85 % and not 8 %.

  The only **exception** to this rule is made in the case of secured claims and claims for which a **set-off** is possible.[61] According to Art 4 (2) sentence 2 (i) of the EIR, the rights of the creditors who have obtained partial satisfaction after the opening of insolvency proceedings by virtue of a right *in rem* or through a set-off are determined by the *lex fori concursus*. The EIR is silent on whether these secured claims, if the security or the set-off does not cover the total amount of the claim, must be lodged for the total original amount or for the residual amount only; this must be resolved by the *lex fori concursus*.[62]
- A claim will only be taken into account in the distribution if the creditors of the same ranking were satisfied in these proceedings at the same quota as the holder of the claim in the first proceedings.

  Example: German creditor X obtained 5 % of his claim in proceedings opened in Member State Y. He may only take part in the distribution in proceedings in Member State Z (he also lodged his claim in the proceedings there) once the non-preferred creditors here have also obtained 5 % of their claims.[63]

---

[56] With same result: *Paulus* Komm EuInsVO Art 20 mn 12 fn 8; *Virgós/Garcimartín* Regulation, p 248.

[57] *Virgós/Garcimartín* Regulation, p 248.

[58] *Virgós/Garcimartín* Regulation, p 248; MünchKomm InsO/*Reinhart* Art 20 EuIns-VO mn 6; *Wessels* International Insolvency Law (2006) mn 10774.

[59] *Virgós/Schmit* Explanatory report mn 175.

[60] There is no apparent reason for treating secured creditors' claims for deficiencies (of amounts of their preferential payment) differently as proposed by *Balz* in: *Balz* ZIP 1996, 948, 952.

[61] *Virgós/Garcimartín* Regulation, p 246.

[62] *Virgós/Garcimartín* Regulation, p 246.

[63] *Virgós/Schmit* Explanatory report mn 175; *Pannen/Riedemann/Kühnle* NZI 2002, 303, 305.

- The ranking or the categories of the individual claims is governed in every proceeding by the *lex fori concursus*.

30 If different insolvency laws apply to different insolvency proceedings, it may well happen that the same claim lodged in two different proceedings is allocated a different ranking in each proceeding.[64] In calculating the dividend in such a case, only the quota obtained in the other proceeding – and not the ranking or the category of the claim – is taken into account.[65]

Example: Creditor X's claim in Member State Y is considered a non-preferred claim against the insolvency estate, but in Member State Z it would be considered a preferred claim. Regardless of its ranking, the claim was satisfied in Member State Y at 5 %. In Member State Z, this 5 % will then be compared to the dividend determined pursuant to the laws of Member State Z applicable to preferred claims. If Member State Z provides for a dividend of 25 % for such claims, then creditor X in Member State Z obtains a dividend of 20 % (25 %–5 %).[66]

31 In implementing the distribution procedure, the liquidator is advised to proceed step-by-step for each ranking in case claims have been lodged and partially satisfied in another Member State:[67]

- The **first step** involves checking whether the creditor concerned is "of the same ranking or category".
- If this is the case, then the **second step** involves determining whether the creditor has participated and obtained a dividend in another proceeding.
- In the **third step**, the liquidator must determine the dividend in his own proceedings. The creditors of the same ranking who have already obtained a dividend are excluded from the dividend distribution procedure as long as the dividend to be distributed does not exceed the dividend distributed in the other proceedings.[68]

32 The liquidator should, within the classes of creditors of the same ranking, form sub-classes according to the specific dividends already obtained, and should only take further claims into consideration once the dividends have attained the levels of the other claims with the same ranking.[69]

33 In the example at mn 30, the claim already satisfied in Member State Y will not be taken into consideration until a quota of 5 % has been reached. Only once the claims of the same ranking have been satisfied at 5 % can the liquidator distribute the remaining 20 %, providing that the insolvency estate is not already depleted.

---

[64] *Virgós/Schmit* Explanatory Report mn 175; *Pannen/Riedemann/Kühnle* NZI 2002, 303, 305. Although it will seldom happen that ordinary (non-preferred) claims against the insolvency estate will be allocated different rankings, examples of this do exist: wage claims pursuant to art L 143-10 of the French Employment Law Code are privileged, unlike in Germany, and therefore must be satisfied preferentially. In contrast to German law, English law does not treat claims of shareholders or affiliated companies as substituted equity and therefore does not subordinate them. On this, see the High Court of Justice of London, 9 June 2006 in the matter Collins & Aikman NZI 2006, 654 → cf Table of Cases Art 3 of the EIR Appendix A mn 5) and the comments by *Meyer-Löwy/Plank* NZI 2006, 622.

[65] *Virgós/Schmit* Explanatory report mn 175.

[66] *Virgós/Schmit* Explanatory report mn 175; *Pannen/Riedemann/Kühnle* NZI 2002, 303, 305.

[67] *Virgós/Schmit* Explanatory report mn 176.

[68] *Paulus* Komm EuInsVO Art 20 mn 11.

[69] *Beck* NZI 2007, 1, 6.

3.3 No Duty to Return Dividends

The attempt made by Art 20 (2) of the EIR to ensure an equal treatment of creditors is not quite perfect: creditors who have rightfully obtained a higher dividend in an insolvency proceeding are not obliged to transfer the difference to those creditors who have been forced to accept a lower dividend in another insolvency proceeding.[70] **34**

Example: Creditor W obtains in secondary insolvency proceedings in Member State X a dividend of 15 %. Creditor Y, on the other hand, obtains a dividend of 5 % in different secondary insolvency proceedings in Member State Z. Although this violates the principle of equal treatment of creditors, creditor Y has no claim against creditor X since neither Art 20 (2) of the EIR nor Art 20 (1) of the EIR (the dividend having been rightfully obtained) imposes a duty to return dividends.[71] **35**

In the early stages of development of the EIR, some criticized the fact that proceeds from a dividend obtained in foreign insolvency proceedings were not to be paid over.[72] Others argue that the multiple lodgement sanctioned by Arts 32 and 39 of the EIR makes little sense if the advantages resulting from it are ultimately beneficial to the creditors as a whole but not to the creditor who took the initiative to make the lodgement.[73] Recital 21 of the EIR also provides that a creditor should be able to keep what he has received in the course or an insolvency proceeding. What must be taken into account here, however, is the fact that major creditors in particular are able to take advantage of their right to lodge their claims in every proceeding, but small creditors will hardly be in a position to afford the costs of foreign legal representation.[74] The protection of the small creditors is thus being safeguarded by Art 32 (2) of the EIR, which allows the lodging of the claims via the liquidator in the main insolvency proceedings.[75] **36**

Article 21
Publication

1. The liquidator may request that notice of the judgment opening insolvency proceedings and, where appropriate, the decision appointing him, be published in any other Member State in accordance with the publication procedures provided for in that State. Such publication shall also specify the liquidator appointed and whether the jurisdiction rule applied is that pursuant to Article 3(1) or Article 3(2).

2. However, any Member State within the territory of which the debtor has an establishment may require mandatory publication. In such cases, the liquidator or any au-

[70] D-K/D/Ch-*Duursma-Kepplinger/Chalupsky* Art 20 mn 3; *Paulus* Komm EuInsVO Art 20 mn 14.

[71] D-K/D/Ch-*Duursma-Kepplinger/Chalupsky* Art 20 mn 3.

[72] *Lüer* Zur Neuordnung des deutschen Internationalen Insolvenzrechts, in Stoll (ed), Stellungnahmen und Gutachten zur Reform des deutschen Internationalen Insolvenzrechts, p 96, 118.

[73] *Kolmann* Kooperationsmodelle im internationalen Insolvenzrecht (2001), 355; approving: D-K/D/Ch-*Duursma-Kepplinger/Chalupsky* Art 20 mn 3.

[74] *Lüer* Zur Neuordnung des deutschen Internationalen Insolvenzrechts, in Stoll (ed), Stellungnahmen und Gutachten zur Reform des deutschen Internationalen Insolvenzrechts, p 96, 120; *Lüke* ZZP 111 (1998), 301; *Kolmann* Kooperationsmodelle im internationalen Insolvenzrecht (2001), 315.

[75] *Smid* Europäisches Internationales Insolvenzrecht, p 135.

thority empowered to that effect in the Member State where the proceedings referred to in Article 3(1) are opened shall take all necessary measures to ensure such publication.

Contents

Index

Bibliography

Heidelberger Kommentar zur Insolvenzordnung, 4th edn (2006), Eickmann/Flessner/Irschlinger/Kirchhof/Kreft/Landfermann/Marotzke/Stephan (eds); *Kübler/Prütting* Kommentar zur Insolvenzordnung (March 2006); Münchener Kommentar zur Insolvenzordnung, vol 1 (2001); *Nerlich/Römermann* (eds) Insolvenzordnung (InsO), Kommentar (May 2003); *Virgós/Schmit* Erläuternder Bericht zu dem EU-Übereinkommen über Insolvenzverfahren, in Stoll (ed), Vorschläge und Gutachten (1997), p 32.

1. Objects of the Rule

1 Art 21 of the EIR deals with the **publication** of the opening of insolvency proceedings and other orders and matters related thereto (see mn 5 et seq below). Its central importance arises in response to the protectionary provisions (of commercial transactions) found in **Art 24 of the EIR**, i.e. where obligations are being honoured for the benefit of the debtor instead of for the liquidator. In cases where the debtor honours an obligation to a third party, publication only plays a role if the law governing the insolvency proceedings (see Art 4 (2) sentence 2 (c) of the EIR) couples the protection of commercial transactions to a publication, or if the law of the place where property is situated (or where a register is kept) that is referred to in **Art 14 of the EIR** links the validity of a disposition to publication. A publication also serves as a warning to those engaging in commercial transactions. It is a substantive-law rule having immediate effect in the EU Member States.[1]

[1] MünchKomm InsO/*Reinhart* Art 21 EuInsVO mn 1; Kübler/Prütting-*Kemper* EuInsVO Art 21 mn 1.

2. Publication Upon Request

2.1 The liquidator's Right of Request

The liquidator has a statutory right to request publication, which means there is no need for providing proof of it; what must be proven, of course, is his appointment as the liquidator[2] if this is not already known to the official authorities. Such proof must be provided in the manner contemplated by Art 19 of the EIR. The request must be made to the authorities of the Member State that are, pursuant to the law of the State in which publication is being sought, responsible for this. In addition to deciding which authority is responsible, the law of this State also determines the procedures for the publication.[3] The term "liquidator" is defined in Art 2 (b) of the EIR in conjunction with Annex C thereto. **2**

The responsible authority in **Germany** is the court with local jurisdiction, Art 102 Sec 5 (1) *EGInsO*. For the requirements of such request, see the discussions on this (Art 102 Sec 5 EGInsO at mn 2 et seq). **3**

Although Art 21 (1) of the EIR puts the making of a request at the liquidator's discretion – on Art 21 (2) see mn 11 et seq below – this cannot be interpreted as giving him a free hand as to whether to make a request or not. One would expect that, even when the requirements for the second subsection have not been met, he would have to make a request if he knows that there are debtors of the insolvent debtor in a Member State. **4**

2.2 Content of the Publication

a) **Basic principles.** Subsection 1 stipulates the minimum information that – independent of national laws – must be included in a publication;[4] the failure to include these would render the publication invalid. On the nature of this information, see mn 7 to 10 below. National laws may demand the inclusion of additional information. **5**

b) **Publication in Germany.** This is regulated in Art 102 Sec 5 (1) *EGInsO*. **6**

See the discussions on this (Art 102 Sec 5 EGInsO at mn 8 et seq).

c) **Minimum requirements.** The German version of Art 21 (1) of the EIR refers first of all to the "*wesentlicher Inhalt*" (essential contents) of the judgement opening insolvency proceedings. (The English wording here merely refers to the "notice" of the judgement opening insolvency proceedings.) "Essential" must mean: **7**

- identification of the debtor,
- the time at which proceedings were opened, and
- the body (authority) making the decision.

Whether the reasons for opening proceedings must also be stated[5] seems doubtful, this being irrelevant to what Art 21 of the EIR is trying to achieve (mn 1 above). **8**

Also to be stated is whether main insolvency proceedings pursuant to Art 3 (1) of the EIR or independent territorial insolvency proceedings pursuant to Art 3 (2) of the EIR are at issue. **9**

---

[2] Kübler/Prütting-*Kemper* EuInsVO Art 21 mn 2. Ambiguous in this respect: MünchKomm InsO/*Reinhart* Art 21 EuInsVO mn 2.

[3] *Virgós/Schmit* Explanatory report mn 181.

[4] Same opinion: MünchKomm InsO/*Reinhart* Art 21 EuInsVO mn 2; HK-InsO/*Stephan* Art 21 EuInsVO mn 2; Kübler/Prütting-*Kemper* EuInsVO Art 21 mn 4. Contra: Nerlich/Römermann-*Mincke* Komm InsO Art 21 EuInsVO mn 5.

[5] See Kübler/Prütting-*Kemper* EuInsVO Art 21 mn 4.

10 A reference to the appointed liquidator is found in both the first and second sentences of Art 21 (1) of the EIR. This must be generally understood to mean that the specifying of such person is a requirement. His appointment is either a part of the opening decision, which means that the information is required pursuant to sentence 1. Or it is required pursuant to sentence 2 if, for instance, the *lex fori concursus* provides for the appointment of a liquidator in a separate procedure, or if another liquidator is being appointed when the one initially appointed withdraws.

3. Compulsory Publication

11 Art 21 (2) of the EIR enables the Member States to provide for compulsory publication in their national laws, i.e. independent of the liquidator's request. This is only the case, however, if the debtor maintains an establishment within the meaning of Art 2 (h) of the EIR in such State.

12 The powers afforded by Art 102 Sec 5 (2) *EGInsO* have been resorted to in Germany.

13 Should the national law in question contain a rule referred to in subsection 2, then the authorities deemed responsible by such rule are under an official obligation to make the publication. The responsible authorities of the opening State as per Art 3 (1) of the EIR and the liquidator are under the obligation described in the second sentence of Art 21 (2) of the EIR to "take all necessary measures". This can (only) mean an obligation to provide information.[6]

14 Subsection 1 of Art 21 of the EIR also applies to the **contents** of a compulsory publication.

Article 22
Registration in a public register

1. The liquidator may request that the judgment opening the proceedings referred to in Article 3(1) be registered in the land register, the trade register and any other public register kept in the other Member States.

2. However, any Member State may require mandatory registration. In such cases, the liquidator or any authority empowered to that effect in the Member State where the proceedings referred to in Article 3(1) have been opened shall take all necessary measures to ensure such registration.

Contents

[6] Kübler/Prütting-*Kemper* EuInsVO Art 21 mn 7; HK-InsO/*Stephan* Art 21 EuInsVO mn 5.

Index

Bibliography

Duursma-Kepplinger/Duursma/Chalupsky Europäische Insolvenzverordnung, Kommentar (2002); *Hanisch* Das Recht grenzüberschreitender Insolvenzen: Auswirkungen im Immobiliensektor, ZIP 1992, p 1125; *Eickmann/Flessner/Irschlinger/Kirchhof/Kreft/Landfermann/Marotzke/Stephan* (eds) Heidelberger Kommentar zur Insolvenzordnung, 4th edn (2006); *Kübler/Prütting* Kommentar zur Insolvenzordnung (March 2006); *Nerlich/Römermann* (eds) Insolvenzordnung (InsO), Kommentar (May 2003); *Virgós/Schmit* Erläuternder Bericht zu dem EU-Übereinkommen über Insolvenzverfahren, in Stoll (ed), Vorschläge und Gutachten (1997), p 32; *Wimmer* Anmerkung zur Vorlage des irischen Supreme Court in Sachen Parmalat, ZinsO 2005, p 119; *Wimmer* (ed) Frankfurter Kommentar zur Insolvenzordnung, 4th edn (2006).

1. Objects of the Rule

Art 22 of the EIR deals with the registration of the opening of proceedings in public registers (on this, see mn 5 and 8 below). Its protectionary function – similar to Art 21 of the EIR in this respect – lies in the **protection of third parties acting in good faith** before an entry has (yet) been made in the land register or in a similar register, and, after registration, the **protection of the insolvency estate from being diminished by such an acquisition**; its general purpose is to warn third parties of an invalid or avoidable legal transaction. 1

Art 22 of the EIR is a **substantive-law rule** having immediate effect in the EU Member States.[1] 2

2. Scope of Application

While Art 21 of the EIR applies to proceedings pursuant to Art 3 (1) of the EIR as well as those pursuant to Art 3 (2) of the EIR, Art 22 of the EIR only applies to main insolvency proceedings pursuant to Art 3 (1) of the EIR. In the case of territorial insolvency proceedings, only the assets situated in the State of the opening of proceedings are being seized/attached so that there is no need for registration in other Member States. 3

Problematic are the cases referred to by *Kemper*[2] where assets are being removed from the State in which territorial proceedings have been opened to the territory of another Member State. And because the attachment/seizure remains in effect,[3] there is still 4

[1] Kübler/Prütting-*Kemper* EuInsVO Art 22 mn 3.

[2] Kübler/Prütting-*Kemper* EuInsVO Art 22 mn 2.

[3] Kübler/Prütting-*Kemper* EuInsVO Art 17 mn 11.

the need for the protection referred to in mn 1 above. In these cases, Art 18 (2) of the EIR could be interpreted in favour of a right of request pursuant to subsection 1. Since, due to their nature, only moveable property, ships, or aircraft may be involved here, this will only be an option if the law of the place where the property is situated knows this kind of a register.

3. Registration Upon Request

3.1 The Liquidator's Right to Request

5 The liquidator (Art 2 (b) of the EIR) in the main insolvency proceedings has a statutory right of request, which means there is no need for providing proof of it; what must be proven is his appointment as a liquidator. This proof must be provided in the manner contemplated by Art 19 of the EIR. The request must be made to the authorities of the Member State that are, pursuant to the law of this State, responsible for this.

6 According to Art 102 Sec 6 (1) *EGInsO*, the responsible authority in Germany is the court that has local jurisdiction pursuant to Art 102 Sec 1 *EGInsO*. This court requests registration in the register kept by the respective body.

7 If the Member States has no such law, the liquidator is entitled to make his request directly to the authority that keeps the register.

3.2 Registers Included

8 Art 22 of the EIR basically encompasses all **public registers** known to the Member State.[4] The scope of their authority and their powers, the procedures, and the content of the registrations are determined by the law of the State in which registration is being sought.[5]

3.3 Preclusion of Registration and Substitution

9 a) For obvious reasons, a registration that is tailored to a register known in the opening State but unknown in the State in which the property is situated cannot be made.[6]

10 b) Because the registering authority is entitled to (incidentally) review the recognisability of the opened proceedings,[7] registration is precluded if the requirements of Art 16 of the EIR have not been satisfied or if there has been an infringement of public policy (Art 26 of the EIR).

11 c) The term **"substitution"** (***Anpassung***) involves the contents of (i.e. information contained in) a registration.[8] The concept presupposes that a request has been duly made and that no reasons exist to preclude registration (mn 9 and 10 above). Assuming that a registration is permitted, then the law of the State of the opening of proceedings is presumed to determine the contents of the registration. And if this content also coincides with the law of the registering State (which is rather unlikely), then the registration is

---

[4] Kübler/Prütting-*Kemper* EuInsVO Art 22 mn 3.

[5] Kübler/Prütting-*Kemper* EuInsVO Art 22 mn 3; FK-InsO/*Wimmer* Anhang I nach § 358 mn 108; Nerlich/Römermann-*Mincke* Komm InsO Art 22 EuInsVO mn 2; HK-InsO/*Stephan* Art 22 EuInsVO mn 2.

[6] Kübler/Prütting-*Kemper* EuInsVO Art 22 mn 4.

[7] *Virgós/Schmit* Explanatory Report mn 96.

[8] D-K/D/Ch-*Duursma-Kepplinger/Chalupsky* Art 22 mn 8; *Hanisch* ZIP 1992, 1125, 1127.

made using this content. In any other case, the registration must be reworded to comply as closely as possible with registrations of the opening State. But in the words of *Hanisch*:[9] "No more or no less should be demanded of the national law than is required by the foreign law." But in order to make a substitution at all, the foreign prohibition must be at least basically similar – systematically and functionally – to its national equivalent.

4. Compulsory Registration

Like Art 21 of the EIR, Art 22 (2) of the EIR allows Member States to make registration as well compulsory (to be executed *ex officio*). The comments made on Art 21 of the EIR at mn 11 therefore apply here as well. **12**

Germany has made no use of this. **13**

5. Judgements Opening Proceedings

The provisions of Art 22 of the EIR presuppose – as does the EIR in general – the existence of validly opened insolvency proceedings. However, some Member States allow – as early as the proceedings prior to the opening of insolvency proceedings – the ordering and the registration of measures restricting (debtor) disposals.[10] The need to prevent asset-diminishing disposals by the debtor is as important at such an early stage of the proceedings as it is after insolvency proceedings have been opened. **14**

Wimmer[11] therefore advocates a broad interpretation of "the time of the opening of proceedings" in Art 2 (f) of the EIR to include the time at which – even if only temporary – the debtor has been divested of the powers of administration and disposal. This approach should be supported since it is the best way to bring about that which Art 22 of the EIR is trying to accomplish (safeguarding of commercial transactions). And that the decision restricting the (debtor's) powers of disposal need not be a final one is also supported in the wording of Art 2 (f) of the EIR itself.

Article 23
Costs

The costs of the publication and registration provided for in Articles 21 and 22 shall be regarded as costs and expenses incurred in the proceedings.

Contents

[9] *Hanisch* ZIP 1992, 1125, 1127.

[10] For instance, under German law according to sec 21 subpara 2 No 2, sec 23 subpara 2, sec 32 InsO.

[11] *Wimmer* ZInsO 2005, 119, 126.

Index

Bibliography

Kübler/Prütting Kommentar zur Insovenzordnung (March 2006); *Virgós/Schmit* Erläuternder Bericht zu dem EU-Übereinkommen über Insolvenzverfahren, in Stoll (ed), Vorschläge und Gutachten (1997), p 32.

1. Objects of the Rule

1 Art 23 of the EIR allocates to the insolvency estate of the main proceedings all of the costs of publication and for the seizure/attachment of the insolvency assets in the Member States via the measures set out in Arts 21 and 22 of the EIR. It goes without saying that costs incurred in the State of the main insolvency proceedings will be allocated pursuant to the law governing the insolvency proceedings.

2. Contents of the Rule

2.1 Costs Included

2 **"Costs"** within the meaning of this provision refers to all of the fees and expenses charged by the responsible authorities or by the bodies engaged by such authorities (e.g. the German *Grundbuchamt* (Land Title Registry) to which requests are made by the insolvency court, see Art 22 EIR at mn 1 and 8) according to the fee/cost schedules in effect there. It is irrelevant whether the particular authority has acted in response to a request (Art 21 (1), Art 22 (1) of the EIR) or on its own accord where the publication or registration is compulsory (Art 21 (2) and Art 22 (2) of the EIR).[1]

3 **"Expenses"** means all expenditures incurred by the liquidator to bring about the publication and/or the registration. This generally involves translation and postage costs; in some cases, the provision may comprise travelling costs or the costs of a lawyer retained by the liquidator in a Member State to lodge an appeal, for example, where the responsible authorities there refuse to act.

4 The costs of **translating** and **certifying** the liquidator's appointment (Art 19 sentence 2 of the EIR) are also covered by this provision, these being expenses necessary for bringing about publication/registration.[2]

---

[1] *Virgós/Schmit* Explanatory report mn 186; Kübler/Prütting-*Kemper* EuInsVO Art 23 mn 2.

[2] Kübler/Prütting-*Kemper* EuInsVO Art 23 mn 3.

2.2 Costs of the Insolvency Estate

The referred to costs and expenses are "regarded as costs and expenses incurred in the proceedings". This means that they are to be borne by the insolvency estate, and it also makes clear that such costs are being awarded the procedural-law status that the law governing the insolvency proceedings awards to procedural costs, which as a rule benefit from **preferential satisfaction**. **5**

Art 24
Honouring of an obligation to a debtor

1. Where an obligation has been honoured in a Member State for the benefit of a debtor who is subject to insolvency proceedings opened in another Member State, when it should have been honoured for the benefit of the liquidator in those proceedings, the person honouring the obligation shall be deemed to have discharged it if he was unaware of the opening of proceedings.

2. Where such an obligation is honoured before the publication provided for in Article 21 has been effected, the person honouring the obligation shall be presumed, in the absence of proof to the contrary, to have been unaware of the opening of insolvency proceedings; where the obligation is honoured after such publication has been effected, the person honouring the obligation shall be presumed, in the absence of proof to the contrary, to have been aware of the opening of proceedings.

Contents

Index

Bibliography

Duursma-Kepplinger/Duursma/Chalupsky Europäische Insolvenzverordnung, Kommentar (2002); Frankfurter Kommentar zum Insolvenzrecht (2005); *Haß/Huber/Gruber/Heiderhoff* EU-Insolvenzverordnung, Kommentar (2005); *Israel* European Cross-Border Insolvency Regulation (2005);

Kübler/Prütting Kommentar zur Insolvenzordnung (March 2006); Münchener Kommentar zur Insolvenzordnung, vol 3 (2003); Münchener Kommentar zum Bürgerlichen Gesetzbuch, vol 11 (2006); *Nerlich/Römermann* (eds) Insolvenzordnung (InsO), Kommentar (May 2003); *Paulus* Europäische Insolvenzverordnung, Kommentar (2006); *Smid* Deutsches und Europäisches internationales Insolvenzrecht, Kommentar (2004); *Virgós/Garcimartín* The European Insolvency Regulation: Law and Practice (2004); *Virgós/Schmit* Erläuternder Bericht zu dem EU-Übereinkommen über Insolvenzverfahren, in Stoll (ed), Vorschläge und Gutachten (1997), p 32; *Wessels* International Insolvency Law (2006).

1. Overview

1 Art 24 of the EIR is a **substantive law rule**[1] that safeguards the **good faith** of **third party debtors** (on the prerequisites for this, see mn 8 et seq).

2 Pursuant to Art 16 of the EIR, a judgement opening insolvency proceedings must be recognised **automatically** in all Member States, i.e. directly and without formalities. A prior **publication** of the opening judgement is not mandatory, but is, according to Art 21 of the EIR, at the absolute discretion of the liquidator. It is possible therefore that some of the persons concerned may in fact be unaware of the opening of proceedings and may, **in good faith**, act in a manner inconsistent with these new circumstances.[2] Debtors of the insolvent debtor (i.e. third party debtors) who have not been informed of the opening of insolvency proceedings might make payment (honour an obligation) to the debtor when they should have made such payment to the liquidator.

3 In this regard, and in keeping with Recital 30 of the EIR, Art 24 (1) of the EIR contains a **protective norm in favour of the bona fide third party debtor** who, being unaware of the opening of an insolvency proceeding, honours an obligation to an insolvent debtor and not to the liquidator.[3] In spite of the opening of insolvency proceeding and the resulting divestment of the debtor, such an obligation is deemed to have been **discharged** if the third party debtor concerned was unaware of the opening of proceedings.[4]

4 **Art 24 (1) of the EIR** is not a conflict of laws rule, but is rather a **substantive law norm** that must be applied in each Member State irrespective of national law.[5] Whether or not the national law contains a similar norm is irrelevant. But if the national insolvency

---

[1] D-K/D/Ch-*Duursma-Kepplinger-Chalupsky* Art 24 mn 2; *Wessels* International Insolvency Law (2006) mn 10791; MünchKomm BGB/*Kindler* IntInsR mn 550; Nerlich/Römermann-*Mincke* Komm InsO Art 24 mn 1; *Smid* Komm EuInsVO Art 24 mn 3; Haß/Huber/Gruber/Heiderhoff-*Gruber* Art 24 EuInsVO mn 2; MünchKomm InsO/*Reinhart* Art 24 EuInsVO mn 1; *Paulus* Komm EuInsVO Art 24 mn 1.

[2] Recital 30 of the EIR; *Virgós/Schmit* Explanatory Report mn 187; *Virgós/Garcimartín* Regulation, p 205.

[3] *Paulus* Komm EuInsVO Art 24 mn 1; D-K/D/Ch-*Duursma-Kepplinger-Chalupsky* Art 24 mn 1; *Wessels* International Insolvency Law (2006) mn 10799; Kübler/Prütting-*Kemper* EuInsVO Art 24 mn 1; MünchKomm BGB/ *Kindler* IntInsR mn 549; Nerlich/Römermann-*Mincke* Komm InsO Art 24 mn 1; *Smid* Komm EuInsVO Art 24 mn 1; Haß/Huber/Gruber/Heiderhoff-*Gruber* Art 24 EuInsVO mn 1.

[4] *Virgós/Schmit* Explanatory Report mn 187.

[5] D-K/D/Ch-*Duursma-Kepplinger-Chalupsky* Art 24 mn 2; Kübler/Prütting-*Kemper* EuIns-VO Art 24 mn 1; *Wessels* International Insolvency Law (2006) mn 10791; MünchKomm BGB/*Kindler* IntInsR mn 550; Nerlich/Römermann-*Mincke* Komm InsO Art 24 mn 1; *Smid* Komm EuInsVO Art 24 mn 3; Haß/Huber/Gruber/Heiderhoff-*Gruber* Art 24 EuInsVO mn 2; MünchKomm InsO/*Reinhart* Art 24 EuInsVO mn 1; *Paulus* Komm EuIns-VO Art 24 mn 1.

law does contain such a norm, as is the case with Sec 82 *InsO*, then this norm is superseded by Art 24 of the EIR.[6]

Through the two **legal presumptions** contained in it, **Art 24 (2) of the EIR** regulates which party has the **burden of proof** for proving the good faith of the third party debtor, see mn 15 et seq. These presumptions are intended to make the rendering of such proof easier: depending on whether the obligation is honoured before or after the publication provided for in Art 21 of the EIR, there is a presumption either of good or bad faith on the part of the third party debtor. **5**

2. Obligation-Discharging Payment to Insolvent Debtor

2.1 General

Art 24 of the EIR creates a **defence for third party debtors** towards the liquidator.[7] **6**
If, being **unaware** of the opening of insolvency proceedings, an obligation is honoured for the benefit of the debtor instead of for the liquidator, this payment is deemed to have **discharged** the obligation. The debtor's claim is extinguished and can no longer be asserted by the liquidator. However, if the third party debtor was aware of the opening of proceedings, the payment made by him is disregarded: he must honour the obligation again and this time for the benefit of the liquidator.

In the case of a payment to the debtor that discharges the obligation, the question **7**
of whether or not the liquidator has a **recourse claim against the insolvent debtor** is a matter for the respective national law.[8] If the payment made to the debtor does not discharge the obligation, then the same applies to the question of **whether** and **how** the **third party debtor can reclaim payment from the (insolvent) debtor.**

2.2 Prerequisites for an Obligation-Discharging Payment to the Debtor

2.2.1 After the opening of insolvency proceedings

Art 24 of the EIR presupposes that **insolvency proceedings have been opened.**[9] These **8**
may be **main** as well as **secondary insolvency proceedings.**[10] **Opening of proceedings** means, pursuant to Art 2 (f) of the EIR, the time at which the judgement opening proceedings becomes effective, whether it is a final judgement or not (on this, see Art 2 of the EIR mn 24 et seq). **Insolvency proceedings** are those proceedings contemplated in Art 2 (a) in connection with Annex A of the EIR (on this, see Art 2 of the EIR mn 2 et seq).

2.2.2 In another Member State

According to the wording of Art 24 (1) of the EIR, the honouring of an obligation for **9**
the benefit of the debtor can only discharge an obligation if it was made in **another**

6 MünchKomm InsO/*Reinhart* Art 24 EuInsVO mn 1.

7 Kübler/Prütting-*Kemper* EuInsVO Art 24 mn 10.

8 MünchKomm BGB/*Kindler* IntInsR mn 552; Kübler/Prütting-*Kemper* EuInsVO Art 24 mn 3; *Smid* Komm EuInsVO Art 24 mn 2.

9 MünchKomm BGB/*Kindler* IntInsR mn 552; Kübler/Prütting-*Kemper* EuInsVO Art 24 mn 3; *Smid* Komm EuInsVO Art 24 mn 2.

10 *Paulus* Komm EuInsVO Art 24 mn 3; Kübler/Prütting-*Kemper* EuInsVO Art 24 mn 1.

Member State, i.e. in one other than the one of the opening of proceedings.[11] If the obligation has been honoured in the Member State of the opening of proceedings, then the question as to whether the payment made to the debtor discharges the obligation is determined pursuant to the respective ***lex fori concursus***, in Germany pursuant to Sec 82 *Ins*O.[12] In relation to **non-EU States**, the national conflict of laws rules dealing with insolvency apply (e.g. Sec 350 *Ins*O)[13]; Art 24 of the EIR does not apply here as it explicitly refers to another *Member State*.

10 In order to decide whether an obligation was honoured in another Member State, **the place of performance** must first be **ascertained**. There is a dispute amongst legal writers as to whether the relevant place is where the third party debtor was contractually obliged to honour the obligation[14] or where he **in fact** honoured it.

11 According to the Explanatory Report, the **place of performance** means, for the purposes of Art 24 (1) of the EIR, the place where the obligation has **in fact** been honoured by the third party debtor.[15] This is the preferable approach considering that the wording of Art 24 (1) of the EIR ("Where an obligation has been honoured in a Member State for the benefit of a debtor") refers explicitly to the place where the actual honouring of the obligation was made. This is a practical way of dealing with this since the Member State in which the obligation is actually honoured is relatively easy to ascertain. Besides, it also has the advantage of circumventing the ascertainment problems arising *inter alia* from the decisions of the ECJ on Art 5 No 1 of the 1968 Brussels Convention (now Council Regulation (EC) No 44/2001).[16] In the decision **Tessili/Dunlop** of 1976, the ECJ held that the place of performance of the obligation within the meaning of Art 5 (1) of the Brussels Convention "is to be decided in accordance with the law which governs the obligation in question according to the rules of conflicts of laws of the court before which the matter is brought".[17] If the **actual place of performance** is considered decisive, then any private international law or contractually determined place of performance is irrelevant for the application of Art 24 (1) of the EIR.[18]

2.2.3 For the benefit of the debtor

12 Art 24 of the EIR requires that the third party debtor honour an obligation **for the benefit of the debtor** instead of the liquidator. Included are only claims of the insolvency estate.[19] The issue as to whether the particular obligation should have been honoured for the benefit of the liquidator is a matter for determination by the *lex fori concursus*.

---

11 *Israel* European Cross-Border Insolvency Regulation (2005) 267; Haß/Huber/Gruber/Heiderhoff-*Gruber* Art 24 EuInsVO mn 7.

12 D-K/D/Ch-*Duursma-Kepplinger-Chalupsky* Art 24 mn 8.

13 MünchKomm BGB/*Kindler* IntInsR mn 551; D-K/D/Ch-*Duursma-Kepplinger-Chalupsky* Art 24 mn 2; Haß/Huber/Gruber/Heiderhoff-*Gruber* Art 24 EuInsVO mn 8 und 9.

14 FK-InsO/*Wimmer* Anhang I nach § 358 mn 72.

15 *Virgós/Schmit* Explanatory Report Nr 188; Zustimmend: Nerlich/Römermann-*Mincke* Komm InsO Art 24 mn 4 (refering however to sec 269 BGB); *Israel* European Cross-Border Insolvency Regulation (2005) 267; *Smid* Komm EuInsVO Art 24 mn 5; Haß/Huber/Gruber/Heiderhoff-*Gruber* Art 24 EuInsVO mn 2; D-K/D/Ch-*Duursma-Kepplinger-Chalupsky* Art 24 mn 7; Kübler/Prütting-*Kemper* EuInsVO Art 24 mn 5; *Paulus* Komm EuInsVO Art 24 mn 2; MünchKomm InsO/*Reinhart* Art 24 mn 1.

16 *Israel* European Cross-Border Insolvency Regulation (2005) 267.

17 ECJ dated 16 Oct 1976 (Industrie Tessili Italiana Como ./. Dunlop AG) EC reports 1976, 1473.

18 *Israel* European Cross-Border Insolvency Regulation (2005) 267.

19 Kübler/Prütting-*Kemper* EuInsVO Art 24 mn 4.

2.2.4 Unaware of the opening of proceedings

The obligation owed by the third party debtor is discharged if he was unaware of the opening of insolvency proceedings. Only a **positive knowledge** of the opening of proceedings, and not a mere **negligent lack of knowledge** of such, will negate such a discharge, as is clearly implied by the wording of Art 24 of the EIR.[20] **13**

Art 24 (2) of the EIR contains two presumptions for determining whether or not the third party debtor who honoured the obligation was unaware of the opening of insolvency proceedings (see mn 15 et seq). **14**

3. Burden of Proof

Art 24 (2) of the EIR contains **two rebuttable presumptions**; these simplify proving knowledge of the opening of insolvency proceedings. Central to these presumptions is the **publication** pursuant to Art 21 of the EIR: depending on whether the obligation was honoured before or after the publication, there is a presumption in favour of either good or bad faith on the part of the third party debtor. **15**

These presumptions may be rebutted by the liquidator or by the third party debtor who honoured the obligation.[21] However, providing proof to the contrary will be difficult in practice. **16**

Art 24 (2) of the EIR emphasizes the significance of Art 21 of the EIR, which regulates publication of the notice of the judgement opening insolvency proceedings (see Art 21 of the EIR mn 1). Although the making of such a publication is at the absolute discretion of the liquidator (Art 21 (1) of the EIR), each Member State is entitled to make such publication mandatory (Art 21 (2) of the EIR). This optional publication can be advantageous to the liquidator, as it prevents third party debtors in other Member States from honouring obligations for the benefit of the debtor in a manner that discharges the obligation. **17**

3.1 Honouring an Obligation Before Publication Pursuant to Art 21 EIR

If the obligation is honoured for the benefit of the debtor **before** the publication provided for in Art 21 of the EIR, the person honouring the obligation is presumed, pursuant to Art 24 (2) sentence 1 EIR, in the absence of proof to the contrary, to have been **unaware** of the opening of insolvency proceedings. The honouring of the obligation for the benefit of the debtor results in the discharging of the obligation. **18**

Even if no publication has been made, the **liquidator** is still entitled to prove positive knowledge of the third party debtor.[22] This could be the case if the liquidator has distributed a **circular letter**.[23] If the liquidator can provide **evidence rebutting the presumption,** the third party debtor cannot profit from the discharge of the obligation. **19**

---

[20] D-K/D/Ch-*Duursma-Kepplinger-Chalupsky* Art 24 mn 12; Kübler/Prütting-*Kemper* EuInsVO Art 24 mn 6; *Paulus* Komm EuInsVO Art 24 mn 4; MünchKomm BGB/*Kindler* IntInsR mn 557; *Smid* Komm EuInsVO Art 24 mn 4; Haß/Huber/Gruber/Heiderhoff-*Gruber* Art 24 EuInsVO mn 3.

[21] Cf Kübler/Prütting-*Kemper* EuInsVO Art 24 mn 8 und 9.

[22] Kübler/Prütting-*Kemper* EuInsVO Art 24 mn 8; D-K/D/Ch-*Duursma-Kepplinger-Chalupsky* Art 24 mn 14.

[23] MünchKomm BGB/*Kindler* IntInsR mn 560.

3.2 Honouring an Obligation After Publication Pursuant to Art 21 of the EIR

20 If the obligation is honoured **after** the publication provided for in Art 21 of the EIR, the person honouring the obligation is presumed, pursuant to Art 24 (2) sentence 2 of the EIR, in the absence of proof to the contrary, to have been **aware** of the opening of proceedings. In such a case, the honouring of the obligation for the benefit of the debtor does not result in the discharge of the obligation. The third party debtor must honour the obligation once again and this time for the benefit of the liquidator.

21 Since Art 24 (2) sentence 2 of the EIR is a rebuttable presumption only, it is open to the **third party debtor** to provide evidence **rebutting the presumption**, i.e. to prove that he was unaware of the opening of proceedings. From a practical viewpoint, however, it is very difficult[24] to prove a "negative" fact, i.e. the absence of something.[25]

3.3 Place of Publication

22 Art 24 of the EIR does not say in which Member State the publication pursuant to Art 21 of the EIR is to take place.[26] Art 21 (1) of the EIR itself merely states that the decision may "be published in any other Member State". It is certain, however, that a publication in the Member State of the opening of proceedings will not be determinative,[27] such a publication being unable to reach foreign third party debtors. In addition, the wording of Art 21 of the EIR also demands a publication in *another* Member State.

23 The Explanatory Report holds that the publication must take place in the Member State in which the party honouring the obligation is domiciled, or in the Member State in which the party is obliged to fulfil its obligation, as the case may be.[28]

24 Legal writers have interpreted this in different ways. Some argue that the publication must take place **cumulatively** in the Member State in which the third party debtor is domiciled and in the Member State of the place of contractual performance.[29] This approach should be rejected, however: in cases where the domicile and the place of contractual performance are not the same, it would be very difficult for the liquidator to stop the making of an obligation-discharging payment by the third party debtor for the benefit of the (insolvent) debtor.

25 Other writers hold that the Member State relevant for Art 24 (2) of the EIR is the same one as in Art 24 (1) of the EIR[30] (see mn 11), i.e. the place where the third party debtor actually honours the obligation. This solution has the advantage of simplifying the determination of the place of performance, the Member State in which the obligation has actually been honoured being relatively easy to ascertain. Such an interpretation could, however, be taken advantage of by a third party debtor who, in order to profit from the presumption in Art 24 (2) sentence 1 of the EIR, deliberately honours the obligation in a Member State in which no publication took place. Because of this risk of

[24] MünchKomm BGB/*Kindler* IntInsR mn 561; D-K/D/Ch-*Duursma-Kepplinger-Chalupsky* Art 24 mn 17.

[25] Nerlich/Römermann-*Mincke* Komm InsO Art 24 mn 3; Kübler/Prütting-*Kemper* EuInsVO Art 24 mn 9.

[26] *Wessels* International Insolvency Law (2006) mn 10793.

[27] Nerlich/Römermann-*Mincke* Komm InsO Art 24 mn 5.

[28] *Virgós/Schmit* Explanatory Report Nr 187; also: D-K/D/Ch-*Duursma-Kepplinger-Chalupsky* Art 24 mn 11.

[29] *Wessels* International Insolvency Law (2006) mn 10792; MünchKomm BGB/*Kindler* IntInsR mn 556.

[30] Kübler/Prütting-*Kemper* EuInsVO Art 24 mn 7; *Israel* European Cross-Border Insolvency Regulation (2005) 268.

manipulation, the Member State relevant for Art 24 (1) of the EIR should not be used for Art 24 (2) of the EIR.

In interpreting Art 24 of the EIR, it must kept in mind that the purpose of this norm is the protection of debtors who are satisfying their obligations in good faith. In this context, the publication provided for in Art 21 of the EIR also has the function of informing third party debtors of the opening of insolvency proceedings so that they do not make payment to the insolvent debtor. For teleological reasons, the publication would have to be made in a Member State in which it could reach third party debtors who may make payments.[31] Therefore, the Member State of the third party debtor's residence/domicile or, **alternatively**, the Member State of the place of performance may be considered. However, whether the **actual**[32] or the **contractual** place of performance is decisive is still unresolved. The first solution facilitates an easier ascertainment of the place of performance, but it also entails a certain amount of risk of manipulation (see above mn 25). The third party debtor could choose a Member State in which no publication was made in order to make an obligation-discharging payment to the debtor. To avoid such manipulations, the **contractual place of performance** should be taken into account. However, in determining the place where performance is supposed to have been made, one is again confronted with the difficulties following from the decisions of the ECJ (see mn 11). According to these decisions, the place of performance is determined pursuant to the law that, according to the conflict of laws rules of the opening court, governs the obligation.[33] **26**

Best practice: In order to avoid the making of obligation-discharging payments by third party debtors to the debtor, the liquidator should request a publication of the judgement opening insolvency proceedings in as many Member States as possible. **27**

Article 25
Recognition and enforceability of other judgments

1. Judgments handed down by a court whose judgment concerning the opening of proceedings is recognised in accordance with Article 16 and which concern the course and closure of insolvency proceedings, and compositions approved by that court shall also be recognised with no further formalities. Such judgments shall be enforced in accordance with Articles 31 to 51, with the exception of Article 34(2), of the Brussels Convention on Jurisdiction and the Enforcement of Judgments in Civil and Commercial Matters, as amended by the Conventions of Accession to this Convention.

The first subparagraph shall also apply to judgments deriving directly from the insolvency proceedings and which are closely linked with them, even if they were handed down by another court.

The first subparagraph shall also apply to judgments relating to preservation measures taken after the request for the opening of insolvency proceedings.

---

[31] Also: Kübler/Prütting-*Kemper* EuInsVO Art 24 mn 7, but with different result.

[32] Nerlich/Römermann-*Mincke* Komm InsO Art 24 mn 5; Moss/Fletcher/Isaacs-*Moss/Smith*, Regulation, mn 8.194; Haß/Huber/Gruber/Heiderhoff-*Gruber* Art 24 EuInsVO mn 6.

[33] ECJ dated 6 Oct 1976 (Industrie Tessili Como ./. Dunlop AG) 12/76, EC reports 1976, 1473.

2. The recognition and enforcement of judgments other than those referred to in paragraph 1 shall be governed by the Convention referred to in paragraph 1, provided that that Convention is applicable.

3. The Member States shall not be obliged to recognise or enforce a judgment referred to in paragraph 1 which might result in a limitation of personal freedom or postal secrecy.

→ Cf Art 21 (1) (a), Art 20 (1) (a) UNCITRAL Model Law

Contents

Index

Bibliography

Balz Das neue Europäische Insolvenzübereinkommen, ZIP 1996, p 948; *Bork* (ed) Handbuch des Insolvenzanfechtungsrechts (2006); *Carstens* Die Internationale Zuständigkeit im europäischen Insolvenzrecht (2005); *Duursma-Kepplinger/Duursma/Chalupsky* Europäische Insolvenzverordnung, Kommentar (2002); *Haß/Huber/Gruber/Heiderhoff* EU-Insolvenzverordnung, Kommentar (2005); *Haubold* Europäisches Zivilverfahrensrecht und Ansprüche im Zusammenhang mit Insolvenzverfahren, IPRax 2002, p 157; *Hinkel/Flitsch* Comments on OLG Frankfurt dated 26.1.2006 – 15 U 200/05, EWiR 2006, p 237; *Homann* System der Anerkennung eines ausländischen Insolvenzverfahrens, KTS 2000, 343; *Israel* European Cross-Border Insolvency Regulation (2005); *Kübler/Prütting* Kommentar zur Insolvenzordnung (March 2006); *Leipold* Zuständigkeitslücken im neuen

Europäischen Insolvenzrecht, in Lüke/Mikami/Prütting (eds), FS Ishikawa (2001), p 221; *Moss/Fletcher/Isaacs* (eds) The EC Regulation on Insolvency Proceedings (2002); Münchener Kommentar zum Bürgerlichen Gesetzbuch, vol 11 (2006); Münchener Kommentar zur Insolvenzordnung, vol 2 (2003); Münchener Kommentar zur Insolvenzordnung, vol 3 (2003); *Nerlich/Römermann* Insolvenzordnung (InsO), Kommentar (April 2006); *Paulus* Europäische Insolvenzverordnung, Kommentar (2006); *Paulus* Die Europäische Insolvenzverordnung und der deutsche Insolvenzverwalter, NZI 2001, p 505; *Paulus* Anfechtungsklagen in grenzüberschreitenden Insolvenzverfahren, ZInsO 2006, 295; *Runkel* (ed) Anwaltshandbuch – Insolvenzrecht (2005); *Smid* Deutsches und Europäisches internationales Insolvenzrecht, Kommentar (2004); *Virgós/Garcimartín* The European Insolvency Regulation: Law and Practice (2004); *Virgós/Schmit* Erläuternder Bericht zu dem EU-Übereinkommen über Insolvenzverfahren, in Stoll (ed), Vorschläge und Gutachten (1997), p 32; *Von Boehmer* (Deutsches) Internationales Insolvenzrecht im Umbruch: Grundfragen grenzüberschreitender Insolvenzen, unter Berücksichtigung der UNCITRAL-Modellbestimmungen über grenzüberschreitende Insolvenzverfahren (2006); *Wessels* International Insolvency Law (2006).

1. Overview

Art 25 of the EIR applies to both **main and territorial proceedings.**[1] It regulates the **recognition of other judgements**, i.e. judgements other than the **judgement opening proceedings.**[2] These include judgements concerning the course and closure of insolvency proceedings, the so-called insolvency-related judgements, and judgements on preservation measures.[3] Art 25 of the EIR supplements Arts 16 and 17 of the EIR, which separately regulate the recognition of the **judgement opening proceedings** because of its importance to the entire insolvency proceedings.[4] 1

Art 25 of the EIR also uniformly regulates the **enforceability** of all judgements that are governed by the EIR. The heading of Art 25 of the EIR – "Recognition and enforceability of other judgements" – is therefore misleading. The provisions of Art 25 of the EIR dealing with 2

- **recognition** apply to **other judgements** only,
- but those dealing with **enforceability** also apply to **judgements opening proceedings**, contrary to the heading of Art 25 of the EIR, see mn 39.

Art 25 of the EIR **aims** to provided for a conflict-free and **gapless coordination** of the EIR and Council Regulation (EC) No 44/2001[5] by ensuring that every possible judgement is governed by one of these European regulations.[6] For this reason, Art 25 (2) of the EIR subjects those judgements that are not specifically provided for in the EIR to Council Regulation (EC) No 44/2001, provided that this Regulation applies. 3

---

1 Kübler/Prütting-*Kemper* EuInsVO Art 25 mn 2.

2 *Virgós/Garcimartín* Regulation, p 205; Kübler/Prütting-*Kemper* EuInsVO Art 25 mn 1; MünchKomm BGB/*Kindler* IntInsR mn 562.

3 *Wessels* International Insolvency Law (2006) mn 10794.

4 Kübler/Prütting-*Kemper* EuInsVO Art 25 mn 1.

5 *Virgós/Schmit* Explanatory report mn 197; D-K/D/Ch-*Duursma-Kepplinger* Art 25 mn 50; Moss/Fletcher/Isaacs-*Moss/Smith*, Regulation, mn 8.197; *Virgós/Garcimartín* Regulation, p 208; *Leible/Staudinger* KTS 2000, 531, 566; *Wessels* International Insolvency Law (2006) mn 10809; *Paulus* Komm EuInsVO Art 25 mn 2; MünchKomm BGB/*Kindler* IntInsR mn 590.

6 MünchKomm BGB/*Kindler* IntInsR mn 590.

2. Types of Judgements Pursuant to the EIR

4 There are five types of judgements in the EIR.[7] The criterion for assuming jurisdiction and the basis of recognition differs for each type of judgement. By contrast, enforceability is uniformly regulated in Art 25 (1) of the EIR subpara 1 sentence 2, subpara 2 and subpara 3, and in Art 25 (2) of the EIR. The following chart summarizes the types of judgements that can be rendered pursuant to insolvency proceedings.

5

Type of Judgement	Jurisdiction	Basis of Recognition
Judgements opening proceedings	Art 3 of the EIR	Art 16 of the EIR
Judgements concerning insolvency proceedings	Art 3 of the EIR	Art 25 (1) sentence 1 of subpara 1 of the EIR
Insolvency-related judgements	Art 3 of the EIR (by analogy)	Art 25 (1) subpara 2 of the EIR
Preservation measures	Art 3 of the EIR	Art 25 (1) subpara 3 of the EIR
Other judgements	Varies	Art 25 (2) of the EIR: Council Regulation (EC) No 44/2001

6 The structure of Art 25 of the EIR reflects the decisions of the ECJ on the 1968 Brussels Convention (now Council Regulation (EC) No 44/2001).[8] Because several decisions had restricted the scope of applicability of the 1968 Brussels Convention, it became necessary to clarify this issue in the EIR. The definitions of the individual **categories of judgements** are virtually taken word for word from the headnotes of the judgements of the ECJ, see mn 18, 28.

3. Recognition

3.1 Judgements Concerning Insolvency Proceedings

3.1.1 Judgements concerned

7 According to Art 25 (1) sentence 1 of subpara 1 of the EIR, **judgements concerning the course and closure of insolvency proceedings** rendered by a court whose opening judgement is recognised in accordance with Art 16 of the EIR, as well as **compositions** approved by such a court, must be recognized without any further formalities.

[7] *Wessels* International Insolvency Law (2006) mn 10540.

[8] *Israel* European Cross-Border Insolvency Regulation (2005) 268; see:
- ECJ (Gourdain ./. Nadler) EC reports 1979, 733 = RIW 1979, 273, 274 et seq;
- ECJ dated 27 Mar 1979 143/78, De Cavel/ De Cavel, EC reports 1979, 1055.

The terms **"judgement"** and **"court"** are legally defined in Art 2 (d) and (e) of the EIR and are to be construed broadly. The term "court" in particular must be understood in a functional sense.[9] **8**

According to Art 25 (1) sentence 1 of subpara 1 of the EIR, judgements concerning insolvency proceedings must be rendered by the court whose judgement to open proceedings is recognized in accordance with Art 16 of the EIR. **9**

Judgements concerning the course of insolvency proceedings are those rendered by the court during the course of proceedings for the purpose of conducting hearings/negotiations, for structuring a phase of the proceedings, or for fostering the progression of the proceedings,[10] e.g. the **appointment** or **dismissal of the liquidator** or the **imposing of certain disposal restrictions** on the debtor.[11] **Judgements concerning the closure of insolvency proceedings** are those that formally end insolvency proceedings in their entirety or individual parts of proceedings,[12] e.g. in Germany the setting aside of the insolvency proceedings pursuant to Sec 200 *InsO* or the staying of the proceedings pursuant to Sec 207 (lack of assets), Sec 212 (reason for opening proceedings has ceased), or Sec 213 (with the consent of the creditors) *InsO*.[13] **10**

Also covered by Art 25 (1) sentence 1 of subpara 1 of the EIR are **compositions** approved by a court whose judgement to open proceedings is recognized in accordance with Art 16 of the EIR.[14] This is only one **example** of a judgement to end insolvency proceedings.[15] Also covered are **insolvency plans**[16] or **other mutually agreed ways of ending proceedings** pursuant to the respective *lex fori concursus*, to name a few.[17] What is required, however, is the **court approval of the composition**; a "company voluntary arrangement" under English law, which is valid without a court order, would not fall within this.[18] **11**

Judgements opening proceedings do not, on the other hand, constitute judgements concerning insolvency proceedings, the recognition of such proceedings already being comprehensively provided for by Art 16 of the EIR.[19] A classification of judgements opening insolvency proceedings as judgements concerning insolvency proceedings within the meaning of Art 25 (1) sentence 1 of subpara 1 of the EIR would lead to a double regulation of the recognition of judgements opening proceedings. The wording of Art 25 (1) sentence 1 of subpara 1 of the EIR – "whose judgment concerning the opening of proceedings is recognised in accordance with Art 16" – is a further indication that the judgements concerning insolvency proceedings are different from judgements opening such proceedings. **12**

---

[9] D-K/D/Ch-*Duursma-Kepplinger* Art 25 mn 7; MünchKomm BGB/*Kindler* IntInsR mn 562.

[10] Kübler/Prütting-*Kemper* EuInsVO Art 25 mn 3.

[11] *Homann* KTS 2000, 343, 345.

[12] Kübler/Prütting-*Kemper* EuInsVO Art 25 mn 3.

[13] Nerlich/Römermann-*Mincke* Komm InsO Art 25 EuInsVO mn 1.

[14] *Virgós/Schmit* Explanatory report mn 191; *Virgós/Garcimartín* Regulation, p 206.

[15] Kübler/Prütting-*Kemper* EuInsVO Art 25 mn 3.

[16] *Pannen* in Runkel (ed), AHB-Insolvenzrecht (2005) § 16 mn 279.

[17] Kübler/Prütting-*Kemper* EuInsVO Art 25 mn 3; MünchKomm BGB/*Kindler* IntInsR mn 563; Nerlich/Römermann-*Mincke* Komm InsO Art 25 EuInsVO mn 1; *Leible/Staudinger* KTS 2000, 531, 566.

[18] MünchKomm InsO/*Reinhart* Art 25 EuInsVO mn 3.

[19] Kübler/Prütting-*Kemper* EuInsVO Art 25 mn 1 et seq.

3.1.2 Automatic recognition

13 According to the wording of Art 25 (1) sentence 1 of subpara 1 of the EIR, judgements concerning insolvency proceedings are to be recognized without any *further* formalities. This could be interpreted to mean that there are at least a minimum of formalities. The word "also" is a reference, however, to the provisions on recognition of the opening judgement (Art 16 et seq of the EIR), for which **automatic recognition** takes place (see Art 16 of the of the EIR mn 2). Just like the opening judgement, judgements concerning the insolvency proceedings will therefore be automatically recognized; hence there is **no recognition procedure.**[20] Both a review of the judgement by the recognizing State and a review on the merits are inadmissible. A **public notification** of opened insolvency proceedings (Art 21 of the EIR) **is not a prerequisite** to recognition.[21]

3.2 Insolvency-related Proceedings

14 According to Art 25 (1) sentence 1 of subpara 2 of the EIR, subpara 1 (see mn 7 et seq) also applies to judgements **deriving directly from the insolvency proceedings and which are closely linked** with them, even if these judgements were rendered by **another court** (so-called **insolvency-related proceedings**). As in the case of judgements opening proceedings and judgements concerning insolvency proceedings, these insolvency-related proceedings must be automatically recognised as soon as the respective judgement becomes effective.

15 Insolvency-related judgements could arguably be subsumed under Art 25 (1) sentence 1 of subpara 1 of the EIR, since they are also being made, to an extent, in the course of insolvency proceedings. In contrast to Art 25 (1) sentence 1 of subpara 1 of the EIR, Art 25 (1) subpara 2 of the EIR expressly stipulates that the insolvency-related judgement may also be handed down by another court. "Another court" is to be understood as a court other than the court with jurisdiction pursuant to Art 3 of the EIR.[22] Art 25 (1) subpara 2 of the EIR thus has a broader sphere of application than the first subparagraph.

16 The question as to which proceedings fall within this must be decided on an individual basis pursuant to the criterion "**closely linked**" in Art 25 (1) subpara 2 of the EIR.[23]

17 Legal academics have described this provision as puzzling[24] due to its failure to regulate two important issues. These are:

- the judgements that are to be classified as insolvency-related proceedings (see mn 18 et seq), and
- the court that has international jurisdiction for these (on this, see Art 3 of the EIR mn 96 et seq).

3.2.1 Judgements concerned

18 The reason for the express regulation of insolvency-related proceedings in Art 25 (1) subpara 2 of the EIR is, as mentioned briefly above, the judgement of the ECJ in

[20] *Virgós/Schmit* Explanatory report mn 191; D-K/D/Ch-*Duursma-Kepplinger* Art 25 mn 15; MünchKomm BGB/*Kindler* IntInsR mn 564; Nerlich/Römermann-*Mincke* Komm InsO Art 25 EuInsVO mn 1; *Virgós/Garcimartín* Regulation, p 205.

[21] Kübler/Prütting-*Kemper* EuInsVO Art 25 mn 5.

[22] *Virgós/Garcimartín* Regulation, p 208.

[23] Kübler/Prütting-*Kemper* EuInsVO Art 25 mn 7.

[24] For example: *Leipold* in FS Ishikawa, p 224; D-K/D/Ch-*Duursma-Kepplinger* Art 25 mn 21.

Gourdain vs Nadler in 1979.[25] In this judgement, the ECJ interpreted Art 1 (2) (b) of the 1968 Brussels Convention (which laid down the scope of applicability of the Convention – now Art 1 (2) (b) of Council Regulation (EC) No 44/2001) as also excluding judgements related to insolvency proceedings from the application of the Convention if they derive directly from these proceedings and if they remain within the close bounds of the bankruptcy or composition proceedings. The rulings of these judgements are now expressly found in the EIR.

What remains problematic is distinguishing between the sphere of applicability of Council Regulation (EC) No 44/2001 and that of the EIR. In principle, all judgements on claims that could be asserted even without insolvency proceedings should be governed by Council Regulation (EC) No 44/2001, and all judgements that in any way whatsoever presuppose insolvency proceedings should be governed by the EIR.[26] The Gourdain vs Nadler decision of the ECJ also provides **three criteria** for **classifying insolvency-related proceedings:**[27] **19**

- the exclusive jurisdiction of the insolvency court;
- the liquidator's standing to sue on the claim;
- the allocation of the proceeds of the lawsuit to the creditors as a whole.

But whether a judgement is to be considered an insolvency-related proceeding can only be decided in the **individual case.**[28]

Examples of insolvency-related proceedings are: **20**

- **actions to avoid (avoidance actions)**[29] acts detrimental to the creditors as a whole,
- bankruptcy-law related lawsuits seeking to impose **personal liability on the managing director**[30] (e.g. the French *action en comblement du passif*[31]),
- lawsuits concerning the **priority of a claim,**
- disputes between the liquidator and the debtor concerning the **inclusion of an asset in the insolvency estate,**
- an action for **(official) recognition of a claim in the schedule of creditors' claims,**
- the **approval of an insolvency plan** (Sec 248 *Ins*O),[32]
- a judgement concerning a **discharge of residual debt** (Sec 300 *Ins*O),[33]
- the **approval of a debt adjustment plan** (Sec 308 *Ins*O), and
- **actions involving the liquidator's liability** for damages, the direct and sole reason for these being the carrying out of the insolvency proceedings.[34]

---

25 *Virgós/Schmit* Explanatory report mn 195; ECJ (Gourdain ./. Nadler) EC reports 1979, 733 = RIW 1979, 273, 274 et seq.

26 Nerlich/Römermann-*Mincke* Komm InsO Art 25 EuInsVO mn 4.

27 Kübler/Prütting-*Kemper* EuInsVO Art 25 mn 6.

28 Kübler/Prütting-*Kemper* EuInsVO Art 25 mn 7.

29 D-K/D/Ch-*Duursma-Kepplinger* Art 25 mn 54; *Haubold* IPRax 2002, 157, 163; also: *Paulus* NZI 2001, 505, 512; *Paulus* Komm EuInsVO Art 25 mn 8; Kübler/Prütting-*Kemper* EuInsVO Art 3 mn 10; *Carstens* Die internationale Zuständigkeit im europäischen Insolvenzrecht p 110; Nerlich/Römermann-*Mincke* Komm InsO Art 25 EuInsVO mn 5.

30 *Paulus* Komm EuInsVO Art 25 mn 8; differencing: MünchKomm BGB/*Kindler* IntInsR mn 579.

31 Cf ECJ "(Gourdain ./. Nadler)" EC reports 1979, 733 = RIW 1979, 273, 274 et seq.

32 *Paulus* Komm EuInsVO Art 25 mn 5.

33 *Paulus* Komm EuInsVO Art 25 mn 8.

34 Cf *Virgós/Schmit* Explanatory report mn 196; *Paulus* Komm EuInsVO Art 25 mn 5; MünchKomm InsO/*Reinhart* Art 25

21 Examples of proceedings that are **not insolvency-related:**

- **criminal prosecutions** that can be pursued in conjunction with insolvency proceedings,[35] e.g. insolvency (criminal) offences pursuant to Sec 283 et seq *StGB* (German Criminal Code), because such offences are not being pursued directly because of the insolvency proceedings;
- actions to **recover property** in the possession of the debtor,[36]
- actions to determine the **legal validity or the amount of a claim** pursuant to general laws.[37]

22 **The concept of "insolvency-related proceedings"** must be construed **strictly.**[38]

3.2.2 International jurisdiction for insolvency-related proceedings

23 The EIR does not regulate the **international jurisdiction** for insolvency-related proceedings. In order to avoid **conflicts of jurisdictions** and contradictory assessments, it seems appropriate to determine the **international jurisdiction for insolvency-related proceedings analogous** to that of the opening of proceedings,[39] since what is involved here is an unintended regulatory gap (for a detailed discussion on this, see Art 3 of the EIR mn 110 et seq).

24 The scope of application of Art 3 of the EIR would thus cover both:

- determining international jurisdiction for the opening of proceedings, and
- (by way of analogous application) determining jurisdiction for insolvency-related proceedings, the so-called ***vis attractiva concursus* under European law.**[40]

An invocation of the corresponding provisions of Council Regulation (EC) No 44/2001[41] and the application of national provisions concerning jurisdiction, which have been discussed in the legal literature as a way to solve the issue of international jurisdiction for insolvency-related proceedings, should be rejected (see Art 3 of the EIR mn 100, 109).

3.3 Preservation Measures

25 According to Art 25 (1) subpara 3 of the EIR, Art 25 (1) subpara 1 of the EIR also applies to the recognition and the enforceability of **preservation measures taken after the request to open** insolvency proceedings but **prior to the opening of proceedings.**[42] Preservation measures ordered after the opening of insolvency proceedings constitute

---

EuInsVO mn 5; Nerlich/Römermann-*Mincke* Komm InsO Art 25 EuInsVO mn 5.

[35] *Virgós/Garcimartín* Regulation, p 206.

[36] MünchKomm BGB/*Kindler* IntInsR mn 579.

[37] MünchKomm BGB/*Kindler* IntInsR mn 579; *Paulus* Komm EuInsVO Art 25 mn 8.

[38] D-K/D/Ch-*Duursma-Kepplinger* Art 25 mn 51.

[39] Also: *Paulus* Komm EuInsVO Art 25 mn 21; *Carstens* Die internationale Zuständigkeit im europäischen Insolvenzrecht p 110.

[40] Cf Haß/Huber/Gruber/Heiderhoff-*Haß/Herweg* Art 3 EuInsVO mn 23; Kübler/Prütting-*Kemper* EuInsVO Art 3 mn 11; *Paulus* ZInsO 2006, 295, 298; *Paulus* Komm EuInsVO Art 25 mn 21; *Carstens* Die internationale Zuständigkeit im europäischen Insolvenzrecht p 110; *Hinkel/Flitsch* EWiR 2006, 237 et seq; contra: OLG Frankfurt ZIP 2006, 769, 771.

[41] D-K/D/Ch-*Duursma-Kepplinger* Art 25 mn 35; *Smid* Komm EuInsVO Art 25 mn 10; Haß/Huber/Gruber/Heiderhoff-*Gruber* Art 25 EuInsVO mn 25 und 26; *Adolphsen* in Bork (ed), Handbuch des Insolvenzanfechtungsrechts p 661.

[42] *Virgós/Garcimartín* Regulation, p 208; MünchKomm BGB/*Kindler* IntInsR mn 585.

judgements concerning insolvency proceedings within the meaning of Art 25 (1) sentence 1 of subpara 1 of the EIR.[43] This is to ensure that all preservation measures necessary for safeguarding the future effectiveness of the particular proceedings fall within the scope of application of the EIR commencing at the point in time of the request to open insolvency proceedings.[44] Like judgements concerning the insolvency proceedings, these preservation measures are being automatically recognised and enforced pursuant to the provisions of Council Regulation (EC) No 44/2001.

The EIR makes no provision, however, for **preservation measures taken prior to the making of the request for insolvency proceedings** (so-called *ante causam* preservation measures).[45] One way of closing this regulatory gap would be to have the EIR govern insolvency-related preservation measures and Council Regulation (EC) No 44/2001 govern other preservation measures; but in no instance should national regulations be invoked.[46] **26**

Art 25 (1) subpara 3 of the EIR concerns preservation measures taken exclusively in anticipation of **main insolvency proceedings,** as such measures ultimately produce cross-border effects.[47] No cross-border preservation measures can be ordered prior to the opening of secondary insolvency proceedings (although local ones can be, see Art 18 of the EIR mn 31 et seq), because the sole exception to the territorial restriction of secondary insolvency proceedings (Art 18 (2) sentence 1 of the EIR) may only be effected after proceedings have been opened. **27**

The reason for this rule stems from the decision of the ECJ of 27 March 1979 (De Cavel vs De Cavel).[48] In this decision, the court ruled that judicial decisions on provisional preservation measures that are ordered in the course of a divorce proceeding do not fall within the scope of application of the 1968 Brussels Convention, because it is not the legal nature of such measures themselves that determines whether or not they fall within the scope of the Convention but rather the nature of the claims being secured by them.[49] Preservation measures ordered prior to the opening of insolvency proceedings for the purposes of ensuring the effectiveness thereof are thus excluded from the scope of applicability of the 1968 Brussels Convention (now Council Regulation (EC) No 44/2001), because Council Regulation (EC) No 44/2001 expressly excludes insolvency proceedings from the scope of its application (Art 1 (2) (b) of Council Regulation (EC) No 44/2001).[50] In light of the practical significance of preservation measures to insolvency proceedings, the drafters of the EIR considered it logical to expressly include such measures within the scope of the EIR's applicability.[51] **28**

Art 25 (1) subpara 3 of the EIR contains no provision regarding the **international jurisdiction** to order such preservation measures; it merely stipulates that preservation measures ordered by the competent court commencing with the request to open insolvency proceedings must be automatically recognized.[52] **29**

Preservation measures may be ordered by the court with jurisdiction pursuant to **Art 3 (1) of the EIR** irrespective of the Member State in which the assets or the persons concerned (debtor or creditor) are situated.[53] **30**

---

[43] *Virgós/Garcimartín* Regulation, p 208.
[44] *Virgós/Schmit* Explanatory report mn 198.
[45] *Virgós/Garcimartín* Regulation, p 208.
[46] *Virgós/Garcimartín* Regulation, p 209.
[47] *Virgós/Garcimartín* Regulation, p 208.
[48] ECJ dated 27 Mar 1979 143/78, De Cavel/De Cavel, EC reports 1979, 1055.
[49] ECJ dated 27 Mar 1979 143/78, De Cavel/De Cavel, EC reports 1979, 1055 No 8.
[50] *Virgós/Schmit* Explanatory report mn 199.
[51] *Virgós/Schmit* Explanatory report mn 199.
[52] D-K/D/Ch-*Duursma-Kepplinger* Art 25 mn 57.
[53] *Virgós/Schmit* Explanatory report mn 78.

31 In dispute is whether Art 25 (1) subpara 3 of the EIR also applies with respect to the **powers of the provisional liquidator.**[54] However such an approach runs contrary to the unequivocal wording of Art 25 (1) subpara 3 of the EIR, which refers exclusively to judicial decisions.[55] The wording of Recital 16 of the EIR also speaks against such an approach: it states that the court with jurisdiction for the main insolvency proceedings is supposed to be able to order provisional and protective measures.[56] According to Recital 16 of the EIR, the **provisional liquidator** is only supposed to be able, in another Member State in which an establishment belonging to the debtor is found, to **apply for** preservation measures that are possible under the laws of such State.

32 The most recent decision of the **ECJ** may, however, have modified the scope of application of Art 25 (1) subpara 3 of the EIR. This provision was originally enacted to deal with the case where preservation measures had been ordered after the request for insolvency but prior to the opening of the insolvency proceedings. In its **Eurofood/Parmalat** decision (→ cf Table of Cases Art 3 of the EIR Appendix A mn 10), the ECJ ruled that:

- a decision of a **court of a Member State**
- that is made pursuant to a **request to open a proceeding listed in Annex A of the EIR**, such request being based on the insolvency of the debtor,
- constitutes a **judgement to open insolvency proceedings** within the meaning of this provision
- if it leads to the **divestment** of the debtor and
- pursuant to which a **liquidator listed** in Annex C of the EIR is appointed.

Preliminary insolvency proceedings can therefore be regarded as the opening of proceedings within the meaning of the EIR (see Art 3 of the EIR mn 91 et seq). Preservation measures ordered by such a provisional liquidator can no longer be subsumed under Art 25 (1) subpara 3 of the EIR but are rather judgements concerning insolvency proceedings within the meaning of Art 25 (1) sentence 1 of subpara 1 of the EIR. By this, the scope of application of Art 25 (1) subpara 3 of the EIR is being restricted.

33 Depending on which law applies, the nature of preservation measures may vary considerably.[57] Examples of these are:

- interim judgements containing orders to perform or refrain from certain acts,
- appointing a provisional liquidator, or
- seizures/attachments of assets.[58]

34 An example of a preservation measure with extra-territorial consequences effective throughout the Community is the ordering of a **provisional restraint on disposition** – which deprives the debtor of the power to dispose of his assets – by the court with jurisdiction pursuant to Art 3 (1) of the EIR pursuant to a request to open insolvency proceedings and upon submission of satisfactory proof of an attempt to fraudulently conceal assets.[59]

---

[54] See also for instance: *Paulus* NZI 2001, 505, 510; *Paulus* Komm EuInsVO Art 25 mn 10; contra: MünchKomm BGB/*Kindler* IntInsR mn 587.

[55] MünchKomm BGB/*Kindler* IntInsR mn 587; Nerlich/Römermann-*Mincke* Komm InsO Art 25 EuInsVO mn 17.

[56] Nerlich/Römermann-*Mincke* Komm InsO Art 25 EuInsVO mn 17.

[57] *Virgós/Schmit* Explanatory report mn 78; Nerlich/Römermann-*Mincke* Komm InsO Art 25 EuInsVO mn 19.

[58] *Virgós/Schmit* Explanatory report mn 78.

[59] *Virgós/Schmit* Explanatory report mn 200.

Should the enforcement of a preservation measure be requested in a Member State whose laws do not contemplate such measure, such measure must be adapted to the law of the enforcing State.[60] 35

4. Enforcement

4.1 General

Enforcement means "compulsory execution" and implies the exercising of a state's coercive powers for ensuring compliance.[61] For reasons of state sovereignty, a Member State may **not** exercise its public authority in the form of an enforcement in the sovereign territory of another Member State; the exercising of coercive acts is reserved to the local authorities of the State in which the enforcement is to be carried out.[62] Thus, in order to enforce judgements in other Member States made pursuant to insolvency proceedings, an approval must be obtained; this is done by way of a so-called **exequatur procedure.**[63] 36

Enforcement is not dealt with directly in the EIR. Art 25 (1) sentence 2 of subpara 1 of the EIR refers here to **Arts 31 to 51 (with the exception of Art 34 (2)) of the 1968 Brussels Convention**, which was replaced by Council Regulation (EC) No 44/2001 on 1 March 2002.[64] **Arts 38 to 52 of Council Regulation (EC) No 44/2001** now apply (Art 68 (2) of Council Regulation (EC) No 44/2001) in lieu of the provisions stated in the EIR.[65] It is debatable whether the exception of Art 34 (2) of the 1968 Brussels Convention (grounds for refusing recognition and enforcement) has been replaced by an exception of the corresponding provision, Art 41, of Council Regulation (EC) No 44/2001. In contrast to the 1968 Brussels Convention, Art 41 of Council Regulation (EC) No 44/2001 provides that there is no longer a right to refuse enforcement. In particular, no review pursuant to Arts 34 and 35 of Council Regulation (EC) No 44/2001 takes place, which means that the exception of Art 34 (2) of the 1968 Brussels Convention in Art 25 (1) sentence 2 of subpara 1 of the EIR has been rendered invalid[66] due to the fact that Council Regulation (EC) No 44/2001 no longer contemplates any grounds for refusing enforcement. Not to be overlooked, however, is that according to Art 45 (1) of Council Regulation (EC) No 44/2001, the declaration of enforceability may be refused or revoked in an appeal procedure for one of the reasons specified in Arts 34 and 35 of Council Regulation (EC) No 44/2001. For teleological reasons, the exception of Art 34 (2) of the 1968 Brussels Convention must now apply to Art 45 (1) of Council Regulation (EC) No 44/2001 in order to ensure that Arts 25 (3) and Art 26 of the EIR remain the sole 37

---

[60] Nerlich/Römermann-*Mincke* Komm InsO Art 25 EuInsVO mn 19.

[61] *Virgós/Schmit* Explanatory report mn 190.

[62] *Virgós/Schmit* Explanatory report mn 190.

[63] *Virgós/Schmit* Explanatory report mn 190.

[64] Council Regulation (EC) No 44/2001 of 22 December 2000 on jurisdiction and the recognition and enforcement of judgments in civil and commercial matters, OJ L 12 pp 0001–0023.

[65] Prevailing opinion: D-K/D/Ch-*Duursma-Kepplinger* Art 25 mn 6; MünchKomm BGB/*Kindler* IntInsR mn 562; *Paulus* Komm EuInsVO Art 25 mn 13; *Smid* Komm EuInsVO Art 25 mn 2; Moss/Fletcher/Isaacs-*Moss/Smith*, Regulation, mn 8.198; Nerlich/Römermann-*Mincke* Komm InsO Art 25 EuInsVO mn 9; Haß/Huber/Gruber/Heiderhoff-*Gruber* Art 25 EuInsVO mn 3; contra: MünchKomm InsO/*Reinhart* Art 25 EuInsVO mn 6, who approves the applicability of Arts 31 to 51 of the Council Regulation (EC) No 44/2001.

[66] Also Nerlich/Römermann-*Mincke* Komm InsO Art 25 EuInsVO mn 11; *Paulus* Komm EuInsVO Art 25 mn 13.

grounds for refusing enforcement.[67] This is because the EIR has its own mechanism for refusing the recognition or enforcement of judgements,[68] which is much narrower than Council Regulation (EC) No 44/2001.

4.2 Judgements Concerned

38 Art 25 (1) sentence 2 of subpara 1 of the EIR regulates the **enforcement** of all judgements that are subject to the EIR (thus **including the judgement opening insolvency proceedings**).[69] Unlike recognition, the enforcement of judgements is **uniformly regulated**. The wording of this provision is, however, not completely clear: "such judgements" in sentence 2 apparently refers to the judgements listed in sentence 1, i.e. judgements concerning the course and closure of insolvency proceedings as well as court-approved compositions. This certainly does not include judgements opening insolvency proceedings, which for systematic reasons are not judgements concerning insolvency proceedings. Even the heading of Art 25 of the EIR itself – "Recognition and enforceability of other judgements" – excludes *a priori* judgements opening insolvency proceedings.

39 Prevailing opinion nevertheless holds that, with respect to all of the legal consequences going beyond the opening itself, **judgements opening insolvency proceedings** are also to be enforced in accordance with Art 25 (1) sentence 2 of subpara 1 of the EIR.[70] In Germany, Art 102 Sec 8 of the *EGInsO* also presumes the applicability of Art 25 (1) sentence 2 of subpara 1 of the EIR if the judgement opening insolvency proceedings must be enforced by way of compulsory execution (on this, see Art 102 Sec 8 *EGInsO* mn 1). Such is the case when the *lex fori concursus* empowers the liquidator to demand the surrender of property in the custody of the debtor, or if the liquidator wishes to liquidate property belonging to the insolvency estate.

40 A minority opinion holds that it is not necessary to enforce the judgement opening insolvency proceedings because – due to its nature – it does not contain any enforceable elements.[71] However the judgement opening proceedings may indeed do more than merely modify a legal right/status. In German law, Sec 148 (2) sentence 1 *InsO* holds that the judgement opening proceedings is a judicially enforceable instrument pursuant to which the liquidator may demand the surrender of property in the custody of the debtor by way of compulsory execution.[72]

---

[67] See *Virgós/Garcimartín* Regulation, p 209; Nerlich/Römermann-*Mincke* Komm InsO Art 25 EuInsVO mn 15; *Paulus* Komm EuInsVO Art 25 mn 13; dissenting opinion: Moss/Fletcher/Isaacs-*Moss/Smith*, Regulation, mn 8.198 and *Wessels* International Insolvency Law (2006) mn 10796 who advocate an exception of Art 45 (2) of Council Regulation (EC) No 44/2001 (prohibition on reviewing substance of the matter), because the corresponding provision was contained in Art 34 (3) and not in Art 34 (2) of the 1968 Brussels Convention.

[68] *Virgós/Garcimartín* Regulation, p 211.

[69] MünchKomm BGB/*Kindler* IntInsR mn 565.

[70] *Virgós/Schmit* Explanatory report mn 189; *Virgós/Garcimartín* Regulation, p 209; D-K/D/Ch-*Duursma-Kepplinger* Art 25 mn 4 und 5; *Smid* Komm EuInsVO Art 25 mn 1; *Balz* ZIP 1996, 948, 953; MünchKomm BGB/*Kindler* IntInsR mn 565; Kübler/Prütting-*Kemper* EuInsVO Art 3 mn 14; *von Boehmer* (Deutsches) Internationales Insolvenzrecht im Umbruch: Grundfragen grenzüberschreitender Insolvenzen, unter Berücksichtigung der UNCITRAL-Modellbestimmungen über grenzüberschreitende Insolvenzverfahren (2006), 87; *Virgós/Garcimartín* Regulation, p 209; *Wessels* International Insolvency Law (2006) mn 10807.

[71] MünchKomm InsO/*Reinhart* Art 25 EuInsVO mn 1; Haß/Huber/Gruber/Heiderhoff-*Gruber* Art 25 EuInsVO mn 1.

[72] MünchKomm InsO/*Füchsl/Weishäupl* § 148 mn 61.

4.3 Enforcement Pursuant to Council Regulation (EC) No 44/2001

Art 25 (1) sentence 2 of subpara 1 of the EIR makes no provision for **enforcement**; it rather refers this matter to Arts 38 to 52 of Council Regulation (EC) No 44/2001. **41**

According to Arts 38 and 39 of Council Regulation (EC) No 44/2001, the **exequatur procedure** commences with the making of an application by an interested party to the competent court/authority. The court with **jurisdiction** is the court at: **42**

- the **place of domicile of the debtor**, or
- the **place where (compulsory) enforcement takes place** (Art 39 (2) of Council Regulation (EC) No 44/2001).

An **official copy** of the judgement and a **certificate** in accordance with Annex V of Council Regulation (EC) No 44/2001 must be submitted. Once these formalities have been completed, the judgement must, as laid down in Art 41 of Council Regulation (EC) No 44/2001, be declared immediately enforceable without any review under Arts 34 and 35 of Council Regulation (EC) No 44/2001; a review of the substance of the judgement is equally prohibited (Art 45 (2) of Council Regulation (EC) No 44/2001).[73] The court issues a so-called **certificate (clause) of enforceability**.[74] Either party is entitled to **appeal** the decision made on the application for a declaration of enforceability (Art 43 of Council Regulation (EC) No 44/2001). Only in the appeal proceedings is the court entitled pursuant to Art 45 (1) of Council Regulation (EC) No 44/2001 to review the judgement whose enforcement is being sought. But because Article 34 (2) of the 1968 Brussels Convention was originally excepted from Art 25 (1) sentence 2 of subpara 1 of the EIR, this does not apply to the enforcement of judgements falling within the scope of applicability of the EIR (see mn 37).

To be kept in mind, however, is that Council Regulation (EC) No 44/2001 only regulates the first phase of the enforcement procedure, i.e. the obtaining of the **exequatur**. The **actual enforcement** is carried out subsequent to this by the **competent public authority of the particular State** according to this State's laws on enforcing similar national judgements.[75] The customary procedures for compulsory executions prescribed by the particular national laws are being employed, which, if necessary, are to be modified in order to ensure the *effet utile* of Council Regulation (EC) No 44/2001.[76] **43**

5. Other Judgements Within the Meaning of Art 25 (2) of the EIR

5.1 General

According to Art 25 (2) of the EIR, the recognition and enforcement of **other judgements** are subject to the 1968 Brussels Convention (now Council Regulation (EC) No 44/2001) provided that this Convention is applicable. Art 25 (2) of the EIR is intended to ensure a gapless interlocking of the EIR and Council Regulation (EC) No 44/2001.[77] For this reason, the exclusion of insolvency proceedings in Art 1 (2) (b) of **44**

[73] Nerlich/Römermann-*Mincke* Komm InsO Art 25 EuInsVO mn 12.

[74] MünchKomm BGB/*Kindler* IntInsR mn 567.

[75] *Virgós/Schmit* Explanatory report mn 190; *Virgós/Garcimartín* Regulation, p 211.

[76] *Virgós/Schmit* Explanatory report mn 190.

[77] *Virgós/Schmit* Explanatory report mn 197; D-K/D/Ch-*Duursma-Kepplinger* Art 25 mn 50; Moss/Fletcher/Isaacs-*Moss/Smith*, Regulation, mn 8.197; *Virgós/Garcimartín* Regulation, p 208; *Leible/Staudinger* KTS 2000, 531, 566; *Wessels* International Insolvency Law (2006) mn 10809; *Paulus* Komm EuInsVO Art 25 mn 2; MünchKomm BGB/*Kindler* IntInsR mn 590.

Council Regulation (EC) No 44/2001 should be construed in a way that accords with the definition of insolvency proceedings in the EIR and with the criteria listed in Art 25 of the EIR.[78] Art 25 (2) of the EIR is therefore an **allocation provision.**[79]

45 Art 25 (2) of the EIR has a clarifying function to formally ensure that no kind of judgement remains unregulated.

46 The international jurisdiction for these other judgements is determined pursuant to Art 5 (3) of Council Regulation (EC) No 44/2001, the recognition and enforcement of these pursuant to Chapter III of the same.

5.2 Judgements Concerned

47 **Other judgements** are those judgements that cannot be classified as judgements opening proceedings, judgements concerning insolvency proceedings, insolvency-related judgements, or judgements on preservation measures.

48 **Examples** of these are:

- actions concerning the legal validity or the amount of a claim pursuant to general law, or
- actions concerning the legal validity and the effectiveness of a right *in rem*,
- actions to recover property in the possession of the debtor, and
- general actions that the debtor could have asserted even if insolvency proceedings had not been opened.[80]

6. Art 25 (3) of the EIR

49 Art 25 (3) of the EIR releases the Member States from their obligation to recognize pursuant to Art 25 (1) of the EIR if the judgement concerned would result in a **limitation of personal freedom** or **of postal secrecy**. This limitation does not refer to the insolvent debtor only but also to any other person who could be affected by it.[81]

50 Art 25 (3) of the EIR grants a **discretion**, as clearly implied from the negative formulation "shall not be obliged".[82] Because it concerns an issue that directly affects fundamental liberties, the Member States have chosen in this area to safeguard their discretionary powers with respect to recognition and enforcement.[83]

51 In light of Art 26 of the EIR, which contains a general proviso in cases involving public policy, Art 25 (3) of the EIR could be considered superfluous (on this, see Art 26 of the EIR mn 31 et seq as well). This is because limitations of personal freedom or of postal secrecy already constitute breaches of public policy;[84] a recognition or enforcement of judgements that have come about under such circumstances could therefore also be refused pursuant to Art 26 of the EIR.

---

[78] *Virgós/Schmit* Explanatory report mn 197.

[79] MünchKomm InsO/*Reinhart* Art 25 EuInsVO mn 8; D-K/D/Ch-*Duursma-Kepplinger* Art 25 mn 49.

[80] *Virgós/Schmit* Explanatory report mn 196.

[81] *Virgós/Schmit* Explanatory report mn 193.

[82] *Paulus* Komm EuInsVO Art 25 mn 12; D-K/D/Ch-*Duursma-Kepplinger* Art 25 mn 12.

[83] *Virgós/Schmit* Explanatory report mn 193; *Virgós/Garcimartín* Regulation, p 218.

[84] Contra: MünchKomm InsO/*Reinhart* Art 25 EuInsVO mn 8; MünchKomm BGB/*Kindler* IntInsR mn 591.

According to its wording, however, **Art 26 of the EIR** only concerns: **52**

- judgements opening insolvency proceedings, and
- judgements handed down in the context of an insolvency proceeding, i.e. judgements pursuant to Art 25 (1) sentence 1 of subpara 1 of the EIR.

Excluded from the ambit of Art 26 of the EIR are:

- insolvency-related judgements and
- judgements on preservation measures

whose recognition and enforcement can therefore only be refused on the basis of **Art 25 (3) of the EIR** (see Art 26 of the EIR at mn 32).

This means that the **grounds for refusing to recognize and enforce insolvency-related judgements** and **preservation measures** are more narrow than for other judgements, because the recognition or enforcement may only be refused if there is a limitation of personal freedom or of postal secrecy. **53**

The grounds for refusing recognition found in Art 25 (3) of the EIR is also a substantive rule that exists independent of national law and national concepts of public policy.[85] But in light of Arts 5 and 8 of the CPHRFF, it is rather unlikely that a Member State would not consider a limitation of personal freedom or of postal secrecy as breaches of public policy. **54**

Article 26
Public policy

Any Member State may refuse to recognise insolvency proceedings opened in another Member State or to enforce a judgment handed down in the context of such proceedings where the effects of such recognition or enforcement would be manifestly contrary to that State's public policy, in particular its fundamental principles or the constitutional rights and liberties of the individual.

→ Cf Art 6 UNCITRAL Model Law

Contents

[85] MünchKomm BGB/*Kindler* IntInsR mn 592; MünchKomm InsO/*Reinhart* Art 25 EuIns-VO mn 8.

Index

Bibliography

Carstens Die internationale Zuständigkeit im europäischen Insolvenzrecht (2005); *Dammann/Podeur* L'affaire Daisytek: l'épilogue. Application par la Cour de cassation du règlement européen relatif aux procédures d'insolvabilité, Banque & Droit 2006 (109), p 3; *Duursma-Kepplinger/Duursma/Chalupsky* Europäische Insolvenzverordnung, Kommentar (2002); *Haß/Huber/Gruber/Heiderhoff* EU-Insolvenzverordnung, Kommentar (2005); *Kebekus* Comments on AG Nürnberg dated 1.10.2006, ZIP 2007, 84; *Kübler/Prütting* Kommentar zur Insolvenzordnung (March 2006); *Leible/Staudinger* Die europäische Verordnung über Insolvenzverfahren, KTS 2000, p 533; *Moss/Fletcher/Isaacs* (eds) The EC Regulation on Insolvency Proceedings (2002); Münchener Kommentar zum Bürgerlichen Gesetzbuch, vol 11 (2006); *Pannen/Riedemann* EWiR 2005, p 177; *Pannen/Riedemann* EWiR 2005, p 701; *Paulus* Europäische Insolvenzverordnung, Kommentar (2006); *Paulus* Der EuGH und das moderne Insolvenzrecht, NZG 2006, p 609; *Smid* Deutsches und Europäisches Internationales Insolvenzrecht, Kommentar (2004); *Vallender* Aufgaben und Befugnisse des deutschen Insolvenzrichters in Verfahren nach der EuInsVO, KTS 2005, p 283; *Virgós/Garcimartín* The European Insolvency Regulation: Law and Practice (2004); *Virgós/Schmit* Erläuternder Bericht zu dem EU-Übereinkommen über Insolvenzverfahren, in Stoll (ed), Vorschläge und Gutachten (1997), p 32; *Wessels* International Insolvency Law (2006).

1. Overview

1 An underlying principle of the EIR is the **automatic recognition** of judgements in the other Member States (Art 16 of the EIR). This applies to:

- **judgements opening insolvency proceedings,**
- **judgements concerning the course and closure of insolvency proceedings** (Art 25 (1) subpara 1 of the EIR),
- the so-called **insolvency-related judgements** pursuant to Art 25 (1) subpara 2 of the EIR, and
- **preservation measures** pursuant to Art 25 (1) subpara 3 of the EIR, on this see mn 3.

"**Automatic**" means that the courts of the recognizing State are not entitled to review the judgement. Thus no **review on the merits** takes place (prohibition of the ***révision au fond***);[1] the only review made is to determine whether the court opening proceedings assumed jurisdiction pursuant to Art 3 of the EIR.[2] The question is not whether, in the opinion of the court of the second State, the court opening proceedings had in fact international jurisdiction pursuant to the EIR but only whether this court in fact assumed international jurisdiction.[3] The sole exception to the principle of automatic recognition in the EIR is the **public policy proviso** in Art 26 of the EIR, which holds that a foreign judgement does not have to be recognized or enforced if this is incompatible with the public policy of the Member State in which the recognition or enforcement is being sought.[4]

According to Art 26 of the EIR, the recognizing State has a **discretion** (in contrast to Art 34 of Council Regulation (EC) No 44/2001) whether or not to refuse recognition of the judgement.[5] This is inferable from the wording of Art 26 of the EIR ("may"); on this, see mn 14 as well. **2**

According to its wording, **Art 26 of the EIR** does **not** apply to: **3**

- the so-called **insolvency-related judgements** pursuant to Art 25 (1) subpara 2 of the EIR, or
- **preservation measures** pursuant to Art 25 (1) subpara 3 of the EIR.[6]

2. Subject Matter of the Public Policy

As to **what falls within public policy** is defined by the national laws of the various Member States,[7] the result being that the same set of acts will not necessarily be considered an infringement of public policy in all Member States.[8] According to its wording, Art 26 of the EIR protects fundamental principles or constitutionally guaranteed rights and liberties. It covers both the **procedural-law aspects** (on this, see mn 5 et seq) as well as the **substantial-law aspects of public policy** (on this, see mn 9 et seq).[9] **4**

2.1 Procedural-Law Aspects of Public Policy

An infringement of the **procedural-law aspects of public policy** occurs if the foreign insolvency proceeding is incompatible with the fundamental principles of the law of the recognizing or enforcing State.[10] The public policy proviso protects, for example, the **5**

---

1 *Smid* Komm EuInsVO Art 26 mn 2.

2 *Virgós/Schmit* Explanatory report mn 202; *Virgós/Garcimartín* Regulation, p 212; MünchKomm BGB/*Kindler* IntInsR mn 593; *Leible/Staudinger* KTS 2000, 533, 568; *Vallender* KTS 2005, 283, 301.

3 *Vallender* KTS 2005, 283, 317.

4 *Virgós/Schmit* Explanatory report mn 202; *Virgós/Garcimartín* Regulation, p 213; *Smid* Komm EuInsVO Art 26 mn 2; *Wessels* International Insolvency Law (2006), mn 10811.

5 *Carstens* Die internationale Zuständigkeit im europäischen Insolvenzrecht (2005), 94; *Paulus* Komm EuInsVO Art 26 mn 1.

6 Contra: D-K/D/Ch-*Duursma-Kepplinger* Art 26 mn 15.

7 *Paulus* Komm EuInsVO Art 26 mn 6.

8 *Virgós/Schmit* Explanatory report mn 205; *Virgós/Garcimartín* Regulation, p 214; MünchKomm BGB/*Kindler* IntInsR mn 600.

9 *Virgós/Schmit* Explanatory report mn 206; *Virgós/Garcimartín* Regulation, p 215; Kübler/Prütting-*Kemper* EuInsVO Art 26 mn 5; D-K/D/Ch-*Duursma-Kepplinger* Art 26 mn 6.

10 *Virgós/Schmit* Explanatory report mn 203; Kübler/Prütting-*Kemper* EuInsVO Art 26 mn 5.

participants' or the interested parties' right to defend themselves in a proceeding.[11] Insolvency proceedings must therefore guarantee a minimum of procedural mechanisms for producing just decisions, i.e. certain **procedural guarantees** must be present.[12] The **right to a fair trial** as understood in Art 6 CPHRFF could serve as a benchmark for this.[13] According to this article, in the determination of his civil rights and obligations or of any criminal charge against him, everyone is entitled to a fair and public hearing within a reasonable time by an independent and impartial tribunal established by law. The judgement must also be pronounced publicly.

6 Legal writers and judicial precedent are unanimous in their opinion that an infringement of the **right to be heard** constitutes an infringement of public policy and is therefore grounds to refuse recognition within the meaning of Art 26 of the EIR.[14]

7 In the Eurofood/Parmalat decision (→ cf Table of Cases Art 3 of the EIR Appendix A mn 10), the ECJ had to decide whether a Member State is obliged pursuant to Art 16 of the EIR to recognize proceedings opened in another Member State if the decision opening the proceedings infringes the procedural methods guaranteed by the public policy of the State in which recognition is being sought. To answer this question, the ECJ referred to its earlier decisions on the 1968 Brussels Convention. The court had held in 2000 that, because it operates as an obstacle to fulfilling one of the fundamental goals of the Convention – namely facilitating the reciprocal recognition of judgements – the public policy clause of this Convention can only apply in exceptional cases.[15] The ECJ ruled in another case that the public policy clause can only apply if the recognition or enforcement of the foreign judgement infringes a fundamental principle of law, thus making it incompatible with the laws of the enforcing State. The infringement must be a manifest breach of a fundamental legal norm of the law of the enforcing State, or a manifest breach of a right recognized as fundamental by such law.[16] According to the ECJ, these decisions may be invoked for interpreting Art 26 of the EIR.[17] With respect to fundamental procedural rights, the ECJ has already ruled that everyone has a right to a fair trial.[18] The right to **receive the documents of the proceedings**, and the right to be **heard in accordance with the law** are of paramount importance to obtaining a fair trial.[19] A Member State may thus refuse recognition if, in the rendering of it, the judgement opening proceedings manifestly infringes a person affected by such proceeding's fundamental right to be heard in accordance with the law.[20]

8 In addition to the right to be heard in accordance with the law, the procedural-law aspects of the public policy proviso pursuant to Art 26 of the EIR also protect the **right**

[11] *Virgós/Schmit* Explanatory report mn 206.

[12] Kübler/Prütting-*Kemper* EuInsVO Art 26 mn 5.

[13] *Paulus* Komm EuInsVO Art 26 mn 8; *Smid* Komm EuInsVO Art 26 mn 7.

[14] *Virgós/Garcimartín* Regulation, p 215; Kübler/Prütting-*Kemper* EuInsVO Art 26 mn 5; *Carstens* Die internationale Zuständigkeit im europäischen Insolvenzrecht (2005), 94; *Paulus* Komm EuInsVO Art 26 mn 13; *Paulus* NZG 2006, 609, 613; Haß/Huber/Gruber/Heiderhoff-*Gruber* Art 26 EuInsVO mn 7; D-K/D/Ch-*Duursma-Kepplinger* Art 26 mn 7; MünchKomm BGB/*Kindler* IntInsR mn 602.

[15] ECJ dated 28 Mar 2000 – C-7/98, EC reports 2000 I-1935 = ZIP 2000, 859.

[16] ECJ dated 28 Mar 2000 – C-7/98, EC reports 2000 I-1935 = ZIP 2000, 859.

[17] ECJ C-341/04 dated 2 May 2006, ZInsO 2006, 485 No 64.

[18] ECJ dated 17 Dec 1998 C-185/95 P, EC reports 1998, I-8417; ECJ dated 11 Jan 2000 C-174/98 P and C-189/98 P, EC reports 2000, I-1; ECJ dated 28 Mar 2000 – C-7/98, EC reports 2000, I-1935.

[19] ECJ C-341/04 dated 2 May 2006, ZInsO 2006, 485 No 65 (→ cf Table of Cases Art 3 of the EIR Appendix A mn 10).

[20] ECJ C-341/04 dated 2 May 2006, ZInsO 2006, 485 No 67 (→ cf Table of Cases Art 3 of the EIR Appendix A mn 10).

to participate in the proceedings.[21] This right plays a key role in the case of a **reorganization plan**. The procedural-law aspects of the particular public policy would then be infringed if the creditors were denied the opportunity to participate in the insolvency proceedings. This participation could, however, take the form of a so-called "class representation".[22]

2.2 Substantive-Law Aspects of Public Policy

The **substantive-law aspects of public policy**[23] comprise primarily two elements: the **principle of freedom from discrimination**[24] and the **protection of private ownership.**[25] The principle of freedom from discrimination on the grounds of nationality is one of the fundamental principles of EU legislation, as clearly set out in Art 12 of the EEC Treaty.[26] This has been affirmed in the EIR in Recital 21 and in Art 39 of it. The recognition of a judgement may thus be refused if such judgement prejudices a creditor solely because his/its domicile/registered office is in another Member State.[27] **9**

Public policy is also infringed if insolvency proceedings are used as a pretext for an **expropriation** that otherwise breaches the fundamental rights of the opening State, or if the creditors are forced to sacrifice their interests in a way that is clearly inequitable or arbitrary.[28] But such constellations are hardly to be expected in the EU.[29] **10**

3. Restrictive Interpretation of the Public Policy Proviso

The EIR is based on the **principle of mutual trust** and on the general presumption that judgements from other Member States are made in conformance with the law. In light of this, the public policy proviso can only be applied in exceptional cases.[30] This is emphasized in Recital 22 of the EIR: the permissible grounds for refusing recognition should be reduced to the minimum necessary.[31] **11**

The necessary **restrictive** interpretation of the public policy proviso stems from the wording of Art 26 of the EIR, which is worded to cover the most narrow scope of application possible and which is considerably different from other comparable provisions (e.g. Art 34 of Council Regulation (EC) No 44/2001). Firstly, it is not the recognition or the enforcement itself that must infringe public policy but rather the **effects** of these. This forces the court wishing to refuse recognition to make a concrete analysis of the consequences of such recognition.[32] Should this recognition infringe public policy in theory only, but not in fact, then Art 26 of the EIR does not apply. Through the supplement "where the effects", the scope of applicability of the public policy proviso is being restricted even more. **12**

The infringement of public policy must also be **"manifest"**. This means that the infringement must be so clear that an informed party would immediately recognize this.[33] **13**

---

[21] *Virgós/Garcimartín* Regulation, p 216; D-K/D/Ch-*Duursma-Kepplinger* Art 26 mn 7.

[22] *Virgós/Garcimartín* Regulation, p 216.

[23] On this, see also *Paulus* Komm EuInsVO Art 26 mn 10 et seq.

[24] *Paulus* Komm EuInsVO Art 26 mn 15.

[25] *Virgós/Garcimartín* Regulation, p 217.

[26] *Virgós/Garcimartín* Regulation, p 217.

[27] *Virgós/Garcimartín* Regulation, p 217.

[28] *Virgós/Garcimartín* Regulation, p 217.

[29] *Virgós/Garcimartín* Regulation, p 217.

[30] *Virgós/Schmit* Explanatory report mn 204; D-K/D/Ch-*Duursma-Kepplinger* Art 26 mn 3; *Leible/Staudinger* KTS 2000, 533, 567; *Virgós/Garcimartín* Regulation, p 214.

[31] There is a presumption that every foreign judgement is compatible with domestic public policy, *Paulus* Komm EuInsVO Art 26 mn 10.

[32] Cf *Virgós/Schmit* Explanatory report mn 204; *Virgós/Garcimartín* Regulation, p 214.

[33] Kübler/Prütting-*Kemper* EuInsVO Art 26 mn 4; D-K/D/Ch-*Duursma-Kepplinger*

14 In contrast to Art 34 of Council Regulation (EC) No 44/2001, Art 26 of the EIR leaves the recognition of the judgement to the **discretion** of the court.[34] According to Art 26 of the EIR, "any Member State may refuse", whereas Art 34 of Council Regulation (EC) No 44/2001 states that "a judgement shall not be recognised ...". In the absence of any "automatism", a judgement can be recognized in cases of doubt.

15 According to the German wording of Art 26 of the EIR ("*soweit*" = in so far as/to the extent to which), the refusal to recognize may result in a dismissal of the judgement **as a whole** or **in part.**[35] The refusal to recognize is therefore not necessarily a refusal of the whole judgement.

16 Legal writers also demand that the judgement under review also demonstrate an adequate **national connection** to the recognizing Member State.[36] This will not be found merely because the judgement produces legal effects in the particular national territory.[37] Rather, national protected interests must be affected by the foreign judgment.[38] This is the case, for example, if a party to the proceedings is a national of the recognizing Member State, or if he resides permanently in this Member State.[39]

17 Art 16 (1) sentence 2 of the EIR contains an express restriction to the public policy proviso.[40] According to this provision, a judgement must still be recognized even if insolvency proceedings cannot be opened in the recognizing State against the assets of the debtor due to a lack of legal capacity (e.g. businessperson/non-businessperson). Hence the debtor's **lack of insolvency capacity** in the recognizing State may not be relied on to establish an infringement of public policy for the purposes of refusing recognition of a judgement rendered in another Member State.[41]

18 Even an assumption of **international jurisdiction** based on an obviously incorrect ascertainment of the location of the COMI[42] does not, according to the prevailing opinion, allow for a refusal to recognize.[43] Allowing such would, according to this opinion, undermine the system of the EIR.[44] The prejudiced party's only recourse in such a situation is an appeal pursuant to the national laws of the State of the opening of proceedings.[45]

19 Furthermore, **relocations of domicile** or **foreign incorporations** do **not** constitute **infringements** of public policy, nor does a use of the EIR for the purposes of **forum shopping.**[46]

Art 26 mn 3; MünchKomm BGB/*Kindler* IntInsR mn 612.

[34] *Carstens* Die internationale Zuständigkeit im europäischen Insolvenzrecht (2005), 94; Moss/Fletcher/Isaacs-*Moss/Smith*, Regulation, mn 8.204.

[35] *Virgós/Schmit* Explanatory report mn 209; Haß/Huber/Gruber/Heiderhoff-*Gruber* Art 26 EuInsVO mn 6; Kübler/Prütting-*Kemper* EuInsVO Art 26 mn 9; *Paulus* Komm EuInsVO Art 26 mn 19.

[36] *Virgós/Garcimartín* Regulation, p 217; D-K/D/Ch-*Duursma-Kepplinger* Art 26 mn 3; Kübler/Prütting-*Kemper* EuInsVO Art 26 mn 8.

[37] Kübler/Prütting-*Kemper* EuInsVO Art 26 mn 8.

[38] Kübler/Prütting-*Kemper* EuInsVO Art 26 mn 8.

[39] Kübler/Prütting-*Kemper* EuInsVO Art 26 mn 8; D-K/D/Ch-*Duursma-Kepplinger* Art 16 mn 3.

[40] *Virgós/Garcimartín* Regulation, p 212.

[41] *Virgós/Schmit* Explanatory report mn 208.

[42] On the concept of COMI, see in-depth Art 3 EuInsVO mn 15 et seq.

[43] D-K/D/Ch-*Duursma-Kepplinger* Art 16 mn 5; *Wessels* International Insolvency Law (2006) mn 10812; Moss/Fletcher/Isaacs-*Moss/Smith*, Regulation, mn 8.205; *Paulus* Komm EuInsVO Art 26 mn 16; *Smid* Komm EuInsVO Art 26 mn 13; *Leible/Staudinger* KTS 2000, 533, 568.

[44] *Virgós/Schmit* Explanatory report mn 205.

[45] ECJ C-341/04 2.5.2006, ZInsO 2006, 485, No 43; *Smid* Komm EuInsVO Art 26 mn 13.

[46] *Paulus* Komm EuInsVO Art 26 mn 16.

4. Judicial Precedents

The issue of public policy infringements has been the topic of discussion in many judicial decisions of the Member States. But according to the most current information, recognition of a judgement opening proceedings has been refused pursuant to Art 26 of the EIR in one case only. 20

4.1 Judgements Negating an Infringement of Public Policy

- *AG* Cologne, order of 23 January 2004, ZIP 2004, 471 (Automold): There are no indications of an infringement of public policy, even though insolvency proceedings have been opened in England against the German debtor. (→ cf Table of Cases Art 3 of the EIR Appendix A mn 2). 21
- *AG* Düsseldorf, order of 7 April 2004, ZIP 2004, 866 (ISA/Daisytek): Even though the managing director of the debtor company did not herself make the request to open insolvency proceedings and was not heard prior to the opening, recognition of the English judgement cannot be refused on the basis of infringing German public policy. (→ on this, cf Table of Cases Art 3 of the EIR Appendix A mn 15).
- *AG* Saarbrücken, order of 25 February 2005, ZIP 2005, 2027[47] (HTB-Orange Ltd): Establishing a company in a Member State whose laws afford the shareholders more freedom, and setting up branch establishments in other Member States, does not infringe German public policy. According to well-established precedent of the ECJ, creditor protection in particular – as a form of safeguarding economic interests – does not fall within public safety and order.
- *OLG* Düsseldorf 9 July 2004, ZIP 2004, 1514 NZI 2004, 628 (ISA/Daisytek)[48]: There are no apparent grounds for refusing recognition based on an infringement of German public policy pursuant to Art 26 of the EIR, even though main insolvency proceedings were opened in England against the assets of a German company. (→ on this, cf Table of Cases Art 3 of the EIR Appendix A mn 15).
- *OGH* Vienna 17 March 2005, NZI 2005, 465: An incorrect assumption of jurisdiction pursuant to Art 3 (1) of the EIR to open insolvency proceedings by a court of a Member State does not *per se* constitute an infringement of public policy. (→ on this, cf Table of Cases Art 3 of the EIR Appendix A mn 13).
- *Cour de cassation,* 27 June 2006[49]: The *Cour de cassation* had to decide on a possible infringement of public policy. Art L 621-1 of the *Code de commerce* provides that, prior to the opening of preventative insolvency proceedings (*procédure de sauvegarde*), the **workers' council representative must be heard.** Failure to hear this person can, under French law, result in the annulment of the judgement opening proceedings. In its decision, the *Cour de cassation* held, however, that the failure to hear the workers' representative prior to the opening of proceedings does not constitute a manifest infringement of the fundamental right of a person involved in such a proceeding to be heard in accordance with the law, the ECJ thereby citing the Eurofood judgement word for word. But what is actually meant in this case is not clear: does it mean that the workers' representative is simply not directly affected by the opening of proceedings, or, if he/she is affected, that the failure to be heard does not in itself amount to

[47] Explanatory note by *Pannen/Riedemann* EWiR 2005, 701.

[48] On this, see *Pannen/Riedemann* EWiR 2005, 177.

[49] Cour de cassation dated 27 Jun 2006, Dalloz 2006 AJ 1816; see on this *Dammann/Podeur* Banque & Droit 2006 (109), 3 (Daisytek).

an infringement of the right to be heard in accordance with the law due to the fact that the applicable law grants workers' representatives a right of appeal?[50] What is certain in any case is that Art L 621-1 of the *Code de commerce* is not one of the protected fundamental rights.[51]

4.2 Judgements Affirming an Infringement of Public Policy

22 The only example where a court **effectively refused recognition** based on an infringement of public policy was done on 15 August 2006 by the *AG* Nuremberg.[52] The court held that the opening of English main insolvency proceedings against the assets of **Hans Brochier Holdings Ltd** (→ on this, cf Table of Cases Art 3 of the EIR Appendix B No 97, 98, 100, 101), which operated almost exclusively in Germany, was not to be recognized because:

- the court had not made an independent review of its jurisdiction, but decided to open insolvency proceedings based solely on the unsubstantiated allegations of the requesting party,
- the judgement was based on representations of the requesting party that were contrary to the facts,
- the judgement lacked merit, and
- the liquidator was not impartial, as he had been appointed on application of the managing director of the insolvency debtor and was being advised by the long-standing legal advisors of the insolvency debtor.

23 The *AG* Nuremberg concluded from this that a recognition of the main insolvency proceedings opened in England would infringe German public policy.[53] This decision must, however, be understood within the context of English insolvency law. Since the enactment of the insolvency law reform on 15 September 2003, the directors of a company are authorized to open administration proceedings (so-called "out of court appointment") without the participation of a court. In this case, it was so obvious that the appointment of the liquidator was done with an intent to deceive and was so contrary to the facts that afterwards the High Court of Justice of London refused to locate the COMI in England and regarded the appointment of the liquidator as invalid.[54]

5. Consequences of Refusing to Recognize

24 The consequences of a **refusal to recognize** are not regulated in the EIR. Art 26 of the EIR merely provides that recognition or enforcement may be refused. There is consensus, however, that the refusal to recognize a judgement in a Member State may relate to the judgement **in whole or to parts** of it[55] (see mn 15), although a partial recognition is only possible if the judgement is severable.[56]

[50] *Dammann/Podeur* Banque & Droit 2006 (109), 3, 6.

[51] *Dammann/Podeur* Banque & Droit 2006 (109), 3, 6.

[52] AG Nuremberg dated 15 Aug 2006 – 8004 IN 1326 – 1331/06 ZIP 2007, 81.

[53] AG Nuremberg dated 15 Aug 2006 – 8004 IN 1326 – 1331/06 ZIP 2007, 81.

[54] High Court of Justice London dated 15 Aug 2006 – Nr 5618/2006; see on this *Kebekus* ZIP 2007, 84, 85.

[55] *Virgós/Garcimartín* Regulation, p 219; *Carstens* Die internationale Zuständigkeit im europäischen Insolvenzrecht (2005), 96; D-K/D/Ch-*Duursma-Kepplinger* Art 26 mn 16; *Smid* EuInsVO Komm Art 26 mn 12; *Paulus* Komm EuInsVO Art 26 mn 19.

[56] MünchKomm BGB/*Kindler* IntInsR mn 616.

The **refusal to recognize** has various consequences depending on whether it concerns an individual judgement or a judgement opening proceedings. **25**

In the case of a refusal to recognize an **individual judgement**, only this particular judgement produces no effects in the Member State concerned; the foreign insolvency proceedings remain effective for all other purposes in the State in which recognition was being sought. For example, if a creditor is excluded from the distribution for reasons that infringe the public policy of the recognizing Member State, than this creditor can collect on his claim in the recognizing State, if necessary by way of compulsory execution, since the divestment (of the debtor) does not apply to him in this State.[57] **26**

If, to the contrary, a **judgement opening proceedings** is not recognized because it infringes public policy, the **local assets** of the debtor are **not affected** by the **divestment** ensuing from the non-recognized insolvency proceedings.[58] It is thus still possible to implement individual (regular) execution measures. With respect to further consequences, three possibilities are conceivable: **27**

1. If there are individual assets only, then insolvency proceedings pursuant to the EIR cannot be opened. If national law provides the same, the creditors may implement individual (regular) execution measures.
2. But if there is an establishment in the State refusing recognition, then independent territorial insolvency proceedings pursuant to Art 3 (4) (a) of the EIR may be opened. This is because the non-recognition of main insolvency proceedings is equivalent to the inability to open insolvency proceedings within the meaning of this provision.
3. If the court refusing recognition holds that the COMI of the debtor lies within its territory, the court may open main insolvency proceedings pursuant to Art 3 (1) of the EIR, which would trigger a "positive" conflict of jurisdictions, i.e. both courts claiming jurisdiction.[59] *Carstens*[60] is of another opinion, however, arguing that main insolvency proceedings could only be opened if, as a result of the non-recognition, the judgement is regarded as a legal nullity. But this is not the case. Despite the non-recognition, the judgement would remain effective in the State in which proceedings were opened.

The fact that the judgement remains effective in the original State does not, however, hinder the non-recognizing court from opening main insolvency proceedings. Thus the *AG* Nuremberg in the **Brochier** case[61] (→ on this, cf Table of Cases Art 3 of the EIR Appendix B mn 97, 98, 100, 101) decided to open main insolvency proceedings against a company operating in Germany in the form of an English limited liability company[62] after the court had refused to recognize the English judgement opening proceedings because it infringed public policy.[63] This is a case involving a "positive" conflict of jurisdictions (both courts claiming jurisdiction) that cannot be resolved by the principle of priority: the first State relies on its having priority, and the second State regards the first judgement as ineffective. Whether such a conflict of jurisdictions will cause difficulty depends on the positions taken by the various other Member States affected by the insolvency proceedings. If the first insolvency proceedings are not recognized in these other **28**

---

57 *Virgós/Garcimartín* Regulation, p 220.

58 *Virgós/Garcimartín* Regulation, p 219; *Carstens* Die internationale Zuständigkeit im europäischen Insolvenzrecht (2005), 96.

59 *Carstens* Die internationale Zuständigkeit im europäischen Insolvenzrecht (2005), 96.

60 *Carstens* Die internationale Zuständigkeit im europäischen Insolvenzrecht (2005), 96.

61 NZI 2007, 187.

62 AG Nürnberg 1.10.2006

63 AG Nürnberg 15.8.2006.

Member States either, then the second proceedings will produce their effects there. What is very problematic is the situation where some States refuse to recognize the first proceedings and others accept it, this being diametrically opposed to the goals of the EIR, i.e. the facilitation of a proper functioning of the internal (EU) market (Recital 2 of the EIR).

29 In the **Brochier** case referred to above (mn 22)[64], the conflict of jurisdictions was resolved in that the High Court of Justice of London on 15 August 2006 nullified the appointment of the English liquidator, the court holding that the COMI was not located in England.[65]

30 In light of the restrictive interpretation of the public policy proviso, the problems arising in conjunction with a refusal to recognize are more of a theoretical nature and will probably seldom occur. The fact that this potential conflict of jurisdictions has not been regulated does not represent a regulatory gap; it is rather in accord with the remaining provisions of the EIR. One way of resolving a possible conflict of jurisdictions would be for the participating liquidators to agree to so-called protocols[66] (on protocols, see the chapter on protocols in this commentary).

6. Relationship to Art 25 (3) of the EIR

31 According to Art 25 (3) of the EIR, the Member States are not obliged to recognize or enforce judgements as understood by Art 25 (1) of the EIR if the judgement would result in a limitation of **personal freedom** or of **postal secrecy**. This raises the question of the relationship between this provision and Art 26 of the EIR.

32 Like Art 26 of the EIR, Art 25 (3) of the EIR grants the courts of the Member States an option. According to the wording of the latter, the Member States are "not obliged" to recognize the judgement. This option also aims to keep the scope of application of Art 25 (3) of the EIR as narrow as possible. Art 25 (3) of the EIR is drafted even **narrower** than Art 26 of the EIR in two respects:

- Firstly, Art 25 (3) of the EIR relates **only** to **judgements concerning the course and closure of insolvency proceedings, insolvency-related judgements** within the meaning of Art 25 (1) subpara 2 of the EIR, and judgements relating to **preservation measures** taken after the request for opening insolvency proceedings pursuant to Art 25 (1) subpara 3 of the EIR. **Judgements opening proceedings** are therefore **excluded** from the scope of application of Art 25 (3) of the EIR and are subject exclusively to Art 26 of the EIR. Judgements concerning the course and closure of insolvency proceedings are thus regulated twice: both in Art 25 (3) of the EIR and in Art 26 of the EIR.
- Secondly, Art 25 (3) of the EIR can only serve as a reason to refuse recognition if the recognition would cause a limitation of **personal freedom** or of **postal secrecy**.

33 Art 25 (3) of the EIR is therefore somewhat odd because, although it concerns public policy, it treats it as a separate matter. Every limitation of personal freedom or of postal secrecy is an infringement of the public policy contemplated by Art 26 of the EIR.[67] Accordingly, the approach that regards Art 26 of the EIR and Art 25 (3) of the EIR as two mutually independent impediments to recognition and enforcement should be

---

[64] NZI 2007, 187.

[65] Decision No 5618/2006, unreported.

[66] *Paulus* Komm EuInsVO Art 26 mn 19.

[67] Contra: MünchKomm BGB/*Kindler* IntInsR mn 591.

rejected,[68] since an application of Art 25 (3) of the EIR is conditioned in each and every case on an infringement of public policy.

Another view regards the relationship between Art 25 (3) of the EIR and Art 26 of the EIR as one of *lex specialis* to *lex generalis*.[69] According to this approach, if a judgement cannot be recognized because of Art 25 (3) of the EIR, then recourse to Art 26 of the EIR becomes superfluous.[70] But this is not true here, because such a relationship could only be presumed if the scope of application of the alleged *lex specialis* (Art 25 (3) of the EIR) was already contained within that of the *lex generalis*. However, as already mentioned, this is not the case: Art 26 of the EIR does not relate to judgements referred to in Art 25 (1) subpara 2 and subpara 3 of the EIR; reversely, Art 25 (3) of the EIR does not apply to judgments opening insolvency proceedings. For this reason, Art 25 (3) of the EIR cannot be regarded as the *lex specialis*. **34**

The existence of Art 25 (3) of the EIR alongside the general public policy proviso in Art 26 of the EIR cannot be explained for historical reasons either. It is true that Art 25 (1) sentence 2 of subpara 1 of the EIR expressly excludes the application of Art 34 (2) of the 1968 Brussels Convention (now Arts 34 and 34 of Council Regulation (EC) No 44/2001), which made it necessary for the EIR to enact its own public policy proviso.[71] But this does not justify the necessity of Art 25 (3) of the EIR, because Art 26 of the EIR would have been more than adequate for this purpose. **35**

Art 25 (3) of the EIR simply **broadens** Art 26 of the EIR:[72] it provides a way for refusing the recognition of insolvency-related judgements and of judgements relating to preservation measures taken after the request for opening insolvency proceedings as well. **36**

Viewed logically, this splitting of the public policy proviso into two provisions still remains incomprehensible. It is also unclear why personal freedom and postal secrecy only – and not other fundamental rights – are being protected by this broadening of Art 26 of the EIR. **37**

In light of the latest ruling of the ECJ, Art 26 of the EIR and not Art 25 (3) of the EIR could also apply to judgements relating to preservation measures taken after the request to open insolvency proceedings as contemplated by Art 25 (1) subpara 3 of the EIR. In the Eurofood/Parmalat decision[73] (→ see cf Table of Cases Art 3 of the EIR Appendix A mn 10), the ECJ held that a judgement that is made in response to a request stemming from the debtor's insolvency to open one of the proceedings set out in Annex A of the EIR constitutes the opening of insolvency proceedings within the meaning of this provision if such judgement leads to the divestment of the debtor and if, pursuant to it, one of the liquidators named in Annex C of the EIR is appointed. **Preliminary insolvency proceedings** can therefore be regarded as the opening of proceedings within the meaning of the EIR. Preservation measures taken by a provisional liquidator can no longer be subsumed under Art 25 (1) subpara 3 of the EIR but rather under Art 26 of the EIR. **38**

---

[68] MünchKomm BGB/*Kindler* IntInsR mn 591.

[69] *Virgós/Schmit* Explanatory report mn 208; D-K/D/Ch-*Duursma-Kepplinger* Art 26 mn 15.

[70] D-K/D/Ch-*Duursma-Kepplinger* Art 26 mn 15.

[71] Cf *Virgós/Schmit* Explanatory report mn 192.

[72] Also: *Paulus* Komm EuInsVO Art 25 mn 11.

[73] ECJ C-341/04 dated 2 May 2006, ZInsO 2006, 485.

7. Portugal's Declaration

39 The Portuguese Republic has made a **unilateral declaration** regarding the application of Art 37 of the EIR.[74] According to this, Art 37 of the EIR – which allows for the **conversion** into winding-up proceedings of independent territorial insolvency proceedings that were opened prior to main insolvency proceedings – is to be so construed that such conversion does not prevent a judicial assessment of the situation involved in the local proceedings (as in Art 36 of the EIR), nor does it prevent the taking into account of the interests of public order (that are being referred to in Art 26 of the EIR). If a request is made pursuant to Art 37 to convert independent territorial insolvency proceedings, Portugal retains the right to invoke Art 26 to reject the conversion as an infringement of public policy.[75]

---

[74] OJ 2000 No C 183/1.

[75] D-K/D/Ch-*Duursma-Kepplinger* Art 26 mn 16.

Chapter III

Secondary Insolvency Proceedings

Article 27
Opening of proceedings

The opening of the proceedings referred to in Article 3(1) by a court of a Member State and which is recognized in another Member State (main proceedings) shall permit the opening in that other Member State, a court of which has jurisdiction pursuant to Article 3(2), of secondary insolvency proceedings without the debtor's insolvency being examined in that other State. These latter proceedings must be among the proceedings listed in Annex B. Their effects shall be restricted to the assets of the debtor situated within the territory of that other Member State.

→ Cf Art 21 UNCITRAL Model Law

Contents

Index

Bibliography

Balz Das neue Europäische Insolvenzübereinkommen, ZIP 1996, p 948; *Balz* The European Union Convention on Insolvency Proceedings 70 American Bankruptcy Law Journal (1996), p 485; *Beck* Verwertungsfragen im Verhältnis von Haupt- und Sekundärinsolvenzverfahren nach der EuInsVO, NZI 2006, p 609; *Duursma-Kepplinger/Duursma* Das Schicksal von dinglichen Sicherungsrechten sowie des Eigentumsvorbehalts nach der Insolvenzverordnung, wbl 2002, p 59; *Duursma-Kepplinger/Duursma/Chalupsky* Europäische Insolvenzverordnung, Kommentar (2002); *Ehricke* Die Zusammenfassung von Insolvenzverfahren mehrerer Unternehmen desselben Konzerns, DZWiR 1999, p 356; *Ehricke* Die neue Europäische Insolvenzverordnung und grenzüberschreitende Konzerninsolvenzen, EWS 2002, 101; *Ehricke* Das Verhältnis des Hauptinsolvenzverwalters zum Sekundärinsolvenzverwalter bei grenzüberschreitenden Insolvenzen nach der EuInsVO, ZIP 2005, p 1104; *Ehricke/Ries* Die neue Europäische Insolvenzverordnung, JuS 2003, p 313; *Eidenmüller* Europäische Verordnung über Insolvenzverfahren und zukünftiges deutsches internationales Insolvenzrecht, IPRax 2001, p 2; *Fritz/Bähr* Die Europäische Verordnung über Insolvenzverfahren – Herausforderung an Gerichte und Insolvenzverwalter, DZWiR 2001, p 221; *Gottwald* Grenzüberschreitende Insolvenzen, 1997; *Hanisch* Stellungnahme zu der Frage, ob und gegebenenfalls in welcher Weise ein in seiner Wirkung territorial beschränktes Sonderinsolvenzverfahren über das Inlandsvermögen eines Schuldners vorzusehen ist, wenn dieser den Mittelpunkt seiner hauptsächlichen Interessen im Ausland hat, in Stoll (ed): Vorschläge und Gutachten zur Umsetzung des EU-Übereinkommens über Insolvenzverfahren im deutschen Recht, 1997, p 202; *Herchen* Das Übereinkommen über Insolvenzverfahren der Mitgliedstaaten der Europäischen Union vom 23.11.1995 (2000); *Herchen* Die Befugnisse des deutschen Insolvenzverwalters hinsichtlich der „Auslandsmasse“ nach In-Kraft-Treten der EG-Insolvenzverordnung (Verordnung des Rates Nr. 1346/2000), ZInsO 2002, p 345; *Herchen* International-Insolvenzrechtliche Kompetenzkonflikte in der Europäischen Gemeinschaft, ZInsO 2004, p 61; *Huber* Internationales Insolvenzrecht in Europa ZZP 114 (2001), p 133; *Kemper* Die Verordnung (EG) Nr. 1346/2000 über Insolvenzverfahren, ZIP 2001, p 1609; *Kolmann* Kooperationsmodelle im Internationalen Insolvenzrecht – Empfiehlt sich für das deutsche internationale Insolvenzrecht eine Neuorientierung (2001); *Leible/Staudinger* Die europäische Verordnung über Insolvenzverfahren, KTS 2000, p 533; *Lüke* Das europäische internationale Insolvenzrecht ZZP 111 (1998), p 275; *Mankowski* Konkursgründe beim inländischen Partikularkonkurs, ZIP 1995, p 1650; *Mankowski* Klärung von Grundfragen des europäischen Internationalen Insolvenzrechts durch die Eurofood-Entscheidung?, BB 2006, p 1753; *Meyer-Löwy/Plank* Entbehrlichkeit des Sekundärinsolvenzverfahrens bei flexibler Verteilung der Insolvenzmasse im Hauptinsolvenzverfahren, NZI 2006, p 622; *Meyer-Löwy/Poertzgen* Eigenverwaltung (§§ 270 InsO) löst Kompetenzkonflikt nach der EuInsVO, ZInsO 2004, p 195; *Morscher* Die europäische Insolvenzverordnung (2002); *Paulus* „Protokolle“ – ein anderer Zugang zur Abwicklung grenzüberschreitender Insolvenzen, ZIP 1998, p 977; *Paulus* Das inländische Parallelverfahren nach der Europäischen Insolvenzverordnung, EWS 2002, p 497; *Paulus* Zuständigkeitsfragen nach der Europäischen Insolvenzverordnung, ZIP 2003, p 1725; *Paulus* Comments on OLG Vienna dated 09.11.2004 – 28 R 225/04w, NZI 2005, p 62; *Penzlin/Riedemann* Comments on High Court of Justice Birmingham dated 18.04.2005, 2375 to 2382/05, NZI 2005, p 469; *Penzlin/Riedemann* Comments on High Court of Justice Birmingham dated 11.05.2005, 2375 – 2382/05, NZI 2005, p 517; *Reinhart* Sanierungsverfahren im internationalen Insolvenzrecht (1995); *Reisch/Winkler* Die Tücken der Eröffnung eines Parallelverfahrens nach der EuInsVO, ZIK 2004, p 118; *Ringstmeier/Homann* Masseverbindlichkeiten als Prüfstein des internationalen Insolvenzrechts, NZI 2004, p 354; *Rosch* Grenzüberschreitende Insolvenzen im Lichte der Verordnung (EG) Nr. 1346/2000, ELR 2000, p 378; *Sabel* Hauptsitz als Niederlassung im Sinne der EuInsVO, NZI 2004, p 126; *Scheel* Konzerninsolvenz – eine vergleichende Darstellung des US-amerikanischen und des deutschen Rechts (1995); *Schollmeyer* Gegenseitige Verträge im internationalen Insolvenzrecht (1997); *Smid* Vier Entscheidungen englischer und deutscher Gerichte zur europäischen internationalen Zuständigkeit zur Eröffnung von Hauptinsolvenzverfahren, DZWiR 2003, p 397; *Smid* Judikatur zum internationalen Insolvenzrecht, DZWiR 2004, p 397; *Spahlinger* Sekundäre Insolvenzverfahren bei grenzüberschreitenden Insolvenzen, eine vergleichende Untersuchung zum deutschen, US-amerikanischen, schweizerischen und europäischen Recht (1998); *Thieme* Vermögensgerichtsstände, Inlandsbezug und

Partikularkonkurs, Jahresheft der Internationalen Juristenvereinigung Osnabrück (1995/1996), p 44; *Trunk* Internationales Insolvenzrecht (1998); *Vallender* Die Voraussetzungen für die Einleitung eines Sekundärinsolvenzverfahrens nach der EuInsVO, InVo 2005, p 41; *Vallender* Aufgaben und Befugnisse des deutschen Insolvenzrichters in Verfahren nach der EuInsVO, KTS 2005, p 283; *Weller* Inländische Gläubigerinteressen bei internationalen Konzerninsolvenzen ZHR 169 (2005) p 570; *Wimmer* Die Besonderheiten von Sekundärinsolvenzverfahren unter besonderer Berücksichtigung des Europäischen Insolvenzübereinkommens, ZIP 1998, p 982; *Wimmer* Die Verordnung (EG) Nr. 1346/2000 über Insolvenzverfahren, ZInsO 2001, p 97.

1. General

1 Once main insolvency proceedings have been opened at the place where the debtor has its centre of main interests, which must be recognized pursuant to Article 16 et seq of the EIR, the only proceedings that may then be opened in another Member State with the exception of Denmark are territorially restricted insolvency proceedings within the meaning of Art 3 (2) and (3) of the EIR (secondary insolvency proceedings).[1] The 3rd sentence of Article 27 and the 2nd sentence of Article 3 (2) of the EIR restrict the insolvency law effects of such secondary insolvency proceedings[2] in territorial terms[3] to the Member State in whose territory secondary insolvency proceedings have been opened. Art 27 of the EIR does not apply to independent territorial insolvency proceedings.[4]

2 The prerequisite for opening secondary insolvency proceedings is the existence of an establishment within the meaning of Art 2 (h) of the EIR in the territory of the relevant Member State. By making the opening of secondary insolvency proceedings dependent upon the existence of an establishment, and given the broad definition of "establishment" in Art 2 (h) of the EIR, the Regulation was able to compromise between the concept of a multiplicity of proceedings and a unified proceeding.[5] Although the Regulation places particular emphasis on the principles of unified proceedings and the universality of them, the coupling of the admissibility of such proceedings to the – broadly defined – establishment of the debtor pays tribute to the considerable disparities between the national insolvency law regimes of the individual Member States and the divergent weighing of interests found in them.[6] There are also pragmatic reasons for allowing territorial insolvency proceedings.[7] This, however, does not resolve the issue as to whether such proceedings are useful from the decisive point of view of the joint and several creditors, which is what really counts.

3 In terms of insolvency law, the main effect of the opening of secondary insolvency proceedings is the separation of the insolvency estate situated in the territory of the secondary insolvency proceedings from the insolvency estate of main proceedings.[8]

---

1 *Virgós/Schmit* Explanatory Report mn 211.

2 These rare cases where territorial insolvency proceedings are opened prior to the opening of main insolvency proceedings (Art 3 (4) of the EIR) are referred to as *independent territorial insolvency proceedings*. Territorial insolvency proceedings in a broader sense, may be regarded as the generic term.

3 D-K/D/Ch-*Duursma-Kepplinger* Art 27 mn 71.

4 *Paulus* Komm EuInsVO Art 27 mn 3; see also mn 15 below and the comments on Art 28 of the EIR mn 8.

5 See *Ehricke* ZIP 2005, 1104, 1105; *Wimmer* ZIP 1998, 982, 985; FK-InsO/*Wimmer* Anhang I nach § 358 mn 87.

6 Critical: D-K/D/Ch-*Duursma-Kepplinger* Art 27 mn 3; *Herchen* Das Übereinkommen über Insolvenzverfahren der Mitgliedstaaten der Europäischen Union vom 23.11.1995 (2000) p 51; *Lüke* ZZP 111 (1998) 275, 297.

7 On this, see: mn 11 et seq below.

8 For the relevant point in time, see mn 61 et seq below.

2. Functions of Territorially Restricted Insolvency Proceedings

Territorially restricted insolvency proceedings essentially serve three functions.[9] The protective function of territorial insolvency proceedings (cf mn 5 et seq below), the assistance provided by secondary insolvency proceedings (cf mn 12 et seq below), and the substitution function of independent territorial insolvency proceedings (cf mn 15 et seq below). **4**

2.1 Protective Function of Territorial Insolvency Proceedings

2.1.1 Protection of national interests and creditors

The protection of national interests is facilitated through the Regulation by opening secondary insolvency proceedings. From that point of time the debtor's assets situated within the territory of the secondary insolvency proceedings are removed from the ambit of the *lex fori concursus universalis* and are subject of the *lex fori concursus secundarii.*[10] The Regulation thereby achieves two purposes: On the one hand, the private international law rule is applied to which local creditors have adapted themselves within the framework of their business relations to the debtor. They are spared having to familiarize themselves with foreign (insolvency) laws in a language generally foreign to them.[11] On the other hand, it minimizes possible conflicts between the *lex fori concursus universalis* and any other laws of the country of the secondary insolvency proceedings, e.g. laws applicable to individual legal relationships affected by the insolvency proceedings, which may arise because of a lack of coordination between the two legal systems. **5**

All of the debtor's creditors have the capacity to file an application to open proceedings, not just those whose claims can show a connection to the country of the secondary insolvency proceedings.[12] The protective function afforded by the secondary insolvency proceedings does not justify restricting in general the right to file an application to open proceedings to only certain local creditors. A conclusion to the contrary can neither be inferred from the wording of Art 29 (b) of the EIR nor from the purpose of secondary insolvency proceedings. If the drafters of the Regulation would had intended a corresponding provision, in the view of the specific restriction of the entitlement to file a request for opening a proceeding as in Art 4 (b) of the EIR in respect of independent territorial insolvency proceedings, then they would have made provision for it for secondary insolvency proceedings as well. Even though there is a territorial restriction of the assets of the secondary insolvency proceedings, the liabilities linked to it are universal in nature.[13] A review of whether the interests of the requesting creditor warrant protection is a sufficient way to protect against an excessive limitation of the principles of universal and unified proceedings. **6**

In the case of a cross-border reorganization, which both in legal and practical terms must ensue from the main insolvency proceedings, the opening of secondary insolvency proceedings is not necessarily a disadvantage;[14] a territorial reorganization plan pre- **7**

---

[9] *Virgós/Schmit* Explanatory Report mn 32 et seq; D-K/D/Ch-*Duursma-Kepplinger* Art 27 mn 7 et seq; *Lüke* ZZP 111 (1998) 275, 297 et seq.

[10] *Virgós/Schmit* Explanatory Report mn 32; D-K/D/Ch-*Duursma-Kepplinger* Art 27 mn 9 et seq; *Lüke* ZZP 111 (1998) 275, 298 et seq.

[11] Haß/Huber/Gruber/Heiderhoff-*Heiderhoff* Art 27 EuInsVO mn 4; see also: *Weller* ZHR 169 (2005) 570, 584 et seq.

[12] For a detailed discussion on this, see the comments on Art 29 of the EIR mn 25 et seq.

[13] On this, see: mn 85 et seq below.

[14] See Arts 33 and 34 of the EIR and the comments on these.

pared in conformity with the *lex fori concursus secundarii* and coordinated with the reorganization plan in the main proceedings can more readily accommodate "lighter" national characteristics, e.g. the ranking order of claims pursuant to the *lex fori concursus secundarii*, thus increasing local acceptance of the insolvency procedures.

2.1.2 Practical structuring possibilities

8 Where the creditors as a whole are comprised predominately of institutional creditors (e.g. banks) with only few small creditors, it may sometimes suffice to include certain national or local interests in a reorganization plan in main insolvency proceedings. Provided that the *lex fori concursus universalis* allows this, treating certain classes of creditors in a "special" manner, i.e. in derogation of the *lex fori concursus universalis,* in order to comply with national or local interests may make sense in order to prevent a request to open secondary insolvency proceedings.[15] Special treatment may, for example, take the form of deviating in the reorganization plan from the ranking order prescribed by the *lex fori concursus universalis,* forming for certain classes of creditors the ranking order pursuant to "their" *lex fori concursus secundarii.*[16]

9 But it should not be overlooked that affording special treatment to certain classes of creditors may also enable them to virtually bargain for the waiver, or the cumbersomeness, of the opening of secondary insolvency proceedings.

10 In the case of secondary insolvency proceedings pursuant to German law, extortionate requests of this kind can be prevented by an in-depth examination by the court of both the general interest to take legal action and the special interest in the opening of secondary insolvency proceedings.[17] Such an insolvency request is inadmissible and must therefore be denied. The liquidator of the main insolvency proceedings' right to be heard prior to the opening of secondary insolvency proceedings[18] not only satisfies general rules of procedural law in such a case, but it is also vital to the clarification of facts and the determination of an actual misappropriation of justice.

11 Cross-border insolvency proceedings can be dealt with pragmatically and efficiently in some cases through reorganization by a sale of the business enterprise, which emanates from the main insolvency proceedings, by coordinating the sale of the debtor's enterprise, including any foreign establishments, and a subsequent (in time) opening of secondary insolvency proceedings. The sale contract must, in such cases, be concluded prior to the opening of secondary insolvency proceedings in order to achieve a reorganization through a sale of the business enterprise as a whole. If the sale contract allocates a specific and appropriate portion of the purchase price to the individual establishments and to the assets sold in the Member State of the establishment, then this portion of the purchase price can be paid to the liquidator in the secondary insolvency proceedings in the event of the opening of secondary insolvency proceedings coordinated with the liquidator of main insolvency proceedings. Distribution to the creditors can then be effected by the secondary insolvency proceedings in accordance with the *lex fori con-*

---

[15] See High Court of Justice Birmingham NZI 2005, 467 et seq; NZI 2005, 515 et seq ("MG Rover"); on this: *Penzlin/Riedemann* NZI 2005, 469 et seq; *Penzlin/Riedemann* NZI 2005, 517 et seq; Table of Cases Art 3 of the EIR Appendix A mn 1.

[16] See High Court of Justice London, NZI 2006, 654 et seq ("Collins & Aikman"); on this: *Meyer-Löwy/Plank* NZI 2006, 622 et seq; also Table of Cases Art 3 of the EIR Appendix A mn 1.

[17] See the comments on Art 29 of the EIR mn 29 et seq.

[18] On this, see: mn 78 below.

cursus secundarii. However, whether the portion of the purchase price allotted to the respective establishment may actually be transferred to the insolvency estate of the secondary insolvency proceedings is a legally problematic issue that must be determined pursuant to the *lex fori concursus universalis*. Since the contract selling the business enterprise is attributed to the main insolvency proceedings, the total purchase price would arguably have to form part of the insolvency estate of the main proceedings. The share of the purchase price allocated to the establishments does not become part of the insolvency estate of the secondary insolvency proceedings on account of the divestment occasioned by the opening of the secondary insolvency proceedings. According to the line of reasoning applied here, the divestment occasioned by the opening of the secondary insolvency proceedings can no longer affect the assets connected to the establishment because the business enterprise has already been transferred to the purchaser. It is therefore of particular practical importance not to make a request for insolvency proceedings too early in the Member States where establishments are situated. Once a request is made, coordinating the chronological sequence of events becomes considerably more difficult because of the very limited means that the requesting parties (e.g. the liquidators in the main insolvency proceedings) and third parties can influence the date on which the proceedings are opened, which vary depending on the particular *lex fori concursus secundarii*.

2.2 Assistance Provided by Secondary Insolvency Proceedings

Secondary insolvency proceedings also provide assistance to the main insolvency proceedings.[19] In order to accomplish this, Art 29 (a) of the EIR affords the liquidator of main insolvency proceedings an independent right to request the opening of secondary insolvency proceedings. **12**

It may, for example, be more efficient in insolvency cases involving a complex asset structure to administer the estate in coordinated main and secondary insolvency proceedings rather than in one single main insolvency proceeding.[20] But whether this is actually ever contemplated is highly doubtful. If the liquidator of the main proceedings needs the assistance of knowledgeable persons in the pertinent legal fields in another Member State, such persons need not necessarily be liquidators of secondary insolvency proceedings. Local advisors may equally be consulted. This applies even more where – as in the case of German secondary insolvency proceedings – the liquidators of main insolvency proceedings have virtually no way of influencing which liquidator the court is going to appoint. Nevertheless, it may make sense to request the assistance of both local advisors and a liquidator of secondary proceedings should the cooperation between the liquidator of the main proceedings and local creditors, institutions, government authorities, etc. prove difficult, where the liquidator's status is not being given the respect theoretically envisioned by the Regulation (Article 18 (1) of the EIR). **13**

One of the primary reasons for the liquidator of the main insolvency proceedings to request the opening of secondary insolvency proceedings is because of the inclusion in the insolvency proceedings – via Art 5 of the EIR – of protected foreign secured rights.[21] Second- **14**

[19] Recitals 19 and 25; *Virgós/Schmit* Explanatory Report mn 33; D-K/D/Ch-*Duursma-Kepplinger* Art 27 mn 11; *Lüke* ZZP 111 (1998) 275, 298 et seq.

[20] D-K/D/Ch-*Duursma-Kepplinger* Art 27 mn 11; *Herchen* ZInsO 2002, 345, 351; *Wimmer* ZIP 1998, 982, 985; justifiably critical: *Smid* Komm EuInsVO Art 27 mn 7.

[21] In detail: *Herchen* Das Übereinkommen über Insolvenzverfahren der Mitgliedstaaten der Europäischen Union vom 23.11.1995 (2000) p 73 et seq; see also: *Wimmer* ZInsO 2001,

ary insolvency proceedings do not – probably not even if the *lex fori concursus secundarii* governed – allow the full value of such objects to be included in the assets available for distribution, although the objects may generally be used for continuing the business operations of the debtor's enterprise pursuant to Art 31 (3) and Art 33 (1) of the EIR.[22]

2.3 Substitution Function of Independent Territorial Insolvency Proceedings

15 For the sake of completeness, the so-called substitution function of independent territorial insolvency proceedings pursuant to Art 3 (4) of the EIR is worth mentioning.[23] But it must be emphasized again that Art 27 of the EIR does not apply to territorial insolvency proceedings.[24]

16 According to Art 3 (4) (a) of the EIR, independent territorial insolvency proceedings may be opened if the opening of main insolvency proceedings is impossible in the Member State whose courts have international jurisdiction pursuant to Art 3 (1) of the EIR. This may be the case particularly where the debtor lacks insolvency capacity pursuant to the *lex fori concursus universalis*.[25] The wording of Art 3 (4) (a) of the EIR, however, also includes the situation where main insolvency proceedings cannot be opened due to insufficiency of assets. If the potential assets of independent territorial insolvency proceedings admissible pursuant to Art 3 (4) (a) of the EIR were included to determine whether there were sufficient assets to cover the costs of the proceedings, and the conclusion is reached that they are not sufficient, but if such assets are sufficient to cover the costs of territorial insolvency proceedings, then it would seem correct to nevertheless allow the opening of the independent territorial insolvency proceedings.[26] Such a case clearly illustrates the substitution function of independent territorial insolvency proceedings.[27]

17 Often cited as an example of a debtor who lacks insolvency capacity is the natural person who is not a merchant and whose centre of main interests is located in France. It is not possible under French law to conduct insolvency proceedings in respect of the assets of such persons.[28] These cases will have little practical relevance, however, since it is extremely unlikely that such debtors will be disposed of the requisite establishment, provided that the term "establishment" is not interpreted too broadly.[29]

97, 101; *Duursma-Kepplinger/Duursma* wbl 2002, 59, 62 et seq.

[22] See the comments on Art 1 of the EIR mn 40 et seq and on Art 33 of the EIR mn 11 et seq and 15.

[23] On this, see: *Virgós/Schmit* Explanatory Report mn 30; D-K/D/Ch-*Duursma-Kepplinger* Art 27 mn 8; *Lüke* ZZP 111 (1998) 275, 298.

[24] See mn 1 above and the comments on Art 28 of the EIR mn 8.

[25] E.g. in case of a debtor with a public-law legal form; see D-K/D/Ch-*Duursma-Kepplinger* Art 3 mn 88 et seq.

[26] On this, see the comments on Art 3 of the EIR mn 127 et seq.

[27] D-K/D/Ch-*Duursma-Kepplinger* Art 3 mn 89; *Kolmann* Kooperationsmodelle im Internationalen Insolvenzrecht – Empfiehlt sich für das deutsche internationale Insolvenzrecht eine Neuorientierung (2001) p 334.

[28] *Virgós/Schmit* Explanatory Report mn 85; *Balz* ZIP 1996, 948, 949; D-K/D/Ch-*Duursma-Kepplinger* Art 27 mn 8; Haß/Huber/Gruber/Heiderhoff-*Haß/Herweg* Art 3 EuInsVO mn 50; Haß/Huber/Gruber/Heiderhoff-*Heiderhoff* Art 27 EuInsVO mn 5; in Moss/Fletcher/Isaacs-*Moss/Smith*, Regulation, mn 8.05, 8.218.

[29] On this, see mn 22 et seq; going too far, however, is the example of a summer residence in a foreign country that is occasionally let and that occasionally employs a caretaker cited in D-K/D/Ch-*Duursma-Kepplinger* Art 27 mn 20; *Paulus* EWS 2002, 497, 499; *Kolmann* Kooperationsmodelle im Internationalen Insolvenzrecht – Empfiehlt sich für das deutsche internationale Insol-

The ability to file a request to open independent territorial insolvency proceedings that is provided to local creditors through Art 3 (4) (b) of the EIR is merely an expression of the protective function of territorial insolvency proceedings.[30] 18

3. Prerequisites of Opening Secondary Insolvency Proceedings

3.1 Main Insolvency Proceedings

3.1.1 Opening of main insolvency proceedings

In order to open secondary insolvency proceedings it is imperative that main insolvency proceedings, which recognition is mandatory pursuant to Art 16 et seq (Annex A of the Regulation), have been opened in another Member State. In this regard, the court of the secondary insolvency proceedings only needs to examine whether the judgement ordering the opening of the insolvency proceedings is valid and whether the recognition of the order violates public policy (Art 26 of the EIR). It is irrelevant whether or not the foreign reason for the insolvency is known to the insolvency law of the court of the secondary insolvency proceedings.[31] For the other requirements in conjunction with an establishment, see the discussions under mn 23 below; for discussions regarding the costs to cover the proceedings, see the comments on Art 30 of the EIR. 19

Effectiveness of the opening of proceedings does not mean whether it is formally or substantively final and absolute (*res judicata*), but whether pursuant to the *lex fori concursus universalis* it gives rise to its immediate legal effects. The fact that the judgement may be appealed against in the country in which the proceedings are opened does not deter from this.[32] However, provisional main insolvency proceedings will not suffice.[33] This is so even in light of the decision of the ECJ in the Eurofood/Parmalat case.[34] Even the appointment of a provisional liquidator[35] – for example in German main insolvency proceedings – can be viewed as the opening of insolvency proceedings within the meaning of the Regulation,[36] the court of the main insolvency proceedings must still fully convince itself of the de facto insolvency of the debtor, i.e. of the existence of a reason to open insolvency proceedings pursuant to the *lex fori concursus universalis*. In this lies the actual justification, via Art 27 of the EIR, for doing away with the examination of the reason to open insolvency proceedings by the court of the secondary insolvency proceedings. For the appointing of a temporary administrator, as is the case in German insolvency law, such a conviction is generally not required. 20

Even if the prior judgement opening insolvency proceedings does not contain an indication that the court was aware of the cross-border dimension of the insolvency case, nor that it intended to open main insolvency proceedings within the meaning of the Regulation, there must still be an assumption that main insolvency proceedings have been opened. This follows from the special status afforded to independent territorial insolvency proceedings (Art 3 (4) of the EIR), which are to be viewed as the exception, 21

---

venzrecht eine Neuorientierung (2001) p 328.

[30] See mn 5 et seq above.

[31] *Paulus* Komm EuInsVO Art 27 mn 5.

[32] *Virgós/Schmit* Explanatory Report mn 147; D-K/D/Ch-*Duursma-Kepplinger* Art 16 mn 10 et seq; *Fritz/Bähr* DZWiR 2001, 221, 225.

[33] *Vallender* InVO 2005, 41, 42, 45; doubting this *Mankowski* BB 2006, 1753.

[34] NZI 2006, 360 et seq.

[35] Even the so-called weak temporary administrator of German law will suffice: *Herchen* NZI 2006, 435 et seq.

[36] On this: *Herchen* ZIP 2005, 1410 et seq.

i.e. as alternative proceedings, and from the universal nature of the effects of the divestment pursuant to the insolvency laws of the Member States.[37] Since such universal effects constitute the rule and the territorial (self-)limitation the exception, the exceptional case would in case of doubt have to be justified in law by some special reason, which is not present in such cases.

3.1.2 Termination of the main insolvency proceedings

22 If the main insolvency proceedings are stayed or terminated after the opening of secondary insolvency proceedings, secondary insolvency proceedings are to be continued provided that the continuation is permitted pursuant to the provisions of the *lex fori concursus secundarii*. Decisive here are the legal consequences contemplated by the *lex fori concursus secundarii* when the reason for the insolvency no longer exists; more precisely, when the reason for the (de facto) insolvency was the opening of the main insolvency proceedings whose recognition is mandatory.[38] It may be necessary to stay such proceedings.[39] Absent such a provision in the *lex fori concursus secundarii*, the termination alone of the main insolvency proceedings does not constitute a legally sufficient reason for terminating the secondary insolvency proceedings as well.[40] A provision of this kind, which would have to be included in the Regulation as a substantive law rule, does not exist.

3.2 Establishment

3.2.1 Establishment within the meaning of Article 2 (h) of the EIR

23 In order to open secondary insolvency proceedings, there must be an establishment in the Member State at whose courts a request is being made to open secondary proceedings. This requirement is laid down in the first sentence of Art 3 (2) of the EIR. Art 2 (h) of the EIR defines "establishment" as any place of operations where the debtor carries out a non-transitory economic activity with human means and goods. The fact that assets of the debtor are situated in the Member State where the request is being made does not suffice.[41] The legislators of the Regulation consciously refrained from creating jurisdiction based on the existence of assets.[42]

24 There is a wide consensus in favour of a broad interpretation of the term "establishment".[43] The reasons for this are found in the historical origins of the Regulation. Affording establishment a broad interpretation was meant to compensate those Member States that advocated an asset-dependent establishment of jurisdiction.[44] However,

---

[37] On this, see: *Herchen* Das Übereinkommen über Insolvenzverfahren der Mitgliedstaaten der Europäischen Union vom 23.11.1995 (2000) 40 et seq.

[38] On this, see: mn 30 et seq below.

[39] For German law, see the stay of the debtor's request pursuant to sec 212 et seq InsO.

[40] *Mankowski* BB 2006, 1753, 1757 et seq.

[41] OLG Vienna NZI 2005, 56, 60; concurring: *Paulus* NZI 2005, 62 et seq; *Virgós/Schmit* Explanatory Report mn 70; D-K/D/Ch-*Duursma-Kepplinger* Art 27, mn 20; *Kemper* ZIP 2001, 1609, 1613; *Leible/Staudinger* KTS 2000, 533, 547; in Moss/Fletcher/Isaacs-*Moss/Smith*, Regulation, mn 8.61.

[42] For a detailed discussion on the history of the Regulation, see: in FK-InsO/*Wimmer* Anhang I nach § 358 mn 87.

[43] For instance, *Weller* ZHR 169 (2005), 570, 586; critical view *Thieme* IJVO 1995/1996, 44, 83 et seq; see also *Rosch* ELR 2000, 378, 379.

[44] See OLG Vienna NZI 2005, 56, 60; *Balz* ZIP 1996, 948, 949; D-K/D/Ch-*Duursma-Kepplinger* Art 27 mn 20; in Haß/Huber/Gruber/Heiderhoff-*Heiderhoff* Art 27

neither the broad definition of Art 2 (h) of the EIR nor prevailing opinion rejecting a narrow interpretation is appropriate. This provision is merely the statutory enactment of that which is admitted in Recital 11, namely that as a result of the diversity of the legal regimes of the Member State, it is impossible to have one universal, unified proceeding. However a restrictive interpretation does not necessarily contradict the Regulation's legislative intent;[45] the legislator's intention is already reflected in the wording of the definition in Art 2 (h) of the EIR and does not have to reveal itself by way of a broad interpretation. One frequently cited example therefore goes too far: In this case, the debtor's holiday residence in another Member State that he occasionally lets out and for which he occasionally employs a caretaker is already deemed an establishment.[46] The restriction laid down by the Higher Regional Court (*OLG*) of Vienna should be followed. The court held that the fact that the debtor himself carries out an activity in another Member State is not sufficient on its own to affirm the employment of personnel within the meaning of Art 2 (h) of the EIR.[47] The *OLG* Vienna also held, however, that a single office with one employee will suffice. In light of the definition in Art 2 (h) of the EIR, this is clearly correct.

3.2.2 Establishment at the corporate domicile or at the reputed centre of interests of the debtor

In cases involving cross-border insolvencies of corporate groups, the corporate domicile of the parent company will often be used for determining international jurisdiction for opening main insolvency proceedings concerning the assets of subsidiaries of the group whose corporate domiciles – either pursuant to their incorporating statutes or their place of registration – are located in another Member State.[48] If main insolvency proceedings have been opened in respect of the assets of the group subsidiary, such proceedings must be recognized in compliance with Art 16 et seq. A false assumption of international jurisdiction is not a violation of public policy (Art 26 of the EIR) and therefore does not impair recognition.[49] **25**

In such cases, the court in the location of the corporate domicile – either pursuant to their incorporating statutes or their place of registration – or at the reputed centre of **26**

EuInsVO mn 7; *Wimmer* ZIP 1998, 982, 985; *Wimmer* in FK-InsO, Anhang I nach § 358, mn 87.

45 But see: D-K/D/Ch-*Duursma-Kepplinger* Art 27 mn 21; *Kolmann* Kooperationsmodelle im Internationalen Insolvenzrecht – Empfiehlt sich für das deutsche internationale Insolvenzrecht eine Neuorientierung (2001) 328.

46 D-K/D/Ch-*Duursma-Kepplinger* Art 27 mn 20; *Paulus* EWS 2002, 497, 499; *Kolmann* Kooperationsmodelle im Internationalen Insolvenzrecht – Empfiehlt sich für das deutsche internationale Insolvenzrecht eine Neuorientierung (2001) 328.

47 OLG Vienna NZI 2005, 56, 60; on this, see: *Paulus* NZI 2005, 62 et seq.

48 On this, see in particular the comments on Art 3 of the EIR mn 35 et seq, mn 46 et seq; some examples of this are: "ISA/Daisytek" High Court of Justice Leeds ZIP 2003, 1362; ZIP 2004, 963; on this: *Paulus* EWiR Art 3 EuInsVO 3/2003, 709 et seq; *Smid* DZWiR 2003, 397; *Herchen* ZInsO 2004, 61 et seq; "Hettlage" AG Munich ZIP 2004, 962; "MG Rover" High Court of Justice Birmingham, NZI 2005, 467 et seq; NZI 2005, 515 et seq; on this: *Penzlin/Riedemann* NZI 2005, 469 et seq; *Penzlin/Riedemann* NZI 2005, 517 et seq; "EMTEC" Tribunal de Commerce de Nanterre EWiR, Art 3 EuInsVO, 4/2006, 207 et seq; with comments: *Penzlin* "Eurofood/Parmalat" High Court of Dublin ZIP 2004, 1223 et seq; on this: *Herweg/Tschauner* EWiR Art 3 EuInsVO 5/2004, 599 et seq.

49 Examples of discussions of public policy in judicial decisions: OLG Vienna NZI 2005, 56, 58 et seq (denied); AG Düsseldorf ZIP 2004, 632 (incorrectly affirmed).

interests of the group subsidiary is not in general prevented from opening secondary insolvency proceedings. The corporate domicile can be an "establishment" within the meaning of Art 2 (h) of the EIR as long as the actual requirements of Art 2 (h) of the EIR have been satisfied.[50] The corporate domicile stipulated in the incorporating statute is not sufficient on its own.[51] By reinterpreting the (from the perspective of the court at the corporate domicile, reputed) head office as an establishment, the court is not making a contradiction since the centre of main interests within the meaning of Art 3 (1) of the EIR, the 1st sentence that was ascertained by the court in the judgement opening the main insolvency proceedings must be recognized as part of the decision to open proceedings.[52] Such a corporate domicile cannot, therefore, legally be the centre of main interests since only one such centre is conceivable by the Regulation. Thus, if the requirements for an establishment have been satisfied, then there may be an establishment at the location of the corporate domicile.

27 The previously discussed[53] functions of secondary insolvency proceedings, which are to protect national creditors or national interests and to provide assistance in some cases,[54] also speak in favour of allowing secondary insolvency proceedings at the location of the corporate domicile.[55]

3.2.3 A subsidiary as an establishment

28 A legally independent subsidiary does not constitute an establishment within the meaning of Art 2 (h) of the EIR.[56] If the subsidiary itself is insolvent, then the centre of its main interests as understood by Art 3 (1) of the EIR must be determined independently and, where applicable, a request to open main insolvency proceedings must be made and proceedings opened. The Regulation contains no provisions allowing, in the case of insolvencies of corporate groups, a legally independent subsidiary to be classified as an establishment of the parent company.[57]

29 Shares held by the debtor in a foreign subsidiary constitute assets of the debtor to be included in the insolvency seizure/attachment.[58] Shares are generally included in the

---

[50] AG Cologne ZIP 2004, 471; AG Düsseldorf ZIP 2004, 623, 625; Landesgericht Klagenfurt NZI 2004, 677; Landesgericht Innsbruck ZIP 2004, 1721; *Duursma-Kepplinger* NZI 2003, 87, 90; Haß/Huber/Gruber/Heiderhoff-*Heiderhoff* Art 27 EuInsVO mn 9; *Paulus* ZIP 2003, 1725, 1728; *Sabel* NZI 2004, 126, 127; *Weller* ZHR 169 (2005), 570, 586 et seq; *Wimmer* ZInsO 2005, 119, 124; FKInsO/*Wimmer*, Anhang I nach § 358 mn 88; dissenting opinion: in Kübler/Prütting-*Kemper* Art 102 sec 3 EGInsO mn 6; doubtful: Cour d'Appel de Versailles, judgement of 4 Sep 2003 – No 03/05038 – "ISA/Daisytek"; on this: *Mankowski* EWiR Art 3 EuInsVO 5/2003, 1239 et seq.

[51] Possibly leaning in this direction: Landesgericht Klagenfurt NZI 2004, 677, 678.

[52] FK-InsO/*Wimmer* Anhang I nach § 358 mn 88.

[53] See mn 5 et seq above.

[54] As was the case in AG Cologne ZIP 2004, 417 where all of the debtor's creditors and employees were domiciled in Germany.

[55] Haß/Huber/Gruber/Heiderhoff-*Heiderhoff* Art 27 EuInsVO mn 9; *Sabel* NZI 2004, 126, 127.

[56] D-K/D/Ch-*Duursma-Kepplinger* Art 27 mn 25; *Ehricke* EWS 2002, 101, 104 et seq; *Gottwald* Grenzüberschreitende Insolvenzen (1997) 21 et seq; Haß/Huber/Gruber/Heiderhoff-*Heiderhoff* Art 27 EuInsVO mn 8; *Huber* ZZP 114 (2001), 133, 143; *Smid* DZWiR 2004, 397, 400; *Vallender* InVO 2005, 41, 43 et seq; *Vallender* KTS 2005, 283, 303; see also: *Paulus* EWS 2002, 497, 501.

[57] *Virgós/Schmit* Explanatory Report mn 76; D-K/D/Ch-*Duursma-Kepplinger* Art 1 mn 48; Art 27 mn 26; *Gottwald* Grenzüberschreitende Insolvenzen (1997) 23; Haß/Huber/Gruber/Heiderhoff-*Haß/Herweg* Art 3 EuInsVO mn 55 et seq.

[58] D-K/D/Ch-*Duursma-Kepplinger* Art 27

insolvency estate of the main proceedings. If the corporate domicile of the subsidiary is located in a Member State (Art 2 (g) of the EIR) in which secondary insolvency proceedings have been opened in respect of the assets of the parent company, then such shares will become part of the insolvency estate of the secondary insolvency proceedings.

3.3 Reasons for Opening Insolvency Proceedings

3.3.1 Reasons for opening secondary insolvency proceedings

According to the 1st sentence of Art 27 of the EIR, the court seized with the issue of opening secondary insolvency proceedings no longer examines whether there is a reason for opening insolvency proceedings pursuant to the *lex fori concursus secundarii*.[59] The de facto insolvency of the debtor has already been established by the opening of main insolvency proceedings whose recognition is mandatory pursuant to Art 16 et seq of the EIR. The ascertainment of (de facto) insolvency through the opening of main insolvency proceedings, whose recognition is mandatory, is in itself an independent reason for opening secondary insolvency proceedings.[60] It is irrelevant whether the reasons for opening insolvency proceedings according to the *lex fori concursus universalis* are comparable to those of the *lex fori concursus secundarii*.[61] **30**

If the (de facto) insolvency based on the opening of main insolvency proceedings, the recognition of which is imperative, is understood to be an independent reason for opening secondary insolvency proceedings, then this amounts to a modification of the substantive insolvency law regulations of the *lex fori concursus secundarii*: the reasons for opening insolvency proceedings under national law are replaced by the opening of main insolvency proceedings under European law, the recognition of which is mandatory. This is the same reasoning behind the opinion held by some who hold that the recognition of foreign main insolvency proceedings replaces the reason for opening insolvency proceedings under the provisions of the *lex fori concursus secundarii*.[62] **31**

It is also acknowledged that Art 27 sentence 1 of the EIR does not constitute an evidentiary rule commanding an irrebuttable presumption, although such an interpretation could certainly be inferred from the wording.[63] Speaking against such an inference **32**

---

mn 27; *Eidenmüller* NJW 2004, 3455, 3458; in Haß/Huber/Gruber/Heiderhoff-*Haß/Herweg* Art 3 EuInsVO mn 42; Haß/Huber/Gruber/Heiderhoff-*Heiderhoff* Art 27 EuInsVO mn 8; *Huber* ZZP 114 (2001), 133, 142; *Kolmann* Kooperationsmodelle im Internationalen Insolvenzrecht – Empfiehlt sich für das deutsche internationale Insolvenzrecht eine Neuorientierung (2001) 329.

[59] See also mn 19 et seq above.

[60] Similar: Haß/Huber/Gruber/Heiderhoff-*Heiderhoff* Art 27 EuInsVO mn 6; *Morscher* Die europäische Insolvenzverordnung (2002), p 49; *Wimmer* ZIP 1998, 982, 986; FK-InsO/*Wimmer* Anhang I nach § 358 mn 92; obvious dissenting opinion: *Beutler/Debus* EWiR Art 3 EuInsVO 3/2005, 217 et seq.

[61] Concurring: *Smid* Komm EuInsVO Art 27 mn 18; see also: *Lüke* ZZP 111 (1998), 275, 302 et seq; critical of this: *Kolmann* Kooperationsmodelle im Internationalen Insolvenzrecht – Empfiehlt sich für das deutsche internationale Insolvenzrecht eine Neuorientierung (2001) 336 et seq; *Wimmer* ZIP 1998, 982, 986.

[62] D-K/D/Ch-*Duursma-Kepplinger* Art 27 mn 33; *Kolmann* Kooperationsmodelle im Internationalen Insolvenzrecht – Empfiehlt sich für das deutsche internationale Insolvenzrecht eine Neuorientierung (2001) 337.

[63] FK-InsO/*Wimmer* Anhang I nach § 358 mn 92; with respect to a comparable provision in German autonomous international insolvency in sec 356 (3) InsO see: FK-InsO/*Wimmer* Anhang I nach § 356 mn 15.

is the fact that, in the court's examination of (de facto) insolvency, neither the assets and liabilities of the debtor's that have to be included nor the reasons for opening main and secondary insolvency proceedings have to be identical. However, if the ascertainment of (de facto) insolvency in the main insolvency proceedings is to serve as evidence in secondary insolvency proceedings, an evidentiary rule must be presumed that logically presupposes that the actual issues and requirements are identical in both proceedings.

33 Neither can Art 27 sentence 1 of the EIR be construed as a rule of international procedural insolvency law,[64] i.e. it cannot be viewed as a provision regarding the recognition of foreign judgements.[65] Since the insolvency law regimes of the individual Member States do not permit the opening of insolvency proceedings in the absence of a reason, the legal systems of the individual Member States need to be modified. The recognition of the opening of main insolvency proceedings does not in itself satisfy this since the assets and liabilities to be included for the determination of de facto insolvency in main insolvency proceedings may differ from those to be taken into account in secondary insolvency proceedings.[66] Therefore, an understanding of Art 27 sentence 1 of the EIR purely as a provision recognizing foreign judgements will not satisfy this requirement.

34 Substantively, the correctness of interpreting Art 27 of the EIR as an independent reason for opening insolvency proceedings, which has been created through material integration, follows from the fact that the Regulation confers on an establishment within the meaning of Art 2 (h) of the EIR legal personality, albeit limited, for the opening of secondary insolvency proceedings. However, such an establishment remains a legally dependent part of the debtor that is merely clothed in part with legal personality; it is irrelevant whether the debtor has the legal form of a legal entity, a natural person, or a company. At the point in time at which secondary insolvency proceedings are opened, the de facto insolvency pursuant to the *lex fori concursus universalis* of the subject "debtor" – who has legal capacity for an insolvency – has already been ascertained and includes the assets and liabilities of future secondary insolvency proceedings.[67] Art 16 et seq of the EIR stipulates that the decision (i.e. the ascertainment of de facto insolvency) must be recognized in the territory of the secondary insolvency proceedings. Therefore, the inclusion of the insolvency estate situated in the country of the secondary proceedings in insolvency proceedings, be these main or secondary insolvency proceedings, has already taken place at the time of the opening of the main insolvency proceedings.

3.3.2 Digression: Reason for opening territorial insolvency proceedings

35 Because of the absence of opened main insolvency proceedings, it is more difficult to ascertain the reason for opening insolvency proceedings in the case of independent territorial insolvency proceedings than it is for secondary insolvency proceedings. Art 27 of the EIR does not apply in the case of independent territorial insolvency proceedings.[68]

36 It must be kept in mind that the reason for opening insolvency proceedings is to be determined pursuant to the provisions of the *lex fori concursus particularis*. The question

[64] On the wording, see: *Herchen* Das Übereinkommen über Insolvenzverfahren der Mitgliedstaaten der Europäischen Union vom 23.11.1995 (2000) 26.

[65] But see: FK-InsO/*Wimmer* Anhang I nach § 358 mn 92.

[66] On this, see: mn 35 et seq below.

[67] Similar: D-K/D/Ch-*Duursma-Kepplinger* Art 27 mn 35.

[68] *Paulus* Komm EuInsVO Art 27 mn 7.

involved both with the inability to pay debts (*Zahlungsunfähigkeit*) and with over-indebtedness (*Überschuldung*) is whether this should be measured on a territorial or on a universal basis, or a mixture of both. If the law of the respective Member State only recognizes the inability to pay as a reason for opening insolvency proceedings,[69] then this solely is the decisive factor.

The establishment must be presumed as the reference entity for evaluating the inability to pay.[70] Such an evaluation must take into account any establishment-related liabilities and any liquidity capable for consideration pursuant to the *lex fori concursus secundarii* that, pursuant to the seizure/attachment effects of the opening order, belongs to the future assets in the insolvency. Whether or not the debtor is sufficiently liquid at the centre of its main interests or in other establishments is irrelevant if such liquid funds are not at the disposal of the establishment to pay the debts owing. Otherwise, the creditors of the establishment would be denied the special protection of territorial insolvency proceedings afforded them by Art 3 (4) (b) of the EIR. Such creditors would be forced to rely on the regular execution procedures in a foreign country. **37**

In light of the fact that assets situated in other Member States are not included in the distributable estate of the territorial insolvency proceedings, it would seem inappropriate to evaluate the inability to pay either on a worldwide basis[71] or based on the main and the European establishments;[72] this would also not be in line with the primary aims of territorial insolvency proceedings, this being the safeguarding of the interests of national creditors.[73] In a decision of the German Federal Supreme Court (*BGH*) dealing with what constitutes ceased payments of a worldwide operating company, the court held that the (main) establishment at the centre of the main interests and the European establishments had to be taken into consideration.[74] However, because the court did not deal with the Regulation's territorial scope of application, this decision also fails to supply a proper basis for evaluation in cases falling with the Regulation's sphere of application.[75] **38**

The territorial indivisibility of the debtor's legal capacity in no way lends support to a worldwide-based evaluation[76] since the recognition of the insolvency proceedings con- **39**

---

69 For example Belgian law (*Verdonck* in Münchener Kommentar zur InsO, vol 3, 2003, Belgium mn 26) and French law (*Augustin* in Münchener Kommentar zur InsO, vol 3, 2003, France mn 4); different in German law for example in sec 17 InsO (insolvent) and sec 19 InsO (overindebted).

70 See also: *Eidenmüller* IPRax 2001, 2, 12; *Hanisch* in Stoll (ed) Vorschläge und Gutachten zur Umsetzung des EU-Übereinkommens über Insolvenzverfahren im deutschen Recht 1997, p 202, 205 comments on the issue as to whether and, if applicable, in which way special insolvency proceedings, with limited territorial effects, in respect of a debtor's national assets are to be regarded when the centre of the debtor's main interests is situated in a foreign country.

71 See *Lüer* Kölner Schrift zur Insolvenzordnung 2nd edn 2000, p 297, 314 et seq; *Mankowski* ZIP 1995, 1650 et seq; *Reischl/Winkler* ZIK 2004, 118, 120.

72 FK-InsO/Wimmer Anhang I nach § 358 mn 94; *Wimmer* ZIP 1998, 983, 986.

73 See also: *Eidenmüller* IPRax 2001, 2, 12.

74 BGH ZIP 1991, 1014, 1015.

75 If the protection of national creditors is correctly placed at the centre of the discussion, then it would appear appropriate to be guided by rules that alleviate regular cross-border execution procedures. For instance, the Convention on Jurisdiction and the Enforcement of Judgments in Civil and Commercial Matters done at Lugano on 16 September 1988 or the Council Regulation (EC) No 44/2001 of 22 December 2000 on Jurisdiction and the Recognition and Enforcement of Judgments in Civil and Commercial Matters.

76 Held by: D-K/D/Ch-*Duursma-Kepplinger* Art 3 mn 100.

cerning the establishment presupposes at least a certain degree of legal independence on the part of the establishment, enough at least for the purposes of the insolvency proceedings contemplated by the Regulation. The universal nature of the liabilities of the territorial insolvency proceedings[77] equally fails to support an establishment-based evaluation. This would only be an argument if participation in subsequent main insolvency proceedings and other secondary insolvency proceedings was not possible.

40 Over-indebtedness is a relatively unsuitable reason for opening territorial insolvency proceedings, the concept of over-indebtedness being based on the legal entity's accounting.[78] Should over-indebtedness nevertheless constitute a reason for opening insolvency proceedings pursuant to the *lex fori concursus secundarii* invoked for the decision, this is not modified by the Regulation. However, if it is presumed – as it is here – that the establishment has only limited legal personality for insolvency law purposes, then neither over-indebtedness nor the inability to pay can be evaluated in relation to the establishment. In this case, the establishment-related liabilities are to be set off against the assets situated in the Member State in which the establishment is situated.[79]

41 A worldwide-based evaluation of over-indebtedness must be ruled out as is an evaluation that sets off the assets of the establishment against the entire worldwide liabilities.[80]

3.4 Other Requirements of the Lex Fori Concursus Secundarii

42 Another requirement for opening secondary insolvency proceedings is that the party making the request must be empowered to do so. This stems partly from the insolvency laws of the individual Member States and partly from the Regulation.[81]

43 Whether the debtor has insolvency capacity or not must be answered solely by the *lex fori concursus secundarii*. This follows from Art 4 (1), (2)(a) of the EIR, and from Art 28 of the EIR. The fact that main insolvency proceedings will still be recognized in compliance with Art 16 (1) sentence 2 of the EIR even if the opening of insolvency proceedings in respect of the debtor's assets would be inadmissible pursuant to the laws of the respective Member State does nothing to change this. This is regulated in German law in Sections 11 and 12 *InsO*.

44 The issue of jurisdiction within a sovereign state is also a matter for the *lex fori concursus secundarii*.[82] This is regulated in German law in Sections 2 and 3 *InsO*.

---

[77] On this, see: mn 78 below; but see: *Mankowski* ZIP 1995, 1650, 1656.

[78] *Eidenmüller* IPRax 2001, 2, 12.

[79] Dissenting opinion (the establishment-related assets only): D-K/D/Ch-*Duursma-Kepplinger* Art 3 mn 103; *Mankowski* ZIP 1995, 1650, 1654; FK-InsO/*Wimmer* Anhang I nach § 358 mn 95.

[80] Justifiably critical on this point: D-K/D/Ch-*Duursma-Kepplinger* Art 3 mn 103; *Mankowski* ZIP 1995, 1650, 1654; FK-InsO/*Wimmer* Anhang I nach § 358 mn 95; *Wimmer* ZIP 1998, 983, 986.

[81] On this, see the comments on Art 29 of the EIR mn 1 et seq.

[82] On this and on Austrian law, see: D-K/D/Ch-*Duursma-Kepplinger* Art 27 mn 40 et seq.

4. Effects of the Opening of Proceedings

4.1 Assets

4.1.1 Territorial restriction of the assets of the secondary insolvency proceedings

Upon the opening of main insolvency proceedings, a unified and universal insolvency estate (assets) comes into existence. The opening of secondary insolvency proceedings causes a reduction of these assets in the amount of the debtor's assets situated in the territory of the Member State where secondary insolvency proceedings are opened. The unified insolvency estate is divided amongst the main and the secondary insolvency proceedings. **45**

Under certain circumstances, the dividing of the assets may alter the insolvency estate as a whole. **46**

The insolvency estate may increase if the debtor's assets situated in the country where secondary insolvency proceedings are opened contains property encumbered with third party rights *in rem* within the meaning of Art 5 of the EIR. If permitted by the *lex fori concursus secundarii*, this property will be included in the assets of the secondary insolvency proceedings even though – at least with respect to the value of it seen from an economic viewpoint – it was (partly) excluded from the assets of the main insolvency proceedings because of Art 5 (1) of the EIR.[83] **47**

Where the *lex fori concursus universalis* excludes certain property of the debtor's assets from the effects of the seizure/attachment (Art 4 (2) sentence 2 (b) of the EIR), property that is, however, situated in the territory of the country of the secondary insolvency proceedings, then this property will become part of the insolvency estate of the secondary insolvency proceedings as long as this is permissible according to the *lex fori concursus secundarii* (Art 4 (2) sentence 2 (b) and 28 of the EIR). This will also result in an increase of the insolvency estate. **48**

The following is not a case where the insolvency estate is being diminished:[84] where the *lex fori concursus secundarii* stipulates that, although it is situated in the territory of the country of the secondary proceedings as understood in Art 2 (g) of the EIR, certain property of the debtor's assets is to be excluded from the insolvency estate although such property was part of the assets of the main insolvency proceedings, then the effects of any seizure/attachment ensuing from the main insolvency proceedings continues in effect despite the opening of secondary insolvency proceedings. The setting aside of the effects of such a seizure/attachment would necessitate the enactment of a regulation. However, neither the Regulation nor generally the *lex fori concursus universalis* contains such a regulation. Articles 5 (1), 7 (1), and Articles 3 (2) sentence 2 and 17 (2) sentence 1 of the EIR merely restrict the effects of the seizure/attachment of the main insolvency proceedings to the extent to which the seizure/attachment of the secondary insolvency proceedings covers the debtor's assets. However, neither these regulations nor Articles 4 (2) sentence 2 (b) and 28 of the EIR may be interpreted as facilitating the creation of insol- **49**

[83] On this, see the comments on Art 5 of the EIR mn 10 et seq. This ultimately depends on whether art 5 (1) of the EIR precludes the divestment of such assets and creates insolvency-immune assets of the debtor, or if it aims at preserving (only) the economic value of the owner's rights *in rem* pursuant to the provisions of the *lex fori concursus secundarii* where applicable; see *Herchen* Das Übereinkommen über Insolvenzverfahren der Mitgliedstaaten der Europäischen Union vom 23.11.1995 (2000) 81 et seq; Haß/Huber/Gruber/Heiderhoff-*Huber* Art 5 EuInsVO mn 15 et seq.

[84] Unclear: D-K/D/Ch-*Duursma-Kepplinger* Art 27 mn 54.

vency-immune assets of the debtor because of the divergent provisions on the ascertainment of the insolvency estate in the substantive laws of the *lex fori concursus universalis* and the *lex fori concursus secundarii.*[85] According to Art 4 (2) sentence 2 (b) of the EIR, the *lex fori concursus secundarii* only determines which property is to form part of the insolvency estate; it does not determine which property is to be excluded from the effects of the seizure/attachment ensuing from the order opening the main insolvency proceedings. Finally, Articles 35 and 20 (2) of the EIR, as well as the universal nature of the liabilities of the secondary insolvency proceedings,[86] all speak in favour of upholding the effects of the seizure/attachment emanating from the main insolvency proceedings; they clearly illustrate that, despite a territorial division of the assets, the debtor's worldwide or Community assets constitute a common fund from which claims can be satisfied.[87]

4.1.2 Liabilities of the insolvency estate

50 The liabilities of the insolvency estate, i.e. the debt claims for which the insolvency estate is fully liable, must be satisfied out of that insolvency estate in which the liquidator who established the liabilities had powers of disposition.[88] Any contrary view, for example that the debtor's worldwide assets constitute a fund from which the insolvency-estate liabilities and the procedural costs of all insolvency proceedings opened pursuant to the Regulation are to be satisfied, thwarts an efficient handling of insolvency proceedings when there is a multiplicity of proceedings; the liquidator would hardly be in a position to decide whether the total insolvency estate was sufficient to cover additional insolvency estate liabilities, for example the liabilities related to a continuance of business operations.[89]

51 The following cases are undisputed: the insolvency estate of the secondary proceedings is solely liable for insolvency-estate liabilities established in opening proceedings prior to the secondary insolvency proceedings or after the opening of secondary proceedings.[90] If insolvency estate liabilities are established by the liquidator in the main insolvency proceedings after the opening of secondary insolvency proceedings, the insolvency estate of the secondary proceedings is not liable.[91] The same applies to the costs of proceedings: for the costs of the secondary insolvency proceedings, its insolvency estate alone is liable. If costs are incurred by the main insolvency proceedings subsequent to the opening of secondary insolvency proceedings, the part of the insolvency estate of the secondary proceedings that has been separated in the interim from the estate of the main insolvency proceedings is not liable for these costs.

52 What is problematic is how to treat insolvency-estate liabilities and the procedural costs of the main insolvency proceedings when such liabilities are established prior to the opening of secondary insolvency proceedings and before the separation of the insolvency estate of secondary insolvency proceedings from that of the main insolvency proceedings.[92]

---

[85] On this, see also: Haß/Huber/Gruber/Heiderhoff-*Huber* Art 5 EuInsVO mn 15 et seq.

[86] On this, see: mn 78 below and the comments on Art 30 of the EIR mn 2 et seq.

[87] D-K/D/Ch-*Duursma-Kepplinger* Art 27 mn 56; *Herchen* Das Übereinkommen über Insolvenzverfahren der Mitgliedstaaten der Europäischen Union vom 23.11.1995 (2000) 53.

[88] D-K/D/Ch-*Duursma-Kepplinger* Art 27 mn 57 et seq; *Ringstmeier/Hohmann* NZI 2004, 354 et seq; FK-InsO/*Wimmer* Anhang I nach § 358 mn 96.

[89] See: D-K/D/Ch-*Duursma-Kepplinger* Art 27 mn 57; *Herchen* Das Übereinkommen über Insolvenzverfahren der Mitgliedstaaten der Europäischen Union vom 23.11.1995 (2000) 51.

[90] *Paulus* Komm EuInsVO Art 28 mn 5 et seq, 7.

[91] *Paulus* Komm EuInsVO Art 28 mn 5 et seq, 7.

[92] Cf *Beck* NZI 2007, 1, 2 et seq.

The favoured solution is the formation of partial estates, especially a third (fictitious) partial estate.[93] The (fictitious) third estate comprises the debtor's worldwide assets. Next to this is the insolvency estate of the main proceedings after the opening of secondary insolvency proceedings and the insolvency estate of the secondary proceedings. Using this approach, it would appear correct to limit the assets of the third (fictitious) insolvency estate to the property that was included in the debtor's assets at the time of the opening of the secondary insolvency proceedings. However this is not clearly stated by the advocators of this line of reasoning. The time at which the insolvency-estate liabilities were established cannot be the decisive point in time, unless this corresponds with those provisions of the *lex fori concursus universalis* dealing with the liability of the insolvency assets for insolvency-estate liabilities. This is hardly imaginable, however, and is not in line with German law for example. What is certain is that a later increase of the insolvency estate of the secondary proceedings will not be taken into account. **53**

Some supporters of the aforementioned solution are in favour of imposing full liability on that part of the third insolvency estate attributable to the insolvency estate of the secondary proceedings,[94] while others are in favour of limiting liability to that part of insolvency-estate liabilities equivalent to the part of the estate of secondary proceedings attributable to the third (fictitious) estate.[95] **54**

In my opinion the first version is preferable, but with a restriction and a certain degree of refinement. It must be kept in mind that the liquidator in the main insolvency proceedings in the phase prior to the opening of proceedings must consider whether the insolvency estate contains sufficient assets to cover the costs of the proceedings. In the phase after the opening of proceedings but prior to establishing the insolvency-estate liabilities, a determination must be made whether the insolvency estate is sufficient to cover these insolvency-estate liabilities. If secondary insolvency proceedings have not been opened, the liquidator in the main insolvency proceedings is not obliged when making his determination to consider the possibility of such secondary insolvency proceedings being opened.[96] This is made clear through a simple logical consideration: where substantial portions of the debtor's assets are situated in a Member State that has international jurisdiction for secondary insolvency proceedings, then the only thing that could lead to the assets being insufficient to cover the costs of the future main insolvency proceedings is the opening of these secondary proceedings. This means that both the main and the secondary insolvency proceedings could not be opened. The debtor's insolvency **55**

[93] D-K/D/Ch-*Duursma-Kepplinger* Art 28 mn 57; *Reinhart* Sanierungsverfahren im internationalen Insolvenzrecht 1995, 295 et seq; similar: *Ringstmeier/Hohmann* NZI 2004, 354 et seq; *Lüke* ZZP 111 (1998), 275, 306; *Paulus* Komm EuInsVO Art 28 mn 5 et seq, 7; FK-InsO/*Wimmer* Anhang I nach § 358 mn 96.

[94] *Ringstmeier/Hohmann* NZI 2004, 354, 358.

[95] D-K/D/Ch-*Duursma-Kepplinger* Art 28 mn 57; *Reinhart* Sanierungsverfahren im internationalen Insolvenzrecht 1995, p 295 et seq; *Lüke* ZZP 111 (1998), 275, 306; FK-InsO/*Wimmer* Anhang I nach § 358 mn 96.

[96] But see: FK-InsO/*Wimmer* Anhang I nach § 358 mn 96. What must be taken into account, however, are independent territorial insolvency proceedings that are already opened. If the main proceedings have not yet been opened, but secondary insolvency proceedings have already been requested, then its assets also do not need to be deducted. Firstly, a request at the point in time of the examination is inadmissible because the opening of secondary insolvency proceedings necessitates previously opened main insolvency proceedings. Secondly, it has not been determined whether proceedings will be opened at all even if main insolvency proceedings are opened prior to the decision of the court invoked to make the decision.

would have to be dealt with in territorial insolvency proceedings pursuant to Art 3 (4) of the EIR without including the assets situated at the centre of the debtor's main interests. Such an outcome is not only inappropriate, it is also contrary to the goal expressed in Recital 12 of the EIR, namely to deal with insolvency cases first and foremost in a universal main insolvency proceeding. It is also contrary to the objectives of secondary insolvency proceedings,[97] which do not exactly include the thwarting of main insolvency proceedings.

56 Although when examining whether the procedural costs can be covered, the liquidator in main insolvency proceedings is not obliged to take into account the possibility that the main insolvency estate may be diminished by the insolvency estate of subsequent secondary proceedings, the fact still remains that not only is there a latent risk that the insolvency estate will be diminished by the opening of secondary insolvency proceedings, but that the opening of such proceedings is even condoned by the system. Looked at from the perspective of both the State of the opening proceedings, in its capacity as creditor for the procedural costs, and the other creditors of the insolvency estate, the only secure funds liable for the satisfaction of their claims are the debtor's assets situated in the State in which the main insolvency proceedings are opened, or those situated in those States where there is no international jurisdiction pursuant to Art 3 (2) of the EIR.

57 This, together with the principle that the liabilities of the insolvency estate must be satisfied out of the insolvency estate in which the liquidator who established the liabilities had powers of disposition, justify limiting the liability of the insolvency estate of the secondary proceedings to covering any shortages of payments in respect of the insolvency-estate liabilities and the procedural costs of the main proceedings. Liability is therefore neither joint and several, nor is it proportionate to the partial insolvency estates.

58 The respective creditors of the insolvency-estate liabilities or of the procedural costs must assert their claims against the liquidator in the secondary insolvency proceedings.

59 Because of the recognition of the insolvency-law effects of the main insolvency proceedings, the classification as insolvency-estate liabilities or as procedural costs pursuant to the *lex fori concursus universalis* must also be recognized in the secondary proceedings. The liability of the insolvency estate of the secondary proceedings is effected by ranking the insolvency-estate liabilities and the procedural costs established pursuant to the *lex fori concursus universalis* in the ranking system of the *lex fori concursus secundarii.* The liabilities are to be allocated the same priority that would be allocated to insolvency-estate liabilities and to procedural costs in the secondary insolvency proceedings. Should the assets of the secondary proceedings be insufficient to satisfy all of the insolvency-estate liabilities and all of the procedural costs, then satisfaction will be effected in equal shares. However, this too must be permitted by the *lex fori concursus secundarii.*[98]

4.1.3 Insufficiency of assets in main proceedings caused by the opening of secondary proceedings

60 Despite the fact that, as demonstrated, the insolvency estate of the secondary proceedings is liable for certain liabilities of the insolvency estate and the procedural costs of the main proceedings, the division of the estate caused by the opening of secondary insolvency proceedings may lead to an insufficiency of the insolvency estate in the main

[97] See mn 5 et seq above.

[98] In German law, see sec 209 InsO.

proceedings.[99] The manner in which insufficiency of assets in the main insolvency proceedings is dealt with is determined by the *lex fori concursus universalis*.

4.1.4 Assets of the debtor situated in the Member State of the secondary proceedings

The *situs* of the various assets of the debtor is regulated in Art 2 (g) of the EIR.[100] **61**

4.1.5 Decisive point in time for ascertaining assets

The time at which proceedings are opened is decisive for the effects in terms of insolvency law of the seizure/attachment (Art 1 (1) = divestment); such seizure/attachment partially or completely divests the debtor of his powers of disposition and vests these in the liquidator.[101] **62**

A subsequent cross-border shifting of the *situs* of property will not alter the property's allocation to the one or the other insolvency estate. This is illustrated by Art 18 (2) sentence 1 of the EIR. According to this section, the liquidator in territorial insolvency proceedings is entitled to assert in any other Member State that moveable property was removed to the territory of the other Member State after the opening of insolvency proceedings. This provision does not clothe the liquidator with anything akin to a substantive-law power to act in other Member State, it is merely a confirmation of such power.[102] The justification for this is found in the substantive-law entitlement to the insolvency estate that is conferred on the liquidator via the seizure/attachment of the estate. **63**

In some cases, however, an earlier point in time is decisive. Art 18 (2) sentence 2 of the EIR empowers the liquidator in secondary insolvency proceedings to bring an avoidance action in any of the remaining Member States. Because of its connection to Art 18 (1) of the EIR in the Regulation, the Regulation makes it clear that an avoidance action may be made to reverse a removal of assets to another Member State. Art 18 (2) sentence 2 of the EIR does not, however, mean that assets removed outside the State where proceedings are opened will be subject to any divestment ensuing from secondary insolvency proceedings. **64**

Doubtful is whether the various national laws on the avoidance of transactions detrimental to the creditors (that are made by the insolvent prior to the opening of the proceedings) cover the actual elements of such cases. In German insolvency law, the elements of Section 129 et seq *InsO* allowing such an avoidance would not cover such cases where there is an intentional change of the governing legal regime to the detriment of the creditors of a secondary insolvency proceeding for the purposes of benefiting creditors of other secondary or main insolvency proceedings. Absent comparable interests involved in avoidance cases pursuant to Section 129 et seq *InsO* and those involved in the other legal regime, an application by way of analogy can also not be considered. There is no detriment to the creditors because every creditor is entitled to participate in all other **65**

[99] See *Lüke* ZZP 111 (1998), 275, 306; FK-InsO/*Wimmer* Anhang I nach § 358 mn 96; regarding the consequences for the secondary insolvency proceedings, see mn 22 above.

[100] On this, see the comments on Art 2 mn 29 et seq; D-K/D/Ch-*Duursma-Kepplinger* Art 2 mn 15 et seq.

[101] *Smid* Komm EuInsVO Art 28 mn 28; see also: D-K/D/Ch-*Duursma-Kepplinger* Art 28 mn 71.

[102] Misunderstood: FK-InsO/*Wimmer* Anhang I nach § 358 mn 85.

insolvency proceedings, i.e. in proceedings in another Member State to which assets have been removed.

4.1.6 Insufficiency of assets in secondary insolvency proceedings

66 Where the *lex fori concursus secundarii* prescribes that the insolvency estate must be examined to ascertain whether it is sufficient to cover the costs of the proceedings, then this ascertainment must be based on the assets situated in the territory of the State of the secondary insolvency proceedings at the time of the opening of such proceedings.[103]

67 Whether those assets that can be reclaimed back to the insolvency estate of the secondary proceedings in conjunction with an avoidance action (Art 18 (2) sentence 2 of the EIR) are to be taken into account when deciding whether there is a sufficiency of assets is a decision for the *lex fori concursus secundarii*.[104] Under German insolvency law, such assets may be taken into account in full or in part under certain circumstances; the decision is based on the chances of success of the avoidance action and the creditworthiness of the party opposing it.

68 If the assets are insufficient to cover the costs of the proceedings, the requesting party may be asked to make an advance payment of costs and expenses (Art 30 of the EIR).[105]

4.1.7 Transfers of ownership between the assets of the main and secondary insolvency proceedings

69 Transfers of ownership between the various insolvency estates are not possible[106] if the seizure/attachment ensuing from the opening of insolvency proceedings does not change the legal status of the debtor entity with respect to its assets.[107]

70 Legally possible, however, are transfers of ownership where the opening of insolvency proceedings in effect clothes the debtor's assets with legal proprietary rights of their own, the insolvency estate itself acquiring legal capacity and thus becoming the legal entity with respect to the assets.[108]

71 Where such transfers of ownership are not legally possible, one potential way of transferring the asset from the insolvency estate of the secondary proceedings to that of the main insolvency proceedings may be for the liquidator of the secondary insolvency proceedings to release (*Freigabe*) the asset.[109] The object becomes a part of the insolvency estate of the main proceedings at the moment of its release, provided that the *lex fori concursus universalis* condones the inclusion of these kinds of objects in the insolvency estate.[110]

72 In the case of a transfer of objects from the insolvency estate of the main proceedings to that of the secondary proceedings, however, a release is not a solution. Should it nevertheless happen that an asset is transferred prior to the release to the territory of the

[103] See mn 62 et seq above.

[104] Against taking these into account: D-K/D/Ch-*Duursma-Kepplinger* Art 28 mn 39.

[105] On this, see the comments on Art 30 of the EIR mn 1 et seq.

[106] *Lüke* ZZP 111 (1998), 275, 306 et seq.

[107] As is the case in German law in sec 80 (1) InsO, which merely provides for a transfer of the powers of administration and disposal to the liquidator.

[108] As is the case in Swedish law; see: in MünchKomm InsO/*Csatho* Sweden mn 2.

[109] With respect to releases, see: mn 81 et seq below.

[110] Under German law, for instance, certain assets of the debtor, namely assets that may not be seized/attached in regular execution procedures, are excluded from the effects of the insolvency seizure/attachment (sec 36 InsO).

secondary insolvency proceedings, then it will be subject to the effects of the seizure/attachment emanating from these. The same conclusion should be reached, in my opinion, even if the *lex fori concursus secundarii* prescribes that assets acquired after the opening of insolvency proceedings do not form part of the insolvency estate; the date of acquisition of the debtor's assets, and not the date of the change of territory, should be the relevant date.[111]

Whether a transfer of assets from one insolvency estate to another is permitted pursuant to insolvency law, and whether and under which conditions a transfer of assets complies with the insolvency law obligations of the respective liquidators, is a decision for the respective *lex fori concursus*. **73**

4.1.8 Contracts "between" the insolvency estates of the main and the secondary proceedings

The liquidators of the main and secondary insolvency proceedings may enter into agreements with each other "as representatives of their respective insolvency estates".[112] Such a transaction does not constitute a transaction concluded by someone with himself as a representative of another,[113] which under certain circumstances may be prohibited pursuant to the *lex fori concursus*.[114] This follows from the recognition provisions of Art 16 et seq of the EIR, which make it clear that, although the identity of the insolvent legal entity continues to exist, the particular insolvency proceedings are legally independent. The individual liquidator represents the interests of "his creditors" vis-à-vis all the other liquidators as well.[115] There is therefore no danger of "transacting with himself". This is clearly illustrated in the provisions of Articles 32 (2), 33 (1), 34 (1) sentence 2 of the EIR. Furthermore, the cooperation contemplated by Art 31 et seq of the EIR between the liquidator in the main and secondary insolvency proceedings would be virtually impossible if agreements between the individual insolvency estates were prohibited, or if the *lex fori concursus* demanded that such agreements had to be approved by the insolvency court, the creditors, or by a creditors' committee. **74**

4.1.9 Ongoing contractual relationships

According to the definition in Art 2 (g) of the EIR, any claims are part of the insolvency estate if the third-party debtor's centre of main interests is in the State of the secondary insolvency proceedings. Because ongoing contractual relationships as such do not fall within the definition of assets, the question arises as to which law should apply to them. The Regulation contains no substantive law provision on this. This is an insolvency law question (Art 4 (2) (e) of the EIR) that is to be answered by reference to a uniform conflict of laws provision on claims and contracts as such.[116] **75**

It would be unacceptable to allocate these matters exclusively to the main insolvency proceedings. In the documentation related to the Regulation, it is clear that secondary **76**

---

[111] *Lüke* ZZP 111 (1998), 277, 307 who apparently views a release in both directions as basically a pragmatic solution.

[112] The use of so-called "protocols" is a practical solution for dealing with cross-border insolvency; see *Paulus* ZIP 1998, 977 et seq; as an example, see the protocol of the "Nakash" case in ZIP 1998, 1013 et seq.

[113] *Reinhart* Sanierungsverfahren im internationalen Insolvenzrecht (1995) p 296 et seq; *Lüke* ZZP 111 (1998), 277, 306.

[114] On German law, see: sec 181 BGB.

[115] D-K/D/Ch-*Duursma-Kepplinger* Art 28 mn 83.

[116] *Trunk* Internationales Insolvenzrecht (1998), p 249; *Weller* ZHR 169 (2005), 570, 588 et seq.

insolvency proceedings are intended to deal not only with national assets but legal relationships as well.[117] This is made clear by Art 4 (2) (e) of the EIR, which also applies to secondary insolvency proceedings.[118] Allocating such matters exclusively to the main insolvency proceedings would also conflict with the functions of territorial insolvency proceedings.[119]

77 The allocation must be made pursuant to general conflict of laws principles. Contractual relationships are to be governed by the legal system most closely related to them. Decisive here is not the location of the debtor's claim, the location of the subject matter of the contract, or the *lex causae* of the contract[120] but rather the qualified relationship which the characteristic obligation of the contract has to the debtor's establishment, as suggested by *Weller*.[121] Such a relationship exists if the performance characteristic to the contract is rendered by or for the debtor's establishment. The involvement of the establishment must ensue from the contractual arrangement.

4.2 Liabilities

78 The liabilities of the secondary insolvency proceedings are universal in nature.[122] The same applies to independent territorial insolvency proceedings. This follows from Art 32 (1) of the EIR for main and secondary insolvency proceedings, and for territorial insolvency proceedings indirectly from Art 36 of the EIR in conjunction with Art 32 (1) of the EIR.[123] This means, in effect, that every creditor is entitled to participate in main, secondary, and independent territorial insolvency proceedings.

5. Recognition

5.1 General

79 The opening of secondary insolvency proceedings[124] must be recognized in all Member States, i.e. its recognition is universal. Recognition is effected automatically pursuant to Art 16 (1) and 17 (2) of the EIR and is subject only to the public policy of the respective Member State. The effects of secondary insolvency proceedings may not be questioned in any Member State. An erroneous determination of international jurisdiction, e.g. a Member State thinks that there has been an incorrect finding of the existence of an establishment, is as irrelevant here as it is in respect of the recognition of main insolvency proceedings.[125]

---

117 *Virgós/Schmit* Explanatory Report mn 139.

118 See the comments on Art 28 of the EIR mn 2, 6.

119 See mn 6 et seq above.

120 On this, see: *Schollmeyer* Gegenseitige Verträge im internationalen Insolvenzrecht (1997), p 170; *Trunk* Internationales Insolvenzrecht (1998), p 249 et seq.

121 *Weller* ZHR 169 (2005), 570, 590 et seq.

122 On this, see the comments on Art 32 of the EIR mn 13, as well as *Balz* 70 American Bankruptcy Law Journal (1996), 485, 521, 525; *Gottwald* Grenzüberschreitende Insolvenzen (1997), 27 et seq; *Lüke* ZZP 111 (1998), 275, 300.

123 On this, see the comments on Art 32 of the EIR mn 6 et seq, 13.

124 The provision applies of course to independent territorial insolvency proceedings as well. See D-K/D/Ch-*Duursma-Kepplinger* Art 16 mn 9; misunderstood: *Smid* Komm EuInsVO Art 28 mn 5.

125 *Smid* Komm EuInsVO Art 16 mn 10; *Herchen* ZInsO 2004, 61, 64 et seq; dissenting opinion: AG Düsseldorf ZIP 2003, 1362; on this: *Paulus* ZIP 2003, 1725 et seq; *Paulus* EWiR, Art 3 EuInsVO 2/03, 709 et seq; *Mankowski* EWiR, Art 3 EuInsVO 3/03, 767 et seq; the AG Düsseldorf abandoned its opinion in the interim

The main impact of the recognition of secondary insolvency proceedings is the suspension of the insolvency-related divestment of the debtor's assets that was occasioned by the opening of main insolvency proceedings.[126] The suspension is effected the moment that secondary insolvency proceedings are opened. The fact that effects of the seizure of assets in the main insolvency proceedings are only suspended, is because of the universal effects of main insolvency proceedings. These universal effects continue and, pursuant to Articles 16 and 17 of the EIR, must be recognized if and "as long as" (Art 17 (1) of the EIR) there has been no seizure/attachment of assets in secondary insolvency proceedings. **80**

5.2 Release of Property From the Insolvency Estate

The suspension of the seizure/attachment of assets in the main insolvency proceedings has practical significance in the case of a release of property from the insolvency estate under German law. Powers of administration and disposal in respect of assets that have been released by the liquidator in secondary proceedings do not revert back to the debtor but are transferred to the liquidator in main insolvency proceedings.[127] This follows if a functional approach is taken to Art 17 (1) of the EIR. The debtor has no chance – not even temporarily – of regaining his powers of administration and disposal. The wording of Art 17 (1) of the EIR could possibly be construed in the manner just mentioned since a release does not affect the opening of the Art 3 (2) of the EIR proceedings that are referred to in Art 17 (1) of the EIR. However, the obligation prescribed by Art 35 of the EIR to transfer any surplus in the secondary proceedings to the main proceedings illustrates that any of the debtor's assets not required in secondary proceedings must first be used for the benefit of the main insolvency proceedings. **81**

If, for example, a German liquidator in secondary insolvency proceedings were to release contaminated property in order to prevent the insolvency estate being made liable under public law for the costs of cleaning up the polluted soil,[128] the property would become part of the insolvency estate of the main proceedings. In such a case, it is a matter for the *lex fori concursus universalis* to decide whether, and to what extent, a claim for reimbursement of the clean-up costs may be asserted in the insolvency proceedings, i.e. in this constellation, in the main insolvency proceedings. **82**

6. Winding-up Proceedings (Articles 27 sentence 3, 3 (3) sentence 2, 2 (c) of the EIR)

According to the provisions of Art 27 sentence 3, Art 3 (3) sentence 2, and Art 2 (c) of the EIR in conjunction with Annex B, the aim of secondary insolvency proceedings is the winding-up of the debtor's assets.[129] An exhaustive list of the types of proceedings permitted in the particular Member States is found in Annex B. The choice of the listed **83**

after a change of judges: see AG Düsseldorf NZI 2004, 269, 270.

126 AG Cologne NZI 2004, 151, 153; concurring: OLG Düsseldorf ZIP 2004, 1514 et seq; D-K/D/Ch-*Duursma-Kepplinger* Art 28 mn 73; *Weller* ZHR 169 (2005), 570, 584 et seq mn 94.

127 D-K/D/Ch-*Duursma-Kepplinger* Art 28 mn 62 et seq; *Lüke* ZZP 111 (1998), 275, 307; see also: mn 44 et seq above, 79.

128 See *Uhlenbruck* in Uhlenbruck InsO 12th edn 2003, sec 35, mn 25.

129 On this, see the comments on Art 33 of the EIR mn 2 and on Art 34 of the EIR mn 5, 16.

proceedings illustrates that the proceedings may – but do not have to – be terminated via a winding-up of the debtor's assets.[130]

84 With respect to the so-called unified proceedings listed in Annex B, i.e. insolvency proceedings with an unpredictable outcome that may end either with a winding-up or a reorganization plan, the issue arises as to whether this amounts to an encroachment on those particular national substantive (insolvency) laws that do not allow proceedings to be terminated by a reorganization. This would mean for German insolvency law that reorganizing insolvency plans would not be permitted.[131] It must, however, be possible to end proceedings by way of reorganizing insolvency plan since Art 34 (1) sentence 2 of the EIR expressly deals with reorganization plans that are not proposed by the liquidator in main insolvency proceedings, simply making them subject to his approval.[132]

85 Without doubt, Articles 27 sentence 3, 3 (3) sentence 2, and 2 (c) of the EIR do not preclude the termination of secondary insolvency proceedings through reorganizations by way of transfers (sales). From the perspective of the debtor, this involves a winding-up pursuant to an asset deal, i.e. a sale of the business operations of the debtor's branch establishment.[133]

7. Procedural issues

7.1 The Liquidator of the Main Insolvency Proceedings' Right to be Heard

86 Allowing the liquidator of the main insolvency proceedings the opportunity of being heard prior to pronouncing the judgement opening insolvency proceedings is not only expedient, but it also fosters the quality and the cross-border acceptance of the judgement opening secondary insolvency proceedings. Depending on the particular *lex fori concursus secundarii*, this can take place by telephone.

87 The need for granting such an opportunity to be heard follows from the loss of the debtor's powers of administration and disposal of his assets, this being transferred to the liquidator in the main proceedings concurrently with the opening of the main insolvency proceedings. If the *lex fori concursus secundarii* requires that the debtor be heard prior to the opening of secondary insolvency proceedings, then the liquidator in the main insolvency proceedings will be heard in his stead since the opening of secondary insolvency proceedings constitutes a measure affecting the powers of administration and disposal of the debtor's assets.

---

[130] *Balz* 70 American Bankruptcy Law Journal (1996), 485, 523; D-K/D/Ch-*Duursma-Kepplinger* Art 28 mn 65; *Gottwald* Grenzüberschreitende Insolvenzen (1997) p 43 et seq; *Kolmann* Kooperationsmodelle im Internationalen Insolvenzrecht – Empfiehlt sich für das deutsche internationale Insolvenzrecht eine Neuorientierung (2001), 331.

[131] But this would not apply to insolvency plans aimed at a winding-up; see comments on Art 34 of the EIR mn 16.

[132] Concurring: *Ehricke/Ries* JuS 2003, 313, 319; in Haß/Huber/Gruber/Heiderhoff-*Heiderhoff* Art 28 EuInsVO mn 12; *Lüke* ZZP 111 (1998), 275, 307; *Morscher* Die europäische Insolvenzverordnung (2002), 48; *Paulus* EWS 2002, 497, 502; Münch Komm InsO/*Reinhart* Art 37 mn 2; *Spahlinger* Sekundäre Insolvenzverfahren bei grenzüberschreitenden Insolvenzen, (1998), p 254.

[133] See comments on Art 33 of the EIR mn 1, 14, and on Art 34 of the EIR mn 3, 16.

7.2 Identity of the Liquidators in the Main and Secondary Insolvency Proceedings

The requirements relating to the person of the liquidator in secondary insolvency proceedings and to his appointment are matters for the *lex fori concursus secundarii* (see Art 4 (2) (c), Art 28 of the EIR). **88**

At first glance it may appear expedient to have the same liquidator for both the main and the secondary insolvency proceedings, this facilitating optimal information exchanges and for cooperation and coordination purposes between the main and secondary insolvency proceedings.[134] It is doubtful, however, whether this actually leads to a more cost-effective handling of insolvency proceedings where costs are charged according to statutory fee scales, as in Germany for example. Even if the costs are calculated according to the time expended, it is hard to imagine a liquidator in the main insolvency proceedings who is so familiar with the *lex fori concursus secundarii* that additional expenditures for work in a number of legal systems, or for the involvement of national legal advisors, can be dispensed with. The physical distance between the head office and the (branch) establishments is also a factor that generally detracts from the efficiency of the insolvency proceedings. **89**

The Regulation contains however no express provisions forbidding the appointment of the liquidator in main insolvency proceedings; such provisions are also not likely to be found in the respective *lex fori concursus secundarii* either. Absent linguistic and legal knowledge in the state of the secondary proceedings, the liquidator in the main insolvency proceedings will normally not have the qualification requested in Sec 56 *InsO* from the liquidator appointed in the German insolvency proceedings.[135] However looked at conceptually, particularly the relationship between the main and secondary insolvency proceedings, it is to be inferred that the Regulation does not allow the liquidators of the main and secondary of the EIR insolvency proceedings to be one and the same person.[136] This is seen clearly in the provisions of Articles 32 (2), 33 (1), and 34 (1) sentence 2 of the EIR, which illustrate that the liquidators in the main proceedings and those in the secondary insolvency proceedings have to represent the opposing interests of potentially different classes of creditor. Even if the creditors of both proceedings are identical on account of Art 32 (2) sentence 1 of the EIR, this does not necessarily preclude conflicts of interests between the various proceedings. Differences in the ranking orders of the *lex fori concursus universalis* and the *lex fori concursus secundarii* in respect of the same claim may result in the same creditors obtaining different results in the main and secondary insolvency proceedings. **90**

7.3 Debtor in Possession Arrangement According to Sec 270 et seq *InsO* in German Secondary Insolvency Proceedings

The debtor in possession constellation (*Eigenverwaltung*) contemplated by German insolvency law (Sec 270 et seq *InsO*), whereby the powers of administration and disposal **91**

---

[134] D-K/D/Ch-*Duursma-Kepplinger* Art 28 mn 83; *Kolmann* Kooperationsmodelle im Internationalen Insolvenzrecht – Empfiehlt sich für das deutsche internationale Insolvenzrecht eine Neuorientierung (2001), 351; *Lüke* ZZP 111 (1998), 275, 304; *Vallender* KTS 2005, 283, 311 et seq.

[135] *Beck* NZI 2006, 609, 617.

[136] Concurring: *Beck* NZI 2006, 609, 617; D-K/D/Ch-*Duursma-Kepplinger* Art 28 mn 83; *Kolmann* Kooperationsmodelle im Internationalen Insolvenzrecht – Empfiehlt sich für das deutsche internationale Insolvenzrecht eine Neuorientierung (2001), 351; *Lüke* ZZP 111 (1998), 275, 304; concurring: *Virgós/Schmit* Explanatory Report mn 236 et seq; dissenting opinion: *Ehricke* DZWiR 1999, 356 et seq; *Vallender* KTS 2005, 283, 311 et seq; see also: *Scheel* Konzerninsolvenz – eine vergleichende Darstellung des US-amerikanischen und des deutschen Rechts (1995), 40 et seq.

are retained by the debtor and are not vested in the liquidator upon the opening of the insolvency proceedings, appears to have been left open by the regulatory drafters in the case of secondary insolvency proceedings as well.[137] The provisions of sec 270 et seq *InsO* form part of the *lex fori concursus secundarii* invoked via Art 4 (1) and Art 28 of the EIR. Neither German law nor the Regulation expressly stipulates that such a debtor in possession arrangement is inadmissible in conjunction with secondary insolvency proceedings. What characterizes secondary insolvency proceedings that are constituted as debtor in possession proceedings is – as in the Automold decision of the *Amtsgericht* Cologne[138] – that the liquidator in the main insolvency proceedings, to whom the powers of administration and disposal over the debtor's assets has been transferred, also has these powers with respect to an establishment covered by the secondary insolvency proceedings. The liquidator in the main proceedings is merely being supervised by the custodian (*Sachwalter*) appointed by the insolvency court of the secondary proceedings (Sec 274 *InsO*). All that is required is that the *lex fori concursus universalis* confers on him such powers to administer and dispose of the debtor's assets.

92 However, whether the debtor in possession arrangement is admissible in secondary insolvency proceedings is disputed[139], and rightly so.[140] The conflict of interests arising from the "double role"[141] played by the liquidator in the main insolvency proceedings – having powers of administration and disposal in "his" main insolvency proceedings as well as in the secondary proceedings – is one of the detriments envisioned by Sec 270 (2) No 3 *InsO* that would preclude the ordering of debtor in possession proceedings. As already discussed in mn 90 in conjunction with the issue of having the same person act as the liquidator in the main and in the secondary insolvency proceedings, the way the Regulation is conceived – particularly the interaction between the main and secondary insolvency proceedings – simply does not allow a transfer of the powers of administration and disposal to the same person (liquidator) in both main and secondary insolvency proceedings. The argument frequently put forth by those advocating the debtor in possession arrangement in secondary insolvency proceedings, namely that such an arrangement promotes a uniform processing of the main and secondary insolvency proceedings, is exactly what is contemplated by the Regulation in the coordination and cooperation provisions of Art 31 et seq of the EIR.

8. Cross-border Effects of Territorial insolvency Proceedings

93 Territorial insolvency proceedings may, to a limited extent, have a cross-border impact; the terms "territorial insolvency proceedings" are being used here as a generic term for secondary and independent territorial insolvency proceedings.

---

[137] AG Cologne, ZIP 2004, 472 – "Automold", cf Table of Cases Art 3 of the EIR Appendix A mn 1; *Meyer-Löwy/Poertzgen*, ZinsO 2004, 197; *Sabel*, NZI 2004, 127, *Smid*, DZWiR 2004, 397, 406 et seq; critical HamburgerKomm-*Undritz* Art 27 mn 12 et seq.

[138] AG Cologne, ZIP 2004, 472 – "Automold".

[139] In detail *Beck* NZI 2006, 609, 616 et seq; critical also HamburgerKomm-*Undritz* Art 27 mn 13.

[140] However, the argument that the debtor in possession arrangement is not permitted in insolvency proceedings aimed at winding-up does not hold up in my opinion (in this direction, Beck NZI 2006, 609, 616 with further substantiation). If it was correct, then such an arrangement would in fact already be considered inadmissible based on the fact that art 3 (3) stipulates that secondary insolvency proceedings must be winding-up proceedings.

[141] HamburgerKomm-*Undritz* Art 27 mn 13.

8.1 Article 18 (2) of the EIR

The jurisdiction of the liquidator in the territorial proceedings is restricted to the State in which the territorial proceedings are opened; this follows from the physical restriction of the territorial proceedings. An exception to this is found in Art 18 (2) in cases where assets are removed to a foreign country. Reference is made here to the comments on Art 18 of the EIR at mn 16 et seq as above on mn 63 et seq. **94**

8.2 Compensation of Lost Wages for the Debtor's Employees Pursuant to German Social Security Law

Territorial proceedings seldom have a cross-border impact on employees' claims to insolvency money pursuant to Section 183 (1) of the German Social Security Code III ("*SGB III*"). The claim of a person employed in Germany to payment of compensation of lost wages from the government authority *Bundesagentur für Arbeit* presupposes the existence of an insolvency event, namely the opening of insolvency proceedings. Via section 183 (1) sentence 2 *SGB III*, a foreign insolvency event is put on equal footing with a national insolvency event. The wording of Section 183 *SGB III* does not differentiate between foreign proceedings with universal effects and those with territorial effects. **95**

For logical reasons, however, it must be an unwritten requirement that the foreign insolvency proceedings have to affect employment relationships for which the *Bundesagentur für Arbeit* and the German governmental authorities responsible for insolvency money are responsible. Since the *Bundesagentur* is responsible when an employee habitually works in Germany, there must be an event giving rise to cross-border effects; these effects may emanate not only from foreign universal insolvency proceedings but also, as an exception, from foreign territorial insolvency proceedings.[142] If the employee of the foreign establishment that is subject to the territorial insolvency proceedings is primarily engaged in Germany, then, because of the provisions of Art 10 of the EIR, Section 183 (1) *SGB III* applies to employees and their claims for compensation of lost wages if German law governs the employment contract.[143] If, in conjunction with this constellation, foreign main insolvency proceedings are subsequently opened, i.e. the territorial proceedings that were opened were independent territorial proceedings, then the duration for which the compensation of lost wages is to be paid is determined in accordance with the earlier insolvency event, i.e. the opening of the territorial proceedings. **96**

Should the opening of the foreign main insolvency proceedings take place before the opening of the German secondary insolvency proceedings (as the case may be after Art 36 of the EIR as a transformed independent territorial insolvency proceeding), the foreign insolvency occurrence limits the period during which compensation of lost wages due to insolvency are granted.[144] **97**

---

[142] See Directive 2002/74/EC of the European Parliament and of the Council of 23 September 2002 amending Council Directive 80/987/EEC on the approximation of the laws of the Member States relating to the protection of employees in the event of the insolvency of their employer, OJ L 270 of 8 Oct 2002, p 10 et seq; Council Directive 80/987/EEC of 20 October 1980 on the approximation of the laws of the Member States relating to the protection of employees in the event of the insolvency of their employer, OJ L 283 of 28 Oct 1980, p 23 et seq; on this: D-K/D/Ch-*Duursma-Kepplinger* Art 10 mn 16 et seq, 21 et seq; ECJ C-117/96 (Mosbaek), ECR 1997, I-5017, NZA 1997, 1155; ECJ C-198/98 (Everson/Barras Bell Lines Ltd), ECR 1999, I-8903, NZA 2000, 959.

[143] *Paulus* Komm EuInsVO Art 10 mn 6 et seq.

[144] Concurring: the *deutsche Bundesagentur für Arbeit* (according to *Kebekus* ZIP 2007, 84 et seq, 87); *Kebekus* ZIP 2007, 84 et seq, who pleads *de lege ferenda* for a change.

Article 28
Applicable law

Save as otherwise provided in this Regulation, the law applicable to secondary proceedings shall be that of the Member State within the territory of which the secondary proceedings are opened.

Contents

Index

Bibliography

Balz Das neue Europäische Insolvenzübereinkommen ZIP 1996, p 948; *Buchberger* Das System der „kontrollierten" Universalität des Konkursverfahrens nach der Europäischen Insolvenzverordnung, ZIK 2000, p 149; *Herchen* Das Übereinkommen über Insolvenzverfahren der Mitgliedstaaten der Europäischen Union vom 23.11.1995 (2000); *Huber* Die Europäische Insolvenzverordnung, EuZW 2002, p 490; *Kammel* Die Bestimmung der zuständigen Gerichte bei grenzüberschreitenden Konzerninsolvenzen, NZI 2006, p 334; *Kemper* Die Verordnung (EG) Nr. 1346/2000 über Insolvenzverfahren, ZIP 2001, p 1609; *Kolmann* Kooperationsmodelle im Internationalen Insolvenzrecht – Empfiehlt sich für das deutsche internationale Insolvenzrecht eine Neuorientierung 2001; *Knof/Mock* Comments on ECJ dated 02.05.2006 – C-341/04, ZIP 2006, p 911; *Leible/Staudinger* Die europäische Verordnung über Insolvenzverfahren, KTS 2000, p 533; *Lüke* Das europäische internationale Insolvenzrecht, ZZP 111 (1998), p 275; *Morscher* Die europäische Insolvenzverordnung 2002; *Sabel* Hauptsitz als Niederlassung im Sinne der EuInsVO? NZI 2004, p 126; *Thieme* Vermögensgerichtsstände, Inlandsbezug und Partikularkonkurs, Jahresheft der Internationalen Juristenvereinigung Osnabrück (1995/1996), p 44; *Wimmer* Die Besonderheiten von Sekundärinsolvenzverfahren unter besonderer Berücksichtigung des Europäischen Insolvenzübereinkommens, ZIP 1998, p 982.

1. General

According to Art 28 of the EIR, secondary insolvency proceedings are governed by the law of the Member State in whose territory the proceedings were opened: the *lex fori concursus*, or more precisely: the *lex fori concursus secundarii*. It involves a referral to the respective national substantive and procedural insolvency laws.[1] 1

2. Declaratory Provision

For the purposes of secondary insolvency proceedings, Art 28 of the EIR has a declaratory function only since it merely reiterates the basic conflict of laws principle found in Art 4 (1) of the EIR.[2] Because Art 4 (1) of the EIR is not restricted to main insolvency proceedings, but applies to both main insolvency proceedings and to secondary and independent territorial insolvency proceedings as well, the regulation contained in Art 28 of the EIR is superfluous.[3] It therefore already follows from Art 4 (1) of the EIR and from the coordinated multiplicity of proceedings contemplated by the Regulation[4] that, within the territory of secondary insolvency proceedings, the territorial sphere of application of the *lex fori concursus universalis* is subordinate to the applicability of the *lex fori concursus secundarii*. In legal terms, this means a complete ousting of the *lex fori concursus universalis*[5] and not merely a superimposition on it that would result in a subsidiary application of the *lex fori concursus universalis* in the case of a gap in the rules of the *lex fori concursus secundarii*.[6] Art 28 of the EIR clearly illustrates the solution chosen by the Regulation in the event of conflicting effects of the *lex fori concursus universalis* and the *lex fori concursus secundarii*.[7] 2

3. Applicability to Independent Territorial Insolvency Proceedings

On the face of its wording, Art 28 of the EIR only applies to secondary insolvency proceedings within the meaning of Art 3 (3) of the EIR.[8] Since Art 4 (1) of the EIR also applies to independent territorial insolvency proceedings, the issue of applicability beyond the wording of Art 28 of the EIR to these proceedings is irrelevant;[9] what is 3

---

1 Moss/Fletcher/Isaacs-*Moss/Smith*, Regulation, mn 8.78; *Smid* Komm EuInsVO Art 28 mn 2.

2 *Virgós/Schmit* Explanatory Report mn 89, 225; *Morscher* Die europäische Insolvenzverordnung 2002, p 51.

3 D-K/D/Ch-*Duursma-Kepplinger/Chalupsky* Art 4 mn 3; Moss/Fletcher/Isaacs-*Moss/Smith*, Regulation, mn 8.77; MünchKomm InsO/*Reinhart* Art 4 EuInsVO mn 1; in Haß/Huber/Gruber/Heiderhoff-*Haß/Herweg* Art 4 EuInsVO mn 5.

4 On this, see: Introduction mn 34 et seq.

5 *Paulus* Komm EuInsVO Art 28 mn 4 correctly points out that this will of course only apply to the same extent as the scope of the secondary insolvency proceedings themselves. Should an object in the insolvency estate of the secondary insolvency proceedings be released, then this object will immediately fall within the insolvency estate of the main insolvency proceedings (on this: OLG Vienna NZI 2005, 56, 61 et seq.; *Lüke* ZZP 111 (1998), 275, 306 et seq).

6 Held by: *Paulus* Komm EuInsVO Art 28 mn 4, Art 17 mn 4 et seq; example of dissenting opinion: *Sabel* NZI 2004, 126, 127; *Huber* EuZW 2002, 490, 495.

7 *Smid* Komm EuInsVO Art 28 mn 1.

8 Regarding the problem of a certain ambiguity of the wording, see: *Paulus* Komm EuInsVO Art 27 mn 3.

9 This issue is discussed by Haß/Huber/Gruber/Heiderhoff-*Heiderhoff* Art 28 EuInsVO mn 4; see also: *Paulus* Komm

relevant, however, is whether and which other provisions of Chapter III of the EIR apply to independent territorial insolvency proceedings.[10]

4. Referral to Substantive Law Provisions

4 Although unlike Art 4 (1) of the EIR, the wording of Art 28 of the EIR speaks of "the law" and not the "insolvency law of the Member State", there is no substantial difference.[11] Both instances involve a referral to the substantive provisions of the *lex fori concursus* and not to the foreign law in its entirety.[12] A referral to the foreign law in its entirety *(Gesamtverweisung)* would involve a referral to the particular conflict of laws rules pertaining to insolvency in the concerned Member State.

5 An interpretation of Art 28 of the EIR as a referral to the foreign law in its entirety is also incorrect for the simple reason that it would then contradict Art 4 (1) of the EIR; this provision regulates the law which is to govern main, secondary, and independent territorial insolvency proceedings.[13] According to Recital 23 of the EIR, the Regulation is intended to create uniform conflict of laws rules for main insolvency proceedings as well as for secondary and independent territorial insolvency proceedings. To interpret Art 28 of the EIR, because of the wording "the law of the Member State", as a referral to the foreign law in its entirety would be contrary to this legislative intent.

6 If a strict approach was taken to the difference in wording between Art 4 (1) of the EIR and Art 28 of the EIR, then the missing reference in Art 28 of the EIR to the "effects" of the insolvency proceeding could be understood as restricting the possibility of qualifying national laws as insolvency laws. In contrast to Art 4 (1) of the EIR, Art 28 of the EIR invokes the *lex fori concursus* in respect of the "insolvency proceedings", but not "their effects". The result would be that certain national laws would not form part of the referral even though they qualify as insolvency laws. To draw such a material conclusion from the differences in wording would be contrary to the intentions of the drafters of the Regulation. As clearly evidenced by the matters outlined in Art 4 (2) of the EIR, i.e. to qualify them as insolvency law matters which are therefore subjected to the *lex fori concursus*, applies equally to Articles 4 (1) and 28.

5. Application of the Provisions of Chapter III to Independent Territorial Insolvency Proceedings

7 Some provisions of Chapter III are applicable to independent territorial insolvency proceedings.[14] In detail:

EuInsVO Art 28 mn 2 who assumes that it applies to both secondary and independent territorial insolvency proceedings.

10 On this, see: mn 7 et seq below.

11 On this, see: *Paulus* Komm EuInsVO Art 28 mn 2, 3.

12 D-K/D/Ch-*Duursma-Kepplinger/Chalupsky* Art 28 mn 5; Moss/Fletcher/Isaacs-*Fletcher*, Regulation, mn 4.04; dissenting opinion: *Buchberger* ZIK 2000, 149.

13 Moss/Fletcher/Isaacs-*Fletcher*, Regulation, mn 4.01.

14 D-K/D/Ch-*Duursma-Kepplinger/Chalupsky* Art 28 mn 2; MünchKomm InsO/*Reinhart* Art 4 mn 2; critical in respect of art 28 of the EIR: Haß/Huber/Gruber/Heiderhoff-*Heiderhoff* Art 28 mn 2.

5.1 Article 27 of the EIR

Art 27 of the EIR does not apply to independent territorial insolvency proceedings.[15] **8**
Since in the case of territorial insolvency proceedings there are no opened main insolvency proceedings, the de facto insolvency of the debtor – which is established by the opening of main insolvency proceedings whose recognition is mandatory pursuant to Art 16 et seq of the EIR – has not yet been judicially determined. It is up to the court with international jurisdiction for the territorial insolvency proceedings to determine whether pursuant to the *lex fori concursus particularis* there are grounds for opening insolvency proceedings.

5.2 Article 29 of the EIR

Art 29 (a) of the EIR, which grants the liquidator of main insolvency proceedings **9**
the right to request the opening of secondary insolvency proceedings, does not apply to territorial insolvency proceedings.[16] The provision presupposes that main insolvency proceedings have already been opened.

Even in light of the opinion of the Advocate General in Eurofood IFSC Ltd.,[17] in **10**
whose legal opinion the mere appointment of a temporary administrator may already constitute the opening of insolvency proceedings that must be recognized by the other Member States pursuant to Art 16 of the EIR, the wording of Art 29 (a) of the EIR, which is unequivocal in this respect, cannot be so broadly interpreted as to provide the temporary administrator with a right to request the opening of insolvency proceedings.[18] This would be the only way that Art 29 (a) of the EIR could have any meaning for territorial insolvency proceedings.

Art 29 (b) of the EIR also does not apply. The provision has no inherent significance **11**
for secondary or for independent territorial insolvency proceedings since Art 29 (b) of the EIR is merely a more concrete form of Art 4 (2) sentence 1 of the EIR. The issue of entitlement to request the opening of insolvency proceedings is determined pursuant to the particular *lex fori concursus* invoked via Art 4 of the EIR. There is no need to extend the application of Art 29 (b) of the EIR beyond its wording to include independent territorial insolvency proceedings.

5.3 Article 30 of the EIR

Based on its wording alone, Art 30 of the EIR cannot be applied to independent terri- **12**
torial insolvency proceedings. The *lex fori concursus particularis* invoked via Art 4 (1) of the EIR regulates both whether the covering of the costs of the proceedings is a prerequisite to opening an independent territorial insolvency proceeding, and whether and from whom an advance payment of costs and expenses, or appropriate security for costs, may be requested.

If, however, Art 30 of the EIR is accorded the meaning suggested by the Explanatory **13**
Report, its applicability to independent territorial insolvency proceedings is at least wor-

[15] On this, see: mn 31 et seq below.

[16] *Paulus* Komm EuInsVO Art 29 mn 1.

[17] NZI 2006, 360 et seq; on this, see: *Kammel* NZI 2006, 334 et seq; *Knof/Mock* ZIP 2006, 911 et seq.

[18] See Art 29 of the EIR mn 20; *Virgós/Schmit* Explanatory Report mn 226, 262; D-K/D/Ch-*Duursma-Kepplinger/Chalupsky* Art 29 mn 9; Haß/Huber/Gruber/Heiderhoff-*Heiderhoff* Art 29 mn 2, Art 38 mn 1; *Kolmann* Kooperationsmodelle im Internationalen Insolvenzrecht – Empfiehlt sich für das deutsche internationale Insolvenzrecht eine Neuorientierung 2001, 335; *Leible/Staudinger* KTS 2000, 533, 570.

thy of discussion and should, in the result, be endorsed. According to the Explanatory Report,[19] the *lex fori concursus secundarii* should only be allowed to require the covering of the costs of secondary insolvency proceedings if such requirement is not restricted to secondary insolvency proceedings within the meaning of the EIR, but also applies in the case of purely national insolvency proceedings.[20] Such a restriction cannot, however, be gleaned from the wording of Art 30 of the EIR.[21] But since there is no objective reason for setting up higher hurdles for the opening secondary insolvency proceedings than there are for national insolvency proceedings, nor for independent territorial insolvency proceedings in relation to secondary insolvency proceedings, this interpretation of Art 30 of the EIR should apply to both kinds of proceedings. However, because its language speaks to the contrary, it is not possible to read into the wording of Art 30 a compulsory directive to the national insolvency law legislators either with respect to independent territorial or secondary insolvency proceedings.

14 Unlike the meaning attributed to it by the Explanatory Report[22] and the prevailing opinions in support of this,[23] the wording of Art 30 of the EIR speaks rather in favour of viewing the ability to require advance payments or appropriate security as an incorporated substantive law provision, and not merely – on account of Art 4 of the EIR – an unnecessary referral to the *lex fori concursus*. If this were correct, insolvency courts would be able to request advance payments or appropriate security even if the governing *lex fori concursus* did not provide for such. But since it is not appropriate in this respect to treat independent territorial insolvency proceedings differently than secondary insolvency proceedings, Art 30 of the EIR should be subjected to a broader interpretation and apply here to independent territorial insolvency proceedings as well.

5.4 Articles 31 to 35, Article 36, and Article 37 of the EIR

15 Articles 36 and 37 of the EIR explicitly regulate the treatment of independent territorial insolvency proceedings subsequent to the opening of main insolvency proceedings.

16 Art 36 states that Articles 31 to 35 of the EIR, which initially only apply to secondary insolvency proceedings, apply – subject to any modifications or restrictions necessitated by the particular progress of the proceedings – to (formerly) independent territorial insolvency proceedings as soon as the main insolvency proceedings are opened.[24] Prior to the opening of main insolvency proceedings, Art 35 of the EIR does not apply to independent territorial insolvency proceedings.[25]

17 Art 34 (2) of the EIR, however, is not to be applied to independent territorial insolvency proceedings since it merely repeats that which is laid down in Art 17 (2) of the EIR, which itself applies to both independent territorial and secondary insolvency proceedings.[26]

---

[19] *Virgós/Schmit* Explanatory Report mn 228.

[20] Haß/Huber/Gruber/Heiderhoff-*Heiderhoff* Art 30 EuInsVO mn 1; Moss/Fletcher/Isaacs-*Moss/Smith*, Regulation, mn 8.225; *Wimmer* ZIP 1998, 987.

[21] Haß/Huber/Gruber/Heiderhoff-*Heiderhoff* Art 30 EuInsVO mn 1; obvious dissenting opinion: D-K/D/Ch-*Duursma-Kepplinger/Chalupsky* Art 30 mn. 2.

[22] *Virgós/Schmit* Explanatory Report mn 228.

[23] D-K/D/Ch-*Duursma-Kepplinger/Chalupsky* Art 30 mn 2; Haß/Huber/Gruber/Heiderhoff-*Heiderhoff* Art 30 mn 1; concurring: Moss/Fletcher/Isaacs-*Moss/Smith*, Regulation, mn 8.225; clear dissenting opinion: MünchKomm InsO/*Reinhart* Art 30 EuInsVO mn 1.

[24] Moss/Fletcher/Isaacs-*Fletcher*, Regulation, mn 8.262; see comments on Art 32 of the EIR mn 12 et seq; Art 36 of the EIR mn 2 et seq.

[25] See the comments on Art 35 of the EIR mn 3, 7.

[26] See the comments on Art 34 of the EIR mn 43 et seq; MünchKomm InsO/*Reinhart* Art 17 EuInsVO mn 4.

5.5 Article 38 of the EIR

The inclusion of Art 38 of the EIR in Chapter III of the EIR is in itself incorrect, and encourages those adhering to the prevailing opinion[27] to draw faulty conclusions based on systematic arguments in respect of the scope of its application.[28] **18**

Art 38 of the EIR does not deal with any problem specific to either secondary or independent territorial insolvency proceedings, but rather provides the temporary administrator of future main insolvency proceedings with a wider scope of possibilities for requesting preservation measures in all other Member States, whether or not a request to open territorial insolvency proceedings has been made there. **19**

Art 38 of the EIR will of course not apply if independent territorial insolvency proceedings have already been opened. **20**

6. Restriction of the *lex fori concursus secundarii/particularis* by the Substantive Insolvency Law Provisions of the EIR

6.1 General

The invoking of the *lex fori concursus secundarii* is expressly subject to the other provisions of the Regulation. This undoubtedly means the provisions of Chapter III, which deals explicitly with "Secondary Insolvency Proceedings". There has been little discussion, however, on whether provisions of the Regulation besides those in Chapter III (could) also constitute "other provisions". Where other provisions of the Regulation apply not only to main but also to secondary insolvency proceedings, this constitutes a modification of the respective national substantive insolvency law invoked via Art 28 of the EIR, thereby standardizing the various national insolvency law regimes. **21**

6.2 General Comments on Articles 5 to 15 of the EIR

The Explanatory Report[29] only speaks expressly about the impediment to contesting the insolvency [i.e. contesting by the insolvency creditors to transactions of/dispositions of the insolvent prior to the opening of the insolvency proceedings that are detrimental to the creditors] that is regulated in Art 13 of the EIR in cross-border cases, i.e. where there is a discrepancy between the *lex fori concursus* and the *lex causae,* and states that this impediment should apply to both main and secondary insolvency proceedings.[30] Although the Report has no legally binding authority – one reason being that it was not rendered in respect of the Regulation but in respect of the Convention on Insolvency Proceedings of 23 November 1995, which is identically worded in this respect – as a report rendered in respect of a convention pursuant to Art 293 EEC Treaty, it had to be **22**

---

[27] *Virgós/Schmit* Explanatory Report mn 262; D-K/D/Ch-*Duursma-Kepplinger/Chalupsky* Art 38 mn 10; Haß/Huber/Gruber/Heiderhoff-*Heiderhoff* Art 38 EuInsVO mn 2; *Leible/Staudinger* KTS 2000, 533, 570; dissenting opinion: *Herchen* Das Übereinkommen über Insolvenzverfahren der Mitgliedstaaten der Europäischen Union vom 23.11.1995 (2000), p 162; Moss/Fletcher/Isaacs-*Moss/Smith*, Regulation, mn 8.272; MünchKomm InsO/*Reinhart* Art 38 EuIns-VO mn 1.

[28] See comments on Art 38 of the EIR mn 1, 10 et seq.

[29] *Virgós/Schmit* Explanatory Report mn 39.

[30] Concurring: D-K/D/Ch-*Duursma-Kepplinger/Chalupsky* Art 28 mn 13, 18 et seq; Haß/Huber/Gruber/Heiderhoff-*Gruber* Art 13 EuInsVO mn 15; Haß/Huber/Gruber/Heiderhoff-*Heiderhoff* Art 28 EuInsVO mn 4.

approved of by the European Community Council. It therefore can be concluded that it reflects the legal opinion of the legislator and must be taken into account for the purposes of interpretation. This is in line with the ECJ's treatment of reports rendered in respect of conventions pursuant to Art 293 EEC Treaty.[31]

23 The fact that Art 13 of the EIR is the only provision mentioned in the Explanatory Report should not lead to the conclusion that it is the only provision that applies to secondary as well as to main insolvency provisions. Rather, each provision of the EIR must be examined in the individual circumstances to determine whether it is to apply to secondary insolvency proceedings as well.[32] In addition to systematic and wording-based arguments, it must also be kept in mind that the matters outlined in Art 5 et seq of the EIR address a particularly risky situation that, although especially pertinent in main insolvency proceedings, can arise just the same in secondary insolvency proceedings: a discrepancy between the *lex fori concursus* and the law applicable to the underlying legal relationships. The source of this particular risk is found not so much in the universal effects of the main insolvency proceedings,[33] but more so in the universal nature of the facts and circumstances common to an insolvency to which the Regulation is able to respond with either a territorially-limited proceeding or a universal insolvency proceeding.

24 Viewed systematically, the fact that Articles 5 to 15 of the EIR are included in Chapter I "General Provisions" is reason enough for considering their application. Secondary insolvency proceedings are also "collective insolvency proceedings" within the meaning of Art 1 of the EIR (see Annexes A and B to the EIR) to which the general provisions are to apply.

25 Another systematic argument follows from the reiteration in Art 28 of the EIR of the basic conflict of laws principle found in Art 4 of the EIR. Articles 5 to 15 of the EIR constitute exceptions to the general application of the *lex fori concursus*. As such, they are linked most closely with the *lex fori concursus*-rule articulated in Art 28 of the EIR.

6.3 Article 13, Articles 6, 8, 9, 10, 11, 14, 15 of the EIR

26 In the case of Art 13 of the EIR, it is not only the aforementioned systematic reasons that speak in favour of an application of Art 13 of the EIR to secondary insolvency proceedings but also the legislative intent of the Regulation itself. According to Recital 23 of the EIR, the Regulation is intended to create uniform conflict of laws rules for main insolvency proceedings as well as for secondary and independent territorial insolvency proceedings. It would be adverse to this legislative intent if the (non)contestability of a legal position, which arises from the *lex causae*, depends on whether the legal position is being contested by the liquidator of the main insolvency proceedings or by the liquidator of the secondary proceedings. If it was held that Art 13 of the EIR does not apply to secondary insolvency proceedings, then the ability to contest in the insolvency is determined solely pursuant to the *lex fori concursus secundarii*. The non-contestability pursuant to the *lex causae* would be irrelevant. These considerations apply equally to the provisions of Articles 6, 8, 9, 10, 11, 14 and 15 of the EIR.[34] These provisions are also to be applied in secondary insolvency proceedings.

---

[31] *Herchen* Das Übereinkommen über Insolvenzverfahren der Mitgliedstaaten der Europäischen Union vom 23.11.1995, (2000), p 83.

[32] Concurring: *Morscher* Die europäische Insolvenzverordnung 2002, p 51.

[33] But see: Haß/Huber/Gruber/Heiderhoff-*Heiderhoff* Art 28 EuInsVO mn 4.

[34] *Balz* ZIP 1996, 948, 950; *Kolmann* Kooperationsmodelle im Internationalen Insolvenzrecht – Empfiehlt sich für das deutsche internationale Insolvenzrecht eine Neuorien-

6.4 Article 7 (2) of the EIR

Art 7 (2) of the EIR deserves special mention in this context. Unlike Art 7 (1) of the EIR,[35] Art 7 (2) of the EIR is considered by some to apply to secondary insolvency proceedings.[36] According to this line of reasoning, Art 7 (2) of the EIR – as an insolvency law provision – provides that the expectant right of the "conditional purchaser" (of goods subject to a reservation of title) is immune from the insolvency of the "conditional seller" (of goods subject to a reservation of title) even if secondary insolvency proceedings were opened in the State in which the goods are situated. **27**

This is incorrect. Art 7 (2) of the EIR does not apply to secondary insolvency proceedings. Firstly, the unequivocal wording of Art 7 (2) of the EIR does not support such an interpretation. If the immunity of the conditional purchaser's expectant right from the insolvency of the conditional seller (Art 7 (2) of the EIR) was intended to be more extensive than the retention of title in the insolvency of the conditional purchaser, then this would have to have been more explicitly regulated, which is not found in subsection 2 whose wording is modelled upon subsection 1. Secondly, the particular danger threatening cross-border insolvency cases of which Art 7 (2) of the EIR is a response to[37] – namely a discrepancy between the *lex fori concursus* and the *lex rei sitae* – does not exist in the case of secondary insolvency proceedings. **28**

6.5 Article 12 of the EIR

Based on both its wording and in terms of its intent and purpose, Art 12 of the EIR is to be applied to secondary insolvency proceedings. Art 12 of the EIR stipulates that Community trademarks, Community patents, or other similar rights established by Community law may be "included only in the proceedings referred to in Art 3 (1) of the EIR", i.e. they are specifically not to be included in secondary insolvency proceedings.[38] **29**

6.6 Articles 5, 7 (1) of the EIR

Articles 5 and 7 (1) of the EIR are not applicable in secondary insolvency proceedings.[39] Although it is true that the facts upon which Articles 5 and 7 (1) of the EIR are based may also be present in secondary insolvency proceedings, i.e. assets in which creditors or third parties hold specific rights *in rem* may be situated outside of the country of the opened proceedings. It is nevertheless unnecessary to provide for the legal consequences such as those contemplated by Articles 5 and 7 (1) of the EIR in the case of territorially restricted proceedings because such proceedings have no legal effect on assets located in other Member States due to the inability to legally enforce any decisions made pursuant to them. **30**

---

tierung 2001, p 330 et seq; D-K/D/Ch-*Duursma-Kepplinger/Chalupsky* Art 28 mn 9 et seq; *Morscher* Die europäische Insolvenzverordnung (2002), p 51; MünchKomm InsO/*Reinhart* Art 28 mn 1; similar: Haß/Huber/Gruber/Heiderhoff-*Heiderhoff* Art 28 EuInsVO mn 4.

[35] See mn 30 below.

[36] D-K/D/Ch-*Duursma-Kepplinger/Chalupsky* Art 7 mn 27 et seq, Art 28, mn 18; *Morscher* Die europäische Insolvenzverordnung (2002), p 41; *Smid* Komm EuInsVO Art 28 mn 3; in doubt: Haß/Huber/Gruber/Heiderhoff-*Huber* Art 7 EuInsVO mn 17.

[37] See mn 23 above.

[38] D-K/D/Ch-*Duursma-Kepplinger/Chalupsky* Art 28 mn 17.

[39] Concurring: *Morscher* Die europäische Insolvenzverordnung (2002), p 51.

6.7 Article 27 of the EIR

31 Because of its inclusion in Chapter III of the EIR, it is clear that Art 27 of the EIR applies to secondary insolvency proceedings.[40] In effect, the court faced with the issue of opening secondary insolvency proceedings need no longer review whether there is a reason to open insolvency proceedings pursuant to the *lex fori concursus secundarii*. The de facto insolvency of the debtor is automatically determined through the prior opening of the main insolvency proceedings, the recognition of which is mandatory pursuant to Articles 16 and 17 of the EIR; the opening of the main insolvency proceedings constitutes an autonomous reason for opening the secondary insolvency proceedings.[41] This modifies the substantive insolvency law provisions of the *lex fori concursus secundarii* by substituting the reasons for opening pursuant to national law with the European reason for opening, i.e. the opening of the main insolvency proceedings whose recognition is mandatory.

32 The substantive correctness of this understanding of Art 27 of the EIR follows from the fact that, even though the Regulation grants to an establishment as defined in Art 2 (h) of the EIR (restricted) legal personality in terms of insolvency law for the purposes of opening secondary insolvency proceedings, the establishment itself remains a legally dependent part of the debtor and is merely clothed in part with legal personality; it is irrelevant whether the debtor, in terms of its legal nature, is a legal entity, a natural person, or a company. With respect to a "debtor" who is the legal subject of an insolvency, the de facto insolvency is already determined at the point in time of the opening of the secondary insolvency proceedings and includes the assets and liabilities of future secondary insolvency proceedings. Articles 16 and 17 of the EIR stipulate that the decision (i.e. the determination of de facto insolvency) must be recognized in the territory of the secondary insolvency proceedings.

6.8 Article 29 of the EIR

33 Art 29 (a) of the EIR of the EIR grants the liquidator of main insolvency proceedings the right to request the opening of secondary insolvency proceedings regardless of whether this is provided for in the particular *lex fori concursus secundarii*.

34 The temporary administrator in main insolvency proceedings is not empowered to request the opening of insolvency proceedings. Even in light of the decision of the ECJ in the action Eurofood/Parmalat[42] which held that the mere appointment of a temporary administrator may already constitute the opening of insolvency proceedings that must be recognized by the other Member States pursuant to Art 16 of the EIR, the wording of Art 29 (a) of the EIR, which is unequivocal in this respect, cannot be so broadly interpreted as to provide the temporary administrator with a right to request the opening of insolvency proceedings.[43]

---

40 On this, see: mn 8 above.

41 On this, see: Art 27 of the EIR mn 19 et seq; similar: *Wimmer* ZIP 1998, 982, 986; Haß/Huber/Gruber/Heiderhoff-*Heiderhoff* Art 27, mn 6; *Morscher* Die europäische Insolvenzverordnung (2002), p 49; obvious dissenting opinion: *Beutler/Debus* EWiR 3, 217, 218.

42 NZI 2006, 360 et seq; on this, see: *Kammel* NZI 2006, 334 et seq; *Knof/Mock* ZIP 2006, 911 et seq.

43 See Art 29 of the EIR mn 20 and mn 10 above; *Virgós/Schmit* Explanatory Report mn 226, 262; D-K/D/Ch-*Duursma-Kepplinger/Chalupsky* Art 29 mn 9; Haß/Huber/Gruber/Heiderhoff-*Heiderhoff* Art 29 EuInsVO mn 2, Art 38 EuInsVO mn 1; *Kolmann* Kooperationsmodelle im Internationalen Insolvenzrecht – Empfiehlt sich für das deutsche internationale Insolvenzrecht eine Neuorientierung (2001), p 335; *Leible/Staudinger* KTS 2000, 533, 570.

6.9 Article 32 of the EIR

Prevailing opinion holds that Art 32 (1) of the EIR, in conjunction with Art 39 of the EIR, modify national substantive insolvency laws and thereby the *lex fori concursus secundarii* invoked in each case. The provision substantively regulates which group of creditors is allowed to lodge claims in secondary insolvency proceedings. According to it, every creditor is entitled to lodge its claim(s) both in the main and in every secondary insolvency proceeding.[44] **35**

Art 32 (2) of the EIR also grants to the liquidator in main insolvency proceedings the right to lodge the claims lodged in his proceedings in the secondary insolvency proceedings as well. **36**

6.10 Chapter IV (Articles 39 to 42) of the EIR

Articles 39 to 42 of the EIR contain substantive law provisions for informing the creditors and the lodging of their claims. These provisions do not distinguish between main insolvency proceedings on the one side and secondary insolvency proceedings or independent territorial insolvency proceedings on the other; they apply equally in both cases.[45] **37**

Article 29
Right to request the opening of proceedings

The opening of secondary insolvency proceedings may be requested by:
a) the liquidator in the main proceedings,
b) any other person or authority empowered to request the opening of insolvency proceedings under the law of the Member State within the territory of which the opening of secondary proceedings is requested.

Contents

---

[44] D-K/D/Ch-*Duursma-Kepplinger/Chalupsky* Art 28 mn 7 et seq; Haß/Huber/Gruber/Heiderhoff-*Heiderhoff* Art 29 EuInsVO mn 2, Art 32 EuInsVO mn 1; *Lüke* ZZP 111 (1998), 275, 300 et seq; Moss/Fletcher/Isaacs-*Moss/Smith*, Regulation, mn 8.236; *Wimmer* ZIP 1998, 982, 987; dissenting opinion: *Thieme* Jahresheft der Internationalen Juristenvereinigung Osnabrück (1995/1996), p 44, pp 86 et seq.

[45] *Virgós/Schmit* Explanatory Report mn 264; D-K/D/Ch-*Duursma-Kepplinger/Chalupsky* Art 39, mn 3; Haß/Huber/Gruber/Heiderhoff-*Heiderhoff* Art 28 EuInsVO mn 4, Art 39 EuInsVO mn 3; *Kemper* ZIP 2001, 1619.

Index

Bibliography

Dawe Der Sonderkonkurs des deutschen internationalen Insolvenzrechts 2005; *Duursma-Kepplinger* Aktuelle Entwicklungen in Bezug auf die Auslegung der Vorschriften über die internationale Eröffnungszuständigkeit nach der Europäischen Insolvenzverordnung, DZWiR 2006, p 177; *Duursma-Kepplinger/Duursma/Chalupsky* Europäische Insolvenzverordnung, Kommentar (2005); *Habscheid* Antrags- und Beteiligungsrecht im gesonderten (Art 102 III EGInsO) und im sekundären Insolvenzverfahren (Art 27 ff EuInsÜ), NZI 1999, p 299; *Herchen* Das Übereinkommen über Insolvenzverfahren der Mitgliedstaaten der Europäischen Union vom 23.11.1995 (2000); *Herchen* Das Prioritätsprinzip im Internationalen Insolvenzrecht, ZIP 2005, p 1410; *Herchen* Wer zuerst kommt, mahlt zuerst! Die Bestellung eines „schwachen" vorläufigen Insolvenzverwalters als Insolvenzverfahrenseröffnung i.S.d. EuInsVO, NZI 2006, p 435 et seq; *Kemper* Verordnung (EG) Nr 1346/2000 über Insolvenzverfahren, ZIP 2001, p 1609; *Leible/Staudinger* Die europäische Verordnung über Insolvenzverfahren, KTS 2000, p 533; *Leipold* Miniatur oder Bagatelle: das internationale Insolvenzrecht im deutschen Reformwerk 1994, in Gerhardt (ed), Festschrift für Wolfram Henckel, 1995, 533; *Liersch* Comments on AG Düsseldorf dated 12.03.2004 – 502 IN 126/03, NZI 2004, p 271; *Lüke* Das europäische internationale Insolvenzrecht, ZZP 111 (1998), p 275; *Metzger* Die Umsetzung des Istanbuler Konkursübereinkommens in das neue deutsche Internationale Insolvenzrecht (1994); *Paulus* Die europäische Insolvenzverordnung und der deutsche Insolvenzverwalter, NZI 2001, p 505; *Morscher* Die europäische Insolvenzverordnung (2002); *Paulus* A Theoretical Approach to Cooperation in Transnational Insolvencies: A European Perspective, European Business Law Review 2000, p 435; *Moss/Fletcher/Isaacs* (eds) The EC Regulation on Insolvency Proceedings (2002); *Spahlinger* Sekundäre Insolvenzverfahren bei grenzüberschreitenden Insolvenzen, Eine vergleichende Untersuchung zum deutschen, US-amerikanischen, schweizerischen und europäischen Recht 1998; *Thieme* Grundsätze des EG-Konkursübereinkommens, Allgemeine Stellungnahme zum Entwurf von 1980, in Stoll (ed), Stellungnahmen und Gutachten zur Reform des deutschen internationalen Insolvenzrechts 1992, 213; *Vallender* Die Voraussetzungen für die Einleitung eines Sekundärinsolvenzverfahrens nach der EuInsVO, InVo 2005, 41.

1. General

1 Art 29 of the EIR deals with the right to request the opening of secondary insolvency proceedings.

2 The idiosyncrasies of the right to request the opening of independent territorial insolvency proceedings – which Art 29 of the EIR does not apply to[1] – are found in Art 3 (4)

[1] *Paulus* Komm EuInsVO Art 29 mn 1.

of the EIR. Additional requirements for opening such proceedings are also set out there.

Art 29 (a) of the EIR establishes a right on the part of the liquidator in the main insolvency proceedings to request the opening of proceedings. This right to request the opening provided for in the Regulation[2] either augments the respective insolvency laws of the particular States through the incorporation of substantive law, or supersedes any contrary and identical provisions contained therein.[3] **3**

Art 29 (b) of the EIR on the other hand simply clarifies that the right to request the opening of insolvency is otherwise – i.e. both with respect to the parties entitled to request the opening of proceedings pursuant to Art 29 of the EIR and with respect to all other requirements for making such a request – determined by the *lex fori concursus secundarii*.[4] This follows already from Art 4 (1), (2) sentence 1 of the EIR. Any other person or authority that is empowered pursuant to the laws of the State of the secondary insolvency proceedings is entitled to request the opening of insolvency proceedings. **4**

2. Request to Open Proceedings by the Liquidator in the Main Proceedings

2.1 Right of Request of the Liquidator in the Main Insolvency Proceedings

Central to the concept of a coordinated multiplicity of proceedings is the right of the liquidator in the main insolvency proceedings to request the opening of proceedings. The dogmatic justification for such right to request stems from the universal effect of the transfer of the debtor's power to dispose of his assets from the debtor to the liquidator in the (main) insolvency proceedings.[5] However, the actual regulating of the right of the liquidator in the main insolvency proceedings to request the opening of proceedings is found in Art 4 (1) of the EIR. Art 29 (a) of the EIR has a mere clarifying function. Most importantly, the right to request allows him to include rights *in rem* as defined in Art 5 of the EIR in the insolvency-related winding-up or reorganization of the debtor's assets. Unless secondary insolvency proceedings are opened, which would subject the rights pursuant to Art 5 of the EIR to the *lex fori concursus secundarii*, these rights would remain untouched by the effects of the main insolvency proceedings.[6] **5**

According to the definition in Art 2 (b) sentence 2 of the EIR, each person listed in Annex C must actually be regarded as a liquidator entitled to make a request within the meaning of Art 29 (a) of the EIR. This is, however, only partially correct. The temporary administrator of the German Insolvency Act (Section 21 (2) No. 1, Section 22 *InsO*), who is also named in Annex C, is not entitled to make a request.[7] **6**

The same applies to the custodian (*Sachwalter* – Section 273 *InsO*) in German law in so-called "debtor in possession" proceedings who, despite the opening of insolvency proceedings, does not acquire powers of administration and disposal in respect of the **7**

---

[2] For details see mn 5 below.

[3] MünchKomm InsO/*Reinhart* Art 29 EuInsVO mn 1; *Smid* Komm EuInsVO Art 29 mn 1.

[4] Haß/Huber/Gruber/Heiderhoff-*Heiderhoff* Art 29 EuInsVO mn 1; Moss/Fletcher/Isaacs-*Moss/Smith*, Regulation, mn 8.225; MünchKomm InsO/*Reinhart* Art 28 EuInsVO mn 2.

[5] *Dawe* Der Sonderkonkurs der deutschen internationalen Insolvenzrechts 2005, p 150 et seq.

[6] For the meaning of this term, see: *Herchen* Das Übereinkommen über Insolvenzverfahren der Mitgliedstaaten der Europäischen Union vom 23.11.1995 (2000), 81 et seq.

[7] On this, see: mn 20 below.

debtor's assets.[8] The debtor is therefore entitled to request the opening of proceedings provided that he is accorded the right to do so by the *lex fori concursus secundarii.*[9]

2.2 Admissibility of the Request to Open Insolvency Proceedings made by the Liquidator in the Main Proceedings

8 The admissibility of the request to open insolvency proceedings made by the liquidator in the main insolvency proceedings must be determined pursuant to the *lex fori concursus secundarii* (Art 4 (1), (2) sentence 1 of the EIR). In this respect, the provisions of the latter regime are being substantively modified or superseded by Articles 27 and 29 (a) of the EIR.

9 The request to open insolvency proceedings is to be deemed as a request made by the debtor himself since the liquidator in the main insolvency proceedings is acting on behalf of the debtor and – subject to the opening of independent territorial or secondary insolvency proceedings – is awarded legal competence in respect of the worldwide insolvency estate.[10] If the requirements of the *lex fori concursus secundarii* for making insolvency requests are different depending on whether the request is being made by the debtor or by the creditors, as in the case of German law in Sections 13 and 14 *InsO*, then the rules governing the former will apply.

10 In German secondary insolvency proceedings, the admissibility of the request to open insolvency proceedings requires the submission of the reason for opening insolvency proceedings in a substantiated and comprehensible form. A conclusive submission of facts and the furnishing of prima facie evidence that is required when giving evidence in a civil process (Section 294 *ZPO*) – which is required when a creditor requests the opening of proceedings[11] – is not necessary.[12] What is therefore required (but also sufficient) is a submission of facts from which it is comprehensively evident that, in addition to showing that the court has international and territorial jurisdiction, main insolvency proceedings as understood by the Regulation have been opened[13] and the party making the request has been appointed its liquidator.[14]

2.3 Individual Aspects of the Substantiation of the Request to Open Insolvency Proceedings made by the Liquidator in the Main Proceedings

11 Although the reason for opening insolvency proceedings arises from the Regulation itself,[15] i.e. it does not make a referral in this respect to the insolvency laws of the Member States, the procedural-law aspects in conjunction with substantiating the request are determined by the *lex fori concursus secundarii.*[16]

12 To substantiate the request to open German secondary insolvency proceedings, the court must be convinced of the existence of the opening requirements. The court itself

---

[8] *Smid* Komm EuInsVO Art 29 mn 4 correctly points out that for this reason the *commissario giudiziale* in the Italian *ammistrazione controllata* (articles 187 et seq, 188 c. 3 *codice fallimentare*) is not included in Annex C of the EIR; concurring in effect: *Vallender* InVo 2005, 41, 46 who makes the debtor's right to request a prerequisite, and who generally affirms such right.

[9] *Smid* Komm EuInsVO Art 29, mn 4 10.

[10] *Smid* Komm EuInsVO Art 29 mn 3.

[11] On this, see: mn 25 et seq below.

[12] BGHZ 153, 205.

[13] AG Cologne NZI 2006, 57.

[14] Dissenting opinion: *Smid* Komm EuInsVO Art 29 mn 3 who holds that it is not necessary to make a submission of facts showing the reasons for opening.

[15] See Art 27 of the EIR mn 19 et seq, 30 et seq.

[16] Along the same lines: *Mankowski* EWiR, Art 3 EuInsVO, 1/06, 109, 110.

is obliged here on its own motion (Section 5 *InsO*) to review the matter; it may, for example, demand from the requesting party a certified copy of the order ordering the main insolvency proceedings.[17] This follows from Art 19 of the EIR as well. However despite the court's obligation to review the matter on its own motion, certified translations may not be demanded. Sentences 2 and 3 of Art 19 of the EIR allow for uncertified translations only, thereby restricting the scope of Section 5 *InsO*.

2.4 Obligation of the Liquidator in the Main Insolvency Proceedings to Make a Request

Whether or not the liquidator in the main insolvency proceedings makes a request pursuant to Art 29 (a) of the EIR to open insolvency proceedings is basically at his discretion.[18] However, this discretionary right to make a request will be converted to an obligation to do so where the provisions of the *lex fori concursus universalis* reduce the discretion to such an extent that alone the making of the request constitutes proper conduct on the part of the liquidator, or where the court or the creditors may, and in fact do, put the liquidator under such an obligation. The failure to make the request pursuant to Art 29 (a) of the EIR in this situation may result in claims for damages against the liquidator pursuant to the *lex fori concursus universalis*.[19] **13**

3. Other Parties Entitled to Request

3.1 Any Other Person or Authority

Any other person or authority that is empowered pursuant to the laws of the State of the secondary insolvency proceedings is entitled to request the opening of insolvency proceedings. Art 29 (b) of the EIR is not a substantive law provision, but rather a pure conflict of laws rule.[20] The reference to "every other ... authority" has little significance where German law governs as the *lex fori concursus secundarii*. *Paulus* is correct in his criticism[21] that this conflict of laws solution is a "disturbance factor"; he prefers the proposal of the European Parliament whereby the liquidator in the main insolvency proceedings must consent to the request to open secondary insolvency proceedings. **14**

The exclusive right to make the request granted to the German Federal Financial Supervisory Authority (*BaFin*) by Section 46 (b) of the Banking Act (*KWG*) in the case of insolvent credit institutions (Section 1 (1) *KWG*) does not fall within Art 29 (b) since insolvency proceedings respecting the assets of credit institutions are, pursuant to Art 1 (2), excluded from the sphere of application of the Regulation. Furthermore, pursuant to Section 46e (2) *KWG*, the opening of secondary and territorial insolvency proceedings in respect of the assets of some types of credit institutions – namely deposit banking institutions (Section 1 (3d) sentence 1 *KWG*) and electronic money institutions (Section 1 (3d) sentence 4 *KWG*) – is prohibited in Germany by operation of law. **15**

---

[17] See Moss/Fletcher/Isaacs-*Moss/Smith*, Regulation, mn 8.222; *Smid* Komm EuInsVO Art 29 mn 7.

[18] For the liquidator's discretion to request the conversion of independent territorial insolvency proceedings into secondary insolvency proceedings pursuant to art 37, see Art 37 of the EIR mn 10.

[19] E.g. sec 60 InsO.

[20] Dissenting opinion: *Morscher* Die europäische Insolvenzverordnung 2002, p 52.

[21] *Paulus* Komm EuInsVO Art 29 mn 2; *Paulus* A Theoretical Approach to Cooperation in Transnational Insolvencies: A European Perspective, European Business Law Review 2000, 435, 436.

16 The same applies to insurance companies; Section 88 (1) of the German Insurance Companies Supervision Act *(VAG)* confers upon the supervisory authorities an exclusive right to request the opening of insolvency proceedings. Insurance companies are excluded from the Regulation's sphere of applicability. Not to be overlooked is that the opening of secondary and insolvency proceedings is also prohibited in Germany by operation of law, namely by Section 88 (1b) *VAG*.

17 A distinction is to be made in the case of financial service institutions (Section 1 (1a) *KWG*).

18 Art 1 (2) of the EIR excludes the opening of insolvency proceedings in respect of the assets of "securities companies that provide services involving the holding of monetary funds or securities on behalf of third parties" from the sphere of applicability of the Regulation. As to which undertakings are to be subsumed under this category is not a decision for the respective *lex fori concursus*; the wording is rather to be construed pursuant to Community law, whereby the legal instruments enacted in this area by the Council of the European Union are to be consulted for purposes of interpretation and systematic construction.[22] If one consults the definition in Art 1 No. 2 and Annex A (particularly Nos. 2 and 3) of Council Directive 93/22/EEC, the exceptions provided for in Art 1 (2) of the EIR include only those financial services institutions that carry out financial portfolio administration (Section 1 (1a) No. 3 *KWG*) or that trade for their own account (Section 1 (1a) No. 4 *KWG*) as it is only these forms of financial service providers that involve the holding of monetary funds or securities for third parties.

19 With respect to the remaining forms of financial service institutions, the right to request the opening of insolvency proceedings is conferred on the *BaFin* pursuant to Art 29 (b) of the EIR. Where main insolvency proceedings are opened in respect of the assets of such a financial service provider, the *BaFin* may request the opening of secondary insolvency proceedings in respect of its German establishment. This means that, in effect, the *BaFin*'s right to request the opening of secondary insolvency proceedings in respect of the German establishment – via the right conferred on it by Art 29 (a) of the EIR as a liquidator in main insolvency proceedings to request the opening of secondary proceedings – extinguishes the exclusivity granted by the *KWG*.

3.2 Temporary Administrator

20 According to overriding prevailing opinion, the temporary administrator in main insolvency proceedings is not empowered to request the opening of secondary insolvency proceedings.[23] This follows firstly from the wording of Art 29 (a) of the EIR, which only

---

[22] Haß/Huber/Gruber/Heiderhoff-*Huber* Art 1 EuInsVO mn 8: credit institutions: First Council Directive 77/780/EEC of 12 December 1997 amended by Council Directive 95/26/EC; insurance companies: Council Directive 73/239/EEC of 24 July 1973 amended by Council Directive 95/26/EC for non-life insurance; First Council Directive 79/267/EEC of 5 March 1979 as amended by Council Directive 95/26/EC for life insurance companies; securities companies: Directive 93/22/EEC of 10 May 1993 as amended by Council Directive 95/26/EC; undertakings for collective investment: Council Directive 85/611/EEC as amended by Council Directive 95/26/EC.

[23] *Virgós/Schmit* Explanatory Report mn 78; *Duursma-Kepplinger* DZWIR 2006, 177 et seq; Haß/Huber/Gruber/Heiderhoff-*Heiderhoff* Art 29 EuInsVO mn 1; *Leible/Staudinger* KTS 2000, 533, 570; Münch-Komm InsO/*Reinhart* Art 29 EuInsVO mn 1; *Vallender* InVO 2005 41, 42, 45; HK-InsO/*Stephan* Art 29 EuInsVO mn 2; dissenting opinion: *Smid* Komm EuInsVO Art 29 mn 5 who would grant the temporary administrator the right to request if a general prohibition of disposition pursuant to sec 21 (2)

mentions the liquidator although the Regulation also knows the temporary administrator (see Art 38 of the EIR). Secondly, the opening of secondary insolvency proceedings necessitates the opening of main insolvency proceedings (see Art 27 of the EIR). The reason for opening that is regulated in Art 27 of the EIR[24], i.e. the opening of main insolvency proceedings, cannot exist as long as a temporary administrator has been appointed.[25] This particular line of reasoning should still be upheld in spite of the decision of the ECJ in the Eurofood/Parmalat[26] case. Even if the appointment of a temporary administrator[27] in German main insolvency proceedings can be viewed as the opening of insolvency proceedings within the meaning of the EIR[28], this still necessitates a decision to be made by the court of the main insolvency proceedings based on the court having to be fully convinced of the de facto insolvency of the debtor, i.e. of the existence of a reason to open insolvency proceedings pursuant to the *lex fori concursus universalis*. This is the actual justification for being able – pursuant to Art 27 of the EIR – to do away with the examination of the reason to open insolvency proceedings by the court of the secondary insolvency proceedings. For the appointing of a temporary administrator, as is the case in German insolvency law, such a conviction is generally not required.

3.3 Debtor

3.3.1 No express provision in the Regulation

The Regulation fails to expressly accord the debtor a right to request the opening of insolvency proceedings. Based on the referral in Art 29 (b) of the EIR to the *lex fori concursus secundarii*, it follows that, in principle, the issue of whether the debtor has a right to request the opening of insolvency proceedings in a case where mandatorily recognizable main insolvency proceedings have already been opened must be answered pursuant to the law of the individual national State.[29] **21**

3.3.2 Loss of the powers of administration and disposal pursuant to the *lex fori concursus*

Where the national law derives the debtor's right to request the opening of insolvency proceedings from his jurisdiction over his property (powers of administration and disposal) in the insolvency estate affected by the insolvency proceedings, the debtor's right to request an opening is extinguished if he is divested of these rights because of the effects of the – mandatorily recognizable (Articles 16, 17 of the EIR) – main insolvency proceedings. Although this issue is unsettled,[30] any other interpretation fails to appreciate the legal **22**

No 2, 1st alternative InsO has been imposed on the debtor.

24 *Smid* Komm EuInsVO Art 29 mn 2.

25 *Vallender* InVO 2005, 41, 42, 45.

26 NZI 2006, 360 et seq.

27 Even the so-called weak temporary administrator of German law will suffice: *Herchen* NZI 2006, 435 et seq.

28 On this *Herchen* ZIP 2005, 1410 et seq.

29 For German law, see: sec 13 (1) sentence 2, sec 15 InsO.

30 D-K/D/Ch-*Duursma-Kepplinger/Chalupsky* Art 29 mn 5, 8; *Paulus* Komm EuInsVO Art 29 mn 6 et seq; *Smid* Komm EuInsVO Art 29 mn 9; HK-InsO/*Stephan* Art 29 EuInsVO mn 4; FK-InsO/*Wimmer* Anhang I nach § 358 mn 99; goes further: *Dawe* Der Sonderkonkurs der deutschen internationalen Insolvenzrechts 2005, 151 et seq; dissenting opinion: AG Cologne ZIP 2004, 471, 473; also indirectly: AG Cologne ZIP 2005, 1566; see also: AG Cologne NZI 2006, 57 with comments by *Mankowski* EWiR art 3 EuInsVO 1/06, 109; Haß/Huber/Gruber/Heiderhoff-*Heiderhoff* Art 29 EuInsVO mn 4; *Kemper* ZIP 2001, 1609, 1613; *Liersch* NZI 2004, 271; *Lüke* ZZP 111 (1998), 275, 302; *Paulus* NZI 2001, 505, 514; *Vallender* InVo 2005, 41, 46; FK-InsO/*Wimmer* Anhang I zu Art 102 EGInsO mn 386;

effects on property when insolvency proceedings are opened. There is actually no need to expressly deny the right to request the opening of insolvency proceedings – either via the *lex fori concursus universalis* or through the *lex fori concursus secundarii*.[31] This remains so even in the case of insolvency of companies or legal entities where the *lex fori concursus universalis* allows their executive bodies to essentially remain in office, and empowers them with partial authority respecting the internal corporate structures of the debtor company. The right to request the opening of insolvency proceedings is derived from the jurisdiction (power) over the property which has been conferred on the liquidator.

23 Where German law governs, the right to request the opening of insolvency proceedings does not remain with the executive bodies of the debtor. Upon the opening of insolvency proceedings, these parties are divested of this jurisdiction over the property in favour of the liquidator (Section 80 (1) *InsO*).[32] Therefore neither the debtor nor its executive bodies is empowered to request the opening of secondary insolvency proceedings once German main insolvency proceedings have been opened.[33]

24 The counterargument,[34] namely that Art 29 (b) of the EIR would be robbed of all meaning if the debtor or its executive bodies are not also empowered to request the opening of proceedings – effectually independent of the *lex fori concursus secundarii* – fails to appreciate the nature of a conflict of laws rule, and Art 29 (b) of the EIR is nothing else but. Art 29 (b) of the EIR cannot be "robbed of all meaning" since the only legal effect it has is to invoke the national laws of a particular State. The actual content of the law being invoked in an actual case is irrelevant to the interpretation of Art 29 (b) of the EIR. But the Regulation equally fails to conclusively preclude the debtor from requesting the opening of secondary insolvency proceedings.[35] This opinion also neglects understand that Art 29 (b) of the EIR is a conflict of laws rule that invokes, without any restriction whatsoever, the laws of the particular *lex fori concursus secundarii* concerning the powers to request. It also fails to provide a satisfactory solution for example to the situation of the "debtor in possession" *(Eigenverwaltung)* in German main insolvency proceedings (Section 270 et seq *InsO*) according to which the debtor expressly retains powers of administration and disposal and is merely supervised by the custodian

---

concurring: *Morscher*, Die europäische Insolvenzverordnung 2002, 52.

[31] But see: AG Cologne ZIP 2004, 471.

[32] The reference occasionally found in this regard to the effect that at least section 354 (1) InsO does not stand in the way of the debtor's right to make a request for opening, see for example AG Cologne ZIP 2004, 471, is irrelevant in this connection since it is a provision of autonomous, international insolvency law that, in respect of independent territorial insolvency proceedings, excludes the debtor's right to request the opening of insolvency proceedings if main insolvency proceedings have been opened in a non-EU State. Equally unhelpful is a reference to section 356 (2) InsO the wording of which could imply that, in spite of mandatorily recognizable main insolvency proceedings having been opened in a non-EU State, the request by a debtor to open secondary insolvency proceedings could still be allowed. However this provision also stems from autonomous, international insolvency law to which art 29 (b) of the EIR makes no referral. From the reasons for adoption in the legislative draft to section 356 InsO, it can also be indirectly gleaned that the debtor in particular was not to have a right to request an opening (ZIP 2002, 2331, 2342).

[33] For the effects on the duty to make the request of the managing director of a German limited liability company (GmbH), see: *Paulus* Komm EuInsVO Art 29 mn 9 et seq.

[34] Especially: AG Cologne ZIP 2004, 471, 473; left open: AG Cologne NZI 2006, 57 with comments by *Mankowski* EWiR Art 3 EuInsVO, 1/06, 109.

[35] But see: *Dawe* Der Sonderkonkurs der deutschen internationalen Insolvenzrechts, 2005, 151 et seq.

(Sachwalter). The very intent and purpose of the "debtor in possession" constellation commands that the debtor retain the right to open secondary insolvency proceedings.

3.4 Creditors in the Insolvency Proceedings

3.4.1 Basic principle

Based on the referral in Art 29 (b) of the EIR to the *lex fori concursus secundarii*, the latter regime determines whether creditors in the insolvency are entitled to request the opening of secondary insolvency proceedings.[36] **25**

3.4.2 Admissibility of the request for opening secondary insolvency proceedings under German law

In the case of German secondary insolvency proceedings, Art 29 (b) of the EIR makes a referral to Section 13 (1) sentence 2 and Section 14 *InsO*. Under German insolvency law, the request of a creditor to open insolvency proceedings is admissible if the requesting insolvency creditor can substantiate, by way of prima facie evidence, his claims against the debtor, the reasons for opening insolvency proceedings, and a legal interest in the opening of the insolvency proceedings (Section 14 (1) *InsO*). **26**

The substantiation by way of prima facie evidence must include – in addition to conclusively submitting the claim, the reasons for opening the proceedings, and the legal interest in opening the insolvency proceedings – proof of such matters in the forms contemplated by the German Code of Civil Procedure *(ZPO)* including the making of an affirmation in lieu of an oath *(eidesstattliche Versicherung)* (Section 294 *ZPO*). **27**

For the submission and the substantiation of the reason for opening the insolvency proceedings, it suffices if a submission is made that main insolvency proceedings have been opened pursuant to the Regulation in another Member State.[37] A certified copy of the order ordering the opening of the main insolvency proceedings can be submitted as proof.[38] This arises indirectly from Art 19 of the EIR. From Art 19 sentences 2 and 3 of the EIR it can be inferred that a certified translation is not required; an uncertified translation will suffice. **28**

Section 14 (1) *InsO*, which is invoked in the case of German secondary insolvency proceedings, also requires – as already stated above in marginal notes 26 and 28 – the submission and substantiation of a legal interest in the opening of insolvency proceedings. If construed strictly, the referral to Section 14 (1) *InsO*, where the creditor requests the opening of German secondary insolvency proceedings, must be read to mean that a legal interest in the opening of *secondary* insolvency proceedings must be submitted and substantiated.[39] In effect, Section 14 *InsO*, apart from providing a general protection of legal interests – which is actually no more than protection from misuse of insolvency proceedings – must also be viewed as providing protection of a special legal interest, namely the opening of secondary insolvency proceedings. **29**

---

[36] For German law, see: sec 13 (1) sentence 2 InsO, 14, 15 (1) InsO.

[37] *Mankowski* EWiR, Art 3 EuInsVO, 1/06, 109, 110.

[38] See Moss/Fletcher/Isaacs-*Moss/Smith*, Regulation, mn 8.222; *Smid* Komm EuInsVO Art 29 mn 7.

[39] *Leipold* Miniatur oder Bagatelle: das internationale Insolvenzrecht im deutschen Reformwerk 1994, in Gerhardt (ed), FS Henckel 1995, 533, 541; dissenting opinion: *Habscheid* NZI 1999, 299, 300 et seq; *Dawe* Der Sonderkonkurs der deutschen internationalen Insolvenzrechts 2005, pp 157, 159, 161 who does not agree that sec 14 (1) InsO creates an interest in the opening of German *secondary* insolvency proceedings, and wishes to restrict the right to open proceedings to creditors whose claims have a strong national connection.

30 For a finding in favour of a special legal interest, the creditor must submit and substantiate by way of prima facie evidence that his participation in the foreign main insolvency proceedings is impossible, unjustified, or it is unreasonable to expect this of him. In the case of a creditor in the insolvency of an establishment, there is a basic presumption in favour of a special legal interest. However should the creditor already be participating in the foreign main insolvency proceedings, this presumption is reversed.[40]

31 Prevailing opinion holds, however, that a special legal interest in the opening of secondary insolvency proceedings does not have to be submitted and substantiated.[41] This is incorrectly supported by a reference to German autonomous international insolvency law (Section 335 et seq *InsO*). If there is a German debtor establishment whose centre of main interests is situated in a non-EU country, then German autonomous international insolvency law (see Section 354 (2) *InsO*) waives the need for the creditor in the insolvency to prove a legal interest in the opening of secondary insolvency proceedings. Apart from the fact that Section 354 *InsO* is not applicable within the sphere of the Regulation's application,[42] it also does not allow the conclusion to be drawn that a legal interest need not be demonstrated in European international insolvency cases. The reason for the waiver in Section 354 (2) *InsO* is, because of a lack of trust in the insolvency law regimes of non-EU countries, to make the opening of German secondary insolvency proceedings easier for national creditors.[43]

32 The history of the Regulation itself is equally unhelpful to support a waiver of the legal interest requirement. Although the original idea to expressly stipulate the need for demonstrating a special legal interest in the case of requests made by creditors for opening secondary insolvency proceedings was discarded,[44] the only conclusion that can be drawn from this is that the requirement cannot be found in the Regulation itself. The Regulation does not, however, preclude the invoking of such provisions of the Member States via conflict of laws rules.[45]

33 The fact that a creditor in insolvency proceedings whose request to open insolvency proceedings was denied because of his failure to demonstrate a special legal interest is

[40] *Dawe* Der Sonderkonkurs der deutschen internationalen Insolvenzrechts 2005, p 161.

[41] Haß/Huber/Gruber/Heiderhoff-*Heiderhoff* Art 29, mn 5; *Metzger* Die Umsetzung des Istanbuler Konkursübereinkommens in das neue deutsche Internationale Insolvenzrecht 1994, 174 et seq; *Smid* Deutsches und Europäisches Internationales Insolvenzrecht 2004, art 29, mn 8; *Thieme* in Stoll (ed), Stellungnahmen und Gutachten zur Reform des deutschen internationalen Insolvenzrechts 1992, 213, 230; *Spahlinger* Sekundäre Insolvenzverfahren bei grenzüberschreitenden Insolvenzen, Eine vergleichende Untersuchung zum deutschen, US-amerikanischen, schweizerischen und europäischen Recht 1998, 323 et seq.

[42] This can already be seen in the asset-related jurisdiction awarded in sec 354 (1) InsO, which is foreign to the EIR. But see: Haß/Huber/Gruber/Heiderhoff-*Heiderhoff* Art 29 mn 5; *Smid* Komm EuInsVO Art mn 8; dissenting opinion: *Dawe* Der Sonderkonkurs der deutschen internationalen Insolvenzrechts 2005, p 156.

[43] This is, on the other hand, only different in autonomous international insolvency law if the international jurisdiction is based not on a national establishment (sec 354 (1) InsO), but merely on assets located inland (sec 354 (1) InsO) the reason being that such exorbitant types of jurisdiction are considered as problematic in terms of international procedural law, and the requirement that there be a special interest ensures that these will be used restrictively.

[44] See art 22 (2) of the Draft Convention on Bankruptcy, Winding-Up, Arrangements, Composition and Similar Proceedings from 1992 ZIP 1992, 1197.

[45] Recital 18 of the Regulation and the opinion in *Virgós/Schmit* Explanatory Report mn 227, are most likely meant to be understood in this way.

still allowed to take part in secondary insolvency proceedings that have been opened pursuant to another request does not speak against the requirement of having to demonstrate a special legal interest.[46] This in no way results in a discrepancy between the right to request the opening of proceedings and the right to take part in them: the negating of a special interest of a creditor in one case does not result in completely divesting him his right to make the request.

In the case of German secondary insolvency proceedings, to require that a creditor **34** making the request have a special interest is in line not only with the wording of the law, but also with the principle of universality on which the Regulation is based – the secondary insolvency proceedings should be the exception, and the settlement of the insolvency case in a universal proceeding the rule.[47] The absence of a requisite special legal interest, a broad interpretation of the term establishment in Art 2 (h) of the EIR, and the lack of ascertaining the de facto insolvency of the debtor (Art 27 of the EIR) would result in a surge of secondary insolvency proceedings and would counteract the legislative intent of the Regulation.

In conclusion, a restricted invocation of Section 14 (1) *InsO* via conflict of laws rules **35** that does away with the need to demonstrate a legal interest, as discussed above,[48] cannot be implied from the Regulation.

3.4.3 International jurisdiction

In addition to the submission and, where necessary, the required proof of facts from **36** which the admissibility of the creditor's request to open secondary insolvency proceedings arises, the creditor must submit all of the facts establishing the international jurisdiction of the court invoked pursuant to Art 3 (2) of the EIR. Most importantly, the existence of an establishment within the meaning of Art 2 (h) of the EIR must be conclusively submitted.

If the insolvency court affirms the admissibility of the request to open German se- **37** condary insolvency proceedings and the creditor in the insolvency makes a conclusive submission of the facts demonstrating the existence of an establishment within the meaning of Art 2 (h) of the EIR, the international jurisdiction must still be reviewed by the court on its own motion and investigated further if necessary.[49]

4. Time Limit for Request

The Regulation does not stipulate any time limit within which the request to open **38** secondary insolvency proceedings must be made. The adoption of such a time limit into the national laws of the individual Member States would, at least in the case of the liquidator in the main insolvency proceedings pursuant to Art 29 (a) of the EIR, have to be regarded as prohibited. The right to make a request is exhausted by Art 29 of the EIR (a) with respect to the sphere of applicability of the Regulation. National laws affecting the legal status of the liquidator in the main proceedings that is conferred on him pursuant to Community law encroach on Community law and thus infringe its superiority.

[46] But see: *Habscheid* NZI 1999, 299, 301.

[47] Recitals 11, 12 and 17 of the EIR suggest this. In depth: *Dawe* Der Sonderkonkurs der deutschen internationalen Insolvenzrechts 2005, p 155 et seq.

[48] See mn 29 above.

[49] AG Cologne NZI 2006, 57 with comments by *Mankowski* EWiR, Art 3 EuInsVO, 1/06, 109.

Article 30
Advance payment of costs and expenses

Where the law of the Member State in which the opening of secondary proceedings is requested requires that the debtor's assets be sufficient to cover in whole or in part the costs and expenses of the proceedings, the court may, when it receives such a request, require the applicant to make an advance payment of costs or to provide appropriate security.

Contents

Index

Bibliography

Beutler/Debus Comments on Landesgericht Klagenfurt, EWiR 3/2005, p 217; *Duursma-Kepplinger/Duursma/Chalupsky* Europäische Insolvenzverordnung, Kommentar (2002); *Haß/Huber/Gruber/Heiderhoff* EU-Insolvenzverordnung, Kommentar (2005); *Kolmann* Kooperationsmodelle im Internationalen Insolvenzrecht – Empfiehlt sich für das deutsche internationale Insolvenzrecht eine Neuorientierung (2001); *Morscher* Die europäische Insolvenzverordnung (2002); *Moss/Fletcher/Isaacs* (eds) The EC Regulation on Insolvency Proceedings (2002); Münchener Kommentar zur Insolvenzordnung, vol 3 (2003); *Paulus* Europäische Insolvenzverordnung, Kommentar (2006); *Vallender* Die Voraussetzungen für die Einleitung eines Sekundärinsolvenzverfahrens nach der EuInsVO, InVo 2005, p 41; *Virgós/Schmit* Erläuternder Bericht zu dem EU-Übereinkommen über Insolvenzverfahren, in Stoll (ed), Vorschläge und Gutachten (1997), p 32.

1. General

1 From a European point of view, Art 30 of the EIR is largely superfluous on account of its predominantly clarifying nature,[1] if the wording of it is taken seriously. The provision merely confirms what the Regulation already states in Art 4 (2) sentence 1 and sentence 2 (i) of the EIR: the *lex fori concursus secundarii* determines whether the opening of secondary insolvency proceedings may be made dependent on the requesting party having to provide an advance payment of costs and expenses or appropriate security.[2] The *lex fori concursus secundarii* must, however, provide that proceedings may only be opened if the costs, including expenses, of such proceedings are able to be covered in

[1] Haß/Huber/Gruber/Heiderhoff *Heiderhoff* Art 30 EuInsVO mn 1; *Morscher* Die europäische Insolvenzverordnung 2002, p 51; MünchKomm InsO/*Reinhart* Art 30 EuInsVO mn 1.

[2] *Virgós/Schmit* Explanatory Report mn 228; D-K/D/Ch-*Duursma-Kepplinger/Chalupsky* Art 30 mn 2, fn 2.

whole or in part by the insolvency estate.[3] Art 30 of the EIR therefore also empowers the Member States to enact such a regulation in their national insolvency law regimes.[4]

Art 30 of the EIR is not an autonomous – substantive law – provision pursuant to which national courts would be competent to require an advance payment or the provision of security if this is not contemplated by the respective *lex fori concursus secundarii*.[5] **2**

From the point of view of German law, Art 30 of the EIR has no practical significance. According to Sec 26 (1) sentence 1 *Ins*O, the opening of insolvency proceedings must be denied for insufficiency of assets if the assets are not sufficient to cover costs. German law does not contain a provision requiring an advance payment or a provision of security. Sec 26 (1) sentence 2 *Ins*O only allows the requesting party, the creditors, and third parties the opportunity to advance a sufficient sum of money to cover the costs of the proceedings. Since Sec 26 *Ins*O is an integral part of the *lex fori concursus secundarii* invoked via Art 4 and 28 of the EIR, it goes without saying that in German secondary insolvency proceedings the same opportunity is awarded the creditors, third parties, and the liquidator in the main proceedings in their capacities as requesting parties pursuant to Art 29 (a) of the EIR. **3**

According to the Explanatory Report to the Convention on Insolvency Proceedings, Art 30 of the EIR is to be so construed that where sufficiency of assets is not already a prerequisite to opening insolvency proceedings pursuant to the respective national law, then that national law may not prescribe sufficiency of assets as a prerequisite exclusively for secondary insolvency proceedings.[6] Although it is an approach very much worthy of support, such an understanding of Art 30 of the EIR cannot be readily inferred from the wording itself.[7] But in light of the principle of Community trust, such support certainly can be found by an interpretation of its wording. Because the Regulation in Art 30 speaks of "the costs and expenses of the proceeding", and not the costs and expenses of the secondary insolvency proceedings, it indicates albeit cautiously that only those national laws on advance payments and the provision of security that are aimed at all types of insolvency proceedings (within the meaning of Annex A of the EIR) of the particular Member State will be acceptable from the point of view of the Regulation. A separate law on this that is aimed only at secondary insolvency proceedings will not be accepted by the Regulation. **4**

---

[3] On this, see the case of the Landgericht Klagenfurt NZI 2004, 677 et seq with comments by *Beutler/Debus* EWiR Art 3 EuInsVO 3/2005, 217.

[4] But see: mn 4 et seq below.

[5] *Virgós/Schmit* Explanatory Report mn 228; D-K/D/Ch-*Duursma-Kepplinger/Chalupsky* Art 30, mn 2; *Kolmann* Kooperationsmodelle im Internationalen Insolvenzrecht – Empfiehlt sich für das deutsche internationale Insolvenzrecht eine Neuorientierung 2001, p 338; indirectly: Moss/Fletcher/Isaacs-*Moss/Smith*, Regulation, mn 8.225; possible dissenting opinion: Landesgericht Klagenfurt NZI 2004, 677, 678; rejecting this: *Beutler/Debus* EWiR 3/2005, 217 et seq.

[6] *Virgós/Schmit* Explanatory Report mn 228; on this: *Heiderhoff* Haß/Huber/Gruber/Heiderhoff *Heiderhoff* Art 30 EuInsVO mn 1.

[7] Concurring: Haß/Huber/Gruber/Heiderhoff *Heiderhoff* Art 30 EuInsVO mn 1; obvious dissenting opinion: *Duursma* D-K/D/Ch-*Duursma-Kepplinger/Chalupsky* Art 30 mn 2; Moss/Fletcher/Isaacs-*Moss/Smith*, Regulation, mn 8.225.

2. Parties Under the Obligation to Provide Advance Payment or Security

5 Despite its near practical irrelevance, Art 30 of the EIR may to a marginal extent be regarded as incorporating substantive law.[8] If in some individual Member States only requesting parties who are simultaneously creditors in the insolvency may be put under an obligation to provide an advance payment or security, then the insolvency laws of these individual States will be augmented by Art 30 of the EIR in such a way that advance payments or security may also be required from the liquidator in the main insolvency proceedings. The liquidator does not generally step into the shoes of a creditor in the insolvency even though he is entitled pursuant to Art 32 (2) of the EIR to lodge the claims of the creditors taking part in the main insolvency proceedings. It does however confer on him a status for procedural purposes only – comparable to a creditor in the insolvency – from which an obligation to provide advance payments cannot be readily inferred. However an obligation to make an advance payment may arise not from his procedural status in the other insolvency proceedings but rather from the obligation he owes to "his creditors" on whose behalf he has deemed the lodging of the claims in the other proceedings as expedient (see Art 32 of the EIR) if the execution of the other insolvency proceedings is dependent on this advance payment and if such proceedings are expedient in light of the burden caused by such a payment.

6 The question as to whether the liquidator in the main insolvency proceedings is entitled to satisfy the advance payment or the security out of the insolvency estate of the main insolvency proceedings must be answered pursuant to the *lex fori concursus universalis*.[9]

3. Amount of the Advance Payment or the Security

7 The appropriateness of the security is roughly equivalent to the amount that would be demanded in the case of an advance payment. This in turn is to be calculated based on the anticipated costs of the proceedings plus expenses, or based on the amount by which the existing insolvency estate is short of these costs. The levying of a security surcharge is acceptable. The conclusion to be drawn here is that the ratio of the existing assets to the amount of the advance payment/extent of the security is irrelevant, and it does not constitute a formula for deciding whether an advance payment or a security may be required in order to allow the opening of proceedings.[10]

8 The amount of the advance payment or the extent of the security is to be calculated using the same standard that is used in non cross-border insolvency proceedings governed by the respective national insolvency laws.[11]

9 A conscious use of the discretionary power to determine the amount of the advance payment or the security – which is conferred on the competent insolvency courts by the *lex fori concursus secundarii* – to impede the opening of secondary insolvency proceedings may be regarded as an infringement of Community law giving rise to an action for breach of the Treaty (Art 227 EC-Treaty) or a liability suit against the state (government body).[12]

[8] Similar: MünchKomm InsO/*Reinhart* Art 30 EuInsVO mn 1.

[9] *Vallender* InVo 2005, 41, 45.

[10] D-K/D/Ch-*Duursma-Kepplinger/Chalupsky* Art 30 mn 2.

[11] *Paulus* Komm EuInsVO Art 30 mn 4 holds that demanding a bank guarantee specifically from a national bank is contrary to European law.

[12] Held by: D-K/D/Ch-*Duursma-Kepplinger/Chalupsky* Art 30 mn 4; *Smid* Komm EuInsVO Art 30 mn 7.

4. Insufficiency of Assets

The issue as to whether the assets are sufficient, i.e. sufficient to cover at least the costs of the proceedings plus expenses, must be determined for the secondary insolvency proceedings[13] in accordance with the *lex fori concursus secundarii*. This follows indirectly from Art 30 as well as from Art 4 (2) sentence 1 sentence 2 (i) of the EIR. The assets upon which the calculation is to be based are those situated in the territory of the State in which the establishment is located. This is the logical result on the one hand of insolvency proceedings that are restricted to a certain territory, and follows on the other hand from the fact that it is specifically these particular assets that are being excluded from the assets in the main insolvency proceedings.[14] Claims based on Art 18 (2) sentence 1 of the EIR for the return of objects removed to the territory of another Member State subsequent to the opening of the proceedings are to be taken into account as are trans-border claims to set aside (see Art 18 (2) sentence 2 of the EIR).[15] For assessing the (nominal) value of such claims, the value is to be reduced proportionate to their chances of successful recovery. **10**

Article 31
Duty to cooperate and communicate information

1. Subject to the rules restricting the communication of information, the liquidator in the main proceedings and the liquidators in the secondary proceedings shall be duty bound to communicate information to each other. They shall immediately communicate any information which may be relevant to the other proceedings, in particular the progress made in lodging and verifying claims and all measures aimed at terminating the proceedings.

2. Subject to the rules applicable to each of the proceedings, the liquidator in the main proceedings and the liquidators in the secondary proceedings shall be duty bound to cooperate with each other.

3. The liquidator in the secondary proceedings shall give the liquidator in the main proceedings an early opportunity of submitting proposals on the liquidation or use of the assets in the secondary proceedings.

→ Cf Art 25 (1), (2) UNCITRAL Model Law

Contents

[13] For main insolvency proceedings, see: Art 27 of the EIR mn 16 and 60 et seq; D-K/D/Ch-*Duursma-Kepplinger/Chalupsky* Art 30 mn 5–8.

[14] *Smid* Komm EuInsVO Art 30 mn 3.

[15] Dissenting opinion: D-K/D/Ch-*Duursma-Kepplinger/Chalupsky* Art 30 mn 9.

Index

Bibliography

Ahrens Rechte und Pflichten ausländischer Insolvenzverwalter im internationalen Insolvenzrecht (2002); *Balz* The European Union Convention on insolvency proceedings, American Bankruptcy Law Journal 70 (1996), p 485; *Balz* Das neue Europäische Insolvenzübereinkommen, ZIP 1996, p 948; Blersch, Jürgen/Goetsch, Hans W. Berliner Kommentar, InsO (January 2007); *Bork* Einführung in das Insolvenzrecht, 3rd edn (2002); *Duursma-Kepplinger/Duursma/Chalupsky* Europäische Insolvenzverordnung, Kommentar (2002); *Ehricke* Das Verhältnis des Hauptinsolvenzverwalters zum Sekundärinsolvenzverwalter bei grenzüberschreitenden Insolvenzen nach der EuInsVO, ZIP 2005, p 1104; *Ehricke* Verfahrenskoordination bei grenzüberschreitenden Unternehmensinsolvenzen, in Basedow et al (eds), Aufbruch nach Europa, 75 Jahre Max-Planck-Institut für Privatrecht (2001), p 337 et seq; *Ehricke* Die Zusammenarbeit der Insolvenzverwalter bei grenzüberschreitenden Insolvenzen nach der EuInsVO, WM 2005, p 397; *Eidenmüller* Der nationale und der internationale Insolvenzverwaltungsvertrag, ZZP 114 (2001), p 3; *Eidenmüller* Europäische Verordnung über Insolvenzverfahren und zukünftiges deutsches internationales Insolvenzrecht, IPRax 2001, p 2; *Erman* Bürgerliches Gesetzbuch (2004); *Göpfert* In re Maxwell Communications – ein Beispiel einer „koordinierten" Insolvenzverwaltung in parallelen Verfahren, ZZPInt 1 (1996), p 269; *Gitlin/Silverman* International Insolvency and the Maxwell Communication Corporate Case, in: International Bankruptcies: Developing Practical Strategies, Commercial Law and Practice Course Handbook-Series, August 5, 1992, p 7; *Hanisch* Grenzüberschreitende Insolvenz, Drei Lösungsmodelle im Vergleich, in Heldrich/Uchida (eds), Festschrift für Hideo Nakamura, Tokyo 1996, p 221 et seq; *Herchen* Das Übereinkommen über Insolvenzverfahren der Mitgliedstaaten der Europäischen Union vom 23.11.1995, Eine Analyse zentraler Fragen des Internationalen Insolvenzrechts unter besonderer Berücksichtigung dinglicher Sicherungsrechte (2000); *Kemper* Die Verordnung (EG) Nr. 1346/

2000 über Insolvenzverfahren, ZIP 2001, p 1609; *Kübler/Prütting* Kommentar zur Insolvenzordnung (March 2006); *Lüke* Das europäische internationale Insolvenzrecht, ZZP 111 (1998), p 275; *Moss/Fletcher/Isaacs* (eds) The EC Regulation on Insolvency Proceedings: A Commentary and Annotated Guide (2002); Münchener Kommentar zur Insolvenzordnung, vol 3 (2003); *Nielsen/Sigal/Wagner* The Cross-Border Insolvency Concordat: Principles to Facilitate the Resolution of International Insolvencies, American Bankruptcy Law Journal 70 (1996), p 533; *Pannen/Kühnle/Riedemann* Die Stellung des deutschen Insolvenzverwalters in einem Insolvenzverfahren mit europäischem Auslandsbezug, NZI 2003, p 72; *Pannen/Riedemann* Cooperation is key, eurofenix 2005, p 20; *Paulus* Europäische Insolvenzverordnung, Kommentar (2006); *Paulus* Das inländische Parallelverfahren nach der Europäischen Insolvenzverordnung, EWS 2002, p 497; *Paulus* Änderungen des deutschen Insolvenzrechts durch die Europäische Insolvenzverordnung, ZIP 2002, p 729; *Runkel* (ed) Anwaltshandbuch – Insolvenzrecht (2005); *Smid* Deutsches und Europäisches Internationales Insolvenzrecht (2004); *Staak* Mögliche Probleme im Rahmen der Koordination von Haupt- und Sekundärinsolvenzverfahren nach der Europäischen Insolvenzverordnung (EuInsVO), NZI 2004, p 480; *von Staudinger* Kommentar zum Bürgerlichen Gesetzbuch mit Einführungsgesetz und Nebengesetzen (2004); *Virgós/Garcimartín* The European Insolvency Regulation: Law and Practice (2004); *Virgós/Schmit* Erläuternder Bericht zu dem EU-Übereinkommen über Insolvenzverfahren, in Stoll (ed), Vorschläge und Gutachten (1997), p 32; *Wessels* Current Topics of International Insolvency Law (2004); *Wittinghofer* Der nationale und internationale Insolvenzverwaltungsvertrag – Koordination paralleler Insolvenzverfahren durch ad hoc-Vereinbarungen (2004).

1. Overview

In order to ensure the best possible and most efficient administration of the debtor's assets in the case of parallel (concurrent) insolvency proceedings, a close cooperation based on mutual trust between the **liquidators of the main and secondary insolvency proceedings** is indispensable.[1] This also conforms to the ideas expressed in Recital 20 of the EIR. **1**

In this context, Art 31 of the EIR lays down a **series of duties** for liquidators.[2] It therefore represents a **substantive-law allocation of responsibility**. Art 31 of the EIR prescribes a duty to cooperate and communicate information between the liquidators of the main and secondary insolvency proceedings.[3] **2**

"**Cooperation**" is to be regarded as an umbrella term of Art 31 of the EIR, which is then subdivided into a **duty to communicate information** within the meaning of Art 31 (1) of the EIR (see mn 6 et seq) and a **duty to cooperate in a narrower sense** within the meaning of Art 31 (2) of the EIR (mn 32). **3**

Art 31 (3) of the EIR makes it clear that, with respect to the duty to cooperate and communicate information, the secondary insolvency proceedings **serve the needs** of the main insolvency proceedings.[4] The liquidator in the secondary insolvency proceedings is put under an obligation to give the liquidator in the main proceedings the opportunity of **4**

---

[1] BK-InsO/*Pannen* Art 31 mn 1; *Paulus* Komm EuInsVO Art 31 mn 3; *Wessels* Current Topics of International Insolvency Law, p 30; *Hanisch* Grenzüberschreitende Insolvenz, 221, 239.

[2] *Ehricke* ZIP 2005, 1104, 1108.

[3] BK-InsO/*Pannen* Art 31 EuInsVO mn 2; *Pannen/Riedemann* eurofenix 2005, 20.

[4] D-K/D/Ch-*Duursma-Kepplinger/Chalupsky* Art 31 mn 1; *Ehricke* Verfahrenskoordination bei grenzüberschreitenden Unternehmensinsolvenzen in *Basedow*, Aufbruch nach Europa, 337, 346; Kübler/Prütting-*Kemper* EuInsVO Art 31 mn 8; *Wessels* Current Topics of International Insolvency Law, p 30.

submitting proposals for the liquidation.[5] Art 31 (3) of the EIR is therefore a **special provision on communication and cooperation**[6] (on this mn 40 et seq).

5 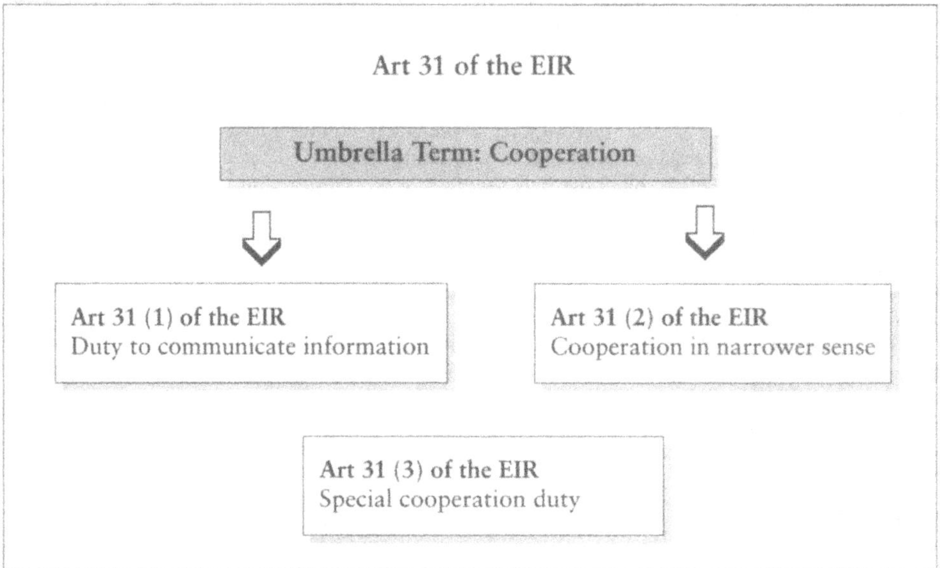

2. Duty to Communicate

6 The liquidators' duties to cooperate and communicate information pursuant to Art 31 of the EIR mirrors the interconnected nature of the main and secondary insolvency proceedings, the main insolvency proceedings having a **dominant role** in this, see Recital 20 sentence 3 of the EIR. The secondary insolvency proceedings are to be subordinated to the needs of the main proceedings, provided that this is compatible with the aims of the secondary insolvency proceedings.[7] *Smid* even goes so far as saying that the purpose of

---

[5] D-K/D/Ch-*Duursma-Kepplinger/Chalupsky* Art 31 mn 18. An express duty on the part of the liquidator of the secondary proceedings to actually accept or implement the proposals cannot be inferred from art 31 of the EIR.

[6] D-K/D/Ch-*Duursma-Kepplinger/Chalupsky* Art 31 mn 5; *Virgós/Schmit* Explanatory Report mn 233. In-depth see also BK-InsO/*Pannen* Art 31 mn 11 et seq. The liquidator in the secondary insolvency proceedings must, in effect, inform the liquidator in the main insolvency proceedings of the planned usage or liquidation of property.

[7] *Pannen/Riedemann* eurofenix 2005, 20 (The project "CoCo" [Communication and Cooperation between Liquidators] of the Academic Wing of INSOL Europe is also presented in this contribution; on this, see the chapter on protocols at mn 23 as well). Despite the interconnected nature of the main and secondary insolvency proceedings, and the superior position of the liquidator in the main proceedings, the latter does not rule over the secondary insolvency proceedings, *Ehricke* Verfahrenskoordination bei grenzüberschreitenden Unternehmensinsolvenzen in *Basedow*, Aufbruch nach Europa, 337, 344; *Balz* Am. Bankr.L.J 70 (1996), 485, 526. With respect to the administration and disposal of the respective insolvency estates, the powers of the liquidators generally remain separate, these being subject to the provisions of the respective *lex fori concursus* (art 28 of the EIR).

the cooperation is to foster the interests of the main insolvency proceedings.[8] The co-operation should not, however, be viewed as a "one way street". The liquidator in the secondary insolvency proceedings can, and will, normally profit from the exchange of information.

According to Art 31 (1) sentence 2 of the EIR, the liquidators of the main and **7**
secondary insolvency proceedings are under a duty to **immediately communicate to each other any information** that may be relevant to the other proceedings. In order to effectively coordinate parallel insolvency proceedings, it is crucial that the same information is available to the various liquidators.[9] Particularly the liquidator in the main insolvency proceedings needs the information from the territorial proceedings.[10] The **duty to communicate information** simultaneously forms the **basis** of the liquidator's supplementary[11] duty of **mutual cooperation**[12] in Art 31 (2) of the EIR; it also **makes it possible** for the liquidator in the main proceedings to **intervene** in the secondary insolvency proceedings in the ways contemplated in Arts 32 to 38 of the EIR.[13]

Some have criticized (with respect to the provision in the 1995 Draft Convention on **8**
Insolvency Proceedings, on this, see the Introduction at mn 10) the duty to cooperate and communicate information as being more suited to winding-up proceedings than to cross-border reorganisations.[14] They argue that such duties only ensure that the interests of national creditors can be asserted across the borders, and that an administration's procedural interests are able to be taken into account in the parallel proceedings. Such duties alone do not ensure, a close coordination of two reorganisation proceedings concerning a holding company whose subsidiaries have experienced different economic fates.[15] According to the cooperation provisions, the parallel insolvency proceedings would be conducted to a large extent independent of the other pursuant to the law applicable in the place of the particular proceedings.[16]

This criticism is justified to some extent since Art 31 of the EIR, taken on its own, **9**
does not adequately guarantee an actual coordination of proceedings. The so-called **"protocols"** could play an important role here; on this, see the chapter on protocols at mn 1 et seq and the country report for England at mn 106 et seq.[17] These are **formalized agreements** between liquidators or other participants in the proceedings for the purposes of coordinating parallel (concurrent) insolvency proceedings. They make it possible to autonomously identify and stipulate the key points of the common administration.[18]

---

8 *Smid* Komm EuInsVO Art 31 mn 8.

9 *Ehricke* Verfahrenskoordination bei grenzüberschreitenden Unternehmensinsolvenzen in Basedow (ed), Aufbruch nach Europa, 337, 345; D-K/D/Ch-*Duursma-Keppling er/Chalupsky* Art 31 mn 7.

10 D-K/D/Ch-*Duursma-Kepplinger/Chalupsky* Art 31 mn 7.

11 Disagreeing with the term "supplementary": *Smid* Komm EuInsVO Art 31 mn 12 who holds that subs 1 and 2 are separate rules with their own requirements.

12 *Ehricke* Verfahrenskoordination bei grenzüberschreitenden Unternehmensinsolvenzen in Basedow (ed), Aufbruch nach Europa, 337, 345.

13 D-K/D/Ch-Duursma-Kepplinger/Chalupsky Art 31 mn 7.

14 *Göpfert* ZZPInt 1 (1996), 269, 279.

15 *Göpfert* ZZPInt 1 (1996), 269, 279.

16 *Göpfert* ZZPInt 1 (1996), 269, 279.

17 *Eidenmüller* Der nationale und der internationale Insolvenzverwaltungsvertrag, ZZP 114 (2001), 3 et seq, *Gitlin/Silverman* International Insolvency and the Maxwell Communication Corporate Case, in International Bankruptcies: Developing Practical Strategies, Commercial Law and Practice Course Handbook-Series, August 5, 1992, 7 et seq; *Göpfert* ZZPInt 1 (1996), 269 et seq; *Nielsen/Sigal/Wagner* The Cross-Border Insolvency Concordat, Am.Bankr.L.J. 70 (1996), 533 et seq; *Wittinghofer* Der nationale und internationale Insolvenzverwaltungsvertrag.

18 *Ehricke* ZIP 2005, 1104, 1111.

From the practitioner's point of view, even though protocols have the advantage of enabling parallel proceedings to be similarly conducted, they may also introduce a certain degree of rigidity, since they restrict the flexibility of the respective liquidators.[19] In German law, it is uncertain whether liquidators and courts would be allowed to enter into such contracts at all, and whether German courts can be involved with them.[20] For an in-depth discussion on protocols, see the country report for England at mn 106 et seq and the chapter on protocols.

2.1 (Secondary) Liquidator

10 According to the wording of Art 31 (1) sentence 1 of the EIR, the duties to communicate information are restricted to the **liquidators** in the parallel proceedings.[21] The duty is only owed between the liquidators in a **main/secondary insolvency proceeding relationship.**[22] Art 31 (1) sentence 1 of the EIR **does not obligate the liquidators of the various secondary insolvency proceedings** to communicate information to each other.[23] The primary goal of Art 27 et seq of the EIR is to secure the dominance of the main insolvency proceedings, this being an irrelevant issue when only territorial insolvency proceedings are involved.[24]

11 Some are of the opinion[25] that, although the **duty to communicate information** exists primarily between the liquidators of the main and secondary insolvency proceedings and only subsidiarily between the individual liquidators in the various secondary proceedings, since there are usually no points of contact between these proceedings, should a need for communication ever arise between the liquidators in the secondary insolvency proceedings, then there would also be a **duty** here pursuant to Art 31 (1) of the EIR to exchange information, provided that it furthers the efficiency of the proceedings. Others are of the opinion that there is a **possibility** of cooperation between the liquidators in the secondary insolvency proceedings, and that Art 31 of the EIR should also be applied analogously to the liquidators of the various secondary insolvency proceedings.[26] This would mean that there would also be a ***duty* to exchange information.** There may certainly be a need for the liquidators of the secondary insolvency proceedings to exchange information, for instance in conjunction with the equalization of dividends contemplated

---

[19] Also *Ehricke* WM 2005, 397, 402.

[20] Although sec 80 InsO confers on the liquidator the powers of administration and disposal over the debtor's assets, it is still questionable whether such an administration contract can be entered into independent of the wishes of the creditors. Even "protocols" are difficult to implement in Germany. They are borrowed from US law; insolvency courts there accept arrangements made between liquidators, including these as schedules to "procedural orders", which the courts then hand out to the liquidators. The use of the courts to anchor agreements entered into by the liquidators is not possible in Germany because of the different status that German insolvency courts have. E.g. see also *Ehricke* WM 2005, 397, 402.

[21] *Herchen* Das Übereinkommen über Insolvenzverfahren der Mitgliedstaaten der Europäischen Union, p 147; BK-InsO/*Pannen* Art 31 mn 2; D-K/D/Ch-*Duursma-Kepplinger/Chalupsky* Art 31 mn 6.

[22] Kübler/Prütting-*Kemper* EuInsVO Art 31 mn 2; *Pannen* in: Runkel (ed), AHB-Insolvenzrecht (2005) § 16 mn 621; *Pannen/Riedemann* eurofenix 2005, 20.

[23] *Balz* ZIP 1996, 948, 954; Kübler/Prütting-*Kemper* EuInsVO Art 31 mn 2; *Pannen* in Runkel (Hrsg), AHB-Insolvenzrecht (2005) § 16 mn 621; **contra:** D-K/D/Ch-*Duursma-Kepplinger/Chalupsky* Art 31 mn 8; *Ehricke* WM 2005, 397, 399.

[24] *Pannen* in Runkel (ed), AHB-Insolvenzrecht (2005) § 16 mn 621.

[25] D-K/D/Ch-*Duursma-Kepplinger/Chalupsky* Art 31 mn 8.

[26] *Ehricke* WM 2005, 397, 399.

by Art 20 (2) of the EIR or in respect of avoidance actions (Art 4 (2) sentence 2 (m), Art 13 of the EIR), so that it should be ***possible* to cooperate** with one another. But the mandatory exchange of information between the liquidators of the secondary insolvency proceedings is not, based on the unequivocal wording of Art 31 of the EIR, formulated as an obligation.

The liquidator in the main insolvency proceedings may, however, be under a duty to inform a liquidator in a secondary proceeding on the status of another secondary insolvency proceeding.[27] From the duty set out in Art 31 (1) of the EIR, *Paulus* infers that the liquidator in the main insolvency proceedings procures – and is even obliged to procure – the information that the liquidator in the secondary insolvency proceedings needs, this including the information needed to compile the property of the insolvency estate.[28] **12**

2.2 Courts

The **addressees of the duty to cooperate** pursuant to Art 31 of the EIR are the liquidators within the meaning of Annex C of the EIR.[29] Inverting the rule in Art 31 of the EIR will not, however, allow the conclusion to be drawn that the **courts** are not allowed to cooperate.[30] The goal of Art 31 et seq of the EIR is to ensure the most meaningful cooperation possible between the main and secondary insolvency proceedings, i.e. one that facilitates the optimal administration of the debtor's assets. The duty imposed on the liquidators pursuant to Art 31 (1) of the EIR to communicate information to each other is necessary for the efficient conducting and coordinating of the various proceedings. There is no apparent reason why a cooperation between the insolvency courts involved in the proceedings should not foster such an efficient conducting of the proceedings.[31] The problem arising from this is whether such communication by the insolvency courts should also be a **duty,** or whether it should be on a **voluntary basis** only. The EIR contains no provision of its own on this.[32] **13**

The ***OLG* Vienna** (→ cf Table of Cases Art 3 of the EIR Appendix B No 63) ruled in its decision of 9 November 2004[33] that Art 31 of the EIR, over and above the wording of it, also imposes an obligation on the courts to cooperate. The *OLG* refers in its decision to *Duursma-Kepplinger/Chalupsky,*[34] although the latter do not actually seem to mean a duty to cooperate but simply would like to give the courts the **possibility** of cooperating.[35] **14**

A **duty** on the part of the courts to cooperate cannot be inferred from the EIR.[36] What is certain is that the courts cannot be regarded as liquidators (administrators) **15**

[27] Kübler/Prütting-*Kemper* EuInsVO Art 31 mn 2.

[28] *Paulus* EWS 2002, 497, 504.

[29] *Smid* Komm EuInsVO Art 31 mn 10.

[30] *Eidenmüller* IPRax 2001, 2, 9; BK-InsO/*Pannen* Art 31 mn 2.

[31] Cf also *Ehricke* WM 2005, 397, 401; *Herchen*, Das Übereinkommen über Insolvenzverfahren, p 147.

[32] According to information received, such a cooperation supposedly took place in a more informal fashion in the preliminary stages of AG Cologne, ZIP 2004, 471 ("Automold" → cf Table of Cases Art 3 of the EIR Appendix A mn 2), *Ehricke* WM 2005, 397, 401.

[33] OLG Vienna dated 9 Nov 2004 – 28 R 225/04, NZI 2005, 56 with explanatory note by *Paulus* S 62 f.

[34] OLG Vienna dated 9 Nov 2004; NZI 2005, 56, 61.

[35] D-K/D/Ch-*Duursma-Kepplinger/Chalupsky* Art 31 mn 6; going further: *Herchen*, who also considers a cooperation within the meaning of art 31 of the EIR between the insolvency courts as necessary. In the insolvency opening procedure, the insolvency court is the "decisive organ"; cf *Herchen* Das Übereinkommen über Insolvenzverfahren, p 149.

[36] Also: *Ehricke* WM 2005, 397, 401; *Pannen/Riedemann* eurofenix 2005, 20.

within the meaning of the EIR, one reason being that not every Member State has included the insolvency court in its list of liquidators in Annex C of the EIR.[37] Austria for instance included the *Konkursgericht* (bankruptcy court) in Annex C, but Germany did not include its *Insolvenzgericht* (insolvency court). The wording of Annex C of the EIR is exhaustive with respect to the "liquidators" that may be taken into consideration for the purposes of the EIR, which means that Art 31 (1) of the EIR cannot be applied analogously to insolvency courts.[38] A subsumption of insolvency courts within the definition of liquidator in Art 2 (b) of the EIR would, because of other provisions of the EIR that concern liquidators, lead to problems.[39]

16 Without some kind of legal grounds and without any provision for it in the EIR, it is difficult to impose a **duty to cooperate** – and **consequences** for not complying with such a duty to cooperate – on the **insolvency courts.**[40] Art 31 of the EIR does not, however, operate to prevent the ***possibility* of cooperation** between the courts involved.[41]

2.3 Subject Matter and Limitations of the Duty to Communicate Information Within the Meaning of Art 31 (1) of the EIR

17 According to Art 31 (1) of the EIR, the liquidators in the main and secondary insolvency proceedings are obliged to communicate information to each other. This duty exists **for the entire duration** of the insolvency proceedings.[42]

2.3.1 "Immediately"

18 Art 31 (1) sentence 2 of the EIR demands that the information be communicated **immediately** without defining this term in any more detail. The German understanding of "immediately" generally means **"without undue delay"** (statutory definition in Sec 121 *BGB*). This statutory definition applies in Germany to the entire area of private and public law; the times within which the parties under the obligation must react vary, however, depending on the context.[43] An **upper limit of 14 days** is the basic rule for determining whether an action has been done without undue delay.[44]

19 Deciding whether an act has been done **"without undue delay"** within the context of the EIR is difficult: in the case of cross-border insolvencies in the European Union, there are usually language barriers that must first be overcome.[45] This affects the determination of whether an act has been done "immediately" pursuant to Art 31 (1) sentence 2 of the EIR, since documents or reports of a liquidator, which contain the required information for the other liquidators, first have to be **translated** either into the native language of the liquidator receiving it or into one of the official languages.[46]

2.3.2 Translation costs

20 The issue of who bears the **costs of translations** is a problematic one. One view holds that the costs connected with a translation should be borne by the **insolvency estate pro-**

---

[37] D-K/D/Ch-*Duursma-Kepplinger/Chalupsky* Art 31 mn 6.

[38] *Staak* NZI 2004, 480, 483.

[39] *Staak* NZI 2004, 480, 483; *Pannen/Riedemann* eurofenix 2005, 20.

[40] *Staak* NZI 2004, 480, 483.

[41] *Ehricke* WM 2005, 397, 401; *Pannen/Riedemann* eurofenix 2005, 20.

[42] *Kemper* ZIP 2001, 1609, 1618; BK-InsO/*Pannen* Art 31 mn 6.

[43] Staudinger-*Singer* § 121 BGB mn 8.

[44] OLG Hamm dated 9 Jan 1990 – 26 U 21/89M, NJW-RR 1990, 523; Erman-*Palm,* § 121 BGB mn 3; Staudinger-*Singer*, § 121 BGB mn 8.

[45] *Pannen/Riedemann* eurofenix 2005, 20.

[46] *Staak* NZI 2004, 480, 482.

viding the information, even if the information was given at the request of the foreign creditor.[47] It seems to make more sense, however, to hold the liquidator receiving the information responsible for its translation, who in his own interests would tend to deal with this quickly. The liquidator who is passing on the information is of course duty bound to pass along vital information to the other liquidators as soon as he has obtained knowledge of such.[48] The **receiving insolvency estate** will then have to bear the costs of the translation.

2.3.3 Examples of the duty to communicate information

Communicating information means that the liquidators must – unsolicited – make the required information available to each other; but this also means that information must be (actively) requested or that a **request for information must be complied with.**[49] Art 31 (1) sentence 2 of the EIR sets out what the subject matter of the duty to communicate information may entail. The progress and the verifying of the lodged claims and all measures aimed at terminating the proceedings, such as **21**

- composition or plan proposals or
- requests to stay the proceedings,

are given as examples of information relevant to the respective other proceedings. These are intended to make clear that the duty to communicate information only relates to **essential measures and information.**

According to the Virgós/Schmit-Report,[50] the communication of information be- **22**
tween the various liquidators relates especially to:[51]

- the insolvency estate (what is meant is a list of assets and a notification in the event of an insufficiency of assets),[52]
- the planned or filed lawsuits to reclaim parts of the insolvency estate, e.g. avoidance actions or payment actions,
- the lodged claims,
- the verifying of the claims,
- the order of priority of the creditors,
- the planned reorganization measures,
- the proposed composition measures,
- a discharge of residual debt,
- the proposals for the distribution of dividends,
- the specific phase of the proceedings.[53]

Art 31 (1) of the EIR also places the liquidators under a **duty to render accounts to** **23**
each other.

---

47 MünchKomm-InsO/*Reinhart* Art 31 EuInsVO mn 2.

48 *Staak* NZI 2004, 480, 482.

49 Kübler/Prütting-*Kemper* EuInsVO Art 31 mn 2.

50 On its importance, see Introduction at mn 42.

51 *Virgós/Schmit* Explanatory Report mn 230; *Virgós/Garcimartín* The European Insolvency Regulation: Law and Practice (2004) p 233 (mn 436); *Pannen/Kühnle/Riedemann* NZI 2003, 72, 76.

52 D-K/D/Ch-*Duursma-Kepplinger/Chalupsky* Art 31 mn 9.

53 On this see also: *Ahrens* Rechte und Pflichten ausländischer Insolvenzverwalter im internationalen Insolvenzrecht, p 311; BK-InsO/*Pannen* Art 31 mn 8; Moss/Fletcher/Isaacs-*Moss/Smith*, Regulation, mn 8.228; Kübler/Prütting-*Kemper* EuInsVO Art 31 mn 3.

24 In order to avoid the unnecessary taxing of the workload of the liquidators through a multitude of communication duties, and to safeguard the legal autonomy of the proceedings, it is advisable to reduce the information to facts/circumstances that concern **significant parts of the insolvency estate** or to **decisions that are important** to the conducting of the proceedings.[54]

2.3.4 Procedures for exchanging information

25 Left open is the issue as to which procedures the liquidators must use to request and pass on information. For practical reasons, the exchange of information will take place:

- in a **personal meeting,**
- by **telephone,**
- via **e-mail,** or
- by **post** (in the procedural language agreed on).[55]

It may also be necessary to have professional **translations** prepared, which can be very costly and time consuming.[56] As stated above (see mn 20), it would seem reasonable that the insolvency estate receiving the translations bear the costs of these. Reference is also made here to "CoCo" (Communication and Cooperation between Liquidators), an initiative of the Academic Wing of INSOL Europe (on this, see mn 57 and the chapter on protocols at mn 23): Guidelines for the cooperation and communication of information in the case of cross-border insolvencies are being prepared by this body.[57]

26 Some have suggested the setting up of a **special server**, a **part of a server**, or a **common chat room** accessible to the participating liquidators only.[58] The **creation of an information pool** in data processing systems, in which both liquidators store the data necessary for their administration and which is accessible to both of them, has also been suggested.[59] From a practitioner's point of view, however, the technical implementation of the latter proposals would likely prove difficult.

2.3.5 Enforceability of the right to receive information

27 Art 31 (1) of the EIR grants the liquidators **substantive-law rights to receive information** from the other liquidators.[60] According to Art 18 (1) of the EIR in conjunction with Art 31 (1) of the EIR, the liquidators in the main and secondary insolvency proceedings may **bring an action for information** pursuant to the national laws of the respective State and the procedural law of the other Member State. A breach of the duty to communicate information may also render the liquidator liable pursuant to the *lex fori concursus*.[61]

---

54 D-K/D/Ch-*Duursma-Kepplinger/Chalupsky* Art 31 mn 9; *Wimmer* ZIP 1998, 987.

55 *Staak* NZI 2004, 480, 481; *Ehricke* Verfahrenskoordination bei grenzüberschreitenden Unternehmensinsolvenzen in: Basedow (ed), Aufbruch nach Europa, 337, 351; *Paulus* Komm EuInsVO Art 31 mn 9.

56 *Staak* NZI 2004, 480, 481.

57 A description of the project is available at: http://bobwessels.nl/download/project_insol_europe.pdf. The Guidelines are available on the Internet site: http://bobwessels.nl/worldpress, as well as in Annex 5. The Guidelines were presented at the INSOL Europe conference in Bucharest in 2006.

58 *Staak* NZI 2004, 480, 481; *Paulus*, ZIP 2002, 729, 735.

59 *Ehricke* Verfahrenskoordination bei grenzüberschreitenden Unternehmensinsolvenzen in Basedow (ed), Aufbruch nach Europa, 337, 351 et seq. Concurring *Paulus* Komm EuInsVO Art 31 mn 9.

60 *Smid* Komm EuInsVO Art 31 mn 16.

61 Kübler/Prütting-*Kemper* EuInsVO Art 31 mn 5.

2.3.6 Limitations of the duty to communicate information

2.3.6.1 Constraints pursuant to Art 31 (1) sentence 1 of the EIR

The duty to communicate information is subject to the **respective national laws on data-protection and on professional and trade secrets.**[62] **28**

If the laws of a Member State forbid the transmission of information, such as the laws relating to the protection of electronically stored person-related data (the data-protection acts of Austria (*DSG*) and Germany (*BDSG*) for instance), Art 31 of the EIR cannot be invoked for the purpose of disregarding these national data-protection laws. Such national laws restrict the **scope of the duty to communicate information** that one liquidator owes to the other (Art 31 (1) sentence 1 of the EIR). However, a close examination will have to be made in each case to determine whether the **transmission** of administration-related information **for a specific purpose** from one liquidator to another actually violates the objects of the data-protection provisions.[63] **29**

Art 31 (1) sentence 1 of the EIR **only relates to reservations** prescribed by the laws of sovereign states only. It does not include instructions given by the creditors to the liquidators not to pass on certain information. The creditors would otherwise be able to hinder the exchange of information between the parallel proceedings.[64] **30**

2.3.6.2 Other constraints

As with all other provisions of the EIR, the duty to cooperate and communicate information in Art 31 of the EIR only produces effects as between the Member States of the EU.[65] If non-EU ancillary proceedings are being conducted concurrently with main and secondary insolvency proceedings within the European Community, the cooperation and communication provisions of the EIR apply to the liquidators of these latter two proceedings only and not to the non-EU liquidator.[66] **31**

3. Duty to Cooperate

The key provision for coordinating the main and secondary insolvency proceedings is Art 31 (2) of the EIR. According to it, the liquidator in the main insolvency proceedings and the liquidator in the secondary proceedings are, subject to the rules applicable to the individual proceedings, under a duty to **cooperate** in a manner that goes beyond the mere provision of information. Hence the duty to cooperate **supplements** the **duty to communicate information.**[67] **32**

The object of Art 31 (2) of the EIR is simply to ensure the cooperation between several liquidators; it makes no provision for the cooperation between the insolvency courts of the various Member States, or between the **insolvency courts** and any foreign liquidators, see mn 16. Although Art 31 (2) of the EIR does not prevent the **possibility** of courts cooperating with each other, the wording of the EIR does also not allow the inference of a **duty to cooperate** with each other. **33**

---

[62] Moss/Fletcher/Isaacs-*Moss/Smith*, Regulation, mn 8.229; *Virgós/Schmit* Explanatory Report mn 231; *Ehricke* ZIP 2005, 1104, 1110; *Paulus* Komm EuInsVO Art 31 mn 11.

[63] *Balz* ZIP 1996, 948 (954); BK-InsO/*Pannen* Art 31 mn 9.

[64] *Ehricke* ZIP 2005, 1104, 1111.

[65] Basically: *Pannen* in Runkel (ed), AHB-Insolvenzrecht (2005) § 16 mn 26.

[66] D-K/D/Ch-*Duursma-Kepplinger/Chalupsky* Art 31 mn 2.

[67] Kübler/Prütting-*Kemper* EuInsVO Art 31 mn 6.

3.1 Examples of Cooperation

34 In the interests of an efficient and undisturbed conducting of the various insolvency proceedings, the liquidators are obliged to coordinate their procedures with each other, to coordinate the implementation of the procedural phases, and to make the work as easy for each other as possible.[68] More detailed information on what is actually entailed by the duty to cooperate is found neither in the Explanatory Report to the 1995 Draft Convention on Insolvency Proceedings nor in the recitals to the EIR.

35 One example of the Art 31 (2) duty to cooperate is the **procurement of documents** that could be relevant to the foreign proceeding.[69] In practice, the cooperation will focus primarily on the following things:

- the **carrying out of liquidation transactions** (e.g. selling participating interests[70]),
- the **exercising of voting rights,**
- the **presentation of an insolvency plan** (whether/when/contents[71]),
- the **exercising of a (performance) option in the case of reciprocal contracts,**
- the **assertion of avoidance claims,**
- the **assumption of credit or the provision of security**, or
- the **filing of further insolvency requests** in respect of other establishments.[72]

3.2 Limits to the Duty to Cooperate

36 According to Art 31 (2) of the EIR, the duty to cooperate is subject to the rules applicable to the individual proceedings. This is generally understood to mean all of the provisions of the national law that governs the insolvency proceedings.[73]

37 The creditors' rights to structure certain matters in the particular insolvency proceedings must also be taken into account here.[74] For instance, a German liquidator could be prevented from cooperating if faced with an **especially important transaction pursuant to Sec 160 *InsO*** for which the creditors' consent must be sought.[75]

3.3 Sanctions

38 The EIR is silent as to **consequences of not complying with the cooperation duty**, or for complying with it too late.[76] According to the Virgós/Schmit Report, the applicable national law also governs the issue of the liquidator's liability for breaching his duties pursuant to Art 31 of the EIR.[77] The enforcement of the duty to cooperate and communicate information is thus governed by the *lex fori concursus* via the insolvency court in

---

68 *Virgós/Schmit* Explanatory Report mn 232.

69 FK-InsO *Wimmer* Art 102 EGInsO mn 141.

70 *Virgós/Garcimartín* The European Insolvency Regulation: Law and Practice, p 234 (mn 441); *Eidenmüller* ZZP 114 (2001), 3, 10 et seq; Kübler/Prütting-*Kemper* EuInsVO Art 31 mn 6.

71 *Eidenmüller* ZZP 114 (2001), 3, 11.

72 *Ehricke*, Verfahrenskoordination bei grenzüberschreitenden Unternehmensinsolvenzen in Basedow, Aufbruch nach Europa, 337, 346.

73 *Ehricke* ZIP 2005, 1104, 1111; Kübler/Prütting-*Kemper* EuInsVO Art 31 mn 7.

74 The various legal regimes differ extremely on the issue of creditor autonomy, which means that obstacles to cooperation are to be expected; *Ehricke* ZIP 2005, 1104, 1111.

75 *Ehricke* ZIP 2005, 1104, 1111.

76 D-K/D/Ch-*Duursma-Kepplinger/Chalupsky* Art 31 mn 25.

77 *Virgós/Schmit* Explanatory Report mn 234; BK-InsO/*Pannen* Art 31 mn 3.

charge of supervising the liquidator.[78] **Another view** holds that the enforcement in Germany could not take place via the court's supervision, because the insolvency court is only entitled to supervise the propriety of the proceedings pursuant to *national* insolvency law.[79] It would only be different if, as a result of the liquidator's breach of duty, the national insolvency estate suffered harm.[80] Speaking against this view, however, is the fact that the EIR constitutes law that is directly applicable in Germany.

From the **German perspective, Sec 58 et seq *InsO*** may be invoked in the case of a breach of the duties laid down in Art 31 of the EIR.[81] In addition to the supervisory control exercised by the insolvency court, there is also the possibility of imposing personal liability on the liquidator for his unlawful conduct. The basic principles concerning the personal liability of the liquidator are regulated in German law primarily in Sec 60 et seq *InsO*. A liquidator who culpably breaches the duties imposed on him pursuant to the *InsO* is liable in damages to all other participants in accordance with Sec 60 (1) sentence 1 *InsO*. "**Participants**" are those persons to whom the liquidator owes certain insolvency-specific duties, even if such persons do not directly participate in the proceedings.[82] According to this substantive-law definition of "participant", a liquidator in a foreign main or secondary insolvency proceeding could also be a party with a claim pursuant to Sec 60 (1) *InsO*. This is, of course, conditioned on the German liquidator having breached an **insolvency-specific duty**. According to the wording of Sec 60 (1) *InsO*, the liability of the liquidator is linked to the breach of such duties "owed by him pursuant to this law (i.e. the *InsO*)".[83] For this reason, one opinion holds that liability cannot – at least not under Sec 60 (1) sentence 1 *InsO* – be imposed on the liquidator for a breach of the duty to cooperate and communicate information pursuant to Art 31 of the EIR, the Community-law duty lying outside the area protected by national law.[84] Although this view does follows the wording of the provision, it narrows the scope of applicability of this liability-imposing norm too much, thus preventing the ability to sanction breaches of not insignificant duties imposed by the EIR, and especially the ability to enforce compliance with the same. This provision should thus be interpreted in conformity with Community law in a way that allows the duties laid down in the EIR to fall within the protection afforded by Sec 60 *InsO*.[85] **39**

4. Art 31 (3) of the EIR

Art 31 (3) of the EIR puts into **concrete terms** the cooperation between the liquidator in the secondary and main insolvency proceedings, and it emphasizes the **dependency** of the secondary insolvency proceedings on the main proceedings.[86] The liquidator in the **40**

[78] D-K/D/Ch-*Duursma-Kepplinger/Chalupsky* Art 31 mn 25; *Herchen* Das Übereinkommen über Insolvenzverfahren, p 147; contra *Lüke* ZZP 111 (1998), 275, 305.

[79] *Lüke* ZZP 111 (1998), 275, 305.

[80] *Lüke* ZZP 111 (1998), 275, 305.

[81] Contra Kübler/Prütting-*Kemper* EuInsVO Art 31 mn 12.

[82] *Bork* Einführung in das Insolvenzrecht, mn 58.

[83] Cf MünchKomm InsO/*Reinhart* Art 31 EuInsVO mn 1; contra Kübler/Prütting-*Kemper* EuInsVO Art 31 mn 5.

[84] MünchKomm InsO/*Reinhart* Art 31 EuInsVO mn 1. Questionable here is therefore the extent to which an analogous application of sec 60 (1) sentence 1 InsO can be considered here at all.

[85] In favour of the inclusion of the EIR-duties, see *Ehricke* Verfahrenskoordination bei grenzüberschreitenden Unternehmensinsolvenzen, in Basedow, Aufbruch nach Europa, 2001, p 337, 349.

[86] *Ehricke* Verfahrenskoordination bei grenzüberschreitenden Unternehmensinsolvenzen, in Basedow, Aufbruch nach Europa, 2001,

main proceedings is entitled to create **guidelines** for the conducting of the secondary insolvency proceedings, without there being a **right to give directions.**[87]

41 The liquidator in the secondary insolvency proceedings is under a duty to give the liquidator in the main proceedings the **opportunity of submitting proposals on the liquidation or use of the assets in the secondary proceedings.** The liquidator in the secondary insolvency proceedings must therefore inform the liquidator in the main proceedings on **every planned liquidation or use of the assets of the insolvency estate.**[88] The liquidator in the main proceedings is thereby put in a position to, for example, prevent the sale of assets in the secondary insolvency proceedings and to request a stay of liquidation pursuant to Art 33 of the EIR.

42 In the German version of the EIR, the liquidator in the secondary insolvency proceedings' duty arises at an "early opportunity", this conferring a discretionary power on the liquidator in secondary proceedings.[89]

43 Art 31 (3) of the EIR **only applies to significant parts** of the insolvency estate, or to **important decisions** in connection with the secondary insolvency proceedings (e.g. discontinuing the operations of the establishment). If this was not the case, there is a danger that the work of the liquidator in the secondary insolvency proceedings would be blocked.[90]

44 Art 31 (3) of the EIR regulates neither

- the **form** in which **the proposals** are to be made to the secondary insolvency proceedings nor
- the **degree** to which the proposals **are binding.**[91]

45 Arts 33 and 34 of the EIR prescribe specific ways that the liquidator in the main insolvency proceedings can influence the secondary insolvency proceedings; these are the only **binding ways of influencing** available to the liquidator in the main insolvency proceedings. The **proposals** made pursuant to Art 31 (3) of the EIR are **not binding.**[92] After reviewing these, the liquidator in the secondary insolvency proceedings should present them to the creditors to be voted on.[93] The decision reached by the creditors' meeting has priority over the proposal made by the liquidator in the main insolvency proceedings.[94]

---

p 337, 346; Kübler/Prütting-*Kemper* EuInsVO Art 31 mn 8; *Paulus* Komm EuInsVO Art 31 mn 18.

[87] *Paulus* Komm EuInsVO Art 31 mn 18.

[88] BK-InsO/*Pannen* Art 31 mn 11.

[89] Kübler/Prütting-*Kemper* EuInsVO Art 31 mn 10. According to Paulus [*Paulus* Komm EuInsVO Art 31 mn 20], the notification of a German liquidator in secondary insolvency proceedings must always be effected prior to the so-called *Berichtstermin* (comprehensive reporting hearing).

[90] *Virgós/Schmit* Explanatory Report mn 233.

[91] Kübler/Prütting-*Kemper* EuInsVO Art 31 mn 9; BK-InsO/*Pannen* Art 31 mn 14.

[92] In *Ehricke's* opinion, the liquidator in the secondary insolvency proceedings should generally follow the proposals. *Ehricke,* Verfahrenskoordination bei grenzüberschreitenden Unternehmensinsolvenzen, in Basedow, Aufbruch nach Europa, 2001, p 337, 343. As here Kübler/Prütting-*Kemper* EuInsVO Art 31 mn 9.

[93] Kübler/Prütting-*Kemper* EuInsVO Art 31 mn 9.

[94] *Paulus* Komm EuInsVO Art 31 mn 21.

Article 32
Exercise of creditors' rights

(1) Any creditor may lodge his claim in the main proceedings and in any secondary proceedings.

(2) The liquidators in the main and any secondary proceedings shall lodge in other proceedings claims which have already been lodged in the proceedings for which they were appointed, provided that the interests of creditors in the latter proceedings are served thereby, subject to the right of creditors to oppose that or to withdraw the lodgement of their claims where the law applicable so provides.

(3) The liquidator in the main or secondary proceedings shall be empowered to participate in other proceedings on the same basis as a creditor, in particular by attending creditors' meetings.

→ Cf Arts 26, 30 UNCITRAL Model Law

Contents

Index

Bibliography

Balz The European Union Convention on Insolvency Proceedings, 70 American Bankruptcy Law Journal (1996), p 485; *Dawe* Der Sonderkonkurs des deutschen internationalen Insolvenzrechts 2005; *Kemper* Die Verordnung (EG) Nr. 1346/2000 über Insolvenzverfahren, ZIP 2001, p 1609; *Keppelmüller* Österreichisches Internationales Konkursrecht (1997); *Kodek* Internationale Bindungswirkungen der konkursrechtlichen Forderungsfeststellung, ZIK 2005, p 6; *Lüke* Das europäische internationale Insolvenzrecht, ZZP 111 (1998), p 275; *Pannen/Kühnle/Riedemann* Die

Stellung des deutschen Insolvenzverwalters in einem Insolvenzverfahren mit europäischem Auslandsbezug, NZI 2003, p 72; *Thieme* Vermögensgerichtsstände, Inlandsbezug und Partikularkonkurs, Jahresheft der Internationalen Juristenvereinigung Osnabrück (1995/1996), p 44; *Weller* Inländische Gläubigerinteressen bei internationalen Konzerninsolvenzen, ZHR 169 (2005), p 570; *Wimmer* Die Besonderheiten von Sekundärinsolvenzverfahren unter besonderer Berücksichtigung des Europäischen Insolvenzübereinkommens, ZIP 1998, p 982.

1. General

1 Art 32 of the EIR regulates the exercising of creditors' rights in secondary insolvency proceedings. The provision applies via Art 36 of the EIR with certain modifications also to independent territorial insolvency proceedings opened after the opening of main insolvency proceedings.[1]

2. Exercising of Creditors' Rights by the Creditors (Subsection 1)

2 The most important of the creditors' rights is the right, through the lodging of insolvency claims, to participate in an insolvency proceeding. In general, the circle of creditors who are entitled to lodge claims and the qualifying of such claims as insolvency claims, which thereby entitles them to be lodged, are determined pursuant to the respective *lex fori concursus secundarii*; this is stated clearly in Art 4 (2) sentence 2 (g) and (h) of the EIR.[2]

3 Art 32 (1) of the EIR (in conjunction with Art 39 of the EIR) modifies national substantive insolvency laws and thereby the *lex fori concursus secundarii* invoked in each case.[3]

4 Art 32 (1) of the EIR constitutes a substantive law provision regulating the circle of creditors allowed to lodge claims in secondary insolvency proceedings.[4]

5 It also establishes the right to make multiple lodgings.[5]

2.1 Entitlement to Lodge Claims

6 According to Art 32 (1) of the EIR, every creditor is entitled to lodge claims both in main and in all secondary insolvency proceedings in the nominal amount of the claim in each case.[6]

---

1 On this, see below mn 12 et seq, 32 et seq and Art 28 EuInsVO mn 15 et seq.

2 D-K/D/Ch-*Duursma-Kepplinger/Chalupsky* Art 4 mn 21.

3 D-K/D/Ch-*Duursma-Kepplinger/Chalupsky* Art 4 mn 21; Haß/Huber/Gruber/Heiderhoff-*Heiderhoff* Art 32 EuInsVO mn 1; *Lüke* ZZP 111 (1998), 275, 300 et seq.

4 Concurring: *Paulus* Komm EuInsVO Art 32 mn 1.

5 Concurring: *Paulus* Komm EuInsVO Art 32 mn 3.

6 *Balz* 70 American Bankruptcy Law Journal (1996), 485, 525; D-K/D/Ch-*Duursma-Kepplinger/Chalupsky* Art 28 mn 7 et seq; Art 27 mn 44 et seq; Haß/Huber/Gruber/Heiderhoff-*Heiderhoff* Art 29 EuInsVO mn 2, Art 32 mn 1; *Lüke* ZZP 111 (1998), 275, 300 et seq; Moss/Fletcher/Isaacs-*Moss/Smith*, Regulation, mn 8.236; *Wimmer* ZIP 1998, 982, 987; dissenting opinion: *Dawe* Der Sonderkonkurs des deutschen Internationalen Insolvenzrechts 2005, 161 et seq, 174 et seq; *Thieme* Jahresheft der Internationalen Juristenvereinigung Osnabrück (1995/1996), p 44, p 86 et seq; *Keppelmüller* Österreichisches Internationales Konkursrecht 1997, p 426.

Any restricting of the circle of parties entitled to lodge claims based on their habitual residence, domicile, or registered office that is prescribed by the *lex fori concursus secundarii* is prohibited pursuant to Art 39 of the EIR if it involves a Member State (with the exception of Denmark). Art 39 of the EIR is therefore a uniform, substantive-law provision.[7] Claims lodged by creditors from non-EU countries and Denmark that are allowed under the respective *lex fori concursus* will of course not be precluded by Art 39 of the EIR.[8] **7**

Art 32 (1) of the EIR prohibits any restrictions prescribed by the *lex fori concursus secundarii* to the circle of parties entitled to lodge claims because of nationality,[9] the *lex causae* governing the claim,[10] or because of any special local (national) characteristics of a claim involving a preferred right, a secured right (on movable property), its public-law nature, or its association with the establishment.[11] **8**

2.2 Scope of Incorporation of Substantive Law

Little discussion has been devoted to the extent of the incorporation – through Art 32 (1) of the EIR – of the various substantive national insolvency laws. **9**

One question, for example, is whether creditors with subordinate insolvency claims within the meaning of Section 39 of the German *InsO* – regardless of which *lex causae* governs these – are allowed to lodge their claims pursuant to Art 32 (1) of the EIR in German secondary insolvency proceedings without complying with Section 174 (3) sentence 1 *InsO*, i.e. without the court having made a prior demand to lodge subordinate claims?[12] The question becomes even more difficult in light of the "equitable treatment of creditors" principle[13] in a case where, for example, there is no restriction pursuant to the *lex fori concursus* to lodging a claim in the main insolvency proceedings, but where such a claim will only be allowed in German secondary insolvency proceedings if the insolvency court has made a prior demand for it – which practically never happens. In light of the provisions of Art 4 (2) sentence 2 (g) of the EIR, such a question would have to be answered in the negative. According to this, the *lex fori concursus* invoked in each case determines whether the claim qualifies as an insolvency claim – and is therefore a determination of the basic admissibility of the lodged claim – without regard to the person of the creditor. Although because of its substantive law character Art 32 (1) of the EIR must be viewed as partially restricting of Art 4 (2) sentence 2 (g) and (h) of the EIR, the wording of it only prohibits the incorporation of those substantive laws of the *lex fori concursus secundarii* whose restriction of the circle of creditors entitled to lodge claims is founded in the person of such creditor. National laws that restrict the right to lodge a claim – e.g. for reasons found in the legal nature of the claim itself and the resulting ranking of it as a subordinate insolvency claim within the meaning of Section 39 *InsO* – are still allowed.[14] A repayment claim arising from a **10**

---

[7] Moss/Fletcher/Isaacs-*Moss/Smith*, Regulation, mn 8.274.

[8] Moss/Fletcher/Isaacs-*Moss/Smith*, Regulation, mn 8.238.

[9] Concurring in this respect: *Keppelmüller* Österreichisches Internationales Konkursrecht 1997, p 426.

[10] D-K/D/Ch-*Duursma-Kepplinger/Chalupsky* Art 32 mn 4.

[11] *Lüke* ZZP 111 (1998), 275, 300 et seq.

[12] "The claims of subordinate creditors may only be lodged if the insolvency court has specifically demanded the lodgement of these claims."

[13] This is being ensured primarily through the equalization of dividends provided for in art 20 (2) of the EIR.

[14] Moss/Fletcher/Isaacs-*Moss/Smith*, Regulation, mn 8.235, 8.277; in my opinion the Report also points in this direction at mn 235, 238, 267.

shareholder's loan in lieu of shareholder's equity that is lodged for example in English main insolvency proceedings as an insolvency claim,[15] may consequently only be lodged as a subordinate insolvency claim pursuant to Section 39 (1) No 5 *InsO* – notwithstanding Art 32 (1) of the EIR – in German secondary insolvency proceedings once the insolvency court has demanded this.

11 Equally unaffected by Art 32 (1) of the EIR are time limits/preclusive periods for lodging and excluding claims prescribed by the respective *lex fori concursus*.[16] These involve procedural issues regarding the lodging of claims which, according to Art 4 (2) sentence 2 (h) of the EIR, continue to be governed by the *lex fori concursus secundarii* and in respect of which Art 32 (1) of the EIR is silent.[17] The same applies to provisions dealing with the costs of lodging and reviewing claims, and the consequences of a belated lodgement of a claim and its costs.[18]

2.3 Application of Articles 32 and 39 of the EIR to Independent Territorial Insolvency Proceedings

12 Art 39 of the EIR applies to main, secondary, and independent territorial insolvency proceedings;[19] in the latter case even where main insolvency proceedings have not yet been opened. Neither the wording nor the systematic positioning of the provision in the Regulation allows for any other interpretation.

13 Art 32 (1) of the EIR also applies to independent territorial insolvency proceedings that are opened subsequent to the opening of the main insolvency proceedings, provided that the stage of progress of the territorial proceedings permits this (Art 36 of the EIR). Art 32 of the EIR also confers a substantive law right on every creditor to lodge his claim(s) in the territorial insolvency proceedings as well.[20]

14 If, however, the *lex fori concursus secundarii* restricts the circle of parties entitled to lodge claims because of their nationality,[21] based on the *lex causae* governing the claim,[22] or because of any special local (national) characteristics of the claim involving a preferred right, a secured right (on movable property), its public-law nature, or its association with the establishment,[23] then the issue arises as to whether Art 32 (1) of the

---

[15] On this, see: Rule 2.69 The Insolvency Rules 1986; but see also: sec 74 (2) (f) Insolvency Act 1986.

[16] *Virgós/Schmit* Explanatory Report mn 238; Moss/Fletcher/Isaacs-*Moss/Smith*, Regulation, mn 8.277; MünchKomm InsO/*Reinhart* Art 32 EuInsVO mn 3 who supports *de lege ferenda* an integration in this respect.

[17] In this regard, also see the purported written-form requirement of art 39 of the EIR, which is generally being so understood that the written form, as an admissible form, stands on equal footing in terms of procedural law with the form requirements of the respective *lex fori concursus*; see for example: Moss/Fletcher/Isaacs-*Bogdan*, Regulation, mn 8.277; Report mn 265, 267, 270, 273.

[18] See D-K/D/Ch-*Duursma-Kepplinger/Chalupsky* Art 39 mn 6; *Virgós/Schmit* Explanatory Report mn 268.

[19] D-K/D/Ch-*Duursma-Kepplinger/Chalupsky* Art 39 mn 3; Haß/Huber/Gruber/Heiderhoff-*Heiderhoff* Art 39 mn 3; *Kemper* ZIP 2001, 1609, 1619; *Virgós/Schmit* Explanatory Report mn 264; see also Art 28 of the EIR mn 37 et seq.

[20] In depth: D-K/D/Ch-*Duursma-Kepplinger/Chalupsky* Art 27 mn 47 et seq; Moss/Fletcher/Isaacs-*Bogdan*, Regulation, mn 8.71; dissenting opinion: *Dawe* Der Sonderkonkurs des deutschen Internationalen Insolvenzrechts 2005, 161 et seq, 174 et seq; *Thieme* Jahresheft der Internationalen Juristenvereinigung Osnabrück (1995/1996), 44, 86 et seq.

[21] Concurring in this respect: *Keppelmüller* Österreichisches Internationales Konkursrecht 1997, p 426.

[22] D-K/D/Ch-*Duursma-Kepplinger/Chalupsky* Art 32 mn 4.

[23] *Lüke* ZZP 111 (1998), 275, 300 et seq.

EIR also precludes such restrictions in independent territorial insolvency proceedings as well. It should be remembered at this point that Art 39 of the EIR only prohibits restrictions of the circle of parties entitled to lodge claims resulting from the *lex fori concursus secundarii,* and because of their habitual residence, domicile, or registered office.[24] Any attempt to broaden the meaning of Art 39 of the EIR based on the principle of equitable treatment of creditors would have to fail in light of the fact that Art 39 of the EIR – as opposed to domicile, habitual residence, and registered office – explicitly fails to mention nationality and the *lex causae.*[25] It also seems more reasonable to include restrictions based on nationality and *lex causae* in Art 32 of the EIR, whose wording is broader. Also, because of the "conversion"[26] of independent territorial insolvency proceedings to secondary insolvency proceedings that takes place pursuant to Art 36 upon the opening of main insolvency proceedings, Art 32 of the EIR should already be applied to territorial insolvency proceedings that are pending prior to the opening of main insolvency proceedings.[27] If this is not done, then restrictions to the lodging of claims based on nationality and the *lex causae*, which stem from the *lex fori concursus particularis*, can only be excluded via Art 32 of the EIR if it should happen that the time limits for lodging claims, which continue to be governed by the *lex fori concursus particularis*, have already expired, or if additional costs were incurred on account of the belated lodgement (see Section 177 (1) sentence 2 *Ins*O).

3. Exercising of Creditors' Rights by the Liquidator (Subsections 2 and 3)

3.1 Objective of the Rule

Art 32 (2) of the EIR grants to the liquidators in main and in the secondary insolvency **15**
proceedings the right to lodge the claims that have been lodged in their proceedings in all other insolvency proceedings provided that it is expedient for "their" creditors. This is subject to the creditor's right to object to or withdraw the lodged claim. According to subs. 3, the liquidator is authorized to participate on the same basis as a creditor commencing with the other proceedings.

The aim of the provision on the one hand is to simplify the exercising of creditors' **16**
rights; this, taken together with the equalization of dividends stipulated by Art 20 (2) of the EIR, lends support to the equitable treatment of creditors. On the other hand, the reciprocal lodging and safeguarding of the creditors' rights (subsection 3) is intended to strengthen the liquidator's ability to influence the other insolvency proceedings.[28] Despite a multiplicity of insolvency proceedings, the ideal goal here is to approximate a uniform and universal insolvency proceeding through a coordination of the various proceedings.

3.2 Incorporation of Substantive Law

Through the creation of the (reciprocal) rights of the liquidators in the main and **17**
secondary insolvency proceedings to lodge claims, Art 32 (2) of the EIR modifies the

---

[24] See mn 7 above.

[25] D-K/D/Ch-*Duursma-Kepplinger/Chalupsky* Art 39 mn 5; possible dissenting opinion regarding the *lex causae*: *Virgós/Schmit* Explanatory report mn 266.

[26] D-K/D/Ch-*Duursma-Kepplinger/Chalupsky* Art 36 mn 3; Recital 17 of the EIR; *Virgós/Schmit* Explanatory report mn 254; Moss/Fletcher/Isaacs-*Fletcher*, Regulation, mn 8.262.

[27] Also concurring: Haß/Huber/Gruber/Heiderhoff-*Heiderhoff* Art 32 EuInsVO mn 1.

[28] *Virgós/Schmit* Explanatory report mn 239.

insolvency laws of the various Member States. In this regard, an incorporation of the substantive law of the Member States is taking place.

18 Through Art 32 (2) of the EIR, as a uniform provision of international procedural insolvency law, every creditor is afforded the right to oppose the lodging of his claim by the liquidators in other insolvency proceedings. This right to oppose is not subject to the consent of the respective *lex fori concursus* that governs the proceedings pursuant to which the lodging is made.[29]

19 The right to withdraw a lodged claim is subject to the provisions on this found in the *lex fori concursus*, which has jurisdiction regarding the form (content) of creditors' rights (Art 4 (2) sentence 2 (h) of the EIR). In this respect, Art 32 (2) of the EIR does not incorporate a substantive law provision.

3.3 Duty to Lodge Claims

20 The overwhelming opinion on this point is that Art 32 (2) of the EIR creates a duty on the part of the liquidator to lodge claims if the lodging of such claim is expedient.[30] It is widely presumed that this duty only exists if, and in the manner in which, such expediency is being affirmed generally and unequivocally for the creditors as a whole, or in respect of certain classes of creditors.[31] The presumption of a duty to lodge claims is rebutted if the lodging of such claim is only expedient in the eyes of certain individual creditors.[32] The only possibility left open to such creditors is to lodge their claims on their own behalf.

21 The wording of Art 32 (2) of the EIR supports this widely accepted restriction of the liquidator's duty to lodge claims in that it assumes an expediency, and therefore a review of such expediency, from the point of view of a majority of creditors. A majority of creditors here means, on the one hand, the entirety of creditors in the proceeding whose liquidator has to decide whether to lodge the claims in another proceeding and, on the other hand, the classes of creditors that are also formed pursuant to, or at least contemplated by, the *lex fori concursus* that governs this proceeding. Art 20 (2) of the EIR presupposes that the forming of classes of creditors is permitted. As supported by the Explanatory Report, the liquidator is not under a duty to review expediency from an individual perspective; such a perspective also lacks practicability.[33] Such a restricting of the test to be applied for the review can also not be readily inferred from the wording of Art 32 (2) of the EIR.[34] A restricting of the test would anyway not exonerate the liquidator, once a decision to lodge claims has been made, to specify the individual claims being lodged and to submit them in compliance with the requirements of the insolvency laws governing the proceedings in which the claims are being lodged.[35]

---

[29] But see: Haß/Huber/Gruber/Heiderhoff-*Heiderhoff* Art 32 EuInsVO mn 2; dissenting opinion: Moss/Fletcher/Isaacs-*Moss/Smith*, Regulation, mn 8.243; *Kemper* ZIP 2001, 1609, 1620.

[30] Restricting this: HamburgerKomm-*Undritz* Art 32 mn 6; *Weller* ZHR 169 (2005), 570, 585 (fn 102): "only if such expediency is *general and unequivocal* for one class of creditors".

[31] *Virgós/Schmit* Explanatory report mn 239; D-K/D/Ch-*Duursma-Kepplinger/Chalupsky* Art 32 mn 9, 11; *Kemper* ZIP 2001, 1609, 1620; *Pannen/Kühnle/Riedemann* NZI 2003, 72, 76; *Weller* ZHR 169 (2005), 570, 584.

[32] Possible dissenting opinion: Moss/Fletcher/Isaacs-*Moss/Smith*, Regulation, mn 8.239.

[33] On this: D-K/D/Ch-*Duursma-Kepplinger/Chalupsky* Art 32, mn 11.

[34] See also mn 29 below.

[35] *Paulus* Komm EuInsVO Art 32 mn 10.

3.4 Expediency of Lodging Claims

The requirement of expediency regulates the duties between the liquidator and the creditors who have lodged claims in his insolvency proceedings. **22**

Whether the lodging of a claim is expedient or not is determined in accordance with the prospective dividend and the anticipated costs of lodging the claim. If someone's prospective dividend is equal to or less than the dividend in his own proceeding, the lodging of the claim in the other proceeding is prohibited due to a lack of expediency pursuant to the dividend equalization rule contained in Art 20 (2) of the EIR. The same applies if the net proceeds, i.e. the insolvency dividend minus the costs of lodging the claim, are not expected to exceed the dividend in the own proceedings. **23**

Whether or not the lodging of a claim is expedient is a decision for the liquidator alone. This follows from the creditor's right established in the Regulation to oppose the lodging of a claim by the liquidator; the creditors in the insolvency can express their differences of opinion through their right to oppose the lodging or – if permitted – their right to withdraw the lodged claim. **24**

If a claim has been lodged subsequently and the collective lodging of claims has already taken place in the other proceedings pursuant to Art 32 (1) of the EIR, then expediency must be negated if additional costs ensuing from the subsequent lodging are incurred by those lodging the claims in the other proceedings, as is the case for example pursuant to Section 177 (1) sentence 2 *InsO* in German insolvency proceedings. The administrative expenses incurred by the office of the liquidator should not on their own – considering the rather inferior significance afforded to the subsequent lodging of claims – be sufficient to negate expediency. **25**

The liquidator of another proceeding is not entitled to reject the lodging of a claim on the basis of a lack of expediency, even though the question of expediency is ascertained primarily on the basis of the prospective dividend and the costs in his proceedings the judging of which can best be made by him because of his proximity to the facts and circumstances of the particular case. The right to reject the lodging of a claim is determined either by the respective *lex fori concursus* (Art 4 (2) sentence 2 (h) of the EIR), or by a corresponding substantive law provision in the Regulation. In respect of the latter, no such provision exists; in respect of the former, German law also fails to provide for this. Such a power would also undermine the reciprocal rights granted to liquidators to lodge claims. A different conclusion may be reached, however, if expediency is to be negated for reasons that constitute an autonomous right to reject the lodgement pursuant to the *lex fori concursus* of the proceedings in which the lodging is effected. An example of this would be an incurable belated lodging of a claim.[36] **26**

Where a liquidator contests a claim lodged in his own proceedings, there is in my opinion no duty to lodge in the other proceedings. For logical reasons, there could be no finding of expediency in such a case. This does not change the fact that, when making his decision to lodge claims, the liquidator is under an obligation to base this decision not on individual claims but rather with reference to all of the prospective claims, or at least certain classes of them, that will then as a whole be lodged or rejected.[37] This construction can be complied with by allocating all of the contested claims in one's own proceedings to one specific class. This also applies in the case of a so-called *vorläufiges Bestreiten*, i.e. provisional challenge, in German law, which involves contesting in a legal **27**

---

[36] On this, see: *Virgós/Schmit* Explanatory report mn 239 and mn 29 below.

[37] *Paulus* Komm EuInsVO Art 32, mn 8 et seq; dissenting opinion mn 29 below.

sense.[38] The necessity of determining expediency, which is demanded of the liquidator pursuant to Art 32 (1) of the EIR, would be stretched too far if he was to be put under an obligation to review whether the legal grounds for his contesting of the claim also constitute valid legal grounds pursuant to the *lex fori concursus* of the proceedings in which the lodging of the claim is being contemplated. This review can be made by the concerned creditor through his own determination of expediency, who can then lodge the claim himself depending on the outcome of his review.

28 Should, however, the liquidator decide to refrain from lodging certain claims, be they contested or uncontested, because in his opinion they lack expediency, he would presumably be under a duty to inform the concerned creditors of this.

3.5 Nature of the Lodgement

29 A legal obligation to lodge – in a uniform manner – all claims or classes of claims the lodging of which the liquidator has found expedient cannot be gleaned from the wording of the Regulation. Therefore no collective lodging must be made.[39] For reasons of simplicity, however, this is of course the generally preferred practice. In our opinion,[40] and in the opinion of others, the liquidator's obligation to review the expediency of the lodging by referring to all of the claims as a whole, or based on classes of claims, finds its justification solely in the interests of an efficient and effective cross-border lodging of claims by liquidators,[41] but not in the wording of the Regulation.

3.6 The Liquidator of the "Other" Proceedings' Duty to Review

30 The liquidator making the lodgement will of course only lodge those claims in other proceedings that he himself deems justified.[42] With respect to all other claims, he will instruct the creditors of their right to lodge claims themselves.

31 With respect to the claims that have been lodged, the issue arises as to whether these must be reviewed, i.e. recognized, by the liquidator receiving them.[43]

32 The duty to review, and the scope of such review, are determined pursuant to the *lex fori concursus*. This law determines whether a claim officially recognized in another insolvency proceeding as part of the schedule of creditors' claims must be recognized, and whether this releases the liquidator from his duty to review.

33 The Regulation itself contains no provisions on this. Even if the claim recognized in an insolvency proceeding is afforded *res judicata* status, as is the case in German law (see Section 178 (3) *Ins*O), it does not constitute recognition pursuant to Art 25 of the EIR due to the absence of a judgement within the meaning of Art 25 of the EIR.[44] When recognizing a claim, the German insolvency court is not making a judgement, it is merely acting in an authenticating capacity.

34 A recognition pursuant to Art 32 et seq of Council Regulation (EC) 44/2001 must also fail if not because of Art (2) (b) of it,[45] than certainly because of the restriction found in Art 32 ("any judgment given by a court or tribunal of a Member State").

---

[38] See HambKommentar-*Herchen* § 179 mn 14.

[39] Dissenting opinion: *Paulus* Komm EuInsVO Art 32 mn 8.

[40] Above mn 21.

[41] For example, see: D-K/D/Ch-*Duursma-Kepplinger/Chalupsky* Art 32 mn 11.

[42] See mn 27 above.

[43] On this, see also: *Paulus* Komm EuInsVO Art 32 mn 11 et seq; *Kodek* Internationale Bindungswirkungen der konkursrechtlichen Forderungsfeststellung ZIK 2005, 6.

[44] *Kodek* Internationale Bindungswirkungen der konkursrechtlichen Forderungsfeststellung ZIK 2005, 6.

[45] Musielak ZPO/*Weth* Art 32 EuGVVO mn 1.

Special rules of recognition for claims recognized as part of the schedule of creditor's claims, as provided for by Section 1061 of the German *ZPO* in the case of foreign arbitral awards, are equally missing in German law. **35**

The foregoing submissions also apply in the case of claims that are already legally enforceable (by execution) prior to the opening of the insolvency proceedings. These are to be dealt with pursuant to the provisions of the law that the *lex fori concursus* of the other insolvency proceedings deems competent for the issues of lodgement, review, and recognition of claims that are legally enforceable (by execution). In order to be treated as a legally enforceable claim, it must be recognized as such by Council Regulation (EC) 44/2001, or by other provisions of national or supranational law. **36**

If the lodged claim has been recognized pursuant to an action for a declaratory judgement, which is being conducted in response to the liquidator's contesting of the claim, then in my opinion such recognition falls within Art 25 of the EIR.[46] Both the right and the duty to review may (partially) be rendered inapplicable by the recognition made in the other proceedings provided that the subject matter of the declaratory action is restricted to the recognition of the claim in terms of its merit and the amount of it.[47] There is, however, still a duty to review in the sense of reviewing how specific insolvency-law related issues are to be taken into account in relation to the recognition of claims as part of the schedule of creditors' claims,[48] e.g. the priority of the claim pursuant to insolvency law, or whether it is an insolvency claim at all, i.e. whether the claim may be lodged in the insolvency proceedings in the first place. If the claim was contested in the other proceedings, then the objections made there must be disregarded on account of the judgement recognizing the claim as far as such recognition is final (*res judicata*). If the recognition of the claim covers the legal grounds and the amount of the claim, then a contesting of such claim in respect of the legal grounds and the amount will no longer be successful. This is not the case, however, with respect to such issues as priority or qualification as an insolvency claim since such issues are matters for resolution pursuant to a different insolvency statute. For example, a declaratory judgement passed pursuant to German (insolvency) law can have no bearing on an objection made in secondary insolvency proceedings in France where the claim is being contested on the grounds that it does not qualify as an insolvency law claim pursuant to French law. **37**

3.7 Opposing or Withdrawal of the Lodging by the Creditor

The exercising of the right anchored in the Regulation to oppose the lodging or the withdrawal of a claim – if permitted by the *lex fori concursus* – is presumably of little practical relevance. **38**

Such a right may conceivably be used, however, to avoid procedural costs where for example the creditor, as opposed to the liquidator who is entitled to lodge claims, does not find it expedient to lodge claims in other insolvency proceedings because of a negligible prospective dividend.[49] **39**

---

[46] Dissenting opinion: *Kodek* Internationale Bindungswirkungen der konkursrechtlichen Forderungsfeststellung ZIK 2005, 6.

[47] *Paulus* Komm EuInsVO Art 32 mn 12; dissenting opinion: *Kodek* Internationale Bindungswirkungen der konkursrechtlichen Forderungsfeststellung ZIK 2005, 6.

[48] For the specific insolvency-law related issues that must be reviewed in German law in addition to the justification of the claim in terms of its merits and the amount of it, see: HamburgerKomm-*Herchen* § 179, mn 17.

[49] Moss/Fletcher/Isaacs-*Bogdan*, Regulation, mn 8.243.

40 Another reason to oppose or withdraw the lodgement may be to avoid any negative legal effects imposed by the *lex fori concursus* on the claim or on secured rights connected with it, which would then be recognizable in other Member States in appropriate circumstances.[50]

3.8 Participation Rights (Article 32 (3) of the EIR)

41 Via Art 32 (3) of the EIR, every liquidator of main and secondary insolvency proceedings is afforded the right to participate in any further insolvency proceedings on the same basis as a creditor. The right to attend creditors' meetings is particularly emphasized by subs. 3.

42 Since creditors are well-known for their disinterest in the insolvency proceedings, in particular for their absence at creditors' meetings, the aim of this provision is primarily to compensate for this.[51] Any doubts as to the scope of the powers of a liquidator in other insolvency proceedings must be answered in light of this aim. An approach favouring a wide range of powers is very much in place here. Only by conferring on the liquidator the same rights afforded to the creditor pursuant to the *lex fori concursus* of the other proceedings in which the liquidator wishes to exercise the creditors' rights, can the supervision and control of the insolvency proceedings, which is generally done by the creditors but is missing due to their absence, be safeguarded.

The particulars of the liquidator's participation rights are not provided for in the Regulation. They may be – and should be for the purposes of avoiding legal uncertainty and delays in proceedings – regulated by the Member State in the respective *lex fori concursus*.[52] Art 32 (3) of the EIR simply sets out a minimum of competence; the respective *lex fori concursus* may go beyond this.[53]

43 There should be no doubt that, based on the Regulation, a right to be heard and to ask questions follows from the liquidator's right to participate in the creditors' meeting.[54] To enable the liquidator to exercise these rights, he must – like every other creditor and regardless of whether he has lodged the claims of "his creditors" pursuant to Art 32 (2) of the EIR – be kept informed about the progress of the proceedings, particularly about the holding and the dates/deadlines of creditors' meetings.

44 In my opinion, the treating of the liquidator as the creditor's equal for the purposes of the proceedings confers on the liquidator the right to contest lodged claims provided that the insolvency law concerned grants such a right to the creditor. The liquidator may, for example, find it appropriate to contest a lodged claim if he had contested that claim in "his insolvency proceedings" but the liquidator in the other proceedings does not. If the legal grounds for the objection are valid grounds for contesting in both insolvency

---

50 See for example Rule 6.116 (1) Insolvency Rules 1986 (England and Wales) pursuant to which the failure to disclose a secured right can lead to the loss of it. However pursuant to Rule 4.96 (3), introduced through the Insolvency (Amendment) Rules 2002, this does not apply to secured rights protected by art 5. On this: Moss/Fletcher/Isaacs-*Moss/Smith*, Regulation, mn 8.243.

51 *Virgós/Schmit* Explanatory report mn 240.

52 Moss/Fletcher/Isaacs-*Moss/Smith*, Regulation, mn 8.240; HK-InsO/*Stephan* Art 32 EuInsVO mn 7; *Virgós/Schmit* Explanatory report mn 240.

53 HK-InsO/*Stephan* Art 32 EuInsVO mn 7.

54 Haß/Huber/Gruber/Heiderhoff-*Heiderhoff* Art 32 EuInsVO mn 3; Moss/Fletcher/Isaacs-*Moss/Smith*, Regulation, mn 8.240; *Paulus* Komm EuInsVO Art 32 EuInsVO mn 16; HK-InsO/*Stephan* Art 32 EuInsVO mn 7; *Virgós/Schmit* Explanatory report mn 240.

proceedings, then the liquidator will even be held to be under an obligation to contest the claim in both proceedings, in the one instance as a liquidator and in the other as a "creditor within the meaning of Art 32 (3) of the EIR". The liquidator's obligation to safeguard the interests of "his insolvency creditors", which is anchored in the Regulation, can be inferred from the element of expediency in relation to the creditors that is required by Art 32 (2) of the EIR. The duty to contest certain claims follows from this obligation. The right to participate laid down in Art 32 (3) of the EIR simultaneously creates a right to contest lodged claims; the legal justification for this can be found in the wording of subs. 3, which is so loosely worded as to allow such an interpretation, and can also be inferred from the aims of the Regulation itself.

Unresolved is whether and under which conditions a liquidator is empowered to exercise voting rights in another insolvency proceeding. One thing that may be said with a degree of certainty is that his voting powers, provided that he is afforded a right to vote at all, would have to be restricted – as per the provisions of the particular *lex fori concursus* of the other proceedings – to the claims that have been lodged by him. The same reasoning arising from Art 32 (3) of the EIR that justifies the liquidator's right to contest lodged claims[55] can be applied to justify the liquidator's right to vote based on the claims lodged by him.[56] This is expressly regulated in German law in Section 341 (3) *InsO*. However it merely confirms that which already applies pursuant to the Regulation. The reference in the Report to the fact that the drafters of the predecessor convention to the Regulation decided, in the course of their deliberations, to refrain from including a provision allowing a right to vote has no bearing on this interpretation. From this opinion, no intention contrary to the interpretation favoured here can be ascribed to the drafters of the Regulation; such an intention can neither be gleaned from the wording of subs. 3 nor is it in line with the aims of this section. **45**

In order to avoid any difficulties in exercising voting power, liquidators would be advised to obtain express authorization to vote from "their creditors" whose claims they are lodging in the other proceedings, provided that this is permitted by the insolvency laws of the other proceedings.[57] **46**

Whether a right to vote actually ensues from a lodged claim, and in which amount, is a decision for the *lex fori concursus*; e.g. whether, because of an objection, the claim lodged does not give rise to a right to vote or only to an extent less than the nominal amount of the claim. **47**

Since individual claims do not forfeit their independence through a lodgement pursuant to Art 32 (2) of the EIR, each claim must be assessed separately. This, being a mere practical inconvenience, will not be negated simply by the fact that it may be very tedious in some cases to determine voting rights and assess voting results. **48**

Although it will rarely happen, if there is a conflict in respect of the exercising of the voting rights ensuing from the same claim due to the presence of a creditor for whom **49**

---

[55] Above mn 45, 47.

[56] Affirming: HK-InsO/*Stephan* Art 32 EuInsVO mn 7; hesitant: Haß/Huber/Gruber/Heiderhoff-*Heiderhoff* Art 32 EuInsVO mn 3; Moss/Fletcher/Isaacs-*Moss/Smith*, Regulation, mn 8.240; rejecting: D-K/D/Ch-*Duursma-Kepplinger/Chalupsky* Art 32 mn 1; *Paulus* Komm EuInsVO Art 32 mn 16; HamburgerKomm-*Undritz* Art 32 mn 8; MünchKomm InsO/*Reinhart* Art 32 EuInsVO mn 4 who supports *de lege ferenda* a right to vote.

[57] Haß/Huber/Gruber/Heiderhoff-*Heiderhoff* Art 32 EuInsVO mn 3; HK-InsO/*Stephan* Art 32 EuInsVO mn 7.

this claim has also been lodged by the liquidator pursuant to subs. 2, then the vote cast by the creditor will override, the liquidator's voting right being a mere derivative of the creditor's original right to vote.

4. Applicability of Article 32 of the EIR to Independent Territorial Insolvency Proceedings Opened Subsequent to Main Proceedings (Article 36)

50 Via Art 36 of the EIR, the provisions of Art 32 of the EIR also apply to independent territorial insolvency proceedings pursuant to Art 3 (4) of the EIR if main insolvency proceedings within the meaning of Art 3 (1) of the EIR will be opened subsequently.

51 The application of Art 32 (1) of the EIR via Art 36 of the EIR is largely irrelevant on account of the provisions of Art 39 of the EIR. Every creditor is entitled to lodge claims in territorial insolvency proceedings.[58]

52 With respect to subsections 2 and 3, the referral in Art 36 of the EIR is primarily of importance if the time limits for lodging the claim in the other insolvency proceedings have not yet expired, or if subsequent lodgings are permitted pursuant to the *lex fori concursus*. Any obligations imposed on the parties who are lodging claims to bear the costs incurred by the subsequent lodgings, for already held assessment meetings, etc. must be taken into account by the liquidator in his review of expediency.

Article 33
Stay of liquidation

(1) The court, which opened the secondary proceedings, shall stay the process of liquidation in whole or in part on receipt of a request from the liquidator in the main proceedings, provided that in that event it may require the liquidator in the main proceedings to take any suitable measure to guarantee the interests of the creditors in the secondary proceedings and of individual classes of creditors. Such a request from the liquidator may be rejected only if it is manifestly of no interest to the creditors in the main proceedings. Such a stay of the process of liquidation may be ordered for up to three months. It may be continued or renewed for similar periods.

(2) The court referred to in paragraph 1 shall terminate the stay of the process of liquidation:
- **at the request of the liquidator in the main proceedings,**
- **of its own motion, at the request of a creditor or at the request of the liquidator in the secondary proceedings if that measure no longer appears justified, in particular, by the interests of creditors in the main proceedings or in the secondary proceedings.**

→ Cf Arts 27, 29 et seq UNCITRAL Model Law

[58] See mn 14 et seq above.

Contents

Index

Bibliography

Balz Das neue Europäische Insolvenzübereinkommen, ZIP 1996, p 948; *Fritz/Bähr* Die Europäische Verordnung über Insolvenzverfahren – Herausforderung an Gerichte und Insolvenzverwalter, DZWiR 2001, p 221; *Gottwald* Grenzüberschreitende Insolvenzen (1997); *Herchen* Das Übereinkommen über Insolvenzverfahren der Mitgliedstaaten der Europäischen Union vom 23.11.1995 (2000); *Herchen* Die Befugnisse des deutschen Insolvenzverwalters hinsichtlich der „Auslandsmasse" nach In-Kraft-Treten der EG-Insolvenzverordnung (Verordnung des Rates Nr. 1346/2000), ZInsO 2002, p 345; *Johnson* The European Union Convention on Insolvency Proceedings, International Insolvency Review 1996, p 80; *Sommer* Zu den Einflussmöglichkeiten des Hauptverwalters auf das Sekundärinsolvenzverfahren, ZInsO 2005, p 1137; *Paulus* Comments on OLG Vienna dated 09.11.2004 – 28 R 225/04w, NZI 2005, p 62; *Vallender* Aufgaben und Befugnisse des deutschen Insolvenzrichters in Verfahren nach der EuInsVO, KTS 2005, p 283; *Wimmer* Die Besonderheiten von Sekundärinsolvenzverfahren unter besonderer Berücksichtigung des Europäischen Insolvenzübereinkommens, ZIP 1998, p 982.

1. General

The primary objective of Art 33 of the EIR is to ensure the possibility of reorganizing **1**
the debtor's enterprise in the main insolvency proceedings – at least temporarily – by postponing the shattering (breaking up) of an establishment subject to secondary insolvency proceedings. Liquidation in this connection means the disposal (sale) of all or individual parts of the insolvency estate of the secondary insolvency proceedings.[1] The re-

[1] Going further: *Paulus* Komm EuInsVO Art 33 mn 3 et seq who can imagine including reorganization measures in secondary insolvency proceedings. This follows, in my

organization emanating from the main insolvency proceedings may take the shape of a restructuring of the debtor itself – i.e. of the legal entity – or a reorganization by way of a transfer (sale)[2] of the debtor enterprise.[3]

2 To attain this, Art 33 (1) sentence 1 of the EIR grants the liquidator in the main insolvency proceedings the right to request a complete or partial stay of the liquidation from the court of the secondary insolvency proceedings. This is particularly significant in light of Art 3 (3) of the EIR, which expressly stipulates that secondary insolvency proceedings must take the form of winding-up proceedings.[4] The stay of the secondary insolvency proceedings themselves cannot be requested pursuant to Art 33 of the EIR.[5] As presupposed for example by Art 31 (3) of the EIR ("... liquidation or use of the assets ..."), secondary insolvency proceedings, although they are aimed at liquidation, are not comprised solely of liquidation measures.

3 The court must allow the request to stay unless a stay of the liquidation process is manifestly not in the interests of the creditors of the main insolvency proceedings (Art 33 (1) sentence 2 of the EIR). The restricted ability to deny the request, which works to the detriment of the secondary insolvency proceedings, is being compensated for at least in theory by the court's entitlement to order protective measures in favour of the creditors as a whole, or in favour of individual classes of creditors of the secondary insolvency proceedings (Art 33 (1) sentence 1, 2nd half-sentence of the EIR).

4 The provision also elucidates the superior role attributed to the main insolvency proceedings[6] – the interests of the creditors of the main insolvency proceedings are placed in the foreground, the interests of the creditors of the secondary insolvency proceedings merely being afforded court-ordered compensation in the appropriate case (Art 33 (1) sentence 1, 1st half-sentence of the EIR).[7] These creditors are, of course, always free to participate in the main insolvency proceedings (Art 32 (1) and Art 39 of the EIR).

5 The right of the liquidator in the main insolvency proceedings to request a stay of the liquidation process, combined with the right to propose measures to end proceedings (Art 34 of the EIR), constitute the fundamental means by which the coordination of the main and secondary insolvency proceedings is achieved.[8] A proper exercising of such incisive powers presupposes that the liquidator in the main insolvency proceedings is not only being comprehensively informed about the secondary insolvency proceedings, but also that the liquidator in the secondary insolvency proceedings and the insolvency court competent for the secondary insolvency proceedings are being informed about the main insolvency proceedings. This is important to keep in mind when interpreting the scope and the intensity of the duty to inform found in Art 31 (1) of the EIR.[9]

---

opinion, from the combined effect of art 33 and art 34 (3) of the EIR (see the comments on Art 34 of the EIR mn 21 et seq, 57 et seq), but only if the reorganization is to take place pursuant to a reorganization plan.

2 *Herchen* ZInsO 2002, 345, 351; MünchKomm InsO/*Reinhart* Art 33 EuInsVO mn 1.

3 Moss/Fletcher/Isaacs-*Moss/Smith*, Regulation, mn 8.244.

4 MünchKomm InsO/*Reinhart* Art 33 EuInsVO mn 1.

5 Landesgericht Leoben ZIP 2005, 1930 (cf Table of Cases Art 3 of the EIR Appendix A mn 5) with comments by: *Sommer* ZInsO 2005, 1137 et seq; see also: OLG Graz dated 20 Oct 2005, head note in ZIP 2006, 1544 et seq (decision on the appeal to Landesgericht Leoben; cf Table of Cases Art 3 of the EIR Appendix A mn 5); *Paulus* Komm EuInsVO Art 33 mn 2.

6 D-K/D/Ch-*Duursma-Kepplinger/Chalupsky* Art 33 mn 2; Haß/Huber/Gruber/Heiderhoff-*Heiderhoff* Art 33 EuInsVO mn 2; *Herchen* ZInsO 2002, 345 et seq.

7 See D-K/D/Ch-*Duursma-Kepplinger/Chalupsky* Art 33 mn 1.

8 See Recital 20 of the EIR.

9 On this, see: the comments on Art 31 of the

2. Stay of the Liquidation

2.1 Admissibility of the Request

The liquidator in the main insolvency proceedings is empowered to make the request. **6**

The court that opened the secondary insolvency proceedings has jurisdiction. **7**

The request must be made for a complete or a partial stay. In the latter case, the specific assets that are to be suspended from the liquidation must be itemized. A request to stay the secondary insolvency proceedings themselves is inadmissible.[10] It may, however, be able to be interpreted as a request to completely stay the liquidation if such an interpretation of the request accords with the procedural law of the country of the secondary insolvency proceedings.[11] **8**

Finally, the interests of the creditors in the main insolvency proceedings must be submitted to enable the making of a proper decision by the court invoked to make such decision.[12] **9**

Both the temporary administrator and the custodian in German law are not entitled to make a request.[13] **10**

2.2 Justified Grounds for the Request

The court may only deny the request to stay the liquidation if such stay is manifestly not in the interests of the creditors of the main insolvency proceedings (Art 33 (1) sentence 2 of the EIR).[14] It must be inferred from the wording of Art 33 of the EIR ("manifestly") that the court of the secondary insolvency proceedings' duty to review is reduced to checking the existence of the information provided.[15] **11**

The interests of the creditors of the secondary insolvency proceedings are not to be taken into account when reviewing whether there are justified grounds for the request.[16] Such interests are safeguarded through the ordering of protective measures by the court (Art 33 (1) sentence (1), 2nd half-sentence of the EIR). The reasons for denying the request to stay cannot be based on the argument that the creditors involved in both proceedings are completely, or largely, identical, and thus the liquidation in the secondary insolvency proceedings would in any case benefit all of the creditors of the main insolvency proceedings.[17] The ideal concept of coordinated main and secondary insolvency proceedings is, namely, that all of the creditors participate in all proceedings (see Art 32 (1) and (2) of the EIR). In addition, the fact that the liquidation benefits all of the creditors of the main insolvency proceedings says nothing about whether – in the estimation of the liquidator in the main insolvency proceedings, which is decisive here,[18] – there **12**

EIR mn 17 et seq; OLG Vienna NZI 2005, 56, with comments by: *Paulus* NZI 2005, 63 et seq; *Herchen* Das Übereinkommen über Insolvenzverfahren der Mitgliedstaaten der Europäischen Union vom 23.11.1995 (2000), p 149.

[10] See mn 2 et seq above.

[11] See also mn 13 below and mn 20.

[12] *Smid* Komm EuInsVO Art 23 mn 5; OLG Graz dated 20 Oct 2005 (cf Table of Cases Art 3 of the EIR Appendix A mn 5) speaks of a reduced burden to submit in Reasons III.

[13] See the comments on Art 29 of the EIR mn 6, 7, 20.

[14] See *Virgós/Schmit* Explanatory Report mn 242.

[15] OLG Graz dated 20 Oct 2005, in Reasons III., NZI 2006, 660.

[16] *Wimmer* ZIP 1998, 982, 988.

[17] Landesgericht Leoben ZIP 2005, 1930 (decision on the appeal: OLG Graz NZI 2006, 660, dated 20 Oct 2005, 3 R 149/05i; head note in ZIP 2006, 1544 et seq); rejecting: *Sommer* ZInsO 2005, 1137, 1139.

[18] On this, see: mn 13 below.

may not indeed be a better alternative to the liquidation planned in the secondary insolvency proceedings.

13 Because of the wide discretionary powers conferred by the wording of Art 33 (1) of the EIR on the liquidator in the main insolvency proceedings, a request to stay proceedings is seldom denied and is practically limited to cases of misuse.[19] The court is not limited to the contents of the request.[20] If only a partial stay is being applied for, the court is entitled to go beyond this. Because of the discretionary powers afforded to the liquidator in the main insolvency proceedings, a granting of less than that requested will seldom occur since this would also be tantamount to a partial denial of the request.

14 It must be presumed that a stay is in the interests of the creditors of the main insolvency proceedings if the "shattering liquidation" of the debtor's assets that are subject to the secondary insolvency proceedings does less to further the goals of the main insolvency proceedings than a (temporary) stay of the liquidation would. The stay can serve to preserve the debtor enterprise as a whole either through a restructuring of the enterprise, or through a reorganization by way of a transfer – i.e. a liquidation through a sale of the enterprise ("asset deal"). The liquidator in the main insolvency proceedings is authorized to apply for a stay of liquidation pursuant to Art 33 (1) of the EIR even if the liquidation in the secondary insolvency proceedings has not yet commenced or has already been stayed pursuant to the *lex fori concursus secundarii*.[21] It suffices that the liquidation is forthcoming. This is exactly the case with the opening of the secondary insolvency proceedings since these proceedings, as prescribed by the Regulation, must be winding-up proceedings, i.e. they must be geared towards liquidation (see Art 3 (3) sentence 2 of the EIR).[22] The request to stay can then no longer be justified on the basis that it is safeguarding a legal right, and is therefore inadmissible pursuant to the systematic of German procedural law, if the liquidator of the secondary insolvency proceedings conclusively declares to the (temporary) administrator of the main proceedings that he will not commence the liquidation.

15 A partial stay of liquidation is justified if the liquidator in the main insolvency proceedings wishes to secure for the main insolvency proceedings certain assets of the secondary insolvency proceedings for the purposes of continuing the business operations of the main insolvency proceedings,[23] provided of course that the continuation of the business operations is in the interests of the creditors of the main insolvency proceedings. This condition is only met if the stay of the liquidation leads to a measure that ends the proceedings pursuant to Art 34 (1), (2) of the EIR. During the liquidation moratorium, only the liquidator in the main insolvency proceedings and the debtor with the consent of the liquidator in the main insolvency proceedings are entitled to propose such measures (Art 34 (3) of the EIR). The reason for this is that the liquidator in the main insol-

---

[19] Moss/Fletcher/Isaacs-*Moss/Smith*, Regulation, mn 8.246; *Vallender* KTS 2005 283, 304. MünchKomm InsO/*Reinhart* Art 33 EuInsVO mn 2 points out that the court of the secondary insolvency proceedings will often not be able to answer this question on their own due to a lack of sufficient knowledge of the facts of the main insolvency proceedings.

[20] *Vallender* KTS 2005, 283, 304; see also mn 8 above.

[21] On this, see the comments on Art 34 of the EIR mn 60, as well as in German law sec 233 InsO. Concurring: *Sommer* ZInsO 2005, 1137, 1138; OLG Graz ZIP 2006, 1544 et seq; dissenting opinion: Landesgericht Leoben ZIP 2005, 1930 (set aside in this respect by the OLG Graz dated 20 Oct 2005, NZI 2006, 660, cf Table of Cases Art 3 of the EIR Appendix A mn 5).

[22] Stricter: *Paulus* Komm EuInsVO Art 33 mn 2 who holds that the liquidation must at least be contemplated.

[23] *Herchen* ZInsO 2002, 345, 351.

vency proceedings is not afforded any rights of possession, use, and exploitation in respect of objects included in the insolvency estate of the secondary insolvency proceedings.[24] He is therefore not entitled to shift the assets from the secondary insolvency proceedings that are required for the continuation of the business operation in the main insolvency proceedings to the assets of the main insolvency proceedings. In such a constellation, a stay of liquidation in and of itself is generally not in the interests of the creditors of the main insolvency proceedings. This illustrates that the liquidation moratorium contemplated by Art 33 of the EIR is ultimately to facilitate or to pave the way for measures to end the proceedings pursuant to Art 34 of the EIR.[25] It would therefore not suffice, for example, if the sole objective of the request to stay the liquidation is to prevent a sale to a third party in order to sell to the liquidator in the main insolvency proceedings at a lower price. It would only be different if the liquidator of the secondary insolvency proceedings intended to sell to the third party in spite of an offer from the liquidator in the main insolvency proceedings for at least the same amount.

The request to stay the liquidation can also be justified if the planned shattering liquidation in the main insolvency proceedings would bring a larger amount of distributable proceeds were the assets of the secondary insolvency proceedings included in it. **16**

The stay cannot be denied on the grounds that a substantial part of the insolvency estate is situated within the territory of the Member State of the secondary insolvency proceedings.[26] The leading role allocated to the main insolvency proceedings justifies even more so in such cases the influence it has on, and the inclusion of, the fundamental assets in the cross-border uniform proceedings. **17**

2.3 Stay During the Opening Proceedings

The wording of Art 33 (1) of the EIR presupposes that secondary insolvency proceedings have already been opened. The judgement of the ECJ in the Eurofood/Parmalat case[27] on the issue as to whether the appointing of a temporary administrator can constitute the opening of proceedings within the meaning of the Regulation must, however, be taken into account here. In light of this decision, it can be argued that Art 33 (1) of the EIR is to be so construed as to allow a request to stay even in the proceedings to open proceedings.[28] This of course presupposes that a temporary administrator has been appointed in the secondary insolvency proceedings. The fact that the court, pursuant to its supervisory function, is able to prevent the temporary administrator of the secondary insolvency proceedings from implementing certain liquidation measures, as is the case for example in German law (Sections 21 (2) No 1, Section 58 *InsO*), is not sufficient to safeguard the interests of the creditors of the main insolvency proceedings[29] if the *lex fori concursus secundarii* does not confer on the liquidator in the main insolvency proceedings the right to make a request in this respect. Even if the *lex fori concursus secundarii* provides for a right to make a request, this may not suffice if it does not entail **18**

---

[24] Moss/Fletcher/Isaacs-*Bogdan*, Regulation, mn 8.249.

[25] D-K/D/Ch-*Duursma-Kepplinger/Chalupsky* Art 33 mn 5; *Fritz/Bähr* DZWIR 2001, 221, 232.

[26] But see: Landesgericht Leoben ZIP 2005, 1930; rejecting: *Sommer* ZInsO 2005, 1136, 1139; OLG Graz dated 20 Oct 2005, NZI 2006, 660, cf Table of Cases Art 3 of the EIR Appendix A mn 5.

[27] ECJ NZI 2006, 360 et seq; opinion of the Advocate General of the ECJ *Jacobs* ZIP 2005, 1878 et seq.

[28] *Paulus* Komm EuInsVO Art 33 mn 6; dissenting opinion: *Vallender* FS Kreft, 565 et seq, 575; KTS 2005, 283, 305.

[29] But see: *Vallender* KTS 2005, 283, 305.

the broad discretionary powers afforded to the liquidator in the main insolvency proceedings.

19 In light of the objectives of Art 33 (1) of the EIR, i.e. to maintain the status quo in the secondary insolvency proceedings, the provision must be interpreted more broadly in terms of the time period for which it is to apply.[30] Liquidation measures implemented by a temporary administrator – at least in German secondary insolvency proceedings – can well be imagined and are even legally permissible pursuant to the *lex fori concursus secundarii* in some circumstances. Liquidation measures that not only serve, but also go beyond, the preservation of the debtor enterprise correspond to the situation envisioned by Art 33 (1) of the EIR.

2.4 Effects of the Judicial Order to Stay

20 The order to stay proceedings covers liquidation acts within the secondary insolvency proceedings.

21 Generally excluded from the ambit of the stay of the liquidation are those objects situated in the territory of the secondary insolvency proceedings to which security rights *in rem* are attached provided that the enforcing of such rights takes place external to the insolvency proceedings pursuant to the *lex fori concursus secundarii*; an example of this is the so-called *Aussonderungsrecht* (right of separation) known to German and Austrian law (Section 47 *Ins*O respectively Section 11 (2) *KO*), which allows property belonging to third parties to be separated from the insolvency estate.[31] A different result would only be possible if it were provided for by the *lex fori concursus secundarii*.[32]

22 However, where so-called *Absonderungsrechte* – rights of preferential treatment, i.e. rights of secured creditors to separate satisfaction out of certain property – are involved in German secondary insolvency proceedings, a (temporary) stay of liquidation must be ordered in the event of a liquidation of objects to which these rights are attached and pursuant to which the liquidator is granted a right to liquidate (see Section 165 et seq *Ins*O).[33]

23 The staying of the liquidation also does not affect the right of the liquidator in the secondary proceedings to retain possession of the assets found in the insolvency estate and to use – but not liquidate – these for the purposes permitted by the *lex fori concursus secundarii*.[34]

24 The order to stay the liquidation does not result in the avoidance of liquidation measures that have already been implemented: commenced, but not yet completed, liquidation measures are to be stayed but not avoided.[35]

---

[30] Concurring: *Paulus* Komm EuInsVO Art 33 mn 6; dissenting opinion: *Vallender* KTS 2005, 283, 304 et seq.

[31] D-K/D/Ch-*Duursma-Kepplinger/Chalupsky* Art 33 mn 4; Haß/Huber/Gruber/Heiderhoff-*Heiderhoff* Art 33 EuInsVO mn 3; *Herchen* Das Übereinkommen über Insolvenzverfahren der Mitgliedstaaten der Europäischen Union vom 23.11.1995 (2000), pp 155, 156.

[32] *Gottwald* Grenzüberschreitende Insolvenzen (1997), p 44; *Johnson* International Insolvency Review 1996, 80, 106.

[33] On this, see: mn 25 et seq below, 42 et seq.

[34] Haß/Huber/Gruber/Heiderhoff-*Heiderhoff* Art 33 EuInsVO mn 3; *Herchen* Das Übereinkommen über Insolvenzverfahren der Mitgliedstaaten der Europäischen Union vom 23.11.1995 (2000), p 156; *Herchen* ZInsO 2002, 345, 351.

[35] See *Virgós/Schmit* Explanatory report mn 246; D-K/D/Ch-*Duursma-Kepplinger/Chalupsky* Art 33 mn 14; *Herchen* ZInsO 2002, 345, 351; *Smid* Komm EuInsVO Art 23 mn 2.

This means precisely:

A stay of liquidation does not, in principle, affect a lawsuit being conducted by the liquidator in the secondary proceedings to bring about a liquidation since this is being done merely in preparation of the liquidation. **25**

This may be different, however, if the liquidation itself were to ensue from the judgement being sought. An example of this is where the liquidator brings an action against a third party to force that party to declare/consent to something, i.e. to make a so-called *Willenserklärung*; if the action is successful, the declaration/consent is deemed pursuant to Section 894 (1) *ZPO* as having been given once the judgement ordering the party to make the declaration becomes final and absolute *(res judicata)*. In such a case, the action should be deemed suspended analogous to Section 239 (1) or Section 240 *ZPO* on the grounds that the order of the insolvency court staying the proceedings – partially and for a limited period of time – divests the liquidator of the secondary insolvency proceedings of his right to liquidate, this right being a part of his right to dispose of the assets. **26**

The actual liquidation takes place only upon execution of the judgement that was obtained. The insolvency court's order to stay proceedings acquires – provided that compulsory execution measures are being implemented to liquidate assets – the status of an order for a provisional stay of execution within the meaning of Section 775 (1) No 2 *ZPO*. Thus, compulsory execution measures may no longer be initiated, and commenced compulsory execution measures no longer resumed. **27**

Foreclosure proceedings *(Zwangsversteigerung)* in respect of real property situated in Germany represent a special case; such proceedings will not be impaired by the opening of German secondary insolvency proceedings. Foreclosure proceedings are to be provisionally stayed analogous to Section 30d of the German *ZVG* (Law on Foreclosures and Compulsory Administration). The request is to be made separately in addition to the one made pursuant to Art 33 (1) of the EIR to the court having jurisdiction to execute the judgement. Both the liquidator in the main insolvency proceedings and the liquidator in the secondary insolvency proceedings are authorized to make the request. The liquidator in the secondary insolvency proceedings is, pursuant to Section 30d *ZVG*, under an obligation to make a request to implement the order to stay ordered by the insolvency court. **28**

If the insolvency court's order to stay proceedings is not complied with, the liquidator in the main insolvency proceedings may, as a means of redress, either lodge a complaint against an execution measure pursuant to Section 766 *ZPO* or, provided that execution measures have been made by way of a court decision, make a special appeal (subject to a time limit) pursuant to Section 793 *ZPO*. **29**

If the liquidation is effected by way of a private sale (as opposed to a court auction) of an asset and if in preparation of such sale the asset is being appraised by an expert, the liquidator is at liberty to decide whether the appraisal by the expert is to be resumed, this being a measure merely preparatory to liquidation. In making his decision he will have to consider the further costs of the expert assessment, possible postponements of a later liquidation caused by the interruption, and the probability of a later liquidation. **30**

2.5 Duration of the Stay

As outlined in Art 33 (1) sentence 3 of the EIR, the order may be made for a maximum of three months. Although it may be repeated as often as desired, an order may **31** only be granted if it has been requested and only upon a renewed judicial review of both admissibility and the grounds for the request.[36]

2.6 Procedural Issues

32 The form of the decisions made, as well as the permissible means of appealing decisions, are governed by the procedural rules of the deciding court *(lex fori)*.[37] In the case of German secondary insolvency proceedings, the insolvency court decides by way of an order *(Beschluss)* as contemplated by Section 233 sentence 1 *InsO*.[38]

33 The liquidator of the secondary insolvency proceedings must be heard prior to a decision being made.[39] This is not primarily the result of the respective *lex fori*, but rather follows from the wording of Art 33 (1) of the EIR itself. According to Art 33 (1) of the EIR, the liquidator in the main insolvency proceedings is only given the burden of submitting the interests of the creditors in the main insolvency proceedings; it leaves it to the liquidator in the secondary insolvency proceedings to submit and, if necessary, to prove that the stay is not in the interests of the creditors of the main insolvency proceedings. This splitting of the burden of proof is made clear by the fact that Art 33 (1) of the EIR formulates the existence of a – justified – interest of the creditors of the main insolvency proceedings as the rule, the non-existence on the other hand as the exception the existence of which must be proven by the party relying on it.

34 A special appeal (subject to a time limit) against the order of a German insolvency court staying proceedings is granted neither to the creditors nor to the liquidator of the secondary insolvency proceedings. One reason is that the *lex fori* does not provide for such an appeal (see Section 6 *InsO*), another being that a request can always be made to lift the stay.

35 The liquidator in the main insolvency proceedings is equally denied a right of appeal against an unsuccessful stay ordered by a German insolvency court. Section 6 *InsO*, which only grants a right of appeal against decisions of the insolvency court if the special appeal (subject to a time limit) is expressly allowed, is also of no assistance here. Although a different regulation of this would probably be desirable, the legislators had ample opportunity to do so when creating Art 102 Sec 10 *EGInsO* but nevertheless refrained from doing it. The liquidator in the main insolvency proceedings is, however, free to make a renewed request to stay proceedings. Since there is no regulation of this, no court costs are incurred.[40]

---

[36] *Virgós/Schmit* Explanatory Report mn 245; D-K/D/Ch-*Duursma-Kepplinger/Chalupsky* Art 33 mn 16; Moss/Fletcher/Isaacs-*Moss/Smith*, Regulation, mn 8.247.

[37] Moss/Fletcher/Isaacs-*Wessels*, Regulation, mn 8.248.

[38] D-K/D/Ch-*Duursma-Kepplinger/Chalupsky* Art 33 mn 7.

[39] *Paulus* Komm EuInsVO Art 33 mn 14 ("should").

[40] See Part 2, chapter 3 of the appendix 1 to the *Gerichtskostengesetz* (Act on Court Costs).

3. Court Orders in Favour of the Creditors of the Secondary Insolvency Proceedings (Article 33 (1) sentence 1, 2nd half-sentence of the EIR)

3.1 Protective Orders

It lies in the discretionary powers of the court of the secondary insolvency proceedings to decide whether protective measures should be ordered and the content of them.[41] **36**

In deciding on the content of protective measures, it is advisable to make use of such measures provided for in the *lex fori concursus secundarii*. This is, however, not mandatory since Art 33 (1) sentence 1, 2nd half-sentence of the EIR, as a substantive law provision, confers on the insolvency court jurisdiction to order all "suitable measures". Since it contains neither a manifest nor a concealed conflict of laws referral to the express provisions of the *lex fori concursus secundarii*, it is not restricted to it.[42] **37**

The order could contain, for example, the obligation to pay the interest accruing on the insolvency estate of the main insolvency proceedings.[43] It would seem appropriate here to pay interest to those creditors who are prevented from realising their secured rights in objects in the insolvency estate. An example of this in German secondary insolvency proceedings are the holders of so-called *Absonderungsrechte* – rights of preferential treatment – i.e. rights of secured creditors to separate satisfaction out of certain property.[44] To impose an obligation on the main insolvency proceedings to pay interest in such a case would be quite appropriate, the clear legislative intent of this being evident already in Art 102 Sec 10 *EGInsO*.[45] **38**

In the case of unsecured creditors, it may be appropriate to calculate the interest based on the dividend anticipated according to the prognosis of the liquidator of the secondary insolvency proceedings at the time at which the liquidation is stayed. **39**

Absent an agreement between the creditor and debtor on the interest rate, an appropriate interest rate would be the statutory interest rate for arrears/defaulted payment. **40**

The imposing of an obligation to compensate for loss of value of the assets of the secondary insolvency proceedings during the term of the stay is also conceivable.[46] If the stay was later lifted and the liquidation resumed, the insolvency estate of the main insolvency proceedings would have to compensate the loss of value of the insolvency estate of the secondary insolvency proceedings. The practical difficulty here is that the value of the assets would have to be ascertained at the time of the stay and at the time at which the stay is lifted. **41**

Finally, the securing of the aforementioned obligation to compensate could take the form of a suretyship or a guaranty at the expense of the insolvency estate of the main insolvency proceedings.[47] **42**

---

41 *Virgós/Schmit* Explanatory Report mn 244; D-K/D/Ch-*Duursma-Kepplinger/Chalupsky* Art 33 mn 9.

42 Dissenting opinion: Haß/Huber/Gruber/Heiderhoff-*Heiderhoff* Art 33 EuInsVO mn 3; unclear: MünchKomm InsO/*Reinhart* Art 33 EuInsVO mn 2.

43 MünchKomm InsO/*Reinhart* Art 33 EuIns-VO mn 2.

44 Guidance is found here in sec 169 InsO.

45 On this, see: mn 43 et seq.

46 *Smid* Komm EuInsVO Art 33 mn 8; similar: *Balz* ZIP 1996, 948, 954.

47 See *Balz* ZIP 1996, 948, 954; *Herchen* Das Übereinkommen über Insolvenzverfahren der Mitgliedstaaten der Europäischen Union vom 23.11.1995 (2000), p 156.

3.2 Article 102 Sec 10 *EGInsO*

43 If the stay of liquidation covers objects to which preferential rights (*Absonderungsrechte*) are attached, Art 102 Sec 10 *EGInsO* prescribes, in the case of secondary insolvency proceedings governed by German law, the payment of the interest owed out of the "insolvency estate". Where the preferred creditor and the debtor have not agreed on the interest rate, then the statutory interest rate for arrears/defaulted payment[48] is owing.[49] A court order is (at first glance) not necessary.

44 Construed in light of Art 33 (1) sentence 1, 2nd half-sentence of the EIR, the wording of Art 102 Sec 10 *EGInsO* could be so understood that "insolvency estate" means the insolvency assets of the main insolvency proceedings.

45 The provisions of Art 102 Sec 10 *EGInsO* must, however, be qualified as insolvency law provisions. Pursuant to Art 4 (1) of the EIR, Art 102 Sec 10 *EGInsO* does not apply to foreign main insolvency proceedings and is not capable of ordering any payment from the assets of the main insolvency proceedings for the simple fact that the provision does not form part of the *lex fori concursus universalis*.

46 Consequently, Art 102 Sec 10 *EGInsO* can only apply in one instance, namely if "insolvency estate" is read to mean the insolvency assets of German secondary insolvency proceedings.[50] But this would be incorrect. What is intended by Art 33 (1) sentence 1, 2nd half-sentence of the EIR is that the insolvency estate which is responsible for, or which profits from, the stay – i. e. the insolvency estate of the main insolvency proceedings – must compensate the insolvency estate that is disadvantaged by the stay.[51] An obligation to pay interest can only be imposed on them via an order made pursuant to Art 33 (1) sentence 1, 2nd half-sentence of the EIR.[52] Art 102 Sec 10 *EGInsO* cannot be applied based on the higher ranking afforded to the (applicability of) European law through Art 33 (1) sentence 1, 2nd half-sentence of the EIR. Art 33 (1) of the EIR creates a balanced system for weighing and accounting for the various interests in that the stay of liquidation is ordered in favour of the creditors of the main insolvency proceedings who then, on the secondary level, must compensate for the costs of the creditors of the secondary insolvency proceedings whose interests are overridden through the stay of liquidation in the secondary insolvency proceedings. Art 102 Sec 10 *EGInsO* is contrary to such a compensating and thus conflicts with the overriding provisions of Community law.

---

48 Sec 288 BGB or sec 352 HGB.

49 See the reasons of the German legislator for the government draft of a law to amend international insolvency law: Art 102 Sec 10 EGInsO, ZIP 2002, 2331, 2334.

50 Concurring: *Paulus* Komm EuInsVO Art 33 mn 14; dissenting opinion: Braun/*Liersch* InsO § 357 mn 10. The provisions of sec 169 InsO, which is similar in its wording, also provide that the interest obligation is imposed on the proceedings in which the interruption of the liquidation occurs. However, sec 169 covers a different situation. There the interruption of the liquidation was caused in the same proceedings in which they actually occurred.

51 Already held by: *Herchen* Das Übereinkommen über Insolvenzverfahren der Mitgliedstaaten der Europäischen Union vom 23.11.1995 (2000), p 156.

52 MünchKomm InsO/*Reinhart* Art 33 EuInsVO mn 2 holds that such an order made to the liquidator in the main insolvency proceedings is only required if the interest obligation cannot be satisfied out of the insolvency assets of the secondary insolvency proceedings.

3.3 No Protective Measures Ordered

If the court stays the liquidation in the secondary insolvency proceedings pursuant to Art 33 (1) of the EIR, the ordering of protective measures is generally not necessary when insolvency claims lodged in the secondary insolvency proceedings are also lodged in the main insolvency proceedings. Orders made by the insolvency court of the secondary proceedings, either in respect of the creditors as a whole or in respect of certain classes of creditors of the secondary insolvency proceedings, should take into account whether the claim of an insolvency creditor has also been lodged in the main insolvency proceedings. The stay of the liquidation in the secondary insolvency proceedings, which was in effect (also) approved in his interests as a creditor in the main insolvency proceedings, would otherwise lead to a double benefit. **47**

A multiple benefiting of individual creditors by staying the liquidation in the secondary insolvency proceedings in their interests on the one hand, and by ordering protective measures on the other hand, would be contrary to the aforementioned[53] system of weighing and accounting for the interests contemplated by Art 33 (1) of the EIR. Furthermore, the ordering of a protective measure in favour of such creditors would conflict with the equitable treatment of creditors principle of insolvency law. Art 20 (2) of the EIR makes this quite clear in that the benefits obtained by a creditor in a proceeding compared to other creditors must be equalized in other proceedings. **48**

It is therefore appropriate to exclude those groups of creditors who have claims lodged in several proceedings from the benefit of protective measure orders. **49**

4. Lifting the Stay of Liquidation

Art 33 (2) of the EIR regulates those cases in which the stay of liquidation is to be terminated by the court of the secondary insolvency proceedings. **50**

The case set out in the first dash, i.e. a request by the liquidator in the main insolvency proceedings, poses no problem. He would also be entitled to withdraw the request since his exclusive right to make the request ensues solely from the interests of the insolvency estate of the main insolvency proceedings, which he is the representative of. Third parties' interests in staying the liquidation that would deprive the liquidator in the main insolvency proceedings of his right to make and to withdraw the request are not to be taken into account in conjunction with Art 33 of the EIR. The court is only afforded a "formality right" in this respect, i.e. the right to review whether the applicant is indeed the liquidator of the main insolvency proceedings. There is no discretion to decide whether the stay should be lifted. **51**

The second dash also allows a termination by the court on its own motion, at the request of a creditor, or upon a request by the liquidator in the secondary insolvency proceedings. **52**

The creditors of the main insolvency proceedings, as well as those in the secondary insolvency proceedings who are affected by the stay, are entitled to make a request.[54] Although this is not explicit in the wording here itself, it is implied through the reference at the end of the second dash to the interests of the creditors of the main and secondary insolvency proceedings. Creditors of other secondary insolvency proceedings who have **53**

---

[53] Mn 45.

[54] Dissenting opinion: *Smid* Komm EuInsVO Art 33 mn 10: only creditors of the secondary insolvency proceedings.

not simultaneously lodged their claims in the main insolvency proceedings, or in the secondary insolvency proceedings affected by the stay, have no right to make a request; their interests are not affected by the stay of the liquidation.

54 The test to be applied by the court in deciding whether to lift the stay of liquidation is – seemingly – different than the one to be used for granting the stay in subsection 1: the stay is to be lifted if it becomes apparent that it "no longer appears justified, in particular, by the interests of creditors in the main proceedings or in the secondary proceedings."

55 Applying a strictly literal interpretation, the use of the word "or" means that the stay should not be lifted if either the interests of the main insolvency proceedings or the interests of the secondary insolvency proceedings justify its continuance.[55] The reference to the interests of the creditors of the secondary insolvency proceedings, which are not to be taken into account in deciding on the stay of the liquidation itself but in respect of protective measures only, does not at first appear very plausible in this context. The wording of this provision in general is unfortunate. It is difficult to imagine a real situation where a stay of liquidation on its own – namely without considering the protective measures ordered pursuant to subs. (1) – would be in the interests of the creditors of the secondary proceedings, i.e. it is hard to imagine a situation where a stay would be justified by the interests of the creditors of the secondary insolvency proceedings. What is obviously meant is that the order staying liquidation must be lifted if the stay is contrary to the interests of the creditors of the secondary insolvency proceedings. Such an interpretation then begs the question whether a lifting of a protective measure is also justified if it, albeit contrary to the interests of the creditors in the secondary insolvency proceedings, nevertheless continues to be in the interests of the creditors of the main proceedings.[56] In my opinion this is not what is meant. To interpret Art 33 (2) of the EIR in this way is contrary to both the objectives and the logic of Art 33 of the EIR; it also fails to accord with the correct understanding of its wording, which turns on a prejudicing of the interests of the creditors in the secondary insolvency proceedings because of the stay of liquidation. As long as such a prejudicing of the interests of the creditors in the secondary insolvency proceedings can be offset by the ordering of protective measures, then the sole issue for consideration is whether the stay of liquidation is in the interests of the creditors of the main insolvency proceedings. A simple logical observation confirms this: If a stay of liquidation continues to be in the interests of the creditors of the main insolvency proceedings and the order staying liquidation may still be lifted pursuant to Art 33 (2) 2nd dash of the EIR, then the liquidator in the main insolvency proceedings would be entitled to request the stay once again and would in fact be granted it. And because of the insolvency-related duty owed to the creditors of the main insolvency proceedings, he is also obliged to do this. More accurately, the stay of liquidation may only be lifted pursuant to the 2nd dash of subs (2) if it is prejudicial to the interests of the creditors in the secondary insolvency proceedings and (1) this prejudicing of their

[55] Same conclusion: Haß/Huber/Gruber/Heiderhoff-*Heiderhoff* Art 33 EuInsVO mn 6; Moss/Fletcher/Isaacs-*Moss/Smith*, Regulation, mn 8.247; *Smid* Komm EuIns-VO Art 33 mn 10; dissenting opinion: D-K/D/Ch-*Duursma-Kepplinger/Chalupsky* Art 33 mn 19, 20; concurring: MünchKomm InsO/*Reinhart* Art 33 EuInsVO mn 4.

[56] Same Landesgericht Leoben, NZI 2006, 663; *Beck* NZI 2006, 609, 612; D-K/D/Ch-*Duursma-Kepplinger/Chalupsky* Art 33 mn 19, 20; MünchKomm InsO/*Reinhart* Art 33 EuIns-VO mn 4; dissenting opinion: Haß/Huber/Gruber/Heiderhoff-*Heiderhoff* Art 33 mn 6; Moss/Fletcher/Isaacs-*Moss/Smith*, Regulation, mn 8.247; *Smid* Komm EuInsVO Art 33 mn 10.

interests cannot, or cannot sufficiently, be offset by the ordering of protective measures and (2) the stay of liquidation is not (no longer) in the interests of the creditors of the main insolvency proceedings.

In line with the interpretation preferred here, the reference to the interests of the **56**
creditors of the secondary insolvency proceedings must be so understood that – as long as the stay of proceedings continues to be in the interests of the creditors of the main insolvency proceedings – the lifting of the stay pursuant to Art 33 (2) 2nd dash of the EIR may only be made, and actually must be made, if the measures ordered pursuant to Art 33 (1) sentence 1 of the EIR for the protection of the interests of the creditors of the secondary insolvency proceedings are not being complied with.[57]

Furthermore, the stay of the liquidation must be lifted if the interests of the main **57**
insolvency proceedings no longer justify the stay; in this respect, this is congruent with the conditions in subsection 1. Art 33 (1) sentence 2 of the EIR is to be applied here: the lifting of the stay may only be effected if it manifestly is not (no longer) in the interests of the creditors of the main insolvency proceedings. If the court were to apply another broader test here and were to order the lifting of the stay, then the stay would have to be immediately ordered anew on the request of the liquidator in the main insolvency proceedings: an obviously illogical and uneconomical result.

Article 34
Measures ending secondary insolvency proceedings

(1) Where the law applicable to secondary proceedings allows for such proceedings to be closed without liquidation by a rescue plan, a composition or a comparable measure, the liquidator in the main proceedings shall be empowered to propose such a measure himself.

Closure of the secondary proceedings by a measure referred to in the first subparagraph shall not become final without the consent of the liquidator in the main proceedings; failing his agreement, however, it may become final if the financial interests of the creditors in the main proceedings are not affected by the measure proposed.

(2) Any restriction of creditors' rights arising from a measure referred to in paragraph 1 which is proposed in secondary proceedings, such as a stay of payment or discharge of debt, may not have effect in respect of the debtor's assets not covered by those proceedings without the consent of all the creditors having an interest.

(3) During a stay of the process of liquidation ordered pursuant to Article 33, only the liquidator in the main proceedings or the debtor, with the former's consent, may propose measures laid down in paragraph 1 of this Article in the secondary proceedings; no other proposal for such a measure shall be put to the vote or approved.

→ Cf Arts 25 to 27, 29, 30 UNCITRAL Model Law

[57] See MünchKomm InsO/*Reinhart* Art 33 EuInsVO mn 4.

Contents

Index

Bibliography

Ahrens Rechte und Pflichten ausländischer Insolvenzverwalter 2002; *Ehricke/Ries* Die neue Europäische Insolvenzverordnung, Jus 2003, p 313; *Eidenmüller* Europäische Verordnung über Insolvenzverfahren und zukünftiges deutsches internationales Insolvenzrecht, IPRax 2001, p 2; *Flessner* Insolvenzplan und Restschuldbefreiung im Internationalen Konkursrecht – Stellungnahme zu den Artt. 15 und 16 des Vorentwurfs (VE), in Stoll (eds), Stellungnahmen und Gutachten zur Reform des deutschen Internationalen Insolvenzrecht (1992), p 201; *Herchen* Die Befugnisse des deutschen Insolvenzverwalters hinsichtlich der „Auslandsmasse" nach In-Kraft-Treten der EG-Insolvenzverordnung (Verordnung des Rates Nr. 1346/2000), ZInsO 2002, p 345; *Kemper* Die Verordnung (EG) Nr. 1346/2000 über Insolvenzverfahren, ZIP 2001, p 1609; *Kolmann* Kooperationsmodelle im Internationalen Insolvenzrecht – Empfiehlt sich für das deutsche internationale Insolvenzrecht eine Neuorientierung (2001); *Liersch* Deutsches Internationales Insolvenzrecht, NZI

2003, p 302; *Lüke* Das europäische internationale Insolvenzrecht, ZZP 111 (1998), p 275; *Paulus* Das inländische Parallelverfahren nach der Europäischen Insolvenzverordnung, EWS 2002, p 497; *Reinhart* Sanierungsverfahren im internationalen Insolvenzrecht (1995); *Vallender* Aufgaben und Befugnisse des deutschen Insolvenzrichters in Verfahren nach der EuInsVO, KTS 2005, p 283; *Wehdeking* Reform des Internationalen Insolvenzrechts in Deutschland und Österreich, DZWIR 2003, p 133; *Wimmer* Die Besonderheiten von Sekundärinsolvenzverfahren unter besonderer Berücksichtigung des Europäischen Insolvenzübereinkommens, ZIP 1998, p 982.

1. General

1.1 The Subject Matter of the Provision

Art 34 of the EIR deals with the termination of secondary insolvency proceedings by a reorganization which is designed to preserve the business enterprise, rather than shattering it through a winding-up process. The Regulation speaks of a rescue plan, composition proceedings, or another comparable measure. For the sake of brevity, the term "reorganization plan" will be used collectively in the following. 1

Art 34 of the EIR applies in the case where only the secondary insolvency proceedings are being terminated by a reorganization plan, in the case of coordinated reorganization plans in main and in secondary insolvency proceedings, and in the case of competing reorganization plans proposed by the liquidator in the main insolvency proceedings and by other parties entitled to propose reorganization plans in secondary insolvency proceedings. 2

Art 34 of the EIR is not directed at the so-called "asset deals", i.e. reorganization by means of a sale of the business enterprise to an acquiring party. This type of reorganization constitutes a winding-up for the purposes of insolvency law. 3

1.2 The Practical Significance of the Provision

The practical significance of Art 34 of the EIR lies in its facilitation of an inter-proceeding reorganization of the debtor enterprise through coordinated reorganization plans made on the initiative of the liquidator in the main insolvency proceedings.[1] This is also made apparent by the interlocking nature of Art 34 and 33 via Art 34 (3) of the EIR. During a stay of the liquidation pursuant to Art 33 (1) of the EIR in secondary insolvency proceedings, only the liquidator in the main insolvency proceedings or the debtor with he latter's consent is entitled to propose a reorganization plan ending the proceedings. The liquidator in the main insolvency proceedings is empowered to request a stay of liquidation pursuant to Art 33 (1) of the EIR even if the liquidation in the secondary insolvency proceedings has not yet commenced or has already been stayed pursuant to the *lex fori concursus secundarii*.[2] 4

Considering the concepts underlying the Regulation, the isolated reorganization in the secondary insolvency proceedings constitutes an exception.[3] This is illustrated by a glance at Art 3 (3) sentence 2 of the EIR which stipulates that secondary insolvency proceedings must be winding-up proceedings. It is also required that such a termination 5

[1] See Recital 20 of the EIR; MünchKomm InsO/*Reinhart* Art 34 EuInsVO mn 1; *Smid* Komm EuInsVO Art 34 mn 2; see also: Moss/Fletcher/Isaacs-*Moss/Bayfield*, Regulation, mn 5.80–5.83.

[2] On this, see: mn 60 et seq below.

[3] MünchKomm InsO/*Reinhart* Art 34 EuInsVO mn 3.

of proceedings by way of a reorganization plan in the winding-up proceedings must be permissible pursuant to the *lex fori concursus secundarii*.[4] This is the case in German secondary insolvency proceedings. The German Insolvency Act *(InsO)* sanctions both a winding-up process and an insolvency plan (Sec 217 et seq *InsO*).

6 In practice, the isolated reorganization plan is probably of little relevance since the isolated reorganization of a legally dependent business establishment may not be carried out without reorganizing the responsible legal entity in the main insolvency proceedings.[5] This will still hold even if the *lex fori concursus secundarii* – as is the case with the German Insolvency Act – contemplates both reorganization and winding-up insolvency plans.[6]

1.3 The Declaratory Nature of the Provision

7 Art 34 of the EIR makes it clear that the reorganization plan in the secondary insolvency proceedings serves primarily the interests of the creditors in the main insolvency proceedings. Following directly from this is the explicit necessity of obtaining the consent of the liquidator in the main insolvency proceedings to reorganization plans in the secondary insolvency proceedings (Art 34 (1) 2nd subpara of the EIR). At the very least, the reorganization in the secondary insolvency proceedings must not adversely affect the interests of the creditors in the main insolvency proceedings.

8 Considering that the liquidator in the main insolvency proceedings is being empowered to independently propose a reorganization plan that terminates the secondary proceedings (Art 34 (1) 1st subpara of the EIR) and that the approval of such a plan is principally impossible without his consent (Art 34 (1) 2nd subpara of the EIR), Art 34 of the EIR is a confirmation and a bolstering of the superiority attributed to the main insolvency proceedings over the secondary insolvency proceedings.[7]

2. The Proposal Right of the Liquidator in the Main Insolvency Proceedings (subsection 1, 1st subparagraph)

2.1 In General

9 By means of a uniform substantive law regulation, the first subparagraph of Art 34 (1) of the EIR augments the respective *lex fori concursus secundarii* with an independent right of the liquidator in the main insolvency proceedings to propose a reorganization plan to end the secondary insolvency proceedings.

10 It does not, however, establish an exclusive right of proposal. The right is supplementary to the proposal rights prescribed by the particular *lex fori concursus secundarii*.[8] This will not be the case, however, if a request to stay the liquidation made by the

---

4 MünchKomm InsO/*Reinhart* Art 34 EuInsVO mn 1.

5 Haß/Huber/Gruber/Heiderhoff-*Heiderhoff* Art 34 EuInsVO mn 3; MünchKomm InsO/*Reinhart* Art 34 EuInsVO mn 3. The references regarding structure made by *Liersch* NZI 2003, 302, 311 naturally refer to coordinated reorganization plans in main and in secondary insolvency proceedings.

6 On this, see: mn 16 below.

7 Moss/Fletcher/Isaacs-*Moss/Smith*, Regulation, mn 8.252.

8 *Virgós/Schmit* Explanatory Report mn 248; MünchKomm InsO/*Reinhart* Art 34 EuInsVO mn 1; dissenting opinion: *Paulus* Komm EuInsVO Art 34 mn 2; Art 3 mn 50 et seq; *Vallender* KTS 2005, 283, 305 et seq.

liquidator in the main insolvency proceedings pursuant to Art 33 (1) of the EIR has already been complied with (Art 34 (3) of the EIR).[9]

The provision ensures that the chances of reorganizing the debtor establishment subject to the secondary insolvency proceedings remain intact if it is in the interests of a reorganization of the debtor enterprise in the main insolvency proceedings. **11**

2.2 The Proposal Right of the Temporary Administrator

Even if listed in Annex C of the EIR, no right to make a proposal is conferred on a temporary administrator. The opening of secondary insolvency proceedings, and consequently the ending of these through a reorganization plan, necessitates the opening of the main insolvency proceedings (see Art 27 of the EIR). The reason for opening that is established by Art 27 of the EIR[10], i.e. the opening of main insolvency proceedings, does not exist as long as a temporary administrator has been appointed.[11] **12**

2.3 Proposal Right of the Temporary Administrator and the Custodian in German Main Insolvency Proceedings

The aforementioned submissions will apply equally in the case of German main insolvency proceedings as regarding the so-called "weak" temporary administrator, the "strong" temporary administrator,[12] and to the custodian *(Sachwalter)* under German law.[13] In other words, they have no right to make a proposal. **13**

2.4 Law Governing the Reorganization Plan

The Regulation contains no explicit conflict of laws referral to the law that is to govern a reorganization plan, e.g. with respect to content, form, and procedural aspects (proposal, voting, judicial approval). Since, however, Art 34 of the EIR – regarding the incorporation of the substantive laws of the Member States – restricts itself to the proposal right of the liquidator in the main insolvency proceedings, all remaining issues are governed by the *lex fori concursus secundarii* as contemplated by Art 28 of the EIR and the basic conflict of laws principle underlying the Regulation (see Art 4 (1) of the EIR). **14**

2.5 German Secondary Insolvency Proceedings

For German secondary insolvency proceedings, the 1st subparagraph of Art 34 (1) of the EIR confers upon the liquidator in the main insolvency proceedings the right analogous to Sec 218 *InsO* to initiate a plan.[14] **15**

Considering what the right of proposal is trying to achieve and taking into account the provisions of Art 31 (3) of the EIR, it must be concluded that the right of proposal conferred on the liquidator in the main insolvency proceedings is restricted to proposing an insolvency plan geared towards reorganization. Winding-up plans and plans con- **16**

[9] On this, see: mn 57 et seq below.

[10] *Smid* Komm EuInsVO Art 29 mn 2.

[11] See the comments on Art 29 of the EIR mn 6, 7, 20.

[12] Dissenting opinion: *Smid* Komm EuInsVO Art 34, mn 4.

[13] Sec 273 InsO.

[14] *Paulus* EWS 2002, 497, 506; Haß/Huber/Gruber/Heiderhoff-*Heiderhoff* Art 34 EuInsVO mn 1 who, however, erroneously holds that art 102 sec 9 EGInsO expressly provides for this.

sisting of a mixture of reorganization and winding-up[15], which are both permitted in German law preparatory to a so-called "asset deal", do not constitute reorganization plans within the meaning of Art 34 (1) 1st subparagraph of the EIR.

17 In all other respects, the requirements laid down in Sec 217 et seq *InsO* apply, particularly Sec 219 to 230 *InsO* regarding form and content.[16]

2.6 Binding Nature of the Proposals of the Liquidator in the Main Proceedings

2.6.1 Basic principle

18 According to Art 34 (1) of the EIR – which by creating the proposal right is afforded the status of a substantive law rule and otherwise a conflict of laws rule – the question as to whether the proposal of a reorganization plan made by liquidator in the main insolvency proceedings is binding is determined solely pursuant to the *lex fori concursus secundarii.*[17] Art 34 (1) 1st subparagraph of the EIR merely supplements the respective *lex fori concursus secundarii* by adding a Community-law right to make a proposal.[18]

2.6.2 Pragmatic approach

19 A range of pragmatic measures are also available to the liquidator in the main insolvency proceedings to increase his chances of executing his reorganization plan proposed pursuant to the 1st subparagraph of Art 34 (1) of the EIR.

20 The use of such means is permissible and does not constitute a misappropriation of justice. This follows from the superior significance that Chapter III of the Regulation attributes to the main insolvency proceedings in comparison to the secondary insolvency proceedings and from the goal of Art 34 of the EIR, which is to facilitate the inter-procedural reorganization by means of coordinated reorganization plans. The use of the following leverage-seeking measures in German secondary insolvency proceedings can therefore not be dismissed on a charge of their being adverse to the objectives of insolvency proceedings.[19]

21 If the only option available in the secondary insolvency proceedings is between a winding-up or accepting the reorganization plan proposed by the liquidator in the main insolvency proceedings, then the liquidator in the main proceedings can lend support to his reorganization proposal by making a request – which is generally successful[20] – to stay the liquidation in the secondary insolvency proceedings. He will have to assess here, however, whether the stay of the liquidation is sufficiently convincing in light of the right of the insolvency court of the secondary insolvency proceedings to order protective measures at the expense of the assets of the main insolvency proceedings (Art 33 (1) sentence 1, 1st half-sentence of the EIR).[21] The liquidator in the main insolvency proceed-

---

15 See Uhlenbruck Komm InsO/*Lüer* vor §§ 217–219 InsO mn 41 et seq.

16 See also: *Herchen* ZInsO 2002, 345, 351; *Paulus* EWS 2002, 497, 506; *Smid* Komm EuInsVO Art 29 mn 3, who also refers to the provisions of the "concordato" pursuant to art 124 of the "Codice fallimentare".

17 *Herchen* ZInsO 2002, 345, 351, as well as mn 14 above.

18 Dissenting opinion on art 31 (3) of the EIR: *Herchen* ZInsO 2002, 345, 351; see also the comments on Art 31 of the EIR mn 40 et seq, 45.

19 On the issue of being adverse to the objectives of insolvency, see for example: BGH NZI 2002, 375.

20 See the comments on Art 33 of the EIR mn 11 et seq.

21 See the comments on Art 33 of the EIR mn 36 et seq.

ings is also entitled pursuant to Art 32 (2) of the EIR to lodge the claims that are lodged in the main insolvency proceedings in the secondary insolvency proceedings as well.[22] Since Art 32 (3) of the EIR authorizes him to exercise the voting rights of the creditors of the main insolvency proceedings, he will generally be able to force the acceptance of his reorganization plan.[23] The liquidator is not subject to a vote prohibition according to the rule prohibiting to vote in own matters. There is no such vote prohibition when an insolvency plan is decided, because the claims of all creditors – inclusive the creditors represented by the liquidator – are concerned by such a measure.[24]

If other plans are proposed in addition to the reorganization plan of the liquidator in the main insolvency proceedings, he is free to withhold the consent required of him pursuant to Art 34 (1) 2nd subpara of the EIR to any other reorganization plan. However, in the case of conflicting reorganization plans, the consent of the liquidator in the main insolvency proceedings cannot pursuant to Art 34 (1) 2nd subpara of the EIR be dispensed with. The other reorganization plan, in effect, has an adverse impact on the interests of the creditors of the main insolvency proceedings, which are the only relevant interests, since the acceptance and approval of it would simultaneously preclude the acceptance and approval of the reorganization plan proposed by the liquidator in the main insolvency proceedings.[25] **22**

2.6.3 Secondary insolvency proceedings pursuant to the German Insolvency Act

For the German Insolvency Act *(InsO)* as the *lex fori concursus secundarii* this means that the insolvency court is entitled to reject the insolvency plan pursuant to Sec 231 *InsO* under certain conditions. If the plan is not rejected by the insolvency court, then the majority of the creditors in the secondary insolvency proceedings, both per capita and per quantum of their claims, must consent to it. Should the requisite majority not be reached, then a judicial approval of it may only take place if the requirements of Sec 245 *InsO* and Art 102 (9) *EGInsO* have been satisfied. Such a substantive law modification of the *lex fori concursus secundarii*, i.e. giving special consideration to the interests of the creditors of the main insolvency proceedings, is not provided for by the Regulation. **23**

3. The Consent of the Liquidator in the Main Insolvency Proceedings (subsection 1, 2nd subparagraph)

3.1 Underlying Principle

According to the 2nd subparagraph of Art 34 (1) of the EIR, the termination of secondary insolvency proceedings through a reorganization plan may only be approved if the liquidator in the main insolvency proceedings gives his consent. If he withholds his consent, the plan may only be approved if the financial interests of the creditors in the main insolvency proceedings are not adversely affected by the reorganization plan. **24**

---

[22] Provided that this has not already been done and if, pursuant to the *lex fori concursus secundarii,* this is still admissible considering the stage of the proceedings.

[23] See comments on Art 32 of the EIR mn 2 et seq, 6 et seq.

[24] Uhlenbruck Komm InsO/*Uhlenbruck* § 76 mn 24.

[25] On this, see: mn 34, 40 below.

3.2 Subject Matter of the Consent

25 Consent must be sought in respect of both the reorganization plan proposed by the party entitled to make a proposal pursuant to the *lex fori concursus secundarii*, as well as to the plan proposed by the liquidator in the main insolvency proceedings himself.

26 The consent to the reorganization plan proposed by the liquidator in the main insolvency proceedings is generally a mere formality. This may be different, however, where there are coordinated reorganization plans in the main and in the secondary insolvency proceedings, thus making it necessary to modify the reorganization plan in the secondary insolvency proceedings because of modifications made in the main insolvency proceedings. The liquidator in the main insolvency proceedings may withhold his consent in such a case if a modifying of the reorganization plan is no longer possible pursuant to the *lex fori concursus secundarii*, for example where a voting procedure has already taken place.[26] If the consent cannot be substituted by the court, then the reorganization-plan proceedings must be brought to an end.[27] The liquidator in the main insolvency proceedings is then able pursuant to Art 34 (1) 1st subpara of the EIR to propose a new reorganization plan. The fact that he cannot be denied this by the *lex fori concursus secundarii* is illustrated by Art 33 (1) of the EIR.[28] If the *lex fori concursus secundarii* stipulates that the winding-up proceedings must be resumed subsequent to the failure of a reorganization plan, then the liquidator in the main insolvency proceedings could request a stay of such proceedings and could exercise his exclusive right to propose a reorganization plan pursuant to Art 34 (3) of the EIR.

3.3 Granting Consent

27 As a uniform substantive law provision, Art 34 (1) 2nd subpara of the EIR supplements the respective *lex fori concursus secundarii* with a consent requirement of the liquidator in the main insolvency proceedings, which must be observed by the court on its own motion.

28 In terms of the German Insolvency Act, the 2nd subparagraph of Art 34 (1) of the EIR augments the provisions of Sec 248 *InsO*. This section provides for the approval of the insolvency plan by the insolvency court.[29]

29 The declaration of consent must be made to the insolvency court with jurisdiction in the secondary insolvency proceedings.

30 If consent is withheld, the insolvency court is not entitled to approve the reorganization plan unless it is a situation in which the court is allowed, as an exception, to substitute its consent.

3.4 Substitution of Consent by the Court

3.4.1 Basic principle

31 Provided that the financial interests of the creditors of the main insolvency proceedings are not being adversely affected by the reorganization plan, the court may substitute the missing consent with its own.[30] However in light of the dominant status of the main

[26] See for example in German insolvency law sec 240 InsO.

[27] See for example in German insolvency law sec 231 (1) No 2 InsO.

[28] The rejection by the court of the second plan in German secondary proceedings pursuant to sec 231 (2) InsO would for example not be permitted.

[29] *Smid* Komm EuInsVO Art 34 mn 7.

[30] *Smid* Komm EuInsVO Art 34 mn 7; rejecting

insolvency proceedings, the ability to substitute consent appears rather questionable.[31] It is nevertheless a part of the *lex lata* and, as a decision of the Regulation's legislators, must be accepted. The decision to substitute consent must be made no later than the decision to approve.

3.4.2 Practical significance

Since the case outlined above[32] practically never occurs, i.e. that the liquidator in the main insolvency proceedings refuses to consent to a reorganization plan proposed by himself, the main applicability of the substituted consent is found in the area of isolated reorganization plans proposed by those parties entitled to do so pursuant to the *lex fori concursus secundarii*. **32**

In the case of conflicting reorganization plans in secondary insolvency proceedings, it has little practical significance. So long as a – conflicting – reorganization plan that is contrary to the interests of the creditors in the main insolvency proceedings has not been approved by the court, the liquidator in the main insolvency proceedings may prevent its approval via Art 33 (1) of the EIR in conjunction with Art 34 (3) of the EIR. In such a case, only the plan proposed by the liquidator in the main insolvency proceedings may be put to the vote and approved by the court. **33**

3.4.3 Review by the insolvency court

When deciding whether to substitute its consent, the insolvency court must review whether the financial interests of the creditors in the main insolvency proceedings are being adversely affected by the reorganization plan. **34**

Based on its wording, the phrase "financial interests" in Art 34 (1) 2nd subpara of the EIR must be more strictly construed than the phrase "interests of the creditors" in Art 33 of the EIR.[33] Such a restrictive interpretation is justified by the fact that terminating insolvency proceedings through a reorganization plan is a clear manifestation of the autonomy awarded creditors by the insolvency law regimes of the Member States and by the Regulation, the subordination of which to the interests of other parties – in this case the financial interests of the creditors in the main insolvency proceedings[34] – must remain the exception. The insolvency court here is afforded a wider margin for making its decision than it is in respect of its decisions to allow a request to stay pursuant to Art 33 (1) of the EIR and to lift such a stay pursuant to Art 33 (2) of the EIR. **35**

The central function of insolvency proceedings is, from the point of view of the creditors, to attach liability to the debtor's assets for the satisfaction of his obligations. The "financial interests of the creditors in the main insolvency proceedings" are therefore manifested solely in the prospective dividend attributed to their particular claim(s).[35] **36**

---

the possibility of substitution: Uhlenbruck Komm InsO/*Lüer* Art 34 mn 2; *Vallender* KTS 2005, 283, 305 et seq.

[31] On this: *Vallender* KTS 2005, 283, 305 et seq.

[32] See mn 26 above.

[33] *Kemper* ZIP 2001, 1609, 1619.

[34] From the point of view of the secondary insolvency proceedings, the creditors in the main insolvency proceedings will still be regarded as third parties even if individual or all creditors participate in both proceedings. On this, see also mn 42 below.

[35] *Virgós/Schmit* Explanatory Report mn 248, 249; D-K/D/Ch-*Duursma-Kepplinger/Chalupsky* Art 34 mn 10; Haß/Huber/Gruber/Heiderhoff-*Heiderhoff* Art 34 EuInsVO mn 4; *Kolmann* Kooperationsmodelle im Internationalen Insolvenzrecht – Empfiehlt sich für das deutsche internationale Insolvenzrecht eine Neuorientierung 2001, 353; Moss/Fletcher/Isaacs-*Moss/Smith*,

37 The court's primary task is therefore to compare the dividends that the creditors in the main insolvency proceedings can expect (1) from a winding-up in the secondary insolvency proceedings or from the execution of a reorganization plan proposed pursuant to Art 34 (1) of the EIR by the liquidator in the main insolvency proceedings, and (2) from the execution of a reorganization plan consent to which has been withheld.[36] In simpler terms: the financial interests of the creditors in the main insolvency proceedings will be adversely affected if the execution of the reorganization plan, whose consent has been withheld, causes a reduction to the distributable dividends in the main insolvency proceedings.[37]

38 The suggested comparative assessment in the case of conflicting reorganization concepts in the secondary insolvency proceedings means: even if the conflicting reorganization plan, viewed on its own, is not more prejudicial to the financial interests of the creditors in the main insolvency proceedings than a winding-up would be, the interests of the creditors in the main insolvency proceedings will still be presumed to be adversely affected if the reorganization plan of the liquidator in the main proceedings puts the creditors of the main insolvency proceedings in a better position than a winding-up would.

39 Although such an assessment, which involves the making of an in-depth economic comparison on the basis of hypotheses, is commonly thought of as difficult,[38] this is not always necessarily so in insolvency law practice.

40 What is problematic, however, are assessments of conflicting reorganization plans, and cases in which an asset in the secondary insolvency proceedings – for example a license necessary to carry on the business operations in the main insolvency proceedings – is being used to carry on the business operations in the main insolvency proceedings as suggested by the liquidator in the main insolvency proceedings (Art 31 (3) of the EIR), and this use is supposed to come to an end according to the reorganization plan. The assessment to be made here is whether the prospective dividends in the main insolvency proceedings will be diminished by the loss of such use.

41 Where none of these outlined constellations are involved, generally no real difficulties arise in judicial practice. Since there is no surplus in most insolvency proceedings, a reorganization plan that ends proceedings cannot be more detrimental to the insolvency estate of the main proceedings than a winding up. There is, therefore, no adverse impact on the dividends of the creditors in the main insolvency proceedings. The missing consent can then be substituted in both cases. Furthermore, a reorganization plan in insolvency proceedings, which in the case of a winding-up results in a surplus and therefore a 100 % dividend, will have little chance of being accepted. The issue of substituted consent is then rendered superfluous.

42 Whether claims are lodged by individual creditors or by all of the creditors in main and secondary insolvency proceedings does not trigger any particular difficulties in conjunction with the court's assessment respecting the decision to substitute consent.[39] The

---

Regulation, mn 8.254; MünchKomm InsO/*Reinhart* Art 34 EuInsVO mn 2; *Smid* Komm EuInsVO Art 34 mn 7; FK-InsO/*Wimmer* Anhang I nach § 358, mn 117.

[36] *Kolmann* Kooperationsmodelle im Internationalen Insolvenzrecht – Empfiehlt sich für das deutsche internationale Insolvenzrecht eine Neuorientierung 2001, 353; *Smid* Komm EuInsVO Art 34 mn 7.

[37] *Ehricke/Ries* Jus 2003, 313, 319.

[38] *Ahrens* Rechte und Pflichten ausländischer Insolvenzverwalter 2002, 314; Haß/Huber/Gruber/Heiderhoff-*Heiderhoff* Art 34 EuInsVO mn 4.

[39] But see: Haß/Huber/Gruber/Heiderhoff-*Heiderhoff* Art 34 EuInsVO mn 4, 6; incomprehensible: MünchKomm InsO/*Reinhart* Art 34 EuInsVO mn 3.

reference figure for the comparison is not the individual creditors in the main insolvency proceedings, but rather the entirety of the creditors of the main insolvency proceedings. It is immaterial if, via the substituted consent and approval of the reorganization plan, some individual creditors – because of their participation in both proceedings – are being put in a worse position altogether than they would be in in the case of a winding-up in the secondary insolvency proceedings.[40] Firstly, such an understanding corresponds more closely to the wording of Art 34 (1) 2nd subpara of the EIR *("if the financial interests of the creditors in the main proceedings are not affected ...")* than it does to Art 17 (2) of the EIR *("only in the case of those creditors who have given their consent")*, which refers to the individual creditors; it is equally in line with Art 34 (2) of the EIR *("without the consent of all the creditors having an interest")*, which also refers to the creditors as a whole. Secondly, the duty to transfer a surplus in the secondary insolvency proceedings to the main insolvency proceedings (Art 35 of the EIR) illustrates that the financial interests are to be judged from the point of view of the creditors as a whole. The duty to transfer the surplus is a manifestation of the *"financial interests of the creditors of the main insolvency proceedings"* and benefits the creditors as a whole.

4. Scope of the Reorganization Measures (Article 34 (2) of the EIR)

4.1 Relationship between Articles 34 (2) and 17 (2) of the EIR

Due to the large degree of similarity between their wordings and subject matters, the interaction between Articles 34 (2) and 17 (2) of the EIR should first be clarified. Although Art 34 (2) is a repetition of that which is stated in Art 17 (2) of the EIR, it restricts itself to secondary insolvency proceedings only, whereas Art 17 (2) of the EIR applies to both territorial and secondary insolvency proceedings.[41] **43**

Furthermore, Articles 17 (2) of the EIR and 34 (2) of the EIR can be – ostensibly – distinguished in respect of two other points. **44**

Firstly, Art 17 (2) of the EIR speaks of assets situated in a Member State. Art 34 (2) of the EIR on the other hand concerns assets not covered by the secondary insolvency proceedings. The wording of Art 34 (2) of the EIR could also be read to refer to assets in non-EU countries, or put more precisely, to the imposition of liability for insolvency obligations on assets in non-EU countries and on assets outside the ambit of the insolvency proceedings. The wording of Art 17 (2) of the EIR refers only to assets in Member States. Since Art 34 (2) of the EIR operates to territorially limit the encroachments ensuing from the reorganization in the secondary insolvency proceedings to the debtor's assets to which liability for insolvency obligations is attached, there is no reason why the exclusion of restrictions (to the creditors' rights) through Art 34 (2) of the EIR should not relate to the debtor's worldwide assets and assets outside the ambit of the insolvency proceedings.[42] These restrictions are a matter for the main insolvency proceedings, the **45**

[40] Dissenting opinion: Haß/Huber/Gruber/Heiderhoff-*Heiderhoff* Art 34 EuInsVO mn 4 who holds that, in this case, the substituting of the consent and the approval of the reorganization plan is inadmissible.

[41] MünchKomm InsO/*Reinhart* Art 17 EuInsVO mn 4; see also: FK-InsO/*Wimmer* Anhang I after § 358, mn 119; obvious dissenting opinion: D-K/D/Ch-*Duursma-Kepplinger/Chalupsky* Art 34 mn 13, Art 17, mn 18.

[42] Dissenting opinion: *Eidenmüller* IPRax 2001, 1, 9 et seq; *Wimmer* ZIP 1998, 982, 988; FK-InsO/*Wimmer* Anhang I nach § 358, mn 119.

idea behind the Regulation being that the (financial) healing should emanate from these proceedings and should be aimed first and foremost at reducing the insolvency liabilities.

46 Secondly, pursuant to Art 34 (2) of the EIR, restrictions should only have effects beyond national borders if all of the creditors concerned have consented. Prevailing opinion holds that a restriction in conjunction with assets not covered by the secondary insolvency proceedings should still be ineffective vis-à-vis creditors who have given their consent if such restrictions have been objected to by individual creditors.[43] According to this opinion, the objection itself, or the failure of one creditor with a lodged claim to take part in the vote, already suffices to exclude the effects beyond the national borders for all creditors. Although this interpretation may be the more likely choice if the wording of Art 34 (2) of the EIR is considered in isolation,[44] it amounts in effect to a "veto right" that affects outside third parties and as such goes too far;[45] it practically precludes any reorganization plan from succeeding in secondary insolvency proceedings. However, since both Art 34 (2) of the EIR and Art 17 (2) of the EIR apply to secondary insolvency proceedings and have the same subject matter, it is correct to afford both provisions the same meaning. Authoritative for this interpretation is Art 17 (2) of the EIR since it applies equally to secondary and territorial insolvency proceedings. There is no material reason to distinguish between secondary and territorial insolvency proceedings in respect of their requirements regarding the transborder effects of a restriction of creditors' rights. Art 34 (2) of the EIR must therefore be interpreted within the meaning of Art 17 (2) of the EIR:[46] an objection made by an individual creditor affects only this individual creditor.

4.2 Article 34 (2) of the EIR

47 It follows from the territorial (self-)limiting of the *lex fori concursus secundarii* that the effects of a reorganization plan in secondary insolvency proceedings have no impact on the debtor's assets which are not covered by the secondary insolvency proceedings, for example real property comprised within the insolvency estate of the main insolvency proceedings. This can already be found in Art 3 (2) sentence 2 and Art 27 sentence 3 of the EIR. Art 34 (2) of the EIR makes it clear that the territorial (self-)limitation of the effects of the secondary insolvency proceedings also concerns the liability side of the debtor's assets.

48 According to its wording, Art 34 (2) of the EIR deals with the "restriction of creditors' rights" in relation to the "debtor's assets not covered by these proceedings". This is addressed to the debt claims against the debtor and the liability of the insolvency estate for these claims.[47] In order to precisely define the subject matter of Art 34 (2) of the EIR with respect to the restricting of claims by a reorganization plan, a distinction must be drawn between the legal essence (substance) of a claim pursuant to substantive

---

[43] D-K/D/Ch-*Duursma-Kepplinger/Chalupsky* Art 34 mn 13; concurring: *Virgós/Schmit* Explanatory Report mn 250; Haß/Huber/Gruber/Heiderhoff-*Heiderhoff* Art 34 mn 4; FK-InsO/*Wimmer* Anhang I nach § 358, mn 119; critical: MünchKomm InsO/*Reinhart* Art 34 EuInsVO mn 2.

[44] This absurd legal consequence is provided for in German secondary insolvency proceedings through art 102 sec 9 EGInsO which forbids the approval of a plan if it is objected to by individual concerned parties.

[45] *Eidenmüller* IPRax 2001, 1, 9 et seq.

[46] *Eidenmüller* IPRax 2001, 1, et seq ("teleological reduction of Art 34 (2)").

[47] The wording gives the impression, however, that the debtor's assets situated outside of the country of the secondary insolvency proceedings are to be included in the reorganization plan.

law and the imposition of liability on a (specific) insolvency asset for a claim. The latter is being referred to here as the "asset-linked liability for the claim".

In respect of the legal essence of claims and the asset-linked liability for the claims, **49** the following arises from a territorial (self-)limitation of the secondary insolvency proceedings:

The subject matter of Art 34 (2) of the EIR is the – legally imperative universal – **50** restriction of the legal essence of claims, but not the restriction of the transborder effects of the asset-linked liability for the claims. Any restricting of the asset-linked liability for claims through a reorganization plan in secondary insolvency proceedings may only affect the debtor's assets comprised within the secondary insolvency proceedings; such restrictions therefore lack any transborder effect since neither the *lex fori concursus secundarii* nor the creditors participating in the secondary insolvency proceedings are empowered, or possess the legal mechanisms, to affect the asset-linked liability for the claims in the main proceedings and in any other secondary insolvency proceedings.[48] There is actually no need for the regulation in Art 34 (2) of the EIR.

The purpose underlying Art 34 (2) of the EIR is to guaranty the substantive-law legal **51** essence of claims against the debtor. The restricting of claims through a reorganization plan in the secondary insolvency proceedings requires not only that the concerned creditors participate in these proceedings – through the lodging of their claim(s) – but also that they give their consent to the restrictions foreseen by the reorganization plan. If it were possible – contrary to what is prescribed by Art 34 (2) of the EIR – to restrict the substantive-law legal essence of a claim without the consent or against the will of the concerned creditor in the secondary insolvency proceedings, then it is imperative that such restrictions have a transborder effect; this is so because it is impossible to contain such substantive restrictions – for example a partial discharge of 30 % of the nominal value of a claim – within borders. A territorial splitting of the legal essence of a claim is impossible.[49] The indirect consequence of such a – imperatively, universally effective – restriction of the substantive-law legal essence of a claim is the simultaneous restriction of the – insolvency-relevant – asset-linked liability for such a claim since such liability cannot be greater than the substantive-law essence of a claim. A transborder, direct restriction of the substantive-law legal essence of a claim – and therefore an indirect restriction of the asset-linked liability for claims – would be incongruous with the territorial (self-)limitation of the secondary insolvency proceedings.

Where, however, a creditor consents to the restriction of the legal essence of his **52** claim, then such restriction is effective in respect of the debtor's universal assets. This is simply a consequence of the creditors' autonomy expressed by the reorganization plan that brings the proceedings to an end.

This interpretation of Art 34 (2) of the EIR, as safeguarding the substantive-law legal **53** essence of claims, simultaneously illustrates that restrictions to the legal essence of claims – including those of creditors who are not participating in the main proceedings

---

[48] Provisions of the *lex fori concursus secundarii* that restrict the asset-linked liability for claims that are not lodged in the secondary insolvency proceedings, for example sec 254 (1) sentence 3 InsO, have no force since liability cannot be linked to assets in the secondary insolvency proceedings for claims that have not been lodged in these proceedings.

[49] In-depth discussion: *Lüke* ZZP 111 (1998), 275, 307 et seq; *Flessner* in Stoll (ed), Stellungnahmen und Gutachten zur Reform des deutschen Internationalen Insolvenzrecht 1992, pp 201, 205; *Reinhart* Sanierungsverfahren im internationalen Insolvenzrecht 1995, 299 et seq, 301 et seq; MünchKomm InsO/*Reinhart* Art 34 EuInsVO mn 3.

and whose consent has not been given – are a matter for the reorganization plan in the main insolvency proceedings. This of course presupposes that the *lex fori concursus universalis* permits it.

54 Through this, individual creditors who do not, by waiving claims, participate in the reorganization through coordinated reorganization plans – which emanate from the main insolvency proceedings, are against the will of the minority, and which may be executed pursuant to the rules of the *lex fori concursus universalis* – are prevented from avoiding the universal restriction of claims, which is necessary for the reorganization, by seeking refuge in the secondary insolvency proceedings.

4.3 German Secondary Insolvency Proceedings[50]

55 In terms of its function, the insolvency plan contemplated by the German Insolvency Act fits seamlessly into Art 34 (2) of the EIR as outlined above: a restriction of claims arising from an insolvency plan does not, pursuant to Sec 254 *InsO*, encroach on the substantive-law legal essence of the claims. Although such claims continue to exist pursuant to substantive law both in terms of their legal essence and their value, there are no legal grounds for their satisfaction or enforcement.[51]

56 In order to prevent the possibility allowed for by the Regulation of a territorial splitting of the asset-linked liability a claim that is – universally - uniform in terms of its legal essence,[52] the German legislator introduced the requirement in Art 102 Sec 9 *EGInsO* that for reorganization plans containing encroachments on claims by means of a deferred payment, a discharge of debt, or through any other restrictions, all creditors affected must consent to it. Through this, encroachments – permissible pursuant to Art 34 (2) of the EIR that form part of a reorganization plan – on the asset-linked liability of claims of creditors who participate in the secondary insolvency proceedings, but do not consent to the reorganization plan, are precluded. Since the restriction of claims is generally instrumental to a reorganization plan, the approval of a reorganization insolvency plan as per Sec 217 et seq *InsO* is practically impossible.[53]

5. Stay of the Liquidation and the Debtor's Proposal (subsection 3)

57 The liquidator in the main insolvency proceedings is empowered to prevent the isolated reorganization in the secondary insolvency proceedings through a request to stay pursuant to Art 33 (1) of the EIR.

58 For the duration of the stay, only the liquidator in the main proceedings, or the debtor with the former's consent, is entitled to initiate a reorganization by submitting a reorganization plan.[54] No other reorganization plans may be proposed, put to a vote, or approved by a court.

59 The right to make the request to stay pursuant to Art 33 (1) of the EIR, in order to establish an exclusive right of the liquidator in the main insolvency proceedings to bring

[50] See comments on Art 102 Sec 9 EGInsO mn 2.

[51] Uhlenbruck Komm InsO/*Lüer* § 254 mn 8.

[52] See the reasons for art 102 sec 9 of the governmental draft act to amend international insolvency law of 23 Oct 2002, BT-Drucksache 15/16 of 25 Oct 2002, printed in ZIP 2002, 2331, 2334.

[53] On this, see: Haß/Huber/Gruber/Heiderhoff-*Heiderhoff* Art 34 EuInsVO mn 2, 6; *Wehdeking* DZWIR 2003, 133, 188.

[54] See the comments on Art 33 of the EIR mn 15, and *Virgós/Schmit* Explanatory Report mn 251; Moss/Fletcher/Isaacs-*Moss/Smith*, Regulation, mn 8.255.

about a reorganization plan, must be construed broadly. Only such a broad interpretation can do justice to the objective of the Regulation, this being the facilitation of a reorganization emanating from the main insolvency proceedings and extending to other proceedings.[55] This is supported by Art 34 of the EIR, which allows the liquidator in the main insolvency proceedings to influence the secondary insolvency proceedings.

Logically, the liquidator in the main insolvency proceedings must also be held authorized to request a stay pursuant to Art 33 (1) of the EIR even if liquidation measures have not yet commenced in the secondary insolvency proceedings.[56] Support for this broad interpretation of the right to make the request arising from Art 33 (1) of the EIR is found both in its wording and in the purpose of the stay, namely the safeguarding of the status quo of the insolvency estate of the secondary insolvency proceedings; from the moment secondary insolvency proceedings are opened, there is a permanent danger that the status quo will be altered through liquidation measures which are possible at any given time. **60**

Due to the coupling of Art 34 (3) to Art 33 (1) of the EIR, the request to stay must still be allowed even if the liquidation has already been stayed pursuant to the *lex fori concursus secundarii*, which may happen for example in German secondary insolvency proceedings pursuant to Sec 233 *InsO*. Since it is alone the stay of proceedings based on a request pursuant to Art 33 (1) of the EIR that upgrades the proposal right in Art 34 (1) 1st subpara of the EIR to an exclusive proposal right of the liquidator in the main insolvency proceedings, there is both a legal interest in the request to stay, as well as the interest – required by Art 33 (1) of the EIR for the making of the request – of the creditors in the main insolvency proceedings to stay the proceedings provided that it furthers the inter-procedural reorganization. **61**

Article 35
Assets remaining in the secondary proceedings

If by the liquidation of assets in the secondary proceedings it is possible to meet all established claims under those proceedings, the liquidator appointed in those proceedings shall immediately transfer any assets remaining to the liquidator in the main proceedings.

Contents

Index

[55] See Recital 20 of the EIR, as well as *Virgós/Schmit* Explanatory report mn 243.

[56] See the comments on Art 33 of the EIR mn 14.

Bibliography

Rajak The Inter-Relationship between Main an Secondary Bankruptcies, International Insolvency Institute (2004).

1. General

1 Art 35 of the EIR deals with the rather theoretical situation in which there is a surplus remaining after satisfying all of the established claims in the secondary insolvency proceedings. Due to the fact that creditors may lodge their claims in the secondary insolvency proceedings as well as in the main insolvency proceedings, the possibility of there being a surplus is rendered nearly non-existent.[1]

2 Art 35 of the EIR places the liquidator in the secondary insolvency proceedings under an obligation to transfer any assets remaining in his proceedings after the distribution to the liquidator in the main insolvency proceedings; the liquidator in the main insolvency proceedings is thereby entitled to such surplus, this ensuing directly from Community law.[2] The subject matter of the provision is substantive in nature. The insolvency court or the creditors are, pursuant to the *lex fori concursus secundarii,* responsible for supervising the liquidator's compliance with the obligation. International procedural-law rules empower the liquidator in the main insolvency proceedings to bring an action against the liquidator in the secondary insolvency proceedings to transfer the surplus.[3]

3 Art 35 of the EIR also makes clear the superiority of the main insolvency proceedings over the secondary insolvency proceedings.[4] The absence of a comparable provision that would obligate the liquidator in the main insolvency proceedings to transfer a remaining surplus to the liquidator(s) in the secondary insolvency proceedings is an unequivocal demonstration of this superior status.[5] The absence of a comparable provision must be accepted as *de lege lata.* The Regulation should, however, be amended in this regard as it is unacceptable that a surplus remaining in the main insolvency proceedings should be distributed to the debtors[6] when there are creditors in the secondary insolvency proceedings whose claims have not been satisfied. Although a regulation of this on the Community law level would very much be in place here, amendments on the national insolvency law level should also be legally possible since it is not apparent that the Regulation intended to conclusively preclude such an obligation to transfer a surplus.

4 As with Art 20 (2) of the EIR, this provision must also be viewed in light of the concept of an equitable treatment of creditors. The absence in Art 20 (2) of the EIR at the level of the individual creditors of an obligation to "transfer" the portion of a dividend that exceeds the dividend of creditors in other proceedings is, in contrast to this, being established at the level of the various insolvency proceedings through Art 35 of the EIR.

---

[1] *Virgós/Schmit* Explanatory report mn 252, 253; D-K/D/Ch-*Duursma-Kepplinger/Chalupsky* Art 35 mn 2; in Haß/Huber/Gruber/Heiderhoff-*Heiderhoff* Art 35 EuInsVO mn 1; Moss/Fletcher/Isaacs-*Moss/Smith*, Regulation, mn 8.260.

[2] *Rajak* The Inter-Relationship between Main an Secondary Bankruptcies, 14; *Smid* Komm EuInsVO Art 35 mn 6.

[3] *Smid* Komm EuInsVO Art 35 mn 6.

[4] D-K/D/Ch-*Duursma-Kepplinger/Chalupsky* Art 35 mn 1; Haß/Huber/Gruber/Heiderhoff-*Heiderhoff* Art 35 EuInsVO mn 1.

[5] Moss/Fletcher/Isaacs-*Moss/Smith*, Regulation, mn 8.260.

[6] Or for example in the case of the German Insolvency Act, to the shareholders of the debtor pursuant to company law winding-up provisions (sec 199 sentence 2 InsO).

Because the provision lacks practical relevancy, it should be viewed primarily as lending support to the principle of equitable treatment of creditors.

2. Surplus

Whether a de facto surplus remains after satisfying all of the established claims is to be determined pursuant to the respective *lex fori concursus secundarii*. In addition to liquid funds, a surplus may also comprise any non-liquidated assets of the debtor.[7] **5**

3. Immediate Transfer

The surplus must be transferred immediately to the liquidator in the main insolvency proceedings. Where the German Insolvency Act governs, this means immediately after the termination of the proceedings subsequent to a completed final distribution (Sec 200 (1) *Ins*O). **6**

4. Main Insolvency Proceedings

The obligation to transfer presupposes the existence of main insolvency proceedings. If they do not exist, because the surplus was achieved in independent territorial insolvency proceedings (see Art 3 (4) (a) of the EIR), then the surplus must be transferred to the debtor provided that this is prescribed by the *lex fori concursus particularis*.[8] Art 35 of the EIR is not relevant in this case.[9] The same would also have to apply if (previously opened) main insolvency proceedings are terminated and there is no possibility of a subsequent distribution, i.e. assets of the debtor are discovered subsequent to the termination of the main insolvency proceedings and, for legal reasons, they can no longer be distributed to the creditors. This may be the case where, upon an appeal by the debtor, the order ordering the opening of insolvency proceedings is conclusively *(res judicata)* set aside. However if main insolvency proceedings are terminated through a conclusive distribution, and if the *lex fori concursus universalis* allows subsequent distributions, then the obligation to transfer, in light of the aims of Art 35 of the EIR, is still in place. **7**

5. Characteristics of German Secondary Insolvency Proceedings

Where German secondary insolvency proceedings are stayed with the consent of the creditors (Sec 213 *Ins*O), Art 35 of the EIR cannot apply since the established claims have not been satisfied within the proceedings, or because the claims had not been established at all. Although the surplus assets are not to be transferred by the liquidator in the secondary insolvency proceedings to the liquidator in the main insolvency proceedings, they will – once the proceedings have been stayed – be caught within the confiscation powers of the main insolvency proceedings and can be included in its insolvency estate (see Art 18 (1) sentence 2 of the EIR). The same applies in the case of a stay due to **8**

---

[7] Moss/Fletcher/Isaacs-*Moss/Bayfield*, Regulation, mn 5.84.

[8] On this, see also: *Rajak* The Inter-Relationship between Main an Secondary Bankruptcies, 14.

[9] *Paulus* Komm EuInsVO Art 35, mn 1.

insufficiency of assets (Sec 207 *InsO* – assets insufficient to cover the costs of the proceedings), and a stay after the notification of inadequacy of assets (Sec 211 *InsO*). It may well happen in such cases that assets are returned to the debtor, e.g. in the case of assets that cannot be liquidated and objects that have not been released or liquidated.[10] But since all of the creditors have not been satisfied, one cannot speak of a surplus as understood in Art 35 of the EIR, nor has there been full satisfaction as required by it.

9 A stay pursuant to Sec 212 *InsO* based on the fact that the reason for opening the proceedings has ceased is not possible since main insolvency proceedings (Art 27 sentence 1 of the EIR) have already been opened.

Article 36
Subsequent opening of the main proceedings

Where the proceedings referred to in Article 3(1) are opened following the opening of the proceedings referred to in Article 3(2) in another Member State, Articles 31 to 35 shall apply to those opened first, in so far as the progress of those proceedings so permits.

Contents

Bibliography

Eidenmüller Europäische Verordnung über Insolvenzverfahren und zukünftiges deutsches internationales Insolvenzrecht, IPRax 2001, p 2; *Gottwald* Grenzüberschreitende Insolvenzen 1997; *Herchen* Das Übereinkommen über Insolvenzverfahren der Mitgliedstaaten der Europäischen Union vom 23.11.1995 (2000); *Kolmann* Kooperationsmodelle im Internationalen Insolvenzrecht – Empfiehlt sich für das deutsche internationale Insolvenzrecht eine Neuorientierung (2001); *Wimmer* Die Besonderheiten von Sekundärinsolvenzverfahren unter besonderer Berücksichtigung des Europäischen Insolvenzübereinkommens, ZIP 1998, p 982.

1. General[1]

1 Under certain conditions, Art 3 (4) of the EIR allows the opening of independent territorial insolvency proceedings prior to the opening of main insolvency proceedings. From both a pragmatic and a dogmatic point of view, it represents an exception to the rule that main insolvency proceedings should be opened first, and in the ideal case only these should be opened. However since the Regulation has opted for a coordinated mul-

[10] See sec 207 (3) sentence 2 InsO according to which the liquidator is no longer under an obligation to liquidate.

[1] On this, see also the comments on Art 32 of the EIR mn 1, 12 et seq, 32 et seq, Art 28 of the EIR mn 15 et seq; for the applicability of art 31 et seq of the EIR to isolated territorial insolvency proceedings, see the comments on Art 28 of the EIR mn 16.

tiplicity of proceedings, rather than one unified insolvency proceeding, it must regulate the effects of the subsequent opening of main insolvency proceedings on the coordination with previously opened territorial insolvency proceedings. This is accomplished through Art 36 of the EIR. According to Art 36 of the EIR, Art 31 to 35 of the EIR are applicable to the territorial insolvency proceedings opened first to the extent possible considering the progress of those proceedings.[2]

2. Requirements and Effects

Once the main insolvency proceedings are opened, the heretofore independent territorial insolvency proceedings are converted to secondary insolvency proceedings.[3] **2**

As laid down in Art 36 of the EIR, the provisions of Art 31 et seq of the EIR on co- **3** ordinating main and secondary insolvency proceedings are to be applied to the extent possible considering the progress of those proceedings. Derogations from the provisions of Art 31 et seq of the EIR are therefore only permitted if it is unavoidable in light of the particular status of the proceedings.

Support for the restrictive interpretation of Art 36 of the EIR can be found on the **4** one hand by a comparison to the wording of the Convention on Insolvency Proceedings of the Member States of the European Union of 23 November 1995,[4] which in this connection used the word "necessary".[5] In addition, Recital 17 of the EIR presumes that "if the main insolvency proceedings are opened, the territorial proceedings become secondary", i.e. as a rule, Art 31 et seq of the EIR are to apply.

The cooperation provisions of Art 31 et seq of the EIR will no longer need to be **5** applied once the aim of the cooperation becomes unachievable. An application of Art 31 et seq of the EIR in the manner contemplated by Art 36 of the EIR then becomes impossible. In order to answer the question as to when this is the case, a distinction must be drawn between reorganization and winding-up proceedings.

If the isolated territorial insolvency proceedings are winding-up proceedings, the **6** primary interest of the main insolvency proceedings is in receiving a surplus (Art 35 of the EIR). As long as a surplus – which is theoretically conceivable but extremely seldom –

---

2 On this, see: "Declaration by Portugal concerning the application of Articles 26 and 37 of Council Regulation (EC) No 1346/2000 of 29 May 2000 on insolvency proceedings" OJ of 30 June 2000, C 183/01: "Article 37 of Council Regulation (EC) No 1346/2000 on insolvency proceedings, which mentions the possibility of converting territorial proceedings opened prior to the main proceedings into winding-up proceedings, should be interpreted as meaning that such conversion does not exclude judicial appreciation of the state of the local proceedings (as is the case in Article 36) or of the application of the interests of public policy as provided for in Article 26."

3 See Recital 17 of the EIR; *Virgós/Schmit* Explanatory report mn 254; Moss/Fletcher/Isaacs-*Fletcher*, Regulation, mn 8.262; *Gottwald* Grenzüberschreitende Insolvenzen (1997), p 26, fn 75; HamburgerKomm-*Undritz* Art 36 mn 1.

4 On this, see: *Herchen* Das Übereinkommen über Insolvenzverfahren der Mitgliedstaaten der Europäischen Union vom 23.11.1995 (2000).

5 *Wimmer* ZIP 1998, 982, 988 holds that the word "necessary" is an editorial error, and that derogations from the provisions of art 31 et seq of the EIR are therefore only permissible if it is unavoidable in light of the progress of the particular proceedings; concurring: *Virgós/Schmit* Explanatory report mn 255; on this, see: D-K/D/Ch-*Duursma-Kepplinger/Chalupsky* Art 36 mn 2; *Eidenmüller* IPRax 2001, 2, 8.

has not yet been exhausted pursuant to the *lex fori concursus particularis*, i.e. it is still within the powers of disposition of the liquidator in the territorial insolvency proceedings, then the cooperation provisions of Art 31 et seq of the EIR must still be applied.[6]

7 If the isolated territorial insolvency proceedings are reorganization proceedings, the liquidator in the main insolvency proceedings must first decide whether he wishes to exercise his Art 37 of the EIR right to demand the conversion of the territorial insolvency proceeding to a winding-up proceeding.[7] Once the conversion has been effected, the aforementioned submissions apply.

8 If the liquidator in the main insolvency proceedings does not demand a conversion to winding-up proceedings, or if it is just not effected, the application of Art 31 et seq of the EIR is limited.[8]

9 Particularly the cooperation and communication obligations of Art 31 of the EIR should still be capable of application until the end of the territorial insolvency proceedings.[9] The exercising of creditors' rights pursuant to Art 32 of the EIR is possible as long as the transactions of the creditors spoken of in Art 32 of the EIR are permitted by the *lex fori concursus particularis*. Because of the absence of a liquidation process in reorganization proceedings, the application of Art 33 and 35 of the EIR would have to be excluded. The same applies to Art 34 (3) of the EIR based on the reference to Art 33 of the EIR.

10 Art 34 (1) of the EIR, particularly the second sentence, is equally incapable of being applied. An approval of the reorganization plan in the territorial insolvency proceedings cannot be made dependent on the consent of the liquidator in the main insolvency proceedings. Taken together, Art 34 (1) and 37 of the EIR operate to force the liquidator in the main insolvency proceedings, in such a case, to request that the reorganizing territorial insolvency proceedings be converted to winding-up proceedings pursuant to Art 37 of the EIR. After the conversion, he may if necessary propose a rescue plan, composition, or a comparable measure in accordance with Art 34 (1) sentence 1 of the EIR.

11 Art 34 (2) of the EIR does, however, apply. On closer examination, the provision can be regarded as a manifestation of the principle of coordinated multiple proceedings – universal main proceedings and territorial insolvency proceedings – and therefore must apply to the interaction between the universal and territorially limited proceedings. Subsection 2 embodies the general idea that the debtor's assets outside of the territory of the territorial insolvency proceedings may not – even indirectly – be drawn into these proceedings, and if they are then only with the consent of the affected creditors.

---

[6] An incorrect conclusion in the opinion of *Smid* Komm EuInsVO Art 36 mn 2 who finds that the goal of the cooperation is without merit as early as the phase when the insolvency estate is being distributed.

[7] On this, see: Moss/Fletcher/Isaacs-*Fletcher*, Regulation, mn 8.262.

[8] Concurring: Moss/Fletcher/Isaacs-*Moss/Smith*, Regulation, mn 8.262.; D-K/D/Ch-*Duursma-Kepplinger/Chalupsky* Art 36, mn 4; obvious dissenting opinion: *Kolmann* Kooperationsmodelle im Internationalen Insolvenzrecht – Empfiehlt sich für das deutsche internationale Insolvenzrecht eine Neuorientierung (2001), p 332; *Smid* Komm EuInsVO Art 36 mn 3.

[9] MünchKomm InsO/*Reinhart* Art 36 EuInsVO mn 1.

Article 37
Conversion of earlier proceedings

The liquidator in the main proceedings may request that proceedings listed in Annex A previously opened in another Member State be converted into winding-up proceedings if this proves to be in the interests of the creditors in the main proceedings.

The court with jurisdiction under Article 3(2) shall order conversion into one of the proceedings listed in Annex B.

Contents

Index

Bibliography

Kolmann Kooperationsmodelle im Internationalen Insolvenzrecht – Empfiehlt sich für das deutsche internationale Insolvenzrecht eine Neuorientierung (2001); *Morscher* Die europäische Insolvenzverordnung (2002); *Wimmer* Die Besonderheiten von Sekundärinsolvenzverfahren unter besonderer Berücksichtigung des Europäischen Insolvenzübereinkommens, ZIP 1998, p 982.

1. General

Art 37 of the EIR regulates the conversion of (independent) territorial insolvency proceedings structured as reorganization proceedings pursuant to Annex A of the EIR to winding-up proceedings pursuant to Annex B of the EIR. The conversion is effected through the court of the territorial insolvency proceedings (solely) upon request of the liquidator in the main insolvency proceedings and only if it is in the interests of the creditors in the main insolvency proceedings. Whether or not to make the request is at the discretion of the liquidator in the main insolvency proceedings. **1**

The right of the liquidator in the main proceedings to request the conversion makes particularly clear that the territorial insolvency proceedings are subordinate to the main insolvency proceedings and subordinate to the interests of the creditors in these proceedings.[1] The interests of these creditors is the decisive factor for the competent court when **2**

[1] *Virgós/Schmit* Explanatory report mn 210, 258; D-K/D/Ch-*Duursma-Kepplinger/Chalupsky* Art 37 mn 7.

deciding to order a conversion. It is of course preferable that the conversion be made with the consent of the liquidator of the territorial insolvency proceedings.[2]

3 Art 37 of the EIR is only relevant in those Member States that differentiate between reorganization and winding-up proceedings.[3] Thus the provision has no practical relevance for German territorial insolvency proceedings.[4] The German Insolvency Act contemplates only one uniform insolvency proceeding, which can be terminated either through a winding-up or a reorganization via an insolvency plan. This is acknowledged by the Regulation on the one hand by the fact that insolvency proceedings are listed in Annex A of the EIR as insolvency proceedings within the meaning of the definition in Art 2 (a) of the EIR and in Annex B of the EIR as winding-up proceedings within the meaning of the definition in Art 2 (c) of the EIR, and on the other hand by the fact that a conversion pursuant to Art 37 of the EIR must be made from a proceeding listed in Annex A to a proceeding listed in Annex B of the EIR. In the case of German territorial insolvency proceedings, Art 37 of the EIR can also not be construed in a way which allows the liquidator in the main proceedings to request the interruption of insolvency-plan proceedings in favour of winding-up proceedings pursuant to the Insolvency Act since a winding-up via insolvency-plan proceedings is also possible.[5] It is also hard to imagine that insolvency-plan proceedings in territorial insolvency proceedings could ever lead to the reorganization of the debtor, which has to have a universal effect.[6]

4 Portugal has made a unilateral declaration[7] of interpretation of Art 37 of the EIR pursuant to which Portuguese courts, for the purposes of safeguarding important local interests within the meaning of Art 26 of the EIR, are entitled to resort to the *ordre public* rule if these interests have not been sufficiently taken into consideration in the application of Art 37 of the EIR.[8] According to this, when deciding whether the conversion should be ordered, Portuguese courts may also in addition to the interests of the creditors in the main insolvency proceedings take the "situation of the local proceedings" into account, which probably means, like in Art 36 of the EIR, the state of the proceeding. This declaration is presumably not legally binding. This is only one possible, tenable interpretation.

---

[2] *Paulus* Komm EuInsVO Art 37 mn 3 et seq goes further and finds that the discretion may only be considered as properly exercised if this mutual consent has been obtained.

[3] On this, see: *Morscher* Die europäische Insolvenzverordnung 2002, p 55. D-K/D/Ch-*Duursma-Kepplinger/Chalupsky* Art 37 mn 4 find that it is of limited relevance for Austria.

[4] Haß/Huber/Gruber/Heiderhoff-*Heiderhoff* Art 37 EuInsVO mn 1.

[5] MünchKomm InsO/*Reinhart* Art 37 EuInsVO mn 1; obvious dissenting opinion: *Smid* Komm EuInsVO Art 37 mn 5 in whose opinion the German insolvency court, upon a request based on art 37 of the EIR, must refuse to approve the insolvency plan in territorial insolvency proceedings.

[6] MünchKomm InsO/*Reinhart* Art 37 EuInsVO mn 1 with further references; *Wimmer* ZIP 1998, 982, 989.

[7] Declaration made by Portugal to the application of Articles 26 and 37 of the Regulation (EC) No. 1346/2000 of 29 May 2000 on Insolvency Proceedings, OJ EC of 30 June 2000, C 183/01: "Article 37 of Council Regulation (EC) No 1346/2000 on insolvency proceedings, which mentions the possibility of converting territorial proceedings opened prior to the main proceedings into winding-up proceedings, should be interpreted as meaning that such conversion does not exclude judicial appreciation of the state of the local proceedings (as is the case in Article 36) or of the application of the interests of public policy as provided for in Article 26."

[8] *Virgós/Schmit* Explanatory report mn 210; D-K/D/Ch-*Duursma-Kepplinger/Chalupsky* Art 37 mn 3; Moss/Fletcher/Isaacs-*Moss/Smith*, Regulation, mn 8.268; *Smid* Komm EuInsVO Art 37 mn 2.

2. Scope of Application

Art 37 of the EIR is applicable only to those independent territorial insolvency proceedings contemplated by Art 3 (4) of the EIR.[9] This does not follow directly from the wording of Art 37 of the EIR, but rather from the logic of Art 37 and 3 (3) sentence 2 of the EIR and by construing the two articles as a whole. After the opening of main insolvency proceedings, only winding-up proceedings within the meaning of Annex B of the EIR may be opened (see Art 2 (c) of the EIR as well). A comparison of Annex A and B of the EIR makes it clear that winding-up proceedings are to be considered the opposite of reorganization proceedings. The insolvency proceedings pursuant to Annex A of the EIR that are referred to in Art 37 of the EIR – which clearly includes winding-up proceedings – can therefore only involve reorganization proceedings. **5**

Another requirement is that the territorial insolvency proceedings must be listed in Annex A of the EIR. If the type of proceeding is not listed there, then it does not fall within the sphere of application of the Regulation (see Art 1 (1) in conjunction with Art 2 (a) of the EIR).[10] Such proceedings are not capable of hindering the extension of the effects of the main insolvency proceedings to the territory of these proceedings; the assets in the State of the territorial insolvency proceedings are subject to the confiscation powers of the main insolvency proceedings. Based on the automatic *(ex lege)* and thus mandatory recognition resulting from Art 16 and 17 of the EIR, it is necessary to stay the proceedings that have already been opened since these proceedings will be divested of their entire assets through the confiscation powers of the main insolvency proceedings. Where the national law is silent on this,[11] a stay of proceedings analogous to Art 102 Sec 4 (1) sentence 1 *EGInsO* in German law would be in order. This provision may be directly applied to stay main insolvency proceedings pursuant to Art 3 (1) of the EIR in favour of prior-ranking main insolvency proceedings in another Member State.[12] **6**

3. Competent Court

According to Art 37 sentence 2 of the EIR, the competent court is the court that has jurisdiction pursuant to Art 3 (2) of the EIR. This referral is unfortunate both from a systematic point of view and in terms of its wording; Art 3 (2) of the EIR alone deals with international jurisdiction, coupling this to the existence of an establishment as defined in Art 2 (h) of the EIR. Considering that – in the constellation envisioned by Art 37 of the EIR – territorial insolvency proceedings pursuant to Art 3 (4) and (3) of the EIR have already been opened, the issue of international jurisdiction for the conversion is reduced to a question of allocating jurisdiction for the conversion as between the insolvency court of the main proceedings and the insolvency court of the territorial insolvency proceedings. This is all that Art 37 of the EIR deals with. Art 37 of the EIR therefore **7**

---

9 Moss/Fletcher/Isaacs-*Moss/Smith*, Regulation, mn 8.265; D-K/D/Ch-*Duursma-Kepplinger/Chalupsky* Art 37 mn 4.

10 *Virgós/Schmit* Explanatory Report mn 261; D-K/D/Ch-*Duursma-Kepplinger/Chalupsky* Art 37 mn 9.

11 See D-K/D/Ch-*Duursma-Kepplinger/Chalupsky* Art 37 mn 9.

12 In the alternative, the liquidator in the main insolvency proceedings may request secondary insolvency proceedings pursuant to art 3 (2) of the EIR. However, it is necessary to stay the territorial insolvency proceedings prior to their opening because of the inclusion of the State of the territorial insolvency proceedings in the main insolvency proceedings. On this, see also: HamburgerKomm-*Undritz* Art 37 mn 5.

allocates jurisdiction in the matter to the court that opened the territorial insolvency proceedings.

4. Requirements for a Conversion

4.1 Request

8 A conversion may only be made pursuant to a request by the liquidator in the main insolvency proceedings.[13] The main insolvency proceeding must therefore not be terminated.[14] Whether or not to make the request is at the discretion of the liquidator in the main insolvency proceedings. The consent of the liquidator in the territorial insolvency proceedings is not required. Such a requirement is not found in the unequivocal wording of the provision nor by referring to Recital 19 of the EIR and the special function of territorial insolvency proceedings, which is the safeguarding of national interests.[15] This does not, however, relieve the court of its obligation to review the grounds for the request.

9 Based on the unequivocal wording of the provision, the ordering of a conversion by the court on its own motion is not possible; this is so, even if the liquidator in the main insolvency proceedings erroneously fails to make the request in a case where a conversion is undoubtedly in the interests of the creditors of the main insolvency proceedings.[16] This right to make the request, as a substantive law provision, directly modifies the national insolvency law regimes of the Member States, and excludes a conversion *ex officio*, even if it would possible pursuant to the *lex fori concursus secundarii.*[17]

10 The decision whether or not to make an Art 37 of the EIR request is at the discretion of the liquidator in the main insolvency proceedings. The German term "kann"[18] not only awards him the power to make the request, but also the discretion whether or not to exercise such power.[19] In the case of a misjudgement, however, he may be liable for damages under the particular national law.[20] Under German law, the exercising of the discretion in observance of the interests of the creditors in his proceedings constitutes an insolvency-specific obligation within the meaning of Sec 60 *InsO*.

11 When making the request, the liquidator in the main insolvency proceedings must submit[21] and, if needed, prove[22] that the conversion is in the interests of the creditors in the main insolvency proceedings.

12 The temporary administrator under German law is not afforded a right to make a request based on the fact that he is not listed in Annex C of the EIR. Any other view

[13] See the references by Moss/Fletcher/Isaacs-*Moss/Smith*, Regulation, mn 8.266, fn 197 to the English provisions on dealing with such requests in the Insolvency (Amendment) Rules 2002.

[14] On the consequences of the termination, see Art 27 of the EIR mn 22.

[15] But see: *Paulus* Komm EuInsVO Art 37 mn 3, 5.

[16] D-K/D/Ch-*Duursma-Kepplinger/Chalupsky* Art 37 mn 6; Haß/Huber/Gruber/Heiderhoff-*Heiderhoff* Art 37 mn 2, fn 4; FK-InsO/*Wimmer* Art 102 EGInsO mn 168, *Smid* Komm EuInsVO Art 37 mn 3.

[17] See Moss/Fletcher/Isaacs-*Moss/Smith*, Regulation, mn 8.266.

[18] In English "may".

[19] D-K/D/Ch-*Duursma-Kepplinger/Chalupsky* Art 37 mn 2, 5; *Wimmer* ZIP 1998, 982, 989.

[20] D-K/D/Ch-*Duursma-Kepplinger/Chalupsky* Art 37 mn 6 Art 31 mn 26 et seq.

[21] *Smid* Komm EuInsVO Art 37 mn 5.

[22] *Virgós/Schmit* Explanatory Report mn 258; Moss/Fletcher/Isaacs-*Moss/Smith*, Regulation, mn 8.266.

would be incorrect since, because of the request, territorial insolvency proceedings would most likely be irreversibly converted into winding-up proceedings even though it is not yet certain whether main insolvency proceedings will ever be opened at all.[23] For the same reasons, the decision of the ECJ in the Eurofood/Parmalat case[24] also does not allow any other conclusion.

4.2 Test to be Applied by the Insolvency Court

Prevailing opinion holds[25] that the competent insolvency court is not to blindly order the conversion without examining the facts itself, although the choice of the word "order" could certainly be so understood.[26] **13**

According to this opinion, the competent insolvency court must review whether the conversion is in the interests of the creditors in the main insolvency proceedings, and is not limited to merely examining whether the liquidator's assumption (that the conversion is in the interests of the creditors in the main insolvency proceedings) is tenable or whether it is an erroneous exercise of discretion. But since the Regulation provides no guidelines for the court's decision, the only possibility in this respect is to resort to the *lex fori concursus secundarii*. The decision to convert the proceedings is, because of the effects of the conversion, comparable to the decision to open insolvency proceedings and should not be put on the same footing as an act of the liquidator in proceedings that are already opened; in the latter case, the German insolvency court is only obliged to examine the (formal) legality, but not the expediency, of the act. In order to open German insolvency proceedings, the court must be convinced of the existence of a reason to open such proceedings, i.e. it must be convinced of the de facto insolvency of the debtor. The court must equally be convinced that the conversion is in the interests of the creditors in the main insolvency proceedings. **14**

4.3 Conversion in the Interests of the Creditors of the Main Insolvency Proceedings

The Regulation does not provide any guidelines for deciding whether the conversion is proper or not within the meaning of Art 37 of the EIR. **15**

A finding in favour of a conversion would have to be made in a case where winding-up proceedings would produce a surplus pursuant to Art 35 of the EIR whose transfer to the main insolvency proceedings would increase the dividend to be distributed there.[27] This seems logical provided that the increase is not too minimal. But since the Regulation is silent as to any guidelines for measuring this, and the setting of any limit would appear arbitrary, it must be presumed that any dividend increase suffices, even if it is extremely small. **16**

Also conceivable is the case where the reorganization of the debtor in the main insolvency proceedings requires a specific asset that is subject to the secondary insolvency proceedings and that is needed there for the reorganization of the establishment. Only a winding-up proceeding, i.e. through a liquidation, would enable the liquidator in the main insolvency proceedings to acquire this asset for the main insolvency proceedings. **17**

---

[23] But see: *Smid* Komm EuInsVO Art 37 mn 4.

[24] NZI 2006, 360 et seq.

[25] *Duursma* D-K/D/Ch-*Duursma-Kepplinger/Chalupsky* Art 37 mn 5; Moss/Fletcher/Isaacs-*Moss/Smith*, Regulation, mn 8.267; see also: Rules 1.33, 2.61, 5.33 Insolvency (Amendment) Rules 2002; dissenting opinion: *Smid* Komm EuInsVO Art 37 mn 7.

[26] See Moss/Fletcher/Isaacs-*Moss/Smith*, Regulation, mn 8.267.

[27] *Smid* Komm EuInsVO Art 37 mn 5.

Such a conversion would also be done in the interests of the creditors in the main insolvency proceedings.

18 A conversion is not to be regarded as not being in the interests of the creditors in the main insolvency proceedings merely because the main insolvency proceedings are being conducted as reorganization proceedings. A conversion in such a case may still be in the interests of the creditors in the main insolvency proceedings if, for example, in order to accomplish a reorganization in the main insolvency proceedings, it is necessary to close an establishment situated in another Member State that is subject to territorial insolvency proceedings.[28]

5. Conversion Proceedings

19 The Regulation contains no rules concerning the conversion proceeding.[29] This is not surprising. Although Community law is the suitable instrument for ordering the conversion, it is not suited for creating abstract rules to govern every conceivable constellation of conversion from proceedings in Annex A to those in Annex B of the EIR. The detailed regulation of the conversion is a matter for the national law regimes. Due to the absence of any practical relevance for converting German territorial insolvency proceedings, German law contains no such provisions.[30]

6. Absence of Conversion

20 If the liquidator in the main insolvency proceedings does not request the conversion, or if the court does not order it, the territorial insolvency proceedings are to be resumed as secondary insolvency proceedings pursuant to the provisions of Art 36 of the EIR.[31]

Article 38
Preservation measures

Where the court of a Member State which has jurisdiction pursuant to Article 3(1) appoints a temporary administrator in order to ensure the preservation of the debtor's assets, that temporary administrator shall be empowered to request any measures to secure and preserve any of the debtor's assets situated in another Member State, provided for under the law of that State, for the period between the request for the opening of insolvency proceedings and the judgment opening the proceedings.

→ Cf Art 19 UNCITRAL Model Law

[28] This example by FK-InsO/*Wimmer* Art 102 EGInsO mn 166. D-K/D/Ch-*Duursma-Kepplinger/Chalupsky* Art 37 mn 2 who points out that although such a closure constitutes a particular hardship for the affected employees and business partners, it is nevertheless anchored in the logic of the Regulation which prescribes in art 3 (3) sentence 2 that secondary insolvency proceedings must be winding-up proceedings.

[29] Critical: *Kolmann* Kooperationsmodelle im Internationalen Insolvenzrecht – Empfiehlt sich für das deutsche internationale Insolvenzrecht eine Neuorientierung 2001, p 333.

[30] See mn 3 above.

[31] See the comments on Art 36 of the EIR mn 2 et seq.

Contents

Index

Bibliography

Duursma-Kepplinger Aktuelle Entwicklungen in Bezug auf die Auslegung der Vorschriften über die internationale Eröffnungszuständigkeit nach der Europäischen Insolvenzverordnung, DZWiR 2006, p 177; *Fritz/Bähr* Die Europäische Verordnung über Insolvenzverfahren – Herausforderung an Gerichte und Insolvenzverwalter, DZWiR 2001, p 221; *Herchen* Das Übereinkommen über Insolvenzverfahren der Mitgliedstaaten der Europäischen Union vom 23.11.1995 (2000); *Lüke* Das europäische internationale Insolvenzrecht, ZZP 111 (1998), p 275; *Paulus* Die europäische Insolvenzverordnung und der deutsche Insolvenzverwalter, NZI 2001, p 505; *Wimmer* Anmerkungen zum Vorlagebeschluß des irischen Supreme Court in Sachen Parmalat, ZInsO 2005, p 119.

1. General

As a substantive law provision, Art 38 of the EIR confers on the temporary administrator of the main insolvency proceedings, for the purposes of securing and preserving the debtor's assets in any other Member State[1] in which assets of the debtor are situated, 1

[1] In dispute; see mn 10 et seq below.

an autonomous procedural right to request the execution of any measures that are provided for by the Member State for the time between the request to open insolvency proceedings and its opening.

2 Because such measures are designed to maintain the status quo, the request for preservation measures pursuant to the *lex fori concursus territorialis* also serves to pave the way for secondary insolvency proceedings, provided that such proceedings are not prohibited by the Regulation.

3 Supplementary to other means of preserving the assets of the debtor, and thus improving the chances of recovery of the creditors as a whole, some of the insolvency law regimes of the Member States provide for the appointment of the temporary administrator referred to in Art 38 of the EIR as a preservation measure.[2]

4 In addition to Art 38 of the EIR, the preservation measures ordered by the insolvency court of the main insolvency proceedings (see Art 25 (1) subpara 3 of the EIR)[3] must be recognized and enforced if need be; the "appointing of a temporary administrator" represents just one of these means of securing and preserving the insolvency estate.

5 The temporary administrator's powers to secure and preserve the insolvency estate are governed primarily by the *lex fori concursus universalis*. It is correct that the powers conferred on the temporary administrator pursuant to the *lex fori concursus universalis* relate to the debtor's assets worldwide. The automatic recognition of the appointment of the temporary administrator and his powers in the other Member States is provided for in the Regulation through Art 25 (1) subpara 3 in the same manner as Art 18 of the EIR does in respect of the (final) liquidator.[4]

6 Nevertheless, the *lex fori concursus universalis* does not create a right to request judicial measures in the sovereign territories of foreign countries. Art 38 of the EIR therefore widens[5] the scope of the temporary administrator's procedural powers in this respect. It also compensates for the fact that, neither pursuant to the intentions of the drafters of the Regulation[6] nor to prevailing legal opinion, is the temporary administrator of the main proceedings granted the right to request the opening of secondary insolvency proceedings.[7]

7 The enforcement of a preservation measure in another Member State in compliance with its (ordinary) *lex fori concursus territorialis*[8] will probably be enforced more readily

---

[2] For example: German law (sec 21 et seq InsO), Austrian law (sec 73 KO), Irish law (sec 226 (1) Companies Act 1963), and Czech law; for English law see: Moss/Fletcher/Isaacs-*Moss/Bayfield*, Regulation, mn 5.88; otherwise see the country reports in this commentary and in the Münchener Kommentar zur Insolvenzordnung, vol 3, 2003.

[3] On this: mn 48 et seq below and Art 25 of the EIR mn 25 et seq.

[4] *Virgós/Schmit* Explanatory report mn 198, 262; Haß/Huber/Gruber/Heiderhoff-*Gruber* Art 25 EuInsVO mn 12; D-K/D/Ch-*Duursma-Kepplinger* Art 25 mn 59, 60; Moss/Fletcher/Isaacs-*Moss/Smith*, Regulation, mn 8.269; *Paulus* NZI 2001, 505, 510; *Wimmer* ZInsO 2005, 119, 126; see also: FK-InsO/*Wimmer* Anhang I nach § 358, mn 35, 132 et seq; dissenting opinion: *Smid* Komm EuInsVO Art 38 mn 3.

[5] *Martini* ZInsO 2002 905, 910.

[6] See *Virgós/Schmit* Explanatory Report mn 119.

[7] See Art 29 of the EIR mn 6, 19, and Haß/Huber/Gruber/Heiderhoff-*Gruber* Art 29 EuInsVO mn 1; *Leible/Staudinger* KTS 2000, 533, 570; MünchKomm InsO/*Reinhart* Art 29 EuInsVO mn 1; HK-InsO/*Stephan* Art 29 EuInsVO mn 2; *Vallender* InVO 2005, 41, 45; dissenting opinion: *Smid* Komm EuInsVO Art 29 mn 5 who would grant the temporary administrator the right to request if a general prohibition of disposition pursuant to sec 21 (2) no 2, 1st alternative InsO has been imposed on the debtor.

[8] The *lex fori concursus territorialis* is being

than one pursuant to the (unknown) *lex fori concursus universalis*, which would be enforceable pursuant to Art 25 (1) subpara 3 of the EIR; the latter measure most likely cannot be introduced into the legal system of the concerned Member State without some kind of modification or without causing some kind of problem.[9]

In some cases, the preservation measures contemplated by the *lex fori concursus territorialis* may even be more advantageous, e.g. they may go further, than those provided for by the *lex fori concursus universalis*.[10] 8

Finally, Art 38 of the EIR makes it clear that the appointment of a temporary administrator must be recognized especially in those Member States whose insolvency law regimes do not provide for temporary administrators.[11] 9

2. Requirements for the Application of Article 38 of the EIR

2.1 Establishment

There is no consensus on whether the power pursuant to Art 38 of the EIR is conferred on temporary administrators of main insolvency proceedings in every Member State, or only in those in which secondary insolvency proceedings may be opened, i.e. where there is an establishment within the meaning of Art 2 (h) of the EIR. 10

Widely held opinion correctly favours the former.[12] The wording of the provision certainly does not allow the inference of a territorial restriction of the temporary administrator's right to request. The purpose of securing assets, whose existence in a Member State is – by its very nature – independent of the existence of an establishment, also rules out a restrictive interpretation of Art 38. This must apply even more so considering that the risk of removing assets that are not connected to an establishment is even greater than in the case of assets connected to a business operation. 11

The minority opinion here, were it adhered to, goes too far since it in effect imposes on the competent court, in its examination of the existence of an establishment, the burden of examining and affirming the admissibility of a (hypothetical) request to open secondary insolvency proceedings.[13] 12

---

referred to here rather than *lex fori concursus secundarii* since, in our opinion, even in those Member States in which the requirements for opening secondary insolvency proceedings have not been satisfied, requests pursuant to art 38 of the EIR are still allowed (see mn 10 et seq below).

[9] *Herchen* Das Übereinkommen über Insolvenzverfahren der Mitgliedstaaten der Europäischen Union vom 23.11.1995 (2000), p 161.

[10] *Lüke* ZZP 111 (1998), 275, 295.

[11] *Wimmer* ZInsO 2005, 119, 126.

[12] Concurring: *Herchen* Das Übereinkommen über Insolvenzverfahren der Mitgliedstaaten der Europäischen Union vom 23.11.1995 (2000), p 162; Moss/Fletcher/Isaacs-*Moss/Bayfield*, Regulation, mn 5.88; Moss/Fletcher/Isaacs-*Moss/Smith*, Regulation, mn 8.269; MünchKomm InsO/*Reinhart* Art 38 EuInsVO mn 1; *Smid* Komm EuInsVO Art 38 mn 10; HamburgerKomm-*Undritz* Art 38 mn 3; dissenting opinion: *Virgós/Schmit* Explanatory report mn 262; *Duursma-Kepplinger* DZWiR 2006, 177 et seq; D-K/D/Ch-*Duursma-Kepplinger/Chalupsky* Art 38 mn 9 et seq; *Fritz/Bähr* DZWIR 2001, 221, 226; Haß/Huber/Gruber/Heiderhoff-*Gruber* Art 38 EuInsVO mn 2; *Leible/Staudinger* KTS 2000, 533, 570; *Paulus* Komm EuInsVO Art 38 mn 2; *Paulus* NZI 2001, 505, 510; *Smid* Deutsches und Europäisches Internationales Insolvenzrecht 2004, art 38, mn 12; FK-InsO/*Wimmer* Anhang I zu Art 102 EGInsO mn 174; undecided: FK-InsO/*Wimmer* Anhang I nach § 358, mn 132 et seq.

[13] FK-InsO/*Wimmer* Anhang I zu Art 102 EGInsO mn 174.

2.2 Establishment and Secured Rights Pursuant to Articles 5 and 7 of the EIR

13 There are, however, certain hesitations to the conferring of an Art 38 of the EIR right of request in all Member States,[14] namely in such Member States where, although no establishment exists, objects are situated to which secured rights within the meaning of Articles 5 and 7 of the EIR are attached.[15] According to Articles 5 and 7 of the EIR, these rights *in rem* are not affected by the opening of main insolvency proceedings. It could similarly be argued that, absent the existence of an establishment pursuant to Art 2 (h) of the EIR, secured rights could not be caught by the insolvency process via the opening of secondary insolvency proceedings. In such circumstances, it is questionable whether requests to order preservation measures are justified pursuant to the *lex fori concursus territorialis* when they are requested in respect of rights protected under Articles 5 and 7 of the EIR. This may be the case in German law, for example, where an application is made pursuant to Section 21 (2) No 3 *InsO* to prevent or temporarily stay the execution of an order to recover possession of the creditor's property – a retention of title – in an object in the debtor's possession.

14 However due to the urgent nature of these measures, preservation measures will have to be allowed even in such circumstances at least where German law governs in respect of foreign proceedings.[16] In the making of such urgent judicial decisions, it is often not possible to conclusively determine whether the rights *in rem* contemplated by Articles 5 and 7 of the EIR have been validly established in the particular assets of the debtor.[17] The purpose of preservation measures, i.e. to maintain the status quo, also provides the court and the liquidator with the opportunity to make the factual and legal assessments required here.

2.3 No Opening of Territorial Insolvency Proceedings

15 It is clear that preservation measures may not be ordered pursuant to the *lex fori concursus particularis* where territorial insolvency proceedings pursuant to Art 3 (4) of the EIR have already been opened in the Member State concerned.[18] An Art 38 of the EIR request that is made to a German insolvency court would have to be denied based on an absence of a need for legal protection.

2.4 Request

16 The ordering of preservation measures pursuant to the *lex fori concursus territorialis* may only be made upon a request to do so. By creating a Community-wide, uniform substantive rule, Art 38 of the EIR not only confers on the temporary administrator in the main insolvency proceedings a special right to make the request, but simultaneously upgrades the request to a requirement for granting the preservation measures pursuant to the respective *lex fori concursus territorialis*; this is so even if the latter – e.g. German law in Sec 21 *InsO* – contemplates the granting of preservation measures on the court's own motion.[19]

---

[14] See mn 10 et seq above.

[15] In-depth discussion: *Herchen* Das Übereinkommen über Insolvenzverfahren der Mitgliedstaaten der Europäischen Union vom 23.11.1995 (2000), pp 163–165.

[16] Even different opinion: *Herchen* Das Übereinkommen über Insolvenzverfahren der Mitgliedstaaten der Europäischen Union vom 23.11.1995 (2000), pp 163–165.

[17] See in Jaeger Komm InsO/*Gerhardt* § 21 mn 4.

[18] *Paulus* NZI 2001, 505, 510.

[19] German law requires, however, that an admissible request to open insolvency pro-

2.4.1 Temporary Administrator in the Main Insolvency Proceedings

The temporary administrator appointed by the court with jurisdiction per Art 3 (1) of the EIR for the (future) main insolvency proceedings is empowered to make the request. Where it later becomes apparent that the jurisdiction pursuant to Art 3 (1) of the EIR was erroneously assumed, see mn 40 et seq below. **17**

Whether or not the temporary administrator is listed as such in Annex C of the EIR is irrelevant. Annex C of the EIR defines only the liquidator for the purposes of the Regulation (see Art 2 (b) of the EIR), but not the temporary administrator.[20] Although the temporary administrators of the Austrian Bankruptcy Act and the German Insolvency Act are included in Annex C of the EIR, these do not really correspond to the definition of a liquidator contained in Art 2 (b) of the EIR; the liquidation of the insolvency estate spoken of in Art 2 (b) of the EIR is contradictory to the basic task of a temporary administrator which is limited to the securing of such estate. **18**

2.4.2 So-called Weak and Strong Temporary Administrator in German Law

Since the temporary administrator *(vorläufiger Insolvenzverwalter)* of the German Insolvency Act is expressly mentioned in Annex C of the EIR, it can be deduced that, in the case of German main insolvency proceedings, both the weak temporary administrator (Sec 21 (1), (2) No 1 and No 2, Sec 22 (2) *InsO*) and the strong temporary administrator (Section 21 (1), (2) No. 1, Section 22 (1) sentence 1 *InsO*) are entitled to make Art 38 of the EIR requests in the other Member States.[21] The legal protection that the Annexes intend to supply does not allow a distinction to be drawn here in respect of the application of Art 38 of the EIR; through Annex C of the EIR, both the weak and the strong temporary administrator are defined without any linguistic differentiation as liquidators within the meaning of the Regulation. The wording of Art 38 of the EIR also allows for no distinction to be made. **19**

2.4.3 Liquidator in the Main Insolvency Proceedings

According to its unequivocal wording, Art 38 of the EIR does not afford the liquidator in the main insolvency proceedings a right to make a request. **20**

The Regulation is silent, however, with respect to the possibilities open to the liquidator in the main insolvency proceedings to affect the preservation measures that were requested by the temporary administrator pursuant to Art 38 of the EIR, granted by the competent court, and still in force at the time of the opening of the main insolvency proceedings.[22] **21**

Since the Regulation in Art 38 of the EIR invokes the *lex fori concursus territorialis* with respect to the ordering of preservation measures, uniform substantive law simply introduces a special right on the part of the temporary administrator to make a request, it would seem logical to entrust matters concerning the effects, widening, restricting, and ending of preservation measures to the *lex fori concursus territorialis* as well. **22**

Depending on which *lex fori concursus territorialis* is invoked, certain modifications to the insolvency law invoked may have to be made in the individual case. In German **23**

---

ceedings has been made at the court from which preservation measures are being sought; see here: mn 33, 34, 46, et seq below.

[20] *Virgós/Schmit* Explanatory report mn 263; D-K/D/Ch-*Duursma-Kepplinger/Chalupsky* Art 38 mn 3.

[21] Possible dissenting opinion: *Smid* Komm EuInsVO Art 38 mn 5.

[22] For the effects of the opening of the main insolvency proceedings, see mn 44 below.

insolvency law, for example, certain legal consequences ensue from a withdrawal of the Art 38 of the EIR request. As the party entitled to make the request, the temporary administrator in the main insolvency proceedings is allowed to withdraw the request. And since the liquidator in the main insolvency proceedings steps into the legal shoes of the temporary administrator of the main proceedings, the same must apply to him.[23]

2.5 Assets in Another Member State

24 The Art 38 of the EIR request presupposes that assets of the debtor are situated in the Member State concerned.

25 The preservation measures ordered pursuant to Art 38 of the EIR in conjunction with the *lex fori concursus territorialis* may only be made in respect of those assets of the debtor that are situated in the Member State in which the request is made. The Regulation prohibits any transborder effects of preservation measures.

3. The Ordering of Preservation Measures Pursuant to the *lex fori concursus territorialis*

3.1 Applicable Law

26 The ordering of preservation measures, i.e. especially whether they are to be ordered at all, the form of the court decision, its content[24], and its further procedural treatment,[25] is governed by the *lex fori concursus territorialis*.[26]

3.2 Applicable Test Pursuant to the *lex fori concursus territorialis*

27 When confronted with Art 38 of the EIR requests, the courts must fully examine whether all of the factual requirements of the *lex fori concursus territorialis* are present. This is imperative since Art 38 of the EIR invokes the *lex fori concursus territorialis* as the law applicable to the ordering of preservation measures.[27]

28 However if the *lex fori concursus territorialis* requires the existence of an admissible, or even a mere pending, request to open insolvency proceedings, this requirement is deemed satisfied by the request to open proceedings that was made to the court having Art 3 (1) of the EIR international jurisdiction in conjunction with the request per Art 38 of the EIR.[28]

---

[23] Report mn 262; D-K/D/Ch-*Duursma-Kepplinger/Chalupsky* Art 38 mn 18.

[24] For German law, see: sec 21, 22 InsO.

[25] E.g. in German law, the notification of the appointment of a temporary administrator and the debtor's restrictions of disposition pursuant to sec 23 InsO. Where preservation measures are ordered pursuant to art 38 of the EIR, sec 23 InsO is to be modified to include special service of the preservation order to the temporary administrator as well.

[26] D-K/D/Ch-*Duursma-Kepplinger/Chalupsky* Art 38 mn 15; FK-InsO/*Wimmer* Anhang I nach § 358, mn 132 et seq.

[27] See D-K/D/Ch-*Duursma-Kepplinger/Chalupsky* Art 38 mn 15.

[28] Likely misunderstood by D-K/D/Ch-*Duursma-Kepplinger/Chalupsky* Art 38 mn 15 who seem to find it necessary that the court seized of the art 38 of the EIR decision must examine the admissibility of the application to open the main insolvency proceedings. However, the reference cited in FK-InsO/*Wimmer* Art 102 EGInsO, mn 174 (= FK-InsO/*Wimmer* Anhang I nach § 358, mn 136) does not support this interpretation.

3.3 Binding of the Insolvency Court to the Article 38 Request

29 Practical problems arise in German insolvency law where the temporary administrator of foreign main insolvency proceedings – which initially seems to be suggested by Art 38 of the EIR based purely on the face of its wording – requests concrete preservation measures from a German insolvency court.

30 Especially in the case of a request to appoint a temporary administrator as a preservation measure, the question arises as to whether the court should exercise its own discretion and divest the debtor of his powers of administration and disposal over his assets (situated in Germany) in favour of the so-called strong temporary administrator (Sec 21 (1), (2) No 1, Sec 22 (1) sentence 1 *InsO*); or whether it should appoint a so-called weak temporary administrator (Sec 21 (1), (2) No 1 and No 2, Sec 22 (2) sentence 1 *InsO*), which binds the validity of the debtor's dispositions to the former's consent.

31 In more general terms, it concerns cases where the insolvency court intends to go either beyond the request made by the temporary administrator, or to order less than what was requested.

32 The core of the legal problem here is the wording of Art 38 of the EIR. The right of request conferred on the temporary administrator in the main insolvency proceedings is formulated as a demand. Preservation measures pursuant to the German *lex fori concursus territorialis*, however, may not be demanded, but only suggested; they must be ordered by the court on its own motion provided that an admissible application to open insolvency proceedings has been made.[29]

33 To facilitate a frictionless interaction between the Regulation on the one hand and the *lex fori concursus universalis* / *lex fori concursus territorialis* on the other, it thus seems both reasonable and necessary to afford an admissible Art 38 of the EIR request the same legal mechanisms as are attributed to admissible applications to open insolvency proceedings: an admissible request gives the court the opportunity to decide, on its own motion, which preservation measures are necessary in its opinion. The actual measures set out in an Art 38 of the EIR request are merely awarded the status of non-binding suggestions.[30] This solution is in line with the view that Art 38 of the EIR not only makes a referral to the legal effects of the *lex fori concursus territorialis*, but also to the particular national substantive requirements of it.[31]

34 For the effects of a withdrawal of the Art 38 of the EIR request, see marginal note 45 et seq below.

3.4 Appointment of the Temporary Administrator of the Main Proceedings as Temporary Administrator in Other Member States

35 The appointing of a temporary administrator in main insolvency proceedings, at his request pursuant to Art 38 of the EIR, as a temporary administrator in another Member State is not per se precluded.[32]

36 As long as the temporary administrator in the main insolvency proceedings satisfies the requirements of the *lex fori concursus territorialis* as to the person and eligibility of temporary administrators, there can be no objection in principle to his appointment.

---

29 Jaeger Komm InsO/*Gerhardt* § 21 mn 81.

30 See Jaeger Komm InsO/*Gerhardt* § 21, mn 81.

31 See mn 27 et seq above.

32 Likely in favour of such preclusion: in MünchKomm InsO/*Reinhart* Art 38 EuInsVO mn 2; but see also Art 29 of the EIR mn 88 et seq.

This applies, however, only in Member States in which secondary insolvency proceedings may not be opened.[33]

37 However, where there is an establishment within the meaning of Art 2 (h) of the EIR in the Member State in which the Art 38 of the EIR request is being made, thus permitting the opening of secondary insolvency proceedings, then any preservation measures, especially the appointing of a temporary administrator, will then be ordered for the purposes of maintaining the status quo, and therefore preparatory to the opening of future secondary insolvency proceedings. In light of the ability of the main insolvency proceedings to affect the secondary insolvency proceedings, especially pursuant to Chapter III of the Regulation, there is potential here for a conflict of interests between the two proceedings, and therefore for their liquidators as well. It is therefore prohibited in German law (Sec 56 *InsO*), for example, to appoint the liquidator in the main proceedings as the liquidator in the secondary insolvency proceedings. As a logical consequence, it must be considered improper to appoint a temporary administrator of main insolvency proceedings to temporary administrator of German secondary insolvency proceedings.

4. Term of Validity of Preservation Measures

4.1 Underlying Principle

38 The term of validity of preservation measures ordered pursuant to Art 38 of the EIR in conjunction with the *lex fori concursus territorialis* is determined by the *lex fori concursus territorialis*.

4.2 Opening of Secondary Insolvency Proceedings

39 Where preservation measures are ordered in a Member State in which there is international jurisdiction to open secondary insolvency proceedings, and such proceedings are in fact opened, the validity of such preservation measures ends upon the opening of such proceedings. This ensues from the respective *lex fori concursus territorialis* whose preservation measures pursuant to the wording of Art 38 of the EIR may neither be requested nor ordered if they are not limited in time to the period between the request to open and the opening of the insolvency proceedings.

4.3 Terminating the Temporary Administration in the Main Proceedings

40 The preservation measures ordered pursuant to the *lex fori concursus territorialis* must be stayed if main insolvency proceedings are not opened and the office of the temporary administrator comes to an end.[34] In the case of German main insolvency proceedings, this could take the form of: a final (non-appealable) denial of the request to open proceedings because of insufficiency of assets, a final dismissal of the request to open insolvency proceedings because it is inadmissible or lacks merit, the valid withdrawal of the request to open insolvency proceedings, or the valid declaration by the party making the request that the request is no longer necessary. Also belonging to this category is the case where jurisdiction pursuant to Art 3 (1) of the EIR was erroneously assumed and this becomes apparent prior to the opening of proceedings. The proceed-

[33] In dispute is whether an art 38 of the EIR request is permissible here at all; see mn 10 et seq.

[34] Haß/Huber/Gruber/Heiderhoff-*Gruber* Art 38 EuInsVO mn 4; FK-InsO/*Wimmer* Anhang I nach § 358, mn 134; unclear: *Virgós/Schmit* Explanatory report mn 262.

ings must then be stayed or converted to the opening of territorial insolvency proceedings. The powers conferred on the liquidator by Art 38 of the EIR either come to an end or are converted. It is irrelevant whether the need to stay Art 38 of the EIR preservation measures ensues from the *lex fori concursus territorialis* invoked through the Regulation since the issue can arguably be resolved by the Regulation itself. According to its own logic, Art 38 of the EIR presupposes the existence of, at the very least, pending main insolvency proceedings in order to justify the granting and the confirmation (continuance) of preservation measures pursuant to the respective *lex fori concursus territorialis*.[35] The goals contemplated by Art 38 of the EIR – to secure and preserve the debtor's assets – taken in light of Art 38 of the EIR and Chapter III of the Regulation together, means securing and preserving for the benefit of the creditors as a whole in one universal main insolvency proceeding. The fact that secondary insolvency proceedings can be opened changes nothing here; the coordination and cooperation provisions of Chapter III of the Regulation sanction the opening of such secondary proceedings, as well as their subordination to the main insolvency proceedings. Thus, preservation measures requested and ordered pursuant to Art 38 of the EIR presuppose that proceedings to open main insolvency proceedings are either pending or that main insolvency proceedings have already been opened.

If, pursuant to a request made by a foreign temporary administrator prior to the **41** stay or conversion of his proceedings, preservation measures have already been taken for example in Germany pursuant to German law by invoking Art 38 of the EIR, then Art 102 (4) subsection 2 *EGInsO* should be applied analogously[36] to the legal effects ensuing from such preservation measures.[37] The validity of any such preservation measures would then not be subsequently disputed.

If the temporary administration ordered in accordance with the *lex fori concursus* **42** *universalis* is ended without a termination of the proceedings to open insolvency proceedings,[38] then the ending of the measures must be determined in accordance with the *lex fori concursus territorialis*. Central to the decision under German law is whether the preservation measures ordered continue to be necessary until, at least, a final (non-appealable) decision is made in the proceedings to open insolvency proceedings.

4.4 No Opening of Secondary Insolvency Proceedings

If secondary insolvency proceedings are not requested in spite of the existence of **43** international jurisdiction to do so in a Member State of an establishment, or if they are not opened for any other reason, the *lex fori concursus territorialis* alone determines the term (length) of validity of the preservation measures.

4.5 Opening of Main Insolvency Proceedings

The opening of main insolvency proceedings does not operate to terminate preservation **44** measures; such measures are also not to be stayed simply because main insolvency proceedings have commenced. The underlying aims of Art 38 of the EIR – i.e. the universal

---

[35] See mn 1 et seq above, as well as Recital 16 of the EIR.

[36] For example, a temporary administrator could have been appointed as a preservation measure under German law who has been granted powers of disposition over the debtor's assets in Germany. Any dispositions made pursuant to this power continue to be effective.

[37] *Paulus* Komm EuInsVO Art 38 mn 4.

[38] This can happen, for example, if the order appointing the temporary administrator is set aside without the request to open insolvency proceedings being denied or dismissed.

securing and preservation of the insolvency estate and, if permitted, the preparation of secondary insolvency proceedings – are not robbed of their justification simply because main insolvency proceedings are opened.

4.6 Powers of the Court with Art 3 (1) of the EIR Jurisdiction

45 The power conferred by the Regulation on the court with Art 3 (1) of the EIR jurisdiction does comprise the power to instruct the court that ordered the preservation measures to either stay or permit the continuance of such measures.[39] Such a power can also not be implied from the fact that, by operation of law, the universal effects of the proceedings to open main insolvency proceedings (Art 25 (1) subpara 3 of the EIR) and of the main insolvency proceedings themselves (Art 16 and 17 of the EIR) must be recognized in other Member States. Through the referral to the *lex fori concursus territorialis*, Art 38 of the EIR confers upon the courts of the other Member States an autonomous, request-dependent decision making competence; any such power to instruct another court, which would amount to a direct encroachment on the sovereignty of the Member States, would have to be expressly regulated (see for example Art 18 (3) of the EIR).

4.7 Withdrawal of the Art 38 of the EIR Request

46 It is, however, conceivable, that a court with Art 3 (1) of the EIR jurisdiction may indirectly exercise a power to give instructions pursuant to the *lex fori concursus universalis* against the temporary administrator to attain a withdrawal of the Art 38 of the EIR request. Since an Art 38 of the EIR request made to a German insolvency court replaces the admissible request to open insolvency proceedings, which is a prerequisite to ordering preservation measures pursuant to Sec 21 of the German *InsO*, the withdrawal of the Art 38 of the EIR request must also be treated like the withdrawal of a request to open insolvency proceedings made to a German court. In both cases, the withdrawal automatically effects a stay of the preservation measures. This applies although, in the case of requested secondary insolvency proceedings in Germany, the request to grant preservation measures is only regarded as a suggestion to the insolvency court.[40]

47 Where, however, a request to open secondary insolvency proceedings in Germany is allowed, the insolvency court is obliged to decide on the preservation measures on its own motion. The withdrawal of Art 38 of the EIR preservation measures – whether declared by the temporary administrator or the final[41] liquidator in the main insolvency proceedings – is thereby rendered irrelevant.

5. Preservation Measures Pursuant to the *lex fori concursus universalis*

48 In addition to preservation measures ordered pursuant to Art 38 of the EIR in conjunction with the *lex fori concursus territorialis*, preservation measures ordered by the court that is competent for the main insolvency proceedings pursuant to the *lex fori concursus universalis* also serve to secure and preserve the universal insolvency estate.

49 Supposing that preservation measures pursuant to Art 38 of the EIR may only be ordered in Member States in which an establishment within the meaning of Art 2 (h) of the EIR is situated,[42] preservation measures available in the proceedings to open main

[39] But see: *Virgós/Schmit* Explanatory report mn 262; D-K/D/Ch-*Duursma-Kepplinger/Chalupsky* Art 38 mn 18.

[40] See mn 29 et seq, 32 et seq above.

[41] See mn 20 et seq above.

[42] See mn 10 et seq above.

insolvency proceedings, in respect of assets in other Member States, will be limited to preservation measures available according to the *lex fori concursus universalis* (see Art 4 (1) of the EIR, Art 25 (1) subpara 3 of the EIR).

The main difference between preservation measures pursuant to Art 38 of the EIR **50**
and those available under the *lex fori concursus universalis* is that the former are limited to a specific territory, whereas the latter have universal effect.[43]

Preservation measures ordered by a court with Art 3 (1) jurisdiction must be recognized **51**
in all other Member States without the imposition of any other formalities (Art 25 (1) subpara 3, subpara 1 sentence 1 of the EIR). Enforcement in the other Member States is made in accordance with Art 31 to 51 (with the exception of Art 34 (2)) of the 1968 Brussels Convention on Jurisdiction and the Enforcement of Judgments in Civil and Commercial Matters (Art 25 (1) subpara 1, sentence 2 of the EIR).[44]

---

[43] For other – obvious – distinctions, see the overview by D-K/D/Ch-*Duursma-Kepplinger* Art 38 mn 13.

[44] See Art 25 of the EIR mn 25 et seq.

Chapter IV

Provision of Information for Creditors and Lodgement of Their Claims

Article 39
Right to lodge claims

Any creditor who has his habitual residence, domicile or registered office in a Member State other than the State of the opening of proceedings, including the tax authorities and social security authorities of Member States, shall have the right to lodge claims in the insolvency proceedings in writing.

→ Cf Art 13 UNCITRAL Model Law

Contents

Index

Bibliography

Balz Das neue Europäische Insolvenzübereinkommen, ZIP 1996, p 948; *Blersch/Goetsch/Haas* Insolvenzrecht, Berliner Kommentar; *Duursma-Kepplinger/Duursma/Chalupsky* Europäische Insolvenzverordnung, Kommentar (2002); *Haß/Huber/Gruber/Heiderhoff* EU-Insolvenzverordnung, Kommentar (2005); *Kübler/Prütting* Kommentar zur Insolvenzordnung (March 2006); *Moss/Fletcher/Isaacs* (eds) The EC Regulation on Insolvency Proceedings (2002); Münchener Kommentar zum Bürgerlichen Gesetzbuch, vol 11 (2006); *Pannen/Riedemann/Kühnle* Zur Stellung der Gläubiger nach der Europäischen Verordnung über Insolvenzverfahren, NZI 2002, p 303; *Paulus* Europäische Insolvenzverordnung, Kommentar (2006); *Smid* Deutsches und Europäisches Internationales Insolvenzrecht (2004); *Virgós/Schmit* Erläuternder Bericht zu dem EU-Übereinkommen über Insolvenzverfahren, in Stoll (ed), Vorschläge und Gutachten (1997), p 32; *Virgós/Garcimartín* The European Insolvency Regulation: Law and Practice (2004); *Wessels* International Insolvency Law (2006).

1. Overview

Arts 32[1] and 39 of the EIR grant **every creditor**, whose habitual domicile, residence, or registered office is in the EU, the right to lodge his claims in every insolvency proceeding pending in the EU.[2] Art 39 of the EIR is a **substantive-law provision** of Community law[3] independent of the applicable national insolvency law (*lex fori concursus*).[4] 1

The right of every creditor to lodge his claim in the insolvency proceedings is a direct consequence of the principle of universality. Only by allowing a claim to be lodged in all proceedings is the universal effect of the insolvency proceedings compatible with the **principle of equal treatment of creditors.**[5] 2

Art 39 of the EIR applies to both **main and territorial proceedings.**[6] 3

The right conferred by Art 39 of the EIR on foreign creditors to lodge their claims means that the lodgement of such claim cannot be denied on the grounds that the creditor is domiciled in another Member State, or that the claim is subject to the public law provisions of another Member State.[7] 4

2. Creditors

The right to lodge a claim pursuant to Art 39 of the EIR is, according to the wording, available **to all creditors** that have their habitual residence, domicile, or registered office in a Member State other than the opening State. 5

This includes both **legal entities** and **natural persons.**[8] 6

By contrast, Art 39 of the EIR makes no provision for **creditors domiciled in the Member State of the opening of proceedings.** Any rights they may have to lodge their claims are determined by the *lex fori concursus*.[9] 7

The EIR also makes no provision for the rights of creditors domiciled in **non-EU countries.**[10] The right of these creditors to lodge claims is governed by the laws of the respective individual State,[11] for example in Germany by Sec 341 *Ins*O, which grants every creditor the right to lodge his claims. 8

Whether the creditors have the **nationality** of a Member State is, however, irrelevant for an application of Art 39 of the EIR; hence, the creditor need **not be a European citizen.**[12] 9

---

1 On the relationship between arts 32 and 39 of the EIR, see mn 23.

2 *Pannen/Riedemann/Kühnle* NZI 2002, 303.

3 *Virgós/Schmit* Explanatory report mn 265; D-K/D/Ch-*Duursma* Art 39 mn 5; Kübler/Prütting-*Kemper* EuInsVO Art 39 mn 1; MünchKomm BGB/*Kindler* IntInsR mn 817; contra: *Smid* Komm EuInsVO Art 39 mn 1: procedural law.

4 Kübler/Prütting-*Kemper* EuInsVO Art 39 mn 1.

5 MünchKomm BGB/*Kindler* IntInsR mn 817.

6 Haß/Huber/Gruber/Heiderhoff-*Heiderhoff* Art 39 EuInsVO mn 3; Kübler/Prütting-*Kemper* EuInsVO Art 39 mn 2; Moss/Fletcher/Isaacs-*Moss/Smith*, Regulation, mn 8.274; *Smid* Komm EuInsVO Art 39 mn 1; *Paulus* Komm EuInsVO Art 39 mn 2.

7 *Virgós/Schmit* Explanatory report mn 266.

8 Kübler/Prütting-*Kemper* EuInsVO Art 39 mn 3.

9 *Virgós/Schmit* Explanatory report mn 269.

10 Moss/Fletcher/Isaacs-*Moss/Smith*, Regulation, mn 8.278; *Wessels* International Insolvency Law (2006) mn 10911.

11 *Virgós/Schmit* Explanatory report mn 269; Kübler/Prütting-*Kemper* EuInsVO Art 39 mn 3.

12 *Virgós/Garcimartín* Regulation, p 148; MünchKomm BGB/*Kindler* IntInsR mn 819.

10 The EIR contains no definition of **habitual residence, domicile,** or **registered office.** Council Regulation (EC) No 44/2001 may be referred to for determining habitual residence and the registered office.[13] According to Art 59 of Council Regulation (EC) No 44/2001, domicile is ascertained pursuant to the procedural law of the forum.[14] The concept of "habitual residence" is to be construed more broadly than "domicile" – it is based on a situation at the time of the lodging of the claim that is – without having to be formalized (as does "domicile" for instance) - discernible to outside third parties.[15] The concept of "registered office" is to be understood as the effective administrative head office.[16]

11 The creditor may, in cases of doubt, have **to prove** that his habitual residence, domicile, or registered office is in a Member State other than the State of the opening of proceedings.[17]

12 The right to lodge claims contemplated in Art 39 of the EIR also applies to **tax authorities**[18] and **social security authorities**[19] of the Member States; any provisions to the contrary found in the Member States is superseded by Art 39 of the EIR.[20] The explicit inclusion of these authorities was made for the sake of clarity[21] and is also in line with Recital 21 of the EIR. Any specific **ranking** of the claims of tax authorities or social security authorities is governed by the *lex fori concursus*.[22]

13 There is some opinion in Germany that the ***Bundesagentur für Arbeit*** (Federal Employment Agency) and its foreign counterparts are also encompassed by Art 39 of the EIR with regard to employees' wage claims that have devolved upon it.[23] Art 39 of the EIR does not, however, grant foreign public authorities the priority that they may enjoy in their native countries; these bodies will most likely attempt to have secondary insolvency proceedings opened.[24]

3. Derogation From the *lex fori concursus*

14 Art 39 of the EIR is a substantive-law provision on lodging claims that derogates from Art 4 (2) sentence 2 (h) of the EIR (lodging, verification, and admission of claims are governed by the *lex fori concursus*).[25] It does not, however, provide any **deadlines** for lodging claims, the **consequences of a late lodgement**, the **admissibility** and the **substantiation of a lodgement.** Pursuant to Art 4 (2) sentence 2 (h) of the EIR, such

---

[13] Kübler/Prütting-*Kemper* EuInsVO Art 39 mn 3.

[14] Kübler/Prütting-*Kemper* EuInsVO Art 39 mn 3.

[15] Kübler/Prütting-*Kemper* EuInsVO Art 39 mn 3.

[16] Kübler/Prütting-*Kemper* EuInsVO Art 39 mn 3.

[17] *Wessels* International Insolvency Law (2006) mn 10920.

[18] Because art 39 of the EIR does not specify the types of claims, it raises the question whether all types of fines fall within it. On this, see: *Wessels* International Insolvency Law (2006) mn 10913.

[19] It was standard practice in some Member State to deny participation by foreign tax authorities and foreign social security authorities for reasons based on public policy. On this, see also: *Balz* ZIP 1996, 948, 955; MünchKomm BGB/*Kindler* IntInsR mn 818.

[20] MünchKomm BGB/*Kindler* IntInsR mn 818.

[21] *Virgós/Schmit* Explanatory report mn 265; *BK-Pannen* Art 39 EuInsVO mn 2.

[22] MünchKomm BGB/*Kindler* IntInsR mn 818; *Paulus* Komm EuInsVO Art 39 mn 4.

[23] *Paulus* Komm EuInsVO Art 39 mn 4.

[24] Moss/Fletcher/Isaacs-*Moss/Smith*, Regulation, mn 8.276.

[25] *Virgós/Schmit* Explanatory report mn 265; *Wessels* International Insolvency Law (2006) mn 10911.

matters are governed by the *lex fori concursus*.[26] The *lex fori concursus* also governs the costs associated with the lodging and verification of the claim. A prudent creditor will therefore take the provisions on costs into consideration and will weigh these against the benefits of lodging a claim.[27] He will ascertain the priority of his claim according to the *lex fori concursus* and the size of the insolvency estate available for distribution.[28]

Art 39 of the EIR is made complete by Art 41 of the EIR (Content of the lodgement of a claim) and Art 42 of the EIR (Languages); both of these also derogate from the general applicability of the *lex fori concursus*.[29] **15**

According to Art 39 of the EIR, creditors have the right to lodge their claims **in writing**. The words "have the right" are not made in reference to "in writing" but rather with reference to "lodge", i.e. the creditor is not given a choice as to whether he "has the right to" lodge the claim in writing, he is given the choice as to whether he "has the right to" lodge the claim at all. If a creditor does decide to lodge his claim, then this lodgement must be made in writing. **16**

Some are of the opinion that Art 39 of the EIR is **exhaustive** with respect to the requirements for lodging claims.[30] But such an interpretation cannot be implied from the wording of it, and it is also hard to justify this in light of the contents of Art 41 of the EIR (Content of the lodgement of a claim) and especially Art 42 (2) of the EIR (necessity of a heading in the official language of the State of the opening of proceedings). Furthermore, the written form constitutes only one of its formal aspects; other form requirements must be determined pursuant to the *lex fori concursus*.[31] **17**

The written form also includes electronic transmissions that allow permanent recordings, such as **e-mails** (see Art 23 (2) of the Council Regulation (EC) No 44/2001).[32] **18**

Prevailing legal opinion regards the written-form requirement as an **upper limit of form requirements** that the Member States may not go beyond.[33] Art 39 of the EIR partially repeals and replaces any other provisions requiring personal attendance or imposing additional requirements.[34] The lodgement of the claim in duplicate required by Sec 104 (3) of the **Austrian** ***KO*** is thus superseded by Art 39 of the EIR.[35] The same holds true in France for Art L 622-25 of the ***Code de commerce***, which requires that creditors make an assurance that the claim exists. Some are of the opinion that this written-form requirement does not prohibit the laws of the individual States from imposing other, less stringent forms of lodging claims on the creditors.[36] **19**

Such a view is not, however, directly justified by the wording of Art 39 of the EIR. Though the Explanatory Report states that, despite the wording of Art 39 of the EIR, **20**

---

[26] *Virgós/Schmit* Explanatory report mn 267; *Paulus* Komm EuInsVO Art 39 mn 7; BK-*Pannen* Art 39 EuInsVO mn 5; D-K/D/Ch-*Duursma* Art 39 mn 6.

[27] *Virgós/Schmit* Explanatory report mn 268; D-K/D/Ch-*Duursma* Art 39 mn 6; BK-*Pannen* Art 39 EuInsVO mn 5.

[28] *Virgós/Schmit* Explanatory report mn 268.

[29] *Virgós/Schmit* Explanatory report mn 273.

[30] *Smid* Komm EuInsVO Art 39 mn 3; Haß/Huber/Gruber/Heiderhoff-*Heiderhoff* Art 39 EuInsVO mn 3.

[31] Moss/Fletcher/Isaacs-*Moss/Smith*, Regulation, mn 8.277; Kübler/Prütting-*Kemper* EuInsVO Art 39 mn 5.

[32] MünchKomm BGB/*Kindler* IntInsR mn 821; BK-*Pannen* Art 39 EuInsVO mn 6.

[33] D-K/D/Ch-*Duursma* Art 39 mn 4; Haß/Huber/Gruber/Heiderhoff-*Heiderhoff* Art 39 EuInsVO mn 2; Kübler/Prütting-*Kemper* EuInsVO Art 39 mn 5; MünchKomm BGB/*Kindler* IntInsR mn 821; *Paulus* Komm EuInsVO Art 39 mn 6; *Smid* Komm EuIns-VO Art 39 mn 3.

[34] *Paulus* Komm EuInsVO Art 39 mn 6.

[35] D-K/D/Ch-*Duursma* Art 39 mn 4.

[36] *Virgós/Schmit* Explanatory report mn 270; D-K/D/Ch-*Duursma* Art 39 mn 4; Haß/Huber/Gruber/Heiderhoff-*Heiderhoff* Art 39 EuInsVO mn 2; MünchKomm BGB/*Kindler*

less stringent form requirements are permissible,[37] it does not explicitly prohibit national laws from imposing stricter form requirements. With regard to Art 41 of the EIR, which regulates the content of the lodgement of a claim and which – similar to Art 39 of the EIR – derogates from the general applicability of the *lex fori concursus,* the Explanatory Report states that the laws of an individual State law may not impose additional requirements on the content of the lodgement of a claim of a foreign creditor since the very aim of this provision is to make it easier for creditors in the EU to exercise their rights.[38] The same applies to Art 39 of the EIR, which is also aimed at alleviating the lodgement of claims by foreign creditors. Art 39 of the EIR must therefore be so understood that **any form requirement stricter** than the requirement that the claim be lodged in writing **will not be tolerated.**[39] Stricter language requirements, such as those insisting that claims may only be lodged in the official language of the State of the opening of proceedings, are already expressly precluded via Art 42 (2) of the EIR.

21 Such an approach may lead to foreign creditors being placed in a better position than domestic creditors, for whom Art 39 of the EIR does not apply. For instance, German creditors may lodge their claims in Austrian insolvency proceedings with a single copy, whereas Austrian creditors must lodge theirs in duplicate. This clearly violates the principle of equal treatment of creditors (Recital 21 of the EIR). In order to avoid this, it would be preferable to **teleologically restrict the more stringent national laws** in favour of the national creditors as well.

22 Permitting a lodgement less stringent for the creditor, as is suggested in the Explanatory Report, would be quite unlikely in practice: an oral lodgement, in particular, would be highly impractical.

4. Relationship to Art 32 of the EIR

23 According to Art 32 of the EIR, every creditor can register his claim in the **main insolvency proceedings** and in each **secondary insolvency proceeding.** The object of this provision is different than Art 39 of the EIR. Whereas Art 32 of the EIR aims to ensure the unified nature of insolvency proceedings despite the opening of secondary insolvency proceedings, Art 39 of the EIR grants every creditor the fundamental right to lodge his claims whether territorial proceedings have been opened or not.[40]

Article 40
Duty to inform creditors

1. As soon as insolvency proceedings are opened in a Member State, the court of that State having jurisdiction or the liquidator appointed by it shall immediately inform known creditors who have their habitual residences, domiciles or registered offices in the other Member States.

IntInsR mn 821; *Paulus* Komm EuInsVO Art 39 mn 6; *Smid* Komm EuInsVO Art 39 mn 3; *Wessels* International Insolvency Law (2006) mn 10911.

[37] *Virgós/Schmit* Explanatory report mn 270.
[38] *Virgós/Schmit* Explanatory report mn 273.
[39] Also: D-K/D/Ch-*Duursma* Art 39 mn 4.
[40] *Paulus* Komm EuInsVO Art 39 mn 2.

2. That information, provided by an individual notice, shall in particular include time limits, the penalties laid down in regard to those time limits, the body or authority empowered to accept the lodgement of claims and the other measures laid down. Such notice shall also indicate whether creditors whose claims are preferential or secured in rem need lodge their claims.

→ Cf Art 14 UNCITRAL Model Law

Contents

Index

Bibliography

Duursma-Kepplinger/Duursma/Chalupsky Europäische Insolvenzverordnung, Kommentar (2002); Hamburger Kommentar zum Insolvenzrecht (2006) (ed *Schmidt, A.*); *Haß/Huber/Gruber/Heiderhoff* EU-Insolvenzverordnung, Kommentar (2005); *Kübler/Prütting* Kommentar zur Insolvenzordnung (March 2006); *Moss/Fletcher/Isaacs* (eds) The EC Regulation on Insolvency Proceedings (2002); Münchener Kommentar zum Bürgerlichen Gesetzbuch, vol 11 (2006); Münchener Kommentar zur Insolvenzordnung, vol 3 (2003); *Nerlich/Römermann* Insolvenzordnung, Kommentar (September 2005); *Pannen/Riedemann/Kühnle* Zur Stellung der Insolvenzgläubiger nach der Europäischen Verordnung über Insolvenzverfahren (EuInsVO), NZI 2002, p 303; *Pannen/Riedemann* Die deutschen Ausführungsbestimmungen zur EuInsVO – Ein Überblick zu den Regelungen des Art 102 EGInsO nF, NZI 2004, p 301; *Paulus* Europäische Insolvenzverordnung, Kommentar (2006); *Smid* Deutsches und Europäisches Internationales Insolvenzrecht (2004); *Virgós/Garcimartín* The European Insolvency Regulation: Law and Practice (2004); *Virgós/Schmit* Erläuternder Bericht zu dem EU-Übereinkommen über Insolvenzverfahren, in Stoll (ed), Vorschläge und Gutachten (1997), p 32; *Wessels* International Insolvency Law (2006).

1. Overview

Parallel to the **creditors' right to lodge their claims**, Art 40 of the EIR places the court **1**
or the liquidator under a **duty to inform the creditors**. Such a duty is necessary because without being informed that proceedings were opened, the creditors would hardly have an

opportunity to exercise their right to lodge claims. Although Art 21 of the EIR facilitates the public notification of the opening judgement, it is at the liquidator's discretion whether or not to do so. A **central European register** for insolvency proceedings that documents all opened proceedings does not (yet) exist.[1]

2 Art 40 of the EIR regulates, for the entire Community, the **form** and **content** of the duty to inform.[2] It is therefore a **provision of specific substantive law.**[3]

3 Art 40 of the EIR lays down a **minimum standard**[4] and applies to both the **main** and the **secondary insolvency proceedings.**[5] The *lex fori concursus* governs all aspects not regulated by Art 40 of the EIR. Art 40 of the EIR presupposes **opened insolvency proceedings** within the meaning of Art 2 (a) of the EIR in a Member State[6] (on this, see Art 2 of the EIR mn 24 et seq).

2. Affected Creditors

4 According to its wording, Art 40 of the EIR, like Art 39 of the EIR, only **concerns those creditors** whose habitual residence, domicile, or registered office is in a Member State other than the State of the opening of proceedings. The duty to invite the lodging of claims is **not**, therefore, owed to **domestic creditors** or **creditors in non-EU countries.**[7] It should be noted, however, that domestic creditors in most Member States are already being adequately informed of the opening of insolvency proceedings through their own national laws (in German law pursuant to Sec 29 in conjunction with Sec 30 *InsO*; in France according to Art *96 Décret n° 2005-1677 of 28 December 2005*).[8] As to whether and how creditors of non-EU countries are to be invited to lodge their claims is a matter for the *lex fori concursus.*[9]

5 As with Art 39 of the EIR (see Art 39 of the EIR mn 21), the fact that Art 40 of the EIR does not apply to **domestic creditors** contains a **risk** that **domestic and foreign creditors will be treated unequally** should the law of the individual State fail to provide the invitation to lodge claims. Where necessary, a teleological reduction of this area of national law must then be made.[10]

6 By speaking of "**known creditors**" only, Art 40 (1) of the EIR is imprecise. The extent of the **investigations** that must be carried out by the court or the liquidator is therefore a

---

[1] Moss/Fletcher/Isaacs-*Moss/Smith*, Regulation, mn 8.280.

[2] Art 102 sec 11 EGInsO (see the comments there) regulates the informing of the creditors within the framework of insolvency proceedings opened in Germany. See also *Pannen/ Riedemann* NZI 2004, 301, 305.

[3] D-K/D/Ch-*Duursma* Art 40 mn 1; Kübler/ Prütting-*Kemper* EuInsVO Art 40 mn 1; MünchKomm BGB/*Kindler* IntInsR mn 822.

[4] *Virgós/Garcimartín* Regulation, p 148; D-K/D/Ch-*Duursma* Art 40 mn 1; Nerlich/ Römermann-*Mincke* Art 40 EuInsVO mn 1; *Paulus* Komm EuInsVO Art 40 mn 5.

[5] Kübler/Prütting-*Kemper* EuInsVO Art 40 mn 2; *Paulus* Komm EuInsVO Art 40 mn 2; *Smid* Komm EuInsVO Art 40 mn 1.

[6] Kübler/Prütting-*Kemper* EuInsVO Art 40 mn 3.

[7] *Virgós/Schmit* Explanatory report mn 271; D-K/D/Ch-*Duursma* Art 40 mn 2; Haß/Huber/Gruber/Heiderhoff-*Heiderhoff* Art 40 EuInsVO mn 1; MünchKomm BGB/*Kindler* IntInsR mn 823; *Wessels* International Insolvency Law (2006) mn 10915.

[8] *Virgós/Schmit* Explanatory report mn 271.

[9] *Virgós/Schmit* Explanatory report mn 271; Haß/Huber/Gruber/Heiderhoff-*Heiderhoff* Art 40 EuInsVO mn 1; *Wessels* International Insolvency Law (2006) mn 10915.

[10] See also MünchKomm BGB/*Kindler* IntInsR mn 823; Nerlich/Römermann-*Mincke* Art 40 EuInsVO mn 3.

matter for the *lex fori concursus*. "Known creditors" are those creditors contained in the debtor's files and documents as found by the liquidator.[11]

3. Method of Informing

7 The creditors must be informed **in writing.**[12] Although this requirement is not expressly stated in Art 40 of the EIR (as it is in Art 39 of the EIR – lodgement of a claim), it can be directly inferred from the requirement imposed by Art 42 (1) of the EIR that a notice bearing a heading in all official EU languages must be sent.[13] The requisite **language** is regulated in Art 42 (1) of the EIR. According to Art 42 (1) of the EIR, the invitation to lodge a claim must be made in the **official language** or one of the official languages of the State of the opening of proceedings, albeit using the form with the heading – "Invitation to lodge a claim. Time limits to be observed" – in all of the official languages of the institutions of the European Union.

8 Unlike Arts 39 and 41 of the EIR (Lodgement of a claim), national laws may impose additional information requirements on the invitation to lodge a claim.[14] This is understandable considering that the object of Arts 39 to 42 of the EIR is to protect foreign creditors. The imposition of stricter national-law requirements on the invitation to lodge a claim will always be to the advantage of the creditors of the other Member States anyway.

9 It is questionable here whether the invitation to lodge a claim must be **served** within the meaning of European **Council Regulation (EC) No 1348/2000.**[15] One line of argument favours service of all invitations to lodge a claim, service then being carried out pursuant to the provisions of Council Regulation (EC) 1348/2000.[16] Against such an approach is the argument that such service would result in excessive costs to the detriment of the insolvency estate, which would mean that service pursuant to Council Regulation (EC) No 1348/2000 would never be required.[17] This argument is not convincing however. Service according to Council Regulation (EC) No 1348/2000 does not necessarily lead to higher costs: Art 14 of Council Regulation (EC) 1348/2000 allows each Member State to effect service of judicial documents directly by post to persons residing in another Member State.

10 A rejection of an **automatic application** of Council Regulation (EC) No 1348/2000 should rather be made based on the fact that a special system for informing creditors has already been created by Arts 40 and 42 (2) of the EIR independent of Council Regulation (EC) No 1348/2000.[18] Art 40 (2) of the EIR provides that the information must be provided by sending individual notices. There is therefore no need for service and thus no need for an automatic application of Council Regulation (EC) No 1348/2000.[19]

---

[11] *Virgós/Garcimartín* Regulation, p 148; *Wessels* International Insolvency Law (2006) mn 10915.

[12] *Paulus* Komm EuInsVO Art 40 mn 4.

[13] *Paulus* Komm EuInsVO Art 40 mn 5; Kübler/Prütting-*Kemper* EuInsVO Art 40 mn 4.

[14] *Virgós/Schmit* Explanatory report mn 272; Moss/Fletcher/Isaacs-*Moss/Smith*, Regulation, mn 8.280; Kübler/Prütting-*Kemper* EuInsVO Art 40 mn 5.

[15] Council Regulation (EC) No 1348/2000 of 28 May 2000 on the service in the Member States of judicial and extrajudicial documents in civil or commercial matters, OJ L 160 p 37.

[16] D-K/D/Ch-*Duursma* Art 40 mn 9.

[17] *Smid* Komm EuInsVO Art 40 mn 7.

[18] *Virgós/Garcimartín* Regulation, p 149.

[19] *Virgós/Garcimartín* Regulation, p 149.

11 Individual national laws may, however, impose additional requirements on the invitation to lodge a claim, which will likely take the form of a service of it. Whether service is required at all is a matter for the applicable *lex fori concursus*.[20] But if service is required, then it must be effected in compliance with Council Regulation (EC) No 1348/2000, since Art 1 (1) of this regulation provides its mandatory application in civil and commercial matters.[21] This is the case in Germany: Art 102 Sec 11 *EGInsO* provides that creditors must be informed via a served notice. Service to creditors in other Member States must be effected in compliance with Council Regulation (EC) No 1348/2000.

4. Contents of the Information

12 According to Art 40 (2) of the EIR, the information is to be made by sending an individual **notice**[22] that must indicate in particular:

- the time limits that must be observed;
- the penalties laid down in regard to those time limits;
- the body or authority empowered to accept the lodgement of claims;
- the other measures laid down;
- whether the creditors whose claims are preferential or secured *in rem* need to lodge their claims.

13 The German form goes further than the requirements of Art 40 (2) of the EIR in that it includes comprehensive information on lodging claims in Germany. This is nevertheless in line with the EIR as Member States are entitled to require additional information.[23] According to the wording of Art 42 (2) of the EIR, the content requirements listed there are merely "in particular". They are therefore only **minimum information** requirements that may be supplemented.[24]

5. Party With the Duty to Inform

14 According to the wording of Art 40 of the EIR, creditors are to be informed either by the competent **court** (legal definition in Art 2 (d) of the EIR) or by the **appointed liquidator.**[25] As to which body is obliged to inform the creditors is determined by the *lex fori concursus*.[26] If the *lex fori concursus* is silent on such requirements, then, in adherence to the doctrine of ***effet utile***, both the court and the liquidator must inform the creditors.[27] In Germany it is the liquidators who, pursuant to Sec 8 (3) *InsO*, are generally commissioned with effecting service on the creditors.[28]

---

20 Kübler/Prütting-*Kemper* EuInsVO Art 40 mn 4.

21 With same result: Kübler/Prütting-*Kemper* EuInsVO Art 40 mn 4; see also likewise MünchKomm BGB/*Kindler* IntInsR mn 827.

22 The German form in almost all of the EU's official languages is available at www.bmj.bund.de and is printed in the commentary to Art 42 of the EIR. The French form is printed at the end of the Country Report on France.

23 *Virgós/Schmit* Explanatory report mn 272.

24 Kübler/Prütting-*Kemper* EuInsVO Art 40 mn 5; MünchKomm BGB/*Kindler* IntInsR mn 826.

25 *Wessels* International Insolvency Law (2006) mn 10915; *Pannen/Riedemann/Kühnle* NZI 2002, 303.

26 D-K/D/Ch-*Duursma* Art 40 mn 3; MünchKomm BGB/*Kindler* IntInsR mn 825.

27 MünchKomm BGB/*Kindler* IntInsR mn 825.

28 HamburgerKomm-*J.-S. Schröder* § 30 InsO mn 12.

The Explanatory Report on the 1995 Draft convention on insolvency proceedings (so-called Virgós/Schmit Report, on this see also Introduction mn 42) obviously assumes that the liquidator is the party affected by this duty since it speaks in two places of a "duty of the liquidator" without any mention of the court.[29] **15**

The creditors must be informed **immediately**. According to German law, this means without culpable delay.[30] **16**

6. Sanction

The consequences of not complying with Art 40 of the EIR are unclear. The typical loss resulting from not informing a creditor is the non-satisfaction of his claim caused by the delayed or failed lodgement of it.[31] It would also lead to increased costs incurred for the commonly required second verification procedure.[32] But because the EIR adheres to the principle of proportionality, Art 40 of the EIR contains no sanctions.[33] Therefore any **sanctioning** of the insolvency court or the liquidator must be made pursuant to the respective *lex fori concursus*. **17**

The liquidator in Germany may be held personally liable through an analogous application of Sec 60 *InsO*. This liability could manifest itself in claims for damages.[34] The liability of the insolvency court could be based on the liability imposed on public authorities and officials (*Staatshaftungsrecht*).[35] **18**

7. Judicial Decisions

The 2005 decision of the ***Cour d'appel* of Orléans**[36] in the matter "R. Jung GmbH" deals with the failure to inform creditors pursuant to Art 40 of the EIR. Reorganization proceedings were opened against the assets of a French company. A German creditor had lodged his claim within the time limits without, however, indicating that he was the managing director of the affected company. He only informed the court of this after the time limit had expired. The lodgement of the claim was thus rejected. The *Cour d'appel* of Orléans reversed this decision, however, on the following grounds: Art 40 of the EIR places the liquidator under a duty to inform the creditors of other Member States via the form contemplated by Art 42 (2) of the EIR. And because this was not done here, the expiration of the time limit did not apply to the German creditor. **19**

---

[29] In mn 271 und 272; see *Wessels* International Insolvency Law (2006) mn 10915.

[30] D-K/D/Ch-*Duursma* Art 40 mn 2; *Smid* Komm EuInsVO Art 41 mn 3; Kübler/Prütting-*Kemper* EuInsVO Art 40 mn 3; MünchKomm BGB/*Kindler* IntInsR mn 824. See also: *Wessels* International Insolvency Law (2006) mn 10915.

[31] MünchKomm BGB/*Kindler* IntInsR mn 829.

[32] MünchKomm BGB/*Kindler* IntInsR mn 829.

[33] *Smid* Komm EuInsVO Art 40 mn 4; D-K/D/Ch-*Duursma* Art 40 mn 5.

[34] *Smid* Komm EuInsVO Art 40 mn 4; MünchKomm InsO/*Reinhart* Art 40 EuInsVO; MünchKomm BGB/*Kindler* IntInsR mn 828.

[35] MünchKomm BGB/*Kindler* IntInsR mn 828; *Smid* Komm EuInsVO Art 40 mn 5.

[36] Cour d'appel of Orléans dated 9 Jun 2006 (R. Jung GmbH), on this, see *Wessels* International Insolvency Law (2006) mn 10915.

Article 41
Content of the lodgement of a claim

A creditor shall send copies of supporting documents, if any, and shall indicate the nature of the claim, the date on which it arose and its amount, as well as whether he alleges preference, security in rem or a reservation of title in respect of the claim and what assets are covered by the guarantee he is invoking.

→ Cf Art 14 UNCITRAL Model Law

Contents

Index

Bibliography

Duursma-Kepplinger/Duursma/Chalupsky Europäische Insolvenzverordnung, Kommentar (2002); *Gottwald* Insolvenzrechtshandbuch, 3rd edn (2006); *Haß/Huber/Gruber/Heiderhoff* EU-Insolvenzverordnung, Kommentar (2005); *Kübler/Prütting* Kommentar zur Insolvenzordnung (March 2006); Münchener Kommentar zum Bürgerlichen Gesetzbuch, vol 11 (2006); *Paulus* Europäische Insolvenzverordnung, Kommentar (2006); *Moss/Fletcher/Isaacs* (eds) The EC Regulation on Insolvency Proceedings (2002); *Nerlich/Römermann* Insolvenzordnung, Kommentar (September 2005); *Smid* Deutsches und Europäisches Internationales Insolvenzrecht (2004); *Virgós/Garcimartín* The European Insolvency Regulation: Law and Practice (2004); *Virgós/Schmit* Erläuternder Bericht zu dem EU-Übereinkommen über Insolvenzverfahren, in Stoll (ed), Vorschläge und Gutachten (1997), p 32; *Wessels* International Insolvency Law (2006).

1. Overview

1 According to Art 4 (2) sentence 2 (h) of the EIR, the *lex fori concursus* governs the lodging, the verification, and the admission of the claims. By prescribing for the whole Community the content of the lodgement of a claim, Art 41 of the EIR, like Arts 39 and 42 (2) of the EIR, represents an **exception** to the applicability of the *lex fori concursus*.[1]

[1] *Virgós/Schmit* Explanatory report mn 273.

Art 41 of the EIR determines the substantive-law content of the lodgement of the claim and is thus a **specific provision of substantive law.**[2] **2**

The object of Art 41 of the EIR is to clearly define or individualize the lodged claims, which is particularly important if the creditor lodges the same claim in several insolvency proceedings.[3] **3**

National laws may not impose conditions or requirements (such as a certification, etc.) on the content of the lodgement of claims of foreign (EU) creditors more onerous than that required by Art 41 of the EIR.[4] **4**

Art 41 of the EIR applies to **main and territorial insolvency proceedings.**[5] **5**

2. Affected Creditors

Unlike Arts 39 and 40 of the EIR, Art 41 of the EIR, according to its wording, is not restricted to creditors that have their habitual residence, domicile, or registered office in a Member State other than the State of the opening of proceedings. However, prevailing opinion holds that Art 41 of the EIR – interpreted within the context of Chapter IV of the EIR as a whole and Art 39 of the EIR in particular – does **not** regulate the content of claims lodged by **domestic creditors.**[6] Art 41 of the EIR is to be restricted systematically to creditors from a Member State other than the State of the opening of proceedings. **6**

The Regulation does not apply to creditors from **non-EU countries.** The content of the lodgement of these claims is therefore governed not by Art 41 of the EIR but by the respective country's autonomous international insolvency laws (in Germany Sec 335 *InsO* applies in conjunction with Sec 174 *InsO*).[7] Whether or not the creditors are nationals of a Member State has no bearing on the applicability of Art 41 of the EIR.[8] **7**

3. Content of the Lodgement of a Claim

Although Art 39 of the EIR provides that claims are to be lodged **in writing,** the Member States are entitled to impose form requirements on claim lodgements that are less stringent for the creditors.[9] According to Art 41 of the EIR, the creditor is also to **8**

[2] Kübler/Prütting-*Kemper* EuInsVO Art 41 mn 1; MünchKomm BGB/*Kindler* IntInsR mn 830.

[3] *Virgós/Schmit* Explanatory report mn 273; MünchKomm BGB/*Kindler* IntInsR mn 835; Nerlich/Römermann-*Mincke* Art 41 EuInsVO mn 2; *Wessels* International Insolvency Law (2006) mn 10921.

[4] Haß/Huber/Gruber/Heiderhoff-*Heiderhoff* Art 41 EuInsVO mn 1; Moss/Fletcher/Isaacs-*Moss/Smith*, Regulation, mn 8.282; Nerlich/Römermann-*Mincke* Art 41 EuInsVO mn 1; *Paulus* Komm EuInsVO Art 41 mn 2; *Virgós/Schmit* Explanatory report mn 273; *Wessels* International Insolvency Law (2006) mn 10921.

[5] Kübler/Prütting-*Kemper* EuInsVO Art 41 mn 2.

[6] D-K/D/Ch-*Duursma* Art 41 mn 1; Haß/Huber/Gruber/Heiderhoff-*Heiderhoff* Art 41 EuInsVO mn 1; Kübler/Prütting-*Kemper* EuInsVO Art 41 mn 3; MünchKomm BGB/*Kindler* IntInsR mn 833; *Smid* Komm EuInsVO Art 41 mn 1; *Virgós/Garcimartín* Regulation, p 148; *Wessels* International Insolvency Law (2006) mn 10920.

[7] D-K/D/Ch-*Duursma* Art 41 mn 2.

[8] *Virgós/Garcimartín* Regulation, p 148.

[9] *Virgós/Schmit* Explanatory report mn 270; D-K/D/Ch-*Duursma* Art 39 mn 4; *Smid* Komm EuInsVO Art 39 mn 3; Haß/Huber/Gruber/Heiderhoff-*Heiderhoff* Art 39 EuIns-VO mn 2.

send **copies** of supporting documents, if there are any. The wording "**if any**" illustrates that the submission of copies is not a requirement of lodgement.[10]

9 The creditor must also provide information on:

- the **nature of the claim**, e.g. whether it is a contractual claim or a claim under tort law;[11]
- the **date on which the claim arose**, which is ascertained pursuant to the law governing the claim;
- the **amount** of the claim.

The creditor must further state whether, in respect of the claim, he has

- a **preference**,
- a **security *in rem***, or
- a **reservation of title**, and
- which **assets** are covered by the guarantee he is invoking.

10 Whether or not a **preference** exists is determined pursuant to the *lex fori concursus.*[12] French law for instance provides that employees' wage claims for the past 60 days must be satisfied first (Art L 143-10 *Code du travail*).

11 Whether a **security *in rem*** exists either on moveable or immoveable property is determined, on the other hand, pursuant to the *lex rei sitae.*[13] This follows from Art 5 of the EIR, which provides that third-party rights *in rem* are not affected by the opening of proceedings. The applicable law is thus determined pursuant to the rules of private international law, which in nearly all legal systems provides that the *lex rei sitae* governs (in Germany: Art 43 *EGBGB*).

12 Whether a **reservation of title** exists is also determined pursuant to the *lex rei sitae.*[14] This follows from Art 7 of the EIR, which provides that the rights of a conditional seller are not affected by the opening of proceedings.

13 Like Art 39 of the EIR, and for the same teleological reasons applicable there (see Art 39 of the EIR mn 21), Art 41 of the EIR is to be construed in a way that **prohibits** national laws from imposing **additional conditions or requirements** on the content of the lodgement of the claim.[15] Art 41 of the EIR therefore overrides for instance Art 98 of the *Décret n° 2005-1677* (which determines the content of the lodgement of the claim under French law), which obligates the creditors in the lodgement of their claims to state how the interest is calculated and the court invoked if the claim is being judicially contested. But according to the logic of Chapter IV of the EIR, this only applies to creditors from other Member States. In order to prevent these creditors from being put in a better position than domestic creditors, which would violate the principle of equal treatment of creditors, national laws that are more onerous for the creditors must – like with Art 39 of the EIR – be teleologically restricted in respect of their scope of application.

---

10 Nerlich/Römermann-*Mincke* Art 41 EuIns-VO mn 1.

11 *Paulus* Komm EuInsVO Art 41 mn 3.

12 Kübler/Prütting-*Kemper* EuInsVO Art 41 mn 5.

13 Kübler/Prütting-*Kemper* EuInsVO Art 41 mn 5.

14 Kübler/Prütting-*Kemper* EuInsVO Art 41 mn 5.

15 D-K/D/Ch-*Duursma* Art 41 mn 3; *Paulus* Komm EuInsVO Art 41 mn 2; Haß/Huber/Gruber/Heiderhoff-*Heiderhoff* Art 41 EuIns-VO mn 1; *Wessels* International Insolvency Law (2006) mn 10921.

The question also arises – again like Art 39 of the EIR (see Art 39 of the EIR mn 19 et seq) – whether content requirements less stringent for the creditors should be allowed. The Explanatory Report (Virgós/Schmit Report, see on this Introduction mn 42) is silent on this point.[16] But viewed in teleological terms, Arts 39 and 41 of the EIR pursue the same goal: making it easier for creditors from other Member States to lodge their claims.[17] Since, in conjunction with Art 39 of the EIR, national laws may prescribe less stringent forms of claim lodgements (see Art 39 of the EIR mn 19 et seq), the same should apply to the content of such lodgements.[18] Art 41 of the EIR therefore represents an **upper limit** of that which may be required of creditors in connection with the lodgement of their claims.[19] **14**

According to Art 4 (2) sentence 2 (h) of the EIR, the *lex fori concursus* governs the verification and the admission of the claims.[20] **15**

Article 42
Languages

1. The information provided for in Article 40 shall be provided in the official language or one of the official languages of the State of the opening of proceedings. For that purpose a form shall be used bearing the heading "Invitation to lodge a claim. Time limits to be observed" in all the official languages of the institutions of the European Union.

2. Any creditor who has his habitual residence, domicile or registered office in a Member State other than the State of the opening of proceedings may lodge his claim in the official language or one of the official languages of that other State. In that event, however, the lodgement of his claim shall bear the heading "Lodgement of claim" in the official language or one of the official languages of the State of the opening of proceedings. In addition, he may be required to provide a translation into the official language or one of the official languages of the State of the opening of proceedings.

Contents

Index

---

16 But on art 39 of the Draft convention on insolvency proceedings (1995) see: *Virgós/ Schmit* Explanatory report mn 270.

17 *Virgós/Schmit* Explanatory report mn 273.

18 Dissenting opinion: Gottwald/*Eickmann* InsR-Handb (2006), § 63 mn 11 – According to *Eickmann*, art 41 of the EIR augments sec 174 (1) sentence 2 InsO by requiring copies of supporting documents and by demanding that the lodgement includes the date on which the claim arose.

19 Nerlich/Römermann-*Mincke* Art 41 EuInsVO mn 1.

20 *Virgós/Schmit* Explanatory report mn 274.

Bibliography

Balz Das neue Europäische Insolvenzübereinkommen, ZIP 1996, p 948; *Duursma-Kepplinger/ Duursma/Chalupsky* Europäische Insolvenzverordnung, Kommentar (2002); *Kübler/Prütting* Kommentar zur Insolvenzordnung (March 2006); *Leible/Staudinger* Die europäische Verordnung über Insolvenzverfahren, KTS 2000, p 533; Münchener Kommentar zum Bürgerlichen Gesetzbuch, vol 11 (2006); *Nerlich/Römermann* Insolvenzordnung, Kommentar (September 2005); *Paulus* Europäische Insolvenzverordnung, Kommentar (2006); *Smid* Deutsches und Europäisches Internationales Insolvenzrecht (2004); *Virgós/Schmit* Erläuternder Bericht zu dem EU-Übereinkommen über Insolvenzverfahren, in Stoll (ed), Vorschläge und Gutachten (1997), p 32.

1. Overview

1 Art 42 of the EIR is a **specific provision of substantive law**[1] and applies to **main and secondary insolvency proceedings**. It provides the creditors with a **minimum of language protection**, and it supplements Arts 39 and 40 of the EIR. According to Art 39 of the EIR, every creditor from a Member State is entitled to lodge his claim in the insolvency proceedings. According to Art 40 of the EIR, the liquidator or the insolvency court must inform the known creditors in other Member States of the opening of proceedings. Art 42 of the EIR does not apply to **domestic creditors** or to creditors from **non-EU countries**.

2 In view of the multiplicity of languages in the European Union (currently 23 official languages[2]), it is necessary to **regulate the language to be used** for the invitation to lodge a claim and for the lodgement of the actual claim. Art 42 (1) of the EIR concerns the invitation to lodge claims, whereas Art 42 (2) of the EIR concerns the lodgement of the claim itself.[3]

2. Invitation to Lodge a Claim

3 Art 42 (1) of the EIR provides that the invitation to lodge a claim pursuant to Art 40 of the EIR must be made in the official language or one of the official languages of the State of the opening of proceedings, using a form bearing the heading "Invitation to lodge a claim. Time limits to be observed" in **all of the official languages** (for the German form, see mn 11). Without such a heading, creditors would find it very difficult to understand that the document sent is an invitation to lodge a claim, which – in breach of the principle of equal treatment of creditors – would deprive them of the opportunity to lodge their claims (see Recital 21 of the EIR). The heading is therefore supposed

---

[1] Kübler/Prütting-*Kemper* EuInsVO Art 42 mn 1.

[2] Bulgarian (minority language in Greece and Romania), Danish (minority language in Germany and Sweden), German (minority language in Belgium, Denmark, France, Italy, Poland, Romania, Slovakia, Slovenia, the Czech Republic, and Hungary), English, Estonian, Finnish, French, Greek, Irish, Italian, Latvian, Lithuanian, Maltese, Dutch, Polish (minority language in Latvia, Lithuania, Romania, and the Czech Republic), Portuguese, Romanian (minority language in Bulgaria and Hungary), Swedish, Slovakian (minority language in Austria, Poland, Romania, the Czech Republic, and Hungary), Slovenian (minority language in Italy, Austria, and Hungary), Spanish, Czechoslovakian, Hungarian (minority language in Austria, Romania, Slovakia, and Slovenia).

[3] MünchKomm BGB/*Kindler* IntInsR mn 836.

to help the creditors to understand what the document is, and thereby safeguard their interests.[4]

4 The body of the invitation itself does not have to be translated into the other official languages.[5] If the State of the opening of proceedings has more than one official language, it suffices if the information is made in one of these official languages.[6] According to the wording of Art 42 (1) of the EIR, the information may be provided in one of the official languages of the State of the opening of proceedings. This is not necessarily one of the official languages of the European Union, as is the case with the Irish language for example.[7]

5 If a creditor is compelled to have the body of the invitation (to lodge a claim) translated, the costs incurred for this are borne by him alone.[8] He is not entitled to a translation.[9] For this reason, legal writers advocate the introduction of a multilingual form that is standardized for the EU similar to the one already found in the Annex to Regulation (EC) No 805/2004[10].[11]

3. Lodgement of a Claim

6 Art 42 (2) of the EIR regulates which language must be used for the **lodgement of a claim**. According to it, any creditor from a Member State other than the State of the opening of proceedings is entitled to lodge his claim

- in the official language or one of the official languages of the State of the opening of the insolvency proceedings,[12] or
- in the official language or one of the official languages of the State in which the creditor has his habitual residence, domicile, or registered office.[13]

7 The lodgement must, however, bear the heading "Lodgement of claim" in the official language or one of the official languages of the State of the opening of proceedings. This requirement has a dual purpose. Firstly, it makes the lodging of claims easier for foreign creditors, which helps to avoid both delays in lodging claims and unnecessary costs.[14] Secondly, the heading written in the language of the State of the opening of proceedings allows the liquidator to understand what the document is about.[15]

8 The use of one of the official languages of the European Union is not required: a creditor located in Ireland can therefore lodge his claim in Irish.[16]

9 According to Art 42 (2) of the EIR, the liquidator is entitled to request a **translation** of the lodgement into the official language of the State of the opening of proceedings.

---

[4] *Virgós/Schmit* Explanatory report mn 275; Kübler/Prütting-*Kemper* EuInsVO Art 42 mn 3; *Paulus* Komm EuInsVO Art 42 mn 1.

[5] MünchKomm BGB/*Kindler* IntInsR mn 839.

[6] MünchKomm BGB/*Kindler* IntInsR mn 839.

[7] D-K/D/Ch-*Duursma* Art 42 mn 3.

[8] MünchKomm BGB/*Kindler* IntInsR mn 840.

[9] Nerlich/Römermann-*Mincke* Art 42 EuInsVO mn 1.

[10] Regulation (EC) No 805/2004 of the European Parliament and of the Council of 21 April 2004 creating a European Enforcement Order for uncontested claims, OJ L 143 p 15.

[11] MünchKomm BGB/*Kindler* IntInsR mn 840.

[12] This follows in the German version from the use of the word "*auch*" (also). See Kübler/Prütting-*Kemper* EuInsVO art 42 mn 4.

[13] Kübler/Prütting-*Kemper* EuInsVO Art 42 mn 4.

[14] *Virgós/Schmit* Explanatory report mn 276.

[15] Moss/Fletchers/Isaacs-*Moss/Smith*, Regulation, mn 8.290; MünchKomm BGB/*Kindler* IntInsR mn 841.

[16] D-K/D/Ch-*Duursma* Art 42 mn 6.

The native-language version of the lodgement is decisive, however, for determining compliance with form and deadlines.[17] What is unclear is the question of who bears the **translation costs.** Prevailing opinion holds that it is the creditor who must bear these costs.[18] The creditor does not, however, bear the consequences of **translation errors.**[19] The creditor's non-compliance with the liquidator's request for a translation does not legally prejudice him.[20] The liquidator will simply have the translation made at the creditor's expense.[21]

4. German Form of the Invitation to Lodge a Claim

10 The form required by Art 42 (1) of the EIR for Germany is found at www.bmj.bund.de.[22] The form includes information on German insolvency law and is available in almost all of the official languages of the European Union. This allows the invitation to lodge a claim to be made directly in the language of the respective creditor, which saves the costs of a translation. Printed below is the English-language version of the German form.

Aufforderung zur Anmeldung einer Forderung. Etwaige Fristen beachten![23]
Opfordring til anmeldelse af fordringer. Vær opmærksom fristerne! *
Invitation to lodge a claim. Time limits to be observed! *
Kutse nõudeavalduse esitamiseks. Arvestage kehtestatud tähtaegu! *
Kehotus saatavan ilmoittamiseen. Noudatettavat määräajat! *
Invitation à produire une créance. Délais à respecter! *
Πρόσκληση για αναγγελία απαιτήσεως. Προσοχή στις προθεσμίες! *
Invito all'insinuazione di un credito. Termine da osservare! *
Aicinājums iesniegt prasījumu pieteikumus. Ievērot varbūtējos termi¯Hus! *
Kvietimas pateikti reikalavimą. Privalomieji terminai! *
Oproep tot indiening van schuldvorderingen. In acht te nemen termijnen! *
Sejħa sabiex tissottometti talba. Il-perijodi ta' Ŝmien stupulati għandhom jiău osservati *.
Wezwanie do zgłoszenia wierzytelności. Proszę nie zapominać o konieczności dotrzymania ew. terminów! *
Aviso de reclamação de créditos. Prazos legais a observar! *
Výzva na prihlásenie pohl'adávky. Všimnite si prípadné termíny! *
Poziv k prijavi terjatve. Roki, ki jih je treba upoštevati! *

[17] *Balz* ZIP 1996, 948, 955; D-K/D/Ch-*Duursma* Art 42 mn 7; Kübler/Prütting-*Kemper* EuInsVO Art 42 mn 5; MünchKomm BGB/*Kindler* IntInsR mn 843; *Leible/Staudinger* KTS 2000, 533, 571.

[18] MünchKomm BGB/*Kindler* IntInsR mn 845; D-K/D/Ch-*Duursma* Art 42 mn 13; *Paulus* Komm EuInsVO Art 42 mn 7; *Smid* Komm EuInsVO Art 42 mn 4.

[19] D-K/D/Ch-*Duursma* Art 42 mn 9; MünchKomm BGB/*Kindler* IntInsR mn 844.

[20] Kübler/Prütting-*Kemper* EuInsVO Art 42 mn 5; Nerlich/Römermann-*Mincke* Art 42 EuInsVO mn 2.

[21] Kübler/Prütting-*Kemper* EuInsVO Art 42 mn 5; Nerlich/Römermann-*Minck*, Art 42 EuInsVO mn 2.

[22] The French form of the invitation to lodge and the claim lodgement is printed at the end of the Country Report on France.

[23] With this form, the obligation to inform creditors pursuant to art 40 in conjunction with art 42 (1) of Council regulation (EC) No 1346/2000 of 29 May 2000 on insolvency proceedings (OJ L 160/1) is fulfilled.

Convocatoria para la presentación de créditos. Plazos aplicables!
Anmodan att anmäla fordran. Tidsfrister att iaktta!*
Výzva k uplatnění pohledávky Případné lhůty musejí být dodrženy!*
Felhívás egy követelés bejelentésére. Esetleges hatíridıket figyelembe venni!*

As you may have gathered from the accompanying order of the insolvency court, insolvency proceedings have been opened regarding the assets of the debtor named therein, which also serves the uniform satisfaction of creditors' claims.

Every creditor, including the tax authorities and social insurance institutions of the Member States, may **lodge a written claim in the insolvency proceeding.** This also applies to creditors whose habitual residence, domicile, or registered office is in a different Member State than the State in which the insolvency proceeding was opened (Article 39 of the Council Regulation on Insolvency Proceedings). Creditors may also lodge their claims in the official language or one of the official languages of such other State. In this case, the claim must at least contain the **heading "*Anmeldung einer Forderung*" ("Lodgement of a Claim") in the German language.** The creditor may be required to provide a translation of the claim in German (Article 42 para. 2 of the Council Regulation on Insolvency Proceedings).

The lodgement of the claim must take place **within the time period set forth in the accompanying order opening the insolvency proceedings** (§ 28 para. 1 of the Insolvency Statute).

Claims that are first lodged **after the expiration of the filing period,** may require an **additional verification proceeding.** The **costs arising therefrom shall be borne by the creditor who lodged an untimely claim** (§ 177 para. 1 of the Insolvency Statute).

The lodgement of the claim shall not be made to the insolvency court but **to the insolvency administrator set forth in the accompanying order opening the insolvency proceedings** (§ 174 of the Insolvency Statute). If a custodian or trustee is appointed (§§ 270, 313 of the Insolvency Statute), the lodgement of the claim shall be made there.

In the lodgement, the creditor shall state the **form, the date the claim arose, and the amount of the claim** and shall be accompanied by, as applicable, available **supporting documents, as well as certificates of the lodgement, upon which the claim is based** (Article 41 of the Council Regulation on Insolvency Proceedings; § 174 para 1 of the Insolvency Statute).

In addition to the lodgement, **the basis for the claim** and, if applicable, the **facts, from which, in the opinion of the creditor, it appears to be based on an unauthorised intentional act committed by the debtor** (§ 174 para. 2 of the Insolvency Statute). The grant of discharge from residual debt shall remain unaffected by unauthorised acts intentionally committed by the debtor, when the creditor lodged a corresponding claim with information regarding this legal basis and the acts upon which it is based (§ 302 nr 1 of the Insolvency Statute).

All claims are to be asserted in fixed amounts stated **in Euros** and at the end the total amount shall be summarised. **Claims in foreign currency must be converted to Euros** at the exchange rate applicable at the time the proceeding was opened. Claims that are not based upon money or whose value is uncertain must be lodged with their estimated value (§ 45 of the Insolvency Statute).

Interest, in principle, may be claimed **only for the period up until the opening of the insolvency proceedings** (the date of the accompanying opening order). The interest rate and time period upon which it is calculated shall be provided and it shall be stated as a fixed amount.

Subordinate claims (for example, interest that accrued after the opening of the proceeding or claims based upon services provided free of charge by the debtor) **shall only be lodged to the extent the insolvency court expressly invited lodgement of these claims in the order opening the insolvency proceedings.** Upon the lodgement of such claims, the lower rank shall be indicated and the lower rank to which the creditor is entitled shall be designated (§ 174 para 3 of the Insolvency Statute).

To the extent creditors claim **security rights in moveable property or rights of the debtor,** they must **promptly inform the insolvency administrator** thereof. At the same time, the object in which a security right is claimed and the form and basis upon which the security right and the secured claim arise, shall be described. **Whoever culpably refrains from or delays such notification, is liable for the damages resulting therefrom** (§ 28 para 2 of the Insolvency Statute).

Creditors who, based upon a lien or other security right **may demand separate satisfaction, are creditors in the insolvency insofar as the debtor is also personally liable to him,** such as based on a loan or purchase agreement. **This personal claim may be lodged.** It will only be considered in the distribution of the insolvency assets, however, insofar as they waive their rights to separate satisfaction or that it has failed (§ 52 of the Insolvency Statute).

Anyone entitled to claim the separation of an object from the assets involved in the insolvency proceedings based upon a real property right or a personal property right (such as, as owner) **shall not be included as a creditor in the insolvency proceedings. Entitlement to separation of such object from the assets shall not be lodged in the insolvency proceeding,** but rather, according to the statutes that apply outside of the insolvency proceedings (§ 47 of the Insolvency Statute).

Chapter V

Transitional and Final Provisions

Article 43
Applicability in time

The provisions of this Regulation shall apply only to insolvency proceedings opened after its entry into force. Acts done by a debtor before the entry into force of this Regulation shall continue to be governed by the law which was applicable to them at the time they were done.

Contents

Index

Bibliography

Dammann L'application du règlement CE n° 1346-2000 après les arrêts Staubitz-Schreiber et Eurofood de la CJCE, Dalloz 2006, p 1752; *Duursma-Kepplinger/Duursma/Chalupsky* Europäische Insolvenzverordnung, Kommentar (2002); *Haß/Huber/Gruber/Heiderhoff* EU-Insolvenzverordnung, Kommentar (2005); *Herchen* Das Prioritätsprinzip im internationalen Insolvenzrecht, ZIP 2005, p 1401; *Knof/Mock* Comments on ECJ dated 17.1.2006 – C-1/04, ZIP 2006, p 189; *Laukemann* Rechtshängigkeit im europäischen Insolvenzrecht, RIW 2005, p 104; *Mankowski* Klärung von Grundfragen des europäischen Internationalen Insolvenzrechts durch die Eurofood-Entscheidung? BB 2006, 1753, p 1757; Münchener Kommentar zum Bürgerlichen Gesetzbuch, vol 11 (2006); *Paulus* Europäische Insolvenzverordnung Kommentar (2006); *Schmidt, J.* Perpetuatio fori im europäischen internationalen Insolvenzrecht, ZInsO 2006, p 88; *Smid* Deutsches und Europäisches Internationales Insolvenzrecht (2004); *Stoll* (ed) Vorschläge und Gutachten zur Umsetzung des EU-Übereinkommens über Insolvenzverfahren im deutschen Recht (1997); *Virgós/Schmit* Erläuternder Bericht zu dem EU-Übereinkommen über Insolvenzverfahren, in Stoll (ed), Vorschläge und Gutachten (1997), p 32; *Wessels* Current Topics of International Insolvency Law (2004); *Wessels* International Insolvency Law (2006).

1. Overview

1 Art 43 of the EIR regulates the **time of applicability** of the EIR.[1] In this respect it supplements Art 1 of the EIR, which outlines the **scope of application in terms of subject matter**. But since the EIR is silent as to the **territorial scope of its application**, it must be assumed that it only applies to matters having a so-called **qualified foreign connection** (on this, see Art 3 of the EIR mn 67).[2]

2 The EIR only applies to insolvency proceedings opened after its entry into force. Acts done by the debtor before the entry into force of the EIR (see Art 47 of the EIR "Entry into force") continue to be governed by the law which was applicable to such acts at the time they were carried out. Behind both Arts 43 and 47 of the EIR is the idea that existing situations and relationships that were already governed by the explicit laws of a Member State at the time at which the new provisions of the EIR came into force are not supposed to be altered.[3]

2. Content

2.1 Insolvency Proceedings

3 According to Art 43 (1) of the EIR, the EIR only applies to insolvency proceedings opened after its entry into force. Pursuant to Art 47 of the EIR, the EIR came into force on 31 May 2002.

4 In the ten Member States that joined the European Union on 1 May 2004, Art 2 of the **Act of Accession**[4] stipulates that the EIR is applicable commencing on the date of accession.[5] For the Member States Bulgaria and Romania, which joined on 1 January 2007, Art 2 of the **Accession Protocol**[6] stipulates that the acts of the institutions of the European Union adopted prior to accession, which includes the EIR, apply as of the date of accession.

5 Whether proceedings were opened before or after the EIR came into force is ascertained pursuant to the legal definition of "the time of the **opening of proceedings**" in Art 2 (f) of the EIR.[7] According to Art 2 (f) of the EIR, it is irrelevant whether or not the opening judgement is conclusive or *res judicata*.[8] A judgement that is not *res judicata* will therefore suffice, i.e. it is already **effective**, even if it only produces effects in the

---

1 D-K/D/Ch-*Duursma* Art 43 mn 1.

2 D-K/D/Ch-*Duursma* Vorbemerkung mn 30.

3 *Virgós/Schmit* Explanatory report mn 303.

4 Act concerning the conditions of accession of the Czech Republic, the Republic of Estonia, the Republic of Cyprus, the Republic of Latvia, the Republic of Lithuania, the Republic of Hungary, the Republic of Malta, the Republic of Poland, the Republic of Slovenia and the Slovak Republic and the adjustments to the Treaties on which the European Union is founded of 23 Sept 2003, OJ L 236 p 33.

5 *Paulus* Komm EuInsVO Art 43 mn 1.

6 Protocol concerning the conditions and arrangements for admission of the Republic of Bulgaria and Romania to the European Union of 21 June 2005, OJ L 157 p 29.

7 *Virgós/Schmit* Explanatory report mn 305.

8 *Smid* Komm EuInsVO Art 2 mn 16.

opening State.[9] Whether or not a judgement is effective is a matter for determination by the *lex fori concursus*.[10]

Since the ECJ's decision in **Eurofood/Parmalat**, the **ordering of temporary administration** can also be regarded as the **opening of proceedings**, see Art 3 of the EIR mn 91 et seq and Art 2 of the EIR mn 24 et seq: the appointment of a **provisional liquidator**[11] also constitutes the **opening of proceedings** within the meaning of Art 16 of the EIR.[12] **6**

Problematic for determining the time of the opening of proceedings are the so-called **relation back principles**, which exist in English, Irish, Welsh, and Czech law (on this see Art 3 of the EIR mn 89 et seq).[13] The opening of insolvency proceedings in such constellations is retroactive to the point in time at which the request was made.[14] However, the ECJ's decision in Eurofood/Parmalat (→ cf Table of Cases Art 3 of the EIR Appendix A mn 10) is to be so understood that **retroactive fictions of national law** are to be disregarded, for a detailed discussion on this see Art 3 of the EIR mn 89 et seq.[15] **7**

Even before its actual entry into force, the EIR had already been applied (as an interpretation aid for the previously applicable law).[16] The Dutch ***Hoge Raad der Nederlande***, for instance, had already applied Art 4 and Art 13 of the EIR on 24 October 1997[17] in a German/Dutch case.[18] **8**

What causes problems are those cases in which **several proceedings** were opened and some of which, because of the time of their opening, do not fall within the scope of the EIR's applicability.[19] If insolvency proceedings against a certain debtor's assets were opened before the EIR came into force, then proceedings opened after the EIR came into force are **not** governed by the EIR regardless of whether the proceedings opened later are main or secondary insolvency proceedings.[20] **9**

Insolvency proceedings opened prior to the coming into force of the EIR are governed either by the autonomous international insolvency-law provisions of the respective State or by international conventions. Art 43 (2) of the EIR also contains a transitional provision for this, providing that conventions between the Member States continue to have effect with regard to proceedings opened before the entry into force of the EIR. **10**

---

9 *Paulus* Komm EuInsVO Art 2 mn 15; MünchKomm BGB/*Kindler* IntInsR mn 848.

10 *Paulus* Komm EuInsVO Art 2 mn 15.

11 It is irrelevant whether a strong or weak liquidator is appointed as long as this is provided for in law, as is the case in German law (sec 21, 22 InsO). Of sole importance is that a decision has been made to appoint a liquidator.

12 ECJ dated 2 May 2006 – C-341/04 (Eurofood IFSC Ltd.), NZI 2006, 360 et seq (→ cf Table of Cases Art 3 of the EIR Appendix A mn 10 – Eurofood/Parmalat); cf also Advocate General *Jacobs* in his Opinion, ZIP 2005, 1641; *Laukemann* RIW 2005, 104, 112.

13 Haß/Huber/Gruber/Heiderhoff-*Huber* Art 2 EuInsVO mn 3.

14 For instance High Court Dublin "Eurofood/ Parmalat" ZIP 2004, 1223 (→ cf Table of Cases Art 3 EuInsVO Appendix A mn 10 – Eurofood/Parmalat); Court of Prague dated 26 Apr 2005 ZIP 2005, 1431, see Table of Cases Art 3 of the EIR Appendix A mn 1, on this, see *Herchen* ZIP 2005, 1401.

15 *Mankowski* BB 2006, 1753, 1757.

16 *Wessels* Current topics of international Insolvency Law, p 196.

17 Netherlands Supreme Court dated 24 Oct 1997 (NIPR 1998, 114). On this *Wessels* Current topics of international Insolvency Law, p 195.

18 Further examples in *Wessels* Current topics of international Insolvency Law, p 196 et seq and *Wessels* International Insolvency Law (2006) mn 10926.

19 MünchKomm BGB/*Kindler* IntInsR mn 849.

20 *Virgós/Schmit* Explanatory report mn 304; D-K/D/Ch-*Duursma* Art 43 mn 14; Kübler/ Prütting-*Kemper* EuInsVO Art 43 mn 2; *Wessels* International Insolvency Law (2006) mn 109927.

2.2 Acts by the Debtor

11 According to Art 43 (2) of the EIR, acts done by a debtor before the entry into force of the EIR continue to be governed by the law which was applicable to them at the time they were done. Art 43 (2) of the EIR is relevant in cases where the act was done before the EIR came into force but insolvency proceedings associated with the act were opened pursuant to Art 3 of the EIR.

12 For determining the **time at which the EIR entered into force**, the comments on Art 43 (1) of the EIR can be referred to. Which acts of the debtor are affected and the moment at which these were done are determined in the given case by the law that applies[21] pursuant to the rules of private international law.

13 "***Rechtshandlungen des Schuldners***" (English: "acts done by a debtor") within the meaning of the German version of Art 43 (2) of the EIR are not restricted to acts connected with avoidance actions, a conclusion which can be drawn from other (language) versions of the EIR.[22]

3. Judicial Precedent

14 Art 43 of the EIR has played a decisive role to date in three particular judgements. Because the EIR entered into force nearly five years ago, it is unlikely that there will be any new decisions dealing with the interpretation of Art 43 of the EIR.

15
- **DAM Italia Di Borgward Industrials BV**: Insolvency proceedings in this case[23] were opened in the Netherlands prior to 31 May 2002 against the assets of the Dutch Borgward Industrials BV. This company had an establishment in Italy. The Italian court decided – contrary to prevailing opinion[24] – that the transitional provision in Art 43 of the EIR did not preclude the opening of secondary insolvency proceedings in Italy. The court ruled that the opening of insolvency proceedings in a foreign country that are to be regarded as main insolvency proceedings on account of the coming into force of the EIR does not prohibit the opening of secondary insolvency proceedings.
- **New Deal**: Reorganisation proceedings were opened on 4 April 2002 against the assets of the debtor in France. The same French court opened winding-up proceedings on 3 October 2002 against the debtor's assets. A dispute was pending at that time between the debtor and Yamaha in Amsterdam. On 25 August 2005, the Court of Appeal of Amsterdam[25] ruled that the EIR did not apply to the earlier reorganisation proceedings, but that it did apply to the later winding-up proceedings.
- **Staubitz-Schreiber** (→ cf Table of Cases Art 3 of the EIR Appendix A mn 17): Art 43 sentence 1 of the EIR lays down the rule determining the time at which the EIR becomes applicable. This provision is to be so understood that the EIR is applicable as long as no decision has been made on a request to open insolvency proceedings by the time of the EIR's entry into force on 31 May 2002, even if the request had been filed

[21] *Virgós/Schmit* Explanatory report mn 306.

[22] *Paulus* Komm EuInsVO Art 43 mn 3.

[23] Court of Lodi dated 27 Sep 2002, unpublished, quoted according to *Wessels* International Insolvency Law (2006) mn 10929.

[24] See also *Wessels* International Insolvency Law (2006) mn 10929.

[25] Court of Appeal of Amsterdam dated 25 Aug 2005 (Nr 2094/03), quoted according to *Wessels* International Insolvency Law (2006) mn 10929.

prior to this point in time. Such was the situation in the **Susanne Staubitz-Schreiber** case. Although the claimant had filed her request on 6 December 2001, a decision to open insolvency proceedings had not been made by 31 May 2002.[26]

Article 44
Relationship to Conventions

1. After its entry into force, this Regulation replaces, in respect of the matters referred to therein, in the relations between Member States, the Conventions concluded between two or more Member States, in particular:

(a) the Convention between Belgium and France on Jurisdiction and the Validity and Enforcement of Judgments, Arbitration Awards and Authentic Instruments, signed at Paris on 8 July 1899;

(b) the Convention between Belgium and Austria on Bankruptcy, Winding-up, Arrangements, Compositions and Suspension of Payments (with Additional Protocol of 13 June 1973), signed at Brussels on 16 July 1969;

(c) the Convention between Belgium and the Netherlands on Territorial Jurisdiction, Bankruptcy and the Validity and Enforcement of Judgments, Arbitration Awards and Authentic Instruments, signed at Brussels on 28 March 1925;

(d) the Treaty between Germany and Austria on Bankruptcy, Winding-up, Arrangements and Compositions, signed at Vienna on 25 May 1979;

(e) the Convention between France and Austria on Jurisdiction, Recognition and Enforcement of Judgments on Bankruptcy, signed at Vienna on 27 February 1979;

(f) the Convention between France and Italy on the Enforcement of Judgments in Civil and Commercial Matters, signed at Rome on 3 June 1930;

(g) the Convention between Italy and Austria on Bankruptcy, Winding-up, Arrangements and Compositions, signed at Rome on 12 July 1977;

(h) the Convention between the Kingdom of the Netherlands and the Federal Republic of Germany on the Mutual Recognition and Enforcement of Judgments and other Enforceable Instruments in Civil and Commercial Matters, signed at The Hague on 30 August 1962;

(i) the Convention between the United Kingdom and the Kingdom of Belgium providing for the Reciprocal Enforcement of Judgments in Civil and Commercial Matters, with Protocol, signed at Brussels on 2 May 1934;

(j) the Convention between Denmark, Finland, Norway, Sweden and Iceland on Bankruptcy, signed at Copenhagen on 7 November 1933;

(k) the European Convention on Certain International Aspects of Bankruptcy, signed at Istanbul on 5 June 1990;

(l) the Convention between the Federative People's Republic of Yugoslavia and the Kingdom of Greece on the Mutual Recognition and Enforcement of Judgments, signed at Athens on 18 June 1959;

(m) the Agreement between the Federative People's Republic of Yugoslavia and the Republic of Austria on the Mutual Recognition and Enforcement of Arbitral Awards

---

[26] ECJ dated 17 Jan 2006 – C-1/04 "Susanne Staubitz-Schreiber", ZIP 2006, 188 et seq, with explanatory note by *Knof/Mock* ZIP 2006, 189; *Schmidt* ZInsO 2006, 88; *Dammann* Dalloz 2006, 1752, 1758.

and Arbitral Settlements in Commercial Matters, signed at Belgrade on 18 March 1960;

(n) the Convention between the Federative People's Republic of Yugoslavia and the Republic of Italy on Mutual Judicial Cooperation in Civil and Administrative Matters, signed at Rome on 3 December 1960;

(o) the Agreement between the Socialist Federative Republic of Yugoslavia and the Kingdom of Belgium on Judicial Cooperation in Civil and Commercial Matters, signed at Belgrade on 24 September 1971;

(p) the Convention between the Governments of Yugoslavia and France on the Recognition and Enforcement of Judgments in Civil and Commercial Matters, signed at Paris on 18 May 1971;

(q) the Agreement between the Czechoslovak Socialist Republic and the Hellenic Republic on Legal Aid in Civil and Criminal Matters, signed at Athens on 22 October 1980, still in force between the Czech Republic and Greece;

(r) the Agreement between the Czechoslovak Socialist Republic and the Republic of Cyprus on Legal Aid in Civil and Criminal Matters, signed at Nicosia on 23 April 1982, still in force between the Czech Republic and Cyprus;

(s) the Treaty between the Government of the Czechoslovak Socialist Republic and the Government of the Republic of France on Legal Aid and the Recognition and Enforcement of Judgments in Civil, Family and Commercial Matters, signed at Paris on 10 May 1984, still in force between the Czech Republic and France;

(t) the Treaty between the Czechoslovak Socialist Republic and the Italian Republic on Legal Aid in Civil and Criminal Matters, signed at Prague on 6 December 1985, still in force between the Czech Republic and Italy;

(u) the Agreement between the Republic of Latvia, the Republic of Estonia and the Republic of Lithuania on Legal Assistance and Legal Relationships, signed at Tallinn on 11 November 1992;

(v) the Agreement between Estonia and Poland on Granting Legal Aid and Legal Relations on Civil, Labour and Criminal Matters, signed at Tallinn on 27 November 1998;

(w) the Agreement between the Republic of Lithuania and the Republic of Poland on Legal Assistance and Legal Relations in Civil, Family, Labour and Criminal Matters, signed in Warsaw on 26 January 1993.

2. The Conventions referred to in paragraph 1 shall continue to have effect with regard to proceedings opened before the entry into force of this Regulation.

3. This Regulation shall not apply:

(a) in any Member State, to the extent that it is irreconcilable with the obligations arising in relation to bankruptcy from a convention concluded by that State with one or more third countries before the entry into force of this Regulation;

(b) in the United Kingdom of Great Britain and Northern Ireland, to the extent that is irreconcilable with the obligations arising in relation to bankruptcy and the winding-up of insolvent companies from any arrangements with the Commonwealth existing at the time this Regulation enters into force.

Contents

Index

Bibliography

Duursma-Kepplinger/Duursma/Chalupsky Europäische Insolvenzverordnung, Kommentar (2002); *Kübler/Prütting* Kommentar zur Insolvenzordnung (March 2006); *Leible/Staudinger* Die europäische Verordnung über Insolvenzverfahren, KTS 2000, p 533; *Moss/Fletcher/Isaacs* (eds) The EC Regulation on Insolvency Proceedings (2002); Münchener Kommentar zum Bürgerlichen Gesetzbuch, vol 11 (2006); *Nerlich/Römermann* Insolvenzordnung (September 2005); *Paulus* Europäische Insolvenzverordnung, Kommentar (2006); *Smid* Deutsches und Europäisches Internationales Insolvenzrecht (2004); *Virgós/Schmit* Erläuternder Bericht zu dem EU-Übereinkommen über Insolvenzverfahren, in Stoll (ed), Vorschläge und Gutachten (1997), p 32; *Wessels* International Insolvency Law (2006).

1. Overview

Art 44 of the EIR clarifies the relationship of the EIR to other international conventions that regulate the private international law aspect of cross-border insolvency proceedings.[1] Such a provision was necessary in light of the numerous international conventions on cross-border insolvency proceedings that had already been concluded between various Member States and between the Member States and non-EU countries before the EIR came into force. The fact that Art 249 (2) of the EEC Treaty provides that the EIR is binding in its entirety and that it is directly applicable in all Member States does not mean that it automatically overrides previous international conventions. An express regulation was therefore needed to confer on the EIR its overriding status in the European legal system. The list of international conventions was extended in conjunction with the expansion of the EU in 2004 to include certain Eastern European countries.[2] **1**

2. Relationship of the EIR to Intra-Community Conventions

Art 44 (1) of the EIR regulates the relationship between the EIR and the conventions that were concluded between two or more Member States, i.e. bilateral or multilateral conventions. **2**

Art 44 (1) of the EIR contains a detailed list of 23 conventions that have been replaced by the EIR. This list is **not exhaustive**, as illustrated by the words "in particular".[3] **3**

There is little likelihood that other intra-Community conventions have been overlooked. Art 44 (1) of the EIR was worded so to make sure that other conventions that only touch on insolvency law incidentally are caught by it.[4] **4**

---

[1] *Virgós/Schmit* Explanatory report mn 307.
[2] MünchKomm BGB/*Kindler* IntInsR mn 852.
[3] D-K/D/Ch-*Duursma* Art 44 mn 3; Kübler/Prütting-*Kemper* EuInsVO Art 44 mn 2; *Paulus* Komm EuInsVO Art 44 mn 1; MünchKomm BGB/*Kindler* IntInsR mn 852.
[4] *Paulus* Komm EuInsVO Art 44 mn 1; D-K/D/Ch-*Duursma* Art 44 mn 3.

5 The **German version** contains two oversights, one with respect to the **Nordic Convention**[5] (Art 44 (1) (j) of the EIR). Contrary to the wording of the EIR, this convention was concluded on 7 November 1933 and not on 7 November 1993. Secondly, Iceland was a party to this convention and not Ireland. Versions in other languages (e.g. English, French, or Spanish) are correct here.

6 According to the wording of Art 44 (1) of the EIR, the EIR only replaces the listed conventions within the **scope of its subject matter**. The scope of the EIR's application in terms of subject matter is set out in Art 1 of the EIR (see the discussions on Art 1 mn 6 et seq): the EIR does not apply to insolvency proceedings concerning of insurance undertakings, credit institutions, investment undertakings which provide services involving the holding of funds or securities for third parties, or to collective investment undertakings (for details on this, see Art 1 of the EIR mn 22 et seq).

7 The law previously in force, which includes the conventions listed in Art 44 (1) of the EIR in the given case, continues to govern these **areas excepted** from the scope of the EIR's application.[6] The conventions also continue to apply to **proceedings** that are **not listed in Annexes A and B to the EIR.**[7]

8 But in those areas where the EIR does apply, the old conventions do not apply subsidiarily.[8] The EIR is **not a *lex specialis***[9] but rather completely **supersedes** the conventions.[10] The old law **cannot** be invoked, for instance, in the event of a **regulatory gap** in the EIR. Jurisdiction for the so-called insolvency-related proceedings pursuant to Art 25 (1) subpara 2 of the EIR, which is not regulated in the EIR, may not for example be determined by reference to the old conventions but rather by way of analogy to Art 3 of the EIR (see Art 3 of the EIR mn 110 et seq).

3. Transitional Provision

9 Art 44 (2) of the EIR defines the **time of applicability** of the EIR in relation to insolvency proceedings opened before its entry into force. The conventions listed in Art 44 (1) of the EIR continue, where applicable, to apply to these proceedings. This provision aims to ensure legal certainty by preventing changes being made to the legal status of existing situations and relationships that were already governed by the explicit laws of a Member State at the time at which the new provisions of the EIR came into force.[11] Art 44 (2) of the EIR thereby supplements Art 43 of the EIR, which regulates the time when the EIR becomes applicable.

10 In light of the content of Art 43 of the EIR, it is doubtful whether Art 44 (2) of the EIR was necessary at all. Because according to Art 43 of the EIR, the EIR only applies to insolvency proceedings that were opened after it came into force. It can already be inferred from this that the old laws, and thus the international conventions, apply to proceedings opened prior to the EIR's entry into force. Art 44 (2) of the EIR has therefore a mere **clarifying function.**

---

[5] On this, see Introduction mn 24 et seq.

[6] D-K/D/Ch-*Duursma* Art 44 mn 9; *Smid* Komm EuInsVO Art 44 mn 3; MünchKomm BGB/*Kindler* IntInsR mn 852.

[7] Nerlich/Rommermann-*Mincke* Art 44 EuInsVO mn 1.

[8] D-K/D/Ch-*Duursma* Art 44 mn 4; *Smid* Komm EuInsVO Art 44 mn 2.

[9] Contra MünchKomm BGB/*Kindler* IntInsR mn 852.

[10] D-K/D/Ch-*Duursma* Art 44 mn 5, also: MünchKomm BGB/*Kindler* IntInsR mn 852.

[11] Cf *Virgós/Schmit* Explanatory report mn 303.

11 Regarding the **ascertainment of the point in time of the entry into force of the EIR** and of the opening of insolvency proceedings, see the discussions on this in Art 43 of the EIR mn 1 et seq.

4. Relationship of the EIR to Conventions with Third Countries

12 Art 44 (3) of the EIR deals with the problem of compatibility of the EIR with conventions concluded between a Member State and a **third country** (not-EU country).[12] **Third countries** are countries that are not Member States of the European Union. According to Arts 1 and 2 of the Protocol on the position of Denmark annexed to the Treaty on European Union, **Denmark** did not participate in the adoption of the EIR with the result that the EIR does not apply for it.[13] The **Netherlands Antilles** and **Aruba** are also considered third countries.[14]

13 According to Art 44 (3) (a) of the EIR, the EIR does not apply to the extent that it is irreconcilable with the obligations arising in relation to bankruptcy from a convention concluded by that State with one or more third countries before the entry into force of the EIR.

14 According to Art 44 (3) (b) of the EIR, the EIR does not apply in the United Kingdom of Great Britain and Northern Ireland to the extent that is irreconcilable with the obligations arising in relation to bankruptcy and the winding-up of insolvent companies from any arrangements with the Commonwealth existing at the time the EIR enters into force. This provision is a reference to Sec 426 of the Insolvency Act 1986 pursuant to which English courts are obliged to assist insolvency proceedings from Commonwealth states.[15]

15 In order to decide whether or not the application of the EIR is **reconcilable** with the obligations from other conventions, it must be determined whether the legal effects produced by a particular application exclude the other.[16] If that is the case, Art 43 (3) of the EIR ensures that the old conventions between a Member State and a non-EU country will have precedence.[17] This is in adherence to the principle of *pacta sunt servanda* (contracts must be respected). Art 44 (3) of the EIR therefore has a clarifying function only.

16 Even though the EIR applies if a debtor's COMI (see Art 3 of the EIR mn 15 et seq) is located in the sovereign territory of a Member State, it only applies if the relationships are between Member States; it does not apply to relationships between Member States and non-EU countries (see Art 3 of the EIR mn 58 et seq).[18]

17 The question is whether there is any competence remaining to the EU Member States to enter into agreements with non-EU countries. According to the so-called **AETR doctrine**, the Member States are not entitled, either individually or jointly, to enter into agreements with non-EU countries that interfere with the areas in which the Community has adopted legislation implementing common policy provided for in the EEC Treaty.[19] According to the so-called **"relaxed AETR doctrine"**,[20] the Member States only forfeit

---

12 *Virgós/Schmit* Explanatory report mn 10.

13 Recital 33 of the EIR.

14 *Wessels* International Insolvency Law (2006) mn 10937.

15 Moss/Fletcher/Isaacs-*Moss/Smith*, Regulation, mn 8.294.

16 *Virgós/Schmit* Explanatory report mn 310; MünchKomm BGB/*Kindler* IntInsR mn 856.

17 D-K/D/Ch-*Duursma* Art 44 mn 21; MünchKomm BGB/*Kindler* IntInsR mn 856.

18 *Virgós/Schmit* Explanatory report mn 310.

19 ECJ 22/70, EC reports 1971, 263, AETR.

20 ECJ Opinion 1/94 EC reports 1994, I-5267 mn 77.

their entitlement to conclude such agreements to the extent to which such agreements interfere with common legislation in force.[21]

18 The EIR does not deal with non-EU countries and does not apply to such matters. The European Union has not yet enacted any legislation in this connection with which conventions between Member States and non-EU countries could interfere. It therefore remains open to the Member States to enter into agreements with non-EU countries dealing with cross-border insolvency proceedings,[22] provided that such agreements do not interfere with any of the provisions of the EIR.[23]

Article 45
Amendment of the Annexes

The Council, acting by qualified majority on the initiative of one of its members or on a proposal from the Commission, may amend the Annexes.

Contents

Index

Bibliography

Duursma-Kepplinger/Duursma/Chalupsky Europäische Insolvenzverordnung, Kommentar (2002); *Haß/Huber/Gruber/Heiderhoff* EU-Insolvenzverordnung, Kommentar (2005); *Moss/Fletcher/Isaacs* (eds) The EC Regulation on Insolvency Proceedings (2002); Münchener Kommentar zum Bürgerlichen Gesetzbuch, vol 11 (2006); *Paulus* Europäische Insolvenzverordnung Kommentar (2006); *Virgós/Schmit* Erläuternder Bericht zu dem EU-Übereinkommen über Insolvenzverfahren, in Stoll (ed), Vorschläge und Gutachten (1997), p 32.

21 D-K/D/Ch-*Duursma* Art 44 mn 30; MünchKomm BGB/*Kindler* IntInsR mn 858.

22 D-K/D/Ch-*Duursma* Art 44 mn 31; MünchKomm BGB/*Kindler* IntInsR mn 858; contra *Leible/Staudinger* KTS 2000, 533, 539.

23 Nerlich/Rommermann-*Mincke* Art 44 EuInsVO mn 4; cf also explanation of the Council (2000/C 183/02).

1. Overview

Art 45 of the EIR regulates the **amending of the three Annexes A, B, and** C to the EIR, which list respectively for each Member State the "insolvency proceedings" falling within Art 2 (a) of the EIR, "winding-up proceedings" within Art 2 (c) of the EIR, and "liquidator" within Art 2 (b) of the EIR. Since **national laws** undergo new **developments** from time to time, it must be possible to amend the Annexes to adapt to these. However, if it is too easy to make such amendments, certainty of the law could be jeopardized. The EIR therefore requires a qualified majority of the Council for the amendment of the Annexes.[1] **1**

2. Mechanism to Amend the Annexes

An amendment of the Annexes must be made on the initiative of one of the members **2**
of the Council or by a proposal from the Commission. According to the wording of Art 45 of the EIR, this is at the Council's **discretion**: it "may" amend the Annexes.[2] Such an amendment must be decided by the members of the Council with a qualified majority. The qualified majority is calculated in accordance with Art 205 (2) of the EEC Treaty. According to this, resolutions are passed by the Council with a minimum of 232 votes, which entails the consent of at least two thirds of its members.[3] Although calculation problems could arise due to Denmark's special position, these will not be discussed further here because they have nearly no practical relevance whatsoever.[4]

An amendment can be made against the will of the Member State concerned,[5] which **3**
is important where the initiative is taken by the Commission.[6]

According to Art 54 of the 1995 Draft convention on insolvency proceedings (on **4**
this convention, see Introduction mn 10), each contracting state was entitled to amend Annexes A, B and C at any time. This was restricted by the fact that the "new" insolvency or winding-up proceedings had to meet the requirements of the respective definitions in the convention.[7] The contracting state was supposed to make a declaration to the Secretary-General of the Council of the European Union as to how it wished to amend the Annex.[8] Each amendment to the Annexes had to be approved, although it was not necessary that every state expressly declare its approval. In absence of an objection within the three months following this, the amendment was to be deemed approved. In order to rule out any differences of opinion between contracting states, the requisitioning of a review conference was possible.[9]

The **amendment procedure** provided for in Art 45 of the EIR has been criticised by **5**
legal writers.[10] In their opinion, requiring a qualified majority gives rise to a certain degree of cumbersomeness, which could prevent the making of timely amendments.[11]

---

1 Haß/Huber/Gruber/Heiderhoff-*Heiderhoff* Art 45 EuInsVO mn 1; *Paulus* Komm EuInsVO Art 45 mn 1; D-K/D/Ch-*Duursma* Art 45 mn 2.

2 *Paulus* Komm EuInsVO Art 45 mn 2.

3 In the version of December 29, 2006, OJ C 321 E/136.

4 See D-K/D/Ch-*Duursma* Art 45 mn 6–10.

5 Moss/Fletcher/Isaacs-Moss/Smith, Regulation, mn 8.296.

6 MünchKomm BGB/*Kindler* IntInsR mn 861.

7 *Virgós/Schmit* Explanatory report mn 319; MünchKomm BGB/*Kindler* IntInsR mn 860.

8 *Virgós/Schmit* Explanatory report mn 320.

9 *Virgós/Schmit* Explanatory report mn 322.

10 *Paulus* Komm EuInsVO Art 45 mn 1.

11 *Paulus* Komm EuInsVO Art 45 mn 1.

They therefore suggest to either make corrections *de lege ferenda*, or that the Council set up a working group responsible for such amendments.[12] But the number of amendments that have been made up to now (see mn 7 et seq) proves that these fears are unfounded. There is therefore no reason to derogate from the wording of Art 45 of the EIR.

3. Prior Amendments to the Annexes

6 The three Annexes have been changed on several occasions. Pursuant to the EU **enlargement on 1 May 2004**, the proceedings and liquidators of the new Member States (Czech Republic, Republic of Estonia, Republic of Cyprus, Republic of Latvia, Republic of Lithuania, Republic of Hungary, Republic of Malta, Republic of Poland, Republic of Slovenia, and the Slovak Republic)[13] were included in Annexes A, B, and C.[14] The last **enlargement of the EU on 1 January 2007** has not yet resulted in any amendments to the EIR. Many amendments to the Annexes made by Member States that were already in the EU prior to the coming into force of the EIR have been made to reflect developments in their national laws. A comparison of the current version of the EIR[15] to the first version shows the following amendments:

3.1 Annex A: insolvency proceedings within the meaning of Art 2 (a) of the EIR

7 There are three new insolvency proceedings in **Belgium**:

- *De vrijwillige vereffening/la liquidation volontaire*
- *De gerechtelijke vereffening/la liquidation judiciaire*
- *De voorlopige ontneming van beheer, bepaald in artikel 8 van de faillissementswet/Le dessaisissement provisoire, visé à l'article 8 de la loi sur les faillites*

8 The three former insolvency proceedings in **Spain**:

- *Concurso de acreedores*
- *Quiebra*
- *Suspensión de pagos,*

have been replaced by one single proceeding, the *concurso*.

9 In **France**, the *procédure de sauvegarde* was added.

10 In **Italy**, the *amministrazione controllata* was deleted from Annex A to the EIR.

11 In **Portugal**, the *processo de insolvência* was added.

12 In the **United Kingdom**, administration proceedings, including appointments made by filing prescribed documents with the court, have been added to Annex A.

---

[12] *Paulus* Komm EuInsVO Art 45 mn 1.

[13] Act concerning the conditions of accession of the Czech Republic, the Republic of Estonia, the Republic of Cyprus, the Republic of Latvia, the Republic of Lithuania, the Republic of Hungary, the Republic of Malta, the Republic of Poland, the Republic of Slovenia and the Slovak Republic and the adjustments to the Treaties on which the European Union is founded, OJ L 236 p 33.

[14] Haß/Huber/Gruber/Heiderhoff-*Heiderhoff* Art 45 EuInsVO mn 2.

[15] Last amended by Council Regulation (EC) No 694/2006 of 27 April 2006 amending the lists of insolvency proceedings, winding-up proceedings and liquidators in Annexes A, B and C to Regulation (EC) No 1346/2000 on insolvency proceedings, OJ L 121 p 1.

3.2 Annex B: winding-up proceedings within the meaning of Art 2 (c) of the EIR

In Belgium, the two new winding-up proceedings have been added: **13**

- *De vrijwillige vereffening/La liquidation volontaire*
- *De gerechtelijke vereffening/La liquidation judiciaire*

In Spain, the three former winding-up proceedings: **14**

- *Concurso de acreedores*
- *Quiebra*
- *Suspensión de pagos basada en la insolvencia definitiva*,

have been replaced by one single proceeding, the *concurso*.

In **Italy**, the *concordato preventivo con cessione dei beni* was added. **15**

In **Portugal**, the *processo de insolvência* was added to Annex B. **16**

In the **United Kingdom**, the winding-up through administration, including appointments made by filing prescribed documents with the court, was added to Annex B. **17**

3.3 Annex C: liquidators within the meaning of Art 2 (b) of the EIR

In **Belgium**, two new liquidators were added to the Annex: **18**

- *De vereffenaar/Le liquidateur*
- *De voorlopige bewindvoerder/L'administrateur provisoire*

In **Spain**, the former types of liquidators: **19**

- *Depositario-administrador*
- *Interventor o Interventores*
- *Síndicos*
- *Comisario*,

have been replaced by one single liquidator, the *administradores concursales*.

In **France**, the *représentant des créanciers* was replaced by the *liquidateur*. **20**

In **Austria**, the *vorläufiger Verwalter* is no longer included in Annex C to the EIR. **21**

The *liquidatore giudiziale* in **Italy**, the *administrador da insolvência* in **Portugal**, and the *provisional liquidator* in the **United Kingdom** have been added to Annex C to the EIR. **22**

It is astounding that all three Annexes of the latest version of the EIR for Germany still refer to the *Konkursordnung* (Bankruptcy Act), to the *Vergleichsordnung* (Act on Composition Proceedings), and to the *Gesamtvollstreckungsordnung* (Insolvency Act in the former East Germany). On the one hand Art 104 of the *EGInsO* provides that the *InsO* (the "new" German Insolvency Act) applies to all insolvency proceedings opened after 31 December 1998. On the second hand, Art 43 in conjunction with Art 47 of the EIR provides that the EIR only applies to insolvency proceedings opened after 31 May 2002. Therefore the inclusion of the *Konkursordnung*, the *Vergleichsordnung*, and the *Gesamtvollstreckungsordnung* in the Annexes to the EIR was, from the outset, never really necessary.[16] **23**

[16] *Paulus* Komm EuInsVO Art 45 mn 3.

Article 46
Reports

No later than 1 June 2012, and every five years thereafter, the Commission shall present to the European Parliament, the Council and the Economic and Social Committee a report on the application of this Regulation. The report shall be accompanied if need be by a proposal for adaptation of this Regulation.

Bibliography

Duursma-Kepplinger/Duursma/Chalupsky Europäische Insolvenzverordnung, Kommentar (2002); *Kübler/Prütting* Kommentar zur Insolvenzordnung (March 2006); *Moss/Fletcher/Isaacs* (eds) The EC Regulation on Insolvency Proceedings (2002); *Virgós/Schmit* Erläuternder Bericht zu dem EU-Übereinkommen über Insolvenzverfahren, in Stoll (ed), Vorschläge und Gutachten (1997), p 32.

1 In order to ensure its continual development, the EIR contains in Art 46 of the EIR a built-in adaptation mechanism in the form of a report that must be presented by the Commission to the European Parliament, the Council and the Economic and Social Committee no later than 1 June 2012. This report serves as a means to evaluate the application of the EIR and may include proposals for adapting the EIR.[1]

2 A provision similar to Art 46 of the EIR is rarely found in national legislation.[2]

3 Art 53 of the 1995 Draft convention on insolvency proceedings (on this convention, see the Introduction at mn 10) included the holding of a conference to review or evaluate the convention, but only upon application by a contracting state.[3] Only if one of the contracting states had not filed an application within ten years of the coming into effect of the 1995 Draft convention on insolvency proceedings would the President of the Council have to have called a meeting.[4]

Article 47
Entry into force

This Regulation shall enter into force on 31 May 2002.

This Regulation shall be binding in its entirety and directly applicable in the Member States in accordance with the Treaty establishing the European Community.

1 Art 47 of the EIR regulates the date on which the Regulation enters into force, namely 31 May 2002. Therefore the presumption in Art 254 (2) EEC Treaty – which holds that a regulation that does not specify the date it comes into force on the twentieth day following its publication – does not apply.

[1] D-K/D/Ch-*Duursma* Art 46 mn 1; Kübler/Prütting-*Kemper* EuInsVO Art 46 mn 1.

[2] Moss/Fletcher/Isaacs-*Moss/Smith*, Regulation, mn 8.297.

[3] *Virgós/Schmit* Explanatory report mn 317.

[4] *Virgós/Schmit* Explanatory report mn 318.

The date that the EIR came into force is significant for one main reason: according to Art 43 of the EIR, the EIR only applies to those insolvency proceedings that are opened after its coming into force. For acts carried out by the debtor prior to the coming into force of the EIR, the law that was applicable to such acts when they were carried out continues to govern. As to which law is applicable is determined either pursuant to the provisions of private international law of the respective Member States, or pursuant to international agreements that, although they were replaced by the EIR when it came into force, still – pursuant to Art 44 (2) of the EIR – govern proceedings opened before the EIR came into force. **2**

In the ten Member States that joined the European Union on **1 May 2004** (Czech Republic, Republic of Estonia, Republic of Cyprus, Republic of Latvia, Republic of Lithuania, Republic of Hungary, Republic of Malta, Republic of Poland, Republic of Slovenia, and the Slovak Republic), Art 2 of the Act of Accession[1] stipulates that the acts adopted by the institutions of the European Union and the European Central Bank before accession are, from the date of accession, binding and applicable in these States under the conditions laid down in those Treaties and in this Act. The EIR therefore applies in these Member States as of 1 May 2004. **3**

For the Member States Bulgaria and Romania, which joined on **1 January 2007**, Art 2 of the accession protocol[2] stipulates that the acts adopted by the institutions of the European Union before accession, which includes the EIR, are binding as of the date of accession. **4**

Art 249 (2) of the EEC Treaty provides that the EIR, being a regulation, has general application; it is binding in its entirety and applies directly in all Member States. Art 47 (2) of the EIR merely repeats the wording of the EEC Treaty. **5**

For the Annexes A, B and C of the EIR, see Annex 1 p 819 et seq.

[1] Act concerning the conditions of accession of the Czech Republic, the Republic of Estonia, the Republic of Cyprus, the Republic of Latvia, the Republic of Lithuania, the Republic of Hungary, the Republic of Malta, the Republic of Poland, the Republic of Slovenia and the Slovak Republic and the adjustments to the Treaties on which the European Union is founded, OJ L 236 p 33.

[2] Protocol concerning the conditions and arrangements for admission of the Republic of Bulgaria and Romania to the European Union of 21 June 2005, OJ L 157 p 29.

PART 2

Article 102 of the German Act Introducing the Insolvency Act (EGInsO) Implementing Regulation (EC) 1346/2000 on Insolvency Proceedings

Preliminary Comments on Article 102 *EGInsO*

Bibliography

Breutigam/Blersch/Goetsch/Haas Insolvenzrecht, Berliner Kommentar (August 2006); *Smid* Deutsches und Europäisches intenationales Insolvenzrecht, Kommentar (2004).

1 Sections 1 to 11 of Art 102 of the German *EGInsO* – enacted through the Act of 14 March 2003 amending international insolvency law[1] – primarily serve the implementation of European Council Regulation (EC) 1346/2000 of 29 May 2000 on insolvency proceedings (hereinafter "EC-Regulation" or "EIR"). Although pursuant to Art 249 of the EC-Treaty the EC-Regulation has immediate effect in each Member State of the European Union, and therefore there is no need for express adoption of it, it was nevertheless necessary to modify German procedural rules (e.g. jurisdiction of the courts, publication, stays of proceedings, etc.) in the case of insolvency proceedings with a European connection.

In the event of a conflict, however, the provisions of the EC-Regulation prevail.

2 Where the EC-Regulation does not apply, for example in insolvency cases having no connection to an EU Member State, then autonomous German international insolvency law applies, which is regulated in Sections 335–358 of the German *InsO* (Insolvency Act). However these provisions may also be applied **additionally** in insolvency cases with a connection to an EU Member State should the EC-Regulation or Art 102 of the German *EGInsO* fail to contain a rule covering the issue involved, e.g. the issue of exercising voting rights by a foreign liquidator in respect of the claims registered with him (Sec 341 (3) *InsO*).[2]

Article 102 EGInsO
Section 1 Local Jurisdiction

1. If the German courts in insolvency proceedings acquire international jurisdiction pursuant to Art 3 (1) of European Council Regulation (EC) 1346/2000 of 29 May 2000 (OJ L160/1), where no national jurisdiction pursuant to Section 3 of the *InsO* would

[1] BGBl vol I, 345.

[2] *Smid* Komm EuInsVO prelim. comments on Art 102 EGInsO mn 4; BK-InsO/*Pannen* prelim. comments on Art 102 EGInsO mn 9.

be established, then the insolvency court in whose district the centre of a debtor's main interests is situated acquires exclusive jurisdiction.

2. If the German courts acquire jurisdiction pursuant to Art 3 (2) of the EC Regulation, then the insolvency court in whose district the debtor's establishment is situated acquires exclusive jurisdiction. Section 3 (2) of the *InsO* applies accordingly.

3. Notwithstanding the jurisdiction established by subsections (1) and (2), for any decisions or other measures executed pursuant to the EC-Regulation, any national insolvency court in whose district assets of the debtor are located has jurisdiction. The governments of the individual German federal states are, in the interests of the expedient enhancement or faster conclusion of proceedings, authorized to order that decisions or measures executed pursuant to the EC Regulation for the districts of several insolvency courts are to be assigned to one of these alone. The governments of the federal states are entitled to delegate their authorization to the Administration of Justice (*Landesjustizverwaltung*) of the respective federal state.

Contents

Index

Bibliography

Breutigam/Blersch/Goetsch/Haas Insolvenzrecht, Berliner Kommentar (January 2006); *Duursma-Kepplinger/Duursma/Chalupsky* Europäische Insolvenzverordnung, Kommentar (2002); *Ehricke* Die Umsetzung der Finanzsicherheitenrichtlinie (Richtlinie 2002/47/EG) im Rahmen des Diskussionsentwurfs zur Änderung der Insolvenzordnung, ZIP 2003, p 1065 und ZIP 2003, p 1068; Hamburger Kommentar zum Insolvenzrecht (2006) (ed *Schmidt, A.*); Heidelberger Kommentar zur Insolvenzordnung, 4th edn (2006) (eds *Eickmann/Flessner/Irschlinger/Kirchhof/Kreft/Landfermann/ Marotzke/Stephan*); *P. Huber* Internationales Insolvenzrecht in Europa, ZZP 114 (2001), p 133; *U. Huber* Inländische Insolvenzverfahren über Auslandsgesellschaften nach der Europäischen Insolvenzverordnung, in Festschrift Gerhardt (2004), p 397 et seq; *Klöhn* Statische oder formale Lebenssachverhalte als „Interessen" iSd Art. 3 I 1 EuInsVO? – Zum Mittelpunkt der hauptsächlichen Interessen einer im Ausland gegründeten Gesellschaft bei Einstellung ihrer werbenden Tätigkeit im Inland, NZI 2006, p 383; *Knof* Internationale Zuständigkeit bei Abwicklungstätigkeiten nach Einstellung der werbenden Tätigkeit einer GmbH, comments on AG Hamburg dated 16.8.2006, NZI 2006, p 653; *Knof* Europäisches Insolvenzrecht und Schuldbefreiungs-Tourismus, ZInsO 2005, p 1017; *Knof Perpetuatio fori* und Attraktivkraft des Erstantrags im Europäischen Insolvenzrecht?, ZInsO 2006, p 754; *Leible/Staudinger* Die europäische Verordnung über Insolvenzverfahren, KTS 2000, p 533; *Mankowski* Grenzüberschreitender Umzug und das center of main interest im europäischen Internationalen Insolvenzrecht, NZI 2005, p 368; *Mankowski* Mittelpunkt der hauptsächlichen Interessen bei Verlegung des Wohnsitzes nach Antragstellung, comments on ECJ dated 17.1.2006 – C-1/04 Susanne Staubitz-Schreiber, NZI 2006, S 153; *Mankowski* Bestimmung des Mittelpunkts der hauptsächlichen Interessen nach Zeitpunkt der Verfahrenseröffnung, comments on Court of Appeal Civil Division dated 27.7.2005 – [2005] EWCA Civ 974, NZI 2005, p 571; *Moss/Fletcher/Isaacs* (eds) The EC Regulation on Insolvency Proceedings (2002); Münchener Kommentar zur Insolvenzordnung, vol 1 (2001); *Pannen/Riedemann* Der Begriff des „centre of main interests" iSd Art 3 I 1 EuInsVO im Spiegel aktueller Fälle aus der Rechtsprechung, NZI 2004, p 646; *Pannen/Riedemann* Die deutschen Ausführungsbestimmungen zur EuInsVO – Ein Überblick zu den Regelungen des Art 102 EGInsO nf, NZI 2004, p 301; *Paulus* Europäische Insolvenzverordnung, Kommentar (2006); *Schmidt, J.* Perpetuatio fori im europäischen internationalen Insolvenzrecht, ZInsO 2006, p 88; *Smid* Deutsches und Europäisches internationales Insolvenzrecht, Kommentar (2004); *Smid* Auswirkungen des europäischen internationalen Insolvenzrechts auf die Praxis der deutschen Insolvenzgerichte, InVo 2005, p 437; *Vallender* Die Insolvenz von Scheinauslandsgesellschaften, ZGR 2006, p 425; *Vallender* Aufgaben und Befugnisse des deutschen Insolvenzrichters in Verfahren nach der EuInsVO, KTS 2005, p 283; *Waechter* Der Entwurf des MoMiG und die Auswirkungen auf inländische Zweigniederlassungen von Auslandsgesellschaften, GmbHR 2006, p 793; *Wimmer* Einpassung der EU-Insolvenzverordnung in das deutsche Recht durch das Gesetz zur Neuregelung des Internationalen Insolvenzrechtes, in Gerhardt/Haarmeyer/Kreft (eds), FS Kirchhof (2003), p 521.

1. Purpose of Art 102 Sec 1 *EGInsO*

Digressing from the German provision on jurisdiction found in Sec 3 *InsO*, Art 102 Sec 1 (1) *EGInsO* regulates the jurisdiction of courts in cross-border insolvency cases in which a German court, although having acquired international jurisdiction, has no local jurisdiction. Art 102 Sec 1 (2) *EGInsO* grants jurisdiction to a German insolvency court for secondary insolvency proceedings. Art 102 Sec 1 (3) *EGInsO* grants jurisdiction to German insolvency courts for the execution of measures in support of foreign insolvency courts or foreign liquidators, e.g. publicizing the proceedings. Art 102 Sec 1 (3) sentence 2 *EGInsO* allows for a concentration of jurisdiction for proceedings pursuant to the EIR at one single insolvency court of a German federal state by way of an ordinance issued by the particular state's authorities. This provision is in line with Recital 15 sentence 2 of the EIR. 1

2. Contents of the Rule

2.1 Local Jurisdiction for Main Insolvency Proceedings

2.1.1 Distinction between sec 3 (1) *InsO* and Art 3 (1) of the EIR

2 As to which insolvency court has jurisdiction within Germany is regulated in Sec 3 (1) *InsO*. According to Sec 3 (1) sentence 2 *InsO*, the "centre of the debtor's independent economic activities" is the overriding factor in determining jurisdiction. This differs from the rule in Art 3 (1) of the EIR according to which international jurisdiction is determined by where the debtor has its "centre of his main interests".[1] These differences in wording actually refer to two different connecting factors. The "economic activities" in German insolvency decisions involves an investigation *ex officio* to determine whether the business of the company is actually being conducted at a particular location, i.e. whether management decisions are being made there,[2] or whether, viewed objectively, perceivable business transactions are being executed from the location in question;[3] the mere storage of business documents for example will not constitute "economic activities". The decisive point in time for determining jurisdiction, and consequently the "centre of main interests", is the receipt of the request at the insolvency court (request is then pending).[4]

2.1.2 Scope of application of Art 102 Sec 1 *EGInsO*

3 According to Art 102 Sec 1 *EGInsO*, the jurisdiction of the German insolvency court, in cases where no German court would acquire jurisdiction pursuant to Sec 3 *InsO* and in these cases only,[5] is to be determined pursuant to Art 3 (1) of the EIR. The "centre of main interests" to be ascertained pursuant to this also allows economic interests to be taken into consideration: the determination of the competent court in cases of cross-border insolvencies of corporate groups will therefore be easier,[6] i.e. where subsidiary companies, although their registered offices are situated in another EC Member State, are nevertheless fully controlled by the "managerial authority" of the parent company. However, the exercising of this "managerial authority" must be ascertainable by outside third parties, which follows from the definition in Recital 13 of the EIR.[7] Where the registered office and the alleged centre of administration are not in the same location,

---

[1] See the comments to Art 3 of the EIR mn 29 et seq.

[2] BayObLG ZInsO 2001, 517; BayObLG, ZInsO 2003, 1045; LG Dessau ZIP 1998, 1007; MünchKomm InsO-*Ganter* § 3 mn 11 and mn 14.

[3] BayObLG ZInsO 2003, 902; BayObLG ZInsO 2003, 1142; OLG Düsseldorf NZI 2000, 601; OLG Braunschweig NZI 2000, 266; OLG Hamm ZInsO 1999, 533; OLG Schleswig NZI 2004, 264.

[4] ECJ ZInsO 2006, 86 with concurring comments by *J. Schmidt*, 88; AG Celle NZI 2005, 410; OLG Cologne NZI 2003, 567; OLG Frankfurt NZI 2002, 499; OLG Naumburg ZIP 2001, 753; OLG Hamm NZI 2000, 220; *Mankowski* NZI 2005, 368, 369 with further substantiation; Advocate General ECJ ZIP 2005, 1641; dissenting opinion on German insolvency law: regarding the creditor's request, the day of serving the debtor: OLG Düsseldorf ZVI 2004, 31 = NZI 2004, 146 = ZInsO 2004, 507; on international insolvency law: fn 7 in *Mankowski*, as cited above, 369.

[5] BK-InsO/*Pannen* Art 102 § 1 mn 5; HK-InsO/*Stephan* Art 102 § 1 mn 4.

[6] *Smid* Komm EuInsVO Art 102 § 1, mn 3.

[7] See AG Mönchengladbach ZInsO 2004, 561 = ZIP 2004, 1064 with concurring comments by *Bähr/Riedemann*; Tribunale di Parma "Eurofood Decision" ZIP 2004, 1220; Tribunale di Parma dated 15 Jun 2004, ZIP 2004, 2298; *Vallender* KTS 2005, 283, 292; limiting: *Paulus* Komm EuInsVO Art 3 mn 31; in-depth: Art 3 of the EIR mn 43, 45, 53, 54.

the burden of proof lies with the party making the request even though the court itself, pursuant to Sec 5 (1) *InsO*, is obliged *ex officio* to investigate such circumstances. This can be decided by way of *non liquet*, i.e. if neither side is able to prove the issue, the party with the burden of proof is deemed to have failed.[8]

2.1.3 Main area of application: discontinuance of the economic activities

In the case of a "Ltd." operating exclusively in Germany, jurisdiction in favour of the German insolvency court will be found even if the economic activities have ceased prior to the making of the request to open insolvency proceedings,[9] although the time of the making of the request should remain decisive. The "interests" within the meaning of Art 3 of the EIR are not always equivalent to "activities".[10] The object of the rule is to create predictability of international jurisdiction for creditors in insolvency cases (Recital 4 of the EIR).[11] "Interests" in this sense also includes things like the necessity of terminating employment relationships, the existence of obligations, or the *situs* of the debtor's realizable property (i.e. the lingering effects of more permanent factors).[12] The determination of the court's jurisdiction must not depend on any arbitrary conduct in relation to the making of the request by the responsible executive bodies of the company either at the time of or subsequent to the discontinuance of business activities. If, however, the company is still being actively wound up at the time at which the request is made, then the place in which the winding-up is made is decisive for determining jurisdiction.[13] This is not the case if the winding-up is only an internal activity or a passive reaction.[14] Decisive is also the belief of the creditors at the time of making the particular business investment, i.e. which insolvency law did they believe would be applied in the event of insolvency; however, jurisdiction will not be determined purely on the number of creditors in the country in which the request is being made or in the country of the registered office.[15] **4**

Therefore, in case of business activities of natural persons, jurisdiction is determined by the place of these business activities.[16] Should this person have a different domicile, this has no bearing on the jurisdiction.

2.1.4 Area of application: discrepancy between residence and place of employment

This also solves the problem in insolvency cases involving natural persons whose main occupation is not of a self-employed nature and whose domicile and place of employment are not in the same location, or in other words natural persons whose secondary occupation only is of a self-employed nature. Pursuant to Art 3 of the EIR, domicile – as the habitual residence[17] and therefore the *situs* of the "main interests" – is deemed here **5**

[8] *Vallender* KTS 2005, 283, 295; *U. Huber* FS Gerhardt, 397, 406.

[9] AG Hamburg ZIP 2005, 2275 = NZI 2006, 120; concurring in the outcome: *Klöhn* NZI 2006, 383; contra *Schall*, ZVI 2007, 236.

[10] Dissenting opinion: AG Celle NZI 2005, 410.

[11] *Klöhn* NZI 2006, 383.

[12] Critical: *Klöhn* NZI 2006, 383; on this, see: LG Leipzig ZInsO, 378 where the debtor is the owner of real estate and lessor in Germany; only the business documents were taken to France.

[13] AG Hamburg ZInsO 2006, 559 = ZIP 2006, 1105.

[14] AG Hamburg dated 16 Aug 2006, ZIP 2006, 1643 = ZInsO 2006, 1006.

[15] But see: *Knof* NZI 2006, 653, 654.

[16] BGH dated 22 Mar 2007, ZInsO 2007, 440, *Moss/Fletcher/Isaacs*, The EC Regulation in Insolvency Proceedings: A Commentary and Annotated Guide, 2002, 169; Advocate General ECJ, ZIP 2005, 1641, 1645, no 64.

[17] High Court of Justice London, NZI 2007, 361, with approving comment by *Paulus* NZI

as decisive for determining jurisdiction.[18] Particularly in insolvency cases involving natural persons, the legislator wished to avoid the linking of the jurisdiction issue purely to the business activities of the debtor.[19] In the case of natural persons whose main activities are not of a business nature, this centre is generally their habitual residence at the time of making the request,[20] which need not be the same as the "domicile".[21] One must therefore agree with the opinion[22] which implores the need for a "residency concept" of the debtor's based purely on objective criteria (dwelling, where one's life is centred, family, permanent relationships to persons/place), since the German term "*Wohnsitz*" (domicile) contains a subjective element and allows for multiple domiciles (Sec 7 (2) *BGB* – German Civil Code). This place of residence must, however, actually be substantiated by the debtor, the insolvency court being obliged to thoroughly investigate this if necessary.[23] If the reason for the permanent residence is to work in the foreign country, then a domicile cannot be assumed in Germany.[24]

By contrast, neither the composition of the creditors and their registered offices/domiciles nor the point in time at which the obligations were created nor the work place is relevant for determining jurisdiction since they could not reliably be ascertained and discerned by an outside third party.[25]

2.1.5 Change of domicile

6 Although through an actual and timely change of domicile *before* the making of the request a debtor may end up in a place governed by insolvency laws more favourable to him (e.g. where the law allows a discharge of residual debt in the case of natural persons[26]), jurisdiction, in the case of a natural person whose main activities are of a business nature, is determined by the place of these business activities (and these activities cannot be transferred so easily).[27] It is different, however, when the director of a "Ltd." has no activities in England, but has his residence there; in such a case, the residence is decisive.[28] The determination of a territorial insolvency at the location of an establishment requires that the establishment meets the definition of this found in Art 2 (h) of the EC-Regulation, namely that it is made up of a combination of human means and goods. In the case of natural persons, this is generally not the case.[29]

7 A change of domicile subsequent to the making of the request is irrelevant to the issue of jurisdiction. By way of an order of 27 November 2003,[30] the German Federal

2007, 367; D-K/D/Ch-*Duursma-Kepplinger* Art 3 mn 22; *Huber* ZZP 114 (2001), 140; AG Celle NZI 2005, 410 = ZInsO 2005, 895.

18 *Wimmer* FS Kirchhof, 521, 524; BK-InsO/*Pannen* Art 102 § 1 mn 5.

19 *Wimmer* FS Kirchhof, 523.

20 See mn 1 at the end; *Mankowski* NZI 2005, 368, 369; for a dissenting opinion see Court of Appeal, NZI 2005, 571 (time of opening proceedings is decisive) with a declining opinion *Mankowski*, 575.

21 AG Celle ZInsO 2005, 895 = NZI 2005, 410.

22 *Knof* ZInsO 2005, 1017 et seq.

23 *Mankowski* NZI 2005, 368, 372.

24 AG Hamburg dated 2 Mar 2007, ZVI 2007, 182.

25 *Knof* ZInsO 2005, 1017, 1022; *Mankowski* NZI 2005, 368, 369, 370; *J. Schmidt* ZInsO 2006, 88, 89; *Mankowski* NZI 2006, 154.

26 For the absence of such in Spanish law: Advocate General ECJ ZIP 2005, 1641, 1646, fn 39.

27 *Moss/Fletcher/Isaacs* The EC Regulation in Insolvency Proceedings: A Commentary and Annotated Guide, 2002, 169; Advocate General ECJ ZIP 2005, 1641, 1645, no 64.

28 High Court of Justice London, dated 20 Dec 2006, NZI 2007, 361.

29 *Mankowski* NZI 2005, 575, 576; on the concept of establishment when not only the own staff is employed: AG Munich dated 5 Feb 2007, NZI 2007, 358, with approving comments by *Mankowski*, NZI 2007, 360.

30 ZIP 2004, 94 = ZVI 2003, 655 = NZI 2004, 139 = ZInsO 2004, 34 = DZWiR 2004, 83.

Supreme Court (*BGH*) submitted the question to the ECJ whether a change of the centre of main interest (in this case a change of the place of residence to Spain) subsequent to the making of the request, but before the opening of proceedings, would also result in a transfer of jurisdiction to the insolvency court of the Member State of the new location. Based on various applications of 6 September 2005[31], the Advocate General of the ECJ decided in favour of jurisdiction of the court at which the request was made.[32] It held that, as contemplated by Recital 2 of the EIR, the principle of "efficiency of proceedings" (*Verfahrenseffizienz*) applies, and therefore concluded that a change of jurisdiction during the opening proceedings would be incompatible with this. The ECJ affirmed this,[33] referring to Recital 4 of the EIR, which in the court's opinion discourages the transferring of the registered office/domicile for the purposes of obtaining a more favourable position in another legal system, and to Recital 8 of the EIR, which aims at improving the efficiency and effectiveness of cross-border proceedings in the interests of creditors who, at the time of taking on the obligation, assessed the risks of doing so in relation to the place where the debtor had his registered office/domicile, and they should be able to rely on this. The Federal Supreme Court of Germany has also affirmed a residual jurisdiction in favour of the court at which a request is made both in the case of a relocation subsequent to the making of the request (decision of 9 February 2006) and upon receipt of several subsequent additional requests to open proceedings after the transferring of the centre of the economic interests (decision of 2 March 2006).[34] In the court's opinion, the proceedings properly initiated in Germany are still pending and are not terminated even after the debtor has relocated to a foreign country. The German insolvency court, which has jurisdiction first, precludes other foreign courts from assuming jurisdiction and thereby prevents "forum shopping" (Recitals 2, 4, and 8 of the EIR).

2.2 Local Jurisdiction for Territorial Insolvency Proceedings

Art 102 Sec 1 (2) *EGInsO* presupposes German jurisdiction pursuant to Art 3 (2) of the EIR. It regulates jurisdiction within Germany for territorial insolvency proceedings. As in the case of Art 3 (2) of the EIR, the location of the establishment is also decisive for determining jurisdiction. Other assets of the debtor, e.g. real estate or bank accounts that is/are not situated at the location of the establishment, are not capable of establishing jurisdiction for the opening of territorial insolvency proceedings.[35] **8**

Where the debtor operates several establishments, Art 102 Sec 1 (2) sentence 2 *EGInsO* with its reference to Sec 3 (2) *InsO* makes it clear that the German insolvency court at which the first request was made (principle of priority) acquires jurisdiction. If there is one managerial authority for several establishments, then the German insolvency court at the location of the main establishment has jurisdiction.[36] **9**

---

[31] ZIP 2005, 1641 with comments by *Brenner*, 1646 = NZI 2005, 544.

[32] For a consenting opinion see *Knof* ZInsO 2005, 1017, 1023; for a dissenting opinion see *Leible/Staudinger* KTS 2000, 533, 545.

[33] ECJ ZInsO 2006, 86 with a consenting opinion *J. Schmidt*, 88 = ZIP 2006, 188 with a consenting opinion *Knof/Mock*, 189; consenting *Vogl* EWiR 2006, 141; consenting *Mankowski* NZI 2006, 154; summing up: *Duursma-Kepplinger* ZIP 2007, 896.

[34] BGH dated 9 Feb 2006, ZInsO 2006, 321 and dated 2 Mar 2006, ZIP 2006, 767 = ZInsO 2006, 431; critical: *Knof* ZInsO 2006, 756.

[35] BK-InsO/*Stephan* Art 102 § 1 mn 5; *Smid* Komm EuInsVO Art 102 § 1 mn 4.

[36] BK-InsO/*Pannen* Art 102 § 1 mn 9; HamburgerKomm-*Undritz* Art 102 § 1 mn 9; *Wimmer* FS Kirchhof, 524.

2.3 Local Jurisdiction for Supporting Measures

10 The support of German insolvency courts is often required for proceedings opened pursuant to the EIR in a foreign country. This may involve measures such as publication (Art 21 of the EIR) or registration in public registers (Art 22 of the EIR). According to Art 102 Sec 1 (3) sentence 1 *EGInsO*, the insolvency court in whose district assets of the debtor are located is responsible for this. In the case of publications, the party making the request, usually the foreign liquidator, has a free choice as to which of the insolvency courts with a "connection to the assets" he wishes employ; however in the case of registrations in the register, he should choose the insolvency court in the district where the register of the concerned assets is kept. This is advisable if only for practical reasons, despite the ambiguous wording of the legislation that states that an – even far-distant – insolvency court may be resorted to in whose district "any" asset of the debtor is situated.

11 None of the German federal states have yet made use of the concentration power to create special German "EC-Regulation insolvency courts" granted by Art 102 Sec 1 (3), sentence 2 and 3 *EGInsO*.[37]

3. Best Practice

12 In the case of uncertainty as to the jurisdiction of a court, it is well-advised to clarify the issue orally in advance with the prospective insolvency court (insolvency judge) prior to the making of the request. Later referrals (to other courts) and disputes over jurisdiction take up valuable time and may delay or even foil any necessary, expedient protective (preservation) measures. Sensible insolvency judges will not refuse such a clarifying discussion in advance.

Article 102 EGInsO
Section 2 Reasons for the Opening Order

Where it is presumed that assets of the debtor are situated in another Member State of the European Union, the order opening the insolvency proceedings (*Eröffnungsbeschluss* – "opening order") should briefly describe the actual findings and legal considerations substantiating jurisdiction pursuant to Article 3 of Regulation (EC) 1346/2000 for German courts.

Contents

[37] HK-InsO*Stephan* Art 102 § 1 mn 10.

Index

Bibliography

Breutigam/Blersch/Goetsch/Haas Insolvenzrecht, Berliner Kommentar (January 2006); *Ehricke* Die Zusammenarbeit der Insolvenzverwalter bei grenzüberschreitenden Insolvenzen nach der EuInsVO, WM 2005, p 397; Heidelberger Kommentar zur Insolvenzordnung, 4th edn (2006) (eds *Eickmann/Flessner/Irschlinger/Kirchhof/Kreft/Landfermann/Marotzke/Stephan*); *Herchen* Das Übereinkommen über Insolvenzverfahren der Mitgliedstaaten der Europäischen Union vom 23.11.1995 (2000); *Kebekus* Hauptinsolvenzverfahren, Sekundärinsolvenzverfahren, Mittelpunkt der hauptsächlichen Interessen/EMBIC I, EWiR 2004, S 705; *Kübler/Prütting* Kommentar zur Insolvenzordnung (March 2006); *Paulus* Zuständigkeitsfragen nach der Europäischen Insolvenzverordnung, ZIP 2003, p 1725; *Penzlin/Riedemann* Klarstellung der Befugnisse englischer Hauptinsolvenzverwalter – MG Rover II, comments on High Court of Justice Birmingham dated 11.5.2005, NZI 2005, p 517; *Smid* Deutsches und Europäisches internationales Insolvenzrecht, Kommentar (2004); *Vallender* Aufgaben und Befugnisse des deutschen Insolvenzrichters in Verfahren nach der EuInsVO, KTS 2005, p 283; *Wehdeking* Reform des Internationalen Insolvenzrechtes in Deutschland und Österreich, DZWiR 2003, p 133; *Wimmer* Einpassung der EU-Insolvenzverordnung in das deutsche Recht durch das Gesetz zur Neuregelung des Internationalen Insolvenzrechtes, in Gerhardt/Haarmeyer/Kreft (eds), FS Kirchhof (2003), p 521.

1. Purpose of Art 102 Sec 2 *EGInsO*

Art 102 Sec 2 *EGInsO* stipulates the necessity of substantiating the jurisdiction of the German insolvency court when it opens main insolvency proceedings pursuant to the EIR. It therefore supplements the provisions of Sec 27 *InsO*. German opening orders generally do not contain the reasons upon which they are based. Therefore if the German insolvency court acknowledges an international connection, then the order must make clear that insolvency proceedings are being opened as main proceedings within the meaning of the EIR. Foreign insolvency courts may otherwise assume that mere territorial insolvency proceedings are being opened. **1**

2. Contents of the Rule

2.1 Reasons for Granting the Order

The proceedings must be opened as main proceedings within the meaning of the EIR when it is apparent from the ascertained facts and circumstances that assets of the debtor may be situated in another Member State.[1] A substantiated possibility of foreign assets is sufficient – this following from the wording of the provision "where it is pre- **2**

[1] *Smid* Komm EuInsVO Art 102 § 2 mn 2;
BK-InsO*Pannen* Art 102 § 2 mn 4.

sumed" – for finding that international insolvency proceedings are necessary.[2] Appropriate investigations must be carried out by the expert to be appointed by the insolvency court, and the results must be discussed in his expert report.[3] If necessary, the German court must also review whether a request to open secondary insolvency proceedings should be reinterpreted as a request to open main insolvency proceedings.[4] Such a reinterpretation must however be based on the facts available and may not be made for the purposes of "winning a competition" to open insolvency proceedings".[5]

2.2 Drafting the Opening Order

3 Because it has a declaratory effect on other foreign courts, the opening order must make it clear directly in the wording of it that main insolvency proceedings as per the EIR are being opened. It is therefore advisable to state expressly in the operative part of the order that the proceedings are being opened "as main proceedings with in the meaning of Regulation (EC) 1346/2000 of 29 May 2000", therefore ensuring its publication in this way (Sec 9 and 30 *InsO*). After the operative part, under "Reasons", the relevant criteria and considerations upon which the court bases its international jurisdiction are to be stated. The court's opinion as to why it has jurisdiction pursuant to Art 3 (1) of the EIR must be stated here in unequivocal terms, the "centre of main interests" must be substantiated in detail if necessary, and the possibility of another foreign insolvency court having jurisdiction must be reviewed.[6] Although the provision uses the word "*soll*" (should), this must be interpreted as a "must".[7] A failure to state the reasons for jurisdiction does not, however, result in a nullification of the order[8] nor does it constitute a violation of the public policy principle set out in Art 26 of the EIR,[9] but it may expose the court to public-authority liability claims (*Amtshaftungsansprüche*) should a foreign court open main proceedings at a future point in time based on an assumption that the German proceedings were territorial insolvency proceedings.[10] The failure to state the reasons also infringes the obligation to observe the principle of Community trust contemplated by Recital 22 of the EIR.[11]

3. Best Practice

4 Should the German insolvency court obtain knowledge that other insolvency proceedings against the same debtor are simultaneously pending at a foreign court, or should it obtain such knowledge during the course of the proceedings to open insolvency proceedings *(Eröffnungsverfahren)*, then the principle of Community trust demands that the participating insolvency judges informally exchange information prior to the making of any decisions that are binding in the proceedings.[12] Reference is made here to the

---

[2] HK-InsO*Stephan* Art 102 § 2 mn 7; Kübler/Prütting-*Kemper* EGInsO Art 102 § 2 mn 4.

[3] *Vallender* KTS 2005, 283, 287.

[4] AG Mönchengladbach ZIP 2004, 1064 with comments by *Bähr/Riedemann* ZIP 2004, 1066; Kübler/Prütting-*Kemper* EGInsO Art 102 § 3 mn 5.

[5] *Kebekus* EWiR 2004, 705, 706.

[6] Example: High Court of Justice Birmingham NZI 2005, 467; AG Mönchengladbach ZIP 2004, 1064 with comments by *Bähr/Riedemann* ZIP 2004, 1066.

[7] *Smid* Komm EuInsVO Art 102 § 2 mn 3; *Wehdeking* DZWiR 2003, 133, 136.

[8] BK-InsO/*Pannen* Art 102 § 2 mn 2; Kübler/Prütting-*Kemper* EGInsO Art 102 § 2 mn 5; *Wimmer* FS Kirchhof, 521, 525; *Vallender* KTS 2005, 283, 312.

[9] OLG Vienna NZI 2005, 56; affirmed by OGH NZI 2005, 465.

[10] BK-InsO/*Pannen* Art 102 § 2 mn 2.

[11] *Smid* Komm EuInsVO Art 102 § 2 mn 3.

[12] *Paulus* ZIP 2003, 1725, 1726 regarding the

"Guidelines Applicable to Court-to-Court Communications in Cross-Border Cases"[13] of the American Law Institute and to Art 27 of the UNCITRAL Model Law.[14] A provision equivalent to Art 31 of the EIR is missing.[15] However, will be difficult because of the language differences. *Paulus* relates that in the "BenQ-Holding" case, the judges involved communicated via a translator.[16]

Provided that the proceedings before the German court are indeed "ripe" for opening, the German court does not have to wait in making its opening decision until a decision is made in proceedings pending elsewhere.[17]

The German court must also consider whether it is sensible and appropriate to delineate and explain the powers of the German (provisional) liquidator in the order or in a separate explanatory order for the purposes of transparency and enforceability vis-à-vis foreign courts.[18] If necessary, the insolvency court may also empower the liquidator to conclude a "liquidator contract" or "protocol" that stipulates mutual co-operation obligations with a foreign liquidator.[19]

Article 102 EGInsO
Section 3 Avoiding Conflicts of Jurisdiction

(1) Where the court of another Member State of the European Union has opened main insolvency proceedings and as long as these proceedings are pending, any petition made to a national insolvency court to open such proceedings in respect of the assets forming part of the insolvency assets is inadmissible. Any proceedings opened in contravention of sentence 1 may not be continued. The liquidator of the foreign main insolvency proceedings also has a right to appeal against the opening of the national proceedings.

(2) If the court of a Member State of the European Union has refused to open insolvency proceedings claiming that the German courts have jurisdiction pursuant to Article 3 (1) of Regulation (EC) 1346/2000, a German insolvency court may not refuse to open insolvency proceedings by claiming that the courts of the other Member State have jurisdiction.

Contents

so-called "protocols" in the Maxwell case; *Vallender* KTS 2005, 283, 321.

13 See http://www.iiiglobal.org/international/projects/German_package.pdf; German version in KTS 2005, 121.

14 See also *Vallender* KTS 2005, 283, 322.

15 *Vallender* KTS 2005, 283, 321; *Ehricke* WM 2005, 397, 401; for a dissenting opinion see *Herchen* Das Übereinkommen über Insolvenzverfahren der Mitgliedstaaten der Europäischen Union (2000), 146 et seq. *Paulus* Komm EuInsVO Art 31 mn 5 et seq considers it as a regulatory gap of the Regulation.

16 EWiR 2007, 143.

17 *Vallender* KTS 2005, 283, 314.

18 Example: High Court of Justice Birmingham, NZI 2005, 515; comments agreeing with this: *Penzlin/Riedemann* NZI 2005, 517 et seq.

19 *Vallender* KTS 2005, 283, 324.

Index

Bibliography

Breutigam/Blersch/Goetsch/Haas Insolvenzrecht, Berliner Kommentar (January 2006); *Fritz/Bähr* Die Europäische Verordnung über Insolvenzverfahren – Herausforderung an Gerichte und Insolvenzverwalter, DZWiR 2001, p 221; Heidelberger Kommentar zur Insolvenzordnung, 4th edn (2006) (eds *Eickmann/Flessner/Irschlinger/Kirchhof/Kreft/Landfermann/Marotzke/Stephan*); *Herchen* Wer zuerst kommt, mahlt zuerst!, NZI 2006, p 435; *Kammel* Die Bestimmung der zuständigen Gerichte bei grenzüberschreitenden Konzerninsolvenzen, NZI 2006, p 334; *Kübler/Prütting* Kommentar zur Insolvenzordnung (March 2006); *Laukemann* Rechtshängigkeit im europäischen Insolvenzrecht, RIW 2005, p 104; *Leible/Staudinger* Die europäische Verordnung über Insolvenzverfahren, KTS 2000, p 533; *Kebekus* Hauptinsolvenzverfahren, Sekundärinsolvenzverfahren, Mittelpunkt der hauptsächlichen Interessen/EMBIC I, EWiR 2004, p 705; *Knof* Europäisches Insolvenzrecht und Schuldbefreiungs-Tourismus, ZInsO 2005, p 1017; *Knof/Mock* Zuständigkeit des Insolvenzgerichts auch bei COMI-Verlegung des Schuldners zwischen Antragsstellung und Insolvenzeröffnung („Susanne Staubitz-Schreiber"), comments on ECJ dated 17.1.2006, ZIP 2006, p 189; *Knof/Mock* Comments on ECJ dated 2.5.2006, ZIP 2006, p 911; *Liersch* Nach der Eurofood-Entscheidung des EuGH: Genugtuung, aber auch viel Nachdenklichkeit, NZI 6/2006, V; *Mankowski* Comments on AG Cologne dated 1.12.2005, EWiR 2006, p 109; *Mankowski* Zulässigkeit der Verweisung durch deutsches Insolvenzgericht an ausländisches Gericht, AG Hamburg, Beschluss vom 9.5.2006, NZI 2006, p 486; *Meyer-Löwy/Poertzgen* Eigenverwaltung (§§ 270 ff InsO) Löst Kompetenzkonflikte nach der EuInsVO, ZInsO 2004, p 195; *Mock* Safe Harbour für Qualifikationsprobleme bei der Insolvenzantragspflicht? NZI 2006, p 24; *Oberhammer* Europäisches Insolvenzrecht in praxi – „Was bisher geschah", ZInsO 2004, p 761; *Paulus* Zuständigkeitsfragen nach der Europäischen Insolvenzordnung, ZIP 2003, p 1725; *Poertzgen/Adam* Die Bestimmung des „centre of main interests" gem Art 3 Abs 1 EuInsVO, ZInsO 2006, p 505; *Sabel* Hauptsitz als Niederlassung im Sinne der EuInsVO? NZI 2004, p 126; *Schilling/Schmidt* Comments on LG Hamburg dated 18.8.2005 – 326 T 34/05, EWiR 2006, p 15; *Schilling/Schmidt* COMI und vorläufiger Insolvenzverwalter – Problem gelöst?, ZInsO 2006, p 113; *Smid* Vier Entscheidungen englischer und deutscher Gerichte zur europäischen internationalen Zuständigkeit zur Eröffnung von Hauptinsolvenzverfahren, DZWiR 2003, S 397; *Smid* Deutsches und Europäisches internationales Insolvenzrecht, Kommentar (2004); *Vallender* Aufgaben und Befugnisse des deutschen Insolvenzrichters in Verfahren nach der EuInsVO, KTS 2005, p 283; *Vallender/Fuchs* Die Antragspflicht organschaftlicher Vertreter einer GmbH vor dem Hintergrund der Europäischen Insolvenzverordnung, ZIP 2004, p 829; *Wagner* Insolvenzantragstellung nur im EU-Ausland? Zivil- und strafrechtliche Risiken für den GmbH-Geschäftsführer, ZIP 2006, p 1934.

1. Purpose of Art 102 Sec 3 *EGInsO*

Art 102 Sec 3 *EGInsO* implements the principle of priority laid down in Art 16 of the EIR for avoiding conflicts of jurisdiction. 1

2. Contents of the Rule

2.1 Principle of Priority – Art 102 Sec 3 (1) sentence 1 *EGInsO*

Supplementary to the German rule found in Section 14 *InsO*, Art 102 Sec 3 (1) sentence 1 *EGInsO* provides an additional criterion for allowing insolvency requests: according to this, the German insolvency court in a proceeding with a connection to another European country must examine whether proceedings have validly been opened at an earlier point in time in another country where the EIR applies. This follows from the principle of Community trust (Recital 22 of the EIR), which states that the decisions of other courts are to be automatically recognized and which also aims to ensure the effectiveness of Art 16 (1) of the EIR. Although the insolvency court is obliged *ex officio* to review the facts and circumstances upon which the alleged jurisdiction is based (Sec 5 *InsO*), the party making the request is under an obligation to give the court the opportunity in the approval/admission proceedings *(Zulassungsverfahren)* to make a preliminary investigation to determine whether other prior foreign proceedings have been opened.[1] Therefore, in proceedings with a connection to a foreign country, the party making the request must provide the court with information as to whether or not main insolvency proceedings concerning the assets of the debtor have been opened in another country; because there is no European insolvency register, the court has no other way of ascertaining this.[2] Since the courts are under no obligation comparable to Art 31 of the EIR to cooperate or to provide information to each other, a request that fails to provide this additional information will not be allowed.[3] 2

The reference in the act to a "valid" opening decision refers to the issue to be examined by the German insolvency court, i.e. whether it can refuse to recognize the foreign opening decision based on an incompatibility with the public policy of the court at which the request is being made (i.e. the German court) (Art 26 of the EIR – infringement of public policy).[4] In recent times, a narrow construction of Art 26 of the EIR has been recommended since disadvantaged creditors can appeal themselves before the opening court.[5] The finding of a public policy infringement, however, does not invalidate the opening decision made by the court opening the proceedings[6] but rather results in a denial of recognition of this proceeding in Germany.[7] 3

There is also no way for the German court to review the foreign opening order. For the national, legally representative organs of the debtor, the making of the foreign insolvency request is sufficient to satisfy their obligation to make an insolvency request; there 4

[1] *Vallender* KTS 2005, 283, 295.

[2] AG Cologne NZI 2006, 57.

[3] De lege ferenda: *Leible/Staudinger* KTS 2000, 533, 569.

[4] On this: AG Düsseldorf ZIP 2003, 1363 = DZWiR 2003, 437 with critical comments by *Smid* DZWiR 2003, 397; ECJ dated 2 May 2006 ZInsO 2006, 484 = ZIP 2006, 907.

[5] On this narrow construction, see *Duursma-Kepplinger* DZWiR 2006, 177; *Duursma-Kepplinger* ZIP 2007, 896, 901; *Andres/Grund* NZI 2007, 137, *Knof* ZInsO 2007, 629, 635.

[6] *Vallender* KTS 2005, 283, 298; *Duursma-Kepplinger* ZIP 2007, 896, 901.

[7] AG Nürnberg, NZI 2007, 185; *Andres/Grund* NZI 2007, 137, 141; *Knof* ZInsO 2007, 629, 635.

is therefore no right in need of legal protection that would justify a second national insolvency request on account of the statutory obligations to do so.[8] However, the request must be made to the foreign court that has jurisdiction.[9] The obligation to make the request is, however, only satisfied if the insolvency proceedings in the foreign country encompass the entire assets of the debtor, which is why a request to open territorial insolvency proceedings will not suffice.[10]

5 According to the position taken by the Advocate General of the ECJ[11] on a question referred to it by the Supreme Court of Ireland,[12] a decision to open insolvency proceedings is already "effective" as soon as "insolvency proceedings" are initiated by a foreign insolvency court (so-called issue of retroactive effect). According to one opinion, the mere making of the request bans all other insolvency courts from opening insolvency proceedings,[13] whereas another opinion holds that only effectively opened proceedings can do this.[14] "Insolvency proceeding" was qualified by the Advocate General as only coming into existence once "provisional liquidators with powers to take possession" had been deployed. Item 152 of the opinion of the Advocate General speaks of a "provisional liquidator with the effect in law of depriving the directors" and of a "combined" measure, i.e. a measure with all of the implications set out in item 152 of the opinion.

6 German law however recognizes two forms of provisional liquidators ("temporary administrator" in the EIR): those with approval powers whose competence is determined at the "absolute discretion" of the court (Sec 21 (2) No. 2, 2nd alternative and 22 (2) *InsO*). These are called "weak" provisional liquidators. In contrast to these are the so-called "strong" provisional liquidators pursuant to Sec 21 (2), No. 2, 1st alternative and 22 (1) sentence 1 *InsO*. The latter steps completely into the legal shoes of either the debtor or of the party who has been granted powers to legally represent it. The legal implications described by the Advocate General relate solely to the German "strong" provisional liquidator pursuant to Sec 21(2), No. 2 *InsO*, because only a protective order such as that contemplated by the German *InsO* can deprive the managing director of a debtor company of his rights. Such measures would therefore "ban" foreign courts from opening their own insolvency proceedings within the meaning of Art 3 and 16 of the EIR.[15] In its decision of 2 May 2006, the ECJ largely follows the position taken by the Advocate General[16] and finds that the combination of the transfer of the power to dispose of

---

[8] AG Cologne ZIP 2005, 1566; ZIP 2004, 471; BK-InsO/*Pannen* § 335 mn 21; *Vallender/Fuchs* ZIP 2004, 829, 833; *Sabel* NZI 2004, 126, 127; *Meyer-Löwy/Poertzgen* ZInsO 2004, 195, 197; an obviously dissenting opinion AG Mönchengladbach ZIP 2004, 1064; *Wagner* ZIP 2006, 1934.

[9] *Wagner* ZIP 2006, 1934, 1941; *Vallender/Fuchs* ZIP 2004, 829, 831.

[10] *Mock* NZI 2006, 24.

[11] ZIP 2005, 1878 et seq.

[12] NZI 2004, 505=ZIP 2004, 1969 = ZInsO 2005, 159.

[13] *Laukemann* RIW 2005, 104, 110; *Oberhammer* ZInsO 2004, 761, 763; *Knof* ZInsO 2005, 1017, 1024; *Knof/Mock* ZIP 2005, 189, 191.

[14] LG Hamburg ZVI 2005, 549 = ZInsO 2005, 1052.

[15] Concurring: *Schilling/Schmidt* EWiR 2006, 15 comment on LG Hamburg ZInsO 2005, 1052; no differentiation between the various types of provisional liquidators: *Schilling/Schmidt* ZInsO 2006, 113, 115; *Poertzgen/Adam* ZInsO 2006, 505, 508; *Kammel* NZI 2006, 334, 337; **undecided:** *Liersch* NZI Heft 6/2006, NZI-aktuell, V; **dissenting opinion:** *Knof/Mock* ZIP 2006, 911, 912 who hold that the ordering of a "weak" provisional liquidator already has a blocking effect; concurring: *Herchen* NZI 2006, 435; against a preliminary effect in general: *Vallender* KTS 2006, 505, 508.

[16] ZInsO 2006, 484; *Schmidt* ZIP 2007, 405, on the reception in the USA, summing up: *Duursma-Kepplinger*, ZIP 2007, 896.

the debtor's assets *and* the appointment of a liquidator, which is listed in Annex C of the EIR, consitutes an effective decision within the meaning of Art 3 (3) and 16 (1) of the EIR, and thus has a blocking effect. Therefore German courts should state explicitly in the order appointing a "strong" provisional liquidator that the order has a blocking effect within the meaning of Art 16 of the EIR. Unresolved however is the status of proceedings that have nevertheless been opened in another Member State.[17] According to Art 25 (1) of the EIR, the preservation measures taken by an insolvency court in a foreign country must be recognized and their enforcement facilitated. The provisional liquidator may, pursuant to Art 38 of the EIR, apply for any protective measure that would be permissible in opening proceedings pursuant to the law of the country where these are being requested.

According to the view of the law taken by the Advocate General and the ECJ,[18] a court acting at a later point in time may only then open main proceedings if the court acting first had disregarded fundamental procedural rules ("fair procedures and fair hearing"), e.g. the right to be heard (Art 26 of the EIR). He also held that the provisional liquidator already appointed by the other court, if one had been appointed, must also be heard. The German courts must then also consider whether foreign courts have already decisively initiated "insolvency proceedings", which is why the local court in Cologne (*AG Köln*) obligates the party making the request to include such facts in its pleadings.[19] This is because no European insolvency register exists at the current time.[20] **7**

2.2 Prohibition of Continuation – Art 102 Sec 3 (1) sentence 2 *EGInsO*

If, contrary to Art 102 Sec 3 (1) sentence 1 *EGInsO*, German insolvency proceedings are opened subsequent to an effective foreign opening order, e.g. because the German court did not obtain knowledge of the earlier opening until a later point in time, then the German proceedings must be stayed pursuant to Art 102 Sec 4 *EGInsO*. But in order to determine whether the proceedings conflict at all, the foreign proceedings must also have been opened "in respect of the assets forming part of the insolvency assets". Although this refers to the insolvency assets in the German proceedings, Art 4 (2) (b) of the EIR provides that the determination of which assets form part of the insolvency assets is made according to the laws of the country in which the proceedings were first opened. As long as the German proceedings were expressly opened as territorial insolvency proceedings pursuant to Art 3 (2) and 4 of the EIR, there is no need for staying the proceedings since the EIR provides for parallel proceedings – the main proceedings and the territorial insolvency proceedings. The wording of the provision, like Art 102 Sec 4 (1) *EGInsO*, is therefore subject to a restrictive interpretation.[21] An inadmissible request for main insolvency proceedings may in such cases be reinterpreted as secondary insolvency proceedings provided that the conditions for this are met and the party making the request actually or alternatively, desires this.[22] This is conditioned however on there being an *establishment* within Germany territory.[23] **8**

---

[17] *Liersch* NZI Heft 6/2006, NZI-aktuell, V.
[18] ECJ dated 2 May 2006, ZInsO 2006, 484.
[19] NZI 2006, 57 with consenting comments by *Mankowski* EWiR 2006, 109.
[20] *Fritz/Bähr* DZWiR 2001, 221, 233.
[21] *Smid* Komm EuInsVO Art 102 § 3, mn 3.
[22] *Paulus* ZIP 2003, 1725, 1728; *Kebekus* EWiR 2004, 705, 706; HK-InsO/*Stephan* Art 102 § 3 with an incorrect reference to AG Mönchengladbach ZIP 2004, 1064; Kübler/Prütting-*Kemper* EGInsO Art 102 § 3 mn 5; BK-InsO/*Pannen* Art 102 § 3 mn 2.
[23] Regarding the term "establishment", see Art 2 of the EIR mn 19 and AG Munich ZIP 2007, 495, with approving note by *Mankowski* NZI 2007, 360.

2.3 Right of Appeal – Art 102 Sec 3 (1) sentence 3 *EGInsO*

9 To facilitate compliance with the principle of priority, the liquidator of the foreign insolvency proceedings has, supplementary to Sec 34 *InsO*, a special right to appeal the opening order.

2.4 Avoidance of a Mutual Negation of Jurisdiction – Art 102 Sec 3 (2) *EGInsO*

10 This section lays down a kind of "reversed principle of priority". The German insolvency court may not deny its jurisdiction because another insolvency court falling within the scope of the EIR has denied its jurisdiction, the German court considering the other court competent. The German court may, however, deny jurisdiction by claiming that the *situs* of the centre of main interests of the debtor company is in a third country.[24]

11 Although an "international" referral does not have a binding effect on the court to which the referral should be made, the principle of Community trust can be relied on in cases falling within the scope of application of the EIR.[25]

Article 102 EGInsO
Section 4 Staying Insolvency Proceedings in Favour of the Courts of Another Member State

(1) If the insolvency court is prohibited from continuing insolvency proceedings already opened pursuant to Section 3 (1), then the court must *ex officio* stay the proceedings in favour of the courts of the other Member State of the European Union. Prior to staying the proceedings, the insolvency court should hear the liquidator, the creditors' inspection committee *(Gläubigerausschuss)*, if one has been appointed, and the debtor. If the insolvency proceedings are stayed, then every creditor in the insolvency proceedings has a right of appeal.

(2) Anything effected pursuant to the insolvency proceedings that has already taken place prior to the staying of these proceedings and that is not restricted to the duration of them remains in effect even if it conflicts with anything effected by insolvency proceedings opened in another Member State of the European Union that, pursuant to the EC-Regulation, extends to a national territory. This also applies to any legal acts carried out during the stayed proceedings by or with the liquidator in the exercise of his office.

(3) Prior to the stay of proceedings pursuant to subsection 1, the insolvency court must inform the court of the other Member State of the European Union at which the proceedings are pending of the impending stay of proceedings; the information should state how the opening of the proceedings to be stayed was publicized, in which public books and registers the opening is registered, and who the liquidator is. The order staying the proceedings must name the court of the other Member State in whose favour the proceedings are being stayed. An official copy of the order staying the proceedings must be sent to this court. Section 215 (2) of the *InsO* does not apply.

---

[24] HK-InsO/*Stephan* Art 102 EGInsO § 3 mn 7.

[25] AG Hamburg ZInsO 2006, 559 = ZIP 2006, 1105 = NZI 2006, 486; rejecting comment: *Mankowski* NZI 2006, 487 on account of a lack of legal regulation of this and a lack of binding effect; dissenting opinion: *Vallender* KTS 2005, 293, 298; OLG Linz ZIK 2004, 178.

Contents

Index

Bibliography

Beck Verwertungsfragen im Verhältnis von Haupt- und Sekundärinsolvenzverfahren nach der EuInsVO, NZI 2006, p 609; *Breutigam/Blersch/Goetsch/Haas* Insolvenzrecht, Berliner Kommentar (January 2006); Frankfurter Kommentar zum Insolvenzrecht (2005); Heidelberger Kommentar zur Insolvenzordnung, 4th edn (2006) (eds *Eickmann/Flessner/Irschlinger/Kirchhof/Kreft/Landfermann/ Marotzke/Stephan*); *Kübler/Prütting* Kommentar zur Insolvenzordnung (March 2006); *Pannen/ Riedemann* Die deutschen Ausführungsbestimmungen zur EuInsVO – Ein Überblick zu den Regelungen des Art 102 EGInsO nF, NZI 2004, p 301; *Smid* Deutsches und Europäisches internationales Insolvenzrecht, Kommentar (2004); *Westphal* Comments on AG Düsseldorf dated 7.4.2004, EWiR 2004, p 909.

1. Purpose of Art 102 Sec 4 *EGInsO*

Art 102 Sec 4 *EGInsO* regulates the procedure to be taken to stay proceedings that 1
were opened as main insolvency proceedings contrary to Art 3 (3) of the EIR and Art 102 Sec 3 (1) *EGInsO*. It establishes an obligation to hear the German parties and an obligation to provide information to the court rightfully entitled to open main insolvency proceedings. According to Sec 3 (2) (g) and 19a No 1 of the German *RPflG* (law governing senior court officers), the judge has the right to make the decision.

2. Contents of the Rule

2.1 Stay of Proceedings – Art 102 Sec 4 (1) and (2) *EGInsO*

2.1.1 Hearing the German parties – Art 102 Sec 4 (1) *EGInsO*

As soon as the German insolvency court obtains knowledge that main insolvency 2
proceedings falling within the scope of the EIR have been opened – and that these are effective and have been opened at an earlier point in time – in respect of the same assets, then pursuant to Art 102 Sec 3 (1) sentence 2 *EGInsO* the German proceedings may not

be continued. Such proceedings must be stayed *ex officio.*[1] Prior to staying the proceedings, the insolvency court must hear the German parties to the proceedings in compliance with Art 102 Sec 4 (1) sentence 2 *EGInsO*, namely the liquidator, the creditors' inspection committee (if one has been appointed), and the debtor or the party(ies) granted powers to legally represent it. Because the creditors have a right of appeal pursuant to Art 102 Sec 4 (1) sentence 3 *EGInsO*, they must be served separately with the order staying the proceedings in compliance with Sec 4 *InsO* in conjunction with Sec 329 (3) of the German Civil Procedure Code (*ZPO)*. According to Sec 8 (3) *InsO*, service may still be made to the liquidator. In addition, the stay of proceedings must be publicized for the attention of all possible creditors (Sec 215 (1) *InsO* in conjunction with Sec 200 (2) sentences 2 and 3 *InsO*).[2]

2.1.2 Right of appeal

3 According to Art 102 Sec 4 (1) sentence 3, only the creditors in the insolvency proceedings are entitled to appeal against the order staying the proceedings. They are being denied the opportunity of participating in German main insolvency proceedings. Secured creditors (*Absonderungsberechtigte Gläubiger*), i.e. creditors with a right to preferential claims, have no right of appeal.[3] The correct method of appeal is the "*sofortige Beschwerde*", i.e. a special kind of appeal subject to a time limit, within the meaning of Sec 6 *InsO* and Sec 567 et seq *ZPO*.[4] It is difficult to understand why the legislator did not also affort the liquidator and the debtor a right of appeal since they too may possibly be denied the benefits of a national proceeding, the liquidator being denied further - remuneration as well.

2.1.3 Relationship to the foreign insolvency court

4 Prior to staying the proceedings, the foreign insolvency court must also be informed (Art 102 Sec 4 (3) sentence 1 *EGInsO*). This information must include the type and place of publication of the previous national proceedings and the name of the German liquidator. There is no specified form for doing this and it may be made in the German language.[5] The aim here is to facilitate a well-prepared and uninterrupted transition of the legal effects of the seizure/attachment of the assets. The foreign liquidator in the main proceedings is then able to make the publications required by Art 21 (1) of the EIR and, for the purposes of securing the assets, is able to contact the liquidator of the stayed proceedings. For this reason, the information is to be provided in a timely manner prior to the issuing of the order staying the proceedings. It is therefore incorrect if the foreign court first receives the name of the German liquidator in the official copy of the order staying proceedings.[6] The order staying proceedings must be sent to the foreign insolvency court (Art 102 Sec 4 (3) sentence 2 *EGInsO*) but does not have to be served on it.[7]

---

1 Example: AG Düsseldorf ZIP 2004, 866.

2 FK-InsO/*Wimmer* Art 102 EGInsO § 4 mn 3; Kübler/Prütting-*Kemper* EGInsO Art 102 § 4 mn 5.

3 *Smid* Komm EuInsVO Art 102 EGInsO § 4 mn 2.

4 HK-InsO/*Stephan* Art 102 EGInsO § 4 mn 4; FK-InsO/*Wimmer* Art 102 EGInsO § 4 mn 4; Kübler/Prütting-*Kemper* EGInsO Art 102 § 4 mn 7: analogous to sec 216 InsO.

5 HK-InsO/*Stephan* Art 102 EGInsO § 4 mn 8; Kübler/Prütting-*Kemper* Art 102 EGInsO § 4 mn 14.

6 But see: FK-InsO/*Wimmer* Art 102 EGInsO § 4 mn 11.

7 Kübler/Prütting-*Kemper* Art 102 EGInsO § 4 mn 16.

According to Art 102 Sec 4 (3) sentence 2 *EGInsO*, the foreign court must be named expressly in the order staying proceedings. What is most likely meant here is not only the naming of the court but also the actual proceedings in whose favour the stay has been made, stating the specifics of the court file number, the debtor's name, debtor's address, etc. The reason for this is to provide the national creditors with the information on the foreign proceedings. **5**

2.2 Effects of the Stay of Proceedings – Art 102 Sec 4 (2) *EGInsO*

Art 102 Sec 4 (2) *EGInsO* provides that the stay of proceedings does *not have a retroactive effect*. The provision differentiates between procedural consequences that only apply during the German proceedings (e.g. prohibitions of (individual) execution (*Vollstreckungs-verbote)*, suspension of limitation periods, directives issued by the insolvency court, interruptions of proceedings, the offices of the liquidator and the members of the creditors' inspection committee) and those that have legal implications extending beyond the termination of the proceedings (e.g. liquidation measures taken by the German liquidator (Sec 159 et seq *InsO*), contracts, contractual-performance obligations (Sec 103 *InsO*), tenancy cancellations (Sec 109 *InsO*)). These continuing effects of the German insolvency proceedings and the legal acts transacted by and with the German liquidator (Art 102 Sec 4 (2) sentence 2 *EGInsO*) remain in effect and even supersede anything ordered to the contrary in the foreign main insolvency proceedings that has national effect. The reason for this is the safeguard the reliance placed on national legal transactions.[8] Excluded from the category of permanent effects are those that do not require an act of the liquidator such as terminating powers of attorney, contracts, business management contracts, etc. (Sec 115 et seq *InsO*).[9] Although the terminated proceeding is then opened as secondary insolvency proceedings, the previous obligations against the whole insolvency estate still remain in effect. After the opening of secondary insolvency proceedings, only the estate of the secondary insolvency proceedings is bound by the subsequent obligations.[10] **6**

2.3 Transition of the Divestment

The staying of the national proceedings should not cause the debtor to regain the power to dispose of his assets. Art 102 Sec 4 (3) sentence 3 *EGInsO* therefore expressly provides that the German provision found in Sec 215 (2) *InsO does not apply*; if it did, this very thing would occur. Rather, because of the German court's obligation to provide information and through the reference to the foreign main insolvency proceedings, the foreign liquidator is put in a position – due to the uninterrupted transition of the legal effects of the divestment pursuant to Art 17 (1) of the EIR – to effect his own preservation measures; it is also being made clear that from then on the legal effects of the divestment are determined pursuant to the *lex fori concursus* of the other country opening proceedings. The German insolvency court must, by way of analogy to Sec 215 (1) and 31 to 33 *InsO,* delete the insolvency notification in the German registers.[11] Analogous to Sec 209 and 25 (2) *InsO*, the national liquidator is still obliged, in close cooperation with the foreign liquidator, to satisfy the preferential creditors (*Massegläubiger),* i.e. **7**

---

[8] Kübler/Prütting-*Kemper* EGInsO Art 102 § 4 mn 11; FK-InsO/*Wimmer* Art 102 EGInsO § 4 mn 7.

[9] Kübler/Prütting-*Kemper* EGInsO Art 102 § 4 mn 10.

[10] *Duursma-Kepplinger* ZIP 2007, 752.

[11] HK-InsO/*Stephan* Art 102 EGInsO § 4 mn 7.

creditors whose claims are to be discharged directly (fully) by the liquidator.[12] Although he has no other preservation duties in respect of the assets once the order staying proceedings has become final and absolute,[13] the liquidator may not hand over any of the assets to the debtor.

3. Best Practice

8 As soon as the foreign liquidator has been informed of the impending stay of the German insolvency proceedings, he must make the publication and registration applications in favour of the foreign main insolvency proceedings to the German insolvency court / registration court pursuant to Art 21 (1) and 22 of the EIR; this makes the debtor's divestment pursuant to the foreign proceedings publicly effective. Decisions regarding preservation measures must, according to Art 25 (1) of the EIR, be declared enforceable.[14] Simultaneous to the issuing of the order staying proceedings, secondary insolvency proceedings may be opened upon the appropriate request pursuant to Art 29 (a) of the EIR in the interests of a comprehensive safeguarding of the national assets.[15] The foreign liquidator in the main insolvency proceedings then has the right, pursuant to Art 31 (3) and 33 of the EIR, to request the stay of the liquidation of certain property in the secondary insolvency proceedings.[16]

Article 102 EGInsO
Section 5 Publication

1. The request for publication of the notice of the judgments in accordance with Article 21 (1) of Regulation (EC) No 1346/2000 shall be addressed to the court having jurisdiction in accordance with section 1. The court may require a translation which shall be certified by a person empowered to do so in one of the Member States of the European Union. Section 9 subpara 1 and 2 and section 30 subpara 1 of the Insolvency Law shall apply mutatis mutandis.

2. If the debtor has an establishment on domestic territory, publication shall be effected ex officio in accordance with subs. 1. If the opening of the insolvency proceedings has been published, termination shall be published in the same manner.

Contents

[12] FK-InsO/*Wimmer* Art 102 EGInsO § 4 mn 13; *Pannen/Riedemann* NZI 2004, 301, 303.

[13] BK-InsO/*Pannen* Art 102 EGInsO § 4 mn 13; dissenting opinion: FK-InsO/*Wimmer* Art 102 EGInsO § 4 mn 12.

[14] OLG Düsseldorf ZInsO 2004, 867 = NZI 2004, 628.

[15] AG Düsseldorf ZIP 2004, 866 with comments by *Westpfahl* EWiR 2004, 909; on the conflicts between secondary and main insolvency proceedings: *Beck* NZI 2006, 609.

[16] On this: OLG Graz NZI 2006, 660; LG Leoben NZI 2006, 663.

Index

Bibliography

Heidelberger Kommentar zur Insolvenzordnung, 4th edn (2006) (eds *Eickmann/Flessner/Irschlinger/Kirchhof/Kreft/Landfermann/Marotzke/Stephan*); *Kübler/Prütting* Kommentar zur Insolvenzordnung (March 2006); *Pannen/Riedemann* Die deutschen Ausführungsbestimmungen zur EuInsVO – Ein Überblick zu den Regelungen des Art 102 EGInsO n f, NZI 2004, p 301; *Trunk* Regelungsschwerpunkt eines Ausführungsgesetzes zum Europäischen Insolvenzübereinkommen, in Stoll (ed), Vorschläge und Gutachten (1997), p 32.

1. Purpose of Art 102 Sec 5 *EGInsO*

Art 102 Sec 5 *EGInsO* implements the provisions of Art 21 of the EIR into German law. Art 102 Sec 5 (1) *EGInsO* provides for publication upon the foreign liquidator's request as referred to in Art 21 (1) of the EIR; Art 102 Sec 5 (2) *EGInsO* refers to compulsory publication provided for by Art 21 (2) of the EIR. Art 102 Sec 5 (2) sentence 2 *EGInsO* also provides for publication of the termination of the insolvency proceedings, which, although not being required by Art 21 of the EIR, is absolutely reasonable. 1

2. Publication Upon Request

2.1 Jurisdiction

In Germany, a request for publication according to Art 21 (1) of the EIR is to be addressed to the court having jurisdiction pursuant to Art 102 Sec 1 (3) *EGInsO*[1], i.e. the insolvency court in whose district the centre of a debtor's main interests is situated. If this involves more than one jurisdiction, a request for publication has to be filed with each individual court unless a concentration order pursuant to Art 102 Sec 1 (3) *EGInsO* has been issued. If a request for publication is received by a court not having jurisdiction, 2

[1] Same opinion: Kübler/Prütting-*Kemper* EGInsO Art 102 § 5 mn 2. This concerns "other measures" within the meaning of subsection 3, loc cit.

the request must be forwarded *ex officio* to the court having jurisdiction (Art 102 Sec 6 (3) *EGInsO*). This task is to be performed by a court officer (the "*Rechstpfleger*") pursuant to Sec 3 (2) (g), Sec 19a of the German Judicial Officers Act (*RPflG*)).

2.2 Examination of Request

3 a) The liquidator, i.e. a person or body as listed in Annex C of the EIR (see Art 2 (b) of the EIR), is authorized to submit a request.

4 b) Debatable is whether the court addressed has to examine whether the recognition requirements of proceedings according to Art 16 of the EIR have been fulfilled in this case too[2]. While this has to be affirmed in the cases referred to in Art 102 Sec 6 *EGInsO* (see Art 102 Sec 6 *EGInsO* mn 7), a mere publication does not require such an examination. The registration of the opening of insolvency proceedings in a land register for instance is equivalent to an official announcement of a restraint on disposal which has a direct effect on the domestic legal relations concerning property and which influences the decisions of such Land register. Such a registration is only possible if the proceedings triggering it can be recognized in Germany. Publication, by contrast, does not have direct domestic legal effects. It merely warns persons involved in business dealings; whether or not they take notice of such warning or act upon it is up to them.

5 c) The insolvency court may request that evidence be furnished of the liquidator's appointment, unless such appointment already follows from the notice of judgment to be published.

6 d) The liquidator must furnish the information required for the publication (see mn 8 et seq below).

7 e) Art 102 section 5 (1) sentence 2 *EGInsO* provides that the court may request a translation of the notice of the judgment opening proceedings. This is at the court's lawful discretion. The translation is to be certified by a person authorized to do so in one of the Member States of the European Union (i.e. not necessarily in Germany!). Art 55 (2) of Council Regulation (EC) on Jurisdiction and the Recognition and Enforcement of Judgments in Civil and Commercial Matters applies in this regard.[3] The person submitting the request is free to choose a translator; the translator does not have to be admitted by the court to which the request is submitted.

2.3 Content, Form

8 a) What is to be publicized pursuant to the German version of Art 21 (1) of the EIR is the "*wesentlicher Inhalt*" (essential content) of the judgement opening insolvency proceedings (on this see Art 21 of the EIR at mn 5 et seq).

9 In addition, it must be stated whether main insolvency proceedings according to Art 3 (1) of the EIR or territorial insolvency proceedings according to Art 3 (2) of the EIR exist. Furthermore, the liquidator appointed has to be named.

10 b) As regards the form of the publication, Art 102 Sec 5 (1) sentence 3 *EGInsO* refers to Sec 9 (1), (2) and Sec 30 *InsO*; foreign proceedings are to be publicized in the same way as national proceedings. Publication is to be effected:

---

[2] In the affirmative: Kübler/Prütting-*Kemper* EGInsO Art 102 § 5 mn 3. Negating: *Trunk* in Stoll, Vorschläge und Gutachten zur Umsetzung des EU-Übereinkommens über Insolvenzverfahren im deutschen Recht (1997), 232, 242.

[3] HK-InsO/*Stephan* EGInsO Art 102 § 5 mn 4; Kübler/Prütting-*Kemper* EGInsO Art 102 § 5 mn 5; *Pannen/Riedemann* NZI, 2004, 301, 303.

- in the gazette ("Blatt") for official publications of the court to which the request is submitted or in an electronic information and communication system (Internet)[4] of such court, and
- in the German Federal Gazette ("*Bundesanzeiger*").

The insolvency court may order further publications according to Sec 9 (2) sentence 1 *InsO*. **11**

If the liquidator is free to arrange for further publications in other media on his own initiative[5], then this may be correct; however, this has little in common with the purpose of Art 21 of the EIR since publications of this kind will have no bearing on the situations described in Art 24 of the EIR. **12**

2.4 Costs

Any costs payable to judicial authorities (see No 9004 of the Cost Schedule – Court Fees Act (*KV-GKG*)) are borne by the applicant according to Sec 24 *GKG*. However, Art 23 of the EIR provides that such costs are payable out of the insolvency estate (regarding the publication of termination, see mn 14 below). **13**

2.5 Judgment Cancelling (terminating) Insolvency Proceedings

Art 21 of the EIR does not regulate the publication of the termination of insolvency proceedings. *Kemper*, by way of analogy to Art 102 Sec 5 (1) *EGInsO*, affirms the entitlement to file make such a request provided that the liquidator is authorized to do so according to the law governing the insolvency proceedings[6]. However, a recourse to the law governing the insolvency proceedings is unnecessary as Art 102 Sec 5 (2) sentence 2 *EGInsO* refers to Sec 5 (1) and extends the authorization to file a request to the *actus contrarius*. This cannot be interpreted as an infringement of Art 21 of the EIR. **14**

3. Ex officio Publication

3.1 Prerequisites

Art 102 Sec 5 (2) *EGInsO*, in compliance with Art 21 (2) of the EIR, provides that publication must be effected *ex officio* if the debtor has an establishment within the meaning of Art 2 (h) of the EIR on domestic territory. **15**

3.2 Jurisdiction

Art 102 Sec 1 (3) *EGInsO* in conjunction with Sec 1 (2) provides that the court in whose district the debtor's establishment is situated has jurisdiction.[7] **16**

In all other respects, mn 3 above applies. **17**

---

[4] The Ordinance on Publications on the Internet during Insolvency Proceedings of 12 February 2002 insofar applies (BGBl I 677). Sec 1 sentence 1 of the Ordinance provides that this type of publication and the system must be determined by the "Landesjustizverwaltung" of the respective German federal State.

[5] Kübler/Prütting-*Kemper* EGInsO Art 102 § 5 mn 6; *Trunk* in Stoll Vorschläge und Gutachten zur Umsetzung des EU-Übereinkommens über Insolvenzverfahren im deutschen Recht (1997), 241.

[6] Kübler/Prütting-*Kemper* EGInsO Art 102 § 5 mn 7.

[7] Kübler/Prütting-*Kemper* EGInsO Art 102 § 5 mn 9.

3.3 Procedure

18 The publication procedure is to be carried out *ex officio*. However, this requires that the court having jurisdiction (see mn 2 above) gains knowledge of the opening of main insolvency proceedings. According to Art 21 (2) sentence 2 of the EIR a liquidator in main insolvency proceedings is obliged to notify the insolvency court having jurisdiction (see Art 21 of the EIR, mn 2 et seq).

3.4 Content, Form

19 Mn 8 et seq apply in this respect as well.

3.5 Costs

20 Although the basic rule is that found in mn 13 above, Sec 24 *GKG* is of course not applicable in case of an *ex officio* procedure. In this case, the debtor is liable (i.e. the insolvency estate of the debtor) according to Sec 23 *GKG*. This should also apply to the costs of the publication of termination. This publication, at least according to German understanding, is the *actus contrarius* of the publication of the opening of proceedings, when one considers what the publication provisions are trying to accomplish. If the costs of publication are to be borne by the insolvency estate according to international law, this should apply to the publication of the termination of proceedings as well; both types of publication have the same goal in mind.

Art 102 EGInsO
Section 6 Entry in Public Books and Registers

1. The request for registration in accordance with Article 22 of Regulation (EC) No 1346/2000 shall be addressed to the court with jurisdiction in accordance with section 1. The latter shall request the authority keeping the register for registration if in accordance with the law of the Member State of the opening of proceedings the opening of the proceedings is also entered. Section 32 supara. 2 second sentence of the Insolvency Law shall not apply.

2. The form and content of the entry shall be in accordance with German law. If the law of the Member State of the opening of proceedings provides for entries unknown to German law, the insolvency court shall select an entry which comes closest to that of the Member State of the opening of proceedings.

3. If the request in accordance with subs. 1 or in accordance with section 5 subpara 1 is received by a court not having jurisdiction, the latter shall forward the application without delay to the court having jurisdiction, and shall inform the person filing the request thereof.

Contents

Index

Bibliography

Flessner Ausländischer Konkurs und inländischer Arrest, in Festschrift für Merz (1992), p 93; Heidelberger Kommentar zur Insolvenzordnung, 4th edn (2006) (eds *Eickmann/Flessner/Irschlinger/Kirchhof/Kreft/Landfermann/Marotzke/Stephan*); *Pannen/Riedemann* Die deutschen Ausführungsbestimmungen zur EuInsVO – Ein Überblick zu den Regelungen des Art 102 EGInsO nf, NZI 2004, p 301.

1. Purpose of Art 102 Sec 6 *EGInsO*

Art 102 Sec 6 *EGInsO* implements the provisions of Art 22 of the EIR into German law. The German legislator refrained, however, from making registration mandatory (Art 22 (2) of the EIR). **1**

2. Register Entries

2.1 The Principle of Filing a Request

While national insolvency law generally require that most registrations in public registers are to be effected by the insolvency court *ex officio* (see Sec 32 subpara 2 sentence 1, Sec 33 *InsO*), Art 102 Sec 6 *EGInsO* takes a conciliatory approach: a **request** must be made before a registration will be effected. However, the request cannot be made to the authority keeping the register; the applicant is not authorized to make a request to the authority keeping the register (Art 102 Sec 6 sentence 3 *EGInsO*). Rather, the request must be made to the insolvency court (see mn 4 below), which will then submit a request to the authorities keeping the registers in accordance with the registry rules applicable from time to time. The procedure is thus being implemented into national law without ignoring the need for a request required by Art 22 of the EIR. **2**

The main reason for interposing the insolvency court is the requisite review of the recognition of the opened proceedings[1] (see mn 7 below). **3**

2.2 Competence for Request and Submission of Request

In Germany, a request pursuant to Art 22 (1) of the EIR must be made to the court with jurisdiction pursuant to Art 102 Sec 1 subpara 3 *EGInsO*, i.e. to the insolvency court in whose district assets of the debtor are situated. If the debtor's assets are **4**

[1] Explanation contained in RegE BT-Drucks 15/16 p 16.

distributed amongst several districts, then all of these courts must be addressed, each with regard to the registry authorities competent in its district. The prevention of contradictory judgments addressed by *Stephan*[2] is therefore ensured within the scope of Art 102 Sec 1 subpara 3 *EGInsO* in one district only, but not throughout Germany.

5 Directly submitting a request to the authority keeping the register is inadmissible; however, such request must be forwarded to the insolvency court with jurisdiction as required by Art 102 Sec 6 subpara 3 *EGInsO*.

2.3 The Procedure Before the Insolvency Court

6 a) The liquidator, i.e. a person or body of the Member States as referred to in Annex C of the EIR, is authorized to submit a request (see Art 2 (b) of the EIR). The insolvency court may request that the liquidator's appointment be evidenced according to Art 19 of the EIR.

7 b) The insolvency court must examine whether the requirements per Art 16 of the EIR for the recognition of the foreign proceedings have been fulfilled, and must ensure that no infringement of public policy (Art 26 of the EIR) has been made.

8 c) The insolvency court must also examine whether an entry in a particular register is provided for by the law governing the insolvency proceedings as well as an entry in the same or in a similar German register is only admissible if this condition is fulfilled (see Art 102 Sec 6 (1) sentence 2 *EGInsO*[3]). The law governing the insolvency proceedings need only contemplate such a registration; it is not necessary that the actual registration in the registry already have been made.

9 d) Finally, the insolvency court must review the content of the registration, As German law is applicable according to Art 102 Sec 6 (2) sentence 1 *EGInsO*, the content of the registration being sought here must be compared to the content of a registration being sought pursuant to the law governing the insolvency proceedings. Entry in a register may be allowed by the law of the Member State of the opening of proceedings that is unknown to German law. In this case, the insolvency court orders a registration that comes closest to the registration provided for by the Member State of the opening of proceedings (so-called adaptation/substitution) (see initially Art 22 of the EIR mn 11).

10 At any rate, in the event of registrations to be made in the **land register,** the restrictions imposed on the foreign debtor must directly affect the legality of legal acts in foreign insolvency proceedings has a direct impact on the effectiveness of legal acts; for restrictions giving rise to personal sanctions only (e.g. contempt of court) a subsitution is not possible.[4]

2.4 Registrations

11 a) If insolvency proceedings have been opened **in Germany**, their registration in the public registers will be effected in different ways: the registration in the commercial registeror in registers for cooperatives ("*Genossenschaft*"), partnerships, or associations is effected *ex officio*; Sec 31 *InsO* provides for a duty of notification of the insolvency court in any of the above cases. In contrast, an entry in the land register, the register of ships, the ship construction register, the aircraft register and the trademark register will only be effected upon the insolvency court's request or the liquidator's application

---

[2] Cf HK-Inso/*Stephan* Art 102 EGInsO § 6 mn 4.

[3] *Pannen/Riedemann* NZI 2004, 301, 304.

[4] *Flessner* in Festschrift Merz (1992) 93, 95.

(Sec 32, 33 *InsO*, Sec 29 subpara 3 of the German Trademark Act (*MarkenG*)). This differentiation is not adhered to in the case of registrations of foreign insolvency proceedings: if the insolvency court to which the liquidator's request was addressed deems the entry admissible according to the submissions made at mn 6 et seq above, then it will request registration from the authority keeping the register in any of the above cases. A registration made pursuant to a liquidator's direct request is as inadmissible (Art 102 Sec 6 (1) sentence 3 *EGInsO*) as a registration effected *ex officio*.

b) The form and content of the registration are governed by German law subject to **12**
an adaptation needed (see mn 9 above).

Article 102 EGInsO
Section 7 Appeal

An immediate appeal shall be admissible against the judgment of the insolvency court in accordance with Section 5 or Section 6. Section 7 of the Insolvency Law shall apply mutatis mutandis.

Contents

Index

Bibliography

Heidelberger Kommentar zur Insolvenzordnung, 4th edn (2006) (eds *Eickmann/Flessner/Irschlinger/Kirchhof/Kreft/Landfermann/Marotzke/Stephan*); *Hess* Neues deutsches und europäisches Zustellungsrecht NJW 2002, p 2417; *Keidel/Kuntzel/Winkler* Freiwillige Gerichtsbarkeit (2005); *Kübler/Prütting* Kommentar zur Insolvenzordnung (March 2006); *Kuntze/Ertl/Hermann/Eickmann* Grundbuchrecht, 5th edn (1999); *Meikel* Grundbuchrecht, 9th edn (2004); *Schlosser* EU-Prozessrecht (2003).

1. Purpose of Art 102 Sec 7 *EGInsO*

1 Given the importance attributed to publications and registrations, a foreign liquidator must be able to take action against declining or restricting judgments of the insolvency court. Thus the legal rule establishes a right of appeal against judgments of the insolvency court as the "competent body" within the meaning of Art 21, 22 of the EIR.

2 However, the differentiation between proceedings that is prescribed for bringing about registrations (see Art 102 Sec 6 *EGInsO* mn 11) may also lead to the authority keeping the register giving a declining or restricting judgment. The judgment is challengeable according to the provisions generally applicable to these registration procedures (see mn 8 below).

2. Appeal Against the Judgment of the Insolvency Court

2.1 Sofortige Beschwerde

3 a) The **admissibility** of a "*sofortige Beschwerde*" (special appeal subject to a time limit) follows from Art 102 Sec 7 sentence 1 *EGInsO*. The appeal is subject to Sec 6, 4 *InsO*, Sec 567 et seq of the German Code of Civil Procedure (*ZPO*).

4 b) (Only) the foreign liquidator has a **right of appeal**. His grievance, if he was the party making the request, is a formal grievance, i.e. in the cases set forth in Art 102 Sec 5 subpara 1 and Sec 6 *EGInsO*. In the case of Art 102 Sec 5 subpara 2 *EGInsO*, a refusal or restriction of publication would give rise to a substantive grievance as it may be vitally important for preserving the insolvency estate.

5 c) The **time limit for giving notice of appeal** is two weeks according to Sec 569 subpara 1 sentence 1 *ZPO*. Sec 6 subpara 2 *InsO* provides that it begins to run upon the pronouncement – which is not applicable in the present case – or upon service of the judgment to be challenged. As the judgment is always served on the foreign liquidator, service of the judgment is always effected in another EU Member State and will then be subject to the EC Regulation on the Service in the Member States of Judicial and Extrajudicial Documents in Civil or Commercial Matters.[1] According to Art 4 (1) of the aforesaid EC Regulation, formal service to the foreign receiving authority is arranged by the forwarding authority, i.e. the insolvency court itself, according to the Law Implementing Community Law Regulations on Service in the Member States.[2] The foreign receiving authority then effects service (Art 7 of the EC Regulation on the Service in the Member States of Judicial and Extrajudicial Documents in Civil or Commercial Matters). The foreign receiving authority will then issue an acknowledgment of service according to Art 10 of the aforesaid EC Regulation including the date of service, this date being decisive for calculating the time limit for giving notice of appeal.

---

[1] Council Regulation (EC) No 1348/2000 of 29 May 2000 on the Service in the Member States of Judicial and Extrajudicial Documents in Civil or Commercial Matters (Official Journal L 160 p 37). The aforesaid EC Regulation also applies to service during insolvency proceedings (*Schlosser* EuZVO Art 1 mn 2; *Hess* NJW 2002, 2417).

[2] Law Implementing Community Law Regulations on the Service in the Member States of Judicial and Extrajudicial Documents in Civil or Commercial Matters (Law Implementing Community Law Regulations on Service in the Member States) of 9 July 2001 (Federal Law Gazette I p 1536).

Sec 8 subpara 1 *InsO* provides that service by ordinary mail is admissible as well; it shall be effected by registered letter with return receipt according to the aforesaid EC Regulation, Sec 2 of the Law Implementing Community Law Regulations on Service in the Member States (see also Sec 183 subpara 1 *ZPO*). The return receipt evidences service at the time of delivery stated on the return receipt. **6**

d) The appeal is filed by submitting a written notice of appeal to the insolvency court or the appellate court (Sec 569 subpara 1, 2 *ZPO*). The insolvency court has to decide whether to supply intermediate relief ("*Abhilfe*") (Sec 572 subpara 1 *ZPO*). The appellate court is generally the "*Landgericht*" (Regional court) (Sec 71 subpara 1 of the German Judicature Act (*GVG*)). However, contrary to *Kemper's*[3] opinion, the application of Sec 119 subpara 1 (1) (c) *GVG* is not generally excluded. It may be correct that this provision does not apply when European Community law applies to the decision (e.g. in deciding whether an "establishment" within the meaning of the EIR exists). It should be applicable, however, where European Community law refers to foreign law that only applies there (e.g. whether the law governing the insolvency proceedings contemplates a particular registration at all (Art 102 Sec 6 subpara 1 sentence 2 *EGInsO*) or the content of such registration (Art 102 Sec 6 subpara 2 sentence 2 *EGInsO*)). **7**

2.2 Appeal on Points of Law

Sentence 2 provides the appeal on points of law ("*Rechtsbeschwerde*") is to be used to challenge the "*sofortige Beschwerde*". However, it is only admissible if the legal matter is fundamentally important or if a judgment is required for purposes of advancing the law or for ensuring consistency of court decisions. **8**

The appeal on points of law must be filed to the appellate court (= German Federal Court of Justice Sec 133 *GVG*) within a strict time limit of one month from service of the judgment on the appeal. Such notice can only be effectively given by a lawyer admitted to the Federal Court of Justice (Sec 78 subpara 1 sentence 4 *ZPO*). **9**

3. Appeal Against a Judgment of the Authority Keeping the Register

3.1 Generals

The request filed by the insolvency court (Art 102 Sec 6 subpara 1 sentence 1 *EGInsO*) is not absolutely binding on the authority keeping the register according to the relevant codes of procedure. Although the authority requested does not have to examine whether the request was legally admissible, it does have to examine, in general, whether the form and content of the request complies with statutory provisions[4], i.e. in the present case, whether it fulfils the requirements of Sec 29 subpara 3, 38 of the German Land Registry Act (*GBO*). **10**

What is problematic is the treatment of registration matters. In ordinary national proceedings, the insolvency court does not submit a formal request to the registry court but merely informs it of the various decisions it has made (Sec 31 *InsO*). The registry court decides on the opening, execution and the result of its proceedings *ex officio*. The formality of a request submitted to the land registry clearly differs from the above **11**

---

[3] Kübler/Prütting-*Kemper* EGInsO Art 102 § 7 mn 4.

[4] Details concerning the land register: *Meikel/Roth* Grundbuchrecht, 9th ed § 38 GBO mn 13 et seq; *Kunze/Ertl/Hermann/Eickmann* Grundbuchrecht, 5th ed § 38 GBO mn 67 et seq. The same should apply with regard to registry courts (see mn 11).

(Sec 32 *InsO*, 38 *GBO*). Requests pursuant to Art 102 Sec 6 *EGInsO* constitute "alien elements" to the official procedures of the commercial register (and similar proceedings). Even if the main purpose of this rule is to shift the decision on recognition, a controversy is nevertheless possible that may result from the recourse to the law governing the insolvency proceedings or from any decisions on substitution (see Art 102 Sec 6 *EGInsO* mn 9). Therefore, the principle of *ex officio* proceedings cannot apply in Art 102 Sec 6 *EGInsO* circumstances; the same concept that underlies Sec 38 *GBO* must therefore apply here as well.

12 In light of the purpose behind the allocation of tasks found in Art 102 Sec 6 *EGInsO*, no review of the decision substituting a registration should be allowed to take place.

13 If the Land Registry (registry court, etc.) refuses or restricts the registration, then this decision can be appealed using the appeal procedures provided for by the particular civil procedure code.[5] In particular, the following types of appeal may be considered: Sec 71 *GBO* (land register), Sec 19 et seq of the Act relating to Matters of Voluntary Jurisdiction (*FGG*) (registration matters).

3.2 Right of Appeal

14 a) The authority making a request, i.e. the insolvency court in the present case, always has the right to appeal. This has been generally acknowledged with regard to Sec 38 *GBO*[6] and should apply in the other areas as well.[7]

15 b) In addition, participants whose legal position is being prejudiced are also entitled to appeal even if they do not have a right of appeal themselves.[8] Therefore the foreign liquidator is also entitled to make an appeal.

Article 102 EGInsO
Section 8 Enforcement of the Judgment Opening Proceedings

1) If the liquidator of main insolvency proceedings in accordance with the law of the Member State of the opening of proceedings is empowered on the basis of the judgment on the opening of proceedings to enforce by way of execution surrender of the assets in the keeping of the debtor, Article 25 (1) first subparagraph of Regulation (EC) No 1346/2000 shall apply to the declaration of enforceability on domestic territory. The first sentence shall apply mutatis mutandis to the disposition of objects from the estate by way of execution.

2) Section 6 subpara 3 shall apply mutatis mutandis.

[5] Kübler/Prütting-*Kemper* EGInsO Art 102 § 7 mn 6; in HK-InsO/*Stephan* Art 102 EGInsO § 7 mn 3. See also explanation contained in RegE BT-Drucks. 15/16, p 16.

[6] OLG Hamm Rpfleger 1985, 396; OLG Düsseldorf Rpfleger 1988, 140; *Kuntze/Ertl/Hermann/Eickmann* § 71 GBO mn 77; *Meikel/Streck* § 71 GBO mn 140.

[7] Regarding the right of appeal of public authorities (courts) according to the Act relating to Matters of Voluntary Jurisdiction (*FGG*) see *Keidel/Kuntze/Winkler* § 20 FGG mn 24 et seq, particularly mn 36.

[8] See references in fn 6.

Contents

Index

Bibliography

Balz Das neue Europäische Insolvenzübereinkommen, ZIP 1996, p 948; *Dassler/Schiffhauer/Gerhardt* Gesetz über die Zwangsversteigerung und die Zwangsverwaltung (1991); *Eickmann* Zwangsversteigerungs- und Zwangsverwaltungsrecht, 2nd edn (2004); *Gottwald* FamRZ 2002, p 1423; Heidelberger Kommentar zur Insolvenzordnung, 4th edn (2006) (eds *Eickmann/Flessner/Irschlinger/Kirchhof/Kreft/Landfermann/Marotzke/Stephan*); *Haas* in FS Gerhardt (2004); *Hub* Die Neuregelung der Anerkennung und Vollstreckung in Zivil- und Handelssachen und das familienrechtliche Anerkennungs- und Vollstreckungsverfahren, NJW 2001, p 3145; *Kropholler* Europäisches Zivilprozessrecht, 7th edn (2002); *Kübler/Prütting* Kommentar zur Insolvenzordnung (March 2006); Münchener Kommentar zur Insolvenzordnung, vol 1 (2001); Münchener Kommentar zur Insolvenzordnung, vol 3 (2003); *Muth* Die Zwangsversteigerung auf Antrag des Insolvenzverwalters, ZIP 1999, p 945; *Pannen/Riedemann* Die deutschen Ausführungsbestimmungen zur EuInsVO – Ein Überblick zu den Regelungen des Art. 102 EGInsO nF, NZI 2004, 301, p 303; *Paulus* Die europäische Insolvenzverordnung und der deutsche Insolvenzverwalter NZI 2001, p 505; *Steiner/Eickmann* Zwangvollstreckungsgesetz, 9th edn (1986); *Stöber* Zwangsversteigerungsgesetz, 18th edn (2006); *Storz* Praxis der Zwangsversteigerungsverfahren, 10th edn (2007); *Thomas/Putzo* Zivilprozessordnung, 27th edn (2005).

1. Purpose of Art 102 Sec 8 *EGInsO*

This provision – in implementation of Art 18 (3) and Art 25 (1) of the EIR – regulates 1
the enforcement in Germany of judgments opening insolvency proceedings that have been rendered by a foreign insolvency court of a Member State. It involves the taking of of property belonging to the insolvency estate (see mn 20 et seq below) as well as the liquidation of this property by way of compulsory execution (see mn 27 et seq below).

2. Exequatur Proceedings

2.1 Principle

2 The subject-matter of exequatur proceedings is not the implementation of the enforcement measures required, which according to Art 18 (3) of the EIR are subject to German insolvency law and German law of enforcement of civil judgments[1], but the authorization required for such enforcement.[2]

3 Art 102 Sec 8 subpara 1 *EGInsO* provides that the enforcement of judgments opening proceedings rendered by the foreign insolvency court of a Member State is subject to Art 25 (1) subpara 1 of the EIR. As regards the declaration of enforceability, Art 25 (1) subpara 1 of the EIR refers to Art 31 to 51 (with the exception of Art 34 (2)) of the Brussels Convention on Jurisdiction and the Enforcement of Judgments in Civil and Commercial Matters. The 1968 Brussels Convention was replaced by Council Regulation (EC) on Jurisdiction and the Recognition and Enforcement of Judgments in Civil and Commercial Matters[3] effective as of 1 March 2002. Art 68 (2) of the aforesaid Council Regulation provides that references to the 1968 Brussels Convention are to be deemed as references to the Council Regulation (EC) No 44/2001. Consequently, **Art 38 to 52** (with the exception of Art 45 (1)) of the Council Regulation (EC) No 44/2001 apply (so-called simplified exequatur).

4 However, according to Art 68 (1) of the Council Regulation (EC) No 44/2001, the 1968 Brussels Convention has not been replaced in Denmark, the Channel Islands, the Isle of Man and the British sovereign territories of Cyprus.

2.2 Application

5 Art 38 (1) of the Council Regulation (EC) No 44/2001 provides that a request of the foreign liquidator is required, whose appointment has to be evidenced according to Art 19 of the EIR. The provisions of the German Act on the Recognition and Enforcement of Foreign Judgments (*AVAG*) also apply; Sec 1 subpara 1 (2) (b) of the *AVAG* expressly provides that the Council Regulation (EC) No 44/2001 applies. According to Sec 4 subpara 2 of the *AVAG*, the application may be filed with the competent court (see mn 8 below) in writing or it may be made orally at the court registry ("*Geschäftsstelle*"), which will then officially record this. If the application is not made in German (see Sec 184 of the German Judicature Act (*GVG*)), then the court may request a certified translation (Sec 4 subpara 3 of the *AVAG*).

6 An official copy of the judicially enforceable title, i.e. usually of the judgment on the opening of proceedings (Art 40 (3), 53 of the Council Regulation (EC) No 44/2001), two copies thereof (Sec 4 subpara 4 of the *AVAG*), and the certificate required by Art 54 of the Council Regulation (EC) No 44/2001, which must be prepared using the form in Annex V, are to be attached. A translation of the certificate may be required pursuant to Art 55 (2) of the Council Regulation (EC) No 44/2001, however it will usually be unne-

[1] Kübler/Prütting-*Kemper* EGInsO § 8 mn 3, 10.
[2] *Pannen/Riedemann* NZI 2004, 301, 304.
[3] Council Regulation (EC) No 44/2001 of 22 December 2000 on Jurisdiction and the Recognition and Enforcement of Judgments in Civil and Commercial Matters (OJ 2001 L 12/1), amended by Regulation (EC) No 1496/2002 of 21 August 2003 (Official Journal L 225/13) and the Treaty of Accession of 23 September 2003 (Official Journal 236/715).

cessary as it has the same structure and content in all Member States; the information to be supplied is easily understandable.[4]

Art 40 (2) sentence 2 of the Council Regulation (EC) No 44/2001 provides that the applicant "must" appoint a representative to accept service on his behalf in the application. However, Sec 5 of the *AVAG* and Sec 184 subpara 1 sentence 2, subpara 2 of the German Code of Civil Procedure (*ZPO*)[5] apply so that, irrespective of the imperative wording, the application may not be treated as inadmissible (incomplete) simply because it fails to appoint a representative for accepting service. **7**

2.3 Court's Jurisdiction

Annex II to the Council Regulation (EC) No 44/2001 provides that the presiding judge of a chamber of the "*Landgericht*" (Regional court) is competent with regard to subject-matter. If the application is addressed to "*Landgericht*" then it will not be deemed as inadmissible.[6] Moreover, Sec 6 subpara 3 would apply in this case. **8**

Art 39 (2) of the Council Regulation (EC) No 44/2001 provides that the court with jurisdiction at the place of the debtor's domicile (Art 59, 60 of the Council Regulation (EC) No 44/2001) or at the place of intended enforcement has local jurisdiction. The first alternative will, in general, be irrelevant as the (foreign) insolvency proceedings will have been opened there. Sec 6 subpara 3 also applies in this case, subpara 2. **9**

2.4 Court Procedure

If the application submitted to the court is admissible – provided that the basic requirement has been fulfilled, i.e. enforceability of the judgment submitted (see Art 25 of the EIR mn 41 et seq) – a declaration of enforceability has to be immediately issued according to Art 41 of the Council Regulation (EC) No 44/2001 (Art 41 of the Council Regulation (EC) No 44/2001). A review pursuant to Art 34, 35 does not take place. **10**

The court delivers a judgment according to Sec 8 of the *AVAG*, which is then executed by the clerk of the court registry according to Sec 9 of the *AVAG*. **11**

2.5 Appeal

a) The debtor may "appeal" against a judgment allowing enforceability and the applicant against a judgment refusing enforceability (Art 43 of the Council Regulation (EC) No 44/2001). The provisions of Art 43 form an independent system of appeal.[7] Sec 11 to 14 of the *AVAG* apply in addition unless they are excluded by Sec 55 subpara 1 of the *AVAG*. **12**

b) **Debtor's right of appeal:** The appeal is **limited in time** according to Art 43 (5) of the Council Regulation (EC) No 44/2001; the one-month time limit commences upon service in the event that the debtor has his domicile **within the Member State in which enforcement is being sought** (Art 59, 60 of the Council Regulation (EC) No 44/2001). If the debtor **has his domicile in a EU Member State other than the one in which enforcement is being sought**, the time limit will be two months as from service. If the debtor has his domicile in a non-EU Member State, then the time limit will be one month as from service unless Sec 10 subpara 2 of the *AVAG* provides for a longer time limit. **13**

---

[4] Likewise: Thomas/Putzo-*Hüßtege* ZPO Art 53 EuGVVO mn 5.

[5] BGH ZIP 1999, 617.

[6] LG Hamburg IPRspr 1975 No 160, 161.

[7] Thomas/Putzo-*Hüßtege* Art 43 EuGVVO mn 1.

14 Service is to be effected *ex officio* (Sec 10 subpara 1 of the *AVAG*), within Germany according to Sec 166 et seq *ZPO*, in EU Member States according to the Council Regulation on the Service in the Member States[8], in non-EU Member States according to the Hague Convention of 15 November 1965 on the Service Abroad of Judicial and Extrajudicial Documents in Civil and Commercial Matters provided that the Member State has acceded to said Convention, otherwise in accordance with the Hague Convention of 1 March 1954.

15 Service must be in due form; Sec 189 *ZPO* does not apply.[9]

16 c) **Applicant's right of appeal:** The applicant's right of appeal is **unlimited** in time; Art 43 (5) of the Council Regulation (EC) No 44/2001 provides that a limitation is only possible with respect to an appeal "against the declaration of enforceability".

17 d) The court of appeal is the "*Oberlandesgericht*" (higher Regional court) according to Art 43 (2) in conjunction with Annex III of the Council Regulation (EC) No 44/2001.

18 e) The appeal procedure is subject to Art 43 (3), (4) of the Council Regulation (EC) No 44/2001 in conjunction with Art 13 of the *AVAG*. Art 45 of the Council Regulation (EC) No 44/2001 provides that the appellate court may only refuse the declaration of enforceability on the grounds set forth in Art 34 and 35. Prevailing opinion concludes from this that the debtor will be denied an appeal that contends a lack of jurisdiction (on the part of the *Landgericht* concerned) or an absence of the formalities found in Art 41, 53.[10]

19 f) An appeal can be lodged against the judgment given on the appeal according to Annex IV of the Council Regulation (EC) No 44/2001 (Art 44). This is the German "*Rechtsbeschwerde*" (appeal on a point of law) found in Sec 574 subpara 1, 2 *ZPO*. The court to which such an appeal must be made is the German Federal Court of Justice.

3. Enforcement Measures

3.1 Protection of the Estate After the Opening of Proceedings

20 The "judgments concerning the course of insolvency proceedings" referred to in Art 25 of the EIR primarily include the judgment on the opening of insolvency proceedings provided that the content of the judgment is enforceable according to the law governing the insolvency proceedings (see Art 25 of the EIR mn 39).

21 The rules applicable to the enforcement proceedings are those provided for by German law (see Art 18 (3) of the EIR).

22 If a surrender of property belonging to the insolvency estate is to be enforced by way of compulsory execution, then this must be done in conformity with the procedure provided for by Sec 883 et seq *ZPO*.

23 First, the existence of a (judicially enforceable) **title** is required. The property to be surrendered is to be set out in such title. However, according to the prevailing opinion

[8] Council Regulation (EC) No 1348/2000 of 29 May 2000 on the Service in the Member States of Judicial and Extrajudicial Documents in Civil or Commercial Matters (OJ L 160 p 37).

[9] BGHZ 120, 305.

[10] *Hub* NJW 2001, 3145, 3147; *Gottwald* FamRZ 2002, 1423. Contra: *Kropholler* Europäisches Zivilprozeßrecht Art 43 mn 6, 27.

this is unnecessary in case of an execution according to Sec 148 subpara 2 *InsO*[11]; a description of the property to be surrendered in the execution request addressed to the bailiff is deemed sufficient.

In addition, the German law of enforcement of civil judgments requires that the title be endorsed with a **court certificate of enforceability**, i.e. the certificate of readiness for enforcement (Sec 750 subpara 1 *ZPO*). Enforceability as such is already certified by the form according to Annex V to Art 54 of the Council Regulation (EC) No 44/2001 (see mn 6 above), the court certificate of enforceability with regard to the title according to Sec 9 of the *AVAG* is added to this. **24**

Finally, **service** of title is required by the German law of enforcement of civil judgments. Service of title is effected by the exequatur court according to Sec 10 of the *AVAG*; the order pursuant to Sec 8 of the *AVAG*, the judiciary enforceable title (here: the judgment opening insolvency proceedings), and the court certificate of enforceability per Sec 9 of the *AVAG* are being served. **25**

According to German law, the judgment opening insolvency proceedings also makes an **eviction** possible (Sec 885 *ZPO*) with regard to domestic or business premises owned by the debtor.[12] A judgment concerning authorization according to Sec 758 subpara 1 *ZPO* is not required.[13] **26**

If property belonging to the insolvency estate is in the possession of **third parties**, execution against this property **cannot** be made on the basis of the judgment opening insolvency proceedings. This follows already from Sec 8 itself ("... in the custody of the debtor ...") as well as from Sec 148 subpara 2 *InsO*: The liquidator can only enforce the surrender of such assets through ordinary judical proceedings even if the law governing the insolvency proceedings allow this on the basis of the judgment opening proceedings. **27**

3.2 Realization of the Assets by Way of Execution

a) **General.** The effects of main insolvency proceedings do not suspend the rules of the Member State where action is to be taken (see Art 18 (3) of the EIR where the "procedures for the realization of assets" are expressly referred to). The laws of the Member State where realization is to be effected are to be taken into account when realizing assets; the legal procedure must be chosen which comes as close as possible to the provisions of the law governing the insolvency proceedings.[14] This is important because the realization of assets by the liquidator via compulsory execution measures is not always provided for by German insolvency law; it is also uncommon. **28**

b) **Immovable property.** If the property is encumbered with some kind of of real-property charge, which is usually the case, individual creditors usually effect a foreclosure sale. According to prevailing opinion, which should be rejected[15], the liquidator may join in such foreclosure proceedings, i.e. participate in this (Sec 28 of the German Foreclosure Sales Act (*ZVG*)). **29**

---

[11] Kübler/Prütting-*Holzer* §148 InsO mn 15; MünchKomm-InsO/*Füchsl/Weishäupl* § 148 InsO mn 63, 70.

[12] See references in fn 11.

[13] Kübler/Prütting-*Holzer* see fn 11, HK-InsO/Irschlinger § 148 InsO mn 8.

[14] *Balz* ZIP 1996, 948, 952; *Paulus* NZI 2001, 505, 511; *Haas* in FS Gerhardt 2004, pp 319, 338.

[15] *Bauer/Stürner* Vollstreckungs- u Insolvenzrecht vol II mn 15.11; *Dassler/Schiffhauer/Gerhardt* ZVG § 172 Ann 6c, Kübler/Prütting-*Kemper* InsO § 165 mn 24; *Muth* ZIP 1999, 945, 950; contra: *Storz* Praxis der Zwangsversteigerung A 3.1; *Stöber* ZVG § 172 mn 6.1; *Steiner/Eickmann* ZVG § 172 mn 31.

30 This participation in the foreclosure proceedings should, in general, be sufficient for the purposes of the law governing the insolvency proceedings. A judicially enforceable title is required for participating in such procedure.

31 However, apart from of a foreclosure proceeding being effected by creditors, the liquidator may effect a foreclosure proceeding in his own right (Sec 172 *ZVG*, Sec 165 *InsO*). This so-called "liquidator's foreclosure proceeding" constitutes an independent type of procedure where highly encumbered property may also be sold via foreclosure particularly because of the possibilities found in Sec 174a *ZVG*.[16] It is to be preferred to an ordinary foreclosure from an insolvency point of view. The liquidator does **not** need a judicially enforceable **title** in order to apply for this special procedure[17]; merely his capacity as liquidator and the classification as assets have to be evidenced, the latter evidence being furnished through the notification of insolvency in the Land Registery. One could therefore argue that exequatur proceedings are **dispensable** in these cases. It should be sufficient if the liquidator brings about the registration of the insolvency notification according to Art 102 Sec 6 *EGInsO*; the request for entry addressed to the Land Registry by the insolvency court shows that the foreign proceedings have been recognized. The liquidator will then merely have to furnish the court having jurisdiction over the execution with evidence of his capacity as liquidator.

32 c) **Movable property**. Realization by way of execution does not exist in this respect in German insolvency law.

33 Realization by way of execution presupposes an attachment/seizure (see Sec 814 *ZPO*) which, however, only takes place in case of execution being effected by a creditor based on money claims. The most the liquidator can do is to recover possession from the debtor (see chapter 2, 4 of book 8 of the German Code of Civil Procedure).

34 According to German insolvency law, the realization of movable assets is made either by private sale or by private or public auction according to Sec 383 subpara 3 of the German Civil Code (*BGB*).[18] If the law governing the insolvency proceedings prescribes the realization of assets by way of execution, then a normal sale through an **auction** is preferable to some kind of compulsory execution. An auction can be achieved by instructing the bailiff according to Sec 244 to 246 of the German Instructions to Bailiffs (*GVGA*).[19] A judicially enforceable title is not required.

35 d) **Debt claims and rights.** If a third-party debtor does not pay voluntarily, debt claims and rights may only be realized by way of compulsory execution.

Article 102 EGInsO
Section 9 Insolvency Plan

If an insolvency plan provides for deferred payment, a discharge (of debt), or any other diminution of the creditor's rights, then it may only be ratified by the insolvency court if all of the affected creditors have approved it.

---

16 As to details see *Eickmann* Zwangsversteigerungs- und Zwangsverwaltungsrecht § 26.

17 Prevailing opinion, see *Stöber* § 172 mn 5; *Steiner/Eickmann* § 172 mn 13. This also applies to foreign liquidators, LG Krefeld NJW-RR 1992, 1407 and 1535.

18 HK-InsO/*Flessner* § 159 InsO mn 8.

19 Notaries (sec 20 subs 3 National Rules and Regulations for German Notaries (*BNotO*)) and public auctioneers appointed according to sec 346 German Industrial Code (*GewO*) are competent as well.

Contents

Index

Bibliography

Beck Verwertungsfragen im Verhältnis von Haupt- und Sekundärinsolvenzverfahren nach der EuInsVO, NZI 2006, p 609; *Breutigam/Blersch/Goetsch/Haas* Insolvenzrecht, Berliner Kommentar (January 2006); Frankfurter Kommentar zum Insolvenzrecht (2005); Hamburger Kommentar zum Insolvenzrecht (2006) (ed *Schmidt, A.*); Heidelberger Kommentar zur Insolvenzordnung, 4th edn (2006) (eds *Eickmann/Flessner/Irschlinger/Kirchhof/Kreft/Landfermann/Marotzke/Stephan*); *Kübler/Prütting* Kommentar zur Insolvenzordnung (March 2006); *Meyer-Löwy/Plank* Entbehrlichkeit des Sekundärinsolvenzverfahrens bei flexibler Verteilung der Insolvenzmasse im Hauptinsolvenzverfahren, NZI 2006, p 622; Münchener Kommentar zur Insolvenzordnung, vol 3 (2003).

1. Purpose of Art 102 Sec 9 *EGInsO*

According to Art 34 (1) in conjunction with Art 31 (3) of the EIR, the liquidator in the main insolvency proceedings may submit a reorganisation ("rescue") plan to the secondary insolvency proceedings.[1] This constellation is the key focus of the provision. Although in terms of its wording the provision deals with every kind of insolvency plan being proposed in main or secondary insolvency proceedings (Art 3 (3), Art 27 et seq of the EIR), or in independent territorial insolvency proceedings (Art 3 (4) of the EIR) pursuant to Section 217 et seq *InsO*, it is supposed to apply to secondary insolvency proceedings only.[2] It therefore implements Art 34 of the EIR and at the same time narrows Art 34 (2) of the EIR by introducing an approval requirement in addition to those required by Sec 248 in conjunction with Section 250 *InsO* for approving the insolvency plan: the approval of *all* of the affected creditors. An analogous provision is found in Sec 355 (2) *InsO* in respect of non-European international insolvency law. 1

[1] On conflicts between the main and secondary insolvency proceedings: *Beck* NZI 2006, 609; *Meyer-Löwy/Plank* NZI 2006, 622.

[2] Kübler/Prütting-*Kemper* Art 102 EGInsO § 9 mn 1; BK-InsO/*Pannen* Art 102 EGInsO § 9 mn 1; dissenting opinion: FK-InsO/*Wimmer* Art 102 EGInsO § 9 mn 3: in the case of independent territorial insolvency proceedings only.

2. Contents of the Rule

2.1 Scope of Application

2 Art 34 (1) of the EIR widens the circle of parties who are entitled as per Sec 218 *InsO* to propose an insolvency plan to include the liquidator in the main insolvency proceedings. The insolvency plan being proposed may only deal with the distribution of the national insolvency assets.[3] German insolvency law applies (Art 28 of the EIR). Sec 221 *InsO* states that the German insolvency plan is to regulate the legal positions of the "parties". This includes all of the categories of creditors (Sec 223 to 226 *InsO*).

2.2 Affected Creditors

3 Affected creditors are all of those creditors who were able to register their claims in a national secondary insolvency proceeding. The provision modifies the national rules found in Sec 243 to 246 *InsO* if the insolvency plan stipulates a deferred payment, a discharge (of debt), or any other diminution of the rights of these creditors.[4] According to Sec 254 (1) *InsO*, the plan creates legal rights/relationships. According to sentence 3 of this section, the plan would also govern creditors who have not registered their claims or who have objected to the plan. Such an insolvency plan could therefore also be used to encroach on the rights of foreign creditors since it may stipulate, for example, that the claims of individual creditors be partially discharged. According to Sec 254 (3) *InsO*, they would then no longer be able to participate in the main insolvency proceedings as they would only be entitled to a mere unenforceable obligation (*Naturalobligation*) at most; the foregoing assumes that their approval had been substituted pursuant to Sec 245 and 248 *InsO*.[5] This should be prevented.

2.3 General Approval Hurdle

4 For the reasons set out above the provision demands the approval of all affected creditors in the case of encroachments on assets external to those directly comprised by the secondary insolvency proceedings. As a "cross-border, uniform insolvency plan",[6] the plan must apply to all creditors or to none at all.[7] There are two dangers intrinsic to secondary proceedings: the possible inclusion, through the plan, of debtor's assets in the foreign country, and the creation of a majority of foreign creditors via the possibilities found in German insolvency law provisions (Sec 244, 245, 254 *InsO*) in the plan proceedings. Therefore the wording in Art 34 (2) of the EIR – "effect in respect of the debtor's assets not covered by those proceedings" – must be read broadly since a German insolvency plan, although it can not regulate the debtor's assets situated in a foreign country, could indeed encroach on the claims of the foreign creditors. This should not be possible without the approval of all of them.

5 *Wimmer* points out that such an approval hurdle is not necessary if the insolvency plan is based on a coordinated "master plan" that stipulates the distribution of the debtor's entire assets, subdividing them into groups of "sub-assets".[8] In such cases of

[3] HK-InsO/*Stephan* Art 102 EGInsO § 9 mn 3.
[4] Kübler/Prütting-*Kemper* Art 102 EGInsO § 9 mn 4 at the end.
[5] FK-InsO/*Wimmer* Art 102 EGInsO § 9 mn 1.
[6] MünchKomm InsO/*Reinhart* Art 34 EuInsVO mn 3.
[7] HamburgerKomm-*Undritz* § 355 mn 5.
[8] FK-InsO/*Wimmer* Art 102 EGInsO § 9 mn 3.

"coordinated" insolvency plans, a group of creditors should not be allowed to form an objecting majority in the national insolvency proceedings.[9] The possibility of forming such a majority is actually inconsistent with Art 17 (2) sentence 2 of the EIR, and for this very reason the implementation of this provision through Art 102 Sec 9 *EGInsO* is justified. Therefore, Art 102 Sec 9 *EGInsO* does not make the approval hurdle dependent on whether foreign assets are affected by the provisions of the plan, but rather lays down a general approval hurdle for insolvency plan proceedings that contain discharges (of debts), payment respites, etc.[10]

Article 102 EGInsO
Section 10 Suspension of Realization

If, upon request by the liquidator of the main insolvency proceedings, the realization of an object in which a right to separate satisfaction exists is stayed in secondary domestic insolvency proceedings in accordance with Article 33 of Regulation (EC) No 1346/2000, the creditor shall continue to be paid the interest owed from the estate.

Contents

Index

Bibliography

Böttscher Gesetz über die Zwangsversteigerung und die Zwangsverwaltung, 4th edn (2005); *Dassler/Schiffhauer/Gerhardt* Gesetz über die Zwangsversteigerung und die Zwangsverwaltung (1991); *Eickmann* Zwangsversteigerungs- und Zwangsverwaltungsrecht, 2nd edn (2004); Heidelberger Kommentar zur Insolvenzordnung, 4th edn (2006) (eds *Eickmann/Flessner/Irschlinger/Kirchhof/Kreft/Landfermann/Marotzke/Stephan*); *Hintzen* Höhe des Zinsausgleiches nach Einstellung der Zwangsversteigerung, ZInsO 2000, p 205; *Hintzen* Insolvenz und Immobiliarzwangsvollstreckung, Rpfleger 1999, p 256; *Kübler/Prütting* Kommentar zur Insolvenzordnung (March 2006); *Liersch* Deutsches internationales Insolvenzrecht, NZI 2003, p 302; *Pannen/Riedemann* Die deutschen Aus-

[9] But see: FK-InsO/*Wimmer* Art 102 EGInsO § 9 mn 3 at the end.

[10] Kübler/Prütting-*Kemper* Art 102 EGInsO § 9 mn 4; HamburgerKomm-*Undritz* Art 102 § 9 mn 1.

führungsbestimmungen zur EuInsVO – Ein Überblick zu den Regelungen des Art. 102 EGInsO nF, NZI 2004, p 301; *Schmidt* InVo 1999, p 76; *Smid* Deutsches und Europäisches internationales Insolvenzrecht, Kommentar (2004); *Steiner/Eickmann* Zwangsvollstreckungsgesetz; *Stöber* Zwangsversteigerungsgesetz, 18th edn (2006); *Wenzel* Die Rechtsstellung des Grundpfandrechtsgläubigers im Insolvenzverfahren, NZI 1999, p 102.

1. Purpose of Art 102 Sec 10 *EGInsO*

1 Art 102 Sec 10 *EGInsO* presupposes that main insolvency proceedings (Art 3 (1) of the EIR) as well as – in Germany – secondary insolvency proceedings (Art 3 (2), (3) of the EIR) have already been opened. Given the conceptional superiority of the main insolvency proceedings, Art 33 (1) of the EIR provides that, upon receipt of a request filed by the liquidator in the main proceedings, realization will be stayed in whole or in part in the secondary insolvency proceedings. Art 33 (1) sentence1 2nd half-sentence provides that in this case the court may require the liquidator to take any suitable measures to safeguard the interests of the creditors in the secondary proceedings. Art 102 Sec 10 *EGInsO* makes use of this for the benefit of creditors with a right to separate satisfaction ("*Absonderungsrecht*"). This rule is similar to national law provisions (Sec 169 *InsO*, Sec 30 of the German Foreclosure Sales Act (*ZVG*)) that grant the creditor adequate compensation for a delay in realization.

2. Suspension of Realization

2.1 Prerequisites, Procedure

2 With regard to the requirements for ordering a suspension of realization, see the comments on Art 33 of the EIR.

3 Realization is suspended by way of an order issued by the national court that opened secondary insolvency proceedings. This task is to be ordered by a court officer ("*Rechtspfleger*") (see Sec 3 (2) (g), 19a of the German Judicial Officers Act (*RPflG*)).

4 Insofar as movable property is concerned, the order is to be served on the liquidator in the secondary proceedings; in the case of real property (which includes ships or aircraft), suspension is effected vis-à-vis the liquidator in the secondary insolvency proceedings and, provided that foreclosure proceedings are already pending, vis-à-vis the court that is also competent for the foreclosure proceeding as well. The aforesaid court has to temporarily suspend the proceedings by issuing an order that upholds the decision of the insolvency court ("*Vollzugsbeschluss*").[1]

[1] "Such dependent execution orders" are issued whenever a trial court or a general court competent for execution has issued an order of suspension of execution according to sec 775 (1) or (2) German Code of Civil Procedure (*ZPO*): RGZ 70, 399; *Dassler/Muth* § 30 ZVG mn 20; *Böttcher* § 28 ZVG mn 50; *Steiner/Eickmann* § 28 ZVG mn 129. As the situation referred to by art 33 of the EIR is similar, one should proceed accordingly. sec 30d ZVG does not apply because the insolvency court is expressly authorized to render a decision according to art 33 of the EIR.

2.2 The Requirement of Interest Payment

a) The paying of interest must be ordered in favor of creditoirs with a right to separate satisfaction whenever the order of suspension (also) includes persons with a right to separate satisfaction. Whether a right to separate satisfaction exists is a matter for national law, i.e. Sec 49 to 51 *InsO*. **5**

It is doubtful whether the paying of interest can also be ordered in favor of unsecured creditors.[2] Interest claims for the period following the opening of insolvency proceedings constitute subordinate insolvency claims according to Sec 39 subpara 1 (1) *InsO*, which will not be satisfied until all other claims have been settled.[3] There inclusion in Art 102 Sec 10 *EGInsO* would turn them into preferential debts of the insolvency estate ("*Masseschulden*") with regard to the period concerned. **6**

b) In the case of **movable** property, the **amount** of interest payable should be determined according to Sec 169 *InsO*[4]: if an agreement on the amount of interest has been concluded, then this amount will be decisive, otherwise statutory default interest according to Sec 288 of the German Civil Code (*BGB*) is payable. **7**

As regards **immovable property**, the amount of interest should consistently conform to Sec 30e *ZVG* especially since the wording ("... interest owed ...") of Art 102 Sec 10 *EGInsO*, Sec 169 *InsO*, and Sec 30e *ZVG* is identical. It is disputed whether the term"owed" in Sec 30e *ZVG* refers to the so-called "*dingliche Zinsen*" (a secured amount of interest registered in the land register) or the interest payable pursuant to the loan agreement.[5] The first view ("*dingliche Zinsen*") is correct.[6] **8**

c) As interest payment is to be effected "on an ongoing basis", payment is to be effected on a recurrent basis. Given a period of suspension of three months only, a mode other than **monthly** payment can hardly be considered[7]. **9**

d) The liquidator in the main insolvency proceedings has to effect payment out of the estate of the main insolvency proceedings.[8] **10**

2.3 Other requirements

The interest payment requirement is generally regarded as providing only a **minimum of protection**[9]. Therefore, other requirements are to be considered as admissible, which may also be ordered in favor of unsecured creditors. **11**

---

[2] Opinion obviously held by *Smid* Komm EuInsVO Art 33 mn 8.

[3] Sec 39 *InsO* does not apply to "dingliche Zinsen" (secured rights registered in the land register) in connection with rights to separate satisfaction, BGH ZIP 1997, 120.

[4] This obviously corresponds to the explanation contained in RegE BT-Drucks. 15/16 p 1.

[5] "Dingliche Zinsen": *Stöber* ZVG § 30e mn 2.2, *Böttcher* ZVG § 30e mn 4; *Hintzen* ZInsO 2000, 205 and Rpfleger 1999, 256, 260; *Alff* Rpfleger 2000, 228; *Schmidt* InVo 1999, 76. Contractual interest: LG Göttingen Rpfleger 2000, 228; *Wenzel* NZI 1999, 102; Kübler/Prütting-*Kemper* EGInsO Art 102 § 165 mn 38.

[6] See in detail *Eickmann* Zwangsversteigerungs- und Zwangsverwaltungsrecht (2nd edn) § 6 II 5.

[7] Same: HK-InsO-*Stephan* EGInsO Art 102 § 10 mn 7; Kübler/Prütting-*Kemper* EGInsO Art 102 § 10 mn 4.

[8] *Liersch* NZI 2003, 302, 310; Kübler/Prütting-*Kemper* EGInsO Art 102 § 10 mn 4.

[9] Explanation contained in RegE BT-Drucks 15/16 p 17; *Pannen/Riedemann* NZI 2004, 301, 305; Kübler/Prütting-*Kemper* EGInsO Art 102 § 10 mn 5; HK-InsO/*Stephan* EGInsO Art 102 § 10 mn 5.

12 In the case of persons with a right to separate satisfaction, the interest owing is to be secured through the furnishing of collateral security.

13 With respect to all types of creditors, proportional equalization payments could be considered if, because of the suspension, the realization planned in secondary proceedings fails, which diminishes the chances of satisfaction.

Article 102 EGInsO
Section 11 Informing the Creditors

In addition to the order opening the insolvency proceedings, the creditors whose domicile, habitual residence, or registered office is situated in another Member State of the European Union must also be served with a notice informing them of the consequences pursuant to Section 177 *InsO* of making a belated claim application. The provisions of Section 8 *InsO* apply accordingly.

Contents

Index

Bibliography

Frankfurter Kommentar zum Insolvenzrecht (2005); *Vallender* Aufgaben und Befugnisse des deutschen Insolvenzrichters in Verfahren nach der EuInsVO, KTS 2005, 283; *Weller* Forum Shopping im internationalen Insolvenzrecht, IPRax 2004, 412.

1. Purpose of Art 102 Sec 11 *EGInsO*

1 Art 102 Sec 11 *EGInsO* implements Art 40 and 42 (1) of the EIR, i.e. the obligation to inform the foreign creditors, since an automatic, general publication of a proceeding opened pursuant to the EIR is not provided for (see Art 21 of the EIR).

2. Contents of the Rule

2.1 Method of Informing

Immediately after the opening of proceedings, the competent insolvency court or the appointed liquidator must serve the foreign Member State-creditors known to them, but not the national creditors or creditors situated in third (non-EU) countries, with the order opening proceedings and the form sheet created in compliance with Art 42 (1) of the EIR (printed in Art 42 of the EIR mn 10[1]). **2**

Decisive for ascertaining the circle of creditors to be informed is their domicile, habitual residence, or registered office in a Member State; as contemplated by Art 59 of Regulation (EC) 44/2001, the court applies its own laws for determining habitual residence in this situation.

Service is effected *ex officio* and in compliance with Art 14 of Regulation (EC) 1348/2000.[2] According to Art 102 Sec 11 sentence 2 *EGInsO*, service can be made to the liquidator analogous to Sec 8 *InsO*. Creditors whose residence is unknown will not be served (Sec 8 (2) *InsO*).

2.2 Contents of the Information

The foreign creditors should be informed in a reliable manner of the opening of the proceedings and the method of lodging their claims. The order opening the proceedings already contains most of the important information required by the foreign creditors as prescribed by Art 40 (2) of the EIR (registration deadline, form of the registration, place of registration). It must also, however, explain the "consequences of delays". Art 102 Sec 11 EGInsO therefore creates an additional requirement by providing that the creditors are to be informed pursuant to Sec 177 *InsO* about belated claim registrations, i.e. should a liquidator or a creditor in the insolvency proceedings object to the lodging of belated claims, the court will order either a separate verification (of claims) meeting or a verification in writing at the expense of the party in delay. **3**

[1] Also available on the homepage of the BMJ at www.bmj.bund.de.

[2] FK-*Wimmer* Art 102 § 11 mn 4; on this, see also: Art 102 EGInsO Sec 7 mn 5 and 6.

PART 3: Country Reports

Application of the European Insolvency Regulation in France

Contents

Index

Bibliography

Audit La fin attendue d'une anomalie jurisprudentielle: retour à la lettre de l'article 15 du code civil, Dalloz 2006, p 1846; *Bureau* note to Cass com dated March 21, 2006, Bull Joly 2006, § 185; *Bureau* La fin d'un îlot de résistance : Le règlement du Conseil relatif aux procédures d'insolvabilité, RCDIP 2002, p 613; *Chaput* comments on ECJ dated May 2, 2006 (Eurofood), Rev Lamy dr aff Juni 2006, p 26; *Courbe* L'effet international de la faillite: la solution de la Cour de cassation, in Jault- Seseke/Robine (ed), L'effet international de la faillite: une réalité? (2004); *Dammann* Das neue französische Insolvenzrecht, RIW 2006, p 16; *Dammann* La loi de sauvegarde des entreprises, Bull Lamy Sociétés Commerciales novembre 2005; *Dammann* La future procédure de conciliation, pierre angulaire du projet de loi de sauvegarde des entreprises, Rev Lamy dr aff June 2005; *Dammann* Mobility of companies and localisation of assets, arguments in favor of a dynamic and teleological interpretation of the EC Regulation no 1346/200 on Insolvency Proceedings, in Cross-border insolvency and conflicts of jurisdictions, Brussels 2007, 105 et seq; *Dammann* Conflits de juridictions et Forum shopping, Dalloz 2005, p 1779; *Dammann* comments on TC Nanterre dated May 15, 2005, Dalloz 2005, p 1787; *Dammann* La mobilité des sociétés et la localisation des actifs, JCP E, March–April 2006; *Dammann* Vers une interprétation pragmatique du règlement européen des faillites, Banque June 2006; *Dammann* comments on ECJ (Eurofood), Dalloz 2006, p 1752; *Dammann* comments on CA Versailles dated December 15, 2005, Dalloz 2006, p 379; *Dammann* L'évolution du droit européen des procédures d'insolvabilité et ses conséquences sur le projet de loi de sauvegarde, Rev Lamy dr aff April 2005, p 18; *Dammann/Sénéchal* Procédure secondaire du Règlement (CE) n° 1346/2000: mode d'emploi, Rev Lamy dr aff October 2006; *Dammann/Ollivry* Réflexions sur l'aménagement du principe d'universalité de la faillite, JCP E 2006, p 2628; *Dammann/Podeur* L'affaire Daisytek: l'épilogue. Application par la Cour de cassation du règlement européen relatif aux procédures d'insolvabilité, Banque et droit 2006, p 3; *Dammann/Podeur* L'affaire Eurotunnel, première application du règlement CE n° 1346-2000 à la procédure de sauvegarde, Dalloz 2006, p 2329; *Dammann/Podeur* Le mandat ad hoc, une "porte d'entrée" pour l'application au groupes de sociétés du règlement européen relatif aux procédures d'insolvabilité, Rev Lamy dr aff November 2006; *Dammann/Podeur* Les groupes de sociétés face aux procédures d'insolvabilité, Rev Lamy Dr aff May 2007 p 65 et seq; *Dammann/Undritz* Die Reform des französischen Insolvenzrechts im Rechtsvergleich zur InsO, NZI 2005, p 198; *Fasquelle* comments on TC Nanterre dated May 19, 2005, JCP E 2006, p 1412; *Fasquelle* comments on ECJ dated May 2, 2005 (Eurofood), Bull Joly 2006; *Grasmann* Effets nationaux d'une procédure d'exécution collective étrangère (redressement ou liquidation judiciaires, faillite, concordat), RCDIP 1990, p 419; *Henry* comments on Cass com dated March 21, 2006, Dalloz 2006, p 1466; *Jault-Seseke/Robine* comments on TC Nanterre dated December 15, 2006, Bull Joly Sociétés, p 575; *Jault-Seseke/Robine* L'interprétation du Règlement n° 1346/2000 relatif aux procédures d'insolvabilité, la fin des incertitudes?, RCDIP 2006; *Jacquemont* comments on Cour de cassation dated September 4, 2003, JDI 2004, p 142; *Khairallah* comments on Cour de cassation dated November 19, 2002, Dalloz 2003, p 797; *Khairallah* comments on CA Versailles dated September 4, 2003, RCDIP 2003, p 667; *Klein* Frankreichs Insolvenzrechtsreform setzt auf Vorbeugung, RIW 2006, p 13; *Lagarde* comments on Cour de cassation dated March 19, 1979, RCDIP 1981, p 524; *Legros* comments on Cass com dated 21.3.2006, JCP E 2006, p 2072; *Likillimba* comments on Cour d'appel de Versailles dated September 4, 2003, JCP E 1747; *Lienhard* comments on Cass com dated March 21, 2006, Dalloz AJ p 914; *Lienhard* comments on Cour de cassation dated June 27, 2006, Dalloz 2006 AJ p 1816; *Lienhard* comments on TC Nanterre dated December 15, 2006, Dalloz 2006 AJ, p 651; *Lienhard* Procédures d'insolvabilité: déplacement du centre des intérêts principaux du débiteur, comments on ECJ dated January 17, 2006 Dalloz 2006, AJ p 367; *Lienhard* comments on CA Versailles dated December 15, 2005, Dalloz 2006, AJ p 142; *Lienhard* comments on Cour de cassation dated February 5, 2002, Dalloz 2002 AJ p 957; *Lienhard* comments on Cour de cassation dated May 10,

2005, Dalloz 2005, p 1414; *Loussouarn/Borel/de Vareilles-Sommières* Droit international privé, 8th edn; *Mayer* Droit international privé, 6th edn; *Mélin* La faillite internationale (2004); *Mélin* comments on Cour de cassation dated June 27, 2006, JCP E 2006, p 2291; *Mélin* comments on Cour d'appel de Versailles dated September 4, 2003, RJDA 1/04, p 3; *Mélin* comments on TC Nanterre dated May 19, 2005, Act proc coll 2005 Nr 11; *Menjucq* Aspects de droit international privé relatifs aux conflits de compétence et aux conflits de lois, Rev proc coll March 2003, p 49; *Menjucq* comments on Cass com dated December 26, 1999; *Menjucq* comments on ECJ dated May 2, 2006 (Eurofood), JCP 2006 II, No 10089; *Menjucq* comments on Cour de cassation dated June 27, 2006, JCP G 2006 II, No 10147; *Menjucq* Ouverture, reconnaissance et coordination des procédures d'insolvabilité dans le règlement 1346/2000, Bull Joly Soc December 2000, p 1111; *Menjucq* comments on TC Nanterre dated May 19, 2005, JCP G II No 10116; *Menjucq* comments on TC Nanterre dated December 15, 2006, Rev proc coll 2006, p 241; *Menjucq* comments on Cour de cassation dated March 14 2000, Bull Joly sociétés June 2000, p 600; *Oppetit* comments on Cass com dated April 11, 1995 RCDIP 1995, p 742; *Raimon* comments on Cour de cassation dated February 5, 2002, JCP E 2003, p 955; *Rémery* comments on Cass civ dated January 19, 1988, Dalloz 1988, p 565; *Rémery* comments on Cass civ dated February 25, 1986, JCP 1987 II, No 20776; *Rémery* comments on ECJ dated May 2, 2006 (Eurofood), Rev soc 2006, p 360; *Rémery* comments on Cour de cassation dated January 31, 1990, Dalloz 1990, p 461; *Rémery* comments on Cour d'appel de Versailles dated September 4, 2003, Rev des sociétés 2003, p 891; *Rémery* Les aspects européens de la déclaration des créances dans une procédure collective ouverte en France, Rev proc coll March 2003, p 66; *Roussel Galle* comments on Cour de cassation dated November 19, 2002, JDI 2003, p 132; *Soinne* Droit communautaire des entreprises en difficulté: prospective, Rev proc coll March 2003; *Sonnenberger/Dammann* Französisches Handels- und Wirtschaftsrecht, Heidelberg, 3rd edn Kap VIII (in preparation); *Synvet* comments on Cass civ dated February 25, 1986, RCDIP 1987, p 589; *Urbain-Parléani* La faillite des sociétés, Bref aperçu sur le règlement CE n° 1346-2000 du 29 mai 2000 relatif aux procédures collectives, Rev soc January/February 2005; *Vallender/Heukamp* Die Reform des französischen Unternehmensinsolvenzrechts oder: Rette sich, wer kann! InVo 2006, p 1; *Vallens* comments on ECJ dated May 2, 2006 (Eurofood), JCP E 2006, Nr 2071; *Vallens* comments on Cour de cassation dated June 27, 2006, Dalloz 2006, p 2257; *Vallens* Le règlement communautaire sur les procédures d'insolvabilité et les procédures de redressement et de liquidation judiciaire, Rev Lamy dr aff July 2002; *Vallens* comments on CA Versailles dated September 4, 2003, Dalloz 2003, p 2352; *Vallens* comments on TC Nanterre dated December 15, 2006, Dalloz 2006, p 793; *Vallens* Le droit de la faillite en Europe, Les procédures secondaires, Rev proc coll March 2003; *Vallens* comments on Cour d'appel de Versailles dated September 4, 2003, Dalloz 2003, p 2352; *Vallens* comments on ECJ dated January 17, 2006 (Staubitz-Schreiber), Rev des sociétés 2006, p 346; *Vallens* La mise en œuvre du règlement communautaire sur les procédures d'insolvabilité: questions de procédure, Dalloz 2003, p 1426; *Vasseur* comments on Cass com dated April 11, 1995, Dalloz 1995, p 640; *Virgós/Schmit* Erläuternder Bericht zu dem EU-Übereinkommen über Insolvenzverfahren, in Stoll (ed), Vorschläge und Gutachten, p 32; *Witz/Zierau* Französisches internationales Konkursrecht – Neue Tendenzen und Entwicklungen in der Rechtsprechung der Cour de cassation, RIW 1989, p 929.

1. Introduction

This country report provides a brief overview of the various types of civil and commercial insolvency proceedings available in France[1], as well as the basic principles of French autonomous private international law in the area of international insolvency. This overview is confined to the issues that are relevant to the application of the EIR in France. 1

1.1 Various Types of French Insolvency Proceedings

French substantive insolvency law recognizes a distinction between **civil debt restructuring and commercial insolvency proceedings.** 2

1.1.1 Civil debt restructuring proceedings

3 Individuals who are not engaged in business, *i.e.* **consumers**, cannot request the benefit of commercial insolvency proceedings as set forth in the Commercial Code (Code de commerce, CCom). The French Consumer Code provides for civil debt restructuring proceedings *(surendettement des particuliers)* for individuals who demonstrate good faith and are over-indebted with respect to their non-professional obligations. These proceedings were established by the so-called *Loi Neiertz* of December 31, 1989[2] and reformed by the law of August 1, 2003[3]. Art. L 331-1 *et seq* of the Consumer Code provide, under certain conditions, for a relief of indebtedness, comparable in some respects to commercial liquidation proceedings. *Bona fide* over-indebted consumers can benefit from these restructuring proceedings.[4] Private debts of business people, handicraftsmen, farmers or freelancers do not fall within the scope of civil debt restructuring proceedings. The proceeding starts with a conciliation. If the debtor is irremediably over-indebted, a judicial reorganization proceeding, the so-called *procédure de rétablissement personnel*, can be opened. If the judge establishes at the end of the proceeding that the sale of the assets will not cover the costs of the debts, or that the debtor owns only moveable assets necessary for his everyday life or work, the proceeding is closed and a **discharge** of all remaining debts takes place.

4 There are also special proceedings, called *faillite civile*, which apply to natural persons domiciled in the French departments of Haut-Rhin, Bas-Rhin and Moselle (**Alsace-Lorraine**), who are not merchants, farmers, artisans or freelancers.[5]

1.1.2 Commercial insolvency proceedings

5 The various commercial proceedings relating to financial difficulties of businesses are set out in the sixth book of the Commercial Code starting with Art L 611-1, which distinguishes between pre-insolvency and insolvency proceedings. In July 2005[6], the French legislature reformed the law by, *inter alia*, creating new safeguard proceedings and rendering more efficient the existing pre-proceedings, focusing on **tackling the financial difficulties** of the debtor's business at an early stage. The reform became effective on

[1] Cf *Sonnenberger/Dammann* Französisches Handels- und Wirtschaftsrecht, 3rd edn (in preparation).

[2] No 89-1010 and Execution Decree No 90-175.

[3] No 2003-710. The reform was accompanied by Execution Decree No 2004-180 of February 24, 2004, modifying in several aspects Arts R 331-1 *et seq* of the *Code de la consommation*. Cf the Circular of March 24, 1999, JCP III 20076. In 2000, about 150,000 proceedings were opened. The trend is toward increased numbers of proceedings.

[4] Guarantors and co-debtors jointly liable for the obligations of a company can also benefit from these proceedings, provided that they were not involved in the management of the company.

[5] *See* Art L 670-1 *et seq* CCom. In several aspects, these proceedings have been adapted to close the gap with the proceedings of *surendettement des particuliers*.

[6] For comments on the draft law of May 5, 2005, *see Dammann/Undritz* NZI 2005, 198. The law No 2005-845 of July 26, 2005 and the execution decrees are published in Dalloz, Code des procédures collectives, 5th edn (2007). The Decree was codified in March 2007, Arts R 600 *et seq* CCom. For an overview of the new law, *see Klein* RIW 2006, 13, *Dammann*, Rev Lamy soc com November 2005 and RIW 2006, p 16; *Lienhard*, Sauvegarde des entreprises en difficultés, 1st edn, 2006; *Le Corre* Droit et Pratique des Procédures collectives, 3rd ed, 2006. The new law changes the codification numbering of the CCom. The legislature has published an orientation tabulation as an exhibit.

January 1, 2006. The proceedings remain applicable to traders, craftsmen, farmers, civil law legal entities, and, since the reform of 2005, to freelancers, like lawyers or medical practitioners.[7]

There are presently two kinds of pre-insolvency proceedings: nomination of an *ad hoc* conciliator by the president of the commercial court *(mandat ad hoc)*, and conciliation proceedings *(conciliation)*. For companies that are in financial distress but not yet insolvent, the president of the commercial court may, at the debtor's request, nominate a ***mandataire ad hoc*** pursuant to Art L 611-13 *CCom* to bring about a settlement with the main creditors and thus avoid the opening of insolvency proceedings. The ***mandat ad hoc***, originally created in commercial court practice, is very flexible. The president of the commercial court determines the duration of the mandate and the functions of the *mandataire ad hoc*. The resulting settlement need not to be confirmed by the court and remains confidential. The reform of 2005 did not change the *mandat ad hoc*. **6**

Art L 611-4 et seq of the Commercial code regulate **conciliation** proceedings – *conciliation*, which have become more attractive since the 2005 Reform. This proceeding could play a decisive role in the prevention of insolvency proceedings.[8] According to Art L 611-4 of the *CCom*, debtors may request the opening of proceedings, when they encounter actual or foreseeable legal, economic or financial difficulties, and have not been in a state of cessation of payments for more than forty-five days. The proceeding lasts generally four months. In complex situations, as a matter of practice, conciliation proceedings are preceded by the opening of *mandat ad hoc* proceedings. The court conciliator has no power to force concessions from the creditors. Settlement is voluntary. During conciliation proceedings, creditors may not request the opening of normal insolvency proceedings. At the end of the proceedings, the settlement is either subject to a mere confirmation by the court (*constatation*), or, at the debtor's request, to an official homologation (*homologation*). In the case of a *constatation*, the conciliation proceedings remain confidential. A judgment of *homologation* is published, but not the terms of settlement themselves. **7**

The key element of the reform is the new safeguard proceedings, the ***procédure de sauvegarde***, which may be commenced on the petition of the debtor, provided that the debtor is facing financial difficulties that it is unable to overcome on its own and that would lead to a cessation of payments.[9] The proceedings start with an observation period (***période d'observation***). The debtor benefits from an automatic stay of execution proceedings. It remains in possession, is supervised or assisted by a court-appointed trustee and formulates with two creditor committees a safeguard plan (*plan de sauvegarde*) that is subject to the approval of a majority of each committee. At the end of the observation period, the court must determine whether the safeguard plan has a reasonable chance to succeed and sufficiently accounts for the interests of all creditors. The *procédure de sauvegarde* does not provide any opportunity for investors to file a take-over bid for the ongoing business.[10] **8**

---

[7] Civil courts (*Tribunal de Grande Instance*) rather than commercial law courts have jurisdiction over these cases. Public law entities are not subject to insolvency proceedings.

[8] Cf *Dammann* Rev Lamy Dr aff June 2005.

[9] The wording of art L 620-1 CCom can be compared to sec 18 (2) of the German InsO. It is more restrictive than art L 611-4 of the CCom with respect to the opening of conciliation proceedings.

[10] In the framework of a safeguard plan, only parts of the ongoing business may be sold.

9 If the debtor is insolvent, the court normally opens judicial **rehabilitation proceedings** (***redressement judiciaire***). Since the reform of 2005, however, the debtor may instead request the opening of conciliation proceedings. In general, rehabilitation proceedings start with an observation period at the end of which the court decides whether to **liquidate** the debtor (*liquidation judiciaire*) or to **continue its operation** according to a plan of reorganization (***plan de continuation***). Until the reform of 2005, there was a third alternative: the sale of the business to an outside investor (***plan de cession***). Conceptually, the sale of the ongoing business is now integrated into judicial liquidation proceedings, but, under certain conditions, the Court may also order the sale of the ongoing business within the framework of the *redressement judiciaire*. If no rehabilitation appears to be possible, the court immediately opens **liquidation proceedings** (***liquidation judiciaire***) without any prior observation period.[11] In addition, a *liquidation judiciaire simplifiée* may be requested for small companies.[12]

10 **Best practice**: the very flexible *mandat ad hoc* and conciliation play an important role in the area of pre-insolvency debt restructuring of mid-size and large companies in France. It is to be expected that proceedings will generally start with a *mandat ad hoc* that in the end will be converted into a conciliation proceeding (either confidential or official).[13] The success of the proceeding often depends on the skill of the *mandataire*. As an independent expert and with the authority of nomination by the president the commercial court, the *mandataire* or conciliator can obtain concessions from the creditors that the debtor himself could not. This explains the high **success rate**. In the most recent years past, about two-thirds of all proceedings have been concluded through a settlement. Whether or not the *procédure de sauvegarde* will fulfill the hopes of the legislature is an open question. The *Eurotunnel* case can be considered a successful test-case.[14]

11 If the *mandat ad hoc/conciliation* fails, a successful reorganization of the debtor can in most cases be achieved only through a **sale of the business** in an asset deal. Even after the reform, the sale of the business remains, as in the past, the most attractive alternative for investors. In general, the purchaser acquires the business without debts. All employees whose employment is not taken over are dismissed at the expense of the insolvency estate. This is one of the main advantages of a takeover through a *plan de cession*: the employee has no claim against the purchaser for continuation of his employment contract.

1.2 Overview of Autonomous French Private International Law in the Area of International Insolvencies

12 Unlike other continental codifications, neither the French Civil nor Commercial code contains specific provisions regarding international jurisdiction and conflict of laws rules governing international insolvency proceedings. In fact, the autonomous private international law in this area has been developed in **French case law** and legal doctrine.[15]

[11] Art L 640-1 of the CCom.

[12] Cf arts L 644-1 to L 644-6 of the CCom.

[13] *See Dammann* Lamy Dr aff June 2005 p 5.

[14] On this, *see* below at mn 20 et seq. The TC Paris has accepted the safeguard plan in a judgment dated January 1, 2007, Dalloz 2007, 313. Another proceeding has been opened for the well-known daily newspaper *Libération* and was successfully closed in January 2007.

[15] For an overview, *see Dammann/Sonnenberger* Französiches Handels- und Wirtschaftsrecht, No IX 93 *et seq*; Rép International Dalloz, Faillite-*Synvet* (1998) and *Mélin* La faillite internationale (2004). *See also Menjucq* Rev proc coll March 2003

The international jurisdiction of French courts pursuant to Art R 600-1 (1) of the *CCom*[16] corresponds essentially, in spite of different wording, to Art 3 (1) of the EIR. The **registered office of the company** – ***siège de l'entreprise***, or, if there is no registered office in France, the centre of its interests – ***centre principal de ses interest***, is decisive. In the case of artificial persons there is a rebuttable presumption in favor of the registered office as provided for in the EIR. If the registered office is abroad, a centre of interests is assumed to be in France provided there is a secondary establishment (*établissement secondaire*), whether it be a branch, an agency or a mere sales agency.[17] Even isolated assets in France can establish the jurisdiction of French courts.[18] **13**

This international jurisdiction is generally not affected by the opening of insolvency proceedings in a foreign country, but that rule does not hold true when an insolvency proceeding has been opened abroad, in particular in the country of the debtor's registered office, and has been recognized per exequatur in France.[19] Besides, jurisdiction can be based on Art 14 and 15 of the CC (*Code civil*).[20] Particularly important is Art 14, since it allows the opening of proceedings against foreign debtors, provided only that they have French creditors.[21] Following a recent decision of the *Cour de Cassation*, the rule of Art 14 ceases to be mandatory.[22] **14**

An insolvency proceeding opened in the place of the debtor's French registered office has universal effect, according to consistent case law, provided that it is recognized in the States where assets are located.[23] *Lex concursus* is French law.

---

p 49; on the recent developments following the *Khalifa Airways* decision of the *Cour de cassation* on June 6, 2006, *see Dammann/Ollivry* JCP E 2006, 2628.

16 This provision corresponds to a large extent to the wording of art 1 (1) of the decree no 85-1388 of December 27, 1985.

17 Cf Cass civ dated 19 Jan 1988, Dalloz 1988 Jur 565, note by *Rémery*; *Grasmann* RCDIP 1990, 421; *see also* the *BCCI* case, Cass dated 11 Apr 1995, Bull civ IV Nr 126, RCDIP 1995, 742, note by *Oppetit*; Dalloz 1995, 640 note by *Vasseur*, J-Cl Int Fasc 569-10 mn 40 with further references.

18 Cf Cass com dated 26 Oct 1999, Bull Joly p 385, note by *Menjucq* (company with registered office on the Isle of Man, which concluded a financial leasing agreement with respect to real estate assets located in France); Cass com dated 1 Oct 2002, Rev dr soc 2003, somm p 89 (liquidation of an English company which had taken out a loan in order to finance its leasing activities in France).

19 Cass com dated 11 Apr 1995, RCDIP 1995, 742 note by *Oppetit*. For in-depth treatment of this, *see* J-Cl Int Fasc 569-10 Mn 54 *et seq*; Rép dr int, Faillite mn 21.

20 Cf the case of a French creditor who obtained the opening of a liquidation proceeding against an Algerian company, even though the company was not insolvent in Algeria: Cass com dated 19 Mar 1979, RCDIP 1981, 524 note by *Lagarde*. *See also Mélin* mn 20. On Art 15, *see* Cass civ dated 7 Jun 1962, Bull civ 1962 No 506, which plays an important role for the exequatur. Whether or not this decision on Art 15 CC in connection with the *Prieur* decision of the *Cour de cassation* dated 23 May 2006, Dalloz 2006, 1880, is still valid, is doubtful. On this, *see Audit* La fin attendue d'une anomalie jurisprudentielle: retour à la lettre de l'article 15 du code civil, Dalloz 2006 chron, 1846. On the implications of this decision for the autonomous international private law, *see Dammann/Ollivry* JCP E 2006, 2628. This decision has been confirmed by Cass civ dated 22 May 2007, Dalloz 2007 p 1596.

21 Even if there is no office, establishment or even assets. For the importance of a proceeding in France in such cases, *see Lagarde* RCDIP 1981, 524, 534; *Witz/Zierau* RIW 1989, 930.

22 Cf the *Fercometam* decision of Cass civ dated 22 May 2007, Dalloz 2007 p 1596, JCP G 2007 Act 258.

23 *See, e.g.*, the "*Banque Worms*" decision dated 19 Nov 2002, Bull civ I No 275; Dalloz

15 If the foreign decision purports to have universal effect, an exequatur of a French court is necessary. This is particularly true where the divestment of the debtor, the stay of individual claims, preservation and execution measures of a creditor, the powers of the competent insolvency body to administer and to realize the insolvency assets *etc*, are concerned.[24] The stay against opening insolvency proceedings also requires an exequatur.[25] If the exequatur is granted, the opening of foreign insolvency proceedings has the effect for which the relevant insolvency law provides. As long as the exequatur has not been granted, the debtor may freely dispose of his assets in France, and the creditors may pursue individual executions. Note that a subsequent exequatur is to be taken into account when assessing legal situations that have occurred before it.[26]

2. Effects of the EIR on French Law

2.1 Introduction

16 Since May 31, 2002, the EIR has been directly applicable to collective cross-border insolvency proceedings opened with respect to a debtor whose center of main interests is located within the EU Member States and whose assets are located in more than one Member State.[27] The EIR replaces, within the scope of its application, **French autonomous private international law** and **French substantive insolvency law.**

17 The French legislature has not enacted special provisions with respect to the introduction of the EIR into French law, with the exception of Art R 721-26 of the *CCom*, which requires the registration of decisions opening main insolvency proceedings in another Member State in the French commercial register. The French Minister of Justice published a Circular dated March 17, 2003 interpreting the EIR[28], but French courts are not bound by it.[29] Following the *Eurofood* decision of the European Court of Justice dated May 2, 2006[30] and the *Daisytek* decision of the French Supreme Court dated June 27, 2006[31], the French Ministry of Justice has prepared a revised Circular. The Circular,

2003, 797 note *Khairallah* JDI 2003, 132 note *Roussel Galle*. In the case of a branch office, *see* the *Khalifa* decision, Cass com dated 21 Mar 2005, Dalloz 2006, AJ 914 note by *Lienhard*; Dalloz 2006, 1466 note by *Henry*, JCP E 2006, 2072 note by *Legros*; Bull Joly 2006, § 185 note by *Bureau*. On this *Dammann/Ollivry* JCP E 2006, 2628. The universal effect of insolvency proceedings has been recognized by French courts since 1913, *see Courbe* L'effet international de la faillite: la solution de la Cour de cassation, in L'effet international de la faillite: une réalité? Dalloz (2004).

24 *See* Rép dr int, *Faillite* mn 96 et seq.

25 Id; *Jacquet/Delebecque* mn 406.

26 *Kléber* case, Cass civ dated 25 Feb 1986, Rev crit DIP 1987, 589 note *Synvet*; JCP 1987 II 20776 note *Rémery*.

27 The reference to the Member States herein refers to the all EU Member States that are bound by the EIR. The EIR does not apply to the Channel Islands, the Isle of Man or Gibraltar.

28 On July 30, 2003, the Circ was published in the Official Journal of the French Republic p 12939. Published in Code des procédures collectives Dalloz p 966 et seq (2007).

29 *See* the introduction of the Circ.

30 Dalloz 2006 Jur p 1752 note *Dammann*; Rev Soc 2006 p 360 note *Rémery*; JCP 2006, II, 10089 note *Menjucq*; JCP 2006, ed E no 2071 note *Vallens*; Rev Lamy dr aff June 2006, p 26, note *Chaput*.

31 Dalloz 2006 AJ 1816 note *Lienhard*, Banque & Droit 2006 p 3 note *Dammann/Podeur*; Dalloz 2006 Jur 2257, note *Vallens*; JCP G 2006 II 10147, note, Menjucq; JCP E 2006, 2291, note *Mélin*.

dated December 15, 2006, has not yet been published in the Official Journal of the French Republic.[32]

2.2 The Scope of the EIR

2.2.1 The geographic reach of the EIR

The EIR is applicable to insolvency proceedings opened in France with respect to a debtor having assets located in another Member State or having its **center of main interests** within the territory of another Member State. Thus, the Circular excludes the application of the EIR by French courts when the center of a debtor's main interests is located outside the territory of the European Union.[33] The EIR is also not applicable to the establishment in France of an insolvent debtor the center of whose main interests is located outside the EU.[34] Finally, the EIR is not applicable to **assets and creditors of the debtor located outside the Member States**, even when the debtor's center of main interests is located within the EU.[35] **18**

2.2.2 Concept of "centre of main interests" – COMI

As in the other Member States, the interpretation of the concept of "centre of main interests" is very disputed in France. At first, the prevailing opinion held that the **center of main interests**, or **COMI**, is the location of the effective center of management *("le centre effectif de direction des affaires")*.[36] The presumption of a business' COMI being located at the place of the registered office of the debtor should be displaced only if that registered office is fictitious or has been subject to an artful transfer immediately prior to the opening of proceedings.[37] The discussion became more acute when it concerned insolvencies of corporate groups. The problem is whether and when the COMI of a subsidiary can be located at the registered office of its parent company. At first the prevailing opinion strictly rejected such a concentration of insolvency proceedings against companies of a corporate group by a court. The dogmatic reason for this solution was the effective seat theory.[38] The well-known cases of *Daisytek* and *Rover* represented first and foremost a defensive reaction against the "Imperialism of the English insolvency law".[39] The legal scholars almost unanimously considered the opening of English insolvency proceedings against the French subsidiaries of the *Daisytek* and the *Rover* groups as impermissible forum shopping.[40] Some annotators were therefore in favor of a review **19**

---

[32] It has only been published in the Bulletin officiel du Ministère de la justice, February 28, 2007. The following explanations refer to the Circular dated December 15, 2006.

[33] *See* the introduction of the Circ, referring to recitals 14 and 33 of the EIR.

[34] *See* the introduction of the Circ. On the other hand, it would be possible to apply the EIR to a company registered outside the EU, provided that the COMI of such a company is located in France.

[35] *See* the introduction of the Circ.

[36] *See* art 1.2.1 of the Circ.

[37] *See Bureau* RCDIP 2002, 613 et seq mn 27. *Menjucq* Bull Joly Société December 2000, 1111; *Vallens* Rev Lamy dr aff July 2002.

[38] For an in-depth analysis, *see Dammann* Mobility of companies and localisation of assets, arguments in favor of a dynamic and teleological interpretation of the EC Regulation No 1346/2000 on Insolvency Proceedings, in Cross-border insolvency and conflicts of jurisdictions, Brussels 2007, 105 *et seq*.

[39] Formulation of the public prosecutor (*ministère public*) in the *Rover* case.

[40] Cf *Vallens* Dalloz 2003, 2352 comments on Versailles dated 4 Sep 2003. Cf also the critical note by *Menjucq* on TC Nanterre in JCP G II 10116 and *Fasquelle* JCP E 2006, 1412.

of the merits of English decisions in order to refuse recognition to the corresponding English proceeding, if necessary.[41]

20 Some authors have suggested a more flexible and pragmatic approach, in particular within the framework of **insolvency of groups of companies**[42], such as that followed by the Commercial Courts of Nanterre and Paris in the *EMTEC*[43] and *Eurotunnel*[44] cases. In its *EMTEC* decisions dated February 15, 2006, the Commercial Court of Nanterre adopted an interpretation of COMI in opening a French main proceeding broad enough to include eight foreign subsidiaries of the EMTEC group, including the Dutch mother company and the German sister company of the group's main French operating company. The Commercial Court conducted a very thorough analysis of the facts at issue, the European case law and the opinion of Advocate General Jacobs in the *Eurofood* case dated September 27, 2005. Making reference to the concept of headquarters functions, the court found that a multitude of objective criteria led to the conclusion that the COMI of the various foreign subsidiaries of the EMTEC group were located in France and that such location was ascertainable to third parties. In particular, the main French operating company of the EMTEC group centralized placement of all purchase orders, conducted all negotiations with the main suppliers and clients and determined the commercial strategy of the whole group. Thus, the French holding company became the most important creditor of its subsidiaries. In addition, the court heard the representative of the employees of each subsidiary who confirmed that the whole group was administered out of France. The court also stressed the necessity for international cooperation and transparency. Finally, the court indicated that opening of secondary insolvency proceedings with respect to the foreign subsidies of EMTEC-group would appear to be an interesting tool in order to protect local creditors.[45]

21 In the context of the *Eurofood* decision of the ECJ, some legal authors doubt whether the *EMTEC* jurisprudence will be upheld by French courts in the future.[46] The ***Euro-***

41 Cf the comments by *Khairallah* on Cour d'appel Versailles dated 4 Sep 2003, RCDIP 2003, 667, as well as the notes by *Menjucq* and *Fasquelle* (previous footnote).

42 *Dammann* Dalloz 2005 Jur p 1779; comments on TC Nanterre dated 15 May 2005, Dalloz 2005, 1787.

43 TC Nanterre dated 15 Feb 2006, Dalloz 2006 AJ 651, note by *Lienhard*; Dalloz 2006, 793 note by *Vallens*; Rev proc coll 2006, 241, note by Menjucq; Bull Joly Sociétés 2006, 575 § 122, note by *Jault-Seseke/Robine*. The Dutch holding company of the EMTEC-group was merely a letterbox company, created only to acquire the EMTEC-group. For tax reasons, the company also retained EMTEC's trademark and logo.

44 TC Paris dated 2 Aug 2006, *Dammann/Podeur* L'affaire Eurotunnel, première application du règlement n° 1346/2000 à la procédure de sauvegarde, Dalloz 2006, 2329, confirmed by TC Paris dated 15 Jan 2007, Dalloz AJ 313.

45 The idea of a combination of main and secondary proceedings has been suggested by *Dammann* in various publications and public conferences. *See Dammann* La mobilité des sociétés et localisation des actifs, JCP éd E Cahier dr. entrep., March/April 2006; Vers une interprétation pragmatique du règlement européen des faillites, Banque juin 2006; note Eurofood, Dalloz 2006 Jur p 1752; Procédure secondaire du Règlement (CE) n° 1346/2000: mode d'emploi, Rev Lamy dr aff October 2006 (co-author Sénéchal); Mobility of companies and localisation of assets, arguments in favor of a dynamic and teleological interpretation of the EC Regulation No 1346/2000 on Insolvency Proceedings, in Cross-border insolvency and conflicts of jurisdictions, Brussels 2007, 105 *et seq*.

46 For instance: *Menjucq* JCP, II, 10089. Contra: *Lienhard* Dalloz 2006 AJ p 367; *Dammann* Dalloz 2006 Jur p 1752, *Dammann* Vers une interprétation pragmatique du règlement européen des faillites, Banque June 2006.

tunnel* decisions** of the Commercial court of Paris dated August 8, 2006 and January 15, 2007 are very clear in this regard. Referring to the decisions of the ECJ, the judges in Paris declared that the centre of main interests of the Eurotunnel-group was located in Paris. The ***ministère public[47] approved of this argumentation too. Very interesting is the criterion of the **debt-restructuring negotiations**, which have been conducted as a ***mandat ad hoc*** since 2003 under the direction of the Commercial Court of Paris. Since both companies are listed on the stock exchange, the *mandat ad hoc* proceeding was publicly announced. Therefore it was obvious to the creditors participating in the proceedings, who were organized into several committees, as well as to the other creditors, that the centre of main interests of the foreign companies of the group had been transferred to France. The creditors could anticipate that the French pre-insolvency proceeding, voluntarily accepted by the creditors, could be later converted into a "normal" insolvency proceeding. The **criteria of legal certainty and foreseeability of the applicable law**, which had been embraced by the ECJ, were thus satisfied. The same holds true with regard to the factor of necessary **efficiency of insolvency proceedings**. The Judges of the Court of Paris assumed that only a global restructuring of the debts, which amounted to 9 billion Euros could be successful. It would not make sense from an economic point of view to limit the jurisdiction of the Court of Paris to the French companies, since each company of the corporate group is jointly and severally liable.[48]

2.2.3 Concept of "establishment"

According to the Circular, a **branch** (*succursale*), an **office for representation purposes** (*bureau de représentation*) or an **agency** (*agence*) are each deemed to constitute an establishment.[49] The Circular considers that isolated assets, such as money deposited in a bank account, are insufficient to bring about the existence of an establishment in France.[50] An office that has been opened for a single transaction only does not constitute an establishment under the EIR.[51] The Circular, as well as some French authors, consider that a legally-defined subsidiary of a company will not qualify as "establishment".[52] Arguably, it would not be possible for French courts to open secondary insolvency proceedings in favor of a company having its registered office in France which is subject to main insolvency proceedings in another Member State.[53] As shown in the **22**

[47] In France, the public attorney is a party in insolvency proceedings.

[48] Cf the in-depth, approving comments on TC Paris dated 2 Aug 2006 by *Dammann/Podeur* Dalloz 2006, 2329. On the practical importance of the French pre-proceedings, *see Dammann/Podeur* Le mandat ad hoc, une "porte d'entrée" pour l'application aux groupes de sociétés du règlement européen relatif aux procédures d'insolvabilité, Rev Lamy Dr aff November 2006.

[49] *See* art 1.2.2 of the Circ. The definition of the term 'establishment' is close to the one used in French case law to justify opening proceedings in France when the head office of a company is situated abroad. *See, e.g.*, the BCCI case Cass com dated 11 May 1995, Bull civ IV no 126, Rev crit DIP 1995, 742 note *Oppettit*, Dalloz 1995 Jur p 640 note *Vasseur*.

[50] *See also J-Cl* mn 36. The case law referred to above pursuant to which single assets located in France were sufficient to open insolvency proceedings in France is applicable with respect to a debtor whose center of main interests is located within the European Community.

[51] *See Bureau* Rev crit DIP 2002, 634 note no 99.

[52] *See* art 1.2.2 of the Circ. *See* J-Cl mn 37 and *Urbain-Parleani* Rev soc Janvier/février 2005, mn 9 and 22.

[53] Cf JCl mn 37 and *Urbain-Parléani* Rev soc January/February 2005, mn 9 and 22.

Rover and *Daisytek* cases, where UK jurisdictions opened main insolvency proceedings in favor of French subsidiaries, such an interpretation would lead to undesirable results. From a practical point of view, it would appear preferable to permit the opening of secondary insolvency proceedings given such a scenario in order to protect the interests of the employees and other local creditors. Some legal authors have therefore suggested **broadening the interpretation of the term "establishment"**.[54] In the *Rover* case, the Court of appeal of Versailles followed such interpretation.[55] It held that the opening of secondary insolvency proceedings in favor of Rover SAS was generally possible, although the company's registered office was in France. Under the given circumstances of the case, it rejected the request of the public prosecutor finding that such opening would have been costly and useless. The court mentioned that opening of secondary insolvency proceedings had not been requested by any local creditor or employee of the French subsidiary. Judge Norris had accepted in a judgment dated May 11, 2005 the English liquidator's guarantee to the French employees of the same privileges in the main insolvency proceedings that they would have enjoyed under French judicial liquidation proceedings. This stipulation was designed to prevent the court in Nanterre from opening secondary insolvency proceedings at the request of the employees. Consequently, Judge Norris created a kind of "contractual secondary proceedings". The Court of Appeal of Versailles approved this pragmatic approach.[56] The Commercial Court of Nanterre followed a similar course with respect to the Italian subsidiary of the EMTEC-group.[57] The Circular of the Justice Minister has also adopted this interpretation.[58]

2.2.4 Scope of the EIR with respect to the definition of the debtor

23 The EIR applies to insolvency proceedings, whether the debtor is a natural or legal person, a trader or consumer.[59] In France, only insolvency proceedings as defined in the Commercial Code fall within the scope of the EIR; civil debt restructurings[60] are therefore excluded, whereas the *faillite civile*[61] is included, although there are only slight differences between these proceedings.

2.2.5 The scope of the EIR with respect to various types of French insolvency proceedings

24 **Traditionally**, French doctrine had a **restrictive interpretation of the scope of the EIR.**[62] Originally Annex A mentioned two types of French insolvency proceedings: judicial rehabilitation proceedings with the appointment of an administrator (*redressement judiciaire avec nomination d'un administrateur*) and judicial liquidation (*liquidation judiciaire*). The circular of March 17, 2003 interpreted the EIR narrowly, excluding from its scope a certain number of commercial (pre-)insolvency proceedings before the

---

[54] *Dammann* Dalloz 2005 p 1779; *see also Menjucq* JCP 2005 II 10116. For *Fasquelle* it would be conceivable for the subsidiary to be considered an establishment (*see* his comment on the *Eurofood* decision in Bull Joly 2006). This interpretation cannot be accepted.

[55] CA Versailles dated 15 Dec 2005, AJ p 142 note *Lienhard,* Dalloz 2006 Jur p 379 note *Dammann.*

[56] *See* the approving comments of *Dammann* Dalloz 2006 Jur p 379.

[57] *Dammann/Sénéchal* Rev Lamy Dr aff October 2006. On this, *see* below mn 61 et seq.

[58] Cf art 1.2.2 of the Circular.

[59] *See* recital 9 of the EIR.

[60] On this *see* above mn 3.

[61] On this *see* above mn 4.

[62] Cf *Vallens* Rép communautaire Dalloz, Faillite mn 14.

reform of the French material insolvency law in 2005.[63] If one would have continued to apply its reasoning, the new safeguard proceedings (*procédure de sauvegarde*) would not have fallen within the scope of the EIR.[64]

With the reform of 2005, the French government changed its approach. At the request of the French government, Annex A of the EIR was modified on April 27, 2006 to include the new safeguard proceedings (*procédure de sauvegarde*) and to delete the various restrictions with respect to restructuring proceedings.[65] But the *mandat ad hoc* as well as the conciliation proceeding continue to be excluded from the scope of the EIR. The exclusion of the *mandat ad hoc* is certainly justified. The *mandat ad hoc* proceedings can, however, as shown in the *Eurotunnel* case[66], play an important role in the determination of the centre of the debtor's main interests. In light of the contractual nature of the conciliation proceeding, the French Justice Minister has not requested its introduction into Annex A of the EIR.[67] An increasing number of practitioners have suggested reconsideration of this position in order to achieve the recognition of conciliation proceedings throughout Europe. In some cases, the conciliation serves as a substitute for insolvency proceedings that may be requested by an insolvent debtor instead of opening a *redressement judiciaire*. The figures speak for themselves: more than two thirds of all conciliation proceedings are successfully terminated in France. The reform of 2005 has enhanced the attractiveness of these proceedings. During the first nine months after the entry of the reform into force on January 1, 2006, the number of openings of insolvency proceedings has more than doubled.[68] Conciliation proceedings could thus become a model in Europe to resolve financial difficulties of companies. This being said, the French government recently confirmed its position excluding the conciliation proceedings from the scope of the EIR.[69] **25**

---

[63] *Mandat ad hoc*; *règlement amiable*; rehabilitation proceedings (*redressement judiciaire*) with the appointment of an administrator who has been entrusted by the court with a mission limited to the supervision of the debtor; simplified rehabilitation proceedings (*redressement judiciaire simplifié*) where no judicial administrator is appointed; and rehabilitation proceedings (*redressement judiciaire*) that are not opened as a consequence of the occurrence of the insolvency of the debtor, but rather as a sanction for the behavior of the debtor. *See* Art 1.1.2 of the Circ.

[64] *See* J-Cl com mn 23. Under the *procédure de sauvegarde* the debtor is solvent and keeps management control with the administrator merely supervising or assisting it (*see supra*). *Dammann* has proposed to include the *procédure de sauvegarde de lege ferenda* in Annex A, cf Les Echos dated 2 May 2005, AGEFI 4.3.2005 and Rev Lamy dr aff April 2005, p 18.

[65] Council Regulation (CE) 694/2006 OJ L121/1 May 6, 2006. The change was facilitated by the reform of 2005 abrogating various provisions providing for the opening of rehabilitation proceedings as a sanction for the behavior of the debtor. The various exceptions made by the Circular are no longer applicable.

[66] Above mn 19.

[67] During the debates in the French National Assembly on March 8, 2005, the French Minister of Justice declared that the conciliation proceedings were not judicial proceedings within the definition of the EIR.

[68] *Dammann* in particular has been in favor of an inclusion of the conciliation proceedings into Annex A; *see* the comments on ECJ dated 2 May 2006, Dalloz 2006, 1752 et seq (1759), for the reasons.

[69] Cf art 1.1.2 of the Circular. The Minister of Justice has expressly confirmed this position in the answer to a question in Parliament on March 13, 2007, Rép min No 120202, JOANQ 1.5.2007. *See* Dalloz of 18.5.2007 with a note by *Lienhard*.

26 Following the May 2, 2006 ECJ *Eurofood* decision, there is a debate in French doctrine as to the interpretation of the term "a decision to open insolvency proceedings". According to Art 1 (1) of the EIR, insolvency proceedings have four characteristics: they must be collective proceedings, based on the debtor's insolvency, which entail at least partial divestment of the debtor and the prompt appointment of a liquidator.[70] In its *Eurofood* decision the ECJ emphasized two conditions: "a decision to open insolvency proceedings for the purpose of that provision [Art 16 (1 of the EIR)] is a decision handed down by a court of a Member State to which application for such a decision has been made, based on the debtors['] insolvency and seeking the opening of proceedings referred to in Annex A to the Regulation, where that decision involves the divestment of the debtor and the appointment of a liquidator referred to in Annex C to the Regulation. Such divestment implies that the debtor loses the power of management that he has over his assets."[71] According to *Michel Menjucq*, a French judge would have the right to disregard insolvency proceedings listed in Annex A provided that such proceedings do not meet the two conditions set forth by the ECJ and, in particular, the divestment requirement.[72] Consequently, in such a case, domestic insolvency proceeding could be opened in spite of the opening of foreign proceedings that do not match the aforementioned two criteria. Such an interpretation would lead to great legal uncertainty and would trigger important consequences. It could be argued that since the new safeguard proceeding provides for only a partial divestment of the debtor, such proceedings have been wrongly introduced into Annex A. Arguably, the same reasoning could lead a French judge to disregard similar foreign proceedings, such as the German *Eigenverwaltung*, although the *InsO* is listed in Annex A. Some authors strictly reject such interpretation.[73] The ECJ intended to enlarge the proceedings listed in Annex A to also include decisions opening provisionary proceedings leading to the opening at a later stage of proceedings listed in Annex A. In order to include these pre-proceedings, a total divestment of the debtor and the appointment of a liquidator would be required. Allowing a judge to verify whether the proceedings listed in Annex A would comply with the divestment requirement would be impossible in practice and contrary to the purpose of Annex A, which was designed to create legal certainty with respect to the recognition of foreign proceedings and the scope of the application of the EIR. How could a judge monitor whether the conditions of a divestment have been met?[74] In its second *Eurotunnel* decision of January 15, 2007, the Commercial Court of Paris followed this interpretation.[75] The Commercial Courts of Versailles and Creteil also recently shared this view, opening *procédures de sauvegarde* for foreign subsidiaries of a French group of companies by application of the EIR.[76]

2.2.6 The time-wise application of the EIR

27 The EIR is applicable to insolvency proceedings opened after May 31, 2002. The date of opening is defined by the *lex fori concursus*, which could give rise to **uncertainties**

[70] *See* No 46 of the *Eurofood* decision.

[71] *See* No 58 of the *Eurofood* decision.

[72] *Menjucq* JCP 2006 II 10089; similar, Rémery Rev sociétés 2006, 360. Without result: *Jault-Seseke/Robine* RCDIP 2006, p 811.

[73] Cf *Dammann* Dalloz 2006 Jur p 1752; *Dammann* Mobility of companies and localisation of assets, arguments in favor of a dynamic interpretation of the EC Regulation No 1346/2000 on Insolvency proceedings, in Cross-border insolvency and conflicts of jurisdictions, Brussels 2007, 105 *et seq*.

[74] In-depth on this: *Dammann* op cit (previous footnote).

[75] *See* above mn 21.

[76] TC Versailles dated 15 Feb 2007 in the *Webraska* case and TC Créteil dated 24 Apr 2007 in the *HMO* case.

under French law. For example, the resolution of a restructuring plan for breach of the obligations by the debtor may lead to the opening of judicial liquidation proceedings. Such proceedings are deemed to continue the initial rehabilitation proceedings.[77] Consequently, if such rehabilitation proceedings were opened before May 31, 2002, the subsequent liquidation would not fall within the scope of the EIR, even though such liquidation might have been opened after May 31, 2002. On the other hand, if the opening of the liquidation were triggered by the insolvency of the debtor, then the EIR would apply to such proceeding opened after May 31, 2002.[78]

2.2.7 Extension of proceedings in case of fictitiousness or co-mingling of assets

Art L 621-2 of the Commercial Code provides for the extension of insolvency proceedings to a third party debtor if the assets of both debtors have been co-mingled, or if the third party debtor is fictitious. According to case law, it is not necessary for such third party debtor to be insolvent.[79] The assets of the debtors in question are aggregated within the original proceedings. French courts might extend this provision to apply to third party debtors having their (registered) office in another Member State.[80] **28**

The EIR is silent with respect to the extension of insolvency proceedings to a third party debtor located in another Member State. According to the Circular, the EIR applies to extended proceedings since the insolvency of the combined estate is presumed.[81] **29**

If the center of main interests of the third party in question is located in another Member State, French courts would nevertheless be competent to order the extension of the insolvency proceedings to the third party. Such a decision would be a judgment derived directly from the insolvency proceedings as defined in Art 25 of the EIR and would thus be immediately recognized in accordance with Art 16 of the EIR. Any enforcement would be subject to the simplified exequatur procedure of Art 25 of the EIR.[82] *Dammann* has suggested a more restrictive two step approach.[83] The extension of insolvency proceedings to another debtor is a decision triggering more legal consequences than the opening of main insolvency proceedings with respect to a debtor whose registered office is located in another Member state, since both proceedings remain separate. In addition, the prerequisites for substantive consolidation vary considerably under the substantive insolvency laws of the Member States. Consequently, it would seem necessary for a court to first establish its competence with respect to the COMI of such a third party debtor. If, in light of the fraudulent transfer of assets within the group or the fictitious character of the legal entity in question, a French tribunal concludes that the COMI of the third party debtor is located in France, French courts would be competent to open main insolvency proceedings against such debtor. Subsequently, pursuant to French substantive insolvency law, the merger of the proceedings could be ordered by the tribunal and receive recognition within the Member states. **30**

[77] *See* Cass com dated 4 Jan 2000, Bull civ IV no 2. *See* other decisions published by Litec's annotation of the Commercial Code after art L 621-82 no 6.

[78] *See Vallens,* Rev Lamy dr aff July 2002.

[79] *See, e.g.,* Cass com dated 7 Jan 2003, Bull civ 2003 IV no 2. *See also J-Cl* com mn 28 and *Le Corre* mn 22.21.

[80] *See* Cass civ dated 31 Jan 1990, Dalloz 1990, 461 note *Rémery. See Mélin* mn 33; *Soinne* mn 523.

[81] *See* Art 1.1.2 of the Circ dated March 17, 2003. This passage was deleted in the new version.

[82] *See Menjucq* Rev proc coll March 2003 p 54; *J-Cl* com mn 29 and art 1.1.2 of the Circ.

[83] *Dammann* Dalloz 2006 Jur p 1752.

2.2.8 Opening of insolvency proceedings against unlimited partners of the debtor

31 Prior to the reform of 2005, under the old Art L 624-1 of the *CCom*, if a company with unlimited liability[84] became insolvent, **separate rehabilitation proceedings** had to be opened under French law against all its partners. If the center of main interests of a partner of the insolvent partnership was situated in another Member State, according to the circular of March 17, 2003, French courts had no jurisdiction to open any insolvency proceedings, except where the transfer of the COMI to another Member State was fraudulent.[85] The new French Insolvency Law abrogated Art L 624-1.

2.2.9 Opening of insolvency proceedings in France as a sanction for mismanagement of the debtor

32 **Until the reform of 2005**, Art L 624-4 of the Commercial Code allowed a Court to decide to open, as a sanction, insolvency proceedings against managers found liable under French law for all or part of the debts of the insolvent debtor but who have failed to meet their obligations. The Supreme Court extended application of this provision to international insolvency proceedings while retaining its competence to open insolvency proceedings and convert them into judicial liquidations with respect to managers without assets in France.[86] It was unclear whether, as a general rule, insolvency proceedings opened in France on Art 624-4 grounds would fall within the scope of the EIR.[87] This issue no longer exists, because the reform of 2005 abrogated Art L 624-4.

33 Art L 651-2 of the Commercial Code provides that, in case of mismanagement, the *de jure* or *de facto* managers of a company may be compelled[88] to partially or fully assume the debts of the company. Such decisions of French courts would fall within the scope of Art 25 of the EIR.[89]

2.2.10 Opening of secondary insolvency proceedings in France in favor of debtors that are not subject to French commercial insolvency proceedings

34 The definition of the term **'debtor'** under the EIR is broader than that French law provides. Unlike in Germany or the United Kingdom, for instance, French consumers may not be debtors in French commercial insolvency proceedings.[90] It would appear impossible to open secondary insolvency proceedings in France with respect to French nationals who are the subject of main insolvency proceedings in another Member State but who could not be subject to judicial liquidation in France.[91]

---

[84] *See Dammann* (previous footnote).

[85] *See* art 1.1.2 of the circular of March 17, 2003.

[86] *See* Cass Com dated 14 Mar 2000, Bull Joly sociétés June 2000 § 132 p 600 note *Menjucq*.

[87] Art 1.1.2 of the circular of March 17, 2003 generally excluded proceedings opened as a sanction from the scope of the application of the EIR. *Vallens* Rev Lamy dr aff July 2002 suggested the EIR might apply in such a case, since the opening of proceedings could be based on the assumption that the sanctioned manager was insolvent.

[88] The decisions require that in the case of a de facto management "*la commission des actes positifs de gestion effectués en toute indépendance par une personne autre qu'un dirigeant de droit*", cf *Jeantin/Le Cannu* Droit commercial, Entreprises en difficulté, 7 edn (2006) mn 1261 et seq.

[89] *Vallens*, cited by *Niggeman/Blenske* NZI 2003, 478. *See also Virgós-Schmit* Explanatory Report mn 196.

[90] *Supra* mn 3

[91] The Circ (art 4.1.2) opts for a mandatory application of the conditions imposed by French substantive law, save the state of insolvency that is determined by the court opening main proceedings. *See also* J-Cl com mn 50 and *Vallens* Rev proc coll March 2003 p 61.

2.2.11 Exclusion of the application of Art 14 and 15 of the Civil Code

Articles 14 and 15 of the Civil Code provide authority for French claimants and defendants to request the exclusive jurisdiction of French courts.[92] The rules Articles 14 and 15 provide are incompatible with the application of the EIR, which prevails over them.[93] **35**

2.3 Territorial Competence of French Courts Opening Insolvency Proceedings Subject to the EIR

Art R 600-1 (1) of the *CCom* determines the territorial competence of French courts regarding the opening of restructuring and liquidation proceedings. The court's jurisdiction depends upon where the debtor's head office is located: *"siège de son entreprise"*.[94] For companies, the French Supreme court refers to the actual location of the head office. If the office is located abroad, the court is domestically competent when the debtor's main center of interests is located in France, since Art R 600-1 (1) of the CCom's presumption is rebuttable. French case law has expanded application of these rules to determine the international jurisdiction of French insolvency courts. French courts have adopted a rather broad interpretation of the term 'debtor's main center of interests'.[95] **36**

Art 3 (1) of the EIR determines the international competence of French courts with respect to the opening of main insolvency proceedings. French case law transposing the principles of French territorial competence into rules applicable to the international jurisdiction of French courts thus no longer applies, the EIR having superseded it.[96] According to recital no 15, the rules set out in the EIR establish only international jurisdiction, leaving each Member State to establish national rules with respect to its own territorial jurisdiction. Consequently, Art R 600-1 (1) of the *CCom* still applies to determine the competent territorial court within the territory of France. The Commercial Court of Nanterre and the Court of Appeal of Versailles would appear to apply Art 3 of the EIR to determine the local competence of the Court, thus administratively regrouping insolvency proceedings for a French group of companies.[97] The Circular does not set forth any particular provisions harmonizing Art R 600-1 of the *CCom* with the EIR. There is, however, one exception. According to Art R 600-1 (2) of the *CCom*, the original territorial court remains competent for a period of six months in case of a change of the registered office to another jurisdiction. This provision conflicts with the EIR to the extent that the transfer of the registered office is made to the territory of another Member State. The Circular specifically reserves comments on the case in which the transfer of the registered office is exclusively motivated by the intention to harm any or all the creditors.[98] *A contrario*, the rule of Art R 600-1 (2) of the *CCom* continues to apply to the transfer of the registered office within French territory. Finally, the Circular states that if the debtor has several establishments in France, the competent territorial French court is the one where the main establishment is located.[99] **37**

---

92 On this *see* above mn 14.

93 *See Menjucq* Bull Joly soc December 2000, 1112; *see also Vallens* Rev Lamy dr aff July 2002, J-Cl com mn 40.

94 This term refers to the registered office of juridical persons and to the professional domicile of natural persons.

95 *See* above mn 13.

96 *See Mélin* mn 100.

97 Court of Appeal of Versailles dated 11 Jan 2007, *see Dammann/Podeur* Les groupes de sociétés face aux procédures d'insolvabilité, Rev Lamy Dr aff May 2007 p 65 *et seq*.

98 *See* art 1.2.1 of the Circ. In this respect, *Mélin* (mn 103) also reserves comment on the case of the fictitiousness of the registered office.

99 *See* art 1.2.2.1 of the Circ interpreting art 1 (1) of the decree of December 27, 1985.

2.4 Rationale for the Competence of the Court to Open Proceedings

38 In order to limit the risk of conflicting decisions between the courts of two Member States concerning the interpretation of the "center of main interests" and "establishment" concepts, the Circular underlines the importance of French Courts stating and justifying in their decisions opening proceedings the criteria used to establish their competence.[100] In this respect, French courts are not bound by the qualification made in the filing by the debtor or a creditor requesting the opening of main or territorial insolvency proceedings. If a court determines that in reality, contrary to any qualification made in the filing, the center of main interests of the debtor is located within the territory of another EU Member State, the court has the power to open territorial insolvency proceedings, provided such question is discussed at the hearing. It would also be possible for a court, after a hearing, to open main insolvency proceedings even where the opening of territorial insolvency proceedings has been requested. If the claimant requesting the opening of proceedings does not specify the criteria establishing the competence of the court under the EIR, the filing nevertheless remains valid. The courts must discuss the topic at the hearing, thereby allowing an open debate to take place. Following the *Eurofood* decision, such rationale for international jurisdiction would appear to be crucial. In particular, the court must set forth factors which are both objective and ascertainable by third parties to explain how the presumption in favor of the registered office was rebutted. As shown in the *EMTEC* case, it is important for the court to hear the representatives of the employees of a company the registered office of which is located in another Member State, even if neglect of this duty would not constitute a violation of public policy within the meaning of Art 26 of the EIR.[101]

2.5 Avoiding Conflicting Decisions

39 Conflicting decisions have led to heated debates in France that have now been cut-off due to the *Eurofood* decision of the ECJ and the *Daisytek* decision of the Court de cassation. The following explanations provide a short critical overview.

40 At first the situation seemed clear. In order to avoid **positive conflicts** of decisions between courts of two Member States, both of which claim competence to open main insolvency proceedings, recital 22 of the EIR establishes the **principle of mutual trust** among the courts of the Member States and **the rule of priority**. The Circular states that a positive conflict between two or more jurisdictions with respect to the interpretation of Art 3 of the EIR should be avoided by application of the rule of priority. The Circular refers to Art 16 of the EIR, pursuant to which any judgment opening insolvency proceedings handed down by a court of a Member State must be recognized in all the other Member States from the time that it becomes effective in the State whose court opens proceedings. The Circular also emphasizes that the public policy provision contained in Art 26 of the EIR should be interpreted narrowly[102] and should not be used to set aside

---

[100] *See* art 1.2.4 of the Circ.

[101] Cf the *Daisytek* decision of the Court de cassation, dated 27 Jun 2006, No 45.

[102] Traditionally, under French private international law, the public policy exception was interpreted restrictively. In the area of international insolvency, the French supreme court has held, for example, that an avoidance period ("période suspecte") longer than the 18 month long French avoidance period does not constitute an obstacle for the exequatur of a foreign court decision, Cass com dated 5 Feb 2002 Dalloz 2002 AJ 957 note by *Lienhard*, JCP E 2003, 955 note by *Raimon*. On this *see also Dammann/Podeur* Banque et Droit September/October 2006 p 7.

the findings made by a foreign court opening insolvency proceedings with respect to the state of insolvency of the debtor and the location of its office or its establishment.

The ***Daisytek* case** suddenly disturbed this understanding. The problem was no longer to interpret the EIR grammatically, but rather to find a defense against the "imperialism" of English courts' interpretation of the COMI in the case of corporate groups. **41**

On May 16, 2003, the High Court of Leeds opened main insolvency proceedings over Daisytec-ISA Limited, a UK company having its registered office in Bradford, as well as over 13 of its subsidiaries, including the French company SAS ISA Daisytek, whose registered office was in Pontoise. On May 26, 2003, the Commercial Court of Pontoise opened competing main insolvency proceedings for SAS ISA Daisytek. The UK liquidators of Daisytek appealed the French decision (*tierce opposition*). In its decision dated July 1, 2003, the Court of Pontoise rejected the appeal, holding that the Court of Leeds was not complying with Art 3 of the EIR. On September 4, 2003, the Court of appeal of Versailles overruled this judgment.[103] Referring to Art 16 and 17 of the EIR, the Court of appeal held that the High Court of Leeds had ruled that the center of main interests of SAS ISA Daisytek was Leeds, thereby prohibiting the opening of a subsequent and conflicting main insolvency proceeding in France. The court rejected the alleged violation of Article 6 of the European Convention on Human Rights (lack of a fair trial) and the violation of Article 26 of the EIR (violation of public policy). **42**

This decision was criticized by many authors. *Georges Khairallah*[104] held, for example, that the automatic recognition of the judgement opening insolvency proceedings in another Member State pursuant to Art 16 and 17 of the EIR presupposes that the court which opened the insolvency proceeding was competent under to Art 3 of the EIR. This interpretation would allow the court of one Member State to determine whether the court of another Member State was truly competent pursuant to Art 3 of the EIR. Such an interpretation, however, disregards Recital 22 of the EIR: "*The decision of the first court to open proceedings should be recognised in the other Member States without those Member States having the power to scrutinise the court's decision.*" *Michel Menjucq* held that the control can be carried out only if the foreign court could rebut the presumption in favor of the registered office.[105] Although this decision is clearly in accord with the provisions and spirit of the EIR,[106] the Public Prosecutor filed an appeal in the interest of the law to the French Supreme Court.[107] **43**

In the ***Rover* case** a similar problem arose. On April 18, 2005, the High Court of Justice of Birmingham opened main insolvency proceedings over the French subsidiary of the Rover group, Rover SAS. The Public Prosecutor concluded that such opening was contrary to public policy pursuant to Art 26 of the EIR. Consequently, the court-appointed administrator resigned and was replaced by an administrator with a mandate to analyze the financial situation of Rover SAS. The new administrator came to the conclusion that the company was insolvent and recommended judicial liquidation. Finally, the conflict between jurisdictions was resolved by the judgment of the Commercial Court of Nanterre dated May 19, 2005 recognizing the effect of the administration order of the High Court **44**

[103] *See* Dalloz 2003, 2352 note *Vallens*; RJDA 1/04 chron p 3 note by *Mélin*; RCDIP 2003, 667 note by *Khairallah*; JCP E 1747 note by *Likillimba*; JDI 2004, 142 note by *Jacquemont*; Rev sociétés 2003, 891 note by *Rémery*.

[104] Previous footnote.

[105] JCP G 2005, II, 10116.

[106] *See Vallens* Dalloz 2003, 2354 and *Mélin* RJDA 1/04 chron p 3.

[107] The Minister of Justice seems to justify this appeal to the Supreme Court by reference to the possible violation of public policy, Min Answer QE no 40288, dated June 1, 2004, JO 2004, 6104.

of Justice of Birmingham, rejecting the objection of public policy violation under Art 26 of the EIR and, consequently declaring itself incompetent to open a competing judicial liquidation proceedings.[108] The Public Prosecutor filed an appeal against the judgment that was rejected by the Court of appeal of Versailles in its decision dated December 15, 2005.[109]

45 Referring to the *Eurofood* decision of the ECJ, the French Supreme Court rejected the appeal in a decision dated June 27, 2006.[110] The Circular dated December 15, 2006 adopted this interpretation.[111]

46 The Circular does not deal with **negative conflicts**, i.e. when no jurisdiction accepts authority to open main insolvency proceedings under Art 3 (1) of the EIR. French doctrine suggests that in such a scenario, a French court could open territorial insolvency proceedings.[112]

2.6 Forum Shopping and *forum conveniens*

47 Forum shopping is defined by French doctrine as the fraudulent change of jurisdiction-determining circumstances, or the abusive use of a scheme to artificially create a legal forum.[113] If a judge, for opportunistic reasons, retains his competence where, in fact, he should have declined jurisdiction on the basis of the law, one speaks of ***forum conveniens***.[114]

48 Recital 4 of the EIR states that the avoidance of forum shopping is one of the primary goals of the EIR. Unfortunately, Art 3 of the EIR does not contain precise and objective criteria defining the 'COMI'. In its *Eurofood* decision, the ECJ stated that the COMI "must be identified by reference to criteria that are both objective and ascertainable by third parties" without setting forth any examples of such criteria.[115] The EIR is also silent with respect to insolvencies of European groups of companies. Nor does the EIR contain any specific provisions with respect to the consequences of a transfer of the registered office of a debtor immediately before the opening of insolvency proceedings. Finally, the EIR does not make reference to the concept of fraud with respect to a debtor who establishes fictitious companies, co-mingles assets or transfers its registered office into another Member State. Under the EIR, these problems are to be resolved through interpretation of the notion of 'COMI'. The extremely broad interpretation of Article 3 of the EIR could, however, constitute *forum conveniens*.

49 In order to discourage forum shopping within France, Art R 600-1 (2) of the *CCom* provides that the court where the registered office of the debtor is located continues to have jurisdiction over a debtor for a **period of six months** after a transfer of the registered office. As outlined above, the Circular considers that this provision is incompatible with the EIR in the case of a transfer of the registered office of the debtor to another Member State.

[108] *See* Dalloz 2005 Jur p 1787 note *Dammann*; JCP G II 10116 note by *Menjucq*; Act proc coll 2005 No 11 note by *Mélin*; JCP E 2006, 1412 note by *Fasquelle*.

[109] Cf Dalloz 2006 AJ 142 note by *Lienhard*; Dalloz 2006 Jur 379 note by *Dammann*.

[110] Cf Dalloz 2006 AJ p 1816 note by *Lienhard*; Banque & Droit September October 2006 p 3 note by *Dammann/Podeur*; Dalloz 2006 Jur p 2257 note by *Vallens*; JCP G 2006 II 10147 note by *Menjucq*; JCP E 2006, 2291 note by *Mélin*.

[111] Cf art 2 of the Circular.

[112] *See J-Cl* com mn 34. *Mélin* (mn 111) must be approved indicating that such a solution would appear difficult in the case of art 3 (4) (a) of the EIR.

[113] *Mayer* Droit international privé, 6th edn mn 267 and 390 *et seq*.

[114] *See Dammann* Dalloz 2005 Jur p 1779.

[115] *See* No 33 of the *Eurofood* decision.

Traditionally, French case law sanctions the artful transfer of the registered office of a company.[116] As mentioned above, the commercial *redressement judiciaire* is applicable to consumers having their domicile in the French departments of Haut-Rhin, Bas-Rhin and Moselle, enabling them to benefit, under certain conditions, from the discharge of all debts at the end of the proceedings. There is some case law on the subject of the attempted artful transfer of the residence of an individual from Paris to Strasbourg immediately prior to opening of insolvency proceedings in order to benefit from the more favorable insolvency law in force in these three departments in Eastern France.[117] **50**

The Circular invites French courts to disregard the (artful) transfer of a registered office or COMI by a debtor into another Member State immediately prior to the opening of insolvency proceedings, provided that such transfer was exclusively motivated by a desire to adversely affect the rights of any or all of the creditors.[118] Following the *Staubitz-Schreiber* decision of the ECJ dated January 17, 2006[119], it would appear difficult to upheld this interpretation. In practice, however, forum shopping by artificial transfer of the COMI would appear rather difficult since the COMI is based on objective criteria that could not be so easily manipulated.[120] In addition, French judges could refer to the use in the definition of COMI in recital 13 of the EIR of the term "on a regular basis" as characterizing some kind of stability of COMI.[121] The artful manipulation of criteria determining the location of an 'establishment' of a debtor would appear to be even more unlikely since the definition of Art 2 (h) of the EIR refers to non-transitory economic activity with human resources of the debtor.[122] Thus far there has been no case law on the controversial opening of secondary insolvency proceedings in France. **51**

2.7 Termination of Insolvency Proceedings by Incompetent Courts Under the EIR

The Circular is silent with respect to (mandatory) termination of main insolvency proceedings opened by a French court where main insolvency proceedings have already been opened in another Member State for the same debtor. French authors have suggested that in such a case the subsequent proceedings should be converted into secondary insolvency proceedings.[123] In the absence of any French regulation, French doctrine has raised the question as to whether it would be possible to refer by analogy to Art 100 of the New French Code of Civil Procedure.[124] In case of *litispendance* of the same matter pending before two courts which are both competent, this article gives priority to the first jurisdiction and orders the second court, failing a demand by one of the parties, to declare, *ex officio*, its incompetence in favor of the first jurisdiction.[125] This reasoning by **52**

---

116 The fictitious transfer of the registered office of a debtor prior to the opening of insolvency proceedings is without effect on third parties, *see e.g.* Cass Com dated 8 Mar 1988, Bull. civ. IV no 103.

117 *See* art L 628-1 *et seq* of the CCom. The Court of Appeal of Colmar held in its decision dated 2 Oct 2001, RTD com 2001, 983, that the new residence in Strasbourg was fictitious and that the transfer of residence to Strasbourg constituted an attempt at forum shopping.

118 *See* art 1.2.1 of the Circ.

119 Dalloz 2006 Jur p 1752 note *Dammann*; Rev sociétés 2006 p 346 note *Vallens*.

120 *See Dammann* Dalloz 2005 Jur p 1789.

121 *See Dammann* Dalloz 2006 Jur p 1752.

122 *See Bureau* Rev crit DIP 2002 mn 33.

123 See the suggestion by *Vallens* Dalloz 2003, 1422, approved by *Mélin* mn 110.

124 *Vallens* raises this question, Lamy dr aff July 2002.

125 According to case law, art 100 of the NCPC is applicable if the first court is a foreign one. See the cases cited by Litec note of the NCPC after art 100. *See also Loussouarn-Borel-de Vareilles-Sommières* Droit international privé, 8th ed (2004), mn 490-2 *et seq.*

analogy is very interesting. Of course, Art 100 is not applicable since, under the EIR, there is only one possible center of main interests for each debtor within the EU.

53 A liquidator appointed by the court of another Member State that has already opened main insolvency proceedings in favor of the same debtor may file an **appeal *(tierce opposition)*** with the French jurisdiction having subsequently opened competing main proceedings.[126] The liquidator may also file an appeal against a decision of the insolvency court rejecting the filing of *tierce opposition*. The Circular does not specify the legal consequences of the judgment of the Tribunal or the Court of appeal annulling the opening of main insolvency proceedings with respect to acts taken by the local liquidator or decisions made by the insolvency court. It is unclear whether such an annulment has a retroactive effect. There is no case law on this topic.[127] One practical solution would be to "convert" the main proceedings into secondary proceedings with retroactive effect.[128] A second alternative would be to enter into settlement with the liquidator in order to avoid any dispute with respect to the validity of the acts taken before the judgment annulling the opening of the French proceedings.[129]

2.8 Publication of the Decision Opening Main Insolvency Proceedings

54 Art 21 of the EIR allows a liquidator the option to request the publication of the judgment opening insolvency proceedings in any other Member State in accordance with the publication procedures provided for in that State. The Circular considers this provision directly applicable. The competent court **clerk *(greffier)*** is the one in the territory where the establishment of the debtor is situated in France.[130] The clerk of the insolvency court cannot refuse such a request made by a foreign liquidator.[131]

55 In accordance with Art R 621-8 of the *CCom*, the *greffier* of the insolvency court where the debtor's establishment is located is requested to publish the foreign judgment opening main insolvency proceedings in the *BODACC* and another official publication in France. In case of a judgment opening territorial insolvency proceedings in another Member State, the French *greffier* of the Tribunal where the registered French office of the debtor is located is requested to undertake the necessary publication at the request of the liquidator of the territorial insolvency proceedings. According to Art R 621-8 (4) of the *CCom*, the publication is to include the name of the debtor, its place of business, its registration, a description of its business activities, the date of the judgment opening the proceedings, the name and address of the liquidator (representative of the creditors) and the notice to the creditors. In addition, according to the Circular, the publication must contain a reference to the criteria the foreign court used to arrive at the judgment to retain its **jurisdiction under the EIR.**[132]

56 The **effects of the publication** under the EIR differ from substantive French insolvency law. Art 24 of the EIR protects a person honoring an obligation for the benefit of an

[126] *See infra* mn 58.

[127] A recent decision of the French Supreme Court dated 10 May 2005 has established the principle of non retroactive effect of the cancellation of insolvency proceedings on ground of incompetence, Dalloz 2005 p 1414 note *Lienhard*.

[128] *See Dammann* Dalloz 2005 Jur p 1789.

[129] In the *Daisytek* case, the liquidators adopted the settlement approach. On May 26, 2003, the Tribunal of Pontoise opened main proceedings in the form of a *procédure de redressement judiciaire*. On July 17, 2003, the Tribunal ordered the sale of the ongoing business. The English liquidator challenged the validity of the sale. The settlement between the two liquidators recognized the validity of the sale of the business.

[130] *J-Cl* com mn 47.

[131] *See* art 2.1.1 of the Circ.

[132] *See* art 2.1.1 of the Circ.

insolvent debtor following a judgment opening insolvency proceedings in another Member State. Contrary to French law, the co-contractor of an insolvent debtor could prove that he ignored the existence of the opening of the insolvency proceedings even though the judgment has been published. According to the Circular, this provision of Art 24 of the EIR replaces French substantive insolvency law for the benefit of debtors of the insolvent French debtor that are located in another Member State.[133]

2.9 Registration in Public Registers

Art 22 (1) of the EIR provides that the liquidator may request the registration of the judgment opening main insolvency proceedings in the appropriate public register in other Member States.[134] The Circular emphasizes that the French clerks are required to proceed with the inscription of the judgment opening main insolvency proceedings in another Member State in the appropriate register where the establishment of such debtor is located in France.[135] Art R 123-91 of the *CCom* provides for **this mandatory registration with the French commercial register**. According to the decree, such inscription is made at the request of the foreign liquidator who justifies his capacity to this effect.[136] **57**

2.10 Appeal

The Circular emphasizes that potential conflicts of jurisdictions be resolved by appeal proceedings before the judge who opened insolvency proceedings under the EIR.[137] This interpretation was confirmed in the *Daisytek* case by the *Cour de cassation* on June 27, 2006.[138] Liquidators of another Member State becoming aware of the opening of conflicting main proceedings in France are entitled to appeal (*tierce opposition*) such a decision and to appeal a judgment rejecting any *tierce opposition*. The time period for filing a request for *tierce opposition* is relatively short, *i.e.* ten days from the date of the publication of the challenged French judgment in the BODACC.[139] **58**

2.11 Exequatur Proceedings Under Art 25 of the EIR

With respect to the interpretation of Art 18 and 19 of the EIR, the Circular states that if the liquidator of one Member State intends to use the powers provided for by the law of another Member State, it has to establish the proof of such a law if it is requested to do so by the court or the creditors.[140] **59**

---

133 *See* art 2.1.2 of the Circ.

134 In France, the registers are the *registre du commerce et des sociétés*, the *répertoire des métiers*, the *répertoire des entreprises* in the departments of Haut-Rhin, Bas-Rhin and Moselle, and the register at the Tribunal de Grande Instance.

135 *See* art 3.2.1 of the Circ. In the *Daisytek* case, however, the *greffier* of the Commercial Court of Pontoise refused to inscribe the judgment of the High Court of Leeds dated 16 Mar 2003 into the commercial register. The situation was cured following a decision rendered of the Court of Versailles dated 4 Sep 2003.

136 Decree no 2005-77, JO February 2, 2005, adding a new art 36-2 to the *décret* no 84-406 of May 30, 1984.

137 Cf art 3 of the Circular.

138 For the practical consequences see *Dammann/Podeur* Banque & Droit September October 2006, p 5.

139 *See* art 329 (3) of the decree dated December 28, 2005. Article 329 of the decree provides for a 10-day period for appeal following the notification of the judgment.

140 *See* art 2.4.1 of the Circ, although according to art 19 (2) of the EIR, no legislation or other similar formality is required other than a translation into the official language of proof of the liquidator's appointment.

60 Art 25 of the EIR refers to Art 31 through 51, with the exception of Art 34 (2), of the Brussels Convention on Jurisdiction and Enforcement of Judgments in Civil and Commercial Matters. EC Regulation no 44/2001 entered into force on March 1, 2002, modifying the rules under the Brussels Convention. It would appear logical to apply Regulation no 44/2001 with respect to Art 25 of the EIR. The circular of March 17, 2003, however, has opted for a literal interpretation of Art 25 of the EIR.[141] That interpretation has been criticized in French doctrine.[142] It seems that the Minister of Justice has taken these arguments into account. The new version of the Circular dated December 15, 2006, does not contain any opinion on this issue.

2.12 Coordination of Main and Secondary Proceedings in France

61 The practical importance of the **coordination between main and secondary proceedings** has been already underlined.[143] In the *EMTEC* case, the Commercial Court of Nanterre stressed it as well.[144] Unfortunately, the legislature has not reformed liquidation proceedings to introduce any flexibility into the process.[145] Pursuant to Art 34 of the EIR, the liquidator of main insolvency proceedings could propose to close secondary insolvency proceedings by a rescue plan, a composition or a comparable measure rather than liquidation. Until the reform of 2005, French law did not provide any flexibility for such reorganization within judicial liquidation. Since 2005 it has been possible to sell the business in liquidation proceedings (*plan de cession*). Unfortunately it is still impossible to carry out a reorganization of the debtor since these proceedings are not listed in Annex B.[146]

62 The EIR provides for coordination of main and secondary insolvency proceedings only fragmentarily. In the *Sendo* case, the English liquidator of the main insolvency proceedings and the French liquidator of the secondary insolvency proceeding entered into a protocol organizing in great detail the necessary coordination of both proceedings that was officially confirmed by the Commercial Court of Nanterre on June 29, 2006.[147] This protocol is based on the principle of mutual duty to inform and to cooperate. It deals with questions such as the lodging and the resolving of claims and realization on the assets.

63 Under Art 33 of the EIR, at the request of the liquidator of the main insolvency proceedings, the court opening secondary insolvency proceedings must stay the process of liquidation in whole or in part, provided, however, that it may require the liquidator in the main insolvency proceedings to take any suitable measure to guarantee the interests of the creditors in the secondary proceedings. The French legislator has not enacted any provision with respect to the implementation of Art 33 of the EIR into French substantive insolvency law. According to French doctrine, the Tribunal is free to impose adequate guarantees.[148]

---

[141] The Circ makes reference to arts 67 and 68 of the Regulation 44/2001 dated December 22, 2000.

[142] *See J-Cl* com mn 90. *Vallens* Dalloz 2003 chron 1426; *Mélin* mn 141.

[143] *See* mn 20 *et seq*.

[144] *See* mn 20.

[145] Cf *Vallens* Rev proc coll March 2003, 65.

[146] Suggestions have been made in French doctrine to this effect; *see Dammann* Lamy dr aff April 2005 and Lamy dr aff June 2005; *Dammann/Sénéchal* Rev Lamy dr aff October 2006.

[147] *See* Dalloz 2006, 2237. For an in-depth commentary, see *Dammann/Sénéchal* Rev Lamy dr aff October 2006.

[148] *Vallens* Rev pro coll March 2003 p 63.

In the *Sendo* case, the liquidator in the main insolvency proceeding has renounced the right to request the stay of the liquidation for three months. In return, the liquidator in the secondary insolvency proceeding obliged himself not to sell any assets. Both liquidators agreed to give the liquidator in the main insolvency proceeding the opportunity to propose a global solution to the liquidator in the secondary insolvency proceeding. The protocol states that the proposals of the liquidator in the main insolvency proceeding are not binding and that the realization on the assets located in France may be carried out exclusively pursuant to French law. The *EMTEC* case reveals that the coordination of two different jurisdictions does not necessarily result in a coherent solution. In spite of the excellent cooperation between main and secondary insolvency proceedings, and the coordination between the judges, it was nonetheless impossible to adopt a *plan de cession* pursuant to French law within the main insolvency proceeding and at the same time to sell the assets of EMTEC located in Austria pursuant to Austrian law.[149] **64**

2.13 Information Relating to Creditors

Chapter IV of the EIR sets forth provisions for recording creditors' information and lodgment of their claims. Art 40 of the EIR refers to the duty to inform known creditors who have their habitual residences, domiciles or registered offices in another Member State as soon as insolvency proceedings are opened. Art 96 of the decree of December 28, 2005 imposes an obligation upon the representative of the creditors to notify known creditors within 15 days after the opening of proceedings.[150] The Circular interprets the **scope of Art 40 of the EIR** rather broadly, stating that this provision is applicable in the case of the opening of territorial proceedings in France.[151] In addition, the representative of the creditors must inform *all* known creditors, even if their claims do not relate to the activities conducted by the debtor in France. **65**

The notice may be sent by simple letter, although use of registered mail (receipt requested) is recommended.[152] In particular, this notice must indicate time limits, the penalties laid down in regard to those time limits and the body or authority empowered to accept lodgment. Under French law, compliance with Art R 622-21 of the *CCom* is required. Secured creditors and creditors benefiting from preferences or priorities are obliged to declare their claims. Art L 622-24 of the *CCom* provides for a special notice to secured creditors as well as creditors who have concluded a contract with the debtor, and the Circular invites the French liquidator to systematically proceed with such notice by registered mail (return receipt requested). It has been suggested, *de lege ferenda*, to limit the obligations of the representative of the creditors under Art L 622-24 of the *CCom* to those security interests filed in France.[153] **66**

The legal consequences for known creditors not receiving a notice, for example because the debtor does not provide the liquidator with a complete list of creditors, is unclear.[154] The EIR and the Circular are silent on the issue. This question could be resolved in accordance with the principle of *lex fori concursus*. Under French substantive law, the time period for the lodging of claims continues to run, even if the lack of notice is due to the incompleteness of the list of creditors furnished by the debtor.[155] **67**

[149] For practical solutions, see *Dammann/Sénéchal* Rev Lamy dr aff October 2006.
[150] *See* the model annexed hereto.
[151] *See* art 2.2.1.1 of the Circ.
[152] *See* J-Cl com mn 80.
[153] *See Vallens* Rev proc coll March 2003 p 65.
[154] *See* J-Cl com mn 81.
[155] *See* Cass com dated 11 Oct 1988, Bull civ IV no 267; Cass com dated 7 Dec 1999, Bull civ IV no 222.

2.14 Lodgment of Claims

68 The EIR is silent with respect to compliance with any special formalities in lodging claims. The issue is therefore governed by the *lex fori concursus*. In the case of juridical entities, French case law requires a company to specially authorize its representative, since the lodging of claims is comparable to litigating a claim before a court.[156]

69 According to Art 42 (2) of the EIR, a creditor may lodge its claim in the official language of the State of its habitual residence, domicile or registered office, but it must bear the title '*Production de créance*' in order to be admissible in French proceedings.[157] If the creditor does not comply with this formality, it would appear that the lodgment could be considered irregular.

70 According to Art 42 (2) of the EIR, the creditor may be required to provide a translation in the official language of the State where proceedings are opened. The costs for the translation are likely to be born by the creditor.[158] The failure to provide a translation in a timely manner does not itself make the lodgment of the claim void. It would also be possible to request a translation of the main supporting evidence of the claims into French, and the Circular invites the liquidator to make its position clear in this respect in the notice sent to foreign creditors.[159]

71 Under French law, the lodging of a claim must be made within two months after the date the judgment opening the proceedings is published in the *BODACC*. If the creditor has its domicile abroad, this time period is extended by two months.[160] Consequently, the starting point is not the publication of the decision opening proceedings in the Member State of residence of the creditor.[161] In a decision dated June 9, 2005, the Court of Appeal of Orléans held that such time period did not start to run if the creditor who had his place of business in another Member State did not receive the official notice pursuant to Art 40 and 42 (1) of the EIR.[162] If the foreign creditor has elected its domicile within the jurisdiction of the insolvency court of the debtor, there is a risk that it would not benefit from the additional two month time period to lodge its claim.[163]

72 The time period for lodging claims is extended by one month from the date the claim arises out of a current contract that was first continued by the administrator and then terminated.[164] It would appear necessary to so inform a creditor located in another Member State.[165]

73 Until the reform of 2005, compliance with the time limits under substantive French insolvency provisions was very important. Claims that had been lodged late, whether secured or unsecured, were extinguished.[166] The consequence of this provision with respect to secured creditors benefiting from Art 5 and 7 of the EIR is unclear. There is an obligation to lodge these claims under French law and, as a practical matter, it appears advisable for secured creditors to lodge their claims in time to avoid any discussion with respect to the voidance of the security interest that could be opposed within the foreign

---

156 *See* Cass ass plén dated 26 Jan 2001, Bull civ no 1; *see* also J-Cl com mn 83.

157 *See* the model annexed hereto. This rule is more favorable than substantive French law, pursuant to which French language is mandatory.

158 *See* J-Cl com mn 85.

159 *See* art 2.2.2 of the Circ. Such a request would appear to be optional. *J-Cl* com mn 86.

160 *See* art R 622-22 of the CCom.

161 *See* art 3.2.2.1 of the Circ.

162 The decision has not yet been published.

163 *See Réméry* Rev proc coll March 2003 p 73.

164 Art R 622-21 Ccom.

165 *See* J-Cl com mn 87.

166 *See* before the Reform of 2005 art L 621-46 CCom.

foreclosure procedure.[167] This problem ceased to exist with the reform of 2005. The new wording of Art L 622-24 of the Commercial Code no longer refers to the concept of extinction of late claims. These claims remain excluded from any distribution of dividends by the debtor, however, unless the bankruptcy court finds that these late declarations cannot be imputed to these creditors.

One last question concerns the date of conversion of the claim into the currency of the State opening the proceedings. As a general rule, such conversion is to be performed as of the date of the opening of rehabilitation proceedings. In the case of the opening of liquidation proceedings, the claims must be converted as of the date of the opening.[168] **74**

3. Court rulings on the EIR

3.1 *Daisytek* case

Commercial Court of Pontoise dated July 1st 2003 (not published). **75**

Court of Appeal of Versailles dated September 4, 2003, Dalloz 2003, 2352 note *Vallens*; RJDA 1/04 chron p 3. note *Mélin*, Rev crit DIP 2003, 667 note *Khairallah*, JCP éd E p 2012 no 1747 note *Likillimba*, JDI 2004, 142 note *Jacquemont*; Rev Sociétés 2003, 891 note *Rémery*.

French Supreme Court dated June 27, 2006, Dalloz 2006 AJ 1816 note *Lienhard*, Banque & Droit 2006 note *Dammann* in preparation; Dalloz 2006 note *Vallens* in preparation; JCP 2006 note *Menjucq* in preparation.

3.2 *Rover* case

Commercial Court of Nanterre dated May 19, 2005, Dalloz 2005 Jur p 1787 note *Dammann*; JCP éd G II 10116 note *Menjucq*; Act proc coll 2005 Nr. 11 note *Mélin*; JCP ed E 2006 no 1412 note *Fasquelle*. **76**

Court of Appeal of Versailles dated December 15, 2005, Dalloz 2006 AJ p 142 note *Lienhard*, Dalloz 2006 Jur p 379 note *Dammann*.

3.3 *EMTEC* case

Commercial Court of Nanterre dated February 15, 2006, Dalloz 2006 AJ p 651 note *Lienhard*; Dalloz 2006 p 793 note *Vallens*; Rev proc coll 2006 p 241 note *Menjucq*; Bull Joly Sociétés 2006 p 575 § 122 note *Jault-Seseke/Robine*; EWiR Art 3 EuInsVO 4/06 p 2007, note *Penzlin*. **77**

[167] *See Rémery*, Rev proc coll March 2003, p 71; *Dammann* Banque et Droit, June 2005. The Circ (art 2.2.1.2) takes the position that the extinction of late lodged claims in French insolvency proceedings would not affect the rights of the secured creditors under applicable local law in realizing on their security interests in assets located in another Member State pursuant to arts 5 to 7 of the EIR.

[168] There is a debate in French doctrine in cases where the *procédure de redressement judiciaire* is converted into liquidation proceedings, *see* J-Cl com mn 88; *see also Rémméry* Rev proc coll March 2003 p 74.

3.4 *Eurotunnel* case

78 Commercial Court of Paris dated August 2, 2006, *Dammann/Podeur*, L'affaire Eurotunnel, première application du règlement CE n° 1346-2000 à la procédure de sauvegarde, Dalloz 2006 p 2329. Commercial Court Paris January 15, 2007, Dalloz 2007 AJ 313.

3.5 Other decisions

79 Court of Appeal of Orléans dated June 9, 2005 (not published)
Court of Lure dated March 9, 2006, Dalloz 2006 AJ 1044 with note by *Lienhard*.
Commercial Court of Nanterre dated June 29, 2006, Dalloz 2006, 2237.
Commercial Court of Versailles dated February 15, 2007 (not published)
Commercial Court of Creteil dated April 24, 2007, (not published).

4. Literature on the EIR

80 *Adeline* De l'ouverture d'une procédure principale d'insolvabilité, Journal des sociétés, Dossier faillite Internationale, July 2005 No 23; *Beaubrun* Le règlement C.E. n° 1346/2000 du Conseil du 29 mai 2000 relatif aux procédures d'insolvabilité, Defrénois 2005 p 1873; *Béguin/Menjucq* Droit du commerce international, Litec 2005 no 2310 *et seq; Bureau* La fin d'un îlot de résistance : Le règlement du Conseil relatif aux procédures d'insolvabilité, Rev crit DIP 2002, p 613; *Castell* Application du règlement CE 1346/2000 relatif aux procédures d'insolvabilité, Gaz Pal 24/25 February 2006 p 8; *Chaput* L'entrée en vigueur d'un droit communautaire de la faillite (Le règlement du Conseil du 29 mai 2000, relatif aux procédures d'insolvabilité, Dr soc 2000 chron 22 p 4; *Chaput* Le droit européen de l'insolvabilité: de prometteuses lacunes, Lamy Dr aff July 2002; *Coquelet* L'effet international de la faillite: la solution du règlment communautaire relative aux procédures d'insolvabilité, in L'effet international de la faillite: une réalité? Dalloz 2004, p 163; *Coviaux* Présentation générale du règlement 1346/2000 relatif aux procédures d'insolvabilité, Pet Aff November 20, 2001; *Courbe* L'effet international de la faillite : la solution de la Cour de cassation, in L'effet international de la faillite: une réalité ? Dalloz 2004, p 15; *Deharveng* Le droit de la faillite en Europe, Présentation générale, Rev proc coll March 2003 p 46; *Dammann* L'évolution du droit européen des procédures d'insolvabilité et ses conséquences sur le projet de loi de sauvegarde, Bull Lamy dr com March 2005 actualized version in Lamy dr aff Avril 2005 p 18; *Dammann* Le droit français des Faillites: Source d'Incertitudes et d'Opportunités pour les Banques, Banque & Droit juin 2005; *Dammann* La future procédure de conciliation, pierre angulaire du projet de loi de sauvegarde des entreprises, Lamy dr aff June 2005; *Dammann* Conflits de juridictions et Forum Shopping, Dalloz 2005 Jur p 1779; *Dammann* Vers une interprétation pragmatique du règlement européen des faillites, Banque juin 2006; *Dammann* Mobility of companies and localisation of assets, arguments in favor of a dynamic interpretation of the EC Regulation No 1346/2000 on Insolvency proceedings, in Cross-border insolvency and conflicts of jurisdictions, Brussels 2007, 105 *et seq*; *Dictionnaire Permanent*, *(Communier/Vallens)* Insolvabilité et droit européen, March 2004; *Fasquelle* Les faillites des groupes de sociétés dans l'Union européenne: la difficile conciliation entre approches économique et juridique, Bull. Joly Sociétés February 2006 § 30 p 151; *Froehlich* La situation des créanciers au regard des règlements des 29 mai et 22 décembre 2000, Lamy dr aff July 2002; *Hameau/Raimon* Les faillites internationales, Approche européenne, RDAI 2003 p 645; *Idot* Un nouveau droit communautaire des procédures collectives : Le règlement (CE) n° 1346/2000 du 29 mai 2000, JCP éd E 2000 p 1648;

Jacquemont JDI 1, 2004 p 154; *Jault-Seseke/Robine* Le droit européen de la faillite, Dalloz 2004 p 1009; *Jault-Seseke,* Le sort des salariés, in L'effet international de la faillite: une réalité? Dalloz 2004, p 151; *Jobard-Bachellier* Le sort des garanties, in L'effet international de la faillite: une réalité? Dalloz 2004, p 127; *Juris-Classeur* Procédures collectives, Fasc. 3125, Redressement et liquidation judiciaires, droit communautaire, règlement n° 1346/2000 du conseil du 29 mai 2000 relatif aux procédures d'insolvabilité by *Roussel Galle,* April 2004; *Kerckhove* La convention européenne relative aux procédures d'insolvabilité, Revue des procédures collectives No 1996-3; *Khairallah* La compétence internationale du juge de l'insolvabilité, in L'effet international de la faillite: une réalité? Dalloz 2004, p 55; Le Cannu, Effet international de la faillite et principe d'égalité entre créanciers, in L'effet international de la faillite: une réalité? Dalloz 2004, p 95; *Legrand* La défaillance de l'entreprise: le règlement 1346/2000 relatif aux procédures d'insolvabilité, Rev soc 2001, 292; *Lamy* Droit Commercial *(Vallens)* 2004 No 3780; *Mathieu-Bouyssou* Aperçu des règles de droit judiciaire privé relatives aux procédures d'insolvabilité européennes après le règlement communautaire, Dalloz 2002 chron p 2245; *Mélin* La faillite internationale, 2004; *Mélin* Première application du règlement du 29 mai 2000 sur les procédures d'insolvabilité, RJDA 1/04 chron p 3; *Mélin* Conflits de juridictions et procédures européennes d'insolvabilité. Approche critique, Bull Joly August/September 2005 p 927; *Menjucq* Ouverture, reconnaissance et coordination des procédures d'insolvabilité dans le règlement 1346/2000, Bull Joly Société December 2000 p 1109; *Menjucq* La situation des créanciers dans le dans le règlement 1346/2000 sur les procédures d'insolvabilité, RJDA 6/01 p 579; *Menjucq* Ouverture, reconnaissance et coordination des procédures d'insolvabilité dans le règlement 1346/2000, Bull Joly Soc 2000, p 1109 § 278; *Menjucq* Aspects de droit international privé relatif aux conflits de compétence et aux conflits de lois, Rev proc coll March 2003 p 49; *Menjucq* Les groupes de sociétés, in L'effet international de la faillite: une réalité? Dalloz 2004, p 163; *Rémery* Les aspects européen de la déclaration des créances dans une procédure collective ouverte en France, Rev proc coll March 2003 p 66; *Rémery* L'effet à l'étranger des solutions des procédures collectives in L'effet international de la faillite: une réalité? Dalloz 2004, p 109; *Soinne* Droit communautaire des entreprises en difficulté: prospective, Rev proc coll March 2003; *Teboul* Droit communautaire des procédures collectives: la circulaire du 17 mars 2003 sur l'application du règlement sur les procédures d'insolvabilité, Pet Aff, June 20, 2003; *Urbain/Parleani* La faillite des sociétés, Bref aperçu sur le règlement CE n° 1346-2000 du 29 mai 2000 relatif aux procédures collectives, Rev soc janvier/février 2005; *Urban* La protection juridique incertaine des salariés dans une procédure collective transfrontalière, JCP 2006 I 122; *Vallens* Le droit européen de la faillite, DS 1995 chron p 307; *Vallens,* Présentation du règlement communautaire relatif aux procédures d'insolvabilité, Rev Lamy dr aff September 2000; *Vallens* Les créanciers et le règlement 1346/2000, Pét Aff, November 20, 2001; *Vallens* L'exequatur des jugements étrangers de faillite après le règlement communautaire sur les procédures d'insolvabilité, Pet Aff June 13, 2002 p 15; *Vallens,* Le règlement communautaire sur les procédures d'insolvabilité et les procédures de redressement et de liquidation judiciaire, Rev Lamy, dr aff July, 2002; *Vallens* Le droit de la faillite en Europe, Les procédures secondaires, Rev proc coll March 2003; *Vallens* La mise en œuvre du règlement communautaire sur les procédures d'insolvabilité : questions de procédure, Dalloz 2003, chron p 1421; *Vallens* La faillite internationale entre universalité et territorialité : Les enjeux, in L'effet international de la faillite : une réalité ?, Dalloz 2004, p 5.

5. Chart of French Insolvency proceedings

81 **Pre-insolvency proceedings (before *cessation des paiements*)**

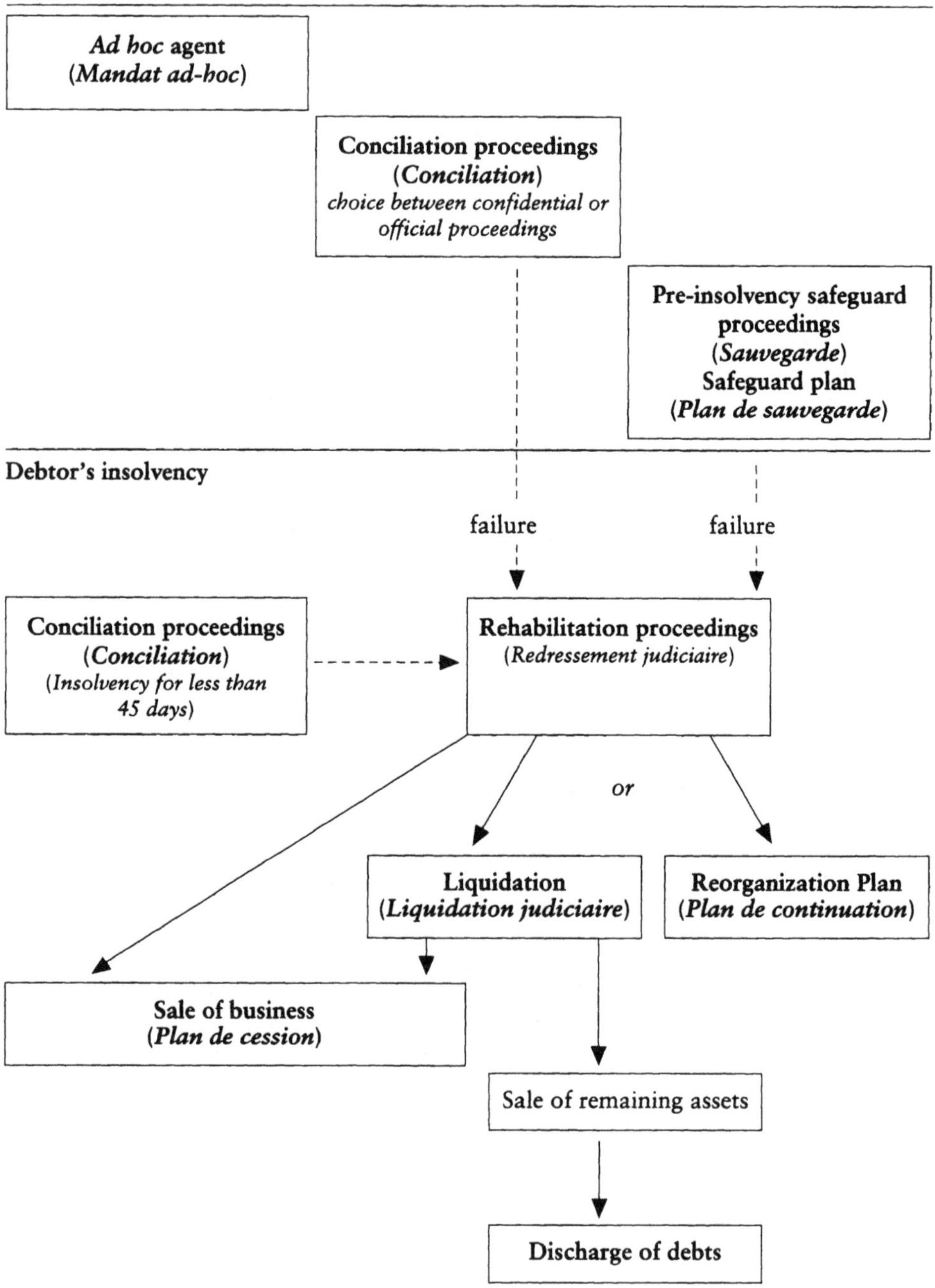

«Convocatoria para la presentación de créditos. Plazos aplicables».
"Opfordring til anmeldelse af fordringer. Vær opmærksom på fristerne."
„Aufforderung zur Anmeldung einer Forderung. Etwaige Fristen beachten!"
«Πρόσκληση για αναγγελία απαιτήσεως. Προσοχή στις προθεσμίες»
'Invitation to lodge a claim. Time limits to be observed'
«Invitation à produire une créance. Délais à respecter»
«Invito all'insinuazione di un credito. Termine da osservare»
„Oproep tot indiening van schuldvorderingen. In acht te nemen termijnen"
«Aviso de reclamação de créditos. Prazos legais a observar»
„Kehotus saatavan ilmoittamiseen. Noudatettavat määräajat"
„Anmodan att anmäla fordran. Tidsfrister att iaktta"

La présente note d'information doit être complétée par la juridiction ou le syndic et envoyée à chaque créancier, sans délai après l'ouverture de la procédure d'insolvabilité.

3. Informations concernant le débiteur

4. Informations concernant la procédure de production des créances

- **Délais à observer:**
- **Sanctions prévues quant à ces délais:**
- **Organe ou autorité habilité à recevoir la production des créances:**
- **Autres prescriptions:**

5. Informations concernant certaines catégories de créances

Les créanciers dont les créances sont garanties par un privilège ou une sûreté réelle:

☐ doivent produire leurs créances
☐ sont exemptés de cette obligation.

Fait à ...., le ....

Signature et/ou cachet ....

«Presentación de crédito»
„Anmeldelse af fordring"
„Anmeldung einer Forderung"
«Αναγγελία απαιτήσεως»
'Lodgement of claim'
«Production de créance»
«Insinuazione di credito»
„Indiening van een schuldvordering"
«Reclamação de crédito»
„Saatavaa koskeva ilmoitus"
„Anmälan av fordran"

6. 1 Données personnelles

7. 2 Informations concernant la créance

- **Nature:**
- **Date:**
- **Montant:** .... EUROS

Prière de fournir une copie des pièces justificatives

8. 3 Pour cette créance, vous revendiquez:

☐ **Un privilège**
☐ **Une sûreté réelle**
☐ **Une réserve de propriété**

Prière de cocher la case appropriée et de décrire ci-dessous les biens sur lesquels porte la garantie: ....

Fait à ...., le ....

Signature ....

The Approach of the Courts of England and Wales to the EC Regulations on Insolvency Proceedings as at September 2006

Contents

Index

Bibliography

Totty & Moss Insolvency; Butterworths Company Law Cases, 1993.

1. Introduction

1 There are four main regimes governing the powers and approach of the English courts to cross-border insolvencies and restructuring:

- These are the EC Regulation on Insolvency Proceedings 2000 ("EIR");
- the Insolvency Act 1986, in particular, Part V which deals with the winding-up of unregistered companies and Section 426 (*Co-operation between courts exercising jurisdiction in relation to insolvency*);
- case law built up over more than 100 years;
- and The Cross-Border Insolvency Regulations 2006, which brought into effect in English law the UNCITRAL Model Law on cross-border insolvency.

2 This chapter mainly considers the approach of the English courts to the EIR, but first briefly considers how English courts, through the interpretation of legislation or use of common law principles, have historically dealt with cross-border insolvency issues.

3 It should be noted that what follows in sections 1, 2 and 3 below now has to be considered in the light of the EIR, which governs the insolvency proceedings of all companies which have their "centre of main interests" or an "establishment" in the European Union ("EU"), except Denmark (see section 5 below).

2. Common Law

4 Over more than 100 years, the English courts have attempted to use principles of international comity to assist the functioning of cross-border insolvencies. *Totty and Moss*[1] claim that English law has "acquired [a] predominantly liberal, and internationalist, character with regard to cross-border recognition and assistance". The English courts have been willing to assert that English insolvency officeholders can control assets overseas, as well as being willing to assist the courts of other jurisdictions in insolvency matters where possible.

5 Before the introduction of the EIR and the concept of centre of main interests (as to which see section 5 below), the English courts talked about a company's domicile when referring to the country of its incorporation or where it principally operated its activities. English case law has developed the concept that an English winding-up of a foreign domiciled company would effectively be ancillary to the main insolvency proceedings in the other country. In the *Felixstowe Dock* case[2], Hirst J. recognised the principle of having a concurrent liquidator in England so that English assets may be dealt with, thus maintaining the principle that English based assets should be dealt with in accordance with English rules.

6 In that case, the company was in Chapter 11 proceedings in the U.S. Two English creditors obtained Mareva injunctions[3] in the English court against the company in an attempt to prevent the company moving its assets out of the English jurisdiction. The company sought the discharge of the injunctions on the basis that they disrupted the ongoing U.S. insolvency process. The order sought was that, on grounds of international

[1] *Totty & Moss* Insolvency para H 9.17.

[2] Felixstowe Dock & Railway Co. v United States Lines Inc. [1989] 2 WLR 109.

[3] A Mareva injunction is a form of freezing order of the assets of a person or company usually used to maintain the status quo and prevent dissipation of those assets while a dispute is settled before the courts.

comity, the English court should recognise the US bankruptcy order and permit distribution of the company's assets in accordance with US bankruptcy law.

The court did not discharge the injunction on the grounds that there was no prejudice to other creditors in maintaining the injunction whilst a discharge of the injunction, on the other hand, would be likely to prejudice English creditors. However, the court recognised that the courts of the country of incorporation should be considered the principal forum for controlling the winding-up. To the extent that there were English assets, there should be an ancillary English liquidator appointed over those assets, and the English liquidation would then proceed under English law rules, working in harmony with the foreign courts. **7**

There are, however, few firm rules as to exactly what is meant by the procedure being "ancillary". A liquidation of an English incorporated company is universal, in that the English courts consider it to cover all of the assets of the company, wherever they are situated, and also to deal with the claims of all creditors wherever they may be. The courts of other jurisdictions, notably the US, tend to take the same approach. However, in an ancillary liquidation of a foreign company, the English courts recognise that their remit is to deal only with those assets within their jurisdiction. The liquidator will usually collect in and realise the English assets and then pay the collected proceeds to the principal liquidator for distribution to all creditors *pari passu*. However, the English court has made clear that it does not have any general jurisdiction to disapply English insolvency law in these situations. **8**

For example, in *Re BCCI SA (No 10)*[4], the Vice Chancellor decided that he could not disapply the mandatory set-off rule which applies in liquidation. In that case, an agreement had been entered into by the liquidators of the UK branch of BCCI with the principal liquidators in Luxembourg and others as to how BCCI's assets should be distributed. **9**

Luxembourg does not have a rule of mandatory set-off in liquidation, and the outcome for certain creditors in England would have been significantly different had the rule been disapplied in England and funds simply transferred to Luxembourg for distribution. The judge decided that funds should be passed to Luxembourg by the English liquidators, but reserves made to ensure that those in the UK who would have had the right to set-off in a purely English liquidation would not suffer as a result of the transfer to Luxembourg. The ancillary nature of the English liquidation did not relieve the English court of its duty to apply English insolvency law to resolve issues arising in the English liquidation. The English approach to ancillary liquidations is summed up very neatly in a paragraph from the judgment in that case[5]: **10**

"This line of authority establishes, in my opinion, at least the following propositions. (1) Where a foreign company is in liquidation in its country of incorporation, a winding-up order made in England will normally be regarded as giving rise to a winding-up ancillary to that being conducted in the country of incorporation. (2) The winding-up in England will be ancillary in the sense that it will not be within the power of the English liquidators to get in and realise all the assets of the company worldwide. They will necessarily have to concentrate on getting in and realising the English assets. (3) Since in order to achieve a *pari passu* distribution between all the company's creditors it will be necessary for there to be a pooling of the company's assets worldwide and for a dividend to be declared out of the assets comprised in that pool, the winding-up in England will be ancillary in the sense, also, that it will be the liquidators in the principal liquidation who will be best placed to declare the dividend and to distribute the assets in the pool **11**

[4] [1997] Ch.D. 213.

[5] Per Richard Scott V-C at p 246.

accordingly. (4) None the less, the ancillary character of an English winding-up does not relieve an English court of the obligation to apply English law, including English insolvency law, to the resolution of any issue arising in the winding-up which is brought before the court. It may be, of course, that English conflicts of law rules will lead to the application of some foreign law principle in order to resolve a particular issue."

12 Of course, in many cases, the practical actions of the liquidators in cross-border insolvencies cannot be brought before the court on each occasion, and therefore a spirit of co-operation between jurisdictions has been needed. In some cases, the English liquidators or administrators have entered into protocols or agreements with their foreign counterparts as to the running of the insolvency or restructuring process. Because of the number of large scale and complex international insolvencies, courts have been forced to recognise the need for co-operation in the interests of creditors of these large corporations, allowing their counterpart insolvency professionals to enter into agreements to harmonise their procedures and eliminate duplication and expense.

13 Probably the first of these of the modern era was in the ***Maxwell Communications Corp plc*** ("MCC") case. In that case, MCC (an English incorporated company, but having a number of US subsidiaries) filed for Chapter 11 protection in the US as well as entering into administration in the UK. The US courts recognised the administrators as the proper controllers of the company, even though an examiner was appointed in the US. The administrators and the examiner then entered into a protocol by which they agreed how each would conduct the administration. This protocol was approved in the English courts, by Mr Justice Hoffman as he then was. Now Lord Hoffman, he has since stated that:

14 "The Protocol was brought before me for approval. I think it took me about 20 minutes to read and approve it. I checked to see whether it contained anything which looked like an obvious mistake. Otherwise the chances are I would have approved whatever it said. I had appointed administrators and it was their duty to take charge of the business and collect the assets according to their professional judgment. They were eminent insolvency accountants who had an experience in the management of insolvent businesses which I certainly did not share. I would ordinarily therefore accept their judgment of the best way to go forward ... In those circumstances, it is hardly surprising that I approved. It involved no conflict between the interests of English creditors and any principle of comity or internationalism."

15 Later in the *MCC* administration, similar, interesting comments came from the Court of Appeal. In *Barclays Bank plc v Homan and others*[6], the administrators were considering how to challenge a payment made to the bank to pay off the company's overdraft shortly before the administration and Chapter 11 filing. The bank attempted to force the administrators to bring preference proceedings against them in the UK rather than the US since they believed that there was a greater chance of their successfully defending any claim in the UK. At first instance, Hoffman J had decided that there were sufficient connecting factors not to make it unjust for the US courts to claim jurisdiction. These were that the moneys used to pay off the overdraft came from the sale of a company owned by MCC's major North American subsidiary and that the administrators were recognised as the corporate governance of MCC for Chapter 11 purposes and were therefore subject to the jurisdiction of the US Courts. The bank appealed, but the Court of Appeal refused to make the order sought by the bank and made the following comment[7]:

[6] [1993] BCLC 680.

[7] Per Leggatt LJ at p 703.

"Hoffman J. recognised the jurisdiction of the United States Bankruptcy Court when he made his order [approving the Protocol]. This court having recognised the United States court in relation to this insolvency, it would, in my judgment, offend against comity for this court now to decree which claims the administrators can, and which they cannot, allege in the United States Court are preferences." **16**

MCC is not the only high profile insolvency case where such agreements have been used in order to facilitate the cross-border process. As mentioned above, in the *BCCI* case, the English liquidators entered into an agreement among them and liquidators in other jurisdictions which, among other things, determined how the distributions to creditors were to be made. This agreement was sanctioned by the English courts, a decision upheld on appeal to the Court of Appeal. **17**

Another example of co-operation is the *Cenargo* case. The Cenargo group of companies operated shipping businesses in the UK, Ireland and in Continental Europe. In reliance on a very limited connection with the US (a bank account in New York), the companies filed for Chapter 11 protection in the US. One creditor objected to this course of action and petitioned, almost immediately thereafter, for provisional liquidation orders in the UK. In theory, this application was a contempt of the automatic stay in Chapter 11 and Cenargo therefore brought contempt proceedings against the petitioning creditors (and the provisional liquidators themselves) in the New York court. **18**

The arguments over which court was better placed to deal with relevant matters was resolved quickly following a conference call between Lightman J. in London and Judge Drain, the judge of the Southern District of New York court with responsibility for the Chapter 11 proceedings. Matters were resolved on a pragmatic basis with the UK proceedings moving forward as an administration rather than a provisional liquidation at the expense of the Chapter 11 case, which seems the correct approach, given the very obvious UK connections of the Cenargo group and the far more tenuous connections with the US. **19**

The English court will consider all the factors in the case before deciding on its approach, which can, of course, differ in each case. For example, there are differing authorities on how the English courts will treat a stay granted in a foreign bankruptcy as regards its operation in the UK. As noted above, in the *Felixstowe Dock* case, the English courts upheld an injunction by creditors to prevent assets from being removed from the jurisdiction and taken to the US for use within the company's Chapter 11 proceedings. The court made clear that it was not bound by the stay imposed by the US courts and that it would be improper to allow the assets to leave the jurisdiction to the prejudice of UK creditors. A few years later, in *Banque Indosuez SA v Ferromet Resources Inc*[8], Hoffman J. refused injunctions to the plaintiff in circumstances where they would have been in breach of the US Chapter 11 stay. The judge specifically mentioned that one of the factors affecting his decision to refuse the injunctions was the existence of the stay. Whilst agreeing that the English courts were not bound by a stay imposed in a US bankruptcy, Hoffman J stated[9] that the court should do "its utmost to co-operate with the United States Bankruptcy Court and avoid any action which might disturb the orderly administration" of the Chapter 11 proceedings. However, it should be stressed that in this case the bank seeking injunctions was itself one of the petitioners for the Chapter 11 proceedings, and arguably had submitted to the jurisdiction of the US courts in this way. Hoffman J considered this to be particularly significant. **20**

---

[8] [1993] BCLC 112.

[9] At p 117.

21 The story of the Turner & Newell group administrations also helps to illustrate some of the limitations on co-operation between different jurisdictions. Turner & Newell was the UK part of the US Federal Mogul group which filed for Chapter 11 protection in order to deal with its liabilities to employees for asbestosis. The UK group went into administration and filed for Chapter 11. In a number of reported decisions, the English courts have resisted attempts by US creditors to force the UK group to follow the US plan of reorganisation which would have adversely affected the interests of domestic creditors. Whilst the courts in the two countries have worked hard to co-operate, the English courts have been careful not to overstep the boundaries of English insolvency law.

22 As Hirst stated in the *Felixstowe Dock* case[10]:

"The court would in principle always wish to co-operate in every proper way with an order ... made by a court in a friendly jurisdiction ... But whether this is appropriate in any given case, and if so the precise nature and extent of such co-operation, must depend on the particular sphere of activity in question and the English law applicable thereto".

3. Insolvency Act 1986

3.1 Part V

23 English courts have long assumed jurisdiction to wind up foreign companies under Part V (sections 220–229) Insolvency Act 1986 and its predecessor statutes. This part of the Insolvency Act 1986 deals with "unregistered companies" which has been interpreted by the courts as including companies incorporated in foreign jurisdictions. The legislation does not give any guidance as to when the English court should assume jurisdiction. This is left to the discretion of the court. In order to assume jurisdiction to wind up foreign companies, the court must decide that there is sufficient connection with England and Wales to make an order appropriate. This will usually be because the debtor company has a branch office or business in England or Wales, there is some property in England or Wales or because there is some benefit to creditors, or perhaps a group of creditors, in doing so. However, it is not necessary that there are assets in the English jurisdiction.[11] The courts have taken a liberal view as to the circumstances in which they will take jurisdiction to wind up a foreign company. In the *Okeanos* case[12], the English court took jurisdiction to wind up a Liberian debtor which had obtained a loan from an English bank. Although the debtor had no assets in the jurisdiction, the debt was governed by English law and was repayable in England. This, coupled with the fact that there was no alternative jurisdiction in which to wind up the debtor and there was evidence the debtor had carried on a business in England, enabled the court to take jurisdiction. As Peter Gibson J stated:[13]

24 "the presence of assets in this country is not an essential condition for the court to have jurisdiction in relation to the winding-up of a foreign company. In my judgment, provided a sufficient connection with the jurisdiction is shown, and there is a reasonable possibility of benefit for the creditors from the winding-up, the court has jurisdiction to wind up the foreign company".

---

[10] At p 123.

[11] Re a Company (No. 003102 of 1991) Ex p Nyckeln Finance Co Ltd [1991] BCLC 539.

[12] International Westminster Bank v Okeanos [1987] 3 WLR 339.

[13] At p 352.

The approach of the English courts was succinctly set out in *Re Real Estate Development Co.*[14] In order for the English court to claim jurisdiction: **25**

1) there must be a sufficient connection with England and Wales to justify making a winding-up order (though it is not necessary for there to be assets in England and Wales);
2) there must be a reasonable possibility of benefit to creditors in the winding-up; and
3) the court must be able to claim jurisdiction over at least one of the parties who has an interest in the assets to be distributed.

Once the court has decided the question of whether it has jurisdiction to wind up a foreign company, it will consider whether to make the winding-up order. The grounds for winding up a foreign company in England and Wales are set out in section 221(5): **26**

- if the company is dissolved, or has ceased to carry on business or is carrying on business only for the purpose of winding up its affairs; or
- if the company is unable to pay its debts. The legislation sets out various circumstances when the company will be deemed unable to pay its debts. These largely mirror the provisions for companies registered in England and Wales, save that a foreign company will also be deemed unable to pay its debts if an action is instituted against it for payment of a debt and the company has not paid the debt or had the action stayed within 3 weeks of service of notice of the action on it; or
- if the court is of the opinion that it is just and equitable that the company should be wound up.

These grounds are more restricted than the grounds for winding-up companies registered in England and Wales. **27**

Provided that the foreign company can be served with a winding-up petition (and subject to the EIR issues described in 4 below), the court will therefore be in a position to take jurisdiction over the debtor company and to wind it up. Where a foreign company has registered a place of business in England and Wales under section 691 of the Companies Act 1985, this makes service straightforward. It should also be noted that by Insolvency Rule 12.12, the usual rules for service out of the jurisdiction do not apply in English insolvency proceedings and the court has discretion to order service "within such time, on such person, at such place and in such manner as it thinks fit".[15] **28**

A liquidation under Part V is then run in accordance with the Insolvency Act 1986 provisions, subject to certain exceptions which are beyond the scope of this chapter. **29**

3.2 Section 426

Section 426(4) Insolvency Act 1986 places a positive obligation on the courts in the UK to "assist the courts having the corresponding jurisdiction in any other part of the United Kingdom or any relevant country or territory". **30**

Accordingly, if a court in a "relevant country or territory", with jurisdiction over insolvency matters, makes a request to the English court for assistance in relation to matters of insolvency specified in the request, then the English court is obliged to assist the foreign court. **31**

The scope of this section may not be as wide as it first appears. The "relevant country or territory" means the Channel Islands or the Isle of Man, or certain countries listed by **32**

[14] [1991] BCLC 210.

[15] Insolvency Rule 12.12(3).

statutory instrument, most of which are former British territories or members of the Commonwealth (notably Australia, Canada, Hong Kong, the Republic of Ireland, New Zealand and South Africa). Significantly, it does not include the US or most European jurisdictions.

33 Historically, the English courts did not have power to make administration orders in relation to foreign incorporated companies. However, in *Re. Dallhold Estates (UK) Pty Ltd*,[16] the English courts decided that section 426 gave them the power to make an administration order in relation to an Australian company at the request of the Australian courts. Similarly, it seems possible that this provision would allow the English courts to make an order sanctioning some form of compromise with creditors or scheme of arrangement at the request of another relevant country's court. However, as noted above, the "relevant countries" for the purposes of this section are limited. When it comes to countries other than "relevant countries", the English courts do not have the power similarly to make such orders (save under the Cross-Border Insolvency Regulations which are discussed below). There is, for example, no equivalent to Section 304 US Bankruptcy Code which would allow the English courts to give effect to a foreign scheme under English law. That said, it is always open to a company with sufficient connection in the UK, or which has an establishment here, to propose an English scheme of arrangement having the same effect as its restructuring process in its home jurisdiction.

34 There has been judicial consideration of what, if any, discretion the English court has in giving assistance to a foreign court when faced with a legitimate request. In other words, while the legislation states that there is an obligation to assist, what actually constitutes assistance? The *Dallhold Estates* case stated that if a request under section 426 has been made by a relevant country, and the necessary conditions for compliance under English law were satisfied, the court is required by section 426 to make the order requested unless there is some compelling reason why that should not be done. This suggests that the court has a discretion on whether to assist, in that assistance could be refused if there was a "compelling reason" to do so. The *Hannover Re* case[17] confirms that the court retains the discretion on the giving of assistance. The court must consider if the requested assistance could properly be granted and, if not possible to do exactly what was requested, must consider whether it could assist in some other way in accordance with any laws the court is authorised to apply. In exercising this discretion, the court can refuse to assist and in so doing does not have to be limited to grounds of public policy for the refusal. The court can take into account any factors which may justify refusal. That said, the English courts will look at the whole circumstances of the case and it would take something extraordinary for the assistance requested not to be given.[18]

35 The principle was expanded further in *England v Smith*[19]. In that case, the Court of Appeal said that the policy of comity was the starting point for any consideration of section 426. Accordingly, it was possible for the English court to order a process which was lawful in the applicant's jurisdiction (in this case, Australia), which would not otherwise be allowed in England.

36 There has also been debate in the courts about which law should be applied by the English court in granting assistance. Should it be the law of the requesting state or English law? Section 426(5) provides that a request for assistance under section 426(4):

---

16 [1992] BCLC 621.

17 Hughes and others v Hannover Rück-versicherungs-Aktiengesellschaft [1997] 1 B.C.L.C. 497.

18 Duke Group Ltd v Carver [2001] B.P.I.R 459.

19 (Re Southern Equities Corp) [2001] Ch 419.

"is authority for the court to which the request is made to apply … the insolvency law which is applicable by either court in relation to comparable matters falling within its jurisdiction. In exercising its discretion under this subsection, a court shall have regard in particular to the rules of private international law". **37**

In *BCCI SA*[20], Rattee J. expressed the view that the discretion was on the part of the requested court to decide whether to apply its own law or the law of the requesting court and that it must have regard to the rules of private international law when deciding how to exercise this discretion. This may, for example, lead to a situation where the English court considers a specific remedy of foreign insolvency law, although not a principle recognised in English law as valid, and still applies that principle if private international law allows it to do so. **38**

4. The Cross-Border Insolvency Regulations 2006

Pursuant to section 14 Insolvency Act 2000, the Secretary of State has now recognised the UNCITRAL Model Law on Cross-Border Insolvency. This was done pursuant to the Cross-Border Insolvency Regulations 2006, which came into force in England and Wales and Scotland on 4 April 2006. The common law principles and section 426 Insolvency Act 1986 (described in sections 1 and 2 above) now have to be considered alongside these regulations. At the EU level, the EIR will apply (see section 5 below). **39**

The UNCITRAL Model Law is designed to assist countries to equip their insolvency laws with a harmonised and fair framework to address instances of cross-border insolvency. The Model Law is intended to cover the classic case where the debtor has assets in more than one state or where some of the creditors of the debtor are not from the state where the insolvency proceeding is taking place. **40**

There is a significant element of overlap between the UNCITRAL Model Law and the EIR as both are designed to respect the differences amongst national procedural laws and do not attempt to provide a substantive unification of insolvency laws. The EIR only governs the co-ordination of insolvency proceedings within the EU and does not deal with cross-border insolvency matters extending beyond Member States of the EU. The Model Law therefore provides a complimentary regime addressing instances of cross-border insolvency and co-operation outside the EU. By virtue of the Cross-Border Insolvency Regulations 2006, the intention was that, along with section 426 Insolvency Act 1986 and the EIR, England and Wales would have a suite of statutory procedures available in cross-border insolvency cases, as well as the flexibility and spirit of co-operation of the common law described above (in section 2). **41**

The Model Law aims to provide direct access to the courts in England and Wales for a person administering a foreign insolvency proceeding, to allow the courts to determine what relief or co-ordination is needed for the optimal carrying out of the insolvency. The foreign representative has the right to initiate an insolvency proceeding in England and Wales in relation to a debtor who is subject to a foreign proceeding[21] and the right to participate in an English insolvency proceeding regarding that debtor[22]. As with the EIR (see section 5 below), the Model Law establishes criteria for determining whether a foreign proceeding is to be recognised and if so whether as a "main" or "non-main" pro- **42**

[20] [1993] BCC 787.

[21] Art 11 of the EIR.

[22] Art 12 of the EIR.

ceeding. This is essentially dependant on whether the foreign proceeding is taking place in the country where the main operations of the debtor business are located.

43 The Model Law sets out the effects of recognition and relief available to a foreign representative[23]. These can include a stay of actions by individual creditors and of enforcement proceedings against the debtor and a suspension of the debtor's right to dispose of or encumber assets. The moratorium provides a respite until appropriate measures can be put in place for the reorganisation or liquidation of the debtor's assets. However, exceptions and limitations to this moratorium will be the same as if the debtor had been wound up under English insolvency law. In particular, this moratorium does not affect specified security rights or the exercise of set-off rights, which will be exercisable in the same way as they would be in an English winding-up. The intention is to give secured creditors greater predictability about the likely outcome in any cases of cross-border insolvency.

44 It is important to note that recognition of foreign proceedings by the English courts does not prevent English creditors from initiating or continuing with insolvency proceedings in England in relation to the debtor.

45 The Model Law also aims to provide a legislative framework for co-operation and co-ordination between courts and insolvency officeholders in different jurisdictions. It provides for the English courts to have the power to co-operate to the maximum extent possible with foreign courts and foreign representatives,[24] and a duty to co-operate is placed on English insolvency officeholders (to the extent it does not conflict with their duties under English insolvency law).[25] Further, the Model Law provides for the co-ordination of insolvency proceedings across jurisdictions, with the intention of co-ordinating decisions that would best achieve the objective in both insolvency proceedings.[26]

46 As the provisions of the Model Law have only just been enacted into English law, there are no reported cases on the approach of the English courts to the Model Law. However, it is believed that the introduction of the Model Law into English law will be a useful tool to assist the courts in their pursuit of cross-border assistance and will be as helpful and important in relation to non-European insolvencies as the EIR has been in relation to European ones.

5. The EIR

5.1 Commencement in England and Wales

47 The EIR came into force in England and Wales on 31st May 2002. By virtue of its nature as a regulation, there was no need for any further ratification or enactment for it to become law in England and Wales. Because the EIR is primary legislation, any existing legislation which is inconsistent with the EIR is automatically repealed and any inconsistent rule of law is automatically superseded. All English courts are required to give effect to the provisions of the regulation. Further, all Member States are required to ensure that their domestic laws are in compliance with EC law. Accordingly, various statutory instruments were enacted in England and Wales in order to make English insolvency legislation compatible with the EIR. These statutory instruments were:

[23] Arts 19–21 of the EIR.
[24] Art 25 of the EIR.
[25] Art 26 of the EIR.
[26] Arts 29–30 of the EIR.

- The Insolvency Act 1986 (Amendment) Regulations 2002 (SI 2002/1037)
- The Insolvency Act 1986 (Amendment) (No 2) Regulations 2002 (SI 2002/1240)
- The Insolvency (Amendment) Rules 2002 (SI 2002/1307)
- The Insolvent Partnerships (Amendment) Order 2002 (SI 2002/1308)
- The Administration of Insolvent Estates of Deceased Persons Order 2002 (SI 2002/1309).

5.2 Amendments to the EIR

A further regulation (EC Council Regulation 603/2005) amending the EIR came into force on 21st April 2005 (the "New Regulation"). The New Regulation was brought into force in order to take account of changes to the domestic insolvency law of certain Member States since the EIR came into force (as well as to encompass into the provisions of the EIR the insolvency proceedings of countries which became Member States of the EU after the EIR came into force). **48**

The New Regulation provided amendments to the definitions of "insolvency proceedings" (Annex A), "winding-up proceedings" (Annex B) and "Liquidator" (Annex C) of the EIR. In England and Wales, the two main amendments provided by the New Regulation can be summarised as follows: **49**

(i) Under English law, it was previously only possible to have an administration by order of the court. Following implementation of the Enterprise Act 2002, it is now possible to appoint an administrator without the necessity for a court order – a filing of papers at court being sufficient. Such a filing can be made by the debtor company, its directors or a secured lender (so long as certain conditions are satisfied). The New Regulation provides that administrations pursuant to such out of court appointments are now "insolvency proceedings" for the purposes of the EIR. As a result, administrations by out of court appointment can be the subject of "main proceedings" and an administrator so appointed, together with his powers, must be recognised in all other Member States (except Denmark). **50**

(ii) The New Regulation makes it a "winding-up proceeding" if there is a "winding-up through administration, including appointments made by filing prescribed documents with the court". This provision allows administration (including by way of the out of court appointment route mentioned in (i) above) as a secondary proceeding as an aid to winding up in the main proceedings, so long as such administration is only being used to wind up a branch in England or Wales. There is some question as to how such an administration would operate, however, since the overriding purpose for administration in England and Wales is the survival of the company as a going concern. The writer is not yet aware of an administration being used for secondary proceedings in England & Wales, but when this occurs it is likely to involve a need for some closer guidance by the court. **51**

One of the inadequacies of the Annexes to the EIR so far as England and Wales is concerned is that no mention is made of a scheme of arrangement pursuant to section 425 Companies Act 1985. This legislation allows a company to propose a compromise with its creditors, which is subsequently sanctioned by the court. A section 425 scheme of arrangement is often used as a rescue tool for English companies and it would therefore have been helpful if such a scheme could have been listed as an "insolvency proceeding" in Annex A to the EIR. This would have allowed section 425 schemes to be easily opened as main proceedings for companies which have their centre of main interests in England (which could have been particularly useful in group company situations). In this situation, it would still be possible to utilise Article 25 of the EIR, which provides that: **52**

53 "Judgments handed down by a court whose judgment concerning the opening of proceedings is recognised in accordance with Article 16 of the EIR and which concern the course and closure of insolvency proceedings, and compositions approved by that court shall also be recognised with no further formalities." (emphasis added)

54 This Article would allow a section 425 scheme to be used as a rescue tool alongside an administration which had been opened as main proceedings. The English court could take jurisdiction to open main proceedings against a debtor which has its centre of main interests in England, and could also sanction a s 425 scheme of arrangement between that debtor and its creditors. In accordance with Article 25 of the EIR, the section 425 scheme, being a composition between the debtor and its creditors which is approved by the court, would have to be recognised in all Member States (except Denmark) without further formalities. This technique could be used to facilitate the rescue of groups of companies, however it would have been preferable to avoid the extra layer of procedure (and therefore cost) of first requiring an administration order to be made in respect of that debtor.

5.3 The EIR in the English Courts – the story so far

5.3.1 Centre of main interests

55 Since the EIR came into effect, the English courts have assumed jurisdiction to make administration or winding-up orders in relation to any company which has its centre of main interests in England and Wales. One of the earliest instances of this exercise of jurisdiction was the *Enron Directo SA* case[27], where the English court made an administration order (thus opening main proceedings) in respect of a company incorporated in Spain. This power arises from Article 3 of the EIR which states:

56 "The courts of the Member State within the territory of which the centre of a debtor's main interests is situated shall have jurisdiction to open insolvency proceedings ..."

57 The English courts then interpreted Article 3 of the EIR as giving them jurisdiction to make an order for winding-up or administration in relation to any company, be it incorporated in a Member State of the EU or otherwise, which has its centre of main interests within England and Wales. This principle was established in *Re. Brac Rent-A-Car International Inc*[28]. BRAC Rent-A-Car International Inc. ("BRAC") went into administration in England on 14 January 2003, following a petition by the company itself. BRAC was incorporated in Delaware and had its registered office in the US. However, BRAC had never traded in the US and its operations were conducted almost entirely in the UK. BRAC was in Chapter 11 proceedings in the US, along with other members of the Budget car rental group of companies. However, BRAC considered that it also needed the protection against creditors in England which an administration order would give. BRAC was registered as an overseas company in England, traded from an address in England and all its employees worked in England under contracts of employment governed by English law. All the contracts necessary for its trading activities were subject to English law, as were the other contracts necessary for it to operate the business, such as for utilities.

58 In considering the question of whether the English court had jurisdiction to grant an administration order over BRAC, the fundamental question was whether the debtors in relation to whom insolvency proceedings governed by the EIR may be taken are limited to those incorporated within the EU or not. The court was persuaded that in general, EU

---

[27] Judgment of Lightman J on 4th July 2002 – unreported.

[28] [2003] EWHC 128 (Ch).

legislation is not limited to companies incorporated within a Member State of the EU. The court decided that the EIR gave jurisdiction to the courts of a Member State to open insolvency proceedings in relation to a company incorporated outside the EU if the centre of that company's main interests was within that Member State. Accordingly, it was prepared to make an administration order in respect of BRAC.

Lloyd J stated that the EIR refers to the "domicile" or registered office of creditors in various places within the regulation. Accordingly, if it had been the intention that only debtors incorporated in a relevant Member State could be affected by the EIR then it would have been straightforward for the regulation to say exactly that. In other words, if such a limitation was intended then it would have been expressly stated in the regulation, or at very least in the long recitals to the regulation. The court also stated that if the EIR was taken to apply only to debtors who are incorporated in a Member State, it would allow debtor companies an opportunity to avoid the workings of the regulation by being incorporated outside the EU, even though their business, assets and operations were based within the EU. Lloyd J considered this would be inconsistent with the aim of the EIR to avoid manipulation and forum-shopping among Member States (as stated in Recital 4 to the EIR)[29]. **59**

The term "centre of a debtor's main interests" is not defined in the EIR, although Recital (13) of the EIR states that the centre of main interests "should correspond to the place where the debtor conducts the administration of his interests on a regular basis and is therefore ascertainable by third parties." There is a presumption that the centre of main interests will be the place of the company's registered office, in the absence of proof to the contrary[30], though the EIR is silent on what constitutes the requisite proof. One difficult issue which has arisen in this regard is the question of how corporate groups can be dealt with, as the EIR does not specifically deal with corporate groups, only single corporate entities. Clearly, this is a shortcoming in the EIR, given the tendancy of multi-national businesses to operate on a group network basis, with a parent company and subsidiaries incorporated in different jurisdictions across the globe. It is often useful (and indeed often provides a better return for creditors), if insolvency proceedings in respect of a group of companies can proceed under the provisions of the laws of just one Member State. In several cases before the English courts, the presumption that a debtor's centre of main interests is the jurisdiction of its registered office has been rebutted, and this has provided a useful tool to allow groups of companies to be put into administration where the head office function and control is run from within England and Wales. **60**

One example of this approach was *Re. Daisytek-ISA Limited & Ors*[31]. Daisytek-ISA Limited ("Daisytek") was a company incorporated in England with a US parent company. The US parent, along with various of its other US subsidiaries filed for Chapter 11 bankruptcy protection in the US. Daisytek was the holding company of a group of companies across Europe which was a pan-European reseller and wholesale distributor of electronic office supplies. Daisytek, along with 10 of its English subsidiaries, 3 of its German subsidiaries and one French subsidiary applied for administration orders to be made in respect of each company. The court heard evidence that the trading companies in the group were managed and controlled as a group and co-ordinated by the head office **61**

[29] Recital 4 to the EIR states "It is necessary for the proper functioning of the internal market to avoid incentives for the parties to transfer assets or judicial proceedings from one Member State to another, seeking to obtain a more favourable legal position (forum shopping)."

[30] Per Article 3 (1).

[31] [2003] BCC 562.

in Bradford, England. Although the German subsidiaries had their registered offices in Germany and conducted their business from premises in Germany, the majority of the administration of the German companies was conducted from the head office in Bradford. In particular, the finance function of the Germany companies was co-ordinated from head office and their financial information was compiled in accordance with English accountancy principles; the German subsidiaries required the approval of head office to buy anything in excess of € 5,000; the head office was consulted in relation to the recruitment of the senior employees of the German subsidiaries; all information, technology and support functions were run from head office; all contracts with pan-European customers and suppliers were negotiated and entered into by the head office; most purchases of the German subsidiaries were under contracts negotiated by head office; all corporate identity and branding were run by head office and the German subsidiaries were required to carry out their business in accordance with the management strategy plan drawn up by the chief executive officer of Daisytek.

62 Accordingly, the court was satisfied that England was the place where each of the German subsidiaries conducted the administration of its interests on a regular basis (as per Recital 13 of the EIR). The court held that the identification of a debtor's centre of main interests required the court to consider both the scale of interests administered at a particular place and their importance as against the scale and importance of that debtor's interests administered at any other place which could be regarded as its centre of main interests.

63 The court also emphasised the fact that Recital 13 required that the centre of a debtor's main interests must be "ascertainable" by third parties, and the most important of these third parties in respect of a trading company are its creditors and potential creditors. In this case, the large majority of potential creditors by value knew that England was where most of the important functions of the German subsidiaries were carried out. In comparison, local functions of the German subsidiaries were very limited. For similar reasons, the court also held that England was the centre of main interests of the French subsidiary. In view of the fact that the other conditions for making an administration order were present (namely that the companies were insolvent and the assets of those companies could be realised for a greater value in administration than in a German or French liquidation), the court proceeded to make administration orders against the German and French subsidiaries.

64 A further example was the Rover Group Decisions in 2005[32]. In April 2005, MG Rover Group subsidiary companies from Germany, The Netherlands, Benelux, Spain, Italy, Portugal, France and Ireland (the "national sales companies") applied for administration orders to be made against them. Each of the national sales companies was a wholly-owned subsidiary (either directly or indirectly) of MG Rover Overseas Holdings Limited, which itself was a subsidiary of MG Rover Group Limited, both of which were English incorporated companies. Cars manufactured by the Group were processed by another English company, MG Rover Exports Limited ("Exports"). Exports then supplied the cars to the national sales companies for onward transmission to car dealerships in the local jurisdictions. The role of the national sales companies was to implement strategic decisions taken by MG Rover Group in its international headquarters in Longbridge, England (the "Head Office").

[32] See for example [2005] EWHC 874 (CHAN).

The court considered whether there was sufficient evidence to rebut the presumption in Article 3 of the EIR that the centre of a debtor's main interests should be the place of its registered office. The court held that there was sufficient evidence presented to it that the centre of main interests of each of the national sale companies was in England and Wales and not in the countries in which they were incorporated. The court took the following circumstances into account: **65**

- the management of the national sales companies was essentially based in England. At least one of the board was a UK resident director and in some cases the national sales company had a board with an English resident majority. Monthly meetings of each board were held alternately between the country of incorporation and England and senior staff of the national sales companies were only appointed or removed with direct authorisation from Head Office. The recruitment and number of all employees for the national sales companies were authorised by Head Office. The court was satisfied that all effective management decisions, other than those which could be described as routinely operative, were taken by Head Office or by personnel appointed or supervised from Head Office in England; **66**
- the financial structure of the group was such that, even though the national sales companies had local capitalisation, Exports operated as a funder for each of them. All the cash collected from local dealers was transferred to Exports, but in practice Exports only took what it needed to meet the immediate funding needs of the national sales companies. Exports therefore effectively provided a group overdraft facility for the national sales companies. Further, the budget for each national sales company was approved and monitored by Head Office in England, as indeed was capital expenditure; **67**
- no national sales company had an autonomous and independent trading existence. Each company was an extension of the sales operation carried out worldwide by Head Office in England. All marketing was designed and carried out by Head Office. The national sales companies were essentially just a gateway through which cars were passed to local markets;
- in all of the national sales companies bar Italy, the chief creditor was Exports in relation to the cars provided from Head Office for onward transmission to dealers. Similarly, in terms of suppliers, MG Rover was by far the largest supplier of products to the national sales companies. Each national sales company could only deal with the MG Rover Group in relation to cars sold through it;
- it was clear that in looking to where debts would be dealt with, debtors would look to England rather than the individual national sales company. The operation of the national sales companies was wholly parasitic on the main operation of manufacture at Head Office; and
- the national sales companies clearly formed a subsidiary network within part of the international group structure of the MG Rover Group. They were not individual discrete commercial undertakings.

In this case the judge seems to have emphasised less the views of third parties as to the centre of main interests and looked more to the management of the companies and their purpose. **68**

As can be seen from these decisions, the English courts have been leaning in favour of the concept of making administration orders in relation to groups of companies where there is one central controlling head office in England, which is known to those dealing with the group to be such, and where it appears to be in the interests of all creditors that there is a co-ordinated insolvency of the group. **69**

70 These decisions also lean towards a subsidiary company's centre of main interests being where its finance and management functions are performed, rather than its place of trading operations. However, the factors to take into account when assessing a company's centre of main interests have not yet been finalised by the English courts and each case will turn on its facts. On 2 May 2006, the European Court of Justice ("ECJ") gave a preliminary ruling on the concept of centre of main interests in the Eurofood case.[33]

71 Amongst other issues, the ECJ considered whether, when considering a subsidiary in a corporate group, the critical factor in ascertaining a centre of main interests is the location of where strategic policy decisions are made or the place where the subsidiary conducts administration of its interests in a manner ascertainable by third parties.

72 In considering this issue, the court emphasised that with respect to corporate groups each distinct legal entity must be analysed separately. The court stressed that objectivity and the possibility of ascertainment by third parties were the criteria to ensure legal certainty and foreseeability. Consequently, the court was of the view that the presumption in favour of the registered office of the company "can be rebutted only if factors which are both objective and ascertainable by third parties enable it to be established that an actual situation exists which is different from that which locating it at that registered office is deemed to reflect" [34].

73 The court later stated[35]: "Where a company carries on its business in the territory of the Member State where its registered office is situated, the mere fact that its economic choices are or can be controlled by a parent company in another Member State is not enough to rebut the presumption laid down by the Regulation". Consequently any debtor or creditor which wanted to rebut the presumption that a debtor's centre of main interests was not the place of its registered office must demonstrate that the elements relied on are objective and ascertainable by third parties.

74 This decision provides welcome guidance on the contentious centre of main interests test. Although the ECJ did not define examples of ascertainable and objective criteria (which would have been helpful given the lack of criteria set out in the regulation itself), its decision goes a long way to counteracting the preference of some debtors to seek jurisdiction based on criteria which are not necessarily ascertainable by third parties, such as the location of board meetings and internal company management functions.

75 Initial hearings seeking jurisdiction for voluntary insolvency proceedings are usually conducted on an ex-parte basis (i.e. there is no person objecting to the debtor's application). In these circumstances the court only hears one side of the story often meaning a decision is made with less than the complete factual picture. The emphasis by the ECJ on the centre of main interests being determinable by third parties may ease the evidential burden on third parties seeking to challenge the claims of the debtor. Creditors usually do not have detailed information concerning the internal workings of the debtor and therefore are at an evidential disadvantage in trying to establish the centre of main interests. By the ECJ emphasising objective factors ascertainable by third parties, publicly available information should become a crucial factor in determining the centre of main interests, putting creditors on a more equal footing with debtors in any dispute.

76 It is interesting to consider whether the *Daisytek* and *MG Rover* cases would have been decided differently by the English courts had they had the benefit of first reading this ruling by the ECJ. Certainly the judge in the *Daisytek* case laid particular emphasis on the perception of third party creditors in determining where the centre of main

[33] Eurofood IFSC Ltd – 2 May 2006 (C-341/04).

[34] At paragraph 34.

[35] At paragraph 36.

interests of the companies was located. On the other hand, in the *MG Rover* case, the judge seemed to place less emphasis on this. He also seemed to view the presumption in Article 3(1) of the EIR as less important than the ECJ later viewed it. In *MG Rover* the judge stated that a presumption such as that the centre of main interests will be the place of its registered office will "rarely be determinative of the question". He went on to say that it will only be determinative "if there is either no evidence or all of the evidence which is adduced is evenly balanced and a court cannot make a rational choice between the two versions". This emphasis seems rather different from the ECJ statement that the presumption "can be rebutted only if factors which are both objective and ascertainable by third parties enable it to be established that an actual situation exists which is different from that which locating it at its registered office is deemed to reflect".

Of course, the judge's decision in *MG Rover* may have been exactly the same even if he had had the benefit of reading the ECJ decision – we do not have sufficient detail of the evidence which was before him to suggest otherwise. However, it does seem likely that in future cases applicants will have to put less emphasis on the location of the debtor's management and more on objective views of third party creditors. **77**

It is common practice in the UK market for lenders to ask for a representation from borrowers in a loan agreement that the borrowers' centre of main interests is where their registered office is located and for an undertaking not to change this without lender consent, or without notifying the lender. This may prove a useful tool in disputing any application for a debtor to open main proceedings in a different jurisdiction, since the representation can be used as objective evidence that a major third party creditor perceived the place of the centre of main interests of the debtor to coincide with that of the registered office. **78**

5.3.2 Forum Shopping

The EIR does not expressly deal with the possibility that a debtor could move its centre of main interests from one state to another. As such, it is in theory possible for a debtor to engage in "forum shopping" by shifting its assets and business to another jurisdiction in the hope of being subject to a more favourable insolvency regime. This is despite Recital 4 of the EIR specifically stating that the purpose of the EIR is to prevent such tactics[36]. The question of whether a debtor could change its centre of main interests was considered by the English Court of Appeal in the case of *Malcolm Brian Shierson v Clive Vlieland-Boddy*[37]. In this case, a bankruptcy order had been made against Mr. Vlieland-Boddy in February 2004 on the basis that his centre of main interests was in England. The petition was based on an award for costs made against Mr. Vlieland-Boddy in respect of an individual voluntary arrangement he had put forward to his creditors, for which it was necessary for him to have his centre of main interests in England and Wales. By the date of the petition for bankruptcy, Mr. Vlieland-Boddy had separated from his wife and was living and working in Spain. After their separation, Mr. Vlieland-Boddy and his wife had charged, then sold, a joint interest in a property (known as Unit 2A Sunrise Business Park) to a company controlled by Mr. Vlieland-Boddy and incorporated in the British Virgin Islands. Mr. Vlieland-Boddy was also on the board and held shares in an English company. The bankruptcy registrar granted the bankruptcy order on the basis that the time for determining a debtor's centre of main interests was the date on which the debts were incurred as this was the time when the **79**

[36] See note 28 supra.

[37] [2005] EWCA Civ 974 – this case concerned an individual debtor but its principles will apply equally to companies.

creditors needed to assess the risk of a debtor's insolvency. In this case, when the debts were incurred it was common ground that Mr. Vlieland-Boddy's centre of main interests was in England and Wales. Accordingly, the bankruptcy proceedings commenced as main proceedings under the EIR.

80 The High Court set aside this bankruptcy order on appeal by Mr. Vlieland-Boddy. The judge in the High Court (Mann J) stated that the relevant time for determining a debtor's centre of main interests or the existence of an establishment was the date of the hearing of the bankruptcy petition or the date of presentation of the petition. Even though it was clear that Mr. Vlieland-Boddy's centre of main interests was England in October 2003, there was evidence before the court that Mr. Vlieland-Boddy was now living and working in Spain. Mann J thought that the registrar had been wrong to look at the position during the period when the debt was incurred and held that Mr. Vlieland-Boddy's main centre of interest was Spain, not England and Wales. Further, merely by being a director and shareholder of an English company did not amount to Mr. Vlieland-Boddy having an "establishment" in England, and therefore secondary proceedings could not be opened against him either. Mr. Shierson appealed against this decision.

81 The Court of Appeal held that a debtor's centre of main interests had to be determined at the time that the court in question was required to decide whether to open insolvency proceedings, and there was nothing in the EIR to prevent a debtor from changing its centre of main interests from time to time. The question was then how much weight is to be given to historical fact or, as Chadwick LJ put it, how ready should the court be to accept that a debtor can change its centre of main interests between the time it incurs debt and the opening of insolvency proceedings. Chadwick LJ stated that the determination has to be made in light of the facts as they are at the relevant time for determination, including historical facts which had led to the position as it is at the time for determination. In making the determination, the court had to have regard to the need for the centre of main interests to be ascertainable by third parties so that the legal risks to which creditors would be subject in the event of the debtor's insolvency can be evaluated in advance. As such, the centre of main interests has to have some element of permanence. As Chadwick LJ said[38]: "The court should be slow to accept that an established centre of main interests has been changed by activities which may turn out to be temporary or transitory". Equally, a debtor is free to choose where he carries on the administration of his interests and there is no outright prohibition on changing the centre of main interests. However, where there were grounds for suspicion that a debtor had sought deliberately to change his centre of main interests in order to alter the insolvency rules that would apply to him in respect of existing debt, the court would need to be satisfied that

- the change that occurred was a change based on substance and
- not an illusion and that the change had the necessary element of permanence.

82 On the facts of this case, the Court of Appeal held that in light of the above, it was impossible to say that Mann J was not entitled to reach the conclusion that Mr. Vlieland-Boddy had permanently moved his centre of main interests to Spain. However, the Court of Appeal also held that, by way of his interest in Unit 2A Sunrise Business Park (of which he was legal owner in February 2004, in addition to the property being rented out), Mr. Vlieland-Boddy possessed an "establishment" in England for the purposes of Article 3(2) of the EIR. As such, the bankruptcy order was restored subject to a variation

[38] At paragraph 55 (3).

that the bankruptcy proceedings in England were changed from main proceedings to secondary proceedings.

Interestingly, Longmore L J and Sir Martin Nourse considered that it was at least arguable that the correct date for determining a debtor's centre of main interests was the date of the service of the bankruptcy petition on the debtor rather than the date of the hearing of the petition, though on the facts of this case it made no difference to the outcome. Their reasoning was that this interpretation would make it difficult for a debtor to change its centre of main interests in the time between service of a petition on it and the hearing of that petition, which could take several months. This view has now been endorsed by the ECJ and will therefore have to be followed by the English courts. In *Susanne Staubitz-Schreiber*[39], the ECJ ruled that a debtor's centre of main interests must be assessed on the date that the application to open insolvency proceedings is filed. This is the case even where the debtor moves his centre of main interests to another Member State of the EU after the filing but before insolvency proceedings are opened. This interpretation is consistent with the intention that the EIR prevent debtors from "forum shopping". **83**

5.3.3 Secondary proceedings

The EIR anticipates that there can also be secondary proceedings where a main insolvency proceeding has previously been opened. The secondary proceedings must always be winding-up proceedings, although, as noted in 5.2 above, that latter category now includes an English law administration provided that it is for the purposes of winding up the debtor company. In order for the English courts to make an order for secondary proceedings in relation to a company which has its centre of main interests in another EU Member State, the company must have an establishment within England and Wales. Establishment is defined as: **84**

"any place of operations where the debtor carries out a non-transitory economic activity with human means and goods."[40] **85**

Bearing in mind the "sufficient connection" test explained at 3.1 above, this necessity for an "establishment" would appear, therefore, to apply a more narrow test to the ability of the English courts to make a winding-up order in relation to a foreign company where that company's centre of main interests is within the EU than if it is outside. As yet, there are no reported cases considering this anomaly. **86**

As a general rule, the English court retains the right to wind up any company incorporated in England, and would usually do so even where the majority of the company's assets and business are conducted in a different country. As mentioned above, the EIR appears to provide that the English courts would not have jurisdiction to wind up an English incorporated company where the centre of main interests of that company is elsewhere and the company has no "establishment" in England and Wales. There is, as yet, no direct judicial interpretation of this provision. However, given the current trend for businesses in Germany, Belgium and some other European countries to incorporate English companies with a view to carrying on business within their own countries (in order to avoid much higher costs of incorporating companies in their own jurisdictions), this matter may come before the English courts for a decision before too long. **87**

The courts which have jurisdiction to open main proceedings also dominate the winding-up or reorganisation process. Article 4(2) of the EIR provides that it is the laws **88**

---

[39] 17 January 2006 (C-1/04).

[40] Art 2 (h) of the EIR.

of the principal state which will determine, amongst other things, which assets form part of the estate; the powers of the liquidator and the debtor; conditions in which set-off may be invoked; the effect of insolvency on current contracts and proceedings brought by other creditors; rules governing lodging, verification and admission of claims; distribution of proceeds from realisation of assets and the ranking of creditor claims; the conditions for and effects of closure of insolvency proceedings, in particular by composition; and rules for the voidness, voidability or unenforceability of acts detrimental to creditors. In these circumstances, the law of the jurisdiction in which main proceedings were opened applies and must be given effect across the EU. There are exceptions to this, in that rights *in rem* are governed by local law, as are rules in relation to immovable property and certain other local rights.

89 Where secondary proceedings are opened, such proceedings are limited to the assets available in that state and the proceedings will be governed by the local law of the jurisdiction in which they were opened. There have, as yet, been few cases where an English company has been subject to secondary proceedings. However, because of the primacy of main proceedings under the EIR (and the law of jurisdiction opening those proceedings), there have been conflicts arising out of the English courts taking jurisdiction to open main proceedings in respect of companies incorporated in other Member States.

5.3.4 Cross-jurisdictional conflicts

90 The EIR does not contain express provisions to resolve conflicts between the courts of different Member States where both consider themselves to be the appropriate jurisdiction for the opening of main proceedings. The EIR relies on these courts to exercise the principals of mutual trust and recognition on which the EIR is founded. As Recital 22 to the EIR states:

91 "This Regulation should provide for immediate recognition of judgments concerning the opening, conduct and closure of insolvency proceedings which come within its scope and of judgments handed down in direct connection with such insolvency proceedings. Automatic recognition should therefore mean that the effects attributed to the proceedings by the law of the State in which the proceedings were opened extend to all other Member States. Recognition of judgments delivered by the courts of the Member States should be based on the principle of mutual trust. To that end, ground for non-recognition should be reduced to the minimum necessary. This is also the basis on which any dispute should be resolved where the courts of two Member States both claim competence to open main insolvency proceedings. The decision of the first court to open insolvency proceedings should be recognised in the other Member States without those Member States having the power to scrutinise the court's decision".

92 In the *Daisytek* case referred to above, the commercial court of Pontoise in France decided to put the French subsidiary of Daisytek into administration proceedings *(redressement judiciare)* in France, despite the fact that the French subsidiary was already in administration in England. The English administrators appealed against this judgment, but their appeal was declined. The French court's opinion was that, just because the holding company of a group was in England, this did not give the English court jurisdiction to open insolvency proceedings against the French subsidiary. The concept of a group of companies had no legal standing and each company was a separate legal entity. Accordingly, only secondary proceedings could be opened in England against the French subsidiary.

Fortunately for the future of the EIR, the Court of Appeal in Versailles reversed this decision, holding that the only test for deciding where main proceedings can be opened is the question of where the debtor's centre of main interests is. The court stated that, if the English court considered there was enough evidence to rebut the presumption that the French subsidiary's centre of main interests was in France (and that it therefore had jurisdiction to open main proceedings by reason of its centre of main interests being in England), then Article 16 of the EIR provided that such a judgment must be recognised in all Member States[41]. In accordance with Article 17 of the EIR[42], the English administration order produced the same effect in France as it did in England, without the need for any further formalities (unless and until secondary proceedings were opened in France). This ruling confirms the principle that once main proceedings have been opened in one Member State, no other Member State has jurisdiction to open main proceedings in respect of the same company. **93**

The French court made a similar decision in the *MG Rover* case, refusing to open main proceedings in respect of MG Rover's French subsidiary on the basis that main proceedings had already been opened in England. These decisions show that the French court is willing to use the principal of mutual respect and recognition on which the EIR is based to accept the primacy of main proceedings and the possibility that each company within a group of companies can be held to have the same centre of main interests. It is hoped that the courts of all Member States will follow this lead. However, similar problems have occurred in jurisdictions other than England and France, and sometimes the courts of those jurisdictions have been unable to solve the problem between themselves using judicial comity. **94**

5.3.5 The approach of the English courts to the "race to the courthouse" difficulties

Shortly after their appointment in the *MG Rover* case, the administrators made an application to court regarding the practical difficulties occasioned by the international jurisdiction provisions of the EIR. By virtue of the administrations proceeding as main proceedings, the national sales companies were subject to the English administration regime, rather than the local law of each companies' jurisdiction of incorporation. It was possible, by virtue of Article 3(2) of the EIR, for secondary proceedings to be opened in respect of each national sales company, as each company possessed an establishment within its territory of incorporation. However, because such proceedings must be winding-up proceedings[43], there was the risk that the main proceedings would be conducted with the aim of rescuing the business as a going concern (as administrations in England) and the secondary proceedings conducted with the aim of immediately closing down the business and realising and distributing its assets. **95**

Norris J. handed down a written judgment on 11 May 2005. In that judgment, he accepted that the powers of the administrators should be set out in a court order, so that the administrators could show this order to the various insolvency practitioners in the **96**

[41] Article 16(1) of the EIR states "Any judgment opening insolvency proceedings handed down by a court of a Member State which has jurisdiction pursuant to Article 3 shall be recognised in all other Member States from the time that it becomes effective in the State of the opening of proceedings ..."

[42] Article 17(1) of the EIR states "The judgment opening the proceedings referred to in Article 3(1) shall, with no further formalities, produce the same effects in any other Member State as under this law of the State of the opening of proceedings, unless the Regulation provides otherwise and as long as no proceedings referred to in Article 3(2) of the EIR are opened in that other Member State".

[43] Article 3(3) of the EIR.

secondary proceedings in order to explain what powers are conferred upon English administrators and what effect the administration had on the rights of third parties in the different jurisdictions. This was highly unusual. An administration order is usually very brief, merely stating that the named administrators are appointed and whether they are to act jointly or individually. Third parties dealing with the administrator are expected to know or be able to look up the statutory provisions setting out their powers. However, this English approach was quite alien to some other jurisdictions, and so the court was also able to assist by making the order in a non-standard, but more helpful form.

97 The court also addressed a specific question of the administrators relating to the various employees of the national sales companies. Article 4(2)(g) and (i) state that claims which are lodged against an insolvent company's estate, rules governing the distribution of proceeds from the realisation of assets and the ranking of claims are matters to be determined by reference to the law of the Member State in which the main proceedings are opened. In this case, this was England by reason of the administration orders made by Norris J in April 2005. Accordingly, the employees of any particular national sales company could only make claims in the administration in accordance with English insolvency law, which does not treat the claims of employees as favourably as some other jurisdictions within the EU. However, if secondary proceedings had been opened against a national sales company, then the law applicable to those secondary proceedings would be that of the Member State in which the secondary proceedings are commenced. An employee of the national sales company could then make such claims against the national sales company as would be allowed in its jurisdiction of incorporation. Norris J. was clearly concerned by this.

98 "The result of this disposal of international jurisdiction under the EU Regulation is that there will be strong pressure from those most favourably treated under local law for the commencement of secondary local proceedings. But the inevitable consequence of that will be the unco-ordinated destruction of the individual businesses in the separate secondary proceedings, and the frustration of the purpose of the primary proceedings, which is the preservation and rescue of the businesses (or their orderly and co-ordinated wind-down with a view to maximising realisations in each)."[44]

99 The question was therefore whether the administrators of a national sales company were able to make payments to the employees of that national sales company in excess of their strict entitlement under English insolvency law. If this was possible, then the desire for such creditors to commence secondary proceedings would be reduced. Paragraph 65 of Schedule B1 of the Insolvency Act 1986 allows an administrator to make distributions to creditors of the company over which he is appointed. Paragraph 13 of Schedule 1 of the Insolvency Act 1986 states that the administrators have power to make any payment which is necessary or incidental to the performance of the administrator's functions. Norris J. stated that this paragraph has conventionally been regarded as enabling the administrators to secure the provision of goods and services for the purposes of administration rather than as authorising a distribution to creditors, though the terms of the paragraph did not in fact confine it to such payments. In any event, the administrators could rely on paragraph 66 of Schedule B1 Insolvency Act 1986 which provides that "the administrator of a company may make a payment otherwise than in accordance with Paragraph 65 or Paragraph 13 of Schedule 1 if he thinks it likely to assist achievement of the purpose of administration". The court held this paragraph

[44] Paragraph 10.

intended to confer the widest powers on an administrator and to supplement the already wide powers of distribution and payment conferred on administrators elsewhere in the Insolvency Act 1986. Further, there was previous authority for allowing administrators to make payments in excess of what the beneficiaries of such payments were entitled to be paid under English law. Previous case law showed that it was possible to make payments to certain creditors which are of benefit to the overall administration even though in doing so those creditors will receive more than they would be strictly entitled to under English law. The court held that the administrators accordingly had the power to make the payments under paragraph 66 and therefore did not need to make any application to court for permission to make payments to foreign employees in this situation. Whilst this led to the anomaly of French employees, for example, receiving presumably greater payments in the English proceedings than their English counterparts, by avoiding secondary proceedings, all creditors received a better outcome.

This concept was considered further in the *Collins & Aikman* case[45]. The Collins & **100**
Aikman group was a supplier of automotive components, with 24 European subsidiaries spread over 10 countries. The group also carried on business within the US, where Chapter 11 proceedings were opened on 17 May 2005. On 15 July 2005, administration orders were made in respect of 24 European group companies on the basis that each of the subsidiaries had its centre of main interests in England. The companies consisted of a Luxembourg holding company, six companies in England and Wales and companies in Spain, Sweden, Germany, Belgium, Italy and The Netherlands. Many of the functions of the group were organised on European-wide basis, and accordingly the administrators adopted a co-ordinated approach to the continuation of the businesses, to the funding of the administrations and to the sale of the businesses and assets of the group, considering that such an approach would lead to the best possible returns to creditors. The administrators were concerned that, should creditors in local jurisdictions be successful in having secondary proceedings opened against any of the European companies, this would make it very difficult to continue to trade the businesses and conduct sales processes on a group-wide basis. To avoid such proceedings, the administrators gave assurances to creditors in the European jurisdictions that, so long as there were no secondary proceedings in the relevant jurisdiction, the creditors' financial positions under the relevant local law would be respected in the English administrations, so far as this was possible. In the main, creditors went along with this proposal and secondary proceedings were only opened in three of the subsidiaries' jurisdictions of incorporation. The administrators considered that this enabled them to realise approximately $ 45 m more than they estimated they would realise.

The administrators then sought directions from the English court as to how the $ 125 m **101**
available for distribution to creditors of the European companies should be distributed, bearing in mind the assurances that they had given the creditors previously. The problem was that the assurances the administrators had given included performance by them of differing provisions of local laws in the various jurisdictions, for example, regarding assessment of which creditors qualified as preferential, and these provisions were different from the provisions of English law, the law of the main proceedings. The administrators took the view that, in line with the decision of the court in the *MG Rover* case, if the English courts gave appropriate directions, full effect could be given to the assurances notwithstanding that this would involve payments to creditors which, had the assurances not been given, would have been alien to or inconsistent with English law.

---

[45] [2006] EWHC 1343 (Ch).

The Court held that the question of whether the administrators were able to honour the assurances given should be considered under three possible routes:

102 *The rule in Ex Parte James*

This is a rule of English law dating back over 100 years, first stated in the case of *Re Condon, Ex Parte James*[46]. The rule essentially states that, as administrators are officers of the Court, an administrator must act in an honest, honourable and high-minded way. Case law developed this principle to the extent that officers of the court must act in an honourable way even if in certain situations this means overriding rights which persons may otherwise be entitled to on a strict application of the rules of law. Lindsay J considered previous cases where the rule had been invoked to allow office holders to honour a previous promise even if a worse realisation to creditors or shareholders would occur as a result of the application of the rule. He decided that the rule could be used to permit an administrator to honour a promise (such as the assurances to creditors) which had procured a better realisation to creditors. However, the rule could not be used where statutory provisions (either expressly or by implication) clearly precluded the course of conduct which the rule would otherwise have supported.

103 *Legislation*

Lindsay J considered the provisions of paragraphs 65 and 66 of Schedule B1 and Schedule 1 of the Insolvency Act 1986, referred to above in relation to the *MG Rover* case. Lindsay J had concerns about the use of paragraph 65 in the circumstances. He considered that, by way of its reference to section 175 of the Insolvency Act 1986 (which deals with preferential debts in an English liquidation), the distribution under paragraph 65 must be restricted to those creditors which were characterised as preferential creditors under English law. Because the distributions to be made pursuant to the administrators' assurances were to be made in jurisdictions which had different provisions as to what constituted a preferential creditor, it would take detailed and time-consuming investigation to establish which creditors would, applying English law, be regarded as preferential. However, he considered that paragraph 65 need not be considered further as paragraph 66 gave the administrators the power to make the distributions to creditors of the European subsidiaries in accordance with their earlier assurances. At the time the administrators gave the assurances to the creditors, there was no doubt that the administrators considered that the giving of those assurances was "likely to assist achievement of the purpose of administration" within paragraph 66. This was because the assurances were made so that no secondary proceedings would be opened, thus potentially jeopardising the co-ordinated sales process of the group as a whole. Lindsay J stated that he did not consider that the legislation intended to create a difference between the administrators' thoughts at the time of giving the assurance and the time of performance of the assurance, nor that it made any difference that in this case the administrators had not given the assurances in contractual form. The court also stated that there was nothing in Article 3 of the EIR which precluded circumstances where local laws may have to be respected rather than the law of the main proceedings.

104 *The inherent jurisdiction of the Court*

The court considered various authorities which stated that the English courts had an inherit jurisdiction to control the actions of administrators. However, all those

[46] (1874) LR 9 Ch App 609.

authorities were prior to the coming into force of the Enterprise Act 2002, which contains many provisions which prescribe what the administrators are or are not able to do in various circumstances. Whilst the Court's inherent jurisdiction would not be eliminated by the statutory provisions, in exercising the inherent jurisdiction the court must look carefully at what the legislation stated and apply its inherent jurisdiction alongside that. The court did not consider it necessary to pursue a more detailed examination of the interaction between statute and the inherent jurisdiction of the Court as in these circumstances, the administrators had power under the statute[47] to make the necessary distributions to comply with the assurances which they had given to creditors.

Accordingly, the court held that it had jurisdiction to direct the administrators to implement the assurances which they had given to creditors and could depart from the ordinary application of English insolvency law in order to do so, even though English law was the law in the main proceedings. **105**

These cases highlight again the willingness of the English court to interpret English law to give practical working to the provisions and ideals of the EIR. It seems likely that the English courts will continue to utilise the provisions of English statutes, together with their inherent jurisdiction and the rules of common law, in order to reduce the pressure to begin secondary proceedings being applied by creditors in overseas jurisdictions. However, these cases can only apply at present in relation to administrations. Whether a court would be as willing in a liquidation to disapply the statutory order of payment of creditors remains to be seen. **106**

5.3.6 Protocols

The EIR has only been in effect for three years and is still at an early stage of development in these trans-European cases. Furthermore, the courts of some countries in Europe have been rather less willing than the English courts to embrace the effects of the EIR and have taken a rather more narrow view of EIR's effect on their own domestic laws (though there are signs this may be changing). In a number of cases, secondary liquidations have been opened and the administrators in the UK have had to work with those liquidators, with varying results. We are not aware of another court sanctioned protocol such as those in *BCCI* or *MCC* being used in relation to a European group of proceedings, although this may well become something necessary in cases where the provisions of the EIR are insufficient to deal with specific issues. We are aware, however, that protocols are being established to act as an informal framework for how the liquidators in specific main proceedings and secondary proceedings will work together within the provisions of the EIR. **107**

One example of such a protocol was that used to assist the pan-European insolvency of the Sendo group of companies[48]. Sendo International Limited ("Sendo") was a company incorporated in the Cayman Islands, which was registered as an overseas company in England and Wales. Sendo's centre of main interests was in England and main proceedings were opened in England on 29th June 2005. Sendo also had branch offices in several countries throughout the EU (and indeed the world), including France. Secondary proceedings were subsequently opened in France and, although there were no specific problems with the operation of the EIR between the English administrators and French liquidator, it was thought sensible to draft a protocol which would outline how the English administrators and the French liquidator intended the proceedings, and their **108**

[47] ie paragraph 66 of Schedule B1 Insolvency Act 1986.

[48] Drafted by the Paris and London offices of White & Case.

mutual cooperation, to work in practice within the framework of the EIR. The protocol covered the practical workings of issues such as the claims of the French creditors of Sendo and the remuneration of the French liquidator, and was registered in the commercial court in Nanterre. We anticipate that such protocols will become increasingly utilised to fill the gaps in the EIR.

6. Annex: SENDO-Protocols of 29. May 2000

109

PROTOCOL AGREEMENT FOR THE COORDINATION OF A MAIN

INSOLVENCY PROCEEDING WITH A SECONDARY INSOLVENCY PROCEEDING

FILED IN CONFORMITY WITH EUROPEAN REGULATION n° 1346-2000 of 29 May 2000

WITNESSETH THE PARTIES HERETO:

That, by a motion on 20 June 2005, the directors of SENDO INTERNATIONAL LIMITED filed before the High Court of Justice in London an insolvency proceeding under Article 3 of the European Regulation on Insolvency Proceedings 2000 (n° 1346/2000) of May 29, 2000 (hereinafter the «(EC) **Regulation**») against SENDO INTERNATIONAL LIMITED,

That by order of 29 June 2005, the High Court of Justice, Chancery Division of London, ruled in favor of the application of a proceeding of judicial administration *(Administration)* to SENDO INTERNATIONAL LIMITED and appointed Alastair P Beveridge and Simon J Appell as Joint Administrators. The appointment of the Joint Administrators was extended to 28 December 2006 by order of the High Court of Justice, Chancery Division, on 20 December 2005.

In a motion filed on 6 July 2005 with the Examining Magistrate of the Commercial Court of Nanterre, the Joint Administrators requested the opening of a secondary proceeding of insolvency against the French establishment of SENDO INTERNATIONAL LIMITED in conformity with Article 29 (a) of the (EC) regulation,

That under a decision dated 3 August 2005, the Commercial Court of Nanterre ruled in favor of the application of a secondary proceeding of judicial liquidation *(liquidation judiciaire)* to the French establishment of SENDO INTERNATIONAL LIMITED and appointed SCP BECHERET-THIERRY-SENECHAL in its capacity as liquidator and Mr. Jérôme MANDRILLON in his capacity as judge in charge of the proceedings,

That this insolvency proceedings is a secondary proceedings under Articles 3.2 and 3.3 of the (EC) Regulation,

WHEREAS:

The Joint Administrators and French Liquidators have come to understand that the (EC) regulation establishes only very general operating principles,

Consequently, the Joint Administrators and the French Liquidators have concluded that they wish to enter into an informal agreement for the purpose of defining a practical means of functioning which would allow for the efficient coordination of the two insolvency proceedings and would respect the general operating principles established by the (EC) regulation,

This protocol is established in respect of the insolvency of SENDO INTERNATIONAL LIMITED only, and the particular circumstances of this company. It is not intended to create a binding precedent and should not be considered appropriate for all other secondary proceedings in France pursuant to the EC Regulations, however may be regarded indicative of achieving good practice. It is established for the purposes of implementing such operating means by the Joint Administrators and the French Liquidators agreeing to act in conformity with the following principles:

- Mutual trust,
- Adherence to the duty to communicate information and to cooperate as defined by Article 32 of the (EC) regulation,
- Precedence of the main proceeding over the secondary proceeding.

THEREFORE THE PARTIES NOW HEREBY AGREE:

That there is a genuine need to establish a practical means of treating the liabilities (I) and the assets (II) of the French branch of SENDO INTERNATIONAL LIMITED.

I- PRACTICAL MEANS OF TREATING THE LIABILITIES OF SENDO INTERNATIONAL LIMITED

I-1. Practical means of treating notification sent to the creditors of SENDO INTERNATIONAL LIMITED

The obligation to notify the creditors is regulated by Article 40 of the (EC) regulation, which holds that «*As soon as insolvency proceedings are opened in one Member State, the court having jurisdiction in such State or the liquidator appointed by such [court] shall immediately inform known creditors who have their habitual residences, domiciles or registered offices in other Member States*». This article further specifies the content of such notification.

Consequently, given the relative lack of precision of Article 40 of the (EC) regulation, the parties consider that this protocol must specify the means of implementation of this article. The practical means agreed upon by the parties are as follows:

• The Joint Administrators in the main proceeding, having a direct contact with the manager and the accounting departments of SENDO INTERNATIONAL LIMITED, as well as direct access to the entirety of the accounting documents of this company, will notify by regular mail and in conformity with the terms and conditions of Article 40.2 of the (EC) regulation all of the debtor's creditors based in France, without exception. Such notice shall be in the form of an individual notice and shall set forth the required formalities and penalties provided by English law and applicable to the main proceedings. It has been agreed in this instance, following the appointment of the French Liquidators, that all French claims are to be notified to the French Liquidators following which the French Liquidators will then make one overall claim in the Administration.

• The French Liquidators shall send a notice:

– To the Joint Administrators in order for them to be able to implement, under Article 32.2 of the (EC) regulation, the overall claims lodged under the main proceedings;

– To any possible liquidators appointed in the context of secondary proceedings filed against SENDO INTERNATIONAL LIMITED in other Member States of the European Union;

– To all known creditors only of the secondary establishment, including those possibly residing abroad, and a list of such creditors shall be provided to the French Liquidators by the head of such establishment. The creditors thus notified shall be qualified as «local» in this protocol agreement. The creditors not known to the secondary establishment shall not be notified by the French Liquidators.

This notice shall respect both Article 40.2 of the (EC) regulation and the terms and conditions of French law, applicable only to the secondary proceedings. Such notice shall specify all of the time periods and formulae to be observed as well as any penalties that may be incurred by creditors and/or foreign liquidators appointed in other secondary proceedings under French law in the case of failure to lodge a claim or the tardy lodging of claims with the liquidator.

The Joint Administrators and the French Liquidators shall exchange their lists of creditors in France that have been notified in order to identify those who have been so notified by both the Joint Administrators and the French Liquidators.

I-2. Practical means of treating the claims lodged by the creditors of SENDO INTERNATIONAL LIMITED

– Under Article 32.1 of the (EC) regulation, any creditor may lodge on its own behalf its claim in the main proceedings and in the secondary proceedings.

– Under Article 32.2 of the (EC) regulation, the Joint Administrators and the French Liquidator must in principle produce the global amount of liabilities claimed with such Joint Administrator or the French Liquidators to the other proceedings. The Joint Administrators and the French Liquidators are nonetheless exempted from such production when such production is not in the interest of the creditors it represents. In the case of SENDO INTERNATIONAL LIMITED, the assets previously situated in France were of minimal value.

Accordingly, the Joint Administrators, given regular notification by the French Liquidators in conformity with I-1 hereinabove, are exonerated from production to the secondary insolvency proceeding of the liabilities for the proceeding for which it was appointed given the poor assets included in the scope of the secondary proceeding. Redistribution among creditors is not possible in the secondary proceeding; therefore the lodgment of claims by the Joint Administrators in the secondary proceedings holds no interest for the creditors they represent.

The French Liquidators must however and given the interest that such represents for the «local» creditors, produce to the Joint Administrators appointed under the Main proceeding, the amount of claims lodged with it.

In conformity with the same rules and regulations, the French Liquidators will produce this amount to all secondary proceedings filed or to be filed against SENDO INTERNATIONAL LIMITED within European territory.

Each of these such productions shall be accompanied by a list providing the names of the creditors with claims which make up this debt. As per Article 41 of the (EC) regulation, in addition to the names of each of these such creditors, the list must also state the creditor's address, the amount and nature of the claim lodged and any possible security interests, or other encumbrances attached thereto.

I-3. Practical means of verification of claims made against SENDO INTERNATIONAL LIMITED

I-3.1. Independence of the proceedings of verification of the liabilities

Whilst it is preferred that each party shall verify the amount and the form of the claims made directly to each such party in conformity with the applicable national legislation, in the case of SENDO INTERNATIONAL LIMITED, it was agreed that the French Liquidators would collect details of claims and subsequent to verifying same, would provide a listing of proved debts to the Joint Administrators.

In conformity with Articles 4.2 (h) and 28 of the (EC) regulation, such verification shall be made independently in conformity with the national legislation applicable to each of the two insolvency proceedings.

I-3.2. Dual-Verification Obligation

Given the European dimension of the insolvency proceedings in question, each of the Joint Administrators and the French Liquidators must check and double check, for each of the claims accepted by each of them if such claim has not been filed twice under I-2 hereof in conformity with Article 32 of the (EC) regulation.

Such verification shall be made by each of the Joint Administrators and French Liquidators by using the list of creditors which is to be annexed to the production made to the other Joint Administrator or French Liquidators in conformity with Article I-2 hereof.

Each claim lodged twice by the foreign liquidator in conformity with Article 32.2 of the (EC) regulation on the one hand and by the creditor itself in conformity with Article 32.1 of the (EC) regulation on the other hand, may be counted only once in the liabilities total for each of the insolvency proceedings.

Each Joint Administrator or French Liquidators shall thus ensure that it does not make multiple distributions to the same creditor in the insolvency proceeding to which it has been appointed.

I-4. Treatment of Legal costs

Article 30 of the (EC) regulation foresees only the theoretical instance of the opening of a secondary insolvency proceedings if the debtor's assets are sufficient to cover in whole or in part the costs and expenses of such proceedings.

Internal French law does not require such financial coverage in the context of French insolvency proceedings prior to the opening of such proceedings.

Nevertheless, to the extent where the opening of the secondary proceeding was requested by the Joint Administrators in conformity with Article 29 of the (EC) regulation, it is hereby stipulated and agreed by the parties that Article 30 of the (EC) regulation shall be applicable.

The financial burden of all legal costs in connection with the opening of the secondary insolvency proceeding filed on French territory, and specifically the fees due to the French Liquidators for the actions and rates for such established by Decree n° 85-1390 of 27 December 1985 setting the remuneration and rates for judicial liquidators in the context of judicial liquidation and bankruptcy proceedings for companies shall be borne from the assets of SENDO INTERNATIONAL LIMITED as an expense of the administration in England. It has been agreed that in the case of the secondary proceedings of SENDO INTERNATIONAL LIMITED, the fees payable as expenses of the administration in England shall be subject to a limit of € 3604,05, to be determined by the judge.

The actions and tariffication for such under Decree n° 85-1390 of 27 December 1985 for the practice of the mission of judicial liquidator are as follows:

- verification of claims lodged (art. 13)
- establishment of statements of wages due (art. 14)
- recovery of the assets created by actions initiated or pursued by the judicial liquidator (art. 18)

Furthermore, the French Liquidators will receive, under Article 12-1 of the Decree n° 85-1390 of 27 December 1985, a fixed fee in the pre-tax amount of 2,287.00 € to be paid from the assets of SENDO INTERNATIONAL LIMITED as an expense of the administration in England.

The amount of the fees that the French Liquidators will receive for its actions, the rates for which are established under Decree n° 85-1390 of 27 December 1985, is set by the judge having jurisdiction in conformity with Articles 16 and 22 of Decree n° 85-1390 of 27 December 1985.

Coverage of the fees of the French Liquidators under the secondary proceeding defined by the application of Decree n° 85-1390 of 27 December 1985 are subsidiary in the event where the recovery of assets included in the scope of the secondary proceeding would allow for all or part of such coverage.

II- PRACTICAL MEANS OF TREATING THE ASSETS OF THE FRENCH BRANCH OF SENDO INTERNATIONAL LIMITED

II-1. Treatment of the recovery of assets in time

II-1.1. Preparation of the transfer by coordination between and among the various proceedings

In conformity with the principles defined by the (EC) regulation:

• The sections of Article 31 of the (EC) regulation relating to the obligation to cooperate and inform, provide that:

– Each Joint Administrator and French Liquidators establishes individually, prior to any disposition of such, a list of assets, limited to those assets in France, entering into the scope of the proceeding for which such Joint Administrator or French Liquidators has been appointed. Once established, this list is produced to the other Joint Administrator or French Liquidators.

– The Joint Administrators shall provide to the French Liquidators in the secondary proceeding, at the earliest opportunity and in any case after receipt of the list cited above, proposals concerning the assets of the debtor in France in conformity with Article 31.3 of the (EC) regulation.

• Article 33.1 of the (EC) regulation provides that the Joint Administrators may request of the court where the secondary proceeding was filed to stay for a three-month period, which period shall be renewable, all judicial liquidation proceedings carried out in the context of the secondary proceeding.

• Article 28 of the (EC) regulation provides that the law applicable to the secondary proceeding is the law of the Member State within whose territory the proceeding was opened.

The parties hereto accept and agree to apply harmoniously the following principles:

– In order to privilege the best means of recovery of the assets of SENDO INTERNATIONAL LIMITED in France or to enable their use in support of adoption of a winding-up arrangement or any comparable measures, the Joint Administrators undertakes not to request, for a three-month period from the date of the pronouncement of the filing of the secondary proceeding, the stay of liquidation proceedings within French territory by the French Liquidators.

An extension of such delay may be made upon agreement by both of the parties hereto.

– In compensation for and, again, to allow a possible transfer of all of the assets, or a winding-up arrangement, the French Liquidators undertake not to proceed, for the same (renewable) three-month period, with the forced recovery of assets entering into the scope of the secondary insolvency proceeding.

If the recovery of such assets is required of the French Liquidator prior to the expiration of this (renewable) three-month period, the French Liquidator shall notify the Joint Administrators that this latter may request the Commercial Court of Nanterre to stay liquidation proceedings in conformity with Article 33 of the (EC) regulation.

– As soon as it has established the list of inventoried assets, and no later than two months from the pronouncement of the opening of the secondary proceeding, the French Liquidators shall produce such list to the Joint Administrators.

– Within one month from the receipt of such list, the Joint Administrators shall submit to the French Liquidators its recovery proposals, and will request the French Liquidators' opinion as to such. If the proposals include all or part of the assets falling under the scope of the secondary proceeding, it must in any case respect, with regard to the recovery of such assets, the provisions of French law, in conformity with Article 28 of the (EC) regulation.

In the absence of agreement, and subject to a stay of the secondary proceeding upon the Joint Administrators' request in conformity with Article 33 of the (EC) regulation, the French Liquidators will recover the assets in the scope of the secondary proceeding in conformity with applicable French law.

II-1.2. Operating proceedings for the disposal of the assets

The proposals that the Joint Administrators in the Main proceeding, makes, must be taken into consideration by the Commercial Court of Nanterre, but are in no way binding; the Commercial Court of Nanterre has supreme jurisdiction to rule on the destiny of the assets included in the scope of the secondary proceeding, opened within French territory.

In the event where the Joint Administrators submits to the French Liquidators a proposal for the global transfer including all assets included in the scope of the secondary proceeding, the French Liquidators will submit such proposal, along with its opinion as to such, to the French court having jurisdiction to authorize or order the transfer of these assets.

In the event where the proposal submitted by the Joint Administrators receives the approval of the French court having jurisdiction to authorize the transfer of the assets included in the scope of the secondary proceeding, the decision of the judge in charge of proceedings (in the case of transfer of isolated assets) or the decision of the Court (in the event of transfer of the business) ruling on the transfer of these assets will appoint the taking-over party selected in the context of the main proceeding. The acts of transfer of the assets shall go through the French Liquidators in conformity with applicable French legislation.

II-2. Treatment of the distribution of the income from the recovery of the assets

Article 20.2 of the (EC) regulation aims to protect equal treatment for each category of creditors by excluding any creditor who has obtained a dividend in one of the insolvency proceedings from distributions made in the context of another proceeding when creditors of the same rank or category as that creditor have not received, in the other proceeding, an equivalent dividend.

Articles 4.2 (i) and 28 of the (EC) regulation provide that operations concerning distribution of the income from the recovery of assets included in the scope of the secondary proceeding are governed by French law.

The parties hereby stipulate that the income from the recovery of assets included in the scope of the secondary proceeding shall be paid, including in the event of a total transfer of the assets as defined in II-1 hereof, to the French Liquidators to be deposited with the *Caisse des dépôts et consignations* for later distribution to those creditors whose claims were entered as a liability in the accounts in the secondary proceeding.

In order to avoid the risk, incurred by the plurality of insolvency proceedings, of granting a creditor an amount that is greater than his or her receivable, each Joint Administrator or French Liquidator is required to send to the other Joint Administrators or French Liquidators of the other proceedings, main or secondary:

– after the payment of sums, the list providing the names of the creditors who have received a dividend. This list shall provide the name and address of each of the creditors paid, the amount and nature of the claim and the amount of the dividend paid.

– prior to any payment, the draft distribution plan based on which the payment of dividends will be made. The Joint Administrators or the French Liquidators to whom this draft is sent shall respond to such within fifteen days from the date of receipt of such draft. Failure to respond within this time period shall be considered as acceptance of the draft plan.

The Joint Administrators or the French Liquidators who carries out the distribution shall enter such amounts as have been paid and notified to him by his foreign colleagues.

In Paris, on June 1, 2006

In 5 original counterparts,

signed by the French liquidators

the Joint administrators

Before Mr. Jérôme MANDRILLON, Bankruptcy Judge with the Commercial Court of Nanterre

Application of the European Insolvency Regulation in Hungary

Characteristics of Hungarian Insolvency Law Particularly in Respect of Issues Relating to Proceedings Opened Pursuant to the EIR

Contents

Index

1. Introduction

1.1 Historical Evolution

The economic boom at the end of the 19th century forced nearly all European countries to enact bankruptcy laws to meet the needs of the developing markets. This was no different in Hungary, which at that time belonged to the Austro-Hungarian Monarchy. 1

The Hungarian Insolvency Act was enacted in 1881 and remained in force until the middle of the 20th century. Certain parts of it are still found in the modern laws today.

2 The post-World War II political regime was reluctant to officially admit that bankruptcy existed at all. For this reason, the communist state attempted to resolve the problem of bankruptcy of state-owned companies and cooperatives in a number of different ways. One common way was to merge companies that were generating losses with prosperous ones. However if worst came to worst, or when large state-owned companies were involved, the state undertook their financial rescue; an economic institution appointed by the state would then attempt to restore stability through an injection of state-funded capital.

3 From 1987 to 1992, a draft-like act based on the **Insolvency Act of 1881** was in place to regulate liquidation proceedings. This act was very incomplete as it failed to provide a remedy for failing enterprises. In practice, the only possibility open to such enterprises was to dissolve the company without a legal successor and distribute its assets amongst the creditors.

1.2 Hungarian Bankruptcy Proceedings

4 The **objective of Insolvency Act XLIX of 1991** (Insolvency Act[1]) on bankruptcy, liquidation, and dissolution proceedings, which is still in force despite a large number of amendments, was to fill this gap: after many decades, insolvency proceedings were introduced once again.

5 The **aim of a bankruptcy proceeding**[2] is to allow the debtor, by declaring bankruptcy, to request a stay from the court in order to enter composition proceedings with his creditors. The proceedings take place out of court, and rather than seeking a reorganisation of the debtor, the parties are provided with an opportunity to enter into an agreement. If an agreement is reached, the debtor is no longer bankrupt and is able to resume his activities; if an agreement is not reached, liquidation may be ordered. The Act naturally contained detailed provisions concerning liquidation proceedings as well, adopting practical solutions for use in conjunction with them.

6 Both Acts deal, however, exclusively with companies; it is still not possible today to open insolvency proceedings in Hungary **in respect of natural persons** (private bankruptcy), private entrepreneurs or non-governmental organisations ("NGOs")[3]. There is no doubt that a modification to the law is needed to allow the opening of insolvency proceedings against such private individuals. Otherwise, there is a risk of social tension particularly amongst individuals. In addition to extending the scope of applicability of the Act to private individuals, an immediate solution should be sought to resolve the inconsistencies found within the Insolvency Act itself and between the Insolvency Act and other statutes, and to remedy the deficiencies found there since both of these problems cause increased difficulty for the activities of companies. Although the new Insolvency Act has been in existence in draft form for years, until it actually enters into force, the most urgent issues are expected to be dealt with through amendments.

---

[1] Bankruptcy and Liquidation Act XVIX, 24.9.1991.

[2] The Hungarian concept of bankruptcy proceedings can be compared to the austrian composition proceedings. The proceeding against an illiquid company, which is usually associated to the concept of bankruptcy, is called unvoluntarily liquidation in hungarian law.

[3] I.e. generally any non-profit association of persons organized for a certain period of time that is not organized by any state (governmental) body, is not dependent on the state, and operates on a voluntary basis.

Needless to say, there is urgent need for action in this area of economic law. In addition to considering the internal problems in this area, the provisions of Council Regulation (EC) No 1346/2000 and the experience gained in conjunction with Hungarian cross-border insolvency cases must also be taken into consideration. This becomes increasingly important in light of the fact that the insolvency acts and legal solutions of the various countries initially give rise to interpretation problems only, but, as time goes on, these become sources of real conflict. Questions of interpretation should undoubtedly be clarified at international level. **7**

2. Insolvency Proceedings Pursuant to the Hungarian Insolvency Act

2.1 Bankruptcy and Liquidation Proceedings

The present Insolvency Act makes provision for two kinds of insolvency proceedings: **8**

- **bankruptcy proceedings** and
- **liquidation proceedings**.

Considering the extremely small number of **bankruptcy proceedings** that have been opened recently in Hungary (less than 50 per year for the entire country), it is safe to say that for all intents and purposes that kind of proceeding does not exist. One reason for this is that the bankruptcy proceeding does not provide immediate protection to the debtor – as the debtor can only be granted the stay well after the publication of commenced proceedings – and the legal provisions cannot be complied with and implemented. Other reasons are the absence of strict civil and criminal law sanctions for failing to timely commence the proceedings (until recently there were no rules governing the duties of chief executives[4]), and it is difficult to prove in a criminal proceeding that the assets have been hidden.

The problem here is not only that the proceedings do not function properly, but that the law does not provide for any alternative (e.g. reorganization, debt-equity-swap, or any other means) for the financially distressed debtor enterprise to negotiate a joint solution with its creditors. **9**

This situation also has an impact on the economy. If there is no regulated way to deal with a bankruptcy, the owners of enterprises may seek to protect their assets in an "unregulated" manner. This may not necessarily mean preserving the enterprise, but rather the transferring its assets to, or channelling its business activity into another company, etc. Since, as a rule, creditors lack information, they generally discover where the assets have gone only after it is too late to take appropriate action. In the absence of documentation, it is also extremely difficult, if not impossible, to prove the facts necessary to obtain an equitable remedy. **10**

2.2 Liquidation Proceedings

For these reasons the **liquidation proceeding** is practically the only insolvency proceeding in Hungary today. It may be commenced by the debtor, a creditor, or certain official authorities pursuant to a special procedure. The overwhelming majority of liquidation proceedings are, however, opened by creditors. **11**

---

[4] The Insolvency Act was amended on July 1, 2006 in respect of the duties of chief executives. Since the amendment is so recent, it is uncertain just how the provisions will be applied. However, the authors have many misgivings about these rules.

12 The proceeding consists of two easily distinguishable phases:

- In the first phase the court examines whether the debtor is insolvent from the point of view of the creditor who commenced the liquidation proceedings. According to the Act[5], insolvency is a question of liquidity, and it allows for the opening of a liquidation proceeding if (a) the debtor fails to settle a debt that he did not contest or acknowledge within 60 days from its due date, (b) an execution ordered against the debtor is unsuccessful, or (c) he fails to meet the obligations assumed in the composition proceedings made pursuant to the bankruptcy proceedings (this last reason, however, needs not be seriously considered since there are practically no bankruptcy proceedings in Hungary). Clearly then, it is very simple to ascertain insolvency.
- The second phase of liquidation proceedings begins once a court's decision to order liquidation proceedings after a finding of insolvency this decision comes into force; from this point on, the debtor's management bodies are divested of their powers. The court's decision confers on the appointed liquidator the sole power to make decisions concerning the assets – he is both empowered and obligated to collect and sell the debtor's assets, and to distribute the proceeds amongst the creditors in accordance with the **compulsory satisfaction order** (ranking of priority of claims, see mn 19). Insolvency proceedings, whose objective is to remove insolvent debtors from the economy, generally function according to the same pattern in all countries.

2.3 Characteristics of Hungarian Liquidation Proceedings

2.3.1 Debtor's Liquidity

13 When a liquidation proceeding is opened, the court examines the debtor's liquidity. Various laws contain different approaches to try and resolve the problem of the opening of proceedings in cases in which the debtor still has assets that which could **satisfy creditors' claims**; care must be taken in such cases, as it is undesirable to liquidate viable companies. One approach would be for the court to compare the **debtor's assets** and the **creditors' claims** with the help of a practitioner. (The disadvantage here is that the process is slow, lengthy, and uncertain as to whether the debtor's assets will be accurately valued compared to market prices at the time of sale). The Hungarian Insolvency Act generally takes another approach: it examines only the non-payment of concrete claims. Although this approach is undoubtedly quicker and clearer, one of its disadvantages is that creditors often use liquidation proceedings to collect their claims, since it is a much more effective weapon against debtors who are reluctant to pay than are litigation proceedings. It does not always have a negative effect, since creditors are able to collect their debts much more quickly if they are able to use the threat of liquidation proceedings than if they had to wait for litigation or execution proceedings; this also improves the liquidity of the creditors' business enterprises. As a result of this phenomenon, the courts competent for liquidation proceedings are overburdened, since liquidation proceedings are not the only cases they handle. (They are also responsible for legal suits, execution proceedings). For this reason, proceedings take much longer.

14 Another disadvantage of this system is that, if a debtor fails to pay attention to his bookkeeping, liquidation proceedings may be opened against him even if his assets are actually much greater than his liabilities, i.e. when he is not bankrupt, but merely inattentive.

---

[5] The recent amendments have also modified the requirements for establishing insolvency. It is now more difficult for creditors to establish insolvency for the purposes of opening liquidation proceedings.

2.3.2 Deletion Procedure

The court opens the proceeding against all debtors – provided that insolvency can be ascertained – irrespective of whether they have assets or not. The principle underlying this norm is that even insolvent companies must terminate their activities in a regulated and controlled manner. This principle was somewhat distorted, however, by the earlier laws which provided that **"mail box" companies** (companies that have disappeared from their registered office and other addresses) should be deleted from the company register without a settlement, but the problems which arose in such cases forced this **deletion procedure** to be made stricter. (The problem is the absence of laws on managerial responsibility; steps have already been taken, and further steps are expected to be taken, to remedy this situation.) 15

2.3.3 Notice of Proceedings and Distribution to the Creditors

The court publishes a notice in the **official gazette** that liquidation proceedings have been opened (this will soon be available on the **Internet** as well). The creditors are invited to lodge their claims with the liquidator within 40 days. In order to be recognized as a creditor, it is necessary to pay the finance department of the court a fee of 1% of the claim (minimum HUF 1,000 and maximum HUF 100,000[6]). This charge may be reimbursed to the creditor if the debtor has as a large amount of assets. (The amount is collected in order to cover the liquidator's minimum fee in cases where the debtor has no assets). The lodging of claims is preclusively barred one year subsequent to publication. The debtor's assets are distributed first to the creditors who lodged their claims within the initial 40 day period; once these have been fully satisfied, a distribution to the extent possible based on the debtor's assets is then made to the creditors who lodged their claims after initial the 40-days, but prior to the end of the one year period. 16

2.3.4 Separation of Encumbered Property from Debtor's Assets

Secured creditors are not allowed to separate encumbered property (collateral) from the debtor's assets; encumbered property is sold by the liquidator and what remains is distributed amongst the creditors after deducting costs. The Act currently gives priority to secured creditors who secured their claims at least one year prior to the commencement of liquidation proceedings; they are guaranteed a payment of 50% of the price attained from the sale of the encumbered property even if there are no other assets to cover the **liquidation expenses**; it is expected in future that secured creditors will be favoured even more.[7] It is quite certain, however, that encumbered property will remain under the administration of, and realized by, the liquidator as part of the debtor's assets. 17

2.3.5 Relationship Between the Liquidator and the Creditors

The relationship between the liquidator and the creditors in the opened liquidation proceedings is unclear. Although the liquidator's position is not clearly outlined in the Act, the role creditors play in the proceedings is even more unsettled. As a result of the ambiguous wording of various court decisions, the status of the **liquidator** is quite curious since sometimes he is regarded as the debtor's representative, and sometimes as an individual in his own right with all the consequences resulting from this. At the same 18

---

[6] 1 EUR = 254, 63 HUF on March 5, 2007.

[7] The latest amendments to the Act also favour the claims of secured creditors.

time, based on the wording of the Act, one can say that once liquidation proceedings begin, practically no one controls the administration of the assets taken over by the liquidator. Also, the Act confers only negligible powers of supervision upon the court decisions only in the case of legal disputes between the parties or in respect of a review of the **annual financial accounts**. In addition, the creditors have no power to control the way the liquidator administers the assets. The Act is also inconsistent in respect of the composition of the creditors' committee, although the committee may be afforded some power. Individual creditors, however, may ask the court to revise their own claims, but only in respect of their recognition and classification in terms of order of satisfaction (ranking); they have no actual power respecting the administration of the assets. Therefore, the fate of the assets, and ultimately the extent of the satisfaction of the creditors' claims, will to a large degree depend on the liquidator's capabilities and honesty.

2.3.6 Order of Satisfaction

19 The **order of satisfaction** (ranking) of the creditors' claims is quite complicated and reflects the influence of various lobby groups. This applies not only to the original ranking of priority, but also to the amendments thereto. The new Act is expected to simplify the situation,[8] i.e. there may be fewer classes of creditors to be considered for the ranking order.

3. Adoption and Application of the EIR

20 On May 1, 2004, Hungary became a fully-fledged member of the European Union. In order to adopt Regulation (EC) 1346/2000 of 29 May 2000 (hereinafter „Regulation"), and to eliminate its inconsistencies with the Hungarian Insolvency Act, the Insolvency Act has been modified to the extent required. However not all amendments have turned out to be appropriate and finding a clear wording is not always possible due to the various approaches taken by the Member States. The creativity of legal professionals will certainly be called for here.

The following examines the **issues** and the various approaches taken to them.

3.1 Scope of Application of the EIR

21 The first important modification was that, apart from an itemized listing of the sphere of application of the Insolvency Act, **main and territorial proceedings** were allowed to be opened in Hungary against companies incorporated in other Member States of the European Union provided that the conditions set out in the Regulation are satisfied. The **scope of application** is restricted in this respect as well: private entrepreneurs, individual persons, NGOs, other associations, or churches may not be debtors in insolvency proceedings in Hungary. As a result of the modification, the circle of debtors may be extended to involve in a proceeding not only companies incorporated in other Member States, but also those which are incorporated outside of the Member States but whose **centre of main interests** (COMI) is within the European Union. This would bring the definition of COMI used in the Regulation in line with that of the Insolvency Act.[9]

---

[8] The amendment will not completely solve the complication of the priority ranking of the creditors' claims.

[9] The amendment will resolve the issue in this manner.

3.2 Jurisdiction and Publication Procedure

A request to **open main or territorial insolvency proceedings** against a company incorporated **in another Member State** can be made only to the **Metropolitan Court of Budapest**, and it is the task of that court to order publication of the request in accordance with Article 21 of the EIR based on the liquidator's request. According to the Regulation, the liquidator can request the publication of the decision opening the insolvency proceedings and the decision appointing him in accordance with the **publication procedure** stipulated by the given Member State. Since such publication is performed in Hungary by the court, a court had to be appointed to carry out this task. The two cases in this area so far have raised the issue as to how the court ordering the publication or how the potential creditors are to gain knowledge of the different proceedings of the various Member States. In the first case[10], a so-called **administration proceeding** was conducted in another Member State, and according to the announcement made by the liquidators, the proceeding commences by the court receiving the application – the filing of the application was even confirmed by the court – so there was no need for a court decision to open the proceeding, i.e. there was no court decision to open the insolvency proceedings or to appoint the administrators. The court ordered publication based on the application, it being obvious however that it cannot have knowledge of all of the procedural regulations of all the Member States and must, therefore, trust the information provided by the liquidator. Should it turn out later that the information provided was incorrect, the liquidator will of course be liable. **22**

3.3 Registration of the Opening of Insolvency Proceedings

Another problem arose in a proceeding[11] based on Article 22 of the EIR in a somewhat different way (according to the law, the Metropolitan Court of Budapest was exclusively competent in this proceeding as well). A liquidator who had been appointed in a bankruptcy proceeding that had been opened in another Member State (Germany) against a private individual requested the court to register the opening of bankruptcy proceedings in Germany on the title of the private individual's real estate in Hungary. The court complied with the request and, based on its decision, the bankruptcy proceeding was registered on the real estate. This registration, however, made it impossible for any one to dispose of the real estate afterward. The purpose of registering the opening of insolvency proceedings is to keep properties of the company intact until it has been determined whether to proceed with a composition or with a sale of assets by the Hungarian liquidator. The effect in this case, however, was not only to prevent the debtor from selling the real estate himself, but also to prevent the German liquidator from disposing of it. The reason is that the effect according to the Hungarian Act on real estate registrations, gives from the registering of the opening of liquidation proceedings is that, from then on, only a Hungarian liquidator may dispose of the real estate. Although insolvency proceedings against a private individual in another Member State are recognized in Hungary, there is no equivalent Hungarian proceeding since it is not legally possible to open insolvency proceedings in Hungary against private individuals. The proceeding conducted abroad simply cannot be translated in a way that reflects its original meaning. According to Art 22 of the EIR, the court has to respond to the request for registration, but registration will go beyond its intended purpose and results in a perma- **23**

---

[10] Metropolitan Court of Budapest 4.5.2005, Fővárosi Bíróság; Eufpk. 01-05-000001/5.

[11] Metropolitan Court of Budapest 13.9.2004, Dauerheim v. Guth, Fővárosi Bíróság; Eufpk. 01-04-000001/6; see also *Marshall* European Cross Border Insolvency, No. 2.080.

nent "freezing" of the property according to Hungarian law. How could this problem be resolved?

24 In Hungary, Register authorities administer the registers autonomously. Thus, one possible solution may be for the court that is ordering the registration to explain to the authority that administers the register how it must treat the registration according to the national laws, i.e. explain what proceeding in the national laws most closely resembles the foreign proceeding as far as its legal effects are concerned. In the given example where it employed this solution, the court had to examine the nature of **the powers conferred on the liquidator** by the court of the Member State that ordered the main proceeding against the individual person. After comparing this with the provisions of its own national laws, the court could then instruct the registrar on the legal consequences and allow him to implement the registration with the interpretation of the court. Therefore not only the registrar, the liquidator, and the debtor, but also everyone else who wishes to acquire rights connected to the real estate will have a clear understanding of the registration – a solution that strengthens credibility and transparency.

3.4 Powers of a Temporary Liquidator

25 Another issue related to Article 22 of the EIR arose in the same proceedings, namely, the powers of the temporary administrator in another Member State. In a proceeding against an individual, the court of the other Member State immediately appointed a temporary administrator with extensive powers who, in this capacity, after assessing the debtor's assets, initially requested registering the proceedings opened in the other Member State against the real estate in Hungary. According to Article 38 of the EIR, a temporary administrator can take measures in order to preserve and maintain assets in another Member State. But since the temporary administrator is unknown to Hungarian law, and the Hungarian Insolvency Act does not empower a temporary administrator to commence a registration procedure, the registration had to wait until the temporary administrator became the **final liquidator**.

3.5 First Experiences of Cross-Border Proceedings

26 In respect of cross-border proceedings, on the debtor's request, the Hungarian court has for the first time ordered the liquidation of a company incorporated in Slovakia, the court having come to the conclusion that the debtor's centre of main interests was in Hungary.[12]

Once again problems arose from discrepancies between the different proceedings available under the various acts, as well as translating them. The literal translation of the Hungarian word "**felszámolás**" is "liquidation", which European law has taken from the Latin term meaning liquidation and termination. However, in Slovakia, a proceeding called a "liquidation" does not mean that the debtor is insolvent, but rather that he merely wishes to terminate his business activities – the owner decides to end his activities and, through its executive bodies, distributes the amount remaining after satisfying the creditors to the owners (this is very much akin to **dissolution proceedings** in Hungary).

27 The first phase of the liquidation proceeding was marked by the liquidator's struggle to have the powers conferred on him by the Hungarian Insolvency Act recognized. Although

[12] Metropolitan Court of Fejer/Székesfehérvár, 14.06.2004, Fővárosi Bíróság; Fpk. 01-04-002916/15, Metropolitan Court of Budapest, 14.6.2004, see *Csia/Martinez Ferber* ZInsO 2004, 861.

the liquidation was registered in the **company register** after a lengthy proceeding at the Court of Registration, the change in the powers of representation on behalf of the company was not. The Hungarian Act, which governed in this case, transfers the relevant powers of representation including powers to dispose of assets, i.e. as affecting third parties, from the chief executive to the liquidator, and this change is registered in the company register. The insolvency law and the corporate procedural system of Slovakia differ from this, and although the liquidator was registered and, after a lengthy struggle, was able to exercise the powers conferred on him by the Hungarian Act in Slovakia, this was not apparent to third parties inspecting the company register there. This is in blatant contradiction to Article 4 (1) of the EIR which states that the law of the Member State where the proceeding was opened is to be applied to the insolvency proceeding and its legal effects. According to Articles 16 (1) and 17 (1) of the EIR, the legal effects of an opened proceeding must be recognized in all other Member States, i.e. in the case under discussion it should have been recognized that the liquidator replaced the debtor's chief executive in respect of powers of representation. However, the law of the other Member State concerned Slovakia does not allow for this.

The other problem was that since pursuant to Article 4 of the EIR Hungarian law **28**
had to apply to the proceedings, the court published the notice to invite creditors to lodge their claims in the Hungarian Official Gazette. Creditors acknowledged by the debtor were invited by the liquidator to lodge their claims based on Articles 40 and 42 of the EIR, but what about potential, unknown creditors from other Member States? A computerized listing of all the insolvency proceedings opened in all the Member States is urgently needed. This would enable a search for proceedings and, apart from providing notification to creditors, would enable them to obtain information about what they need to do, what powers and liabilities they have, what procedural actions are expected, etc.

In the case under discussion, theoretical problems arose in the interpretation of the **29**
Regulation with respect to the **main insolvency proceedings**. Since these can arise at any time, they should be discussed here.

A – primarily technical – problem may arise in connection with the reporting of the **30**
proceedings in the financial (accounting) statements. Not only insolvency acts vary in the different countries, but financial reporting regulations as well. The Hungarian Insolvency Act expressly prescribes a breakdown (itemization) of the balance sheet. The balance sheet of an enterprise that is incorporated and reporting in another Member State may have to be revised not only in terms of the form of its reporting, but also with respect to currency (except if both Member States belong to the Euro zone).

In the case of cross-border proceedings, the liquidator needs to take special care **31**
selling the debtor's assets. The Hungarian Act contains compulsory regulations in this regard. The liquidator must comply not only with these provisions, but also with those stipulated by the Member State in which the debtor wishes to have the sale recognized (Article 18 (3) of the EIR). In the case of particular kinds of property, such as securities, real property, and motor vehicles, the various Member States may have enacted special provisions that the liquidator must also take into consideration.

In case of cross-border proceedings, the order of satisfaction (ranking) of claims is **32**
carried out differently. Once the liquidator has mastered the aforementioned problems, the most important part of the proceedings from the point of view of the creditor has arrived: where does the creditor rank for the satisfaction of his claim(s), and which form should this satisfaction take? Creditors will generally be ranked according to the laws of the Member State that governs the proceeding; however, this rule is superseded by

Article 5 (1) of the EIR, which provides that "the opening of insolvency proceedings shall not affect the rights in rem of creditors or third parties in respect of tangible or intangible, moveable or immovable assets belonging to the debtor which are situated within the territory of another Member State at the time of the opening of proceedings, ...", and Article 5 (2) (a) of the EIR, which states: "the rights referred to in paragraph 1 shall in particular mean: the right to dispose of assets or have them disposed of and to obtain satisfaction, in particular by virtue of a lien or a mortgage". Thus, the Regulation excludes encumbered property from the debtor's assets if it is situated in a Member State other than the one in which the proceedings are taking place. The Regulation therefore supersedes the order of satisfaction (ranking) provisions of the Hungarian Insolvency Act since, as already mentioned, the Hungarian Insolvency Act provides that encumbered property forms part of the liquidation assets to be sold by the liquidator. If the opening of insolvency proceedings in the Member State, where the encumbered property is situated, hinders the secured creditor from exercising his rights in such property, then there is only one way to defeat the effect of Article 5 (1) of the EIR: the liquidator of the main insolvency proceedings must open secondary insolvency proceedings as quickly as possible and prevent the encumbered property from being realized. However, this is only possible when there is an establishment of the debtor in the Member State in which secondary insolvency proceedings should be opened.

33 Rights in encumbered property that is situated in a Member State other than the one in which the main insolvency proceedings are opened raises another issue: must a secured creditor become a creditor in the main insolvency proceedings, i.e. does he have to lodge a claim in the main insolvency proceedings taking place in another Member State, even though his right to be satisfied ensues from the property itself? This issue is also worth considering, as it has become increasingly common for the courts to regard the centre of main interests as not the place where the company carries out its activities, but rather the place where the business and financial decisions are made, in effect, the owner's residence/registered office. It may, however, happen that main insolvency proceedings are opened in a Member State that is more advantageous for the owners, whilst the debtor's assets – perhaps encumbered – are situated in a different Member State. If as a result of this situation, the opening of the main insolvency proceedings does not affect the right of the secured creditor to be satisfied from the encumbered property in another Member State – and according to Article 5 of the EIR it certainly does not – it would seem that the effects of the main insolvency proceedings, in terms of their extending to the entire territory of the European Union, is restricted particularly in light of the aforementioned Article 5 of the EIR.

What happens if the secured creditor does not exercise his rights? What is the timeframe for him to do so?

3.6 Jurisdiction Issues

34 In the case discussed above[13], the Hungarian court opened main insolvency proceedings against an enterprise incorporated in another Member State. The reverse situation has also occurred, i.e. main insolvency proceedings were opened in another Member State against a company incorporated in Hungary, and a Hungarian creditor initiated the opening of the **secondary insolvency proceedings** in Hungary. The question arises as to whether the Metropolitan Court of Budapest has exclusive jurisdiction to open the

[13] Fővárosi Bíróság; Fpk. 01-04-002916/15, Metropolitan Court of Budapest, 14.6.2004, see *Csia/Martinez Ferber* ZInsO 2004, 861.

secondary insolvency proceedings, or whether the request in Hungary must be made to the court with jurisdiction in respect of the **registered office of the company**; the latter court would then decide[14] whether a part of the debtor's company can be regarded as an establishment within the meaning of the Regulation, and therefore whether secondary insolvency proceedings can be opened. According to the law in force, the exclusive jurisdiction afforded the Metropolitan Court of Budapest only applies in respect of enterprises incorporated in another Member State of the European Union, and since the debtor is incorporated in Hungary, there is no **exclusive jurisdiction**; the issue of jurisdiction is then to be decided pursuant to the general provisions on jurisdiction in the Insolvency Act.

If the court with jurisdiction for the establishment comes to the conclusion that the **35**
debtor does not carry out any activities in Hungary with human means and goods (Article 2 (h) of the EIR), then court must deny the request to open the insolvency territorial proceeding. If the requisite establishment does exist there, secondary insolvency proceedings must be opened.

On the surface, it may appear quite easy for foreign managers and corporate owners **36**
to have a company liquidated in a Member State other than the one in which the actual business activities are being performed, that is, in an insolvency regime with whose rules they are familiar. In our opinion, however, the risk of criminal law sanctions, and the uncertainty in other Member States regarding the various regulations concerning corporate executives, has not yet been fully examined. In some Member States, the provisions governing the corporate responsibility of the executive members are rather strict, whilst others prove to be quite lenient. If a company is transferred from a Member State with more relaxed regulations to one with stricter regulations, and main insolvency proceedings are opened in the latter, the executive member in a lawsuit pursuant to the strict rules may be held liable for not having initiated the opening of the proceedings earlier. The criminal law provisions of such a strict regime would also be applicable.

[14] Metropolitan Court of Budapest 10.7.2005, Fővárosi Bíróság; Fpk. 01-05-002932.

The Use of Protocols in Cross Border Insolvency Cases

Contents

Index

1. Overview

1 The purpose of this chapter is to look beyond the law as it relates to the restructuring of an international enterprise and consider how to give practical substance to aims and intentions of the law makers, while at the same time delivering real and sustainable recovery and reconstruction remedies for businesses in difficulty.

2 The point of departure will be the law itself and the particular circumstances under which it is created. Then the default role of the practitioner will be overlaid before moving on to consider the use of protocols as part of the solution. Finally this chapter concludes with a look at the key features of a successful protocol.

2. The Law of the Land

3 It is common practice for many practitioners, especially lawyers, when handling a case in a new territory to reach first for the local law. But the law itself is rarely sufficient to get beyond a preliminary understanding. Not only is the law embedded in the local

culture and enmeshed with other laws, it is often silent on the very detailed practical points that make the difference between success and failure.

It is easy to blame this void on the cloistered world of the draftsmen, drawing as they do on the equally cloistered world of academia to create a law to deal with the world as they imagine it. It is true that this reality is a factor, and one can be sure that the world as anyone imagines it will not be the world as it truly is when the time comes for implementation. Hence, the draftsmen proudly presented the new French law[1] designed to allow consensual restructuring only to find that they had not allowed for the increasing tendency of creditors to sell down their debt into the hands of new players with completely different agendas.[2] **4**

However, one must also have sympathy with the draftsman. Not only is the future shape of commerce impossible to predict, the law itself necessarily has to include compromises. These compromises are required to allow for both political and legal harmony and to cover as many possibilities as can be imagined at the time of drafting. **5**

Two of the most common compromises are reflected in the use of the word "or" and the omission of matters that are subject to material disagreement between the parties. **6**

Nowhere is such inability to predict and need for compromise a problem as much as it is in the creation of international insolvency laws. It is at this point when the whole panoply of historic, cultural and political issues arrives with a thud on the table of negotiation. **7**

Examples abound, but in the sphere of insolvency there are two major legislative initiatives to handle international restructuring: the European Union Cross Border Insolvency Regulation[3] and the UNCITRAL Model Law.[4] The former began as a project in the 1960s, ran the gauntlet of successive enlargement of the Union, became sidetracked by totally extraneous political matters[5] and changed status from a convention to a Regulation before finally seeing light in 2000 for enactment on 31st May 2002. In the process it was substantially changed and above all shrunk to a shadow of its former self to accommodate the compromises necessary to get it onto the statute books. **8**

For example: **9**

Art 2 (d):

"'court' shall mean the judicial body or any other competent body of a member state empowered to open insolvency proceedings or to take decisions in the course of such proceedings ..."

One impact of this tortuous sentence is on a regime such as the UK that routinely allows bodies other than a court in the normally accepted use of the term to open or take decisions during an insolvency. The board of directors of a UK company may very well qualify as a court under the definition in art 2 (d). Equally the liquidator may qualify since he or she takes decisions in the course of proceedings. **10**

The main feature of the Regulation is the idea that the jurisdiction used for the purpose of winding up a company should be that of its Centre of Main Interest – now **11**

---

1 Passed by parliament on 13th July 2005, published 27th July and into force from 1st January 2006.

2 According to insiders this has been a particular feature of the Eurotunnel restructuring.

3 1346/2000.

4 UN resolution 15/158 dated 15th December 1997.

5 Including the dispute over the sovereignty of Gibraltar and the question of control of "Mad Cow" disease.

universally referred to as its CoMI. The negotiations to produce the caps regulation resulted in the definition getting whittled down to one short sentence:

"In the case of a company ... the place of the registered office shall be presumed to be the Centre of Main Interest in the absence of proof to the contrary."[6]

12 This of course led to the inevitable question as to how one provides "proof to the contrary". Within the final emaciated text the only other place to find guidance is Recital 13.[7]

"The Centre of Main Interest should correspond to the place where the debtor conducts the administration of his interests on a regular basis and is therefore ascertainable by third parties."

13 The lack of clarity on the meaning and correct interpretation of "administration of his interests", "a regular basis", "ascertainable" and "third parties" has been a significant factor in the growth of forum shopping, the very thing that the Regulation set out to avoid[8].

14 The UNCITRAL model law fared only slightly better although compared with the EUIR it was, however, only developed in the 1990s and there is plenty of time ahead for confusion.[9] Finally passed in 1997 to great fanfare, by 2004 only seven countries had signed up to it: Eritrea, Japan, South Africa, Mexico, Montenegro, Poland and Romania. In the subsequent two years these were joined by the US[10] and the UK, so at least some of the world's largest trading nations are taking an interest.

15 Notwithstanding international law, very few judges have any familiarity with the law outside their own country. One reason is the woeful provision for funding travel and continuing education programmes on international matters in many countries. It is not unconnected that the US and UK have been the most active in pushing forward the boundaries on cross border insolvency law and are the places from which many judges have travelled to seek out their opposite numbers.

16 Ignorance[11] and, sadly, misplaced belief that local practice is superior to any foreign alternative coupled with the compromised international law has left the practitioner with a major problem.

3. Whither The Practitioner?

17 Very few practitioners make their livelihood outside their immediate legal jurisdiction. Almost certainly trained[12] in the minutiae of their own local law and practice, few will have knowledge of alternative overseas procedures. Furthermore, a significant proportion will owe their livelihood to a local court or judge or regulator with whom they will have worked on many previous cases.

---

[6] Art 3 (1) of the EIR.

[7] While strictly speaking only the 47 articles of the Regulation constitute the law, the accompanying 33 recitals are intended to guide the court in its interpretation of the articles.

[8] Recital 4 of the EIR.

[9] For a discussion of the application of the model law see Khumalo "International Response to the UNCITRAL model Law on Cross Border Insolvency" at www.iiiglobal.og/ organisations/uncitral.

[10] As Chapter 15 US Bankruptcy code.

[11] In the case of ISA France sa, the President of the Commercial Court in Cergy Pontoise, France, was not aware of the Regulation and refused to acknowledge it even when it was pointed out to him.

[12] Whether by formal education or by apprenticeship to another practitioner.

Inevitably the default mode of practitioners is to do nothing that might in any way upset or damage his or her relationship with local work providers or supervisors of his or her work. Thus, it is rare for a practitioner to argue in his local court against the application for a secondary insolvency under EUIR. Furthermore, once appointed under a secondary, a major source of disagreement will arise over the extent to which the secondary liquidator should and can restrict his work to less than that proscribed by local law and practice. Two examples will suffice: **18**

Most laws require a liquidator to examine antecedent transactions. Can that requirement be waived when another liquidator is carrying out the same work from another jurisdiction? **19**

Similarly, liquidators[13] are required to satisfy themselves as to the validity of creditor claims. Does this requirement mean that they cannot allow another practitioner in another location to agree claims on their behalf, perhaps in a different language or format?[14] **20**

Without even touching on the murky waters of professional jealousy and protection of fees, it is clear that the cooperation envisaged in the EIR[15] faces an uphill struggle. **21**

Art 31 is itself silent on what is meant by a duty to cooperate (to what extent? how?), and what the recourse might be for non-cooperation. This guidance was omitted in order to reach a compromise.[16] **22**

It is noticeable that even the highly laudable initiative known as the CoCo project[17] launched by the profession itself to try to define cooperation has run into similar pressures and in the latest draft is only a shadow of the original detailed document. **23**

Some of these issues are to be found when dealing with purely domestic matters but the really complicated problems arise in cross border cases. It is these problems that protocols are designed to overcome. **24**

4. Use Of Protocols

Protocols have been developed as a way of setting out clearly and transparently the rights, roles and responsibilities of practitioners when two (or more) are appointed by different courts to handle the same matter. Each protocol is tailored to the specifics of the particular situation and is often the result of extensive negotiation between the respective practitioners. Where appropriate – that is in practice when one or other of the **25**

---

[13] It is ironic that many of these issues arise in secondary proceedings, which under EUIR have to be liquidation proceedings. Typically the law gives far less discretion to liquidators' actions than to those of practitioners appointed in more rescue-oriented processes.

[14] Notwithstanding that all creditors of the two Parmalat companies in Germany were local Bavarian farmers, the court insisted that all claims be filed in Italian by an Italian lawyer accredited with the Parma court.

[15] Art 31 of the EIR.

[16] The dilemma is clear. If liquidator in country A thinks liquidator in county B is not cooperating but liquidator B is following local practice, the court in country B is unlikely to uphold a complaint. The court in country A cannot impose meaningful sanctions on liquidator B. Result: stalemate! This situation can arise over seemingly trivial matters such as the length of time spent dealing with a matter or the use of deputies to carry out certain work which the other liquidator would have expected the principal to do.

[17] European Communication and Cooperation Guidelines for Cross Border Insolvency developed under the aegis of the academic wing of INSOL Europe cf www.insoleurope.org or www.bobwessels.nl.

practitioners deems it necessary for his or her own protection – one or both courts may endorse the protocol. They may also be laid before various other stakeholders, especially creditors, for approval.

26 However, at a most basic level, the protocol is a private agreement between the two practitioners.

27 It is perhaps not surprising that most protocols have been created in circumstances where the underlying legal systems are broadly similar and, specifically in common law countries, where the level of discretion given to judges and practitioners is high.

28 The US in particular has been the most active in supporting protocols and has issued them in cases involving Canada,[18] UK,[19] Israel[20] and Switzerland[21], among others. A significant factor in the US's liberal use of protocols has been the traditional attitude of senior specialist insolvency judges to see through legal obstacles to focus on achieving an agreed successful outcome. The lack of protocols in other countries, especially those of the European Union conversely reflects not only the Civil law tradition but also the more junior status and lack of special expertise often to be found in continental European courts.[22]

29 Cynics would say that some protocols do little more than set areas of disagreement between competing practitioners and, in a sense merely codify that they have "agreed to disagree," but that would be to undermine the real value that protocols can provide to all concerned.

5. Protocols and EIR

30 The express desire of the EIR to see cooperation between main and secondary liquidators would appear to be perfectly satisfied by the creation of a protocol between the parties. While the Regulation itself does not mention such a possibility, the CoCo project[23] does recommend that one be put in place to cover …

… *"at the very least, the provisions for the coordination of court approval for decisions and actions whenever required and for communications with creditors as required under any applicable law. It should also include a statement of the various cross border issues to be addressed … and any questions in respect of which the liquidators are required to seek agreement in advance from the other liquidators."*[24]

31 The CoCo recommendation is a very good starting point and courts should be encouraging this basic approach in all EIR cases where two or more liquidators are involved.

32 Ideally the protocol needs to cover the following topics:

1. dividing responsibility for realising assets between the parties
2. the allocation of costs between the two estates

---

[18] Olympia & York, Everfresh and many other examples between US and Canada that predated Chapter 15 of the US Bankruptcy code. Canada and US continue to be the main source of new protocols.

[19] Maxwell.

[20] Nakash, interesting as a protocol involving the insolvency of a natural person.

[21] AIOC Resources AG.

[22] Although it should be noted that in recent times some judges, such as Judge Wallender in Cologne, are beginning to raise their profile on the international stage. Such developments are warmly welcomed as it fosters the trust and awareness that is essential to mutual cooperation between courts.

[23] Ibid CoCo Guideline 12.

[24] Ibid CoCo Guideline 12.5

3. the form of communication with creditors
4. the agreement and acceptance of creditor claims
5. the closing timetable
6. general communications

5.1 Realising the Assets

The EUIR sets out clear, if controversial rules.[25] The main point of controversy arises in respect of the third bullet, which states that claims (which has been taken to include, third party and interco receivables, bank deposits, etc.) shall be in the Centre of Main Interests of the party required to pay them. Since the third party is often not itself subject to insolvency proceedings under the regulation, the question arises as to how the CoMI for the third party is to be established. Alternatives include asking the third party to determine its CoMI, allowing one of the liquidators or one of the courts to decide. This topic is usefully covered in the protocol. 33

An additional factor under this same sub paragraph of the Regulation is the question of antecedent, voidable and/or other transactions, which may require investigating. It is possible that the action and the claim arising under that action may be in different jurisdictions and this eventuality may need to be covered under the protocol. 34

It is the location of the assets that determines the estate (main or secondary) into which the subsequent realisations will fall. However, it may be that one or other liquidator is particularly well placed to realise assets on behalf of his or her fellow liquidator because he has the resources, he has particular skills or experience or because the asset falls administratively within a bundle of assets being realised by that particular liquidator. In these circumstances the protocol needs to give the authority for the one liquidator to realise assets on behalf of, and for the estate of, the other. 35

5.2 The Allocation of Costs

This is a subject dear to all practitioners! 36

Estate costs can for this purpose be considered under three broad headings: the costs of communicating with the other liquidator, the ongoing trading costs and the liquidator's own fees and expenses in handling his part of the case. Problems typically arise when the assets in one of the estates are insufficient to cover the costs, or when the costs in one liquidation are disproportionate.

The CoCo guidelines[26] suggest that each liquidator carries his or her own costs within the estate to which he or she is appointed. Where however, one liquidator carries out work on behalf of the other, the protocol should allow for the cross charging of the related costs. This might include simple administrative tasks (e.g., translation) or more complex matters such as realising assets on behalf of the other. Furthermore, where one liquidator seeks the advice of the other (in the spirit of cooperation), there should be recognition for value in the other estate. 37

Ongoing trading costs always present a problem in any insolvency and even more so in a cross border matter. As a general rule the costs should be borne out of the estate in which they occurred. However, in circumstances where the decision to continue trading is for the greater benefit of the business as a whole, there should be a recognition within the protocol that some of the costs will have to be shared between the estates. Normally 38

[25] Art 2 (g) of the EIR.

[26] Ibid CoCo Guideline 11.

the need to continue trading has to be taken at the outset of a case, often before the protocol itself is agreed. In these circumstances the liquidators should document carefully the agreement and approvals between themselves as to the terms and extent of continuing to trade, and courts should be supportive of these agreements. Where however, trading is undertaken by a secondary liquidator without the specific agreement of the liquidator in the main proceedings the trading and attendant costs should be for the account of the secondary proceeding only.

39 The remaining costs, being principally the liquidator's own fees and the fees of his own team (including other advisers) should be for the account of his estate. There is a wide discrepancy in cost and fee structures between firms. However, it is not appropriate and certainly not helpful for liquidators to lodge objections or seek to override the fees of fellow liquidators through the mechanism of the protocol.

5.3 Communication with Creditors

40 The Creditors are the third parties who are often the most inconvenienced and penalised by the onset of insolvency proceedings. It should be part of the role of the liquidators to minimise the additional administrative burden and cost on those creditors.

41 Wherever possible, the communications with creditors should be coordinated and the protocol should allow for deviations from normal practice to allow for this cooperation. Hence, for instance, when the creditors meetings would normally be held in a court room, there should be provision for a single alternative venue (still with the judge in attendance) in which the lead parties according to each jurisdiction have equal standing. Likewise the proceedings should follow the higher level of communication between the liquidations. Hence, if one liquidation requires a creditors meeting within three months and the other within four, the three-month rule should prevail in the protocol. If one liquidation requires full disclosure of, for instance, estate receipts and payments, but it is not normal practice in the other, then such disclosure should be produced for both and on a consolidated basis. The protocol should reflect this approach, as well as the means of allocating costs associated with producing the additional information.

5.4 The Agreement and Acceptance of Claims

42 The Regulation[27] permits a creditor to lodge his claim in the main proceeding and in any secondary proceeding. However it goes on[28] to say:

"the liquidators in the main and any secondary proceedings shall lodge in other proceedings claims which have already been lodged in the proceedings for which they were appointed."

43 A cold read of this sentence might lead one to conclude that the word "not" is missing from this quote. Unfortunately it is not.

44 There are multiple problems here upon which the Regulation gives no guidance and which a protocol is almost certainly necessary to prevent confusion.

45 Article 32.1 allows the creditor to lodge more than one claim. Cleary there will be circumstances when lodging in one estate is more beneficial to the creditor than the other – for instance when to do so would permit a higher ranking. However, multiple filings require very careful coordination between the liquidators to ensure that one is not played off against the other, and to deal with circumstances where one liquidator is minded to reject a claim and the other accept. Even in straightforward circumstances it

[27] Art 32.1 of the EIR.

[28] Art 32.2 of the EIR.

should be possible to agree a procedure between the two liquidations so that only one set of proofs is required. A court approval may be required to override the normal duty of a liquidator to check every claim when the co-liquidator has done so.

The easiest way to deal with this situation is to have a protocol which **46**

a) encourages the creditors to file in one proceeding – with a professional obligation on the liquidators to guide the creditor if asked, as to the most beneficial proceeding,
b) sets up a regular communication between liquidators to compare claims received from the same creditor,
c) determines which liquidator will take responsibility for agreeing the gross quantum of each claim received by both liquidators, that is to deal with disputes such as credit notes,
d) allows the non- reconciling liquidator to be released from his or her obligation to do so, but retaining the right to disqualify the claim in its entirety or in part if local laws (eg set off) so determine.

Article 32.2 present a rather different set of problems not least because it appears to double count when taken with Article 32.1. It sets out a requirement *(the liquidators shall ...)* and that requirement is related to claims received rather than claims agreed. Furthermore the Regulation does not make it clear if the cross claim is to be subject to rigorous cross checking by the recipient liquidator, if it is to be regarded as a single homogenous claim and, where that claim might rank in both the recipient and claiming estate. There will, for instance, be claims received in liquidation A which will have a different ranking in liquidation B and vice versa. A further complication created by the English court has been the growing practice[29] of changing the order of distribution in the main proceeding to reflect local law in an attempt to avoid a secondary in another country. If that attempt is unsuccessful or a secondary is opened in a third jurisdiction it is an open question how the cross claim from the main liquidation should rank in that secondary. **47**

Finally if read literally there is a loop if the liquidator in A must claim in liquidation B for all claims received including that of the liquidator of B! The simple solution attempted in the protocol of ISA Deutschland GmbH[30] was to treat the cross claims as single homogenous claim, not subject to revalidation by the recipient liquidator and ranking as an unsecured claim in the receiving estate with the subsequent distribution ranking as available for all unsecured creditors in the claimant estate. The cross claim was to include all claims received in each estate except the cross claim from the other liquidator and such claims as were already and separately lodged in the other liquidation. **48**

This approach is by no means the intellectually perfect solution but, especially when coupled with the above suggestion re Article 32.1, does have the great merit of practical simplicity. It does however represent a deviation from both the strict letter of the Regulation and possibly the local laws too, and therefore, should be dealt with by agreement between the courts and their respective liquidators through the mechanism of the protocol. **49**

[29] MG Rover, Collins and Aikman.
[30] English main proceedings and German secondary.

5.5 The Closing Timetable

50 For all practical purposes it is better that the main proceeding is the last to close once all the aims of the various proceedings have been completed. Partly this is because of the cross claiming procedures noted above (which may not extend to successor parties if a liquidation has been closed) and partly because without a main proceeding the rules governing a secondary are far from clear.

51 However, local laws often determine the maximum length of any procedure. It follows, therefore, that the shortest such length should determine the maximum length of the combined procedure wherever possible. In circumstances where this is not possible or unlikely, the courts and liquidators should look to an agreement at the earliest possible time to prepare for the necessary extensions.

5.6 General Communication

52 In addition to the foregoing, on a regular basis there will be matters that neither the lawmakers, the courts nor the liquidators will have envisaged at the outset of the case. The solution to each of these is open and prompt communication of the type envisaged by the CoCo project. The protocol should allow for communication at the level of both court and liquidators.

6. Conclusion

53 This article has considered the Regulation from a practical perspective. It has explored the deficiencies in local and European law and, perhaps even more importantly, the systemic issues that make cross border insolvencies so challenging. Protocols are a way of creating an environment in which these challenges can be overcome or at least bypassed.

54 There are many that regard protocols as yet another ground for long drawn out negotiations and it is true that such can be the case.[31] Part of the problem is that protocols remain relatively uncommon and are specifically created on a case-by-case basis. However, with each new cross border use of a protocol comes increasing awareness of the benefits that come when all parties have clarity on each other's roles.

55 The CoCo project and the work of other organisations such as the American Bankruptcy Institute[32] and the International Insolvency Institute[33] is moving the process forward. The next step is to create a standardised protocol which will be both a template and a benchmark to facilitate a much higher level of cooperation across borders to the greater benefit of all concerned. This article has identified some of the topics that such a standard might address and until the standard is achieved some of the complications that practitioners will have to address between themselves.

[31] ISA Deutschland Protocol has taken over three years to negotiate.

[32] www.abiworld.org.

[33] www.iiiglobal.org.

PART 4

UNCITRAL

Model Law on Cross-Border Insolvency

Contents

Index

Bibliography

American Law Institute, Principles of Cooperation and Transnational Insolvency Cases Among the Members of the North American Free Trade Agreement (2003) ("Principles"); Guidelines Applicable to Court-to-Court Communications in Cross Border Cases (May 16, 2000) ("Guidelines"); *Baird* "The Hidden Virtues of Chapter 11: An Overview of the Law and Economics of Financially Distressed Firms" (March 1997) (Chicago Working Papers in Law and Economics No. 43 (2d Series)); Black's Law Dictionary (7th ed. 1999); *Breslau/Heron* Interview with then U.S. President William J. Clinton in The Debriefing: Bill Clinton, *Wired Magazine*, Issue 8.12, December 2000 *available at* http://www.wired.com/wired/archive/8.12/clinton.html (citing generally Robert Wright, Nonzero: The Logic of Human Destiny (2000)); *Bufford/Adler/Brooks/Krieger* International Insolvency (Federal Judicial Center 2001); *Bufford* "International Accord," *Los Angeles Lawyer*, at 33–41 (July–August 2006); International Bar Association, Committee J Cross-Border Insolvency Concordat (adopted by the Council of the Section of Business Law of the International Bar Association on Sept. 17, 1995, and by Council of the International Bar Association on May 31, 1996), *available at* http://www.iiiglobal.org/international/projects/concordat.pdf (last viewed Apr. 4, 2007) ("Concordat"); *Engel* Suggested Clarifications and Reforms for U.S. Chapter 15 and the UNCITRAL Model Law on Cross-Border Insolvency on Which It Is Based: The Pragmatic Cynics'

Concerns (prepared for International Insolvency Institute New York Program, June 12–13, 2006), available at: http://www.iiiglobal.org/country/usa/20060620morrison.pdf (last viewed Mar. 20, 2007); *Farley/Leonard/Birch* Cooperation and Coordination in Cross-Border Insolvency Cases (paper delivered on the INSOL conference in May 2006); *Felsenfeld et al.* A Treatise on the Law of International Insolvency (1999) ("Felsenfeld"); Memorandum re Proposed Chapter 15 of the United States Bankruptcy Code from Daniel M. Glosband to E. Bruce Leonard (Sep. 15, 2003), http://www.iiiglobal.org/international/cross_border/United_States_Daniel%20Glosband.pdf (last visited Apr. 6, 2007) ("Glosband Memorandum"); *Glosband* SPhinX Chapter 15 Opinion Misses the Mark, American Bankruptcy Institute Journal 44, 44–45, 84–85 (Dec./Jan. 2007) ("Glosband"); INSOL, Transcript of the Open Forum at UNCITRAL – INSOL International Second Multinational Judicial Colloquium (March 1997); *Moss/Smith* Moss, Fletcher and Isaacs: The EC Regulation on Insolvency Proceedings (2002); National Bankruptcy Review Commission, Bankruptcy, the Next Twenty Years, National Bankruptcy Review Commission Final Report (1997) ("NBRC Report"); *Radin* Fraudulent Conveyances at Roman Law, 18 Virginia Law Review 109 (1931); *Resnick et al.*, Collier on Bankruptcy (15th ed. rev. 1996 & Supp. 2006) ("Collier"); U.N. G.A., United Nations Commission on International Trade Law, Note by the Secretariat, Cross-border insolvency (1993) (A/CN.9/378/Add.4), UNCITRAL Yb 24 (1993) 248–253; U.N. G.A., United Nations Commission on International Trade Law, 27th Session, Report of the Secretariat, Report on UNCITRAL – INSOL Colloquium on Cross-Border Insolvency (19 May 1994) ("A/CN.9/398"); U.N. G.A., United Nations Commission on International Trade Law, 29th Session, Report of Working Group on Insolvency Law on the work of the eighteenth session (1 December 1995) (A/CN.9/419); U.N. G.A., United Nations Commission on International Trade Law, 29th Session, Report of Working Group on Insolvency Law on the work of the nineteenth session, (25 April 1996) ("A/CN.9/422"); U.N. G.A., United Nations Commission on International Trade Law, 30th Session, Report of Working Group on Insolvency Law on the work of the twentieth session, (24 October 1996) ("A/CN.9/433"); U.N. G.A., United Nations Commission on International Trade Law, 30th Session, Report of Working Group on Insolvency Law on the work of the twenty-first session, (19 February 1997) ("A/CN.9/435"); U.N. G.A., 52d Session, Report of the United Nations Commission on International Trade Law on the work of its thirtieth session, (4 July 1997) ("A/52/17"); U.N. G.A., United Nations Commission on International Trade Law, 30th Session, Guide to Enactment of the UNCITRAL Model Law on Cross-Border Insolvency (1997) (the "Guide") ("A/CN.9/442"); United Nations Commission on International Trade Law, Legislative Guide on Insolvency Law (Adopted by General Assembly on 2 December 2004) (the "Legislative Guide"); U.N. G.A., United Nations Commission on International Trade Law, 38th Session, Note by the Secretariat, Developments in insolvency law: adoption of the UNCITRAL Model Law on Cross-Border Insolvency; use of cross-border protocols and court-to-court communication guidelines; and case law on interpretation of "centre of main interests" and "establishment" in the European Union (14 April 2005) ("A/CN.9/580"); U.N. G.A., 61st Session, Report of the United Nations Commission on International Trade Law on the work of its thirty-ninth session, (14 July 2006) ("A/61/17"); U.N. G.A., United Nations Commission on International Trade Law, Note by the Secretariat, Treatment of Corporate Groups in Insolvency (4 October 2006) ("A/CN.9/WG.V/WP.74/Add.2"); Webster's Ninth New Collegiate Dictionary (1984); *Wessels* International Insolvency Law (2006); *Westbrook* Chapter 15 at Last, 79 American Bankruptcy Law Journal 713 (2005); *Westbrook* Multinational Enterprises in General Default: Chapter 15, the ALI Principles, and the EU Insolvency Regulation, 76 American Bankruptcy Law Journal 1 (Winter 2002).

1. Introduction

This part provides commentary on the Model Law on Cross-Border Insolvency (the "Model Law," or the "Law") promulgated by the **United Nations Commission on International Trade Law** ("**UNCITRAL**," or the "**Commission**"), and its particular enactment in the United States of America (the "**United States**"), a major trading partner of the European Union. The Model Law complements the EC **Regulation on Insolvency** 1

Proceedings by offering a regime for cross-border cases involving non-member states, such as the Untied States.[1]

1.1 United Nations Commission on International Trade Law

2 The United Nations General Assembly created UNCITRAL on 17 December 1966 for "the promotion of the progressive harmonization and unification of the law of international trade ...".[2] In establishing the Commission, the General Assembly sought to encourage uniformity of national trade laws to improve international trade, thereby bettering the living conditions of all peoples in order to promote friendly relations, security, and ultimately, peace.[3] UNCITRAL seeks to accomplish its mandate by preparing "international legislative texts for use by States in modernizing commercial law and non-legislative texts for use by commercial parties in negotiating transactions."[4]

1.2 Development of the Model Law

3 A suggestion that "the Commission should consider undertaking work on international aspects of bankruptcy" arose during the UNCITRAL Congress themed "Uniform Commercial Law in the 21st Century" in 1992.[5] After a preliminary discussion in 1993,[6] the Commission requested "an in-depth study on the desirability and feasibility of uniform rules" governing cross-border insolvency.[7] Before beginning work on the Model Law through its Working Group on Insolvency Law (the **"Working Group"**) in

---

1 United Nations Commission on International Trade Law, Legislative Guide on Insolvency Law (Adopted by General Assembly on 2 December 2004) (the "Legislative Guide") ¶ 19.

2 G. A. Res. 2205 (XXI), at I (Dec. 17, 1966).

3 G.A. Res. 2205 (XXI) (Dec. 17, 1966).

4 U.N. G.A., United Nations Commission on International Trade Law, 30th Session, Guide to Enactment of the UNCITRAL Model Law on Cross-Border Insolvency (1997) (the "Guide," or "Guide to Enactment"), penultimate page. Legislative texts include: United Nations Convention on Contracts for the International Sale of Goods; Convention on the Limitation Period in the International Sale of Goods; UNCITRAL Model Law on International Commercial Arbitration; UNCITRAL Model Law on Procurement of Goods, Construction and Services; United Nations Convention on Independent Guarantees and Stand-by Letters of Credit; UNCITRAL Model Law on International Credit Transfers; United Nations Convention on International Bills of Exchange and International Promissory Notes; United Nations Convention on the Carriage of Goods by Sea, 1978 (Hamburg); United Nations Convention on the Liability of Operators of Transport Terminals in International Trade; and UNCITRAL Model Law on Electronic Commerce. Non-legislative texts include: UNCITRAL Arbitration Rules; UNCITRAL Conciliation Rules; UNCITRAL Notes on Organizing Arbitral Proceedings; UNCITRAL Legal Guide on Drawing Up International Contracts for the Construction of Industrial Works; and UNCITRAL Legal Guide on International Countertrade Transactions.

5 U.N. G.A., United Nations Commission on International Trade Law, 27th Session, Report of the Secretariat, Report on UNCITRAL – INSOL Colloquium on Cross-Border Insolvency (19 May 1994) ("A/CN.9/398") ¶ 1.

6 For a fascinating and insightful insider's view of events leading to the Model Law from an American perspective, *see* Carl Felsenfeld, A Treatise on the Law of International Insolvency 5-20–5-30 (1999) ("Felsenfeld"). For an official American view, *see* Nat'l Bankr. Rev. Comm'n, *Bankruptcy, the Next Twenty Years, National Bankruptcy Review Commission Final Report* 355–56 (1997) (the "NBRC Report").

7 U.N. G.A., 52d Session, Report of the United Nations Commission on International Trade Law on the work of its thirtieth session ¶ 12 (July 1997) ("A/52/17") (citing the Official Records of the General Assembly, Forty-eighth Session, Supplement No. 17 (A/48/17), ¶¶ 302–306).

1995,[8] UNCITRAL solicited advice on the feasibility of harmonizing insolvency norms from two colloquia, from which emerged the idea of limiting the scope of the Law largely to governing cooperation among courts and representatives in cross-border insolvency proceedings, providing court access for foreign insolvency administrators and recognition of foreign insolvency proceedings.[9] The Model Law took form unusually quickly, with representatives of some 76 countries and several international groups participating in the deliberations of the Working Group and Commission.[10]

UNCITRAL adopted the Model Law on 30 May 1997.[11] As of this writing, the following States[12] have reportedly[13] adopted some form[14] of the Law: **Eritrea, Japan** (2000),[15] **Mexico** (2000),[16] **Poland** (2003),[17] **Romania** (2003),[18] **Montenegro** (2002),[19] **Serbia** (2004), **South Africa** (2000),[20] **Great Britain** (2006),[21] **the British Virgin Islands** **4**

---

[8] Guide ¶ 6.

[9] *See* Guide ¶ 5 & n. 3; U.N. G.A., United Nations Commission on International Trade Law, 29th Session, Report of Working Group on Insolvency Law on the work of the eighteenth session ¶ 3 (1 December 1995) ("A/CN.9/419"). While it recognized that maximal judicial cooperation could be effected only by means of a treaty, the Commission decided instead to begin its cross-border insolvency work with a model law, "because of its flexibility," which was thought "best suited to induce in the shortest possible time harmonized modernization of national laws in the area." A/52/17 ¶ 26.

[10] Guide ¶ 8. The Secretariat prepared the Guide based on the deliberations of UNCITRAL and the Working Group. *Id.* ¶ 10. Its purpose is to provide background, explanatory information and useful insights about the Model Law to government officials, legislators, judges, academics and practitioners. *Id.* ¶ 9.

[11] Guide ¶ 8.

[12] The term "State," as used in the Model Law and throughout this part, essentially refers to an entity capable of enacting the Law. The term "enacting State" refers to an entity that has enacted the Law. *Cf.* Guide ¶ 56.

[13] Status of 1997 – Model Law on Cross-border Insolvency, http://www.uncitral.org/uncitral/en/uncitral_texts/insolvency/1997Model_status.html (last visited June 21, 2007) (stating no date for Eritrea). There is no requirement that States report enactment. Guide ¶ 11.

[14] UNCITRAL and the Working Committee expected a relatively high degree of non-uniformity among enactments of the Model Law, because its text relates closely "to the national court and procedural system" of the enacting States, Guide ¶ 12, and may thus require considerable customizing to be appropriately adapted to the respective systems.

[15] Law relating to Recognition and Assistance for Foreign Insolvency Proceedings (Law No. 129 of 2000). U.N. G.A., United Nations Commission on International Trade Law, 38th Session, Note by the Secretariat, Developments in insolvency law: adoption of the UNCITRAL Model Law on Cross-Border Insolvency; use of cross-border protocols and court-to-court communication guidelines; and case law on interpretation of "centre of main interests" and "establishment" in the European Union, n. 3 (14 April 2005) ("A/CN.9/580").

[16] Ley de Concursos Mercantiles, D.O. 12 de Mayo de 2000 (Mex). A/CN.9/580 n. 1.

[17] Law on Insolvency and Restructuring of 28 February 2003. A/CN.9/580 n. 6.

[18] Law No. 637 of 7 December 2002 on Regulating Private International Law Relations in the Field of Insolvency. A/CN.9/580 n. 5.

[19] Law on Business Organization Insolvency, February 2002. A/CN.9/580 n. 2.

[20] Cross-Border Insolvency Act, 42 (2000), art 34 (S. Afr.). A/CN.9/580 n. 4.

[21] Insolvency Act 2000, § 14. A/CN.9/580 n. 8. The United Kingdom has enacted enabling legislation that allows for the Model Law to be implemented by regulation, which came into force in England and Wales on 4 April 2006. Cross-Border Insolvency Regulations 2006 (SI 2006 No 1030); *see also* Country Report Great Britain mn 3; A/CN.9/580 ¶ 2.

(2003),[22] **the overseas territory of the United Kingdom of Great Britain and Northern Ireland** (2005), and the **United States** (2005).[23]

1.3 Chapter 15 of the United States Bankruptcy Code

1.3.1 Enactment

5 In 1994, the Congress of the United States ("Congress") determined "there was benefit in establishing ... a commission to review the [American] bankruptcy system."[24] Therefore, pursuant to the Bankruptcy Reform Act of 1994,[25] it authorized creation of a **"National Bankruptcy Review Commission"** (the "NBRC") to:

- investigate and study issues relating to the Bankruptcy Code;
- solicit divergent views of parties concerned with the operation of the bankruptcy system;
- evaluate the advisability of proposals with respect to such issues; and
- prepare a report to be submitted to the President, Congress and the Chief Justice not later than two years after the date of the first meeting.[26]

6 The NBRC submitted its Final Report on October 20, 1997 and passed out of existence by operation of law on November 19 the same year.[27] Among other suggestions for reforms, the NBRC Report contained recommendations for quick adoption of the recently finalized Model Law, with relatively few modifications, by adding it to the Bankruptcy Code along with certain related amendments to existing law.[28]

7 After passing reform legislation that included the adapted text of the Model Law several times without enactment,[29] Congress once again voted to adopt it as **Title VIII of the Bankruptcy Abuse Prevention and Consumer Protection Act** of 2005 in March 2005,

---

[22] Insolvency Act, 2003. According to the UNCITRAL Secretariat, "The Act, which came into force in August 2004, includes provisions on cross-border insolvency (Part XVIII); this Part has not yet entered into force. Part XIX Orders in Aid of Foreign Proceedings, which has entered into force, allows applications from foreign representatives for various types of relief to aid the foreing [sic] proceedings and specifies the matters to be taken into account by the court in ordering that relief. [T]his Part includes provisions similar to those included in articles 5, 7 and 10 of the Model Law." A/CN.9/580 n. 7.

[23] It has been said that Canadian legislation relating to international insolvency was "inspired by the Model Law." Samuel L. Bufford/Louise DeCarl Adler/Sidney B. Brooks/Marcia S. Krieger, *International Insolvency* 56 (Federal Judicial Center 2001); *see also* J. M. Farley/Bruce Leonard/John N. Birch, *Cooperation and Coordination in Cross-Border Insolvency Cases* 22–36 (paper delivered on the INSOL conference in May 2006) (describing the status of Canadian law on cross-border insolvency). More information about the status of legislation related to the Model Law in various countries as of April 2005 can be found in the Note by the Secretariat on Insolvency Law, United Nations Commission on International Trade Law, Thirty-eighth session, Vienna, 4–15 July 2005, U.N. Doc. A/CN.9/580 ¶ 2 (2005); *see also* Farley/Leonard/Birch 19–21.

[24] Preface to the NBRC Report, at iv.

[25] Pub. L. No. 103–394, 108 Stat. 4107 (Oct. 22, 1994).

[26] *Id.* § 603.

[27] *Id.* § 609.

[28] NBRC Report 351–70.

[29] *See* Memorandum re Proposed Chapter 15 of the United States Bankruptcy Code from Daniel M. Glosband to E. Bruce Leonard 1–2 (Sep. 15, 2003) (the "Glosband Memorandum"). Mr. Glosband was a "primary draftsman" of chapter 15. *Id.* at 1.

and President George W. Bush approved it in April that year.[30] It is codified in large part as chapter 15 ("Ancillary and Other Cross-Border Cases"[31] or "chapter 15") under title 11 (the "Bankruptcy Code") of the United States Code[32] and became generally effective as to cases[33] filed on or after October 17, 2005. Less than three weeks after it came into force, Wolridge Mahon Ltd., the trustee in the Canadian bankruptcy of Ian Gregory Thow, filed what appears to have been the first petition seeking relief under chapter 15.[34]

1.3.2 Authorities

The following note provides an American view of sources to which this part refers. **8**

Aside from the text of chapter 15 itself, several authorities need to be considered in **9** analyzing American law on transnational insolvency. Parts of the Bankruptcy Code outside chapter 15 also apply to "**ancillary cases,**"[35] and many of its other provisions affect cross-border insolvencies in other ways, for example when a plenary American case runs concurrently with a foreign proceeding. Other important provisions of United States federal constitutional, statutory and regulatory law also have roles to play, particularly respecting jurisdiction and venue,[36] but also in resolving questions relating to claims, administration, and procedural fairness. There is also a significant body of court rules governing American practice, of which the most relevant are the Federal Rules of Bankruptcy Procedure, the **Federal Rules of Civil Procedure**[37] and, to a lesser extent, the **Federal Rules of Evidence.**[38] In addition, there are certain ethical rules related to attorney and judicial conduct that further limit and develop concepts found in chapter 15. Case law provides interpretations of the organic law, statutes, regulations and rules, all of which exist against a backdrop of authoritative common law and equity tradition.[39]

---

30 Pub. L. No. 109-8, § 801, 119 Stat. 23 (Apr. 20, 2005).

31 The chapter title "maintain[s] a nostalgic deference to [11 U.S.C.] section 304," which was titled "Cases ancillary to foreign proceedings" and governed relief in aid of foreign insolvencies until repealed with the enactment of chapter 15, while "preserving the UNCITRAL denomination 'Cross-Border,' implying a scope broader than ancillary cases and deleting the UNCITRAL reference to insolvency as superfluous in a law already entitled Bankruptcy Code." Glosband Memorandum at 1-bis.

32 Generally, the last two digits of each section number in chapter 15 correspond to the articles of the Model Law, and chapter 15's "subchapters" correspond to the Model Law's chapters.

33 For an explanation of the term "case," *see infra* mn 52.

34 *In re Thow*, No. 05-30432 (Bankr. W. D. Wash. Nov. 2, 2005) (Brandt, J.).

35 *See* 11 U.S.C. § 103 (a) (setting forth Bankruptcy Code provisions applicable to chapter 15 cases). Note that the provisions of chapter 15 itself incorporate other sections of the Bankruptcy Code in addition to those cited in section 103 (a).

36 *See, e.g.*, 28 U.S.C. §§ 157 (b) (2) (p) (governing authority of bankruptcy judges to hear chapter 15 cases); 1410 (governing venue for chapter 15 cases).

37 *See* Fed. R. Civ. P. 81 (a) (1) (Federal Rules of Civil Procedure apply to bankruptcy proceedings as incorporated by the Federal Rules of Bankruptcy Procedure).

38 *See* Fed. R. Evid. 101 (Federal Rules of Evidence generally applicable to proceedings before United States bankruptcy judges); *see also* Fed. R. Bankr. P. 9017 (same). Note that the Federal Rules of Evidence are technically statutes rather than court rules promulgated under the Rules Enabling Act, 28 U.S.C. §§ 2071–77. *See* Act of Jan. 2, 1975, Pub. L. 93–595; 88 Stat. 1926 (codified at 28 U.S.C. app. (1976)).

39 It should be noted that this tradition includes, to some extent, "international law." *See Maxwell Commc'n Corp. v. Société Générale (In re Maxwell Commc'n Corp.)*, 93 F.3d 1036, 1047 (2d Cir. 1996) (stating that "[i]nternational law, ... including ... questions arising under what is usually called

10 Finally, the federal structure of the American polity also makes the law of individual American states relevant in some contexts, particularly with respect to claims characterization, since most American contract and property law issues from the states.

11 Aside from these primary sources of law, American courts often examine secondary authorities, such as

- non-binding case law,
- legislative history and
- legal commentary.

12 The underdeveloped state of transnational insolvency law in the United States[40] enhances the significance of secondary authority to that area. Moreover, given the **novelty of chapter 15** and the fact that it has displaced the law existing under and alongside former section 304, which previously governed petitions for relief in aid of foreign insolvency proceedings,[41] one can safely say that these other authorities will receive extra attention as courts grapple with unfamiliar new concepts that are not always easy to connect to prior doctrine.[42]

13 In enacting chapter 15, **Congress** also disturbed the ordinary hierarchy of secondary material by giving unusual prominence to two of its categories. The first is the body of foreign law that corresponds in scope to chapter 15. Congress requires courts interpreting chapter 15 to "consider its international origin, and the need to promote an application of [chapter 15] that is consistent with the application of similar statutes adopted by foreign jurisdictions."[43] American courts are thus expressly obliged to take account of foreign law not only for its persuasive reasoning, or to conduct a conflict of laws or choice of forum analysis, or to apply it as *foreign* law, but also for the sake of uniformly applying *United States* law codified in chapter 15 with that of similar laws of other jurisdictions.[44] The second category, consisting of the of UNCITRAL materials related to the Model Law, also obtains its exceptional significance on account of the need to promote uniform application of laws relating to cross-border insolvency. The Report of the United States House of Representatives accompanying chapter 15 specifically notes that the Guide to Enactment that UNCITRAL produced, together with the Working Group and Committee reports it cites, will aid in interpreting chapter 15 on a "uniform basis," as they "explain the reasons for the terms used and often cite their origins as well."[45] According to the House Report, "Not only are these sources persuasive,

---

private international law, or the conflict of laws, and concerning the rights of persons within the territory and dominion of one nation, by reason of acts, private or public, done within the dominions of another nation – is part of our law," and citing *Hilton v. Guyot*, 159 U.S. 113, 163 (1895)).

40 *See Maxwell*, 93 F.3d at 1047 (noting that "[t]he management of transnational insolvencies is concededly underdeveloped").

41 How and when the older law might still apply remains somewhat unclear. *Compare* Samuel L. Bufford, *Internat'l Accord*, 29 August – Los Angeles Lawyer 33, 34 (2006) (stating that "[t]his case law applies only in circumstances not addressed by the explicit provisions of chapter 15") *with* Bob Wessels, *Internat'l Insolvency Law* ¶ 10045 (2006) (stating that "it is commonly understood that the major results of case law under § 304 will be reflected in the interpretations of Chapter 15 provisions").

42 Important secondary authorities are cited herein and listed in the bibliography. For a descriptions of some of those authorities, *see* Jay Lawrence Westbrook, *Chapter 15 at Last*, 79 Am. Bankr. L.J. 713, 714–15 (2005).

43 11 U.S.C. § 1508.

44 *See* mn 129 (discussing section 1508).

45 H. Rep. No. 109–31, 109 Cong., 1st Sess. 109 & n. 1 (2005); *see also* mn 129 (discussing section 1508).

but they advance the crucial goal of uniformity of interpretation. To the extent that the United States courts rely on these sources, their decisions will more likely be regarded as persuasive elsewhere."[46]

1.4 Function – a summary of the case in favour of the Model Law

According to the **Guide to Enactment**, the Model Law "is designed to assist States to equip their insolvency[47] laws with a modern, harmonized and fair framework to address more effectively instances of cross-border insolvency. Those instances include cases where the insolvent debtor has assets in more than one State or where some of the creditors of the debtor are not from the State where the insolvency proceeding is taking place."[48] **14**

The harmonization the Law is designed to achieve differs from the concept of a "substantive unification of insolvency law," an aim the Guide pragmatically disclaims.[49] **15**

Instead, the Model Law offers a set of mechanisms "to be imbedded in the national insolvency law"[50] designed to ameliorate the worst effects of what remains an essentially territorial approach, at least respecting foreign law, to insolvency jurisdiction among nations.[51] **16**

The United Nations General Assembly identified some of the deleterious effects of a lack of harmonizing legislation governing cross-border insolvency: a reduction in "the **17**

---

[46] H. Rep. No. 109–31, 109 Cong., 1st Sess. 110 (2005); *see also In re RSM Richter v. Aguilar (In re Ephedra Prods. Liab. Litig.)*, 349 B.R. 333, 336 (S.D.N.Y. 2006) (noting added relevance of Guide).

[47] "The word 'insolvency,' as used in the title of the Model Law, refers to various types of collective proceedings against insolvent debtors." Guide ¶ 51.

[48] Guide ¶ 1. The United Nations General Assembly noted that "that when a debtor with assets in more than one State becomes subject to an insolvency proceeding, there often exists an urgent need for cross-border cooperation and coordination in the supervision and administration of the insolvent debtor's assets and affairs." G.A. Res. 52/158, at 1, U.N. Doc. A/RES/52/158 (Jan. 30, 1998).

[49] Guide ¶ 3. During two joint UNCITRAL-International Association of Insolvency Practitioners ("INSOL") colloquia (including one for judges), the view arose in that UNCITRAL should limit its goals to "facilitating judicial cooperation, court access for foreign insolvency administrators and recognition of foreign proceedings." Guide ¶ 5 & n. 3. This apparently stemmed from a recognition that "it may not be practical to think of unifying the bankruptcy laws since in the evolution of international law we [are] too far from the time when we could expect countries to have similar bankruptcy laws." U.N. G.A., United Nations Commission on International Trade Law, Note by the Secretariat, Cross-border insolvency ¶ 1, UNCITRAL Yb 24, 248–253, 248 (1993) (A/CN.9/378/Add.4); *see also* U.N. G.A., United Nations Commission on International Trade Law, 30th Session, Report of Working Group on Insolvency Law on the work of the twentieth session ¶ 3, (24 October 1996) A/CN.9/433 (noting same); A/CN.9/419 ¶ 18 (stating that it was "not the goal of the Commission's work to overcome or eliminate [differing policy approaches characterizing national attitudes to matters of insolvency]").

[50] Guide ¶ 67.

[51] Guide ¶ 3; *see also* A/CN.9/398 ¶ 5 (stating "[m]any national insolvency laws claimed, for their own insolvency proceedings, application of the principle of 'universality', according to which a unified administration of the insolvency would be the objective and court orders would be effective with respect to assets located abroad, while failing to accord recognition of universality to foreign insolvency proceedings"). For a discussion of the growing trend toward universality in insolvency law, *see* Felsenfeld § 1 (c).

possibility of rescuing financially troubled but viable businesses" and in effecting "fair and efficient administration of cross-border insolvencies," an increase in the likelihood "that the debtor's assets [will] be concealed or dissipated and hinder reorganizations or liquidations of debtors' assets and affairs that would be the most advantageous for the creditors and other interested persons, including the debtors and the debtors' employees."[52]

18 Thus, the Model Law functions to enable creation of law and processes to coordinate procedures governing insolvency cases that have effects in more than one jurisdiction[53] – law that simply does not exist in most countries.[54]

19 The problem is not so much that existing mechanisms to deal with foreign insolvency cases or foreign assets or creditors in domestic cases conflict; rather, it is that such mechanisms have been either inadequate against the backdrop of increasing cross-border trade, investment and insolvency, or nonexistent. As the Guide to Enactment observes, "[o]nly a limited number of countries have a legislative framework for dealing with cross-border insolvency that is well suited to the needs of international trade and investment."[55] What has existed instead are a variety of insolvency regimes that commonly ignore the existence of foreign insolvency law. When courts and administrators cannot ignore it, as is increasingly becoming the case, they are forced to grapple with it haphazardly, at least as measured in terms of predictability of results, causing detrimental effects on foreign investment and trade.[56] From this perspective, the enactment of the

---

[52] G.A. Res. 52/158, *supra* note 48, at 1; *see also* Guide ¶¶ 13–14 (reiterating these problems and adding that "the absence of predictability in the handling of cross-border insolvency cases impedes capital flow and is a disincentive to cross-border investment"). A good description of the basic cross-border insolvency problem is set forth at the beginning of a fascinating article, J. M. Farley/Bruce Leonard/ John N. Birch, *Cooperation and Coordination in Cross-Border Insolvency Cases* (paper delivered on the INSOL conference in May 2006). The authors describe the benefits of globalization in terms of resource allocation by transnational businesses and point out that the efficient global systems such businesses establish are irrationally compartmentalized by territorial insolvency laws: "The unified international business that was once carried on comes to an end and separate, unconnected remnants of the organization continue until they either starve or implode." *Id.* at 1. They comment that "[i]t is almost as if a cross-border insolvency system had been set up deliberately to *promote* failures and liquidations." *Id.* (emphasis in original). Technological advances and globalization have make quick and efficient resource allocation possible, but where "unforeseen or unfortunate circumstances lead to the need for reorganizations or restructurings," they observe, "the pace of communication among jurisdictions reverts to the 19th century." *Id.* at 2. The result is that "[b]y and large, the stakeholders of the global business are the losers in this technological regression." *Id.*

[53] *See* A/CN.9/398 ¶ 7 (noting that "it was widely felt that it would not be feasible, at least in the foreseeable future, to solve ... problems" associated with fragmentation and compartmentalization of insolvency law along national lines).

[54] *See* A/CN.9/398 ¶ 10 (reporting the observation "that specific provisions in national legislation designed to deal with cross-border insolvency remained the exception"); A/CN.9/419 ¶¶ 16 (noting the "wide lack of provisions dealing with cross-border insolvency") and 58 (identifying as "a fundamental purpose of the project" the introduction of "basic 'enabling' legislative provisions that would create the capacity for judicial cooperation and recognition of foreign insolvency proceedings, as there was currently a lack of such capacity in many national laws").

[55] Guide ¶ 15.

[56] Guide ¶¶ 15–17 (providing examples); A/CN.9/398 ¶ 6 (noting "fragmentation and compartmentalization along national lines" and that the resulting "gaps and inadequacies" caused reliance "at best ... on *ad hoc* protocols or agreements among the parties

Model Law in *some* form is desirable quite apart from the uniformity that it offers, though uniformity certainly has its own positive effects on predictability and reliability.[57]

Having considered substantive harmonization of insolvency law or an attempt to create a comprehensive cross-border insolvency treaty or convention too ambitious and impractical as a first steps,[58] the Commission opted for the next best thing: a **flexible system** allowing for a "**primary/secondary jurisdiction structure**," and, where that is not possible or desirable, a cooperative "**concurrent/parallel proceedings structure.**"[59] In enacting the Model Law, a state, without surrendering any of its sovereignty to a reciprocal agreement, is therefore in essence acknowledging **20**

- not only the existence of foreign insolvency regimes, but
- that there may be value in recognizing certain effects of foreign insolvency proceedings within its own territory, and is empowering its courts and administrators to seek to extract that value.[60]

In this spirit, the Model Law concentrates on the concepts of access, recognition, co- **21**
operation and coordination,[61] "establishing a limited number of basic principles and

involved ... in an atmosphere of legal uncertainty that resulted from an inadequate legislative framework for cooperation").

57 *Compare* Guide ¶ 20 (setting forth examples of how the Model Law may be adapted to fit into existing national law) *with* Guide ¶¶ 21 (encouraging uniformity and pointing out that, among other things, it "will make it easier for the enacting States to obtain cooperation from other States in insolvency matters"), 50 (advising that a uniform text will make "the national law as transparent as possible for foreign users of the national law"). At one point, there was consideration of titling the instrument "model legislative provisions" rather than "model law" with the idea that parts of it could be incorporated into law already existing in the enacting State. U.N. G.A., United Nations Commission on International Trade Law, 29th Session, Report of Working Group on Insolvency Law on the work of the nineteenth session ¶ 17, (25 April 1996) (A/CN.9/422). Similarly, there was consideration of drafting a treaty or convention, which, if it came into force, would assure more uniformity and address the concern in some countries with reciprocity. *See, e.g.*, A/CN.9/433 ¶¶ 17–19.

58 A/CN.9/433 ¶ 20.

59 *See* Farley/Leonard/Birch at 3 (coining and expounding on the these terms and noting that, as a result of the influence of local creditors, formal primary/secondary jurisdiction structures may in some cases only appear as such while in fact being "examples of the concurrent/parallel model").

60 In short, the Model Law is intended to facilitate "non-zero sum game solutions." As former U.S. President Clinton has explained, "The more complex societies get and the more complex the networks of interdependence within and beyond community and national borders get, the more people are forced in their own interests to find non-zero-sum solutions. That is, win-win solutions instead of win-lose solutions ... Because we find as our interdependence increases that, on the whole, we do better when other people do better as well – so we have to find ways that we can all win, we have to accommodate each other. And, on balance, that's a humanizing and elevating development." Interview by Karen Breslau and Katrina Heron with then U.S. President William J. Clinton in The Debriefing: Bill Clinton, *Wired Magazine*, Issue 8.12, December 2000 *available at* http://www.wired.com/wired/archive/8.12/clinton.html (citing generally Robert Wright, Nonzero: The Logic of Human Destiny (2000)).

61 *See supra* mn 3; *see also* Samuel L. Bufford, *International Accord*, Los Angeles Lawyer, July–August 2006 at 33, 34 (listing same three themes for American enactment of the Model Law, *viz* "more timely, effective, and efficient procedures" for recognition, "accreditation of a representative in a U.S. case to participate in foreign courts and proceedings," and cooperation by American courts and authorized estate representatives with foreign courts and estate representatives).

threshold rules … [to] facilitate efficiency and speed in responding to cross border insolvency cases … ."[62] A more detailed discussion of those principles and rules follows below.

2. Specific Provisions

22 The Model Law is organized into five Chapters consisting of a total of 32 Articles introduced by a Preamble.

2.1 Preamble

The purpose of this Law is to provide effective mechanisms for dealing with cases of cross-border insolvency so as to promote the objectives of:

(a) Cooperation between the courts and other competent authorities of this State and foreign States involved in cases of cross-border insolvency;

(b) Greater legal certainty for trade and investment;

(c) Fair and efficient administration of cross-border insolvencies that protects the interests of all creditors and other interested persons, including the debtor;

(d) Protection and maximization of the value of the debtor's assets; and

(e) Facilitation of the rescue of financially troubled businesses, thereby protecting investment and preserving employment.

2.1.1 General

23 The language of the Preamble is not intended to create substantive rights, but rather to serve as an interpretive guide to the rest of the Model Law.[63] Nevertheless, the initial principle it sets forth is that the Law exists to create "**mechanisms.**" It therefore stands to reason that the Law must be read to give the mechanisms effect. The reference to "dealing with cases of cross-border insolvency" hints at the kinds of situations that come within the scope of the Law, for which Article 1 provides further explanation. The remainder of the Preamble enumerates five objectives to provide direction by illuminating the ends the mechanisms were created to serve and to aid in determining how the mechanisms should function individually and interact with each other.

24 What is now subparagraph (b) originally listed "encouraging and providing a predictable environment for trade and investment in the enacting state" as an objective. The Working Group modified that language because "it did not constitute an appropriate statement of the scope of the draft model legislative provisions, which were actually aimed at achieving greater legal certainty in cross-border insolvencies."[64]

25 The language of subparagraph (c) results from a modification of an earlier draft which spoke in terms of protecting "the interests of creditors from the enacting state, as well as

[62] A/CN.9/419 ¶ 18.

[63] Guide ¶ 54; A/52/17 ¶ 136; A/CN.9/422 ¶ 19. The Guide suggests that the language of the Preamble could be included as a list of objectives within the body of a statute or in a separate document while still fulfilling its role as interpretive guide, where such an alternative is customary in the place of enactment. *Id.* ¶ 55; *see also* A/52/17 ¶ 136.

[64] A/CN.9/433 ¶ 27; *see also* Wessels ¶ 10189 (noting debate about whether the Model Law provides certainty).

the interests of foreign creditors."[65] The changes were made so as not to inadvertently imply that the interests of foreign creditors should be treated differently from those of creditors from the enacting state[66] and to take into account the potential need to protect other interested parties who are not creditors.[67] Bracketed text in an earlier version which read, "[whether or not resident, domiciled or with a registered office in the enacting State]," was replaced with the word "all" in front of "creditors and other interested persons," which "was considered to be sufficient for the purpose of clarifying that the model legislative provisions were intended to protect the interests of creditors without any form of discrimination based on nationality, residence, domicile or other factors."[68] Nevertheless, a suggestion that non-discrimination against foreign creditors be an objective[69] was not adopted. The words "including the debtor" were also a late innovation not included in earlier drafts.[70]

Eventually dropped was an early addition to what is now subparagraph (d) that **26**
would have promoted the facilitation of "the gathering of information about the debtor's assets and affairs,"[71] which seems an odd omission given that one of the "key objectives" that the UNCITRAL Legislative Guide on Insolvency Law sets forth is "ensuring a transparent and predictable insolvency law that contains incentives for gathering and dispensing information,"[72] though the Model Law predates Legislative Guide.

UNCITRAL's Report on the work of its thirtieth session describes some controversy **27**
about whether to include the final phrase of subparagraph (e).[73] Some participants expressed the view that that phrase should not be included since no provision of the Model Law is "directly concerned with protecting investment or preserving employment," that facilitating the "conduct of insolvency proceedings with cross-border elements" was the primary objective of the Law, that rescue of the debtor's business might not always be possible, and that "the interests of creditors, referred to in subparagraph (c), might not always be compatible with protecting investment and preserving employment."[74] In adopting the present text, "it was observed [among other things] that an objective such as the one mentioned in subparagraph (e) was in line with a number of national insolvency laws, ... [t]he preamble to the draft Model Provisions contained a statement of basic policy objectives and not of mandatory objectives," that "[i]t would be incorrect to regard those objectives as being contradictory only because, in individual cases, some of them might take precedence over the others," and "that the protection of investment and

[65] A/CN.9/422 ¶ 20.
[66] *Id.* ¶ 20.
[67] *Id.* ¶ 21.
[68] A/CN.9/433 ¶¶ 23–25.
[69] *Id.* ¶ 22. *But see* mn 155 *et seq* (discussing Article 13 and the principle of equality of creditors).
[70] U.N. G.A., United Nations Commission on International Trade Law, 30th Session, Report of Working Group on Insolvency Law on the work of the twenty-first session (Vienna, 12–39 May 1997) ¶ 100, A/CN.9/435 (19 February 1997).
[71] *Id.* ¶¶ 22–23.
[72] Legislative Guide 13; *see also* Douglas G. Baird, The Hidden Virtues of Chapter 11: An overview of the Law and Economics of Financially Distressed Firms 5, 34–35 (March 1997) (Chicago Working Papers in Law and Economics No. 43 (2d Series)) (discussing the value of an ability to gather information in terms of reducing transaction costs in insolvency situations). Nevertheless, Article 21 (1) (d) does provide an information-gathering mechanism. *See* mn 224 (discussing Article 21).
[73] A/52/17 ¶¶ 137–38; *see also* Wessels ¶ 10189 (evaluating subparagraph (e) as "evidence of support for a rescue culture").
[74] A/52/17 ¶ 136.

the preservation of employment were not independent objectives, but rather expected consequences from the rescue of financially troubled businesses."[75]

2.1.2 United States Law

Section 1501(a)[76]

The purpose of this chapter is to incorporate the Model Law on Cross-Border Insolvency so as to provide effective mechanisms for dealing with cases of cross-border insolvency with the objectives of –

(1) cooperation between –

(A) courts of the United States, United States trustees, trustees, examiners, debtors, and debtors in possession; and

(B) the courts and other competent authorities of foreign countries involved in cross-border insolvency cases;

(2) greater legal certainty for trade and investment;

(3) fair and efficient administration of cross-border insolvencies that protects the interests of all creditors, and other interested entities, including the debtor;

(4) protection and maximization of the value of the debtor's assets; and

(5) facilitation of the rescue of financially troubled businesses, thereby protecting investment and preserving employment.

28 The placement of chapter 15's purpose statement draws on the Guide's advice that the language of the Preamble may be included within the body of the enacted statute,[77] a feature unique within the Bankruptcy Code, which contains no other formally demarcated statement of purpose.[78]

29 The language of the American enactment generally follows that of the Model Law, but there are some variations.[79]

---

75 A/52/17 ¶ 137.

76 The title of section 1501 is "Purpose and scope of application." Only section 1501 (a) corresponds to the Preamble of the Model Law, however. The remaining subsections correspond to Article 1 of the Model Law.

77 *See supra* note 63.

78 *See In re SphinX, Ltd.*, 315 B.R. 103, 112 (Bankr. S.D.N.Y. 2006) (noting uniqueness), *aff'd*, 371 B.R. 10 (S.D.N.Y. 2007).

79 Maintaining linguistic uniformity with the Model Law was a general policy behind drafting chapter 15. *See* Westbrook, 79 Am. Bankr. L. J. at 719–20 ("Chapter 15 was drafted to follow the Model Law as closely as possible, with the idea of encouraging other countries to do the same."); *In re Tri-Continental Exch. Ltd.*, 349 B.R. 627, 633 (Bankr. E.D. Cal. 2006) (citing Westbrook). Notable for not having been changed, for example, is the Model Law term "insolvency," which was *not* replaced by "bankruptcy," the term more often used in America even in commercial contexts. In fact, the word "bankruptcy" does not appear in chapter 15, nor does it appear in the definition of "foreign proceeding" in chapter 1 of the Bankruptcy Code, as it did before the definition was amended upon adoption of the Model Law. *See* 11 U.S.C. § 101 (23). The word "nonbankruptcy" does appear in chapter 15 twice, however. *See* 11 U.S.C. §§ 1502 (8), 1509 (e).

First, section 1501 (a) specifically references the Model Law, incorporating it as a specific means toward the end of providing mechanisms to promote the numbered objectives. Second, the language of section 1501 (a) (1) (A) provides U.S.-specific names for the "courts and other authorities" of the Model Law's Preamble.[80] **30**

Finally, the word **"entities"** replaces **"persons"** in section 1501 (a) (3). Under the Bankruptcy Code's definitions, an "entity" may include a "person,"[81] so "entity" better conveys the intended expansive breadth of the usage of "person" in the Model Law and thus usually replaces "person" in the American enactment.[82] **31**

2.2 Chapter I. General Provisions

2.2.1 Article 1 – Scope of application

> **1. This Law applies where:**
>
> ***(a)* Assistance is sought in this State by a foreign court or a foreign representative in connection with a foreign proceeding; or**
>
> ***(b)* Assistance is sought in a foreign State in connection with a proceeding under *[identify laws of the enacting State relating to insolvency]*; or**
>
> ***(c)* A foreign proceeding and a proceeding under *[identify laws of the enacting State relating to insolvency]* in respect of the same debtor are taking place concurrently; or**
>
> ***(d)* Creditors or other interested persons in a foreign State have an interest in requesting the commencement of, or participating in, a proceeding under *[identify laws of the enacting State relating to insolvency]*.**
>
> **2. This Law does not apply to a proceeding concerning *[designate any types of entities, such as banks or insurance companies, that are subject to a special insolvency regime in this State and that this State wishes to exclude from this Law]*.**

→ *Cf* Art 1 of the EIR

2.2.1.1 Situations in which the Model Law applies

Paragraph 1 identifies the **four insolvency-related**[83] **situations**[84] in which the provisions of the Model Law are meant to apply, *viz* **32**

[80] Courts "*of* the United States" is a reference to federal courts as opposed to those of individual American states. *Cf.* 15 U.S.C. §§ 1502 (8), 1509, 1510 and 1524 (all referring to courts "*in* the United States"). "United States trustees" are officers of the executive branch of the Federal government charged, *inter alia*, with overseeing and sometimes performing administrative functions in bankruptcy cases. *See* 28 U.S.C. § 586 (setting forth duties of United States trustees). For an explanation of the term "examiner," *see* mn 117 (discussing section 1505). The next section of chapter 15 defines "debtor" and "trustee." 11 U.S.C. § 1502 (1), (6); *see also* mn 102, 103 (discussing the terms "debtor," "trustee" and "debtor in possession").

[81] *See* 11 U.S.C. §§ 101 (15) (defining "entity"), (41) (defining "person").

[82] H. Rep. No. 109–31, 109th Cong., 1st Sess. 107 (2005).

[83] *See* A/CN.9/422 ¶¶ 30–31 and the paragraphs referenced therein for a discussion of the use of the term "insolvency" in Article 1.

[84] The Working Group expressed the view that paragraph 1's function was "to describe clearly and succinctly the situations covered

- when a court faces a request from a foreign court or representative seeking assistance in an enacting State,
- when a court or administrator is seeking assistance in a foreign state in connection with an insolvency proceeding in the enacting State,
- when insolvency proceedings respecting the same debtor are simultaneously occurring in the enacting State and elsewhere, or
- when interested persons in foreign States wish to commence or otherwise participate in insolvency proceedings in the enacting State.[85]

33 Although Article 1 is entitled "Scope of application," the text of the first paragraph is meant to be explanatory rather than limiting. The evidence is set forth in the Working Group's Report of its 21st Session,[86] in which objections were raised to including the first paragraph of the "scope" article on the grounds that it created no "rights or obligations and merely listed situations regulated elsewhere," that it was intended to be explanatory and could be construed "as limiting the scope of the remaining articles," and that it is "unusual for a legislative text to define its own scope of application by providing examples of situations covered by its provisions."[87] One can certainly imagine other situations in which the Law might apply.[88] Although the response to these objections was to retain the first paragraph "to provide such explanation of the scope," the Working Group did note that it could be excluded in enactment by States not finding the paragraph necessary.[89] Therefore, although all seemed to have agreed that paragraph 1 is explanatory, and therefore presumably not an exhaustive list of all situations to which the Law might apply, one must ultimately investigate the circumstances of enactment to get a full picture of what a particular legislature might have meant to accomplish by including or omitting it. In any event, each of the remaining provisions of the Model Law, particularly those in paragraph 2 and the definitions in Article 2, limit and refine rather than explain its scope.[90]

34 In each situation, the Law is concerned with "collective proceedings against insolvent debtors,"[91] whether the proceedings be "compulsory or voluntary, corporate or individual," oriented toward liquidation or reorganization, or administered by a third person or the debtor itself.[92]

35 The term **"assistance,"** as used in Article 1 (1) (a) and (b), covers the subjects of requests of *courts* or *insolvency administrators* "for taking a measure encompassed by the draft Model Provisions." *See* A/CN.9/433 ¶ 30.

---

[85] *See generally* Guide ¶ 22; note that the text of the Model Law itself avoids the undefined term "insolvency proceeding," to which the Guide refers, instead defining only "foreign proceeding" in Article 2 (a) and substituting what might be called domestic insolvency proceedings by reference to the actual law of the enacting State, as, for example, in Article 1. The Working Group did discuss defining "insolvency proceeding" but ultimately decided it was unnecessary and might cause "the misimpression that the text aimed at substantive unification of insolvency cases," *see* A/CN.9/422 ¶¶ 30–31, 46–47, especially since the term "insolvency proceeding" may already have a technical meaning in some legal systems. Guide ¶¶ 52, 71.

[86] The second paragraph, which appears to have been added after the report appeared, is clearly limiting. *See* A/CN.9/435 ¶ 179.

[87] A/CN.9/435 ¶ 102.

[88] Additional situations were suggested, *see* A/CN.9/435 ¶ 104–05, but did not attract sufficient support for inclusion. *Id.* ¶ 106.

[89] A/CN.9/435 ¶ 102.

[90] *See* A/CN.9/422 ¶ 28 (noting the merit of stating the scope generally before "describing it in more detail in the definitions").

[91] Guide ¶ 51.

[92] Guide ¶¶ 23–24.

in the Model Law," whether mentioned specifically or covered by broad formulation.[93]

2.2.1.1.1 In-bound requests for assistance by foreign courts and foreign representatives

Article 1 (1) (a)'s recital of in-bound requests for assistance as within the scope of the Model Law corresponds to the Law's objective "to provide expedited and direct access for foreign representatives to the courts of [an] enacting State."[94] The mechanisms that support the principle of direct assess include **simple proof requirements** for seeking recognition of and relief in foreign proceedings (Article 15) and **standing provisions** for foreign representatives to commence (Article 11) or participate in (Article 12) insolvency proceedings or to intervene in other proceedings involving their debtors (Article 24) in the enacting State.[95] **36**

A foreign proceeding must possess certain attributes to fall within the scope of the Model Law, including **37**

- a "basis in insolvency-related law of the originating State;
- involvement of creditors collectively;
- control or supervision of the assets and affairs of the debtor by a court or another official body; and
- reorganization or liquidation of the debtor as [its] purpose."[96]

These requirements are found in the Article 2 (a) definition of "**foreign proceeding.**"[97] Similarly, the term "**foreign representative**" is defined in Article 2 (d).[98] **38**

Whether and what kind of assistance will be forthcoming depends largely upon whether the foreign proceeding is "recognized"[99] (though a court may grant interim relief pending its decision whether or not to grant recognition[100]) and the type of recognition granted, which may be recognition as either a foreign "main" or "non-main" proceeding.[101] For example, recognition as a foreign "main" proceeding gives rise to the "stay and suspension" provisions, which stay "proceedings concerning the debtor's assets, rights, obligations or liabilities" and execution against its assets, and suspend the "right to transfer, encumber or otherwise dispose of" any of its assets.[102] **39**

Article 21 sets forth the most important forms of relief that may be granted in aid of foreign proceedings, authorizing a court to grant the stays and suspension of Article 20 in "non-main" proceedings, to provide for information gathering, and to entrust the debtor's assets – even the distribution thereof – to a foreign court designee. Foreign representatives may also obtain standing to pursue certain Paulian or avoidance actions or to intervene in other proceedings in the enacting State involving the debtor.[103] **40**

---

93 Guide ¶ 59.

94 Guide ¶ 28 (pointing out that the Law avoids the need to rely "on letters rogatory or other forms of diplomatic or consular communications").

95 Guide ¶ 29 (listing same examples and noting that the Law also ensures that merely seeking recognition is not submitting to jurisdiction).

96 Guide ¶ 23.

97 *See* mn 62 *et seq* (discussing Article 2 (a)).

98 *See* mn 87 *et seq* (discussing Article 2 (b)).

99 *See* Arts 15–17, discussed in mn 172 *et seq.*

100 Guide ¶ 30 (citing Article 19).

101 *See* Art 20 and mn 213 *et seq* (discussing Article 20); Guide ¶¶ 31–32 (summarizing key elements of relief granted in foreign main proceedings).

102 *See* Art 20 and mn 213 *et seq* (discussing Article 20).

103 *See* Arts 24–25 and mn 252 *et seq*, 258 *et seq* (discussing Articles 24–25).

2.2.1.1.2 Out-bound requests for assistance from a court or insolvency administrator

41 Out-bound requests for assistance are also included within the scope of the Law to bridge the gap in the law of some countries which might not otherwise provide their courts the authority they need to seek such assistance.[104] One mechanism the Law provides for such assistance is set forth in Article 25,[105] which empowers courts to communicate (directly or through representatives) with foreign courts. Another is in Article 5,[106] which authorizes local administrators to seek assistance in foreign States.

42 It bears repeating[107] that, according to the Guide to Enactment,[108] the term "**assistance**" in subparagraph (b), as in subparagraph (a), indicates that the situation to which it refers arises in the context of a request from "a court or an insolvency administrator" as opposed to one from a domestic creditor or other interested person, even though the language of the subparagraph does not explicitly so state.

43 A special provision mirroring subparagraph (d) for out-bound requests of creditors and other interested persons to participate in foreign proceedings was suggested but not adopted.[109]

2.2.1.1.3 Cooperation and coordination in concurrent proceedings

44 Article 1 (1) (c) is concerned with "coordination of concurrent proceedings in two or more states."[110] Lack of coordination increases the chances that assets will vanish because of fraud or otherwise become unavailable, or that opportunities to preserve value by rationalized liquidation or reorganization will be lost, perhaps by simple lack of communication.[111] The results may be detrimental not only to creditors, but also to non-creditors interested in possibly rescuing the enterprise, such as management, employees, customers, suppliers and indirect beneficiaries of going concerns, e.g., taxing entities and other participants in the local economy.

45 The Model Law seeks to provide a "legislative framework ... for pursuing cooperation with foreign courts"[112] with the objective of fostering "coordinated decisions that would best achieve the objectives of both [or all] proceedings."[113] Courts in various jurisdictions have varying constraints on their ability, or perceived ability, to cooperate with foreign courts absent such a framework; thus, specific legislative authorizations aim to bridge whatever legal gaps to cooperation may exist.[114]

46 Chapter IV of the Model Law addresses cooperation with foreign courts and foreign representatives.[115] Article 25 directly references Article 1 in this respect, providing that "[i]n matters referred to in article 1, the court shall cooperate ... with foreign courts and representatives" and "is entitled to communicate directly with, or to request information or assistance directly from, foreign courts or foreign representatives."[116] Article 26 correspondingly references Article 1 in requiring that administrators or trustees under the insolvency law of the enacting State cooperate with foreign courts and representa-

---

104 A/CN.9/422 ¶ 26.
105 *See* mn 258 *et seq* (discussing Article 25).
106 *See* mn 113 *et seq* (discussing Article 5).
107 *See* mn 35.
108 Guide ¶ 59.
109 A/CN.9/435 ¶ 104, 106.
110 Guide ¶ 22.
111 Guide ¶ 17.
112 Guide ¶ 38.
113 Guide ¶ 44.
114 Guide ¶¶ 39, 174; *see also id.* ¶¶ 175–76 (discussing differing bases of international cooperation in cross-border insolvencies), 178 (discussing a number of points on the importance of ensuring courts have the flexibility and discretion to cooperate).
115 Guide ¶ 174 (referring to cross-border cooperation as a "core element of the Model Law").
116 *See* mn 258 *et seq* (discussing Article 25).

tives and authorizes such administrators or trustees to communicate directly with them.[117] Article 27 sets forth examples of means of cooperation.[118] In addition to these Chapter IV provisions, Article 5 equips administrators or trustees in the enacting State to serve as foreign representatives in foreign proceedings, thereby clearing another potential obstacle to cooperation based on lack of standing.[119]

Chapter V provides mechanisms to deal with "concurrent proceedings," i.e., insolvency proceedings occurring in more than one State at the same time. Article 28 limits the ability to commence insolvency proceedings in the enacting State after a "foreign main" proceeding has been recognized and restricts the effects of such proceedings to the territory of the enacting State except as necessary to implement cooperation and coordination under Articles 25–27.[120] Chapter IV "cooperation and coordination" is affirmatively required to be sought when a foreign proceeding and a proceeding under the insolvency law of the enacting State take place concurrently, however, regardless of the order of commencement.[121] Article 30 similarly requires such "cooperation and coordination" "in matters referred to in Article 1, in respect of more than one foreign proceeding regarding the same debtor," particularly where either or both seek relief in the enacting State.[122] Finally, Articles 31 and 32 modify insolvency proceedings in enacting States based on the occurrence of certain events in foreign proceedings. Article 31 provides that recognition of a foreign main proceeding constitutes proof that a debtor is insolvent for purposes of opening an insolvency proceeding in the enacting State.[123] Article 32 limits (to some extent) the ability of creditors to obtain greater recovery by participating in more than one concurrent proceeding.[124] **47**

2.2.1.1.4 Foreign creditors and other interested foreign persons

Subparagraph (d) did not appear in the earliest drafts of Article 1. The Working Group added it at its 20th Session and noted that, in addition to the situations described in subparagraphs (a)–(c), there existed the situation "where creditors in a foreign State had an interest in requesting the opening of, or in participating in, an insolvency proceeding in the enacting State."[125] **48**

The primary mechanisms to effect the protection that the Article 1 (1) (d) scope provision mentions are found in Articles 13,[126] which generally provides foreign creditors the same rights to commence or participate in insolvency proceedings in the enacting State as domestic creditors have, and 22,[127] which requires that the court be satisfied that "the interests of the creditors and other affected persons, including the debtor"[128] are adequately protected in granting relief upon application for recognition under Article 19 or discretionary relief under Article 21. The court is also empowered to **49**

- modify,
- terminate or
- attach appropriate conditions to the relief

---

[117] *See* mn 269 *et seq* (discussing Article 26).
[118] *See* mn 271 *et seq* (discussing Article 27).
[119] *See* mn 113 *et seq* (discussing Article 5).
[120] *See* mn 280 *et seq* (discussing Article 28).
[121] Art 29; *see also* mn 284 *et seq* (discussing Article 29).
[122] *See* mn 293 *et seq* (discussing Article 30).
[123] *See* mn 297 *et seq* (discussing Article 31).
[124] *See* mn 302 *et seq* (discussing Article 32).
[125] A/CN.9/433 ¶ 31. As noted above, *see* note 109 and accompanying text, a suggestion for a special provision mirroring subparagraph (d) for out-bound requests of creditors and other interested persons to participate in foreign proceedings was not adopted. A/CN.9/435 ¶¶ 104, 106.
[126] *See* mn 155 *et seq* (discussing Article 13).
[127] *See* mn 240 *et seq* (discussing Article 22).
[128] Article 22 (1).

as necessary.[129] If requested relief is "manifestly contrary to the public policy" of the enacting State, the court may refuse to take action by invoking Article 6.[130]

50 In addition, Article 14 provides for insolvency-related notification to foreign creditors.[131] The Model Law does not address questions of appropriate notice to other "interested persons," leaving that and related questions to the procedural law of the enacting State.[132]

2.2.1.2 Exclusion of certain entities

51 Although it generally applies to any proceeding that meets the Article 2 (a) definition of "foreign proceeding,"[133] the Model Law allows enacting States to exclude certain kinds of entities from becoming debtors within its scope.[134] The bracketed language mentions banks and insurance companies as examples because of the special regulations that customarily apply to them.[135] The Guide to Enactment grudgingly suggests that non-traders or natural persons may also be candidates for exclusion in enacting States that have special or no insolvency regimes that apply to them, or where special provisions exist when a debtor's debt is primarily consumer-related.[136] As the Guide points out, however, the fact that an entity is ineligible to be a debtor under the insolvency law of the enacting State does not mean that foreign entities of the same type need necessarily be excluded by inclusion under paragraph 2 for purposes of recognition, especially if they do not carry-out their specially-regulated business in the enacting State, and/or where the state in which the foreign proceeding is occurring does not specially regulate such proceeding.[137] Furthermore, an exclusion need not be absolute: the Law can be adapted so as to leave certain of its features available for application in connection with the insolvency of special entities.[138] Whatever they choose to exclude, the hope is that enacting States will transparently indicate their choices in paragraph 2 for the sake of foreign users of the enacted Law.[139]

---

129 Article 22 (2), (3); Guide ¶ 35.

130 Guide ¶ 36; *see also* mn 119 *et seq* (discussing Article 6).

131 *See* mn 160 *et seq* (discussing Article 14).

132 Guide ¶ 37.

133 Guide ¶ 60; *see also* mn 60 *et seq* (discussing Article 2).

134 A/CN.9/422 ¶¶ 44–45 (stating consensus that exclusions as to debtor type are best left to national law without encouraging broad resort to a "public policy" exception).

135 Guide ¶ 25. Banks and insurance companies are typical subjects of special insolvency regimes: heavily regulated because of the need to protect a large number of consumers or because of extraordinary actions that need to be undertaken in connection with their insolvency. *Id.* ¶ 61 (noting the need to prevent massive withdrawals of deposits as an example); A/CN.9/419 ¶¶ 34–35 (discussing special needs of banks and insurance companies); A/CN.9/422 ¶ 42 (same). The Guide also indicates there may be reason to exclude other debtors whose needs call for "special solutions in cross-border insolvency cases," such as public utility companies. *Id.* ¶ 62.

136 Guide ¶ 66. *But see id.* ¶ 52 (stating that "the Model Law is designed to be applicable to proceedings regardless of whether they involve a natural person or a legal person as the debtor"); A/CN.9/422 ¶ 40 (same). Though controversial, the availability of an exclusion for consumer debtors living in the enacting State appears to have been necessary to allow for participation of States with special legislation for consumer protection to avoid the impression that the Law extends the same insolvency regime to consumers as to non-consumers. *See* A/52/17 ¶¶ 142–145 (discussing controversy); A/CN.9/419 ¶ 33 (same); A/CN.9/422 ¶ 41 (same); A/CN.9/433 ¶ 36 (same).

137 Guide ¶ 63; A/CN.9/422 ¶ 43 (same).

138 Guide ¶ 64.

139 Guide ¶ 65. Prudent use of the exclusion provision may also prevent overuse of

2.2.1.3 United States Law

Section 1501 (b)–(d) [140]

(b) This chapter applies where –

(1) assistance is sought in the United States by a foreign court or a foreign representative in connection with a foreign proceeding;

(2) assistance is sought in a foreign country in connection with a case under this title;

(3) a foreign proceeding and a case under this title with respect to the same debtor are pending concurrently; or

(4) creditors or other interested persons in a foreign country have an interest in requesting the commencement of, or participating in, a case or proceeding under this title.

(c) This chapter does not apply to –

(1) a proceeding concerning an entity, other than a foreign insurance company, identified by exclusion in section 109 (b);

(2) an individual, or to an individual and such individual's spouse, who have debts within the limits specified in section 109 (e) and who are citizens of the United States or aliens lawfully admitted for permanent residence in the United States; or

(3) an entity subject to a proceeding under the Securities Investor Protection Act of 1970, a stockbroker subject to subchapter III of chapter 7 of this title, or a commodity broker subject to subchapter IV of chapter 7 of this title.

(d) The court may not grant relief under this chapter with respect to any deposit, escrow, trust fund, or other security required or permitted under any applicable state insurance law or regulation for the benefit of claim holders in the United States.

2.2.1.3.1 General application of chapter 15

Section 1501 (b) corresponds to Article 1 (1) of the Model Law. As with most of **52**
chapter 15, the language "largely tracks the language of the Model Law with appropriate United States references," [141] the words "pending" and "country," for example, replacing

the public policy exception of Article 6, desirable because such overuse could lead to overly broad and ultimately counterproductive interpretations of that provision. *See* A/52/17 ¶¶ 142, 147, 149 (discussing possibility of overuse); A/CN.9/433 ¶ 36 (same). Examples of exclusions enacted thus far: "entities such as banking and insurance institutions (e.g. Romania, Poland); financial and investment institutions, commodity exchange members, clearing houses, brokerage companies and traders (e.g. Romania); persons who hold or have held prescribed financial services licenses of a designated type (e.g. British Virgin Islands); and consumers (e.g. Mexico). Reflecting the scope of its insolvency law, one country has limited the provisions to proceedings concerning 'merchants' (Mexico)." A/CN.9/580 ¶ 4.

140 The title of section 1501 is "Purpose and scope of application." Section 1501 (a) corresponds to the Preamble of the Model Law. The remaining subsections correspond to Article 1.

141 H. Rep. No. 109–31, 109th Cong., 1st Sess. 106 (2005).

"taking place" and "State," respectively, as they generally do in the rest of chapter 15. Similarly, "**case under this title**" or "case or proceeding under this title" replace the bracketed language of Article 1. Title 11 is a reference to the Bankruptcy Code, which is codified as title 11 of the United States Code. A "case" in American *bankruptcy* jurisprudence equates roughly to the term "**insolvency proceeding.**"

> [E]very petition under the Bankruptcy Code commences a bankruptcy "case." Such a case provides a vehicle for all other matters relating to that bankruptcy debtor to take place. The term "proceeding," in contrast, refers to a particular action raised or commenced within a case, including motions and adversary proceedings … . A proceeding in a bankruptcy case is the functional equivalent of a case in a non-bankruptcy court.[142]

53 Chapter 15 replaces the repealed "internationally renowned"[143] section 304 of the Bankruptcy Code,[144] which previously governed "**ancillary cases,**" i.e., proceedings

- in which a representative of a foreign court filed a petition before an American bankruptcy court
- respecting a debtor who "ha[d] assets in [the United States] …
- in order to administer [such] assets …,
- to prevent dismemberment by local creditors of [such] assets …, or
- for other appropriate relief."[145]

54 Courts were given "maximum flexibility" to grant "appropriate relief" based on principles of comity[146] set forth in the statute.[147] The general "philosophy of former

---

[142] *In re Artimm*, 278 B.R. 832, 838 (Bankr. C.D. Cal. 2002) (internal citations omitted).

[143] Wessels ¶ 10206.

[144] 11 U.S.C. § 304 (2000) (repealed). Section 304 provided:
(a) A case ancillary to a foreign proceeding is commenced by the filing with the bankruptcy court of a petition under this section by a foreign representative.
(b) Subject to the provisions of subsection (c) of this section, if a party in interest does not timely controvert the petition, or after trial, the court may –
(1) enjoin the commencement or continuation of –
(A) any action against –
(i) a debtor with respect to property involved in such foreign proceeding; or
(ii) such property; or
(B) the enforcement of any judgment against the debtor with respect to such property, or any act or the commencement or continuation of any judicial proceeding to create or enforce a lien against the property of such estate;
(2) order turnover of the property of such estate, or the proceeds of such property, to such foreign representative; or
(3) order other appropriate relief.
(c) In determining whether to grant relief under subsection (b) of this section, the court shall be guided by what will best assure an economical and expeditious administration of such estate, consistent with –
(1) just treatment of all holders of claims against or interests in such estate;
(2) protection of claim holders in the United States against prejudice and inconvenience in the processing of claims in such foreign proceeding;
(3) prevention of preferential or fraudulent dispositions of property of such estate;
(4) distribution of proceeds of such estate substantially in accordance with the order prescribed by this title;
(5) comity; and
(6) if appropriate, the provision of an opportunity for a fresh start for the individual that such foreign proceeding concerns.

[145] H. Rep. No. 95–595, 1st Sess. 324–25 (1977); S. Rep. No. 95–989, 2d Sess. 35 (1978).

[146] The United States Supreme Court defined "comity" in *Hilton v. Guyot*, 159 U.S. 113, 163–64 (1895):
"Comity" in the legal sense is neither a matter of absolute obligation, on the one hand, nor of mere courtesy and good will

§ 304 [wa]s deference to the country where the main insolvency case [wa]s located and flexible cooperation in administration of assets."[148] It "was designed to operate in aid of a main case pending abroad."[149]

As is clear from the description of Article 1 (1) above,[150] chapter 15's scope is broader, but Congress has preserved the "ancillary" position of a case thereunder. As the House Report explains,[151] **55**

> Cases brought under chapter 15 are intended to be ancillary to cases brought in a debtor's home country, unless a full United States bankruptcy case is brought under another chapter. Even if a full case is brought, the court may decide under section 305 to stay or dismiss the United States case under the other chapter and limit the United States' role to an ancillary case under this chapter. If the full case is not dismissed, it will be subject to the provisions of this chapter governing cooperation, communication and coordination with the foreign courts and representatives. In any case, an order granting recognition is required as a prerequisite to the use of sections 301 and 303 by a foreign representative.

The major practical **differences** between a **plenary** and an **ancillary bankruptcy case** are that the commencement of the former creates **56**

- an estate comprised of essentially all of the debtor's property, "wherever located and by whomever held," under the jurisdiction of the court[152] and
- an automatic stay of actions against the debtor and the property of the estate,[153]

whereas commencement of the latter has no such effects, though a foreign representative may request **injunctive relief** upon filing a petition for recognition[154] and may be entitled **to a more limited stay** and related powers if the foreign proceeding is recognized as a foreign main proceeding.[155]

Further, in contrast to the Model Law, a recognized foreign representative has no power to prosecute Paulian, or "avoidance," actions in an ancillary case but may do so **57**

upon the other. It is rather the recognition which one nation allows within its territory to the legislative, executive or judicial acts of another nation, having due regard both to international duty and convenience, and to the rights of its own citizens, or of the other persons who are under the protection of its laws.

147 11 U.S.C. § 304 (c) (2004) (repealed).

148 *In re Artimm*, 335 B.R. 149, 157 (Bankr. C.D. Cal. 2005).

149 *Id.*

150 Note that chapter 15 differs in certain details from the general description of the Model Law above. This commentary describes the major differences in the section-by-section explanations below.

151 H. Rep. No. 109–31, 109th Cong., 1st Sess. 106 (2005) (internal footnote omitted). Sections 301 and 303 provide for voluntary and involuntary commencement of most full (or "plenary") cases. *See* 11 U.S.C. §§ 301, 303.

152 *See* 11 U.S.C. § 541 (a).

153 *See* 11 U.S.C. § 362 (a).

154 *See* 11 U.S.C. § 1519 (a) and mn 202 *et seq* (discussing Article 19).

155 *See* 11 U.S.C. § 1520 and mn 213 *et seq* (discussing Article 20). Ancillary cases in the United States thus differ somewhat from "secondary proceedings" under the European Insolvency Regulation, in that the former have no existence independent of a foreign insolvency proceeding and exist only to support such proceedings. Depending on the level of deference a secondary proceeding affords a foreign main proceeding, however, secondary proceedings and ancillary proceedings may perform similar functions. *See generally* Jay Lawrence Westbrook, *Multinational Enterprises in General Default: Chapter 15, the ALI Principles, and the EU Insolvency Regulation*, 76 Am. Bankr. L. J. 1, 11 (Winter 2002).

only in the context of a plenary case and usually only if recognized as the representative of a foreign main proceeding.[156]

2.2.1.3.2 Exclusions

58 Section 1501 (c) corresponds to Article 1 (2). Section 1501 (c) (1) refers to a list of entities that may not be debtors under the main liquidation chapter (chapter 7) of the Bankruptcy Code.[157] The list includes, *inter alia*,

- **railroads, domestic insurance companies, various kinds of domestic lending institutions**, and
- **certain foreign lending institutions with branches or agencies in the United States**,[158]

all of which have separate, specialized insolvency rules. The section 109 (b) list of excluded entities also includes foreign insurance companies "engaged in such business in the United States," but, as the text of section 1501 (c) (1) indicates, these are not excluded from the application of chapter 15,[159] except that no chapter 15 relief can be granted respecting security required "under any applicable State insurance law ... for the benefit of claim holders in the United States."[160] Section 1501 (c) (3) excludes proceedings under the Securities Investor Protection Act of 1970[161] as well as those involving certain stockbrokers and **commodity brokers** as debtors. Finally, chapter 15 does not apply to individual **consumers** who are citizens (or lawfully admitted permanent resident aliens) of the United States. The debt ceilings under section 109 (e) change periodically, but at this writing they are $ 307,675 for noncontingent, liquidated unsecured debts and $ 922,975 for those that are secured.[162]

59 According to the House Report accompanying the enactment of chapter 15, "Foreign representatives of foreign proceedings which are excluded from the scope of chapter 15 may seek comity from courts other than the bankruptcy court since the limitations of section 1509 (b) (2) and (3) would not apply to them."[163] This is important because section 1509 (c) limits access and relief available to unrecognized foreign representatives,[164] and section 103 (k) (2) of the Bankruptcy Code makes section 1509 applicable whether or not a bankruptcy case is pending.[165] It thus appears Congress does not intend for section 1509 to occupy the field that common law comity otherwise fills with respect to the kinds of foreign proceedings section 1501 (c) excludes.

---

[156] *See* 11 U.S.C. § 1523 and mn 247 *et seq* (discussing Article 23); *see also* 11 U.S.C. § 103 (a) (setting forth the specific parts of the Bankruptcy Code that apply to chapter 15 cases).

[157] *See* 11 U.S.C. § 109 (b).

[158] *See* 12 U.S.C. § 3101 (containing definitions of "foreign bank," "branch," and "agency").

[159] *See also In re Tri-Continental Exch. Ltd.*, 349 B.R. 627, 632 (Bankr. E.D. Cal. 2006) (recognizing winding-up proceedings under the St. Vincent and the Grenadines ("SVG") Companies Act of international insurance companies organized under the laws of SVG and doing business in, among other places, the United States, as foreign main proceedings).

[160] 11 U.S.C. § 1501 (d).

[161] 15 U.S.C. § 78aaa *et seq.*

[162] 11 U.S.C. § 109 (e).

[163] H. Rep. No. 109–31, 109th Cong., 1st Sess. 106 (2005).

[164] *See* 11 U.S.C. § 1509 (b), (c) and mn 134 *et seq* (discussing Article 9).

[165] 11 U.S.C. § 109 (k).

2.2.2 Article 2 – Definitions

For the purposes of this Law:

***(a)* "Foreign proceeding" means a collective judicial or administrative proceeding in a foreign State, including an interim proceeding, pursuant to a law relating to insolvency in which proceeding the assets and affairs of the debtor are subject to control or supervision by a foreign court, for the purpose of reorganization or liquidation;**

***(b)* "Foreign main proceeding" means a foreign proceeding taking place in the State where the debtor has the centre of its main interests;**

***(c)* "Foreign non-main proceeding" means a foreign proceeding, other than a foreign main proceeding, taking place in a State where the debtor has an establishment within the meaning of subparagraph *(f)* of this article;**

***(d)* "Foreign representative" means a person or body, including one appointed on an interim basis, authorized in a foreign proceeding to administer the reorganization or the liquidation of the debtor's assets or affairs or to act as a representative of the foreign proceeding;**

***(e)* "Foreign court" means a judicial or other authority competent to control or supervise a foreign proceeding;**

***(f)* "Establishment" means any place of operations where the debtor carries out a non-transitory economic activity with human means and goods or services.**

→ Cf Art 2 of the EIR

2.2.2.1 General

Article 2 contains the **definitions** of several terms the Model Law uses. The definitions apply only to the Law, not to terms already existing in national insolvency law, and are for use only in "cross-border scenarios."[166] The Guide to Enactment notes that "[t]he definitions of proceedings or persons emanating from foreign jurisdictions avoid the use of expressions that may have different technical meanings in legal systems and instead describe their purpose or function" in order "to avoid inadvertently narrowing the range of possible foreign proceedings that might obtain recognition and to avoid unnecessary conflict with terminology ..."[167] **60**

The definitions, particularly those in subparagraphs[168] (a) and (d), serve to limit the scope of the Law, for the attributes they define are required for recognition under **61**

[166] Guide ¶ 67.

[167] Guide ¶ 71; *see also* A/CN.9/419 ¶ 17 (expressing the need to avoid terminological or conceptual formulations that would be likely to engender difficulties); A/CN.9/422 ¶ 35 (observing that the definitions in Article 2 ought to be "phrased as much as possible in functional terms rather than by utilizing terms which might have particular and diverging definitions in national laws"). Several proposed definitions were ultimately not included in Article 2. *See, e.g.,* A/CN.9/422 ¶¶ 39 ("administrator"); 45 ("debtor"); 47 ("insolvency proceeding"); 58 ("opening of foreign proceedings"); 61 ("reorganization"); 64 ("rights in rem").

[168] While there appears to be no reason to call the subdivisions of Article 2 "subparagraphs" as opposed to "paragraphs," this part adopts the term "subparagraph" from the Model Law itself. *See, e.g.,* Art 17 (1) (a)–(b).

Article 17, and thus for the full cooperation of and access to the courts of the enacting State.[169]

2.2.2.2 United States Law

Section 1502 – Definitions

For the purposes of this chapter, the term

(1) 'debtor' means an entity that is the subject of a foreign proceeding;

(2) 'establishment' means any place of operations where the debtor carries out a non-transitory economic activity;

(3) 'foreign court' means a judicial or other authority competent to control or supervise a foreign proceeding;

(4) 'foreign main proceeding' means a foreign proceeding pending in the country where the debtor has the center of its main interests;

(5) 'foreign nonmain proceeding' means a foreign proceeding, other than a foreign main proceeding, pending in a country where the debtor has an establishment;

(6) 'trustee' includes a trustee, a debtor in possession in a case under any chapter of this title, or a debtor under chapter 9 of this title;

(7) 'recognition' means the entry of an order granting recognition of a foreign main proceeding or foreign nonmain proceeding under this chapter; and

(8) 'within the territorial jurisdiction of the United States', when used with reference to property of a debtor, refers to tangible property located within the territory of the United States and intangible property deemed under applicable nonbankruptcy law to be located within that territory, including any property subject to attachment or garnishment that may properly be seized or garnished by an action in a Federal or State court in the United States.

2.2.2.3 Definition of "foreign proceeding"

2.2.2.3.1 General

62 Together with the definition of foreign representative in subparagraph (d), the definition of "**foreign proceeding**" in subparagraph (a) largely defines the scope of the key provisions of the Model Law. To achieve "**recognition**" under Article 17 (1), a proceeding must meet the definition in subparagraph (a).[170] Recognition, in turn, unlocks the **access**, **assistance** and **cooperation mechanisms** the Model Law was designed to provide.[171]

63 The Model Law allows the word "proceeding," which forms the basis of the definition of "foreign proceeding," to remain undefined. Perhaps Professor Felsenfeld begins to capture its meaning with his suggestion that "fundamental to resolving issues of international bankruptcy is the availability of places, typically – but not necessarily – court-

[169] Guide ¶ 68.

[170] *See* Art 17 (1) (a) (requiring for recognition that a proceeding be "a proceeding within the meaning of subparagraph (a) of article 2").

[171] *See* discussion at mn 3.

rooms, where the issues may be heard."[172] In Article 2 (a), of course, the **place** is a "foreign" one. To this the Model Law definition adds the possibility of official and authoritative (as opposed to private) resolution, which Professor Felsenfeld's suggestion anticipates, with the words, "judicial or administrative."

Another element of the definition is the phrase "pursuant to a law relating to insolvency," a reference to the source of the authority for the proceedings, important because it permits "the recognizing court to avoid examining *de novo* whether the proceeding [is] an insolvency proceeding."[173] Although the language of the definition does not use the formula "insolvency proceedings,"[174] the Guide to Enactment states that "it is intended in subparagraph (a) to refer broadly to proceedings involving companies in severe financial distress."[175] Given the Guide's caution that the term "**insolvency proceedings**" should not exclude natural persons as debtors,[176] one should not read too much into the reference to "**companies.**" The explanation is meant to emphasize that "insolvency" is not intended to carry a narrow meaning as to a type of debtor that national law sometimes assigns it, but rather to refer as the subject of the proceedings to an entity in "**severe financial distress.**"[177] This also appears to leave open the possibility that the debtor need not be "insolvent" in terms of having liabilities exceeding the value of its assets or even a present inability to pay its debts as they mature. **64**

The word "**collective,**" in conjunction with the idea that the debtor's assets and affairs are subject to the control of a foreign court[178] "for the purpose of ... liquidation," conjures up the image of **collective execution** familiar in insolvency practice.[179] The explicit mention of "reorganization" in addition to "liquidation" as a possible purpose of the foreign insolvency legislation is noteworthy, particularly for enacting States whose domestic insolvency legislation does not provide for reorganizations.[180] The legal mechanisms necessary to enable a debtor to reorganize may bring requests for unusual **65**

---

172 Felsenfeld, at 5–23 (discussing the concept of "access and recognition").

173 A/CN.9/419 ¶ 106.

174 There was discussion in the Working Group about especially defining the term "insolvency proceeding," but it was deemed unnecessary. *See supra* note 85.

175 Guide ¶ 71.

176 *Id.* ¶ 52.

177 A/CN.9/435 ¶ 109 (discussing the problem of languages that have connotations of "insolvency" which are narrower than the broad meaning intended).

178 Note that the term "foreign court" is itself defined in subparagraph (e) in a broad sense to include administrative authorities, if competent. *See* discussion at mn 94 *et seq*, *infra*.

179 In commencing its work, the Working Group emphasized "the importance of indicating the essential elements of the proceedings to be covered"; suggestions included "that the proceedings to be encompassed should be of a collective character, should involve supervision of the debtor by an independent party and should not cover financial adjustment measures undertaken by parties purely on a private basis, without court or administrative involvement." A/CN.9/419 ¶ 19.

180 *See, e.g.,* A/CN.9/419 ¶ 32 (discussing same). Inclusion of reorganization was part of the first of three characteristics for which there was a "widely held view" during the early deliberations of the Working Group (the other two of which are discussed above): that "it should be an insolvency proceeding in the broad sense, so as to cover both liquidation and reorganization proceedings; it should be a collective proceeding, in the sense that representation of the mass of creditors would be involved; and it should be a proceeding that was somehow officially sanctioned, whether by a court or an administrative body." *Id.* ¶ 96; *see also* A/CN.9/422 ¶ 48 (including as the "basic elements" of the definition "insolvency in a broad sense covering liquidation and reorganization, a collective character involving representation of the mass of creditors, and official sanction").

actions before courts that ordinarily supervise only liquidations.[181] Use of the term "reorganization" is itself intended to broadly include an array of proceedings with the economic effect of maintaining a going concern in some form.[182]

66 The discussion thus far has been restricted to the limiting language of the Article 2 (a). The text is meant to be otherwise inclusive. For example, it states that a "foreign proceeding" includes **"an interim proceeding."** The inclusion was meant to ensure that the provisional proceedings that often or always occur in some countries not be excluded from consideration as **"foreign proceedings"** when they otherwise meet the requirements of Article 2 (a) merely because they are provisional or interim in nature, because the objectives of the Model Law apply to them as well.[183]

67 The inclusive language for **interim proceedings** and proceedings whose purpose is **reorganization** indicates that other particularities of foreign law ought not become bases for exclusion so long as the proceeding otherwise meets the criteria of Article 2 (a).[184] Thus, it should not matter whether a proceeding that otherwise meets the criteria is "**compulsory or voluntary,**[185] corporate or individual" or one "in which the debtor retains some measure of control over its assets,"[186] as in the case of an American **debtor in possession**[187] or German ***Eigenverwaltung.***[188] Naturally, conflicts will arise as a consequence of the territoriality principle. Indeed, before work on the Model Law began, the UNCITRAL Secretariat noted in its Report on the UNCITRAL – INSOL Colloquium on Cross-Border Insolvency, as an "example of difficulties that might arise in the context of a reorganization proceeding, ... the case in which one jurisdiction envisages a 'debtor in possession' continuing to exercise management functions, while, under the law of another State in which a contemporaneous insolvency proceeding is being

---

181 Notably, reorganization precedes liquidation in the text, probably indicating the "logical progression of possible steps" or the "increasing trend toward greater attempts at reorganization." A/CN.9/419 ¶ 107.

182 The Working Group rejected the words "adjusting the debts of a debtor" because they "might not be universally understood as a reference to reorganization proceedings, which were intended to be covered." A/CN.9/419 ¶ 97. It avoided listing kinds of reorganization proceedings, such as compositions, because doing so risked "excluding some types of proceedings intended to be covered." *Id.* ¶ 108 (noting that "the broad category of 'reorganization', which might be read more as an economic than a legal term, would widely be understood as encompassing composition and other such proceedings"); A/CN.9/422 ¶ 59 ("reorganization" encompasses composition arrangements).

183 Guide ¶ 69; A/CN.9/433 ¶ 38 (describing Working Group's agreement that interim proceedings be included in the definition); A/CN.9/435 ¶ 110 (reiterating need to include interim proceedings); *see also* Art 3 of the EIR and the text describing it at mn 91 *et seq* in part 1.

184 *See, e.g.,* A/CN.9/419 ¶ 98 (stating that the Working Group was "urged to adopt an approach that would be as inclusive as possible, and to avoid including numerous conditions in the definition to the degree that the definition should limit the achievement of the goal of facilitating recognition of foreign insolvency proceedings").

185 A suggestion was made within the Working Group that the suggested phrase "voluntary or compulsory" was "superfluous since both those types of proceedings were implicit in the term 'collective proceeding'." A/CN.9/422 ¶ 49.

186 Guide ¶ 24. This is remarkable because of the fact that in many countries, the removal of assets from the control of the debtor is a hallmark of insolvency procedure. A/CN.9/419 ¶ 30.

187 *See* 11 U.S.C. §§ 1101 (defining "debtor in possession") and 1107 (generally granting debtors in possession the same rights as trustees).

188 *See* §§ 270–85 of the German Insolvency Act [InsO] (governing debtor-administered cases).

conducted with respect to the same debtor, existing management is displaced or the debtor's business is to be liquidated."[189] The point is to establish criteria for recognizing the (other) fora in which the issues are being heard and open the way for **access and co-operation** between or among the fora in resolving the issues. In any event, enacting States may always at least exclude particular kinds of debtors from the scope of the enacted version of the Model Law by use of Article 1 (2).[190]

2.2.2.3.2 United States Law

The following definition is not part of chapter 15 but is rather found in chapter 1 of the Bankruptcy Code:[191] **68**

> **The term "foreign proceeding" means a collective judicial or administrative proceeding in a foreign country, including an interim proceeding, under a law relating to insolvency or adjustment of debt in which proceeding the assets and affairs of the debtor are subject to control or supervision by a foreign court, for the purpose of reorganization or liquidation.**

The only change to the Model Law is the addition of the words "or adjustment of debt," which was apparently intended to make clear that "insolvency" of the debtor, either in the sense of **debts exceeding assets** or in the sense of **financial embarrassment**, is not a requirement to meet the definition. **69**

The inclusion of reorganization as a purpose in the definition of "foreign proceeding" is considered particularly important in the United States.[192] **70**

2.2.2.4 Definition of "foreign main proceeding"

2.2.2.4.1 General

The decision to recognize a foreign proceeding carries with it an obligation to adjudge whether it is a "**foreign main proceeding**" or a "**foreign non-main proceeding.**"[193] The determination turns on the Article 2 (b) definition of "foreign main proceeding," which is reproduced *verbatim* in Article 17 (2) (a) and focuses on the question of the State in which the debtor has the "**centre of its main interests,**" or "**COMI,**" as opposed to a mere "**establishment.**" The dichotomy is meant to make the **level of relief ordinarily available** to a foreign representative depend upon the jurisdictional basis supporting the foreign proceeding for which recognition is sought.[194] **71**

Unlike the term "establishment," which is defined in Article 2 (f), the phrase "centre of a debtor's main interests" is not further defined in the Model Law. Although Article 16 (3) provides a statutory presumption that "the debtor's **registered office,** or **habitual residence** in the case of an individual," is the centre of its main interests, the presumption operates only "[i]n absence of proof to the contrary."[195] Thus, although the location of a debtor's COMI will in many cases be presumed or obvious, it may sometimes **72**

---

[189] A/CN.9/398 ¶ 5.

[190] Guide ¶ 25.

[191] 11 U.S.C. § 101 (23).

[192] *See, e.g.*, Bufford at 34 (noting that having reorganization deemed "a fundamental goal of chapter 15" was a feature "especially important to U.S. interests").

[193] *See* Art 17 (2) (stating that the foreign proceeding "shall" be recognized as either a foreign main or non-main proceeding); *see also* mn 189 *et seq* (discussing same).

[194] *See* related discussion at mn 168 *infra*.

[195] *See* mn 180 *et seq* (discussing Article 16).

be unclear.[196] The definition of "foreign main proceeding" uses the definite article "the" in front of both the words "State" and "centre" to indicate that a debtor may have only **one COMI**, and that it may exist **in only one State.**[197] A number of factors may come into play in determining the COMI, such as the place of the debtor's incorporation, its decision-making "nerve centre," the place in which it has most of its assets[198] or in which its primary operations are located, or perhaps where it has its greatest or most profitable sales or service presence. A complicating circumstance may be the existence of a corporate group, which leads to an inquiry into the degree to which economic reality should overshadow legal form in determining the COMI, particularly where group structure may be manipulated for forum shopping.[199] A possible guiding principle is that determination of the COMI ought to be based on the reasonable expectations of creditors dealing with the debtor.[200]

73 There is no indication, however, that the COMI may be defined by reference to the availability of certain features or remedies in a State's insolvency law, including its similarity to that of the enacting State. Nor does a determination of where the COMI of a debtor lies appear to be an "action" within the **"public policy" exception** of Article 6, though that exception could apply to the decision on whether to grant any recognition at all.[201]

---

[196] A/52/17 ¶ 153 (noting lack of clarity but also remarking that interpretation in the context of the European Union Convention on Insolvency Proceedings, Art 3 (1), O.J. L 160/1 (June 30, 2000), would be useful); *cf* A/CN.9/419 ¶ 17 (citing "domicile" as a term to be avoided in drafting because it is difficult of determination and capable of creating uncertainty).

[197] *Cf* A/CN.9/435 ¶¶ 186–87 (noting agreement as to "principle 1" in the formulation of provisions for concurrent proceedings, "There can only be one main proceeding. The court shall decide which proceeding is the main proceeding.").

[198] It should be noted that while presence of assets may be one factor to consider in determining the centre of a debtor's main interests, it seems unlikely that that factor alone can rebut the presumption of Article 16 (3) that the location of a debtor's registered office determines its COMI, since presence of assets alone is insufficient to prove even an establishment. *See* mn 97 *et seq* (discussing definition of "establishment"), mn 180 (discussing presumption).

[199] *See* G. Larry Engel, Suggested Clarifications and Reforms for U.S. Chapter 15 and the UNCITRAL Model Law on Cross-Border Insolvency on Which It Is Based: The Pragmatic Cynics' Concerns at 16–20 (prepared for International Insolvency Institute New York Program, June 12–13, 2006), available at: http://www.iiiglobal.org/country/usa/20060620morrison.pdf (last viewed Mar. 20, 2007) (discussing manipulation of the COMI concept through creation of "strategic intermediate holding companies").

[200] The COMI concept also appears in the preamble to the European Council Regulation on Insolvency Proceedings 2000, Council Regulation (EC) No. 1346/2000 of 29 May 2000 ¶ 13, providing that the COMI "should correspond to the place where the debtor conducts the administration of his interests on a regular basis and is therefore ascertainable by third parties." This guidance and EU case law will undoubtedly influence the determination of just what COMI means for Model Law purposes given Article 8's injunction to regard the international origin and need to promote uniformity in application in interpreting it. *See* Art 8 and mn 126 *et seq* (discussing Article 8); *see also* Guide ¶ 72 (noting that expression "centre of main interests" is used in the (European Union) Convention on Insolvency Proceedings). For a discussion of the COMI concept in EU jurisprudence, *see* Art 3 of the EIR and the text describing it at mn 15 *et seq* in part 1.

[201] *See* Art 17 (1) (subjecting the decision on whether to grant recognition to Article 6, which contains the Model Law's public policy exception) and mn 188 (discussing same).

A separate question is the extent to which enacting States will uniformly interpret what a COMI is, both abstractly and with respect to a particular debtor. Unlike in the EIR, there is no Model Law rule that a court must recognize a foreign proceeding as a foreign main proceeding only because another court has done so or has already found that the COMI is in a particular place.[202] Article 8, however, does require courts in enacting States to have "regard" for the Law's "international origin and to the need to promote uniformity in its application and the observance of good faith."[203] **74**

Recognition of a foreign proceeding as a foreign main proceeding causes the automatic effects set forth in Article 20 (1)[204] to apply and generally entitles the proceeding to more deference than might be available to a foreign non-main proceeding.[205] **75**

2.2.2.4.2 United States Law

The wording of the section 1502 (4) definition of "**foreign main proceeding**" is nearly identical to the Model Law definition. According to the legislative history, the changes were made to "comport with United States terminology," so they were meant to have little substantive effect.[206] **76**

[Reserved] **77**

The term "center of main interests" ("COMI") "has not heretofore been used in United States jurisprudence."[207] At least two bankruptcy courts have examined the concept in published opinions explaining their decisions to recognize two foreign proceedings under chapter 15. In the first, the bankruptcy court for the Eastern District of California in ***In re Tri-Continental Exchange Ltd.*** recognized St. Vincent and the Grenadines ("SVG") liquidation proceedings of insurance companies organized under the laws of SVG as "foreign main proceedings" even though most of companies' clients were located in the United States and Canada.[208] The court acknowledged its obligation under section 1508[209] to consider the international origin of the term COMI, which, as noted **78**

---

[202] *See* Art 3 of the EIR and the text describing it at mn 88 *et seq*, and Art 16 of the EIR and the text describing it at mn 1 *et seq* in part 1.

[203] *See* mn 126 *et seq* (discussing Article 8).

[204] *See* mn 213 *et seq* (discussing Article 20).

[205] *See* Arts 19 (4) (conditioning grant of provisional relief on non-interference with foreign main proceeding), 21 (3) (generally limiting relief available to representatives of foreign non-main proceedings), 23 (2) (limiting relief respecting Paulian actions available to representatives of foreign non-main proceedings), 28 (restricting effects of a plenary insolvency proceeding opened after recognition of a foreign main proceeding), 29 (c) (limiting relief available to representatives of foreign non-main proceedings during pendency of insolvency proceedings in the enacting State), 30 (generally prioritizing relief accorded to a representative of a foreign main proceeding above that to be accorded to a representative of a foreign non-main proceeding involving the same debtor), 31 (allowing for presumption of insolvency of debtor based on recognition of a foreign main proceeding respecting the debtor) and mn 202 *et seq* (discussing Article 19), mn 224 *et seq* (discussing Article 21), mn 247 *et seq* (discussing Article 23), mn 280 *et seq* (discussing Article 28), mn 284 *et seq* (discussing Article 29), mn 293 *et seq* (discussing Article 30) and mn 297 *et seq* (discussing Article 31).

[206] H. Rep. No. 109–31, 109th Cong., 1st Sess. 107 (2005). For example, "State" was likely changed to avoid what might be interpreted as a reference to one of the states of the United States.

[207] *In re Tri-Continental Exch. Ltd.*, 349 B.R. 627, 633 (Bankr. E.D. Cal. 2006).

[208] *Id.*

[209] Section 1508 corresponds to Article 8. *See* mn 126 *et seq* (discussing section 1508).

above,[210] came from the EU Convention on Insolvency.[211] Based on its investigation, the court equated the term roughly to what has been known in American jurisprudence as the debtor's **"principle place of business."**[212] In *Tri-Continental*, the debtors' only offices were located in SVG, where they had employed about 20 individuals.[213] Insurance contracts and other correspondence were sent from SVG to clients and "consultants" in North America.[214] Premium checks were collected at drop boxes in the United States, sent in bulk to SVG, endorsed there and returned to the United States for deposit in American accounts, from which the debtors transferred most of the funds to off-shore accounts.[215] By the time the court recognized the SVG proceedings, however, the debtors had ceased conducting business and no longer had employees.[216]

79 In the second reported case, ***In re SPhinX, Ltd.***, the bankruptcy court for the Southern District of New York provided a list of factors, "singly or combined, [that] could be relevant" to determining a COMI:

- "the location of the debtor's headquarters;
- the location of those who actually manage the debtor (which conceivably could be the headquarters of a holding company);
- the location of the debtor's primary assets;
- the location of the majority of the debtor's creditors or of a majority of the creditors who would be affected by the case; and/or
- the jurisdiction whose law would apply to most disputes."[217]

80 According to the court, however, such factors should not be applied mechanically, but should instead "be viewed in light of chapter 15's emphasis on protecting the reasonable interests of parties in interest pursuant to fair procedures and the maximalization of the debtor's value."[218] Because it is "their money," reasoned the court, "one generally should defer … to the creditors' acquiescence in or support of a proposed COMI."[219]

81 Also observing section 1508's mandate to consider the international origin of the Model Law, the *SPhinX* court turned for guidance to the recent decision of the European Court of Justice ("ECJ") interpreting the European Council's Insolvency Regulation in ***Bondi v. Bank of America, N.A.*** *(In re Eurofood IFSC Ltd.)*.[220] That court opined that the presumption that the COMI is within the state where the debtor has its registered office "can be rebutted only if factors which are both objective and ascertainable by

[210] *See supra* notes 196, 200.

[211] *Tri-Continental Exch.* at 634.

[212] *Id.* (citing Westbrook, 79 Am. Bankr. L. J. at 719–20); *see also* Black's Law Dictionary 1211 (7th ed. 1999) (defining "principal place of business" as the "place of a corporation's chief executive offices, which is typically viewed as the 'nerve center'"). The court also took note of section 1516 (c), which corresponds to Article 16 (3) and sets forth a presumption that a debtor's COMI corresponds to its "registered office." *Id.* at 634–35. *See* mn 184 for a discussion of section 1516 (c).

[213] *Id.* at 630.

[214] *Id.*

[215] *Id.*

[216] *Id.*

[217] *In re SPhinX, Ltd.*, 351 B.R. 103, 117 (Bankr. S.D.N.Y. 2006), *aff'd*, 371 B.R. 10 (S.D.N.Y. 2007).

[218] *Id.* Where a dispute exists, noted the court, the concept of cooperation between courts would ultimately be more important "than artificially choosing one proceeding as a 'primary' proceeding." *Id.* at 118.

[219] *Id.* at 117.

[220] Case 314/04, 2006 E.C.R. C-341/04, 2006 WL 1142304 (E.C.J. May 2, 2006). For a detailed discussion of this case, *see* Table of Cases Art 3 of the EIR Appendix A mn 10.

third parties enable it to be established that an actual situation exists which is different from that which locating it at that registered office is deemed to reflect."[221] According to the *SPhinX* court, "*Eurofood* ... left open whether the presumption may be rebutted in respect of a debtor that conducts some business in the location where it is registered (even if, as in the case of the SPhinX Funds, most, if not all, of that business in that location pertains to simply maintaining its registered status, and the rest of its business is conducted elsewhere), although the ECJ strongly indicated that if third parties would objectively locate the administration of such a debtor's interests elsewhere, the presumption would be rebutted."[222]

Despite the effective rebuttal of the presumption of a Cayman Island **COMI** that it seemed to acknowledge the ECJ would find as the result of objective inquiry, the *SPhinX* court's examination of the will of the most interested parties, the debtors' investors, who could be considered either as its largest group of creditors (if seen as fraud victims) or as equity holders (in which case the debtors would be solvent), and who "tacitly supported" the petition for recognition as a foreign main proceeding, would normally have left it "inclined to find the Debtor's COMI in the Cayman Islands and recognize the proceedings as foreign main proceedings ..."[223] In the case before it, however, the court recognized the Cayman proceeding as a foreign nonmain proceeding because it found that the petition had been filed with the improper purposes of forum shopping and using the automatic stay that ensues upon recognition of a foreign main proceeding[224] to delay related litigation in order to obtain bargaining leverage, and because no undue prejudice would come to any party by recognition of the Cayman proceedings as foreign nonmain proceedings, since the court had discretion to apply any relief obtainable in a foreign main proceeding to a foreign nonmain proceeding.[225] **82**

Severe criticism has attended the *SPhinX* decision, primarily because of the *SPhinX* court's **consideration of subjective factors**, such as the desires of the parties in interest, in discerning the location of the COMI, which under chapter 15 ought to be determined on a **purely objective basis**.[226] **83**

---

221 *Id.*, slip op. at 6.

222 *SPhinX* at 118–19. The *SPhinX* court also examined "pragmatic considerations" focusing on the degree of assistance an insolvency court in a state purported to be the COMI would require from courts in other states to administer the case. *SPhinX* at 119.

223 *Id.* at 121.

224 *See* 11 U.S.C. § 1520; *see also* mn 218 *et seq* (discussing section 1520).

225 *Id.* at 121–22; *see also* mn 232 *et seq* (discussing section 1521).

226 *See* Daniel M. Glosband, *SPhinX Chapter 15 Opinion Misses the Mark*, Am. Bankr. Inst. J. 44, 44–45, 84–85 (Dec./Jan. 2007). In addition to the *Eurofood* decision, Glosband cites to other European case law: *Dasytek* [2003] BCC 562; *Ci4Net* [2005] BCC 277; *Collins & Aikman* (Lawrence Collins J. 15 July 2005); *Hettlage ZIP* 20/2004 p 962; *Mliekotej sro ("Parmalat Slovakia")*, (Unrep, 14 June 2004, Municipal Court of Fejer/Szekesfehevar); *MPOTEC GmbH* [2006] BCC 681; *Eurotunnel Fin. Ltd.* (Paris Commercial Court, 2 August 2006); *Op. of Advocate-General Jacob in Eurofood* [2005] BCC 1,0201, ¶¶ 111–12. Glosband at 45. In another opinion recently issued, Judge Lifland, an author of the Model Law and chapter 15, declined to recognize two Cayman Islands exempted limited liability companies similar to those in the *SPhinX* case based on an objective finding that the companies conducted administration of their interests in the United States and thus had their COMIs there, even though no objection to recognition of the Cayman proceedings as foreign main proceedings had been raised. *See In re Bear Stearns High-Grade Structured Credit Strategies Master Fund, Ltd.*, 374 B.R. 122 (Bankr. S.D.N.Y. 2007) (amended decision). Other aspects of the *SPhinX*

2.2.2.5 Definition of "foreign non-main proceeding"

2.2.2.5.1 General

84 The alternative to recognition of a foreign proceeding as a foreign main proceeding is recognition of it as a **foreign non-main proceeding.**[227] The key parts of the Article 2 (c) definition of a foreign non-main proceeding are

(i) a foreign proceeding

(ii) that is not a foreign main proceeding and

(iii) the existence of an establishment in the State in which the foreign proceeding is taking place.

85 Thus, other than observing that foreign main proceedings and foreign non-main proceedings are mutually exclusive, the discussion of the definition of foreign non-main proceedings really boils down to examining the definitions of "foreign proceeding" (Article 2 (a)),[228] "foreign main proceeding" (Article 2 (b))[229] and "establishment" (Article 2 (f)).[230]

2.2.2.5.2 United States Law

86 The chapter 15 definition is not substantially different from that of the Model Law.

2.2.2.6 Definition of "foreign representative"

2.2.2.6.1 General

87 With respect to "**foreign representatives,**" the important things for purposes of recognition under Articles 17 (which specifically references the definition of "foreign representative"[231]) and 18,[232] and the access and powers that come with it, are that the person or body

(1) be authorized in a foreign proceeding

(2) to administer the reorganization or liquidation or to act as a representative of the foreign proceeding.

88 As to the latter point, like the definition of "foreign proceeding," the first alternative definition of "foreign representative" in Article 2 (d) is meant to describe the ***function*** of the representantive,[233] i.e., to administer the debtor's assets or affairs, so none of the

---

decision are discussed at mn 104, 193 *et seq.* (discussing sections 1502 (7) (definition of "recognition") and 1517 (decision to recognize foreign proceedings), respectively).

[227] Art 17 (2) (b); *see also* mn 189 (discussing same).

[228] *See* mn 62 *et seq* (discussing definition of "foreign proceeding").

[229] *See* mn 71 *et seq* (discussing definition of "foreign main proceeding").

[230] *See* mn 97 *et seq* (discussing definition of "establishment").

[231] Art 17 (1) (b).

[232] *See* Art 18 (a) (requiring a foreign representative to report "[a]ny substantial change in the status of the recognized foriegn proceeding or the status of the foreign reperesentative's appointment").

[233] *See* A/CN.9/419 ¶ 112 (expressing concern "that defining 'foreign representative' by reference to various specific terms and titles ... might create uncertainty in jurisdictions where the expressions would be unfamiliar and might have the unintended effect of being unduly restrictive, since the list would inevitably be incomplete" and supporting basing "the definition on the functions of the foreign representative").

terms in that part of the definition (except the term "foreign proceeding") should be understood to carry technical freight from national insolvency law or other sources.[234] Thus, the foreign representative may be a "person *or* body," and may be appointed on a long-term *or* "interim basis."[235] Likewise the purpose of the foreign proceeding may be liquidation *or* reorganization. The definition includes "debtors in possession"[236] but excludes other individuals or bodies which, though connected to the insolvency proceeding, do not directly administer the assets or affairs of the debtor, such as judges, accountants or supervising commissioners,[237] unless they are authorized to act as foreign representatives.

The alternative functional definition, requiring a direct authorization to act specifically "as a representative of the foreign proceeding," does, of course, carry a technical, legal meaning in the authorizing State. With respect to States that have also enacted the Model Law, such grant is legislative and may be found in the respective Article 5 enactment.[238] **89**

As to the authorization itself, the question is only whether an appointment to act in one or both of the above-described capacities exists. The procedural propriety of the foreign representative's appointment in the originating country is not before the recognizing court.[239] **90**

Whether directly responsible for administering the liquidation or reorganization of the debtor or only appointed to represent the foreign proceeding commenced for those purposes, the Model Law regards the foreign representative as the "representative of the collectivity of creditors" for purposes of standing.[240] **91**

2.2.2.6.2 United States Law

As with "foreign proceeding," the Bankruptcy Code's definition of "foreign representative" is in chapter 1 rather than chapter 15:[241] **92**

---

234 Guide ¶ 71. *See also* A/CN.9/419 ¶ 36–39 (discussing "the extent and manner in which the recognizing court might wish to assure itself that the foreign representative had authority from the jurisdiction of the recognized proceeding to act abroad" and arguing for "a functional definition of 'foreign representative' rather than one using specific terminology"). The idea of a "functional definition" seems to mean that courts should decide what "functions" fall within the scope of the definition by reference to the Model Law itself and, by extension, to the Guide to Enactment, the various Commission and Working Group reports and to case law and commentary that analyze these without reference to national law, thus developing a unique, consensual, "Model Law" meaning for the term, however technical it may thus become.

235 A/CN.9/422 ¶ 52 (recording agreement in the Working Group that "interim" office holders be included); A/CN.9/433 ¶ 38 (same).

236 A/CN.9/419 ¶ 116; A/CN.9/422 ¶ 51 (discussing debtors in possession as potentially problematic for some states but pointing out that in a broad range of proceedings debtors maintain some control).

237 A/CN.9/419 ¶ 115.

238 *See* mn 113 *et seq* (discussing Article 5).

239 A/CN.9/419 ¶ 117 (deleting the word "duly" to make clear that the question of the whether the appointment was made in in accordance with the procedural law of the originating jurisdiction is not intended to be placed before the recognizing court).

240 A/CN.9/433 ¶ 114.

241 11 U.S.C. § 101 (24).

The term "foreign proceeding" means a collective judicial or administrative proceeding in a foreign country, including an interim proceeding, under a law relating to insolvency or adjustment of debt in which proceeding the assets and affairs of the debtor are subject to control or supervision by a foreign court, for the purpose of reorganization or liquidation.

93 This is essentially identical to the Model Law definition. Of special significance to the United States was the inclusion of **debtors in possession** in the definition.[242]

2.2.2.7 Definition of "foreign court"

2.2.2.7.1 General

94 In keeping with the functional focus of defining terms, the definition of "**foreign court**" merely serves as a drafting device to capture non-judicial authorities that may supervise some foreign proceedings and courts that act in that capacity in a single defined term.[243] It therefore tracks Article 2 (d) of the EIR.[244] The point was to capture insolvency proceedings that are "somehow officially sanctioned" as opposed to private arrangements.[245]

95 The definition suffers from some circularity in that it focuses on **supervision** of "foreign proceedings," which are defined in part by reference to supervision by "foreign courts."[246]

2.2.2.7.2 United States Law

96 The United States definition is the same as that of the Model Law.

2.2.2.8 Definition of "establishment"

2.2.2.8.1 General

97 By defining "**establishment,**" subparagraph (f) essentially completes the definition of "foreign non-main proceeding" in subparagraph (c), which specifically refers to subparagraph (f).[247] The definition is imported nearly verbatim from Article 2 (h) of the EIR, adding only the words "or services" to the definition of establishment appearing there.[248] Its interpretation will thus undoubted be heavily influenced by European practice.

98 To have an establishment in a State, the debtor must have a "place of operations" and "carry out **a non-transitory economic activity**" there, which seems to require something more than a mere presence of assets.[249] The use of the indefinite article "a" indi-

242 *See* Bufford, at 33–34.
243 Guide ¶ 74; A/CN.9/422 ¶ 49.
244 *Cf* Art 2 of the EIR and the explanatory text at mn 17 *et seq*; Guide ¶ 74.
245 *See, e.g.,* A/CN.9/419 ¶ 29.
246 Art 2 (a).
247 Art 2 (c). Aside from Article 2, the term "establishment" appears only in Article 17 (2) (b), which requires that a foreign proceeding be in a State in which the debtor has an "establishment" within the definition of Article 2 (f) to be recognized as a foreign non-main proceeding. *See also* mn 189 *et seq* (discussing Article 17).
248 Art 2 (h) of the EIR; *see also* Guide ¶ 75 (stating the term was "inspired by" Article (2) (h) of the European Union Convention on Insolvency Proceedings); A/52/17 ¶ 158 (noting the term was "closely modeled" on the EU Convention).
249 *See* Glosband at 45 (noting that the definition of "establishment" "arose from the

cates that the **activity** must be unitary as opposed to serial, and the adjective "non-transitory" requires that it be persistent.[250] The modifier "economic" generally means that the activity must involve production, distribution and/or consumption of "goods or services,"[251] and "with human means" probably indicates employees work there.[252] According to one drafter of the Model Law, "Put concisely, there must be a place of business for there to be an 'establishment,'" so a mere "drop box" presence is insufficient.[253]

2.2.2.8.2 United States Law

The chapter 15 definition of "**establishment**" omits the concluding phrase, "with human means and goods or services." The legislative history gives no reason for the omission. **99**

Assuming other requirements are met, American law recognizes the mere presence of assets (without an establishment) in the United States as sufficient to commence a plenary case.[254] Accepting the contrary Model Law rule for ancillary cases may preclude recognition of such American cases in countries that grant recognition based on reciprocity. **100**

2.2.2.9 United States Law – Other Definitions

Section 1502 contains a number of additional definitions that apply to chapter 15 not found in the Model Law. **101**

2.2.2.9.1 "Debtor"

The section 1502 (1) definition of "**debtor**"[255] applies only to the use of the term in chapter 15 and should be distinguished from the general definition of the term that is used in the rest of the Bankruptcy Code, where it "means person ... concerning which a case under this title has been commenced."[256] The specialized definition eliminates **102**

---

rejection, in relation to the EC Regulation, of the presence of assets as a sufficient basis for taking local jurisdiction," citing Moss & Smith, Moss, Fletcher and Isaacs: The EC Regulation on Insolvency Proceedings ¶ 8.26 (Oxford University Press, Dec. 2002)).

250 Webster's Ninth New Collegiate Dictionary 1254 (1984).

251 Webster's Ninth New Collegiate Dictionary 395 (1984).

252 There is a question about whether enterprises operating in an electronic environment can be said to have an establishment in a particular place. The Working Group apparently discussed the issue in the context of a suggestion that the words "with human means and goods" might be interpreted as excluding such enterprises, A/CN.9/435 ¶ 113, but the words remained in the text without further explanation.

253 Glosband, at 45; *see also In re Bear Stearns High-Grade Structured Credit Strategies Master Fund, Ltd. (In Provisional Liquidation)*, 374 B.R. 122, 129 (Bankr. S.D.N.Y. 2007) (amended decision) (holding that carrying-out only those activities necessary to maintain registration is insufficient to meet the definition of establishment under United States law).

254 *But see* 11 U.S.C. § 1528 and mn 280 *et seq* (discussing Article 28) (discussing some limitations on such cases). Although they may be commenced, jurisdictionally weak cases may be subject to suspension or dismissal. *See* 11 U.S.C. § 305 (governing abstention from exercise of jurisdiction).

255 *See also* 11 U.S.C. § 101 (15) (defining "entity").

256 11 U.S.C. § 101 (13).

the need "to refer repeatedly to 'the same debtor as in the foreign proceeding'" in chapter 15.[257]

2.2.2.9.2 "Trustee"

103 The definition of "**trustee**" is another drafting device. A **debtor in possession** or a **debtor under chapter 9** functions as a trustee, i.e., as "the person or body administering a reorganization or liquidation"[258] under United States law.[259] To avoid the need to add mention of them with every use of the term "trustee," that term is defined to include them for chapter 15 purposes.

2.2.2.9.3 "Recognition"

104 According to the legislative history, the definition of "**recognition**" "supplements the Model Law definitions and merely simplifies drafting of various other sections of chapter 15."[260] The definition also makes clear that there can be no recognition aside from that of a foreign main or nonmain proceeding.[261]

2.2.2.9.4 "within the territorial jurisdiction of the United States"

105 Congress defined this phrase for use "where the Model Law and ... chapter [15] intend to refer only to property within the territory of the enacting state."[262] It is necessary because the United States generally asserts "insolvency jurisdiction over property outside its territorial limits ... ."[263]

---

257 H. Rep. No. 109–31, 109th Cong., 1st Sess. 107 (2005).

258 *See* Art 5.

259 *See* 11 U.S.C. §§ 701 (c) (confirming that interim trustees are trustees in chapter 7 cases), 902 (5) (including municipal debtors in the definition of trustee in chapter 9 cases), § 1107 (discussing rights, powers and duties of debtors in possession).

260 H. Rep. No. 109–31, 109th Cong., 1st Sess. 107 (2005).

261 The definition of "recognition" thus seems to contradict the conclusion of the court's opinion in *In re SPhinX, Ltd.*, 351 B.R. 103, 115 (Bankr. S.D.N.Y. 2006), *aff'd*, 371 B.R. 10 (S.D.N.Y. 2007), that the decision to recognize a foreign proceeding as a foreign main proceeding is separate (and can therefore be delayed) from the decision to recognize the proceeding as a foreign proceeding at all. *See* Glosband at 45 (noting that such separation "result[ed] in the court ignoring whether the [debtors' foreign proceedings] are foreign proceedings that are eligible for chapter 15 recognition ... [under] the definitional requirements of § 1502 as foreign main proceedings or foreign nonmain proceedings") (internal quotation marks omitted); *see also In re Bear Stearns High-Grade Structured Credit Strategies Master Fund, Ltd. (In Provisional Liquidation)*, 374 B.R. 122, 126 (Bankr. S.D.N.Y. 2007) (amended decision) (noting that recognition is a "simple single step process ... to determine recognition as either a main or nonmain proceeding or nonrecognition"). Other aspects of the *SPhinX* decision are discussed at mn 79 *et seq* (discussing section 1502 (4) (definition of "foreign main proceeding") and mn 193 *et seq* (discussing section 1517 (decision to recognize foreign proceedings)).

262 H. Rep. No. 109–31, 109th Cong., 1st Sess. 107 (2005).

263 *Id.*; *see also* 28 U.S.C. § 1334 (e) (providing United States district courts in bankruptcy cases jurisdiction "of all the property, wherever located, of the debtor as of the commencement of such [a] case, and of property of the estate"). United States bankruptcy courts are units of such district courts. 28 U.S.C. § 151.

2.2.3 Article 3 – International obligations of this State

To the extent that this Law conflicts with an obligation of this State arising out of any treaty or other form of agreement to which it is a party with one or more other States, the requirements of the treaty or agreement prevail.

→ *Cf* Art 44 (3) (a) of the EIR

2.2.3.1 General

Article 3 is modelled after similar provisions in other UNCITRAL model laws.[264] Its purpose is to establish the "**principle of supremacy** of international obligations of the enacting State over internal law."[265] Examples include some treaties which provide for legalization of documents, which may conflict with Article 16 (2)[266] (establishing presumption of authenticity of documents submitted in support of an application for recognition without need for legalization) or govern communication between courts,[267] which may conflict with Article 25 (2)[268] (entitling courts to communicate directly with foreign courts), or other treaties dealing with cross-border insolvency.[269] **106**

The Guide to Enactment provides drafting suggestions to deal with particularities in how different legal systems treat international obligations in relation to national laws, the thrust of which is to establish the "principle of supremacy" while "tak[ing] steps to avoid an unnecessarily broad interpretation of international treaties"[270] which could impair the benefits of uniformity. **107**

2.2.3.2 United States Law

Section 1503 – International obligations of the United States

To the extent that this chapter conflicts with an obligation of the United States arising out of any treaty or other form of agreement to which it is a party with one or more other countries, the requirements of the treaty or agreement prevail.

The language of section 1503 follows that of Article 3 with only minor changes. The House Report confirms that international agreements should be read to avoid conflict with the text of chapter 15, particularly where "the international obligation addres- **108**

264 Guide ¶ 76.

265 Guide ¶ 76; A/CN.9/422 ¶ 67 (stating that inclusion of Article 3 was "useful because it would draw the attention of enacting States to the need for clarity on the relationship of treaty obligations").

266 *See* mn 180 *et seq* (discussing Article 16).

267 A/CN.9/435 ¶ 115 (citing these examples).

268 *See* mn 258 *et seq* (discussing Article 25).

269 It is, of course, possible that the treaty may allow local law to prevail. *See, e.g.,* Guide ¶ 115 (citing to the Convention Abolishing the Requirement of Legalisation for Foreign Documents (1961), Art 3 (2), as example). In addition to the EIR, other multilateral regional treaties regulating cross-border insolvency include the Montevideo Treaties of 1889 and 1940 (in Latin America), the Convention among Denmark, Finland, Iceland, Norway and Sweden regarding Bankruptcy (concluded in 1933 and amended in 1977 and 1982), and the European Convention on Certain International Aspects of Bankruptcy (among the members of the Council of Europe) (Istanbul, 1990). A/CN.9/398 ¶ 10.

270 Guide ¶¶ 76–78 (discussing, *inter alia*, the self-executing treaty doctrine).

ses a subject matter less directly related than the Model Law to a case before the court."[271]

2.2.4 Article 4 – *[Competent court or authority]*[1]

The functions referred to in this Law relating to recognition of foreign proceedings and cooperation with foreign courts shall be performed by *[specify the court, courts, authority or authorities competent to perform those functions in the enacting State]*.

Footnote [1]: A State where certain functions relating to insolvency proceedings have been conferred upon government-appointed officials or bodies might wish to include in article 4 or elsewhere in chapter I the following provision:

Nothing in this Law affects the provisions in force in this State governing the authority of *[insert the title of the government-appointed person or body]*.

2.2.4.1 General

109 Article 4 serves as both a marker for users of the enacted Law, particularly foreign courts and foreign representatives, pointing to the authority or authorities competent to perform a function related to recognition or cooperation in a particular enacting State,[272] and, more importantly, as a **means** to channel the jurisdiction to perform such functions to the particular courts or other authorities identified.[273] The optional footnote suggests an avenue for enacting States to enable officials whose authority is not affected by the Model Law to perform "certain tasks related to the general supervision of the process of dealing with insolvency cases" despite such jurisdictional channeling, though if such officials are referred to in the bracketed language of Articles 25 and 26, they "may be subjected to a **duty to cooperate**" as those articles provide.[274]

110 The Model Law employs the phrase "recognition of foreign proceedings" for the first time in Article 4.[275] Article 17, which provides the criteria for such recognition, makes submission of the application for recognition "to the court referred to in Article 4" one of the criteria.

---

[271] H. Rep. No. 109–31, 109th Cong., 1st Sess. 107 (2005).

[272] *See* Guide ¶ 80 (stating that "value of Article 4 ... would be to increase the transparency and ease of use of the insolvency legislation for the benefit of, in particular, foreign representatives and foreign courts"); A/CN.9/435 ¶ 120 (stating that the provision "helped the foreign representative identify the authority to which he or she had to submit a request for recognition or cooperation"). In its early deliberations, the Working Group stated that "it might be helpful to state that there should be court access and to provide for an indication by enacting States themselves of which of their courts would be competent in these matters." A/CN.9/419 ¶ 69.

[273] The Guide to enactment warns that "implementing legislation should not unnecessarily limit the jurisdiction of other courts ... in particular to entertain requests by foreign representatives for provisional relief." Guide ¶ 81.

[274] Guide ¶ 81. If such officials also serve as "administrators in individual insolvency cases," they "would be covered by the Model Law." Guide ¶ 83.

[275] The phrase does not appear again until Article 12, which entitles a foreign representative to participate in a proceeding under the insolvency laws of the enacting State, and, after that, not again until it is fully treated in Chapter III, which regulates what is necessary for recognition of a foreign proceeding and provides for its effects.

Because the system of courts and other authorities competent to deal with various aspects of the Model Law are quite diverse across the community of nations, each enacting State is expected to appropriately tailor Article 4 **to meet its needs.**[276] Thus, uniformity of text is not a primary concern with respect to Article 4. **111**

2.2.4.2 United States Law

> **Section 1504 – Commencement of ancillary case**
>
> **A case under this chapter is commenced by the filing of a petition for recognition of a foreign proceeding under section 1515.**

Court jurisdiction in the United States is the subject of the United States Judicial Code,[277] and section 1509 also serves to channel jurisdiction to bankruptcy courts,[278] so section 1504's function is different than Article 4 of the Model Law; its role is to supply the mechanism to commence an **ancillary case.**[279] United States district courts have **exclusive subject matter jurisdiction** over all bankruptcy cases, though they may share jurisdiction over some matters connected to bankruptcy cases with other courts.[280] Generally, bankruptcy courts are units of the district courts over which bankruptcy judges preside, exercising jurisdiction in the first instance by referral from district court judges, though decisions not dealing with core bankruptcy issues may be regarded as recommendations to a district court judge, who in that event makes a final decision (subject to appeal).[281] Congress expressly deemed **recognition** and other matters under chapter 15 to be "core" bankruptcy matters.[282] **112**

> A foreign representative may commence chapter 15 case in the judicial district[283]

> (1) in which the debtor has its principial place of business or principal assets in the United States;
>
> (2) if the debtor does not have a place of business or assets in the United States, in which there is pending against the debtor an action or proceeding in a Federal or State court; or
>
> (3) in a case other than those specified in paragraph (1) or (2), in which venue will be consistent with the interests of justice and convenience of the parties, having regard to the relief sought by the foreign representative.

---

[276] Guide ¶ 80; *see also* A/CN.9/433 ¶ 45 (stating that Article 4 "should not suggest how the enacting State might describe the allocation of jurisdiction").

[277] 28 U.S.C. §§ 1–4001.

[278] *See* mn 136 *et seq* (discussing section 1509).

[279] *See* mn 52 for an explanation of the term "case." Note that "cases" are commenced with "petitions" under the Bankruptcy Code, so the word "petition" in chapter 15 substitutes for Model Law term "application" when it is used in conjunction with recognition.

[280] 28 U.S.C. § 1334 (a), (b).

[281] *See generally* 28 U.S.C. §§ 151, 157.

[282] 28 U.S.C. § 157 (b) (2) (P).

[283] 28 U.S.C. § 1410.

2.2.5 Article 5 – Authorization of *[insert the title of the person or body administering reorganization or liquidation under the law of the enacting State]* to act in a foreign State

A *[insert the title of the person or body administering a reorganization or liquidation under the law of the enacting State]* is authorized to act in a foreign State on behalf of a proceeding under *[identify laws of the enacting State relating to insolvency]*, as permitted by the applicable foreign law.

→ *Cf* Art 18 of the EIR

2.2.5.1 General

113 Article 5 is a legislative grant of the **authority necessary** to meet the second alternative in the Article 2 (d) definition of a "foreign representative," i.e., one "authorized to act as a representative of the foreign proceeding," and thus provides an avenue to meet the Article 17 (1) (b) requirement for recognition of the enacting State's insolvency proceedings as a "foreign proceedings" in other enacting States. To the extent that the enacting State grants Article 5 authorization to "person[s] or body[ies] who administer the reorganization or the liquidation of [a] debtor's assets or affairs," as the language in the first set of brackets suggests, it is theoretically unnecessary for that purpose with respect to other enacting States, since the functional, first alternative of the Article 2 (d) definition should cover such persons or bodies in any event. Nevertheless, as the final phrase of Article 5 superfluously warns, the efficacy of the authorization is subject to the limitations of the relevant foreign law,[284] which may not include the Model Law, so the express authorization may enable the authorized representative to act even in jurisdictions that have not enacted the Model Law[285] in ways that would otherwise be impossible, thus removing "an obstacle to effective ... cooperation in cross-border cases."[286] Furthermore, it is possible that the "identity and functions of a representative may not be self-evident"[287] in foreign jurisdictions, whether or not they have enacted the Model Law. The **legislative grant of Article 5** allows courts in such jurisdictions to assure themselves of the representative's authority to act without investigating whether the representative's functions match those set forth in the Article 2 (d) definition, which may also enhance the representative's ability to act expeditiously when necessary.[288]

114 In this regard, it should also be noted that the representative is entitled to act only "on behalf of a proceeding" under the insolvency law of the enacting State. Though it

[284] *See also* A/CN.9/422 ¶ 72 (noting that Article 5 "was not intended to grant powers to the locally appointed administrator to take actions, including actions such as repatriation of assets, without authoriztion of the local court").

[285] Guide ¶ 85 (pointing out that while foreign law determines how an authorized representative may exercise the power to act, "the authority to act in a foreign country does not depend on whether that country has enacted legislation based on the Model Law").

[286] Guide ¶ 84. Indeed, the Guide to Enactment encourages States to enact Article 5 even if their "administrators are already equipped to act as foreign representatives ... in order to provide clear statutory evidence of that authority." *Id.; see also* A/CN.9/422 ¶ 73 (stating that Article 5 "would help to fill a gap found in some national laws, and would generally be in line with the aim of facilitating cooperation and coordination").

[287] A/CN.9/419 ¶ 37.

[288] A/CN.9/419 ¶ 37 (noting the need to act quickly to protect assets as an example).

seems odd for a *proceeding* to require representation, this formulation is used repeatedly throughout the Model Law[289] and appears aimed at raising the profile of an application for recognition from that of merely recognizing a foreign administrator or similar actor to one recognizing an action of a foreign sovereign.[290] Thus, it should be understood that the application, while typically presented to the Article 4 (or equivalent) court by an insolvency administrator, carries with it, inasmuch as the administrator comes from an enacting State fortified by Article 5 authority, the dignity of a request of a *foreign court*[291] for recognition of its proceedings, thus drawing on traditional notions of comity, including courtesy and respect for the courts and laws of other sovereigns, to enhance the chances of obtaining "recognition" and cooperation. It follows that recognition of a foreign proceeding, after consideration of an application for recognition presented by the foreign representative under Article 5 authority, implicitly includes "recognition of the foreign representative,"[292] though the Model Law never uses that phrase.

Article 5 does not itself make clear the precise bounds of its grant of authority, but **115** the Guide to Enactment indicates that they encompass "action of the type dealt with in the Model Law ... ."[293] It does include an authorization to directly communicate with foreign courts and foreign representatives "in the exercise of its functions and subject to the supervision of the court" and carries a duty of maximum possible cooperation with them.[294]

2.2.5.2 United States Law

Section 1505 – Authorization to act in a foreign country

A trustee or another entity (including an examiner) may be authorized by the court to act in a foreign country on behalf of an estate created under section 541. An entity authorized to act under this section may act in any way permitted by the applicable foreign law.

Section 1505 differs somewhat from Article 5 in that rather than directly granting **116** an entity power to act, it authorizes the court to grant that power. This change was "to ensure that the court has knowledge and control of possibly expensive activities, but it will also have the collateral benefit of providing further assurance to foreign courts

289 *See, e.g.*, Art 17 (governing decision to recognize a foreign proceeding).

290 *See* A/CN.9/419 ¶ 39 (noting that "to some extent the questions that might be raised in the mind of a recognizing court as to the authority of a foreign representative to act abroad might be diminished if the application for recognition were to come from the foreign court rather than from the foreign representative").

291 In the Article 2 (e) sense of that term, which includes competent non-judicial proceedings that exist in some States.

292 *See* A/CN.9/435 ¶ 121 (considering "that the recognition of a foreign representative [is] covered by reference to the recognition of a foreign proceeding").

293 Guide ¶ 85. Earlier drafts listed examples of powers a representative might seek to exercise, *see, e.g.*, A/CN.9/433 ¶ 46, but the prevailing view of the Working Group "was that the text should express only the principle that the insolvency administrator is authorized to act in a foreign State without enumerating the types of measures or relief the administrator might be seeking," *id.* ¶ 47, and it "considered that the purpose of Article 5 was not to specify the details of the authority of an insolvency administrator but to lay down the principle of the administrator's authority to act abroad." *Id.* ¶ 48.

294 Art 26; *see also* mn 269 (discussing same).

that the United States debtor or representative is under judicial authority and supervision."[295]

117 An **examiner** is an official a court may appoint in cases in which the debtor remains in possession of its assets, whose function may be, *inter alia*, to investigate allegations of debtor fraud or mismanagement.[296] Since the term "trustee" includes debtors in possession,[297] examiners may be appointed in chapter 15 cases "to act in a foreign country on behalf of an [American bankruptcy] estate,"[298] particularly in countries in which communication and cooperation would be enhanced by a representative other than the debtor's management.[299]

118 The estate created under section 541 of the Bankruptcy Code consists roughly of **property** of the debtor **at the time the bankruptcy case commenced**, though other property may be added or removed as the case proceeds.[300] The court oversees administration of property of the estate for the benefit of creditors and other interested parties.

2.2.6 Article 6 – Public policy exception

Nothing in this Law prevents the court from refusing to take an action governed by this Law if the action would be manifestly contrary to the public policy of this State.

→ *Cf* Art 26 of the EIR

2.2.6.1 General

119 Article 6 is the **"public policy"** exception widely known in multilateral instruments and national insolvency law dealing with cross-border cases.[301] The Model Law does not define **"public policy,"** since the concept is by nature peculiar to each State.[302] In order to reduce the scope of the exception to "matters of fundamental importance for the enacting State," Article 6 employs the term "manifestly" to modify "contrary."[303] Therefore, "public policy," in the sense it is used in Article 6, should not be understood as "mere technicalit[ies] of a mandatory nature."[304]

---

295 H. Rep. No. 109–31, 109th Cong., 1st Sess. 108 (2005).

296 *See* 11 U.S.C. §§ 1104 (c), 1106 (b).

297 *See* 11 U.S.C. § 1502 (6); *see also* mn 103 (discussing same).

298 *See* 11 U.S.C. § 1106 (b).

299 Examples include instances in which the foreign court would prefer to interact with a representative other than the debtor or where an examiner has special expertise. H. Rep. No. 109–31, 109th Cong., 1st Sess. 109 (2005).

300 *See generally* 11 U.S.C. § 541.

301 A/CN.9/419 ¶ 40.

302 Guide ¶ 86; A/52/17 ¶ 171.

303 Guide ¶ 89. A/CN.9/419 ¶ 40. The Working Group believed that a "more restrictive formulation" was unsupportable "in view of the extent to which the details of the notion of public policy differed from State to State." *Id.* The Guide to Enactment points to a trend (positive from its perspective) of recognizing a distinction "between the notion of public policy as it applies to domestic affairs [and] the notion … as it is used in matters of international cooperation and the question of recognition of effects of foreign laws," the latter of which "would be unduly hampered if public policy would be understood in an extensive manner." Guide ¶ 88; *see also* A/52/17 ¶ 171 (discussing dichotomy and concern that use of the "domestic" sense of the term "public policy" would result in very few foreign decisions ever being recognized, "since most foreign proceedings would, in one or the other aspect, depart from procedures which, internally, constituted matters governed by imperative rules").

304 A/52/17 ¶ 172; A/CN.9/433 ¶ 160.

Under the section entitled "Fitting the Model Law into existing national law," the Guide to Enactment expresses the expectation "that the **public policy exception** will rarely be used."[305] Nevertheless, it remains available if the other provisions of the Model Law that can be employed to protect the legitimate interests of local creditors or other interested persons prove insufficient.[306] Courts should be able to draw a negative inference from the availability of Article 1 (2), providing for possibility of excluding some entities as debtors from the scope of the Model Law, that when the legislative authority of the enacting State did not make use of the provision to exclude a particular kind of entity, it may not have intended that Article 6 be used in its stead to achieve that effect.[307] **120**

2.2.6.2 United States Law

> **Section 1506 – Public policy exception**
>
> **Nothing in this chapter prevents the court from refusing to take an action governed by this chapter if the action would be manifestly contrary to the public policy of the United States.**

This section is essentially identical to Article 6. In a recent case, a court in the Southern District of New York adopted the view set forth above that "'manifestly contrary to the public policy of the United States' should be 'narrowly interpreted,' as 'the word "manifestly" in international usage restricts the **public policy exception** to the most fundamental policies of the United States.'"[308] It held that, procedurally, the "fundamental" public policy of the United States requires only a "**fair and impartial proceeding.**"[309] On that basis, the court held that lack of entitlement to a **jury trial** with respect to claims did not destroy the fairness and impartiality of a Canadian bankruptcy proceeding, even though it might reduce the claimants' "bargaining power."[310] Section 1506 did not, therefore, prevent the court from recognizing and enforcing the Canadian claims procedure.[311] **121**

2.2.7 Article 7 – Additional assistance under other laws

> **Nothing in this Law limits the power of a court or a *[insert the title of the person or body administering a reorganization or liquidation under the law of the enacting State]* to provide additional assistance to a foreign representative under other laws of this State.**

2.2.7.1 General

Article 7 serves to protect the "**additional assistance**" already available to foreign representatives under the law of the enacting State at the time of enactment of the Model **122**

---

[305] Guide ¶¶ 20 (f).

[306] Guide ¶¶ 35–36.

[307] *See supra* note 139.

[308] *In re RSM Richter v. Aguilar (In re Ephedra Prods. Liab. Litig.)*, 349 B.R. 333, 336 (S.D.N.Y. 2006) (citing H. Rep. No. 109–31, 109th Cong., 1st Sess. 108 (2005) and Guide ¶ 89).

[309] *Id.* at 337 (hinting that examples include notice, a right to legal counsel, a right to present evidence and witnesses, a right to examine evidence offered against one's case, and a right to appeal).

[310] *Id.*

[311] *Id.*

Law, it not being "the purpose of the Model Law to displace those provisions to the extent that they provide assistance that is additional to or different from the type of assistance dealt with in the Model Law."[312]

2.2.7.2 United States Law

Section 1507 – Additional assistance

(a) Subject to the specific limitations stated elsewhere in this chapter the court, if recognition is granted, may provide additional assistance to a foreign representative under this title or under other laws of the United States.

(b) In determining whether to provide additional assistance under this title or under other laws of the United States, the court shall consider whether such additional assistance, consistent with the principles of comity, will reasonably assure

(1) just treatment of all holders of claims against or interests in the debtor's property;

(2) protection of claim holders in the United States against prejudice and inconvenience in the processing of claims in such foreign proceeding;

(3) prevention of preferential or fraudulent dispositions of property of the debtor;

(4) distribution of proceeds of the debtor's property substantially in accordance with the order prescribed by this title; and

(5) if appropriate, the provision of an opportunity for a fresh start for the individual that such foreign proceeding concerns.

123 Although the language of this section is quite different than that of Article 7, its aims are similar. Subsection (a) seeks to ensure that enactment of chapter 15 does not unintentionally displace forms of "assistance" otherwise available under other laws of the United States. Subsection (b) requires the court to consider the same factors courts considered under former section 304, which chapter 15 replaced, in determining whether to grant such assistance.[313]

124 The American enactment is carefully worded, however, and the **House Report** accompanying the legislation confirms that while section 1507 "is intended to permit the further development of international cooperation begun under section 304, ... [it] is not to be the basis for denying or limiting relief otherwise available under [chapter 15]."[314]

125 Thus, it appears that for purposes of the most relevant and important relief afforded under chapter 15, especially by its provisions respecting entrustment of the administra-

[312] Guide ¶ 90.

[313] *See supra* note 144 (setting forth text of former section 304). Note that the new text raises comity to the heading rather than including it as a factor itself, since many courts construing former section 304 agreed that the other factors were subsidiary factors included in the concept of comity. Glosband Memorandum at 5–6; H. Rep. No. 109–31, 109th Cong., 1st Sess. 109 (2005).

[314] H. Rep. No. 109–31, 109th Cong., 1st Sess. 109 (2005). Glosband relates that section 1507 represents a marriage of the perspectives of those who saw Article 7 as a means to incorporate section 304 jurisprudence "notwithstanding the anticipated ... replacement of that section by Chapter 15" and those who feared it might be used as "an open invitation to evade the strictly specified requirements for relief contained in Chapter 15." Glosband Memorandum at 4.

tion and even distribution of the debtor's property to a foreign representative,[315] the old law has no applicability of its own. The factors of section 1507 (b), including those dealing with specifics such as paragraphs (3) (prevention of preferential or fraudulent transfers) and (4) (substantial accord with the American distribution scheme), have been replaced primarily with the rubric, "sufficient protection" of creditors' interests, about the meaning of which one can anticipate heated debate.[316]

2.2.8 Article 8 – Interpretation

In the interpretation of this Law, regard is to be had to its international origin and to the need to promote uniformity in its application and the observance of good faith.

2.2.8.1 General

Article 8 makes explicit for purposes of the Model Law the principle that interpreta- **126**
tion should lead to uniform application. The principle follows logically from the goal of uniformity that presumably exists when a legislature enacts a uniform law, particularly when the uniform law is authored by UNCITRAL, which was established in part to "further the progressive harmonization and unification of the law of international trade by ... promoting ways and means of ensuring a uniform interpretation and application of international conventions and uniform laws in the field of the law of international trade."[317] Uniform application and good faith promote transparency and predictability, which is important if foreign representatives, courts, creditors and other interested parties are to be able to operate under local law equitably and with minimal disruption and expense. In short, it contributes to a workable international system that ultimately benefits all.

It seems significant that Article 8 uses the words **"uniform application"** rather than **127**
"uniform interpretation." The enacted Model Law should be interpreted to achieve uniform, predictable *results* in harmony with the goals set forth in the Preamble and thus with those achieved in other enacting States. Use of the phrase "uniform interpretation" might have implied a process of mechanically importing meanings derived from foreign law into the law of the enacting State without consideration of differences in the legislation and legal systems involved, leading to unpredictable results.

Article 8 was modeled on article 3 (1) of the **UNCITRAL Model Law on Electronic** **128**
Commerce.[318] Abstracts of judicial decisions (and some arbitral awards) are available on the Commission's "<u>C</u>ase <u>L</u>aw <u>o</u>n <u>U</u>NCITRAL <u>T</u>exts" ("CLOUT") system to facilitate uniform application.[319]

---

[315] *See generally* 11 U.S.C. §§ 1519–22 (governing relief in conjunction with recognition).

[316] 11 U.S.C. §§ 1521 (b), 1522 (a); *see also* mn 235 *et seq* (discussing "sufficient protection") and mn 261 *et seq* (discussing interplay of the House Report language with the concept of cooperation). Note that the Model Law refers to "sufficient" protection as "adequate" protection. *See* Arts 21 (2); 22 (1); *see also* mn 234 (discussing distinction between "sufficient" and "adequate protection").

[317] G.A. Res. 2205 (XXI), at II (8) (d) (Dec. 17, 1966).

[318] Guide ¶ 91.

[319] Guide ¶ 92.

2.2.8.2 United States Law

> **Section 1508 – Interpretation**
>
> **In interpreting this chapter, the court shall consider its international origin, and the need to promote an application of this chapter that is consistent with the application of similar statutes adopted by foreign jurisdictions.**

129 While the language of section 1508 is somewhat different from that of Article 8, the **legislative history** indicates that "[c]hanges to the language were made to express the concepts more clearly in United States vernacular."[320] The legislative history promotes the use of the Guide and Working Group and Commission reports to encourage **uniform interpretation**, as well as reference to foreign court decisions interpreting Model Law provisions, noting that they are not only persuasive, but that they "advance the crucial goal of uniformity of interpretation," which enhances their importance.[321]

2.3 Chapter II. Access of foreign representatives and creditors to courts

130 Chapter II is largely a series of **enabling provisions** giving foreign representatives and foreign creditors **access to courts** in the enacting State and empowering those courts "to cooperate with the courts in the originating State of a ... foreign proceeding."[322]

131 Articles 9–12 focus on foreign representatives as defined in Article 2 (d). Access for **foreign representatives** exists for three broad purposes under the Model Law:

(1) to seek **"recognition"** of a foreign proceeding, which makes available avenues for relief and cooperation,
(2) to seek **provisional relief** and
(3) to commence an insolvency proceeding in the enacting State, which opens avenues for relief without the need for prior "recognition."[323]

132 A comparison of the wording Articles 11, 12 and 13 establishes some context for the vocabulary each uses. Article 11 provides for the foreign representative's standing to **"commence"** an insolvency proceeding in the enacting State. Article 12 grants the representative standing to **"participate"** in such an insolvency proceeding. The heading of Article 13 refers to **"access"** for foreign creditors to such a proceeding, and the text

---

[320] H. Rep. No. 109–31, 109th Cong., 1st Sess. 109 (2005).

[321] *Id.* at 309–10; *see also* mn 8 *et seq* (discussing authorities); *In re RSM Richter v. Aguilar (In re Ephedra Prods. Liab. Litig.)*, 349 B.R. 333, 336 (S.D.N.Y. 2006) (noting added relevance of Guide); *In re SPhinX, Ltd.*, 351 B.R. 103, 118 (Bankr. S.D.N.Y. 2006) (invoking section 1508's mandate in discussion of the concept of the center of a debtor's main interests and citing to *Bondi v. Bank of America, N.A. (In re Eurofood IFSC Ltd.)*, Case 314/04, slip op. at 6, 2006 E.C.R. 1-3813, 2006 WL 1142304 (E.C.J. May 2, 2006), (*cf* Table of Cases Art 3 of the EIR Appendix A mn 10), and *Cambridge Gas Transport Corp. v. Official Committee of Unsecured Creditors (of Navigator Holdings PLC)*, [2006], 3 All E.R. 829)), *aff'd*, 371 B.R. 10 (S.D.N.Y., 2007); *In re Tri-Continental Exch. Ltd.*, 349 B.R. 627, 633 (Bankr. E.D. Cal. 2006) (noting same mandate).

[322] *See* A/CN.9/422 ¶ 114.

[323] *See* A/CN.9/422 ¶ 147. Note, however, that in the final version of the Model Law, the right to *participate* in collective proceedings requires recognition, *see* Art 12 and discussion thereof at mn 151 *et seq*, though the right to *commence* them does not. *See* Art 11 and discussion thereof at mn 144 *et seq*.

states that they should have the same rights "regarding the commencement of, and participation in," such proceedings. Thus, "access" is the broadest concept, including both commencement and participation.

Articles 13–14 focus on access for foreign creditors, thus promoting objective *(c)* of the Preamble, *viz,* fair and efficient administration of cross border insolvencies, including protection of the interests of creditors.[324] It should be noted at the outset that the Model Law does not define the term **"foreign creditor."** Instead, it "deal[s] with th[e] notion ... within the specific context of the provision to which it relate[s]."[325] Thus, its meaning may change within the Model Law, depending on how it is used. **133**

2.3.1 Article 9 – Right of direct access

A foreign representative is entitled to apply directly to a court in this State.

2.3.1.1 General

The "crucial"[326] but limited focus of Article 9 is to provide a **foreign representative** with expedited and direct court access, i.e., without having to obtain accreditation or consular action,[327] which have been proven "often inadequate for dealing with the urgent circumstances presented in cross-border insolvencies and for taking expedient action to preserve assets from dissipation."[328] The goal of Article 9 is to facilitate "a coordinated, cooperative approach to cross-border insolvency and make[] fast action possible."[329] Thus, direct **access** seems to clothe the foreign representative with some measure of legal personhood in the enacting State, even before recognition,[330] though it **134**

324 *See* mn 23 *et seq* (discussing the Preamble).

325 A/CN.9/435 ¶ 158.

326 A/CN.9/433 ¶ 51.

327 Guide ¶¶ 28, 93; A/52/17 ¶ 177 (reporting agreement of the Commission that the article "was limited to expressing the principle of direct access by the foreign representative to courts of the enacting State, thus freeing the representative from having to meet formal requirements such as licences or consular actions"); A/CN.9/435 ¶ 130 (reporting agreement in the Working Group "that the purpose of the article was to allow direct access by the foreign representative to courts of the enacting State, thus freeing the foreign representative of formalities such as any diplomatic or consular channels"); A/CN.9/422 ¶ 146 (stating the benefit of direct access is avoiding "the need to rely on cumbersome and time-consuming letters rogatory or other forms of diplomatic or consular communication that might otherwise have to be used"); A/CN.9/433 ¶ 51 (noting "that the main purpose of Article [9] was to allow direct access by the foreign representative to the appropriate courts of the enacting State, thus bypassing diplomatic or consular channels that might normally be used for judicial assistance purposes"); *see also* A/CN.9/422 ¶ 145 (stating that the use of the word "directly" is "intended to make it clear that the foreign representative was being given direct access to the court competent for deciding applications for recognition of foreign proceedings").

328 A/CN.9/422 ¶ 146. This accords with Principle 3 (A) of the International Bar Association, Committee J Cross-Border Insolvency Concordat (adopted by the Council of the Section of Business Law of the International Bar Association on Sept. 17, 1995, and by Council of the International Bar Association on May 31, 1996), available at http://www.iiiglobal.org/international/projects/concordat.pdf (last viewed Apr. 4, 2007) (the "Concordat") (expressing a general right to access for foreign official representatives). The Concordat is discussed in mn 273 *et seq* (discussing Article 27).

329 Guide ¶ 28.

330 Note, for example, that standing to apply to commence an insolvency proceeding in the enacting State, even before recognition, is

is unclear to what extent, if any, such personhood displaces the debtor, its management and/or any creditors.

135 Access is available to apply for **recognition** and **relief**[331] and is distinguished from the concept of procedural "standing" or "legitimation" for requesting specified relief.[332] Other parts of the Model Law and other law of the enacting State will govern standing to request specified relief.[333]

136 According to the Guide to Enactment, the enacting State's version of Article 4 will identify and/or provide for the particular court or other authority competent to consider and dispose of the application.[334] The appropriate forum may depend upon the kind of relief sought (recognition or some form of cooperation).[335] Given Article 4's broad function of identifying and channeling jurisdiction for recognition and cooperation among "courts" and/or "authorities" and the Guide's reference to Article 4 in connection with the right to direct access, the word "court" in Article 9 probably includes non-court authorities identified in Article 4. States will, of course, have the opportunity to clarify that point when they enact the Law.

---

available under Article 11. *See* Guide ¶ 99. The same is true for purposes of seeking pre-recognition relief under Article 19, though in that case, at least, an application for recognition must be submitted. *See* mn 202 *et seq.* (discussing Article 19); *see also* A/CN.9/433 ¶ 114 (referring to the unrecognized foreign representative as "the representative of the collectivity of creditors").

[331] A/CN.9/419 ¶ 77.

[332] *See, e.g.* A/CN.9/433 ¶ 72 (stating that the substantive rule contained in what is now Article 11 (providing a foreign representative standing to commence an insolvency proceeding in the enacting State) was "a substantive rule with a broader scope than the right of direct access ...").

[333] For example, Article 11 grants standing to foreign representatives to commence insolvency proceedings in the enacting State, *see* mn 144 *et seq* (discussing Article 11), Article 12 grants them standing to "participate" in insolvency proceedings in the enacting State, *see* mn 151 (discussing Article 12), Article 15 (1) grants them standing to seek recognition, *see* mn 172 *et seq* (discussing Article 15 (1)), Article 19 grants them standing to request relief upon application for recognition but before recognition occurs, mn 202 *et seq* (discussing Article 19), Article 21 grants them standing to seek appropriate relief after recognition, *see* mn 224 *et seq* (discussing Article 21), Article 23 grants them standing to seek to avoid certain acts detrimental to creditors, *see* mn 247 *et seq* (discussing Article 23), and Article 24 grants them conditional standing to intervene in some individual actions in which the debtor is a party, *see* mn 252 *et seq* (discussing Article 24).

[334] Guide ¶ 93; *see also* A/CN.9/433 ¶ 57 (noting agreement in the Working Group that reference should be made in the text of an early draft of Article 9 to the Article 4 court). *But see* A/CN.9/435 ¶ 113 (noting that the prevailing view of the Working Group was that "the article should be limited to expressing the principle of direct access by the foreign representative to courts of the enacting State, without dealing with the competence of the courts or with relief that they could grant" and pointing out "that the foreign representative might have to apply for relief to a court other than the court referred to in article 4 (for example, when the competence of the court was determined according to the location of the asset with respect to which provision relief was sought)").

[335] *See* mn 109 *et seq* (discussing Article 4).

2.3.1.2 United States Law

Section 1509 – Right of direct access

(a) A foreign representative may commence a case under section 1504 by filing directly with the court a petition for recognition of a foreign proceeding under section 1515.

(b) If the court grants recognition under section 1517, and subject to any limitations that the court may impose consistent with the policy of this chapter

(1) the foreign representative has the capacity to sue and be sued in a court in the United States;

(2) the foreign representative may apply directly to a court in the United States for appropriate relief in that court; and

(3) a court in the United States shall grant comity or cooperation to the foreign representative.

(c) A request for comity or cooperation by a foreign representative in a court in the United States other than the court which granted recognition shall be accompanied by a certified copy of an order granting recognition under section 1517.

(d) If the court denies recognition under this chapter, the court may issue any appropriate order necessary to prevent the foreign representative from obtaining comity or cooperation from courts in the United States.

(e) Whether or not the court grants recognition, and subject to sections 306 and 1510, a foreign representative is subject to applicable nonbankruptcy law.

(f) Notwithstanding any other provision of this section, the failure of a foreign representative to commence a case or to obtain recognition under this chapter does not affect any right the foreign representative may have to sue in a court in the United States to collect or recover a claim which is the property of the debtor.

Chapter 15 incorporates the **principle of direct access** for a foreign representative as set forth in Article 9[336] but also channels access through the control of the bankruptcy court exercising recognition jurisdiction, direct access to which exists under subsection (a).[337] Generally, **recognition**[338] under section 1517[339] is necessary for further access, but an exception exists under subsection (f) when the foreign representative is prosecuting an action "to collect or recover a claim which is the property of the debtor," though subsection (f) does not itself create a right to prosecute such claims. For most other purposes, however, the legal personality of a foreign representative (in such capacity) in the United States is established only by recognition, at which time the foreign representative can sue or be sued and is entitled to **comity** or **cooperation** (but not necessarily **relief**) in courts *in* the United States, i.e., federal and state or other non-federal courts, though subsection (e), which corresponds to a similar provision concerning bankruptcy trustees,[340] makes clear that the foreign representative is subject to nonbankruptcy law in any event.[341] **137**

[336] Particularly in subsection (b) (2).

[337] *See* mn 112 for a summary discussion of jurisdiction and proper venue.

[338] *See* 11 U.S.C. § 1502 (7) (defining recognition); *see also* mn 104 (discussing definition).

[339] *See* mn 186 *et seq* (discussing recognition determination).

[340] *See* 28 U.S.C. § 959.

[341] The references to sections 306 and 1510 are to the Bankruptcy Code provisions govern-

138 The aim of this policy is "to make clear that chapter 15 is intended to be the exclusive door to ancillary assistance to foreign proceedings,"[342] and the gatekeeper is the bankruptcy court, which possesses expertise over insolvency matters and is properly empowered and charged to keep apprised of developments in the chapter 15 case of the debtor concerned. "The goal is important in a Federal system like that of the United States with many different courts, state and federal, that may have pending actions involving the debtor or the debtor's property. This section, therefore, completes for the United States the work of article 4 of the Model Law ('competent court') as well as that of article 9."[343] Subsections (c) and (d) are simply control measures toward this end,[344] and the rest of chapter 15 generally supports the concept by making relief for foreign representatives rely upon "recognition."[345]

139 Perhaps the first reported decision invoking chapter 15 concerned section 1509. In ***United States v. J.A. Jones Construction Group, LLC***,[346] a magistrate judge considered an interim receiver's letter requesting a stay of litigation pending before her in accordance with Canadian bankruptcy law.

140 The court concluded it had no authority to consider such a request without recognition under chapter 15, though it did grant a 60-day stay for the receiver to seek chapter 15 relief "given the comity that American courts should accord foreign bankruptcy proceedings ..."[347] Even the grant of that short stay seems inappropriate, however, since section 1519 (a) makes provisional relief, including a stay of litigation, available with bankruptcy court approval to foreign representatives during the period between the time of filing a petition for recognition and the granting of recognition.[348]

2.3.2 Article 10 – Limited jurisdiction

The sole fact that an application pursuant to this Law is made to a court in this State by a foreign representative does not subject the foreign representative or the foreign assets and affairs of the debtor to the jurisdiction of the courts of this State for any purpose other than the application.

---

ing limited appearances and jurisdiction, respectively. *See also* mn 143 (discussing same).

342 H. Rep. No. 109–31, 109th Cong., 1st Sess. 110 (2005).

343 *Id. See also* Glosband Memorandum at 7 ("These provisions will halt the separate development of possibly inconsistent law under free standing comity principles and will preclude forum shopping by a foreign representative who has been denied recognition or relief by a bankruptcy court." (footnote omitted)).

344 The Bankruptcy Code specifically provides that section 1509 "applies whether or not a case under [the Bankruptcy Code] is pending." 11 U.S.C. § 103 (k) (2). Before the enactment of section 1509, ancillary proceedings under former section 304 (replaced by chapter 15) were not the "exclusive remedy for a trustee or representative of [a foreign debtor] who wishe[d] to stay or enjoin creditor actions in the United States." *Cunard Steamship Co. v. Salen Reefer Servs. AB*, 773 F.2d 452, 454–56 (2d Cir. 1985).

345 *See, e.g.*, 11 U.S.C. §§ 1511, 1528 (standing to commence a plenary bankruptcy case), 1512 (standing to participate in a bankruptcy case), 1520 (governing effects of recognition of a foreign main proceeding), 1521 (governing relief that may be granted upon recognition), 1523 (governing availability of Paulian, or "avoidance" actions), 1524 (governing intervention by a foreign representative in state or federal courts), 1507 (obtaining "additional assistance" under the Bankruptcy Code or laws of the United States).

346 333 B.R. 637 (E.D.N.Y. 2005).

347 *Id.* at 639 (citing section 1509 (b) (2)).

348 *See* mn 202 *et seq* (discussing pre-recognition relief).

2.3.2.1 General

This so-called **"safe conduct" rule**[349] removes a practical obstacle to, and thus strengthens, the direct access that Article 9 provides by explicitly guarantying that merely making an application[350] "pursuant to this Law" creates no basis for jurisdiction over "the foreign representative or the foreign assets and affairs of the debtor" except with respect to the application itself. It does not, however, remove jurisdiction that already may have existed or that later comes to exist over the foreign representative or the assets or affairs of the debtor by virtue of circumstances or actions aside from making an application under the Model Law.[351] The Guide to Enactment, paragraph 95, states that the "limitation on jurisdiction over the foreign representative is ... not absolute. It is only intended shield the foreign representative to the extent necessary to make court access a meaningful proposition."[352] While this language is not particularly reassuring, it is meant only to note that other grounds for jurisdiction are not negated by Article 10.[353] In short, an application under the Model Law is not, in itself, a jurisdictional trigger that exposes assets outside the court's jurisdiction to its jurisdiction, except within the scope of the application (and thus, at most, within the scope of the Model Law, i.e., most expansively, matters relating to insolvency). **141**

The practical obstacle that Article 10 is meant to remove is not only an actual jurisdictional threat but a perceived one. Thus, the Guide suggests that even States in which making an application pursuant to the Model Law would provide no basis for expansive jurisdiction over the foreign representative or the assets or affairs of the **142**

349 Guide ¶ 94. A version of the "safe conduct" rule is incorporated into the Concordat (discussed at mn 273 (commentary on Article 27)), which states that an "official representative shall be subject to jurisdiction in all fora for any matter related to the insolvency proceedings, but appearing in a forum shall not subject him/her to jurisdiction for any other purpose in the forum state." Concordat, Principle 3 (A). This formulation is broader than that under the Model Law, which limits jurisdictional exposure to the scope of the application, reflecting the Model Law's more cautious approach and signaling that it does not go so far as to completely acknowledge the Concordat's "guiding principle ... that all common creditors should be treated as creditors of a single world-wide estate ... ." Concordat, Commentary on Principle 3.

350 The Guide to Enactment speaks in terms of a "petition" or "application for recognition," *id.* ¶¶ 29 (e), 94, or "an appearance in the courts of the enacting State for the purpose of requesting recognition." *Id.* ¶ 95. The text of Article 10 does not, however, limit the scope of the application to one seeking recognition. In fact, paragraph 95 of the Guide notes that a "foreign representative who applies for relief in the enacting State will be subject to conditions that the court may order in connection with relief granted (article 22, paragraph 2)." Article 22 (2) includes relief under Article 19 (*see* Art 22 (2)), which provides for the possiblity of relief *prior to* recognition. *See also* A/CN.9/422 ¶ 161 (noting the Working Group's agreement that an early version of what is now Article 10 "was a particularly useful provision for facilitating cooperation *and* access to recognition" (emphasis added)). Note 333 describes many forms of relief for which a foreign representative may apply "pursuant to this Law."

351 *See, e.g.,* A/CN.9/422 ¶ 162 (citing concern that the provision might be read "as attempting to preclude the courts in the enacting State from asserting jurisdiction on grounds other than the application for recognition, a result that would conflict with national procedural laws"); Guide ¶ 95 (disclaiming such a preclusion).

352 Guide ¶ 95.

353 Guide ¶ 95 (citing examples such as the commission of a tort by the foreign representative and noting that a foreign representative "who applies for relief in the enacting State will be subject to conditions that the court may order in connection with relief granted (article 11, paragraph 2)").

debtor should enact Article 10 for the purpose of providing transparent assurance of nonprejudicial access and to eliminate the concern of such jurisdiction being imposed with its dampening effect on a foreign representative's freedom of action.[354]

2.3.2.2 United States Law

> **Section 1510 – Limited jurisdiction**
>
> **The sole fact that a foreign representative files a petition under section 1515 does not subject the foreign representative to the jurisdiction of any court in the United States for any other purpose.**

143 Section 1510 is worded somewhat differently than Article 10, because it has its origins in section 306 of the Bankruptcy Code, another "safe conduct" provision that formerly applied to petitions for recognition in ancillary cases.[355]

2.3.3 Article 11 – Application by a foreign representative to commence a proceeding under *[identify laws of the enacting State relating to insolvency]*

> **A foreign representative is entitled to apply to commence a proceeding under *[identify laws of the enacting State relating to insolvency]* if the conditions for commencing such a proceeding are otherwise met.**

2.3.3.1 General

144 Article 11 explicitly[356] grants **foreign representatives** standing[357] to commence insolvency proceedings in the enacting State. The entitlement to commence an **insolvency proceeding** in the enacting State is open to foreign representatives of both **foreign main** and **non-main proceedings**, the only limitation being that "the conditions for commencing such a proceeding are otherwise met."[358] Although the Working Group considered the idea, the mere existence of a foreign proceeding was decided to be **insufficient** grounds to open an insolvency proceeding in the enacting State respecting the debtor if it meant overriding other local requirements to commence such a proceeding.[359]

---

[354] *See* Guide ¶ 96.

[355] Section 306 continues to apply when, after recognition, a foreign representative files a petition to commence an involuntary plenary case or seeks dismissal or suspension of a plenary case. *See* 11 U.S.C. § 306; *see also* mn 52 (discussing the meaning of "case"), mn 144 *et seq* (discussing Article 11 power to commence domestic insolvency proceedings).

[356] *See* Guide ¶ 97 (noting that absent explicit provision, the standing of foreign representatives to commence insolvency proceedings may be in doubt).

[357] *See* Guide ¶¶ 29 (b), 98.

[358] Guide ¶ 99.

[359] *Compare* A/CN.9/422 ¶¶ 172–175 (advancing the view that "the mere opening of an insolvency proceeding in one country should be a sufficient condition for the opening of an insolvency proceeding in another country" as being "in line with the broad aims of the model provisions to facilitate judicial cooperation in cross-border insolvency cases with a view to preserving the assets of the debtor's estate and maximizing their value for the benefit of the mass of creditors") *with id.* ¶ 176 (pointing out that "there was no need to accord the foreign representative any special status that would vest in the foreign representative powers additional to those granted to any creditor," in essence "overrid[ing] the local requirements for such a proceeding to

As indicated by the lack of the qualifying phrase, "upon recognition of a foreign proceeding,"[360] **recognition** of the foreign proceeding in which the foreign representative was authorised to act is not a requirement for the representative to obtain standing "because the commencement of an insolvency proceeding might be crucial in cases of urgent need for preserving the assets of the debtor."[361] **145**

Article 11 standing may be limited under Article 28 if a foreign proceeding has been recognized as a **foreign main proceeding** in the enacting State. In that case, an insolvency proceeding may be commenced in the enacting State only if the debtor has assets located there, and the effects of the new proceeding are restricted to only those assets except as Article 28 otherwise provides.[362] **146**

2.3.3.2 United States Law

Section 1511 – Commencement of case under section 301 or 303

(a) Upon recognition, a foreign representative may commence

(1) an involuntary case under section 303; or

(2) a voluntary case under section 301 or 302, if the foreign proceeding is a foreign main proceeding.

---

take place"). This discussion again raises the interesting question of whom exactly a foreign representative represents. Does the language requiring compliance with local law mean the foreign representative must meet the requirements for a voluntary (as a representative of the debtor) or an involuntary (as a representative of creditors) insolvency proceeding in countries in which it is possible to commence either form of proceeding? The confirmation of the continued enforcement of conditions for commencement seems to endorse the view that the foreign representative represents creditors, which would imply that requirements for involuntary commencement should apply. It should also be noted that Article 11 nowhere explicitly states that standing to commence an insolvency proceeding necessarily means that the proceeding need concern the debtor in the foreign proceeding that authorized the foreign representative to act. *But see* A/CN.9/433 ¶ 73 (noting an observation "that the foreign representative's right to request the opening of insolvency proceedings in respect of the debtor did not encompass a right to request the opening of insolvency proceedings in respect of subsidiary companies with a juridical personality of their own, except where such possibility was provided under the laws of the enacting State.").

[360] *Cf* Art 12 (employing the qualifying language).

[361] Guide ¶ 99. There was "strong support" in the Working Group "for making the recognition of the foreign representative a necessary condition for the right to request the opening of insolvency proceedings in the enacting State," particularly given the fact that provisional relief is available with an application for recognition under Article 19. *See* A/CN.9/435 ¶ 142. Those holding this view "noted that the recognition was the procedure whereby the foreign representative was given standing before the courts of the enacting State for the purposes of the draft Model Provisions." *Id.* ¶ 143; *see also* A/CN.9/422 ¶ 153 (viewing recognizing court as "traffic cop" regulating foreign representatives). *Quære* whether a foreign representative who is the equivalent of a debtor in possession requires recognition. The answer may lie in the characterization of the debtor's legal personality according to the law of the state in which the bankruptcy is proceeding, or, if it is a different state with different law, under the law of the state of the debtor's incorporation or centre of its main interests.

[362] *See* Art 28 and mn 280 *et seq* (discussing same).

(b) The petition commencing a case under subsection (a) must be accompanied by a certified copy of an order granting recognition. The court where the petition for recognition has been filed must be advised of the foreign representative's intent to commence a case under subsection (a) prior to such commencement.

147 While its function is essentially the same as that of Article 11, section 1511 is more restrictive in that it allows only foreign representatives of ***recognized*** **foreign proceedings** standing to commence **plenary cases.**[363] A foreign representative of a recognized foreign *main* proceeding may commence a voluntary case,[364] a benefit because the commencement of a **voluntary case** constitutes an order for relief.[365] Commencement of an **involuntary case** is less advantageous because the petition for relief may be controverted.[366] Grounds for relief exist where the debtor is generally not paying its debts as they mature or, in some instances, where a custodian has been appointed to take possession of the debtor's property.[367]

148 On the other hand, the so-called "**safe conduct**" **rule,**[368] which provides that merely appearing in a bankruptcy court in connection with a petition to commence an involuntary case is not a submission by a foreign representative to the court's jurisdiction for other purposes, does not apply to voluntary cases,[369] though decisional law might protect the foreign representative in some cases.[370] A representative of a **recognized foreign main proceeding** could file an involuntary proceeding, and would even have the benefit of a rebuttable presumption of the debtor's insolvency by virtue of the "main" recognition,[371] but ultimate relief might remain at risk.

149 The ability to commence a plenary case may be important to obtaining relief unavailable in ancillary proceedings. The most important example is the ability to pursue certain Paulian, or in American terminology, "**avoidance**" **actions.** Unlike the Model Law, chapter 15 expressly excludes the power to revoke certain inequitable transactions of debtors that prejudice creditors and the corresponding power to recover the transferred value from the scope of relief available to foreign representatives in **ancillary**

---

363 *But see In re Bear Stearns High-Grade Structured Credit Strategies Master Fund, Ltd. (In Provisional Liquidation)*, No. 07-12383 (BRL), slip op. at 17–18 & n. 15 (Bankr. S.D.N.Y. Sep. 5, 2007) (amended decision). (opining that a foreign representative denied recognition could nonetheless commence an involuntary plenary case). The amended *Bear Stearns* opinion finds inconsistency between section 1511, which begins with the qualifying phrase "upon recognition," and section 303 (b) (4), which has no qualifier (other than section 1511). *See* mn 52 for a discussion of the meaning of "case").

364 Section 302 provides for commencement of joint plenary cases of married spouses, and section 301 governs commencement of other voluntary plenary cases. 11 U.S.C. §§ 301–02. The title to section 1511 omits reference to section 302.

365 11 U.S.C. §§ 301 (b), 302 (a).

366 11 U.S.C. § 303 (h).

367 *Id.*

368 *See* 11 U.S.C. § 306; *see also* mn 141 *et seq* (discussing a similar rule for ancillary cases under Article 10).

369 The Collier treatise favors extending the rule to voluntary cases. *See* 8 Alan N. Resnick *et al*, *Collier on Bankruptcy* ¶ 1510.01 (15th ed. rev. 1996 & Supp. 2006) ("[S]ections [301 and 302] are not specifically within the language and protective umbrella of section 306 and probably should be.").

370 *See* H. Rep. No. 95–595, 95th Cong., 1st Sess. 325–26 (noting that certain jurisdictional "ambush techniques" have been frequently rejected at common law in other contexts).

371 *See* 11 U.S.C. § 1531; *see also* mn 297 *et seq* (discussing the Article 31).

cases,[372] although it specifically provides that recognized foreign representatives may prosecute such actions in **plenary cases**.[373] To the extent a plenary case is not already pending,[374] a foreign representative may wish to commence one for that purpose,[375] though in doing so, it may "risk losing control over much of that case to a trustee or debtor in possession."[376]

Subsection (b) consists of "housekeeping" measures made necessary by the "many **bankruptcy court districts** [in the United States] and the importance of full information and coordination among them."[377] Sections 1528 and 1529 govern coordination between ancillary and plenary proceedings involving the same debtor.[378] **150**

2.3.4 Article 12 – Participation of a foreign representative in a proceeding under *[identify laws of the enacting State relating to insolvency]*

Upon recognition of a foreign proceeding, the foreign representative is entitled to participate in a proceeding regarding the debtor under *[identify laws of the enacting State relating to insolvency]*.

2.3.4.1 General

Article 12 grants a **foreign representative** standing to "**participate**"[379] in insolvency proceedings in the enacting State respecting the debtor[380] that is the subject of the foreign proceeding in which the representative was authorized to act.[381] Article 12 does **151**

[372] *See* 11 U.S.C. § 1521 (a) (7); *see also* mn 292 *et seq* (discussing § 1521).

[373] *See* 11 U.S.C. § 1523; *see also* 247 *et seq* (discussing Article 23).

[374] *See* 11 U.S.C. § 1512 (governing right of recognized foreign representative to participate in bankruptcy cases); *see also* mn 151 (discussing Article 12).

[375] Perhaps the most famous case in the United States of this sort was *In re Axona International Credit & Commerce Ltd.*, 88 B.R. 597 (Bankr. S.D.N.Y. 1988), *aff'd*, 115 B.R. 442 (S.D.N.Y. 1990), *appeal dismissed*, 924 F.2d 31 (2d Cir. 1991), in which a foreign representative of proceedings in Hong Kong commenced a plenary proceeding in the United States, prosecuted and settled a preference claim there, and then obtained an order suspending the American case and permitting turnover of the settlement proceeds for distribution in Hong Kong.

[376] Glosband Memorandum at 9.

[377] H. Rep. No. 109–31, 109th Cong. 1st Sess. 111 (2005).

[378] *See* mn 280 *et seq* (discussing Article 28) and mn 284 *et seq* (discussing Article 29).

[379] The Guide to Enactment indicates that the enacting State may wish to use a term other than "participate" that it may deem more appropriate. Guide ¶ 102. The Concordat provides for a right of an "official representative" "to appear in all proceedings in any fora." Concordat (Principle 3 (A)). The Concordat is discussed at mn 273 (discussing Article 27).

[380] Although Article 11 (providing a foreign representative standing to commence an insolvency proceeding in the enacting State) does not specify a particular debtor, Article 12 refers to the debtor that is the subject of the proceeding in which intervention is sought, and the Guide to Enactment makes clear that that debtor is the same debtor that is the subject of the foreign proceeding that authorized the foreign representative to act. Guide ¶ 100 (stating that the "purpose of article 12 is to ensure that, when an insolvency proceeding concerning a debtor is taking place in the enacting State, the foreign representative of a proceeding concerning *that* debtor will be given procedural standing").

[381] Article 12 thus embodies Principle 3 (A) of the Committee J Cross-Border Insolvency Concordat, which states that "[i]f there is more than one forum, the official representatives appointed by each forum shall ...

not define a precise role or status for the foreign representative in the enacting State or "vest the foreign representative with any specific powers or rights."[382] The standing it grants is merely "procedural," allowing the foreign representative "to make petitions, requests or submissions concerning issues such as protection, realization or distribution of assets of the debtor or cooperation with the foreign proceeding."[383] It is not clear how far the standing available to a foreign representative extends to roles normally reserved for the domestic insolvency administrator, such as

- prosecuting avoidance litigation or
- other claims of the debtor's estate within the enacting State,
- buying,
- selling, or
- abandoning property,
- borrowing money, etc.

These issues are presumably left for coordination pursuant to Articles 28 and 29,[384] which generally favor the plenary proceeding. Article 12 may be contrasted with Article 24, which grants a foreign representative the right to "intervene in any proceedings in which the debtor is a party."[385]

2.3.4.2 United States Law

> **Section 1512 – Participation of a foreign representative in a case under this title**
>
> **Upon recognition of a foreign proceeding, the foreign representative in the recognized proceeding is entitled to participate as a party in interest in a case regarding the debtor under this title.**

152 This section follows the language of Article 12 closely, except that it makes clear by use of the defined term "debtor"[386] that the "case"[387] must concern the same debtor as

have the right to appear in all proceedings in any fora." Concordat, Principle 3 (A). According to the commentary thereto, the main purpose of foreign representative participation is the "coordination of both the administration and claims processing," presumably of the "single world-wide estate" of the debtor. As discussed in footnote 349, the concept of the "single world-wide estate" goes further than anything set forth in the Model Law, but coordination between or among administrations is certainly a goal.

[382] Guide ¶ 101.

[383] Guide ¶ 100. As the words "such as" indicate, this is not meant to be an exhaustive list, *see also* A/CN.9/435 ¶ 150 (stating that use of the word "participate" is meant to "capture in a flexible way the various purposes for which the foreign representative might appear in an insolvency proceeding in the enacting State").

[384] *See* mn 280 *et seq* (discussing the Article 28) and 284 *et seq* (discussing the Article 29).

[385] *See* Art 24 and mn 252 *et seq* (discussing same). The Working Group avoided the use of the word "intervene" in Article 12 (using instead "participate") because it considered participation in a collective proceeding "fundamentally different" from intervention in an individual proceeding in terms of "the conditions for, and the nature of, the foreign representative's appearance in the two situations." *See* A/CN.9/435 ¶ 149.

[386] *See* 11 U.S.C. § 1502 (1) (defining "debtor" as "an entity that is the subject of a foreign proceeding"); *see also* mn 102 (discussing the definition of "debtor").

[387] *See* mn 52 (discussing the meaning of "case").

the recognized foreign proceeding for standing to obtain. On its face, the provision allows for participation in ancillary as well as plenary cases.

As with Article 12, the scope of **participation** is not addressed. The Bankruptcy Code does not define "party in interest" but does list examples for cases under chapter 11, "including the debtor, the trustee, a creditors' committee, an equity security holders' committee, a creditor, an equity security holder, or any indenture trustee."[388] Parties in interest "may raise and may appear and be heard on any issue" in a chapter 11 case.[389] At any rate, it seems clear that standing to participate is distinct from standing to commence or initiate a proceeding, as can be seen by the separate provision in section 1511 to commence a case[390] and the distinct section 1523 grant of standing to recognized foreign representatives "to *initiate*" avoidance, or Paulian, actions.[391] **153**

Congress has also expressly empowered foreign representatives of recognized foreign proceedings to seek **dismissal** (or **suspension**) of bankruptcy cases in the United States "if the purposes of chapter 15 ... would be best served by such dismissal or suspension."[392] **154**

2.3.5 Article 13 – Access of foreign creditors to a proceeding under *[identify laws of the enacting State relating to insolvency]*

1. Subject to paragraph 2 of this article, foreign creditors have the same rights regarding the commencement of, and participation in, a proceeding under *[identify laws of the enacting State relating to insolvency]* as creditors in this State.

2. Paragraph 1 of this article does not affect the ranking of claims in a proceeding under *[identify laws of the enacting State relating to insolvency]*, except that the claims of foreign creditors shall not be ranked lower than *[identify the class of general nonpreference claims, while providing that a foreign claim is to be ranked lower than the general non-preference claims if an equivalent local claim (e.g. claim for a penalty or deferred-payment claim) has a rank lower than the general non-preference claims]*[2]

Footnote [2]: The enacting State may wish to consider the following alternative wording to replace paragraph 2 of article 13 (2):

2. Paragraph 1 of this article does not affect the ranking of claims in a proceeding under *[identify laws of the enacting State relating to insolvency]* or the exclusion of foreign tax and social security claims from such a proceeding. Nevertheless, the claims of foreign creditors other than those concerning tax and social security obligations shall not be ranked lower than *[identify the class of general non-preference claims, while providing that a foreign claim is to be ranked lower than the general non-preference claims if an equivalent local claim (e.g. claim for a penalty or deferred-payment claim) has a rank lower than the general non-preference claims]*.

→ *Cf* Art 39 of the EIR

---

[388] *See* 11 U.S.C. § 1109 (b).

[389] *Id.*

[390] *See* 11 U.S.C. § 1511 (a).

[391] *See* 11 U.S.C. § 1523 (a) (emphasis added); *see also* mn 247 *et seq* (discussing section 1523) and mn 147 *et seq* (discussing commencement of a plenary case under section 1511 in order to initiate avoidance actions).

[392] 11 U.S.C. § 305.

2.3.5.1 General

155 Article 13 establishes the general **principle of equality of foreign creditors** *vis-à-vis* local creditors in **accessing** insolvency proceedings in the enacting State.[393] **Access** means both "**commencing**"[394] and "**participating**" in such proceedings and does not depend on the existence or non-existence of insolvency proceedings respecting the same debtor in other places. The Model Law does not have a counterpart to the Article 10 **"safe conduct" rule** that would benefit foreign creditors by limiting the jurisdiction of the court of the enacting State respecting them.[395]

156 While the principle of equality among creditors does not generally affect **ranking or priorities of claims**,[396] foreign creditor claims may not be ranked lower than "general nonpreference" claims except where equivalent local claims are ranked below that level. The Guide to Enactment recognizes that "[f]ew States currently have provisions assigning special ranking to foreign creditors,"[397] but if any such discrimination does occur, paragraph 2 provides a floor to limit its effects. Footnote 2 provides an alternative paragraph 2 which is essentially the same except that it provides for a complete exclusion of foreign tax and social security claims from the prohibition against discrimination for those States that wish to continue discriminating against those kinds of claims.[398]

157 Note that Article 32 sets forth a so-called **"hotchpotch"** rule to at least partially offset any inequitable advantage a creditor may obtain by receiving dividends respecting a claim asserted in an insolvency proceeding in the enacting State from the proceeds of other insolvency proceedings respecting the same debtor and claim in other States.[399]

[393] Guide ¶ 103. Article 13 partially incorporates principles of the Concordat, discussed in more detail at mn 273. The Concordat prohibits discrimination against non-local creditors (Principle 2 (D)) and states that, "All creditors should have the right to appear in any forum to the same extent as creditors of the forum state, regardless of whether they have filed claims in that particular forum … ." Concordat, Principle 3 (C).

[394] Foreign creditors generally have the same rights to commence even non-main proceedings as domestic creditors do, though this may be limited pursuant to Article 3 where other international obligations govern. *See, e.g.,* European Council Reg. No. 1346/2000 of 29 May 2000 on Insolvency Proceedings, Art 3 (4) (b), 2000 O. J. (L 160) 1 (generally limiting right to commence territorial insolvency proceedings to local creditors). The Working Group also observed that the "court of the enacting State retained the prerogative to decline to exercise jurisdiction, if the creditor lacked sufficient connection with the enacting State." A/CN.9/433 ¶ 85.

[395] In this respect the Model Law parts company with the Concordat, which states that access should be available to foreign creditors "without [them] subjecting themselves to jurisdiction in that forum (including with respect to recovery against a creditor under voiding rules or otherwise in excess of a creditor's claim)." Concordat, Principle 3 (C).

[396] The Working Group "widely felt" that the provision on equal treatment of creditors should not be "read as attempting to override traditional forms of discrimination found in some national legislation as to the recognition, or lack thereof, of privileges or priorities of foreign creditors," which, it was felt, "would be beyond the border of what would be feasible or desirable as an aim for an instrument in the form of model legislative provisions rather than a convention." A/CN.9/422 ¶ 184. Another view expressed was that "the rule of non-discrimination would be meaningless if, in the absence of … a minimum standard, the court of the enacting State remained free to exclude all foreign claims." A/CN.9/433 ¶ 80 (suggesting that the Model Law "should provide that claims of foreign creditors had at least to be treated in the same manner as local non-priority claims").

[397] Guide ¶ 104.

[398] Guide ¶ 105.

[399] *See* mn 302 *et seq* (discussing Article 32).

The ability to participate in proceedings in foreign States allows creditors who remain disadvantaged despite the hotchpotch rule to go further in obtaining a fully equitable position *vis-à-vis* similarly situated creditors worldwide.

2.3.5.2 United States Law

Section 1513 – Access of foreign creditors to a case under this title

(a) Foreign creditors have the same rights regarding the commencement of, and participation in, a case under this title as domestic creditors.

(b)

(1) Subsection (a) does not change or codify present law as to the priority of claims under section 507 or 726, except that the claim of a foreign creditor under those sections shall not be given a lower priority than that of general unsecured claims without priority solely because the holder of such claim is a foreign creditor.

(2)

(A) Subsection (a) and paragraph (1) do not change or codify present law as to the allowability of foreign revenue claims or other foreign public law claims in a proceeding under this title.

(B) Allowance and priority as to a foreign tax claim or other foreign public law claim shall be governed by any applicable tax treaty of the United States, under the conditions and circumstances specified therein.

Section 1513 generally follows the Model Law, adopting a modified form of the alternative provision in the footnote to Article 13 respecting foreign public law claims. Sections 507 and 726 establish a ranking scheme for privileged, or in American terminology, "priority" claims.[400] "The law as to priority for foreign claims that fit within a class given priority treatment ... is unsettled."[401] Section 1513 leaves the unsettled state of the law undisturbed, though the House Report states that the section's "general principle of national treatment should be an important factor to be considered."[402] **158**

The Bankruptcy Code is also silent respecting the status of foreign public law claims, but the common law rule is that such claims are generally unenforceable;[403] they are therefore accorded no share in bankruptcy distributions. Section 1513 neither changes current law nor arrests its development, including development in the form of tax treaties.[404] **159**

---

400 11 U.S.C. §§ 507 (applying generally), 726 (applying to chapter 7 liquidation cases).

401 H. Rep. No. 109-31, Pt. 1, 109th Cong., 1st Sess. 111 (2005). Thus, for example, it is unclear whether a foreign wage claim is entitled to priority as an American wage claim might be. *See, e.g.*, 11 U.S.C. § 507 (a) (4).

402 H. Rep. No. 109–31, Pt. 1, 109th Cong., 1st Sess. 111 (2005).

403 *Id.* at 112.

404 The NBRC Report addressed treatment of foreign tax claims by recommending that Congress "leave the question open explicitly by saying that nothing in the provision is intended to either endorse or to repudiate current law and by instructing the Treasurer to include in future tax-treaty negotiations the mutual recognition of revenue claims in insolvency proceedings." *Id.* at 366.

2.3.6 Article 14 – Notification to foreign creditors of a proceeding under *[identify laws of the enacting State relating to insolvency]*

1. Whenever under *[identify laws of the enacting State relating to insolvency]* notification is to be given to creditors in this State, such notification shall also be given to the known creditors that do not have addresses in this State. The court may order that appropriate steps be taken with a view to notifying any creditor whose address is not yet known.

2. Such notification shall be made to the foreign creditors individually, unless the court considers that, under the circumstances, some other form of notification would be more appropriate. No letters rogatory or other, similar formality is required.

3. When a notification of commencement of a proceeding is to be given to foreign creditors, the notification shall:

(*a*) Indicate a reasonable time period for filing claims and specify the place for their filing;

(*b*) Indicate whether secured creditors need to file their secured claims; and

(*c*) Contain any other information required to be included in such a notification to creditors pursuant to the law of this State and the orders of the court.

→ *Cf* Art 40 et seq of the EIR

2.3.6.1 General

160 Article 14 gives wider effect to the **access** and **equal treatment** granted foreign creditors[405] in Article 13 by setting **noticing standards** to give **practical effect** to the opportunity to participate in insolvency proceedings in the enacting State.[406] The provision is meant to help redress the common problems foreign creditors face: receiving information about the proceedings too late or not at all as well as handicaps resulting from language problems, distance and a "lack of understanding of the foreign proceedings."[407]

161 Paragraph 1 mandates that creditors with known foreign addresses[408] receive the same **notification** (if any) as creditors in the enacting State whenever such notification is required under the insolvency laws of the enacting State.[409] The court is also given authority to take **steps toward notifying** "any" creditors with unknown addresses, which seems to imply that such steps should be reasonably even-handed with respect to domestic and foreign creditors, even while taking into account the diminishing marginal returns of any specific step with respect to a particular geographic region and respecting

405 Article 14, like Article 13, covers creditors as opposed to other "interested persons." *See* Guide ¶ 37 (noting that "[q]uestions of notice to interested persons ... are in general not regulated in the Model Law ... [and] are governed by the procedural rules of the enacting State").

406 Guide ¶ 106.

407 A/CN.9/419 ¶ 84.

408 The mandatory portion of paragraph 2 refers only to "known creditors." The Working Group suggested that such creditors would become "known" by examination of the debtor's books, records and correspondence, and that national law often requires debtors to provide lists of known creditors. A/CN.9/433 ¶ 87.

409 The "main purpose" of such notification is to inform foreign creditors "of the commencement of the insolvency proceeding and of the time-limit to file their claims." Guide ¶ 106.

the customs of some countries, in which there is no tradition of requiring administrators to seek out creditors.[410] Paragraph 2 complements this principle by making **individual notification** the default mode, thus leveling out disadvantages arising from foreign creditors' lack of regular access to notice by publication in local print media or postings in local places, while allowing the court to prescribe other forms of notification in exceptional cases where appropriate.[411] Paragraph 2 also sets aside any requirement for **letters rogatory** or other formality that may normally be necessary to serve notice, thus simplifying the process of notification to foreign creditors and reducing the time and expense thereof. To the extent dispensing with formal requirements conflicts with an international obligation, Article 3 provides that the international obligation will prevail.[412]

Paragraph 3 focuses on the **timing** and **content** of **notices** of commencement to be delivered to foreign creditors of insolvency proceedings in the enacting State. The provision mandates that a "reasonable time period for filing claims" and a specific place for their filing be set forth, a statement as to whether secured creditors need file secured claims and "any other information required to be included in such a notification" to domestic creditors under the law of the enacting State or orders of the court must also be included.[413] These requirements should help make claims processing more transparent to foreign creditors and alleviate disadvantages they face related to the additional time that may be required to notify them. **162**

With respect to **secured claims**, the Guide to Enactment points out a serious division among nations in treating security interests.[414] Some may deem creditors who file claims in solvency proceedings as having thereby waived the **security** or **privileges** related thereto, while others may attach similar consequences to failing to file.[415] Secured creditors will wish to refer to local law (and perhaps seek local counsel) to determine the precise effects of filing a claim in a particular proceeding on their security interests. **163**

2.3.6.2 United States Law

Section 1514 – Notification to foreign creditors concerning a case under this title

(a) Whenever in a case under this title notice is to be given to creditors generally or to any class or category of creditors, such notice shall also be given to the known cred-

---

[410] *See* A/CN.9/419 ¶ 84 (noting that while some "national systems imposed an obligation on the administrator to seek out claims and to agree on the amount of payment, ... in other systems the burden [is] essentially ... on claimants and no obligation [is] imposed on the administrator to make reservation for claims ... not brought forward").

[411] Guide ¶ 107.

[412] *See* mn 106 *et seq* (discussing Article 3); *see also* Guide ¶¶ 108–109 (noting that the court must decide on the best way to effect notice and observing that most treaties governing notice will not conflict with paragraph 2 because their goal is "typically to facilitate communication and not to preclude use of notification procedures that are even simpler than those" they establish).

[413] These will hopefully include the precise steps required to effectively file a claim or avoid waiving one. For example, the Working Group noted that such notices might include "whether a meeting of creditors would be held and whether failure to attend would result in waiver of a claim ... ." A/CN.9/419 ¶ 85.

[414] Guide ¶ 111.

[415] *Id.* (advising enacting States to include a provision in Article 14 (3) (b) requiring the notification to explain the effects of filing a claim on security interests relating thereto).

itors generally, or to creditors in the notified class or category, that do not have addresses in the United States. The court may order that appropriate steps be taken with a view to notifying any creditor whose address is not yet known.

(b) Such notification to creditors with foreign addresses described in subsection (a) shall be given individually, unless the court considers that, under the circumstances, some other form of notification would be more appropriate. No letter or other formality is required.

(c) When a notification of commencement of a case is to be given to foreign creditors, such notification shall

(1) indicate the time period for filing proofs of claim and specify the place for filing such proofs of claim;

(2) indicate whether secured creditors need to file proofs of claim; and

(3) contain any other information required to be included in such notification to creditors under this title and the orders of the court.

(d) Any rule of procedure or order of the court as to notice or the filing of a proof of claim shall provide such additional time to creditors with foreign addresses as is reasonable under the circumstances.

164 In addition to its desirability from the creditor perspective, adequacy of notice is essential to the binding effects of bankruptcy in the United States, including those of its **plans** and **discharges**.[416] Thus, section 1514's requirements should be considered with care. It follows Article 14 fairly closely, adjusting its terminology as necessary for United States practice.[417]

165 "Subsection (d) replaces the reference to a 'reasonable time period' in Model Law Article 14 (3) (a),"[418] which requires courts and rules to provide "creditors with foreign addresses" additional time as reason dictates. **Interim Rule** 2002 (p) was added to Rule 2002 to allow courts to direct that notice by other means (such as email, fax or **private courier**) supplement notice by mail, or to increase the time for creditors with foreign addresses to respond to the notice.[419] The Interim Rule also requires (unless the court orders otherwise) that creditors with foreign addresses be given at least 30 days' notice of a deadline to file proofs of claim.[420]

2.4 Chapter III – Recognition of a foreign proceeding and relief

166 Chapter III focuses on the **procedure**, **effects** and **relief** associated with **recognition** of a foreign proceeding. "Recognition of a foreign proceeding" is an "express decision of the competent court"[421] in the recognizing State[422] to recognize a foreign sovereign's

[416] *See generally* American Law Institute, Transnational Insolvency Cooperation Among the NAFTA Countries – Guidelines Applicable to Court-to-Court Communications in Cross-Border-Cases 1 (2003) (the "Principles"), Procedural Principle 27 and the comments thereto.

[417] *See, e.g.*, mn 52 (discussing the meaning of "case").

[418] H. Rep. No. 109–31, 109th Cong., 1st Sess. 112 (2005).

[419] *See* Fed. R. Bankr. P. (Interim) 2002 (p) (1) and the 2005 Advisory Committee Note thereto.

[420] Fed. R. Bankr. P. (Interim) 2002 (p) (2).

[421] A/CN.9/419 ¶ 62.

[422] *See* Art 4 (identifying the court(s) or authority(ies) competent to recognize

interest in the insolvency administration of property within the recognizing court's jurisdiction that triggers the applicability of most,[423] though not all,[424] of the provisions of the Model Law that may make relief available to the foreign representative.[425] Although therefore certainly pivotal to a foreign representative's efforts in an enacting State, recognition is, in and of itself, not as decisive an event as the term might imply to those familiar with its technical meaning in the context of foreign judgments[426] or as far-reaching in effect as the recognition contemplated under European Council Regulation on Insolvency Proceedings.[427] For example, a foreign proceeding may lose its recognized status if **the grounds for granting recognition have ceased to exist** or **never existed**, and the precise effects of recognition mostly depend on the law of the recognizing State other than the enacted Model Law and are subject to modification or termination.[428] Nevertheless, recognition under the Model Law does entail a decision-making process similar to that many States employ to determine whether they should recognize

---

foreign proceedings) and mn 109 *et seq* (discussing Article 4).

423 Particularly those set forth in Articles 20–24. *See also* note 345.

424 *See, e.g.,* Arts 11 (granting foreign representatives standing to commence insolvency proceedings in the enacting State even where the foreign proceeding which authorized the foreign representative to act has not been recognized in the enacting State) and 19 (providing for provisional relief upon an application for recognition but before recognition occurs). Note also that the applicability of the Chapter IV cooperation and communication provisions (Arts 25–27) do "not require a previous formal decision to recognize … ." Guide ¶ 177.

425 Importantly, "recognition of a foreign representative … [is] covered by reference to the recognition of a foreign proceeding." A/CN.9/435 ¶ 121; *see also* A/52/17 ¶ 200 (noting "that, under the Model Provisions, the recognition of a foreign representative [does] not occur independently from the recognition of the foreign proceeding in which the foreign representative has been appointed").

426 *See, e.g.,* Guide ¶ 16 (noting "recognition of foreign insolvency proceedings might not be considered as a matter of recognizing a foreign 'judgement', for example, if the foreign bankruptcy order is considered to be merely a declaration of status of the debtor or if the order is considered not to be final"); *see also* A/52/17 ¶ 208 (expressing that, "in the system of the Model Provisions, the recognition of a foreign proceeding did not entail that the foreign proceeding would have in the enacting State the full range of legal effects that it had in the originating jurisdiction"); A/CN.9/433 ¶ 102 (observing that "the term 'recognition' [is] a technical term used for giving effect to foreign judicial decisions, that under the draft Model Provisions 'recognition' meant only recognition of foreign proceedings, and that in the European Union Convention on Insolvency Proceedings the effects of recognition of foreign proceedings [are] much broader that in the draft Model Provisions"). Indeed, at least one voice in the Working Group expressed the view that "it was unnecessary to introduce in the Model Provisions the notion of "recognition" of foreign insolvency proceedings, "the purpose of which was to obtain relief provided elsewhere in such Provisions." A/CN.9/433 ¶ 100. The relief specified could be made subject to the same safeguards, it was suggested, in the article that provided for it "without a special procedure for 'recognition.'" *Id.* Later, the utility of recognition was affirmed because it "could play an important part in the provision designed to secure an opportunity for foreign representatives to seek cooperation and assistance in the enacting State." A/CN.9/422 ¶ 79. Nevertheless, early drafts of the Model Law expressed recognition in terms of recognizing "a foreign judgement opening insolvency proceedings." *See* A/CN.9/422 ¶ 76.

427 Council Regulation 1346/2000 of 29 May 2000 on Insolvency Proceedings, 2000 O.J. (L 160) 1; *see generally* A/CN.9/433 ¶ 102 and Art 16 of the EIR mn 1 *et seq* (discussing recognition).

428 *See* Art 17 (4) and mn 186 *et seq* (discussing Article 17).

foreign judgments.[429] The necessity of a provision on recognition was considered in light of the goal of the Model Law "to open as wide a door to cooperation as would be appropriate, while at the same time not prejudicing the rights of local creditors under the insolvency laws of the enacting State."[430] It thus attempts to reduce the friction at the center of the cross-border insolvency knot without specifying (for example with choice of law rules) exactly how it should be unwound.

167 The concept of recognition in the Model Law can be analyzed by separately examining its causes and effects. The first part of Chapter III deals with what is required to cause recognition of a foreign proceeding in the enacting State, including application procedures[431] (Art 15), potential presumptions respecting the application and decisions concerning recognition (Art 16), recognition decision criteria and timing rules (Art 17) and provisions establishing informational duties of the foreign representative after submission of the application for recognition (Art 18). While these procedures are considerably streamlined and tailored to meet the frequent urgency of insolvency proceedings, particularly with respect to gathering and protecting assets of the debtor, it should be emphasized that recognition is not completely automatic. It is "given upon request of the foreign representative" and can be granted only if the foreign representative presents the requisite evidence.[432] On the other hand, the grounds for denying recognition are limited; in particular, it is not the duty of the recognizing court to "reconsider the grounds on which the foreign court decided to open th[e] foreign proceeding."[433]

168 The Model Law allows for recognition of a foreign proceeding as either a **"main"** or **"non-main" proceeding**, depending on the strength of the connection between the debtor and the state in which the foreign proceeding is occurring. In this sense, the difference may be said to be "jurisdictional," bearing in mind, however, that the Model Law is *not* concerned with jurisdiction in the context of whether the foreign court is or was empowered under the law of its own State to open its proceeding.[434] Recognition as a **"foreign main proceeding"** causes some automatic effects "centering on the need quickly to protect assets against dissipation and to allow time for a comprehensive assessment to be made of the situation"[435] and makes available other relief at the discretion of the court that is generally broader, more universal and less territorial than that attending recognition of a foreign proceeding as a "foreign non-main proceeding," which has no substantive mandatory effects[436] but enables a court to make other **relief** – usually

---

[429] *See* A/CN.9/433 ¶ 100 (noting that "recognition [is] a useful concept since it clarif[ies] the nature of the decision-making process leading to relief ... .").

[430] A/CN.9/422 ¶ 79.

[431] Significantly, "[p]rocedural matters related to notice of the filing of an application for recognition or of the decision to grant recognition are not dealt with in the Model Law; they remain to be governed by other provisions of law of the enacting State." Guide ¶ 30 (emphasis added); *see also* Guide ¶¶ 121, 164 (noting same); A/CN.9/419 ¶¶ 65–68, 84–87, 170 (describing early discussions in the Working Group respecting notice considerations, including notice upon termination of a foreign proceeding).

[432] A/CN.9/433 ¶ 101.

[433] A/CN.9/433 ¶ 101.

[434] This corresponds to what the European Council regulation on insolvency proceedings refers to as "international" vs. "territorial" jurisdiction. *See, e.g.*, Council Regulation 1346/2000 of 29 May 2000 on Insolvency Proceedings, Recital 15, 2000 O.J. (L 160) 1.

[435] A/CN.9/419 ¶ 55; *see also id.* ¶ 57 (noting the "need of preserving the possibility that local assets could be considered for inclusion in a coordinated or comprehensive solution to the insolvency").

[436] A/52/17 ¶ 69 (stating the proposition "that there should be no mandatory effects for a foreign non-main proceeding").

with narrower, more local application than is the case with foreign main proceedings – available at its discretion. At one point the Working Group summarized the scheme with the following principles: "recognition of both main and non-main proceedings; availability of appropriate relief in both types of proceedings; primacy of the main proceeding over the non-main proceedings; limits as to the consequences of non-main proceedings; and coordination between main and non-main proceedings."[437]

Articles 20–24 govern **169**

- the effects of recognition, including automatic effects of recognition of a foreign proceeding as a foreign main proceeding (Art 20),
- authorization to grant appropriate relief upon recognition of foreign proceedings as either main or non-main foreign proceedings (Art 21),
- provisions to protect creditors and other interested persons (Art 22),
- special provisions relating to Paulian actions (Art 23) and
- a provision governing the right of a foreign representative of a recognized foreign proceeding to intervene in actions in the enacting State to which the debtor is a party (Art 24).

These effects of recognition, even the "automatic" effects of recognition of a foreign *main* proceeding (Art 20), do not mechanically import the law of the foreign jurisdiction into that of the recognizing jurisdiction,[438] which is another reason that the term "recognition" may mislead. Each case in which foreign law might be made to apply in the enacting State either requires the approval of a court in the enacting State or may at least be challenged as inappropriate when circumstances dictate a different course, e.g., when creditors' interests are not "adequately protected."[439] **170**

Aside from these provisions, Article 19 authorizes a court to grant provisional relief from the time of filing of an application for recognition until the time of decision on the application, particularly where there is a need to expeditiously gather and protect assets (or potential assets) of the debtor.[440] **171**

---

[437] A/CN.9/433 ¶ 150. The idea of primacy of a main proceeding is also addressed in the Concordat (Principle 1). (The Concordat is described in more detail at mn 273 (discussing Article 27).) The Working Group did recognize, however, that it would not always be possible to subordinate foreign main proceedings to foreign non-main proceedings. *See* A/CN.9/433 ¶ 155 (noting "that there were in particular two situations where it was not possible to adjust measures in non-main proceedings to the measures in the main proceeding: where it was not clear in which State was centre of the debtor's main interests; and where it was not possible (e.g., for political reasons) to open the proceedings in the State where the debtor had the centre of its main interests, or where a main proceeding could not be opened sufficiently quickly in that State").

[438] *See* Guide ¶ 143 (stating that "[r]ecognition therefore, has its own effects rather than importing the consequences of the foreign law into the insolvency system of the enacting State").

[439] *See* Arts 21 (2); 22 (1); Guide ¶ 159 (stating "principle underlying the Model Law that recognition of a foreign proceeding does not mean extending the effects of the foreign proceeding as they may be prescribed by the law of the foreign State. Instead, recognition of a foreign proceeding entails attaching to the foreign proceeding consequences envisaged by the law of the enacting State"); *see also* Art 6 (providing that actions the Law requires need not be taken if doing so would be manifestly contrary to the "public policy" of the enacting State).

[440] *See* mn 202 *et seq* (discussing Article 19).

2.4.1 Article 15 – Application for recognition of a foreign proceeding

1. A foreign representative may apply to the court for recognition of the foreign proceeding in which the foreign representative has been appointed.

2. An application for recognition shall be accompanied by:

***(a)* A certified copy of the decision commencing the foreign proceeding and appointing the foreign representative; or**

***(b)* A certificate from the foreign court affirming the existence of the foreign proceeding and of the appointment of the foreign representative; or**

***(c)* In the absence of evidence referred to in subparagraphs *(a)* and *(b)*, any other evidence acceptable to the court of the existence of the foreign proceeding and of the appointment of the foreign representative.**

3. An application for recognition shall also be accompanied by a statement identifying all foreign proceedings in respect of the debtor that are known to the foreign representative.

4. The court may require a translation of documents supplied in support of the application for recognition into an official language of this State.

→ *Cf* Art 16 *et seq* of the EIR

2.4.1.1 General

172 Although Article 9 provides the foreign representative "access" to the courts of the enacting State,[441] **recognition of the foreign proceeding** that has authorized the foreign representative to act is a requirement for most of the relief the Model Law provides.[442] Paragraph 1 of Article 15 expressly grants the foreign representative standing to apply for such recognition. Article 4 identifies the court to which the application should be presented.[443]

173 The remainder of Article 15 sets forth simple minimum requirements[444] for materials supporting the application. Paragraph 2 requires evidence of the existence of the foreign proceeding from which the foreign representative derives authority to act and evidence of appointment of the foreign representative.[445] To avoid uncertainty, the preferred forms of evidence are set forth in subparagraphs (a) and (b).[446] Other evidence is acceptable only "in absence of" a certified copy of the decision commencing the foreign pro-

441 *See* mn 134 *et seq* (discussing Article 9).

442 *See* notes 423, 424 (discussing relief available with and without recognition).

443 *See* mn 109 *et seq* (discussing Article 4).

444 The simple, minimalist approach is deliberate. Indeed, the Guide to Enactment states that "it is desirable not to encumber the process with additional requirements … ." Guide ¶ 112; *see also* A/CN.9/419 ¶ 180 (stating that the simple application and the presumptions set forth in Article 16 "are based on the view that no unnecessary obstacles should be placed in the way of the foreign representative acquiring the ability to act expeditiously in order to preserve assets").

445 The court considering recognition is "entitled to presume that documents submitted in support of the application … are authentic … ." Art 16 (2); *see also* mn 180 *et seq* (discussing Article 16).

446 A/CN.9/419 ¶ 182. Certification is considered equivalent to a decision because, in some countries, it is possible to commence an insolvency proceeding without a "decision." A/CN.9/433 ¶ 64; *see, e.g.,* 11 U.S.C.

ceeding and appointing the foreign representative or a certificate from the foreign court affirming the existence of the foreign proceeding and the appointment of the foreign representative.[447] The existence of the foreign proceeding and appointment of the foreign representative may be evidenced by a single document or by separate documents.[448] The requirements of paragraph 2 are particularly prominent, because meeting them is part of the express list of items that trigger recognition under Article 17.[449]

Paragraph 3 requires a statement identifying any other foreign proceedings respecting **174**
the debtor known to the foreign representative. This affirmative duty to inform aids the court in determining appropriate relief and in coordinating its proceedings with those of other courts.[450] There is no express requirement to apprise the court of the existence or insolvency status of entities affiliated with the debtor by ownership or control, but doing so certainly accords with the purpose of the Law.[451] Article 18 (b) imposes a continuing duty upon the foreign representative to inform the court of such other foreign proceedings as become known to the foreign representative after the filing of the application for recognition.[452]

Under paragraph 4, the court may require **translations** of the supporting documents. **175**

As noted above,[453] rules governing notice requirements for recognition or the recog- **176**
nition proceeding lie outside the scope of the Model Law, so other law in each enacting State must be consulted to discover the existence and content of any such requirements.

The minimalist **application requirements** of Article 15 do not prohibit a foreign **177**
representative from presenting more or other evidence in support of the application. Indeed, it may be in the representative's best interest to so. For example, a foreign representative may wish to present evidence as to the location of an establishment or the centre of the debtor's main interest to aid the court in determining whether the foreign proceeding should be recognized as a foreign main proceeding or a foreign non-main proceeding.[454]

---

§ 301 (providing for commencement of a voluntary "case" by the filing of an appropriate petition).

447 The Working Group seems to have anticipated that subparagraph (c) situations might occur "in emergency situations, [where] an interim or only recently appointed representative might not be in a position to produce the documentation required ... ." A/CN.9/433 ¶ 61.

448 A/CN.9/419 ¶ 181.

449 *See* Art 17 (1) (c) and mn 186 *et seq* (discussing Article 17). Note also that Article 18 (a) requires the foreign representative to promptly apprise the court of any substantial change in the status of the foreign proceeding or the foreign representative's appointment, *see* mn 199 *et seq* (discussing Article 18), which follows from the non-perennial nature of recognition. *See* Art 17 (4) (providing that nothing in Articles 15–18 prevent modification or termination of recognition "if it is shown that the grounds for granting it were fully or partially lacking or have ceased to exist.").

450 Guide ¶¶ 117–18. *See* Art 30 (requiring the court to seek cooperation and coordination under Chapter IV) and mn 293 *et seq* (discussing Article 30).

451 *See* Preamble (promoting, *inter alia*, the objectives of cooperation between the courts of the enacting and foreign States "involved in cases of cross-border insolvency," "[g]reater legal certainty for trade and investment," "[f]air and efficient administration of cross-border insolvencies that protects the interests of all creditors and other interested persons," and "[f]acilitation of the rescue of financially troubled businesses, thereby protecting investment and preserving employment").

452 *See* 199 *et seq* (discussing Article 18).

453 *See* note 431 and accompanying text (discussing same).

454 *See* Art 17 (2) and mn 186 *et seq* (discussing same); *see also infra* note 457 (discussing

2.4.1.2 United States Law

Section 1515 – Application for recognition

(a) A foreign representative applies to the court for recognition of a foreign proceeding in which the foreign representative has been appointed by filing a petition for recognition.

(b) A petition for recognition shall be accompanied by

(1) a certified copy of the decision commencing such foreign proceeding and appointing the foreign representative;

(2) a certificate from the foreign court affirming the existence of such foreign proceeding and of the appointment of the foreign representative; or

(3) in the absence of evidence referred to in paragraphs (1) and (2), any other evidence acceptable to the court of the existence of such foreign proceeding and of the appointment of the foreign representative.

(c) A petition for recognition shall also be accompanied by a statement identifying all foreign proceedings with respect to the debtor that are known to the foreign representative.

(d) The documents referred to in paragraphs (1) and (2) of subsection (b) shall be translated into English. The court may require a translation into English of additional documents.

178 The wording of section 1515 is almost exactly the same as that of Article 15. The minor variations highlight an important subtlety, however: the union in chapter 15 of the Model Law concept of recognition (or, at least, application for recognition) with the American notion of the **"ancillary case."** Thus, under chapter 15, an application for recognition ("A foreign representative *applies* ... *for recognition*") is nothing other than the petition commencing an ancillary case familiar to American jurists under former practice.[455]

179 Aside from that, the only substantive change to the Article 15 text is that subsection (d) of section 1515 normalizes (to some extent) the requirement for English translations of documents supporting the petition.

2.4.2 Article 16 – Presumptions concerning recognition

1. If the decision or certificate referred to in paragraph 2 of article 15 indicates that the foreign proceeding is a proceeding within the meaning of subparagraph *(a)* of article 2 and that the foreign representative is a person or body within the meaning of subparagraph *(d)* of article 2, the court is entitled to so presume.

---

lack of presumption respecting existence of an "establishment").

[455] *Cf* 11 U.S.C. § 1504 ("A case under this chapter is commenced by the filing of a petition for recognition of a foreign proceeding under section 1515."); *see also* mn 112 (discussing section 1504, jurisdiction and venue); mn 193 (setting forth a brief comparative summary of prior practice and chapter 15 recognition). For an explanation of the term "case," *see* mn 52. "Petition" is the standard term for a request to open a "case" under the Bankruptcy Code.

2. The court is entitled to presume that documents submitted in support of the application for recognition are authentic, whether or not they have been legalized.

3. In the absence of proof to the contrary, the debtor's registered office, or habitual residence in the case of an individual, is presumed to be the centre of the debtor's main interests.

→ *Cf* Art 16 of the EIR

2.4.2.1 General

Article 16 sets forth a number of **presumptions** meant to aid the court in its recognition decision-making process, which furthers the goal underlying Article 17 (3)'s instruction that an application for recognition "be decided upon at the earliest possible time."[456] They generally allow the court to come to its Article 17 decisions absent any evidence beyond that which Article 15 requires the foreign representative to provide.[457] The phrase "is entitled to presume" in paragraphs 1 and 2 make the respective presumptions an entitlement but not a requirement for the court.[458] Thus, for example, a court having little familiarity with insolvency proceedings in particular countries may, despite its entitlements to presume, require evidence to assure itself of the propriety of recognition,[459] though it should minimize demands for evidence so as to avoid defeating the purpose of the presumptions, i.e., streamlining the recognition process to meet the special, often time-sensitive needs of cross-border insolvency cases.[460] Naturally the court's decision respecting the presumptions will also be affected by presentation of evidence that calls them into question.[461] The entitlement to presume the truth of affirmative indications in "the decision[s] or certificate[s] referred to in paragraph 2 of article 15" that the foreign proceeding and foreign representative meet the Article 2 definitions of those terms also applies to documents submitted under Article 15 (2) (c).[462] **180**

Paragraph 2 allows the court to dispense with any requirement for **legalization**.[463] According to the Guide to Enactment, this will give the court flexibility to act when it **181**

[456] *See* Art 17 (3) and mn 186 *et seq* (discussing same); *see also* Guide ¶ 122 (stating that the presumptions "allow the court to expedite the evidentiary process").

[457] Note, however, that no presumption exists with respect to whether an "establishment" of a debtor exists in the State in which the foreign proceeding is occurring, so some further evidence may be necessary for the court to determine whether a foreign proceeding may be recognized as a foreign non-main proceeding, even if there is no objection thereto. *See* Art 17 (2) and mn 186 *et seq* (discussing same).

[458] *See* Guide ¶ 114 (implying that it follows from such language that "the court retains discretion to decline to rely on the presumption" in the context of paragraph 2); A/52/17 ¶¶ 205–06 (discussing same).

[459] *See* Guide ¶ 122 (stating the presumptions "do not prevent, in accordance with the applicable procedural law, calling for or assessing other evidence if the conclusion suggested by the presumption is called into question by the court or an interested party").

[460] *See, e.g.*, A/CN.9/435 ¶ 171 (stating that paragraph 1 is designed "to expressly enable the court to make decisions based on the presumptions" it establishes, "so as to avoid litigation or obviate the need for lengthy arguments as to the nature of the foreign proceeding and the appointment of the foreign representative").

[461] Guide ¶ 122.

[462] Guide ¶ 116.

[463] Guide ¶ 123. "'Legalization' is a term often used for the formality by which a diplomatic or consular agent of the State in which the document is to be produced certifies the authenticity of the signature, the capacity in which the person signing the

can assure itself of the authenticity of the evidence without legalization but allow it to demand often time-consuming legalization procedures when necessary.[464] If an international agreement binds the enacting State to require legalization, Article 3 provides that such obligations override the provisions of the Model Law.[465]

182 The Model Law expresses the presumption respecting the centre of the debtor's main interests ("COMI") in paragraph 3 in mandatory language but prefaces it with the phrase "[i]n the absence of proof to the contrary," making it more vulnerable to negation, a logical result of the large number of potential factors that may come into play in determining that question when the answer is unclear.[466] The term "registered office" was chosen, as opposed to "registered seat," for "purposes of consistency with the wording used in the European Union Convention on Insolvency Proceedings."[467]

2.4.2.2 United States Law

Section 1516 – Presumptions concerning recognition

(a) If the decision or certificate referred to in section 1515 (b) indicates that the foreign proceeding is a foreign proceeding and that the person or body is a foreign representative, the court is entitled to so presume.

(b) The court is entitled to presume that documents submitted in support of the petition for recognition are authentic, whether or not they have been legalized.

(c) In the absence of evidence to the contrary, the debtor's registered office, or habitual residence in the case of an individual, is presumed to be the center of the debtor's main interests.

183 Section 1516 "follows article 16 with minor changes."[468] In the United States, "registered office" is synonymous with "place of incorporation or the equivalent for an entity that is not a natural person."[469]

184 "[A]lthough the court is entitled to shift the burden to the extent indicated in section 1516," the word "proof" in Article 16 is changed to "evidence" in section 1516 (c) – where the presumption is not discretionary – to make clear that the ultimate burden of persuasion remains on the foreign representative.[470]

---

document has acted and, where appropriate, the identity of the seal or stamp on the document." *Id.* ¶ 113.

464 Guide ¶ 114; *see also* A/CN.9/433 ¶ 62 (stating "that the negation of 'legalization' requirements was meant to avoid time-consuming notarial or consular procedures ill-suited for dealing with cross-border insolvency cases, because they lacked the required element of speedy treatment of applications by foreign representatives").

465 The Guide to Enactment notes that treaties on legalization often leave in effect "laws and regulations that have abolished or simplified legalization procedures." Guide ¶ 115 (citing the Convention Abolishing the Requirement of Legalisation for Foreign Documents (1961), adopted under the auspices of the Hague Conference on Private International Law, as an example).

466 *See* mn 71 *et seq* (discussing definition of "foreign main proceeding").

467 A/CN.9/435 ¶ 170; *see also* Council Regulation 1346/2000 of 29 May 2000 on Insolvency Proceedings, Art 3 (1), 2000 O.J. (L 160) 1.

468 H. Rep. No. 109–31, 109th Cong., 1st Sess. 112 (2005).

469 *Id.* at 113.

470 *Id.* at 112–13.

Generally, in American federal practice,[471] a presumption imposes on the party against whom it is directed the burden of going forward with *evidence* to rebut or meet the presumption, but does not shift to such party the burden of proof in the sense of the risk of nonpersuasion, which remains throughout the trial upon the party on whom it was originally cast. 185

2.4.3 Article 17 – Decision to recognize a foreign proceeding

1. Subject to article 6, a foreign proceeding shall be recognized if:

(*a*) The foreign proceeding is a proceeding within the meaning of subparagraph (*a*) of article 2;

(*b*) The foreign representative applying for recognition is a person or body within the meaning of subparagraph (*d*) of article 2;

(*c*) The application meets the requirements of paragraph 2 of article 15; and

(*d*) The application has been submitted to the court referred to in article 4.

2. The foreign proceeding shall be recognized:

(*a*) As a foreign main proceeding if it is taking place in the State where the debtor has the centre of its main interests; or

(*b*) As a foreign non-main proceeding if the debtor has an establishment within the meaning of subparagraph (*f*) of article 2 in the foreign State.

3. An application for recognition of a foreign proceeding shall be decided upon at the earliest possible time.

4. The provisions of articles 15, 16, 17 and 18 do not prevent modification or termination of recognition if it is shown that the grounds for granting it were fully or partially lacking or have ceased to exist.

→ *Cf* Art 16 et seq of the EIR

2.4.3.1 General

Article 17 sets forth **criteria** for the court's decisions respecting **recognition of foreign proceedings** (paragraphs 1 and 2) and requires it to make the decisions "at the earliest possible time" (paragraph 3) but provides that it may modify its choices as new information comes to light (paragraph 4). 186

---

[471] Fed. R. Evid. 301 (emphasis added). *See also In re Tri-Continental Exch. Ltd.*, 349 B.R. 627, 635 (Bankr. E.D. Cal. 2006) ("In effect, the registered office (or place of incorporation) is evidence that is probative of, and that may in the absence of other evidence be accepted as a proxy for, 'center of main interests.'"). One court has held that the absence of objections would not prevent it from finding that the section 1516 (c) presumption was overcome where the foreign representative's own evidence rebutted the presumption. *See In re Bear Stearns High-Grade Structured Credit Strategies Master Fund, Ltd. (In Provisional Liquidation)*, 374 B.R. 122, 130 (Bankr. S.D.N.Y. 2007) (amended decision). For discussion of what might be required to rebut the presumption, *see* mn 76 *et seq* (discussing section 1502 (4)'s definition of "foreign main proceeding").

187 Application of paragraph 1 is startlingly simple. In essence, if the foreign proceeding and foreign representative meet the Model Law's definitions of those terms,[472] recognition should follow.[473]

188 There is no requirement that the court review the propriety of the commencement of the foreign proceeding or appointment of the foreign representative under the law of the originating State.[474] Nor is reciprocal treatment from the foreign jurisdiction a requirement for recognition of its insolvency proceedings.[475] The sufficiency of the connection between the debtor and the originating State to bear the effects of recognition finds basic

---

[472] *See* mn 62 *et seq* and 87 *et seq* (discussing the definitions of "foreign proceeding" and "foreign representative"). Note especially that those terms apply to interim proceedings and to representatives appointed on an interim basis. *Id.*

[473] *See* Guide ¶ 124 (stating that "[t]he purpose of article 17 is to indicate that, if recognition is not contrary to the public policy of the enacting State and if the application meets the requirements set out in the article, recognition will be granted as a matter of course"); A/52/17 ¶¶ 30 (stating that "the purpose of the article ... was to indicate that, if recognition was not contrary to the public policy of the enacting State, if the application was submitted to the competent court and if the application met the requirements set out in article [15], the court was obligated to grant recognition"); 31 (expressing that "the purpose of articles [15–17] ... was to establish a system of quasi-automatic recognition where the conditions established by the Model Provisions were met").

[474] *See* Guide ¶ 125 (noting that "[a]part from the public policy exception (see article 6), the conditions for recognition do not include those that would allow the court considering the application to evaluate the merits of the foreign court's decision by which the proceeding has been commenced or the foreign representative appointed"); *see also* A/CN.9/419 ¶¶ 185 (noting that "an examination of whether the foreign proceeding had been opened in accordance with the detailed procedural requirements of the foreign jurisdiction ... was generally felt ... beyond the authority of the recognizing court"); A/CN.9/433 ¶ 101 (stating that while recognition should not be considered automatic, "the court seized with a request for recognition of a foreign proceeding should not reconsider the grounds on which the foreign court decided to open that foreign proceeding"). Specifically considered but not adopted was a proposed requirement that a foreign representative provide specific assurance of its authority "to act abroad, in particular with respect to assets located abroad." A/CN.9/419 ¶¶ 36–38, 179. The idea was seen as out of line with current practice, appointments generally being phrased in a very general manner, *id.* ¶¶ 36, 113, 179, and it was pointed out that requiring such specific assurance might interfere with the foreign representative's ability to act quickly to secure and protect assets. A/CN.9/419 ¶¶ 37, 180. If the foreign jurisdiction has enacted the Model Law, the court can look to Article 5, which provides for such specific authorization. *See* 113 *et seq* (discussing Article 5).

[475] The Working Group did consider such a requirement, suggesting it might "foster greater harmonization of the law by increasing pressure on States to include in their own laws provisions on cross-border insolvency." A/CN.9/419 ¶ 42. The idea did not carry the day, however, perhaps because of the uncertainty as to the technical meaning of the term given its wide variety of meanings across the array of existing legal systems and in determining the extent to which reciprocity is available in a given instance. *Id.* ¶ 43 (noting that including a reciprocity factor would be inconsistent with the basic aim of fostering international cooperation). ***But see*** Engel, *passim*, (cautioning that lack of reciprocity amounts to a "unilateral disarmament" by enacting States, reducing the leverage of their creditors in the face of inappropriate forum shopping respecting the commencement of foreign main proceedings that may result in those creditors seeking "alternative leverage" by commencing involuntary domestic bankruptcy filings and reduced liquidity in distressed debt markets).

resolution in the Model Law's distinction between **foreign main and non-main proceedings** in paragraph 2, though the reference to Article 6 in paragraph 1 qualifies mechanical application of the recognition criteria in cases where a court must seriously question any recognition at all on grounds of domestic public policy.[476] The requirements respecting the proper court and minimum evidence amount to mere procedural protections.[477] Note that the minimum evidence that Article 17 (1) (c) mandates, however, does not imply the *adequacy* of such evidence to prove subparagraphs (a) and (b), though such adequacy *may* be presumed.[478]

Paragraph 2 requires the court to categorize the recognized foreign proceeding depending on the nature of the connection of the debtor to the State in which the foreign proceeding is occurring.[479] It explicitly provides for two possibilities: recognition as a **foreign main proceeding** and recognition as a **foreign non-main proceeding**, linking recognition status to the definitions of those terms set out in Article 2.[480] The Model Law **contemplates** that a debtor will have only one **centre of its main interests** ("**COMI**"), and that that COMI will exist in only one State, so that a court may recognize at most only one foreign proceeding as a foreign main proceeding.[481] (If the COMI exists in the enact- **189**

[476] *See* mn 119 *et seq* (discussing Article 6). An example of where Article 6 might be invoked would be a case in which the debtor and foreign representative collude to open foreign proceedings to conceal assets. A/CN.9/419 ¶ 186.

[477] Subparagraph (b) is not merely procedural, since the Model Law bundles the concept of recognizing a foreign proceeding to recognizing a foreign representative. *See* note 425 and accompanying text.

[478] *See* Art 16 (1) (providing entitlement to presume such evidence is adequate) and 180 *et seq* (discussing same).

[479] *See* Guide ¶¶ 30 ("The decision [whether or not to recognize a foreign proceeding] includes a determination whether the jurisdictional basis on which the foreign proceeding was commenced was such that it should be recognized as a 'main' or a 'non-main' foreign insolvency proceeding."), 126 ("Article 17 draws in paragraph 2 the basic distinction between foreign proceedings categorized as the 'main' proceedings and those foreign proceedings that are not so characterized, depending upon the jurisdictional basis of the foreign proceeding … .").

[480] *See* Art 2 (b)–(c) (defining those terms) and mn 71 *et seq* and 84 *et seq* (discussing same). The "redefinition" of the defined terms "foreign main proceeding" and "foreign non-main proceeding" in Article 17 has its origin in early deliberations of the Working Group over the definition of "foreign proceeding," and the extent to which the recognizing court would need to assess the competence of the foreign court in opening the foreign proceeding in terms of jurisdiction, i.e., the sufficiency of its connection to the debtor. *See* A/CN.9/419 ¶¶ 99–105. Eventually it was decided that the resolution of that issue, while necessary, did not belong in the definition of the term "foreign proceeding." A/CN.9/419 ¶ 110.

[481] *See, e.g.,* Guide ¶ 127 (stating that it would be inadvisable "to include more than one criterion for qualifying a foreign proceeding as a main proceeding and provide that on the basis of any of those criteria a proceeding could be deemed a main proceeding. An approach involving such a [sic] 'multiple criteria' would raise the risk of competing claims from foreign proceedings for recognition as the main proceeding"); A/CN.9/422 ¶¶ 83, 88–89 (noting that use of only one factor is "necessary to avoid placing the courts in the enacting State in the position of dealing with multiple claims for recognition as a foreign main proceeding"). The use of the COMI as the criterion "corresponds to the formulation in article 3 of the European Union Convention on Insolvency Proceedings, thus building on the emerging harmonization as regards the notion of 'main' proceeding." Guide ¶ 31; *see also* A/CN.9/422 ¶¶ 89–91 (discussing agreement on the COMI as the deciding factor for recognizing a foreign proceeding as a foreign main proceeding, noting the harmony with the EU terminology, and suggesting that the registered seat be rebuttably

ing State, of course, no foreign proceeding can be a foreign main proceeding.) Foreign non-main proceedings can originate only from States in which the debtor has an **"establishment,"** as defined in Article 2 (f).[482] The Model Law gives no designation to foreign proceedings recognized according to the paragraph 1 criteria that originate from States in which the debtor has neither its COMI nor an establishment, even though the mere presence of assets may be sufficient to open an insolvency proceeding in the enacting State.[483] The Guide to Enactment states that "the Model Law does not envisage recognition of a proceeding commenced in a foreign State" under such circumstances.[484]

190 The categorization of the recognized proceeding is important for purposes of determining the effects it is to have in terms of **relief** provided.[485] Thus, the structure of the Model Law makes gaining recognition a relatively simple, mechanical process, essentially requiring only that the foreign proceeding in question meet the Model Law's definition of that term. The Law further mandates that a distinction be made between **foreign main** and **non-main proceedings**, assigning certain more or less mandatory effects and limitations to each kind of proceeding. As a survey of the remaining articles of Chapter III makes clear, however, court discretion plays a large role in the details of applying the effects and tailoring the relief the Model Law makes available through the recognition process.

---

presumed the COMI); *cf* Council Regulation 1346/2000 of 29 May 2000 on Insolvency Proceedings, Art 3, 2000 O.J. (L 160) 1.

[482] *See* Guide ¶¶ 73 ("Thus, a foreign non-main proceeding susceptible to recognition under article 17, paragraph 2, may be only a proceeding commenced in a State where the debtor has an establishment in the meaning of article 2, subparagraph (f)."); 75 (noting that, "for a foreign non-main proceeding to be recognized, the debtor must have an establishment in the foreign state").

[483] *See* Guide ¶ 73 (noting that "the effects of an insolvency proceeding commenced on the basis of the presence of assets only are normally restricted to the assets located in that State"); A/52/17 ¶ 154 (recording the Commission's decision "that a foreign non-main proceeding susceptible to recognition under article [17] should only be a proceeding commenced in a State where the debtor had an establishment in the meaning of article 2 (f)"). The Commission was aware of the seeming conflict with Article 28, which allows the commencement of insolvency proceedings in the enacting State after recognition of a foreign proceeding "only if the debtor has assets in [the enacting] State," Art 28, but "noted that the effects of an insolvency proceeding opened on the basis of the presence of assets in the State were, according to [Article 28], normally restricted to the assets located in that State; if other debtor's assets located abroad should, under the law of the enacting State, be administered in that insolvency proceeding, that cross-border issue was to be dealt with as a matter of international cooperation and coordination under [Chapter IV]." A/52/17 ¶ 154; *see also* mn 280 *et seq* (discussing Article 28). *But see* A/52/17 ¶ 202 (noting criticism of the adopted solution).

[484] Guide ¶ 128.

[485] *See* Guide ¶ 31 ("The determination that a foreign proceeding is a 'main' proceeding may affect the nature of the relief accorded to the foreign representative."), 126 (noting that "[t]he relief flowing from recognition may depend upon the category into which a foreign proceeding falls. For example, recognition of a 'main' proceeding triggers an automatic stay of individual creditor actions or executions concerning the assets of the debtor (article 20, subparagraphs 1 (a) and (b)) and an automatic 'freeze' of those assets (article 20, subparagraph 1 (c)), subject to certain exceptions referred to in article 20, paragraph 2"). The two-tiered approach to recognition based on jurisdictional connection represents a flexible compromise as to what the criteria for "recognition" ought to be. A/CN.9/419 ¶¶ 22–25 (outlining the debate).

Paragraph 3 mandates that the court rule upon an application for recognition "at the earliest possible time."[486] Although Article 19 gives the court the option of providing **provisional relief** while it considers the application, recognition generally makes it easier for a foreign representative to gather and protect the debtor's assets and investigate its affairs.[487] The streamlined application requirements set forth in Article 15 and the presumptions in Article 16 should aid the court in making its recognition-related decisions promptly. Moreover, paragraph 4 provides for the possibility of revisiting such decisions if the grounds upon which it relied "were fully or partially lacking or have ceased to exist,"[488] so they may not need be considered permanent, depending upon the procedural law of the enacting State.[489] **191**

As noted above,[490] requirements for notice of recognition (or the recognition proceeding) lie outside the scope of the Model Law, so other law in each enacting State must be consulted to discover the existence and content of any such requirements.[491] **192**

2.4.3.2 United States Law

Section 1517 – Order granting recognition

(a) Subject to section 1506, after notice and a hearing, an order recognizing a foreign proceeding shall be entered if

(1) such foreign proceeding for which recognition is sought is a foreign main proceeding or foreign nonmain proceeding within the meaning of section 1502;

(2) the foreign representative applying for recognition is a person or body; and

(3) the petition meets the requirements of section 1515.

(b) Such foreign proceeding shall be recognized

(1) as a foreign main proceeding if it is pending in the country where the debtor has the center of its main interests; or

(2) as a foreign nonmain proceeding if the debtor has an establishment within the meaning of section 1502 in the foreign country where the proceeding is pending.

---

[486] Japan, Mexico and Poland have omitted this requirement. A/CN.9/580 ¶ 9.

[487] *See* Guide ¶ 125 ("The foreign representative's ability to obtain early recognition (and the consequential ability to invoke in particular articles 20, 21, 23 and 24) is often essential for the effective protection of the assets of the debtor from dissipation and concealment.").

[488] Examples the Guide to Enactment gives include when the nature of the foreign proceeding has changed, e.g., from a reorganization to a liquidation, or circumstances in which conditions set forth for recognition have not been observed or have not come to pass. Guide ¶ 130.

[489] *See* Guide ¶ 129 (noting that the question of such revisiting "is left to the procedural law of the enacting State other than the provisions implementing the Model Law"). Article 18 obliges foreign representatives, from the time they apply for recognition, to apprise the recognizing court of changes to the status of the foreign proceeding or the foreign representative's appointment as well as the existence of any other foreign proceeding regarding the same debtor of which the foreign representative becomes aware. *See* Art 18 and mn 199 *et seq* (discussing same).

[490] *See* note 431 and accompanying text (discussing same).

[491] *See* Guide ¶ 132.

(c) A petition for recognition of a foreign proceeding shall be decided upon at the earliest possible time. Entry of an order recognizing a foreign proceeding constitutes recognition under this chapter.

(d) The provisions of this subchapter do not prevent modification or termination of recognition if it is shown that the grounds for granting it were fully or partially lacking or have ceased to exist, but in considering such action the court shall give due weight to possible prejudice to parties that have relied upon the order granting recognition. A case under this chapter may be closed in the manner prescribed under section 350.

193 Section 1517 is titled, "Order granting recognition." The concept of recognition, as it exists in chapter 15, was unknown under prior American bankruptcy law.[492] The closest analogue was the commencement of a "case ancillary to foreign proceedings" under former section 304.[493] The opening of the "case"[494] was essentially a jurisdictional exercise without substantive effects of its own.[495] Courts were given "maximum flexibility" to grant "appropriate relief" related to administering assets of debtors subject to foreign bankruptcy cases within the United States based on principles of comity set forth in the statute.[496]

[492] *See* NBRC Report at 358 (noting that "[i]n typical Anglo-American fashion, the United States courts have not focused much on a concept of 'recognition' as such, but upon the specific requests for relief made by foreign representatives").

[493] 11 U.S.C. § 304 (2000) (repealed). *See supra* note 144 for text. It was also possible (but expensive and potentially troublesome) for foreign representatives to commence plenary cases. *See* 11 U.S.C. § 303 (b) (4) (providing for commencement of involuntary plenary cases by foreign representatives); *In re Axona Internat'l Credit & Commerce Ltd.*, 88 B.R. 597 (Bankr. S.D.N.Y. 1988), *aff'd*, 115 B.R. 442 (S.D.N.Y. 1990), *appeal dismissed*, 924 F.2d 31 (2d Cir. 1991) (holding that application of 11 U.S.C. section 303 (b) (4) did not violate constitutionally protected equal protection or due process under the law). As discussed above, commencement of plenary cases by foreign representatives today requires recognition under section 1517. *See* 11 U.S.C. § 1511; *see also* mn 144 *et seq* (discussing standing of foreign representatives to commence domestic insolvency proceedings). *But see In re Bear Stearns High-Grade Structured Credit Strategies Master Fund, Ltd. (In Provisional Liquidation)*, 974 B.R. 122, 132 (Bankr. S.D.N.Y. 2007) (amended decision). (stating in *dicta* that invocation of section 303 (b) (4) (providing that an involuntary plenary case may be commenced by a foreign representative) does not require that the foreign proceeding the foreign representative represents be recognized).

[494] *See* mn 52 for an explanation of the term "case."

[495] *See* Collier ¶ 1515.02 (noting that the new "structure makes the recognition procedure largely objective and not discretionary, in contrast to former section 304, which essentially skipped the formal step of recognition and focused on the factors the court should consider in deciding whether to grant discretionary relief"); *see also* mn 79–83 (discussing objectivity of COMI criteria).

[496] H. Rep. No. 95–595, 1st Sess. 324–25 (1977); S. Rep. No. 95–989, 2d Sess. 35 (1978). *See* 11 U.S.C. § 304 (c) (2000) (repealed) (setting forth principles). Note that "[a]lthough the case law construing section 304 makes it clear that comity is the central consideration, its physical placement as one of six factors in subsection (c) of [former] section 304 is misleading, since those factors are essentially elements of the grounds for granting comity." H. Rep. No. 109–31, 109th Cong. 109 (2005). Section 1507 (b), which adopts the same factors for consideration in granting "additional assistance," rectifies that problem. *Id.*; *see also* mn 123 *et seq* (discussing section 1507).

Nor was it even technically necessary for foreign representatives to use section 304 or bankruptcy courts to obtain some forms of relief.[497]

With the introduction of the Model Law, however, obtaining an order granting recognition is a matter of status and a separate but essential step for a foreign representative seeking aid from courts in the United States.[498]

Section 1517 "closely tracks article 17 ..., with a few exceptions,"[499] the most **194**
important of which make the contrast between the new concept of **recognition** and former practice even more discernible. First, Congress replaced the key phrase "shall be recognized" in Article 17 with "an order recognizing a foreign proceeding shall be entered." Both phrases carry the same meaning under chapter 15 by virtue of the section 1502 (7) definition of "recognition" as "the entry of an order granting recognition of a foreign main proceeding or foreign nonmain proceeding ... ."[500] That definition is essentially reproduced at the end of subsection (c), except that in section 1502 (7), the text makes clear, as mentioned above, that recognition may only be of a **foreign main** or **foreign nonmain proceeding.**[501] Language in section 1517 (a) (1) replacing Article 17 (1) (a)'s requirement that the foreign proceeding meet only the Article 2 (a) definition of "foreign proceeding" with the requirement that the foreign proceeding be (i.e., meet the definition of) either a foreign main proceeding or a foreign nonmain proceeding, reinforces the point. Thus, under chapter 15, it clearly follows that *not* every "**foreign proceeding,**" as defined in section 101 (23),[502] may be entitled to recognition (and thus the relief that may flow from it), because it is possible for a foreign proceeding to be pending in a country in which the debtor has no **establishment**, in which case it is neither a foreign main nor a foreign nonmain proceeding.[503] The same result probably obtains under the Model Law as well, but it is not quite as clear.

---

[497] *See supra* note 344 and accompanying text.

[498] *See* 11 U.S.C. § 1509; *see also* mn 137 *et seq* (discussing section 1509's effect of channeling jurisdiction through single court by means of recognition); H. Rep. No. 109–31, 109th Cong. 113 (2005) ("Consistent with the position of various civil law representatives in the drafting of the Model Law, recognition creates a status ... .").

[499] H. Rep. No. 109–31, 109th Cong., 1st Sess. 113 (2005).

[500] *See* 11 U.S.C. § 1502 (7).

[501] *See* mn 104 (discussing section 1502 (7)).

[502] *See* mn 68 *et seq* (discussing section 101 (23) and the definition of "foreign proceeding").

[503] *See also* H. Rep. No. 109–31, 109th Cong., 1st Sess. 113 (2005) (confirming that a "petition under section 1515 must show that [the foreign] proceeding is a main or a qualifying non-main proceeding in order to obtain recognition"). As noted above, *see supra* note 261, the court in *In re SPhinX* concluded that "in Bankruptcy Code sections 1502 (7), 1504, and 1517 (a) (1) Congress separated the concept of 'recognition' from the concept of 'recognition as a foreign main (or nonmain) proceeding' under 1517 (b)." *In re SPhinX, Ltd.*, 371 B.R. 10, (S.D.N.Y. 2006), *aff'd*, 371 B.R. 10 (S.D.N.Y. 2007). This conclusion seems to contradict sections 1517 (c) and 1502 (7), where the word "an" in front of "order" indicates a single court order constitutes recognition of a foreign proceeding as either main or nonmain. *See also* Glosband at 45, 87 (criticizing the *SPhinX* decision for, among other things, failing to perceive recognition as "a one step process"); *In re Bear Stearns High-Grade Structured Credit Strategies Master Fund, Ltd. (In Provisional Liquidation)*, 374 B.R. 122, 126 (S.D.N.Y. 2007) (amended decision). ("[T]he process of recognition of a foreign proceeding is a simple single step process incorporating the definitions in section 1502 and 101 (23) and (24) to determine recognition as either a main or nonmain proceeding or nonrecognition.") (citations omitted). According to Glosband, "Severing recognition from the application of the definitional requirements of foreign main proceedings and foreign non-main proceedings results in the court

195 Another departure from Article 17's text is section 1517 (a) (3)'s condition to recognition that the petition meet "the requirements of section 1515," which includes *all* its requirements.[504] Article 17 provides only that the requirements of paragraph 2 of Article 15 need be met.

196 Relatedly, section 1517 broadens Article 17's list of provisions that "do not prevent modification or termination of recognition" to include all of subchapter III. With respect to modification and termination, however, the court is admonished to consider whether and how parties have changed position in reliance on recognition. This stands in contrast to the recognition decisions themselves, which are mechanical and objective rather than "dependent upon any findings about the nature of the foreign proceedings of the sort previously mandated by section 304 (c) … ."[505]

197 There are also two procedural additions of note. The first is the phrase, **"after notice and a hearing"** in subsection (a). The Bankruptcy Code expressly construes those words softly to mean "after such notice as is appropriate in the particular circumstances, and such opportunity for a hearing as is appropriate in the particular circumstances … ."[506]

198 The second addition is the last sentence of section 1517, which refers to section 350 of the Bankruptcy Code as prescribing a manner for closing the case. Section 350 does not itself provide a manner of closing but merely instructs courts to close cases after the "estate is fully administered and the court has discharged the trustee,"[507] conditions somewhat ill-fitted to ancillary cases, which have neither estates nor trustees. The House Report that accompanied the legislation states that the reference is "to the routine closing of a case that has been completed and will invoke requirements including a final report from the foreign representative in such form as the Rules may provide or a court may order."[508] Thus, the provision essentially charges the bankruptcy court to take care to close the case and adapt the established pattern for doing so to the features of chapter 15 cases by rule or order.

---

ignoring whether the SPhinX Funds are foreign proceedings entitled to … recognition." *Id.*

504 Section 1517 omits paragraph 1 (d) of Article 17 as unnecessary in the United States, where "a petition submitted to the wrong court will be dismissed or transferred under other provisions of … law." H. Rep. No. 109–31, 109th Cong., 1st Sess. 113 (2005).

505 H. Rep. No. 109–31, 109th Cong., 1st Sess. 113 (2005).

506 11 U.S.C. § 102 (1) (A). Note that a phrase such as "after notice and a hearing" also "authorizes an act without an actual hearing if such notice is given properly and if (i) such a hearing is not requested timely by a party in interest; or (ii) there is insufficient time for a hearing to be commenced before such act must be done … ." 11 U.S.C. § 102 (1) (B). Under an interim procedural rule, 20 days' written notice of a hearing on a recognition petition is required to be mailed to "the debtor, all administrators in foreign proceedings of the debtor, all entities against whom provisional relief is being sought under § 1519 of the [Bankruptcy] Code, all parties to any litigation in which the debtor is a party and that is pending in the United States at the time of the filing of the petition, and such other entities as the court may direct." Fed. R. Bankr. P. 2002 (q) (1) (Interim). The notice must state "whether the petition seeks recognition as a foreign main proceeding or foreign nonmain proceeding." *Id.*

507 11 U.S.C. § 350.

508 H. Rep. No. 109–31, 109th Cong., 1st Sess. 114 (2005).

2.4.4 Article 18 – Subsequent information

From the time of filing the application for recognition of the foreign proceeding, the foreign representative shall inform the court promptly of:

***(a)* Any substantial change in the status of the recognized foreign proceeding or the status of the foreign representative's appointment; and**

***(b)* Any other foreign proceeding regarding the same debtor that becomes known to the foreign representative.**

→ *Cf* Art 16 et seq of the EIR

2.4.4.1 General

Article 18 charges foreign representatives with a continuing duty to keep the court informed of substantial changes to the status of the recognized foreign proceeding and the foreign representative's appointment as well as the existence of any other foreign proceeding of which the foreign representative becomes aware. The obligation to inform in subparagraph (a) should enable the court to wisely exercise its powers to decide whether **recognition** remains appropriate and, if so, whether recognition as a **main** or **non-main foreign proceeding** is most fitting, as circumstances change.[509] In addition, information provided will aid the court in deciding whether relief that has been granted ought to be modified or whether further investigation is necessary.[510] Thus, only "substantial" changes need be reported. The Guide to Enactment implies that the test for substantiality consists of modifications such as "would affect the decision granting relief or the decision recognizing the proceeding,"[511] linking the subparagraph (a) duty to the Article 15 application requirement to provide evidence of the existence of the foreign proceeding and the appointment of the foreign representative.[512] **199**

The Guide to Enactment refers to the subparagraph (b) duty to inform the court of new foreign proceedings as an extension of the Article 15 (3) obligation to inform the court of all other foreign proceedings respecting the debtor of which the foreign representative is aware at the time of application and notes that such information will aid the court in its own duty to seek cooperation and coordination under Chapter IV.[513] **200**

[509] Article 17 (4) permits the court to revisit its decisions respecting recognition. *See* mn 186 *et seq* (discussing Article 17); *see also* Guide ¶ 70 (noting that the purpose of the Article 18 obligation is to allow the court to modify or terminate the consequences of recognition).

[510] Curiously, Article 18 (a) includes the word "recognized" to modify "foreign proceeding" even though a court would undoubtedly profit from information about a change in status of a foreign proceeding after an application for recognition has been filed but before the decisions on recognition have been reached.

[511] Guide ¶ 133 (citing termination of the foreign proceeding, change from a reorganization to a liquidation or *vice versa*, and decisions respecting interim proceedings and appointments as examples of substantive changes).

[512] *See* mn 172 *et seq* (discussing Article 15).

[513] *See* Guide ¶ 134 (citing Article 30 with respect to the duty to seek cooperation and coordination).

2.4.4.2 United States Law

Section 1518 – Subsequent information

From the time of filing the petition for recognition of a foreign proceeding, the foreign representative shall file with the court promptly a notice of change of status concerning

(1) any substantial change in the status of such foreign proceeding or the status of the foreign representative's appointment; and

(2) any other foreign proceeding regarding the debtor that becomes known to the foreign representative.

201 Section 1518 follows the text of Article 18 almost exactly, adding only a requirement to "file with the court ... a notice of change of status" in place of "inform the court," which makes the notice a public record under American law, "open to examination by an entity at reasonable times without charge,"[514] and removing the words "recognized" from before "foreign proceeding" as it appears in Article 18 (a)[515] and "same" before "debtor," which is specifically defined in chapter 15, as it appears in Article 18 (b).

2.4.5 Article 19 – Relief that may be granted upon application for recognition of a foreign proceeding

1. From the time of filing an application for recognition until the application is decided upon, the court may, at the request of the foreign representative, where relief is urgently needed to protect the assets of the debtor or the interests of the creditors, grant relief of a provisional nature, including:

***(a)* Staying execution against the debtor's assets;**

***(b)* Entrusting the administration or realization of all or part of the debtor's assets located in this State to the foreign representative or another person designated by the court, in order to protect and preserve the value of assets that, by their nature or because of other circumstances, are perishable, susceptible to devaluation or otherwise in jeopardy;**

***(c)* Any relief mentioned in paragraph 1 *(c)*, *(d)* and *(g)* of article 21.**

2. *[Insert provisions (or refer to provisions in force in the enacting State) relating to notice.]*

3. Unless extended under paragraph 1 *(f)* of article 21, the relief granted under this article terminates when the application for recognition is decided upon.

4. The court may refuse to grant relief under this article if such relief would interfere with the administration of a foreign main proceeding.

→ *Cf* Art 16 et seq of the EIR

[514] 11 U.S.C. § 107 (a). Note that procedures are available to file papers under seal under certain circumstances. *See generally* 11 U.S.C. § 107 (b).

[515] *See supra* note 510.

2.4.5.1 General

Article 19 authorizes the court to grant an unrecognized foreign representative (who nevertheless has court access under Article 9 and implicit standing from paragraph 1 to request it) **provisional relief** from the time the representative files an application for **recognition** of the foreign proceeding that has authorized the foreign representative to act until the court passes on the application. **202**

While the gist of its function and a number of its qualifications are clear from the text, certain questions respecting Article 19 remain unanswered. First, it is unclear which court is meant by **"the court"** in paragraphs 1 and 4. Article 4 expressly identifies only the court that performs the "functions referred to in this Law relating to recognition of foreign proceedings and cooperation with foreign courts."[516] The Guide to Enactment points out that the "competence for the various judicial functions dealt with in the Model Law may lie with different courts"[517] and states that "[i]n defining jurisdiction in matters mentioned in article 4, the implementing legislation should not unnecessarily limit the jurisdiction of other courts in the enacting State, in particular to entertain requests by foreign representatives for provisional relief."[518] **"Provisional relief"** is not mentioned in Article 4, but perhaps the Commission means that it should be considered as "relating to recognition." In any event, one hopes that each enacting State will make clear, either in Article 4 or elsewhere, which court or courts are available for foreign representatives to seek Article 19 relief.[519] **203**

A second question that arises is the precise meaning of "**may**" as it appears in paragraph 1 (and the heading) of Article 19 as opposed to its meaning in paragraph 4. In paragraph 1, the "may" "authorizes the court to grant the type of relief that is usually available only in **collective insolvency proceedings** (i.e. the same type of relief available under article 21),"[520] but rest of paragraph 1 imposes several limitations on the authorization. A "request of the foreign representative" is necessary to trigger the Article 19 authorization.[521] Any **relief** granted must be "urgently needed to protect the assets of the debtor or the interests of the creditors." Both these requirements testify to the collective nature of the relief, and the phrases "urgently needed" and "of a provisional nature," both modifying "relief," attest to a minimalist quality of such relief in terms of its purpose, i.e., "protection," and "interim"[522] duration, as further detailed under paragraph 3. Finally, the authorization to grant **relief** exists only for the time after the filing of an **204**

---

516 Art 4; *see also* mn 109 *et seq* (discussing Article 4).

517 Guide ¶ 80.

518 Guide ¶ 81.

519 *See generally* A/CN.9/419 ¶ 69 (suggesting that enacting States provide an indication "of which of their courts would be competent in these matters"); A/CN.9/433 ¶ 19 (noting that "the court" "might be any court in the enacting State competent to issue provisional measures and not necessarily the court that, according to article 4, had jurisdiction related to recognition of foreign proceedings and cooperation with foreign courts").

520 Guide ¶ 136, "as opposed to the 'individual' type of relief that may be granted before the commencement of insolvency proceedings under rules of civil procedure (i. e. measures covering specific assets identified by a creditor)." *Id.*

521 Article 9 provides access to the appropriate court(s) for the foreign representative. *See* mn 134 *et seq* (discussing Article 9); A/CN.9/419 ¶ 77 (noting agreement of the Working Group in providing the foreign representative access to obtain appropriate protective measures).

522 Guide ¶ 30.

application[523] for recognition until the application is decided. In addition to these paragraph 1 limitations, paragraph 2 may further narrow the authorization of the court to grant pre-recognition relief by adding additional requirements related to notice.[524] Furthermore, Article 22 (1) provides that the court "must be satisfied that the interests of the creditors and other interested persons, including the debtor, are adequately protected,"[525] Article 29 (a) (i) requires that any Article 19 relief be consistent with an insolvency proceeding regarding the same debtor in the enacting State,[526] and Article 30 (a) requires that any Article 19 relief be consistent with an already recognized foreign main proceeding regarding the same debtor.[527]

205 Grammatically, the "may ... if" formula in paragraph 4 at first glance makes the "may" in paragraph 1 appear to mean "must ... unless," with reference to the condition of paragraph 4, i.e., interference with the administration of a foreign main proceeding. To avoid contradiction with the paragraph 1 meaning of "may" as a "discretionary"[528] authorization, the paragraph 4 meaning of "may" must be intended to convey, by contrast, that one reason – among an array of possible reasons – to refuse to grant relief that the court "may" grant under paragraph 1, is that the contemplated relief would interfere with the administration of a **foreign main proceeding**. In essence, then, Article 19's purpose is to authorize a court (or courts), subject to several scope limitations, to preserve the *status quo* until the Article 17 decisions respecting recognition

523 The requirement that an application be filed appears to have been intended to be mean that all application requirements set forth in Article 15 be fulfilled for the application to be considered filed. *See* A/CN.9/433 ¶ 60 (noting "that the proof referred to in article [15] was required for the purposes of the application for recognition or provisional measures").

524 *See* Guide ¶ 138. The precise requirements are left open to non-uniform formulation in accordance with the policy of the Model Law to leave notice procedures to each enacting State without attempting to set a uniform standard respecting them. *See supra* note 431. Note that some States might provide for provisional relief on an *ex parte* basis to achieve maximum effectiveness (by way of surprise) in ensuring assets do not dissipate because of a notice tip-off, or to protect the reputation of the debtor pending recognition. *See* A/CN.9/419 ¶ 176 (discussing same). In considering notice issues, the court ought also take account of its duty under Article 22 (1) to be satisfied that the legitimate interests of others are adequately protected before granting relief. *See* Art 22 (1) and mn 240 *et seq* (discussing Article 22).

525 *See* Art 22 (1) and mn 240 *et seq* (discussing Article 22).

526 *See* Art 29 (a) (i) and mn 284 *et seq* (discussing Article 29).

527 *See* Art 30 (a) and mn 293 *et seq* (discussing Article 30). Note that the principle of limited relief for non-main proceedings is also reflected in Arts 21 (3) (respecting post-recognition relief), 28 (limiting domestic proceedings after recognition of foreign main proceedings), 29 (c) (governing concurrent foreign and domestic proceedings respecting the same debtor) and 30 (governing coordination of more than one foreign proceeding). Guide ¶¶ 160, 191.

528 *See* Guide ¶¶ 141 (noting that "relief under articles 19 and 21 is discretionary" in contrast to the effects provided by Article 20), 154 (stating that "article 21 relief is discretionary, as is pre-recognition relief under article 19"); A/52/17 ¶ 35 (noting discretionary nature of Article 19 relief); A/CN.9/435 ¶¶ 18 (considering that "the court granting pre-recognition relief should be able to tailor the relief to the needs of the foreign representative"), 20 (noting lack of need "to subject the issuance of relief under article [19] to any exception or limitations applicable under the law of the enacting State," as with Article 20, as Article 19 relief is discretionary).

occur, but in doing so, to take into account the needs of administration of a foreign main proceeding (presumably respecting the same debtor).[529]

The list of relief in paragraph 1 is not exhaustive, as can be seen by following the cross reference in subparagraph (c) to "any relief mentioned in paragraph 1 (g) of article 21," which authorizes "[g]ranting any additional relief that may be available to [reorganization or liquidation administrators] under the laws of [the enacting] State."[530] The Guide to Enactment does, however, point out the contrasts in the relief listed with that set forth in the list of post-recognition discretionary relief in Article 21, noting that it is of the "same type" (collective) but "somewhat more narrow,"[531] i.e., provisional, in that subparagraph (a) "restricts the stay to execution proceedings"[532] and subparagraph (b) "is restricted to perishable assets and assets susceptible to devaluation or otherwise in jeopardy."[533] In addition, as with relief under Article 21, Article 22 (2) provides the court express authority to "subject relief granted under article 19 ... to conditions it considers appropriate."[534] **206**

---

[529] *See generally* Guide ¶ 140 (noting that paragraph 4 "pursues the same objective as the one underlying article 30, subparagraph (a), namely that, if there is a foreign main proceeding pending, any relief granted in favour of a foreign non-main proceeding must be consistent (or should not interfere) with the foreign main proceeding"); *see also id.* ¶¶ 158, 160 (noting that the objective of Article 21 (3) "is to admonish the court that relief in favour of a foreign non-main proceeding should not give unnecessarily broad powers to the foreign representative and that such relief should not interfere with the administration of another insolvency proceeding, in particular the main proceeding," and that the "idea underlying article 21, paragraph 3, has been reflected also in article 19, paragraph 4 (prerecognition relief), article 29, subparagraph (c) (coordination of a foreign proceeding with a local proceeding) and article 30 (coordination of more than one foreign proceedings)"). Articles 15 (3) and 18 (b), each of which requires information from the foreign representative upon and after filing an application for recognition, respectively, to inform the court of any foreign proceedings of which the foreign representative is or becomes aware, also support that objective. Guide ¶ 140. It should be noted that the Model Law does not expressly forbid pre-recognition relief outside the scope of Article 19. It merely places the limitations set forth above on the Article 19 authorization. It is possible that other law in the enacting State may form a basis for pre-recognition relief. *See, e.g.,* A/CN.9/422 ¶ 112 (noting that in the unlikely event "that a foreign representative might not be able to apply for recognition simultaneously with a request for provisional relief ... th[e] question ... should be left for the laws of the enacting State").

[530] Art 21; *see also* Guide ¶ 154 (noting with respect to Article 21 that the list is "not exhaustive and the court is not restricted unnecessarily in its ability to grant any type of relief that is available under the law of the enacting State and needed in the circumstances of the case").

[531] Guide ¶ 136. The Working Group decided it was useful to provide a list of discretionary relief to be available in every enacting State, as some states may not have authorization for such relief, while at the same time keeping the possibilities of other forms of relief broad and flexible by maintaining the parallelism between the lists of relief in Articles 19 and 21. A/CN.9/435 ¶ 18.

[532] Early drafts of the Model Law envisioned a broader stay. *See, e.g.,* A/CN.9/435 ¶ 22 (discussing proposal to restrict the subparagraph (a) stay to execution); A/52/17 ¶ 42 (accepting the proposal for the stay of executions as opposed to a broader stay and agreeing that the Guide should state that the term "execution" should be broadly interpreted).

[533] Guide ¶ 137 (observing that "[o]therwise, the measures available under article 19 are essentially the same as those available under article 21"). *See* Art 21 and mn 224 *et seq* (discussing Article 21).

[534] *See* Art 22 (2) and mn 240 *et seq* (discussing Article 22). The Working Group, in considering whether to make pre-recognition

207 It should be remembered that the position of the foreign representative, which may include interim insolvency administrators and debtors in possession,[535] is particularly tenuous before recognition. Thus, the Article 18[536] duty to keep the court informed of changes in the status of the foreign proceeding and the appointment of the foreign representative plays an important role enabling the court to maintain, if necessary by modification or termination,[537] the deliberately minimalist nature of pre-recognition relief described above.[538]

208 In addition, the court has a duty to review Article 19 relief and modify or terminate it to the extent it is inconsistent with either an intervening domestic insolvency proceeding[539] or an intervening recognition of a foreign main proceeding[540] regarding the debtor that is the subject of the application for recognition.

2.4.5.2 United States Law

Section 1519 – Relief that may be granted upon filing petition for recognition

(a) From the time of filing a petition for recognition until the court rules on the petition, the court may, at the request of the foreign representative, where relief is urgently needed to protect the assets of the debtor or the interests of the creditors, grant relief of a provisional nature, including

(1) staying execution against the debtor's assets;

(2) entrusting the administration or realization of all or part of the debtor's assets located in the United States to the foreign representative or another person authorized by the court, including an examiner, in order to protect and preserve the value of assets that, by their nature or because of other circumstances, are perishable, susceptible to devaluation or otherwise in jeopardy; and

(3) any relief referred to in paragraph (3), (4), or (7) of section 1521 (a).

(b) Unless extended under section 1521 (a) (6), the relief granted under this section terminates when the petition for recognition is granted.

---

relief available even in cases in which no application for recognition has been filed, noted that doing so "would require that the Model Provisions specify the circumstances and conditions (such as a security deposit by the foreign representative or other conditions currently provided in some national laws) under which such relief might be granted." A/CN.9/433 ¶ 111. Thus, while the Model Law itself is silent as to the kind of conditions that might be appropriate, the ultimate decision to require the filing of an application for recognition as one condition to obtain Article 19 relief might imply that other conditions that cast doubt on the legitimate status foreign representative or foreign proceeding pending recognition are inconsistent with the goals of the Law.

535 *See* Art 2 (d) (defining "foreign representative") and mn 87 *et seq* (discussing Article 2 (d)).

536 *See* Art 18 and mn 199 *et seq* (discussing Article 18).

537 *See* Art 22 (3) (allowing the court to modify or terminate Article 19 relief) and mn 240 *et seq* (discussing Article 22).

538 *See* A/CN.9/433 ¶ 113 (noting the Working Group's decision that an interim foreign representative should be able to request provisional relief "with appropriate safeguards concerning a duty ... to notify the court of the conditions of his or her appointment").

539 *See* Art 29 (b) (i) and mn 284 *et seq* (discussing Article 29).

540 *See* Art 30 (b) and mn 293 *et seq* (discussing Article 30).

(c) It is a ground for denial of relief under this section that such relief would interfere with the administration of a foreign main proceeding.

(d) The court may not enjoin a police or regulatory act of a governmental unit, including a criminal action or proceeding, under this section.

(e) The standards, procedures, and limitations applicable to an injunction shall apply to relief under this section.

(f) The exercise of rights not subject to the stay arising under section 362 (a) pursuant to paragraph (6), (7), (17), or (27) of section 362 (b) or pursuant to section 362 (n) shall not be stayed by any order of a court or administrative agency in any proceeding under this chapter.

"This section generally follows article 19 ...."[541] Some changes were made to **209** harmonize its provisions with American law. In paragraph 2 of subsection 1(a), "designated" is changed to "authorized," since in the United States, courts generally do not designate fiduciaries but only authorize them to act.[542] Paragraph 3 parallels Article 19 respecting the Article 21 provisions, but also imports the American peculiarities concerning them.[543]

Section 1519 (e) provides that the "standards, procedures, and limitations applicable **210** to injunction[s]" govern section 1519 relief.[544] These include the **notice procedures** meant to be inserted in Article 19 (2).

Subsection (d) restricts the effect of a section 1519 injunction as indicated, which **211** parallels certain of the exclusions from the **automatic stay** that attends the filing of petitions in plenary cases in the United States.[545] As the words "under this section" indicate, however, excluded acts may not be immune from other forms of injunctive relief. A substantial body of case law has developed respecting "non-automatic" injunctions granted via the general power of the court.[546] That law might have applicability to certain police and regulatory actions in some cases.

While the acts identified in subsection (d) are excluded only from section 1519 relief, **212** no stay can issue from a chapter 15 case respecting the rights identified in subsection (f), which mostly relate to certain financial contracts.

[541] H. Rep. No. 109–31, 109th Cong., 1st Sess. 114 (2005).

[542] *See* Glosband Memorandum at 4 (distinguishing between designations and authorizations). For an explanation of the term "examiner," *see* mn 116 *et seq* (discussing section 1505).

[543] *See* mn 232 *et seq* (discussing section 1521).

[544] The House Report, No. 109–31, 109th Cong., 1st Sess. 114 (2005), implies that the procedures to be employed for section 1519 injunctions are those of Federal Rule of Bankruptcy Procedure 7065, which makes Federal Rule of Civil Procedure 65 generally applicable to bankruptcy cases with modifications respecting the giving of security.

[545] *See* 11 U.S.C. § 362 (a) (providing for general stay of certain acts upon the filing of a bankruptcy petition), (b) (1), (4) (excluding criminal proceedings and police and regulatory actions from the automatic stay).

[546] *See generally* 11 U.S.C. § 105 (providing for general powers of the court); H. Rep. No. 109–31, 109th Cong., 1st Sess. 114 (2005) (stating that section 1519 "does not expand or reduce the scope of section 105 as determined by cases under section 105" and that section 105 remains as the only basis for relief against police and regulatory actions).

2.4.6 Article 20 – Effects of recognition of a foreign main proceeding

1. Upon recognition of a foreign proceeding that is a foreign main proceeding,

***(a)* Commencement or continuation of individual actions or individual proceedings concerning the debtor's assets, rights, obligations or liabilities is stayed;**

***(b)* Execution against the debtor's assets is stayed; and**

***(c)* The right to transfer, encumber or otherwise dispose of any assets of the debtor is suspended.**

2. The scope, and the modification or termination, of the stay and suspension referred to in paragraph 1 of this article are subject to *[refer to any provisions of law of the enacting State relating to insolvency that apply to exceptions, limitations, modifications or termination in respect of the stay and suspension referred to in paragraph 1 of this article]*.

3. Paragraph 1 *(a)* of this article does not affect the right to commence individual actions or proceedings to the extent necessary to preserve a claim against the debtor.

4. Paragraph 1 of this article does not affect the right to request the commencement of a proceeding under *[identify laws of the enacting State relating to insolvency]* or the right to file claims in such a proceeding.

2.4.6.1 General

213 Article 20 introduces the stay and **suspension measures** set forth in paragraph 1 upon recognition of a foreign proceeding as a foreign *main* proceeding. Those measures constitute the **minimum**[547] **relief**[548] that recognition as a foreign main proceeding affords under the Model Law.[549] The precise scope of the relief, as well as the availability of

[547] *See* Guide ¶¶ 32 ("Such stay and suspension are 'mandatory' (or 'automatic') in the sense that either they flow automatically from the recognition of a foreign main proceeding or, in the States where a court order is needed for the stay or suspension, the court is bound to issue the appropriate order"); 141 ("While relief under articles 19 and 21 is discretionary, the effects provided by article 20 are not, for they flow automatically from recognition of the foreign main proceeding"); A/CN.9/435 ¶ 28 (noting the aim of "establishing a minimum catalogue of effects of foreign main proceedings, which ... apply uniformly in all [enacting] States"). One result of the automatic nature of Article 20's effects may be that there will be no "actions" to which the public policy exception of Article 6 (allowing courts to refuse to take actions contrary to public policy) might apply, though the analysis may differ respecting enacting States that require court orders to implement such effects.

[548] Note that the list in Article 20 (1) is one the title describes as *effects* of recognition rather than forms of *relief. See also* A/CN.9/435 ¶ 25 (recording agreement in the Working Group that the title be changed to refer to effects rather than relief). The Guide sometimes calls it "relief," however. *See, e.g.,* Guide ¶ 32.

[549] Early drafts of the Model Law included automatic effects for all recognitions, without distinguishing between foreign main and non-main proceedings. *See, e.g.,* A/CN.9/422 ¶ 94. The Working Group later reached a consensus that automatic effects ought to flow only from recognition of insolvency proceedings in the debtor's home country as opposed, for example, to a place in which the debtor merely had assets, as the bare presence of assets was thought an insufficient basis for allowing automatic

grounds to modify or eliminate it, however, are non-uniform,[550] as the bracketed language in paragraph 2 indicates.[551] Furthermore, Article 20 does not apply at all if an insolvency proceeding regarding the same debtor is already occurring in the enacting State when the application for recognition is filed.[552] On the other hand, relief that goes beyond the Article 20 minimum is available – at the court's discretion – as provided in Articles 21, 23 and 24.[553]

The general aim of the automatic measures is to prevent individual actions by or against the debtor from frustrating the opportunity to create a cooperative, cross-border effort to pursue the general objectives of insolvency law as set forth in the Preamble.[554] Those objectives amount to settling the affairs of the debtor, through either reorganization or liquidation, in a way that provides optimal benefits for the collectivity of creditors and other interested parties in terms of both equity and maximum total returns.[555] **214**

---

stay and suspensions measures, which were said to be "tantamount to opening a local insolvency proceeding." *Id.* ¶¶ 101, 103.

550 The effects of recognition that paragraph 1 requires are not the result of the law of the State in which the foreign main proceeding is taking place but rather independent effects of recognition based on the Model Law, i.e., the law of the enacting State. *See* Guide ¶ 143 ("Recognition, therefore, has its own effects rather than importing the consequences of the foreign law into the insolvency system of the enacting State. If recognition should in a given case produce results that would be contrary to the legitimate interests of an interested party, including the debtor, the law of the enacting State should provide possibilities for protecting those interests, as indicated in article 20, paragraph 2 ..."). Thus, they may be more extensive than the law of the foreign jurisdiction provides, particularly if the foreign main proceeding is still an "interim" proceeding. *Id.* ¶¶ 143–44; A/52/17 ¶¶ 50, 53 (stating it is necessary to possibly impose harsher results in an enacting State than in the State in which the debtor maintains the center of its main interests, i.e., where the foreign main proceeding is occurring, even if still in "interim form," in order to obtain the benefits of "organizing an orderly and fair cross-border insolvency proceeding").

551 Paragraph 2 exists in part to give legislatures in enacting States with legal systems that require statutory grounds for a court to override the automatic statutory effects of recognition the opportunity to provide them. *See* A/52/17 ¶¶ 86–88.

552 *See* Art 29 (a) (ii) and mn 284 *et seq* (discussing Article 29).

553 *See* Arts 21, 23 and 24 and mn 224 *et seq*, 247 *et seq*, 252 *et seq*, respectively (discussing Articles 21, 23 and 24). Moreover, "additional assistance" may be available under other law of the enacting State. *See generally* Art 7 and mn 122 (discussing Article 7).

554 *See* Guide ¶ 143 ("The automatic consequences envisaged in article 20 are necessary to allow steps to be taken to organize an orderly and fair cross-border insolvency proceeding."); A/CN.9/422 ¶ 99 (stating that "what was envisaged was the creation of a breathing space to permit the possibility of cross-border insolvency"); A/CN.9/433 ¶ 116 (noting "the main purpose of the stay of individual actions was to prevent the debtor's assets from being dispersed through enforcement measures ordered in individual actions"). The Working Group saw automatic consequences upon recognition as the step necessary to make significant progress beyond what was available in many states without enactment of the Model Law, the ability to ask a court for assistance, or by relying on comity or treaty relationships. A/CN.9/422 ¶ 100.

555 *See generally* mn 23 *et seq* (discussing the Preamble); *see also* Guide ¶ 32 (stating that "[t]he stay of actions or of enforcement proceedings is necessary to provide 'breathing space' until appropriate measures are taken for reorganization or fair liquidation of the assets of the debtor" and that "[t]he mandatory moratorium triggered by the recognition of the foreign main proceeding provides a rapid 'freeze' essential to prevent fraud and to protect the legitimate interests of the parties involved until the court has an opportunity to notify all concerned and to assess the situation").

Except for paragraph 3's set-aside for actions or proceedings "necessary to preserve a claim against the debtor,"[556] subparagraph (a) of paragraph 1 stays **individual actions**[557] and **proceedings**[558] but is silent respecting **collective proceedings**, which seems to imply they may continue.[559] Paragraph 4 expressly allows proceedings under the insolvency laws of the enacting State to be commenced (and claims to be filed in them),[560] though the commencement and effects of insolvency proceedings in the enacting State are subject to Article 28, which sets forth restrictions on such proceedings after recognition of a foreign main proceeding involving the same debtor.[561] Subparagraph (b) **stays any executions** that subparagraph (a) does not cover.

215 Subparagraph (c) suspends any "right to transfer, encumber or otherwise dispose of any assets of the debtor" in order to preserve such assets for reorganization or orderly liquidation.[562] That apparently leaves the debtor (or other custodian) with a right to possess and use the debtor's property subject again to any scope limitations set forth in paragraph 2.

216 The paragraph 1 provisions are, on their face, universal rather than territorial, but the reservations of particular enacting States – to be reflected in paragraph 2 – may limit their scope, and foreign representatives may encounter the usual difficulties in obtaining recognition of the effects of such measures outside the enacting State's territory, the same difficulties that give the Model Law its reason to exist. As just noted,[563] the Model Law leaves paragraph 2 for enacting States to reference local insolvency law provisions that limit the scope of paragraph 1 **relief**[564] or that allow for its **modification** or **termi-**

---

556 The stay is not intended to disadvantage local creditors' claims. A/CN.9/422 ¶ 107. This exception is conceived to prevent valid claims, especially but not exclusively those of local creditors, from becoming time-barred after recognition. Guide ¶ 151. Although actions on such claims may be commenced, they are then immediately stayed from continuing. *Id.* Practitioners should note that choice of law rules might mandate application of law requiring the filing of such a claim to meet an unfamiliar time limitation, even if filing such a claim might not be necessary under the law of the enacting State. *Id.*; A/52/17 ¶ 57.

557 "Individual actions" includes those before arbitral tribunals. *See* Guide ¶ 145 (noting, in addition, that Article 20 thus "establishes a mandatory limitation to the effectiveness of an arbitration agreement"). Note that in Japan and Mexico, the stay applies only to executions against the debtors asset's rather than to actions against the debtor itself. A/CN.9/580 ¶ 11.

558 The term "individual proceedings" is meant to include "enforcement measures initiated by creditors outside the court system." Guide ¶ 146.

559 *See also* A/CN.9/439 ¶ 29 (noting that the article "is intended to protect the interests of all creditors by staying individual actions and suspending the transfer of assets of the debtor and that the scope was "only intended to avoid dissipation of the debtor's assets that would result from individual actions against the assets of the debtors being allowed to run simultaneously to the foreign proceedings," but not "to prevent the opening of a local collective proceeding").

560 *See also* Arts 11 (providing for foreign representative standing to commence local insolvency proceedings, if appropriate) and 12 (providing a foreign representative standing to appropriately participate in local insolvency proceedings) and mn 144 *et seq*, 151 (discussing Articles 11 and 12).

561 *See* Art 28 and mn 280 *et seq* (discussing Article 28).

562 *See* Guide ¶ 32 ("The suspension of transfers is necessary because in a modern, globalized economic system it is possible for multinational debtors to move money and property across boundaries quickly.").

563 *See supra* note 551.

564 The Guide to Enactment lists "exceptions for secured claims, payments by the debtor made in the ordinary course of business, set-off, execution of rights in rem," prosecution of post-commencement (or post-re

nation.[565] In addition, Article 29 provides that "the stay and suspension referred to in paragraph 1 of article 20 shall be modified or terminated pursuant to paragraph 2 of article 20 if inconsistent with" an insolvency proceeding in the enacting State commenced after recognition.[566]

The Model Law does not provide **remedies** for violations of the stay **and suspension provisions.** The legal effect of a violation or attempted violation must therefore be sought in other law of the enacting State.[567] **217**

2.4.6.2 United States Law

Section 1520 – Effects of recognition of a foreign main proceeding

(a) Upon recognition of a foreign proceeding that is a foreign main proceeding

(1) sections 361 and 362 apply with respect to the debtor and the property of the debtor that is within the territorial jurisdiction of the United States;

(2) sections 363, 549, and 552 apply to a transfer of an interest of the debtor in property that is within the territorial jurisdiction of the United States to the same extent that the sections would apply to property of an estate;

(3) unless the court orders otherwise, the foreign representative may operate the debtor's business and may exercise the rights and powers of a trustee under and to the extent provided by sections 363 and 552; and

(4) section 552 applies to property of the debtor that is within the territorial jurisdiction of the United States.

(b) Subsection (a) does not affect the right to commence an individual action or proceeding in a foreign country to the extent necessary to preserve a claim against the debtor.

(c) Subsection (a) does not affect the right of a foreign representative or an entity to file a petition commencing a case under this title or the right of any party to file claims or take other proper actions in such a case.

---

cognition) claims and "completion of open financial market transactions" as examples. Guide ¶¶ 33, 148; *see also* A/52/17 ¶ 48 (discussing same). The Working Group's Report on Insolvency Law on the Work of Its Twentieth Session also notes examples of exceptions to the stay on individual actions that enacting States might have regarding individual debtors: "civil status, alimony, and various administrative and criminal procedures." A/CN.9/433 ¶ 118. Note that Article 22, which requires the courts to be satisfied that the interests of creditors and other interested persons are adequately protected when considering relief under Articles 19 and 21, does *not* apply to Article 20 relief, raising considerably the profile of the paragraph 2 scope limitations.

565 The Article 18 duty of the foreign representative to keep the court informed of changes to the status of the foreign proceeding and the foreign representative's appointment will also aid the court in determining when to exercise its power to modify or terminate Article 20 relief. *See* Art 18 and mn 199 *et seq* (discussing Article 18); *see also* Guide ¶ 144 (referencing Article 18).

566 *See* Art 29 (b) (ii) and 284 *et seq* (discussing Article 29).

567 *See* Guide ¶ 147 (stating, as to Article 20 (1) (c), that "sanctions vary, depending on the legal system"). The Guide does voice a preference for setting aside *vel non* acts taken in violation of the stay and suspense provisions. *Id.*; *see also* A/CN.9/435 ¶¶ 36–37 (discussing same).

218 The effects of **foreign main proceeding recognition** set forth in section 1520 are generally more expansive than those in Article 20. Section 1520 (a) (1)'s reference to section 362 introduces "the U.S. automatic stay, in all its details"[568] to cases[569] **ancillary to foreign main proceedings**, except that it applies only "to the debtor and property of the debtor that is located within the territorial jurisdiction of the United States,"[570] rather than worldwide, as is true under American law in plenary bankruptcy cases.[571] Section 362 includes scope and remedy provisions relating to the stay as well as a procedure to obtain relief from the stay. Cause for relief includes a lack of "adequate protection" for an interest (often a security interest) in the (debtor's) property.[572] "**Adequate protection**" is a technical term that refers to the protection due the holder of a perfected interest in property of a bankruptcy estate from a loss of value of the interest owing to certain effects of bankruptcy administration (e.g., depreciation during the automatic stay, the sale, lease or use of the property, or the imposition of encumbrances on the property). Section 361, which section 1520 (a) (1) also makes applicable to cases ancillary to **foreign main proceedings**, allows that adequate protection may be provided by periodic payments, replacement liens or other forms of protection of "indubitable equivalence."[573] Thus, the references to sections 361 and 362 correspond to and fulfill the functions of the provisions of Article 20 (1) (a)–(b), (2).

219 Section 1520 (a) (2) and (4) import sections 363 (governing the **use, sale** and **lease of property** of the estate), 549 (governing avoidance (or revocation) of **unauthorized transfers** occurring after commencement of a bankruptcy case) and 552 (governing **attachment of security interests on property** acquired by a bankruptcy estate after commencement of the bankruptcy case)[574] for application in the ancillary case, but again, only to property of the debtor (not the "estate") and only within the territorial jurisdiction of the United States.[575] These provisions correspond to Article 1 (c) and generally limit post-recognition transfers of interests in the debtor's property in the United States to those made in the ordinary course of the debtor's business unless the court otherwise allows. Outside the compass of the "**ordinary course**" **rule** is property of the debtor that is so-called "**cash collateral**," which includes cash and cash equivalents in which entities other than the debtor have an interest.[576] Using, selling or leasing cash collateral requires either consent of the other interested entity(ies) or an order of the court.[577] Use, lease and sale of any property in which others have an interest may be conditioned on pro-

568 *In re Artimm*, 335 B.R. 149, 159 (Bankr. C.D. Cal. 2005).

569 For an explanation of the term "case," *see* mn 52.

570 *See* 11 U.S.C. § 1502 (8) (defining "within the territorial jurisdiction of the United States"). Note that by its terms, section 362 protects "property of the estate," 11 U.S.C. § 362 (a), which refers to the estate created under 11 U.S.C. section 541 in plenary cases. Section 1520 refers instead to the property of the debtor, since no estate is created in chapter 15. *See* 11 U.S.C. § 103 (a) (not including section 541 in the list of provisions applying to chapter 15).

571 Thus, according to the House Report accompanying the enactment of chapter 15, "the foreign representative would have to commence a case under another chapter of the Bankruptcy Code to obtain extraterritorial effects." H. Rep. No. 109–31, 109th Cong., 1st Sess. 115 (2005).

572 11 U.S.C. § 362 (d) (1).

573 11 U.S.C. § 361.

574 *See* 11 U.S.C. §§ 363, 549, 552.

575 *See In re Tri-Continental Exch. Ltd.*, 349 B.R. 627, 639 (Bankr. E.D. Cal. 2006) ("An automatic consequence of recognition of a foreign main proceeding is that § 363 applies.") (citing 11 U.S.C. § 1520 (a) (2)).

576 *See* 11 U.S.C. § 363 (a), (c) (2).

577 *Id.*; *Tri-Continental Exch.*, 349 B.R. at 639.

vision of "adequate protection" of the interest[578] and subject to other rules based on the type of property and non-debtor interest concerned.[579]

According to the House Report that accompanied the enactment of chapter 15, section 1520 (a) is also intended to add "to the powers of the foreign representative of a foreign main proceeding an automatic right to operate the debtor's business and exercise the power of a trustee under sections 363 and 542 [sic?], unless the court orders otherwise."[580] This "automatic" right, i.e., unless "the court orders otherwise,"[581] does not appear in the Model Law and represents a substantial benefit to the foreign representative of a recognized foreign main proceeding acting in the United States. **220**

The text of subsection (b) is similar to Article 20 (3), but the American version clearly limits the right to commence an action outside the United States to only the action necessary to preserve a claim. American law automatically tolls statutes of limitation within the United States until at least "30 days after notice of the termination or expiration of the stay," so the subsection (b) protection need not extend to actions or proceedings in the United States.[582] **221**

Subsection (c) corresponds to Article 20 (4), explicitly exempting any right of the foreign representative or any entity to commence or take proper actions in other United States bankruptcy cases from the scope of the **automatic stay**. Since it is the recognition of the **foreign main proceeding** that triggers the stay under section 1520, the foreign representative of that proceeding will have standing under section 1511 to commence a plenary case and under section 1512 to participate in one.[583] Other foreign representatives will have to obtain recognition to **commence** or **participate** in such cases.[584] **222**

It should be noted that the provisions of the Bankruptcy Code related to certain specifically defined financial contracts[585] apply in ancillary proceedings and that the **223**

---

578 11 U.S.C. § 363 (e).

579 *See generally* 11 U.S.C. § 363.

580 H. Rep. No. 109–31, 109th Cong., 1st Sess. 115 (2005). There appears to be a drafting error involved with the reference to section 542, which generally requires entities in possession of valuable property of the bankruptcy estate to turn the property over to the trustee. 11 U.S.C. § 542. Section 542 does not appear in section 1520, nor is it part of the general list of provisions that apply in chapter 15 cases, *see* 11 U.S.C. § 103 (a), although a foreign representative may request turnover pursuant to section 1519 (a) (3) or 1521 (a) (7). This same passage of the House Report also refers as its subject to section 1520 (a) (2), though the power to "operate the debtor's business and ... exercise the rights and powers of a trustee" is announced in section 1520 (a) (3); thus, the correct references are to sections 552 and 1520 (a) (3). Section 1520 (a) (3) is itself troublesome in that the authorization to operate the business is only "to the extent provided by sections 363 and 552," but section 363 (c) (1), which grants a trustee the power to enter into business transactions and use the debtor's assets in the ordinary course of business without notice or a hearing, does so only "[i]f the business of the debtor is authorized to be operated under section 721, 1108, 1203, 1204, or 1304 ... ." It seems that list ought to have been amended to include section 1520 (and sections 1519 and 1521 as well).

581 11 U.S.C. § 1520 (a) (3). Note that the court's right to order otherwise is supplemented by an ability to subject the right to operate to conditions, "including the giving of security or the filing of a bond." 11 U.S.C. § 1522 (b); *see also* mn 243 *et seq* (discussing section 1522).

582 11 U.S.C. § 108 (c); H. Rep. No. 109–31, 109th Cong., 1st Sess. 115 (2005).

583 *See* mn 147 *et seq* (discussing section 1511), mn 152 *et seq* (discussing section 1512).

584 *Id.*

585 *See* 11 U.S.C. §§ 555–57, 559–62.

"enforcement of contractual provisions of such contracts and agreements in accordance with their terms will not be stayed or otherwise limited" under chapter 15.[586]

2.4.7 Article 21 – Relief that may be granted upon recognition of a foreign proceeding

1. Upon recognition of a foreign proceeding, whether main or non-main, where necessary to protect the assets of the debtor or the interests of the creditors, the court may, at the request of the foreign representative, grant any appropriate relief, including:

***(a)* Staying the commencement or continuation of individual actions or individual proceedings concerning the debtor's assets, rights, obligations or liabilities, to the extent they have not been stayed under paragraph 1 *(a)* of article 20;**

***(b)* Staying execution against the debtor's assets to the extent it has not been stayed under paragraph 1 *(b)* of article 20;**

***(c)* Suspending the right to transfer, encumber or otherwise dispose of any assets of the debtor to the extent this right has not been suspended under paragraph 1 *(c)* of article 20;**

***(d)* Providing for the examination of witnesses, the taking of evidence or the delivery of information concerning the debtor's assets, affairs, rights, obligations or liabilities;**

***(e)* Entrusting the administration or realization of all or part of the debtor's assets located in this State to the foreign representative or another person designated by the court;**

***(f)* Extending relief granted under paragraph 1 of article 19;**

***(g)* Granting any additional relief that may be available to *[insert the title of a person or body administering a reorganization or liquidation under the law of the enacting State]* under the laws of this State.**

2. Upon recognition of a foreign proceeding, whether main or non-main, the court may, at the request of the foreign representative, entrust the distribution of all or part of the debtor's assets located in this State to the foreign representative or another person designated by the court, provided that the court is satisfied that the interests of creditors in this State are adequately protected.

3. In granting relief under this article to a representative of a foreign non-main proceeding, the court must be satisfied that the relief relates to assets that, under the law of this State, should be administered in the foreign non-main proceeding or concerns information required in that proceeding.

→ *Cf* Art 16 et seq of the EIR

2.4.7.1 General

224 Article 21 authorizes the court to grant "**any appropriate relief**" upon **recognition** of a foreign (main or non-main) proceeding. Unlike the automatic "effects" of recognition

[586] 11 U.S.C. § 561 (d).

of a proceeding as a foreign *main* proceeding under Article 20,[587] Article 21 relief, as the word "may" indicates, depends in part upon the court's discretion exercised in light of individual case circumstances.[588] Standing to request such relief is invested in the foreign representative, and as with Article 19 provisional relief, relief available under Article 21 is subject to the satisfaction of the court that "the interests of the creditors and other interested persons, including the debtor, are adequately protected."[589] The court's discretion also includes express power to subject the relief to **appropriate conditions.**[590]

Paragraph 1 itself places further restraints on the court's authority to grant the requested relief. In addition to being "appropriate," the relief must be "necessary to protect the assets of the debtor or interests of the creditors." There is no indication from the text that "creditors" means local creditors only. Instead, the general principle of the Model Law to refrain from discriminating between local and foreign creditors mandates that relief be geared toward creditors in common. In addition, grant of "relief is also subject to compliance with the procedural requirements of the enacting State and to applicable notification requirements"[591] and may be limited or excluded on **public policy** grounds.[592] **225**

Paragraph 1 contains a non-exhaustive[593] list of possible forms of **relief** similar to those found in Article 19.[594] The first three subparagraphs set forth forms of relief that correspond to the effects of recognition of a foreign main proceeding described in Article 20.[595] Subparagraph (b) is also congruous with Article 19 (1) (a),[596] subpara- **226**

587 *See* Art 20 and mn 213 *et seq* (discussing Article 20).

588 *See* Guide ¶ 154 (noting that "[p]ost-recognition relief under article 21 is discretionary").

589 *See* Art 22 (1) and mn 240 *et seq* (discussing Article 22).

590 *See* Art 22 (2) and mn 240 *et seq* (discussing Article 22).

591 Guide ¶ 20 (d). As stated at the beginning of the discussion of Chapter III, the Model Law does not address notice requirements. *See supra* note 431. One procedural matter the Law does partially address is the requirement in some countries of "special qualification or licensing" for persons acting as insolvency administrators; thus, Article 21 (1) (e) and (2) speak in terms of entrusting the foreign representative or "another person" with administration and distribution, respectively. *See* A/CN.9/433 ¶ 129 (noting that for this reason, the wording of the provisions allowing for preservation, administration or management of the debtor's assets should give the court flexibility to appoint someone other than the foreign representative).

592 *See* Art 6 and mn 119 *et seq* (discussing Article 6); Guide ¶ 20 (e) (stating that both recognition itself and discretionary relief are subject to certain public policy restrictions under Article 6).

593 Though not exhaustive, such relief is limited to relief available under the law of the *enacting* State. Guide ¶ 154 ("[T]he list is not exhaustive and the court is not restricted unnecessarily in its ability to grant any type of relief that is available under the law of the *enacting* State and needed under the circumstances of the case") (emphasis added); *see also* A/CN.9/433 ¶ 133 (noting that the possibility that a court might issue measures pursuant to foreign law was widely thought to be unrealistic and that an early reference to such a possibility should be deleted).

594 *See* Guide ¶ 137 (observing, with some reservations, that "the measures available under article 19 are essentially the same as those available under article 21").

595 *See* Art 20 and mn 213 *et seq* (discussing the corresponding Article 20 provisions); *see also* Guide ¶ 155 ("The explanation relating to the use of the expressions 'individual actions' and 'individual proceedings' in article 20, subparagraph 1 (a) and to coverage of execution proceedings ... applies also to article 21, subparagraph 1 (a)."). Note that protections analogous to those set forth in Article 20 (2)–(3) do not exist in such form with respect to Article 21.

graphs (c), (d)[597] and (g) are specifically referenced as possible forms of provisional relief under Article 19,[598] subparagraph (e) is a less restricted version of Article 19 (1)'s subparagraph (b),[599] and subparagraph (f) is merely an opportunity to extend Article 19 **provisional relief** that would otherwise expire upon recognition.[600]

227 While Article 21 relief is normally of a "less urgent nature"[601] than the provisional relief available under Article 19 and the automatic effects of Article 20, it expressly includes the relief typically situated at the crux of debate on cross-border insolvency issues: distribution of the debtor's assets located within the enacting State.[602] The debate results from the tension between the principle of non-discrimination with respect to foreign creditors vis-à-vis similarly situated local creditors and conflict of laws among jurisdictions regarding the precise rights and relative priorities of various kinds of creditors and what it means to "adequately protect" them. While the Working Group seems to have come to a consensus that paragraph 1 relief refers to relief under local law,[603] the choice of law rule respecting paragraph 2 is less clear. In failing to provide a choice of law rule for distribution, Article 21 does not go far in resolving the clash between local-foreign creditor equality and adequate protection of local creditor interests. While the Model Law requires that the court be satisfied that the interests (not rights) of creditors in the enacting State are "adequately protected" before granting relief,[604] it does not identify what those interests are or under which insolvency law(s) they should be treated,[605] though the implication of including protection for creditors in the *enacting*

because of its discretionary nature, though there is the possibility of seeking a modification to any Article 21 relief under Article 22 (3). *See* A/CN.9/435 ¶ 54.

596 *See* Art 19 (1) (a) and mn 202 *et seq* (discussing Article 19).

597 The Commission noted that in granting the provisional relief, "the court would be guided by its own rules on procedure on the taking of evidence and would not introduce discovery mechanisms unknown in the enacting State." A/52/17 ¶ 43. There is no reason this logic would not carry through in granting post-recognition relief.

598 *See* Art 19 (1) (c) and mn 202 *et seq* (discussing Article 19).

599 *See* Art 19 (1) (b) and mn 202 *et seq* (discussing Article 19). Note that "administration and realization" appear to include "all acts which a person appointed by the court to preserve and manage the assets of an insolvent debtor [i]s authorized to perform under the laws of the enacting State, including the right to commence legal proceedings concerning the preservation of the debtor's assets." *See* A/CN.9/433 ¶ 131. *But see* Art 23 (respecting Paulian or avoidance actions) and mn 247 *et seq* (discussing Art 23).

600 *See* Art 19 (3) (providing that such provisional relief terminates automatically unless so extended) and mn 202 *et seq* (discussing Article 19).

601 *See* A/CN.9/422 ¶ 111; *cf* Art 19 (1) (requiring provisional relief to be "urgently needed" in order to be granted).

602 Like the relief set forth in Article 21 (1) (e), paragraph 2 relief is, in contrast to the other forms of relief set forth in Article 21, expressly territorial, referring only to the debtor's assets "located in this State."

603 *See supra* note 593.

604 This protection is in addition to the broader protection for the "interests of creditors and other interested persons, including the debtor," that Article 22 affords. *See* Art 22 (1) and mn 240 *et seq* (discussing Art 22).

605 Traditionally, at least two dynamics have come into play. A contest may develop between local and foreign interests in jurisdictions in which the legal tradition has been to favor local creditors, for example, by allowing distribution to foreign creditors only after all local debts have been fully satisfied. Article 13 (2) is meant to end any such tradition. The more common problem, however, has less to do with the origin of a claim than with its priority classification in competing distribution schemes. Foreign and domestic creditors holding claims of a certain type may align themselves together

State is that distribution under paragraph 2 will generally occur according to the law of the state that opened the foreign proceeding,[606] but only if it is granted recognition as a **foreign main proceeding.**[607] Some courts may examine the choice of law rules existing in the law of the enacting State as well as any other law that might suggest when and under what conditions distribution may occur other than as it would in a domestic insolvency proceeding.[608] In short, the discretionary nature of paragraph 2 gives little indication of how assets must be distributed in a cross-border insolvency. Therefore, parties transacting business with persons who have the **centres of their main interests** outside the enacting State ought to consider the possibility of distribution under foreign law, or some hybrid of foreign and domestic law, if such a person becomes subject to insolvency proceedings.[609]

A similar and related issue is the question of which law determines what the **"debtor's assets"** are under Article 21 (1) (e) and (2) (as well as under Article 19 (b)), and **228**

---

against holders of a different type of claim if the priorities of each kind of claim are differently treated under the laws of countries involved. This dynamic, together with the difficulties in determining where the centre of a debtor's main interests is located, and thus where the foreign main proceeding should occur, *see* mn 186 *et seq* (discussing Art 17), gives rise to forum-shopping dangers, particularly where a debtor is part of corporate group. For a good discussion of these dangers, *see* Engel at 16–19 (noting that "centre of main interests" is "a vague concept that excites the appetites of some forum-shoppers" and that in the context of a corporate group may depend "on the level in the group at which the insolvency is focused"). Engel fears the Model Law's protection of creditors against "main proceeding" forum-shopping may be so weak as to lead them to seek to open expensive and inefficient domestic insolvency proceedings to defend themselves, ultimately leading away rather than toward its efficiency goals. *Id.*

[606] An early draft of the Model Law stated that "the court may permit the foreign representative to administer, realize and distribute assets of the debtor *in the foreign proceeding.*" A/CN.9/435 ¶ 24 (emphasis added). It appears that the provision for adequate protection of local creditor interests was added precisely because it was thought such creditors would seek to open a local insolvency proceeding to shelter their rights from foreign law. *Id.* ¶ 39. At the same time, however, the Working Group was concerned that the principle of equality of similarly-situated creditors be respected. *Id.* ¶ 40.

[607] This accords with the general logic of universalism as well as Principle 2 of the Concordat, which provides for turnover and distribution in the "main" proceeding, but only after payment of secured and "privileged" local claims. Concordat (Principle 2 (B)). For a more general discussion of the Concordat, see mn 273 (commenting on Article 27).

[608] As a practical matter, the local law limitations on the automatic stay in the case of foreign main proceedings, *see* Art 20 (2) and mn 213 *et seq* (discussing Article 20), and the requirement of adequately protecting creditors' interests in granting provisional or post-recognition relief, *see* Art 22 (1) and mn 240 *et seq* (discussing Art 22), may result in the removal of some assets from the court's jurisdiction before it considers distribution.

[609] The possibility of distribution of a single debtor's assets in multiple insolvency proceedings is also partially addressed by (i) Article 13, which provides "foreign creditors" with the "same rights regarding ... participation" in a local proceeding as creditors in the enacting State, and thus the possibility of cross-filing (though the degrees of reciprocity may be an issue), *see* mn 155 *et seq* (discussing Article 13), and (ii) Article 32, which prevents a creditor who has received partial distributions in other insolvency proceedings from participating in a local proceeding until the other creditors participating in the local proceeding with claims "of the same class" have received a ratable distribution of the same proportion as that of the "cross-filing" claimholder. *See* mn 302 *et seq* (discussing Article 32).

which such assets may not be subject to full administration, realization or distribution, either under exemption provisions or because of the rights of third parties. Article 22 (1) provides that interests of such parties, including the debtor, be protected.

229 Paragraph 3 further limits grants of Article 21 **relief** respecting foreign non-main proceedings in that such relief must "relate to assets" that, under the law of the enacting State, should be administered in the **foreign proceeding** or "concern" information required in that proceeding.[610] The vagueness of these requirements may be somewhat redeemed by the express reference to local law,[611] but only to the extent that local law is clear (i) as to what should be administered in and what information concerns a foreign non-main proceeding and (ii) that the Model Law itself provides no basis for importation of foreign law on those questions. In any event, paragraph 3 is at least an indicator that the court should take into account the interests and expectations of those who may be relying on the law of the place in which the debtor has its centre of main interests.[612]

230 These requirements, stemming from the **principle of limited relief for non-main proceedings**, surface again in the context of the court's duty to seek **cooperation** and **coordination** when a foreign non-main proceeding and an insolvency proceeding in the enacting State respecting the same debtor are occurring concurrently.[613] Similarly, when an insolvency proceeding has already been commenced in the enacting State at the time the application for recognition is filed, any Article 21 relief, regardless of whether at the request of a representative of a foreign main or non-main proceeding, must be consistent with the local proceeding, and if the local proceeding is commenced afterward, the court

[610] *See* A/CN.9/435 ¶¶ 50–53 (noting, among other things, that a representative of a foreign non-main proceeding would normally require information relating only to the assets located in the State where the foreign non-main proceeding had been opened or seek measures aimed only at repatriating assets that were improperly removed). *But see* A/52/17 ¶ 70 (reporting that a proposal to reference only assets "that were originally located in the State where the foreign proceeding had been opened and which had been improperly transferred abroad" was "found to be too restrictive, as the foreign representative might, for instance, have a legitimate claim to administer assets originally located in the enacting State or which were lawfully transferred thereto").

[611] The Guide to Enactment notes that the local law reference "reflects the principle underlying the Model Law that recognition of a foreign proceeding does not mean extending the effects of the foreign proceeding as they may be prescribed by the law of the foreign State. Instead, recognition of a foreign proceeding entails attaching to the foreign proceeding consequences envisaged by the law of the enacting State." Guide ¶ 159.

[612] *See* Guide ¶ 158 ("The objective is to admonish the court that relief in favour of a foreign non-main proceeding should not give unnecessarily broad powers to the foreign representative and that such relief should not interfere with the administration of another insolvency proceeding, in particular the main proceeding [which occurs where the debtor has its centre of main interests, *see* Art 17 (2) (a)]."). The provisions of Article 28, which restrict the commencement and effects of a local insolvency proceeding after recognition of a foreign main proceeding, are similar to those in paragraph 3; thus, the development of law around one provision should aid in interpreting the other. *See* A/52/17 ¶ 99 (noting relationship between paragraph 3 and Article 28) and mn 280 *et seq* (discussing Article 28).

[613] *See* Art 29 (c) and mn 284 *et seq* (discussing Article 29); *see also* Guide ¶¶ 160 ("The idea underlying article 21, paragraph 3, has been reflected also in article 19, paragraph 4 (prerecognition relief), article 29, subparagraph (c) (coordination of a foreign proceeding with a local proceeding) and article 30 (coordination of more than one foreign proceeding)"), 191 (making similar comment).

must review any Article 21 relief granted and modify or terminate it as necessary to make it consistent with the local proceeding.[614] Any Article 21 relief granted to the representative of a foreign non-main proceeding must also be reviewed and modified or terminated as necessary to make it consistent with a subsequent recognition of a foreign main proceeding respecting the same debtor or must be consistent with any relief granted the representative of a foreign main proceeding already recognized; to the extent subsequent foreign non-main proceedings are recognized, the court must grant, modify or terminate Article 21 relief as necessary to facilitate coordination between or among them.[615]

Under Article 22 (3), the court has discretion to modify or terminate Article 21 relief.[616] **231**

2.4.7.2 United States Law

Section 1521 – Relief that may be granted upon recognition

(a) Upon recognition of a foreign proceeding, whether main or nonmain, where necessary to effectuate the purpose of this chapter and to protect the assets of the debtor or the interests of the creditors, the court may, at the request of the foreign representative, grant any appropriate relief, including –

(1) staying the commencement or continuation of an individual action or proceeding concerning the debtor's assets, rights, obligations or liabilities to the extent they have not been stayed under section 1520 (a);

(2) staying execution against the debtor's assets to the extent it has not been stayed under section 1520 (a);

(3) suspending the right to transfer, encumber or otherwise dispose of any assets of the debtor to the extent this right has not been suspended under section 1520 (a);

(4) providing for the examination of witnesses, the taking of evidence or the delivery of information concerning the debtor's assets, affairs, rights, obligations or liabilities;

(5) entrusting the administration or realization of all or part of the debtor's assets within the territorial jurisdiction of the United States to the foreign representative or another person, including an examiner, authorized by the court;

(6) extending relief granted under section 1519 (a); and

(7) granting any additional relief that may be available to a trustee, except for relief available under sections 522, 544, 545, 547, 548, 550, and 724 (a).

(b) Upon recognition of a foreign proceeding, whether main or nonmain, the court may, at the request of the foreign representative, entrust the distribution of all or part of the debtor's assets located in the United States to the foreign representative or another person, including an examiner, authorized by the court, provided that the court is satisfied that the interests of creditors in the United States are sufficiently protected.

---

[614] *See* Art 29 (a) (i), (b) (i) and mn 284 *et seq* (discussing Article 29).

[615] *See* Art 30 and mn 293 *et seq* (discussing Article 30).

[616] *See* Art 22 (3) and mn 240 *et seq* (discussing Article 22).

(c) In granting relief under this section to a representative of a foreign nonmain proceeding, the court must be satisfied that the relief relates to assets that, under the law of the United States, should be administered in the foreign nonmain proceeding or concerns information required in that proceeding.

(d) The court may not enjoin a police or regulatory act of a governmental unit, including a criminal action or proceeding, under this section.

(e) The standards, procedures, and limitations applicable to an injunction shall apply to relief under paragraphs (1), (2), (3), and (6) of subsection (a).

(f) The exercise of rights not subject to the stay arising under section 362 (a) pursuant to paragraph (6), (7), (17), or (27) of section 362 (b) or pursuant to section 362 (n) shall not be stayed by any order of a court or administrative agency in any proceeding under this chapter.

232 Section 1521 generally follows but also makes several changes and additions to Article 21. The first addition is the phrase "to effectuate the purpose of this chapter," which modifies the words "where necessary" in subsection (a). These new words should lead courts back to the Preamble[617] for guidance on the necessity of requested relief. Effectuating the purpose of chapter 15 is certainly an appropriate focus, and its relative breadth, which includes and makes redundant the other modifying phrase, "to protect the assets of the debtor or the interests of the creditors,"[618] seems aimed at maintaining the flexibility judges enjoyed under prior law to fashion relief appropriate to the particular circumstances of each case before them.[619]

233 To maintain consistency with pre-chapter 15 law, Congress excluded most[620] of the "avoidance powers" trustees possess under the Bankruptcy Code from the relief a court

[617] 11 U.S.C. § 1501 (a).

[618] *See* 11 U.S.C. § 1501 (a) (3)–(4) (including "fair and efficient administration of cross-border insolvencies that protects the interests of all creditors, and other interested entities, including the debtor" and "protection and maximalization of the value of the debtor's assets" as objectives of incorporating the Model Law).

[619] *Compare* H. Rep. No. 95-595, 95th Cong., 1st Sess. 324–25 (1977); S. Rep. No. 95–989, 95th Cong., 2d Sess. 35 (1978) (stating that the guidelines in former section 304 were "designed to give the court the maximum flexibility in handling ancillary cases") *with* H. Rep. No. 109–31, 109th Cong., 1st Sess. 116 (2005) (stating that section 1522 "gives the bankruptcy court broad latitude to mold [section 1519 and section 1521] relief to meet specific circumstances"); *see also In re SPhinX, Ltd.*, 351 B.R. 103, 112–14 (Bankr. S.D.N.Y. 2006) (noting that "[a]lthough chapter 15 replaced section 304 of the Bankruptcy Code, which previously governed cases ancillary to foreign proceedings, chapter 15 maintains – and in some respects enhances – the 'maximum flexibility' ... that section 304 provided bankruptcy courts in handling ancillary cases in light of principles of international comity and respect for the laws and judgments of other nations," and that flexibility "is inherent in the various forms of relief that the court may grant" and listing examples), *aff'd*, 371 B.R. 10, (S.D.N.Y. 2007).

[620] The section 1521 (a) (7) list of exclusions does not include section 549, which grants, *inter alia*, the power to "avoid a transfer of property of the estate." 11 U.S.C. § 549. Although no "estate" is created in a chapter 15 case, section 549 applies "to a transfer of an interest of the debtor in property that is within the territorial jurisdiction of the United States to the same extent that [it] would apply to property of the estate" after recognition of a foreign main proceeding. 11 U.S.C. § 1520 (a) (2); *see also* mn 218 *et seq* (discussing section 1520);

may make available to a recognized foreign representative under section 1521 (a) (7).[621] Section 1523 grants recognized foreign representatives **standing to pursue these and other**[622] **Paulian actions**, but only in plenary cases. If no plenary case respecting the debtor exists, the foreign representative may commence one if it wishes to pursue avoidance actions.[623]

Subsection (b), which corresponds to Article 21 (2), changes the word "designated" to "authorized"[624] and adds the words, "including an examiner,"[625] as in section 1519 (a) (2). The word "adequately" in Article 21 (2) is changed to "sufficiently" in section 1521 (b) because of the existing technical meaning of the phrase "adequate protection" in American bankruptcy law,[626] and the same change occurs in section 1522 (1).[627] **234**

Providing "**sufficient protection**" and being "necessary to effectuate the purpose of ... chapter [15] and protect the assets of the debtor or the interests of the creditors"[628] are the criteria sections 1521 and 1522 set forth to grant section 1521 relief.[629] Without context, however, the bare standard of "sufficiency" is not very helpful analytically. The House Report accompanying the enactment of chapter 15 states that section 1521 "does not expand or reduce the scope of relief currently available in ancillary cases under sections 105 and 304 ...,"[630] which seems to indicate that the same considerations that have until now governed the grant of **comity**, codified in former section 304, remain to guide decision-making under section 1521. To set out that the scope of relief available under section 1521 (b) remains unchanged seems to mean, for example, that entrustment of the debtor's property to the foreign representative for distribution will not be granted where the distribution scheme of the foreign court is not in substantial accord with the American distribution scheme.[631] The trouble is that another passage of the same Report, commenting on section 1507 "additional assistance,"[632] indicates that while the authority for relief "*beyond* that permitted under sections 1519–1521" is "subject to **235**

H. Rep. No. 109–31, 109th Cong., 1st Sess. 115 (2005) (noting in discussion of section 1521 (a) (7) that "[t]he avoiding power in section 549 and the exceptions to that power are covered by section 1520 (a) (2)").

621 11 U.S.C. § 1521 (a) (7) (excepting sections 522, 544, 545, 547, 548, 550 and 724 (a)).

622 11 U.S.C. § 553 (authorizing and governing recovery of certain setoffs). The omission of section 553 from the section 1521 (a) (7) exclusions appears to have been an oversight.

623 *See* mn 249 *et seq* (discussing section 1523). For an explanation of the term "case," *see* mn 52.

624 *See* mn 209 (discussing change).

625 For an explanation of the term "examiner," *see* mn 117 (discussing section 1505).

626 *See* mn 218 (discussing meaning of "adequate protection").

627 H. Rep. No. 109–31, 109th Cong., 1st Sess. 115 (2005) (stating that "adequately" was changed to "sufficiently" in sections 1521 (b) and 1522 (a) to avoid confusion with the "adequate protection" concept in U.S. law); *see also In re Tri-Continental Exch. Ltd.*, 349 B.R. 627, 636 (Bankr. E.D. Cal. 2006) (noting same and citing House Report).

628 11 U.S.C. § 1521 (a).

629 Each section makes "sufficient protection" of the relevant interest(s) a condition for granting relief. For purposes of relief in the form of entrustment of debtor assets for distribution, the interests of creditors in the United States are entitled to the protection. 11 U.S.C. § 1521 (b). For all other forms of section 1521 (or section 1519) relief, the "interests of creditors [in general] and other interested entities, including the debtor" are entitled to protection. 11 U.S.C. § 1522 (a).

630 H. Rep. No. 109–31, 109th Cong., 1st Sess. 116 (2005).

631 11 U.S.C. § 304 (c) (4) (2000) (repealed). *See supra* note 144 for text of former section 304.

632 *See* mn 123 *et seq* (discussing section 1507, where, with the repeal of former section 304, the considerations of comity are now codified).

the conditions for relief heretofore specified ... under section 304," those conditions are "*not* to be the basis for denying or limiting relief otherwise available under [chapter 15]."[633] This second passage seems to suggest that lack of substantial accord with the American distribution scheme alone is no longer an obstacle to relief.[634]

236 The still sparse case law addressing chapter 15 **relief** does, to some extent, hearken back to notions of **comity** that existed under former section 304. One court points out that while "recognition of a foreign main proceeding may ... serve to indicate that the reasonable interests of creditors and the maximization of value, *as well as considerations of international comity*, generally support the bankruptcy court's deference to such proceeding ..., the Bankruptcy Code does not expressly mandate ... across the board deference, nor would recognition of a foreign main proceeding necessarily be binding on choice of law determinations."[635] Although only as *dicta*, another bankruptcy judge has remarked that the "**sufficient protection**" requirement is *more* demanding than the "language of § 304 (c)," which "require[d] that the court be 'guided by what will best assure an economical and expeditious administration of [the] estate,' consistent with the six factors articulated in § 304 (c)," and that in the case that was before him, the "sufficient protection" under section 1521 (b) "cover[ed] essentially the same ground ... as three of the factors in § 304 (c):

- the just treatment of all holders of claims against the bankruptcy estate,
- the protection of U.S. claimants against prejudice and inconvenience in the processing of claims ...,
- and the distribution of proceeds of the [foreign] estate substantially in accordance with the order prescribed by U.S. law."[636]

---

[633] H. Rep. No. 109–31, 109th Cong., 1st Sess. 109 (2005) (emphasis added); *see also supra* note 314 and accompanying text (discussing same).

[634] A third passage from the Report, commenting on section 1522 ("Protection of creditors and other interested persons"), states that that section allows the bankruptcy court "broad latitude to mold relief, including appropriate responses if it is shown that the foreign proceeding is seriously and unjustifiably injuring United States creditors." H. Rep. No. 109–31, 109th Cong., 1st Sess. 116 (2005). "Serious and unjustifiable injury" appears to be the flipside of the "sufficient protection" coin, but the phrase provides little further guidance, for the terms "serious" and "unjustifiable" beg the question as much as the term "sufficient."

[635] *In re SPhinX, Ltd.*, 351 B.R. 103, 115–16 (Bankr. S.D.N.Y. 2006), *aff'd*, 371 B.R. 10, (S.D.N.Y. 2007) (emphasis added); *see also* mn 243 *et seq* (noting the *SPhinX* court's observations about the meaning of "sufficient protection" under section 1522 (a)). Note that the reference to choice of law analysis is also essentially a reference to comity in the Second Circuit, where the *SPhinX* court sits. *See Maxwell Commc'n Corp. v. Societe Generale (In re Maxwell Commc'n Corp.)*, 93 F.3d 1036, 1047–48 (2d Cir. 1996) (stating that "comity is exercised with reference to prevalent doctrines of international law ..., [which] correspond to familiar choice of law principles").

[636] *In re Artimm*, 335 B.R. 149, 160 (Bankr. C.D. Cal. 2005) (internal citations omitted). Glosband may support this view. He indicates that some feared Article 7 might be used as "an open invitation to evade the strictly specified requirements for relief contained in Chapter 15" by use of the section 304 jurisprudence that chapter 15 was meant to replace. Glosband Memorandum at 4. *See also supra* note 314. Judge Bufford, who authored the *Artimm* decision, has also written that the pre-chapter 15 "case law applies only in circumstances not addressed by the explicit provisions of chapter 15." Bufford, at 34. *But see* Wessels ¶ 10045 (stating that "it is commonly understood that the major results of case

It should be noted that courts may also look to foreign opinions in determining the meaning of **"sufficient protection."**[637] **237**

Subsection (c) does not substantively change the language of Article 21 (3). The House Report states that it "is designed to limit relief to assets having some direct connection with the **foreign non-main proceeding**, for example where they were part of an operating division in the jurisdiction of the foreign non-main proceeding when they were fraudulently conveyed and then brought to the United States."[638] **238**

Section 1521's additions of subsections (d), (e) and (f) match similar provisions in section 1519, all of which import American law respecting injunctions in bankruptcy to chapter 15 with certain modifications. Aside from the observations made in the discussion of section 1519 above,[639] little need be added except to note that, although the issue was undisputed, one bankruptcy court has recognized that permanent injunctive relief may be granted pursuant to section 1521 (a).[640] **239**

2.4.8 Article 22 – Protection of creditors and other interested persons

1. In granting or denying relief under article 19 or 21, or in modifying or terminating relief under paragraph 3 of this article, the court must be satisfied that the interests of the creditors and other interested persons, including the debtor, are adequately protected.

2. The court may subject relief granted under article 19 or 21 to conditions it considers appropriate.

3. The court may, at the request of the foreign representative or a person affected by relief granted under article 19 or 21, or at its own motion, modify or terminate such relief.

2.4.8.1 General

Article 22 narrows the scope of the court's discretion to grant relief under Articles 19 and 21. Paragraphs 2 and 3 flow relatively obviously from the discretionary nature of the relief the court is entitled to grant under Articles 19 and 21,[641] which are themselves discretionary in nature. In addition, paragraph 3 provides interested parties express **240**

law under § 304 will be reflected in the interpretations of Chapter 15 provisions"). According to the *Collier* treatise, section 1521 (b) "is not intended to provide priority or preferential treatment to United States creditors, but is intended to assure that they are not prejudiced by the turnover beyond being subject to the same situation as creditors in the country in which the distribution will be made." *Collier* ¶ 1521.03 (providing examples).

[637] *See* 11 U.S.C. § 1508 (requiring bankruptcy courts to consider "the international origin [of chapter 15], and the need to promote an application of [it] that is consistent with the application of similar statutes adopted by foreign jurisdictions"); *see also* mn 126 *et seq* (discussing Article 8).

[638] H. Rep. No. 109–31, 109th Cong., 1st Sess. 115–16 (2005).

[639] *See* mn 209 *et seq* (discussing section 1519).

[640] *See In re Petition of Ho Seok Lee*, 348 B.R. 799 (Bankr. W.D. Wash. 2006) (overruling procedural objection respecting need for an adversary proceeding to grant motion permanently enjoining creditor from seeking recovery of any debt of the debtor (or its subsidiary) in excess of the amounts provided in the debtor's Korean insolvency plan).

[641] *See* Arts 19 and 21 and mn 202 *et seq* and 224 *et seq* (discussing Articles 19 and 21).

standing to seek modification or termination of relief granted to or requested by the foreign representative.[642]

241 The most important feature of Article 22 is the paragraph 1 requirement that the court be satisfied that the interests of "the creditors" and others are protected, which provides much of the substance corresponding to the Article 1 (d) statement of the scope of the Model Law respecting creditors and other interested persons.[643] As in Article 21 (2), the Model Law uses the word "interests" rather than "rights," and again, as in that Article, the questions arise as to what interests are worthy of protection and how, or more specifically, under what law, that of the enacting State or that of a foreign state, such protection must be sought.[644] Unlike Article 21 (2), all the creditors and interested persons may seek protection under Article 22 (1), not merely the local creditors, though the Guide to Enactment does particularly mention them.[645] Article 22 introduces no other principles to resolve the tension between the **principle of equality among foreign and domestic creditors** and adequate protection of (especially local) creditors' rights, particularly rights *in rem* or those arising under local preference (priority) rules, except perhaps that in using the phrase "the creditors," it may be referring to the collectivity of creditors rather than to individual creditors.[646] The Guide merely states that "there should be a balance between relief that may be granted to the foreign representative and the interests of the persons that may be affected by such relief ... [, which] balance is essential to achieve the objectives of cross-border insolvency legislation."[647]

242 The Guide to Enactment also makes clear that Article 22 "is intended to operate in the context of the procedural system of the enacting State."[648]

2.4.8.2 United States Law

Section 1522 – Protection of creditors and other interested persons

(a) The court may grant relief under section 1519 or 1521, or may modify or terminate relief under subsection (c), only if the interests of the creditors and other interested entities, including the debtor, are sufficiently protected.

(b) The court may subject relief granted under section 1519 or 1521, or the operation of the debtor's business under section 1520 (a) (3), to conditions it considers appropriate, including the giving of security or the filing of a bond.

642 Guide ¶ 162.

643 *See* Art 1 (d) and mn 32 *et seq* (discussing Article 1 (d)).

644 *See* Art 21 (2) and mn 224 *et seq* (discussing Article 21).

645 *See* Guide ¶ 35 (stating parenthetically that Article 22 (1) is designed to protect the interests of local creditors "in particular"). The Model Law does not use the term "local creditors," and the Guide to Enactment points out that the term would be difficult to define and that an attempt to do so reveals "that there is no justification for discriminating creditors on the basis of criteria such as place of business or nationality." Guide ¶ 163.

646 An earlier draft stated that "the court must be satisfied that creditors *collectively* and the debtor are protected against undue prejudice and will be given a fair opportunity to assert their claims and defences." A/CN.9/435 ¶ 72.

647 *See* Guide ¶¶ 161–62, 164.

648 Guide ¶ 162. These requirements include notice procedures. *Id.* ¶ 164; *see also supra* note 431 and accompanying text (discussing notice).

(c) The court may, at the request of the foreign representative or an entity affected by relief granted under section 1519 or 1521, or at its own motion, modify or terminate such relief.

(d) Section 1104 (d) shall apply to the appointment of an examiner under this chapter. Any examiner shall comply with the qualification requirements imposed on a trustee by section 322.

Section 1522 does not substantially change Article 22. The wording of subsection (a) differs somewhat from Article 22 (1) in order to conform to American usage and definitions. Thus, "**persons**" is changed to "**entities**,"[649] and "adequately protected" to "sufficiently protected."[650] As noted above,[651] the meaning of "sufficient protection" is not yet clear in American law. The *SPhinX* court did make the following observations about subsection (a) in general:[652] **243**

> Two aspects of section 1522 (a) are notable. First, Congress directed the court to focus on the interests of *all* creditors and other interested parties, not just those of U.S. parties. Second, section 1522 (a) implements and harmonizes with section 1501 (a)'s policy statement: in light of section 1501 (a), the Court shall protect the parties' interests by implementing fair, efficient and, it is hoped, cooperative procedures designed to maximize the value of the debtor's assets for distribution. **244**

Subsection (b) adds references to operation of the debtor's business, which is generally allowed a foreign representative of a recognized foreign main proceeding[653] and expressly includes the giving of security or the filing of a bond as possible conditions to allowing such operation. **245**

Subsection (c) is not substantively different from Article 22 (3), and subsection (d) merely incorporates special rules that apply to appointments of **examiners** in bankruptcy.[654] **246**

2.4.9 Article 23 – Actions to avoid acts detrimental to creditors

1. Upon recognition of a foreign proceeding, the foreign representative has standing to initiate *[refer to the types of actions to avoid or otherwise render ineffective acts detrimental to creditors that are available in this State to a person or body administering a reorganization or liquidation]*.

2. When the foreign proceeding is a foreign non-main proceeding, the court must be satisfied that the action relates to assets that, under the law of this State, should be administered in the foreign non-main proceeding.

→ *Cf* Art 16 et seq of the EIR

[649] *See* mn 31 (discussing definitions of "person" and "entity").

[650] *See* mn 234 (discussing same change in section 1521 (b)); mn 218 (discussing concept of "adequate protection").

[651] *See* mn 232 *et seq* (discussing section 1521).

[652] *In re SPhinX, Ltd.*, 351 B.R. 103, 113 (Bankr. S.D.N.Y. 2006), *aff'd*, 371 B.R. 10, (S.D.N.Y. 2007).

[653] *See* 11 U.S.C. § 1520 (a) (3) and mn 218 *et seq* (discussing section 1520).

[654] For an explanation of the term "examiner," *see* mn 117 (discussing section 1505).

2.4.9.1 General

247 In addition to the other provisions of the Model Law granting standing,[655] Article 23 clothes the foreign representative with the power to pursue **Paulian actions** within the recognizing state, though without creating "substantive rights regarding such actions."[656] Essentially, **Paulian actions** are actions to avoid or revoke transactions of debtors that have alienated their property to the prejudice or disadvantage of their creditors; such actions often include a restitutive process.[657] Importantly, authorization under Article 23 exists to bring only such actions as are available within the enacting State "to a person or body administering a reorganization or liquidation." Thus, actions available only to individual creditors, as opposed to the collectivity of creditors in the context of an insolvency proceeding, are excluded.[658]

248 The Model Law provides no choice of law rule respecting the Article 23 authorization.[659] The "types of actions ... available" may depend upon the conflict of laws rules of the enacting State.[660] While private international law and notions of due process in some states would seem to generally require that the law of the place where the debtor has the **centre of its main interests** prevail (thus taking into account the expectations of the parties),[661] many legal systems strongly resist the notion of applying foreign law, particularly where it conflicts with local law.[662] Thus, because the kinds of **revocatory actions** available and the predicates and procedure required to maintain them vary greatly from state to state, the lack of a **uniform choice of law rule** may increase uncertainty in commercial relationships to the extent that the opportunity to shop for jurisdictions whose choice of law rules will result in favourable law respecting Paulian actions is enhanced.[663] Paragraph 2 may – depending on the effect of the law of the enacting State in making the determination – discourage such forum shopping, but only by foreign representatives of foreign non-main proceedings. That paragraph requires courts to refuse to grant requests of "non-main" foreign representatives to pursue **Paulian actions** within the enacting State if the assets concerned should not be administered in

---

655 *See supra* note 333 (discussing standing provisions).

656 Guide ¶ 166.

657 These actions appear to have their roots in Roman law and exist in both civil and common law jurisdictions. *See generally* Max Radin, *Fraudulent Conveyances at Roman Law*, 18 Va. L. Rev. 109 (1931). There may be some controversy over whether Article 23 covers both revocation *and* restitution or revocation only. *Compare* Transcript of Open Forum at UNCITRAL – INSOL International Second Multinational Judicial Colloquium, comments of Lord Justice Millet, 6 *with id.*, comments of Neil Cooper, 7 (March 1997).

658 Guide ¶ 165.

659 *See* Guide ¶ 166 (noting that "[t]he provision is drafted narrowly in that it does not create any substantive right regarding such actions and also does not provide any solution involving conflict of laws").

660 *See* A/CN.9/435 ¶ 64 (expressing the view that "the question of the applicable law to determine the requirements and other substantive rules for the commencement of [Paulian] actions should be left for the rules on the conflict of laws of the enacting State").

661 *See* Transcript of Open Forum at UNCITRAL – INSOL International Second Multinational Judicial Colloquium, comments of Lord Justice Millet, 6 (March 1997).

662 *Id.*, comments of Neil Cooper, 7.

663 The Guide to Enactment seems to recognize these dangers but prioritizes the need to protect the integrity of the debtor's assets above them. *See* Guide ¶ 167; *see also* A/52/17 ¶ 214 (discussing same issue and noting strong opposition to inclusion of what is now Article 23 into the Model Law).

the foreign non-main proceeding, a logical extension of the rule of Article 21 (3), which applies the same principles to bare "assets."[664]

2.4.9.2 United States Law

> **Section 1523 – Actions to avoid acts detrimental to creditors.**
>
> **(a) Upon recognition of a foreign proceeding, the foreign representative has standing in a case concerning the debtor pending under another chapter of this title to initiate actions under sections 522, 544, 545, 547, 548, 550, 553, and 724 (a).**
>
> **(b) When a foreign proceeding is a foreign nonmain proceeding, the court must be satisfied that an action under subsection (a) relates to assets that, under United States law, should be administered in the foreign nonmain proceeding.**

Section 1523 corresponds closely to Article 23 in that it confers standing on a recognized foreign representative to commence **Paulian** or, as they are more commonly called in America, **avoidance actions**, under the provisions to which subsection (a) refers. As the text suggests, however, those provisions do not apply in chapter 15 cases.[665] The legislative history notes that this "limitation reflects concerns raised by the United States delegation during the UNCITRAL debates that a simple grant of standing to bring avoidance actions neglects to address very difficult choice of law and forum issues."[666] Since the section 1523 grant of standing neither creates substantive rights nor provides guidance on the questions of choice of law or forum,[667] however, the House Committee's explanation is somewhat puzzling. In any event, since they were drafted to be employed in plenary cases, the requirement that one exist to invoke avoidance actions allows the provisions to which subsection (a) refers and the existing jurisprudence surrounding them to be applied mostly without modifications, though it may take away from the efficiency and cost effectiveness the Model Law was intended to promote in instances where no plenary case already exists.[668] If no plenary case exists, the foreign representative must commence one to exercise avoidance powers. Section 1511 (a) grants foreign **249**

[664] *See* Art 21 (3) and mn 224 *et seq* (discussing Article 21). Paragraph 2 thus makes clear that Paulian actions are to be viewed as valuable assets available for distribution to creditors. *See also* A/52/17 ¶ 216 (describing the paragraph 2 provision as analogous to Article 21 (3)).

[665] *See* 11 U.S.C. §§ 103 (a) (omitting the provisions set forth in section 1523 (a) from an exclusive list of Bankruptcy Code provisions that apply to chapter 15 cases) and 1521 (a) (7) (permitting a bankruptcy court to grant a foreign representative "any additional relief that may be available to a trustee, except for relief available under sections 522, 544, 545, 547, 548, 550, and 724 (a)"). Note, however, that sections 549 (providing power to avoid certain post-bankruptcy transfers) and 552 (preventing attachment of certain security interests) may have limited application in some chapter 15 cases. *See* 11 U.S.C. §§1520 (a) (governing effects of recognition of foreign main proceedings respecting such sections); 1519 (a) (3) (provisional relief), 1521 (a) (7) (discretionary relief for recognized foreign representatives); *see also* mn 218 *et seq* (discussing section 1520), mn 209 *et seq* (discussing section 1519), mn 232 *et seq* (discussing section 1521) and mn 52 (discussing the meaning of "case").

[666] H. Rep. No. 109–31, 109th Cong., 1st Sess. 115 (2005).

[667] *Id.* (citing paragraph 155 of the Guide).

[668] *See* Transcript of Open Forum at UNCITRAL – INSOL International Second Multinational Judicial Colloquium, comments of Neil Cooper, 7 (March 1997) (pointing out that opening plenary proceedings may be inefficient and expensive).

representatives standing to commence plenary cases, but by its terms, only upon recognition,[669] and only the foreign representative of a foreign *main* proceeding may open a *voluntary* case.[670] The foreign representative of a foreign nonmain proceeding may commence an *involuntary* case but may face difficult and expensive hurdles in maintaining it.[671]

250 Although an American bankruptcy court is normally more deferential to foreign proceedings in ancillary cases, recognition entitles foreign proceedings and representatives to cooperation in concurrent cases. If the foreign proceeding is a foreign main proceeding, section 1528 will generally restrict the effects of the subsequent plenary case concerning the chapter 15 debtor to its assets in the United States,[672] and the rest of subchapter V (governing concurrent proceedings) of chapter 15 will also apply.[673] Even so, a trustee or examiner (and possibly one or more committees) may hold views on the management of the case that diverge from those of the foreign representative. Moreover, the court may dismiss the plenary case or suspend its proceedings if it finds that "the purposes of chapter 15 ... would be best served by such dismissal or suspension,"[674] or dismiss individual avoidance actions on the basis of comity and conflict of laws principles.[675] In short, the risks of commencing a plenary case must also be carefully evaluated and taken into account in weighing the costs and benefits of pursuing Paulian actions in the United States.[676]

251 A comprehensive description of the causes of action available in the United States under the sections set forth in subsection (a) is beyond the scope of this work, but two points are important to mention. First, section 550 is the **restitutive provision** for avoided transfers in American bankruptcy cases, and section 1523 (a) brings it within the grant of standing. Its scope is broad, exposing not only the initial transferee in the avoided transaction to liability, but also subsequent transferees of the alienated property, though exceptions exist for those taking for value in good faith and without knowledge of the voidability of the transaction.[677] This **chain of transferee liability** feature of

[669] There may be an argument that a foreign debtor in possession can open a voluntary case as a section 101 (13) debtor without recognition if it meets all the other commencement requirements.

[670] 11 U.S.C. § 1511 (a); *see also* mn 144 *et seq* (discussing Article 11) and 11 U.S.C. §§ 301–02 (providing for commencement of voluntary plenary cases).

[671] *See* 11 U.S.C. § 303; *see also* mn 144 *et seq* (discussing Article 11 and involuntary cases).

[672] *See* mn 280 *et seq* (discussing Article 28).

[673] *See* mn 279 *et seq* (discussing Chapter V of the Model Law together with subchapter V of chapter 15, including the requirement to cooperate).

[674] 11 U.S.C. § 305 (a).

[675] For an important example of the American approach to such principles in the context of avoidance actions, *see Maxwell Commc'n Corp. v. Société Générale (In re Maxwell Commc'n Corp.)*, 93 F.3d 1036 (2d Cir. 1996) (dismissing American preference actions in parallel United States and English proceedings where differences between English and American avoidance laws made it impossible to distribute the debtor's assets in a manner consistent with both sets of rules, England had a closer connection to the transfers, the debtor and its creditors, and cooperation between the courts might have been derailed by selfish application of American rules).

[676] A debtor and/or its creditors contemplating insolvency proceedings should also take these considerations into account in determining whether to commence a plenary case in the United States and, if so, whether to do so before or after petitioning for the opening of insolvency proceedings elsewhere.

[677] *See* 11 U.S.C. § 550.

American avoidance law may make it attractive to some foreign representatives. Second, although Article 23 generally covers only collective insolvency as opposed to individual creditor actions, section 1523 (a)'s inclusion of section 544 (b), which expressly provides that a **trustee** "may avoid any transfer of an interest of the debtor in property or any obligation incurred by the debtor that is voidable under applicable law by a creditor holding an unsecured claim,"[678] makes pursuit of such individual actions available to foreign representatives in American bankruptcy cases.

2.4.10 Article 24 – Intervention by a foreign representative in proceedings in this State

Upon recognition of a foreign proceeding, the foreign representative may, provided the requirements of the law of this State are met, intervene in any proceedings in which the debtor is a party.

→ *Cf* Art 16 et seq of the EIR

2.4.10.1 General

Article 24's grant of standing to recognized foreign representatives to intervene in non-insolvency proceedings of the debtor is the last in a series of standing provisions[679] that flesh out the Model Law's scope provision relating to in-bound requests for assistance.[680] The grant is not absolute but rather contingent upon the foreign representative otherwise meeting the intervention requirements of the enacting State.[681] Thus, it exists only "to avoid the denial of standing to the foreign representative to intervene in proceedings merely because the procedural legislation may not have contemplated the foreign representative among those having such standing."[682] The term "proceedings" includes extra-judicial proceedings.[683] **252**

The text of the provision does not make clear the extent to which the foreign representative may displace the debtor or any local insolvency administrator in such proceedings. The Guide to Enactment states that the "word 'intervene' in the context of article 20 [sic] is intended to refer to cases where the foreign representative appears in court and makes representations in proceedings,"[684] which seems something less than a substitution.[685] **253**

[678] 11 U.S.C. § 544 (b).

[679] *See supra* note 333.

[680] *See* Art 1 (1) and mn 32 *et seq* (discussing Article 1 (1)).

[681] *See* Guide ¶ 170 ("Article 24, which is limited to providing procedural standing, makes it clear (by stating 'provided the requirements of the law of this State are met') that all other conditions of the local law for a person to be able to intervene remain intact.").

[682] Guide ¶ 168.

[683] Guide ¶ 169.

[684] Guide ¶ 169.

[685] *See* A/CN.9/435 ¶ 81 (expressing an opinion in the Working Group that "the words 'to intervene', as used in article 20 [Article 24 of the adopted version], did not mean 'to substitute'"); *see generally* mn 151 (discussing the importance of the difference between participation and intervention).

2.4.10.2 United States Law

Section 1524 – Intervention by a foreign representative

Upon recognition of a foreign proceeding, the foreign representative may intervene in any proceedings in a State or Federal court in the United States in which the debtor is a party.

254 Another consequence of the **access** a foreign representative gains by virtue of **recognition**[686] is the right to intervene. The right may be narrower in the United States enactment than that contemplated under the Model Law in that the added phrase "in any proceedings in State or Federal court in the United States" qualifies the word "proceedings." Thus, while the explicit right to intervene under section 1524 extends to both state and federal courts, other proceedings are not included, though it is not clear the omission implies a statutory exclusion of any pre-existing right to intervene in such proceedings.

255 The American enactment also omits the Model Law phrase "provided the requirements of the law of this State are met." The House Report accompanying the enactment of chapter 15 does not directly address the omission, though it does state that "[r]ecognition being an act under Federal bankruptcy law, it must take effect in state as well as Federal courts."[687] There may procedural issues related to this federally granted right to intervene in the proceedings of individual American states. How they are resolved may depend on the circumstances of the case, particularly whether the recognized foreign representative is deemed to have assumed the **legal personality** of the debtor or **title** to or administration of its property interests at issue. As to this question, the House Report states that '[t]his section does not require substituting the foreign representative for the debtor, although that result may be appropriate in some circumstances."[688]

2.5 Chapter IV – Cooperation with foreign courts and foreign representatives

256 "Cooperation between the courts and other competent authorities of [an enacting] State and foreign States involved in cases of cross-border insolvency" is the first objective of the Model Law.[689] Chapter IV, consisting of Articles 25–27, functions as a "basic enabling provision to make possible judicial cooperation."[690] Despite the status of such **cooperation** as a "core element of the Model Law,"[691] its provisions do not define the term. A definition of "cooperation," it was feared, might limit the legal development of the concept.[692] Instead, Article 27 provides a non-exhaustive, indicative list of the kinds of measures cooperation might involve.[693] In a broad sense, of course, the Model Law itself can be viewed as a series of cooperative mechanisms. Apart from establishing key foundational principles, however, the mechanisms of the Model Law mostly just set the stage for cooperation in pursuing them. Chapter IV gets to the heart of the matter by

---

686 *See* H. Rep. No. 109–31, 109th Cong., 1st Sess. 110 (2005) (noting "that chapter 15 is intended to be the exclusive door to ancillary assistance to foreign proceedings"); mn 136 *et seq* (discussing access under Article 9).

687 H. Rep. No. 109–31, 109th Cong., 1st Sess. 116 (2005).

688 *Id.*

689 Preamble; *see also* mn 23 *et seq* (discussing the Preamble).

690 A/CN.9/419 ¶ 119.

691 Guide ¶ 173.

692 A/CN.9/419 ¶ 122.

693 *Id.* ¶ 123 (discussing possibility of "an indicative or illustrative, i.e., non-exhaustive, list of possible cooperation measures").

issuing a legislative mandate to cooperate to the courts and insolvency administrators of enacting States, but leaves the forms of cooperation for them to determine within the bounds of the legal traditions involved and in light of the purposes set forth in the Preamble and the specific facts at hand.[694]

So long as adequate **procedural safeguards** exist *vis-à-vis* the parties, legal systems that allow for judicial cooperation with foreign courts on the basis of **international comity** should have little problem incorporating the Chapter IV provisions.[695] Courts that cooperate internationally only on the basis of **reciprocity**, a notion the Model Law does not incorporate, may have more difficulty finding applications for the command to "cooperate to the maximum extent possible."[696] Nevertheless, some countries may find that a statutory mandate for cooperation suffices to allow for some level of international **communication** and **cooperation** not possible otherwise. **257**

[694] Guide ¶ 177 ("The articles in chapter IV leave certain decisions, in particular when and how to cooperate, to the courts and, subject to the supervision of the courts, to the insolvency administrators.").

[695] A recent judgment of the Privy Council of the United Kingdom reaffirmed the concepts of universality and, on that basis, judicial cooperation, as part of the common law. The case involved an Isle of Man business, "held through offshore companies incorporated in various jurisdictions," that commenced chapter 11 insolvency proceedings in the United States. *Cambridge Gas Transp. Corp. v. The Official Committee of Unsecured Creditors (of Navigator Holdings PLC)*, 3 All E.R. 829, UKPC 26 ¶ 2 (2006). The American court confirmed a creditors' plan of reorganization which essentially vested title to the stock in the creditors. *Id.* ¶ 5. The American court sought the assistance of the High Court of the Isle of Man in implementing the plan by letter of request. *Id.* ¶ 6. A main shareholder, Cambridge Gas Transport Corporation ("Cambridge"), petitioned against enforcement of the plan on the basis that it, a Cayman company, had not submitted to American jurisdiction. *Id.* ¶ 7. Although the High Court agreed with Cambridge and refused assistance on that basis, the Privy Council rejected the argument as hypertechnical, reasoning that since the shares had no economic value and that, in any event, shareholders are bound by the actions of the company (including seeking bankruptcy relief), *id.* ¶ 26, the real parties in interest were all actively involved in the American proceedings. *Id.* ¶ 8. Recognizing that fairness among creditors "requires that, ideally, bankruptcy proceedings should have universal application," *id.* ¶ 16, the Privy Council stated the limits of assistance were established by what would be possible under local law, *id.* ¶ 22, and determined that what the plan proposed was possible under Manx statutes. *Id.* ¶ 24; *see also Maxwell Commc'n Corp. v. Société Générale (In re Maxwell Commc'n Corp.)*, 93 F.3d 1036, 1053 (2d Cir. 1996) (noting that the "collaborative effort" between the English and American courts in the case "exemplifie[d] the 'spirit of cooperation' with which such tribunals, guided by comity, should approach cases touching the laws and interests of more than on country").

[696] *See* A/CN.9/435 ¶ 89; *see also* A/52/17 ¶ 125 (noting that international cooperation among courts is, under many systems, more suitably addressed by treaty providing for reciprocity and perhaps not even possible under a mere national statute, but that Chapter IV is useful even in countries operating under such systems for hortatory purposes); A/CN.9/435 ¶ 88 (noting that adoption of the Model Law does not exclude future work on a model treaty to address such concerns).

2.5.1 Article 25 – Cooperation and direct communication between a court of this State and foreign courts or foreign representatives

1. In matters referred to in article 1, the court shall cooperate to the maximum extent possible with foreign courts or foreign representatives, either directly or through a *[insert the title of a person or body administering a reorganization or liquidation under the law of the enacting State]*.

2. The court is entitled to communicate directly with, or to request information or assistance directly from, foreign courts or foreign representatives.

2.5.1.1 General

258 In many countries, courts "feel constrained from seeking … assistance abroad" without some form of legislative authorization.[697] Article 25 not only grants the court identified in Article 4[698] authorization to cooperate and communicate directly[699] with foreign courts and foreign representatives, but requires[700] cooperation **"to the maximum extent possible,"** that formulation accounting for variations among jurisdictions in rules about how this might be accomplished.[701] Although the text of Article 25 does not articulate who should initiate cooperation, the Guide to Enactment indicates that there is an authorization for the court in the enacting State to seek cooperation for its proceedings[702] "in matters referred to in Article 1," i.e., "all matters covered by the Model Law."[703] Recognition is not necessary for **communication** or Chapter IV **cooperation,**[704] but Article 25 does not provide authority to grant a foreign representative provisional relief measures without reference to an application for recognition.[705] Possible forms of **cooperation** are set forth in Article 27.

259 With respect to paragraph 2, court-to-court **communications** has been described as "a linking of two concurrent court hearings, all conducted in accordance with proper systems and procedures. The only change from a purely domestic hearing is the technological link to the other court."[706] The Guide to Enactment summarizes points on inter-

[697] Guide ¶ 26; A/CN.9/422 ¶ 26.

[698] *See* Art 4 and mn 109 *et seq* (discussing Article 4).

[699] *See* Guide ¶ 179 (noting intent of Article 25 is to allow for direct communication and requests for assistance without "use of time consuming procedures traditionally in use, such as letters rogatory").

[700] Guide ¶ 174 (noting that "articles [25–27] are designed to overcome the widespread problem of national laws lacking rules providing a legal basis for cooperation by local courts with foreign courts in dealing with cross-border insolvencies").

[701] *See* A/CN.9/422 ¶ 136 (noting that the words "to the maximum extent possible" provide a "sufficient degree of flexibility" to account for other relevant factors affecting cooperation); *see also* Guide ¶ 20 (stating that "[t]he Model Law is in the flexible form of model legislation that takes into account differing approaches in national insolvency laws and the varying propensities of States to cooperate and coordinate in insolvency matters").

[702] Guide ¶ 26 (stating "the Model Law authorizes the courts of the enacting State to seek assistance abroad on behalf of a proceeding taking place in the enacting State (article 25)").

[703] Guide ¶ 44.

[704] Guide ¶ 177.

[705] A/CN.9/433 ¶ 53 (stating that the "widely held view [of the Working Group] was that it would not be desirable for the Model Provisions to provide for provisional measures to the foreign representative without reference to an application for recognition").

[706] Farley/Leonard/Birch at 38.

court **communication** arising from the Second UNCITRAL-INSOL Multinational Judicial Colloquium on Cross-Border Insolvency as follows:[707]

(a) communication between courts is possible but should be done carefully and with appropriate safeguards for the protection of substantive and procedural rights of the parties;

(b) communication should be done openly, in the presence of the parties involved (except in extreme circumstances), who should be given advance notice;

(c) communications that might be exchanged are various and include: e.g. exchanges of formal court orders or judgements; supply of informal writings of general information, questions and observations; and transmission of transcripts of court proceedings;

(d) means of communication include, for example, telephone, facsimile, electronic mail facilities and video; and

(e) where communication is necessary and is intelligently used, there could be considerable benefits for the persons involved in, and affected by, the cross-border insolvency.

2.5.1.2 United States Law

Section 1525 – Cooperation and direct communication between the court and foreign courts or foreign representatives.

(a) Consistent with section 1501, the court shall cooperate to the maximum extent possible with a foreign court or a foreign representative, either directly or through the trustee.

(b) The court is entitled to communicate directly with, or to request information or assistance directly from, a foreign court or a foreign representative, subject to the rights of a party in interest to notice and participation.

Section 1525 closely tracks Article 25,[708] mandating inter-court cooperation and **260** authorizing direct **communication**.

With respect to the meaning of "cooperation," it does not appear that sections **261** 1525–27 (subchapter IV of chapter 15) add much to the general principle of comity as it already existed in American practice.[709] Some have raised questions, however, about whether the mandatory nature of section 1525 (a) reduces the wide discretion American courts previously exercised in cooperating with foreign courts in insolvency matters.[710]

[707] Guide ¶ 178.

[708] As the legislative history notes, "[t]he wording of [section 1525] is nearly identical to that of the Model Law." *See* H. Rep. No. 109–31, 109th Cong., 1st Sess. 117 (2005). The word "trustee" substitutes for the bracketed language of Article 25, *see also* 11 U.S.C. § 1502 (6) (defining "trustee") and mn 103 (discussing section 1502 (6)), and there is a discussion of the additional phrase at the end of subsection (b) below.

[709] *See* Guide ¶ 175 ("To the extent that cross-border judicial cooperation in the enacting State is based on the principle of comity among nations, the enactment of articles 25–27 offers an opportunity for making that principle more concrete and adapted to the particular circumstances of cross-border insolvencies."). *See also supra* note 695 (discussing the *Maxwell* case).

[710] *See* Engel at 3–6 (noting the lack of reciprocity as a condition to the requirement of American courts to cooperate as an example of the adoption of chapter 15 constituting a "unilateral disarmament" of United States based creditors).

These concerns may also arise in part from the legislative history describing section 1507, which seems to relegate the comity jurisprudence existing under former section 304 (replaced by chapter 15)[711] to the sphere of decisions about whether to grant "additional assistance:"[712]

> Subsection [(b)] makes the authority for additional relief (beyond that permitted under sections 1519–1521, below) subject to the conditions for relief heretofore specified in United States law under section 304, which is repealed. This section is intended to permit the further development of international cooperation begun under section 304, but is not to be the basis for denying or limiting relief otherwise available under this chapter.

262 While the legislative history seems more definite about the use of such jurisprudence respecting "relief" as "permitted under sections 1519–1521,"[713] it also implies that the "grounds for granting comity" in section 1507 (b) are "not to be the basis for denying relief otherwise available under *this chapter*." The questions, therefore, are whether judicial **"cooperation"** under section 1525 also constitutes "relief otherwise available under ... chapter [15]," and, if so, what is the interplay between the command that cooperation be given "to the maximum extent possible" and what is considered "available."

263 As to the latter question, without the limiting language of the legislative history, one might turn to the principles of **comity** to determine the extent of cooperation possible, since the Guide to Enactment makes reference to comity as the doctrine (other than reciprocity) upon which court-to-court cooperation is built,[714] but the legislative history may give pause to one considering application of comity analysis to a chapter 15 provision other than that for "additional assistance" in section 1507, at least one respecting "relief."

264 Turning then to the former question of the relationship between "cooperation" and "**relief**," the scope of the term "**cooperation**," as stated above,[715] was deliberately left open, but perhaps its construction in American courts will reflect the recommendation to cooperate in an opinion of the United States Court of Appeals for the Third Circuit, which seems to equate inter-court cooperation in insolvency matters as coming to agreement on "how to proceed."[716] In addition, the legislative history quoted above makes clear that since section 1507 "is intended to permit the further development of ***international cooperation*** begun under section 304," "cooperation" includes "additional assistance." Taking into account the examples of cooperation in section 1527, which include measures to facilitate **communication** and **coordination**, it appears that "cooperation" includes these concepts as well.[717] With respect to "relief," one clue may come from the fact that it is possible for a proceeding to meet the definition of "foreign proceeding,"[718]

---

[711] *See supra* note 144 (setting forth text of former section 304).

[712] *See* H. Rep. No. 109–31, 109th Cong., 1st Sess. 109 (2005) and mn 123 *et seq* (discussing section 1507).

[713] *See* mn 235 *et seq* (discussing this passage in the context of relief under sections 1519 and 1521 and "sufficient protection" under sections 1521 and 1522).

[714] *See, e.g.,* Guide ¶ 175.

[715] *See* mn 256.

[716] *Stonington Partners, Inc. v. Lernout & Hauspie Speech Prods. N.V.*, 310 F.3d 118, 133 (3d Cir. 2002). The situation there was one of concurrent proceedings, so the "cooperation" necessary closely resembled what the Model Law calls "coordination."

[717] *See* mn 276 (discussing relationship among communication, coordination and cooperation).

[718] This may occur, for example, when jurisdiction is based only on the presence of assets or non-persistent contacts. *See* 11 U.S.C. § 101 (23), *see also* mn 68 *et seq*

while still being ineligible for "recognition" for lack of an "**establishment.**"[719] While "relief" seems to flow from (or, in the case of section 1519 relief, at least anticipate) recognition, "cooperation," as noted above,[720] is required even when recognition has not been or cannot be granted.[721] It therefore appears that under chapter 15, "cooperation" is a broader concept than that of "relief," operating on a higher, sovereign level,[722] and that therefore, the principles of comity should be freely used to explore the avenues and limits of cooperation in particular cases.

Subsection (b) adopts the basic language of the Model Law but conditions the entitlement of **direct communication** upon respect for the rights of all parties in interest to participate. American courts have previously recognized that there was nothing preventing a court from initiating communication with a foreign court, though no principle of law required it to do so.[723] The obligation to cooperate makes "[t]he right of courts to communicate with other courts in worldwide insolvency cases ... of central importance."[724] **265**

The last phrase of subsection (b), codifying the right of all parties in interest to be heard, invokes a special Bankruptcy Code rule of construction:[725] **266**

> "after notice and a hearing", or a similar phrase
>
> (A) means after such notice as is appropriate in the particular circumstances, and such opportunity for a hearing as is appropriate in the particular circumstances; but
>
> (B) authorizes an act without an actual hearing if such notice is given properly and if
>
> (i) such a hearing is not requested timely by a party in interest; or
>
> (ii) there is insufficient time for a hearing to be commenced before such act must be done, and the court authorizes such act ....

What **notice** is appropriate is left to Federal Rules of Bankruptcy Procedure[726] and other American procedural law, including a federal constitutional guarantee of the **267**

(discussing section 101 (23) and definition of "foreign proceeding").

[719] *See* mn 97 *et seq* (discussing section 1502 (2) and definition of "establishment"); mn 193 *et seq* (discussing section 1517 and concept of recognition).

[720] *See* mn 258 *et seq* (discussing Article 25).

[721] *See, e.g.,* 11 U.S.C. § 1528 (contemplating cooperation between an American bankruptcy court and a foreign insolvency court even where the American proceeding would, under the Model Law, be ineligible for recognition for lack of an establishment).

[722] *See also* Farley/Leonard/Birch at 2 ("There are means by which this increased level of cooperation can be achieved without in any way compromising or infringing upon the local domestic practices and procedures that exist in the courts involved."); *Collier* ¶ 1501.01 ("Chapter 15 then envelops its mechanism for ancillary relief in a broader structure that mandates cooperation with foreign courts and foreign representatives and coordination of multiple proceedings involving a common debtor.").

[723] *See Stonington Partners, Inc. v. Lernout & Hauspie Speech Prods. N.V.*, 310 F.3d 118, 133 (3d Cir. 2002).

[724] H. Rep. No. 109–31, 109th Cong., 1st Sess. 117 (2005).

[725] 11 U.S.C. § 102 (1).

[726] *See* H. Rep. No. 109–31, 109th Cong., 1st Sess. 117 (2005) (noting that "[g]uidelines for such communications are left to the Federal rules of bankruptcy procedure"). Those rules do not yet reflect the 2005 legislative changes to the Bankruptcy Code, but the Advisory Committee on Bankruptcy Rules has devised interim rules for temporary local adoption, including Interim

affected parties' right to "due process,"[727] and certain ethical rules respecting *ex parte* communications.[728]

268 Another authority to which American courts may turn are the Guidelines Applicable to Court-to-Court Communications in Cross Border Cases ("Guidelines"), adopted and promulgated by the American Law Institute (May 16, 2000).[729] Although the Guidelines "contemplate application only between Canada and the United States," they might be adapted to other cases.[730] The Guidelines are not automatically effective; they are intended to be formally adopted by the courts involved before they are applied and are to be adapted to the circumstances of the particular case at bar.[731] "The Guidelines are intended to encourage ... communication [among courts] and to permit rapid cooperation in a developing insolvency case, while ensuring due process to all concerned."[732]

2.5.2 Article 26 – Cooperation and direct communication between the *[insert the title of a person or body administering a reorganization or liquidation under the law of the enacting State]* and foreign courts or foreign representatives

1. In matters referred to in article 1, a *[insert the title of a person or body administering a reorganization or liquidation under the law of the enacting State]* shall, in the exercise of its functions and subject to the supervision of the court, cooperate to the maximum extent possible with foreign courts or foreign representatives.

2. The *[insert the title of a person or body administering a reorganization or liquidation under the law of the enacting State]* is entitled, in the exercise of its functions and subject to the supervision of the court, to communicate directly with foreign courts or foreign representatives.

→ *Cf* Art 32 of the EIR

Bankruptcy Rule 2002 (q) (governing notice of petitions for recognition and notice of a court's intention to communicate with foreign courts and foreign representatives) and Interim Bankruptcy Rule 5012 (governing communication and cooperation with foreign courts and foreign representatives). Essentially, they require 20 days' notice of a court's intent to engage in such communications to the extent the communications may deal with substantive issues; the notice should identify the subject of the communication and be delivered to the debtor, all administrators in foreign proceedings of the debtor, entities against whom provisional relief is sought, parties involved in litigation with the debtor in the United States and others the court determines are appropriate recipients of such notice. Fed. R. Bankr. P. (Interim) 2002 (q) and 5012. "Any entity that wishes to participate in the communication" must notify the court "not later than five days before the scheduled communication." Fed. R. Bankr. P. (Interim) 5012.

727 *See* U.S. Const. amends. V, XIV (guaranteeing "due process"); *Mullane v. Central Hanover Bank & Trust Co.*, 339 U.S. 306 (1950) (holding notice of opportunity to be heard must be "reasonably calculated" to reach parties affected by proceedings).

728 *See, e.g.,* Code of Conduct for United States Judges, Canon 3A (4) (2000) (regulating *ex parte* communications).

729 These may be found in several languages at http://www.iiiglobal.org/international/guidelines.html (last visited on Mar. 22, 2007). For general discussions of the Guidelines, *see* Farley/Leonard/Birch at 36–43; A/CN.9/580 ¶¶ 49–57; Wessels ¶¶ 10074–75.

730 *Id.* at 3.

731 Farley/Leonard/Birch at 38–39.

732 Farley/Leonard/Birch at 38.

2.5.2.1 General

Article 26 is an analogue of Article 25 that applies to insolvency administrators, who in many systems play instrumental roles in moving insolvency proceedings along. It also complements Article 5's grant of authority to the "the person or body administering a reorganization or liquidation under the law of the enacting State ... to act in a foreign State on behalf of a proceeding" under domestic insolvency law[733] and couples it with the duty to cooperate, subject to the court's supervision. As the Model Law does not modify such supervisory functions,[734] the reference to supervision should not be interpreted as a requirement for court authorization for a particular course of action where one would be unnecessary otherwise.[735] Recognition is not a prerequisite for Chapter IV cooperation.[736] The Model Law does not, however, provide authority to grant a foreign representative provisional relief without reference to an application for recognition.[737] **269**

2.5.2.2 United States Law

Section 1526 – Cooperation and direct communication between the trustee and foreign courts or foreign representatives.

(a) Consistent with section 1501, the trustee or other person, including an examiner, authorized by the court, shall, subject to the supervision of the court, cooperate to the maximum extent possible with a foreign court or a foreign representative.

(b) The trustee or other person, including an examiner, authorized by the court is entitled, subject to the supervision of the court, to communicate directly with a foreign court or a foreign representative.

This language of section 1526 varies only slightly from that of Article 26. The legislative history states that the omission of the phrase "in the exercise of its functions" was made only because the language is "unnecessary because it is always implied under United States law."[738] The words "[the] trustee or other person, including an examiner, authorized by the court," substitute for the bracketed language of Article 26.[739] **270**

---

733 *See* mn 113 *et seq* (discussing Article 5).

734 Guide ¶ 180.

735 A/CN.9/422 ¶¶ 133–35 (noting the concern of such an interpretation arising and observing that the words "to the maximum extent possible" address the concern and provide the necessary flexibility to be integrated with existing law).

736 Guide ¶ 177.

737 A/CN.9/433 ¶ 53 (stating that the "widely held view [of the Working Group] was that it would not be desirable for the Model Provisions to provide for provisional measures to the foreign representative without reference to an application for recognition").

738 H. Rep. No. 109–31, 109th Cong., 1st Sess. 117 (2005).

739 *See* 11 U.S.C. § 1502 (6) (defining "trustee") and mn 103 (discussing section 1502 (6)); 11 U.S.C. § 101 (41) (defining "person"). For an explanation of the term "examiner," *see* mn 117 (discussing section 1505).

2.5.3 Article 27 – Forms of cooperation

Cooperation referred to in articles 25 and 26 may be implemented by any appropriate means, including:

(a) **Appointment of a person or body to act at the direction of the court;**

(b) **Communication of information by any means considered appropriate by the court;**

(c) **Coordination of the administration and supervision of the debtor's assets and affairs;**

(d) **Approval or implementation by courts of agreements concerning the coordination of proceedings;**

(e) **Coordination of concurrent proceedings regarding the same debtor;**

(f) [The enacting State may wish to list additional forms or examples of cooperation].

→ *Cf* Art 32 of the EIR

2.5.3.1 General

271 Article 27 is a non-exhaustive, "indicative list of the types of cooperation that are authorized by articles 25 and 26."[740] The thought behind including the list was a desire to communicate a rough meaning for the term "cooperate" without limiting the extent of possible cooperation by precisely defining the term.[741] The Guide to Enactment notes, however, that the "implementation of cooperation would be subject to any mandatory laws of the enacting State."[742]

272 Of particular interest are the kinds of agreements to which paragraph (d) refers, which often become focal points for implementing cooperation. Such agreements, often called "**protocols**," "might be used, for example, to establish the system of corporate governance that will be applied to the debtor in a reorganization proceeding. A **protocol** dealing with corporate governance might address issues such as appointment of directors, procedural rules for boards of directors, judicial review procedures in connection with removal of directors, and recognition of certain rights of the insolvency administrator, including the right to receive information."[743] Other issues protocols might address include "designation of the administrative forum, application of that forum's priority rules, certain rules for cases in which there is more than one administrative forum, and designation of applicable rules for avoidance of transfers of assets that took place in the period preceding insolvency."[744]

---

740 Guide ¶ 181.

741 *See* Guide ¶ 41; A/CN.9/419 ¶ 122.

742 Guide ¶ 182.

743 A/CN.9/398 ¶ 13.

744 A/CN.9/398 ¶ 14 (collecting issues from the "Cross-Border Insolvency Concordat" of Committee J of the Section on Business Law of the International Bar Association); A/CN.9/580 ¶ 23–33 (comparing Concordat principles to Model Law provisions); *see also* A/CN.9/580 ¶ 18 (suggesting insolvency protocols might "settle a particular dispute arising from the different laws in concurrent cross-border proceedings, create a legal framework for the general conduct of the case or coordinate the administration of an insolvent estate in one State with an administration in another State").

Protocols do not necessarily have a prescribed **form**, though some standardization is occurring.[745] One guide in the development of protocols comes from the International Bar Association, whose Section on Business Law (and Committee J – Insolvency and Creditors' Rights[746]) has developed a "Concordat" for use in cross-border cases.[747] The Concordat itself recognizes that it might "be implemented by court orders or formal agreements between official representatives or informal arrangements, depending upon the rules and practices of the particular fora involved."[748] Its purpose is "to provide a framework of general principles for addressing cross-border insolvencies."[749] **273**

The Concordat deals with both procedural and substantive issues, including many the Model Law leaves unresolved, by setting forth ten principles with commentary. For example, it prefers a "single administrative forum with primary responsibility"[750] to "enhanc[e] control of assets, increasing business values, and ensuring fair treatment of creditors" but warns that the identity of such forum must be predictable,[751] which is obviously akin to the idea of a "foreign main proceeding" determined by the centre of the debtor's main interests that the Model Law implements.[752] The Concordat goes further, however, suggesting that payment of secured and **"privileged" claims** be made with local assets followed by turnover of remaining assets to the primary proceeding for distribution (which must not discriminate against "non-local" creditors) and that a discharge issued by the main forum be recognized in any forum.[753] While the Model Law recognizes a broad **principle of non-discrimination in distribution**, it does not provide specific rules to resolve "privileged claims" or recognize foreign discharges.[754] **274**

The above example sheds light on the nature of **protocols**. "They are complementary to the ... Model Law, as the Model Law provides a legislative basis for cross-border cooperation and it is the role of mechanisms such as protocols to tailor the scope and nature of the cooperation to the circumstances of the particular case."[755] **275**

Article 27 also elucidates the relationship between the concept of "**cooperation**" on one hand, and those of "coordination" and "communication" on the other. Under the Model Law, the latter are "means of implementing" the former. Paragraph (e) particularly mentions "[c]oordination of concurrent proceedings regarding the same debtor" as a means of implementing cooperation under Articles 25 and 26. Articles 28, 29 and 30 each require courts in enacting States dealing with concurrent insolvency proceedings to seek cooperation and coordination under Chapter IV for the concurrent proceedings situations they govern.[756] **276**

---

745 A/CN.9/580 ¶¶ 34, 36.

746 Committee J is now called the Section on Insolvency, Restructuring and Creditors' Rights.

747 International Bar Association, Committee J Cross-Border Insolvency Concordat (adopted by the Council of the Section of Business Law of the International Bar Association on Sept. 17, 1995, and by the Council of the International Bar Association on May 31, 1996). For a discussion of the history, theory and practice behind protocols generally and the Concordat specifically, *see* Farley/Leonard/Birch at 6–10; Wessels ¶¶ 10113–17.

748 Concordat (Introduction).

749 *Id.*

750 *Id.* (Principle 1).

751 *Id.* (Principle 1 cmt.)

752 *See* Art 2 (b) (defining "foreign main proceeding").

753 Concordat (Principle 2).

754 *See* Art 13 (providing "same rights" for foreign creditors in insolvency proceedings) and mn 155 *et seq* (discussing Art 13).

755 A/CN.9/580 ¶ 48. A list of cases employing protocols with links to the protocols can be found at http://www.iiiglobal.org/international/protocols.html (last viewed on Apr. 5, 2007).

756 *See* mn 279 *et seq* (discussing Chapter V).

2.5.3.2 United States Law

Section 1527 – Forms of cooperation

Cooperation referred to in sections 1525 and 1526 may be implemented by any appropriate means, including –

(1) appointment of a person or body, including an examiner, to act at the direction of the court;

(2) communication of information by any means considered appropriate by the court;

(3) coordination of the administration and supervision of the debtor's assets and affairs;

(4) approval or implementation of agreements concerning the coordination of proceedings; and

(5) coordination of concurrent proceedings regarding the same debtor.

277 The language of section 1527 is nearly identical to that of Article 27. Paragraph 1 deviates from the Model Law text to explicitly mention possible appointment of an examiner.[757]

278 In addition to the Concordat mentioned above, another source of cooperative principles that has attracted attention in the United States is *Principles of Cooperation Among the NAFTA Countries*, part of a four volume treatise entitled *Transnational Insolvency: Cooperation Among the NAFTA Countries*, which documents a project by American, Canadian and Mexican experts to "develop principles and procedures for managing the general default of an economic enterprise having its center of interest in a NAFTA country and having assets, creditors, and operations in more than one NAFTA country."[758] The principles are of two kinds: "General Principles that reflect the common values of the bankruptcy laws of the three countries as applied to multinational cases," and "Procedural Principles, which embody practical approaches to cooperation within the existing legal competence of the courts without requiring new legislation or treaties."[759] Although primarily concerned with insolvencies involving two or more of the NAFTA countries, "[i]n general terms, they are also applicable to non-NAFTA bankruptcy proceedings."[760] While generally accounting for provisions of the Model Law, it should be borne in mind that the Principles predate the enactment of chapter 15.

2.6 Chapter V – Concurrent proceedings

279 The scope of the Model Law includes situations in which "[a] foreign proceeding and [a proceeding under the insolvency laws of the enacting State] in respect of the same debtor … tak[e] place concurrently …,"[761] or where a court must deal with more than

[757] For an explanation of the term "examiner," *see* mn 117 (discussing section 1505).

[758] American Law Institute: Transnational Insolvency Cooperation among the NAFTA Countries – Guidelines applicable to Court-to-Court Communications in Cross-Border-Cases 1 (2003).

[759] *Id.* at 2. Note that both sets of principles are available at the IIL website at http://www.ali.org/ali/InsolvencyPrinciples.pdf. The treatise also provides explanatory information and summaries of the insolvency law in the NAFTA countries.

[760] Principles, § III.

[761] Art 1 (c).

one foreign proceeding respecting the same debtor. As noted in the introduction, the Law provides for a flexible system that prefers a "**primary/secondary jurisdiction structure,**" but also provides mechanisms for coordinating a cooperative "**concurrent/parallel proceedings structure.**"[762] Chapter V provides the mechanisms to shape coordination in situations closer to the latter structure, recognizing a hierarchy of proceedings but leaving courts in enacting States considerable **flexibility** to cooperate with their foreign counterparts (directly or through their respective representatives) to the maximum extent local law (including the enacted version of the Model Law)[763] and the circumstances of the particular cases before them allow.[764]

2.6.1 Article 28 – Commencement of a proceeding under *[identify laws of the enacting State relating to insolvency]* after recognition of a foreign main proceeding

After recognition of a foreign main proceeding, a proceeding under *[identify laws of the enacting State relating to insolvency]* may be commenced only if the debtor has assets in this State; the effects of that proceeding shall be restricted to the assets of the debtor that are located in this State and, to the extent necessary to implement cooperation and coordination under articles 25, 26 and 27, to other assets of the debtor that, under the law of this State, should be administered in that proceeding.

→ *Cf* Art 32 of the EIR

2.6.1.1 General

Article 28, reflecting the **principle of limited relief** in non-main proceedings,[765] permits a court in the enacting State to commence a domestic insolvency proceeding respecting a debtor in a domestically recognized foreign *main* proceeding[766] *only* when the debtor has assets in the enacting State,[767] and it generally limits the effects of the domestic pro- **280**

[762] *See* mn 14 *et seq* (discussing the function of the Model Law). The ultimate extreme is where two countries each open domestic insolvency proceedings, and each decides its own proceeding is the main proceeding. In such instances, the command to cooperate takes on enhanced significance. *See* A/CN.9/435 ¶ 187 (making that point); *see also* Principles IV.B.S.A.PP 4 n. 77 and accompanying text (noting dichotomy between instances in which there is a single full bankruptcy (with perhaps ancillary proceedings abroad) and those in which there are parallel proceedings). The Concordat (Principle 1) also expresses the idea of primacy of a main proceeding. *See* mn 273–274 (discussing Article 27 and the Cross-Border Insolvency Concordat).

[763] *See* Art 25 (1) (requiring maximum possible cooperation). As noted above, "[c]oordination of concurrent proceedings regarding the same debtor," is a "means of implementing" the Model Law concept of "cooperation." Art 27 (e); *see also* mn 271 *et seq* (discussing concept of "cooperation").

[764] *See generally* A/CN.9/435 ¶¶ 185–200 (describing the Working Group's discussion of principles taken into account in the formulation of Chapter V).

[765] Note that this principle also manifests itself in Articles 19 (4) (respecting pre-recognition relief), 29 (c) (governing concurrent foreign and domestic proceedings respecting the same debtor) and 30 (governing coordination of more than one foreign proceeding). Guide ¶¶ 160, 191.

[766] Although the text does not expressly so state, the Guide makes clear that the proceedings must concern the same debtor for Article 28 to apply. *See, e.g.*, Guide ¶ 184 (referring to the two proceedings as "concerning the same debtor").

[767] Stated another way, "recognition of a foreign main proceeding will not prevent the

ceeding to only those assets. If its law would – but for application of this rule – provide that the domestic proceeding should affect assets abroad, the court may administer those assets only as "necessary to implement cooperation and coordination under articles 25, 26 and 27."[768] The intent of the second part of the rule is to prevent jurisdictional conflict by providing that the effects of the (non-main) domestic proceeding give way as to assets abroad unless otherwise "coordinated" with the foreign court in the recognized main proceeding.[769] It should not be construed as "impos[ing] a division of assets that belonged to one establishment solely on the basis of their territorial location ..., or as precluding disposition of the debtor's assets in the enacting State as a going concern ... [The enacting State also retains] some latitude to determine, in the light of its own laws, which of the assets located in [its] territory ... should be administered in the foreign proceeding."[770] Those will usually be "cooperation and coordination" issues.[771]

281 The Guide to Enactment notes that the "philosophy of the Model Law" would permit a State enacting Article 28 to upgrade the "presence of assets" basis of jurisdiction to commence a local insolvency proceeding after recognition of a foreign main proceeding respecting the same debtor to require a local "**establishment**" instead.[772] This observation may also reflect the incongruence of the Model Law requiring an establishment for recognition of a foreign proceeding but not for opening a domestic proceeding.[773]

282 Article 29, which further and more generally governs **coordination** of a recognized foreign proceeding and a domestic insolvency proceeding, will also apply to the situation to which Article 28 applies.

---

commencement of a local insolvency proceeding concerning the same debtor as long as the debtor has assets in the State." Guide ¶ 184.

[768] Chapter IV (comprised of articles 25, 26 and 27) requires insolvency administrators and courts of the enacting State to co-operate to the maximum extent possible with foreign representatives and foreign courts respecting common debtors. *See id.* and mn 256 *et seq* (discussing concept of "cooperation").

[769] Guide ¶ 187.

[770] A/52/17 ¶ 99; *see also* Guide ¶ 159 (stating "principle underlying the Model Law that recognition of a foreign proceeding does not mean extending the effects of the foreign proceeding as they may be prescribed by the law of the foreign State. Instead, recognition of a foreign proceeding entails attaching to the foreign proceeding consequences envisaged by the law of the enacting State"). Also consider that the principles underlying the provisions of Article 28 are similar to those in Article 21 (3); thus, the development of law around one of these provisions should aid in interpreting the other. *See* A/52/17 ¶ 99 (noting relationship between Articles 21 (3) and 28) and mn 229 *et seq* (discussing Article 21 (3)).

[771] A/52/17 ¶¶ 99, 154.

[772] Guide ¶ 186; *see also* Guide ¶ 42 (discussing same point), Art 2 (f) (defining "establishment") and mn 97 *et seq* (discussing Article 2 (f)). Romania apparently requires the existence of an establishment to open local proceedings following a recognition of foreign main proceedings. A/CN.9/580 ¶ 15.

[773] *See supra* note 483 and accompanying text (discussing the incongruence).

2.6.1.2 United States Law

> **Section 1528 – Commencement of a case under this title after recognition of a foreign main proceeding**
>
> **After recognition of a foreign main proceeding, a case under another chapter of this title may be commenced only if the debtor has assets in the United States. The effects of such case shall be restricted to the assets of the debtor that are within the territorial jurisdiction of the United States and, to the extent necessary to implement cooperation and coordination under sections 1525, 1526, and 1527, to other assets of the debtor that are within the jurisdiction of the court under sections 541 (a) of this title, and 1334 (e) of title 28, to the extent that such other assets are not subject to the jurisdiction and control of a foreign proceeding that has been recognized under this chapter.**

Section 1528 generally follows Article 28 but refines its phrase "should be administered in that proceeding" to provide that the ordinary universal jurisdiction available to bankruptcy courts under United States law[774] in plenary cases,[775] which section 1528 would otherwise restrict to "the territorial jurisdiction of the United States,"[776] might continue to apply to assets "not subject to the jurisdiction and control of a recognized foreign proceeding ...." This provision keeps the bankruptcy court's full jurisdiction available "to the extent necessary to implement cooperation and coordination," while still giving deference to the recognized foreign main proceeding.[777] **283**

2.6.2 Article 29 – Coordination of a proceeding under *[identify laws of the enacting State relating to insolvency]* and a foreign proceeding

> **Where a foreign proceeding and a proceeding under *[identify laws of the enacting State relating to insolvency]* are taking place concurrently regarding the same debtor, the court shall seek cooperation and coordination under articles 25, 26 and 27, and the following shall apply:**
>
> ***(a)* When the proceeding in this State is taking place at the time the application for recognition of the foreign proceeding is filed,**
>
> **(i) Any relief granted under article 19 or 21 must be consistent with the proceeding in this State; and**

---

774 This is the function of the references to section 541 (a) of the Bankruptcy Code (creating, upon commencement of plenary case, an estate comprised of essentially all of the debtor's property, "wherever located and by whomever held") and section 1334 (e) of the Judicial Code (providing United States district courts in bankruptcy cases jurisdiction "of all the property, wherever located, of the debtor as of the commencement of such [a] case, and of property of the estate").

775 The reference to "a case under another chapter of this title" is to a plenary case (e.g., under chapter 7 or 11 of the Bankruptcy Code). *See* mn 52 (discussing meaning of "case").

776 Congress defined this phrase in section 1502 (8). *See* mn 105 (discussing definition).

777 In *dicta*, the court in *In re SPhinX, Ltd.*, 351 B.R. 103, 115 n. 17 (Bankr. S.D.N.Y. 2006), *aff'd*, 371 B.R. 10 (S.D.N.Y. 2007), noted that a "concurrent case under the Bankruptcy Code should generally serve the interests of the foreign main proceeding – subject, of course, to the court's duty to condition or modify relief to protect creditors ...."

(ii) If the foreign proceeding is recognized in this State as a foreign main proceeding, article 20 does not apply;

***(b)* When the proceeding in this State commences after recognition, or after the filing of the application for recognition, of the foreign proceeding,**

(i) Any relief in effect under article 19 or 21 shall be reviewed by the court and shall be modified or terminated if inconsistent with the proceeding in this State; and

(ii) If the foreign proceeding is a foreign main proceeding, the stay and suspension referred to in paragraph 1 of article 20 shall be modified or terminated pursuant to paragraph 2 of article 20 if inconsistent with the proceeding in this State;

***(c)* In granting, extending or modifying relief granted to a representative of a foreign nonmain proceeding, the court must be satisfied that the relief relates to assets that, under the law of this State, should be administered in the foreign non-main proceeding or concerns information required in that proceeding.**

→ *Cf* Art 32 of the EIR

2.6.2.1 General

284 Article 29 requires the court to seek "cooperation and coordination" with the foreign court in accordance with Chapter IV (Articles 25–27)[778] respecting a foreign proceeding and a simultaneously occurring domestic insolvency proceeding and to prevent (or remedy) any inconsistency between the Article 20 effects[779] of and Article 19[780] or 21[781] relief considered in connection with recognition of the foreign proceeding on one hand and the effects of and relief granted in the domestic proceeding on the other. It applies to three possible situations. The first occurs where the two proceedings co-exist **without reference to an application for recognition**, in which case only the command to seek cooperation and coordination is in play. Paragraph (a) covers instances in which the domestic proceeding "is taking place"[782] upon the filing of the application for recognition, and paragraph (b) covers those in which the domestic proceeding "commences" after the filing of the application.[783]

285 In the latter two situations, the effects of recognition of and relief considered respecting the foreign proceeding give way to the domestic one except as modified through cooperation and coordination.[784] At the same time, however, it is clear "that the commen-

[778] Chapter IV requires insolvency administrators and courts of the enacting State to cooperate to the maximum extent possible with foreign representatives and foreign courts respecting common debtors. *See id.* and mn 256 *et seq* (discussing concept of "cooperation").

[779] *See* mn 213 *et seq* (discussing Article 20).

[780] *See* mn 202 *et seq* (discussing Article 19).

[781] *See* mn 224 *et seq* (discussing Article 21).

[782] The Model Law does not make clear whether this reference includes preliminary insolvency proceedings that occur in some jurisdictions. A similar problem attends the reference to "commencement" in paragraph (b).

[783] Article 20 does not apply to stay commencement of domestic insolvency proceedings. Art 20 (4).

[784] *See* Guide ¶ 190 ("[T]he article maintains a pre-eminence of the local proceeding over the foreign proceeding … [but] avoids establishing a rigid hierarchy between the proceedings since this would unnecessarily hinder the ability of the court to cooperate and exercise its discretion …"); *see also* Jay Lawrence Westbrook, *Multinational Enterprises in General Default: Chapter 15,*

cement of a local proceeding does not prevent or terminate the recognition of a foreign proceeding,"[785] thus ensuring the core function of the Model Law, promotion of "[c]ooperation between the courts and other competent authorities of [the enacting] State and foreign States involved in cases of cross-border insolvency,"[786] retains its vitality when it is needed most, *viz*, in the parallel/concurrent proceedings scenario. Article 28 generally restricts the effects of the domestic proceeding to assets located within the enacting State where the domestic proceeding is commenced after recognition of a **foreign main proceeding.**[787]

Article 29 (a) (ii) precludes Article 20 from taking effect at all where the domestic **286**
proceeding is taking place at the time of the filing of the application for recognition. The automatic nature of Article 20 effects makes this measure necessary to ensure that the smooth functioning of the domestic proceeding is not disturbed. Where it has already taken effect (upon recognition of a foreign main proceeding) and a domestic proceeding intervenes, it must be reassessed taking into account the expectations of the parties.[788]

Paragraph (c) serves to manifest the **ordinarily subordinate posture of non-main pro-** **287**
ceedings to both domestic proceedings and foreign main proceedings while maintaining the practical flexibility to coordinate relief, consistent with the law of the enacting State, in furtherance of the objectives of the Model Law.[789]

Note that the foreign representative is required to keep the court abreast of its status **288**
and that of the foreign proceeding, which should aid in coordination.[790]

2.6.2.2 United States Law

Section 1529 – Coordination of a case under this title and a foreign proceeding

If a foreign proceeding and a case under another chapter of this title are pending concurrently regarding the same debtor, the court shall seek cooperation and coordination under sections 1525, 1526, and 1527, and the following shall apply:

(1) If the case in the United States pending at the time the petition for recognition of such foreign proceeding is filed

The ALI Principles, and the EU Insolvency Regulation, 76 Am. Bankr. L.J. 1, 17 (Winter 2002) (stating that "[i]t was the *sine qua non* of achieving the Model Law that local insolvency proceedings involving the same debtor could trump foreign proceedings" and noting that a foreign representative's right to participate in the domestic proceeding under Article 12 mitigates the effect of the principle to some extent); NBRC Report ¶ 2.2.2 (noting that the Model Law "bows to the primacy of local proceedings wherever they may be opened and depends greatly upon a willingness of local officials to cooperate").

785 Guide ¶ 189.

786 Preamble (objective (a)).

787 *See* mn 280 *et seq* (discussing Article 28).

788 *See generally* A/CN.9/435 ¶ 191 (noting the need for flexibility in order to be able to consider fairness, acquired rights and the need to coordinate the concurrent proceedings).

789 The principle of limited relief (e.g., usually restricted to the territory of the state in which the non-main proceeding is occurring) for non-main proceedings is also reflected in Articles 21 (3) (respecting post-recognition relief); 19 (4) (respecting pre-recognition relief), 28 (providing coordination rules for effects of domestic proceedings commenced after recognition of foreign main (but not non-main) proceedings), and 30 (governing coordination of more than one foreign proceeding). Guide ¶¶ 160, 191.

790 Art 18 (a); *see also* mn 199 *et seq* (discussing Article 18).

(A) any relief granted under section 1519 or 1521 must be consistent with the relief granted in the case in the United States; and

(B) section 1520 does not apply even if such foreign proceeding is recognized as a foreign main proceeding.

(2) If a case in the United States under this title commences after recognition, or after the date of the filing of the petition for recognition, of such foreign proceeding

(A) any relief in effect under section 1519 or 1521 shall be reviewed by the court and shall be modified or terminated if inconsistent with the case in the United States; and

(B) if such foreign proceeding is a foreign main proceeding, the stay and suspension referred to in section 1520 (a) shall be modified or terminated if inconsistent with the relief granted in the case in the United States.

(3) In granting, extending, or modifying relief granted to a representative of a foreign nonmain proceeding, the court must be satisfied that the relief relates to assets that, under the laws of the United States, should be administered in the foreign nonmain proceeding or concerns information required in that proceeding.

(4) In achieving cooperation and coordination under sections 1528 and 1529, the court may grant any of the relief authorized under section 305.

289 The principle Article 29 reflects, that "[a] local proceeding should prevail over the effects of recognition of a foreign proceeding and over relief granted to a foreign representative," is not in complete accord with common law principles of universality and comity.[791] As the Privy Counsel of the United Kingdom has recently observed,[792]

> The English common law has traditionally taken the view that fairness between creditors requires that, ideally, bankruptcy proceedings should have universal application. There should be a single bankruptcy in which all creditors are entitled and required to prove. No one should have an advantage because he happens to live in a jurisdiction where more of the assets or fewer of the creditors are situated .... [T]he principle of universality is given effect by recognising the person who is empowered under the foreign bankruptcy law to act on behalf of the insolvent company as entitled to do so in England.

290 In the United States, from 1979 until the enactment of chapter 15, the universality principle was given effect statutorily through former section 304 of the Bankruptcy Code[793] through which foreign representatives, in the context of an ancillary case,[794] had access to much, though not all, **relief** available to bankruptcy trustees (administra-

[791] A/CN.9/435 ¶ 191 (noting discussion of the principle and long-standing common law approach of distinguishing cases in which the local proceeding is the main proceeding from those in which it is a non-main proceeding).

[792] *Cambridge Gas Transp. Corp. v. Official Committee of Unsecured Creditors (of Navigator Holdings PLC)*, [2006], 3 All E.R. 829 ¶¶ 16, 20. For its example that the common law upholds the principle of universality in insolvency proceedings, the Privy Council cites *Solomons v. Ross* (1764) 1 H Bl 131n (decreeing that a bankruptcy in Holland had vested all the debtor's moveables, including debts owed by English debtors, in the Dutch assignees). *Id.* ¶ 16. That case, of course, predates the American revolution.

[793] *See supra* note 144 (setting forth text).

[794] *See* mn 53 (discussing ancillary cases).

tors) in plenary cases. Today ancillary cases are commenced by petitions for **recognition** under section 1515, and recognition under section 1517 may follow to provide the basis for effects and relief in aid of main proceedings and, to lesser degree, non-main proceedings elsewhere.[795]

Therefore, although section 1529 generally follows the language of Article 29 (with a few stylistic changes to comport with American terminology), Congress[796] added the subsection (4) reference to section 305 of the Bankruptcy Code,[797] which allows the court to dismiss or suspend plenary cases[798] if "a petition under section 1515 for recognition of a foreign proceeding has been granted; and ... the purposes of chapter 15 ... would be best served by such dismissal or suspension."[799] Section 305 "relief" appears to be a case of "additional assistance" under section 1507 to which the considerations of comity and the factors of and jurisprudence that developed under former section 304 are meant to be applied in furtherance of cooperation and coordination.[800] **291**

The Collier treatise points out that there is no specific exclusion to the **automatic stay** in the plenary case for filing a petition for recognition (and thus commencing an ancillary case) against the same debtor.[801] It maintains that "the petition for recognition can be characterized as a determination of the status and standing of the foreign proceeding and foreign representative as opposed to an action or proceeding against the debtor."[802] Further, the very existence of such provisions as section 1529 and 1512, which require recognition for a foreign representative to participate in bankruptcy cases **292**

---

795 11 U.S.C. § 1504; *see also* mn 112 (discussing section 1504), mn 178 *et seq* (discussing section 1515), mn 193 *et seq* (discussing section 1517).

796 This seems in keeping with the common law tradition of legislative respect for and willingness to maintain the flexibility of courts in ancillary cases.

797 *See* H. Rep. No. 109–31, 109th Cong., 1st Sess. 106, 117 (2005) (noting that "cases brought under chapter 15 are intended to be ancillary to cases brought in a debtor's home country, unless a full United States bankruptcy case is brought under another chapter. Even if a full case is brought, the court may decide to stay or dismiss the United States case under the other chapter and limit the United States role to an ancillary proceeding," and that section 1529 (4) "is consistent with United States policy to act ancillary to a foreign proceeding"). In the *Axona International Credit* case mentioned above, *see supra* notes 375, 493, the court traced the trend of American common law toward universality and employed section 305 to grant the application of a foreign representative of a Hong Kong proceeding to suspend an involuntary plenary chapter 7 bankruptcy filed by the foreign representative and to turnover the proceeds of assets recovered in the United States to the foreign representative for distribution in Hong Kong under Hong Kong law after the foreign representative used the chapter 7 case to prosecute a preference claim under the U.S. Bankruptcy Code and succeeded in extracting a large settlement from a the U.S.-based creditor. *In re Axona Internat'l Credit & Commerce Ltd.*, 88 B.R. 597 (Bankr. S.D.N.Y. 1988), *aff'd*, 115 B.R. 442 (S.D.N.Y. 1990), *appeal dismissed*, 924 F.2d 31 (2d Cir. 1991).

798 Section 305 does not apply to ancillary cases. 11 U.S.C. § 103 (a) (listing provisions applying to cases under chapter 15 without including section 305).

799 11 U.S.C. § 305 (a) (2). Section 305 (b) provides that a "foreign representative may seek dismissal or suspension under section 305 (a) (2)," and section 306 of the Bankruptcy Code provides that doing so "does not submit such foreign representative to the jurisdiction of any court in the United States for any other purpose, but the bankruptcy court may condition any order under section ... 305 ... on compliance by such foreign representative with the orders of such bankruptcy court." 11 U.S.C. § 306.

800 11 U.S.C. § 1507 (b); *see also* mn 123 *et seq* (discussing section 1507).

801 *Collier* ¶ 1529.02.

802 *Id.*

involving the same debtor,[803] implies that Congress contemplated (and even encouraged) the idea of commencing an ancillary proceeding in appropriate cases not only to allow for better **cooperation** and **coordination** based on recognizing the foreign proceeding and foreign representative, but to allow for deference to the ancillary proceeding under section 305 in appropriate cases.

2.6.3 Article 30 – Coordination of more than one foreign proceeding

In matters referred to in article 1, in respect of more than one foreign proceeding regarding the same debtor, the court shall seek cooperation and coordination under articles 25, 26 and 27, and the following shall apply:

***(a)* Any relief granted under article 19 or 21 to a representative of a foreign non-main proceeding after recognition of a foreign main proceeding must be consistent with the foreign main proceeding;**

***(b)* If a foreign main proceeding is recognized after recognition, or after the filing of an application for recognition, of a foreign non-main proceeding, any relief in effect under article 19 or 21 shall be reviewed by the court and shall be modified or terminated if inconsistent with the foreign main proceeding;**

***(c)* If, after recognition of a foreign non-main proceeding, another foreign non-main proceeding is recognized, the court shall grant, modify or terminate relief for the purpose of facilitating coordination of the proceedings.**

→ *Cf* Art 32 et seq of the EIR

2.6.3.1 General

293 Article 30 requires the court to seek "cooperation and coordination" with the relevant foreign courts in accordance with Chapter IV (Articles 25–27) where more than one foreign proceeding are simultaneously occurring involving the same debtor[804] and to prevent (or remedy) any inconsistency between or among them in connection with Article 19[805] or 21[806] relief. The article confirms the **general hierarchy** in favor of the foreign main proceeding by requiring in subparagraphs (a) and (b) that any relief to be granted or already granted in support of foreign non-main proceedings be consistent with that granted or to be granted in the foreign main proceeding.[807] Subparagraph (c) requires consistency in relief between two **foreign non-main proceedings** without ranking them, for example, temporally.

803 11 U.S.C. § 1512; *see also* mn 152 *et seq* (discussing section 1512).

804 Chapter IV requires insolvency administrators and courts of the enacting State to cooperate to the maximum extent possible with foreign representatives and foreign courts respecting common debtors. *See id.* and mn 256 *et seq* (discussing concept of "cooperation").

805 *See* mn 202 *et seq* (discussing Article 19 (pre-recognition relief)).

806 *See* mn 224 *et seq* (discussing Article 21 (relief that may be granted upon recognition)).

807 *See* Guide ¶¶ 47, 193. Note that the principle of limited relief for non-main proceedings is also reflected in Arts 21 (3) (respecting post-recognition relief); 19 (4) (respecting pre-recognition relief), 28 (providing coordination rules for effects of domestic proceedings commenced after recognition of foreign main proceedings), and 29 (c) (governing concurrent foreign and domestic proceedings respecting the same debtor). Guide ¶¶ 160, 191.

Note that Article 30 applies whether or not a domestic proceeding involving the same debtor is also occurring. If so, the court must follow the provisions of Article 29 as well.[808] Thus, the complete Chapter V general hierarchy ranks domestic proceedings over foreign ones, and foreign main proceedings over **foreign non-main proceedings**, with due regard to the flexibility required to further the objectives of the Model Law under the **principle of cooperation.**[809] **294**

Foreign representatives are required to keep the court informed of their knowledge of other foreign proceedings.[810] **295**

2.6.3.2 United States Law

Section 1530 – Coordination of more than 1 foreign proceeding

In matters referred to in section 1501, with respect to more than 1 foreign proceeding regarding the debtor, the court shall seek cooperation and coordination under sections 1525, 1526, and 1527, and the following shall apply:

(1) Any relief granted under section 1519 or 1521 to a representative of a foreign non-main proceeding after recognition of a foreign main proceeding must be consistent with the foreign main proceeding.

(2) If a foreign main proceeding is recognized after recognition, or after the filing of a petition for recognition, of a foreign nonmain proceeding, any relief in effect under section 1519 or 1521 shall be reviewed by the court and shall be modified or terminated if inconsistent with the foreign main proceeding.

(3) If, after recognition of a foreign nonmain proceeding, another foreign nonmain proceeding is recognized, the court shall grant, modify, or terminate relief for the purpose of facilitating coordination of the proceedings.

Section 1530 follows Article 30 almost exactly, removing the word "same" in front of "debtor," since "debtor" is a defined term in chapter 15,[811] and making other minor changes in favor of American style and legal terminology. **296**

2.6.4 Article 31 – Presumption of insolvency based on recognition of a foreign main proceeding

In the absence of evidence to the contrary, recognition of a foreign main proceeding is, for the purpose of commencing a proceeding under *[identify laws of the enacting State relating to insolvency]*, proof that the debtor is insolvent.

2.6.4.1 General

This provision follows from the concept of **recognition** and the fact that most jurisdictions require that a debtor be "insolvent" for insolvency proceedings to be commenced respecting it. Recognition does not, however, require an examination of the foreign **297**

[808] *See* Guide ¶ 192.

[809] *See also supra* note 437 and accompanying text (discussing supremacy of main over non-main proceedings).

[810] Arts 15 (3); 18 (b); *see also* mn 172 *et seq* (discussing Article 15) and 199 *et seq* (discussing Article 18).

[811] 11 U.S.C. § 1502 (1); *see also* mn 102 (discussing Article 1502 (1)).

court's grounds for opening its proceedings.[812] Thus, the presumption Article 31 establishes is not conclusive and may be overcome by contrary evidence in accordance with the law of the enacting State. The **presumption** is restricted to the purpose of commencing a parallel proceeding in the enacting State.

298 Recognition of foreign non-main proceedings does not have similar effect. According to the Guide to Enactment, "The reason is that an insolvency proceeding commenced in a State other than the State where the debtor has the centre of its main interests does not necessarily mean that the debtor is to be subject to laws relating to insolvency in other States."[813]

299 The intent of the rule is to improve the speed and efficiency with which local proceedings may be opened.[814]

2.6.4.2 United States Law

> **Section 1531 – Presumption of insolvency based on recognition of a foreign main proceeding**
>
> **In the absence of evidence to the contrary, recognition of a foreign main proceeding is, for the purpose of commencing a proceeding under section 303, proof that the debtor is generally not paying its debts as such debts become due.**

300 Section 1531 substitutes section 303, the Bankruptcy Code provision for commencing involuntary plenary bankruptcy cases,[815] for the bracketed language of Article 31 and its insolvency standard for the word "insolvent" at the end. As stated in the discussion of section 1511 above, the foreign representative of a recognized foreign main proceeding may also opt to commence a **voluntary plenary case**, which requires no proof of insolvency, though it may be submitting to the jurisdiction of the bankruptcy court for other purposes in doing so,[816] whereas the Bankruptcy Code provides for a "**limited appearance**" to shelter foreign representatives from assertions of more general jurisdiction based only on appearances "in connection with a petition ... under section 303."[817]

301 The effect of section 1531 itself is that of a "**presumption.**"[818] As with the presumption of section 1516 (c) discussed above, then, the ultimate burden of non-persuasion remains on the foreign representative or other entities filing the section 303 petition to the extent evidence is presented which shows that the debtor is generally paying its debts as they become due.[819]

2.6.5 Article 32 – Rule of payment in concurrent proceedings

> **Without prejudice to secured claims or rights *in rem*, a creditor who has received part payment in respect of its claim in a proceeding pursuant to a law relating to insolvency in a foreign State may not receive a payment for the same claim in a proceeding under**

812 *See supra* note 474 and accompanying text.
813 Guide ¶ 195.
814 Guide ¶¶ 43, 197.
815 11 U.S.C. § 303.
816 *See* mn 147 *et seq* (discussing section 1511).
817 11 U.S.C. § 306 (providing for limited appearance, or "safe conduct").
818 H. Rep. No. 109–31, 109th Cong., 1st Sess. 118 (2005) ("The word 'proof' in this provision here means 'presumption.'").
819 *See* Fed. R. Evid. 301; *see also* mn 185 (discussing section 1516 and setting forth Federal Rule of Evidence 301).

[*identify laws of the enacting State relating to insolvency*] regarding the same debtor, so long as the payment to the other creditors of the same class is proportionately less than the payment the creditor has already received.

→ *Cf* Art 20 of the EIR

2.6.5.1 General

Article 32 is meant to alleviate the negative effect which concurrent insolvency proceedings have on the ability to marshal all assets of a given debtor into a single, worldwide estate.[820] The rule works by equalizing, to the extent possible, the basis of distribution on claims of a like class against the value of a debtor's assets allotted to the class through a local insolvency proceeding by accounting for distributions on the same claims from foreign proceedings concerning the same debtor. Thus, a creditor participating in a local proceeding is entitled to share only in the value allotted to the class of claims to which the creditor's claim belongs to the extent that value exceeds what must be distributed to the other participating holders of claims of the same class in order for them to receive the ratable equivalent on their claims to what the creditor will have received on its claim in all proceedings respecting the same debtor. **302**

For example, if the creditor received $ 7 on a $ 100 claim in a foreign proceeding and the dividend to creditors holding claims in the class to which the creditor's claim belonged were 7 % or less in a domestic insolvency proceeding, the creditor would not be entitled to participate. If the domestic dividend were 10 %, the creditor would be entitled to $ 3. **303**

The rule does not take into account **foreign distributions** received on "secured claims" or **"rights in rem."** According to the Guide to Enactment,[821] **304**

> The words "secured claims" are used to refer generally to claims guaranteed by particular assets, while the words "rights in rem" are intended to indicate rights relating to a particular property that are enforceable also against third parties. A given right may fall within the ambit of both expressions, depending on the classification and terminology of the applicable law. The enacting State may use another term or terms for expressing those concepts.

2.6.5.2 United States Law

Section 1532 – Rule of payment in concurrent proceedings

Without prejudice to secured claims or rights in rem, a creditor who has received payment with respect to its claim in a foreign proceeding pursuant to a law relating to insolvency may not receive a payment for the same claim in a case under any other chapter of this title regarding the debtor, so long as the payment to other creditors of the same class is proportionately less than the payment the creditor has already received.

---

[820] *See* mn 224 *et seq* (discussing Article 21 (2)'s provision authorizing entrustment of the debtor's assets to a foreign representative for distribution and the tension between the principles of effecting equality of among creditors with similar claims and adequately protecting local creditors from unfair foreign distribution and claims resolution procedures).

[821] Guide ¶ 200.

305 Section 1532 has almost exactly the same wording as Article 32 but does not include the word "same" before "debtor," because "debtor" is defined in section 1502 (1).[822] This and other minor changes are not substantive. The rule, known at common law as the **"hotchpot" rule**, is part of the **principle of equality among similarly situated creditors**[823] and is related to the notion of avoiding transfers that disadvantage creditors collectively or disallowing claims of entities who hold funds or property that should belong to the debtor's estate and be available for general distribution.[824]

3. Conclusions

306 As this discussion has shown, the Model Law aims to straighten the path of cross-border insolvency in the limited areas of access to foreign courts for foreign representatives and creditors, recognition of foreign proceedings and cooperation and coordination. Even if it were universally enacted, many cross-border insolvency issues would remain open. UNCITRAL has already begun work on resolving one of the most important of these: the problem of corporate groups, which the Working Group has described as the "tension between the traditional separate legal entity approach to corporate regulation and its implications for insolvency and the facilitation of insolvency proceedings against a group or part of a group in a cross-border situation in a manner that would enable the goal of maximizing value for the benefit of creditors to be achieved."[825] In that connection, it is also examining the area of post-commencement financing.[826] The Model Law also provides no uniform choice of law provisions, which, if they could be developed, would greatly aid in further centralizing proceedings and reducing forum shopping. It was never the intention of the Law to reach these issues, which were considered next steps, perhaps to be addressed at the regional or bilateral level. The centralization that the Model Law attempts to bring about, however, by, among other things, its focus on the concept of the centre of the debtor's main interests, and the present uncertainty respecting the precise meaning of that phrase, makes further development of the law of cross-border insolvency crucial to the stability of the debt markets, manageable investment risks and continued worldwide economic growth.

---

822 *See* mn 102 (discussing definition of "debtor").

823 *See* Principles, General Principle VII, cmt. & n. 258 (discussing "hotchpot" rule). The rule was previously codified as section 508 (a) of the Bankruptcy Code (though the wording was different).

824 *See, e.g.*, 11 U.S.C. § 502 (d) (disallowing claims of entities from whom property is recoverable under certain avoiding rules or Paulian actions).

825 A/CN.9/WG.V/WP.74/Add.2. In summer 2006, the Commission agreed that the topic of corporate groups was ripe for work, and asked the Working Group to begin to consider the issues associated with the topic. A/61/17 ¶¶ 207–209.

826 A/61/17 ¶ 209.

ANNEX

Council Regulation (EC) No 1346/2000
of 29 May 2000
on insolvency proceedings

Official Journal L 160 – 30/06/2000 (P. 0001 – 0018)

THE COUNCIL OF THE EUROPEAN UNION,

Having regard to the Treaty establishing the European Community, and in particular Articles 61(c) and 67(1) thereof,

Having regard to the initiative of the Federal Republic of Germany and the Republic of Finland,

Having regard to the opinion of the European Parliament[1],

Having regard to the opinion of the Economic and Social Committee[2],

Whereas:

(1) The European Union has set out the aim of establishing an area of freedom, security and justice.

(2) The proper functioning of the internal market requires that cross-border insolvency proceedings should operate efficiently and effectively and this Regulation needs to be adopted in order to achieve this objective which comes within the scope of judicial cooperation in civil matters within the meaning of Article 65 of the Treaty.

(3) The activities of undertakings have more and more cross-border effects and are therefore increasingly being regulated by Community law. While the insolvency of such undertakings also affects the proper functioning of the internal market, there is a need for a Community act requiring coordination of the measures to be taken regarding an insolvent debtor's assets.

(4) It is necessary for the proper functioning of the internal market to avoid incentives for the parties to transfer assets or judicial proceedings from one Member State to another, seeking to obtain a more favourable legal position (forum shopping).

(5) These objectives cannot be achieved to a sufficient degree at national level and action at Community level is therefore justified.

(6) In accordance with the principle of proportionality this Regulation should be confined to provisions governing jurisdiction for opening insolvency proceedings and judgments which are delivered directly on the basis of the insolvency proceedings and are closely connected with such proceedings. In addition, this Regulation should contain

---

[1] Opinion delivered on 2 March 2000 (not yet published in the Official Journal).

[2] Opinion delivered on 26 January 2000 (not yet published in the Official Journal).

provisions regarding the recognition of those judgments and the applicable law which also satisfy that principle.

(7) Insolvency proceedings relating to the winding-up of insolvent companies or other legal persons, judicial arrangements, compositions and analogous proceedings are excluded from the scope of the 1968 Brussels Convention on Jurisdiction and the Enforcement of Judgments in Civil and Commercial Matters[3], as amended by the Conventions on Accession to this Convention[4].

(8) In order to achieve the aim of improving the efficiency and effectiveness of insolvency proceedings having cross-border effects, it is necessary, and appropriate, that the provisions on jurisdiction, recognition and applicable law in this area should be contained in a Community law measure which is binding and directly applicable in Member States.

(9) This Regulation should apply to insolvency proceedings, whether the debtor is a natural person or a legal person, a trader or an individual. The insolvency proceedings to which this Regulation applies are listed in the Annexes. Insolvency proceedings concerning insurance undertakings, credit institutions, investment undertakings holding funds or securities for third parties and collective investment undertakings should be excluded from the scope of this Regulation. Such undertakings should not be covered by this Regulation since they are subject to special arrangements and, to some extent, the national supervisory authorities have extremely wide-ranging powers of intervention.

(10) Insolvency proceedings do not necessarily involve the intervention of a judicial authority; the expression "court" in this Regulation should be given a broad meaning and include a person or body empowered by national law to open insolvency proceedings. In order for this Regulation to apply, proceedings (comprising acts and formalities set down in law) should not only have to comply with the provisions of this Regulation, but they should also be officially recognised and legally effective in the Member State in which the insolvency proceedings are opened and should be collective insolvency proceedings which entail the partial or total divestment of the debtor and the appointment of a liquidator.

(11) This Regulation acknowledges the fact that as a result of widely differing substantive laws it is not practical to introduce insolvency proceedings with universal scope in the entire Community. The application without exception of the law of the State of opening of proceedings would, against this background, frequently lead to difficulties. This applies, for example, to the widely differing laws on security interests to be found in the Community. Furthermore, the preferential rights enjoyed by some creditors in the insolvency proceedings are, in some cases, completely different. This Regulation should take account of this in two different ways. On the one hand, provision should be made for special rules on applicable law in the case of particularly significant rights and legal relationships (e.g. rights in rem and contracts of employment). On the other hand, national proceedings covering only assets situated in the State of opening should also be allowed alongside main insolvency proceedings with universal scope.

(12) This Regulation enables the main insolvency proceedings to be opened in the Member State where the debtor has the centre of his main interests. These proceedings have universal scope and aim at encompassing all the debtor's assets. To protect the diversity of interests, this Regulation permits secondary proceedings to be opened to run

[3] OJ L 299, 31.12.1972, p. 32.

[4] OJ L 204, 2.8.1975, p. 28; OJ L 304, 30.10.1978, p. 1; OJ L 388, 31.12.1982, p. 1; OJ L 285, 3.10.1989, p. 1; OJ C 15, 15.1.1997, p. 1.

in parallel with the main proceedings. Secondary proceedings may be opened in the Member State where the debtor has an establishment. The effects of secondary proceedings are limited to the assets located in that State. Mandatory rules of coordination with the main proceedings satisfy the need for unity in the Community.

(13) The "centre of main interests" should correspond to the place where the debtor conducts the administration of his interests on a regular basis and is therefore ascertainable by third parties.

(14) This Regulation applies only to proceedings where the centre of the debtor's main interests is located in the Community.

(15) The rules of jurisdiction set out in this Regulation establish only international jurisdiction, that is to say, they designate the Member State the courts of which may open insolvency proceedings. Territorial jurisdiction within that Member State must be established by the national law of the Member State concerned.

(16) The court having jurisdiction to open the main insolvency proceedings should be enabled to order provisional and protective measures from the time of the request to open proceedings. Preservation measures both prior to and after the commencement of the insolvency proceedings are very important to guarantee the effectiveness of the insolvency proceedings. In that connection this Regulation should afford different possibilities. On the one hand, the court competent for the main insolvency proceedings should be able also to order provisional protective measures covering assets situated in the territory of other Member States. On the other hand, a liquidator temporarily appointed prior to the opening of the main insolvency proceedings should be able, in the Member States in which an establishment belonging to the debtor is to be found, to apply for the preservation measures which are possible under the law of those States.

(17) Prior to the opening of the main insolvency proceedings, the right to request the opening of insolvency proceedings in the Member State where the debtor has an establishment should be limited to local creditors and creditors of the local establishment or to cases where main proceedings cannot be opened under the law of the Member State where the debtor has the centre of his main interest. The reason for this restriction is that cases where territorial insolvency proceedings are requested before the main insolvency proceedings are intended to be limited to what is absolutely necessary. If the main insolvency proceedings are opened, the territorial proceedings become secondary.

(18) Following the opening of the main insolvency proceedings, the right to request the opening of insolvency proceedings in a Member State where the debtor has an establishment is not restricted by this Regulation. The liquidator in the main proceedings or any other person empowered under the national law of that Member State may request the opening of secondary insolvency proceedings.

(19) Secondary insolvency proceedings may serve different purposes, besides the protection of local interests. Cases may arise where the estate of the debtor is too complex to administer as a unit or where differences in the legal systems concerned are so great that difficulties may arise from the extension of effects deriving from the law of the State of the opening to the other States where the assets are located. For this reason the liquidator in the main proceedings may request the opening of secondary proceedings when the efficient administration of the estate so requires.

(20) Main insolvency proceedings and secondary proceedings can, however, contribute to the effective realisation of the total assets only if all the concurrent proceedings pending are coordinated. The main condition here is that the various liquidators must cooperate closely, in particular by exchanging a sufficient amount of information. In

order to ensure the dominant role of the main insolvency proceedings, the liquidator in such proceedings should be given several possibilities for intervening in secondary insolvency proceedings which are pending at the same time. For example, he should be able to propose a restructuring plan or composition or apply for realisation of the assets in the secondary insolvency proceedings to be suspended.

(21) Every creditor, who has his habitual residence, domicile or registered office in the Community, should have the right to lodge his claims in each of the insolvency proceedings pending in the Community relating to the debtor's assets. This should also apply to tax authorities and social insurance institutions. However, in order to ensure equal treatment of creditors, the distribution of proceeds must be coordinated. Every creditor should be able to keep what he has received in the course of insolvency proceedings but should be entitled only to participate in the distribution of total assets in other proceedings if creditors with the same standing have obtained the same proportion of their claims.

(22) This Regulation should provide for immediate recognition of judgments concerning the opening, conduct and closure of insolvency proceedings which come within its scope and of judgments handed down in direct connection with such insolvency proceedings. Automatic recognition should therefore mean that the effects attributed to the proceedings by the law of the State in which the proceedings were opened extend to all other Member States. Recognition of judgments delivered by the courts of the Member States should be based on the principle of mutual trust. To that end, grounds for non-recognition should be reduced to the minimum necessary. This is also the basis on which any dispute should be resolved where the courts of two Member States both claim competence to open the main insolvency proceedings. The decision of the first court to open proceedings should be recognised in the other Member States without those Member States having the power to scrutinise the court's decision.

(23) This Regulation should set out, for the matters covered by it, uniform rules on conflict of laws which replace, within their scope of application, national rules of private international law. Unless otherwise stated, the law of the Member State of the opening of the proceedings should be applicable (lex concursus). This rule on conflict of laws should be valid both for the main proceedings and for local proceedings; the lex concursus determines all the effects of the insolvency proceedings, both procedural and substantive, on the persons and legal relations concerned. It governs all the conditions for the opening, conduct and closure of the insolvency proceedings.

(24) Automatic recognition of insolvency proceedings to which the law of the opening State normally applies may interfere with the rules under which transactions are carried out in other Member States. To protect legitimate expectations and the certainty of transactions in Member States other than that in which proceedings are opened, provisions should be made for a number of exceptions to the general rule.

(25) There is a particular need for a special reference diverging from the law of the opening State in the case of rights in rem, since these are of considerable importance for the granting of credit. The basis, validity and extent of such a right in rem should therefore normally be determined according to the lex situs and not be affected by the opening of insolvency proceedings. The proprietor of the right in rem should therefore be able to continue to assert his right to segregation or separate settlement of the collateral security. Where assets are subject to rights in rem under the lex situs in one Member State but the main proceedings are being carried out in another Member State, the liquidator in the main proceedings should be able to request the opening of secondary proceedings in the jurisdiction where the rights in rem arise if the debtor has an establish-

ment there. If a secondary proceeding is not opened, the surplus on sale of the asset covered by rights in rem must be paid to the liquidator in the main proceedings.

(26) If a set-off is not permitted under the law of the opening State, a creditor should nevertheless be entitled to the set-off if it is possible under the law applicable to the claim of the insolvent debtor. In this way, set-off will acquire a kind of guarantee function based on legal provisions on which the creditor concerned can rely at the time when the claim arises.

(27) There is also a need for special protection in the case of payment systems and financial markets. This applies for example to the position-closing agreements and netting agreements to be found in such systems as well as to the sale of securities and to the guarantees provided for such transactions as governed in particular by Directive 98/26/EC of the European Parliament and of the Council of 19 May 1998 on settlement finality in payment and securities settlement systems[5]. For such transactions, the only law which is material should thus be that applicable to the system or market concerned. This provision is intended to prevent the possibility of mechanisms for the payment and settlement of transactions provided for in the payment and set-off systems or on the regulated financial markets of the Member States being altered in the case of insolvency of a business partner. Directive 98/26/EC contains special provisions which should take precedence over the general rules in this Regulation.

(28) In order to protect employees and jobs, the effects of insolvency proceedings on the continuation or termination of employment and on the rights and obligations of all parties to such employment must be determined by the law applicable to the agreement in accordance with the general rules on conflict of law. Any other insolvency-law questions, such as whether the employees' claims are protected by preferential rights and what status such preferential rights may have, should be determined by the law of the opening State.

(29) For business considerations, the main content of the decision opening the proceedings should be published in the other Member States at the request of the liquidator. If there is an establishment in the Member State concerned, there may be a requirement that publication is compulsory. In neither case, however, should publication be a prior condition for recognition of the foreign proceedings.

(30) It may be the case that some of the persons concerned are not in fact aware that proceedings have been opened and act in good faith in a way that conflicts with the new situation. In order to protect such persons who make a payment to the debtor because they are unaware that foreign proceedings have been opened when they should in fact have made the payment to the foreign liquidator, it should be provided that such a payment is to have a debt-discharging effect.

(31) This Regulation should include Annexes relating to the organisation of insolvency proceedings. As these Annexes relate exclusively to the legislation of Member States, there are specific and substantiated reasons for the Council to reserve the right to amend these Annexes in order to take account of any amendments to the domestic law of the Member States.

(32) The United Kingdom and Ireland, in accordance with Article 3 of the Protocol on the position of the United Kingdom and Ireland annexed to the Treaty on European Union and the Treaty establishing the European Community, have given notice of their wish to take part in the adoption and application of this Regulation.

---

[5] OJ L 166, 11.6.1998, p. 45.

(33) Denmark, in accordance with Articles 1 and 2 of the Protocol on the position of Denmark annexed to the Treaty on European Union and the Treaty establishing the European Community, is not participating in the adoption of this Regulation, and is therefore not bound by it nor subject to its application,

HAS ADOPTED THIS REGULATION:

CHAPTER I

GENERAL PROVISIONS

Article 1

Scope

1. This Regulation shall apply to collective insolvency proceedings which entail the partial or total divestment of a debtor and the appointment of a liquidator.

2. This Regulation shall not apply to insolvency proceedings concerning insurance undertakings, credit institutions, investment undertakings which provide services involving the holding of funds or securities for third parties, or to collective investment undertakings.

Article 2

Definitions

For the purposes of this Regulation:

(a) "insolvency proceedings" shall mean the collective proceedings referred to in Article 1 (1). These proceedings are listed in Annex A;

(b) "liquidator" shall mean any person or body whose function is to administer or liquidate assets of which the debtor has been divested or to supervise the administration of his affairs. Those persons and bodies are listed in Annex C;

(c) "winding-up proceedings" shall mean insolvency proceedings within the meaning of point (a) involving realising the assets of the debtor, including where the proceedings have been closed by a composition or other measure terminating the insolvency, or closed by reason of the insufficiency of the assets. Those proceedings are listed in Annex B;

(d) "court" shall mean the judicial body or any other competent body of a Member State empowered to open insolvency proceedings or to take decisions in the course of such proceedings;

(e) "judgment" in relation to the opening of insolvency proceedings or the appointment of a liquidator shall include the decision of any court empowered to open such proceedings or to appoint a liquidator;

(f) "the time of the opening of proceedings" shall mean the time at which the judgment opening proceedings becomes effective, whether it is a final judgment or not;

(g) "the Member State in which assets are situated" shall mean, in the case of:

- tangible property, the Member State within the territory of which the property is situated,

- property and rights ownership of or entitlement to which must be entered in a public register, the Member State under the authority of which the register is kept,
- claims, the Member State within the territory of which the third party required to meet them has the centre of his main interests, as determined in Article 3 (1);

(h) "establishment" shall mean any place of operations where the debtor carries out a non-transitory economic activity with human means and goods.

Article 3

International jurisdiction

1. The courts of the Member State within the territory of which the centre of a debtor's main interests is situated shall have jurisdiction to open insolvency proceedings. In the case of a company or legal person, the place of the registered office shall be presumed to be the centre of its main interests in the absence of proof to the contrary.

2. Where the centre of a debtor's main interests is situated within the territory of a Member State, the courts of another Member State shall have jurisdiction to open insolvency proceedings against that debtor only if he possesses an establishment within the territory of that other Member State. The effects of those proceedings shall be restricted to the assets of the debtor situated in the territory of the latter Member State.

3. Where insolvency proceedings have been opened under paragraph 1, any proceedings opened subsequently under paragraph 2 shall be secondary proceedings. These latter proceedings must be winding-up proceedings.

4. Territorial insolvency proceedings referred to in paragraph 2 may be opened prior to the opening of main insolvency proceedings in accordance with paragraph 1 only:

(a) where insolvency proceedings under paragraph 1 cannot be opened because of the conditions laid down by the law of the Member State within the territory of which the centre of the debtor's main interests is situated; or

(b) where the opening of territorial insolvency proceedings is requested by a creditor who has his domicile, habitual residence or registered office in the Member State within the territory of which the establishment is situated, or whose claim arises from the operation of that establishment.

Article 4

Law applicable

1. Save as otherwise provided in this Regulation, the law applicable to insolvency proceedings and their effects shall be that of the Member State within the territory of which such proceedings are opened, hereafter referred to as the "State of the opening of proceedings".

2. The law of the State of the opening of proceedings shall determine the conditions for the opening of those proceedings, their conduct and their closure. It shall determine in particular:

(a) against which debtors insolvency proceedings may be brought on account of their capacity;

(b) the assets which form part of the estate and the treatment of assets acquired by or devolving on the debtor after the opening of the insolvency proceedings;

(c) the respective powers of the debtor and the liquidator;

(d) the conditions under which set-offs may be invoked;

(e) the effects of insolvency proceedings on current contracts to which the debtor is party;

(f) the effects of the insolvency proceedings on proceedings brought by individual creditors, with the exception of lawsuits pending;

(g) the claims which are to be lodged against the debtor's estate and the treatment of claims arising after the opening of insolvency proceedings;

(h) the rules governing the lodging, verification and admission of claims;

(i) the rules governing the distribution of proceeds from the realisation of assets, the ranking of claims and the rights of creditors who have obtained partial satisfaction after the opening of insolvency proceedings by virtue of a right in rem or through a set-off;

(j) the conditions for and the effects of closure of insolvency proceedings, in particular by composition;

(k) creditors' rights after the closure of insolvency proceedings;

(l) who is to bear the costs and expenses incurred in the insolvency proceedings;

(m) the rules relating to the voidness, voidability or unenforceability of legal acts detrimental to all the creditors.

Article 5

Third parties' rights in rem

1. The opening of insolvency proceedings shall not affect the rights in rem of creditors or third parties in respect of tangible or intangible, moveable or immoveable assets – both specific assets and collections of indefinite assets as a whole which change from time to time – belonging to the debtor which are situated within the territory of another Member State at the time of the opening of proceedings.

2. The rights referred to in paragraph 1 shall in particular mean:

(a) the right to dispose of assets or have them disposed of and to obtain satisfaction from the proceeds of or income from those assets, in particular by virtue of a lien or a mortgage;

(b) the exclusive right to have a claim met, in particular a right guaranteed by a lien in respect of the claim or by assignment of the claim by way of a guarantee;

(c) the right to demand the assets from, and/or to require restitution by, anyone having possession or use of them contrary to the wishes of the party so entitled;

(d) a right in rem to the beneficial use of assets.

3. The right, recorded in a public register and enforceable against third parties, under which a right in rem within the meaning of paragraph 1 may be obtained, shall be considered a right in rem.

4. Paragraph 1 shall not preclude actions for voidness, voidability or unenforceability as referred to in Article 4 (2) (m).

Article 6

Set-off

1. The opening of insolvency proceedings shall not affect the right of creditors to demand the set-off of their claims against the claims of the debtor, where such a set-off is permitted by the law applicable to the insolvent debtor's claim.

2. Paragraph 1 shall not preclude actions for voidness, voidability or unenforceability as referred to in Article 4 (2) (m).

Article 7

Reservation of title

1. The opening of insolvency proceedings against the purchaser of an asset shall not affect the seller's rights based on a reservation of title where at the time of the opening of proceedings the asset is situated within the territory of a Member State other than the State of opening of proceedings.

2. The opening of insolvency proceedings against the seller of an asset, after delivery of the asset, shall not constitute grounds for rescinding or terminating the sale and shall not prevent the purchaser from acquiring title where at the time of the opening of proceedings the asset sold is situated within the territory of a Member State other than the State of the opening of proceedings.

3. Paragraphs 1 and 2 shall not preclude actions for voidness, voidability or unenforceability as referred to in Article 4 (2) (m).

Article 8

Contracts relating to immoveable property

The effects of insolvency proceedings on a contract conferring the right to acquire or make use of immoveable property shall be governed solely by the law of the Member State within the territory of which the immoveable property is situated.

Article 9

Payment systems and financial markets

1. Without prejudice to Article 5, the effects of insolvency proceedings on the rights and obligations of the parties to a payment or settlement system or to a financial market shall be governed solely by the law of the Member State applicable to that system or market.

2. Paragraph 1 shall not preclude any action for voidness, voidability or unenforceability which may be taken to set aside payments or transactions under the law applicable to the relevant payment system or financial market.

Article 10

Contracts of employment

The effects of insolvency proceedings on employment contracts and relationships shall be governed solely by the law of the Member State applicable to the contract of employment.

Article 11

Effects on rights subject to registration

The effects of insolvency proceedings on the rights of the debtor in immoveable property, a ship or an aircraft subject to registration in a public register shall be determined by the law of the Member State under the authority of which the register is kept.

Article 12

Community patents and trade marks

For the purposes of this Regulation, a Community patent, a Community trade mark or any other similar right established by Community law may be included only in the proceedings referred to in Article 3 (1).

Article 13

Detrimental acts

Article 4 (2) (m) shall not apply where the person who benefited from an act detrimental to all the creditors provides proof that:

- the said act is subject to the law of a Member State other than that of the State of the opening of proceedings, and
- that law does not allow any means of challenging that act in the relevant case.

Article 14

Protection of third-party purchasers

Where, by an act concluded after the opening of insolvency proceedings, the debtor disposes, for consideration, of:

- an immoveable asset, or
- a ship or an aircraft subject to registration in a public register, or
- securities whose existence presupposes registration in a register laid down by law,

the validity of that act shall be governed by the law of the State within the territory of which the immoveable asset is situated or under the authority of which the register is kept.

Article 15

Effects of insolvency proceedings on lawsuits pending

The effects of insolvency proceedings on a lawsuit pending concerning an asset or a right of which the debtor has been divested shall be governed solely by the law of the Member State in which that lawsuit is pending.

CHAPTER II

RECOGNITION OF INSOLVENCY PROCEEDINGS

Article 16

Principle

1. Any judgment opening insolvency proceedings handed down by a court of a Member State which has jurisdiction pursuant to Article 3 shall be recognised in all the other Member States from the time that it becomes effective in the State of the opening of proceedings.

This rule shall also apply where, on account of his capacity, insolvency proceedings cannot be brought against the debtor in other Member States.

2. Recognition of the proceedings referred to in Article 3 (1) shall not preclude the opening of the proceedings referred to in Article 3 (2) by a court in another Member State. The latter proceedings shall be secondary insolvency proceedings within the meaning of Chapter III.

Article 17

Effects of recognition

1. The judgment opening the proceedings referred to in Article 3 (1) shall, with no further formalities, produce the same effects in any other Member State as under this law of the State of the opening of proceedings, unless this Regulation provides otherwise and as long as no proceedings referred to in Article 3 (2) are opened in that other Member State.

2. The effects of the proceedings referred to in Article 3 (2) may not be challenged in other Member States. Any restriction of the creditors' rights, in particular a stay or discharge, shall produce effects vis-à-vis assets situated within the territory of another Member State only in the case of those creditors who have given their consent.

Article 18

Powers of the liquidator

1. The liquidator appointed by a court which has jurisdiction pursuant to Article 3 (1) may exercise all the powers conferred on him by the law of the State of the opening of proceedings in another Member State, as long as no other insolvency proceedings have

been opened there nor any preservation measure to the contrary has been taken there further to a request for the opening of insolvency proceedings in that State. He may in particular remove the debtor's assets from the territory of the Member State in which they are situated, subject to Articles 5 and 7.

2. The liquidator appointed by a court which has jurisdiction pursuant to Article 3 (2) may in any other Member State claim through the courts or out of court that moveable property was removed from the territory of the State of the opening of proceedings to the territory of that other Member State after the opening of the insolvency proceedings. He may also bring any action to set aside which is in the interests of the creditors.

3. In exercising his powers, the liquidator shall comply with the law of the Member State within the territory of which he intends to take action, in particular with regard to procedures for the realisation of assets. Those powers may not include coercive measures or the right to rule on legal proceedings or disputes.

Article 19

Proof of the liquidator's appointment

The liquidator's appointment shall be evidenced by a certified copy of the original decision appointing him or by any other certificate issued by the court which has jurisdiction.

A translation into the official language or one of the official languages of the Member State within the territory of which he intends to act may be required. No legalisation or other similar formality shall be required.

Article 20

Return and imputation

1. A creditor who, after the opening of the proceedings referred to in Article 3 (1) obtains by any means, in particular through enforcement, total or partial satisfaction of his claim on the assets belonging to the debtor situated within the territory of another Member State, shall return what he has obtained to the liquidator, subject to Articles 5 and 7.

2. In order to ensure equal treatment of creditors a creditor who has, in the course of insolvency proceedings, obtained a dividend on his claim shall share in distributions made in other proceedings only where creditors of the same ranking or category have, in those other proceedings, obtained an equivalent dividend.

Article 21

Publication

1. The liquidator may request that notice of the judgment opening insolvency proceedings and, where appropriate, the decision appointing him, be published in any other Member State in accordance with the publication procedures provided for in that State. Such publication shall also specify the liquidator appointed and whether the jurisdiction rule applied is that pursuant to Article 3 (1) or Article 3 (2).

2. However, any Member State within the territory of which the debtor has an establishment may require mandatory publication. In such cases, the liquidator or any authority empowered to that effect in the Member State where the proceedings referred to in Article 3 (1) are opened shall take all necessary measures to ensure such publication.

Article 22

Registration in a public register

1. The liquidator may request that the judgment opening the proceedings referred to in Article 3 (1) be registered in the land register, the trade register and any other public register kept in the other Member States.

2. However, any Member State may require mandatory registration. In such cases, the liquidator or any authority empowered to that effect in the Member State where the proceedings referred to in Article 3 (1) have been opened shall take all necessary measures to ensure such registration.

Article 23

Costs

The costs of the publication and registration provided for in Articles 21 and 22 shall be regarded as costs and expenses incurred in the proceedings.

Article 24

Honouring of an obligation to a debtor

1. Where an obligation has been honoured in a Member State for the benefit of a debtor who is subject to insolvency proceedings opened in another Member State, when it should have been honoured for the benefit of the liquidator in those proceedings, the person honouring the obligation shall be deemed to have discharged it if he was unaware of the opening of proceedings.

2. Where such an obligation is honoured before the publication provided for in Article 21 has been effected, the person honouring the obligation shall be presumed, in the absence of proof to the contrary, to have been unaware of the opening of insolvency proceedings; where the obligation is honoured after such publication has been effected, the person honouring the obligation shall be presumed, in the absence of proof to the contrary, to have been aware of the opening of proceedings.

Article 25

Recognition and enforceability of other judgments

1. Judgments handed down by a court whose judgment concerning the opening of proceedings is recognised in accordance with Article 16 and which concern the course and closure of insolvency proceedings, and compositions approved by that court shall also be recognised with no further formalities. Such judgments shall be enforced in

accordance with Articles 31 to 51, with the exception of Article 34 (2), of the Brussels Convention on Jurisdiction and the Enforcement of Judgments in Civil and Commercial Matters, as amended by the Conventions of Accession to this Convention.

The first subparagraph shall also apply to judgments deriving directly from the insolvency proceedings and which are closely linked with them, even if they were handed down by another court.

The first subparagraph shall also apply to judgments relating to preservation measures taken after the request for the opening of insolvency proceedings.

2. The recognition and enforcement of judgments other than those referred to in paragraph 1 shall be governed by the Convention referred to in paragraph 1, provided that that Convention is applicable.

3. The Member States shall not be obliged to recognise or enforce a judgment referred to in paragraph 1 which might result in a limitation of personal freedom or postal secrecy.

Article 26[6]

Public policy

Any Member State may refuse to recognise insolvency proceedings opened in another Member State or to enforce a judgment handed down in the context of such proceedings where the effects of such recognition or enforcement would be manifestly contrary to that State's public policy, in particular its fundamental principles or the constitutional rights and liberties of the individual.

CHAPTER III

SECONDARY INSOLVENCY PROCEEDINGS

Article 27

Opening of proceedings

The opening of the proceedings referred to in Article 3 (1) by a court of a Member State and which is recognised in another Member State (main proceedings) shall permit the opening in that other Member State, a court of which has jurisdiction pursuant to Article 3 (2), of secondary insolvency proceedings without the debtor's insolvency being examined in that other State. These latter proceedings must be among the proceedings listed in Annex B. Their effects shall be restricted to the assets of the debtor situated within the territory of that other Member State.

[6] Note the Declaration by Portugal concerning the application of Articles 26 and 37 (OJ C 183, 30.6.2000, p. 1).

Article 28

Applicable law

Save as otherwise provided in this Regulation, the law applicable to secondary proceedings shall be that of the Member State within the territory of which the secondary proceedings are opened.

Article 29

Right to request the opening of proceedings

The opening of secondary proceedings may be requested by:

(a) the liquidator in the main proceedings;

(b) any other person or authority empowered to request the opening of insolvency proceedings under the law of the Member State within the territory of which the opening of secondary proceedings is requested.

Article 30

Advance payment of costs and expenses

Where the law of the Member State in which the opening of secondary proceedings is requested requires that the debtor's assets be sufficient to cover in whole or in part the costs and expenses of the proceedings, the court may, when it receives such a request, require the applicant to make an advance payment of costs or to provide appropriate security.

Article 31

Duty to cooperate and communicate information

1. Subject to the rules restricting the communication of information, the liquidator in the main proceedings and the liquidators in the secondary proceedings shall be duty bound to communicate information to each other. They shall immediately communicate any information which may be relevant to the other proceedings, in particular the progress made in lodging and verifying claims and all measures aimed at terminating the proceedings.

2. Subject to the rules applicable to each of the proceedings, the liquidator in the main proceedings and the liquidators in the secondary proceedings shall be duty bound to cooperate with each other.

3. The liquidator in the secondary proceedings shall give the liquidator in the main proceedings an early opportunity of submitting proposals on the liquidation or use of the assets in the secondary proceedings.

Article 32

Exercise of creditors' rights

1. Any creditor may lodge his claim in the main proceedings and in any secondary proceedings.

2. The liquidators in the main and any secondary proceedings shall lodge in other proceedings claims which have already been lodged in the proceedings for which they were appointed, provided that the interests of creditors in the latter proceedings are served thereby, subject to the right of creditors to oppose that or to withdraw the lodgement of their claims where the law applicable so provides.

3. The liquidator in the main or secondary proceedings shall be empowered to participate in other proceedings on the same basis as a creditor, in particular by attending creditors' meetings.

Article 33

Stay of liquidation

1. The court, which opened the secondary proceedings, shall stay the process of liquidation in whole or in part on receipt of a request from the liquidator in the main proceedings, provided that in that event it may require the liquidator in the main proceedings to take any suitable measure to guarantee the interests of the creditors in the secondary proceedings and of individual classes of creditors. Such a request from the liquidator may be rejected only if it is manifestly of no interest to the creditors in the main proceedings. Such a stay of the process of liquidation may be ordered for up to three months. It may be continued or renewed for similar periods.

2. The court referred to in paragraph 1 shall terminate the stay of the process of liquidation:

- at the request of the liquidator in the main proceedings,
- of its own motion, at the request of a creditor or at the request of the liquidator in the secondary proceedings if that measure no longer appears justified, in particular, by the interests of creditors in the main proceedings or in the secondary proceedings.

Article 34

Measures ending secondary insolvency proceedings

1. Where the law applicable to secondary proceedings allows for such proceedings to be closed without liquidation by a rescue plan, a composition or a comparable measure, the liquidator in the main proceedings shall be empowered to propose such a measure himself.

Closure of the secondary proceedings by a measure referred to in the first subparagraph shall not become final without the consent of the liquidator in the main proceedings; failing his agreement, however, it may become final if the financial interests of the creditors in the main proceedings are not affected by the measure proposed.

2. Any restriction of creditors' rights arising from a measure referred to in paragraph 1 which is proposed in secondary proceedings, such as a stay of payment or

discharge of debt, may not have effect in respect of the debtor's assets not covered by those proceedings without the consent of all the creditors having an interest.

3. During a stay of the process of liquidation ordered pursuant to Article 33, only the liquidator in the main proceedings or the debtor, with the former's consent, may propose measures laid down in paragraph 1 of this Article in the secondary proceedings; no other proposal for such a measure shall be put to the vote or approved.

Article 35

Assets remaining in the secondary proceedings

If by the liquidation of assets in the secondary proceedings it is possible to meet all claims allowed under those proceedings, the liquidator appointed in those proceedings shall immediately transfer any assets remaining to the liquidator in the main proceedings.

Article 36

Subsequent opening of the main proceedings

Where the proceedings referred to in Article 3 (1) are opened following the opening of the proceedings referred to in Article 3 (2) in another Member State, Articles 31 to 35 shall apply to those opened first, in so far as the progress of those proceedings so permits.

Article 37[7]

Conversion of earlier proceedings

The liquidator in the main proceedings may request that proceedings listed in Annex A previously opened in another Member State be converted into winding-up proceedings if this proves to be in the interests of the creditors in the main proceedings.

The court with jurisdiction under Article 3 (2) shall order conversion into one of the proceedings listed in Annex B.

Article 38

Preservation measures

Where the court of a Member State which has jurisdiction pursuant to Article 3 (1) appoints a temporary administrator in order to ensure the preservation of the debtor's assets, that temporary administrator shall be empowered to request any measures to secure and preserve any of the debtor's assets situated in another Member State, provided for under the law of that State, for the period between the request for the opening of insolvency proceedings and the judgment opening the proceedings.

---

[7] Note the Declaration by Portugal concerning the application of Articles 26 and 37 (OJ C 183, 30.6.2000, p. 1).

CHAPTER IV

PROVISION OF INFORMATION FOR CREDITORS AND LODGEMENT OF THEIR CLAIMS

Article 39

Right to lodge claims

Any creditor who has his habitual residence, domicile or registered office in a Member State other than the State of the opening of proceedings, including the tax authorities and social security authorities of Member States, shall have the right to lodge claims in the insolvency proceedings in writing.

Article 40

Duty to inform creditors

1. As soon as insolvency proceedings are opened in a Member State, the court of that State having jurisdiction or the liquidator appointed by it shall immediately inform known creditors who have their habitual residences, domiciles or registered offices in the other Member States.

2. That information, provided by an individual notice, shall in particular include time limits, the penalties laid down in regard to those time limits, the body or authority empowered to accept the lodgement of claims and the other measures laid down. Such notice shall also indicate whether creditors whose claims are preferential or secured in rem need lodge their claims.

Article 41

Content of the lodgement of a claim

A creditor shall send copies of supporting documents, if any, and shall indicate the nature of the claim, the date on which it arose and its amount, as well as whether he alleges preference, security in rem or a reservation of title in respect of the claim and what assets are covered by the guarantee he is invoking.

Article 42

Languages

1. The information provided for in Article 40 shall be provided in the official language or one of the official languages of the State of the opening of proceedings. For that purpose a form shall be used bearing the heading "Invitation to lodge a claim. Time limits to be observed" in all the official languages of the institutions of the European Union.

2. Any creditor who has his habitual residence, domicile or registered office in a Member State other than the State of the opening of proceedings may lodge his claim in the official language or one of the official languages of that other State. In that event,

however, the lodgement of his claim shall bear the heading "Lodgement of claim" in the official language or one of the official languages of the State of the opening of proceedings. In addition, he may be required to provide a translation into the official language or one of the official languages of the State of the opening of proceedings.

CHAPTER V

TRANSITIONAL AND FINAL PROVISIONS

Article 43

Applicability in time

The provisions of this Regulation shall apply only to insolvency proceedings opened after its entry into force. Acts done by a debtor before the entry into force of this Regulation shall continue to be governed by the law which was applicable to them at the time they were done.

Article 44

Relationship to Conventions

1. After its entry into force, this Regulation replaces, in respect of the matters referred to therein, in the relations between Member States, the Conventions concluded between two or more Member States, in particular:

(a) the Convention between Belgium and France on Jurisdiction and the Validity and Enforcement of Judgments, Arbitration Awards and Authentic Instruments, signed at Paris on 8 July 1899;

(b) the Convention between Belgium and Austria on Bankruptcy, Winding-up, Arrangements, Compositions and Suspension of Payments (with Additional Protocol of 13 June 1973), signed at Brussels on 16 July 1969;

(c) the Convention between Belgium and the Netherlands on Territorial Jurisdiction, Bankruptcy and the Validity and Enforcement of Judgments, Arbitration Awards and Authentic Instruments, signed at Brussels on 28 March 1925;

(d) the Treaty between Germany and Austria on Bankruptcy, Winding-up, Arrangements and Compositions, signed at Vienna on 25 May 1979;

(e) the Convention between France and Austria on Jurisdiction, Recognition and Enforcement of Judgments on Bankruptcy, signed at Vienna on 27 February 1979;

(f) the Convention between France and Italy on the Enforcement of Judgments in Civil and Commercial Matters, signed at Rome on 3 June 1930;

(g) the Convention between Italy and Austria on Bankruptcy, Winding-up, Arrangements and Compositions, signed at Rome on 12 July 1977;

(h) the Convention between the Kingdom of the Netherlands and the Federal Republic of Germany on the Mutual Recognition and Enforcement of Judgments and other Enforceable Instruments in Civil and Commercial Matters, signed at The Hague on 30 August 1962;

(i) the Convention between the United Kingdom and the Kingdom of Belgium providing for the Reciprocal Enforcement of Judgments in Civil and Commercial Matters, with Protocol, signed at Brussels on 2 May 1934;

(j) the Convention between Denmark, Finland, Norway, Sweden and Iceland on Bankruptcy, signed at Copenhagen on 7 November 1933;

(k) the European Convention on Certain International Aspects of Bankruptcy, signed at Istanbul on 5 June 1990.

2. The Conventions referred to in paragraph 1 shall continue to have effect with regard to proceedings opened before the entry into force of this Regulation.

3. This Regulation shall not apply:

(a) in any Member State, to the extent that it is irreconcilable with the obligations arising in relation to bankruptcy from a convention concluded by that State with one or more third countries before the entry into force of this Regulation;

(b) in the United Kingdom of Great Britain and Northern Ireland, to the extent that is irreconcilable with the obligations arising in relation to bankruptcy and the winding-up of insolvent companies from any arrangements with the Commonwealth existing at the time this Regulation enters into force.

Article 45

Amendment of the Annexes

The Council, acting by qualified majority on the initiative of one of its members or on a proposal from the Commission, may amend the Annexes.

Article 46

Reports

No later than 1 June 2012, and every five years thereafter, the Commission shall present to the European Parliament, the Council and the Economic and Social Committee a report on the application of this Regulation. The report shall be accompanied if need be by a proposal for adaptation of this Regulation.

Article 47

Entry into force

This Regulation shall enter into force on 31 May 2002.

This Regulation shall be binding in its entirety and directly applicable in the Member States in accordance with the Treaty establishing the European Community.

ANNEX A

Insolvency proceedings referred to in Article 2(a)

BELGIË-/BELGIQUE
- Het faillissement//La faillite
- Het gerechtelijk akkoord//Le concordat judiciaire
- De collectieve schuldenregeling//Le règlement collectif de dettes

DEUTSCHLAND
- Das Konkursverfahren
- Das gerichtliche Vergleichsverfahren
- Das Gesamtvollstreckungsverfahren
- Das Insolvenzverfahren

ΕΛΛΑΣ
- Πτώχευση
- Η ειδική εκκαθάριση
- Η προσωρινή διαχείριση εταιρίας. Η διοίκηση και η διαχείριση των πιστωτών
- Η υπαγωγή επιχείρησης υπό επίτροπο με σκοπό τη σύναψη συμβιβασμού με τους πιστωτές

ESPAÑA
- Concurso de acreedores
- Quiebra
- Suspensión de pagos

FRANCE
- Liquidation judiciaire
- Redressement judiciaire avec nomination d'un administrateur

IRELAND
- Compulsory winding up by the court
- Bankruptcy
- The administration in bankruptcy of the estate of persons dying insolvent
- Winding-up in bankruptcy of partnerships
- Creditors' voluntary winding up (with confirmation of a Court)
- Arrangements under the control of the court which involve the vesting of all or part of the property of the debtor in the Official Assignee for realisation and distribution
- Company examinership

ITALIA
- Fallimento
- Concordato preventivo
- Liquidazione coatta amministrativa
- Amministrazione straordinaria
- Amministrazione controllata

LUXEMBOURG
- Faillite
- Gestion contrôlée

- Concordat préventif de faillite (par abandon d'actif)
- Régime spécial de liquidation du notariat

NEDERLAND
- Het faillissement
- De surséance van betaling
- De schuldsaneringsregeling natuurlijke personen

ÖSTERREICH
- Das Konkursverfahren
- Das Ausgleichsverfahren

PORTUGAL
- O processo de falência
- Os processos especiais de recuperação de empresa, ou seja:
- A concordata
- A reconstituição empresarial
- A reestruturação financeira
- A gestão controlada

SUOMI-/FINLAND
- Konkurssi//konkurs
- Yrityssaneeraus//företagssanering

SVERIGE
- Konkurs
- Företagsrekonstruktion

UNITED KINGDOM
- Winding up by or subject to the supervision of the court
- Creditors' voluntary winding up (with confirmation by the court)
- Administration
- Voluntary arrangements under insolvency legislation
- Bankruptcy or sequestration

ANNEX B

Winding up proceedings referred to in Article 2(c)

BELGIË-/BELGIQUE
- Het faillissement//La faillite

DEUTSCHLAND
- Das Konkursverfahren
- Das Gesamtvollstreckungsverfahren
- Das Insolvenzverfahren

ΕΛΛΑΣ
- Πτώχευση
- Η ειδική εκκαθάριση

ESPAÑA
- Concurso de acreedores
- Quiebra
- Suspensión de pagos basada en la insolvencia definitiva

FRANCE
- Liquidation judiciaire

IRELAND
- Compulsory winding up
- Bankruptcy
- The administration in bankruptcy of the estate of persons dying insolvent
- Winding-up in bankruptcy of partnerships
- Creditors' voluntary winding up (with confirmation of a court)
- Arrangements under the control of the court which involve the vesting of all or part of the property of the debtor in the Official Assignee for realisation and distribution

ITALIA
- Fallimento
- Liquidazione coatta amministrativa

LUXEMBOURG
- Faillite
- Régime spécial de liquidation du notariat

NEDERLAND
- Het faillissement
- De schuldsaneringsregeling natuurlijke personen

ÖSTERREICH
- Das Konkursverfahren

PORTUGAL
- O processo de falência

SUOMI-/FINLAND
- Konkurssi//konkurs

SVERIGE
- Konkurs

UNITED KINGDOM
- Winding up by or subject to the supervision of the court
- Creditors' voluntary winding up (with confirmation by the court)
- Bankruptcy or sequestration

ANNEX C

Liquidators referred to in Article 2(b)

BELGIË-/BELGIQUE
- De curator//Le curateur
- De commissaris inzake opschorting//Le commissaire au sursis
- De schuldbemiddelaar//Le médiateur de dettes

DEUTSCHLAND
- Konkursverwalter
- Vergleichsverwalter
- Sachwalter (nach der Vergleichsordnung)
- Verwalter
- Insolvenzverwalter
- Sachwalter (nach der Insolvenzordnung)
- Treuhänder
- Vorläufiger Insolvenzverwalter

ΕΛΛΑΣ
- Ο σύνδικος
- Ο προσωριός διαχειριστής. Η διοικούσα επιτροπή των πιστωτών
- Ο ειδικός εκκαθαριστής
- Ο επίτροπος

ESPAÑA
- Depositario-administrador
- Interventor o Interventores
- Síndicos
- Comisario

FRANCE
- Représentant des créanciers
- Mandataire liquidateur
- Administrateur judiciaire
- Commissaire à l'exécution de plan

IRELAND
- Liquidator
- Official Assignee
- Trustee in bankruptcy
- Provisional Liquidator
- Examiner

ITALIA
- Curatore
- Commissario

LUXEMBOURG
- Le curateur

- Le commissaire
- Le liquidateur
- Le conseil de gérance de la section d'assainissement du notariat

NEDERLAND
- De curator in het faillissement
- De bewindvoerder in de surséance van betaling
- De bewindvoerder in de schuldsaneringsregeling natuurlijke personen

ÖSTERREICH
- Masseverwalter
- Ausgleichsverwalter
- Sachwalter
- Treuhänder
- Besondere Verwalter
- Vorläufiger Verwalter
- Konkursgericht

PORTUGAL
- Gestor judicial
- Liquidatário judicial
- Comissão de credores

SUOMI-/FINLAND
- Pesänhoitaja//boförvaltare
- Selvittäjä//utredare

SVERIGE
- Förvaltare
- God man
- Rekonstruktör

UNITED KINGDOM
- Liquidator
- Supervisor of a voluntary arrangement
- Administrator
- Official Receiver
- Trustee
- Judicial factor

Model Law on Cross-Border Insolvency of the United Nations Commission on International Trade Law *

The General Assembly,

Recalling its resolution 2205 (XXI) of 17 December 1966, by which it created the United Nations Commission on International Trade Law with a mandate to further the progressive harmonization and unification of the law of international trade and in that respect to bear in mind the interests of all peoples, in particular those of developing countries, in the extensive development of international trade,

Noting that increased cross-border trade and investment leads to greater incidence of cases where enterprises and individuals have assets in more than one State, *Noting* also that when a debtor with assets in more than one State becomes subject to an insolvency proceeding, there often exists an urgent need for cross-border cooperation and coordination in the supervision and administration of the insolvent debtor's assets and affairs,

Considering that inadequate coordination and cooperation in cases of cross-border insolvency reduce the possibility of rescuing financially troubled but viable businesses, impede a fair and efficient administration of cross-border insolvencies, make it more likely that the debtor's assets would be concealed or dissipated and hinder reorganizations or liquidations of debtors' assets and affairs that would be the most advantageous for the creditors and other interested persons, including the debtors and the debtors' employees,

Noting that many States lack a legislative framework that would make possible or facilitate effective cross-border coordination and cooperation,

Convinced that fair and internationally harmonized legislation on cross-border insolvency that respects the national procedural and judicial systems and is acceptable to States with different legal, social and economic systems would contribute to the development of international trade and investment,

Considering that a set of internationally harmonized model legislative provisions on crossborder insolvency is needed to assist States in modernizing their legislation governing cross-border insolvency,

1. Expresses its appreciation to the United Nations Commission on International Trade Law for completing and adopting the Model Law on Cross-Border Insolvency contained in the annex to the present resolution;

2. Requests the Secretary-General to transmit the text of the Model Law, together with the Guide to Enactment of the Model Law prepared by the Secretariat, to Governments and interested bodies;

3. Recommends that all States review their legislation on cross-border aspects of insolvency to determine whether the legislation meets the objectives of a modern and efficient insolvency system and, in that review, give favourable consideration to the

* General Assembly resolution 52/158 of 15 December 1997.

Model Law, bearing in mind the need for an internationally harmonized legislation governing instances of cross-border insolvency;

4. Recommends also that all efforts be made to ensure that the Model Law, together with the Guide, become generally known and available.

72nd plenary meeting
15 December 1997

Model Law on Cross-Border Insolvency of the United Nations Commission on International Trade Law

Preamble

The purpose of this Law is to provide effective mechanisms for dealing with cases of cross-border insolvency so as to promote the objectives of:

(*a*) Cooperation between the courts and other competent authorities of this State and foreign States involved in cases of cross-border insolvency;

(*b*) Greater legal certainty for trade and investment;

(*c*) Fair and efficient administration of cross-border insolvencies that protects the interests of all creditors and other interested persons, including the debtor;

(*d*) Protection and maximization of the value of the debtor's assets; and

(*e*) Facilitation of the rescue of financially troubled businesses, thereby protecting investment and preserving employment.

CHAPTER I

General provisions

Article 1

Scope of application

1. This Law applies where:

(*a*) Assistance is sought in this State by a foreign court or a foreign representative in connection with a foreign proceeding; or

(*b*) Assistance is sought in a foreign State in connection with a proceeding under [*identify laws of the enacting State relating to insolvency*]; or

(*c*) A foreign proceeding and a proceeding under [*identify laws of the enacting State relating to insolvency*] in respect of the same debtor are taking place concurrently; or

(*d*) Creditors or other interested persons in a foreign State have an interest in requesting the commencement of, or participating in, a proceeding under [*identify laws of the enacting State relating to insolvency*].

2. This Law does not apply to a proceeding concerning [*designate any types of entities, such as banks or insurance companies, that are subject to a special insolvency regime in this State and that this State wishes to exclude from this Law*].

Article 2

Definitions

For the purposes of this Law:

(*a*) "Foreign proceeding" means a collective judicial or administrative proceeding in a foreign State, including an interim proceeding, pursuant to a law relating to insolvency in which proceeding the assets and affairs of the debtor are subject to control or supervision by a foreign court, for the purpose of reorganization or liquidation;

(*b*) "Foreign main proceeding" means a foreign proceeding taking place in the State where the debtor has the centre of its main interests;

(*c*) "Foreign non-main proceeding" means a foreign proceeding, other than a foreign main proceeding, taking place in a State where the debtor has an establishment within the meaning of subparagraph (*f*) of this article;

(*d*) "Foreign representative" means a person or body, including one appointed on an interim basis, authorized in a foreign proceeding to administer the reorganization or the liquidation of the debtor's assets or affairs or to act as a representative of the foreign proceeding;

(*e*) "Foreign court" means a judicial or other authority competent to control or supervise a foreign proceeding;

(*f*) "Establishment" means any place of operations where the debtor carries out a nontransitory economic activity with human means and goods or services.

Article 3

International obligations of this State

To the extent that this Law conflicts with an obligation of this State arising out of any treaty or other form of agreement to which it is a party with one or more other States, the requirements of the treaty or agreement prevail

Article 4

[*Competent court or authority*][1]

The functions referred to in this Law relating to recognition of foreign proceedings and cooperation with foreign courts shall be performed by [*specify the court, courts, authority or authorities competent to perform those functions in the enacting State*].

---

[1] A State where certain functions relating to insolvency proceedings have been conferred upon government-appointed officials or bodies might wish to include in article 4 or elsewhere in chapter I the following provision:

"Nothing in this Law affects the provisions in force in this State governing the authority of [*insert the title of the government-appointed person or body*]."

Article 5

Authorization of [insert the title of the person or body administering reorganization or liquidation under the law of the enacting State] **to act in a foreign State**

A [*insert the title of the person or body administering a reorganization or liquidation under the law of the enacting State*] is authorized to act in a foreign State on behalf of a proceeding under [*identify laws of the enacting State relating to insolvency*], as permitted by the applicable foreign law.

Article 6

Public policy exception

Nothing in this Law prevents the court from refusing to take an action governed by this Law if the action would be manifestly contrary to the public policy of this State.

Article 7

Additional assistance under other laws

Nothing in this Law limits the power of a court or a [*insert the title of the person or body administering a reorganization or liquidation under the law of the enacting State*] to provide additional assistance to a foreign representative under other laws of this State.

Article 8

Interpretation

In the interpretation of this Law, regard is to be had to its international origin and to the need to promote uniformity in its application and the observance of good faith.

CHAPTER II

Access of foreign representatives and creditors to courts in this state

Article 9

Right of direct access

A foreign representative is entitled to apply directly to a court in this State.

Article 10

Limited jurisdiction

The sole fact that an application pursuant to this Law is made to a court in this State by a foreign representative does not subject the foreign representative or the foreign assets and affairs of the debtor to the jurisdiction of the courts of this State for any purpose other than the application.

Article 11

Application by a foreign representative to commence a proceeding under
[identify laws of the enacting State relating to insolvency]

A foreign representative is entitled to apply to commence a proceeding under [*identify laws of the enacting State relating to insolvency*] if the conditions for commencing such a proceeding are otherwise met.

Article 12

Participation of a foreign representative in a proceeding under
[identify laws of the enacting State relating to insolvency]

Upon recognition of a foreign proceeding, the foreign representative is entitled to participate in a proceeding regarding the debtor under [*identify laws of the enacting State relating to insolvency*].

Article 13

Access of foreign creditors to a proceeding under
[identify laws of the enacting State relating to insolvency]

1. Subject to paragraph 2 of this article, foreign creditors have the same rights regarding the commencement of, and participation in, a proceeding under [*identify laws of the enacting State relating to insolvency*] as creditors in this State.

2. Paragraph 1 of this article does not affect the ranking of claims in a proceeding under [*identify laws of the enacting State relating to insolvency*], except that the claims of foreign creditors shall not be ranked lower than [*identify the class of general non-preference claims, while providing that a foreign claim is to be ranked lower than the general non-preference claims if an equivalent local claim (e.g. claim for a penalty or deferred-payment claim) has a rank lower than the general non-preference claims*].[2]

[2] The enacting State may wish to consider the following alternative wording to replace paragraph 2 of article 13:
"2. Paragraph 1 of this article does not affect the ranking of claims in a proceeding under [*identify laws of the enacting State relating to insolvency*] or the exclusion of foreign tax and social security claims from such a proceeding. Nevertheless, the claims of foreign creditors other than those concerning tax and social security obligations shall not be ranked lower than [*identify the class of general non-preference claims, while providing that a foreign claim is to be ranked lower than the general non-preference claims if an equivalent local claim (e.g. claim for a penalty or deferred-payment claim) has a rank lower than the general non-preference claims*]."

Article 14

Notification to foreign creditors of a proceeding under
[*identify laws of the enacting State relating to insolvency*]

1. Whenever under [*identify laws of the enacting State relating to insolvency*] notification is to be given to creditors in this State, such notification shall also be given to the known creditors that do not have addresses in this State. The court may order that appropriate steps be taken with a view to notifying any creditor whose address is not yet known.

2. Such notification shall be made to the foreign creditors individually, unless the court considers that, under the circumstances, some other form of notification would be more appropriate. No letters rogatory or other, similar formality is required.

3. When a notification of commencement of a proceeding is to be given to foreign creditors, the notification shall:

(*a*) Indicate a reasonable time period for filing claims and specify the place for their filing;

(*b*) Indicate whether secured creditors need to file their secured claims; and

(*c*) Contain any other information required to be included in such a notification to creditors pursuant to the law of this State and the orders of the court.

CHAPTER III

Recognition of a foreign proceeding and relief

Article 15

Application for recognition of a foreign proceeding

1. A foreign representative may apply to the court for recognition of the foreign proceeding in which the foreign representative has been appointed.

2. An application for recognition shall be accompanied by:

(*a*) A certified copy of the decision commencing the foreign proceeding and appointing the foreign representative; or

(*b*) A certificate from the foreign court affirming the existence of the foreign proceeding and of the appointment of the foreign representative; or

(*c*) In the absence of evidence referred to in subparagraphs (*a*) and (*b*), any other evidence acceptable to the court of the existence of the foreign proceeding and of the appointment of the foreign representative.

3. An application for recognition shall also be accompanied by a statement identifying all foreign proceedings in respect of the debtor that are known to the foreign representative.

4. The court may require a translation of documents supplied in support of the application for recognition into an official language of this State.

Article 16

Presumptions concerning recognition

1. If the decision or certificate referred to in paragraph 2 of article 15 indicates that the foreign proceeding is a proceeding within the meaning of subparagraph (*a*) of article 2 and that the foreign representative is a person or body within the meaning of subparagraph (*d*) of article 2, the court is entitled to so presume.

2. The court is entitled to presume that documents submitted in support of the application for recognition are authentic, whether or not they have been legalized.

3. In the absence of proof to the contrary, the debtor's registered office, or habitual residence in the case of an individual, is presumed to be the centre of the debtor's main interests.

Article 17

Decision to recognize a foreign proceeding

1. Subject to article 6, a foreign proceeding shall be recognized if:

(*a*) The foreign proceeding is a proceeding within the meaning of subparagraph (*a*) of article 2;

(*b*) The foreign representative applying for recognition is a person or body within the meaning of subparagraph (*d*) of article 2;

(*c*) The application meets the requirements of paragraph 2 of article 15; and

(*d*) The application has been submitted to the court referred to in article 4.

2. The foreign proceeding shall be recognized:

(*a*) As a foreign main proceeding if it is taking place in the State where the debtor has the centre of its main interests; or

(*b*) As a foreign non-main proceeding if the debtor has an establishment within the meaning of subparagraph (*f*) of article 2 in the foreign State.

3. An application for recognition of a foreign proceeding shall be decided upon at the earliest possible time.

4. The provisions of articles 15, 16, 17 and 18 do not prevent modification or termination of recognition if it is shown that the grounds for granting it were fully or partially lacking or have ceased to exist.

Article 18

Subsequent information

From the time of filing the application for recognition of the foreign proceeding, the foreign representative shall inform the court promptly of:

(*a*) Any substantial change in the status of the recognized foreign proceeding or the status of the foreign representative's appointment; and

(*b*) Any other foreign proceeding regarding the same debtor that becomes known to the foreign representative.

Article 19

Relief that may be granted upon application for recognition of a foreign proceeding

1. From the time of filing an application for recognition until the application is decided upon, the court may, at the request of the foreign representative, where relief is urgently needed to protect the assets of the debtor or the interests of the creditors, grant relief of a provisional nature, including:

(*a*) Staying execution against the debtor's assets;

(*b*) Entrusting the administration or realization of all or part of the debtor's assets located in this State to the foreign representative or another person designated by the court, in order to protect and preserve the value of assets that, by their nature or because of other circumstances, are perishable, susceptible to devaluation or otherwise in jeopardy;

(*c*) Any relief mentioned in paragraph 1 (*c*), (*d*) and (*g*) of article 21.

2. [*Insert provisions* (*or refer to provisions in force in the enacting State*) *relating to notice.*]

3. Unless extended under paragraph 1 (*f*) of article 21, the relief granted under this article terminates when the application for recognition is decided upon.

4. The court may refuse to grant relief under this article if such relief would interfere with the administration of a foreign main proceeding.

Article 20

Effects of recognition of a foreign main proceeding

1. Upon recognition of a foreign proceeding that is a foreign main proceeding,

(*a*) Commencement or continuation of individual actions or individual proceedings concerning the debtor's assets, rights, obligations or liabilities is stayed;

(*b*) Execution against the debtor's assets is stayed; and

(*c*) The right to transfer, encumber or otherwise dispose of any assets of the debtor is suspended.

2. The scope, and the modification or termination, of the stay and suspension referred to in paragraph 1 of this article are subject to [*refer to any provisions of law of the enacting State relating to insolvency that apply to exceptions, limitations, modifications or termination in respect of the stay and suspension referred to in paragraph 1 of this article*].

3. Paragraph 1 (*a*) of this article does not affect the right to commence individual actions or proceedings to the extent necessary to preserve a claim against the debtor.

4. Paragraph 1 of this article does not affect the right to request the commencement of a proceeding under [*identify laws of the enacting State relating to insolvency*] or the right to file claims in such a proceeding.

Article 21

Relief that may be granted upon recognition of a foreign proceeding

1. Upon recognition of a foreign proceeding, whether main or non-main, where necessary to protect the assets of the debtor or the interests of the creditors, the court may, at the request of the foreign representative, grant any appropriate relief, including:

(*a*) Staying the commencement or continuation of individual actions or individual proceedings concerning the debtor's assets, rights, obligations or liabilities, to the extent they have not been stayed under paragraph 1 (*a*) of article 20;

(*b*) Staying execution against the debtor's assets to the extent it has not been stayed under paragraph 1 (*b*) of article 20;

(*c*) Suspending the right to transfer, encumber or otherwise dispose of any assets of the debtor to the extent this right has not been suspended under paragraph 1 (*c*) of article 20;

(*d*) Providing for the examination of witnesses, the taking of evidence or the delivery of information concerning the debtor's assets, affairs, rights, obligations or liabilities;

(*e*) Entrusting the administration or realization of all or part of the debtor's assets located in this State to the foreign representative or another person designated by the court;

(*f*) Extending relief granted under paragraph 1 of article 19;

(*g*) Granting any additional relief that may be available to [*insert the title of a person or body administering a reorganization or liquidation under the law of the enacting State*] under the laws of this State.

2. Upon recognition of a foreign proceeding, whether main or non-main, the court may, at the request of the foreign representative, entrust the distribution of all or part of the debtor's assets located in this State to the foreign representative or another person designated by the court, provided that the court is satisfied that the interests of creditors in this State are adequately protected.

3. In granting relief under this article to a representative of a foreign non-main proceeding, the court must be satisfied that the relief relates to assets that, under the law of this State, should be administered in the foreign non-main proceeding or concerns information required in that proceeding.

Article 22

Protection of creditors and other interested persons

1. In granting or denying relief under article 19 or 21, or in modifying or terminating relief under paragraph 3 of this article, the court must be satisfied that the interests of the creditors and other interested persons, including the debtor, are adequately protected.

2. The court may subject relief granted under article 19 or 21 to conditions it considers appropriate.

3. The court may, at the request of the foreign representative or a person affected by relief granted under article 19 or 21, or at its own motion, modify or terminate such relief.

Article 23

Actions to avoid acts detrimental to creditors

1. Upon recognition of a foreign proceeding, the foreign representative has standing to initiate [*refer to the types of actions to avoid or otherwise render ineffective acts detrimental to creditors that are available in this State to a person or body administering a reorganization or liquidation*].

2. When the foreign proceeding is a foreign non-main proceeding, the court must be satisfied that the action relates to assets that, under the law of this State, should be administered in the foreign non-main proceeding.

Article 24

Intervention by a foreign representative in proceedings in this State

Upon recognition of a foreign proceeding, the foreign representative may, provided the requirements of the law of this State are met, intervene in any proceedings in which the debtor is a party.

CHAPTER IV

Cooperation with foreign courts and foreign representatives

Article 25

Cooperation and direct communication between a court of this State and foreign courts or foreign representatives

1. In matters referred to in article 1, the court shall cooperate to the maximum extent possible with foreign courts or foreign representatives, either directly or through a [*insert the title of a person or body administering a reorganization or liquidation under the law of the enacting State*].

2. The court is entitled to communicate directly with, or to request information or assistance directly from, foreign courts or foreign representatives.

Article 26

Cooperation and direct communication between the [*insert the title of a person or body administering a reorganization or liquidation under the law of the enacting State*] **and foreign courts or foreign representatives**

1. In matters referred to in article 1, a [*insert the title of a person or body administering a reorganization or liquidation under the law of the enacting State*] shall, in the exercise of its functions and subject to the supervision of the court, cooperate to the maximum extent possible with foreign courts or foreign representatives.

2. The [*insert the title of a person or body administering a reorganization or liquidation under the law of the enacting State*] is entitled, in the exercise of its functions and

subject to the supervision of the court, to communicate directly with foreign courts or foreign representatives.

Article 27

Forms of cooperation

Cooperation referred to in articles 25 and 26 may be implemented by any appropriate means, including:

(*a*) Appointment of a person or body to act at the direction of the court;

(*b*) Communication of information by any means considered appropriate by the court;

(*c*) Coordination of the administration and supervision of the debtor's assets and affairs;

(*d*) Approval or implementation by courts of agreements concerning the coordination of proceedings;

(*e*) Coordination of concurrent proceedings regarding the same debtor;

(*f*) [*The enacting State may wish to list additional forms or examples of cooperation*].

CHAPTER V

Concurrent proceedings

Article 28

Commencement of a proceeding under [*identify laws of the enacting State relating to insolvency*] **after recognition of a foreign main proceeding**

After recognition of a foreign main proceeding, a proceeding under [*identify laws of the enacting State relating to insolvency*] may be commenced only if the debtor has assets in this State; the effects of that proceeding shall be restricted to the assets of the debtor that are located in this State and, to the extent necessary to implement cooperation and coordination under articles 25, 26 and 27, to other assets of the debtor that, under the law of this State, should be administered in that proceeding.

Article 29

Coordination of a proceeding under [*identify laws of the enacting State relating to insolvency*] **and a foreign proceeding**

Where a foreign proceeding and a proceeding under [*identify laws of the enacting State relating to insolvency*] are taking place concurrently regarding the same debtor, the court shall seek cooperation and coordination under articles 25, 26 and 27, and the following shall apply:

(*a*) When the proceeding in this State is taking place at the time the application for recognition of the foreign proceeding is filed,

(i) Any relief granted under article 19 or 21 must be consistent with the proceeding in this State; and

(ii) If the foreign proceeding is recognized in this State as a foreign main proceeding, article 20 does not apply;

(*b*) When the proceeding in this State commences after recognition, or after the filing of the application for recognition, of the foreign proceeding,

(i) Any relief in effect under article 19 or 21 shall be reviewed by the court and shall be modified or terminated if inconsistent with the proceeding in this State; and

(ii) If the foreign proceeding is a foreign main proceeding, the stay and suspension referred to in paragraph 1 of article 20 shall be modified or terminated pursuant to paragraph 2 of article 20 if inconsistent with the proceeding in this State;

(*c*) In granting, extending or modifying relief granted to a representative of a foreign nonmain proceeding, the court must be satisfied that the relief relates to assets that, under the law of this State, should be administered in the foreign non-main proceeding or concerns information required in that proceeding.

Article 30

Coordination of more than one foreign proceeding

In matters referred to in article 1, in respect of more than one foreign proceeding regarding the same debtor, the court shall seek cooperation and coordination under articles 25, 26 and 27, and the following shall apply:

(*a*) Any relief granted under article 19 or 21 to a representative of a foreign non-main proceeding after recognition of a foreign main proceeding must be consistent with the foreign main proceeding;

(*b*) If a foreign main proceeding is recognized after recognition, or after the filing of an application for recognition, of a foreign non-main proceeding, any relief in effect under article 19 or 21 shall be reviewed by the court and shall be modified or terminated if inconsistent with the foreign main proceeding;

(*c*) If, after recognition of a foreign non-main proceeding, another foreign non-main proceeding is recognized, the court shall grant, modify or terminate relief for the purpose of facilitating coordination of the proceedings.

Article 31

Presumption of insolvency based on recognition of a foreign main proceeding

In the absence of evidence to the contrary, recognition of a foreign main proceeding is, for the purpose of commencing a proceeding under [*identify laws of the enacting State relating to insolvency*], proof that the debtor is insolvent.

Article 32

Rule of payment in concurrent proceedings

Without prejudice to secured claims or rights *in rem*, a creditor who has received part payment in respect of its claim in a proceeding pursuant to a law relating to insolvency in a foreign State may not receive a payment for the same claim in a proceeding under [*identify laws of the enacting State relating to insolvency*] regarding the same debtor, so long as the payment to the other creditors of the same class is proportionately less than the payment the creditor has already received.

Directive 2001/24/EC of the European Parliament and of the Council of 4 April 2001 on the reorganisation and winding up of credit institutions

Official Journal L 125 – 05/05/2001 (P. 0015 – 0023)

THE EUROPEAN PARLIAMENT AND THE COUNCIL OF THE EUROPEAN UNION,

Having regard to the Treaty establishing the European Community, and in particular Article 47 (2) thereof,

Having regard to the proposal from the Commission[1],

Having regard to the opinion of the Economic and Social Committee[2],

Having regard to the opinion of the European Monetary Institute[3],

Acting in accordance with the procedure laid down in Article 251 of the Treaty[4],

Whereas:

(1) In accordance with the objectives of the Treaty, the harmonious and balanced development of economic activities throughout the Community should be promoted through the elimination of any obstacles to the freedom of establishment and the freedom to provide services within the Community.

(2) At the same time as those obstacles are eliminated, consideration should be given to the situation which might arise if a credit institution runs into difficulties, particularly where that institution has branches in other Member States.

(3) This Directive forms part of the Community legislative framework set up by Directive 2000/12/EC of the European Parliament and of the Council of 20 March 2000 relating to the taking up and pursuit of the business of credit institutions[5]. It follows therefrom that, while they are in operation, a credit institution and its branches form a single entity subject to the supervision of the competent authorities of the State where authorisation valid throughout the Community was granted.

(4) It would be particularly undesirable to relinquish such unity between an institution and its branches where it is necessary to adopt reorganisation measures or open winding-up proceedings.

(5) The adoption of Directive 94/19/EC of the European Parliament and of the Council of 30 May 1994 on deposit-guarantee schemes[6], which introduced the principle

---

1 OJ C 356, 31.12.1985, p. 55 and OJ C 36, 8.2.1988, p. 1.

2 OJ C 263, 20.10.1986, p. 13.

3 OJ C 332, 30.10.1998, p. 13.

4 Opinion of the European Parliament of 13 March 1987 (OJ C 99, 13.4.1987, p. 211), confirmed on 2 December 1993 (OJ C 342, 20.12.1993, p. 30), Council Common Position of 17 July 2000 (OJ C 300, 20.10.2000, p. 13) and Decision of the European Parliament of 16 January 2001 (not yet published in the Official Journal). Council Decision of 12 March 2001.

5 OJ L 126, 26.5.2000, p. 1. Directive as amended by Directive 2000/28/EC (OJ L 275, 27.10.2000, p. 37).

6 OJ L 135, 31.5.1994, p. 5.

of compulsory membership by credit institutions of a guarantee scheme in their home Member State, brings out even more clearly the need for mutual recognition of reorganisation measures and winding-up proceedings.

(6) The administrative or judicial authorities of the home Member State must have sole power to decide upon and to implement the reorganisation measures provided for in the law and practices in force in that Member State. Owing to the difficulty of harmonising Member States' laws and practices, it is necessary to establish mutual recognition by the Member States of the measures taken by each of them to restore to viability the credit institutions which it has authorised.

(7) It is essential to guarantee that the reorganisation measures adopted by the administrative or judicial authorities of the home Member State and the measures adopted by persons or bodies appointed by those authorities to administer those reorganisation measures, including measures involving the possibility of a suspension of payments, suspension of enforcement measures or reduction of claims and any other measure which could affect third parties' existing rights, are effective in all Member States.

(8) Certain measures, in particular those affecting the functioning of the internal structure of credit institutions or managers' or shareholders' rights, need not be covered by this Directive to be effective in Member States insofar as, pursuant to the rules of private international law, the applicable law is that of the home State.

(9) Certain measures, in particular those connected with the continued fulfilment of conditions of authorisation, are already the subject of mutual recognition pursuant to Directive 2000/12/EC insofar as they do not affect the rights of third parties existing before their adoption.

(10) Persons participating in the operation of the internal structures of credit institutions as well as managers and shareholders of such institutions, considered in those capacities, are not to be regarded as third parties for the purposes of this Directive.

(11) It is necessary to notify third parties of the implementation of reorganisation measures in Member States where branches are situated when such measures could hinder the exercise of some of their rights.

(12) The principle of equal treatment between creditors, as regards the opportunities open to them to take action, requires the administrative or judicial authorities of the home Member State to adopt such measures as are necessary for the creditors in the host Member State to be able to exercise their rights to take action within the time limit laid down.

(13) There must be some coordination of the role of the administrative or judicial authorities in reorganisation measures and winding-up proceedings for branches of credit institutions having head offices outside the Community and situated in different Member States.

(14) In the absence of reorganisation measures, or in the event of such measures failing, the credit institutions in difficulty must be wound up. Provision should be made in such cases for mutual recognition of winding-up proceedings and of their effects in the Community.

(15) The important role played by the competent authorities of the home Member State before winding-up proceedings are opened may continue during the process of winding up so that these proceedings can be properly carried out.

(16) Equal treatment of creditors requires that the credit institution is wound up according to the principles of unity and universality, which require the administrative or judicial authorities of the home Member State to have sole jurisdiction and their deci-

sions to be recognised and to be capable of producing in all the other Member States, without any formality, the effects ascribed to them by the law of the home Member State, except where this Directive provides otherwise.

(17) The exemption concerning the effects of reorganisation measures and winding-up proceedings on certain contracts and rights is limited to those effects and does not cover other questions concerning reorganisation measures and winding-up proceedings such as the lodging, verification, admission and ranking of claims concerning those contracts and rights and the rules governing the distribution of the proceeds of the realisation of the assets, which are governed by the law of the home Member State.

(18) Voluntary winding up is possible when a credit institution is solvent. The administrative or judicial authorities of the home Member State may nevertheless, where appropriate, decide on a reorganisation measure or winding-up proceedings, even after voluntary winding up has commenced.

(19) Withdrawal of authorisation to pursue the business of banking is one of the consequences which winding up a credit institution necessarily entails. Withdrawal should not, however, prevent certain activities of the institution from continuing insofar as is necessary or appropriate for the purposes of winding up. Such a continuation of activity may nonetheless be made subject by the home Member State to the consent of, and supervision by, its competent authorities.

(20) Provision of information to known creditors on an individual basis is as essential as publication to enable them, where necessary, to lodge their claims or submit observations relating to their claims within the prescribed time limits. This should take place without discrimination against creditors domiciled in a Member State other than the home Member State, based on their place of residence or the nature of their claims. Creditors must be kept regularly informed in an appropriate manner throughout winding-up proceedings.

(21) For the sole purpose of applying the provisions of this Directive to reorganisation measures and winding-up proceedings involving branches located in the Community of a credit institution of which the head office is situated in a third country, the definitions of “home Member State”, “competent authorities” and “administrative or judicial authorities” should be those of the Member State in which the branch is located.

(22) Where a credit institution which has its head office outside the Community possesses branches in more than one Member State, each branch should receive individual treatment in regard to the application of this Directive. In such a case, the administrative or judicial authorities and the competent authorities as well as the administrators and liquidators should endeavour to coordinate their activities.

(23) Although it is important to follow the principle that the law of the home Member State determines all the effects of reorganisation measures or winding-up proceedings, both procedural and substantive, it is also necessary to bear in mind that those effects may conflict with the rules normally applicable in the context of the economic and financial activity of the credit institution in question and its branches in other Member States. In some cases reference to the law of another Member State represents an unavoidable qualification of the principle that the law of the home Member State is to apply.

(24) That qualification is especially necessary to protect employees having a contract of employment with a credit institution, ensure the security of transactions in respect of certain types of property and protect the integrity of regulated markets functioning in accordance with the law of a Member State on which financial instruments are traded.

(25) Transactions carried out in the framework of a payment and settlement system are covered by Directive 98/26/EC of the European Parliament and of the Council of 19 May 1998 on settlement finality in payment and securities settlement systems[7].

(26) The adoption of this Directive does not call into question the provisions of Directive 98/26/EC according to which insolvency proceedings must not have any effect on the enforceability of orders validly entered into a system, or on collateral provided for a system.

(27) Some reorganisation measures or winding-up proceedings involve the appointment of a person to administer them. The recognition of his appointment and his powers in all other Member States is therefore an essential factor in the implementation of decisions taken in the home Member State. However, the limits within which he may exercise his powers when he acts outside the home Member State should be specified.

(28) Creditors who have entered into contracts with a credit institution before a reorganisation measure is adopted or winding-up proceedings are opened should be protected against provisions relating to voidness, voidability or unenforceability laid down in the law of the home Member State, where the beneficiary of the transaction produces evidence that in the law applicable to that transaction there is no available means of contesting the act concerned in the case in point.

(29) The confidence of third-party purchasers in the content of the registers or accounts regarding certain assets entered in those registers or accounts and by extension of the purchasers of immovable property should be safeguarded, even after winding-up proceedings have been opened or a reorganisation measure adopted. The only means of safeguarding that confidence is to make the validity of the purchase subject to the law of the place where the immovable asset is situated or of the State under whose authority the register or account is kept.

(30) The effects of reorganisation measures or winding-up proceedings on a lawsuit pending are governed by the law of the Member State in which the lawsuit is pending, by way of exception to the application of the lex concursus. The effects of those measures and procedures on individual enforcement actions arising from such lawsuits are governed by the legislation of the home Member State, in accordance with the general rule established by this Directive.

(31) Provision should be made for the administrative or judicial authorities in the home Member State to notify immediately the competent authorities of the host Member State of the adoption of any reorganisation measure or the opening of any winding-up proceedings, if possible before the adoption of the measure or the opening of the proceedings, or, if not, immediately afterwards.

(32) Professional secrecy as defined in Article 30 of Directive 2000/12/EC is an essential factor in all information or consultation procedures. For that reason it should be respected by all the administrative authorities taking part in such procedures, whereas the judicial authorities remain, in this respect, subject to the national provisions relating to them,

---

[7] OJ L 166, 11.6.1998, p. 45.

HAVE ADOPTED THIS DIRECTIVE:

TITLE I

SCOPE AND DEFINITIONS

Article 1

Scope

1. This Directive shall apply to credit institutions and their branches set up in Member States other than those in which they have their head offices, as defined in points (1) and (3) of Article 1 of Directive 2000/12/EC, subject to the conditions and exemptions laid down in Article 2 (3) of that Directive.

2. The provisions of this Directive concerning the branches of a credit institution having a head office outside the Community shall apply only where that institution has branches in at least two Member States of the Community.

Article 2

Definitions

For the purposes of this Directive:

- "home Member State" shall mean the Member State of origin within the meaning of Article 1, point (6) of Directive 2000/12/EC;
- "host Member State" shall mean the host Member State within the meaning of Article 1, point (7) of Directive 2000/12/EC;
- "branch" shall mean a branch within the meaning of Article 1, point (3) of Directive 2000/12/EC;
- "competent authorities" shall mean the competent authorities within the meaning of Article 1, point (4) of Directive 2000/12/EC;
- "administrator" shall mean any person or body appointed by the administrative or judicial authorities whose task is to administer reorganisation measures;
- "administrative or judicial authorities" shall mean such administrative or judicial authorities of the Member States as are competent for the purposes of reorganisation measures or winding-up proceedings;
- "reorganisation measures" shall mean measures which are intended to preserve or restore the financial situation of a credit institution and which could affect third parties' pre-existing rights, including measures involving the possibility of a suspension of payments, suspension of enforcement measures or reduction of claims;
- "liquidator" shall mean any person or body appointed by the administrative or judicial authorities whose task is to administer winding-up proceedings;
- "winding-up proceedings" shall mean collective proceedings opened and monitored by the administrative or judicial authorities of a Member State with the aim of realising assets under the supervision of those authorities, including where the proceedings are terminated by a composition or other, similar measure;
- "regulated market" shall mean a regulated market within the meaning of Article 1, point (13) of Directive 93/22/EEC;

- "instruments" shall mean all the instruments referred to in Section B of the Annex to Directive 93/22/EEC.

TITLE II

REORGANISATION MEASURES

A. Credit institutions having their head offices within the Community

Article 3

Adoption of reorganisation measures – applicable law

1. The administrative or judicial authorities of the home Member State shall alone be empowered to decide on the implementation of one or more reorganisation measures in a credit institution, including branches established in other Member States.

2. The reorganisation measures shall be applied in accordance with the laws, regulations and procedures applicable in the home Member State, unless otherwise provided in this Directive.

They shall be fully effective in accordance with the legislation of that Member State throughout the Community without any further formalities, including as against third parties in other Member States, even where the rules of the host Member State applicable to them do not provide for such measures or make their implementation subject to conditions which are not fulfilled.

The reorganisation measures shall be effective throughout the Community once they become effective in the Member State where they have been taken.

Article 4

Information for the competent authorities of the host Member State

The administrative or judicial authorities of the home Member State shall without delay inform, by any available means, the competent authorities of the host Member State of their decision to adopt any reorganisation measure, including the practical effects which such a measure may have, if possible before it is adopted or otherwise immediately thereafter. Information shall be communicated by the competent authorities of the home Member State.

Article 5

Information for the supervisory authorities of the home Member State

Where the administrative or judicial authorities of the host Member State deem it necessary to implement within their territory one or more reorganisation measures, they shall inform the competent authorities of the home Member State accordingly. Information shall be communicated by the host Member State's competent authorities.

Article 6

Publication

1. Where implementation of the reorganisation measures decided on pursuant to Article 3 (1) and (2) is likely to affect the rights of third parties in a host Member State and where an appeal may be brought in the home Member State against the decision ordering the measure, the administrative or judicial authorities of the home Member State, the administrator or any person empowered to do so in the home Member State shall publish an extract from the decision in the Official Journal of the European Communities and in two national newspapers in each host Member State, in order in particular to facilitate the exercise of the right of appeal in good time.

2. The extract from the decision provided for in paragraph 1 shall be forwarded at the earliest opportunity, by the most appropriate route, to the Office for Official Publications of the European Communities and to the two national newspapers in each host Member State.

3. The Office for Official Publications of the European Communities shall publish the extract at the latest within twelve days of its dispatch.

4. The extract from the decision to be published shall specify, in the official language or languages of the Member States concerned, in particular the purpose and legal basis of the decision taken, the time limits for lodging appeals, specifically a clearly understandable indication of the date of expiry of the time limits, and the full address of the authorities or court competent to hear an appeal.

5. The reorganisation measures shall apply irrespective of the measures prescribed in paragraphs 1 to 3 and shall be fully effective as against creditors, unless the administrative or judicial authorities of the home Member State or the law of that State governing such measures provide otherwise.

Article 7

Duty to inform known creditors and right to lodge claims

1. Where the legislation of the home Member State requires lodgement of a claim with a view to its recognition or provides for compulsory notification of the measure to creditors who have their domiciles, normal places of residence or head offices in that State, the administrative or judicial authorities of the home Member State or the administrator shall also inform known creditors who have their domiciles, normal places of residence or head offices in other Member States, in accordance with the procedures laid down in Articles 14 and 17 (1).

2. Where the legislation of the home Member State provides for the right of creditors who have their domiciles, normal places of residence or head offices in that State to lodge claims or to submit observations concerning their claims, creditors who have their domiciles, normal places of residence or head offices in other Member States shall also have that right in accordance with the procedures laid down in Article 16 and Article 17 (2).

B. Credit institutions having their head offices outside the Community

Article 8

Branches of third-country credit institutions

1. The administrative or judicial authorities of the host Member State of a branch of a credit institution having its head office outside the Community shall without delay inform, by any available means, the competent authorities of the other host Member States in which the institution has set up branches which are included on the list referred to in Article 11 of Directive 2000/12/EC and published each year in the Official Journal of the European Communities, of their decision to adopt any reorganisation measure, including the practical effects which that measure may have, if possible before it is adopted or otherwise immediately thereafter. Information shall be communicated by the competent authorities of the host Member State whose administrative or judicial authorities decide to apply the measure.

2. The administrative or judicial authorities referred to in paragraph 1 shall endeavour to coordinate their actions.

TITLE III

WINDING-UP PROCEEDINGS

A. Credit institutions having their head offices within the Community

Article 9

Opening of winding-up proceedings – Information to be communicated to other competent authorities

1. The administrative or judicial authorities of the home Member State which are responsible for winding up shall alone be empowered to decide on the opening of winding-up proceedings concerning a credit institution, including branches established in other Member States.

A decision to open winding-up proceedings taken by the administrative or judicial authority of the home Member State shall be recognised, without further formality, within the territory of all other Member States and shall be effective there when the decision is effective in the Member State in which the proceedings are opened.

2. The administrative or judicial authorities of the home Member State shall without delay inform, by any available means, the competent authorities of the host Member State of their decision to open winding-up proceedings, including the practical effects which such proceedings may have, if possible before they open or otherwise immediately thereafter. Information shall be communicated by the competent authorities of the home Member State.

Article 10

Law applicable

1. A credit institution shall be wound up in accordance with the laws, regulations and procedures applicable in its home Member State insofar as this Directive does not provide otherwise.

2. The law of the home Member State shall determine in particular:

(a) the goods subject to administration and the treatment of goods acquired by the credit institution after the opening of winding-up proceedings;

(b) the respective powers of the credit institution and the liquidator;

(c) the conditions under which set-offs may be invoked;

(d) the effects of winding-up proceedings on current contracts to which the credit institution is party;

(e) the effects of winding-up proceedings on proceedings brought by individual creditors, with the exception of lawsuits pending, as provided for in Article 32;

(f) the claims which are to be lodged against the credit institution and the treatment of claims arising after the opening of winding-up proceedings;

(g) the rules governing the lodging, verification and admission of claims;

(h) the rules governing the distribution of the proceeds of the realisation of assets, the ranking of claims and the rights of creditors who have obtained partial satisfaction after the opening of insolvency proceedings by virtue of a right in re or through a set-off;

(i) the conditions for, and the effects of, the closure of insolvency proceedings, in particular by composition;

(j) creditors' rights after the closure of winding-up proceedings;

(k) who is to bear the costs and expenses incurred in the winding-up proceedings;

(l) the rules relating to the voidness, voidability or unenforceability of legal acts detrimental to all the creditors.

Article 11

Consultation of competent authorities before voluntary winding up

1. The competent authorities of the home Member State shall be consulted in the most appropriate form before any voluntary winding-up decision is taken by the governing bodies of a credit institution.

2. The voluntary winding up of a credit institution shall not preclude the adoption of a reorganisation measure or the opening of winding-up proceedings.

Article 12

Withdrawal of a credit institution's authorisation

1. Where the opening of winding-up proceedings is decided on in respect of a credit institution in the absence, or following the failure, of reorganisation measures, the authorisation of the institution shall be withdrawn in accordance with, in particular, the procedure laid down in Article 22 (9) of Directive 2000/12/EC.

2. The withdrawal of authorisation provided for in paragraph 1 shall not prevent the person or persons entrusted with the winding up from carrying on some of the credit institution's activities insofar as that is necessary or appropriate for the purposes of winding up.

The home Member State may provide that such activities shall be carried on with the consent, and under the supervision, of the competent authorities of that Member State.

Article 13

Publication

The liquidators or any administrative or judicial authority shall announce the decision to open winding-up proceedings through publication of an extract from the winding-up decision in the Official Journal of the European Communities and at least two national newspapers in each of the host Member States.

Article 14

Provision of information to known creditors

1. When winding-up proceedings are opened, the administrative or judicial authority of the home Member State or the liquidator shall without delay individually inform known creditors who have their domiciles, normal places of residence or head offices in other Member States, except in cases where the legislation of the home State does not require lodgement of the claim with a view to its recognition.

2. That information, provided by the dispatch of a notice, shall in particular deal with time limits, the penalties laid down in regard to those time limits, the body or authority empowered to accept the lodgement of claims or observations relating to claims and the other measures laid down. Such a notice shall also indicate whether creditors whose claims are preferential or secured in re need lodge their claims.

Article 15

Honouring of obligations

Where an obligation has been honoured for the benefit of a credit institution which is not a legal person and which is the subject of winding-up proceedings opened in another Member State, when it should have been honoured for the benefit of the liquidator in those proceedings, the person honouring the obligation shall be deemed to have discharged it if he was unaware of the opening of proceedings. Where such an obligation is honoured before the publication provided for in Article 13 has been effected, the person honouring the obligation shall be presumed, in the absence of proof to the contrary, to have been unaware of the opening of winding-up proceedings; where the obligation is honoured after the publication provided for in Article 13 has been effected, the person honouring the obligation shall be presumed, in the absence of proof to the contrary, to have been aware of the opening of proceedings.

Article 16

Right to lodge claims

1. Any creditor who has his domicile, normal place of residence or head office in a Member State other than the home Member State, including Member States' public authorities, shall have the right to lodge claims or to submit written observations relating to claims.

2. The claims of all creditors whose domiciles, normal places of residence or head offices are in Member States other than the home Member State shall be treated in the same way and accorded the same ranking as claims of an equivalent nature which may be lodged by creditors having their domiciles, normal places of residence, or head offices in the home Member State.

3. Except in cases where the law of the home Member State provides for the submission of observations relating to claims, a creditor shall send copies of supporting documents, if any, and shall indicate the nature of the claim, the date on which it arose and its amount, as well as whether he alleges preference, security in re or reservation of title in respect of the claim and what assets are covered by his security.

Article 17

Languages

1. The information provided for in Articles 13 and 14 shall be provided in the official language or one of the official languages of the home Member State. For that purpose a form shall be used bearing, in all the official languages of the European Union, the heading "Invitation to lodge a claim. Time limits to be observed" or, where the law of the home Member State provides for the submission of observations relating to claims, the heading "Invitation to submit observations relating to a claim. Time limits to be observed".

2. Any creditor who has his domicile, normal place of residence or head office in a Member State other than the home Member State may lodge his claim or submit observations relating to his claim in the official language or one of the official languages of that other Member State. In that event, however, the lodgement of his claim or the submission of observations on his claim shall bear the heading "Lodgement of claim" or "Submission of observations relating to claims" in the official language or one of the official languages of the home Member State. In addition, he may be required to provide a translation into that language of the lodgement of claim or submission of observations relating to claims.

Article 18

Regular provision of information to creditors

Liquidators shall keep creditors regularly informed, in an appropriate manner, particularly with regard to progress in the winding up.

B. Credit institutions the head offices of which are outside the Community

Article 19

Branches of third-country credit institutions

1. The administrative or judicial authorities of the host Member State of the branch of a credit institution the head office of which is outside the Community shall without delay inform, by any available means, the competent authorities of the other host Member States in which the credit institution has set up branches on the list referred to in Article 11 of Directive 2000/12/EC and published each year in the Official Journal of the European Communities, of their decision to open winding-up proceedings, including the practical effects which these proceedings may have, if possible before they open or otherwise immediately thereafter. Information shall be communicated by the competent authorities of the first abovementioned host Member State.

2. Administrative or judicial authorities which decide to open proceedings to wind up a branch of a credit institution the head office of which is outside the Community shall inform the competent authorities of the other host Member States that winding-up proceedings have been opened and authorisation withdrawn.

Information shall be communicated by the competent authorities in the host Member State which has decided to open the proceedings.

3. The administrative or judicial authorities referred to in paragraph 1 shall endeavour to coordinate their actions.

Any liquidators shall likewise endeavour to coordinate their actions.

TITLE IV

PROVISIONS COMMON TO REORGANISATION MEASURES AND WINDING-UP PROCEEDINGS

Article 20

Effects on certain contracts and rights

The effects of a reorganisation measure or the opening of winding-up proceedings on:

(a) employment contracts and relationships shall be governed solely by the law of the Member State applicable to the employment contract;

(b) a contract conferring the right to make use of or acquire immovable property shall be governed solely by the law of the Member State within the territory of which the immovable property is situated. That law shall determine whether property is movable or immovable;

(c) rights in respect of immovable property, a ship or an aircraft subject to registration in a public register shall be governed solely by the law of the Member State under the authority of which the register is kept.

Article 21

Third parties' rights in re

1. The adoption of reorganisation measures or the opening of winding-up proceedings shall not affect the rights in re of creditors or third parties in respect of tangible or intangible, movable or immovable assets – both specific assets and collections of indefinite assets as a whole which change from time to time – belonging to the credit institution which are situated within the territory of another Member State at the time of the adoption of such measures or the opening of such proceedings.

2. The rights referred to in paragraph 1 shall in particular mean:

(a) the right to dispose of assets or have them disposed of and to obtain satisfaction from the proceeds of or income from those assets, in particular by virtue of a lien or a mortgage;

(b) the exclusive right to have a claim met, in particular a right guaranteed by a lien in respect of the claim or by assignment of the claim by way of a guarantee;

(c) the right to demand the assets from, and/or to require restitution by, anyone having possession or use of them contrary to the wishes of the party so entitled;

(d) a right in re to the beneficial use of assets.

3. The right, recorded in a public register and enforceable against third parties, under which a right in re within the meaning of paragraph 1 may be obtained, shall be considered a right in re.

4. Paragraph 1 shall not preclude the actions for voidness, voidability or unenforceability laid down in Article 10 (2) (l).

Article 22

Reservation of title

1. The adoption of reorganisation measures or the opening of winding-up proceedings concerning a credit institution purchasing an asset shall not affect the seller's rights based on a reservation of title where at the time of the adoption of such measures or opening of such proceedings the asset is situated within the territory of a Member State other than the State in which the said measures were adopted or the said proceedings were opened.

2. The adoption of reorganisation measures or the opening of winding-up proceedings concerning a credit institution selling an asset, after delivery of the asset, shall not constitute grounds for rescinding or terminating the sale and shall not prevent the purchaser from acquiring title where at the time of the adoption of such measures or the opening of such proceedings the asset sold is situated within the territory of a Member State other than the State in which such measures were adopted or such proceedings were opened.

3. Paragraphs 1 and 2 shall not preclude the actions for voidness, voidability or unenforceability laid down in Article 10 (2) (l).

Article 23

Set-off

1. The adoption of reorganisation measures or the opening of winding-up proceedings shall not affect the right of creditors to demand the set-off of their claims against the claims of the credit institution, where such a set-off is permitted by the law applicable to the credit institution's claim.

2. Paragraph 1 shall not preclude the actions for voidness, voidability or unenforceability laid down in Article 10 (2) (l).

Article 24

Lex rei sitae

The enforcement of proprietary rights in instruments or other rights in such instruments the existence or transfer of which presupposes their recording in a register, an account or a centralised deposit system held or located in a Member State shall be governed by the law of the Member State where the register, account, or centralised deposit system in which those rights are recorded is held or located.

Article 25

Netting agreements

Netting agreements shall be governed solely by the law of the contract which governs such agreements.

Article 26

Repurchase agreements

Without prejudice to Article 24, repurchase agreements shall be governed solely by the law of the contract which governs such agreements.

Article 27

Regulated markets

Without prejudice to Article 24, transactions carried out in the context of a regulated market shall be governed solely by the law of the contract which governs such transactions.

Article 28

Proof of liquidators' appointment

1. The administrator or liquidator's appointment shall be evidenced by a certified copy of the original decision appointing him or by any other certificate issued by the administrative or judicial authority of the home Member State.

A translation into the official language or one of the official languages of the Member State within the territory of which the administrator or liquidator wishes to act may be required. No legalisation or other similar formality shall be required.

2. Administrators and liquidators shall be entitled to exercise within the territory of all the Member States all the powers which they are entitled to exercise within the territory of the home Member State. They may also appoint persons to assist or, where appropriate, represent them in the course of the reorganisation measure or winding-up proceedings, in particular in host Member States and, specifically, in order to help overcome any difficulties encountered by creditors in the host Member State.

3. In exercising his powers, an administrator or liquidator shall comply with the law of the Member States within the territory of which he wishes to take action, in particular with regard to procedures for the realisation of assets and the provision of information to employees. Those powers may not include the use of force or the right to rule on legal proceedings or disputes.

Article 29

Registration in a public register

1. The administrator, liquidator or any administrative or judicial authority of the home Member State may request that a reorganisation measure or the decision to open winding-up proceedings be registered in the land register, the trade register and any other public register kept in the other Member States.

A Member State may, however, prescribe mandatory registration. In that event, the person or authority referred to in the preceding subparagraph shall take all the measures necessary to ensure such registration.

2. The costs of registration shall be regarded as costs and expenses incurred in the proceedings.

Article 30

Detrimental acts

1. Article 10 shall not apply as regards the rules relating to the voidness, voidability or unenforceability of legal acts detrimental to the creditors as a whole, where the beneficiary of these acts provides proof that:

- the act detrimental to the creditors as a whole is subject to the law of a Member State other than the home Member State, and
- that law does not allow any means of challenging that act in the case in point.

2. Where a reorganisation measure decided on by a judicial authority provides for rules relating to the voidness, voidability or unenforceability of legal acts detrimental to

the creditors as a whole performed before adoption of the measure, Article 3 (2) shall not apply in the cases provided for in paragraph 1 of this Article.

Article 31

Protection of third parties

Where, by an act concluded after the adoption of a reorganisation measure or the opening of winding-up proceedings, a credit institution disposes, for consideration, of:

- an immovable asset,
- a ship or an aircraft subject to registration in a public register, or
- instruments or rights in such instruments the existence or transfer of which presupposes their being recorded in a register, an account or a centralised deposit system held or located in a Member State,

the validity of that act shall be governed by the law of the Member State within the territory of which the immovable asset is situated or under the authority of which that register, account or deposit system is kept.

Article 32

Lawsuits pending

The effects of reorganisation measures or winding-up proceedings on a pending lawsuit concerning an asset or a right of which the credit institution has been divested shall be governed solely by the law of the Member State in which the lawsuit is pending.

Article 33

Professional secrecy

All persons required to receive or divulge information in connection with the information or consultation procedures laid down in Articles 4, 5, 8, 9, 11 and 19 shall be bound by professional secrecy, in accordance with the rules and conditions laid down in Article 30 of Directive 2000/12/EC, with the exception of any judicial authorities to which existing national provisions apply.

TITLE V

FINAL PROVISIONS

Article 34

Implementation

1. Member States shall bring into force the laws, regulations and administrative provisions necessary to comply with this Directive on 5 May 2004. They shall forthwith inform the Commission thereof.

National provisions adopted in application of this Directive shall apply only to reorganisation measures or winding-up proceedings adopted or opened after the date referred to in the first subparagraph. Measures adopted or proceedings opened before that date shall continue to be governed by the law that was applicable to them at the time of adoption or opening.

2. When Member States adopt these measures, they shall contain a reference to this Directive or shall be accompanied by such reference on the occasion of their official publication. The methods of making such reference shall be laid down by Member States.

3. Member States shall communicate to the Commission the texts of the main provisions of national law which they adopt in the field governed by this Directive.

Article 35

Entry into force

This Directive shall enter into force on the date of its publication.

Article 36

Addressees

This Directive is addressed to the Member States.
Done at Luxembourg, 4 April 2001.

For the European Parliament
The President
N. Fontaine
For the Council
The President
B. Rosengren

Directive 2001/17/EC of the European Parliament and of the Council of 19 March 2001 on the reorganisation and winding-up of insurance undertakings

Official Journal L 110 – 20/04/2001 (P. 0028 – 0039)

THE EUROPEAN PARLIAMENT AND THE COUNCIL OF THE EUROPEAN UNION,

Having regard to the Treaty establishing the European Community, and in particular Articles 47 (2) and 55 thereof,

Having regard to the proposal from the Commission[1],

Having regard to the opinion of the Economic and Social Committee[2],

Acting in accordance with the procedure laid down in Article 251 of the Treaty[3],

Whereas:

(1) First Council Directive 73/239/EEC of 24 July 1973 on the coordination of laws, regulations and administrative provisions relating to the taking up and pursuit of the business of direct insurance other than life assurance[4], as supplemented by Directive 92/49/EEC[5], and the First Council Directive 79/267/EEC of 5 March 1979 on the coordination of laws, regulations and administrative provisions relating to the taking up and pursuit of the business of direct life assurance[6], as supplemented by Directive 92/96/EEC[7], provide for a single authorisation of the insurance undertakings granted by the home Member State supervisory authority. This single authorisation allows the insurance undertaking to carry out its activities in the Community by means of establishment or free provision of services without any further authorisation by the host Member State and under the sole prudential supervision of the home Member State supervisory authorities.

---

1 OJ C 71, 19.3.1987, p. 5, and OJ C 253, 6.10.1989, p. 3.

2 OJ C 319, 30.11.1987, p. 10.

3 Opinion of the European Parliament of 15 March 1989 (OJ C 96, 17.4.1989, p. 99), confirmed on 27 October 1999, Council Common Position of 9 October 2000 (OJ C 344, 1.12.2000, p. 23) and Decision of the European Parliament of 15 February 2001.

4 OJ L 228, 16.8.1973, p. 3. Directive as last amended by European Parliament and Council Directive 95/26/EC (OJ L 168, 18.7.1995, p. 7).

5 Council Directive 92/49/EEC of 18 June 1992 on the coordination of laws, regulations and administrative provisions relating to direct insurance other than life assurance and amending Directives 73/239/EEC and 88/357/EEC (third non-life insurance directive) (OJ L 228, 11.8.1992, p. 1).

6 OJ L 63, 13.3.1979, p. 1. Directive as last amended by Directive 95/26/EC.

7 Council Directive 92/96/EEC of 10 November 1992 on the coordination of laws, regulations and administrative provisions relating to direct life assurance and amending Directives 79/267/EEC and 90/619/EEC (third life assurance directive) (OJ L 360, 9.12.1992, p. 1).

(2) The insurance directives providing a single authorisation with a Community scope for the insurance undertakings do not contain coordination rules in the event of winding-up proceedings. Insurance undertakings as well as other financial institutions are expressly excluded from the scope of Council Regulation (EC) No 1346/2000 of 29 May 2000 on insolvency proceedings[8]. It is in the interest of the proper functioning of the internal market and of the protection of creditors that coordinated rules are established at Community level for winding-up proceedings in respect of insurance undertakings.

(3) Coordination rules should also be established to ensure that the reorganisation measures, adopted by the competent authority of a Member State in order to preserve or restore the financial soundness of an insurance undertaking and to prevent as much as possible a winding-up situation, produce full effects throughout the Community. The reorganisation measures covered by this Directive are those affecting pre-existing rights of parties other than the insurance undertaking itself. The measures provided for in Article 20 of Directive 73/239/EEC and Article 24 of Directive 79/267/EEC should be included within the scope of this Directive provided that they comply with the conditions contained in the definition of reorganisation measures.

(4) This Directive has a Community scope which affects insurance undertakings as defined in Directives 73/239/EEC and 79/267/EEC which have their head office in the Community, Community branches of insurance undertakings which have their head office in third countries and creditors resident in the Community. This Directive should not regulate the effects of the reorganisation measures and winding-up proceedings vis-à-vis third countries.

(5) This Directive should concern winding-up proceedings whether or not they are founded on insolvency and whether they are voluntary or compulsory. It should apply to collective proceedings as defined by the home Member State's legislation in accordance with Article 9 involving the realisation of the assets of an insurance undertaking and the distribution of their proceeds. Winding-up proceedings which, without being founded on insolvency, involve for the payment of insurance claims a priority order in accordance with Article 10 should also be included in the scope of this Directive. Claims by the employees of an insurance undertaking arising from employment contracts and employment relationships should be capable of being subrogated to a national wage guarantee scheme; such subrogated claims should benefit from the treatment determined by the home Member State's law (lex concursus) according to the principles of this Directive. The provisions of this Directive should apply to the different cases of winding-up proceedings as appropriate.

(6) The adoption of reorganisation measures does not preclude the opening of winding-up proceedings. Winding-up proceedings may be opened in the absence of, or following, the adoption of reorganisation measures and they may terminate with composition or other analogous measures, including reorganisation measures.

(7) The definition of branch, in accordance with existing insolvency principles, should take account of the single legal personality of the insurance undertaking. The home Member State's legislation should determine the way in which the assets and liabilities held by independent persons who have a permanent authority to act as agent for an insurance undertaking should be treated in the winding-up of an insurance undertaking.

---

[8] OJ L 160, 30.6.2000, p. 1.

(8) A distinction should be made between the competent authorities for the purposes of reorganisation measures and winding-up proceedings and the supervisory authorities of the insurance undertakings. The competent authorities may be administrative or judicial authorities depending on the Member State's legislation. This Directive does not purport to harmonise national legislation concerning the allocation of competences between such authorities.

(9) This Directive does not seek to harmonise national legislation concerning reorganisation measures and winding-up proceedings but aims at ensuring mutual recognition of Member States' reorganisation measures and winding-up legislation concerning insurance undertakings as well as the necessary cooperation. Such mutual recognition is implemented in this Directive through the principles of unity, universality, coordination, publicity, equivalent treatment and protection of insurance creditors.

(10) Only the competent authorities of the home Member State should be empowered to take decisions on winding-up proceedings concerning insurance undertakings (principle of unity). These proceedings should produce their effects throughout the Community and should be recognised by all Member States. All the assets and liabilities of the insurance undertaking should, as a general rule, be taken into consideration in the winding-up proceedings (principle of universality).

(11) The home Member State's law should govern the winding-up decision concerning an insurance undertaking, the winding-up proceedings themselves and their effects, both substantive and procedural, on the persons and legal relations concerned, except where this Directive provides otherwise. Therefore all the conditions for the opening, conduct and closure of winding-up proceedings should in general be governed by the home Member State's law. In order to facilitate its application this Directive should include a non-exhaustive list of aspects which, in particular, are subject to the general rule of the home Member State's legislation.

(12) The supervisory authorities of the home Member State and those of all the other Member States should be informed as a matter of urgency of the opening of winding-up proceedings (principle of coordination).

(13) It is of utmost importance that insured persons, policy-holders, beneficiaries and any injured party having a direct right of action against the insurance undertaking on a claim arising from insurance operations be protected in winding-up proceedings. Such protection should not include claims which arise not from obligations under insurance contracts or insurance perations but from civil liability caused by an agent in negotiations for which, according to the law applicable to the insurance contract or operation, the agent himself is not responsible under such insurance contract or operation. In order to achieve this objective Member States should ensure special treatment for insurance creditors according to one of two optional methods provided for in this Directive. Member States may choose between granting insurance claims absolute precedence over any other claim with respect to assets representing the technical provisions or granting insurance claims a special rank which may only be preceded by claims on salaries, social security, taxes and rights "in rem" over the whole assets of the insurance undertaking. Neither of the two methods provided for in this Directive impedes a Member State from establishing a ranking between different categories of insurance claims.

(14) This Directive should ensure an appropriate balance between the protection of insurance creditors and other privileged creditors protected by the Member State's legislation and not harmonise the different systems of privileged creditors existing in the Member States.

(15) The two optional methods for treatment of insurance claims are considered substantially equivalent. The first method ensures the affectation of assets representing the technical provisions to insurance claims, the second method ensures insurance claims a position in the ranking of creditors which not only affects the assets representing the technical provisions but all the assets of the insurance undertaking.

(16) Member States which, in order to protect insurance creditors, opt for the method of granting insurance claims absolute precedence with respect to the assets representing the technical provisions should require their insurance undertakings to establish and keep up to date a special register of such assets. Such a register is a useful instrument for identifying the assets affected to such claims.

(17) In order to strengthen equivalence between both methods of treatment of insurance claims, this Directive should oblige the Member States which apply the method set out in Article 10 (1) (b) to require every insurance undertaking to represent, at any moment and independently of a possible winding-up, claims, which according to that method may have precedence over insurance claims and which are registered in the insurance undertaking's accounts, by assets allowed by the insurance directives in force to represent the technical provisions.

(18) The home Member State should be able to provide that, where the rights of insurance creditors have been subrogated to a guarantee scheme established in such home Member State, claims by that scheme should not benefit from the treatment of insurance claims under this Directive.

(19) The opening of winding-up proceedings should involve the withdrawal of the authorisation to conduct business granted to the insurance undertaking unless such authorisation has previously been withdrawn.

(20) The decision to open winding-up proceedings, which may produce effects throughout the Community according to the principle of universality, should have appropriate publicity within the Community. In order to protect interested parties, the decision should be published in accordance with the home Member State's procedures and in the Official Journal of the European Communities and, further, by any other means decided by the other Member States' supervisory authorities within their respective territories. In addition to publication of the decision, known creditors who are resident in the Community should be individually informed of the decision and this information should contain at least the elements specified in this Directive. Liquidators should also keep creditors regularly informed of the progress of the winding-up proceedings.

(21) Creditors should have the right to lodge claims or to submit written observations in winding-up proceedings. Claims by creditors resident in a Member State other than the home Member State should be treated in the same way as equivalent claims in the home Member State without any discrimination on the grounds of nationality or residence (principle of equivalent treatment).

(22) This Directive should apply to reorganisation measures adopted by a competent authority of a Member State principles which are similar "mutatis mutandis" to those provided for in winding-up proceedings. The publication of such reorganisation measures should be limited to the case in which an appeal in the home Member State is possible by parties other than the insurance undertaking itself. When reorganisation measures affect exclusively the rights of shareholders, members or employees of the insurance undertaking considered in those capacities, the competent authorities should determine the manner in which the parties affected should be informed in accordance with relevant legislation.

(23) This Directive provides for coordinated rules to determine the law applicable to reorganisation measures and winding-up proceedings of insurance undertakings. This Directive does not seek to establish rules of private international law determining the law applicable to contracts and other legal relations. In particular, this Directive does not seek to govern the applicable rules on the existence of a contract, the rights and obligations of parties and the evaluation of debts.

(24) The general rule of this Directive, according to which reorganisation measures and the winding-up proceedings are governed by the law of the home Member State, should have a series of exceptions in order to protect legitimate expectations and the certainty of certain transactions in Member States other than the home Member State. Such exceptions should concern the effects of such reorganisation measures or winding-up proceedings on certain contracts and rights, third parties' rights in rem, reservations of title, set-off, regulated markets, detrimental acts, third party purchasers and lawsuits pending.

(25) The exception concerning the effects of reorganisation measures and winding-up proceedings on certain contracts and rights provided for in Article 19 should be limited to the effects specified therein and should not include any other issues related to reorganisation measures and winding-up proceedings such as the lodging, verification, admission and ranking of claims regarding such contracts and rights, which should be governed by the home Member State's legislation.

(26) The effects of reorganisation measures or winding-up proceedings on a lawsuit pending should be governed by the law of the Member States in which the lawsuit is pending concerning an asset or a right of which the insurance undertaking has been divested as an exception to the application of the law of the home Member State. The effects of such measures and proceedings on individual enforcement actions arising from these lawsuits should be governed by the home Member State's legislation, according to the general rule of this Directive.

(27) All persons required to receive or divulge information connected with the procedures of communication provided for in this Directive should be bound by professional secrecy in the same manner as that established in Article 16 of Directive 92/49/EEC and Article 15 of Directive 92/96/EEC, with the exception of any judicial authority to which specific national legislation applies.

(28) For the sole purpose of applying the provisions of this Directive to reorganisation measures and winding-up proceedings concerning branches situated in the Community of an insurance undertaking whose head office is located in a third country the home Member State should be defined as the Member State in which the branch is located and the supervisory authorities and competent authorities as the authorities of that Member State.

(29) Where there are branches in more than one Member State of an insurance undertaking whose head office is located outside the Community, each branch should be treated independently with regard to the application of this Directive. In that case the competent authorities, supervisory authorities, administrators and liquidators should endeavour to coordinate their actions.

HAVE ADOPTED THIS DIRECTIVE:

TITLE I

SCOPE AND DEFINITIONS

Article 1

Scope

1. This Directive applies to reorganisation measures and winding-up proceedings concerning insurance undertakings.

2. This Directive also applies, to the extent provided for in Article 30, to reorganisation measures and winding-up proceedings concerning branches in the territory of the Community of insurance undertakings having their head office outside the Community.

Article 2

Definitions

For the purpose of this Directive:

(a) "insurance undertaking" means an undertaking which has received official authorisation in accordance with Article 6 of Directive 73/239/EEC or Article 6 of Directive 79/267/EEC;

(b) "branch" means any permanent presence of an insurance undertaking in the territory of a Member State other than the home Member State which carries out insurance business;

(c) "reorganisation measures" means measures involving any intervention by administrative bodies or judicial authorities which are intended to preserve or restore the financial situation of an insurance undertaking and which affect pre-existing rights of parties other than the insurance undertaking itself, including but not limited to measures involving the possibility of a suspension of payments, suspension of enforcement measures or reduction of claims;

(d) "winding-up proceedings" means collective proceedings involving realising the assets of an insurance undertaking and distributing the proceeds among the creditors, shareholders or members as appropriate, which necessarily involve any intervention by the administrative or the judicial authorities of a Member State, including where the collective proceedings are terminated by a composition or other analogous measure, whether or not they are founded on insolvency or are voluntary or compulsory;

(e) "home Member State" means the Member State in which an insurance undertaking has been authorised in accordance with Article 6 of Directive 73/239/EEC or Article 6 of Directive 79/267/EEC;

(f) "host Member State" means the Member State other than the home Member State in which an insurance undertaking has a branch;

(g) "competent authorities" means the administrative or judicial authorities of the Member States which are competent for the purposes of the reorganisation measures or the winding-up proceedings;

(h) "supervisory authorities" means the competent authorities within the meaning of Article 1 (k) of Directive 92/49/EEC and of Article 1 (l) of Directive 92/96/EEC;

(i) "administrator" means any person or body appointed by the competent authorities for the purpose of administering reorganisation measures;

(j) "liquidator" means any person or body appointed by the competent authorities or by the governing bodies of an insurance undertaking, as appropriate, for the purpose of administering winding-up proceedings;

(k) "insurance claims" means any amount which is owed by an insurance undertaking to insured persons, policy holders, beneficiaries or to any injured party having direct right of action against the insurance undertaking and which arises from an insurance contract or from any operation provided for in Article 1 (2) and (3), of Directive 79/267/EEC in direct insurance business, including amounts set aside for the aforementioned persons, when some elements of the debt are not yet known. The premiums owed by an insurance undertaking as a result of the non-conclusion or cancellation of these insurance contracts and operations in accordance with the law applicable to such contracts or operations before the opening of the winding-up proceedings shall also be considered insurance claims.

TITLE II

REORGANISATION MEASURES

Article 3

Scope

This Title applies to the reorganisation measures defined in Article 2 (c).

Article 4

Adoption of reorganisation measures – Applicable law

1. Only the competent authorities of the home Member State shall be entitled to decide on the reorganisation measures with respect to an insurance undertaking, including its branches in other Member States. The reorganisation measures shall not preclude the opening of winding-up proceedings by the home Member State.

2. The reorganisation measures shall be governed by the laws, regulations and procedures applicable in the home Member State, unless otherwise provided in Articles 19 to 26.

3. The reorganisation measures shall be fully effective throughout the Community in accordance with the legislation of the home Member State without any further formalities, including against third parties in other Member States, even if the legislation of those other Member States does not provide for such reorganisation measures or alternatively makes their implementation subject to conditions which are not fulfilled.

4. The reorganisation measures shall be effective throughout the Community once they become effective in the Member State where they have been taken.

Article 5

Information to the supervisory authorities

The competent authorities of the home Member State shall inform as a matter or urgency the home Member State's supervisory authorities of their decision on any reorganisation measure, where possible before the adoption of such a measure and failing that immediately thereafter. The supervisory authorities of the home Member State shall inform as a matter of urgency the supervisory authorities of all other Member States of the decision to adopt reorganisation measures including the possible practical effects of such measures.

Article 6

Publication

1. Where an appeal is possible in the home Member State against a reorganisation measure, the competent authorities of the home Member State, the administrator or any person entitled to do so in the home Member State shall make public its decision on a reorganisation measure in accordance with the publication procedures provided for in the home Member State and, furthermore, publish in the Official Journal of the European Communities at the earliest opportunity an extract from the document establishing the reorganisation measure. The supervisory authorities of all the other Member States which have been informed of the decision on a reorganisation measure pursuant to Article 5 may ensure the publication of such decision within their territory in the manner they consider appropriate.

2. The publications provided for in paragraph 1 shall also specify the competent authority of the home Member State, the applicable law as provided in Article 4 (2) and the administrator appointed, if any. They shall be carried out in the official language or in one of the official languages of the Member State in which the information is published.

3. The reorganisation measures shall apply regardless of the provisions concerning publication set out in paragraphs 1 and 2 and shall be fully effective as against creditors, unless the competent authorities of the home Member State or the law of that State provide otherwise.

4. When reorganisation measures affect exclusively the rights of shareholders, members or employees of an insurance undertaking, considered in those capacities, this Article shall not apply unless the law applicable to these reorganisation measures provides otherwise. The competent authorities shall determine the manner in which the interested parties affected by such reorganisation measures shall be informed in accordance with the relevant legislation.

Article 7

Information to known creditors – Right to lodge claims

1. Where the legislation of the home Member State requires lodgement of a claim with a view to its recognition or provides for compulsory notification of a reorganisation measure to creditors who have their normal place of residence, domicile or head office in that State, the competent authorities of the home Member State or the administrator

shall also inform known creditors who have their normal place of residence, domicile or head office in another Member State, in accordance with the procedures laid down in Articles 15 and 17 (1).

2. Where the legislation of the home Member State provides for the right of creditors who have their normal place of residence, domicile or head office in that State to lodge claims or to submit observations concerning their claims, creditors who have their normal place of residence, domicile or head office in another Member State shall have the same right to lodge claims or submit observations in accordance with the procedures laid down in Articles 16 and 17 (2).

TITLE III

WINDING-UP PROCEEDINGS

Article 8

Opening of winding-up proceedings – Information to the supervisory authorities

1. Only the competent authorities of the home Member State shall be entitled to take a decision concerning the opening of winding-up proceedings with regard to an insurance undertaking, including its branches in other Member States. This decision may be taken in the absence, or following the adoption, of reorganisation measures.

2. A decision adopted according to the home Member State's legislation concerning the opening of winding-up proceedings of an insurance undertaking, including its branches in other Member States, shall be recognised without further formality within the territory of all other Member States and shall be effective there as soon as the decision is effective in the Member State in which the proceedings are opened.

3. The supervisory authorities of the home Member State shall be informed as a matter of urgency of the decision to open winding-up proceedings, if possible before the proceedings are opened and failing that immediately thereafter. The supervisory authorities of the home Member State shall inform as a matter of urgency the supervisory authorities of all other Member States of the decision to open winding-up proceedings including the possible practical effects of such proceedings.

Article 9

Applicable law

1. The decision to open winding-up proceedings with regard to an insurance undertaking, the winding-up proceedings and their effects shall be governed by the laws, regulations and administrative provisions applicable in its home Member State unless otherwise provided in Articles 19 to 26.

2. The law of the home Member State shall determine in particular:

(a) the assets which form part of the estate and the treatment of assets acquired by, or devolving on, the insurance undertaking after the opening of the winding-up proceedings;

(b) the respective powers of the insurance undertaking and the liquidator;

(c) the conditions under which set-off may be invoked;

(d) the effects of the winding-up proceedings on current contracts to which the insurance undertaking is party;

(e) the effects of the winding-up proceedings on proceedings brought by individual creditors, with the exception of lawsuits pending as provided for in Article 26;

(f) the claims which are to be lodged against the insurance undertaking's estate and the treatment of claims arising after the opening of winding-up proceedings;

(g) the rules governing the lodging, verification and admission of claims;

(h) the rules governing the distribution of proceeds from the realisation of assets, the ranking of claims, and the rights of creditors who have obtained partial satisfaction after the opening of winding-up proceedings by virtue of a right in rem or through a set-off;

(i) the conditions for and the effects of closure of winding-up proceedings, in particular by composition;

(j) creditors' rights after the closure of winding-up proceedings;

(k) who is to bear the cost and expenses incurred in the winding-up proceedings;

(l) the rules relating to the voidness, voidability or unenforceability of legal acts detrimental to all the creditors.

Article 10

Treatment of insurance claims

1. Member States shall ensure that insurance claims take precedence over other claims on the insurance undertaking according to one or both of the following methods:

(a) insurance claims shall, with respect to assets representing the technical provisions, take absolute precedence over any other claim on the insurance undertaking;

(b) insurance claims shall, with respect to the whole of the insurance undertaking's assets, take precedence over any other claim on the insurance undertaking with the only possible exception of:

(i) claims by employees arising from employment contracts and employment relationships,

(ii) claims by public bodies on taxes,

(iii) claims by social security systems,

(iv) claims on assets subject to rights in rem.

2. Without prejudice to paragraph 1, Member States may provide that the whole or a part of the expenses arising from the winding-up procedure, as defined by their national legislation, shall take precedence over insurance claims.

3. Member States which have opted for the method provided for in paragraph 1 (a) shall require that insurance undertakings establish and keep up to date a special register in line with the provisions set out in the Annex.

Article 11

Subrogation to a guarantee scheme

The home Member State may provide that, where the rights of insurance creditors have been subrogated to a guarantee scheme established in that Member State, claims by that scheme shall not benefit from the provisions of Article 10 (1).

Article 12

Representation of preferential claims by assets

By way of derogation from Article 18 of Directive 73/239/EEC and Article 21 of Directive 79/267/EEC, Member States which apply the method set out in Article 10 (1) (b) of this Directive shall require every insurance undertaking to represent, at any moment and independently from a possible winding-up, the claims which may take precedence over insurance claims pursuant to Article 10 (1) (b) and which are registered in the insurance undertaking's accounts, by assets mentioned in Article 21 of Directive 92/49/EEC and Article 21 of Directive 92/96/EEC.

Article 13

Withdrawal of the authorisation

1. Where the opening of winding-up proceedings is decided in respect of an insurance undertaking, the authorisation of the insurance undertaking shall be withdrawn, except to the extent necessary for the purposes of paragraph 2, in accordance with the procedure laid down in Article 22 of Directive 73/239/EEC and Article 26 of Directive 79/267/EEC, if the authorisation has not been previously withdrawn.

2. The withdrawal of authorisation pursuant to paragraph 1 shall not prevent the liquidator or any other person entrusted by the competent authorities from carrying on some of the insurance undertakings' activities in so far as that is necessary or appropriate for the purposes of winding-up. The home Member State may provide that such activities shall be carried on with the consent and under the supervision of the supervisory authorities of the home Member State.

Article 14

Publication

1. The competent authority, the liquidator or any person appointed for that purpose by the competent authority shall publish the decision to open winding-up proceedings in accordance with the publication procedures provided for in the home Member State and also publish an extract from the winding-up decision in the Official Journal of the European Communities. The supervisory authorities of all the other Member States which have been informed of the decision to open winding-up proceedings in accordance with Article 8 (3) may ensure the publication of such decision within their territories in the manner they consider appropriate.

2. The publication of the decision to open winding-up proceedings provided for in paragraph 1 shall also specify the competent authority of the home Member State, the

applicable law and the liquidator appointed. It shall be in the official language or in one of the official languages of the Member State in which the information is published.

Article 15

Information to known creditors

1. When winding-up proceedings are opened, the competent authorities of the home Member State, the liquidator or any person appointed for that purpose by the competent authorities shall without delay individually inform by written notice each known creditor who has his normal place of residence, domicile or head office in another Member State thereof.

2. The notice referred to in paragraph 1 shall in particular deal with time limits, the penalties laid down with regard to those time limits, the body or authority empowered to accept the lodgement of claims or observations relating to claims and the other measures laid down. The notice shall also indicate whether creditors whose claims are preferential or secured in rem need to lodge their claims. In the case of insurance claims, the notice shall further indicate the general effects of the winding-up proceedings on the insurance contracts, in particular, the date on which the insurance contracts or the operations will cease to produce effects and the rights and duties of insured persons with regard to the contract or operation.

Article 16

Right to lodge claims

1. Any creditor who has his normal place of residence, domicile or head office in a Member State other than the home Member State, including Member States' public authorities, shall have the right to lodge claims or to submit written observations relating to claims.

2. The claims of all creditors who have their normal place of residence, domicile or head office in a Member State other than the home Member State, including the aforementioned authorities, shall be treated in the same way and accorded the same ranking as claims of an equivalent nature lodgeable by creditors who have their normal place of residence, domicile or head office in the home Member State.

3. Except in cases where the law of the home Member State allows otherwise, a creditor shall send copies of supporting documents, if any, and shall indicate the nature of the claim, the date on which it arose and the amount, whether he alleges preference, security in rem or reservation of title in respect of the claim and what assets are covered by his security. The precedence granted to insurance claims by Article 10 need not be indicated.

Article 17

Languages and form

1. The information in the notice referred to in Article 15 shall be provided in the official language or one of the official languages of the home Member State. For that

purpose a form shall be used bearing the heading "Invitation to lodge a claim; time limits to be observed" or, where the law of the home Member State provides for the submission of observations relating to claims, "Invitation to submit observations relating to a claim; time limits to be observed", in all the official languages of the European Union.

However, where a known creditor is a holder of an insurance claim, the information in the notice referred to in Article 15 shall be provided in the official language or one of the official languages of the Member State in which the creditor has his normal place of residence, domicile or head office.

2. Any creditor who has his normal place of residence, domicile or head office in a Member State other than the home Member State may lodge his claim or submit observations relating to his claim in the official language or one of the official languages of that other Member State. However, in that event the lodgement of his claim or the submission of observations on his claim, as appropriate, shall bear the heading "Lodgement of claim" or "Submission of observations relating to claims", as appropriate, in the official language or one of the official languages of the home Member State.

Article 18

Regular information to the creditors

1. Liquidators shall keep creditors regularly informed, in an appropriate manner, in particular regarding the progress of the winding-up.

2. The supervisory authorities of the Member States may request information on developments in the winding-up procedure from the supervisory authorities of the home Member State.

TITLE IV

PROVISIONS COMMON TO REORGANISATION MEASURES AND WINDING-UP PROCEEDINGS

Article 19

Effects on certain contracts and rights

By way of derogation from Articles 4 and 9, the effects of the opening of reorganisation measures or of winding-up proceedings on the contracts and rights specified below shall be governed by the following rules:

(a) employment contracts and employment relationships shall be governed solely by the law of the Member State applicable to the employment contract or employment relationship;

(b) a contract conferring the right to make use of or acquire immovable property shall be governed solely by the law of the Member State in whose territory the immovable property is situated;

(c) rights of the insurance undertaking with respect to immovable property, a ship or an aircraft subject to registration in a public register shall be governed by the law of the Member State under whose authority the register is kept.

Article 20

Third parties' rights in rem

1. The opening of reorganisation measures or winding-up proceedings shall not affect the rights in rem of creditors or third parties in respect of tangible or intangible, movable or immovable assets – both specific assets and collections of indefinite assets as a whole which change from time to time – belonging to the insurance undertaking which are situated within the territory of another Member State at the time of the opening of such measures or proceedings.

2. The rights referred to in paragraph 1 shall in particular mean:

(a) the right to dispose of assets or have them disposed of and to obtain satisfaction from the proceeds of or income from those assets, in particular by virtue of a lien or a mortgage;

(b) the exclusive right to have a claim met, in particular a right guaranteed by a lien in respect of the claim or by assignment of the claim by way of a guarantee;

(c) the right to demand the assets from, and/or to require restitution by, anyone having possession or use of them contrary to the wishes of the party so entitled;

(d) a right in rem to the beneficial use of assets.

3. The right, recorded in a public register and enforceable against third parties, under which a right in rem within the meaning of paragraph 1 may be obtained, shall be considered a right in rem.

4. Paragraph 1 shall not preclude actions for voidness, voidability or unenforceability referred to in Article 9 (2) (l).

Article 21

Reservation of title

1. The opening of reorganisation measures or winding-up proceedings against an insurance undertaking purchasing an asset shall not affect the seller's rights based on a reservation of title where at the time of the opening of such measures or proceedings the asset is situated within the territory of a Member State other than the State in which such measures or proceedings were opened.

2. The opening of reorganisation measures or winding-up proceedings against an insurance undertaking selling an asset, after delivery of the asset, shall not constitute grounds for rescinding or terminating the sale and shall not prevent the purchaser from acquiring title where at the time of the opening of such measures or proceedings the asset sold is situated within the territory of a Member State other than the State in which such measures or proceedings were opened.

3. Paragraphs 1 and 2 shall not preclude actions for voidness, voidability or unenforceability referred to in Article 9 (2) (l).

Article 22

Set-off

1. The opening of reorganisation measures or winding-up proceedings shall not affect the right of creditors to demand the set-off of their claims against the claims of the insurance undertaking, where such a set-off is permitted by the law applicable to the insurance undertaking's claim.

2. Paragraph 1 shall not preclude actions for voidness, voidability or unenforceability referred to in Article 9 (2) (l).

Article 23

Regulated markets

1. Without prejudice to Article 20 the effects of a reorganisation measure or the opening of winding-up proceedings on the rights and obligations of the parties to a regulated market shall be governed solely by the law applicable to that market.

2. Paragraph 1 shall not preclude any action for voidness, voidability, or unenforceability referred to in Article 9 (2) (l) which may be taken to set aside payments or transactions under the law applicable to that market.

Article 24

Detrimental acts

Article 9 (2) (l) shall not apply, where a person who has benefited from a legal act detrimental to all the creditors provides proof that:

(a) the said act is subject to the law of a Member State other than the home Member State, and

(b) that law does not allow any means of challenging that act in the relevant case.

Article 25

Protection of third-party purchasers

Where, by an act concluded after the adoption of a reorganisation measure or the opening of winding-up proceedings, an insurance undertaking disposes, for a consideration, of:

(a) an immovable asset,

(b) a ship or an aircraft subject to registration in a public register, or

(c) transferable or other securities whose existence or transfer presupposes entry in a register or account laid down by law or which are placed in a central deposit system governed by the law of a Member State,

the validity of that act shall be governed by the law of the Member State within whose territory the immovable asset is situated or under whose authority the register, account or system is kept.

Article 26

Lawsuits pending

The effects of reorganisation measures or winding-up proceedings on a pending lawsuit concerning an asset or a right of which the insurance undertaking has been divested shall be governed solely by the law of the Member State in which the lawsuit is pending.

Article 27

Administrators and liquidators

1. The administrator's or liquidator's appointment shall be evidenced by a certified copy of the original decision appointing him or by any other certificate issued by the competent authorities of the home Member State.

A translation into the official language or one of the official languages of the Member State within the territory of which the administrator or liquidator wishes to act may be required. No legalisation or other similar formality shall be required.

2. Administrators and liquidators shall be entitled to exercise within the territory of all the Member States all the powers which they are entitled to exercise within the territory of the home Member State. Persons to assist or, where appropriate, represent administrators and liquidators may be appointed, according to the home Member State's legislation, in the course of the reorganisation measure or winding-up proceedings, in particular in host Member States and, specifically, in order to help overcome any difficulties encountered by creditors in the host Member State.

3. In exercising his powers according to the home Member State's legislation, an administrator or liquidator shall comply with the law of the Member States within whose territory he wishes to take action, in particular with regard to procedures for the realisation of assets and the informing of employees. Those powers may not include the use of force or the right to rule on legal proceedings or disputes.

Article 28

Registration in a public register

1. The administrator, liquidator or any other authority or person duly empowered in the home Member State may request that a reorganisation measure or the decision to open winding-up proceedings be registered in the land register, the trade register and any other public register kept in the other Member States.

However, if a Member State prescribes mandatory registration, the authority or person referred to in subparagraph 1 shall take all the measures necessary to ensure such registration.

2. The costs of registration shall be regarded as costs and expenses incurred in the proceedings.

Article 29

Professional secrecy

All persons required to receive or divulge information in connection with the procedures of communication laid down in Articles 5, 8 and 30 shall be bound by professional secrecy, in the same manner as laid down in Article 16 of Directive 92/49/EEC and Article 15 of Directive 92/96/EEC, with the exception of any judicial authorities to which existing national provisions apply.

Article 30

Branches of third country insurance undertakings

1. Notwithstanding the definitions laid down in Article 2 (e), (f) and (g) and for the purpose of applying the provisions of this Directive to the reorganisation measures and winding-up proceedings concerning a branch situated in a Member State of an insurance undertaking whose head office is located outside the Community:

(a) "home Member State" means the Member State in which the branch has been granted authorisation according to Article 23 of Directive 73/239/EEC and Article 27 of Directive 79/267/EEC, and

(b) "supervisory authorities" and "competent authorities" mean such authorities of the Member State in which the branch was authorised.

2. When an insurance undertaking whose head office is outside the Community has branches established in more than one Member State, each branch shall be treated independently with regard to the application of this Directive. The competent authorities and the supervisory authorities of these Member States shall endeavour to coordinate their actions. Any administrators or liquidators shall likewise endeavour to coordinate their actions.

Article 31

Implementation of this Directive

1. Member States shall bring into force the laws, regulations and administrative provisions necessary to comply with this Directive before 20 April 2003. They shall forthwith inform the Commission thereof.

When Member States adopt these measures, they shall contain a reference to this Directive or shall be accompanied by such reference on the occasion of their official publication. The methods of making such reference shall be laid down by Member States.

2. National provisions adopted in application of this Directive shall apply only to reorganisation measures or winding-up proceedings adopted or opened after the date referred to in paragraph 1. Reorganisation measures adopted or winding up proceedings opened before that date shall continue to be governed by the law that was applicable to them at the time of adoption or opening.

3. Member States shall communicate to the Commission the text of the main provisions of domestic law which they adopt in the field governed by this Directive.

Article 32

Entry into force

This Directive shall enter into force on the day of its publication in the Official Journal of the European Communities.

Article 33

Addressees

This Directive is addressed to the Member States.

Done at Brussels, 19 March 2001.
For the European Parliament
The President
N. Fontaine
For the Council
The President
A. Lindh

ANNEX

SPECIAL REGISTER REFERRED TO IN ARTICLE 10 (3)

1. Every insurance undertaking must keep at its head office a special register of the assets used to cover the technical provisions calculated and invested in accordance with the home Member State's rules.

2. Where an insurance undertaking transacts both non-life and life business, it must keep at its head office separate registers for each type of business. However, where a Member State authorises insurance undertakings to cover life and the risks listed in points 1 and 2 of Annex A to Directive 73/239/EEC, it may provide that those insurance undertakings must keep a single register for the whole of their activities.

3. The total value of the assets entered, valued in accordance with the rules applicable in the home Member State, must at no time be less than the value of the technical provisions.

4. Where an asset entered in the register is subject to a right in rem in favour of a creditor or a third party, with the result that part of the value of the asset is not available for the purpose of covering commitments, that fact is recorded in the register and the amount not available is not included in the total value referred to in point 3.

5. Where an asset employed to cover technical provisions is subject to a right in rem in favour of a creditor or a third party, without meeting the conditions of point 4, or where such an asset is subject to a reservation of title in favour of a creditor or of a third party or where a creditor has a right to demand the set-off of his claim against the claim of the insurance undertaking, the treatment of such asset in case of the winding-up of the insurance undertaking with respect to the method provided for in Article 10 (1) (a) shall be determined by the legislation of the home Member State except where Articles 20, 21 or 22 apply to that asset.

6. The composition of the assets entered in the register in accordance with points 1 to 5, at the time when winding-up proceedings are opened, must not thereafter be changed and no alteration other than the correction of purely clerical errors must be made in the registers, except with the authorisation of the competent authority.

7. Notwithstanding point 6, the liquidators must add to the said assets the yield therefrom and the value of the pure premiums received in respect of the class of business concerned between the opening of the winding-up proceedings and the time of payment of the insurance claims or until any transfer of portfolio is effected.

8. If the product of the realisation of assets is less than their estimated value in the registers, the liquidators must be required to justify this to the home Member States' competent authorities.

9. The supervisory authorities of the Member States must take appropriate measures to ensure full application by the insurance undertakings of the provisions of this Annex.

European Communication and Cooperation Guidelines For Cross-border Insolvency

Developed Under the Aegis of Academic Wing of INSOL Europe

by

Professor Bob Wessels and Professor Miguel Virgós

Final Draft May 2007

Guideline 1
Overriding objective

1.1. These Guidelines embody the overriding objective of enabling courts and liquidators to operate efficiently and effectively in cross-border insolvency proceedings within the context of the EC Insolvency Regulation.
1.2. In achieving the objective of Guideline 1.1. the interests of creditors are paramount and are treated equally.
1.3. All interested parties in cross-border insolvency proceedings are required to further the overriding objective as set out above in Guideline 1.1.

Guideline 2
Aim

2.1. The aim of these Guidelines is to facilitate the coordination of the administration of insolvency proceedings involving the same debtor, including through the use of a governance protocol.
2.2. In particular, these Guidelines aim to promote:

(i) The orderly, effective, efficient and timely administration of proceedings;

(ii) The identification, preservation and maximisation of the value of the debtor's assets (which includes the debtor's undertaking or business) on a world-wide basis;

(iii) The sharing of information in order to reduce the costs involved; and

(iv) The avoidance or minimization of litigation, costs and inconvenience to all parties affected by proceedings.

2.3. In individual insolvency proceedings, the Guidelines require cases to be administered with a view:

(i) To ensure that the creditors' interests are paramount and that they are on an equal footing;

(ii) To save expense;

(iii) To deal with the debtor's estate in ways which are proportionate to the amount of money involved, to the importance of the case, to the complexity-of the issues, and to the number of jurisdictions involved; and

(iv) To ensure that the case is dealt with timely and fairly.

Guideline 3
Status

3.1. Nothing in these Guidelines is intended:

(i) To interfere with the independent exercise of jurisdiction by each of the national courts involved, including their respective authority or supervision over a liquidator;

(ii) To interfere with national rules or ethical principles by which a liquidator is bound according to applicable national law and professional rules; or

(iii) To confer substantive rights or to interfere with any function or duty arising out of the EC Insolvency Regulation or to impinge on applicable national law.

Guideline 4
Liquidator

4.1. A liquidator is any appointed person or body whose function is to administer or liquidate assets of which the debtor has been divested or to supervise the administration of its affairs, either in reorganisation or in liquidation proceedings.

4.2. A liquidator is required to act with the appropriate knowledge of the EC Insolvency Regulation and its application in practice.

4.3. A liquidator is required to act honestly, objectively, fairly and expeditiously in dealing with all parties concerned, including the courts.

Guideline 5
Direct Access

5. Any foreign liquidator should be granted direct access to any court necessary for the exercise of legal rights to the same extent that a national liquidator is so permitted.

Guideline 6
Communications

6.1. Liquidators are required to communicate with each other directly and as soon as they are appointed.

6.2. The liquidator appointed in the main proceedings should always take the initiative to start or to continue communications with other liquidators.

6.3. Substantive replies by a liquidator to queries from other liquidators should always be responded to as soon as reasonably practicable.

Guideline 7
Information

7.1. Liquidators are required to provide prompt and full disclosure to all other liquidators involved of all relevant information about the existence and status of the insolvency proceedings in which they have been appointed.

7.2. Liquidators are required to provide information periodically which may be relevant to the other proceedings detailing the conduct of the proceedings.

7.3. Liquidators in possession of such information are required to inform the courts insofar as they are subject to any reporting duties under national law, of any material development in any such other proceedings.

7.4. A foreign liquidator should be permitted to use all legal methods to obtain information that would be available to a creditor or to a liquidator in any national insolvency proceedings.

7.5. To the fullest extent permissible under any applicable law, relevant non-public information should be shared by a liquidator with other liquidators subject to appropriate confidentiality arrangements to the extent that this is commercially and practically sensible.

7.6. The duty to provide information in the meaning of this Guideline includes the duty to provide copies of documents at reasonable costs on request.

Guideline 8
Information by a liquidator in secondary proceedings

8.1. The liquidator in any secondary proceedings should provide all relevant information to the liquidator in main proceedings without any delay so as to facilitate the submission of proposals on the liquidation or use of assets in secondary proceedings.

8.2. The liquidator in any secondary proceedings is encouraged to provide advice to the liquidator in the main proceedings concerning any views on how to best to proceed.

8.3. The liquidator in main proceedings is encouraged to involve liquidators in any secondary proceedings in devising those proposals referred to above in Guideline 8.1.

8.4. Where a reorganisation or rescue plan can be adopted in secondary proceedings which, in attaining the aims pursued under Guideline 2.2 (ii), would give better value to creditors in main proceedings or reduce the overall size of debts, the liquidator in main proceedings and the courts shall take advantage of the opportunity to promote the adoption of this plan.

Guideline 9
Authentication

9.1. Except to the extent provided for under any applicable law, where existing authentication of documents is required, methods should be established so as to permit rapid authentication and secure transmission of faxes and other electronic communications relating to cross-border insolvencies on any basis that permits their acceptance as official and genuine communications by liquidators and courts in other jurisdictions.

9.2. To the extent permissible under national law, courts are encouraged to provide or publish judgments, orders or rulings also in languages other than those regularly used in proceedings or encourage translations to be made as much as possible.

Guideline 10
Language

10.1. Liquidators shall determine the language in which communications take place on the basis of convenience and the avoidance of costs. The court is advised to allow use of other languages in all or part of the proceedings if no prejudice to a party will result.

10.2. Courts are encouraged, to the maximum extent permissible under national law, to accept any documents related to those communications in language decided upon under Guideline 10.1, without the need for a translation into the language of proceedings before them.

Guideline 11
Obligations incurred by and fees of liquidators

11.1. Obligations incurred by the liquidator during proceedings and the liquidator's fees are funded from the assets within those proceedings in which the liquidator is appointed.

11.2. Obligations and fees incurred by the liquidator in the main proceedings prior to the opening of any secondary proceedings but concerning assets to be included in the estate in principle will be funded by the estate corresponding to the secondary proceedings.

Guideline 12
Cooperation

12.1. Liquidators are required to cooperate in all aspects of the case.

12.2. Liquidators ensure that cooperation takes place with other liquidators with a view to minimising conflicts between parallel proceedings and maximising the prospects for the rehabilitation and reorganization of the debtor's business or the value of the debtor's assets subject to realisation, as may be the case.

12.3. Cooperation is intended to address all issues that are important to the actual case.

12.4. Cooperation may be best attained by way of an agreement or "protocol" that establishes decision-making procedures, although decisions may continue to be made informally as long as they are compatible with the substance of any such agreement or "protocol".

12.5. In case where any matter is not specifically provided for within the protocol, the liquidators shall act in a manner designed to promote the overriding objective set out above in Guideline 1.1.

Guideline 13
Cross-Border Sales

13.1. Where during any period of cooperation between liquidators in main and any secondary proceedings assets are to be sold or otherwise disposed of, every liquidator should seek to sell these assets in cooperation with the other liquidators so as to realise the maximum value for the assets of the debtor as a whole.

13.2. Any national court, where required to act, should approve those sales or disposals that will produce such maximum value.

Guideline 14
Assistance in Reorganization

14.1. Where main insolvency proceedings are aimed at ensuring the rehabilitation and reorganisation of the debtor's business, all other liquidators shall cooperate in any manner consistent with the objective of reorganisation or the sale of the business as a going concern wherever possible, mindful of the interests protected by local insolvency proceedings.

14.2. Liquidators should cooperate so as to obtain any necessary post-commencement financing, including through the granting of priority or secured status to lenders providing finance to the debtor and related entities as may be appropriate and insofar as permitted under any applicable law.

Guideline 15
Coordination between secondary proceedings

15. Liquidators in all secondary proceedings are required to comply with these Guidelines.

Guideline 16
Courts

16.1. Courts are advised to seek to give effect to the overriding objective of enabling courts and liquidators to operate efficiently and effectively operate in cross-border insolvency proceedings within the context of the EC Insolvency Regulation, in the meaning of Guideline 1.

16.2. Courts are advised to operate in a cooperative manner to resolve any dispute relating to the intent or application of these Guidelines or the terms of any cooperation agreement or protocol.

16.3. Courts are advised to consider whether an appointment of the liquidator in main proceedings or a nominated agent of such liquidator as a liquidator or a co-liquidator in secondary proceedings would better ensure coordination between different proceedings under the courts' supervision.

16.4. To the maximum extent permissible under national law, courts conducting insolvency proceedings or dealing with requests for assistance or deciding on any matters relating to communications from other courts should cooperate with each other directly, through liquidators or through any person or body appointed to act at the direction of the courts.

16.5. Courts should encourage liquidators to report periodically, as part of national reporting duties, on the way these Guidelines andlor agreed Protocols are applied, including any practical problems which have been encountered.

Guideline 17
Notices

17.1. Notice of any court hearing or the making of any order by a court should be given to each of the liquidators at the earliest possible point in time where the hearing or order is relevant to that liquidator.

17.2. Where a liquidator cannot be present in person before the court, the court is advised to invite the liquidator to communicate any observations to the court prior to any order being made.

17.3. The liquidators should provide for the keeping of an accessible record of notices in the meaning of Guideline 17.1, which shall be regularly updated, to note the dates and relevant descriptions of any legal documents communicated, including those filed or transferred electronically.

Guideline 18
Scope

18. Whilst the aim of these Guidelines is to facilitate the coordination of the administration of insolvency proceedings involving the same debtor (including through the use of a protocol), liquidators or administrators and courts outside the scope of the EC Insolvency Regulation are encouraged, wherever possible, to use these Guidelines so as to facilitate or increase the prospects of cooperation in other proceedings taking place.

Index

Articles bold, marginal numbers light face

www.ingramcontent.com/pod-product-compliance
Lightning Source LLC
LaVergne TN
LVHW081353011026
849161LV00013BA/2802
9783899492071